THE UNIVERSAL EXPERIENCE OF ADOLESCENCE

The Universal Experience
of Adolescence

NORMAN KIELL

INTERNATIONAL UNIVERSITIES PRESS, INC.
New York

For Adele

Contents

Preface

It is my thesis that the great internal turmoil and external disorder of adolescence are universal and only moderately affected by cultural determinants. In spite of many specific differences in content and degree of stress from one culture to another, adolescent development is basically uniform in all societies. The present book attempts to demonstrate the universalities in adolescence as far back in history and in as many literate cultures as there are records. I have used autobiographies, diaries and letters to illustrate my points. The earliest of these personal documents dates from the first century and the data continue through to contemporary times. Countries from which materials have been collected include every Western European nation, Russia, Poland, Lithuania, Hungary, Moravia, England, Scotland, Wales, Ireland, Canada, United States, Brazil, Argentina, Venezuela, Persia, Turkey, Syria, China, Manchuria, Korea, Japan, India, Siam, Australia, Macao, Philippine Islands, and from such societies as Mexican, Canadian and American Indian.

It would be difficult, if not impossible, for one individual to prepare this kind of book without help. I am indebted to Harold P. Blum, M.D., of Hempstead, Long Island, and to Professors Harry Beilin, Martin L. Nass, Solomon Stone and Dr. Carroll A. Felleman, all members of the Brooklyn College faculty, for their reading of selected chapters and for their perceptive suggestions. I am glad to acknowledge the subvention granted me by President Harry D. Gideonse of Brooklyn College for typing the manuscript through funds administered by the Dean of Faculty, Dean Walter H. Mais.

To Mr. Herbert E. Ruben for his technical assistance, to Arthur I. Neuhauser of the *New York Times* for his help on vital statistics, and to Professor Sidney Lind for his insightful encouragement, I owe a debt of gratitude. Perhaps the largest measure of appreciation goes to the members of my family. During the two years of preparation for and writing of the book, my children were models of co-operation and my wife's patience and understanding were infinite. For her editorial work and comments of substance, I am, indeed, past verbal expression of thanks.

April 24, 1962
Freeport, New York

The Universal Experience
of Adolescence

The rotations of the Universe are the same, up and down, from age to age. . . . In a moment earth will cover us all, then earth, too, will change and what ensues will change to eternity and that again to eternity. A man who thinks of the continuous waves of change and alteration, and the swift passage of all mortal things, will hold them in disdain.— MARCUS AURELIUS

Every man is not only himself; . . . men are lived over again; the world is now as it was in ages past; there was none then, but there hath been some one since that parallels him, and is, as it were, his revived self. —RELIGIO MEDICI

The individual human being is intrinsically no more than a link in the chain of countless generations. In his personality—that is, in the sum of his characteristics—are repeated only the characteristics of his ancestors, in endless combinations, though more or less modified by the manner in which he develops his inherited disposition in his individual life. —AUGUST FOREL

*[The adolescent] recapitulates and expands in the second decennium of life the development he passed through during the first five years of life, just as he recapitulates during these first five years the experiences of thousands of years in his ancestry and during the pre-natal period of those millions of years.—*ERNEST JONES

11

It is clear that no autobiography can begin with a man's birth, that we extend far beyond any boundary line which we can set for ourselves in the past or the future, and that the life of every man is an endlessly repeated performance of the life of man.—EDWIN MUIR

The fundamental question [is] unanswered. Do not all cultures have to cope with the natural turbulence of [adolescence], even though it may not be given institutional expression?—RUTH BENEDICT

The six quotations excerpted above give expression to the philosophy and scope of this book. Despite the fear of at least one psychologist (8) that the vanishing adolescent, like the vanishing Indian, will soon no longer be around to vitalize our dull lives; despite the denial of some people of the existence of adolescents; despite the concern of others over the prolongation of adolescence in our culture; and despite the anxieties of still others that the problems of adolescents are more serious now than ever before in the history of civilization, this book will attempt to show that the difficulties of adolescence are universal, have existed with us ever since the child became father of the man, and will probably continue to remain with us.

The relation of the adolescent to his society and the formation and social development of his personality are problems which have been studied intensively in recent years and which continue to be examined sedulously. Some experts believe that the adolescent period is one of great internal turmoil and external disorder resulting, immediately and inevitably, from physiological development. Others believe the biological explanation is untenable and prefer to think the behavior phenomena of the adolescent years are culturally determined.

This book takes the point of view that adolescence is a physiological state "as definitely characterized by domestic explosions and rebellion as typhoid is marked by fevers [3]." Further, these explosions and rebellions are as manifest in Oriental as in Occidental cultures, in primitive societies as in literate, and they were as true in the days of Hadrian's barbarities as they are for the present atom bomb Era of Terror. While cultures, other than Western, may differ from ours in being tighter, more traditional, and more rule-bound, the sources of friction are not much different from our own: family, marriage, money, jobs, religion, identity, frustrated ambition, balked hopes, intolerable failures. Their problems are clay of our vulnerable clay, no matter the generation, notwithstanding the historical age.

What confuses the picture of adolescence in contemporary society is the ambiguity in which the adolescent role itself is defined. But this is equally true in primitive societies, for they accord adult status in great variation: whereas there may be considerable freedom in, say, sexual behavior, there may be stringent restrictions in achieving full economic status. In their highly original and compelling text, Bloch and Niederhoffer (4) demonstrate conclusively the impressive similarity of adolescent crisis in all cultures and in all times. They show this in detail by analyzing the adolescent period in a great variety and in a large number of different societies. The book places major emphasis on this fact: " . . . the adolescent period in all cultures, visualized as a phase of striving for the attainment of adult status, produces experiences which are much the same for all youths, and certain common dynamisms for expressing reaction to such subjectively held experiences. The intensity of the adolescent experience and the vehemence of external expression depend on a variety of factors, including the general societal attitudes towards adolescence, the duration of the adolescent period itself, and the degree with which the society tends to facilitate entrance into adulthood by virtue of institutionalized patterns, ceremonials, rites, and rituals, and socially supported emotional and intellectual preparation. When a society does not make adequate preparations, formal or otherwise, for the induction of its adolescents into the adult status, equivalent forms of behavior arise spontaneously among adolescents themselves, reinforced by their own group structure, which seemingly provides the same psychological content and function as the more formalized rituals found in other societies [4, p. 17]."

In their intensive cross-cultural survey and analysis of a variety of different cultures and societies in order to determine, by direct comparison, whether similarities in adolescent behavior actually exist, Bloch and Niederhoffer (4, pp. 1-2) were particularly impressed by the remarkable similarities of adolescents, not only on different class levels within the same culture, but even within widely divergent cultures. Despite the relativistic conception of group behavior which infuses the entire modern sociological and anthropological tradition, "it was intellectually disconcerting to discover that adolescent groups widely separated in cultural orientation and geographic location maintained certain profound behavioral similarities. As the research unfolded, it was found that such similarities existed even in the absence of cultural contact and diffusion, and frequently, despite the development of widely different cultural traditions."

They ask the question—and answer it in the affirmative—is there any similarity in psychological meaning to the boys of primitive and modern cultures in their subjection to the ordeal of masculine identification and initiation? In "Ego Pathology and Historical Change," Erikson (6) too provides convincing documentation of the significance for the establishment of identity and personality structure of cultural phenomena that are relatively transient and fleeting as compared with the biological processes involved in personality development, crucial for the individual.

In spelling out their hypothesis, Bloch and Niederhoffer state that "practices such as scarification, tattooing, age-grading, the institution of men's clubs, segregation in bachelor huts, indoctrination of young boys, trial by ordeal, and a host of other painful and weird practices which societies have laboriously contrived to discipline their young for the Great Adventure, not only constitute definite and important parts of primitive rites but appear to have almost their direct counterparts in contemporary gang ritual. We may well ask ourselves, therefore, what are the needs which both the primitive neophyte and the young gang tyro on the streets of a modern American city are trying to express by this behavior.

"It is in this light that our hypothesis begins to take on significant form and added emphasis. Although a given social process may take on its essential meaning within the context of a given culture and in terms of the values of that culture, there are certain common psychological experiences which all individuals face in respect to the needs to preserve ego-identity and rapport with their fellows. As different as the meanings of social life may be to individuals all over the world, the basic distinctions of sex and aging will induce characteristic forms of strain in the effort to achieve the desired status which these unavoidable conditions of human existence establish. Irrespective of how a culture regards childhood, adulthood, and old age, the expectancies a society entertains concerning how people should behave in relation to their age-status will create a certain degree of ego strain and conflict for all individuals in their passage through life. . . .

"Because of the special responsibilities which adulthood imposes in all societies, the transition here is normally fraught with far more psychological peril than is true of the other chronological transitions in life. The need to pursue a desired self-image and to establish the necessary supportive props for the ego is a universal condition. The bias of modern social psychologists notwithstanding—that human psychological characteristics reflect by and large the value-structure within which the individual seeks his adjustments—the need to find some sort of equilibrium for the ego is universal. Fear and anxiety strain, irrespective of the conditions that produce them, are common to all men. The efforts the ego makes to fend off this strain are likewise universal, even though the form of self-reconciliation may acquire the unique value characteristics of a specialized environment [4, pp. 28-29]."

Thus, the anthropologists' "corrective" of cultural relativity cannot be contained. When the anthropologist tests psychological formulations which hold in our culture by examining children in other cultures to see if they also apply and are so validated, the result will be positive. The generalization is true that when a child reacts at a particular time and place, under a set of circumstances, he is exhibiting a pattern of behavior holding in all cultures and at all times.

Every man is in certain respects (a) like all other men (b) like some other men (c) like no other man, state Kluckhohn and Murray (10) in their attempt to assess the determinants of personality formation. It is the very obviousness of the universal features of man that tend to make the experts overlook man's common heritage and lot. "It is possible that the most important of the undiscovered determinants of personality and culture are only to be revealed by close attention to the commonplace." They cite every man's need to explore his environment, to experience sexual tensions and other importunate needs as well as to appease them, to adjust, like all social animals, to a condition of interdependence and interaction and to traditionally defined expectations, to experience both gratification and deprivation. "These universalities of human life produce comparable effects upon the developing personalities of men of all times, places, and races." But while man is like no other man, possessing a unique personality, for general scientific purposes the observation of uniformities—uniformities of elements and uniformities of patterns—is of first importance.

This book attempts to show the universal and ageless feelings of the adolescent, using as data autobiographies relating to the adolescent period, and diaries and letters written by adolescents. Like Wilhelm Dilthey, the historian of the human mind, I shall use historical and empirical methods in trying to answer the question of what the adolescent really is. But in addition, I shall apply current psychological principles of adolescent development to reinforce these methods. Dilthey saw history as a means of comprehending man as a thinking, feeling, willing, creating being who lived in the historical stream of life. His philosophy was founded on an "understanding and analyzing psychology" whose starting point was the analysis of consciousness and whose development was necessary for understanding the way of civilization and its functional relation to the totality of spontaneous impulses. In the light of more modern, Freudian psychology, the unconscious motivations of adolescents will be explored here in depth and in context of the data used.

Marie Bonaparte (2) has stated that biographies—by which she means personal documents—of people of the past "bring to light the unity of human nature and are really like family portraits in which we recognize now one and now another of our own features. . . . We like to feel, through space and through time, the beating of hearts that seem to keep time with our own."

When we read the chapters in St. Augustine's *Confessions*, in which he describes his acts of juvenile delinquency—he was fifteen and sixteen years old and the date was 359 A.D.—we are struck by his recognition of the factor which prompted him to his depredations, for it is so akin to a contemporary theory of delinquency. Nearly 1200 years later, but still only in the year 1519, when Benvenuto Cellini was nineteen years old, he described his experience with juvenile delinquency so that, if we substituted the names of the streets and places in an American city, it would read like a current newspaper story. Benvenuto, bullied by some teenagers on a street corner, clouts one of them on the head. The police come and Benvenuto has to appear before the magistrate. He is sentenced and "rebuked," bound over on bail, cannot raise it, escapes his guards, secures a dagger, rushes to the house of the bully and stabs "him in the breast, piercing doublet and jerkin through and through to the shirt, without however grazing his flesh or doing him the least harm in the world [5]." This starts a kind of gang rumble. The similarities are obvious and need not be labored.

Like the *Confessions* of Saint Augustine, Peter Abelard's *Historia Calamitatum: The Story of My Misfortunes* is an authentic revelation of personality and, like the former, it seems to show how unchangeable man is, how consistent unto himself whether he is of the sixth century or the twelfth, or indeed of the twentieth. There is no reason why his autobiography might not have been written in the last decade.

Lucian, the Syrian rhetorician and artist, was born about 120 A.D. In *The Dream,* a fragment of autobiographical material which has come down to us, Lucian relates the problem of vocational choice that had to be made when he was fourteen years old. His Samosatan parents were poor but status conscious folk, who wanted their son placed in a job suitable for a freeborn man. A family meeting was called, including two maternal avuncular stonemasons who maintained the hereditary business. After various propositions were considered for form's sake, Lucian's father was given the opportunity to express publicly his wife's decision—for the boy to join the family business. His fond parents were convinced that the boy's artistic impulses, which had been evident while in school, would now be fully realized. But early on the very first day of his apprenticeship, Lucian broke a marble slab, was beaten and fired by his uncle, and ran sobbing to mother, claiming uncle had dismissed him because of professional jealousy. The protective mother, with all the acumen of the modern parent, sided with Lucian against her brother (11).

Examples of similar situations and affects, from ancient times to the present, can be cited almost endlessly. John of Salisbury (15), describing the intellectual development of adolescents, wrote in 1159, "Since they cannot really obtain true wisdom in all matters, the young strive to obtain a name for being wise, and endeavor to win esteem, which is the very thing that sophistry promises." Perhaps the most detailed and best characterization of adolescence is the following passage.

The young are in character prone to desire and ready to carry any desire they may have formed into action. Of bodily desires it is the sexual to which they are most disposed to give way, and in regard to sexual desire they exercise no self-restraint. They are changeful too, and fickle in their desires, which are as transitory as they are vehement; for their wishes are keen without being permanent, like a sick man's fits of hunger and thirst. They are passionate, irascible, and apt to be carried away by their impulses. They are the slaves, too, of their passion, as their ambition prevents their ever brooking a slight and renders them indignant at the mere idea of enduring an injury. And while they are fond of honor, they are fonder still of victory; for superiority is the object of youthful desire, and victory is a species of superiority. Again, they are fonder both of honor and of victory than of money, the reason why they care so little for money being that they have never yet had experience of want, as the saying of Pittacus about Amphiaraus puts it. They are charitable rather than the reverse, as they have never yet been witnesses of many villainies; and they are trustful, as they have not yet been often deceived. They are sanguine, too, for the young are heated by Nature as drunken men by wine, not to say that they have not yet experienced frequent failures. Their lives are lived principally in hope, as hope is of the future and memory of the past; and while the future of youth is long, its past is short; for on the first day of life it is impossible to remember anything, but all things must be matters of hope. For the same reason they are easily deceived, as being quick to hope. They are inclined to be valorous, for they are full of passion, which excludes fear, and of hope, which inspires confidence, as anger is incompatible with fear, and the hope of something good is itself a source of confidence. They are bashful, too, having as yet no independent standard of honor and having lived entirely in the school of conventional law. They have high aspirations; for they have never yet been humiliated by the experience of life, but are unacquainted with the limiting force of circumstances; and a great idea of one's own deserts, such as is characteristic of a sanguine disposition, is itself a form of high aspiration. Again, in their actions they prefer honor to expediency, as it is habit rather than calculation which is the rule of their lives, and, while calculation pays regard to expediency, virtue pays regard exclusively to honor. Youth is the age when people are most devoted to their friends or relations or companions, as they are then extremely fond of social intercourse and have not yet learned to judge their friends, or indeed anything else, by the rule of expediency. If the young commit a fault, it is always on the side of excess and exaggeration in defiance of Chilon's maxim (μηδὲν ἄγαν); for they carry everything too far, whether it be their love or hatred or anything else. They regard themselves as omniscient and are positive in their assertions; this is, in fact, the reason of their carrying everything too far. Also their offenses take the line of insolence and not of meanness. They are compassionate from supposing all people to be virtuous, or at least better than they really are; for as they estimate their neighbors by their own guilelessness, they regard the evils which befall them as undeserved. Finally, they are fond of laughter and consequently facetious, facetiousness being disciplined insolence [16].

This description of adolescence was written 2300 years ago; the author was Aristotle. Its universality is at once apparent and still pertinent for contemporary meaning. Were we to jump to the nineteenth century and to Nebraska in the United States, we would be easily able to identify with a fifteen-year-old Winnebago Indian when he writes, "In summer we would go out shooting with our bows and arrows and we generally stayed away all day. At evening when we got home, of course we always expected to get a scolding so we always had some excuse made up for the occasion. It really would have been better had we returned earlier in the day, but we always enjoyed the hunting so much that night would overtake us when we were still a long distance from home. Often we would not eat anything all day, but we were quite accustomed to that. Sometimes we would go fishing down a stream that runs nearby and again we would forget the time and not return home until it was very late. We would then get a scolding even if we gave some sort of an excuse [13]." Testing the limits would seem to be a universal practice.

In the year 1928, Wulf Sachs, a South African psychiatrist, began studying natives at an African mental hospital. It was not long before he made what was to him a startling discovery: manifestations of psychoses, in their form, content, origin, and etiology are identical in both natives and Europeans. This discovery made Sachs inquisitive to know if the working fundamental principles of the mind in its normal state was also the same. In getting at the answer, he analyzed an African *nganga* or witch doctor, John, using the free association technique. In all the time that John spent on the couch telling about his mother, "What impressed me most," wrote Dr. Sachs (14), "was the fact that this ordinary so-called primitive African had been influenced by a woman in his early youth, in the same way that we are: the image of the first love remained in him, as in us, for life, consciously or unconsciously playing a role in his destiny."

Meaningful passages about adolescent development, culled from more than two hundred autobiographies, diaries and letters as representative of the best available material, and dating from about 120 A.D. to the present, will be found in succeeding pages. Evidence for the universal application of the recapitulation of the oedipal conflict during adolescence will be established. The search for identity, basic for the adolescent in all cultures and in all times, appears distinctly in these excerpts. The subsidiary problems of adolescence, such as vocational choice and preparation, the compulsion to read and gamble, the need to belong and be accepted by the peer group, will be demonstrated as well. In addition, his intellectual, physical, sexual and emotional development, as revealed in these materials, will further illustrate the universal qualities of the adolescent.

REFERENCES

1. Aurelius, Marcus. *Meditations*. Book IX, Chapter 28.
2. Bonaparte, Marie. A defence of biography. *Int. J. Psychoanal.*, 20: 239, 1939.
3. Benedict, Ruth. *Patterns of Culture*. New York: New American Library, 1934, pp. 22, 26.
4. Bloch, Herbert A., & Niederhoffer, Arthur. *The Gang. A Study in Adolescent Behavior*. New York: Philosophical Library, 1958, pp. 1-2, 17, 28-29.
5. Cellini, Benvenuto. *Autobiography*. Translated by John Aldington Symonds. Garden City, N.Y.: Garden City Publishing Co., 1927, pp. 27-30.
6. Erikson, Erik H. Ego development and historical change. *Psychol. Issues*, 1:18-49, 1959.
7. Forel, August. *Out of My Life and Work*. New York: W. W. Norton & Co., 1937, p. 15.
8. Friedenberg, Edgar Z. *The Vanishing Adolescent*. Boston: Beacon Press, 1959.
9. Jones, Ernest. Some problems of adolescence. *Brit. J. Psychol.*, 13: 31-47, 1922.
10. Kluckhohn, Clyde, & Murray, Henry A. (Eds.). *Personality in Nature, Society and Culture*. New York: Alfred A. Knopf, 1949, pp. 35-37.

11. Lucian. *The Dream, or Lucian's Career,* in Harmon, A. M. (Ed.), *Lucian.* Loeb Classical Library. Cambridge, Mass.: Harvard University Press, 1947, pp. 213-233.
12. Muir, Edwin. *An Autobiography.* New York: William Sloane Associates, 1954, p. 49.
13. Radin, Paul (Ed.). *The Autobiography of a Winnebago Indian.* Berkeley, Calif.: University of California Press, 1920, pp. 398-399.
14. Sachs, Wulf. *Black Hamlet. The Mind of an African Negro Revealed by Psychoanalysis.* London: Geoffrey Bles, 1937, p. 31.
15. Salisbury, John of. *The Metalogicon.* Translated by Daniel D. McGarry. Berkeley, Calif.: University of California Press, 1955, pp. 236-237.
16. Welldon. *Rhetoric of Aristotle.* New York, 1866, pp. 164-166.

Adolescent Psychology and Personal Documents

A   REVIEW   OF   THE   LITERATURE

The universal experience of adolescence is often revealed to us from the records of lives in the great cultural periods of the past. Autobiographies, diaries and letters are source materials for the description of human lives and, since psychology is a science dealing with the behavior and emotions of people, it is possible to draw on both personal documents and psychology in the attempt to understand the archetypal adolescent. Garraty, long interested in the interrelations between the two fields, states, "it seems clear that biography and psychology have always been related disciplines. Early intuitive interrelationships have been supplemented in recent times by more conscious and more scientific efforts in each field to profit from the works of the other [42]."

Through personal documents, it will be seen that adolescence in all cultures is a time of transition in the biosocial status of the individual. If adolescence is defined as that period of life which comes between biological and sociological maturity, the observation of many societies by Bloch and Niederhoffer (15) clearly indicates that the wider the disparity between these two levels of maturity, the greater the area of adolescent problems and the more acute the experience of adolescent strain. Whether the adolescent upheaval is welcome and beneficial as such, whether it is necessary and inevitable, is answered decisively and unanimously in the affirmative in psychoanalytic opinion (34). Ausubel (8) states in his study of the theory and problems of adolescence that the central idea permeating every chapter of his book "is that adolescence is a distinctive stage in personality development precipitated by significant changes in the biosocial status of the child. As a result of these changes, which are discontinuous with preceding biosocial conditions of growth, extensive reorganization of personality structure is required. Our thesis is that this process of reorganization shows certain basic uniformities from one culture to another—despite many specific differences in content and degree of stress—because of various common elements inhering in the general psychology of transition and in the psychological implications of sexual maturity, biological sex role, and the new personality traits associated with adult roles and status in the community."

A survey by Sherif and Cantril (86) of ethnological data indicates "that the problems facing the adolescent vary from culture to culture rendering the transition to adulthood more or less complicated, more or less conflicting, more or less prolonged. . . . However, the basic psychological principles which operate in all of these social settings should be the same." Unconscious attitudes are universal (73). Freud (40) concluded, in his discussion of primitive man and myths, that it seems more acceptable and more probable "that in the psychic life of present-day children, the same archaic moments still prevail, which generally prevailed at the time of primitive civilization. To all appearances, the child, in the development of his psyche, simply recapitulates the evolution of his species, analogous to the recapitulation of his physical development, which has long since been accepted by embryology."

While it is true that culture shapes the (adolescent) personality, the biological also shapes the culture; *and what is biological becomes bedrock.* As Freud (37) declared, "We often feel that, when we have reached the wish for a penis and the masculine protest, we have penetrated all the psychological strata and reached 'bedrock' and that our task is accomplished. And this is probably correct, for in the psychical field the biological factor is really the rock-bottom." This basic tenet is illustrated repeatedly in the selections in the body of the text.

Saint Augustine's *Confessions,* going back more than 1500 years, is generally recognized as marking a milestone in the history of psychology. While there was frequently a tendency to introspection in Saint Augustine's day, he was "the first to perceive the concrete fullness of the inner life; he did not merely subjectively accept the variety of mental processes, nor did he see in them merely elements of a systematic striving after a moral and religious aim, but he regarded them as philosophically interesting processes: 'I became a great question for myself.' While reproducing, even re-living them, he subjected these processes to objective consideration, noting the type of event and the laws of association and succession, and coming up against problems everywhere. . . . Thoughtful observation was united in him both with the criticizing function of the conscience and with the epideictic tendency of the rhetorician, so that he boldly announced to God and the world secret impulses which until then had lain in obscurity. . . . It is to these psychological and moral achievements that his *Confessions* owe the enduring significance of their content and the influence exerted by them on modern literature from Petrarch onward [70]." Misch (69) credits Saint Augustine with giving autobiography an importance that extends beyond the personal element: "Through Augustine, the portrayal of a life-story attained the poetic and philosophic dignity of serving as a reflection of a view of the world, and the development of autobiography among modern peoples toward the philosophic understanding of human life into general literature, and above all into the psychological novel."

Ever since Saint Augustine, personal documents of individuals have provided material for the revelation of personality development. A great number of authors of autobiographies clearly see the link between childhood and youthful experience and adult life. One of the interesting facts about many of the selections in this volume is that they were written long before modern psychology was established; yet the significance given to the pre-adult period by these writers is marked. Today it is generally recognized that one of the better ways of understanding childhood and adolescent behavior is to be able to recall one's own childhood and adolescence.

THE VALIDITY AND RELIABILITY OF PERSONAL DOCUMENTS

To reconstruct one's adolescence is a precarious process, for it is marked by the triple pitfalls of forgetting, distortion, and selective remembering. Both the psychoanalyst and the autobiographer agree on this. Anna Freud, in her treatment of adult cases, is impressed with how seldom she has succeeded in reviving the adolescent experiences of her patients. She explains, "I do not mean to imply that adult patients have an amnesia for their adolescence which resembles in extent or in depth the amnesia for their early childhood. On the contrary, the memories of the events of the adolescent period are, normally, retained in consciousness and told to the analyst without apparent difficulty. Masturbation in preadolescence and adolescence, the first moves toward intercourse, etc., may even play a dominant part in the patients' conscious memories and, as we know well, are made use of to overlay and hide the repressed masturbation conflicts and the buried sexual activities of early childhood. . . . On the other hand, these memories contain no more than the bare facts, happenings and actions, divorced from the affects which accompanied them at the time. What we fail to recover, as a rule, is the atmosphere in which the adolescent lives, his anxieties, the height of elation or depth of despair, the quickly rising enthusiasms, the utter hopelessness, the burning—or at times sterile—intellectual and philosophical preoccupations, the yearning for freedom, the sense of loneliness, the feeling of oppression by the parents, the impotent rages or active hates directed against the adult world, the erotic crushes—whether homosexually or heterosexually directed—the suicidal fantasies, etc. These are elusive mood swings, difficult to revive which, unlike the affective states of infancy and early childhood, seem disinclined to re-emerge and be relived in connection with the person of the analyst [33]."

John A. Rice (75), in his autobiography, states, "A man may remember his childhood with pleasure, but where is one who does not wince at the memory of his adolescence? . . . Women say they cannot remember the pangs of childbirth. Crafty Nature blots them out, lest there be no more. So also one does not remember one's second birth . . . from childhood into youth. [This] second birth . . . becomes in memory a dull pain." In a similar vein, Jean Cocteau declares, "In a way, I was born at the age of twenty. . . . " Floyd Dell, author of the psychologically insightful autobiography, *Homecoming,* called "the period of adolescence . . . so sentient a time and yet so helpless a one that it would not be strange if all boys and girls became poets then. To be grown up in capacity to wish, to love, to suffer, and yet a child in power to deal with the world, is more than the heart can bear, unless there is some magic by which our wishes can be fulfilled —if not in actuality, then in some seeming, true to the heart, assuaging grief and pain."

If, then, adolescence is such a painful period and so largely repressed from conscious memory, to what degree are autobiographies dealing with the phenomenon likely to be either valid or reliable? The case against validity and reliability at first seems very strong. Since much must be omitted, distortions are likely, and inaccuracies unavoidable. It is difficult for the writers to sort out adolescent memories and adolescent dreams. Both are probably in all the autobiographies, for the dreams are always rooted in what becomes the memories. It was the dreams that made the hardships of adolescence endurable. The flourishing fantasy life, the premature ego development, and the early internalization of restrictions all tend to become connected with the family romance and are elaborated into autobiographical distortion. Kris (58) declared that autobiographical memory has different degrees of ego autonomy and can be altered by conflicts, especially when the need for a past becomes pressing, as in adolescence. And Hall (47) advised that "the striking and cardinal fact never to be forgotten in considering its each and every phenomenon and stage is that the experiences of adolescence are extremely transitory and very easily forgotten, so that they are often totally lost to the adult consciousness."

Many autobiographers have recognized this crucial problem of credibility. The first of them was Saint Augustine. "How do you know," he asked in his *Confessions* (7), "when you hear me talk about myself, that I am telling the truth, considering that no man knows what is true of a man, save his own soul?" And he answered his own question, " . . . because love 'believeth all things,' at least as regards those who, being united by it, have become one, therefore shall I confess to Thee, O Lord, that the man may listen to whom I can prove that I wish to confess the truth; but believe me whose ears are opened to me by love."

While Saint Augustine was carried away by the self-abandonment of religious emotion, Rousseau (76) was stimulated by the exquisite torture of his need for self-justification. In describing his adolescence, Rousseau (76) recognized, as well, the fallibility of memory.

This period of my youth is the one of which I have the most confused idea. During this time scarcely anything occurred of sufficient interest to my heart for me to preserve a lively recollection of it; and it is almost unavoidable that, amidst so many wanderings backwards and forwards, so many successive changes, I should transpose times or places. I am writing entirely from memory, without notes, without materials to assist my recollection. There are events in my life which are as fresh in my mind as if they had just happened; but there are also gaps and voids, which I can only fill up by the aid of a narrative which is as confused as the recollection of it which has remained to me. It is, therefore, possible that I have sometimes made mistakes, and I may do so again, in unimportant matters, up to the time when I possess surer information regarding myself; but, in all that is really of essential importance, I feel sure of being an accurate and faithful chronicler, as I shall always endeavour to be in everything—of that the reader may rest assured.

Rousseau then attempted to justify the writing of his *Confessions.* "In pursuance of the undertaking I have entered upon of unreservedly revealing myself to the public, it is imperative that nothing that concerns me should remain obscure or concealed—I must be continually under the eye of the reader—he must follow me through all the wanderings of my heart, into every nook of my being—he must not lose sight of me for a single instant, lest finding the slightest void or chasm in the recital, he should have occasion to ask, 'What was he doing at such a period?' and should accuse me of not daring to confess the whole. I give scope enough to the malignity of men by what I say, without furnishing further food by my silence [77]."

Abraham Cowley (1618-1667), in his brief sketch of himself, stated, "It is a hard and nice subject for a man to write of himself: it grates his own heart to say anything of disparagement, and the reader's ears to hear anything of praise for him[24]." Sir Walter Scott (1771-1832), writing about his youth, took cognizance of the difficulty of remembering the period accurately: "I am inadvertently led to confound dates while I talk of this remote period, for, as I have no notes, it is impossible for me to remember with accuracy the progress of studies, if they deserve the name, so irregular and miscellaneous [83]." While Goethe (1749-1832) called his autobiography *Dichtung und Wahrheit,* Heine (1799-1856) said in his memoirs, "I will tell thee the fairy-tale of my life [57]." Trollope (1815-1882) flatly asserted: "That I, or any man, should tell everything of himself, I hold to be impossible. Who could endure to own the doing of a mean thing? Who is there that has done none [90]?"

Contemporary autobiographers also recognize the problems of credibility, accuracy and repression. Even William Ellery Leonard, sophisticated in the ways of analysis, found it painfully difficult to write about phases of his adolescence. His father had lost his properties and his job as a newspaper editor; circumstances compelled him to accept a pulpit in the small Vermont town of Bolton. The boy had to forfeit his valedictory speech at the Plainfield, New Jersey High School (Class of 1884), and give up his friends. Leonard (61) wrote: "The uprooting, the estrangement, the isolation, the struggles, the despairs of those two next years toward the end of adolescence: I find I have been trying unconsciously to postpone the chronicling."

The author of *Green Mansions,* W. H. Hudson, has said, "It is difficult, impossible . . . for any one to recall his boyhood exactly as it was. It could not have been what it seems to the adult mind, since we cannot escape from what we are, however great our detachment may be; and in going back we must take our present selves with us; the mind has taken a different colour, and this is thrown back upon our past [53]." The problem that confronts an autobiographer even more urgently than other men is posed by Edwin Muir in his autobiography: "How can he know himself? I am writing about myself in this book, yet I do not know what I am. I know my name, the date and place of my birth, the appearance of the places I have lived in, the people I have met, the things I have done. . . . But I know all this in an external and deceptive way. . . . This external approach, no matter how perfect, will never teach me much either about them or myself [71]." In the attempt to recapture his adolescent period, Theodor Reik [74a] wrote, "It is very difficult for me to feel even any clear echo of the emotions which governed my life forty-three years ago." Similarly, Sherwood Anderson (6) wrote in his *Memoirs,* "It is impossible for the man . . . to be quite sure of what could have been in the child's mind."

Selectivity inevitably enters the personal document. Said Havelock Ellis (30), "There has been selection in my narrative. In every such narrative there is inevitably selection . . . I have sought to select the significant (inner) things." And H. G. Wells (91) warned in his autobiography, "You will discover a great deal of evasion and refusal in my story." The last word concerning the perils inherent in autobiographical writing shall be left with George Bernard Shaw (85), who stated in his usual acerbic way, "All autobiographies are lies. I do not mean unconscious, unintentional lies: I mean deliberate lies. No man is bad enough to tell the truth about himself during his lifetime, involving, as it must, the truth about his family and his friends and colleagues. And no man is good enough to tell the truth to posterity in a document which he suppresses until there is nobody left to contradict him."

Despite these warnings, from the honest bewilderment of Scott and Muir to the snide acidulousness of Shaw, and despite the caution of some social scientists that "reliability is, in general, inversely proportional to the time-lapse between event and recollection [45]," there is substantial evidence, both scientific and intuitive, to make a good case for reliability in personal documents. Autobiographies cannot be regarded as objective narratives; there is probably a good deal of conscious and unconscious self-deception in them all. Misch (67) goes so far as to say that when recollections in an autobiography are entirely free from tendentiousness, "it must of necessity be regarded with scepticism. . . . In the reproduction of inward and especially religious experiences, autobiography is a field of auto-delusion. . . . Yet it is just through this welling up from the most intimate contemporary life of the individual, which includes the past within itself, that autobiography acquires its own peculiar power, through which it can attain the truthfulness of poetry without losing its hold on material facts. Empirical contemplation of reality affords a comprehensive view only at moments of exaltation: this heightened awareness, shaping its story, while re-living it, from the present and past seen as a whole, produces a creative objectivation of the autobiographer's mind that cannot be other than true."

Cartwright and French (21), in their study of the reliability of life histories, raised these two questions: (a) To what extent does a given life history present a valid picture of a person? (b) What is the reliability of multiple studies of the same personality? They define reliability as the amount of agreement between independently written life histories of the same individual and validity as the agreement between the experimenter's estimate of the subject's behavior and the subject's actual behavior. The evidence from their experimentation indicates that reliability and validity can be determined for single items of behavior and for such variables as perseverance, ascendance and introversion. "It seemed to be true in general that validity was greater than reliability—a fact showing that two independent studies of the same personality may diverge in their results and yet both have demonstrated validity." The passages in the chapters which follow repeatedly illustrate the validity of the assertion of the universal affective life of adolescents throughout history and in a variety of cultures. There must be reliability and validity when second and fourth century youths and any number from the fifteenth through the twentieth centuries express nearly identical feelings about their struggle for ego identity and maturity, the recapitulation of the oedipal conflict, their suicidal impulses, their compulsion to gamble and to read, their sexual enlightenment, and so on. The similarities in their autobiographical writings which are concerned with adolescence give credibility and consistency to what they recall of the period.

While personal documents need not be taken at face value, the words of Samuel Butler can be kept in mind. "Every man's work whether it be literature or music or pictures or architecture or anything else is always a portrait of himself, and the more he tries to conceal himself, the more clearly will his character appear in spite of himself." Despite distortions, memory slips, and selective remembering, what the autobiographer writes of his adolescence has meaning and significance transcending the posibility of psychical censorship. As phenomenological psychology postulates, the individual's perception of any given situation is for him the ultimate reality. Whatever he remembers of his adolescence is important because of its immediate or directly subsequent effect; whatever is judged to be unessential is forgotten (41). Freud (39) wrote, "I can remember a dream of my own separated by at least thirty-seven years from today and yet as fresh as ever in my memory." The statement comes from his *Interpretation of Dreams,* written in 1899, which means that Freud vividly remembered a dream which occurred when he was six years old.

According to Saul and his colleagues (79), "Earliest memories are absolutely specific, distinctive, and characteristic for each individual; moreover, they reveal, probably more clearly than any other single psychological datum, the central core of each person's psychodynamics, his chief motivations, form of neurosis, and emotional problem. This is the empirical observable fact." Plato, in his *Timaeus,* wrote, "What we learn in childhood takes a wonderful hold on the memory. With respect to myself, I am not certain that I could recall the whole of yesterday's discourse, but I should be very much astonished if anything that I had heard a long time ago were to escape my remembrance." Martin Freud (36), son of Sigmund, echoed this fifteen hundred years later: "I must retrace my steps back [he wrote in his autobiography] to the years between 1896 and 1898—sixty years ago [when he was six to eight years old], a long time it will seem to younger people who, in time, will learn that events of their childhood remain more sharply outlined than much, even of greater significance, that has occurred in their middle years." Whether the remembrance of a happy childhood is myth or truth, it contains elements of both, as Schachtel (80) has pointed out, for it is woven out of wishes, hopes, remembrance and sorrow, and thus has more than one meaning.

Just as there are autobiographers who mistrusted their memories or who recognized the possibilities of distortion, there are still others who made every deliberate attempt to tell their stories as honestly and truthfully as they possibly could. Schopenhauer (81) stated that "The man who writes his own life surveys it as a whole, the particular becomes small, the near becomes distant, the distant becomes near again, the motives that influenced him shrink; he seats himself at the confessional, and has done so of his own free will; the spirit of lying does not easily take hold of him here, for there is also in every man an inclination to truth which has first to be overcome whenever he lies, and which there has taken up a specially strong position." But if we are not so much concerned about lying as we are about perception distorted by lapse of time, age, affect, and unconscious or repressed feelings, then whatever the narrator sets down becomes truth and the basis for study. In the middle of the nineteenth century, Hamerton (49) said in his autobiography, "It has been frequently mentioned that an autobiography must of necessity be an untrue representation of its subject, as no man can judge himself correctly. [But even if this is so], the reader of an autobiography has this advantage, that the writer must be unconsciously revealing himself all along, merely by his way of telling things."

Edward Gibbon (1737-1794), asserted unequivocably in his *Autobiography* that "Truth, naked, unblushing truth, the first virtue of more serious history, must be the sole recommendation of this personal narrative [43]." Ralph Waldo Emerson predicted that "The novels will give way, by and by, to diaries or autobiographies —captivating books, if only a man knew how to choose among what he calls his experiences that which is really his experience, and how to record truth only." Richard Henry Dana, Jr. (25) knew the limits of truth and was constrained to write, "In order to be honest with myself and with any into whose hands this [autobiography] may come, I shall not profess to myself or pretend to them that it is a faithful transcript of the acts, and feelings and thoughts of my life. I shall set down nothing here which is untrue. There will be no fiction and no dressing up of anything; but our Maker knows each man's own soul, knows that there are thoughts and intents of the heart, sometimes put forth in act, which no man would be willing or need or ought to open to all observers." The contemporary philosopher, Berdyaev (11), discussed the meaning of memory in the Preface to his autobiography: "The writing of this kind of book implies the exercise of the most mysterious power in man: that of memory. Memory and oblivion alternate in human life. I forget many things for a time; many things disappear from my consciousness and are yet preserved at a deeper level."

It was Kierkegaard (22) who said, "The subjective is the true—the subjective and not the objective." Chaudhuri, in his *Autobiography of an Unknown Indian,* reflects, "Men do not become aware of the precise quality of their early years until late in life. Aksakov, Renan, Anatole France, Hudson, Tagore, all wrote their autobiographical masterpieces when they were advanced in years—in fact, advanced considerably into, and sometimes beyond, what Dante called *il mezzo del cammin di nostra vita.*" Shumaker (87), who made an exhaustive study of English autobiography, concluded that "it remains probable that of all kinds of historical literature, autobiography, at its best, may come nearest to the reality it tries to represent.... On the whole, the more autobiographies one reads the more respect one is likely to acquire for their reliability. As for the omissions and mistakes of emphasis, they are inseparable from any work which attempts, not 'creation,' but the reproduction of past actuality, and to some extent they can be rectified by cooperation with the author's mental and emotional processes. In any art form, limitation is the condition of achievement."

The recapitulation of the past, dependent upon the thoughts and feelings of the writer, is the basis on which the autobiography is written. Remembrance of the past can never remain passive nor can it be a mere objective record of past events. It is for this reason that autobiographies are frequently regarded as something less than accurate. But as Berdyaev (10) said, "Memory must needs be active; it is characterized by a creative, transfiguring power inherent in it, and involves individual emphasis, partiality and, therefore, prejudice. Memory is selective; it draws out or chooses certain things, both consciously and unconsciously, while leaving others in the background of oblivion. The remembrance of my life in its varied manifestations is for me an avowedly active remembrance, that is to say, a creative effort of my mind apprehending my past in my present. Between the facts of my life and their record in this book there intervenes a creative, cognitive activity whereby these facts acquire significance; and it is this that interests me above everything else."

THE MOTIVATION FOR WRITING PERSONAL DOCUMENTS

Personal documents are for the most part introspective protocols, adapted especially to the study of the complexities of phenomenal consciousness. The psychologist who wishes to make use of autobiographies, diaries and letters must consider the reasons why an individual uses such means. Among the motives that operate, according to Allport (3), are "special pleading; exhibitionism; desire for order; desire for personal perspective; for relief from tension; for therapy; for monetary gain; for fulfilling an assignment; for social re-incorporation; scientific interests; literary delight; hope for public service or reform; and occasionally a hope for a literary immortality." More likely than not, more than one motive is operative, but the most universal aspect, Misch (66) stipulated, is a man's need for self-revelation.

Even as knowledgeable a student of psychology as Phyllis Bottome, the biographer of Alfred Adler, indicates this need (up to a point) in her autobiography, *Search for a Soul* (17): "My reason for writing these memoirs only up to the age of eighteen is that after adolescence we enter a new region of living where we cease to be an object with whom life is still at play, and become subjects playing upon life. When we take a hand in this final game, we no longer want to show it to other players. A veil must come down between what we are and what we wish others to think of us." The need of William Ellery Leonard (60) was "an adventure in humanity. What was so poignantly my subconscious mind reveals itself, by the laws of our common organic structure and development, as the mind of mankind. My own pain, my own struggle, has been, even to myself, a spectacle, a laboratory. And my findings differ in some ominous particulars from the previous record of poets and psychoanalysts. I have been persuaded, in spite of the shrinkings of privacy and the demands of an insistent profession, to set them down: persuaded by the desire to frustrate, by a neat and unexpected turn, those Demonic Forces which, as appearances go, have backed me for so many years against the wall. Beset by phobias, shell-shocked in a civilian war, hampered and harassed, I have done little enough to justify the ambitions that awakened long ago and that have not yet been willing to die. So out of very suffering and very failure I would create value: the value of a scientific document; the value of a work of art. Something, as science and art in one, to help others to human and humane living."

Ernest Jones' motivation for writing his *Free Associations* (56) has a surprising turn. "Any reflective person who contemplates writing an autobiography must take some interest in his motive for so doing; an infliction of oneself on the public seems to call for some apologetic explanation, even if this is itself, more imposition. On putting the question to myself as sincerely as I could, the rather unexpected answer came: 'Gratitude for life.'" When Turgenev (1818-1883) was seventeen, he started an autobiography (92). "I turned seventeen a week ago. I want to write down all I know about myself, my entire life. Why do I do it? For two reasons. First, I have recently read *Les Confessions de Jean Jacques Rousseau* and so I conceived the idea of writing my own confessions. Secondly, having described my life now, I shall not touch this notebook till the age of fifty (if I live that long), and then it will certainly give me pleasure to recall what I thought and dreamed of at the time when I was writing these lines. And so, having made the exordium, which is always necessary, I begin." Unfortunately, as Yarmolinsky tells us, Turgenev gave himself only one unfinished paragraph to reread at the age of fifty.

An impelling need for immortality drove Hazlitt (50) to write his autobiography. "It was when the future seemed barred to my progress and the hope within me died that I began to turn for consolation to the past, gathering up the fragments of my early recollections and putting them in a form that might live. It is thus that, when we find our personal and substantial identity vanishing from us, we strive to gain a reflected and substituted one in our thoughts; we do not like to perish wholly; we wish to bequest at least our names to posterity. As long as we can keep alive our cherished thoughts and nearest interests in the minds of others, we do not appear to have retired altogether from the stage; we still occupy a place in the estimation of mankind, and excite a powerful influence over them, and it is only our bodies that are trampled into the dust or dispersed into air." Freud (38) reluctantly wrote a brief autobiography, not because any "personal experiences of mine are of interest in comparison to my relations with" psychoanalysis but rather because he felt his life was inextricably interwoven with his work.

Berlioz (72) felt he had to correct the record. "The notices of my life which have from time to time appeared are so crowded with errors and inaccuracies as at length to suggest to me that I myself should record those portions of my agitated and laborious career which may be interesting to the lovers of art. Such a restrospective study will afford me the opportunity of giving my opinion on the difficulties which at present beset the career of a composer and of tendering some useful advice to my brethren." John Stuart Mill was similarly prompted to write about his life because of his "unusual and remarkable" education which might be of value to others.

Perhaps Hazlitt was closest to and most conscious of the primary reason for writing autobiography—the need to be preserved in perpetuity. As Marie Bonaparte (16) wrote, "The human longing for survival is not merely the aspiration to be loved in spite of death. There is also the narcissistic desire to go on living in some form or other and in spite of everything. And even the humblest among us, though he cannot hope for monuments or writings to perpetuate his name, aspires at least to have that name carved on a tomb, so that he shall not be altogether 'forgotten.' . . . And since papyrus, even parchment, and paper most of all, fall into dust, man has invented printed books in which thought can be reincarnated from century to century. And so the battle against oblivion, in which, however, man must finally be defeated, still goes on. For man considers that to be forgotten is to die a second and more complete death and this belief will no doubt endure as long as humanity itself."

There is universal agreement that various unconscious factors operate in the personality of the writer and in the motivation of his creations. Beres (12) lists oedipal and preoedipal conflicts, anxiety, guilt, masochism, procreative wishes, and other psychic functions. What he questions is the designation of one group of factors as the explanation of the artist's personality. He points out Sachs' (78) description of the two main unconscious aims of the poet as "the relief of his guilt feelings and the replacement of his narcissism." But Sachs did not develop this into a formula to be applied to all artists. Others (14, 59) have attempted to supply such a formula, but in endeavoring to account for the motivation of writers of autobiographies, the student of this genre is faced with "the insurmountable obstacle that [he] cannot with the tools of psychoanalysis go further than the stage of assumption or plausibility. . . . The validity of the assumption in the biographical study rests on its plausibility, how it fits in with other available data, and how it will fit in with future studies. It is strengthened by the unity, the consistency, and the convergence of the evidence [13]."

THE VALUE OF PERSONAL DOCUMENTS

Autobiography in its primary form has been defined as a continuous, organized story of a life experience, complete or partial [46] with the function of revealing the "living man." Misch (65) breaks down the term into the description *(graphia)*, of an individual human life *(bios)*, by an individual himself *(auto)*. In Allport's (1) psychological phrase, autobiographies, diaries, and letters are uncontrolled protocols that intentionally or unintentionally yield information concerning the structure, dynamics, and functioning of the author's mental life.

The layman's interest in personal documents, so defined, may be voyeuristic, a desire to see the writer exposed in intimate behavior, or his innermost feelings revealed. Or the reader may be projecting his own affective life, or identifying more or less closely with the author. "The inner conflicts of others are . . . regarded as a mirror in which one's own struggles can be viewed clearly and with profit. Identification is sought, and in the comparisons which are drawn between the struggles of others and one's own conflicts, there is much satisfaction. To compare one's feelings and inward experiences with those of others is bound to afford pleasure, for in so doing man finds comfort, resignation, and at times aspiration [62]."

For the psychologist, the study of personal documents can and does give greater understanding of human drives and motivation. Since human life is not readily observable under laboratory conditions, the data provided by personal documents can supplement the more precise and accurate observations which are accessible only in the laboratory. "To the psychiatrist, [personal documents are] of particular interest, as [they give] him a broader view of what the possibilities of human life are; [they] show him that outside the clinical field there are a great many experiences which form part and parcel of the varied texture of human life and which are not monopolized by the patients of the psychiatrist. . . . In their totality, [the data] form a body of psychological information which is of some value [19]."

Redfield (74), in his foreword to Allport's brilliant work, *The Use of Personal Documents in Psychological Science,* states, "It is in large part through the human, or personal document, that we learn what goes on in people's minds." Allport (2) himself must be quoted on the value of such documents. "Personal documents are good if they serve the comparison of lives, one with another, leading to statistical generalizations and to an understanding of uniformities of behavior. But they are good also if standing one by one they provide concrete evidence of the nature of single personal lives from which all psychological science is derived; if they yield evidence of pluralistic causation; if they give clinicians and practitioners a sounder basis for work; and if they enhance the understanding, prediction, and control of individual lives (which is all that science ultimately demands). . . . To the layman, the chief fault with psychological science seems to be its willingness to pile abstraction upon abstraction with little regard for the concrete personal life. In the personal document can be found the needed touchstone of reality. . . . Since there are no facts in psychology that are divorced from personal lives, the human document is the most obvious place to find these facts in their raw state. . . In longitudinal documents we have the possibility of watching the course of development and change in personality; what the ego demands at the start, how it expands in its wants, how it views the world at successive stages. Such information is found in autobiographies and diaries, and . . . such documents are the only way we have of following through the course of development over a period of years."

Ernest Jones (55), in his foreword to Hitschmann's *Great Men,* said that "Freud himself considered that pathographies, i.e., medical studies of the morbid conditions that had affected various famous personages, were of very little value in throwing light on their personality and consequently on their works. He considered, however, that a psychological, and still better a psychoanalytical, investigation of the manner in which their minds had developed from the earliest beginnings would throw much light on the motives that impelled them toward their various acts of creation and would in this way illuminate the inner meaning of their productions. Such studies, therefore, would be of value to the literary critic as well as to psychologists in their studies of exceptional personalities." Hitschmann (52), himself the author of many analytic studies of famous personalities, felt that the personal document "has begun to acquire a different meaning. It is no longer 'the history of the life of a particular person.' To us it means a recorded personality, especially his psychology, development, function of his soul, heredity, constitution, childhood, defense mechanisms, his instincts and their vicissitudes, the ego, the superego—in short, the understanding of a man's work, character and personality. A 'man-record' would be a better word for it. Because the Twentieth Century contains an accelerated interest in the understanding of psychological life, the disciplines of psychoanalysis, anthropology and sociology together represent a 'science of man' as never before. The dynamics of creativity of the unconscious mind in the form of dreams, fantasies and works of art are being registered. The practicing analyst studies personalities as part of his method of therapy. He records these data in his files. Material of this kind, obtained by psychoanalysis is necessary for the man-record of a great and productive individual. Thus, biography is psychoanalysis, and every psychoanalyst collects data for a man-record *(Menschenbild)*, that is to say, every psychoanalysis is a biography."

The difficult question—what is the most interesting of all subjects?—would probably be answered by most people with, "Myself, of course, particularly myself when young." The fascination of childhood remembered in maturity has inspired thousands of novelists and poets, and the turmoil and excitement of adolescence have inspired tens of thousands. While most adults find it hard to recall the emotional and instinctive life of the teens, the recollections of the period to be found in autobiographies are "the best source [47]." Dilthey (28) said that "Autobiography is the highest and most instructive form in which the understanding of life comes before us." Burgess (18) has stated, "In the life-history is revealed, as in no other way, the inner life of the person, his moral struggles, his successes and failures in securing control of his destiny in a world too often at variance with his hopes and ideals." And to return to Misch (68), "When the autobiographer so penetrates with his personality the adventurous episodes of his life of which he tells that his whole self is visible in every scene, a dramatic form, one might say a heroic one, comes into existence."

The material in this book gives credence to what Dilthey, Burgess and Misch say. As Inhelder and Piaget (54) declare, "To fully understand the adolescent's feelings, we have to go beyond simple observation and look at intimate documents such as essays not written for immediate public consumption, diaries, or simply the disclosures some adolescents may make of their personal fantasies. For example, in the recitation obtained by G. Dumas from a high-school class on their evening reveries, the most normal students—the most retiring, the most amiable—calmly confessed to fantasies and fabulations which several years later would have appeared in their own eyes as signs of pathological megalomania. Without going into the detail of this group, we see that the universal aspect of the phenomenon must be sought in the relationship between the adolescent's abstract theories and the life program which he sets up for himself. . . . " Experience as experience, as it occurs independently of any purpose to describe or analyze it, is almost inaccessible both to the humanist and the psychologist. In the words of Cantril and Bumstead (20), "Naïve, on-going human experience seems unreportable, ineffable. But it is the men and women we call 'humanists' who seem to come closest to capturing and conveying these ineffable, unconceptualizable experiences. Hence we return to them over and over again in trying to get a toe hold on our own awareness, or in trying to lift ourselves up to more satisfying levels of experience. . . . Vivid descriptions of human experience by non-scientists may . . . supply protocol data with which the scientist may begin his task of cross-examining nature in his attempt to arrive at a set of constructs in terms of which he can summarize, understand, 'explain,' and better predict the process of human living."

On the basis of nearly five hundred passages from autobiographies, diaries, and letters dealing with various phases of adolescent development, and reproduced here, the generalization that the basic, affective and biosocial life of the adolescent is universal for virtually all cultures and throughout time has been made. These documents enable the investigator to "understand, explain and better predict the process" of adolescent behavior. It is perhaps relevant to add that the majority of personal memoirs are most interesting at the beginning, as character defines itself and struggles to be free. Childhood and youth, remarked Bernard Shaw (84), is "the readablest part of even the worst autobiography. . . . Of Madame de Warens when (Rousseau) was sixteen I have a lively recollection. Of Madame d'Houdetet when he was forty-five I have not the faintest impression." A. A. Milne (64) was similarly moved: "When I read the [auto] biography of a well-known man, I find that it is the first half of it which holds my attention. I watch with fascinated surprise the baby, finger in mouth, grow into the politician, tongue in cheek; but I find nothing either fascinating or surprising in the discovery that the cynicism of the politician has matured into the pomposity of the Cabinet Minister. . . . "

If, as Allport (5) says, certain statements of tendency in human nature seem approximately true for every mortal, then the data revealed in the material of this text should demonstrate conclusively the similarities of adolescent experience. Ausubel (9) points out that "In denying the universality of the adolescent phenomena, the deniers have pointed to the existence of psychosocial problems, to the pressure of cultural differences in the regulation of adolescence. But . . . it is illogical to conclude that because the nature of adolescence varies from culture to culture in certain of its more specific aspects there can be no common factor in its more general characteristics.

The same type of argument has been urged in disputing the stress of adolescence: there are differences among cultures and among individuals in the degree of stress experienced during this age period. And here, too, it hardly seems necessary to point out that a phenomenon does not cease to exist simply because its intensity varies under different conditions."

The uniqueness and the similarities of adolescents in the East and the West, in ancient and contemporary times, and in primitive and industrial cultures, will be seen repeatedly in the materials used in this text. A systematic attempt has been made to use personal documents, not so much as evidence for the principle of the universality of the adolescent phenomenon, but rather to illustrate it.

THE REPRESENTATIVENESS OF PERSONAL DOCUMENTS

One of the criticisms levelled against the use of personal documents, and which has been pointed out by Allport (4), is the unrepresentativeness of the sample. "In personal documents only a minority of people ever undertake to tell about their mental processes or their personalities. Diary writers, it is true, are numerous during adolescent years, but not many make their documents available. Therefore, it is said, generalization on the basis of personal writing is limited to the kind of people who prepare accessible documents." The limitations of the selectivity of the sample, one would thus suppose, would minimize the opportunity to generalize.

Two points can be made to answer this criticism, so far as this book is concerned. First, there are any number of illustrations used which come from the pens of obscure people. They would include, among others, Thomas Bewick, Catherine Havens, David S. Kogan, Mary Howitt, San Kim, Helen Kuo, Emily Shore, and Don C. Talayesva. Secondly, it is not evident in every adolescent that he is destined to bestride the world like a Colossus. Napoleon, as revealed in his letters, and Maimon, Goethe and Mill (among a very few others), in their autobiographies, were exceptions. Erikson (31) states that "The autobiographies of extraordinary (and extraordinarily self-perceptive) individuals are suggestive sources of insight into the development of identity. In order to find the anchor point for the discussion of the universal genetics of identity, however, it would be well to trace its development through the life histories or through significant life episodes of 'ordinary' individuals—individuals whose lives have neither become professional autobiographies nor case histories."

   While this book has not followed Erikson's suggestion completely, it does contain many representations from the lives of 'ordinary' people. And even when use has been made of material from the lives of the famous, it is rather remarkable how their adolescent years predicted little or nothing of later success. This is a verification of the finding of G. S. Hall (48) at the turn of the century: "... all these biographic facts, [derived from autobiographies] reveal nothing not found in questionnaire returns from more ordinary youth, so that for our purpose they are only the latter, writ large because superior minds only utter what all more inwardly feel."

   What does a random sampling of some of the great and famous people on this subject reveal? Schooling for Darwin (26) was "simply a blank." He could not master any language. Memorizing Virgil and Homer was a torture. "When I left school," he wrote in his *Life and Letters* (he was sixteen years old), "I was for my age neither high nor low in it; and I believe that I was considered by all my masters and by my father as a very ordinary boy, rather below the common standard in intellect. To my deep mortification my father once said to me, 'You care for nothing but shooting, dogs, and rat-catching, and you will be a disgrace to yourself and all your family.'" Andre Gide (44) recalled that in school "My stupidity . . . sent the whole class into ecstasies . . . I was simply stupid . . . I was still asleep —unawakened—unborn . . . I have no pretensions to precocity. . . ." Herbert Spencer's uncle (88), in a letter to the fourteen-year-old boy's parents, wrote, "Herbert sets himself to work in any difficulty in a very bungling manner; displaying real ignorance of the nature of his own language, as well as the Latin. He never knew much of English Grammar." To this, Spencer (89) himself later wrote, "I am surprised that it was even possible to say as much even as this, seeing how unteachable I continued always to be. As to my ignorance of English grammar, my uncle's statement might have been properly much stronger. . . ."

   As different a personality from Darwin, Gide, and Spencer as can possibly be imagined is Field Marshal Paul von Hindenburg, the German general and last President of the Second Reich. Yet, during his adolescence, he said (51), "I myself was anything but what is known in ordinary life as a model pupil. . . . I had at first little inclination to devote myself particularly to study." Albert Schweitzer (82) graduated from the *Gymnasium* at Mülhausen in Alsace on June 18, 1893, when he was eighteen years old. "In the written papers I did not cut a brilliant figure," he wrote in his autobiography. But he did attract notice in the subject of history. "My otherwise rather mediocre final certificate was . . . adorned with an 'Excellent' in history. . . . " Freud (36) had a similar scholastic record. When he was seventeen and took the *Matura,* a final examination on leaving school, which consisted of two parts, one written, the other oral, he wrote his friend Emil Fluss about the results. "Since I don't wish to keep you on tenterhooks about something so unattractive: for the five papers I got *exc., good, good, good, fair.* In Latin we were given a passage from Virgil which I had read by chance on my own account some time ago; this induced me to do the paper in half the allotted time and thus to forfeit an *exc.* So someone else got the *exc.,* I myself coming second with *good.* . . . " And he continues, in the letter, to rationalize why he did not get better grades in the other examinations. Surely one would expect the signs of genius to appear in adolescence in the school work of Schweitzer and Freud, but their performances were as unspectacular as those of the more "ordinary" adolescents.

With seeming modesty and humor, Joseph Conrad (23) wrote of his youth, "I admit that I was never an average, able boy. As a matter of fact, I was not able at all." Louis Fischer (32), in his biography of Gandhi, found it hard to believe that "the real Gandhi, the Gandhi of history, did not emerge, did not even hint of his existence in the years of schooling and study. Perhaps it is unfair to expect too much of the frail provincial Indian transplanted to metropolitan London at the green age of eighteen. Yet the contrast between the mediocre, unimpressive, handicapped, floundering M. K. Gandhi, attorney-at-law, who left England in 1891, and the Mahatma leader of millions is so great as to suggest that until public services tapped his enormous reserves of intuition, will power, energy, self-confidence, his true personality lay dormant." There was nothing apparent about Alexandre Dumas (29) in early life to suggest that he would grow up out of the ordinary. "Little by little," he wrote in his memoirs, "Adolphe made me share his own hopes and roused in me the ambition to become, if not a Scribe, at least a Jouy, an Arnault or a Delavigne. It was indeed a great ambition, for I had had no proper schooling and knew nothing, and it was not until much later, in 1833 when I published my *Impressions de Voyage,* that people began to see I had genius. In 1820 [when Dumas was eighteen years old] I must confess I had not a shadow of it."

These dozen random illustrations from the adolescent period of men renowned in later life as great novelists, scientists, artists, soldiers, musicians, physicians or statesmen, all seem to reflect an ordinariness that is startling and not at all far removed from the every-day adolescent life most of us have experienced. The genius one might expect to see, or even the hint of giftedness, was apparent neither to the individuals themselves nor to the people closest to them. This suggests that in their adolescent experiences and development, they were not far, if at all, different, from less gifted adolescents. The criticism, then, that autobiographies are most often the work of those who have been in some area unusually gifted, of men with genius, and thus may not faithfully reflect the population at large, would not seem valid when applied to the adolescent period. The universal experience of adolescence is again demonstrated. It is the exceptional person who may write a personal document, but it is the exceptional that illuminates the normal. The questions, "What am I? Whither am I going? What *is* this place? Are these things *real?* What is the precise relation between myself and the not-self? Was I always, shall I be for ever? Can I be merely of the Now? Such questions as these are perhaps brooded over more frequently than we suspect. But in general they are asked in private, and adjourned [63]."

REFERENCES

1. Allport, Gordon W. *The Use of Personal Documents in Psychological Science.* New York: Social Science Research Council, 1942, pp. xii, 4.
2. *Ibid.,* pp. 59, 143-145.
3. *Ibid.,* pp. 69-75, 178.
4. *Ibid.,* p. 125.
5. *Ibid.,* p. 147.
6. Anderson, Sherwood. *Memoirs.* New York: Harcourt, Brace & Co., 1942, p. 19.
7. Augustine, Saint. *Confessions.* New York: Liveright, 1942, x, 3.

8. Ausubel, David P. *Theory and Problems of Adolescent Development.* New York: Grune & Stratton, 1954, p. xiv.
9. *Ibid.,* p. 49.
10. Berdyaev, Nicholas. *Dream and Reality; An Essay in Autobiography.* New York: Macmillan, 1950, pp. ix-x.
11. *Ibid.,* p. xii.
12. Beres, David. The contribution of psycho-analysis to the biography of the artist. *Int. J. Psycho-Anal.,* 40:29, 1959.
13. *Ibid.,* p. 35.
14. Bergler, Edmund. *The Writer and Psychoanalysis.* Garden City, N.Y.: Doubleday, 1950.
15. Bloch, Herbert A., & Niederhoffer, Arthur. *The Gang. A Study in Adolescent Behavior.* New York: Philosophical Library, 1958, p. 11.
16. Bonaparte, Marie. A defence of biography. *Int. J. Psycho-Anal.,* 20: 240, 1939.
17. Bottome, Phyllis. *Search for a Soul.* New York: Harcourt, Brace, 1948, p. ix.
18. Burgess, E. W. The family and the person. In: *Personality and the Social Group.* Chicago: University of Chicago Press, 1929, p. 133.
19. Campbell, C. Macfie. Psychology and biography. *Amer. J. Psychiat.,* 10:855-856, 1931.
20. Cantril, Hadley, & Bumstead, Charles H. *Reflections on the Human Venture.* New York: New York University Press, 1960, pp. 2, 3.
21. Cartwright, Dorin, & French, John R. P., Jr. The reliability of life history studies. Character and Pers., 8:119, 1939.
22. Chaudhuri, Nirad C. *The Autobiography of an Unknown Indian.* New York: Macmillan, 1951, p. 127.
23. Conrad, Joseph. *Autobiography.* In: *An Introduction to Conrad,* Frank W. Cushwa (Ed.). Garden City, N. Y.: Doubleday, Doran, 1933, p. 25.
24. Cowley, Abraham. Of my self. In: *Abraham Cowley, The Essays and Other Prose Writings,* Alfred B. Gough (Ed.). Oxford: Oxford University Press, 1915, p. 215.
25. Dana, Richard Henry, Jr. *An Autobiographical Sketch (1815-1842).* Hamden, Conn.: Shoe String Press, 1953, p. 30.
26. Darwin, Charles. *The Life and Letters of Charles Darwin.* New York: D. Appleton, 1888, Vol. I, p. 30.
27. Dell, Floyd. *Homecoming. An Autobiography.* New York: Farrar & Rinehart, 1933, p. 79.
28. Dilthey, Wilhelm. Quoted in Hodges, H. A., *Wilhelm Dilthey: An Introduction.* London: Routledge & Kegan Paul, 1944, p. 28.

29. Dumas, Alexandre. *The Road to Monte Carlo*. New York: Charles Scribner's Sons, 1956, p. 44.
30. Ellis, Havelock. *My Life*. Boston: Houghton Mifflin, 1939, p. viii.
31. Erikson, Erik H. The problem of ego identity. *Psychol. Issues*, 1:110, 1959.
32. Fischer, Louis. *The Life of Mahatma Gandhi*. New York: Harper, 1950, pp. 28-29.
33. Freud, Anna. Adolescence. In: *The Psychoanalytic Study of the Child*, Ruth S. Eissler et al. (Eds.). New York: International Universities Press, 1958, Vol. XIII, pp. 259-260.
34. *Ibid.*, p. 263.
35. Freud, Ernst L., (Ed.). *Letters of Sigmund Freud*. New York: Basic Books, 1960, pp. 3-4.
36. Freud, Martin. *Sigmund Freud: Father and Man*. New York: Vanguard Press, 1958, p. 54.
37. Freud, Sigmund. Analysis terminable and interminable, in *Collected Papers*. New York: Basic Books, 1959, Vol. V, pp. 356-357.
38. Freud, Sigmund. *An Autobiographical Study*. New York: Brentano's, 1927.
39. Freud, Sigmund. *The Interpretation of Dreams*. New York: Basic Books, 1958, p. 43.
40. Freud, Sigmund. *The Problem of Lay-Analysis*. New York: Brentano's, 1927, p. 97.
41. Freud, Sigmund. Screen memories, in *Collected Papers*. New York: Basic Books, 1959, Vol. V, p. 47.
42. Garraty, John A. The interrelations of psychology and biography. *Psychol. Bull.*, 51:580, 1954.
43. Gibbon, Edward. *Autobiography*. New York: Dutton Everyman's Library, 1911, p. 1.
44. Gide, André. *If It Die*. New York: Modern Library Paperbacks, 1935, pp. 50, 51, 60.
45. Gottschalk, Louis. The historian and the historical document. In: *The Use of Personal Documents in History, Anthropology and Sociology*, L. Gottschalk et al. (Eds.). New York: Social Science Research Council, 1943, p. 16.
46. Haines, Helen E. *Living with Books*. New York: Columbia University Press, 1950, p. 255.
47. Hall, G. Stanley. *Adolescence*. New York: Appleton-Century-Crofts, 1904, Vol. II, pp. 535-536.
48. *Ibid.*, p. 563.
49. Hamerton, Philip G. *An Autobiography (1834-1858)*. Boston: Roberts Bros., 1897, pp. 1-2.

50. Hazlitt, William. *Hazlitt Painted by Himself.* London: C. & J. Temple, 1948, p. 14.
51. Hindenberg, Paul, Marshal von. *Out of My Life.* New York: Harper & Bros., 1921, Vol. I, p. 16.
52. Hitschmann, Edward. *Great Men.* New York: International Universities Press, 1956, p. 7.
53. Hudson, W. H. *Far Away and Long Ago. A History of My Early Life.* New York: E. P. Dutton & Co., 1918, pp. 225-226.
54. Inhelder, Bärbel, & Piaget, Jean. *The Growth of Logical Thinking: From Childhood to Adolescence.* New York: Basic Books, 1958, p. 344.
55. Jones, Ernest. Foreword to Hitschmann, Edward, *Great Men.* New York: International Universities Press, 1956, p. vii.
56. Jones, Ernest. *Free Associations.* New York: Basic Books, 1959.
57. Karpeles, Gustav, (Ed.). *Heinrich Heine's Memoirs.* London: John Lane Co., 1910, p. 4.
58. Kris, Ernst. The personal myth. A problem in psychoanalytic technique. *J. Amer. Psychoanal. Assoc.,* 4:653-681, 1956.
59. Lee, H. B. On the aesthetic states of the mind. *Psychiatry,* 10:281, 1947.
60. Leonard, William Ellery. *The Locomotive-God.* New York: Century Co., 1927, pp. 3-4.
61. *Ibid.,* p. 127.
62. Longaker, Mark. *Contemporary Biography.* New York: Appleton-Century, 1953, p. 12.
63. Mare, Walter de la. *Early One Morning in the Spring: Chapters on Children and on Childhood As It is Revealed in Particular In Early Memories and in Early Writings.* New York: Macmillan, 1935, p. 165.
64. Milne, A. A. *Autobiography.* New York: E. P. Dutton, 1939, p. ix.
65. Misch, Georg. *A History of Autobiography in Antiquity.* Cambridge, Mass.: Harvard University Press, 1951, Vol. I, p. 5.
66. *Ibid.,* p. 9.
67. *Ibid.,* p. 12.
68. *Ibid.,* Vol. II, p. 374.
69. *Ibid.,* p. 540.
70. *Ibid.,* pp. 635-636.
71. Muir, Edwin. *An Autobiography.* New York: William Sloan Associates, 1954, p. 54.
72. Newman, Ernest (Ed.). *Memoirs of Hector Berlioz.* New York: Alfred A. Knopf, 1932, p. xi.

73. Pearson, Gerald H. J. *Adolescence and the Conflict of Generations.* New York: W. W. Norton, 1958, pp. 16-17.

74. Redfield, Robert. Foreword to Allport, Gordon W., *The Use of Personal Documents in Psychological Science.* New York: Social Science Research Council, 1942, p. viii.

74a. Reik, Theodor. *Fragment of a Great Confession.* New York: Farrar, Straus, 1949.

75. Rice, John A. *I Came out of the Eighteenth Century.* New York: Harper & Bros., 1942, pp. 186, 200.

76. Rousseau, Jean Jacques. *Confessions.* New York: Pocket Books, 1957, p. 78.

77. *Ibid.,* p. 81.

78. Sachs, Hanns. *The Creative Unconscious.* Cambridge, Mass.: Sci-Art Publishers, 1942.

79. Saul, Leon J., Snyder, Thoburn R., & Sheppard, Edith. On earliest memories. *Psychoanal. Quart.,* 25:229, 1956.

80. Schachtel, Ernest G. On memory and childhood amnesia. *Psychiatry,* 10:24, 1947.

81. Schopenhauer, Arthur. Quoted in Johnson, Edgar (Ed.), *One Mighty Torrent.* New York: Macmillan Co., 1955, p. 98.

82. Schweitzer, Albert. *Out of My Life and Thought.* New York: Henry Holt, 1933, p. 4.

83. Scott, Sir Walter. *Memoirs of the Early Life of Sir Walter Scott, Written by Himself.* London: Macmillan, Vol. I, p. 19.

84. Shaw, George Bernard. *Sixteen Self Sketches.* New York: Dodd, Mead, 1949, p. 19.

85. *Ibid.,* p. 71.

86. Sherif, Musafer, & Cantril, Hadley. *The Psychology of Ego-Involvements.* New York: John Wiley, 1947.

87. Shumaker, Wayne. *English Autobiography. Its Emergence, Material and Form.* Berkeley: University of California Press, 1954, pp. 48, 50.

88. Spencer, Herbert. *An Autobiography.* New York: D. Appleton, 1904, Vol. I, p. 122.

89. *Ibid.,* pp. 122-123.

90. Trollope, Anthony. *An Autobiography.* London: Humphrey Milford, 1941, pp. 1-2.

91. Wells, H. G. *Experiment in Autobiography.* New York: Macmillan, 1934, p. 19.

92. Yarmolinsky, Avrahm. *Turgenev.* New York: Orion Press, 1959, p. 29.

CHAPTER ONE

The Common Core
of Psychobiological Problems

The central interest of the psychology of adolescence, Dennis (7) suggests, is to portray the effects of biological adolescence upon the behavior of the individual. If adolescence is a physical phenomenon, marked by rapid physical and physiological growth, then the sexual, emotional, intellectual, and social development of the period are inescapably interwoven with it.

Underlying the typical adolescent manifestations of ambivalence and contradictoriness, sexual drives, egocentrism, instability of behavior, emotional lability, rebellion, need for independence, identity confusion, self-consciousness, vocational disorientation, preoccupation with health, fear of failure, and the myriad other adolescent characteristics are the fundamental and universal biological processes of pubescence. Biologic development brings in its wake great quantitative and qualitative changes, "in both physiologic and psychologic spheres, and as a result of these changes the adolescent ego is confronted with new difficulties. The emotions, because of their close connection with the instinctual life, are more affected by the process of growth than any other part of the personality [8]."

Perhaps it is Ausubel (2) who has rendered the best expression of the common core of psychobiological problems confronting all adolescents in all cultural settings. In the quotation which follows, he asserts that certain physiological and anatomical changes are everywhere associated with the occurrence of adolescence.

In the present era of psychological sophistication it requires no more than a casual acquaintance with the facts of adolescence to realize that this stage of human development is a biosocial phenomenon. Biologically, it is a period of accelerated physical and sexual maturation that man experiences *in common* with all other mammalian species. Its social foundations, however, are manifested in the *contrast* it presents to pubescence in these other species. For everywhere human adolescence is an institutionalized phenomenon, a socially recognized period of transitional status; and the specific form that it takes varies with differences in culturally-held values. The infrahuman pubescent, on the other hand, unostentatiously assumes an adult role in intra-species life as soon as he is physiologically able, without receiving any explicit group invitation or sanction. There is no formalized period of waiting and no socially prescribed form that his new behavior is required to take. The behavioral concomitants of his physiological maturation are regulated by biogenetic factors that are uniform for all members of a given species.

The terms *psychobiological* and *psychosocial,* however, imply concern with only the psychological or behavioral consequences of the biological and social factors influencing adolescent development rather than with the nature of these factors *per se* or with their other ramifications. And consistent with the theoretical orientation we have adopted toward adolescence, we shall consider psychobiological and psychosocial data not as discrete ends in themselves but only in relation to the respective contributions they make toward reshaping personality structure.

The distinction between *psychobiological* and *psychosocial* insofar as human development is concerned rests with the level of generality of a given phenomenon or principle. When a certain amount of uniformity prevails in the *process* of development (irrespective of specific differences in form, content, or degree attributable to cultural variation), it is meaningful to use the former term. The latter term, on the other hand, refers to those of less general aspects of development which reflect the influence of the particular values or social conditions prevailing within a given culture.[1]

That adolescence should be characterized by a common core of psychobiological problems in a wide diversity of cultural settings is hardly

---

[1] The use of the term *psychosocial* in this context differs from the more conventional usage in which reference is made only to the psychological accompaniments or consequences of social factors. As used here, social phenomena can give rise to either psychosocial or psychobiological effects depending on the generality (universality) of the developmental process involved.

surprising. There are a number of reasons for this. First, there are uniformities that spring from the fact that adolescence is universally a transitional stage in personality development. Transitional periods by their very nature share many properties in common and generate characteristic constellations of psychological problems that inevitably arise when individuals are confronted by radical changes in their biosocial status. For example, the very rapidity of growth during adolescence, its unevenness over various aspects of development, the abruptness of its onset, and the anxiety and disorientation attending any sudden shift in status are bound to constitute a set of developmental common denominators regardless of differences in degree conditioned by cultural factors.

A second source of psychobiological uniformity in the problems of adolescent development is to be found in the common group of physiological and anatomical changes that are everywhere associated with the occurrence of adolescence. These changes give rise to new types of drives, emotions, and states of awareness. Granted that these psychological phenomena will assume different forms and be differently regulated in different cultures, the fact remains that there is a universal need for adolescents to adapt to the very presence of these bodily changes and urges, to overcome feelings of bewilderment and uneasiness at their strangeness, and to subject them to control and direction in ways that are compatible with social expectations. For the first time since early childhood, potent, emergent drives of organic origin require initial handling and socialization; and like all other drives, the direction of regulation proceeds from the relatively diffuse, experimental, and non-specific mode of gratification to the more highly differentiated condition where to be adequate the form of need-satisfaction must meet increasingly more stringent requirements of specificity.

Because of the transitional nature of adolescence and the suddenness of the onset of puberty, the individual is aware of his body as he never was before. The body becomes for the adolescent a "symbol of self" (37), and how he looks upon his physical self may determine the kind of self-esteem he feels. In his autobiography, *Poetry and Truth*, Goethe (10) points out, "To no one can his own form be repugnant; the ugliest as well as the most beautiful has the right of enjoying his own presence, and as kind feeling beautifies, and every one looks into the mirror with kind feeling, so it can be maintained that every one must look at himself with complacency even when he wishes to resist the feeling.''

But the adolescent usually has not yet reached that point of emotional stability where he can accept such a philosophy, as the following passages will illustrate. Mozart (25) was fourteen years old when he wrote a letter to his mother and sister indicating his self-consciousness about his height.

Rome, April 14th, 1770

Praise and thanks be to God, I and my wretched pen are well and I kiss Mamma and Nannerl a thousand or 1000 times. I only wish that my sister were in Rome, for this town would certainly please her, as St. Peter's church and many other things in Rome are *regular*. The most beautiful flowers are now being carried past in the street—so Papa has just told me. I am a fool, as everyone knows. Oh, I am having a hard time, for in our rooms there is only one bed and so Mamma can well imagine that I get no sleep with Papa. I am looking forward to our new quarters. I have just now drawn St. Peter with his keys and with him St. Paul with his sword and St. Luke with my sister and so forth. I have had the honour of kissing St. Peter's foot in St. Peter's church and as I have the misfortune to be so small, I, that same old dunce,

WOLFGANG MOZART,
had to be lifted up.

Another great composer, Wagner (35), was so overwhelmed with shame the summer of 1827, when he was fourteen years old, because he was sunburned that he refused to see anybody for two days until he could treat the condition.

The remainder of our journey was very fatiguing, and the joy I felt when I at last beheld Prague from the summit of a hill, at about an hour's distance, simply beggars description. Approaching the suburbs, we were for the second time met by a splendid carriage, from which my sister Ottilie's two lovely friends called out to me in astonishment. They had recognised me immediately, in spite of my terribly sunburnt face, blue linen blouse, and bright red cotton cap. Overwhelmed with shame, and with my heart beating like mad, I could hardly utter a word, and hurried away to my mother's to attend at once to the restoration of my sunburnt complexion. To this task I devoted two whole days, during which I swathed my face in parsley poultices; and not till then did I seek the pleasures of society. When, on the return journey, I looked back once more on Prague from the same hilltop, I burst into tears, flung myself on the earth, and for a long time could not be induced by my astonished companion to pursue the journey. I was downcast for the rest of the way, and we arrived home in Dresden without any further adventures.

A person's physique represents, to a high degree, his image of himself. Marie Bashkirtseff reveals in her diary an essentially skeptical adolescent, with ambitions to conquer the universe, a yearning for recognition as a female and as an artist, full of the ambivalences characteristic of the period, and yet with a realism of perception and self-concept not found in many youths. In this entry from her diary (4), dated August 10, 1876 when she was sixteen years old, she compares her present self to that of her earlier years, and likes what she finds.

A cup of broth, a hot *calatch*, and some fresh caviar, there is an incomparable commencement of a dinner. The *calatch* is a species of bread, but one must go to Moscow to have an idea of it, and the *calatch* of Moscow is almost as celebrated as the Kremlin. With one portion of *assetrine,* I was given two immense slices, which in another country would be divided into four (it is needless to say that I did not eat it all). Furthermore, I had a veal cutlet fifty centimetres square, surrounded with small peas and potatoes, an entire chicken, and a saucer filled with caviar, representing "a half portion."

Uncle Etienne laughed and told the servants that in Italy there would be enough for four. The servant, tall and thin as Gianetto Doria, immovable as an Englishman, answered without budging, and without changing expression, that this was the reason of the small stature and thinness of Italians; but the Russians, he added, like to eat plenty, that is why they are strong. On this, the immovable brute deigned to smile, and went out like a wooden puppet.

The quantity is not the only advantage of the eatables here, for they are of the most exquisite quality. When we eat well, we are in good humor; when we are in good humor, we regard happiness with more joy, and misfortune with more philosophy, and we feel agreeably disposed toward our neighbor. Exaggerated greediness is a monstrosity in a woman, but a little greediness is as necessary as intellect, as dress, without taking into account that good and simple food maintains the health, and consequently youth, the freshness of the skin, and the roundness of the form. Witness my body. Marie Sapogenikoff says, with reason, that, for such a body, a much more beautiful face is required, and. bear in mind that I am far from being homely. When I think of what I shall be when I am twenty, I am filled with delight. At thirteen I was too fat, and was taken for sixteen. Now I am slender, well-formed, and remarkably curved, perhaps too much so. I compare myself to all the statues, and I find nothing so well curved, or so large across the hips as I. Is it a defect? But the shoulders require to have a little more roundness—But what was I saying? Oh, yes, that I asked for tea. I was served a *samovar*, twenty-four pieces of sugar, and cream enough for five cups of tea. Both exquisite. I always liked tea, even when bad. I drank five cups (small) with cream, and three without cream, like a true Russian.

The adolescent's preoccupation with his body, as indicated in Marie's constant narcissistic comparison with all the statues she saw, often produces anxieties, particularly as the uncertainties associated with the youth's sexual development are connected with his physical growth. The anxieties the adolescent has about his body can be persistent and sometimes emotionally disabling. Grant Richards (31) tells how he was worried for years over a possible facial disfigurement after a fight with a fellow thirteen-year-old in 1885.

. . . . More fun—in retrospect—more punishing, and more complete was one fight in which I was a principal. We, another boy and I, had begun scrapping on the way up in the train, and it was settled by our elders that we would fight the matter out that afternoon on the way down. The compartment would make a ring of sufficient size if our aiders and abettors stood on the seats; the arrival of stations would serve as an indication that a round had come to an end. Whether either of us won I cannot say. I do remember that we were both of us a little damaged about the face. I at least had a black eye and Dodson, eliciting some of the truth, had me sit as a culprit in his own room. Not having even the solace of a book to read I took to fingering my bruise, and discovered to my dismay that the bony edge of the eye-socket was (as, I afterwards discovered, it always is) slightly irregular. Had I destroyed the symmetry of my face for ever, just for the fun of a fight? The fact worried me for years. . . .

In more recent times, the adolescent dismay with his appearance is illustrated in the diary entry of David S. Kogan (19). On October

9, 1944, at the age of fifteen, he wrote, "I feel self-conscious. I don't want to be handsome, but I hate my present appearance. Weak, pale, small ears, big nose, 'peach fuzz,' weak chin. Now my mouth is out of shape and I cannot smile, for Dr. Singer put my brace back yesterday." Nearly ten months later, on July 31, 1945, the peach fuzz was to come off and the day "was one of the landmarks in my life, for on this day I took my first shave. We went up to the guest house and there I carefully watched Larry shave himself, and after he finished, I began to lather up my face. Just then Bob, the camp chauffeur, came in and warned me against the move with the wise expression of a man of twenty-five—but it was to no avail. During the whole evening my face felt drawn taut—dry and uncomfortable, but it was an experience I shall never forget [20]."

Most adolescents recall their first shave for it is symbolic of manhood achieved and identifiable masculinity. The youthful beatniks who today sport beards to assert their sex and maturity had their counterparts in previous centuries. Leigh Hunt (1784-1859) had a book of poetry published at the precocious age of fifteen. It met with critical and popular acclaim but at a party he attended, he met with his comeuppance.

> A mortification that I encountered at a house in Cavendish Square affected me less, though it surprised me a good deal more. I had been held up, as usual, to the example of the young gentlemen and the astonishment of the young ladies, when, in the course of the dessert, one of mine host's daughters, a girl of exuberant spirits, and not of the austerest breeding, came up to me, and, as if she had discovered that I was not so young as I pretended to be, exclaimed, "What a beard you have got!" at the same time convincing herself of the truth of her discovery by taking hold of it! Had I been a year or two older, I should have taken my revenge. As it was, I know not how I behaved, but the next morning I hastened to have a beard no longer.
>
> I was now a man, and resolved not to be out of countenance next time. Not long afterwards, my grandfather, sensible of the new fame in his family, but probably alarmed at the fruitless consequences to which it might lead, sent me word, that if I would come to Philadelphia, "he would make a man of me." I sent word, in return, that "men grew in England as well as America," an answer which repaid me for the loss of my repartee at Dr. Raine's [13].

Rudyard Kipling (18) had a similar but not nearly as embarrassing a situation happen to him. At seventeen, he was attending the United Services College which he describes as a "company promoted by poor officers and the like for the cheap education of their sons. . . . It was largely a caste-school—some seventy-five per cent of us had been born outside England and hoped to follow their fathers in the Army." In 1882, he continued, "I was physically precocious. In my last term I had been thrusting an unlovely chin at C——— in form. At last he blew up, protested he could no longer abide the sight, and ordered me to shave. I carried this word to my House-Master. He, who had long looked on me as a cultivated sink of iniquities, brooded over this confirmation of his suspicions, and gave me a written order on a Bideford [the town nearest the college] barber for a razor, etc. I kindly invited my friends to come and help, and lamented for three miles the burden of compulsory shaving. There were no *ripostes*. There was no ribaldry. But why Stalky and Turkey did not cut their throats experimenting with the apparatus I do not understand."

There were no *ripostes* and there was no ribaldry because shaving is a puberty rite, a ceremony of initiation into manhood, a ritual that calls for no levity. The symbolism of the first shave, whether it involves unconscious castration or a maso-sadistic impulse, requires the utmost seriousness for the adolescent as well as an audience to hallow the ceremony. However, the adolescent suffering from acne, blackheads and other skin blemishes, has heightened sensitivity about his appearance and prefers isolation to anyone's company. Havelock Ellis (1865-1939) wrote, in perhaps characteristic British understatement, "My face was not remarkable in adolescence, and the occasional presence of acne pimples was a source of distress which increased the humble self-consciousness I felt concerning my personal appearance [9]."

Today's adolescents are susceptible to every "medication" and every technique suggested for the riddance of the skin eruption. The Brazilian adolescent, Helena Morley (24), was a willing participant nearly seventy years ago in a novel way of taking care of her particular problem. On Tuesday, March 20, 1894, she entered in her diary:

I had a pimple on my face that bothered grandma and Aunt Madge a great deal, and even Dona Gabriela's family. Yesterday Clélia decided to take it off in a way she'd learned. She took a redhot coal and threw it in a glass of water; the coal hissed, she opened it up and put it on the pimple, hot. She did it three or four times and the pimple got soft. Then she squeezed it and enough tallow came out to make a candle. When I got home mama called me an idiot because I let anyone do anything they want to me. I said, "I know if I'm an idiot or not. The pimple was growing and it could have got as big as an orange and the Senhora and papa just kept saying over and over that it wasn't anything. I was the one who was getting homelier every day. I'll let anybody do anything they want to if it's for my good." Last night my face was very swollen and Clélia was very worried, but I told her that it wasn't anything and not to worry. Today it's almost gone already.

Anticipating today's women by two thousand years, the women of ancient Egypt concentrated on eye appeal, using kohl to extend the lines of the eyebrows and lashes to great lengths. They also wore green eyeshadow, so popular with adolescents today, to achieve a sensual style. The Greek satirist, Lucian, wrote in the second century, "You dye your hair, but you will not dye your age, nor will you stretch the wrinkles out of your cheeks. . . . Why are you mad? A paint and wash will never make a Hecuba or a Helen." Beauties of the Roman Empire wanted to be curly-headed blondes. The wealthy wore wigs, imported from Germany, false eyebrows, and painted their faces with white lead, causing the poet Juvenal to lament, "Your charms are enclosed in a hundred different pots, and your face does not go to bed with you. . . . " By the Middle Ages, ideas of beauty had changed drastically. Inspired, perhaps, by a chivalric age, women strove to sanctify their mortal charms. They plucked their eyebrows, shaved their hairlines to ennoble their foreheads and powdered their faces to achieve a pallid look that reached its peak in the Renaissance. Sixteenth-century women took their cues from Queen Elizabeth I. Like her, they used henna on their hair and masked their faces with chalk-white paste, a device that, in the Queen's own case, was possibly intended to conceal a bad complexion. In the extravagance of pre-Revolutionary France, wigs attained the monumentality of seascapes (36), an approximation of which is seen in the current "beehive" coiffure sported by today's adolescent girls—along with dirty white sneakers and no stockings.

The adolescent's sensitivity to his appearance and awareness of his bodily changes are generally reinforced by well-meaning but insensitive adults who insist on making some comment about these changes. Don C. Talayesva (33), the Hopi Indian who was born in Oraibi, Arizona in 1890, discovered this when he was fifteen years old. "When I returned home in the summer, the people joked about my voice, which was changing." Simone de Beauvoir's father "would pass remarks about my complexion, my acne, my clumsiness which only made my misery worse and aggravated my bad habits." Unwittingly, the adult manifests his hostility because of his unconscious anxiety about being replaced by the adolescent. By belittling the tell-tale marks of growing physical maturity, the adult is actually attempting to belittle the heightened sexuality of a possible rival. Thus, in diminishing the growing glamour of the adolescent, the adult is trying to reduce his own anxieties.

Most adolescents are discomfited and disquieted about their bodies because of the bewilderingly unequal rates of growth in different parts and organs of the body. John A. Rice (29), one of the founders of Black Mountain College in North Carolina, wrote that at the age of thirteen he "lived in a between-world, no longer a small boy and not yet nearly a man. My hands and feet grew farther and farther away from my body and set up on their own, reminding me of their distant connection by getting in the way and declining generally to do what they were told. I would have been glad to get rid of them and go handless and footless through life, and did not realize that they were as unhappy as I, hiding themselves under chairs and tables." Rice's personification of his extremities is a reflection of the adolescent's feelings of wonderment at the changes taking place within him, for it seems to him that while these things are happening it is something alien and removed which thus produces a set of almost entirely new sensations. But within a year, at the age of fourteen, Rice (30) was able to say, "When I returned from the fitting school I was a grown-up young man, I told myself. My hands and feet had tentatively decided against secession, my voice no longer jumped suddenly out of register, and I wore long pants without confusion."

According to Inhelder and Piaget (14), "On the average, puberty appears at about the same ages in all races and in all societies, although there is widespread opinion to the contrary." While this statement is generally accepted, it is also recognized that just as there are variations in bodily changes within the individual, so are there differences in the rate of growth from adolescent to adolescent. Adolescents grow unevenly, not at a smooth, consistent pace. When two childhood friends achieve puberty at disparate times, the friendship is bound to suffer because of the effects of the glandular changes on the affective and sexual life. Najmeh Najafi (26), an Iranian girl, illustrates this in her autobiography. "I felt that Safire had been a traitor to our volleyball team by growing up and falling in love. We had had such fun with the volleyball, playing, running, jumping, screaming. But now when we got together to play, the girls would rather sit in a tight little group and talk about marriage, bridal dresses, homes, boys. Mostly about boys. Disgusted, I got up and ran around bouncing the ball myself. 'Are you a boy or a girl?' Safire asked me, half cross. 'Well, one thing, I am not thinking of marriage,' I said."

At whatever age the first menstruation occurs, the girl's reactions are colored by her deeper feelings and fantasies about femininity, sexuality, and the differences between the sexes (21), as the above passage indicates. The achievement of puberty, of which menstruation is one factor, normally brings with it tendencies toward genital and heterosexual interests and activities. Menstruation is generally considered by adolescents to be a distinct dividing line between girls who are sexually mature and those who are still regarded as prepubescent.

In many primitive tribes the menarche is a time for celebration and festivities, as is illustrated in the section from the autobiography of a Papago Indian woman later in this chapter. While it is a "big time" and a "happy time" with the Papagos when a girl comes of age, the first menstrual period of girls in many other cultures is not so celebrated. Rather it is a time of physical and emotional anguish, as Emma Goldman (11) described it happening to her in 1880, in Russia.

The approach of puberty gave me my first consciousness of the effect of men on me. I was eleven then. Early one summer day I woke up in great agony. My head, spine, and legs ached as if they were being pulled asunder. I called for Mother. She drew back my bed-covers, and suddenly I felt a stinging pain in my face. She had struck me. I let out a shriek, fastening on Mother terrified eyes. "This is necessary for a girl," she said, "when she becomes a woman, as a protection against disgrace." She tried to take me in her arms, but I pushed her back. I was writhing in pain and I was too outraged for her to touch me. "I am going to die," I howled, "I want the *Feldscher*" (assistant doctor). The *Feldscher* was sent for. He was a young man, a new-comer in our village. He examined me and gave me something to put me to sleep. Thenceforth my dreams were of the *Feldscher*.

Another commonly recognized characteristic of adolescence is the increased need for nourishment. An enlarged stomach capacity and glandular changes brought on by puberty generally result in a ravenous appetite, although rapid shifts from over-eating to under-eating are common. Catherine E. Havens (12), who began her diary at the age of ten in 1849, at one point in her adolescence made the following entry: "I love cup custards and I ate two before dinner for fear there would not be any left for me, and then I had to eat another at dessert, for fear my sin would find me out, for they all know how fond I am of them, and it made me so sick I can never look at one again."

The adolescent's constant need for food may be a recapitulation of the oral stage of life, when a great deal of pleasure and comfort was obtained by putting things into one's mouth. The gum and betel-nut chewing, the long phone conversations, the endless chatter and discussions on life's meaning, are symptomatic of these oral needs. Harriet Monroe (1860-1936), the great American poetess and editor, was profoundly and morbidly affected by the suicide of a classmate. She was beset by all kinds of psychosomatic ailments during her late childhood and early adolescence. One of the ways in which she coped with the trauma was by stuffing herself with incredibly huge meals and with snacks in between.

Modern specialists might find reason enough for this illness in the heavy unregulated diet I had always indulged in. Those breakfasts of ham and eggs, or chops and potatoes, with hot rolls or steaming piles of buckwheat cakes! Those luncheons between school sessions—more meat and potatoes belike, more fancy breads, with a finish of flaky-crusted pie or rich cake and preserves! Those dinners, with a roast or steak or perhaps game birds cooked by a mistress of the art, topped by a rich pudding. Green vegetables were served at our table, but I would have none of them, and cereals became a later fashion. Berries we ate lavishly, but other fruits were a between-meals indulgence—there was usually a bowl of apples and grapes on the hall table, also a box of candy somewhere around. Today no child would be allowed the amount of meat and pastry which were a matter of course with me. No wonder my body rebelled, starved as it was for vitamins, over-loaded with sweets and proteins [22].

John Cowper Powys (27) recollects "perfectly how one night after some quarrel with Littleton [his younger brother], and when, too, I was burning with an erotic fever that none of the treasures in my gold and ebony chest could assuage, I tried to overcome the two most formidable of human passions—anger and desire—by aban-donment to the vice of pure gluttony. In that one night I ravenously devoured a whole sponge-cake."

The last characteristic of physical development in adolescence which shall be dealt with here and which generates a common psy-chological problem (with particular reference to boys) involves the individual's feelings about his physical prowess, athletic ability, and need to commit acts of daring or recklessness. The universality of these factors is illustrated in the succeeding passages, both in this section and in the following, longer examples. They range in time from the turn of the sixteenth century to the present and in space from Italy to Japan.

Michel de Montaigne (1533-1592), a latter-day Erasmus, wrote in his *Essays* (23), which belong to the kind of autobiographical litera-ture that Cellini introduced to the West and whose contemporary he was, "In truth, the games of children are not games, but should be looked upon as their most serious business." The adolescent pro-clivity to games and feats of daring has its roots in unconscious and unmet needs. The daring may "be motivated by a sense of danger and misgivings which the youthful novice experiences in contem-plating his entrance into a new world, mysterious and strange, and in which he regards himself as an interloper. . . . Recklessness among young boys is frequently practiced as a deliberate attempt to acquire a serious wound so that the scarred tissue can be conspicuously dis-played later on. As a prelude to such a 'mark of distinction,' it is interesting to note the pride with which the young child displays his bandages and wound-wrappings [5]."

An early illustration is to be found in the autobiography of Jerome Cardan, the Italian physician who was born in 1501. By nature timid, afraid of thunder, firearms, swords, swimming and riding, Cardan found compensation in roaming about the streets at night, disguised and armed, despite the drastic prohibitions of the civic authorities. Here is an example of fantasy-building, wherein his conscious shrinking from danger and his lack of self-confidence found compensatory expression in the fantasy of being a bold and venturesome swashbuckler. Cardan (6) wrote:

> At a very early period in my life, I began to apply myself seriously to the practice of swordsmanship of every class, until, by persistent training, I had acquired some standing even among the most daring. I used to exercise myself with sword alone, or with sword and shields of various sizes and shapes—oblong, round, large or small; and I learned to handle as well, dagger, knife, spear, or lance. As a lad, also, with a sword on my hip and a cloak flung dashingly around me, I used to mount a wooden horse. Another feat I acquired was how to snatch an unsheathed dagger, myself unarmed, from the one who held it. I trained myself by running and jumping, for in these exercises I was reasonably strong. My arms were rather too thin for performances demanding much muscle. In riding, swimming, and in the use of firearms I had little confidence in myself; I actually feared the discharge of a gun as if it were the wrath of God; for timid by nature, I stimulated courage by an artificial show of bravery, and to that end myself enrolled in a company of emergency troopers.

Some two hundred and fifty years later, Vittorio Alfieri (1), poet and playwright, considered to be among the top dozen of Italy's great writers after Dante, Petrarch, Ariosto, and Tasso, described some of the "foolish pranks" in which he participated.

> Having contracted a friendship with many youths nearly my own age, who resided in the city with their governors, we frequently hired wretched hacks, and made excursions into the country, during which we were oftener than once in danger of breaking our necks. Not unfrequently did we gallop down from the Hermitage des Camaldules to Turin, the road between which is paved and full of flint stones,—

an enterprise which no consideration would afterwards have tempted me to undertake, even with the best horses. We have frequently pursued, at full gallop, my valet on his Rosinante, instead of a stag, in the wood between the Po and the Doria. Often, having taken the bridle from his horse, did we follow him at full speed, hallooing, and whipping our horses, imitating the sounds of the French horn, leaping over ditches, and fording the Duria at its confluence with the Po; in short, we committed so many foolish pranks that at length no one would lend us his horses at any price.

How similar are Alfieri's "wretched hacks" to the souped-up jalopies of the present-day hot-rodder. And how alike are his galloping "at full speed" to the drag races of today, the cross-country motorcycle brigades, and the boisterous "hallooing" of the attention-seeking adolescent of all generations. For the hot rod addict, the car is the symbolic embodiment of masculine power and physical ability. Even the name, "hot rod," has significant symbolism as an expression of sexual potency. In addition, hot-rodding, drag-racing, and the intuitive appeal of such slogans as "sliding rides" and "torpedo take-off" may be the outcome of unsolved childhood problems, particularly those affecting the relation with parents. The thrill the adolescent feels from swift acceleration may be based on the desire to recapture the past delights of infancy, such as being rocked, tossed, dandled, swung, or just held comfortably in mother's arms. If the young speed demon is an orphan, he may even follow the urge to rejoin dearly loved parents lost through death or other separation. If there is a hidden dream of a dead mother or father, surely a powerful enough dragster or hot-rodder will overcome the limitations of time and space and reach his lost parents.

The need to prove oneself to his peers so as not to be considered effeminate or "chicken" is a time-honored preoccupation and occupation with adolescents. Any marked physical deficiency among boys has a decidedly unfavorable impact upon personality and social adjustment. To participate actively in games and sports leads to prestige among one's peers; the better one is, the higher the status one holds. Jones' frequently cited study (17) showed that boys with good physique and physical fitness were rated high in social prestige and in general level of adjustment. Boys in poor health or with poor physique tended to be unpopular, to have feelings of inferiority, and to show other personal maladjustments.

Herbert Spencer (1820-1903) relates in his *Autobiography* (34) that because of the economic circumstances of his family, he was to be boarded with and educated by an uncle. Rather than submit, the thirteen-year-old boy ran away from home, walking one hundred and fifteen miles in three days without food, until he was caught. John Cowper Powys (28), born in 1872, in regular demonstrations of adolescent stamina, *ran* every Sunday with his younger brother Littleton the ten miles each way to their home and back to school, rain or shine. The boys would leave the Sherborne School after their two o'clock Sunday dinner and return in time for six o'clock tea. Powys makes the claim they were never late once!

When Ernest Jones was a student of fourteen (1893) at Llandovery College in Wales, he too had to face up to the daring recklessness of his classmates but could not himself meet the challenge. He wrote (15), "A large natural bathing pool was reputed to reach the depth of forty feet—at all events no one ever got near the bottom —and the swimming test upstream against a torrent which threatened to dash one against the rocks was a respectable performance, too much so for my limited powers." He fared better, however, in another kind of physical shenanigan: "The feat the boys most enjoyed was swarming down, and afterwards up, a rope let down some thirty feet from our window in the tower of the college. The purpose was to gather mushrooms in the dewy dawn, which in the evening were duly cooked over a fish-tail gas jet [16]."

In the light of the preceding illustrations and the eleven to follow, the long-accepted view that adolescence is "characterized by a common core of psychobiological problems in a wide diversity of cultural settings is hardly surprising [3]." The passages used here may serve to reinforce this thesis and to explain some of the deeper sources of the adolescent's behavior.

John Clare ##
(1793-1864)

The adolescent characteristic of active participation in acts of daring and demonstrable physical prowess is illustrated in this passage from the life of the English poet who earned his livelihood as a laborer, John Clare.* Although during adolescence he was slightly built and could not bear to watch the rustic sports of hunting a "soapt and larded" pig, badger-baiting, cock-fighting and wrestling, he was by no means lacking in bravery and skill in other physical sports and in competing with the boys of his village.

What many heedless escapes from death doth a boy's heedless life meet with! I met with many in mine. Once, when wading in the meadow-pits with a lot of cow-tending boys, we bid to do each other's tasks. We had gone several times and it was my turn to attempt again, when I unconsciously got beside a gravel ledge into deep water. My heels slipt up and I slid down to the bottom. I felt the water choke me and the thunder in my ears, and I thought all was past. But some of the boys could swim and so I escaped. Another time we were swimming on bundles of bulrushes, when, getting to one end, mine suddenly bounced from under me like a cork and I made shift to struggle to a sallow-bush. Catching hold of the branches of it, I managed to get out, but how I did it I know not, for the water was very deep. Yet we had dabbled there Sunday after Sunday without the least fear of danger.

Once, when bird-nesting in the woods, of which I was very fond, we found a large tree on which was a buzzard's nest. It was a very hard tree to climb; there was no twigs to take hold of and it was too thick to swarm. So we consulted for a while, some proposing one thing and some another, till it was decided that a hook tied to the end of a long pole that would reach to the collar of the tree would be the best to get up by. In taking hold of it and swarming, several attempted to no purpose, and at last I tried, though I was rather loath to make the experiment. I succeeded in getting up to the collar, which swelled in such a projection from the tree that I could not make a landing without hazarding the dangerous attempt of clinging with my hands to the grain, and flinging my feet over it. I attempted it and failed; so there I hung with my hands, and my feet dangling in the air. I expected every moment to drop and be bashed to pieces, for I was a great height: but some of my companions below (while some ran away) had the shrewdness to put the pole under me, and by that means I got on the grain just in time before I was exhausted.

*From *A Life of John Clare* by J. W. and Anne Tibble. Reprinted by permission of The Bodley Head, Ltd. 1932. P. 29.

Herbert Spencer
(1820-1903)

Herbert Spencer, one of the founders of modern sociology, had been trained as an engineer, but turned to philosophy and tried to survey the whole range of human thought with the intention of interpreting "the phenomena of life, mind and society in terms of matter, motion and force. . . . There are no phenomena which a society presents but what have their origins in the phenomena of individual human life." It was Herbert Spencer, whom Charles Darwin referred to as "our philosopher," who characterized Darwin's theory as evolutionism, with which Darwin agreed. To Spencer, evolution was universal, at once dominating the fields of biology, psychology, ethics and sociology. He was the first philosopher to maintain the genetic principle, according to which the more developed thing must be interpreted by the less developed one. He was also the first to use the biological standard for human ethics. He complained that "men do not even know that their sensations are their natural guides and (when not rendered morbid by long-continued disobedience) their most trustworthy guides," because he thought that the senses of men were molded in accordance with the all-embracing law of evolution from a less perfect to a more perfect state (33).

This philosophy is reflected, of course, in Spencer's *Autobiography*.* In it, he explores the effect of his rapid physical growth during adolescence on his emotional and intellectual nature and comes to the right conclusion that there is a decided relationship between them—but for the wrong reasons!

Correspondence soon after this refers to some facts which perhaps have a general physiological meaning, and are therefore here worth noting, though otherwise of no interest. I was, it seems, growing rapidly—three inches per year: having previously been rather slow of growth. In a letter to my father which quotes remarks made about my increasing stature, there is a statement respecting my mental condition, which neither I nor those around seem to have suspected had any relation to the rapid growth, though it probably had. Here is a quotation:

---

*Reprinted by permission of Appleton-Century-Crofts, Inc. Vol. I. Pp. 129-130.

"I do not find my mind in as bright a state as I could wish. Just now I feel as though I had lost nearly all my energy. I think it is partly owing to want of competition, for now P—— is gone I have less stimulus to exertion; but I do not think it can be all owing to that and I am at a loss to account for it."

My uncle, too, at the same period comments on my dullness and failure of memory. Certainly this last trait must have been very marked. Not only have I absolutely forgotten some books I read at that time, but until perusal of my letters proved that I had read them, I did not know that I had ever seen them. Was not growth the cause? If excess of muscular effort, as in a pedestrian tour, is apt to leave behind inertness of brain, which for a time makes mental work difficult, it is reasonable to suppose that an unusual draft upon the resources of the system for building up the body, may, in like manner, leave the brain inadequately supplied, and cause feebleness in its action.

It is worth inquiring whether in such cases there is not produced a simultaneous moral effect. If there is such an effect, an explanation is yielded of the fact which the correspondence of the time proves, that there occurred a deterioration in my relations to my uncle and aunt. I got out of favour with them, and I was dissatisfied with my uncle's treatment of me. Is there not reason to think that rapid growth may temporarily affect the emotional nature disadvantageously, in common with the intellectual nature? As in children failure of cerebral nutrition, when caused by inactivity of the alimentary canal, is commonly accompanied by ill-temper; so, it seems not improbable that when the failure of cerebral nutrition is caused by the demands made for increase of the bodily structure, a kindred result may be entailed. Conditions which bring about a defective supply of blood to the brain, tend to throw the higher powers out of action while they leave the lower in action: the later and less evolved faculties feeling the effects of an ebb-tide of blood, more than the earlier and fully evolved ones. Such a relation, if proved to exist, should be taken into account in the treatment of young people.

Maria Chona
(1854[?]-1937[?])

In many primitive tribes the menarche is an occasion for purifying rites comparable to the initiation ceremonies for the adolescent boy. The Papago Indians of southwest Arizona, near the Mexican border, isolate the girls for four days in a "Little House" some distance from the village, forbid them the use of salt with their food, cut the girls' hair shoulder-length so that it should not be longer than the males', dance the nights through to exhaustion, and symbolize the "rebirth" of the individual in a rechristening ceremony. Maria Chona, in her *Autobiography of a Papago Woman,** described these rites in the following excerpt. Her first and last sentences are of particular interest.

When I was nearly as tall as my mother, that thing happened to me which happens to all our women though I do not know if it does to the Whites; I never saw any signs. It is called menses.

Girls are very dangerous at that time. If they touch a man's bow, or even look at it, that bow will not shoot any more. If they drink out of a man's bowl, it will make him sick. If they touch the man himself, he might fall down dead. My mother had told us this long ago and we knew what had happened in our village. . . .

Our mothers watch us, and so mine knew when it came to me. We always had the Little House ready, over behind our own house. It was made of some branches stuck in the ground and tied together at the top, with greasewood thrown over them to make it shady. There was no rain then, for it was winter, but it was cold in that little house. The door was just big enough to crawl through, like our house door, and there was room for you to lie down inside, but not to stand up. My mother made me a new bowl and drinking cup out of clay, and put them in that house. When my mother cooked food at the big house, she would come over and pour some in my bowl, but no meat and nothing with salt in it. My father sharpened a little stick for me to scratch my hair with, because if I touched it, it would fall out. I was so afraid to lose my nice long hair that I kept that stick in my mouth all the time. Even when I was asleep, I had it there.

It is a hard time for us girls, such as the men have when they are being purified. Only they give us more to eat, because we are women. And they do not let us sit still and wait for dreams. That is because we are women, too. Women must work. . . .

I had to stay four days and then I was not dangerous any more. Everything goes by fours with our people, and Elder Brother arranged it that even this thing should be the same. No woman has trouble for more than four days. Then they gave me a bath just as they did to my father. Oh, it was cold in the winter time! I tell the girls who come of

*Edited by Ruth M. Underhill. Reprinted by permission of American Anthropological Association and Ruth M. Underhill. 1936. Vol. 46. Pp. 31-36.

age in the summer they do not know what hardship is. The water even feels nice in summer.

My mother came in the dark of the morning with the water in a big new jar. The women had to run all day to get that water ready for me. I tried to get away, but my mother caught me and made me kneel down. Then she dipped a gourd in the jar and poured that cold water down over my forehead.

Then my mother washed my hair with soapweed fibres. That is the way women should always wash their hair and it will never grow gray. She cut it so it came just to my shoulders, for we women cannot have hair as long as the men; it would get in our way when we work. But we like to have it thick and shiny, and we know that everybody is noticing. There was quite a lapful that my mother cut off, and she saved it to make hair ropes for our carrying baskets. She had new clothes for me; two pieces of unbleached muslin, tied around my waist with a string. We did not know how to sew in those days. We pinned them together over our hips with bought pins, but it was very modest.

Then I could go back to our house, only still I had to use the stick for four days and I could not eat salt. And then they danced me. All that month they danced me, until the moon got back to the place where it had been at first. It is a big time when a girl comes of age; a happy time. All the people in the village knew that I had been to the Little House for the first time, so they come to our house and the singer for the maidens came first of all.

"Come out," said my father on that first night. "Now you must dance or the Leg will drag you out. He's mean."

I did not want to dance; I was sleepy and I had run so far. Always when I had heard the others singing those maiden songs, from far away, I had been wild to go. But now it was my turn and all I wanted to do was sleep. But Luis, the Leg, came into the house and took me by the arm. He always danced next to the maiden, with his arm over her shoulders and the rattle in his other hand. He and I were at one end of a long line of people and his wife at the end of a line opposite. There was first a boy and then a girl, all down the line, with their arms over each other's shoulder and the blankets held along at the back. I told you the boys always liked that dance.

At midnight my mother brought jars of succotash. She had been cooking all day for this dance, and every day after that she cooked and ground corn and baked bread in the ashes. Every morning we gave gifts to Luis and his wife. My cut-off hair and dried beans and cooked food and the hand woven cotton that I wore for a dress. And to the girl friends who danced beside me, I gave my beads and my baskets because these people had suffered and endured sleeplessness with us.

We stopped dancing in the dark of the morning and then my mother said: "Come and get firewood. Do you want to grow up a lazy woman?" So then I went out in the dark to pick up the dead branches and bring them back before I slept. It seemed I slept only an hour before they were saying: "Get up! Get water. Get wood. Grind the corn. If you sleep at this time you will be sleepy all your life."

Oh, I got thin in that time! We girls are like strips of yucca fibre after our coming of age is over. Always running, and mostly gruel and ash bread to eat, with no salt. And dancing every night from the time the sun sets until morning-stands-up. I used to go to sleep on Luis' arm and he pinched my nose to wake me.

Every night they came, the people who were not too sleepy from the night before. And always the young people came. Even Luis did not know songs enough for all that month and other men sang, too. It is a nice thing for a man to know maidens' songs. Every man likes to dance next to the maiden and to hold her on his arm. But Luis was an old man and his wife danced opposite. The wife always does.

At last the moon had come around again and they gave me a bath. It was over. I looked like half of myself. All my clothes were gone. All our dried corn and beans were eaten up. But I was grown up. Now the medicine man could cleanse me and give me a name.

You have to be cleansed as soon as the month is over; you must not wait. A cousin of mine did that once. She meant to be cleansed but she just waited. I think, perhaps, she did not have anything to pay the medicine man. But while she waited, one of her brothers was chopping wood. Something fell on him like a hot coal and killed him. So I went the day after my bath.

My mother and I went to the house of the medicine man early in the morning, with a big basket my mother had made, to pay him. He drew a circle on the ground and made me sit in it, crosslegged, with my back to the rising sun. In front of me he put a little dish. Then he walked away where we could not see him and took something out of a little deerskin bag. It was the clay that he carries to charm the evil away from women. No one ever sees the medicine man dig up that clay and no one knows how he mixes it. But I know, because my brother was a medicine man and because I myself have seen things. He grinds up the bone of a dead man and some owl feathers so that they are fine dust.

He put that clay in a tiny bowl before me, mixed with a little water. Then he walked up and down four times, facing the sun that was behind me. Every time he came up to me he blew over my head and dusted me off with his eagle feathers to brush away the evil. And every time he turned, he made a noise like an owl: hm. The fifth time, he took up the bowl of clay and stirred it around with a little owl feather that was standing in the center of it. Then he put the clay to my mouth. "Drink this up!" So I drank it all.

Then he marked me, the sacred marks that are put on the men who have got salt from the magic ocean; the marks that take away bad luck and bring you a good life. On my breast, on my shoulders, my back, and my belly.

"Your name shall be cha-veela." I did not know before what name he was going to give me; neither did my parents. The medicine man names one from his dreams. Some of my friends had names that could be understood like Leaf Buds, Rustling Leaves, Windy Rainbow, Dawn Murmur. But I have never understood my name and he did not tell me.

After all that work, I did not menstruate again for a year!

H. G. Wells
(1866-1946)

The narcissistic revival during adolescence has its classical manifestations in a preoccupation with the growing body and its functioning. Herbert George Wells, the imaginative novelist and historian, describes vividly in his autobiography* the impact of his scrawny, "contemptible" body on his affective life, in terms of the sexual inhibitions he felt because of it, his fantasies, his self-imposed secretiveness, and the redirection of his sexual needs through compensatory mechanisms.

I want to make my physical presence, at the time I left South Kensington, as real as possible to the reader. I have given five sections to tell how my picture of life in the universe was built up in my brain, I now want to show what sort of body it was that carried this brain about and supplied it with blood and obedient protection. By 1887, it had become a scandalously skinny body. I was five foot five and always I weighed less than eight stone. My proper weight should have been 9 st. 11 lbs., but I was generally nearer to seven, and that in my clothes. And they were exceedingly shabby clothes. It did not add to the charm

---

*Experiment in Autobiography. Reprinted by permission of the executors of the estate of H. G. Wells. 1934, MacMillan Co. Pp. 229-231.

of my costume that frequently I wore a waterproof collar, an invention now happily forgotten again. It was a glossy white rubber-covered thing that cost nothing for laundry. That was the point of it. You washed it overnight with soap and a sponge, and then it was ready in the morning. But after a time it accumulated something rather like the tartar that discolours teeth. It marks one difference that is worth noting between the eighties and the present time, that never a Kensington student, however needy, would have dreamed of appearing in the classroom or laboratory without what could at least be considered a white collar. Now, I suppose, a good half of the Kensington crowd wear open-necked shirts. A certain proportion of us in those days, and all the staff, wore top hats.

I was as light and thin as I have said, because I was undernourished. I ate a hastily poached egg and toast in the morning before going off for my three mile tramp to the schools and I had a meat-tea about five when I got back—and a bread and cheese supper. Most of my time I was so preoccupied with my studies and my intellectual interests that I did not observe what was happening to me, but occasionally and more especially in my third year, I would become acutely aware of my bad condition. I would survey my naked body, so far as my bedroom looking-glass permitted, with extreme distaste, and compare it with the Apollos and Mercuries in the Art Museum. There were hollows under the clavicles, the ribs showed and the muscles of the arms and legs were contemptible. I did not realize that this was merely a matter of insufficient food and exercise. I thought it was an inferior body—perhaps past hope of mending.

To me, in my hidden thoughts, the realization that my own body was thin and ugly was almost insupportable—as I suppose it would be to most young men or women. In the secret places of my heart I wanted a beautiful body and I wanted it because I wanted to make love with it, and all the derision and humour with which I treated my personal appearance in my talking and writing to my friends, my caricatures of my leanness and my unkempt shabbiness, did not affect the profundity of that unconfessed mortification. Each year I was becoming much more positively and urgently sexual and the desire to be physically strong and attractive was intense. I do not know how far my psychology in these matters is exceptional, but I have never been able to consider any sort of love as tolerable except a complete encounter of two mutually desirous bodies—and they have to be reasonably lovely bodies. The circumstances must be beautiful or adventurous or both. I believe this is how things are with nine people out of ten; as natural as hunger and thirst.

The fact that I was slovenly to look upon and with hollows under my collar-bones and with shoulder-blades that stuck out, could not alter these insistent demands of the life in me. No doubt these realizations reinforced those balancing inhibitions and that wariness and fastidiousness which are as natural as the primary cravings, and made me more than normally secretive; but to hold down an urgency is not to diminish it. I had quite another set of motives, ambition, a desire for good intellectual performance and that vague passion for service which expressed itself in my socialism, and I tried, not always successfully, to take refuge in these from my more vital and intimate imperatives.

Beautiful girls and women do not come the way of poor students in London. One was nearer to such beings among the costume hands and counter assistants of the draper's shop. There were a few friendly women fellow-students in the laboratories, but they deliberately disavowed sex in their dress and behaviour. Sex consciousness broke out to visibility only among the Art students, and these we saw but rarely during brief promenades in the Art Museum, which made a kind of neutral territory between the Art Schools and ourselves. On my long march back to Euston Road I would see women walking in the streets, especially along Oxford Street and Regent Street, and sometimes in the light of the shops, one would shine out with an effect of loveliness and set my imagination afire. I would be reminded of Ellen Terry walking in the sunshine upon the lawn at Surly Hall. Or I would see some handsome girl riding in the Row or taking a dog for a run in the park. They were all as inaccessible as the naked women in the Chantry pictures.

Seiji Noma
(1878-1938)

Seiji Noma was a Japanese newspaper and magazine publisher, one of the greatest in contemporary journalism. During his adolescence, he had a need, like his Western age-mates, to demonstrate his strength, engage in contests of physical endurance and ability, and perform acts of reckless daring. His pride in his achievements and his persistence in these activities, despite parental scoldings, were necessary and effective ego-strengtheners during a period of bewilderment and confusion.*

*From *The Nine Magazines of Kodsansha* by Seiji Noma. Reprinted by permission of Methuen & Co., Ltd. 1934. Pp. 20-24.

I had probably reached the zenith of naughtiness between thirteen and fourteen years, when I was on the eve of graduation. I was now in the top class, with none greater than I among my school-fellows, so, conceited and reckless, I strutted about with a haughty swagger. Once for sheer fun I swam across the Watarasegawa in stormy weather, when the river had swollen to a dangerous height, with logs and uprooted trees sweeping down the current. Afterwards my father gave me a terrible scolding. I had other perilous adventures with narrow escapes from death.

I was continually fighting and was proud of the marks of injury from which I was never free. I was champion wrestler of the western boys' camp. The eastern camp was represented by boys of a neighbouring district who were very strong at the sport. The first champion of the eastern camp, Shimoyama by name was one of those whom I could not beat in the ring. In real fighting, however, I was stronger than he and he knew it.

The boys of Sakaino and Shinshiku fell to fighting whenever they met. I had heard that Shimoyama carried an iron rod in his bosom ready for a chance encounter with me, and one day on the way home from school I was waylaid by a gang of boys with Shimoyama at their head. Instantly I rushed at Shimoyama and snatched the dangerous weapon from his bosom. At the same moment I was attacked by two or three boys from behind who seized my legs and made me fall flat on the ground. I was about to be thrashed within an inch of my life but a passing fishmonger rescued me. Such an encounter took place more than once and I may say without false modesty that I always acquitted myself in such a way that Shinshiku had no cause to be ashamed of me.

Helena Morley
(1880-   )

The tiny mining village of Diamantina, Brazil was the birthplace and home for many years of Helena Morley. She was the daughter of a Catholic Portugese mother and a Protestant English mining adventurer. The two passages quoted here* reflect two eternal and universal needs of adolescents: to be physically attractive and to get enough to eat. The entries in Helena's diary indicate her worries about her height, her thinness, her freckles and her appetite. When,

*From *The Diary of "Helena Morley"* edited by Elizabeth Bishop. Reprinted by permission of Farrar, Straus & Cudahy, Inc. Copyright 1957, Elizabeth Bishop. Pp. 110-111.

by the simple manipulation of scissors and the use of cosmetics, she is transformed from a homely girl to a pretty one, her journal entry is replete with joy and gratitude at the change. Frequent references are also made during the three years (1893-1895) she maintained her diary to her unappeased appetite. In the whimsical second entry below, she relates a frustrating experience about food to the equally dissatisfying introjected religious values of her mother.

Thursday, August 24th, 1893

Today I came home looking so different that Renato kept looking at me and saying, "Just look at her face!" Luizinha, who is a thousand times nicer than he is, said, "How pretty you are, Helena! Who fixed you like that?" I said, "Ester did." When I was talking with them on the stoop I said that I knew that I was homely but that it didn't bother me because Mama Tina (Negro nurse. Her proverb is in Negro dialect.) had brought me up knowing that "The homely lives, the pretty lives, they all lives." When I said that I was homely, Ester exclaimed, "You homely? Just let me fix you up and you'll see." I agreed, and she got the scissors and cut my bangs and combed my hair, then she put rice-powder on my face and when I looked in the mirror I saw that I wasn't homely at all. They laughed when I told them that what we do here is to grease our hair with chicken fat to keep it plastered down. She told me that I should wash my hair and then put it in curls and then go there for her to comb it. How nice that I've become friendly with Dona Gabriela's family. They're so kind! If it weren't for them I never would have thought to have my bangs cut and my hair combed in the latest style. Ester thought it was funny when I told her that Mama Tina used to say, "The pretty lives, the homely lives." She said, "It's true, but the pretty ones live better." How happy I am today to be pretty at last!

Friday, September 8th, 1893

When I got to the *chácara* I missed grandma. "Where's grandma? Where are Dindinha and Iaiá? Where did they go?" Elvira answered, "They went to Sinhá Aurélia's. She had a miscarriage and Sinhá Teodora told me to tell you that you're to go there when you get home from school." I said, "Grandma knows we have to study, we have lessons on Saturday mornings. Wouldn't it be better if I stayed here, Elvira, and Emídio went to tell grandma I have to study?" She said, "No. You know that she gets uneasy when you aren't near her."

I thought to myself, "Heavens! I wish mama were here! How can I live like this, always being obedient and suffering, without saying a word!" I went running to Aunt Aurélia's house, hoping they'd give me something to eat, because I was dying of hunger. When I got there my aunts said immediately, "Don't give her anything to eat because it's almost dinner time and she'll spoil her appetite."

If there's one thing I desire in life, it's not to be as hungry as I am. I'm disgracefully hungry. I never had a day in my life when I didn't want to eat a lot. I even asked the doctor if there wasn't some way of not using my food up so fast, and he thought it was funny.

I waited without even talking very much, I was so hungry. Finally it was dinner time and the Negro, Maria, sat all the children on the bench at the big table in the kitchen and was bringing in the plates all ready for each one. When it was my turn she turned to me and asked me, "Sinhá Helena, do you want to eat, too?" I was surprised at the question and I said, "Oh, no, *I* don't want to eat!" thinking that the stupid girl would understand me. I waited for my plate and nothing came. I called to Maria, "Where's my plate?" She answered, "Oh! Didn't you say you didn't want any? Now there isn't anything left."

I was so surprised I couldn't even speak. I did what mama says we should do when we undergo great suffering: offer it as a sacrifice to God, that it may please Him, and help us later when we need it.

I didn't want the dessert, yams and molasses. I don't know whether it was because I really wanted to make a sacrifice or whether I was in a rage. When dinner was over, grandma saw me and said, "You're pale, and your lips are white. What's the matter? Are you sick?" I said, "No, Senhora. Perhaps it's because I didn't have any lunch after school, or any dinner." Grandma said, "I never in my born days!"

Martin Freud
(1889-   )

Of all the customers for nostrums which will "cure" blackheads, acne, or flat-chestedness, "create" muscles where none existed before, or provide long-windedness where one formerly had shallow breath, the adolescent is probably the most gullible. Mail-order houses thrive on the business they get from adolescents. In 1905, when he was fifteen years old, Martin Freud, son of Sigmund, was prompted to write to such a business concern because of his anxiety about his poor physique.* He had been tormented by some anti-Semitic classmates (as his father before him) and he was determined to strengthen his weak and underdeveloped body in order for retributive justice to take place.

I had got hold of a pamphlet on physical development which proved most useful. I do know that these widely advertised books and pamphlets offering readers detailed instructions about physical development are often ridiculed, but I followed the instructions in my book with the happiest results. I had now been given a room of my own in the Bergasse flat and every evening I exercised with great enthusiasm, spending hours slowly strengthening my weak and underdeveloped body—up and down from the floor on my finger tips, deep breathing, jumping and bending my body until I was completely exhausted.

This worked so well that the day came when I felt I might challenge those of my class-mates who, owing to my physical weakness, had felt safe in beating and insulting me. The result was a series of duels, boxing in fact, fought on a nearby enclosed space. These events drew a lot of spectators eager to see the defeat of a weakling, but they soon lost interest, for my opponents were knocked out rather mercilessly and soon decided to leave me in peace. The last of my former tormentors refused to accept the challenge and he had to be dealt with in the intervals between lessons. And thus I gained the reputation of a bully and a ruffian—undeserved, I felt: my conscience was clear since I felt I was attempting nothing more than retrospective self-defence.

Anonymous
(? - ?)

Although the menarche is not accepted in the same way in every culture, what does seem to be a common thread is the ignorance and fear in which it is held. In a diary which Freud called a "gem," an anonymous Austrian girl, nearing her twelfth birthday (sometime, one gathers, near the turn of the century), reveals the horror she felt on learning about the process.**

---

*From *Sigmund Freud: Man and Father*. Reprinted by permission of Vanguard Press, Inc. Copyright 1958. P. 103.

**From *A Young Girl's Diary*. 1921, Thomas Seltzer. Pp. 34-35.

October 10th

I'm in a great funk. I missed my gymnastic lesson yesterday. I was upstairs at Hella's and without meaning it I was so late I did not dare to go. And Hella said I had better stay with her that we would say that our sum was so difficult that we had not got it finished in time. Luckily we really had a sum to do. But I said nothing about it at home, for to-morrow Oswald is going to G. to Herr S's. I thought that I knew all about it but only now has Hella really told me everything. It's a horrible business this . . . I really can't write it. She says that of course Inspee has it already, had it when I wrote that Inspee wouldn't bathe, did not want to bathe; really she had *it*. Whatever happens one must always be anxious about it. *Streams of blood* says Hella. But then everything gets all bl . . . That's why in the country Inspee always switched off the light before she was quite undressed, so that I couldn't see. Ugh! Catch me looking! It begins at 14 and goes on for 20 years or more. Hella says that Berta Franke in our class knows all about it. In the arithmetic lesson she wrote a note: Do you know what being un . . . is? Hella wrote back, of course I've known it for a long time. Berta waited for her after class when the Catholics were having their religion lesson and they went home together. I remember quite well that I was very angry, for they're not chums. On Tuesday Berta came with us, for Hella had sent her a note in class saying that I knew *everything* and she needn't bother about me. Inspee suspects something, she's always spying about and sneering, perhaps she thinks that she's the only person who ought to know anything.

Simone de Beauvoir
(1908-   )

The following illustration is from the pen of perhaps the most brilliant living woman writer in France. Simone de Beauvoir, in this passage from her *Memoirs of a Dutiful Daughter,** expresses the nearly universal feelings of Western adolescent girls at the first menstrual period: the horror, the shame at soiling clothes, the arousal of guilt, the mobilization of anxieties, the sudden conspiratorial relationship with the mother, all of which are commingled with an incomprehensible pride and a feeling of self-consciousness at having achieved womanhood.

---

*Translated by James Kirkup. Reprinted by permission of World Publishing Co. Copyright 1959, World Publishing Co. Pp. 105-108.

That year, when we moved to the Rue de Rennes, I began to have bad dreams. Had I not properly digested the revelations made by Madeleine? Only a thin partition now divided my bed from the one in which my parents slept, and sometimes I would hear my father snoring: did this promiscuity upset me? I had nightmares. A man would jump on my bed and dig his knee into my stomach until I felt I was suffocating; in desperation, I would dream that I was waking up and once again I would be crushed beneath the awful weight of my aggressor. About the same time, getting up became such a painful ordeal that when I thought about it the night before, my throat would tighten and my palms would grow damp with sweat. When I used to hear my mother's voice in the mornings I longed to fall ill, I had such horror of dragging myself out of the toils of sleep and darkness. During the day, I had dizzy spells; I became anemic. Mama and the doctor would say: "It's her development." I grew to detest that word and the silent upheaval that was going on in my body. I envied "big girls" their freedom; but I was disgusted at the thought of my chest swelling out; I had sometimes heard grown-up women urinating with the noise of a cataract; when I thought of the bladders swollen with water in their bellies, I felt the same terror as Gulliver did when the young giantesses displayed their breasts to him.

Now that the mysterious secret was out, forbidden books frightened me less than they used to; I would often let my gaze wander idly over the bits of old newspaper hanging up in the lavatory. In this way I read a fragment of a novelette in which the hero applied his burning lips to the heroine's white breasts. This kiss burned right through me; I was both hero and heroine, and watcher too; I both gave and received the kiss, and feasted my eyes upon it also. If I felt such violent excitement it was surely because my body was already ripe for it; but my daydreams were crystallized around that image; I don't know how many times I lingered over it before I fell asleep. I invented erotic fantasies: I wonder where I could have got them from. The fact that married couples, scantily dressed, share the same bed had not been enough to make me realize that they might embrace or caress one another. I suppose it was my own need that made me imagine them. Therefore I was prey to agonizing desires; with parched mouth, I would toss and turn in my bed, calling for a man's body to be pressed against my own, for a man's hands to stroke my flesh. Desperately I would calculate: "Girls aren't allowed to marry until they're *fifteen!*" And even that was exceptional: I should have to wait much longer than that before I was released from my torment. It would all begin so nicely; in the warmth of the sheets, my fantasies made my heart pound deliciously with racing blood; I almost felt they were going to come true; but no, they fled away; no hand, no mouth came to soothe my itching flesh; my fine calico nightdress became a shirt of nettles. Sleep alone could deliver me from my torment. I never associated these deliriums with the idea of sin: their violence was too much for me and I felt I was the victim rather than the guilty one. Nor did I wonder if other little girls endured such sufferings. I was not in the habit of comparing myself with others.

We were staying with friends during the stifling heat of mid-July; I awoke horror-stricken one morning: I had soiled my nightdress. I washed it and got dressed: again I soiled my underclothes. I had forgotten Madeleine's vague prophecies, and I wondered what shameful malady I was suffering from. Worried and feeling somehow guilty, I had to take my mother into my confidence: she explained to me that I had now become "a big girl," and bundled me up in a very inconvenient manner. I felt a strong sense of relief when I learned that it had happened through no fault of my own; and as always when something important happened to me, I even felt my heart swell with a sort of pride. I didn't mind too much when I heard my mother whispering about it to her friends. But that evening when we joined my father in the Rue de Rennes, he jokingly made reference to my condition: I was consumed with shame. I had imagined that the monstrous regiment of women kept its blemish a secret from the male fraternity. I thought of myself in relationship to my father as a purely spiritual being: I was horrified at the thought that he suddenly considered me to be a mere organism. I felt as if I could never hold up my head again.

I was going through a difficult period: I looked awful; my nose was turning red; on my face and the back of my neck there were pimples which I kept picking at nervously. My mother, overworked, took little trouble with my clothes: my ill-fitting dresses accentuated my awkwardness. Embarrassed by my body, I developed phobias: for example, I couldn't bear to drink from a glass I had already drunk from. I had nervous tics: I couldn't stop shrugging my shoulders and twitching my nose. "Don't scratch your pimples; don't twitch your nose," my father kept telling me. Not ill-naturedly, but with complete absence of tact, he would pass remarks about my complexion, my acne, my clumsiness which only made my misery worse and aggravated my bad habits.

The rich cousin to whom my father owed his position organized a party for his children and their friends. He composed a revue in verse. My sister was chosen to be the leading lady. In a dress of blue tulle spangled with stars, and with her beautiful long hair hanging down her back, she played the Queen of the Night to perfection. After a poetic dialogue with Pierrot Lunaire, she recited rhymed couplets to introduce the young guests who paraded on a platform in their fancy costumes. Disguised as a Spanish lady, I was to strut up and down flirting a fan while Poupette sang to the tune of *Funiculi-funicula* (more or less!):

> *Here comes a lovely señorita*
> *With her head held high* (repeat)
> *The very latest thing from Barcelona*
> *With a Spanish eye* (repeat)
> *Olé! when she dances with the castanets*
> *She stamps her pretty feet . . . etc.*

With everyone's eyes upon me and feeling a hot blush stain my cheeks, I was in agony. A little later I attended the wedding of a cousin in the north; whereas on the occasion of my aunt Lili's marriage I had been enchanted by the figure I cut, this time my appearance appalled me. It was only on the morning of the ceremony, at Arras, that my mother realized my beige crepe-de-Chine dress, fitting tightly over a bust which was no longer that of a child, accentuated my breasts in an obscene fashion. They were then swathed in bandages and firmly flattened, so that all day I had the feeling I was concealing in my bodice some uncomfortable physical disability. During the long, boring ceremony and an interminable banquet I was sadly conscious of what the wedding photographs later confirmed: badly dressed, ungainly, I was hovering shamefacedly between girlhood and womanhood.

Anne Frank
(1929-1945)

While the anonymous Austrian author of *A Young Girl's Diary* anticipated her first menstrual period with fear and dismay, Anne Frank, the gallant Dutch girl, looked forward eagerly to it. "I'm so longing to have it," she wrote in her diary* when she was thirteen years old, "it seems so important." A year and a half later, after having experienced it three times (typical of the irregularity of menstruation at the beginning), she still had a healthy outlook about it, despite "all the pain, unpleasantness, and nastiness."

---

*From *The Diary of a Young Girl* by Anne Frank. Reprinted by permission of Doubleday & Co., Inc. Copyright 1952, Otto H. Frank. Pp. 38, 115-116.

Thursday, 29 October, 1942

I'm allowed to read more grown-up books lately. I'm now reading *Eva's Youth* by Nico van Suchtelen. I can't see much difference between this and the schoolgirl love stories. It is true there are bits about women selling themselves to unknown men in back streets. They ask a packet of money for it. I'd die of shame if anything like that happened to me. Also it says that Eva has a monthly period. Oh, I'm so longing to have it too; it seems so important.

Wednesday, 5 January, 1944

Yesterday I read an article about blushing by Sis Heyster. This article might have been addressed to me personally. Although I don't blush very easily, the other things in it certainly all fit me. She writes roughly something like this—that a girl in the years of puberty becomes quiet within and begins to think about the wonders that are happening to her body.

I experience that, too, and that is why I get the feeling lately of being embarrassed about Margot, Mummy, and Daddy. Funnily enough, Margot, who is much more shy than I am, isn't at all embarrassed.

I think what is happening to me is so wonderful, and not only what can be seen on my body, but all that is taking place inside. I never discuss myself or any of these things with anybody; that is why I have to talk to myself about them.

Each time I have a period—and that has only been three times—I have the feeling that in spite of all the pain, unpleasantness, and nastiness, I have a sweet secret, and that is why, although it is nothing but a nuisance to me in a way, I always long for the time that I shall feel that secret within me again.

David S. Kogan
(1929-1951)

The diary kept by David Kogan reveals the characteristic ambivalences the adolescent feels. In the three entries from his diary which follow,* David's self-concept vacillates from abject rejection to healthy self-acceptance. These extremes seem to be based on his feelings of physical worth and the question of his acceptance by

---

*From *The Diary of David S. Kogan*. Reprinted by permission of Beechhurst Press. 1955. Pp. 29, 30, 38, 83.

his peers on the basis of his ability in athletics. The third entry reports what he himself recognized as "a typical adolescent experience": a hot-rod tour of his community, Yonkers, New York. David recognized the dangers in the jalopy ride while enjoying its thrills. He applied the classic rationalization about the dangers in the remark made in the last sentence of the entry.

Monday, April 20, 1942

Kids my age ignore me, the eighth-graders ignore me. My friends are in the A.S.C., I have no other friends. There are groups within the club. I can't put myself anywhere. I am at the bottom and don't belong.

I know I am not good in most athletics, but after all, I'm playing against kids a year older than me. At best I'm thought of as a misfit, a show-off, a moron. I've been like that since I skipped the second grade. I'll be like that until I am out of school, when age barriers will vanish.

I am now concentrating on getting a strong body. I need one. I'll try to learn to wrestle, box, ju-jitsu, basketball, football, apply strength.

Got a baseball booklet by mail. . . .

Thursday, August 4, 1942

One of the reasons I enjoy myself here [at a summer camp] is that for the first time in more than five years I am with kids my own age. I am as good an athlete as the rest of them, if not better than most. I am respected. The sister group is as old as me. In short—I am more normal than ever. I hope I can come here every year till sixteen, so I can have a five-week rest from bullies, conspiracy, disappointments, uneven fights and the like.

Tuesday, January 16, 1945

I have indulged in a typical adolescent experience today. Was one of seven A.S.C. boys who piled into an old, smoking, bumpy '29 jalopy and toured around Yonkers for about a half hour. It's fun and thrilling, but I suppose quite dangerous. Nevertheless, everyone feels that HE won't get hurt.

REFERENCES

1. Alfieri, Vittorio. *Autobiography*. Boston: James R. Osgood & Co., 1877, pp. 107-108.
2. Ausubel, David P. *Theory and Problems of Adolescent Development*. New York: Grune & Stratton, 1954, pp. 40-42.
3. *Ibid.*, p. 41.
4. Bashkirtseff, Marie. *Journal*. Chicago: Rand McNally & Co., 1889, pp. 212-213.
5. Bloch, Herbert A., & Niederhoffer, Arthur. *The Gang. A Study in Adolescent Behavior*. New York: Philosophical Library, 1958, p. 57.
6. Cardan, Jerome. *The Book of My Life*. New York: E. P. Dutton & Co., 1930, p. 26.
7. Dennis, Wayne. The adolescent. In: Carmichael, Leonard (Ed.), *Manual of Child Psychology*. New York: John Wiley & Sons, 1946, p. 637.
8. Deutsch, Helene. *The Psychology of Women. A Psychoanalytic Interpretation*. Vol. I., New York: Grune & Stratton, 1944, p. 91.
9. Ellis, Havelock. *My Life*. Boston: Houghton Mifflin Co., 1939, p. 132.
10. Goethe, Johann Wolfgang von. *Goethe's Autobiography. Poetry and Truth from My Own Life*. Translated by R. O. Moon. Washington, D.C.: Public Affairs Press, 1949, p. 196.
11. Goldman, Emma. *Living My Life*. Garden City, N. Y.: Garden City Publishing Co., 1931, p. 21.
12. Havens, Catherine E. *Diary of a Little Girl in Old New York*. New York: Henry Collins Brown, 1920, pp. 115-116.
13. Hunt, Leigh. *Autobiography*. Vol. I. Westminster, England: Archibald Constable & Co., 1903, p. 126.
14. Inhelder, Bärbel, & Piaget, Jean. *The Growth of Logical Thinking: From Childhood to Adolescence*. New York: Basic Books, 1958, pp. 335-336.
15. Jones, Ernest. *Free Associations. Memories of a Psycho-Analyst*. New York: Basic Books, 1959, p. 46.
16. *Ibid.*, p. 47.
17. Jones, Harold E. *Motor Performance and Growth*. Berkeley, Calif.: University of California Press, 1949, p. 167.
18. Kipling, Rudyard. *Something of Myself*. Garden City, N. Y.: Doubleday, Doran & Co., 1937, pp. 32-33.
19. Kogan, David S. *The Diary of David S. Kogan*. Edited by Meyer Levin. New York: Beechhurst Press, 1955, p. 71.
20. *Ibid.*, p. 99.

21. Mohr, George J., & Despres, Marian A. *The Stormy Decade: Adolescence.* New York: Random House, 1958, p. 60.
22. Monroe, Harriet. *A Poet's Life.* New York: Macmillan Co., 1938, p. 35.
23. Montaigne, Michel de. *Autobiography.* Edited by Marvin Lowenthal. Boston: Houghton Mifflin Co., 1935, p. 14.
24. Morley, Helena. *The Diary of "Helena Morley."* Edited by Elizabeth Bishop. New York: Farrar, Straus & Cudahy, 1957, pp. 110-111.
25. Mozart, Wolfgang A. *The Letters of Mozart and His Family.* Vol. I. Edited by Emily Anderson. London: Macmillan Co., 1938, p. 189.
26. Najafi, Najmeh, & Hinckley, Helen. *Persia Is My Heart.* New York: Harper & Bros., 1953, p. 125.
27. Powys, John Cowper. *Autobiography.* London: John Lane, 1934, p. 132.
28. *Ibid.,* pp. 130-134.
29. Rice, John A. *I Came Out of the Nineteenth Century.* New York: Harper & Bros., 1942, p. 144.
30. *Ibid.,* p. 149.
31. Richards, Grant. *Memories of a Misspent Youth, 1872-1896.* New York: Harper & Bros., 1933, p. 66.
32. Runes, Dagobert D. (Ed.). *Treasury of Philosophy.* New York: Philosophical Library, 1955, pp. 1120-1121.
33. Simmons, Leo W. (Ed.). *Sun Chief. The Autobiography of a Hopi Indian.* New Haven: Yale University Press, 1942, p. 168.
34. Spencer, Herbert. *An Autobiography.* New York: D. Appleton & Co., 1904, Vol. I, pp. 105-112.
35. Wagner, Richard. *My Life.* New York: Tudor Publishing Co., 1936, p. 21.
36. Weinman, Martha. Beauty and the bees. *New York Times Magazine,* January 24, 1960, pp. 32-33.
37. Zachry, Caroline B. *Emotion and Conduct in Adolescence.* New York: Appleton-Century Co., 1940, p. 34.

CHAPTER TWO

Psychosexual Characteristics

Sex is not only suitable for autobiographies, the Kornhausers have written, it is a condition of it. "For most of us, sex is a large part of life; if not in actuality, then at least in fantasy. The autobiographies of those few who had the honesty and courage to include both in their personal histories are therefore all the more significant for the student of human nature and all those who . . . are striving toward self-fulfillment in their own individual ways [43]."

Writers of autobiographies may be more or less reticent about describing their adult sexual life. They are, however, far more willing to reveal their libidinal impulses during adolescence, as the illustrations in this chapter indicate. These excerpts are astonishingly frank for the most part, demonstrating, perhaps, the universal recognition and acceptance of the reality of the sexual life of the adolescent.

As several of the passages in the preceding chapter show, the onset of physical and physiological changes in puberty bring with them sexual drives hitherto not manifested in significantly meaningful ways. Adolescence does not initiate but only intensifies and brings about nuances of sexual feeling and behavior which did not exist before. The psychological task at this time is to adapt the personality to the new conditions created by the biological changes. This adjustment to puberty includes a struggle between the id and the superego, and therefore internal conflicts. Bernfeld, in his effort to establish a formula for a typology of adolescence, states that all forms of adolescence have a common characteristic: the presence of conflict which is describable in terms of rebellion and compliance (5).

The manner with which the adolescent coped with his infantile sexuality and with the initial oedipal conflict is reflected in his adaptation to the new physical conditions. There is a recrudescence of these earlier childhood conflicts, but, as Fenichel (16) states, in the interim they have become more complicated. "The relatively pleasant equilibrium of the latency period has stabilized certain attitudes hostile to instincts, which may now increase anxiety and instability. During the latency period the instinctual demands themselves have not changed much; but the ego has. It has developed definite patterns of reaction toward external and internal demands. When in adolescence the ego comes into conflict with instinctual drives, the situation is different from what it was in childhood. Contradictory attitudes come to the fore. Side by side or following one another appear genital heterosexual impulses, all kinds of infantile sexual behavior, and attitudes of extreme asceticism, which not only try to suppress all sexuality but everything pleasant as well."

It is thus obvious that there are a variety of ways in which adolescent sexual drives manifest themselves. Since puberty consists of a considerable increase of libido arising suddenly and since the organism is not equipped to bear that burden, to adjust it to the new situation becomes of utmost concern and is managed by the complex changes of emotion and behavior which we call adolescence. On this basis, Bernfeld arrived at a definition of adolescence as the adjustment of the child's personality to puberty, or at least an attempt at one (6).

This chapter consists of five sections, in an effort to illustrate the variety of ways by which adolescents, living in different centuries in Western, Eastern, and primitive cultures, cope with their sexual needs.

SEXUAL AWAKENING

Perhaps the earliest data in the autobiographical literature pertaining to the sexual awakening of the adolescent is to be found in the *Confessions* of Saint Augustine. In Chapters I through III of his Second Book, Augustine calls to mind his "foulness and carnal corruptions," for "out of the dark concupiscence of the flesh and the effervescence of youth exhalations came forth which obscured and overcast my heart, so that I was unable to discern pure affection from unholy desire. Both boiled confusedly within me, and dragged away my unstable youth into the rough places of unchaste desires, and plunged me into a gulf of infamy [3]." The pubertal conflict which Augustine describes so vividly came about as the result of the sudden increase of libido and the great difficulty he experienced in trying to cope with the second phase of the oedipal conflict. For Augustine, the achievement of equilibrium was a long and precarious business, "resolved" only when he took the priestly vows.

Another priest, some seven hundred years later, encountered much the same problems and resolved them in identical fashion. Guibert, Abbot of Nogent-sous Coucy, left in his *Autobiography* not only a remarkable picture of medieval social and economic life but also a portrait of his own affective life, particularly of childhood and adolescence, which reveals tellingly the dynamics of these two age periods. In 1061, when Guibert was eight, his father died. When he was twelve, his fanatically pious mother forsook him for a nunnery, leaving him in the care of a tutor. In the next two years, puberty began and with it came the conflicts and wildness of sexual behavior characterized by Augustine. When opportunity was lacking, Guibert sublimated his sexual appetite through fantasies. "Now with the gradual growth of my little body, as its carnal life began to stir my itching heart with fleshly longings and lusts according to its stature, my mind oft fell to remembering and thinking on what and how great I might have been in the world, in which my imaginings often travelled beyond the truth [32]."

While Augustine and Guibert were able to give expression to their awakened sexual needs, these urges in other adolescents provoke fears and mobilize defense forces that make several important contributions to the psychological picture of this period of life. Anna Freud considers the adolescent ego the center of defense against the dangers involved in the sexual urges (23). In the two passages which follow, we see the repression of the instinctual forces by two adolescents. In the first, Mozart was eighteen years old. In this letter to his sister (50), he showed his first consciousness of the opposite sex, but had to mask even the modest expression of it by writing in Latin.

Munich, December 16th, 1774

I have toothache.

Johannes Chrysostomus Wolfgangus Amadeus Sigismundus Mo-
zartus Mariae Annae Mozartae matri et sorori, ac amicis omnibus,
praesertimque pulchris virginibus, ac freillibus, gratiosisque freillibus
S.P.D.*

In the second illustration, Havelock Ellis reports his sexual stirrings at the age of sixteen in 1875. He had left his native England
for Australia and in his loneliness had attempted friendship with a
neighbor who had several attractive daughters. "Near-by, a retired
sea-captain called Fox was comfortably settled, and once or twice I
was invited to his house. He had several pretty and charming daughters with whom I was on terms of superficial acquaintance. No more,
but without being in love with any one of them I vaguely desired
more, yet felt myself powerless, in my inexperienced awkwardness,
to attain more. All the obscure mysteries of sex stirred dimly and
massively within me; I felt myself groping helplessly among the
difficulties of life [13]." But behind Ellis' awkwardness and inexperience was a degree of sexual impotence which he did not overcome until he was past sixty. In addition, he suffered from an
unpleasant form of deviation, urolagnia, which colored his libidinal
feelings throughout his adolescence and later life. "I had an instinct for exact measurement," Ellis explains; "at the age of twelve,
or earlier, I was measuring the varying lengths of the urinary stream,
and at seventeen I discovered for myself the fact that stature varies
during the day [14]." Behind this preoccupation was an unhappy
relationship with his mother.

Sex is by no means the simple genital act of children. Rather, it is
a highly complex drive with ramifications into every part of the
body and every aspect of the personality. It is "so complex that it
permits of the widest differences between one individual and the
next both in the experiences which cause sexual tension and in its
mode of expression [47]." In the lengthier autobiographical passages which complete this section, the variety of expressions of sexual
awakenings and desires, as seen from the early eighteenth century
to the present, is presented.

---

*Salutem plurimam dicit. Johannes Chrysostomus Wolfgang Amadeus Sigismund
Mozart sends many greetings to Maria Anna Mozart, his mother and his sister, and to
all his friends, and especially to pretty girls and Fräuleins and gracious Fräuleins.

Jean Jacques Rousseau
(1712-1778)

Rousseau freely admits that much of the early material in his *Confessions** is untrustworthy, due to the caprice of memory. Nevertheless, he takes great pains to speak with utmost candor of the ridiculousness and humiliation of his masochistic perversion, exhibitionism, petty thefts, and sexual inadequacy. "Allowing for the masochistic and exhibitionistic components of this self-revelation," Kligerman wonders "what further motive Rousseau could have had for confabulation." In answering his own question, Kligerman suggests that in any case, "verity is not essential in the psychoanalytic examination of character. In autobiography, as in free association, confabulations assume even greater importance in understanding the fantasy life of the author [39]."

At sixteen, Rousseau wrote, "My feverish blood incessantly peopled my brain with girls and women." In attempting to cope with his sexual urgings, he indulged in masturbatory fantasies and a series of exhibitionistic acts which he recorded. This exhibitionism is regarded by Kligerman as an attempt to approach girls and at the same time to maintain a feminine attitude. "We know from Freud's description of the Wolf-man, who like Rousseau developed somatic delusions and a paranoid state, and also from the studies of the masochistic character by Wilhelm Reich, that such persons frequently reach the genital level with a weakly exhibitionistic organization which breaks down with regression to the anal and urethral level [40]."

> Having left Madame de Vercellis' house in almost the same state as I had entered it, I went back to my old landlady, with whom I remained for five or six weeks, during which health, youth, and idleness again rendered my temperament troublesome. I was restless, absent-minded, a dreamer. I wept, I sighed, I longed for a happiness of which I had no idea, and of which I nevertheless felt the want. This state cannot be described; only few men can even imagine it, because most of them have forestalled this fulness of life, at once so tormenting and so delicious, which, in the intoxication of desire, gives a foretaste of enjoyment. My heated blood incessantly filled my brain with girls and

*Reprinted by permission of Pocket Books, Inc. Copyright 1957. Pp. 55-57.

women; but, ignorant of the relations of sex, I made use of them in my imagination in accordance with my distorted notions, without knowing what else to do with them; and these notions kept my feelings in a state of most uncomfortable activity, from which, fortunately, they did not teach me how to deliver myself. I would have given my life to have found another Mademoiselle Goton for a quarter of an hour. But it was no longer the time when childish amusements took this direction as if naturally. Shame, the companion of a bad conscience, had made its appearance with advancing years; it had increased my natural shyness to such an extent that it made it unconquerable; and never, neither then nor later, have I been able to bring myself to make an indecent proposal, unless she, to whom I made it, in some measure forced me to it by her advances, even though I knew that she was by no means scrupulous, and felt almost certain of being taken at my word.

My agitation became so strong that, being unable to satisfy my desires, I excited them by the most extravagant behaviour. I haunted dark alleys and hidden retreats, where I might be able to expose myself to women in the condition in which I should have liked to have been in their company. What they saw was not an obscene object, I never even thought of such a thing; it was a ridiculous object. The foolish pleasure I took in displaying it before their eyes cannot be described. There was only one step further necessary for me to take, in order to gain actual experience of the treatment I desired, and I have no doubt that some woman would have been bold enough to afford me the amusement, while passing by, if I had had the courage to wait. This folly of mine led to a disaster almost as comical, but less agreeable for myself.

One day, I took up my position at the bottom of a court where there was a well, from which the girls of the house were in the habit of fetching water. At this spot there was a slight descent which led to some cellars by several entrances. In the dark I examined these underground passages, and finding them long and dark, I concluded that there was no outlet, and that, if I happened to be seen and surprised, I should find a safe hiding-place in them. Thus emboldened, I exhibited to the girls who came to the well a sight more laughable than seductive. The more modest pretended to see nothing; others began to laugh; others felt insulted and cried out. I ran into my retreat; someone followed me. I heard a man's voice, which I had not expected, and which alarmed me. I plunged underground at the risk of losing myself; the noise, the voices, the man's voice, still followed me. I had always reckoned upon the darkness; I saw a light. I shuddered, and plunged further into the darkness. A wall stopped me, and, being unable to go any further, I was obliged to await my fate. In a moment I was seized by a tall man with a big moustache, a big hat, and a big sword, who was escorted by four or five old women, each armed with a broom-handle, amongst whom I perceived the little wretch who had discovered me, and who, no doubt, wanted to see me face to face.

The man with the sword, seizing me by the arm, asked me roughly what I was doing there. It may be imagined that I had no answer ready. However, I recovered myself; and, in desperation, at this critical moment I invented a romantic excuse which proved successful. I begged him in a suppliant voice to have pity upon my age and condition; I said that I was a young stranger of good birth, whose brain was affected; that I had run away from home, because they wanted to shut me up; that I was lost if he betrayed me; but that, if he would let me go, I might some day be able to reward him for his kindness. Contrary to all expectation, my words and demeanour took effect; the terrible man was touched by them, and, after administering a short reproof, he let me go quietly without questioning me further.

Robert Burns
(1759-1796)

At the age of twenty-eight, Padover relates, when Scotland's greatest poet published his Poems which made him a celebrity and earned him four hundred pounds sterling, he wrote a brief autobiography in the form of a letter to Dr. Moore, "to explain to an astonished literary public the manner of man he was. Son of a poor farmer and himself an overworked laborer at fifteen, Burns was all music and all love and hilarity, as he tells in this touchingly frank description of himself. His was a life dedicated to women, wine and song, and at the age of thirty-seven, having burned his candle at both ends and the middle, he died [53]."

Burns' sexual awakening and indulgences began, according to this document, at the age of seventeen, precipitated in a measure by the rejection of his father. The poet himself attributes this as one cause of his dissipation in the succeeding years. But he is insightful enough to comprehend that other, more natural, forces were at work as well.

This kind of life . . . the cheerless gloom of a hermit, with the unceasing moil of a galley-slave, brought me to my sixteenth year; a little before which period I first committed the sin of Rhyme. You know our country custom of coupling a man and woman together as partners in the labours of harvest. In my fifteenth autumn, my partner was a bewitching creature, a year younger than myself. My scarcity of English denies me the power of doing her justice in that language, but you know the Scottish idiom; she was a *bonnie sweet sonsie lass*. In short, she altogether unwittingly to herself, initiated me in that delicious passion, which in spite of acid disappointment, gin-horse prudence, and bookworn philosophy, I hold to be the first of human joys, our dearest blessing here below! How she caught the contagion I cannot tell; you medical people talk much of infection from breathing the same air, the touch, etc., but I never expressly said I lov'd her. . . . Indeed I did not know myself why I liked so much to loiter behind with her, when returning in the evening from our labours; why the tones of her voice made my heart-strings thrill like an Aeolian harp; and particularly why my pulse beat such a furious ratan when I looked and fingered over her little hand to pick out the cruel nettle-stings and thistles. Among her other love-inspiring qualities, she sung sweetly: and it was her favourite reel to which I attempted giving an embodied vehicle in rhyme.

Thus with me began love and poetry: which at times have been my only, and till within the last twelve months, have been my highest enjoyment. My father struggled on till he reached the freedom in his lease, when he entered on a larger farm. . . .

It is during the time that we lived on this farm, that my little story is most eventful. I was, at the beginning of this period, perhaps, the most ungainly awkward boy in the parish . . . no *solitaire* was less acquainted with the ways of the world.

In my seventeenth year, to give my manners a brush, I went to a country dancing-school. . . . My father had an unaccountable antipathy against these meetings, and my going was what to this moment I repent, in opposition to his wishes. My father, as I said before, was subject to strong passions; from that instance of disobedience in me, he took a sort of dislike to me, which I believe was one cause of the dissipation which marked my succeeding years. . . . The great misfortune of my life was to want an aim. I had felt early some stirrings of ambition, but they were the blind gropings of Homer's Cyclops round the walls of his cave. I saw my father's situation entailed on me perpetual labour. The only two openings by which I could enter the temple of fortune, was the gate of niggardly economy, or the path of little chicaning bargain-making. The first is so contracted an aperture I never could squeeze myself into it . . . the last I always hated . . . there was contamination in the very entrance! Thus abandoned of aim or view in life, with a strong appetite for sociability, as well from native hilarity, as from a pride of observation and remark; a constitutional melancholy or hypochondriasm that made me fly solitude; add to these incentives to social life, my reputation for bookish knowledge, a certain wild logical talent, and a strength of thought, something like the rudiments of good-sense, and it will not seem surprising that I was generally a welcome guest where I visited, or any great wonder that always where two or three met together, there was I among them. But far beyond all other impulses of my heart, was *un penchant à l'adorable moitié du genre humain.* My heart was completely tinder, and was eternally lighted up by some goddess or other; and as in every other warfare in this world, my fortune was various; sometimes I was received with favour, and sometimes I was mortified with a repulse. At the plough, scythe, or reap-hook, I feared no competitor, and thus I set absolute want at defiance; and as I never cared farther for my labours than while I was in actual exercise, I spent the evenings in the way after my own heart. A country lad seldom carries on a love adventure without an assistant confidant. I possessed a curiosity, zeal, and intrepid dexterity, that recommended me as a proper second on these occasions, and I dare say, I felt as much pleasure in being in the secret of half the loves of the parish of Tarbolton, as ever did the statesmen in knowing the intrigues of half the courts of Europe. . . .

Another circumstance in my life which made some alteration in my mind and manners, was, that I spent my nineteenth summer on a smuggling coast, a good distance from home, at a noted school, to learn mensuration, surveying, dialling, etc., in which I made a pretty good progress. But I made a greater progress in the knowledge of mankind. The contraband trade was at that time very successful, and it sometimes happened to me to fall in with those who carried it on. Scenes of swaggering riot and roaring dissipation were till this time new to me, but I was no enemy to social life. Here, though I learnt to fill my glass, and to mix without fear in a drunken squabble, yet I went on with a high hand with my geometry; till the sun entered Virgo, a month which is always a carnival in my bosom, when a charming *fillette* who lived next door to the school, overset my trigonometry, and set me off at a tangent from the sphere of my studies. I however struggled on with my *sines* and *co-sines* for a few days more; but stepping into the garden one charming noon to take the sun's altitude, there I met my angel.

> Like a Proserpine gathering flowers,
> Herself a fairer flower.—

It was in vain to think of doing any more good at school. The remaining week I staid, I did nothing but craze the faculties of my soul about her, or steal out to meet her; and the two last nights of my stay in the country, had sleep been a mortal sin, the image of this modest and innocent girl had kept me guiltless. . . .

Maria Chona
(1854[?]-1937[?])

Although the elders among the Papago Indians of Arizona told the adolescent girls of the tribe neither to think about nor talk to boys, it was difficult if not impossible for Maria Chona to obey the injunction. At the age of thirteen she fantasied a good deal about boys and married life. She listened eagerly to the stories of marital friction which occurred in the tribe and to the couples who came to her father for a judgment.

The restrictive pattern of the Papago, while repressing the libidinal needs of the adolescent Maria, could not prevent her, however, from dreaming about flutes and snakes, typical sexual symbols. She relates some of her dreams in the following passage.*

We women sat in the dark, under the shelter, and told about the strange things we had heard. We told how there is a root which men carry to make the deer come to them and it makes women come, too. It smells strong and sweet, and you can smell it on the sweaty hands of a man beside you in the dance. If it is very strong and has been used in many love matches, sometimes it turns into a man. It walks up beside a woman while she is sleeping and makes her dream.

We told how, in our village, a girl was struck by lightning. Someone must have been menstruating and not have confessed it, said the medicine man. So he called all the girls, took out his crystals and looked at them. "It was the girl herself," he said. "She has killed herself."

We told how, when a woman does not seem to care for any man or a man for any woman, that person is really married to a snake. There was a man in our village who used to go out alone into the desert and

*From *The Autobiography of a Papago Woman* edited by Ruth M. Underhill. Reprinted by permission of American Anthropological Association and Ruth M. Underhill. Copyright 1936. Vol. 46. Pp. 27-30.

disappear in a wash. His parents followed him and found there a little red snake with her baby snakes on her back. They said to their son: "What! have you a family of snakes?" He said: "No, she is a beautiful woman." That is how snakes fool you. The older women used to tell us, too, that if we thought too much about any boy before we were married, that boy would seem to come and make love to us. But it would not be he, it would only be a snake. So girls must not think too much about boys. That was what the old women told us. We must not think about boys and we must not talk to boys. When we were married it would be time enough to speak to a man. Now it was better to work and be industrious.

So I worked. But I used to think while I was sitting under the shelter with my basketry, about whether I would get a good man and whether I would like being married. I used to hear a good deal about married peoples' troubles, because my father was chief in Mesquite Root. Married people who had quarrels brought their troubles to him. There was a post in front of our house where people were beaten who did wrong, and all the village would come to see and talk about what happened. . . .

We girls never saw men except our brothers. And our brothers kept away from us now we were almost maidens. They said that sometime we might become maidens suddenly and then if they touched anything that we had touched, it would take away their strength. So the boys did not play with us any more.

But I used to think about boys when I was—let me see, we do not count our ages—thirteen. Sometimes I thought I heard flutes at night. I do not know if it was really boys playing them or if I only dreamed it. But the music drove me wild. The flute is what our boys play when they want a woman to come to them and I wanted to go.

But my father said to me: "Never talk to a man alone. If one comes to the house when there is no one there but you, then offer him food. If he is a relative, say: 'Wait till I cook you something.' Even if he is a stranger, say: 'You had better eat.' But do not talk while you feed him. And if you have nothing in the house tell him quickly so he will go away and not wait, expecting."

So I did that way and so did the other girls, all except a few wild ones. When we went to the hills to gather fruits, we went all together and an old woman with us. When we went to the pond with jars on our heads to get water, we went in a group. Sometimes there would be boys there watering their horses. The wild girls would throw gravel at them, then laugh and run. I never did that.

He [her father] would not let me go to any feasts at all, not even to the maiden's dances, when they happened in our own village and to my own cousins. When a maiden came of age, the people sometimes danced every night until the moon got back to where it was when they began. The men and women danced with their arms over each other's shoulders. We wore nothing on our bodies above the waist then. The young men liked that. It is said that some young girls did not come home at night. It is said that some babies were dropped in the arroyo and no one knew.

They told me that there were women who went alone to those dances, the wild women, who did not work and who went about painted every day. Corn ears they painted on their breasts and birds and butterflies, each breast different for the men to see. And a woman's breast, in that dance, comes just where a man's hand can reach it.

I began to dream of those wild women. They can haunt you just as the Prisoners do. They make men and women crazy, sometimes so that they run out and die. Then you must make little clay dolls, a man and a woman, and have the medicine man sing over them to quiet the sick person. I was not bad enough for that, but sometimes, when I sat alone at my basketry, it would seem to me that I saw a boy and a girl making love and it made me wild.

And I dreamed strange things. Once my mother sent me after water and I was all alone; the other girls had gone earlier in the day. I had to cross a dry wash. As I came up to it, there I saw a snake three times as thick as a man. That wash was full of caves, and the snake's head was in one of them, his tail in another, with his body stretched all across the wash. When I tried to cross it, he would hit me on the legs. I ran home without the water and my father was angry. My mother came with me to see what was the matter and there was no snake there.

And I kept hearing flutes; flutes in the morning and evening. Such lovely music that I would stand still in the house to listen. I thought my crystals were growing again.

William Butler Yeats
(1865-1939)

Yeats, the great Irish poet, noted that at the age of seventeen, his sexual awakenings, rather than being disturbances or enemies, were "so beautiful that I had to be constantly alone to give them my whole attention." The tendency for the adolescent to isolate himself under such circumstances is explained by Anna Freud (24).

"The most remarkable phenomena in the life of adolescents are at bottom connected with their object-relations. It is here that the conflict between two opposite tendencies is most visible. . . . The repression prompted by the general antagonism to instinct usually selects for its first attack the incestuous fantasies of the pre-pubertal period. The suspicion and asceticism of the ego are primarily directed against the subject's fixation to all the love-objects of his childhood. The result of this is, on the one hand, that the young person tends to isolate himself; from this time on, he will live with the members of his family as though with strangers. But it is not only his relation to external love-objects which attracts the ego's innate antagonism to instinct; his relation to the super-ego suffers likewise. In so far as the super-ego is at this period still cathected with libido derived from the relation to the parents, it is itself treated as a suspicious incestuous object and falls a victim to the consequences of asceticism. The ego alienates itself from the super-ego also. To young people this partial repression of the super-ego, the estrangement from part of its contents, is one of the greatest troubles of adolescence. The principal effect of the rupture of the relation between ego and super-ego is to increase the danger which threatens from the instincts. The individual tends to become asocial." This is, apparently, precisely what happened to Yeats.*

The great event of a boy's life is the awakening of sex. He will bathe many times a day, or get up at dawn and having stripped leap to and fro over a stick laid down upon two chairs and hardly know, and never admit, that he had begun to take pleasure in his own nakedness, nor will he understand the change until some dream discovers it. He may never understand at all the greater change in his mind.

It all came upon me when I was close upon seventeen like the bursting of a shell. Somnambulistic country girls, when it is upon them, throw plates about or pull them with long hairs in simulation of the polter-geist, or become mediums for some genuine spirit-mischief, surrendering to their desire of the marvellous. As I look backward, I seem to discover that my passions, my loves and my despairs, instead of being my enemies, a disturbance and an attack, became so beautiful that I had to be constantly alone to give them my whole attention. I notice that now, for the first time, what I saw when alone is more vivid in my memory than what I did or saw in company.

---

*From *The Autobiography of William Butler Yeats*. Reprinted by permission of The Macmillan Company. 1953. P. 38.

Theodore Dreiser
(1871-1945)

The powerful portrait Dreiser creates here of his own adolescent sexual awakenings and repressions* reflects experiences common to many of this age. The bounding animality, the bragging of sexual exploits based on wishful thinking, the lewd and endless talk, the voyeuristic acts, the preoccupation with "legs, breasts, thighs, [and] underwear," the almost frantic efforts at self-satiation, the unendurable sex-worshipping fancies, and above all, the ingenuous ignorance betrayed, are all reported with profound sympathy and insight. These behavioral patterns speak of the struggle between the id and the superego in the adolescent's bid for adjustment.

There was one other boy who for at least two of these opening years here was almost my inseparable companion. His name was Harry Croxton, and his father traded in sewing machines. He was an innocently wild, irresponsible youth, full of the maddest dreams of adventure for the future: China, India, Mexico, South America. (He finally died in Mexico, a mining engineer and expert representing a company there.) But better yet, he was of an insatiable intellectual turn, and because of him as spur and impetus I was compelled to discuss some of the more serious and driving thoughts concerning sex which were already beginning to haunt him as well as myself.

Indeed, when we were out in the woods, or swimming, or in our secret or unobserved places, nearly always all of these boys would fall to talking of girls. Some of their talk was positively vile. A woman at a window, a child in a yard, a boy and girl or man and woman walking were certain to provoke the most pornographic comments. "Come on over here in the woods!" or "Say, I wouldn't do a thing to her if I had her here." Quite entirely, of course, all of this was the product of a bounding animality, almost wholly restrained in the policed and so orderly world around them, and accordingly its intenseness transmuted itself to thought and comment, only partially satisfying, you may be sure. Legs, breasts, thighs, underwear, wild stories of encounters, of seeing things through windows or keyholes, of boys and girls seen lying together in the depths of the woods, were dwelt on as the most exciting of all things.

On the other hand—and by reason of the temperament of this par-

---

*From *Dawn, A History of Myself* by Theodore Dreiser. Reprinted by permission of World Publishing Company. Copyright 1931, Theodore Dreiser. Pp. 207-210.

ticular youth—another, and for me much more illuminating type of sex discussion was introduced. For whether by reason of the mental direction of either his father or mother—both New Englanders and intellectuals of the country or small town type—he appeared thus early well aware of the physical anatomy of sex—the actual (as then known) physiology as well as, in a modest way, emotional psychology of the organs and their reactions, and also, as then taught, the attendant dangers of masturbation, lack of sanitation, and the various diseases and contagions to which that lack gives rise. And liked to talk about all these things. Only finding, in our gang at least, few if any hearers other than myself, he devoted much of his time and quite all of his discoveries as well as speculations in this field to me. And hearing of a lecture for men only which was soon to come, was determined that I should hear that. But the admission charge—fifty cents—as well as the shame that I felt at that time of explaining to my mother exactly what the fifty cents was for, caused me to give over the idea.

But Croxton, determined on learning all in this field, and having himself attended, returned with news of all he had heard—not much more than previously he had known except this: that he had seen large colored maps of each particular organ, with the mechanics of the same clearly set forth—some of which he roughly sketched and so made very clear to me much more of my own mechanism as well as that of the opposite sex than I had ever guessed—but all with his now repeated warnings of the dangers that accompanied license—a series of facts in regard to contagions and their devastating effects which impressed me not a little.

I was as determined by then to avoid loose or evil women—as my father described them—as I would the devil himself!

None the less, sex, sex, sex! How the hot fire nature had lighted in my body was driving me to almost frantic efforts at self-satiation! And how, for the next two or three years (to say nothing of the next twenty-five) it harried me from hell to hell! Although my mother and father and the pleasant father confessor of our church were constantly counselling me to keep pure in thought and feeling, yet my proper nature was gratifying itself with insistent thoughts and emotions that concerned girls and this sex function. And while I did not even then quite realize fully the immense force and power of male and female contact, still in a vague way, I did, too. I cannot explain the something of vagueness that lingered about all this, only that it must have been evoked by inexperience. Men and women reveled with one another in some way . . . but how? It seemed—and even after young Croxton, if you will believe it—that it must relate more to hugging and kissing than anything else, although I now knew definitely of that *else*. For the lines of a woman's form were beginning to be of blazing import to me, and just that—the pleasure of viewing and caressing it—seemed almost enough—indeed in some of my sex-worshipping fancies, all but too much. Could I endure? Would I have the vitality, the self-repression even, so that I should not faint? For often at the mere sight of an unheralded Venus displayed in a book or some picture that chanced to fall into my hands, my blood ran hot and cold. I was transfixed, fearsome, and invariably looked cautiously about for fear someone might be looking with or at me. Yet assuring myself of being alone, I would make bold to feast my eyes upon the potent lines. Then a veritable feeling of fear or weakness, an actual wave of bashful terror and almost insupportable breathlessness, as I paused to think on what I should do if I were suddenly confronted by such a reality—what—in love—I should be called upon to do! Ah, how devastating as well as rewarding! How fire-sweet and yet fire-injurious, too!

Sing the dark flower of passion that glorifies and terrifies the world! Once—in my youth, at least—we lied so about it. As one might skirt the quaking caldron of a crater, red and glinting with the molten slag below, so humanity throughout the Christian era has gone about it on tiptoe, fearing to examine what it most greatly desired to possess. But since then, what a change! The stage—books—Freud—life!

At that time, though, I found myself on the *qui vive* for every form of life; all was no more than a minor accompaniment to the molten, sputtering main theme pulsating and winding like a great river within the depths of my inner self. Shall I call it passion? It had no least relationship to the actuality which a passion for some one definite individuality evokes. The feverish unrest to see a given face or hear a certain voice! That was wanting. Instead, though, there was a wild, flaming enthusiasm for the color of life itself: all the color which contributes to the settings of sex. The flowers, trees, grass, sky, beautiful homes, bright shops, music, the artistry of clothing—all combined to produce a thrilling harmony which sang of but one thing: love.

Helena Morley
(1880-   )

On August 28, 1894, Helena Morley, the daughter of an English diamond miner and a Brazilian mountain woman, celebrated her fourteenth birthday in her native town of Diamantina, Brazil. Up until the time of her birthday, and for two weeks afterward, little or no mention is made in her diary* of the opposite sex as such. But with the September 12, 1894 entry, a subtle change emerges. She is teased by friends about her lack of interest in boys and marriage; she listens in silence and then cuts them short with a supposedly devastating cliché in an attempt to defend the disinterest.

The lie is given the disinterest, however, in an entry written a short time later. In it, Helena recalls some dreams, in manifest content and in sexual symbolism much like the ones of the Papago Indian girl, Maria Chona. In them, Helena dreams of "being in a field of peanuts, and I kept pulling up the plants and finding silver coins at the roots. . . . But last night's dream was horrible. I dreamed I'd turned into a monkey, and in spite of my grief I could have resigned myself to being a monkey if I hadn't had a tail, but my tail was enormous!"

Wednesday, September 12, 1894

Why do my schoolmates worry so much about my life? I don't know why, since they've never given me anything and wouldn't if I needed it. How I'd like to tell them, "Don't interfere with me; mind your own business." Some friend is always coming with a message from a brother or a cousin or some other boy for me. Fininha brought me a poem her brother had written for me. I keep telling them that I don't want to have a sweetheart, that I don't love anybody, and to leave me alone. Today they began to tease me and call me an old maid. Mariana said, "You're fourteen years old already. If you don't look for a man now, when you're older no one will want you and you'll be an aunt. You're going to be an old maid." I said, "But if I want to be an old maid, what do you care?" She said, "If you don't care, it's all right; but we care, because we like you. That's why." Biela said, "You don't understand Helena. She wants to get married just as much as we do, but she's proud, she wants something special. I bet that if a doctor [any man with a university degree] appeared she wouldn't send him away." The others said, "Then she just keeps sucking her finger. There aren't any doctors here, unless she's waiting for her cousins who are studying in Rio. Anyway, what's the difference between a doctor and the rest of

*From *The Diary of "Helena Morley"* edited by Elizabeth Bishop. Reprinted by permission of Farrar, Straus, & Cudahy, Inc. Copyright 1957, Elizabeth Bishop. Pp. 153 154, 165.

them? They're all men, aren't they?" I listened to it all in silence. To cut the conversation short, I said, "Don't worry so much about me, my friends; remember the saying, 'Marriages and shrouds are made in Heaven.' "

Saturday, October 27th, 1894

If there were diviners of dreams today, the way there were in the time of Joseph of Egypt, what a fine thing it would be! I can never get that story of the seven fat cows and seven lean cows, that meant seven years of plenty and seven years of famine, out of my head. . . .

Even now I suffer from strange dreams and I don't believe the explanation Mama Tina gave me when I was little, even if it would be easier to. When I told her my dreams and asked her to explain them, she used to say, "Dreaming is when the soul doesn't go to sleep with the body and keeps on thinking. If a person is good and lives according to God's will, he has good dreams; if he's in mortal sin, he has bad dreams." I don't want any other girl to suffer what I suffered over my soul's being in mortal sin when I had a bad dream. I told them to Mama Tina, and she put me on my knees to pray. I had no idea what my mortal sin was, but then I remembered that I must have been envious or greedy and I calmed down a little and made resolutions to correct myself.

I suffer a great deal from dreams and one of the worst I had when I was little was the disillusionment I suffered when I died and went to heaven. How horrible heaven was that night! I remember until today the dismal life I led in heaven until I woke up. It was an enormous yard, clean and bare, filled with old women in cloaks, with shawls on their heads, holding their hands up in prayer, not paying any attention to each other. No St. Pedro, no angels, nothing. When they were tired of kneeling they walked around in that enormous yard with their heads bent, still praying. When I woke up and saw I wasn't in heaven, what a relief!

I told this dream to Mama Tina and she explained to me that it was because she'd told me that the road to heaven is full of thorns; but the road to hell is clean and bare, and in my dream I'd changed them around.

Dreaming that I'm at Mass at the Cathedral in the middle of the crowd in my underwear, is something horrible that's always happening to me. Lots of times I've dreamed I was at School in my bare feet, without knowing where to hide them. It's a constant martyrdom. But I've had marvellous dreams, too. I can't count the times I've flown,

without wings, to Boa Vista or over the houses of the city. It's delightful! Or I was in a marvellous palace, like the little girl and the dwarfs.
And I've dreamed of being in a field of peanuts, and I kept pulling up
the plants and finding silver coins at the roots.

But last night's dream was horrible. I dreamed I'd turned into a
monkey, and in spite of my grief I could have resigned myself to being
a monkey if I hadn't had a tail, but my tail was enormous!

If Mama Tina were alive, I wouldn't have to ask her to explain this
dream. I know quite well it was because we were speaking about Siá
Ritinha's monkey at dinner yesterday.

Jawaharlal Nehru
(1889-   )

The sublimation of the adolescent's sexual needs in lofty, highly
intellectual conversations is a common method of coping. Jawaharlal Nehru, while he was a seventeen-year-old student at Trinity
College, Cambridge, and for several years subsequently, used this
mechanism as did most of his friends.*

The asceticism of the adolescent is itself due to an increase in
instinctual danger, a sign of fear of sexuality and a defense against
it. The anxieties and defensive tendencies manifest themselves in
the sophisticated talk such as Nehru describes. By removing himself
from the possibility of sexual contact with the opposite sex, the
adolescent relieves himself of the agony of rejection, or the humiliation of submission, or the revival of overt oedipal feelings.

Cambridge, Trinity College, the beginning of October 1907, my age
seventeen, or rather approaching eighteen. I felt elated at being an
undergraduate with a great deal of freedom, compared to school, to
do what I chose. I had got out of the shackles of boyhood and felt at
last that I could claim to be a grown-up. With a self-conscious air I
wandered about the big courts and narrow streets of Cambridge, delighted to meet a person I knew.

Three years I was at Cambridge, three quiet years with little of
disturbance in them, moving slowly on like the sluggish Cam. They
were pleasant years, with many friends and some work and some play

---

*From *Toward Freedom* by Jawaharlal Nehru. Reprinted by permission of The
John Day Company, Inc. 1936. Pp. 19-20.

and a gradual widening of the intellectual horizon. I took the Natural Science Tripos, my subjects being chemistry, geology and botany, but my interests were not confined to these. Many of the people I met at Cambridge or during the vacations in London or elsewhere talked learnedly about books and literature and history and politics and economics. I felt a little at sea at first in this semi-highbrow talk, but I read a few books and soon got the hang of it and could at least keep my end up and not betray too great an ignorance on any of the usual subjects. So we discussed Nietzsche (he was all the rage in Cambridge then) and Bernard Shaw's prefaces and the latest book by Lowes Dickinson. We considered ourselves very sophisticated and talked of sex and morality in a superior way, referring casually to Ivan Block, Havelock Ellis, Kraft Ebbing or Otto Weininger. We felt that we knew about as much of the theory of the subject as anyone who was not a specialist need know.

As a matter of fact, in spite of our brave talk, most of us were rather timid where sex was concerned. At any rate I was so, and my knowledge for many years, till after I had left Cambridge, remained confined to theory. Why this was so it is a little difficult to say. Most of us were strongly attracted by sex and I doubt if any of us attached any idea of sin to it. Certainly I did not; there was no religious inhibition. We talked of its being amoral, neither moral nor immoral. Yet in spite of all this a certain shyness kept me away, as well as a distaste for the usual methods adopted. For I was in those days definitely a shy lad, perhaps because of my lonely childhood.

Don C. Talayesva
(1890-   )

The autobiography of Don Talayesva, a Hopi Indian chief, was recorded by the anthropologist, Dr. Leo W. Simmons.* At about the time of the Indian's birth, the conflict between the old and new ways of life was becoming acute, expressing itself in Hopi society through the opposition between the "Friendly," who were willing to co-operate with the white man, and the "Hostile," who were determined to resist. Born as a Hopi, reared as a Hopi child, Don was sent to the American school when he was about ten years old, and until twenty he planned and hoped for an American life. At

*In *The Autobiography of a Winnebago Indian* edited by Paul Radin. Reprinted by permission of University of California Press. 1920. Pp. 387, 393-394.

that time a sudden illness opened a violent crisis in his mind; through dreams and visions he became acquainted with his familiar spirit, and in compliance with the warning he returned to his homeland, renounced Christianity, and settled down in the ways and customs of Hopi life.

In the excerpts which follow, Don describes the sexual curiosity and desires he had soon after the achievement of puberty, which occurred for him at about the age of twelve. Despite the sexual excitement he felt, he could not stay awake to appease it, but satisfied himself—for the time—with a rare smile from one or two of the girls.

After a time I passed from this stage of boyhood into another.[1] I began to use a bow and arrow and I spent my time at play, shooting arrows.

Then I found out that my mother had been told, just before I was born, that she would give birth to no ordinary being, and from that time on I felt that I must be an uncommon person.

At about this time my oldest sister married a holy man. My parents gave her in marriage to him. He was a shaman and he thought a great deal of me.

At this stage of life also I secretly got the desire to make myself pleasing to the opposite sex.

Now at that time the Indians all lived in their lodges and the women were always placed in lodges of their own whenever they had their menses. There the young men would court them at night when their parents were asleep. They would then enter these lodges to court them. I used to go along with the men on such occasions for even although I did not enter the lodge but merely accompanied them, I enjoyed it.

At that time my parents greatly feared that I might come in contact with women who were having their menses, so I went out secretly. My parents were even afraid to have me cross the path over which a woman in such a condition had passed.[2] The reason they worried so much about it at that particular time was because I was to fast as soon

---

[1] The physiological and other changes at puberty are definitely noted by the Winnebago and a special word is used to cover the years from approximately twelve to twenty.

[2] A very general belief among the Winnebago. Any contact with menstruating women, or even with objects in any way connected with them, will, it is believed, destroy the power of sacred objects or individuals temporarily sacred. Fasting youths were regarded as such.

as autumn came; and it was for that reason they did not wish me to be near menstruating women, for were I to grow up in the midst of such women I would assuredly be weak and of little account. Such was their reason.

* * * *

It was at this time that I desired to court women and I tried it. However, I did not know the proper thing to say. The young men always went around at night courting. I used to mix with the women in the daytime but when I went to them at night I did not know what to say. A brother of mine, the oldest, seemed to know how to do it. He was a handsome man and he offered to show me how. Then I went with him at night. We went to a girl who was having her menses at that time. She was a young girl. When girls get their menses they always have to live apart. It was to such a one that we went. We were very cautious about the matter for the girls were always carefully watched as their relatives knew that it was customary to court them at such a time. (One of the precautions they used) was to pile sticks and branches about the lodge so that it would be difficult to enter. If a person tried to enter he was likely to make a noise moving the branches and this would awaken the people living in the larger lodge nearby and they might run out to see what was the matter.

It was to such a place that we went. After working at the obstacles placed near the entrance for some time, my brother entered the lodge. I went as close as possible and lay down to listen. He spoke in an audible whisper so that I might hear him. Sure enough I heard him. However after lying there for some time I fell asleep. When I snored my brother would wake me up. Afterwards the girl found out and she sent us both away. Thus we acted every now and then.

After a while I entered the lodges myself. We always had blankets wrapped around us and we took care to have our heads well covered (on such occasions). . . .

There was one old woman who had a daughter and when this daughter had her menses, she stayed in an oblong lodge with just room enough for two persons. She watched her daughter very carefully. Finally she slept with her. We nevertheless bothered her all the time just out of meanness. One night we went there and kept her awake almost all night. However, just about dawn she fell asleep, so we— there were several of us—pulled up the whole lodge, poles and everything, and threw the poles in the thicket. The next morning the two were found sleeping in the open, it was rumored, and the mother was criticised for being over careful.

The reason why some of the (older) people were so careful at that time was because it had been reported that some young men had forced themselves into lodges where they had not been received willingly.

Once I went to see a young girl and arrived there before the people had retired, so I waited near the lodge until they would go to sleep. As I lay there waiting, listening to them, I fell asleep. When I woke up it was morning and as the people got up they found me sleeping there. I felt very much ashamed of myself and they laughed at me. I was not long in getting away. . . .

After a while I began going around with some particular girl and I liked it so much that I would never go to sleep at night. My older brothers were very much the same. We used to sleep during the day.

While we were acting in this manner, our parents saw to it that we had food to eat and clothes to wear. We never helped, for we did nothing but court girls. In the fall the Indians used to pick berries after they all came together. We used to help on such occasions. However, we were generally out all night and were not able to do much in the morning. I used to go out courting and be among the lodges all night, and yet, most of the time, I did not succeed in speaking to any of the girls. However, I did not mind that for I was doing it in order to be among the girls and I enjoyed it. I would even go around telling people that I was really keeping company with some of the girls. I used to say this to some of my men associates. In reality, however, I did not get much more than a smile from one or two of the girls but even that I prized as a great thing.

Najmeh Najafi
(1932[?]-   )

The Persian girl, Najmeh Najafi, speaks here of the cultural and religious pressures of her country on its pubescent boys and girls. Despite the strict separation of the sexes, Najmeh, at fourteen and fifteen, could not deny the quickening of the sexual impulses within. By minor rebellions and through fantasies, she gave expression to them, although the forms were dissatisfying and frustrating. Many years later, she relates, when she saw couples loving each other by the Seine at moonlight, "My legs softened and would not hold me and I felt sick.*"

---

*From *Persia Is My Heart* by Najmeh Najafi as told by Helen Hinckley. Reprinted by permission of Harper & Brothers. Copyright 1953, Najmeh Najafi and Helen Hinckley Jones. Pp. 95-97.

When I was in high school something strange happened to me. I had been very quiet, very good, very obedient, very quick to learn. I had had a tender heart. But, suddenly I was gay, laughing, silly. Maybe I had lost my sensitivity. I do not know. It was a wonderful thing to be living; to walk down the street with my arm around my friend, Naheet.

We were going to the school which we girls called the Bastille. Though the school work was more difficult and the teachers even more stern, I was happy. The Bastille—we named our school for the famous French prison after reading about the French Revolution—was of course a girls' school. Many of the teachers were hard, unlovely women. In America you have a word to describe them—frustrated. In my country they were examples of what happens to the natural softness of women when they do not marry. To us they were cranky, mean, terrible.

Just two streets from our school there was a boys' school. That is why the teachers kept watch over us with both eyes. Even the school schedule was arranged to make the watching easy. If the school sessions began at the same time and ended at the same time in the afternoon, the boys and girls might be friendly. They might even speak to each other. If the boys were dismissed first, they would wait around for the girls. So the girls were excused early.

It was strange how long it took Naheet and me to walk a very little way—say two blocks—down the avenue. We were surprised to have just passed the boys' school when it was dismissed for the day. We never spoke to the boys, but we were learning the language of tossing the head until the curls jumped, of looking with eyes almost covered with shyly lowered lids. Sometimes a brave boy seized a book from us and escaped. We were flattered! We knew we were beautiful and full of charm. Sometimes the younger boys walked on their hands or turned handsprings so that we would notice them. We did.

This never talking together, the boys never discovering that girls are just people and the girls never discovering that boys are just people, is very bad, I think. It is one of the worst things in my country. The care that is taken to keep boys and girls separated makes us think always of sex. People grow hungry for forbidden food even when they are very young.

Already we had read about moonlight on the Seine and of how lovers walk hand in hand. I dreamed that someday it would be moonlight on the Seine for me. Many years later when I did see the Seine by moonlight—how can I tell you? Many men and girls were sitting on the sidewalks, kissing, caressing. I do not have correct words for all the things they were doing. I had read of these things. I had seen them in pictures. But when I saw them with my eyes, my legs softened and would not hold me and I felt sick.

The segregation of sexes in Persia is a bad thing, I think, yet never is it necessary to put the pot on such a hot fire that it must boil over!

I remember one teacher who was especially unlovely. I did not think then, but I do now, that she was especially hungry to be young and to be desired. One day I had my brown hair tied with two blue bows, one behind each ear holding a clump of curls. Our uniforms were not made alike but they were an ugly lifeless color of gray. I had one of mine made with a tiny red piping around the collar and pockets, the other trimmed with a piping of clean, clear blue. The bows on my hair matched this little piping and made the uniform look almost pretty.

"Why do you wear these ribbons?" she asked me.

"I want to be pretty," I said.

She pulled the ribbons from my hair. "They are wicked. They are for the purpose of decoration and decoration of women is for the purpose of bringing sin to the mind of boys."

I was angry and hurt. I knew the words of the Koran as well as she did: "And speak unto the believing women, that they refrain their eyes and preserve their modesty, and display not their ornaments. . . ." I was only a girl, I would never be anything more than a woman. I was angry that I was a woman, but that was one thing I could not change. At least I should be allowed blue bows in my hair.

It seems to me that since I have been in America I have discovered that everything that seemed like sin to the teachers in the advanced school in Persia is pleasure to young people in America. And I think in America boys and girls may make some little mistakes together, little by little, but they will not make the big mistake that can come to one who has had a growing hunger for a long time and suddenly must satisfy it.

HETEROSEXUAL PLAY

With the first anguished awakenings of sex, the adolescent gradually moves on to heterosexual play. His sexual feelings find expression in a variety of ways as did the initial impulses which were illustrated in the previous section. With the usually transient domination of the id during adolescence comes the typical demand for immediate satisfaction of needs. But the satisfaction is frequently hobbled by unresolved superego development. The immature conscience of the adolescent is fogged by conflict, a conflict created by desire on the one hand and by religious or social instruction on the other. During puberty, the adolescent lives in a state of war with himself, an inner conflict which can be tormenting.

Sullivan (58) states that "the change from preadolescence to adolescence appears as a growing interest in the possibilities of achieving some measure of intimacy with a member of the other sex, rather after the pattern of the intimacy that one in preadolescence enjoyed with a member of one's own sex." The adolescent generally proceeds with extreme caution and tentativeness in his attempts to achieve even a limited intimacy with the other sex. Toward the female, Ackerman (1) states, he is indescribably sensitive, sensitive to her as to his own incompleteness. "She is a mirror into which he gazes anxiously to measure his defects and to confess his masculine unfulfillment. His need of her is acute; his fear of her is critical. Sometimes it reaches immense proportions. He yearns to complete himself in her but fears instead to lose himself in her. He watches with hypertrophied alertness her slightest move, her merest gesture. Will she be receptive, will she rebuff him, will she strike out in anger? If he dares approach her, his movements are awkward and fumbling. He is eternally vigilant and with the first sign of danger is poised for an instantaneous leap to his own defense or for complete retreat. His urge is to show himself to her, but the moment danger looms, he flees for cover."

Catherine the Great (1729-1796) recorded in her *Memoirs* the courtship of the Grand Duke of Russia. The following passage is typical. "During my illness the Grand Duke had shown me every attention. When I was better he kept it up. He seemed to like me; but I can neither say that I liked him nor that I disliked him. I only knew how to obey, and my mother had to marry me; I believe in truth however that the Russian crown meant more to me than he. I was sixteen years old at the time. Before he had the small-pox, he was quite handsome, but was very small and child-like. He used to talk to me about his playthings and toy soldiers with which he busied himself early and late. To be polite and agreeable, I listened to him, but I often yawned without exactly knowing why. But I did not go away and leave him and he thought that he ought to talk to me; as he spoke only of things that gave him pleasure, he was well entertained when he talked with me a long time. Many people looked on this as a genuine attraction, especially those who desired my marriage. But we never used between us the language of tenderness; it was surely not my business to bring it into use, my modesty would not have allowed that even if I had felt so inclined, and my natural pride was sufficient to prevent my taking the first steps. But it did not at all occur to him, which, frankly speaking, did not prepossess me in his favor. For no matter how well up a maiden may be, she always likes to hear the words of flattery and tenderness, especially from one to whom she may listen without blushing [12]."

One of the things Catherine indicates is that with the emergence of sex, the individual is forced to assume a masculine or feminine role. Culturally, there are differences along sexual lines. Maleness is a symbol of strength, responsibility, aggressiveness and dominance. Femaleness is identified with dependence, compliance and subservience. How the adolescent identifies with his sex will be the area pursued in the following selections. The latter include representations from France, the United States, Spain, Russia, and England.

Alexandre Dumas
(1802-1870)

In most Western cultures, petting seems to be a constant in adolescent heterosexual play. In almost all of the passages in this section, some expression of this form of activity is described by the autobiographers. Dumas, père, passed the boundary that separated his boyhood from his youth in his sixteenth year, initiated in the rites of petting by "two sophisticated young women." The town of Villers-Cotterets, in which Dumas spent his adolescence, had (surprisingly enough) "the English custom of free and easy associations between the sexes which I have never seen in any other French town.*"

---

*From *The Road to Monte Carlo. A Condensation of the Memoirs of Alexandre Dumas* edited by Jules Eckert Goodman. New York: Charles Scribner's Sons, 1956. Pp. 36-37.

In the fortnight I spent with those two sophisticated young women, I completed my passage across the boundary that separates childhood from youth. In years I was between the children who still played prisoner's base and quoits and the youths who were turning into men. And instead of turning back to the former, I attached myself to the latter. When anyone asked my age I drew myself up to the full height of my sixteen years and told them that I was seventeen.

Almost all the girls in Villers-Cotterets had some more or less serious affair on hand. For some reason we in Villers-Cotterets had the English custom of free and easy associations between the sexes which I have never seen in any other French town. This was all the more surprising since the parents of these girls were respectable and firmly convinced that all barques launched upon the flood of passion were decked with white sails and crowned with orange blossoms. And, strangely enough, this was true with the majority of the lovers who formed our circle.

While I waited patiently for one of these affairs to break up, I went to every party and took part in all the walks and dances. It was an excellent apprenticeship, and after six weeks or so an engagement between a boy named Richou and Adèle Dalvin was broken off by the boy's father.

I had learned much during my six weeks of watching others, and this time I was not involved with a sarcastic and exacting Parisian girl who knew the world much better than I. Adèle was shyer even than I and mistook my pretended courage for the genuine. This gave me great assurance. Now I was the attacker and I soon realized that only by long and patient wooing could I break down Adèle's obstinate resistance. Thus began my study of the delicious struggle of love which asks unceasingly and is not discouraged by an eternity of refusal—a study that has lasted throughout my life.

In the summer we all met at eight o'clock. If the weather was fine, the park invited us. In winter or bad weather we met at Louise Brexette's, where her mother and aunt surrendered the two front rooms to us. They withdrew to a back room and, seated beside a single light, sewed and read aloud from the *Imitation of Christ*. Meanwhile in the front rooms we chatted, squeezed against each other, two to a chair, and repeated the same stories we had told the night before. On Sundays we met at three and walked and danced until midnight. And then there were fetes in neighboring villages to which we went in happy bands—and returned in silent pairs.

Arturo Barea
(1897-1957)

At the age of fifteen, Arturo Barea, the noted Spanish journalist, was employed by a bank to do the routine work of "filling in blanks with stereotyped words, making deductions and sums, always the same, mechanically." What helped pass the days along and make them notable was his relationship with Enriqueta, a twenty-year-old girl who was also an employee of the firm. Barea reveals the sexual sanctions and taboos of middle-class Spain: overt sexual play in full view of others was permissible, up to a point; sexual intercourse in private, for an unmarried girl, never!*

And then there were the girls. In our section there were four women and two men. Three of the girls were old and ugly, and only Enriqueta was young. She was twenty. On some days it was hell. Antonio and I were the only men who counted, for Perahita was elderly and married. But we—there were days when the girls petted us as though we had been babies. Antonio touched their thighs and breasts and they only laughed. They came up to me and dictated figures, and while they did it they bent over the desk, their breasts pushed up on its surface, they leaned on my shoulder, they excited me, and when in the end I stretched out my hand, they squealed: "You naughty boy!"

Perahita laughed at them and at me and made peace. I had to make my excuses.

Enriqueta had a strong smell. Once she pushed the half-sleeve of her blouse up to her shoulder and asked me: "Does it smell? It's too bad, I wash and wash it every day, just look." She showed me her armpit, full of little black curls and a hot smell. I came very near it with my face and touched it with my fingertips. Later, when I came back from the lavatory she gave me a glance, her eyes smiled, and she blushed. I felt that I, too, was blushing and could not do my sums.

Once we both went down into the steel room where the section had worked before. We had to collect the coupons of the State Bonds and began to open drawers and take out bundles. She stood on one of the white steel benches, which looked like those in a clinic. I could smell her. Her stockings were stretched tight over her legs. I began to stroke softly along one of her calves and follow it upwards. We kissed, she

*From *The Forging of a Rebel* by Arturo Barea. Reprinted by permission of the Barea Estate. 1946, Reynal & Hitchcock. Pp. 174-175.

bending down from the bench, I standing below her, with trembling legs and a burning face. We did not go upstairs together, we would have been too much ashamed. After that we used to caress each other even in front of the others. She would come and stand beside my high desk while I was sitting, and dictate to me. I plunged my left hand under her skirt, she went on dictating absurd figures to me, and my right hand went on scribbling.

These things pleased and repelled me. Once I asked her to come with me to the Moncloa. She said very seriously: "Now listen, I'm a decent girl." A decent girl—and once when we went to the pictures together she stroked my whole body with her fingers and never had her fill!

Why was it necessary for women to be virgins when they married? She herself said it was so. She said that we could not be together without her losing her virginity, and she would have to marry sooner or later. What we were doing was just a childish game, it did not matter and was not dangerous. "But otherwise it might happen that I became pregnant," she said. "It's true that you're still a boy, but you can already have children."

What could I have answered? Nothing. The only thing I could do was to make good use of the dark corners where she sought me out. I wanted to stop that sort of thing, but she got so angry that it was impossible.

Philip O'Connor
(1916-   )

The self-styled "public baby" of Britain, Philip O'Connor, relates vividly the ascetic quality of early heterosexual relationships. He describes his love for "Shirt" as uncomfortably exalted; he spurned imaginary offers of intercourse as if he were an anchorite; from the ages of fourteen to seventeen, "we 'loved' for three years in vain; I liked the vanity of it, religiously. . . . " The vague spiritual aspirations which are associated with sex are characteristic of the early period of adolescence.

"Alternating with instinctual excesses and irruptions from the id and with other, apparently contradictory, attitudes, there is sometimes in adolescence an antagonism towards the instincts which far surpasses in intensity anything in the way of repression which we are accustomed to see under normal conditions or in more or less severe cases of neurosis. In the mode of its manifestation and the width of its range it is less akin to the symptoms of pronounced neurotic disease than to the asceticism of religious fanatics. . . . Adolescents are not so much concerned with the gratification or frustration of specific instinctual wishes as with instinctual gratification or frustration as such. Young people who pass through the kind of ascetic phase which I have in mind seem to fear the quantity rather than the quality of their instincts. They mistrust enjoyment in general and so their safest policy appears to be simply to counter more urgent desires with more stringent prohibitions. Every time the instinctive says, 'I will,' the ego retorts, 'Thou shalt not,' much after the manner of strict parents in the early training of little children. . . . There is . . . another point in which this sort of repudiation of instinct differs from ordinary repression. . . . In the repudiation of instinct characteristic of adolescence no loop-hole is left for such substitutive gratification: the mechanism seems to be a different one. Instead of compromise-formations . . . and the usual processes of displacement, regression and turning against the self, we find almost invariably a swingover from asceticism to instinctual excess [which is precisely what happened to Philip O'Connor, as he relates in a later chapter in his *Memoirs**], the adolescent indulging in everything which he had previously held to be prohibited and disregarding any sort of external restrictions. On account of their anti-social character these adolescent excesses are in themselves unwelcome manifestations; nevertheless, from the analytic standpoint they represent transitory spontaneous recovery from the condition of asceticism. Where no such recovery takes place [as in the case of O'Connor] and the ego in some inexplicable way is strong enough to carry through its repudiation of instinct without any deviation, the result is a paralysis of the subject's vital activities—a kind of catatonic condition, which can no longer be regarded as a normal phenomenon of puberty but must be recognized as a psychotic affection [25]." At the age of eighteen, O'Connor was diagnosed as schizophrenic and spent six months in a mental institution.

At school, I'd begun a love affair with 'Shirt.' She was plainly pretty, with pinkish skin, small but very ardent blue eyes, and much simplic-

---

*From *Memoirs of a Public Baby*. Reprinted by permission of Faber & Faber, Ltd. 1958, Farrar, Straus, & Cudahy, Inc. Pp. 132-134.

ity rather spoiled with High School hoydenishness—she pretended to be, or she may even have been, devoted to hockey. We pressed hard against each other; I planned every week her undoing—we met on a bench in the playing fields of her little town—but was as timid as a mouse and most uncomfortably exalted, in the Tennysonian way, as my due reward for timidity. I affected in further compensation a saintly disgust with the sexual act—there was, of course, no question of our trying it (at fourteen) yet I behaved as though she were suggesting these favours and I was spurning them like an anchorite. I kept about forty of her letters; the writing squarish with secret roundness, like her character, and very clear, and very dull the letters were: yet potentially pregnant. I sometimes secretly objected to her slightly dampish skin; and she often had pimples. But her legs seemed nice; I never dared carry out my plotted inspection of them; she thought them very private, and kept her skirt down when crossing stiles. She loved her father but not her stepmother and I agreed when I heard the latter's voice. I think I have always known women who loved their fathers very much. My shyness made my substitute role acceptable to me, and satisfied incestuous proclivities. We 'loved' for three years in vain; I liked the vanity of it, religiously: great rapture accrued to me from failing in many an amatory pursuit, and my first set the tone for this. I knew well the religious steam arising from repression, and contrived 'interesting' characteristics out of it, in imitation of my guardian who was similarly dowered; as a result for a long time satisfaction was death in the aftermath. But truthfully when I was satisfied it was the great size of the world that dismayed me; repression kept me in a cosy cupboard. I increasingly inhabited this vast space of dismayingly exact contours with balloons of memory inflated by repressed sex, to bend it to my 'will,' conducive to my will-lessness. At school I had begun drawing faces that alternated between dead 'nobility' and lively monstrousness; my own character was in accord.

David S. Kogan
(1929-1951)

A more normal exposition of the throes, fumblings, and anguish of early adolescent sex play was recorded by David Kogan in his *Diary*. During his fourteenth and fifteenth years, David progressed from holding hands to heavy necking, from frustration and bewilderment to frank enjoyment. At one point he bemoans the braces on his teeth and his poor physique which interfere with his progress and restrain him from proving his adequacy as a male.*

Saturday, April 22, 1944

Eight-thirty found me on my way to a party in the home of a Lincoln Park girl.

Was acting as usual—dancing awkwardly; then eating; then talking to the stag line, and so forth. Suddenly Sandra takes an interest in me and feeds me the "only dearest one" line. To my surprise she continues. I find myself in a corner with her, my arm around her—we're holding hands, laughing, talking, joking. I was having a wonderful time. It was the first real enjoyment I had with the opposite sex, besides talking to B. D. and looking at Eleanor. But then—just as suddenly she loses all interest in me. I did not see her the rest of the evening. I was in a daze, and the last period went slowly.

Sunday, November 26, 1944

As today was withal dull, I would like to devote a major portion of my space to Judy. She lives across the street, and is one the half dozen most beautiful girls in Yonkers. Gil likes her, and the three of us either sit in her house, or on my porch. She's a knockout, face, hair, legs, and personality plus. Although only fourteen—she could pass for twenty. An expert dancer, she is the master of the caress, and is sexy without getting into trouble, or being considered cheap. She can wittily discuss sex without vulgarity. She comes over not infrequently. We hold hands on the piano and pick out tunes with one finger. Oh, it's times like this, that I wish I had no brace and complex, and some brawn and looks instead.

Sunday, February 11, 1945

Nora, a most ugly girl, invited me to Irma's party last night. I went out of curiosity, hoping I won't be sorry.

It was the different type of affair. We got there at nine and found several couples. They talked for about ten minutes and then out went all the lights. The couples went into passionate positions. Ken had his hand under the brassiere of Dina for quite a while! I just sat there looking. Then I began kissing Nora; was she homely! The gang treated

---

*From *The Diary of David S. Kogan*. Reprinted by permission of Beechurst Press. 1955. Pp. 52, 77, 86.

the affair so casually as with remarks like "Pull down your sweater, Audrey." I liked the indifference, the knowledge that the girls had not any modesty short of relations. It took a lot of the uncertainty and guessing out of it—the girls cooperated. Also, except for Nora, the girls were very beautiful. Yes, I enjoyed the new experience, the action of others, but why did she have to be so homely!

David C. DeJong
(1905-   )

The great test of sexual competency for the adolescent is illustrated in the next few excerpts.* David DeJong failed the test miserably, as this hilarious autobiographical account of his initial attempt at intercourse reveals. At fifteen, DeJong, author of the novels *Old Haven, The Desperate Children,* and others, was busily making preparations for losing his virginity. He was working as a soda jerk in a Grand Rapids, Michigan drug store when "the opportunity for emerging from that cocoon of innocence which enveloped [him] so disgracefully, soon presented itself." As in the case of Sherwood Anderson and many another adolescent, a joint venture with a friend was a requirement in responding to the imperious and irresistible sex drive. But as the anticipated but awful hour for the assignation approached, David's friend confessed that in spite of his boasting he too was virginal. It would seem that the bragging of sexual exploits in many cases represents but the verbally aggressive assertion of masculinity. The steps the two boys take to prevent the consummation of the act indicate the middle-class prohibition against premarital relations and emphasize the conflict the adolescent faces in the realm of sex.

My friend at the business school, beholding me in the throes of such an extravagant romance, simply gave me up, after cursing all females roundly, and threatening to bomb all the Roman Catholic churches in town, no matter how much I tried to convince him that my Ida May Temptation was no Catholic at all. Only a Catholic could behave so treacherously, gaudily and destructively, he shouted.

These soul-shaking frivolities continued unabated for four or five weeks. Naturally all my work, and even my health suffered. The soda

---

*From *With a Dutch Accent* by David Cornel DeJong. Reprinted by permission of Harper & Brothers. Copyright 1944, David Cornel DeJong. Pp. 288-291.

clerk, wild with jealousy, was full both of gloomy warnings and of scorn. "Temptation" only appeared in the store when I was there alone, preferably when I could seat her at the soda fountain and ply her lovely palate with the most amazing concoctions I could whip into shape with ice cream, assorted syrups, nuts and cherries. Then she called me something wonderful which later turned out to be simply "Blue-Eyes" in her own brand of embroidered French.

All this would never do, the soda fountain clerk told me. Because, unlike him, I wasn't even a man yet, and some day this bewitching creature would demand of me the supreme sacrifice that any man could make to any woman, and I would be unprepared. I would fumble and blunder and our lovely romance would be ruined. It was therefore high time that he taught me the facts of life, so that I might become suave and nonchalant about such matters, instead of acting like a romantic bull calf with yellow hair, pimples and outmoded clothes.

The opportunity for emerging from that cocoon of innocence which enveloped me so disgracefully, soon presented itself. Of course, I would have to be unfaithful to Ida May Temptation just once, but that would be all the better in the end. The opportunity generously presented itself as twofold, in the persons of two tarts who wanted to buy new lipsticks. Of course I didn't even show them the brand called Temptation. Oh no, I never would let that sacred name be sullied. However, they finally chose another kind with which they made the gashes which represented their mouths even more lurid and bloody-looking. Brazenly they wafted terrifically heady perfumes toward me, and showed their age and their ageless experience in all their features, words and gestures. I was waiting on them, and they were giving me the once-over. I had broad shoulders, I looked older than my years, and the white store coat hid my poverty. They were starting to make remarks to me which could lead to only one thing. So I called the soda clerk over to be my mentor, and the outcome of it was that that very evening after eleven o'clock we were to descend to the basement rooms of these ladies of the evening, and there I would bid my childhood innocence good-by forever.

It was all pretty awful. Privately I calculated that these fallen women had at least reached the advanced age of twenty, and that certainly I would become diseased forever, and that perhaps I'd never dare to look my mother in the face again. What was worse, Brick, the soda-fountain clerk, didn't seem to be his usual boastful self either. As the day progressed, he became increasingly quiet and preoccupied.

Once he consulted me *sotto voce* as to what I thought was the right sum of money we should pay the women for their services, and were we to pay it when we left or when we came in, and should we put it in their hands, or leave it on the mantel? Naturally, I couldn't advise him. He was the man of the world, and I was merely the innocent victim, the clay that still had to be molded, the vessel still to be tested by fire.

Still later Brick came to me rather abjectly, with shame so obvious upon him that it might well have been represented by insignia on his jacket. He confessed that in spite of all his boasting, he himself was as virginal as I was. Of course, he'd kissed nice girls, but to take this drastic step . . . well, it seemed too drastic, that was all there was to it. But what were we to do? Of course, we argued, we couldn't back out now. That would be neither honorable, gentlemanly, nor even manly. We had set the ball arolling and now we must keep going, or our humiliation might last forever and someday we might become like those slinky, skulking men who frequented public comfort stations. Certainly our time was here, and if we fled from it now, we'd have to pay the penalty forever.

At that point one of us remembered having heard somewhere that in the army soldiers were fed doses of saltpeter when their morals were likely to be endangered. Surely if Uncle Sam (and Brick should know, as he was an American citizen, which I wasn't) could take measures like that, it would be equally manly for us to do likewise. I started hunting for the powdered saltpeter immediately, and Brick mixed two chocolate sodas into which we shook enormous portions of the saltpeter. Quickly we consumed the sodas and started watching each other warily for results. None came. An hour later we thought it advisable to have another soda and increase the dose of saltpeter, and lo and behold, a few minutes later I felt the first twitches of pain in my stomach. These soon increased in intensity so that before long I was shivering and aching from head to foot. I grinned victoriously at Brick, while he waited for his own reaction to set in.

That came much later, obviously because his constitution was hardier than mine. But now it was ten o'clock, and still an hour till closing time, so we decided to have another doctored-up chocolate soda. This time my aches were so magnificent that the hairs seemed to be popping out of my head like tiny field mice. After a while, Brick, too, started doubling over with pain. His being sixteen and more sophisticated certainly seemed to give him an advantage over pain. However, he insisted that it was the fish he'd eaten that day, it being Friday.

At the fated hour of eleven we left the store, and doubled up with pain we directed our steps to the girls' basement apartment. In fact our aches became so great that we made a beeline for our destination, instead of lingering with any further doubts and misgivings. Besides, we didn't quite know when the effects of the saltpeter might start wearing off to leave us vulnerable again. The two females received us somewhat in undress, in feather-trimmed kimonos; they were actually smoking cigarettes—the first women I'd seen do so—and immediately seemed intent on removing our clothes, only realizing then that we were in distress. And no wonder. At that point I felt as if my eyeballs were going to pop out of my head and roll across the carpet like glass balls. Immediately the girls decided that we must have eaten something that didn't agree with us, and that if we were going to be sick, we'd better be sick on the street. Besides, they said it would be much better for us to go home to our mamas.

We had been saved, and our integrity was still intact. The pains from the saltpeter lasted for forty-eight hours, but they were worth it. Besides, Ida May Temptation was all mine, more fully so now that I'd made such a great sacrifice for her, and now I no longer had to listen to Brick's lectures on the course of true love and the probable demands of your best girl.

Anonymous
(1900[?]-[?])

The voyeuristic proclivity of the adolescent as a sublimation of his own sexual needs and gratifications is reported here by an anonymous Austrian girl in her diary. She is equally curious and ignorant about all aspects of sex. When Resi, the maid, calls her older sister, Dora, the tone of her voice impels the girl to go along. What she sees in a neighbor's window and her feelings about it are the subject of this passage.*

Sigmund Freud (28) had this to say about the girl's journal: "This diary is a gem. Never before, I believe, has anything been written enabling us to see so clearly into the soul of a young girl, belonging to our social and cultural stratum, during the years of pubertal development. We are shown how the sentiments pass from the simple egoism of childhood to attain maturity; how the relation-

---

*From *A Young Girl's Diary* (28). Pp. 122-125.

ships to parents and other members of the family first shape themselves, and how they gradually become more serious and more intimate; how friendships are formed and broken. We are shown the
dawn of love, feeling out towards its first objects. Above all, we are
shown how the mystery of the sexual life first presses itself vaguely
on the attention, and then takes entire possession of the growing
intelligence, so that the child suffers under the load of secret knowledge but gradually becomes enabled to shoulder the burden. Of all
these things we have a description at once so charming, so serious,
and so artless, that it cannot fail to be of supreme interest to educa-
tionists and psychologists."

June 1st

We've had such an experience to-day! It's awful; it's quite true then
that one takes off *every stitch* when one is madly fond of anyone. I
never really believed it, and I'm sure Dora did not, although Mad.
hinted it to her; but *it's true*. We've seen it *with our own eyes*. I was
just sitting and reading Storm's The Rider of the Grey Horse and
Dora was arranging some writing paper to take to Franzensbad when
Resi came and said: Fräulein Dora, please come here a moment, I
want you to look at something! From the tone of her voice I saw there
was something up so I went too. At first Resi would not say what it was
but Dora was generous and said: "It's all right, you can say *everything*
before her." Then we went into Resi's room and from behind the
curtain peeped into the mezzanine. A young *married couple* live
there!!! At least Resi says people say they are *not* really married, but
simply live together!!!! And what we saw was awful. She was absolutely naked lying in bed without any of the clothes on, and he was
kneeling by the bedside quite n— too, and he kissed her all over,
everywhere!!! Dora said afterwards it made her feel quite sick. And
then he stood up—no, I can't write it, it's too awful, I shall never forget it. So *that's* the way of it, it's simply frightful. I could never have
believed it. Dora went as white as a sheet and trembled so that Resi
was terribly frightened. I nearly cried with horror, and yet I could not
help laughing too. I was really afraid he would stifle her because he's
so big and she's so small. And Resi says he is certainly much too big
for her, and that he nearly tears her. I don't know why he should tear
her but certainly he might have crushed her. Dora was so terrified she
had to sit down and Resi hurried to get her a glass of water, because
she believed she was going to faint. I had not imagined it was any-

thing like *that,* and Dora certainly had not either. Or she would never
have trembled so. Still I really don't see why she should tremble like
that. There is no reason to be frightened, one simply need not marry,
and then one need never strip off every stitch, and oh dear, poor
Mademoiselle who is so small and the lieutenant is very tall. But just
think if anyone is as fat as Herr Richter or our landlord. Of course
Herr Richter is at least 50, but last January the landlord had *another*
little girl, so something *must have happened.* No, I'm sure it's best not
to marry, for *it* is really too awful. We did not look any more for then
came the worst, suddenly Dora began to be actually sick, so that she
could hardly get back to our room. If she had not been able to, everything would have come out. Mother sent for the doctor directly and
he said that Dora was very much overworked; that it was a good thing
she was going away from Vienna in a few days. No girl ought to study,
it does not pay. Then he said to me: "You don't look up to much
either. What are you so hollow-eyed for?" "I'm so frightened about
Dora," I said. "Fiddlededee," said the doctor, "that does not give anyone black rings round the eyes." So it must be true that one gets to
look ill when one always has to think about *such* things. But how can
one help it, and Hella says: It's awfully interesting to have black rings
under the eyes and men *like* it.

    We were going to make an excursion to-morrow to Kahlenberg and
Hermannskogel, but probably it won't come off. It's 11 already and
I'm fearfully tired from writing so much; I must go to bed. I do hope I
shall be able to sleep, but. . . .

June 3rd

    Father took Hella and me to Kahlenberg; we enjoyed ourselves tre-
mendously. After dinner, when Father was reading the paper in the
hotel, we went to pick flowers, and I told Hella all about what we'd
seen on Friday. She was simply speechless, all the more since she had
never heard what Mad. told us about taking off everything. She won't
marry either, for it's too disagreeable, indeed too horrid.—The doctor
said too: This perpetual learning is poisonous for young girls *in the
years of development.* If he only knew *what* we had seen. Hella is
frightfully annoyed that she was not there. She can be jolly glad, I
don't want to see it a second time, and I shall never forget it all my
life long; what I saw at the front door was nothing to this. Then Hella
went on making jokes and said: "I say, just think if it had been
Viktor." "Oh, do shut up," I screamed, and Father thought we were

quarrelling and called out: "You two seem to be having a dispute in the grand style." If he'd only known what we were talking about!!!

Emma Goldman
(1869-1940)

Emma Goldman, the noted anarchist, first manifested signs of overt rebellion against constituted authority by disobeying her father. She tells how her violation, at the age of fifteen, of the moral standards of her community precipitated guilt feelings, shock and revulsion. These feelings reappeared on her wedding night, three years after the original incident occurred, and were to pursue her for the remainder of her life.*

When I was fifteen, I was employed in a corset factory in the Hermitage Arcade in St. Petersburg. After working hours, on leaving the shop together with the other girls, we would be waylaid by young Russian officers and civilians. Most of the girls had their sweethearts; only a Jewish girl chum of mine and I refused to be taken to the *konditorskaya* (pastry shop) or to the park.

Next to the Hermitage was a hotel we had to pass. One of the clerks, a handsome fellow of about twenty, singled me out for his attentions. At first I scorned him, but gradually he began to exert a fascination on me. His perseverance slowly undermined my pride and I accepted his courtship. We used to meet in some quiet spot or in an out-of-the-way pastry shop. I had to invent all sorts of stories to explain to my father why I returned late from work or stayed out after nine o'clock. One day he spied me in the Summer Garden in the company of other girls and some boy students. When I returned home, he threw me violently against the shelves in our grocery store, which sent the jars of Mother's wonderful *varenya* flying to the floor. He pounded me with his fists, shouting that he would not tolerate a loose daughter. The experience made my home more unbearable, the need of escape more compelling.

For several months my admirer and I met clandestinely. One day he asked me whether I should not like to go through the hotel to see the luxurious rooms. I had never been in a hotel before—the joy and

*From *Living My Life* by Emma Goldman. Reprinted by Permission of Alfred A. Knopf, Inc. 1931. Pp. 21-23.

gaiety I fancied behind the gorgeous windows used to fascinate me as I would pass the place on my way from work.

The boy led me through a side entrance, along a thickly carpeted corridor, into a large room. It was brightly illumined and beautifully furnished. A table near the sofa held flowers and a tea-tray. We sat down. The young man poured out a golden-coloured liquid and asked me to clink glasses to our friendship. I put the wine to my lips. Suddenly I found myself in his arms, my waist torn open—his passionate kisses covered my face, neck, and breasts. Not until after the violent contact of our bodies and the excruciating pain he caused me did I come to my senses. I screamed, savagely beating against the man's chest with my fists. Suddenly I heard Helena's voice in the hall. "She must be here—she must be here!" I became speechless. The man, too, was terrorized. His grip relaxed, and we listened in breathless silence. After what seemed to me hours, Helena's voice receded. The man got up. I rose mechanically, mechanically buttoned my waist and brushed back my hair.

Strange, I felt no shame—only a great shock at the discovery that the contact between man and woman could be so brutal and so painful. I walked out in a daze, bruised in every nerve.

When I reached home I found Helena fearfully wrought up. She had been uneasy about me, aware of my meeting with the boy. She had made it her business to find out where he worked, and when I failed to return, she had gone to the hotel in search of me. The shame I did not feel in the arms of the man now overwhelmed me. I could not muster up courage to tell Helena of my experience.

After that I always felt between two fires in the presence of men. Their lure remained strong, but it was always mingled with violent revulsion. I could not bear to have them touch me.

These pictures passed through my mind vividly as I lay alongside my husband on our wedding night. He had fallen fast asleep.

ADOLESCENT CRUSHES AND FIRST LOVE

The authors of autobiographies seem to take a kind of sad delight in recalling "crushes" and first loves experienced during adolescence. There is a tendency on the part of nearly all of them to use spiritual phraseology in describing this phase of their lives. Cajal refers to it as "the dawn of love." Sudermann begins his narrative with, "Now, ye cymbals and trumpets, sound and clash, for I will sing a mighty song of young love." Dante writes about "the beatitude" denied him, Dreiser of "the reverential ecstasy," Goethe about the "goodness and beauty" of his first love, Alfieri about "tender passion," and so on. In retrospect, apparently, crushes and first loves are, for the adult, primarily sacred and sweet memories over which he can smile ruefully and tenderly. While the process is in effect, however, the individual is plagued by a variety of feelings, not all of which are as pleasurable as memory permits recall. But the autobiographers are sensitive to this, too. First loves are rarely forgotten and never profaned, if the excerpts in this section are evidence, perhaps not so much for the pleasure derived as from the pain experienced.

Being in love is one of the most absorbing emotional experiences that befalls the adolescent. Normally, he falls in love four or five times prior to the love affair that results in marriage (4). These new attachments take the place of the repressed fixations to the love objects of childhood; while they last, the love relations are passionate and exclusive, but they are of short duration (26). When the attachment takes the form of infatuation with an older person of the opposite sex, as is seen in the excerpts from Alfieri, Berlioz, Hall, Ellis, Bashkirtseff, Milne and Daiches, it may represent a substitution for the abandoned parent-objects. Should the attachment manifest itself by intense devotion to an older person of the same sex, it may be considered a continuation of the homosexuality of the latency period.

First love, calf love, puppy love—different times bring different names, but the feelings are generally the same. The episodes reproduced in this section are notable for the purity and intensity of affect expressed, the absorbing quality of the relationship, the overpowering sweetness of the love, the sense of helplessness when the object of desire either does not respond or is unaware of the writer's very existence, the various devices used to attract attention, the gentle melancholy, and sometimes the ambivalent sensations of confidence and awkwardness.

These feelings find expression in autobiographies from the thirteenth century down to the present and range from such widely disparate cultures as the Philippines and the Netherlands.

Dante
(1265-1321)

Dante's extraordinary relationship with Beatrice (1266-1290) has been the subject of much romanticism and legend throughout the centuries. Actually no romance ever existed, for Dante could never bring himself to the point where he could voice his passion for his beloved. "So much guilt tinctured his feelings for Beatrice," Wolberg (63) declares, "that he employed all sorts of subterfuges to conceal from the world his true emotions.

"In his autobiography, *Vita Nuova*, Dante relates his first meeting with Beatrice, when, at the age of nine, he chanced to gaze upon her as she passed by on the street. She inspired tumultuous feelings within him, and thereafter he trembled and shook so when he thought of Beatrice that he dared not allow himself to appear before her until nine years elapsed after their first meeting. The second meeting again consisted of Dante's passing Beatrice on the street. 'I stood sorely abashed,' Dante wrote, 'and by her unspeakable courtesy, which is now guerdoned in the Great Cycle, she saluted me with so virtuous a bearing that I seemed then and there to behold the very limits of blessedness.'

"Thereafter Beatrice served Dante secretly as his muse and guiding star. She inspired in him in his waking hours and lived with him in his dreams. She was, he insisted, 'not the daughter of a mortal man, but of God.'

"Dante's fear of Beatrice was paralleled only by his intense longing to be in her presence. He utilized many artifices to achieve this purpose and, at the same time, he took extraordinary precautions to shroud his motives. For instance he feigned his admiration for female friends of Beatrice in order that his wooing might perchance bring him near his lady. In his enthusiasm Dante overplayed his part and he pretended to love Beatrice's friends with such inspiration that he soon became the subject of scandal and was finally avoided by Beatrice herself who died in her early youth ignorant of Dante's love."

Wolberg goes on to say that Dante's passion for Beatrice was a screen for a deeper erotic relationship, and that his attitude toward her resembles the yearning of the child for the unattainable mother.

The intensity of Dante's craving for Beatrice is apparent in the selections which follow (54).

But the last word here about Dante should perhaps best be left for the comment of a poet. Rossetti (54) called the *Vita Nuova* "the autobiography or auto-psychology of Dante's youth till about his twenty-seventh year. . . . [It is] a book which only youth could have produced, and which must chiefly remain sacred to the young [pp. 25-26]."

And here it is fitting for me to depart a little from this present matter, that it might be rightly understood of what surpassing virtue her salutation was to me. To the which end I say that when she appeared in any place, it seemed to me, by the hope of her excellent salutation, that there was no man mine enemy any longer; and such warmth of charity came upon me that most certainly in that moment I would have pardoned whosoever had done me an injury; and if one should then have questioned me concerning any matter, I could only have said unto him "Love," with a countenance clothed in humbleness. And what time she made ready to salute me, the spirit of Love, destroying all other perceptions, thrust forth the feeble spirits of my eyes, saying, "Do homage unto your mistress," and putting itself in their place to obey: so that he who would, might then have beheld Love, beholding the lids of mine eyes shake. And when this most gentle lady gave her salutation, Love, so far from being a medium beclouding mine intolerable beatitude, then bred in me such an overpowering sweetness that my body, being all subjected thereto, remained many times helpless and passive. Whereby it is made manifest that in her salutation alone was there any beatitude for me, which then very often went beyond my endurance.

And now, resuming my discourse, I will go on to relate that when, for this first time, this beatitude was denied me, I became possessed with such grief that, parting myself from others, I went into a lonely place to bathe the ground with most bitter tears: and when, by this heat of weeping, I was somewhat relieved, I betook myself to my chamber, where I could lament unheard. And there, having prayed to the Lady of all Mercies, and having said also, "O Love, aid thou thy servant," I went suddenly asleep like a beaten sobbing child. And in my sleep, towards the middle of it, I seemed to see in the room, seated at my side, a youth in white raiment, who kept his eyes fixed on me in deep thought. And when he had gazed some time, I thought that he sighed and called to me in these words: *"Fili mi, tempus est ut prae-termittantur simulata nostra"* (My son, it is time for us to lay aside our counterfeiting). And thereupon I seemed to know him; for the voice was the same wherewith he had spoken at other times in my sleep. Then looking at him, I perceived that he was weeping piteously, and that he seemed to be waiting for me to speak. Wherefore, taking heart, I began thus: "Why weepest thou, Master of all honour?" And he made answer to me: *"Ego tanquam centrum circuli, cui simili modo se habent circumferentiae partes: tu autem non sic"* (I am as the center of a circle, to the which all parts of the circumference bear an equal relation: but with thee it is not thus). And thinking upon his words, they seemed to me obscure; so that again compelling myself unto speech, I asked of him: "What thing is this, Master, that thou hast spoken thus darkly?" To the which he made answer in the vulgar tongue: "Demand no more than may be useful to thee." Whereupon I began to discourse with him concerning her salutation which she had denied me; and when I had questioned him of the cause, he said these words: "Our Beatrice hath heard from certain persons, that the lady whom I named to thee while thou journeydst full of sighs is sorely disquieted by thy solicitations: and therefore this most gracious creature, who is the enemy of all disquiet, being fearful of such disquiet, refused to salute thee. For the which reason (albeit, in very sooth, thy secret must needs have become known to her by familiar observation) it is my will that thou compose certain things in rhyme, in the which thou shall set forth how strong a mastership I have obtained over thee, through her; and how thou wast hers even from thy childhood. Also do thou call upon him that knowest these things to bear witness to them, bidding him to speak with her thereof; the which I, who am he, will do willingly. And thus she shall be made to know thy desire; knowing which, she shall know likewise that they were deceived who speak of thee to her. And so write these things, that they shall seem rather to be spoken by a third person; and not directly by thee to her, which is scarce fitting. After the which, send them, not without me, where she may have chance to hear them; but have them fitted with a pleasant music, into the which I will pass whensoever it needeth." With this speech he was away, and my sleep was broken up.

*   *   *   *

. . . I began to be harassed with many and divers thoughts, by each of which I was sorely tempted; and in especial, there were four among them that left me no rest. The first was this: "Certainly the lordship of Love is good; seeing that it diverts the mind from all mean things."

The second was this: "Certainly the lordship of Love is evil; seeing that the more homage his servants pay to him, the more grievous and painful are the torments wherewith he torments them." The third was this: "The name of Love is so sweet in the hearing that it would not seem possible for its effects to be other than sweet; seeing that the name must needs be like unto the thing named; as it is written: *Nomina sunt consequentia rerum*" (Names are the consequents of things). And the fourth was this: "The lady whom Love hath chosen out to govern thee is not as other ladies, whose hearts are easily moved."

* * * *

... it chanced on a day that my most gracious lady was with a gathering of ladies in a certain place; to the which I was conducted by a friend of mine; he thinking to do me a great pleasure by showing me the beauty of so many women. Then I, hardly knowing whereunto he conducted me, but trusting in him (who yet was leading his friend to the last verge of life), made question: "To what end are we come among these ladies?" and he answered: "To the end that they may be worthily served." And they were assembled around a gentlewoman who was given in marriage on that day; the custom of the city being that these should bear her company when she sat down for the first time at table in the house of her husband. Therefore I, as was my friend's pleasure, resolved to stay with him and do honour to those ladies.

But as soon as I had thus resolved, I began to feel a faintness and a throbbing at my left side, which soon took possession of my whole body. Whereupon I remember that I covertly leaned my back unto a painting that ran round the walls of that house; and being fearful lest my trembling should be discerned of them, I lifted mine eyes to look on those ladies, and then first perceived among them the excellent Beatrice. And when I perceived her, all my senses were overpowered by the great lordship that Love obtained, finding himself so near unto that most gracious being, until nothing but the spirits of sight remained to me; and even these remained driven out of their own instruments because Love entered in that honoured place of theirs, that so he might the better behold her. And although I was other than at first, I grieved for the spirits so expelled, which kept up a sore lament, saying: "If he had not in this wise thrust us forth, we also should behold the marvel of this lady." By this, many of her friends, having discerned my confusion, began to wonder; and together with herself, kept whispering of me and mocking me. Whereupon my friend, who knew not what to conceive, took me by the hands, and drawing me forth from among them, required to know what ailed me. Then, having first held me at quiet for a space until my perceptions were come back to me, I made answer to my friend: "Of a surety I have now set my feet on that point of life, beyond the which he must not pass who would return."

Afterwards, leaving him, I went back to the room where I had wept before; and again weeping and ashamed, said: "If this lady but knew of my condition, I do not think that she would thus mock at me; nay, I am sure that she must needs feel some pity." And in my weeping I bethought me to write certain words, in the which, speaking to her, I should signify the occasion of my disfigurement, telling her also how I knew that she had no knowledge thereof: which, if it were known, I was certain must move others to pity.

John Milton *(1608-1674)*

Milton's seventh Elegy, written when he was twenty years old, and the Epilogue to it, composed in 1645, were frequently assumed to be conventional poetic exercises but were, in reality, based on genuine experience. The Epilogue, particularly, in which Milton's protestation that he has outgrown his infatuation is recorded, offers a strong presumption that Elegy VII itself is not a mere Ovidian exercise but the real thing.*

I did not yet know your ordinances, seductive Amathusia, and my breast was still empty of Paphian fire. O'er and o'er I spurned Cupid's shafts, as darts of a mere boy, I spurned your power divine, O mighty Cupid. "Go, boy," said I, "pierce doves, that know naught of fighting —only unmanly wars befit an unmanly captain—or else, tiny lad, lead a proud triumph over sparrows: such trophies are worthy of warfare such as yours. Why guide your idle missiles 'gainst the sons of men? Not one jot of strength has *your* quiver against sturdy heroes." The lad of Cyprus brooked not my words—no other god is more prompt to anger—, and so this savage (god) was hot now with double fires.

It was the springtime, and the light, shining o'er the roof-trees of the houses, had brought to you, May-month, your first day. But mine eyes were seeking still the vanishing night, and brooked not the early morning brightness. Lo, Love stood at my bed, tireless Love, with spangled wings. The rattling of his quiver betrayed the god as he

*From *Milton on Himself* edited by John S. Diekhoff. Reprinted by permission of John S. Diekhoff. 1939, Oxford University Press. Pp. 31-34.

stood beside me; his face, too, betrayed him and his lovely eyes with their sweet threats, and whatever else was worthy of a lad, worthy e'en of Love. Such is the lad of Sigeum, as, on everlasting Olympus, he mixes the brimming goblets for amorous Jove, or the lad who lured the lovely nymphs to his kisses, Thiodamas' son, Hylas, stolen by a Naiad. He had added wrath—and yet this, too, one would have thought, became him—and he had added wild threats, full of gall and bitterness. Thus then he spoke: "Wretch, you had grown wise (in matters of love) more safely through (others') example: now, you will testify yourself to the power of my right arm. You will be numbered among men who have tried and tested my strength; by your sufferings I shall fashion credence for the truth. . . . Whatever else you doubt, my shafts will teach you better (than words), and your own heart, to be assailed by me with no light stroke. Fool, fool, neither will the Muses you love have power to defend you, nor will Phoebus' snake proffer you aid."

So he spake. Then, brandishing his arrow with the golden tip, he flew away, into the warm bosom of Cypris. But savagely, with threatening lips, he thundered against me, whose one thought was of laughter, and who had no fear of the lad.

Sometimes I found delight in the parts of the city where our citizens promenade, sometimes in the neighbouring countryside adjoining country houses. Crowds close compacted, crowds like in faces to goddesses, moved in brilliance to and fro through the midst of the streets and roads. And so the day flashed bright, glorified by a double brightness. Am I beguiling myself? or has Phoebus rays won from this source too? Not grimly did I flee visions so charming; no, I let myself be driven whithersoever youthful impulse bore me. Lacking all prescience, I sent my glances to meet their glances, nor could I withhold my eyes. One by chance I marked, towering (in beauty) over others: that radiance was the beginning of all my woe. So might Venus have wished herself to look to mortals, such the beauty in which the Queen of the Gods herself should have been seen. This lass Cupid, sly rogue, remembering, flung across my path; single-handed, he had before to my hurt woven these wiles. Hard by, too, the sly rogue was in hiding; many a shaft, and a huge load of torches hung from his back. Without delay, he clung now to the maiden's eyelids, now to her face, then settled on her lips, then was seated on her cheeks: whatever part the agile archer traverses, thence—ah me!—in a thousand places he smites my defenceless breast. Straightway unwonted frenzies entered my heart: I burned within with love, aye, all my being was afire.

Meanwhile, the lass who alone of lasses pleased now my tortured soul, was withdrawn from my gaze, ne'er again to return to mine eyes. But I went onward, voicelessly complaining, empty of wit, and, often irresolute, I was minded to retrace my steps. I am cleft asunder: one half of me tarries behind, the other follows my heart's desire; I find pleasure in weeping for the joys so suddenly wrested from me. So Juno's son wept for his lost heaven, after he was flung downward, among the hearths of Lemnos. So Amphiaraüs, when he was carried to Orcus by his panic-stricken steeds, looked back at the sun that had been wrested (from his eyes). What am I to do, a poor unfortunate, by grief o'ermastered? I am not privileged either to lay aside the love I have welcomed, or to pursue it. O may it be vouchsafed to me to look once again on her beloved face, and in her presence to speak words, if only words of sadness! Mayhap she was not fashioned of unyielding adamant, mayhap she would not be deaf to my prayers. Believe me, no other man has e'er burned thus haplessly: I shall be set down as a pattern (of love's woes), yes, I first and alone. Spare me, Cupid, I pray, since you are the winged god of soft love. Let not your deeds be at odds with your gracious office. Now, now at least, your bow is full of terrors for me, O child of a goddess, child not less potent by your fires than by your darts. Your altars shall smoke with my gifts, you shall be for me a very god, god supreme among the powers above. Take away, at last, my frenzies—no, take them not away. I know not why, but the lover, every lover, is so sweetly wretched. Only be gracious and grant that if in days to come any lass is destined to be mine, a single shaft-point shall pierce two hearts destined to love.

Epilogue to Elegy VII

All this once on a time, with warped and twisted mind, and with all true zeal laid prostrate, I wrote, setting up idle trophies of my worthlessness. So utterly, forsooth, mischievous error wrenched me astray and drove me onward, and my untaught youth proved but misguided teacher, until the shades of Academe proffered to me the Socratic streams, and untaught me, (and loosed) the yoke I had let fall (upon my neck). Straightway, from that moment, the fires were quenched, my heart has been unyielding, belted with deep ice. Hence the lad fears the cold for his beloved shafts, and Venus herself dreads might that matches the might of Diomedes.

Vittorio Alfieri
(1749-1803)

Many of the characteristics of the adolescent crush are seen in this passage from Alfieri's *Autobiography* (2). At the age of fifteen,

Alfieri was smitten by an older, married woman. His inordinate, all-consuming adoration of her was unrealizable of achieving a relationship in terms of what the adolescent wants. The exquisiteness of his sufferings, which pursued him for many years until the fire of his fierce passion burned itself out, reflects the intensity and effusiveness which many adolescents experience in this respect.

Having gone to spend a month in the country with two brothers, who were my particular friends and associates in my riding excursions, I for the first time felt, in the most unequivocal manner, the influence of the tender passion. I became smitten with their sister-in-law, the wife of their elder brother, a young, vivacious, and enchanting brunette. In consequence of this statement I fell into a profound melancholy, became restless whether in her presence or when absent from her, and so embarrassed as to prevent me uttering a single syllable, if I casually met her at a little distance from her brothers-in-law, who never quitted her. After our return from the country, I spent whole days in the public walks and in going from one street to another, that I might have the pleasure of beholding her. What superadded to my sufferings was the impossibility of speaking of her, or of ever hearing her name even pronounced. In fine, I became a victim to all the feelings which Petrarch has so inimitably depicted in some of his pieces; feelings which few can comprehend, and which fewer still ever experience. This first attachment, which never produced any serious consequences, is not even now wholly extinguished in my mind. During my unceasing travels for a succession of years it has uniformly continued, without any act of volition or almost perception on my part, to haunt my imagination and to pursue my steps. It seemed like a voice crying from the inmost recesses of my heart, "If thou provest thyself worthy thou mayest render thyself acceptable in the sight of this female; and should circumstances change, thou mayest yet embody what has hitherto been only a shadow."

Johann Wolfgang von Goethe
(1749-1832)

Goethe called his autobiography *Poetry and Truth*, which is significant in itself. As Freud (34) said, on the occasion of receiving the Goethe Prize, " . . . as a poet, Goethe not only indulged in much self-revelation, but was also carefully reticent despite the fullness of autobiographical details." Goethe's autobiography lacks the qualities of emotional revelation and insight into one's self that make a great work. A clue to this is seen in the first paragraph of the following selection,* in which Goethe's detachment from people is indicated.

The plot within the plot device which Goethe used to attract the attention of his first love would be almost a necessity for a man like Goethe, who generally maintained such distance between himself and others. Although he enjoyed considerable freedom of movement through the city, in the intervals of his study, and struck up several acquaintances outside the home among boys and girls, these were certainly far outweighed by his adult contacts, and by his intimacy with his sister who had much less freedom than he (49).

Goethe was fourteen at the time of his first meeting with Gretchen. "The form of that maiden followed me from that moment on every path," he wrote. "It was the first abiding impression that a female had made upon me." But when the affair ended unhappily, he was prompted to write: "My sister consoled me the more earnestly, because she secretly felt the satisfaction of having gotten rid of a rival; and I, too, could not but feel a quiet, half-delicious pleasure, when she did me the justice to assure me that I was the only one who truly loved, understood, and esteemed her."

In a completely unexpected manner I became mixed up in relationships which very nearly brought me into great danger, and at least for a long time into perplexity and distress. My earlier good relationship with that boy whom I have before called Pylades, had continued up to the time of my youth. Certainly we saw each other less often, because our parents did not stand on the best footing with each other, but whenever we met, the old friendly rapture broke out at once. On one occasion we met in the alleys which, between the inner and outer St. Gallengate, offer a very pleasant walk. We had hardly greeted one another when he said to me: "I hold to the same opinion about your verses as ever I did. Those which you recently communicated to me I have read aloud to some pleasant companions, and no one will believe that you have made them yourself." "Never mind," said I; "we will make them and enjoy them, and the others may think and say about them what they like." "There comes the unbeliever now," said my

---

*From *Goethe's Autobiography. Poetry and Truth from My Own Life*. Reprinted by permission of Public Affairs Press. 1949. Pp. 138-144.

friend. "We will say nothing about it," was my answer. "What is the good? We cannot convert them." "Not at all," said my friend; "I cannot let the matter go thus." After a short, indifferent conversation my young comrade, who was all too well intentioned towards me, would not let the matter drop, and said, with some irritation, to him: "Here is now the friend who made the pretty verses for which you will not give him credit." "He will certainly not be offended," answered the other; "for it is an honour which we show him, if we think that more learning is required to make such verses than one of his years possesses." I made some indifferent reply, but my friend continued: "It won't be much trouble to convince you. Give him any subject and he will make a poem on the spot." I agreed, we were both at one, and the third asked me whether I would trust myself to put into verse a nice love-letter which a modest young girl should write to a young man in order to declare her feelings. "Nothing is easier than that," said I, "if we only had writing materials." The other brought out his pocket almanac, in which there were a number of white pages, and I sat down on a seat to write. They walked up and down, and did not leave me out of their sight. I at once grasped the situation in my mind, and thought how nice it would be if some pretty child really felt an affection for me and wished to discover it to me in prose or verse. I therefore began without ceremony my declaration, and finished it in a metre wavering between doggerel and madrigal, with the greatest possible *naïveté,* in a short time. When I read it aloud to them, the sceptic was overcome with admiration, and my friend with delight. The request of the former for the possession of the poem I was less able to refuse, as it was written in his almanac book, and I was glad to see in his hands the documentary proof of my capabilities. He departed with many assurances of admiration and affection, and we wished for nothing more than that we should often meet, and we settled soon to go into the country.

Our party took place, and it was joined by several more young people of the same stamp. These were fellows from the middle, indeed one might say from the lower, class, who were not wanting in intelligence, and who besides, because they had gone through school, were possessed of much knowledge and a certain kind of cultivation. In a large rich city there are all kinds of branches of industry. They got on by writing for the lawyers and by advancing the children of the lower class by more teaching than was common in the elementary schools; with grown-up children, who were to be confirmed, they went through the religious instruction; then they assisted brokers or merchants in some way, and were able to enjoy themselves in a frugal manner in the evening, especially on Sundays and holidays.

On the way, while they highly praised my love-letter, they confessed to me that they had made a very amusing use of it; they had, namely, copied it with a disguised hand, and with a few pertinent allusions it had been sent to a conceited young man, who was convinced that a girl to whom he paid court at a distance was desperately in love with him and sought an opportunity of becoming more nearly acquainted with him. They confided to me at the same time that he wished for nothing more than to be able also to answer her in verse, but neither he nor they possessed the necessary skill, and so they besought me urgently to compose the desired answer. Mystifications are, and will continue to be, an amusement for idle more or less intelligent people. A pardonable naughtiness, a self-complacent malice are a pleasure for those who have neither resources in themselves nor a wholesome external activity. No age is quite free from such amusement. We had often tricked each other in our boyish years; many games turned on such mystifications and tricks; the present jest did not seem to me to go any further: I consented; they communicated to me many special things which the letter was to contain, and we soon brought it home completed.

A short time afterwards I was pressingly invited by my friend to share in an evening meal with that society. The lover was willing this time to bear the expense, and desired expressly to thank the friend who had shown himself such an excellent poetical secretary.

We came together late enough, the meal was most frugal, the wine drinkable, and as regards the conversation it turned almost exclusively upon jokes about the young man who was present, but indeed not very wide awake, and, after repeated reading of the letter, was not far from thinking that he had written it himself.

My natural good nature did not permit of my finding much pleasure in such malicious dissembling, and the repetition of the same subject soon disgusted me. I should certainly have passed a wretched evening had not an unexpected apparition enlivened me. On our arrival the table was already neatly and properly laid; sufficient wine had been put out; we sat down and remained alone, without requiring further service. But when at last the wine ran short, one of them called out for the maid, but instead of her there entered a girl of uncommon and, when one considered her surroundings, of incredible beauty. "What do you require?" said she, after she had bidden them a friendly good evening. "The maid is ill and gone to bed. Can I serve you?"

"There is no wine," said one; "if you could get us a few bottles, it would be very kind." "Now, Gretchen," said the other, "it is only a stone's throw distant." "Why not!" said she, and took a couple of empty bottles from the table and hurried away. Her form, as seen from behind, was even more delicate. The little cap sat so neatly on her small head, which a slender throat united very gracefully with the neck and shoulders. Everything on her seemed choice, and one could survey the whole form more quietly as one's attention was no more exclusively attracted and fascinated by the quiet, honest eyes and lovely mouth. I reproved my comrades for sending the child out alone in the night; they laughed at me, and I was soon consoled when she came back again, for the publican lived only across the street. "Sit down with us," said one of them. She did so, but unfortunately did not come near me. She drank a glass to our good health, and soon withdrew, while she advised us not to remain very long together, and above all not to be so noisy, for the mother was just going to bed. It was not her mother, but the mother of our host.

The form of that maiden followed me from that moment on every path; it was the first abiding impression that a female being had made upon me, and as I couldn't find a pretext for seeing her at home, and would not seek one, I went to church from love of her, and had soon spied out where she sat; and so during the long Protestant service I gazed my fill at her. When I went out, I did not trust myself to address her, still less to accompany her, and was already blessed if she noticed me and seemed to have answered my greeting with a nod. Yet I was not long to be deprived of the happiness of approaching her. They had made that lover, whose poetical secretary I had become, believe that the letter written in his name had been sent to the lady, and had strained his expectation to the uttermost that an answer must soon follow. This also I was to write, and the roguish company entreated me earnestly through Pylades to expend all my wit and employ all my art in order that this piece should be quite elegant and perfect.

In hope of seeing my fair one again, I at once set to work and thought of everything which would be most pleasing to me, if Gretchen were writing to me. I imagined that I had written everything so entirely from her form, her nature, her manner, and her mind that I could not withhold myself from the wish that it really was so, and I lost myself in rapture only at the thought that something similar might be directed from her to me. Thus I mystified myself while I thought I was making game of another, and much pleasure and much discomfort was yet to arise for me from the affair. But when I was once more reminded, I was ready and promised to come, and did not fail at the appointed hour. There was only one of the young people at home; Gretchen sat in the window spinning; the mother was going to and fro. The young man demanded that I should read it aloud to him; I did so, and read it not without emotion, while I glanced away over the paper at the beautiful child, and thought that I noticed a certain uneasiness in her deportment, a light flush on her cheeks; I only expressed myself better and in more lively fashion, that which I wished to hear from herself. The cousin, who had often interrupted me with commendations, asked me to make some alterations. They had reference to some passages which, doubtless, suited more the situation of Gretchen than that of the lady, who was of good family, wealthy, well known and respected in the town. After the young man had mentioned to me the desired changes and had fetched writing materials, he excused himself on account of some business for a short time; I remained sitting on the bench against the wall behind the large table and examined the changes to be made on the large slate, which almost covered the whole table, with a slate pencil which always lay in the window, because on this slate reckonings were often made, many things were noted down, and those coming in and going out even communicated with each other by means of it.

I had for some time written down different things and again rubbed them out, when I exclaimed impatiently: "It won't do!" "So much the better," said the dear girl in a grave tone. "I wished that it would not do at all. You should not meddle in such matters." She stood up from the distaff and, coming to me at the table, gave me a severe lecture, with much good sense and friendliness. "The thing seems an innocent game; it is a game, but not innocent. I have already experienced many cases in which our young people for the sake of such mischief have got into great embarrassment." "What should I do?" I replied. "The letter is written, and they rely on my altering it." "Trust me," she said, "and don't alter it; nay, take it back, put it in your pocket, go away, and try to make the matter straight through your friend. I will also put in a word, for you see, though I am a poor girl, dependent on these relations, who certainly don't do anything bad, but often for pleasure or profit undertake much that is foolhardy, I resisted them and did not copy the first letter as they asked me to do; they copied it with a disguised hand, and, if it is not otherwise, so they can do with this. And you, a young man of good family, well-to-do, independent, why do you let yourself be used as a tool in an affair from which certainly no good and perhaps much unpleasantness may befall you?" I was glad to hear her speaking thus continuously, for generally she uttered only a few words in the conversation. My inclination towards her increased incredibly, I was not master of myself, and replied: "I am not so independent as you think, and what is the good of being well-to-do, when the most precious thing which I wish for is lacking to me?"

She had drawn my idea of the poetic epistle towards her and read it half aloud, in a sweet and graceful manner. "That is very nice," she said, while she stopped at a certain naïve point; "only, it's a pity that it is not destined for a better and real purpose." "That would certainly be very desirable," I exclaimed; "how happy would he be who receives such an assurance of her affection from a girl whom he deeply loves!"

"There is much required for that," she said, "and yet many things are possible."

"For example," I continued, "if anyone who knew, prized, honoured, and adored you, laid before you such a paper and besought you pressingly, warmly, and in a friendly manner, what would you do?" I pushed the paper nearer to her, which she had already pushed back to me. She smiled, reflected an instant, took the pen, and subscribed her name. I was beside myself with delight, jumped up, and wished to embrace. "No kissing," she said; "that is so vulgar, but let us love if we can." I had taken up the paper and put it into my pocket. "No one shall have it," said I, "and the affair is closed. You have saved me."

"Now complete the salvation," she said, "and hurry off before they come and you fall into trouble and embarrassment." I could not tear myself away from her, but she asked me in so kindly a manner, while she took my right hand in both hers and pressed it lovingly. Tears were not far from me; I thought I saw her eyes were moist. I pressed my face upon her hands and hurried away. Never had I in my life found myself in such a state of perplexity. The first feelings of love in an uncorrupted youth take altogether a spiritual direction. Nature seems to wish that one sex should become aware by the senses of goodness and beauty in the other. And so there had arisen for me a new world of the beautiful and excellent by the sight of this maiden and by my love for her.

David Crockett
(1786-1836)

Characteristic of the adolescent's first experience with love is his plaintive belief that no one else has encountered it before with the same intensity of feeling. "For though I have heard people talk about hard loving," Davy Crockett, the American pioneer and politician, wrote in his *Autobiography*, "yet I reckon no poor devil in this world was ever cursed with such hard love as mine has always been when it came to me." He describes here his first heterosexual love experience when he was fifteen years old.* Although his language is colloquial and ungrammatical, his feelings over the raptures of youthful sexuality are pervasive and universal.

The next day I went back to my old friend, the Quaker, and set in to work for him for some clothes; for I had now worked a year without getting any money at all, and my clothes were nearly all worn out, and what few I had left were mighty indifferent. I worked in this way for about two months; and in that time a young woman from North Carolina, who was the Quaker's niece, came on a visit to his house. And now I am just getting on a part of my history that I know I never can forget. For though I have heard people talk about hard loving, yet I reckon no poor devil in this world was ever cursed with such hard love as mine has always been when it came on me. I soon found myself head over heels in love with this girl, whose name the public could make no use of, and I thought that if all the hills about there were pure chink, and all belonged to me, I would give them if I could just talk to her as I wanted to, but I was afraid to begin, for when I would think of saying anything to her my heart would begin to flutter like a duck in a puddle; and if I tried to outdo it and speak, it would get right smack up in my throat and choke me like a cold potato. It bore on my mind in this way till at last I concluded I must die if I didn't broach the subject; and so I determined to begin and hang on a-trying to speak till my heart would get out of my throat one way or t'other. And so one day at it I went, and after several trials I could say a little. I told her how well I loved her; that she was the darling object of my soul and body; and I must have her or else I should pine down to nothing and just die away with the consumption.

I found my talk was not disagreeable to her; but she was an honest girl and didn't want to deceive nobody. She told me she was engaged to her cousin, a son of the old Quaker. This news was worse to me than war, pestilence, or famine; but still I knowed I could not help myself. I saw quick enough my cake was dough, and I tried to cool off as fast

*From *An Autobiography* by David Crockett. New York: A. L. Burt Co., 1902. Pp. 29-30.

as possible, but I had hardly safety-pipes enough, as my love was so hot as mighty nigh to burst my boilers. But I didn't press my claims any more, seeing there was no chance to do anything.

Hector Berlioz
(1803-1869)

In their study of adolescent crushes, Hurlock and Stein (35) found that they are motivated by various reasons, such as a desire for companionship of someone of the same mental status, the appreciation of one gifted with unusual talent, the recognition of facial beauty or bodily grace, or the desire for sympathetic understanding which would incorporate both the mental and physical phases. Crushes fall within the range of normal emotional reactions of the adolescent, but while they last are inordinately all-consuming and absorbing.

So it was with Berlioz during his twelfth and thirteenth years. The moment he set eyes on Estelle, a girl of eighteen, he felt "an electric shock; in fact, I fell in love with her, desperately, hopelessly. I had no wishes, no hopes, I had no idea what was the matter with me, but I suffered acutely and spent my nights in sleepless anguish." Seventeen years later, at the age of thirty, when he returned home and saw the church in the distance, the little white villa and the old tower, the old associations were revived and he was still tormented by ineffable love.*

I was twelve years old before the magic of music was revealed to me; but earlier than that I had experienced the pangs of that great passion which Virgil depicts with so much power. It came about in this wise. My maternal grandfather, who bore the same name as Walter Scott's hero, Marmion, had a country house at Meylan, three miles from Grenoble, near the frontier of Savoy. . . . Above Meylan, and close under the steep wall of the mountain, lies a little white villa buried in gardens and vineyards, with a far-reaching outlook over the valley of the Isère; it is surrounded by rocky hills and woods; behind it rises the bold mass of the great St. Eynard rock; close by is a ruined tower, and it looks as if it were made to be the scene of a romance. This villa belonged to a Madame Gautier, who used to spend the summer there

---

*From *Memoirs* by Hector Berlioz. Reprinted by permission of Alfred A. Knopf, Inc. 1932. Pp. 8-10.

with two nieces, the younger of whom was called Estelle. The name of itself would have attracted me because of its association with Florian's idyl (*Estelle et Némorin*), which I had discovered in my father's library and devoured in secret. The real Estelle was a tall, slight girl of eighteen, with splendid shining eyes, a mass of hair which might have waved on the casque of Achilles, and the feet—I will not say of a Spaniard, but of a thoroughbred Parisian—clad in a pair of pink shoes! You laugh? Well, I had never seen a pair of pink shoes before! I have forgotten the colour of her hair (I think it was black); but whenever I think of her I see a vision of large brilliant eyes and equally brilliant pink shoes.

The moment I set eyes on her I felt an electric shock; in fact, I fell in love with her, desperately, hopelessly. I had no wishes, no hopes, I had no idea what was the matter with me, but I suffered acutely and spent my nights in sleepless anguish. In the daytime I crept away like a wounded bird and hid myself in the maize-fields and the orchards. I was haunted by Love's ghostly companion, Jealousy, and suffered tortures when any man approached my idol; and it makes me shudder even now when I recall the ring of my uncle's spurs as he danced with her.

The spectacle of so young a child overwhelmed with a feeling so far beyond his years, seeemed to afford all our neighbours the keenest amusement. Estelle was the first to discern my feelings, and she was, I am sure, more amused than anyone. One evening there was a large party at my aunt's; prisoner's base was proposed, and the guests were divided into two parties, the men choosing their companions. I was purposely called up first, but I dared not choose, and stood motionless with downcast eyes and beating heart, while they all laughed at me. At last Estelle took me by the hand and said, "Well then, I will choose. I take Mr. Hector!" Alas! the cruel girl, too, was laughing at me, as she stood looking down on me in her beauty. . . .

No, time itself is powerless. . . no after-loves can blot out the first. . . . I was but thirteen when I ceased to see her . . . I was thirty when, on my return from Italy, I caught sight of St. Eynard in the distance, the little white villa and the old tower, through a mist of tears. . . . I still loved her. . . . I heard that she was . . . married . . . and all the rest of it . . . and even that did not cure me. My mother used often to tease me about my childish love, and one day played me a trick which was scarcely kind. A few days after my return from Rome she handed me a letter, which she said she had been asked to deliver to a lady who was to pass through, in the Vienne diligence, in about an hour's time. "Go to the coach office, and, while they are changing the horses, ask for Mdme. F., and give her the letter. It is seventeen years since you saw her, but I am sure if you look at her carefully you will recognise her." . . . I had no suspicion of what awaited me, and when the coach drew up I went to the door and asked for Mdme. F. "It is I," said a voice, which I at once recognised with a throb of pain. Estelle! Estelle! still beautiful, Estelle, the nymph, the hamadryad of St. Eynard and the wooded hills of Meylan! It is indeed she, with her magnificent hair and her winning smile; but ah! where are the little pink shoes? She took the letter. Did she recognise me? Who can tell? The coach drove off, and I returned quivering with excitement to my mother, who, on seeing my face, said, "Ah, I see, Némorin has not forgotten his Estelle!" *His* Estelle! cruel mother!

Hermann Sudermann
(1857-1928)

In this delightful vignette from Sudermann's early adolescence, many universal features of the sacrosanct period of "calf love" will be recognized. Sudermann discusses it with chuckling good humor, but just the same, the wondrousness of the love, the devotion of the adorer, the panic when near the object of desire, and the feelings of dumbness and stupidity, reflect the complexity of the affective life of the adolescent.*

Now, ye cymbals and trumpets, sound and clash, for I will sing a mighty song of young love.

It was not my cousin. After a few days of devoted attachment which the physical presence of a ripening young woman must necessarily bring with it, my feelings for her passed imperceptibly into the gentle affection which one feels for a sister, and never again went beyond it.

But it was another, far more beautiful, far finer, far more secret, a young cherub, a queen of the May.

When my mother was a young girl she was obliged, in order to relieve to some extent the poverty of her widowed mother, to seek her bread abroad, and had crossed the Haff to Elbing and entered Franz Hornig's toy shop as an apprentice. Friendly relations had developed out of this acquaintanceship, and these were carefully kept up, even

---

*From *The Book of My Youth* by Hermann Sudermann. Reprinted by permission of The Bodley Head, Ltd. 1923. Pp. 62-66.

after her marriage, by letters at the New Year and on her birthday, so that I received instructions from her to present myself to Frau Hornig as soon as possible after my arrival, and give my mother's grateful greetings to her old friend, whose husband had meanwhile died.

When my cousin heard of my proposed visit which my shyness postponed from one Sunday to another, she nodded vigorously.

"You will be captured by Klara on the spot. It is true that she is still in the lower second class, although she is over fourteen."

My cousin had herself long since been promoted to adorn the first class. "But she is taller than I am, has already had dancing lessons, and is, generally speaking, very coquettish, very vain, and all the boys in the first class are running after her."

This description of her character did not succeed in frightening me away, even though I was still too young to have an idea that it was dictated by envy. I did not need to be caught first; I was already head over ears in love with her.

By day I avoided the street in which the Hornigs' house stood, although my way to school led through it. But when the dusk fell I crept gently past it, squinting sideways toward the window at which I thought my beloved one must be sitting. I had never seen her with my eyes. I did not *want* to see her, for I was afraid I should sink into the earth if I did so. My heart was already in a tumult whenever I even thought of it. But my mother began to press me. In every letter she wrote she asked me, "Why have you not yet been to see the Hornigs?" And in her last letter she had even written, "Do not write to me again until you can give me an account of your visit." I could not now postpone it any longer. And when the next Sunday afternoon came I gave my brocade cravat a rather more fashionable twist, revived my memory of the intellectual conversation which I considered suitable for my first entry into the great world and which I had long since had by heart (the relative merits of Karl and Franz Moor played a by no means inconspicuous rôle among them), and in God's name marched off to my execution.

But it all passed off splendidly. Old Frau Hornig received me with genuine joy. A pale, yellow, sickly girl, who did not like standing up because she was deformed, gazed at me with secret excitement, and I spouted like a waterfall without being obliged to make heavy claims on my literary knowledge.

As I say, everything passed off splendidly—only Klara happened to be on a picnic to Vogelsang, as a result of which my cousin gave me an extra pocket handkerchief when I went to bed. "You can cry into it until it is soaked," said this sympathetic soul. A fortnight later I received an invitation to the Sunday dinner. "Take care to eat a lot," said the "good aunt" to me as I set out, "so that you still have enough to be able to be without supper." And my cousin grinned. This time *She* was there. Tall, slender, with a brilliant smile, and eyes which were incredibly blue under broad, dark brows which made the blue of the eyes under the shadow of her big eyelashes seem still more incredible. There she stood in front of me, and gave me her hand—to me, an unworthy nothing, a stupid, crooked small boy who was at the bottom of the third class. She gave me her hand as though we were comrades—she, to me; she whom the boys in the first class ran after.

And when the others had greeted me she told me how sorry she was that she had not been at home on the previous occasion, and next time I must certainly come, too.

A flood of self-consciousness overpowered me. Yes, if it were really true that I was not despised by her, not thrown aside as being childish and of no account, then I was already the master of the situation, and in the long run I could compete even with the boys in the first class. We sat down to table; one of her brothers, a young man with curly hair who looked like an artist, who immediately confided to me that he was going to make the business boom again, completed the party.

I was in the seventh heaven. I had never felt my spirit sway so lightly above the earth. And then as the soup was being ladled out I noticed that I had forgotten my pocket handkerchief.

It was all over—my hopes and my dreams vanished. My unaccustomed joy and happiness, my self-confidence, my flood of conversation were all ruined, overwhelmed by the painful question, "How can I get a pocket handkerchief?"

But everything has an end, and so even dinner went by. Dumb, awkward, stammering stupid answers, and only concerned with one thing, namely to conceal my sniffling, I let the minutes pass by, and squinted occasionally toward the door with the hopeless wish that I could take to flight. But when we wished one another "*Gesegnete Mahlzeit*" after many painful pauses and difficult conversational efforts, and we had reached the proper moment where I could turn with a discreet request to the son of the house, I could stand it no longer, told my kind host that I had something very urgent to do at home, and fled as though pursued by the Furies.

And so my rôle in the house of my beloved came to an end. I never dared to cross its threshold again, and never again did I receive an invitation. But I still preserved in my heart, hopelessly and obstinately, my love for the most beautiful and lovely girl on earth all through the period which followed.

When I walked home at night from Biechschmidt's I used to stand for hours in front of her door, but when I saw her coming toward me on the street I turned round or ran over to the other side, and when I could not help meeting her and her smiling glance greeted me, I always had the feeling as if I had gone blind and was going to sink into the earth, so that it seemed a miracle to me afterward that I was able to pass her more or less properly. And my shame, which was thus stirred up again, raged in me for days afterward.

This went on for more than two years. . . .

Havelock Ellis
(1859-1939)

In 1871, when Havelock Ellis was twelve years old, a girl four years his senior was invited to spend a week or two at his house in Wimbledon. Ellis considered her brief visit an epoch-making event in his life. Perhaps it was. His crush on Agnes was not marked by sensuality, but rather, as he himself stated, "a boy's pure passion." Although he never saw Agnes again, "her image moved and lived within me, revealing myself to myself." He sublimated his feelings through the safety of poetic expression; the new ferment which began to work on him prompted him to make the statement about the epochal quality of the relationship.*

According to Fenichel (17), anxiety about libidinal impulses often provokes partial regressions at puberty, which explains the contradictions in adolescent behavior toward objects. "Many relations at this age represent identifications rather than genuine love; and in many ways are used as mere instruments to relieve inner tensions, as good or bad examples, as proofs of one's own abilities, or as reassurances. . . . Objects are easily abandoned if they lose their reassuring significance."

I was twelve years old, and the summer holidays, after my last term at Merton College, had just begun. Half a century earlier (as I discovered five years afterwards in Australia when reading his attractive *Autobiography*), at the same age, in this same village of Merton, a

---

*From *My Life* by Havelock Ellis. Reprinted by permission of Houghton Mifflin Co. Copyright 1939. Pp. 87-89.

man of letters more famous than I am ever likely to be, Leigh Hunt, had met his first love. Here I was now to meet mine.

My mother, though on occasion hospitable, cared little to have strangers staying in the house; a girl or boy cousin would sometimes be invited to spend a week, and left no impress on my imagination. The first stranger not of my kin to stay in the house was a girl of sixteen, the only daughter of my mother's stepbrother, who was in a well-to-do position. Agnes, then, for that was her name, was invited to spend a summer week or two with us at Wimbledon in 1871. She was a dark, pretty, vivacious girl, with long black ringlets, of something the same type, I can now see, as her grandmother, the second Mrs. Wheatley, whom I distinctly remember. Old enough to be a woman in my eyes, and yet young enough to be a comrade and equal, she adapted herself instinctively to the relationship and won my heart immediately. I took not the slightest liberty with her, and never had the slightest impulse to do so, but she, on her part, treated me with an easy familiarity which no woman had ever used with me before, and that fact, certainly, though its significance was then beyond me, undoubtedly had its influence. She would play and romp with me in all innocent unreserve, and when we went out together for long walks, as often happened, she would sometimes make me offer her my arm and treat her as a lady, then again asserting her superiority by treating me to lemonade and at the best places she could find. One day, as we strolled arm in arm through the poppied cornfields which then lay between Merton Station and the college—it was in these fields that I first knew the beauty of poppies—my severe little schoolmaster suddenly came round the corner onto us. Timid though I habitually seemed, I raised my cap without flinching or withdrawing my arm under my master's stern eye, and have ever since prided myself on that early little act of moral courage. He doubtless smiled to himself at thus seeing a handsome girl hanging on his quiet pupil's arm, and he subsequently asked my father who she was, but without, I think, mentioning that detail. Agnes returned home, and, strangely enough, I have never seen her since. I lent her Keats's *Poems* when she left and she lent me *The Wide, Wide World*; we exchanged a few notes, but our correspondence speedily withered, without protest on my part, and probably aided by the fact that, through a trivial circumstance connected with this very visit of Agnes—she had once offered to help in the domestic work and been given some peas to shell which her mother resented as too menial a task for her daughter—a certain permanent coldness developed between her mother and mine, each feeling aggrieved. She is still alive, and though she was even then looking forward to marriage as a near probability (for I heard her talk to our servant to that effect), she still remains single, an only child who has devoted her life to the care of her aged parents.

I never saw Agnes again; I never made any effort to see her; I never mentioned her name; no one knew that I even thought of her. But for four years her image moved and lived within me, revealing myself to myself. I had no physical desires and no voluptuous emotions; I never pictured to myself any joy of bodily contact with her or cherished any sensuous dreams. Yet I was devoured by a boy's pure passion. That she should become my wife—though I never tried to imagine what that meant—was a wild and constant aspiration. I would lie awake in bed with streaming eyes praying to God to grant that this might some day be. I have often felt thankful since that our prayers are not heard.

Under the stress of this passion I became a person, and, moreover, in temper a poet. I discovered the beauty of the world, and I discovered a new vein of emotion within myself. I began to write verse. I began to enjoy art, and, at the same time, Nature. In a still vague and rudimentary way, all my literary activities slowly took on a new character. Hitherto they had been impersonal, displaying indeed a certain research, a certain orderly and systematic spirit, perhaps inborn, yet not definitely personal. Now the personal element took shape. The touch of this careless vivacious girl had placed within me a new ferment which began to work through every fibre of my being. It was an epoch-making event in my life and was soon to be succeeded by another of scarcely less importance.

Marie Bashkirtseff
(1860-1884)

The initial entry in a diary is as revealing and as important as the statements made by a patient in the first session on the analyst's couch. In the second paragraph of the first entry in her *Journal,* twelve-year-old Marie Bashkirtseff poured out her love for the Duke of H———, whom she had seen a dozen times on the street, whom she did not know, and who did not know that she existed. Seven years later, when she reread the several entries in her diary, reproduced here, she claimed her infatuation, in retrospect, produced no effect on her whatever. But during the year of her passion, her feelings were wild and tumultuous, vacillating between the offering of prayers for the Duke and utter detestation when she learned of his marriage. She would blush at the mere mention of his name; life was desolate and barren when the family moved from Nice to Paris and she could no longer entertain even the possibility of seeing her beloved pass in his carriage; her fantasies carried her to impossible levels of achievement, all for the sake of him.

What seemed to her to be rejection by the Duke affected her subsequent relationship with Pietro who courted her a few years later. But behind this unhappy affair lay an inverse oedipal situation. In the preface to her *Journal*,* Marie relates that after two years of marriage, her mother left her father and took the two children to her parental home. Marie was probably a few months old when the parents separated. From the *Journal*, it is hard to tell how often she saw her father. Her early years were spent with three women— her mother, aunt, and grandmother. Her brother, Paul, is mentioned only in passing. The inverse oedipal complex is apparent in several entries.

> *Villa of Acqua-Viva*
> *Promenade des Anglais, Nice*
> *January, 1873. Age, twelve years*

Aunt Sophie is playing on the piano some airs of Little Russia, and that has recalled to me our country. . . . Aunt Sophie is still playing, and the sounds coming to me at intervals, penetrate my soul. I have no lessons to learn for tomorrow, which is Aunt Sophie's birthday. Oh, my God, give to me the Duke of H—! I will love him and make him happy, and I shall be happy, too, and will do good to the poor. It is a sin to think that one can buy the favor of God by good works, but I do not know how to express my meaning.

I love the Duke of H—, and dare not tell him that I love him, and even if I should tell him so, he would not care. When he was here, I had an object in going out, in dressing—but now!—I used to go onto the terrace in the hope of seeing him from afar, for an instant, at least. My God, solace my affliction! I can pray no more; hear my prayer! Thy grace is so infinite, Thy mercy is so great; Thou hast done so much for me! It grieves me to see him no more on the Promenade. His face was so strikingly distinguished among the vulgar faces of Nice.

I dream of glory, of celebrity, of being everywhere known. When

---

*Translated by A. D. Hall. Chicago: Rand McNally, 1889. Pp. 15-21, 88-89, 40-45.

you come upon the stage, to see thousands of people awaiting with throbbing hearts the moment when you shall sing; to know, as you see them before you, that a single note of your voice will bring them all to your feet; to look upon them with a disdainful glance (I am capable of anything)—that is my dream, that is my life, that is my happiness, that is my desire. And then, when I am in the midst of all this, Monsignor, the Duke of H—, will come, like the rest, to throw himself at my feet; but he shall have a reception different from that of the rest. Dear, you will be dazzled by my splendor, and you will love me; you will see my triumph; but, indeed, you are worthy of only such a woman as I hope to be. I am not homely, I am even pretty; yes, rather pretty; I have an exceedingly good form, like a statue; I have fairly pretty hair; I have a very becoming coquettish manner; and I know how to comport myself with men.

I am modest, and would never kiss any man except my husband, and I can boast, besides, of something that not every young girl of from twelve to fourteen years can—of never having kissed nor been kissed by anyone. So, when he shall see a young girl at the very pinnacle of glory possible for a woman to attain, loving him since her childhood with an unchangeable love—a girl modest and pure—he will be astounded, and will long to win me at any price, and will marry me out of very pride. But what am I saying? Why may I not admit that he may really love me? Ah, yes, by the help of God! God has enabled me to discover the means of gaining my beloved—I thank thee, Oh, my God, I thank thee!

Wednesday, March 14th, 1873

This morning I heard the sound of wheels in the Rue de France; I looked out and saw the Duke of H—, driving a four-in-hand in the direction of the Promenade. Oh, goodness, if he is here he will take part in the pigeon-shooting, in April; I shall certainly go!

To-day I saw the Duke of H— again. No other has his grand air; he carries himself just like a king, when he is driving. . . .

I have been so preoccupied that I have almost forgotten (What a shame!) the duke's absence. It seems to me that we are separated by a profound abyss—especially if we go to Russia next summer. It is seriously spoken of. How can I believe that he will ever be mine? He thinks no more about me than of last winter's snow; I do not exist for him. During the winter, while we remain at Nice, I can still hope; but I fear that when we start for Russia, all my hopes must vanish—all that I dreamed possible will fade away. At the thought of losing all this, I feel a dull, steady pain, which is horrible. I am passing a moment of the greatest anguish, and my whole nature is suffering a change. How strange it is! just now I was thinking of the gaiety of the shooting-match, and now my mind is filled with the saddest imaginable ideas.

I am torn by these emotions. Oh, my God, the thought that he will never love me, kills me with desolation. I have no longer any hope, and was mad to long for things so utterly impossible. I wished for too much. But no, I can not abandon myself so! What! I dare yield thus to despair? Does not God, Who can do everything, watch over me? How dare I entertain such thoughts? Is He not everywhere, always watching over us? To Him all is possible. He is omnipotent; for Him there is neither time nor space. I might be in Peru, and the duke in Africa, and if He willed, He could reunite us. How could I, for a minute, think of despairing? How could I, for a second, forget His divine goodness? Do I dare to deny Him merely because He does not grant at once all my desires? No, no! He is more merciful, and will not leave my beautiful soul to wound itself with wicked doubts.

This morning, I pointed out to Mademoiselle Colignon (my governess) a charcoal-seller, and said: "Look how strongly that man resembles the Duke of H—" She answered, laughing, "What a ridiculous notion!" It gave me an intense delight to pronounce his name. But I can see that if one never speaks to any one of the person one loves, the love grows stronger; whereas, if one speaks of him incessantly (which is certainly not my case), the love becomes weaker. It is like a flask of spirits: If it is corked, the odor is strong; but if it is open, it evaporates. It is exactly so with my love; stronger, because I never hear it mentioned. I never speak of it myself, and I keep it entirely to myself.

I am feeling so sad, because I can form no definite idea of my future —that is to say: I know what I would like but I do not know what I shall have. How gay I was last winter! everything looked smiling, and I was hopeful. I love a shadow which I shall possibly never attain. I am so distressed about my gowns that I have cried about them. My aunt took me to two dressmakers; but they do poor work. I shall write to Paris, for I can't wear the gowns they make here; they make me feel too wretched.

Monday, October 13th, 1873

I was studying my lesson when little Heder, my English governess, said to me: "Do you know the duke is to marry the Duchess M—?"

I brought the book nearer my burning face. I felt as if a sharp knife had been thrust through my bosom. I was trembling so I could scarcely hold the book; I was afraid to faint, the book saved me. I pretended to look for something for a few minutes while composing myself. I was reciting my lesson in a choked voice; my breath was quivering; I gathered my courage as once before when I had to jump from the bridge, at the baths, and said I must conquer myself. I wrote a dictation so as not to have to speak.

I went to the piano and tried to play; my fingers were stiff and cold. The princess asked me to go and teach her croquet; with pleasure, I replied, cheerfully; but with my voice and breathing tremulous. The carriage arrived, I ran to get ready; I wore my green dress; my hair is the color of gold; I am white and pink, pretty as an angel or as a woman. We started; the G— house was open; there were workmen, masons, who seemed experts to me; she has gone . . . where? To Russia, I suppose, to make a fortune.

One thought was ever before me—he was going to marry! Is it possible! I was unhappy, not as formerly, when grieving over the wallpaper of one room or the furniture of another; but truly miserable!

I did not know how to tell the princess that he is going to marry (they will know it soon and better I should tell her myself).

I chose a moment when she was sitting on a sofa, the light behind, my face could not be seen. "Do you know the news, princess? (We spoke Russian.) The Duke of H— is about to marry"—at last I had said it , . . without blushing, perfectly calm; but what I felt in my inner self!!!

Ever since that minx told me of that horrible news, I feel out of breath, as if I had been running a whole hour, and the same feeling makes my heart beat painfully.

I played the piano with a will, but half way through the piece my fingers weakened and I had to lean against the back of the chair. I commenced over again—same story—for five minutes, at the least; I tried again and again. Something came up in my throat which prevented respiration. Ten times I jumped from the piano to the balcony. What a state to be in!

We are going out, but Nice is no more Nice, nor G—, either. The view of her villa affects me no more. All that relates to the duke and that is why my heart breaks at the sight of those two empty houses! He was all that attached me to Nice. I hate it now, and can hardly bear it. *Je m'ennuie! Oh je m'enniue!*

Mon âme rêveuse
Ne songe, qu' à lui
Je suis malheureuse
L'espoir a fui.

My God, save me from unhappiness! My God, forgive my sins, spare me! It is all, all over; my face turns purple as I think it is all ended. I am a-weary! Ah, I am a-weary! My dreamy soul thinks but of him. I am unhappy—hope has fled.

I am happy today; the terrible news has not been repeated and I prefer ignorance to sad truth, glad to believe it could not be true!

Friday, October 17th, 1873

I was playing the piano, when the papers were brought in; I take up the *Galignani's Messenger* and the first lines which strike my eyes are about the marriage of the Duke of H—.

The paper did not fall from my hands, on the contrary it remained there as if fixed; I had not strength to stand, but sat down and reread those crushing lines ten times over, to make very sure I was not dreaming. Oh, divine charity! What did I read? My God! What did I read? That night I could not write, I could only throw myself on my knees and weep. Mamma came in; to avoid her seeing me thus, I pretended to go and see about the tea. And I have to take my Latin lesson! Oh, anguish! I can do nothing, I cannot remain quiet. There are no words to express what I feel; but what makes me desperate, what enrages me, what kills me, is jealousy—jealousy and envy; they rend my soul apart, they make me furious, mad! If I could only let my feelings be seen! But I must hide them and seem calm, and that makes me all the more miserable.

When champagne is uncorked, it bubbles, then grows still, but it only bubbles and does not become still if the cork is but half removed. . . . No, that comparison is not correct. I suffer, I am broken down!

I shall probably forget in time. To say my sorrow will be eternal would be ridiculous, nothing is eternal! But the fact remains that just now I can think of nothing else. *He* does not marry, they marry *him*. It is a plot of his mother's. (1880. *All that for a man I had seen a dozen times on the street, whom I did not know, and who did not suspect my existence.*) Oh, I hate him! I do not wish—I do wish to see him with her! They are at Baden, the Baden I loved so well. Those walks where I used to see him, those kiosks, those stores. (*Re-read all this in*

1880; it does not affect me at all any more.) To-day I must alter my prayers in all that related to him, I will not any more ask that I may be his wife. . . .

To part with that prayer seems impossible, killing! I cry like a fool. Come! come! my dear, let us be reasonable.

It is over, ah, well, it is over! I see now we do not do as we wish.

Let me prepare for the anguish of changing the prayer. Oh, it is the most cruel feeling in the world, it is the end of all! Amen!

Saturday, October 18th, 1873

I said my prayers, omitting the prayer for him and for *all*. I felt as if my heart was being torn, as if I could see a beloved dead taken away in his coffin. As long as the coffin is there we are sorrowful, but not yet as much as when we feel the void everywhere.

I see that *he* was the soul of my prayer, for now it is calm, cold reasoning, while before it was quick, passionate, burning! He is dead to me and the coffin has been removed. It was a weeping sorrow, now it is a hard, aching pain. His will be done. I used to waft signs of the cross in all directions for him, not knowing where he was. I did not do so today, and my heart throbs painfully. I am a strange creature, no one suffers as I do, and yet I live, sing, and write. How I have changed since the thirteenth of October—fatal day! Suffering is stamped on my face. His name is no longer a beneficial warmth, but a burning fire; a reproach, an awakening of jealousy, of sadness. It is the greatest misfortune which can befall a woman. I know what it is—sad mockery!

I must commence to think seriously. How I wish I could sing well! But what matters it now?

He was as a light to my soul, and that light has gone out. It is dark, dreary, sad, I know not which way to turn. Before this, in my slight annoyances, I could always find some ray of comfort, some light to guide and give me strength; but now, wherever I may seek, look around, and feel, I find nothing but void and darkness. It is terrible! terrible! when there is nothing in the depth of your soul!

Tuesday, October 21st, 1873

When we came in it was already dinner time, and we received some chiding from mamma for having eaten before dinner. Our charming family interior was disturbed. Paul was scolded by mamma, grandpapa interfered—he always meddles, thus teaching him disrespect for mamma. Paul went away grumbling, like a servant. I followed grandpapa into the corridor and begged of him to interfere no more with mamma's authority, but let her do as she pleases, for it is a crime to prejudice children against their parents, just through want of tact. Grandpapa commenced to cry, that made me laugh; all these wrangles amuse me at first, then I feel sorry for those poor unfortunates who, having no real sorrows, make martyrs of themselves for want of something to do. Heavens! if I were only ten years older! If I were free; but what can one do when bound hands and feet with aunts, grandpapa, lessons, governesses, family? My grief is not sharp and mad any more. Without having weakened, it is more slow, calm, and reasoning.

No, no! Nothing is left me but remembrance. If I should lose that I would be very unhappy.

I speak in such a flowery style, it becomes stupid, and to think I have never spoken to him. I have seen him ten or fifteen times, often from a distance or from the carriage; but I have heard his voice and I shall never forget it! The more I say, the more I want to say; yet, I can not write all I feel. I am like those unfortunate artists who conceive a picture above their capacity to execute.

I loved him and I lost him, that is all I can say, and that tells the whole story.

After dinner I sang, and charmed the whole turbulent family.

Saturday, October 25th, 1873

. . . . A man below my own social position will never please me, all persons of the lower classes *disgust* and annoy me. A poor man loses half of himself. He seems little, miserable, and looks like a trench-digger. Whilst a rich man, independently so, carries himself with a certain ease, an air of pride. Assurance gives him an air of superiority. I admire in H— that air of assurance, capricious, foppish, and cruel. He possesses something of Nero.

Saturday, November 8, 1873

We should never give too much of our society even to those who love us. It is well not to stay too long in any company so as to leave regrets and illusions behind us when we depart. One will thus appear to better advantage, and seem to be worth more. People will then desire to see you return; but do not gratify that desire immediately; make them wait for you, but not too long, however. Anything that costs too much loses by the difficulty with which it is obtained. Something better was anticipated. Or, on the other hand, make them wait a very long time for you—then you will be a queen.

I believe I am feverish. I am so talkative especially when I grieve silently. No one would suspect it. I sing, I laugh, and talk; the more unhappy I feel the gayer I appear. Today I can not move my tongue and have eaten next to nothing.

All I write can never express my feelings; I am stupid, foolish, and grievously offended. I imagine I am being robbed when they take the duke from me; well, really it is as if they appropriated what belongs to me. What a disagreeable state! I do not know how to express myself, all words sound weak; for a mere nothing I use strong expressions, and then, when I wish to speak seriously, I am at a loss. It is as if—No, enough! If I continue to draw conclusions and give instances, I will never finish; thoughts spring up so fast, become confounded, and end by evaporating.

Looking at mamma as I would a stranger, just now, I discovered that she is charming. She is beautiful as the day, notwithstanding her many troubles and sufferings. When speaking, her voice is low and soft; her manners pretty, although simple and natural.

In all my life I have never seen a person who gave so little thought to herself as my mother. She is a perfect child of Nature. Should she give more thoughts to her toilet, she would be the center of admiration. Say what you will, fine dresses count for much; she usually uses odds and ends, or whatever she can find. Today she wore a pretty dress, and upon my word she was charming.

Saturday, November 29th, 1873

I do not have a moment of peace. If I could only hide myself far, far away! where no one could see me, perhaps then I could recover my peace of mind. I feel jealousy, love, envy, deception, wounded self-love, everything that is hideous in this world. . . . Above all, I feel his loss! I love him! Could I reject all that is in my soul! But then, if I do not know what is taking place, I only know I am tormented; that something devours me, suffocates me, and all I say does not express the one-hundredth part of what I feel.

My face covered with one hand, while with the other I hold my cloak which envelops me entirely, even my head, I remain in obscurity, that I may gather my scattered thoughts; I am all confused. Poor head!

One thing troubles me. It is that in a few years I will have forgotten and will laugh at myself.

(1875. *Two years have passed. I do not laugh, neither have I for-*

gotten!)—All these troubles will appear to me like childish affectation. But no, I conjure you, do not forget. When you read these lines turn backward, suppose yourself to be at the age of thirteen, that you are at Nice, that this is taking place at this moment; think that it is a living reality! You will understand! You will be happy!

Sunday, November 30th, 1873

I wish they would marry sooner; I am always so; when there is something disagreeable to take place, instead of putting it off I prefer to hasten it. To leave Paris, I hurried all the others. I knew I must swallow the pill. For the same reason I burned with anxiety to arrive at Nice; I could wait no longer. The suspense was more terrible than the event itself.

Saturday, October 6th, 1877

By the way, do you know whom I met in the Champs Elysees? None other than the Duke of H—, occupying an entire hackney coach. The handsome young man, somewhat stout, with copper-colored hair, and slight moustache, had become a bulky Englishman, with a very flushed face, and small red whiskers extending from the ear to the middle of the cheek.

Four years, however, change a man. At the end of half an hour, I thought no more of him.

Sic transit gloria Ducis.

How foolish I was!

Manuel Quezon
(1878-1944)

Adolescence is notable for its resiliency, for its ability to bounce from depressed moods to elation, for its characteristic rapid shifts of behavior, alternating between restraint and self-indulgence. Manuel Quezon, who was to become the President of the Philippine Islands, points this up in the first paragraph of the selection which follows.* The "tragic incident" he refers to is his clubbing of a Spanish army corporal who had threatened him with death if he did not procure his young and pretty cousin for the corporal's

---

*From *The Good Fight* by Manuel Quezon. Reprinted by permission of Appleton-Century-Crofts, Inc. Copyright 1946, Aurora A. Quezon, Maria Aurora Quezon, Maria Zeneida Quezon, Manuel L. Quezon, Jr. Pp. 23-26.

delectation. Quezon refused, beat up the army man, and was subsequently accused by the latter of being a member of the Katipunan, a secret revolutionary order, and nearly executed. He was confined to the schoolhouse and since his father was the teacher, he became the jailer too. But Quezon was released and permitted to go to Manila to study at the University of Danto Tomas. He was seventeen years old. Between the time he was released and the time he left for Manila, Quezon experienced the first love described here. The peril he had just gone through was apparently not enough to hold back his need for sexual gratification.

Lest the reader may think that my days in Baler had been constantly spent in a gloomy atmosphere of pain for the death of my mother, indignation over the abuses of the Spanish officials, or the anguish resulting from the almost tragic incident with the Cabo de la Guardia Civil and my confinement in the school-house, I desire to tell a little episode of my youth which took place in the midst of these more serious events.

The town of Baler was always famous for having an abundance of beautiful girls. At the time of which I now write, although only seventeen years old, I was no longer indifferent to the attraction of beautiful eyes and well-shaped figures. There was one girl in particular whose eyes were irresistible to me, and I quickly fell in love with her. Courting in the Philippines during the Spanish days was indeed a most trying enterprise. Girls were always chaperoned whenever they attended a dance, nor were they allowed out of the house alone. Letters through the mail, addressed to a girl, were sure to fall into her parents' hands and never reached the addressee. When a girl was visited in her home, she was not permitted to sit near her suitor, and some one was always present so that the conversation could never refer to anything so personal as the object of the call. In my own town the young man would be asked to sit on a bench—and the prevailing rules of etiquette required that one must not walk straight to the bench, but had to do it step by step, stopping after each step, until the invitation to sit was repeated three times. Then at last the tortured victim would have the right to sit down. The girl would sit at the farthest point away, the mother or the chaperon sitting with solemn face between them.

This procedure was too elaborate, too formal, and too burdensome for my impatient temperament. So I never subjected myself to the ancient ritual. There was another permissible manner of courting a girl more agreeable to my inclinations, and that was by serenading. This consisted of standing in front of the girl's house after the family had retired for the evening, and from the street playing melancholy tunes and singing love ditties. Some austere mothers would let the serenaders remain long in the street before inviting them to come up, doubtless in the hope that the intruders would get tired and leave. Usually, however, after the third musical selection, the lamps were lighted and the cavaliers invited to come up. Then would follow an impromptu dance which would last, depending upon the boldness of the suitor, until two or three o'clock in the morning. The music on such occasion consisted usually of only a flute or a violin and a guitar. I chose the serenade as the means of promoting my pretensions, and with two old friends who played the guitar and the flute, I courted the girl of my dreams. She was an orphan, living with her aunt, the most stern and implacable old lady of the town. As soon as the latter noticed that I was paying attention to her niece, her attitude toward me changed radically. She assumed that I would never marry her girl and therefore condemned me *a priori* as a villain. I went about my business unperturbed. She would keep me waiting in front of her house with my musicians as long as courtesy under the code would permit, and then in a rather hard voice and not concealing her displeasure, would ask us to come up, *"if we wanted."* Of course, we did every time and then I would dance with the girl and although one had to hold his partner at least one foot away, I still managed to whisper a word or two indicative of my deep personal feeling. After noticing that the girl was not indifferent to my advances, I used to carry with me whenever I serenaded her, a sheet of paper containing the most romantic letter I have ever produced. She never answered my letters, much less ever said that she reciprocated my love, for that was bad form in those days. Finally, on one occasion, I succeeded in finding her alone and kissed her on the cheek. There was no protest, but it was the end, for fate took me away shortly after this incident.

San Kim
(1905-   )

San Kim, a Korean nationalist and revolutionary, had left his native land in childhood, studied at the University of Tokyo when he was fourteen, and at fifteen was walking the seven hundred miles from Harbin, China, to the Korean Nationalist Military School in Hami-ho, South Manchuria. One of the stops on this journey was in the home of a pastor in the town of Sanywanp'u. It is with the pastor's daughter that Kim falls in love. It is his first experience with love and his feelings are identical with those of the white, western authors of autobiographies and diaries. His behavior is similar to theirs, and even his choice of words closely follows.*

I lived for three weeks in the home of the pastor in this town. He took a fancy to me and offered to adopt me as a son, and said that if I did not want this he would like me to marry his daughter later, anyway. But I refused, saying that I had parents enough already and that I had vowed never to marry. He was very unhappy about my refusal.

I liked his daughter well enough. I was then fifteen, and the interest she showed in me suddenly awakened my awareness of girls. Until that time I had had no consciousness of sex. Now I found myself shy and tongue-tied in her presence. I wanted to talk with her, but every time I came near I felt oppressed and unfree and wanted to run away. I thought she was the prettiest girl I had ever seen, and my heart used to beat fast whenever I looked at her. Though she was only fourteen, I felt that she was mysterious and beyond my understanding. I wanted to know more about her but dared not talk with her on any personal things at all. Instead, I threw myself with silent devotion into helping her with her lessons. I wrote many essays for her and toiled over her mathematics every day.

I began to lose my appetite and to stay awake nights wondering if marriage were so bad after all. I decided that I might come back some day and that if I still liked her I might consider it. But she would have to be worthy of being a hero's wife. By that time, I reasoned, I would no longer fall in love with a pretty face, and unless she measured up to all requirements in education and intelligence, I would naturally not like her at all, and my problem would solve itself.

Anne Frank
(1929-1945)

The final illustration in this section comes from the *Diary of a Young Girl*. In nine entries of her diary, two of which are reprinted here, Anne Frank records the growth and development of her love for Peter Van Daan, another adolescent.** Both are living with their

---

*From *Song of Ariran* by San Kim. Reprinted by permission of The John Day Company, Inc. 1941. P. 44.

**From *The Diary of a Young Girl* by Anne Frank. Reprinted by permission of Doubleday & Co., Inc. Copyright 1952, Otto H. Frank. Pp. 116-118, 141-143.

families in the confined "Secret Annexe," a place hardly conducive to privacy and which has thrown the two together. Anne tells the story of their love in her unassuming way and with her wonderful gift for characterization. It was a shy love, which blossomed briefly, for shortly after the realization of their love for each other came, the Grüne Polizei made a raid on the "Secret Annexe." All the occupants were arrested and sent to German and Dutch concentration camps. In March, 1945, two months before the liberation of Holland, Anne died in the infamous camp at Bergen-Belsen.

Thursday, 6 January, 1944

Dear Kitty,

My longing to talk to someone became so intense that somehow or other I took it into my head to choose Peter.

Sometimes if I've been upstairs into Peter's room during the day, it always struck me as very snug, but because Peter is so retiring and would never turn anyone out who became a nuisance, I never dared stay long, because I was afraid he might think me a bore. I tried to think of an excuse to stay in his room and get him talking, without it being too noticeable, and my chance came yesterday. Peter has a mania for crossword puzzles at the moment and hardly does anything else. I helped him with them and we soon sat opposite each other at his little table, he on the chair and me on the divan.

It gave me a queer feeling each time I looked into his deep blue eyes, and he sat there with that mysterious laugh playing round his lips. I was able to read his inward thoughts. I could see on his face that look of helplessness and uncertainty as to how to behave, and, at the same time, a trace of his sense of manhood. I noticed his shy manner and it made me feel very gentle; I couldn't refrain from meeting those dark eyes again and again, and with my whole heart I almost beseeched him: oh, tell me, what is going on inside you, oh, can't you look beyond this ridiculous chatter?

But the evening passed and nothing happened, except that I told him about blushing—naturally not what I have written, but just so that he would become more sure of himself as he grew older.

When I lay in bed and thought over the whole situation, I found it far from encouraging, and the idea that I should beg for Peter's patronage was simply repellent. One can do a lot to satisfy one's longings, which certainly sticks out in my case, for I have made up my mind to go and sit with Peter more often and to get him talking somehow or other.

Whatever you do, don't think I'm in love with Peter—not a bit of it! If the Van Daans had had a daughter instead of a son, I should have tried to make friends with her too.

I woke at about five to seven this morning and knew at once, quite positively, what I had dreamed. I sat on a chair and opposite me sat Peter . . . Wessel. We were looking together at a book of drawings by Mary Bos. The dream was so vivid that I can still partly remember the drawings. But that was not all—the dream went on. Suddenly Peter's eyes met mine and I looked into those fine, velvet brown eyes for a long time. Then Peter said very softly, "If I had only known, I would have come to you long before!" I turned around brusquely because the emotion was too much for me. And after that I felt a soft, and oh, such a cool kind cheek against mine and it felt so good, so good. . . .

I awoke at this point, while I could still feel his cheek against mine and felt his brown eyes looking deep into my heart, so deep, that there he read how much I had loved him and how much I still love him. Tears sprang into my eyes once more, and I was very sad that I had lost him again, but at the same time glad because it made me feel quite certain that Peter was still the chosen one.

It is strange that I should often see such vivid images in my dreams here. First I saw Grandma so clearly one night that I could even distinguish her thick, soft, wrinkled velvety skin. Then Granny appeared as a guardian angel; then followed Lies, who seems to be a symbol to me of the sufferings of all my girl friends and all Jews. When I pray for her, I pray for all Jews and all those in need. And now Peter, my darling Peter—never before have I had such a clear picture of him in my mind. I don't need a photo of him, I can see him before my eyes, and oh, so well!

Yours, Anne

Sunday, 27 February, 1944

Dearest Kitty,

From early in the morning till late at night, I really do hardly anything else but think of Peter. I sleep with his image before my eyes, dream about him and he is still looking at me when I awake.

I have a strong feeling that Peter and I are really not so different as we would appear to be, and I will tell you why. We both lack a mother. His is too superficial, loves flirting and doesn't trouble much about what he thinks. Mine does bother about me, but lacks sensitiveness, real motherliness.

Peter and I both wrestle with our inner feelings, we are still uncertain and are really too sensitive to be roughly treated. If we are, then my reaction is to "get away from it all." But as that is impossible, I hide my feelings, throw my weight about the place, am noisy and boisterous, so that everyone wishes that I was out of the way.

He, on the contrary, shuts himself up, hardly talks at all, is quiet, day-dreams and in his way carefully conceals his true self.

But how and when will we finally reach each other? I don't know quite how long my common sense will keep this longing under control.

Yours, Anne

THE HOMOSEXUAL COMPONENT IN ADOLESCENCE

A struggle for supremacy between the desire for possession of the infantile love object and the repression acquired during the latency period is the main cause of the characteristic unrest of puberty. A solution is sought in fantasy, accompanied by or resulting in masturbation or homosexual interests. By and large, homosexual activities at adolescence represent normal behavior in experimentation or in developmental tendencies, are usually episodic in occurrence, and leave little or no trace of psychic trauma. Sullivan attributes great developmental value to these attachments of early adolescence. Far from presaging homosexuality in later life, they are notably absent from the case histories of adult homosexuals (57).

Adult homosexuality is considered "abnormal" in many societies, both in the statistical and normative senses of the term. But according to Kluckhohn's (42) summary of the evidence, homosexuality is not everywhere regarded as a variation: " . . . in such groups as the Siwans and Keraki all the males practise homosexuality as boys (passively) and as men (actively); the Marind-Anim also have institutionalized homosexuality." Kinsey's data, as has been frequently pointed out, throw considerable doubt on the assumption that homosexuality is statistically abnormal in the United States.

But, as Jahoda (36) says, "it would be unjustified to jump from such evidence to the conclusion that the plasticity of human nature is infinite or that the concept of mental disease must vary from culture to culture. The discussion of uniformities or differences in men is to a large degree a function of the intention of the observer. As interest turns from the concrete act, say that of homosexuality, to more formal aspects of human behavior or to modifying processes, the likelihood of finding universal features increases. Kluckhohn proposes some universal criteria for all cultures in the judgement of what is abnormal: 'All cultures *must* regard as abnormal individuals whose behavior fails grossly to be predictable in accord with cultural norms, or who are permanently inaccessible to communication, or who consistently lack a minimum of control over their impulse life.' This anthropological approach to the identification of what is abnormal creates at least some common basis for all cultures."

That homosexual practices by adolescents are found in many cultures and in a wide variety of symbolic and active ways is generally agreed upon. For example, pubescent boys have expressed homosexual trends in symbolic fashion by robbing and setting fires in the company of other boys; such unconscious homosexual mechanisms have been noted in the study of pairs of children and adolescents who set fires. The unconscious homosexual tendencies of the prepubertal and pubertal boy find their satisfaction in group horseplay, wrestling, teasing, and like activities which are more on the sadomasochistic level of development (15). Strongly latent and even active homosexual impulses may be found in the hazing of a fraternity initiate, when the victim is stripped and his genitals played with. Among Australian groups, Bloch (7) reports, female mimicry and imitation are sometimes carried to an extreme. "Certain male members of the initiation party may actually invest themselves with female ornaments and dress, and engage in artful simulation before the young novices of feminine mannerisms and characteristics . . . even [proceeding] to the point where simulated amorous advances are made." Identical behavior is seen in college theatricals in the United States, where all-male casts show great gift in ribald imitations of the female sex.

In the Noshizho rites of the Omaha Indians, the boy's vision may cause him to become a transvestite; among the Chaga of East Africa, the young initiates, after circumcision, wear female clothing and are addressed as girls; the Naven ceremonies of the Iatmul contain definite features of transvestitism and other sexually ambivalent conduct (8). The autobiography of Charles James Nowell, a Kwakiutl chief of Vancouver Island, reveals the common homosexual play activity of children and the practice of transvestitism among male adults (18). There are many other examples throughout history:

ancient Greece and subsequently Rome sanctioned homosexual practices; the Emperor Hadrian (117-138) freely celebrated his love for Antinous (30); Frederick the Great, King of Prussia (1740-1786), was also a homosexual (52); the list could be extended readily. But perhaps this is sufficient evidence to indicate the widespread homosexual activity found in a whole variety of cultures.

The prevalence of homosexual activity is explained by Fenichel (17) to some satisfaction. He writes, "It is probably because of social factors that adolescents frequently prefer to meet in homosexual gatherings. In this way, they avoid the exciting presence of the other sex and at the same time avoid being alone; thus they may find the reassurances they are looking for. However, what has been warded off returns, and the friendships that were founded in the hope of avoiding sexual object relationships assume a sexual character more or less obviously. . . . The frequent preference for homosexual objects at this age may be due not only to shyness in regard to the other sex (and to cultural tradition) but also to the continued narcissistic orientation of the greater part of the object needs of that time."

Freud (29) considered the determining factor in the homosexuality of the boy to be his love for and identification with the mother. A contributing factor is the fear of the father as a rival for the mother's affection. This fear causes the boy to renounce his mother and, with her, all women. He then strives to find an object-love in whom he can rediscover himself, and whom he wishes to love as his mother loved him.

According to Ackerman (1), homosexual fear is much more common than is imagined, and is usually indicative of some confusion and fragmentation of the development of personal identity. "It is not generally a sign of sexual deviancy but rather a reflection of the adolescent's struggle to draw pieces of self-image into an integrated picture of the whole person [p. 224]." The narcissistic orientation of childhood may persist into adolescence.

William Ellery Leonard (1876-1944), the American poet and teacher, wrote in his autobiography (45), "At about twelve I had a few months' devotion to a boy friend, analogous to a sorority house crush. I wanted to serve him; I was peculiarly hurt and jealous at inattention. It was not like other boy-friendships. But the prepuberty sex-life of boyhood is quite normally more unstable and plastic than of maturity; plenty of boys have had such crushes, though they are certainly not to be encouraged. Nor are the gross physical contacts of some boys in their early teens to be interpreted as prophetic of peculiarly homosexual tendencies. They are in fact less homosexual than juvenile crushes, though certainly less respectable; and in my case the abysmal privacies of personality made such rendezvous revolting even to my moments of grosser sexual tumult. . . . "

August Forel (1848-1931), the Swiss psychiatrist, writes essentially in the same vein. "One day [he was about thirteen] I came upon a man [in the rivulet near Morges] who was bathing quite naked. The sight of this naked man made a profound impression upon me; a mixture of curiosity, fear and eroticism. About this time, too, the sight of a girl's portrait which was hanging in my father's room gave me certain erotic sensations. But all this was very innocent [22a]."

Frank Harris (44), the sexologist, relates an adolescent homosexual experience which occurred after his friend Strangways astonished him and another friend, Howard, "by telling how he had made up to the nursemaid of his younger sisters and had managed to get into bed with her." His realistic description of what had transpired between him and this girl so fired the imagination of his listeners, that, Harris says, they gave themselves "to a bout of [masturbation] which for the first time thrilled me with pleasure." Harris says that while he and his friend Howard were "playing with themselves," he "kept thinking of Mary's [sex organ] as Strangways had described it, and at length a real orgasm came and shook me; the imagining had intensified the delight."

In the illustrations which follow, nine passages from autobiographies, confessions, and diaries will reflect the struggle of the adolescent to identify himself. The homosexual component manifests itself in these documents in a variety of ways and for a variety of reasons, as was suggested previously. Included are excerpts dating from 400 A.D. to the present and representing Australia, Vancouver Island, Netherlands, England, France, the United States and ancient Italy.

Saint Augustine
(354-430)

The lusts that raged within Augustine are reflected in the following two chapters from his *Confessions*.* There welled up in him a crescendo of wild sexual restlessness which is described in terms unmatched in literature. "These pages refer rather clearly to some adolescent homosexual activity," which occured during Augustine's sixteenth year (41). He had been attending a school in Madaura to "become a persuasive orator," he tells us and then was to matriculate at the University of Carthage. But his father did not have the necessary tuition and Augustine was forced into idleness for the year. It is this period, which Augustine describes, during which he experienced some homosexual activity.

He deplores the wickedness of his youth. I will now call to mind my past foulness, and the carnal corruptions of my soul, not because I love them, but that I may love Thee, O my God. For love of Thy love do I it, recalling, in the very bitterness of my remembrance, my most vicious ways, that Thou mayest grow sweet to me,—Thou sweetness without deception! Thou sweetness happy and assured!—and recollecting myself out of that my dissipation, in which I was torn to pieces, while, turned away from Thee the One, I lost myself among many vanities. For I even longed in my youth formerly to be satisfied with worldly things, and I dared to grow wild again with various and shadowy loves; my form consumed away, and I became corrupt in Thine eyes, pleasing myself, and eager to please in the eyes of men.

Stricken with exceeding grief, he remembers the dissolute passions in which, in his sixteenth year, he used to indulge. But what was it that I delighted in save to love and to be beloved? But I held it not in moderation, mind to mind, the bright path of friendship, but out of the dark concupiscence of the flesh and the effervescence of youth exhalations came forth which obscured and overcast my heart, so that I was unable to discern pure affection from unholy desire. Both boiled confusedly within me, and dragged away my unstable youth into the rough places of unchaste desires, and plunged me into a gulf of infamy. Thy anger had overshadowed me, and I knew it not. I was become deaf by the rattling of the chains of my mortality, the punishment for my soul's pride; and I wandered farther from Thee, and Thou didst "suffer" me; and I was tossed to and fro, and wasted, and poured out, and boiled over in my fornications, and Thou didst hold Thy peace, O Thou my tardy joy! Thou then didst hold Thy peace, and I wandered still farther from Thee, into more and more barren

---

*Reprinted by permission of Liveright Publishers. 1942. Pp. 27-29.

seed-plots of sorrows, with proud dejection and restless lassitude.

Oh for one to have regulated my disorder, and turned to my profit the fleeting beauties of the things around me, and fixed a bound to their sweetness, so that the tides of my youth might have spent themselves upon the conjugal shore, if so be they could not be tranquillized and satisfied within the object of a family, as Thy law appoints, O Lord,—who thus formest the offspring of our death, being able also with a tender hand to blunt the thorns which were excluded from Thy paradise! For Thy omnipotency is not far from us even when we are far from Thee, else in truth ought I more vigilantly to have given heed to the voice from the clouds: "Nevertheless, such shall have trouble in the flesh, but I spare you;" and, "It is good for a man not to touch a woman;" and, "He that is unmarried careth for the things that belong to the Lord, how he may please the Lord; but he that is married careth for the things that are of the world, how he may please his wife." I should, therefore, have listened more attentively to these words, and, being severed "for the kingdom of heaven's sake," I would with greater happiness have expected Thy embraces.

But I, poor fool, seethed as does the sea, and, forsaking Thee, followed the violent course of my own stream, and exceeded all Thy limitations; nor did I escape Thy scourges. For what mortal can do so? But Thou wert always by me, mercifully angry, and dashing with the bitterest vexations all my illicit pleasures, in order that I might seek pleasures free from vexation. But where I could meet with such except in Thee, O Lord, I could not find,—except in Thee, who teachest by sorrow, and woundest us to heal us, and killest us that we may not die from Thee. Where was I, and how far was I exiled from the delights of Thy house, in that sixteenth year of the age of my flesh, when the madness of lust—to the which human shamelessness granteth full freedom, although forbidden by Thy laws—held complete sway over me, and I resigned myself entirely to it? Those about me meanwhile took no care to save me from ruin by marriage, their sole care being that I should learn to make a powerful speech, and become a persuasive orator.

Henry Handel Richardson
(1870-1946)

Henry Handel Richardson is the pseudonym of the Australian woman novelist, Ethel Florence Lindesay Richardson. She is the author of *The Fortunes of Richard Mahoney*, *The Young Cosima*,

Maurice Guest, and *The Getting of Wisdom.* The first-named novel, a trilogy, is a neglected monument of psychological realism. The last-named novel is the one Miss Richardson refers to in the passage from her autobiography, *Myself When Young,* which follows.* In it she recounts a year she spent, at the age of fourteen, with a room-mate, aged eighteen. "It stirred me to my depths, rousing feelings I hadn't known I possessed, and leaving behind it a heartache as cruel as my first."

The Getting of Wisdom contained a very fair account of my doings at school and of those I came in contact with. It must, however, be remembered that both place and people were seen through the eyes of a very young girl and judged accordingly. This fact my early readers did not grasp; and the book was put down as offensive and derogatory. So much so that when I tried to revisit my old school I was refused admittance, and had to content myself with peering through cracks in the paling-fence.

The one episode in the story I deliberately weakened was my head-strong fancy for the girl there called "Evelyn." To have touched this in other than lightly would have been out of keeping with the tone of the book. The real thing was neither light nor amusing. It stirred me to my depths, rousing feelings I hadn't known I possessed, and leaving behind it a heartache as cruel as my first. Along with the new and bit-ter realisation that to live meant to change. No matter how fast one clung, how jealously one tried to stem the flow, in time all things changed and passed.

In those days school-authorities had not begun to look with jaun-diced eyes on girlish intimacies. We might indulge them as we chose; and, even when it must have been clear to the blindest where I was heading, the two of us continued to share a room. Some may see in my infatuation merely an overflow of feelings that had been denied a normal outlet. But there was more in it than that. The attraction this girl had for me was so strong that few others have surpassed it. Nor did it exist on my side only. The affinity was mutual; and that is harder to understand. For she was eighteen and grown-up, and I but a skinny little half-grown.

While it lasted I was as blissfully happy as a mortal could be who lived with one eye on the clock, begrudging each day that went by,

---

*Reprinted by permission of W. W. Norton & Co., Inc. 1948. Pp. 70-73.

and filled with misgivings about the future. For this was Evelyn's last year at school, and her people only waited for it to end, to snatch her from me and launch her in a world where there would be no room for me.—And so it happened. Except that it wasn't she who defaulted, it was I who fell away. She went to considerable lengths to keep things going. But I felt myself an interloper in her family-circle, a sort of pariah dog among her new and stylish friends, I poor, and unsuitably dressed, and always on the watch for slights or patronage. Besides, it was small joy to me to share her. I wanted to have her to myself, by herself, and if I couldn't, then I didn't want her at all. And so we gradually drifted apart.

She stood, however, among the group that assembled on the Williamstown pier to bid us good-bye when we sailed for England. And in the cabin I found a parting gift in the shape of a princely box of *Maria Farina,* "to help you through the voyage." Its contents lasted me for years, and spun a sort of invisible thread between us; for at any time a fresh whiff of the scent was enough to bring her back, together with the gloriously happy and gloriously unhappy memories of the old days.

I never completely lost sight of her. After her marriage she eventually settled in London, and now and again we met. But an Evelyn married, and living in a whirl, bore little likeness to the girl I had loved. If I wanted to recover *her,* I had to fish out one of the old photographs and see her as I then knew her, with her laughing, provocative eyes—dark, velvety eyes under a thatch of sunlit hair—and altogether so lovely that she could pass nowhere unnoticed. I remember how, at a public prize-giving, as she went up to the platform, an old Scotchwoman in the audience was heard to murmur, almost tearfully: "Aye, but *she's* bonny!"

When we met we carefully avoided the past. Once only, I think, was it touched on, when she told me that she had chosen the woman who became her lifelong companion because of a fancied resemblance to me. And then it was I who shied off the subject. Nor do I know what she thought of the portrait I had drawn of her—or the tombstone I had erected to her memory—in *The Getting of Wisdom.* Unlike certain others whom I had pilloried, she bore me no open grudge for it. But then hers was a truly generous nature. In all the time I knew her I never heard her say an unkind word of anyone. Even when hurt, she was quick to excuse and exonerate. And as long as she lived a letter came to me every Christmas, in her unchanged, buoyant hand.

Charles James Nowell
(1870-[?])

Charley Nowell came of a high-ranking Kwakiutl Indian family, the tribes of which are to be found in Vancouver Island. Charley attended the mission school at Alert Bay and there learned to speak English. This made it possible for Clelland S. Ford (18), the noted anthropologist, to take down Charley's life story exactly as it was told him. Charley's older brother, Owadi, was the head chief of the first clan of the Kweka tribe—a position formerly held by his father's brother and, before that, by his father's father. His mother's father was the young brother of Tlakodloas, the head chief of the second clan in the Nimkis tribe. From his birth Charley was trained to take his place as an important chief in Kwakiutl society.

Ford tells us that childhood aggression, in the form of striking, stealing or lying, was severely punished. "Few restrictions, however, were placed upon sexual behavior. From early years, the boys and girls were free to indulge in sex play among themselves. Their sexual practices took place in the woods and were seldom brought to the attention of their parents [19]." In the first passage which follows, Ford appends this footnote: "Although Charley is somewhat vague about the exact age when he began these [homosexual] practices, it must have been soon after he left the cradle. Up to this time, therefore, his sexual experiences must have been negligible. Apparently, however, it did not take him long to learn what his fellows expected of him. Whether or not handling his own genitals preceded this mutual sex play and met with punishment, cannot be known with certainty, but it seems clear that solitary masturbation was not as openly practiced as mutual masturbation [20]."

In the second excerpt from the autobiography, Charley describes a further homosexual experience he had as an early adolescent. Ford presents this background material: " . . . Homosexual behavior is looked upon by Kwakiutl as infantile, and one who practices it is often severely ridiculed. This attitude helps to insure the perpetuation of the group. Homosexual relations do not produce offspring and, therefore, cannot be permitted to replace productive heterosexual relations [21]." Charley's own explanation for the transvestite is that "Men who act like women I think get that way when they are growing up [22]."

When I was four or five years old, we used to play with other little boys. It was the time we used to be too little to go and play with girls. The boys would pretend to marry each other. We used to go and lay together and play with each other's peckers, and this we call "a pecker to pecker." The pecker of one boy goes together with the other boy's pecker. I've heard about some that uses their hands while they are alone, but I don't know who. I never did. I don't know why. It is all right, if you want to. This is called "handling your pecker yourself." We were about three to five then and were too small to take and ask the girls to go in the woods. Although I used to play with the older boys, they only used me as a play child.

*   *   *   *

I only knew well one of these men that wears women's clothing. There are others like that I knows, but they used men's clothing. They are mostly Quatsino Indians. I will tell you about the one I knew. This man, her name was Frances. The first time I saw her, he came to Fort Rupert and I was young. This was long before I was married. The Quatsino Indians came and camped at Fort Rupert on their way to Fraser River. I saw this man with woman's clothing, but she had a man's voice. We went to see the people in the house where they were staying, and she began to look at us, and she spoke to me and says, "You, young fellow, I'm going to have you for my sweetheart." She had long hair like a woman's. They didn't stay long, so I didn't get to know her then. When they came home from Fraser River, they called at Fort Rupert, and they stopped there for a couple of months. During the time, she called me to go and see her at the house where she was, and when I went there, she caught hold of me, and when I went there she throwed me right into her bed. My, she was strong—awful strong! She told me she want me to lie with her. Before that I was told that she was a man, and I was kind of scared to lie down with her, but I couldn't help it because she was so strong and hold me down. She opened her legs and pulled me in, taking hold of my pecker and putting it in. I didn't work; she done all the work. After I went out of the house, I told all the boys that she was a woman, and that I laid down with her, and all the boys went after her because she was free.

John Cowper Powys
(1872-1963)

John Cowper Powys, one of eleven children, is as prolific in literary productivity as his parents were fecund in offspring. He is a noted novelist, critic, biographer and essayist. Among his works are *Wolf Solent*, a novel, *Rabelais, His Life, In Defence of Sensuality, The Meaning of Culture*, and *The Enjoyment of Literature*. The two brief excerpts from his *Autobiography*,* quoted below, give a clue to his literary genre, hinted at, perhaps, in the very titles his books carry. Powys attended the famous Sherborne School, not very far from the parish where his father was minister. The sensual feelings of the fourteen-year-old boy toward two schoolmates are described here delicately and vividly. Although he never "embraced" the boys (they were oblivious to him) he sublimated his adolescent homosexual impulses by scribbling *perdita erotica* and tracing, upon a slip of transparent tissue paper, the outlines of statues from books.

There was at that time at the school-house a boy quite as delicately beautiful as our royal founder himself, and I think it is a credit to my emotion in the presence of such loveliness that merely to be within sight of this boy made me as brave as Socrates. You will hardly believe it, reader, when I tell you that this wretched Powys Ma.—with his incredible depths of funk, with his inability to catch the easiest "catch," or to tackle the feeblest "half-back," with his feeling that the gymnasium was a place of grotesque and monstrous engines of torture, and the bath a kind of icy Giudecca—was wont each day, the moment when the Lower School was bathing, to select his place of undressing and drying *next* to this notoriously beautiful person. My delight in this boy's loveliness was so intense that when I stole timorous, nervous, furtive, and yet ardently satyrish glances at him, as having undressed at my side he stood for a moment in his bathing-drawers meditating his plunge into those blue-green waters, I was totally lost to the world. The boy himself was completely oblivious of me. I never in my life spoke to him, though I must have undressed by his side a hundred times. But it was so delicious a paradise to me merely to snatch quick glances at his lovely form that I altogether forgot that such an unpleasant phenomenon as "ducking" existed anywhere on the earth.

---

*London: John Lane, 1934. Pp. 114-118, 138-140.

It is really extraordinary that the miseries I went through at Sherborne have not made me shrink from that quiet Wessex town as a Spanish Jew might have shrunk from the city of Torquemada. Such however is not at all the case; and as a matter of fact conditions at school have probably changed from what they were then. Once I could not see the straw hat of a Sherborne boy without a sensation as if I were a Helot watching a young Spartan boy go by! But I have outgrown this feeling; and just as many victims of the war must have settled down peacefully in a landscape, full for them of frightful images, so I would willingly spend my declining years at Sherborne; though I should always glance anxiously at the walls of all the "houses" and utter an invocation on behalf of any little "Johnny," turned into a contemptible "Moony," who might be crying in vain to heaven for a drop of pity as small as a wren's eye.

*   *   *   *

To Weymouth, however, in the flesh I often went, in the holidays of those schooldays. I went into lodgings alone there once, as a convalescent from our Sherborne sick-house. One of the most beautiful boys in the school had been with me in that sick-house—not the young Charmides of those rapt occasions at the bath, but a scarcely less lovely boy—and he, with another companion of a less winning appearance but much more flirtatious, had been sent to a country cottage to recruit, not far from the Coastguards.

I had a passion at that time for collecting seaweeds—*there* indeed were colours to ravish anyone; but alas! their gleaming mysteries faded when you took them out of their native pools. But the truth is I have, ever since that time, linked together the scent of salt-water, the swirl of in-rushing waves among jagged rocks, the upheaving swell of a full tide, not only with crimson seaweeds, but with the greenish-black eyes and foam-white skin of this young invader of my native haunts!

It is interesting to note that my superstitious belief in a flaming Hell for wilful sensualists, which troubled me till I went to college, never prevented me from indulging my attraction to beautiful boys as long as I did not actually embrace them. Indeed, as I never *did* embrace them, save in those scribbled *perdita erotica* which I kept in my treasure-box, I had no anticipation of any final payment for these clinging glances in the bonfire of a jealous deity.

But in my lonely convalescence at Weymouth, for, as Nietzsche says, it is in convalescence that we are especially porous to the magic of life, the green-black eyes of B—— Minor were not my only temptation. Twice in that epoch of my life I actually knelt down on the ground to wrestle with my desire to gaze at young people's beautiful legs. I remember the two precise spots where the knees of the General of the "Volentiä Army" were thus bent before his feudal overlord. One was in Redcliff Bay and one was upon Dartmoor. And I said to myself that it was better not to stare at lovely forms, or to embrace velvet-embroidered cushions or pillows dressed up in my own vests, as long as by such abstinence I escaped being boiled alive like a Lodmoor eel in eternal Hell. It was therefore with knees that trembled and shook—have you, reader, ever experienced that breath-catching feeling?—that I would furtively enter that well-known Weymouth Railway Station and casually glancing—or so I trusted it might seem—at the contents of the bookstall, absent-mindedly possess myself of the Summer Number of *Ally Sloper,* and gravely lay down my penny, as if I had been my father himself buying the *Standard.* But far more romantic, though not, I confess, quite so provocative, as the long legs of the Houris in Sloper's Paradise, were the illustrations in certain works of Rider Haggard that I found in a bookshop library behind the statue of George III. How little would authors like it if they knew all the reasons for which their books are taken out of libraries! In my longing to immortalize these tiny little vignettes of classical charm, I even went so far as to *trace,* upon a slip of transparent tissue-paper, their divine outlines, and I can well recall the heavenly security and luxurious leisure with which, in my high-ceilinged eighteenth-century front-room, under the large illuminated candalabra, and safe from all interruption, my pencil followed those delicate curves.

Simone de Beauvoir
(1908-   )

The oddly blended precocity and innocence of the teen-age girl is apparent in the "fanatic" affection Simone de Beauvoir felt for her school-chum, Zaza. The "fevered torment" was probably responsible for the excessive discretion she displayed. While the love lasted, it was passionate, exclusive—but of short duration, typical of most adolescent homosexual love relations. "The abandoned objects are quickly and completely forgotten," Anna Freud (27) reports, "but the form of the relation to them is preserved down to the minutest detail and is generally reproduced, with an exactness which almost suggests obsession, in the relation to the new object. . . . We note another peculiarity of the object-relations at puberty. The adolescent does not aim so much at possessing himself of the object in the ordinary physical sense of the term as at assimilating himself as much as possible to the person who at the moment occupies the central place in his affection." By the time she reached sixteen, Miss de Beauvoir was able to write, "My friendship with Zaza ceased to be the torment it had been."*

. . . I loved Zaza with an intensity which could not be accounted for by any established set of rules and conventions. I did not entirely correspond to the person she took me for; but I couldn't find a way of demolishing that image and revealing my true nature to Zaza; this misunderstanding drove me to despair. In my reply I pretended to take it all very lightly but at the same time reproached Zaza for being so naughty; she sensed that she had hurt me for she wrote asking to be forgiven by return post: I had been the victim, she told me, of a fit of bad temper. This restored my equanimity a little.

Zaza did not suspect how much I idolized her, nor that I had abjured my pride in her favor. At a charity bazaar held in the Cours Désir, a graphologist examined our handwritings; Zaza's appeared to indicate a precocious maturity, sensitivity, culture, and remarkable artistic gifts; mine showed nothing better than infantilism. I accepted this verdict: yes, I was an industrious pupil, a good little girl, and nothing more. Zaza protested against it with a vehemence I found very comforting. She protested again in a short letter against another analysis, just as unfavorable, which I had sent to her, and sketched my portrait in these words: "Rather reserved, a tendency to conform to convention and custom; but the warmest of hearts and an unequaled, kindly indulgence in overlooking the faults of her friends."

It wasn't often we were so frank with one another. Was that my fault? The fact is that it was Zaza who spoke, very sweetly, of *my* reserve: would she have liked a freer relationship with me? My affection for her was fanatical, but she was very reticent toward me; perhaps it was I, after all, who was responsible for our excessive discretion.

Yet I found it very irksome. Though she was brusque and caustic in her manner, Zaza was sensitive; one day she came to school, her face ravaged with weeping because she had learned the evening before of the death of a distant cousin. She would have been deeply touched by the devotion I felt for her: finally I couldn't bear to think that she

*From *Memoirs of a Dutiful Daughter* by Simone de Beauvoir, translated by James Kirkup. Reprinted by Permission of World Publishing Company. Copyright 1959,. World Publishing Company. Pp. 125-128.

knew nothing about it. As it was impossible for me to say anything, I decided I must do something. It would be running great risks: Mama would consider my plan ridiculous; or Zaza herself would think it odd. But the need to express my feelings was so great that for once I felt I must go ahead with it. I revealed my plan to my mother, who approved it. I was to give Zaza for her birthday a bag which I would make with my own hands. I bought some blue-and-red silk brocaded in gold; it seemed to me the height of luxury. Following a pattern in "Practical Fashions," I mounted it on a base of woven straw, and lined it with cerise satin; I wrapped my handiwork in tissue paper. When the day arrived, I waited for Zaza in the cloakroom; I handed her my gift; she looked at me in amazement, then she blushed hotly and her whole face changed; for a moment we stood looking at each other, embarrassed by our emotion, and quite unable to find in our repertory of set responses a single appropriate word or gesture. The next day we met with our mothers. "Now thank Madame de Beauvoir," said Madame Mabille in her most affable tones, "for all the trouble she must have taken." She was trying to bring my unprecedented action within the range of polite grown-up reactions. I realized at that moment that I didn't like her any more. In any case, she failed in the attempt. Something had happened that could not be undone.

But I still wasn't able to relax. Even when Zaza was very friendly toward me, even when she seemed to enjoy being with me, I was afraid of appearing importunate. She only let me have brief glimpses of that secret "personality" which dwelled within her; my notions of what her conversations with herself might be like became an almost religious obsession. One day I went to the Rue de Varennes to get a book that she had promised to lend me; she wasn't at home; I was asked to wait for her in her room, for she was not expected to be long. I looked at the walls covered with blue paper, da Vinci's *Saint Anne,* the crucifix. Zaza had left one of her favorite books open on her desk: the *Essays* of Montaigne. I read the page at which she had left it open, which she would continue reading when I wasn't there: but the printed symbols seemed to me as remote from my understanding as in the days when I didn't know the alphabet. I tried to see the room with Zaza's eyes, to insinuate myself into the internal monologue that was always going on inside her; but in vain. I could touch all the objects that were expressions of her presence; but they did not release her to me; they revealed but at the same time concealed her; it was almost as if they defied me ever to come close to her. Zaza's existence seemed so hermetically sealed that I couldn't get the smallest foothold in it. I took my book and fled. When I met her the next day, she seemed dumfounded by my action: why had I rushed away like that? I couldn't explain it to her. I would not even admit to myself with what fevered torment I paid for the happiness she gave me.

Anne Frank
(1929-1945)

The "Sis Heyster" to whom Anne Frank refers in this entry from her *Diary** was the author of an article on blushing, which Anne had read and was deeply impressed with: "This article might have been addressed to me personally." As she reflects on it, she expresses her acceptance of herself as a "person," and describes her passing homosexual feelings and experience which helped in the process of acceptance.

Wednesday, 5 January, 1944

Sis Heyster also writes that girls of this age don't feel quite certain of themselves, and discover that they themselves are individuals with ideas, thoughts, and habits. After I came here, when I was just fourteen, I began to think about myself sooner than most girls, and to know that I am a "person." Sometimes, when I lie in bed at night, I have a terrible desire to feel my breasts and to listen to the quiet rhythmic beat of my heart.

I already had these kinds of feelings subconsciously before I came here, because I remember that once when I slept with a girl friend I had a strong desire to kiss her, and that I did do so. I could not help being terribly inquisitive over her body, for she had always kept it hidden from me. I asked her whether, as a proof of our friendship, we should feel one another's breasts, but she refused. I go into ecstasies every time I see the naked figure of a woman, such as Venus, for example. It strikes me as so wonderful and exquisite that I have difficulty in stopping the tears rolling down my cheeks.

If only I had a girl friend!

Yours, Anne

MASTURBATION AND NOCTURNAL EMISSION

Victor Tausk (60) defines masturbation as that kind of sexual ma-

---

*From *The Diary of a Young Girl* by Anne Frank. Reprinted by Permission of Doubleday & Co., Inc. Copyright 1952, Otto H. Frank. P. 116.

nipulation of the genitals or of an erogenous zone which has no partner as an indispensable prerequisite, and the aim of which consists in the direct discharge of sexual excitation. He states further that subjects of masturbation are individuals of both sexes in all age groups and in all social strata (61). Gallagher and Harris (31) agree with this estimate of universal masturbatory practice: "Masturbation is common and widespread among the youth of the world, though in some cultures it may be less widespread. . . . " Linn and Schwarz (48) make a further confirmatory statement. "Masturbation is almost universally a part of the normal growth process. The absence of masturbation during adolescence is not only the exception but may indeed be symptomatic of a serious disturbance in emotional development." The illustrations in this final section on the psychosexual development of the adolescent tend to bear out these statements.

The sexual drive of pubertal boys and girls is so powerful that it is generally impossible for them to sublimate it wholly in nonsexual activities. They commonly resort to masturbation as a direct release from sexual tensions. But accompanying the masturbatory act is the inevitable castration anxiety that the second edition of the phallic phase brings with it. Wittels (62) lays "down the rule that all pubescents feel anxious on the occasion of their first orgasm even if the act is no more than masturbation." The fears and guilt feelings which originally were connected with the accompanying oedipal fantasies are displaced in adolescence to the masturbatory activity (17). Thus the psychiatrist views the act as an infantile autoerotic form of sexual behavior by which the individual eventually liberates himself from the incestuous attachments of early childhood.

Fenichel (17) states that "adolescent personalities react differently to these fears and guilt feelings; they may take sides more with the drive and try to fight the anxiety (or the parents representing the prohibition); or they may, more frequently, side with the anxiety and the parents, and try to fight instinctual temptations as well as rebellious tendencies. Often they do both successively or even simultaneously." Philip O'Connor (51) relates in his memoirs, "I oscillated more violently between cold baths and saintliness and masturbation and D. H. Lawrence, with bouts of film-romanticism in between. I used strong tea and my first cigarettes as agents of my increasing debauch."

The emotional problems associated with masturbation lie not so much in the act itself as in the psychologically dangerous and faulty ideas about its consequences (9). Guibert (1053-1124), Abbot of Nogent-Sous-Coucy, wrote in his *Autobiography* (33) that at the age of thirteen or fourteen, "I refrained from secret vice. . . . " This attitude toward masturbation has been a pervasive one in most cultures. Behind the secretiveness and the feeling of immorality are the depressive after-effects of masturbation, the futility of the whole experience, the subsequent loneliness, combined with a sense of guilt and a conviction of weakness in failing to resist temptation (10).

In the illustrations which follow, these characteristic feelings are generally described by almost all of the writers.

Jean Jacques Rousseau (1712-1778)

Fenichel (17) states that the oedipal fantasies are displaced in adolescence to the masturbatory activity. A perfect illustration is found in this excerpt from Rousseau's *Confessions*.* At the age of seventeen, Rousseau returned from Italy to find sanctuary in the home of Madame de Warens, a woman older than he, and one of many with whom he was to fall in love. In cadence more delicate than we might suppose to come from Rousseau's pen, he describes his first orgasm: "My restless temperament had at last made itself felt, and its first outbreak, quite involuntary, had caused me alarm about my health. . . . " But despite the fears aroused and despite the attitude that masturbation was a vice, he continued the practice—to the accompaniment of oedipal fantasies about Mme. de Warens, in whom he always saw "a tender mother, a beloved sister, a delightful friend, and nothing more."

I had returned from Italy not quite the same as I had entered it, but as, perhaps, no one of my age had ever returned from it. I had brought

---

*Edited by Lester G. Crocker. Reprinted by permission of Pocket Books, Inc. 1957. Pp. 69-70.

back, not my mental and moral, but my bodily virginity. I had felt the progress of years; my restless temperament had at last made itself felt, and its first outbreak, quite involuntary, had caused me alarm about my health in a manner which shows better than anything else the innocence in which I had lived up to that time. Soon reassured, I learned that dangerous means of assisting it, which cheats Nature and saves up for young men of my temperament many forms of excess at the expense of their health, strength, and, sometimes, of their life. This vice, which shame and timidity find so convenient, possesses, besides a great attraction for lively imaginations—that of being able to dispose of the whole sex as they desire, and to make the beauty which tempts them minister to their pleasures, without being obliged to obtain its consent. Seduced by this fatal advantage, I did my best to destroy the good constitution which Nature had restored to me, and which I had given time to strengthen itself. Add to this habit the circumstances of my position, living as I was with a beautiful woman, caressing her image in the bottom of my heart, seeing her continually throughout the day, surrounded in the evening by objects which reminded me of her, sleeping in the bed in which I knew she had slept! What causes for excitement! Many a reader, who reflects upon them, no doubt already considers me as half-dead! Quite the contrary; that which ought to have destroyed me was just the thing that saved me, at least for a time. Intoxicated with the charm of living with her, with the ardent desire of spending my life with her, I always saw in her, whether she were absent or present, a tender mother, a beloved sister, a delightful friend, and nothing more. I saw her always thus, always the same, and I never saw anyone but her. Her image, ever present to my heart, left room for no other; she was for me the only woman in the world; and the extreme sweetness of the feelings with which she inspired me did not allow my senses time to awake for others, and protected me against her and all her sex. In a word, I was chaste, because I loved her. Considering these results, which I can only imperfectly describe, let him who can say what was the nature of my attachment for her. For myself, all that I can say about it is that, if it already seems to be very extraordinary, in the sequel it will appear far more so.

G. Stanley Hall
(1846-1924)

The miasma of dread and the morass of guilt feelings the adolescent experiences because of nocturnal emissions or masturbation is reflected in this passage from G. Stanley Hall's *Life and Confessions of a Psychologist.* The absence of parental guidance and the inadequacy of lines of communication concerning sex education (which will be dealt with in the next chapter) prompted the boy to agonies of torment. "So great was my dread of natural phenomena that in the earliest teens I rigged an apparatus and applied bandages to prevent erethism while I slept. . . . " The intense remorse and fear he felt after experimenting with himself was compounded by the harmful ideas of sin and perversion associated with the act. The lessening of self-esteem was reinforced by resolutions never to masturbate again, only to have the resolve broken, the act committed and the cycle of guilt and anxiety repeated all over again.

On a farm one sees much of sex among domestic animals. As a very small boy I had to keep account of the ewes and older sheep that had been reddened by the madder daily rubbed under the forequarters of the buck hired for a week or two to run with the flock till all were covered, a process I often saw long before I knew its meaning. I always drove the sows, often miles, to the boar and was given detailed instructions as to what I must see done and how. This also began in the age of innocence but continued beyond it. I was never kept from seeing all this relation among cattle and even horses. This often caused, in later years at home, an excitement from which I should have been shielded. Again, I often saw and not infrequently helped in the castration of pigs, lambs, calves, and colts, an operation in which one of my uncles was a local expert.

As a child the only name for a certain part of the body, which I long supposed was its proper and adopted designation, was "the dirty place" for this phrase was applied to nothing else. I knew no other name until I went to school, where I was greatly shocked by the obscenities that prevailed and where these parts were much shown, talked of, compared, and experimented with. My father occasionally went in swimming with us and once or twice took occasion to give us crude admonitions on sex hygiene. The thing that sunk deepest was his story of a youth who abused himself and sinned with lewd women and as a result had a disease that ate his nose away until there were only two flat holes in his face for nostrils and who also became an idiot. For a long time, if I had any physical excitation or nocturnal experience I was almost petrified lest I was losing my brains and care-

*Reprinted by permission of Appleton-Century-Crofts, Inc. Copyright 1923, D. Appleton & Co. Pp. 131-133.

fully examined the bridge of my nose to see if it was getting the least bit flat. I understood that any one who swerved in the slightest from the norm of purity was liable to be smitten with some loathsome disease which I associated with leprosy and with the "unpardonable sin" which the minister often dwelt upon.

So great was my dread of natural phenomena that in the earliest teens I rigged an apparatus and applied bandages to prevent erethism while I slept, which very likely only augmented the trouble. If I yielded to any kind of temptation to experimentation upon myself I suffered intense remorse and fear, and sent up many a secret and most fervent prayer that I might never again break my resolve. At one time I feared I was abnormal and found occasion to consult a physician in a neighboring town who did not know me. He examined me and took my dollar, and laughed at me, but also told me what consequences would ensue if I became unchaste. What an untold anguish of soul would have been saved me if some one had told me that certain experiences while I slept were as normal for boys in their teens as are the monthly phenomena for girls. I did not know that even in college and thought myself secretly and exceptionally corrupt and not quite worthy to associate with girls. This had probably much, if not most, to do with my abstention from them and was, I think, the chief factor that brought about my "conversion" in my sophomore year, although this made the struggle for purity far more intense, though I fear but little more successful.

I fear the good Lord on whom I was told, and tried, to cast my burden did not help me much here. Indeed, perhaps in transferring and committing all to Him I trusted my own powers less. Perhaps, again, my profound sense of inferiority here prompted me to compensate by striving all the harder for excellence in other lines, although there was always a haunting sense that if I succeeded in making anything of myself it would be despite this private handicap. I should certainly never dare to marry and have children. It was ineffable relief, therefore, to learn, as I did only far too late, that my life in this sphere had, on the whole, been in no sense abnormal or even exceptional.

Havelock Ellis
(1859-1939)

The unconscious homosexual horseplay (no pun is intended in connection with the excerpt below*) of the adolescent is manifested

---

*From *My Life* by Havelock Ellis. Reprinted by permission of Houghton Mifflin Co. 1939. Pp. 100-101, 157-158.

here on the sadomasochistic level of development. It led the pubertal Ellis to have copious seminal emissions which "were themselves a source of nervous apprehension, for I vaguely felt they were something to be ashamed of; I constantly dreaded their occurrence and feared their detection." The belief that others can tell if the adolescent masturbates or has nocturnal emissions is another source of anxiety to the individual. The hazard of loss of self-esteem, which may have repercussions on the boy's work efficiency, studies, and social relationships, must be reckoned with.

So far as my masters were concerned, my life at Mitcham would have been from first to last a peaceful and happy period of more or less spontaneous mental development. But for a considerable time it was made a hell by the influence of one boy. I shared a large bedroom with two boys, both several years older than I was. One of them was of quiet and inoffensive temperament when left to himself, but he was always willing to become the tool and partner of the third boy. This third boy, Willie Orr, may, for all that I know, have possessed many fine latent qualities. But he was one of those youths whose irresistible impulse it is to bully and dominate those who are too young or too timid to resist them. His father was a colonel in the Indian army; young Orr was probably fond of riding (later he appropriately joined the Indian Frontier Mounted Police, dying young) and in the absence of a horse he conceived the idea of using me in that capacity. In order to carry out the idea in a manner quite satisfactory to himself he made spurs in which pins formed the working portion; every night he mounted my back with his spurs on and rode me round and round the room in my nightshirt, handing me over to the other boy when he was himself tired of the exercise. (I should add that nothing else, nothing of the slightest sexual character, ever took place.) To a shy, sensitive, and reserved boy, one, moreover, who had never been harshly treated, these performances were an acute nervous torture, out of all proportion to any pain actually inflicted. I had no instincts of pugnacity, and the idea of attacking or resisting a robust and brutal boy older and bigger than myself never occurred to me. I performed the required duties much as a real animal would have done, without articulate protest or complaint, until my mother, discovering something amiss with me, made me confess what was going on, and came to interview Mr. Grover. I was then placed in another room, which I shared with a boy of character congenial to my own. But I am inclined to think that the suffering I had silently endured was not without evil influence on my nervous system. I was just then at the critical period of puberty. While subjected to this treatment, at about the age of thirteen, copious seminal emissions began to take place during sleep, once or twice a week, always without dreams or any sensations, and continued, whenever I was alone, for some thirty years. Doubtless my temperament predisposed me to such manifestations, though my thoughts and my habits were, at this period, alike free from any physically sensual tincture, but I incline to think that the state of nervous excitement in which every night I fell asleep was a factor in causing this lack of nervous stability in the new function then developing. The emissions were themselves a source of nervous apprehension, for I vaguely felt they were something to be ashamed of; I constantly dreaded their occurrence and feared their detection.

Of physical desire I was as yet scarcely aware in any definite way except during sleep. That physical efflorescence of sex had begun with me early and often, as I have already told, at first usually without dreams, and it worried me because of the traces left behind. In time I understood what these manifestations meant and accepted them, methodically noting their occurrences in my pocket diary. I endeavoured so far as possible to avoid anything likely to evoke them when asleep, and never, by any physical or mental procedure, sought consciously to produce them when awake. They had occurred, indeed, so frequently asleep that there was not much temptation to produce them when awake. But at Sparkes Creek, where my life, far from any kind of sexual stimulation, was simple and healthy and regular, these nocturnal eruptions probably ceased to give complete relief. At all events, it was at Sparkes Creek that for the first time in my life I experienced the orgasm when awake. I was lying down on my simple bed, one warm pleasant day, reading something which evidently had in it for me some touch of erotic stimulation—I believe it was the *Dames Galantes* of Brantôme—and suddenly I became aware that the agreeable emotion aroused by the book, without any will or any action of my own, was becoming physically translated and fulfilled. I realised what had happened and felt no alarm; evidently there was nothing in the occurrence that was not natural and beautiful, though it was of course easy to imagine circumstances under which it would have been yet more natural and beautiful. It was not until after this event that I ever became definitely conscious of any stirring of physical excitement at the thought or the proximity of an attractive woman.

Emma Goldman
(1869-1940)

The parental attitude toward masturbation links it with a childish habit and creates the fear that the child is not growing into adulthood and independence. What happens when Emma Goldman's mother catches her clutching her genitals in her sleep (she was eleven years old at the time of the incident) is told here.* "Autosexual behavior," wrote Sullivan (59), "commonly called masturbation, has in general been rather severely condemned in every culture that generally imposes marked restrictions on freedom of sexual development. That's very neat, you see; it means that adolescence is going to be hell whatever you do, unless you have wonderful preparation for being different from everyone else—in which case you may get into trouble for being different."

Mother was busy superintending the servants in our large, chaotic house. My sisters, Lena and Helena, fourteen and twelve, were burdened with work. I was left to myself most of the day. Among the stable help there was a young peasant, Petrushka, who served as shepherd, looking after our cows and sheep. Often he would take me with him to the meadows, and I would listen to the sweet tones of his flute. In the evening he would carry me back home on his shoulders, I sitting astride. He would play horse—run as fast as his legs could carry him, then suddenly throw me up in the air, catch me in his arms, and press me to him. It used to give me a peculiar sensation, fill me with exultation, followed by blissful release.

I became inseparable from Petrushka. I grew so fond of him that I began stealing cake and fruit from Mother's pantry for him. To be with Petrushka out in the fields, to listen to his music, to ride on his shoulders, became the obsession of my waking and sleeping hours. One day Father had an altercation with Petrushka, and the boy was sent away. The loss of him was one of the greatest tragedies of my child-life. For weeks afterwards I kept on dreaming of Petrushka, the meadows, the music, and reliving the joy and ecstasy of our play. One morning I felt myself torn out of sleep. Mother was bending over me, tightly holding my right hand. In an angry voice she cried: "If ever I find your hand again like that, I'll whip you, you naughty child!"

---

*From *Living My Life* by Emma Goldman. Reprinted by permission of Alfred A. Knopf, Inc. 1931.

Theodore Dreiser
(1871-1945)

"Poor, ignorant humanity! I wish that all of the religious and moral piffle and nonsense from which I suffered in connection with this matter [of masturbation] could be undone completely for the rest of the world by merely writing about it." So goes the peroration in Dreiser's vivid chapter on the four or five miserable years he spent as an adolescent, morbidly worried about his autoerotic behavior, scared to death of the tell-tale pimples on his face, the undoubted eventuality of brain trouble and of being sexually crippled for life, and plagued by the myriad psychosomatic complaints which were all ascribed to his self-indulgence. The boy fell prey to the lurid advertisements addressed to "Weak Men" and "Victims of Self-Abuse;" he was a willing victim of nostrums and gadgets to secure him from the evil fate awaiting him. He suffered the torments of "nervous depression," accompanied by a whirring in his head and ringing in his ears, which frightened him nearly out of his wits.*

The fallacy that masturbation causes insanity probably originated in observations of mentally institutionalized people who masturbate quite openly, thereby leading to the conclusion that insanity was caused by such activity. The moral condemnation of this practice probably also suggested that any act so abhorrent to the moral standards of the community ought to affect the brain as a punishment for sinning. But if masturbation does cause insanity, most of us would now be in padded cells (11).

About this time it was that, because of my growing sex interest as well as my contact with the baker's daughter and at the same time my inability to front the elusive subtlety of the more attractive girls of the town, I fell into the ridiculous and unsatisfactory practice of masturbation, which finally became a habit that endured—broken, of course, by occasional normal sex relations with passing women and girls—until I married.

One hot summer day, alone in my room after a bath, I sat down on the side of my bed thinking of what I would do if Gusta Phillipson, or Stella Davenant or Nata Weyler, as opposed to my baker girl, were in

---

*From *Dawn. A History of Myself* by Theodore Dreiser. Reprinted by permission of World Publishing Company. Copyright 1931, Theodore Dreiser. Pp. 268-272.

my arms. To me at least they were such torrid flames of beauty! And, in this state of emotion, I suddenly and quite unexpectedly brought on a sensation which, as in the case of my contact with the baker's daughter, thrilled and yet quite terrified me. For I had not intended any such result and had not even assumed that in this case it would occur. When it did, I jumped up fearful lest I had injured myself. I dressed quickly, resolved not to trifle with myself in this fashion again nor to think the thoughts which our local parish priest was always telling me were evil.

Following this came several days of strenuous effort to remain pure in mind and body. But this decision lasted only some three or four days. The physical beauty of girls as well as the delight and relief of the process I had discovered—the only substitute for the sex contact I so much craved—came back to me with overwhelming force. I forgot my good resolutions. No harm had come to me, apparently from either this or my preceding single relationship with a woman. Subsequently I longed, of course, and with flaming eagerness, to find some girl other than the one mentioned with whom I could continue, but in lieu of that, this other, this something that stung and thrilled, must serve. I ran to my room and indulged in the act again. A heavy reaction of mood again followed, but a few days served to efface the memory of anything save the intense delight. For weeks and months, every two or three days at the utmost, I now indulged myself in a kind of fury of passion. I would run to my room or any secret place I had appointed, and there in a kind of excess of passion and delight, give myself over to this form of self-abuse. At the same time, I would combine it with passional thoughts of one of the girls whom I most admired: Carrie Tuttle, Stella Davenant, or Nata Weyler. It has always been a matter of curiosity to me that the personality of Myrtle Trego was never visualized in this connection. It never occurred to me that I could satisfy myself with her in this fashion.

The natural result of this was, first, a radical change in point of view, and, second, and to a lesser extent, a change in my physical condition. For one thing, temporarily my face became blotched and marred by pimples, which caused Harry Croxton to exclaim one day: "What are you doing to yourself, Ted? Your face is all covered with pimples!" Abashed at the thought that my face was advertising my secret, I resolved to quit. But I could not. The pleasure and relief to my desires were too great. Besides, now that Croxton had indicated this facial condition as a sure sign, I noted other boys and girls to be in the same state. Better, though, I came to talk more freely of all this (sex) with Croxton, McNutt and others and to learn of seemingly endless variations of it. Judson Morris, the hunchback son of the book-store man, had secured a number of immoral, fly-by-night pamphlets, which in those days were allowed to pass through the mails undetected and which for the price of ten cents retailed all the delights of the wedding night. John and George Shoup, Gavin McNutt, Beachey Reid and others—quite a circle of the youths of the school—used to gather to read them at Jud's father's corner book store. A Rabelaisian, immoral business, but so it was. Not a morbid crowd either, if I except myself, but rather of a laughing, jesting jovial turn. And incidentally, and coeval with this—very likely because of it—I came to know of books that dealt with sex in a revelatory if more or less classic way: "Tom Jones," "Joseph Andrews," "Moll Flanders"; also passages from Dryden, Pope, Shakespeare's Sonnets. For several years after that my main concern with old or famous books was to find the portions which dealt with sex, though the merit of a conservative work was by no means beyond me.

But after a time—due to my morbidity in connection with it all—a nervous depression. I was sitting one night at the dinner table some three or four months after I had begun this practice, when all of a sudden I was taken with a whirring in my head and ringing in my ears, which frightened me nearly out of my wits. For a few moments I thought I was going to die. Nature's way, apparently, when an internal physical adjustment is to be made, is not to give warning beforehand but to keep up an appearance of normal health until it can no longer possibly be maintained. In this case I cannot even suggest, I fear, the ominous portents of physical change or readjustment that seemed suddenly to play about my mental horizon. If you can imagine a black landscape with a yellow storm in the offing, or a fever victim pursued by spying, lurking devils, or an inferno glimpsed in half light and quaking with strange and hitherto unimagined sights and sounds, you may arrive at some idea of what I endured. If I had not been sitting, I would have fallen. As it was, I put down my knife and fork, placed my hands on the table to steady myself, and closed my eyes. In my brain was spinning a whirligig of spectral lights: yellow, red, green, blue, grey, white. In place of my normal heart-beat was a feeble fluttering, which alternated with a heavy thumping which seemed to spell instantaneous collapse. I tried to get up, but could not. Then after, say, thirty seconds—by which time I was nearly exhausted—the uproar in my ears ceased, my heart beat less feebly, the grinding and clanking in my brain subsided, and I arose and went upstairs, saying I had forgotten something.

In my room, though, I sat and meditated on all this. Sickness! Brain trouble! Total physical collapse, no doubt! The truth was, I was really thinking of those innumerable advertisements addressed to "Weak Men" or "Victims of Self-Abuse," as the advertisements of those days ran, which Croxton and others by their talks had called to my attention and concerning which we used to jest. But now no more. The emaciated, sunken-eyed victims of youthful excess always illustrated by them haunted me. For now was I not one of these? If not as yet, then obviously I was to become one, emaciated, with hair and teeth falling out, eyes sunken, and no hope of any future of any kind save in the particular pills or nostrums advertised or such periods of treatment as could be procured from "Old Dr. Grindle" of Buffalo, New York, or "Old Dr. Grey," of Scranton, Pennsylvania. The particular "swamp root" or tannic acid pills or electric belt or "Neuro-phag" prescribed by these was all that was left. I shook in terror, for I had no money. My mother would not be able to afford sufficient money to permit me to undergo any one of these saving treatments, even though I had sufficient courage to tell her what had befallen me. And then what?

And worse, the whirrings and interior disturbances returned and at seemingly regular intervals for at least a month or two. Also I had the most terrifying dreams, in which ghosts or skeletons walked and threatened imminent destruction. At two in the morning—the zero hour at which the earth seems to suffer a change or period of inhalation or exhalation—I was wont to awake, feeling as though I were about to expire. A peculiar whistling in my ears would begin and might continue for several hours. I had, or imagined I had, all the symptoms of prolonged insomnia, only with this difference: that when I became exhausted, I would fall into a heavy sleep. After much thought, I hit upon the idea of copying out a prescription which I found in somebody's "Family Medical Guide" and asking the most friendly of the two local druggists—the one who was not Myrtle Trego's father—to fill it and charge it for a month. He did so, but with true rural sagacity, mailed the bill to my mother: a bill for $4.25. Now I know, as I half suspected then, that the medicine (like ninety per cent of all medicine) was worthless. It brought me merely a few days' hope, then greater despair, because the night sweats, etc., continued, and there was the necessity of explaining, or attempting to explain, the matter of the bill to my mother. Curiously enough, that strangely sympathetic woman did not press the mystery of the purchase too far. When she saw I was confused and distressed, she let the matter rest.

"If you think something is the matter with you that you don't want to tell me about, why don't you go and see Dr. Woolley?" she said. Her voice was as soft and pleasing as that of a sweetheart.

But one service the author of "The Family Guide" rendered me was to point out the efficacy of cold baths, exercise, sleeping with the windows open, on a hard bed, etc. All this, coupled with the gradual realization that I was not to die at once, gradually led to a modified view of my condition. Perhaps I was only to be crippled sexually for life, as the advertisements I had been reading by the ton invariably asserted. That was bad enough, of course, but after all it was not insanity or death.

Poor, ignorant humanity! I wish that all of the religious and moral piffle and nonsense from which I suffered in connection with this matter could be undone completely for the rest of the world by merely writing about it. What tons of rot have been written and published concerning the spiritual and moral degradation of this practice! Old wives' tales, for the most part. Quacks and thieves printing lying advertisements to sell nostrums to the ignorant, and so terrifying poor fools who stand in no more real physical or mental danger than a man with a taste for green plums! Doctors more religionistic than medical, writing endless silly books on hearsay or because of early asinine terrors of their own! I have often wished that the pagan or Hebraic view of things had prevailed in my own family and that at this age I had been taken in hand and introduced to a bagnio, or that I had possessed sufficient courage to persuade a girl to have physical relations with me. I was of the temperament that required it. As it was, for four or five years I was thrown into the most, at times, gloomy mental state, that is, whenever I thought of my assumed condition, and yet there was no more the matter with me than there is with any healthy, normal boy who takes to this exotic practice.

REFERENCES

1. Ackerman, Nathan W. *The Psychodynamics of Family Life*. New York: Basic Books, 1958, pp. 220-221.
2. Alfieri, Vittorio. *Autobiography*. Boston: James R. Osgood & Co., 1877, pp. 112-113.
3. Augustine, Saint. *Confessions*. New York: Liveright Publishing Co., 1942, pp. 27-28.
4. Bernard, Harold W. *Adolescent Development in American Culture*. Yonkers-on-Hudson, New York: World Book Co., 1957, p. 446.
5. Bernfeld, Siegfried. Types of adolescence. *Psychoanal. Quart.*, 7:246, 1938.

6. *Ibid.*, p. 243.
7. Bloch, Herbert A., & Niederhoffer, Arthur. *The Gang. A Study in Adolescent Behavior.* New York: Philosophical Library, 1958, p. 81.
8. *Ibid.*, pp. 89-90.
9. Brown, Fred & Kempton, Rudolf T. *Sex Questions and Answers.* New York: McGraw-Hill Book Co., 1950, p. 93.
10. *Ibid.*, p. 94.
11. *Ibid.*, p. 92.
12. Catherine the Great. *Memoirs.* New York: Alfred A. Knopf, 1927, pp. 44-45.
13. Ellis, Havelock. *My Life.* Boston: Houghton Mifflin Co., 1939, p. 126.
14. *Ibid.*, p. 99.
15. English, O. Spurgeon, & Pearson, Gerald H. J. *Emotional Problems of Living.* New York: W. W. Norton & Co., 1945, p. 332.
16. Fenichel, Otto. *The Psychoanalytic Theory of Neurosis.* New York: W. W. Norton & Co., 1945, pp. 110-111.
17. *Ibid.*, p. 112.
18. Ford, Clelland S. *Smoke from Their Fires. The Life of a Kwakiutl Chief.* New Haven: Yale University Press, 1941.
19. *Ibid.*, p. 34.
20. *Ibid.*, p. 68.
21. *Ibid.*, p. 69.
22. *Ibid.*, p. 132.
22a. Forel, August, *Out of My Life and Work.* New York: W. W. Norton & Co., 1937, p. 57.
23. Freud, Anna. *The Ego and the Mechanisms of Defence.* New York: International Universities Press, 1946, pp. 149-165.
24. *Ibid.*, pp. 181-182.
25. *Ibid.*, pp. 167-170.
26. *Ibid.*, p. 183.
27. *Ibid.*, pp. 183-184.
28. Freud, Sigmund. Preface, in *A Young Girl's Diary.* New York: Thomas Seltzer, 1921, p. 7.
29. Freud, Sigmund. Three contributions to the theory of sex. In: *The Basic Writings of Sigmund Freud.* New York: Modern Library, 1938, p. 599.
30. Friedenberg, Edgar Z. *The Vanishing Adolescent.* Boston: Beacon Press, 1959, p. 120.
31. Gallagher, J. Roswell, & Harris, Herbert I. *Emotional Problems of Adolescents.* New York: Oxford University Press, 1958, p. 32.

32. Guibert. *The Autobiography of Guibert, Abbot of Nogent-Sous-Coucy.* New York: E. P. Dutton & Co., 1925, p. 62.
33. *Ibid.,* p. 63.
34. Hitschmann, Edward. *Great Men.* New York: International Universities Press, 1956, p. 12.
35. Hurlock, Elizabeth B., & Klein, E. R. Adolescent crushes. *Child Develop.,* 5:79, 1934.
36. Jahoda, Marie. Environment and mental health. *Internat. Soc.Sci. J.,* 11:16, 1959.
37. Jones, Ernest. Some problems of adolescence. *Brit. J. Psychol.,* 13:32-33, 1922.
38. Jones, Ernest. *The Life and Work of Sigmund Freud.* Vol. 2. New York: Basic Books, 1955, p. 267.
39. Kligerman, Charles. The character of Jean Jacques Rousseau. *Psychoanal. Quart.,* 20:237, 1951.
40. *Ibid.,* p. 239.
41. Kligerman, Charles. A psychoanalytic study of the *Confessions* of St. Augustine. *J. Amer. Psychoanal. Assn.,* 5:473, 1957.
42. Kluckhohn, Clyde. Quoted in Jahoda, Marie, Environment and mental health. *Internat. Soc. Sci. J.,* 11:16, 1959.
43. Kronhausen, Eberhard, & Kronhausen, Phyllis. *Pornography and the Law. The Psychology of Erotic Realism and "Hard Core" Pornography.* New York: Ballantine Books, 1959, p. 79.
44. *Ibid.,* p. 112.
45. Leonard, William Ellery. *The Locomotive-God.* New York: Century Co., 1927, p. 99.
46. *Ibid.,* p. 109.
47. Levy, John, & Monroe, Ruth L. *The Happy Family.* New York: Alfred A. Knopf, 1938, pp. 124-125.
48. Linn, Louis, & Schwartz, Leo W. *Psychiatry and Religious Experience.* New York: Random House, 1958, p. 65.
49. McCurdy, Harold C. *The Childhood Pattern of Genius.* Washington, D.C.: Smithsonian Institution, 1959, pp. 532-533.
50. Mozart, Wolfgang A. *The Letters of Mozart and His Family.* Vol. I. Edited by Emily Anderson. London: Macmillan & Co., 1938, p. 365.
51. O'Connor, Philip. *Memoirs of a Public Baby.* New York: British Book Centre, 1958, p. 134.
52. Oppeln-Bronikowski, Friedrich. Eros als Schicksal bei Friedrich dem Grossen und bei Stendahl. Ein sexualpsychologischer Vergleich. *Psychoanal. Bewegung,* 2:314-325, 1930.
53. Padover, S. K. *Confessions and Self-Portraits.* New York: John Day, 1957, pp. 154-157.

54. Rossetti, Dante. *The Vita Nuova.* New York: R. H. Russell, 1901, pp. 46-47, 50, 52, 53, 55.
55. Simmons, Leo W. (Ed.). *Sun Chief. The Autobiography of a Hopi Indian.* New Haven: Yale University Press, 1942, p. 117.
56. Stern, Bernhard J. (Ed.). *Young Ward's Diary.* New York: G. P. Putnam's Sons, 1935, p. v.
57. Sullivan, Harry Stack. *The Interpersonal Theory of Psychiatry.* New York: W. W. Norton & Co., 1953.
58. *Ibid.,* p. 264.
59. *Ibid.,* p. 270.
60. Tausk, Victor. On masturbation. In: Eissler, Ruth S., et al. (Eds.), *The Psychoanalytic Study of the Child.* Vol. VI. New York: International Universities Press, 1951, p. 63.
61. *Ibid.,* p. 64.
62. Wittels, Fritz. The ego of the adolescent. In: Eissler, K. R. (Ed.), *Searchlights on Delinquency.* New York: International Universities Press, 1949, p. 258.
63. Wolberg, Lewis R. *The Divine Comedy* of Dante. *Psychoanal. Rev.,* 30:36, 1943.
64. Yarnell, Helen. Firesetting in children. *Amer. J. Ortho-psychiat.,* 10:272-286, 1940.

CHAPTER THREE

The Sexual Enlightenment
of Adolescents

In 1907, in an open letter to the editor of *Soziale Medizin und Hygiene,* Freud (5) asked rhetorically what could be the aim of withholding from children and young people information about the sexual life of human beings. "Is it a fear of arousing interest in such matters prematurely, before it spontaneously stirs in them? Is it a hope of retarding by concealment of this kind the development of the sexual instinct in general, until such time as it can find its way into the only channels open to it in the civilized social order? Is it supposed that children would show no interest or understanding for the facts and riddles of sexual life if they were not prompted to do so by outside influence? Is it regarded as possible that the knowledge withheld from them will not reach them in other ways? Or is it genuinely and seriously intended that later on they should consider everything connected with sex as something despicable and abhorrent, from which their parents and teachers wish to keep them apart as long as possible?"

Freud declared these arguments one and all equally foolish. In a letter to Edward Hitschmann (6) he found some answers to such arguments: "To my mind it seems that certain things are altogether too much wrapped in mystery. It is well to keep the fantasies of children pure, but their purity will not be preserved by ignorance. On the contrary, I believe that concealment leads a girl or boy to suspect the truth more than ever. Curiosity leads to prying into things which would have aroused little or no interest if they were talked of openly without any fuss. If this ignorance could be maintained I might be more reconciled to it, but that is impossible; the child comes into contact with other children, books fall into his hands which lead him to reflect, and the mystery with which things he has already surmised are treated by his parents actually increases his desire to know more. Then this desire that is only incompletely and secretly satisfied gives rise to excitement and corrupts his imagination, so that the child is already a sinner while his parents still believe he does not know what sin is."

The writings of the autobiographers reinforce what Freud and Hitschmann exposed. The sexual innocence and inhibitions of Catherine the Great during adolescence may have prompted her adult sexual excesses. "Around St. Peter's," she wrote, "the whole Court returned to the city from Peterhof. As nearly as I can remember, it was on the night before the feast day that I hit upon the notion of having all my ladies-in-waiting and chambermaids sleep in my room. For this purpose, I had the beds for myself and the whole company made on the floor and in this way we spent the night. Before we went to sleep there was a great argument among us about the difference between the sexes. I believe that most of us were still entirely innocent; as far as I was concerned I can swear that in spite of my sixteen years [this would be in 1745] I still had no idea wherein the difference consisted. I did still more; I promised my maidens to ask my mother about it the next day. They listened to that and at last we went to sleep. The next day I really asked my mother some questions, for which I was scolded [4]."

The Chinese autobiographer, Helena Kuo (1), stated that "In sex matters we were as ostrich-like as the English; sex was there, but it was never mentioned. I obtained all my knowledge from books, and when I arrived at the age of fourteen, I realized a definite responsibility in life that I would faithfully observe."

The American poet and editor, Harriet Monroe (1860-1936), felt that the secrecy surrounding sex and her ignorance of sexual matters were at the root of an adolescent crisis she experienced: " . . . modern psychologists might trace my crisis back to sex inhibitions, and indeed, if ever a child or young girl was sex inhibited, that was my fate, shut up as I was in an impenetrable shell of self-consciousness. The subject was secretly whispered around by older girls. Boys became mysterious, inhuman—remote repositories of dread whom I could never meet on simple and natural terms. If involuntary emotional feelers rose to their allure, I crushed them back as shameful, pernicious, and would have died rather than confess them. Thus I always played wrong in the game of sex, and ran away, emotionally, from boy friends; thus through the flowering years I grew up afraid of love [13]."

In a great many cultures, sex is still a tabooed topic. Little recognition is given its role in personality. In actuality, personality adjustment and sex adjustment can not be separated, as Monroe illustrates. Sometimes it is difficult if not impossible to say which is cause and which effect, for 'sex' and 'personality' represent a combination of social learning superimposed upon a highly complicated physical structure (3). When Simone de Beauvoir was ten years old, her mother told her and a younger sister "that little babies came out of the anus, quite painlessly. She spoke in a detached tone of voice; but we were not encouraged to make further inquiries; I never again discussed these problems with her, and she never said another word to us about them (2)." Parents, it would seem, are generally unable to communicate with their children about matters of sex. Freud, himself, was no exception: he was a father before he was a psychologist. Martin Freud, his eldest son, in a passage which will be found later in this chapter, relates a family discussion about cattle. "It became clear to father that none of his children knew the difference between a bullock and a bull. 'You must be told these things,' father had exclaimed; but like the majority of fathers, he had done nothing whatever about it." Martin, it will be seen, tried to find out for himself, underscoring the fact that the forbidden acquires lurid coloring from the efforts of the imagination to pierce the mysteries of the taboos.

Even though Freud had every intellectual insight into and understanding of the need to enlighten children about matters of sex, he was powerless—for one reason or another—to do so. Upton Sinclair (14) was subjected to the same kind of secrecy or withholding of information. He was sixteen before he found out the essential facts. "I spent a summer in the country with a boy cousin, a year or two younger than I, and we watched the animals, and questioned the farm-hands. But never did I get one word of information or advice from either father or mother on this subject; only the motion of shrinking away from something dreadful. I recollect how the signs of puberty began to show themselves in me, to my great bewilderment; my mother and grandmother stood helplessly by, like the hen which hatches ducklings and sees them go into the water."

Because of the unwillingness or inability of parents in many societies to inform and educate children about sexual functionings, adolescents are usually much better indoctrinated in the sinfulness of sex than in accurate information about it. In a study of fifty-two adolescent boys, half of whom were involved in antisocial, aggressive behavior and the other half not, Bandura and Walters (1) show the confused and misinformed way in which many parents handle their children's sex education. "Boys had obtained their sex information from various sources, but mainly from their peer group and from reading. Almost all boys in both groups felt their parents either had given them little, or no, sex information or had been too late in giving it. . . . Most parents were reluctant to face the task of imparting adequate sex information." Freud (7) attributes this adult attitude of mystery to prudery and a guilty conscience about sexual matters. "When children do not receive the explanations for which they turn to their elders, they go on tormenting themselves in secret with the problem, and produce attempts at solution in which the truth they have guessed is mixed up in the most extraordinary way with grotesque inventions; or else they whisper confidences to each other which, because of the sense of guilt in the youthful inquirers, stamp everything sexual as horrible and disgusting."

Ethel Mannin's autobiography illustrates the points Freud made. As an adolescent, she and her schoolmates were morbidly interested in parturition, menstruation and procreation. They raked the Bible for information, researched the encyclopedias and home medical works for the meaning of words, and exchanged ignorances together. One day, coming home from Sunday School, a friend pointed out a passage from the Bible which revealed in one thunderous clap of enlightenment where babies come from: "Esau came forth from his mother's belly." She found this "unspeakably dreadful," conjuring up visions of sanguinary major operations. A terrible anger arose in her when she confronted her parents with her new-found knowledge, only to be rebuffed by her mother who told her that she had no business talking about such things. When the girl and her friend subsequently discovered how babies were created, "horror shook us." Both vowed never to marry: one would become a nun, the other a missionary to Africa (12).

The rigid morality of these girls' parents is not, of course, found in all cultures. Where it is, "It is possible for a woman to remain relatively ignorant of sex during her entire life. . . . The sexual act is in disrepute and devoid of dignity . . . [carrying] with it the distinct connotation of something dirty [15]." Even in a more enlightened society, adolescents feel inhibitions about asking questions. In the diary David Kogan (10) kept, the October 7, 1942 entry reads, "We are learning the story of reproduction to the classe's [sic] amazement, but we don't dare ask questions, because we might bring up the wrong subjects, and the teacher might think we know too much." In cultures such as the Alorese and Comanche this kind of difficulty would never occur because sex is considered a natural activity and therefore performed naturally with little or no restrictions imposed on the children. The Cheyennes, on the other hand, are sexually repressed, have very strict notions of proper conduct, and are most sensitive to what other members of the tribe think of them. In the culture of the Russian serf and villager of the seventeenth, eighteenth and nineteenth centuries, where adult sexual behavior was openly displayed, adolescents were enlightened but forbidden to indulge. Gorky described in his autobiography how his grandmother abetted his friendship with a fourteen-year-old neighbor, Ludmilla: " . . . only no tricks [the grandmother warned]. And, in honest words, we were told what 'tricks' were meant. What she told us had the beauty of an inspiration. I was given a full understanding of the mistake of picking the unripened flower and forfeiting, thereby, the fragrance and the fruit. We were free of any urge toward 'tricks,' but we did not hesitate to discuss that tabooed subject. It was virtually forced upon us by the gross forms, offensive to us both, in which the sexual relationship was continuously and tediously exhibited [9]."

When the child or adolescent is enlightened about sexual matters with "the beauty of an inspiration," as was Gorky, then the anxieties attendant to this area are reduced, the individual need not renounce sex and substitute asceticism, nor sublimate his libidinal urges through fanatic devotion to some cause, nor grow up in the ignorant belief that the navel is the center of sexual attraction or that babies are anally produced. How are the strange, inexplicable feelings of rapture to be explained to the pubertal boy who wonders, in all innocence, as did Eric Gill (8), "What marvellous thing was this that suddenly transformed a mere water tap into a pillar of fire— and water into an elixir of life? I lived henceforth in a strange world of contradiction: something was called ugly which was obviously lovely. Strange days and nights of mystery and fear mixed with excitement and wonder—strange days and nights, strange months and years."

The nine excerpts from personal documents which follow reveal the secrecy and mystery surrounding sex, whether the culture is Japanese, Swiss, English, Austrian, American Quaker, or Russian. They illuminate the intense feelings adolescents have on the subject, their great need to know and understand, the abysmal ignorance of their factual knowledge, the exasperations that accrue from the hush-hush dissemblings of parents, and the anxieties and feelings of guilt which develop needlessly as a result of these factors.

Jean Jacques Rousseau*
(1712-1778)

While these petty disputes about trifles lasted, and the time was spent in arguing, mumbling prayers, and doing nothing, a disgusting little adventure happened to me, which very nearly turned out very badly for me.

There is no soul so vile, no heart so barbarous, that it is not susceptible of some kind of attachment. One of the two vagabonds who called themselves Moors conceived an affection for me. He was fond of accosting me, talked to me in his jargon, rendered me slight services, sometimes gave me part of his food, and frequently kissed me with an ardour which was very annoying to me. In spite of the natural alarm which I felt at his gingerbread face decorated with a long scar, and his inflamed countenance which appeared more furious than tender, I endured his kisses, saying to myself: "The poor fellow has conceived a lively friendship for me. I should be wrong to repulse him." He gradually began to take greater liberties, and sometimes made such curious proposals to me, that I thought he was mad. One night, he wanted to

---

*From *Confessions* by Jean Jacques Rousseau. Reprinted by permission of Pocket Books, Inc. 1957. Pp. 40-41.

sleep with me. I refused, saying that my bed was too small. He pressed me to go to his, but I again refused, for the wretch was so dirty and stunk so strongly of chewed tobacco, that he made me quite sick.

Early on the following morning, we were both alone in the assembly-room. He recommenced his caresses, but with such violent movements, that it became quite alarming. At last, he wanted to take the most disgusting liberties with me, and taking hold of my hand, tried to make me take the same with him. I uttered a loud cry, and, jumping back, freed myself from him; and, without exhibiting anger or indignation, for I had not the least idea what it was all about, I expressed my surprise and disgust so energetically, that he left me where I was; but, while he was finishing his efforts, I saw something gluey and whitish shoot towards the fireplace and fall upon the ground, which turned my stomach. I rushed upon the balcony, more moved, more troubled, more frightened than I had ever been in my life, and prepared to find myself ill.

I could not understand what had been the matter with the wretch. I believed that he was attacked by epilepsy, or some other madness even more terrible; and in truth, I know nothing more hideous for any cool-blooded person to see than such filthy and dirty behaviour, and a frightful countenance inflamed by brutal lust. I have never seen another man in a similar condition; but if we are like it when we are with women, their looks must certainly be bewitched, for them not to feel disgusted at us.

I was in a great hurry to go and tell everyone what had just happened to me. Our old stewardess bade me hold my tongue; but I saw that my story had greatly affected her, and I heard her mutter: *Can maledet! brutta bestia!*

August Forel*
(1848-1931)

In the meantime I had gradually been initiated in matters of sex—and this in the smuttiest and most lascivious manner—by the conversation of my comrades, while my parents continued to preserve a prudish silence, so that I felt ashamed, in the face of their uncommunicativeness, to touch upon the subject spontaneously and ask them for information and explanation; on the other hand, in spite of my comrades' talk, I was still far from a complete understanding of

---

*From *Out of My Life and Work* by August Forel. Reprinted by permission of W. W. Norton & Co., Inc. 1937. Pp. 50-51.

the mystery. I had already completed my seventeenth year; that is, I had entered upon the phase of puberty, and my youthful blood was becoming more and more unruly. Intercourse with my comrades, and their often indecorous conversation, constantly provided fresh nourishment for my erotic imagination, so that from time to time I experienced those normal and natural phenomena (nocturnal emissions) which are merely a sign of maturity, but which filled me with indescribable dread, as they were new to me, and I did not know what to make of them. Suddenly I made up my mind to consult a doctor for whom I had conceived a liking. Very kindly and understandingly he explained that the phenomena which had so alarmed me were normal physiological processes, of which I need take no further notice, and whose occurrence, if I quietly left everything to Nature, would automatically regulate itself. He also gave me a harmless prescription; I left him completely reassured and obediently followed his sensible advice. I am still grateful to him in that he did not do what so many physicians would have done in his position, and in my case, namely, send me to a house of ill-fame; the more so, as even the venereal diseases and the slough of prostitution inspired me with nausea and aversion.

*Etsu Sugimoto**
(1874-1950)

I think it was my third year in school that a wave of excitement over love stories struck Tokyo. All the schoolgirls were wildly interested. When translations were to be had we passed them from hand to hand through the school; but mostly we had to struggle along in English, picking out love scenes from the novels and poems in our school library. Enoch Arden was our hero. We were familiar with loyalty and sacrifice on the part of a wife, and understood perfectly why Annie should have so long withstood the advances of Philip, but the unselfishness of the faithful Enoch was so rare as to be much appreciated.

The hearts of Japanese girls are no different from those of girls of other countries, but for centuries, especially in Samurai homes, we had been strictly trained to regard duty, not feeling, as the standard of relations between man and woman. Thus our unguided reading sometimes gave us warped ideas on this unknown subject. The impression I received was that love as pictured in Western books was interesting

*From *A Daughter of the Samurai* by Etsu Sugimoto. Reprinted by permission of Doubleday & Co., Inc. Copyright 1925. Pp. 131-132.

and pleasant, sometimes beautiful in sacrificing like that of Enoch Arden; but not to be compared in strength, nobility, or loftiness of spirit to the affection of parent for child, or the loyalty between lord and vassal.

Had my opinion been allowed to remain wordless, it probably would never have caused me annoyance, but it was destined to see the light. We had a very interesting literature society which held an occasional special meeting, to which we invited the teachers as guests. With an anxious pride to have a fine entertainment, we frequently planned our programme first and afterward selected the girls for the various tasks. The result was that sometimes the subject chosen was beyond the capacity of the girl to handle. At one time this rule brought disaster to me, for we never shirked any duty to which we were assigned.

On this occasion I was asked to prepare a three-page essay in English, having one of the cardinal virtues for the subject. I puzzled over which to select of Faith, Hope, Charity, Love, Prudence, and Patience; but recalling that our Bible teacher frequently quoted "God is Love," I felt that there I had a foundation, and so chose as my topic, "Love." I began with the love of the Divine Father, then, under the influence of my late reading, I drifted along, rather vaguely, I fear, on the effect of love on the lives of the celebrated characters in history and poetry. But I did not know how to handle so awkward a subject, and reached my limit in both knowledge and vocabulary before the three pages were filled. Faithfulness to duty, however, still held firm, and I wrote on, finally concluding with these words: "Love is like a powerful medicine. When properly used it will prove a pleasant tonic, and sometimes may even preserve life; but when misused, it can ruin nations, as seen in the lives of Cleopatra and the beloved Empress of the Emperor Genso of Great China."

At the close of my reading one teacher remarked, "This is almost desecration."

It was years before I understood what the criticism meant.

Helen Thomas Flexner*
(1871-1956)

In surmounting the hazard of Lot and his daughters I was not so fortunate. When pious parents urged their children as a religious duty

---

*From *A Quaker Childhood* by Helen T. Flexner. Reprinted by permission of Yale University Press. 1940. Pp. 139-142.

to read the Bible through from the first chapter of Genesis to the last sentence of Revelations they must have forgotten the terrible story of incest that lurked near the beginning of Genesis for them to come upon before their zeal had abated. Like many another child I was brought up short by this story. The first reading bewildered me just because the narrative was so simple and so clear. What those eight verses of the Bible seemed to mean, they could not possibly mean. I read them over until I was convinced that Moab and Ammon were in fact the children of Lot and his two daughters. Horrifying as it was, I was forced to accept this as true, and in so doing I clearly perceived that there was some simple fact connected with the birth of children of which I was totally ignorant. I could not by any manner of means make out what it could be.

Sex was never discussed in our family. The word itself was much too shocking to be mentioned. Nursery experience had made me familiar as a tiny child with the physical differences between little boys and girls. I accepted it along with everything else and thought nothing of it. In the same spirit I accepted the current explanation that when a baby arrives the doctor brings it. My complete faith made me laugh Peggie White to scorn for believing that a stork and not the doctor brings the baby. There were no storks in Maryland, I pointed out. Peggie's belief was ridiculous, while mine was supported by evidence. But Peggie stood up for her side. How did I know, she asked, that storks do not fly about at night? Had I ever watched for them? Babies were born at night when we were asleep. Let me deny that, if I could. So we argued each for the truth of her own explanation, each profoundly convinced by her own argument.

Once I had asked my mother what kind of child "an illegitimate child" might be, having heard the term by chance. "A child whose parents are wicked is called an illegitimate child," she had informed me and dropped the subject. Later I learned from some conversation or other that the mother of an illegitimate child was not the wife of its father. This seemed very queer to me—I could not puzzle it out since I knew that only married women had children. However, I did not like to bother my mother with further questions. Something in her manner of answering before put me off. Now the story in the Bible, which by definition could not be wrong, had settled certain things for me. It made no mention of either a stork or a doctor or of marriage. Obviously no one of them was necessary. I decided to find some older person who would explain to me the real truth about the birth of children.

The easiest thing to do was to sound out my sister Margaret. She enjoyed being appealed to, and was not likely to laugh at me. Of course she might not know herself, but there was no harm in trying. I decided to ask Margaret. So the very next afternoon at the time when she always studied her lessons I climbed the stairs to her room. I found her, as I expected, seated before her table hard at work over her books and I stood beside her while I explained my errand. She expressed surprise at my question, but answered it quite willingly. She had herself been informed by Grace of the facts I wanted to know, she told me, and went on to explain them with a youthful bluntness that gave me a shock. Was she quite sure that what she said was true, I asked? Yes, she was sure, because Grace, enlightened first by a gossiping girl at school, had rushed in indignation for denial to my mother, and my mother had confirmed the truth of what the girl said, though she blamed her severely for discussing such matters. Had Margaret talked with my mother about them? I asked. No, she had not. Grace had told her that my mother had been terribly embarrassed when answering her questions. Margaret did not want to trouble my mother.

For my part I had no inclination to discuss the subject further. I never mentioned it to Grace nor did I speak of it again to Margaret. Least of all could I pass on my information to Peggie White, since that would be to do the very thing my mother so disapproved in Grace's friend. My mother's attitude had stamped the whole subject of the birth of children as not to be spoken about, as somehow shameful. Whenever it obtruded, I thrust it out of my mind. None the less, without being conscious of curiosity I noted sharply any chance bit of information that came my way and left it to fit automatically into the general pattern. I do not now remember in what way I learned that my mother had forced herself to forewarn her sons of the temptations with which they would be confronted in the world. This duty to the boys, which both my parents felt imperative, my father, I was told, refused to undertake. It could best be performed by the boy's mother, he said. Girls never thought of such things, nice girls that is. So I turned my mind away from them, and in time the information Margaret had given me ceased to haunt me.

Leon Trotsky (1877-1940)*

In the evenings before it was dark I sometimes went for walks with Moissey Filippovitch, and when he was in a good humor we talked

*From *My Life. An Attempt at an Autobiography*. New York: Charles Scribner's Sons, 1931. Pp. 62-63.

about all sorts of things. On one occasion he told me the story of the opera "Faust," which he liked very much. As I eagerly followed the story, I hoped that one day I might hear the opera on the stage. From a change in his tone, however, I became aware that the story was approaching a delicate point. I was quite disturbed by his embarrassment and began to fear that I should not hear the end of the story. But Moissey Filippovitch recovered his calm and continued: "Then a baby was born to Gretchen before marriage. . . ." We both felt relieved when we had passed this point; after that the story was safely brought to its conclusion.

I was in bed with a bandaged throat, and by way of consolation was given Dickens' "Oliver Twist." The remark of the doctor in the nursing home about the woman's not having a wedding-ring perplexed me utterly.

"What does it mean?" I asked Moissey Filippovitch. "What has the wedding-ring to do with it?"

"Oh," said he, somewhat haltingly, "it is simply that when people are not married, they wear no wedding-ring."

I recalled Gretchen. And the fate of Oliver Twist was spun out in my imagination from a ring which did not exist. The forbidden world of human relations burst into my consciousness fitfully from books, and much that I had heard spoken of in a casual, and usually coarse and gross manner, now through literature became generalized and ennobled, rising to some higher plane.

At that time, public opinion was stirred up over Tolstoy's "Power of Darkness," which had just appeared. People discussed it with great earnestness and were unable to come to any definite conclusion. Pobedonostzev succeeded in inducing Czar Alexander III to prohibit the play from being performed. I knew that Moissey Filippovitch and Fanny Solomonovna, after I had gone to bed, read the play in the adjoining room. I could hear the murmur of their voices. "May I read it, too?" I asked. "No, dear, you are too young for that," came the answer, and it sounded so categorical that I made no attempt to argue. At the same time I noticed that the slim new volume found its way to the familiar bookshelf. Seizing an opportunity when my guardians were out, I read Tolstoy's play in a few hurried installments. It impressed me much less vividly than my mentors apparently feared it would. The most tragic scenes, such as the strangling of the child and the conversation about creaking bones, were accepted not as a terrible reality, but as a literary invention, a stage trick; in other words, I did not really grasp them at all.

During a vacation in the country, while I was exploring a bookshelf high up under the ceiling, I came across a booklet brought home from Elizavetgrad by my elder brother. I opened it and instantly sensed something extraordinary and secret. This was a court report of a murder case in which a little girl was the victim of a sexual crime. I read the book, strewn with medical and legal details, with my mind all astir and alarmed, as if I had found myself in a wood at night, stumbling against ghostlike, moonlit trees and not able to find my way out. Human psychology, particularly in the case of children, has its own buffers, brakes, and safety-valves—an extensive and well-devised system which stands guard against untimely and too drastic shocks.

Eric Gill*
(1882-1940)

So much at this stage for Holy Poverty. There remain Chastity and Obedience. I suppose in respect of chastity we were brought up in the ordinary tradition of middle-class, Victorian nonconformity. This of course meant complete secrecy as regards sex and, if not secrecy at least complete politeness as regards organs of drainage. We rebelled against neither convention and until the very end of the period of which I am writing I never penetrated the veil of secrecy. It was, though not frequently indulged in, an enjoyable pastime to stand with my younger brothers in a row on the top of the brick wall which ran along the bottom of the field beside our house and compete to discover which of us was best in aim and which could "do it" farthest; but we were never caught at this game. We used to visit new public conveniences rather in the manner of little dogs trying a hitherto untried gate post. As a boy of about twelve years old, I and another boy, while we were "changing" in the dormitory after football, showed one another our nether eyes. This, though our interest was, without doubt, potentially sexual, was hardly more than curiosity. . . .

We emerged from childhood without rational defenses. . . .

One may say this and yet not be blaming either parents or children. The histories of sexual secrecy and private disgust are about as long as the history of man, and their physical basis is fear, fear almost amounting to panic. We are, as our ancestors were, simply and desperately afraid of what the young things will do. We dare not cultivate a rational attitude towards physical drainages for fear of what games the children will be up to—so we make a great to-do with disgust. . . .

---

*From *Autobiography* by Eric Gill. Reprinted by permission of Jonathan Cape, Ltd. 1940. Pp. 49-55.

As I have said, it was not until I was nearly at the end of my school-days that I penetrated the veil of secrecy. This was partly by accidental discovery and partly the result of a cousin's information. The information, comically enough, was, in the main point, entirely wrong and therefore innocuous. He told me that the navel was, so to say, the centre of attraction, and the flower of the plant! And as I have always wondered what navels were for (and no one would tell me) this seemed a very reasonable explanation. And as I had for a long time felt very affectionately towards his sister, I thought longingly and lovingly upon her umbilical ornament and basked in this error for several months. But my accidental discoveries caused me black misery for the next seven years. Black misery indeed! but what with prayer and fast-ing and a not too unreasonable amount of indulgence in between while I managed to achieve a sort of accidental balance. But this sort of biology is not a history of adventures and it is not to form an item in the case book of the late Havelock Ellis. I want to discover what things and persons have an influence on me and what opinions I have arrived at in consequence. . . . In this business of human sex and its relation to life and work, it is obvious that the relationship is both real and important. It must, obviously, make a lot of difference to men and women whether they live lives of puzzledom and repression, false valuations and romantic sentiment, untruth and bad conscience, or whether they escape all such troubles and go through life clear-headed and happy; and it is obvious that, among all the things that are influ-ential in our lives to mar or make our happiness, the instinct of mating is one of the most important.

I have done my best to describe my parents and the environment of my childhood. Such as I am their influence was important and so was that of our chapel, our town and our hills. My judgment of persons and things is neither important nor relevant; I am only concerned to describe them justly. So in this matter if I tell you what I was taught you will know what I had to put up with, and in the matter of sex the only thing I was properly taught as a child was that it was a secret. So when I found out the secret, the last possible thing to be done was to confide in our parents or teachers. We tried doing things, both I and my brothers. We were only told not to do so again and that if we dis-obeyed in respect of a certain mysterious prohibition, the consequence would be in the first place a thrashing and, if we persisted, "consump-tion," madness or death. And this was not because my father was a fierce and cruel ogre, for he was precisely the opposite, but simply be-cause he had been brought up that way himself and was not only deeply inhibited but also desperately afraid. So we left it at that and carried on a new and secret life unhelped—and also undeterred. We were given no responsible advice and had access to no reliable reading matter; we were only put off with vagueness and sentimental nonsense about not tampering with sacred things. Why "sacred" we were never told, for the very things which, up to then, we had been brought up to suppose had no relationship to anything but drainage and which were therefore more or less despicable, were now vaguely hinted to be objects of sanctity! So we were undeterred; for when your parents and teachers are quite obviously being unreasonable and even ridiculous they seriously undermine your respect for their admonitions.

But how shall I ever forget that strange, inexplicable rapture of my first experience? What marvellous thing was this that suddenly transformed a mere water tap into a pillar of fire—and water into an elixir of life? I lived henceforth in a strange world of contradiction: something was called filthy which was obviously clean; something was called ugly which was obviously lovely. Strange days and nights of mystery and fear mixed with excitement and wonder—strange days and nights, strange months and years. It was a blessing that this intellectual puzzlement and emotional exaltation was balanced by a good healthy rabelaisianism. Jokes and rhymes took the edge off the parental and pedagogic solemnity and my own.

And in spite of the black misery of bad conscience I was happy. For my conscience was somewhat like the law of gravity; it operated in inverse proportion to distance and in spite of all that we were told (though that was remarkably little and that little was nothing but "don't"), I saw, more or less clearly that what they called "unnatural" was natural enough, and bound to happen in one way if not another.

The awful thing seems to be the way they try to frighten you. Luckily for me I wasn't a very frightenable subject, and I realized without stating it that the teetotallers had no right to call themselves temperate.

*Martin Freud**
(1889-   )

We were both of an age when curiosity about the facts of life, with some emphasis on the female form, then so heavily disguised and even distorted by the prevailing fashions, allowed us to wonder out loud to

---

*From *Sigmund Freud: Man and Father* by Martin Freud. Reprinted by permission of Vanguard Press. 1958. Pp. 79-80.

each other just what was hidden by all these frills and furbelows. My friend had, of course, seen the many statues of stately nude ladies in bronze, marble, masonry or stucco, many bearing aloft candelabra, which adorned his home city of Munich. Vienna, being similarly decorated, placed our discussions on a level. I recall summing up my attitude by saying, "No real lady would appear in public like that," adding that I thought the display of sculpture in both cities nothing but a swindle.

Our discussions were, of course, inconclusive and, in consequence, our curiosity remained. An opportunity to satisfy it came one day, and we seized upon it.

Two tall, red-headed Bavarian *Dirndls* (young girls) had occupied the bathing-hut next to ours, and when we heard sounds which suggested they were preparing for a dip, we decided to dive through our porthole, to swim out a little way and then to return, taking a quick peep through the porthole of theirs. We had not, however, reckoned with the beach-master's excellent knowledge of morbid adolescent curiosity. He saw what we were up to at once, ordering us back quite rudely and threatening to tell our parents. The threat seriously alarmed my companion, who knew how heavily he might be punished; he panicked and raced back through the water to our hut without a single glance. I was less frightened and, while ostensibly obeying the beach-master, I took a quick glance through the porthole and rejoined my nervous friend.

The girls were standing on the platform quite unclothed, but the picture they offered was not fascinating to my eyes. They were long, thin, white and angular, even bony, I thought, with no suggestion of seductive curves. Today I might think their heads of glorious red hair enchanting; but then this glory had no effect on me. I said to my friend, "I saw them; it's all a swindle. Girls with their clothes off are just like boys with their clothes off. It's nothing but a swindle," I repeated. Incidentally, we never bothered to decide who wanted to swindle us.

The beach-master's threat had not alarmed me in any way. I think my father would have laughed had he been told. I remember, however, that before this quite shocking incident there had been a discussion in the family about cattle when it became clear to father that none of his children knew the difference between a bullock and a bull. "You must be told these things," father had exclaimed; but, like the majority of fathers, he had done nothing whatever about it. If the beach-master had reported our escapade, he might have been forced to explain.

Vera Brittain*
(1898[?]-   )

So far as I can now judge, at eighteen I was at least as interested in social problems and in what were then always referred to as "the facts of life" as most of my contemporaries, though my sexual curiosity was always a bad second to my literary ambition. Yet when the War broke out, I did not clearly understand what was meant by homosexuality, incest or sodomy, and was puzzled by the shadow that clung to the name of Oscar Wilde, whose plays I discovered in 1913 and read with a rapturous delight in their epigrams.

Nearly all the older girls with whom I went to school had been addicted to surreptitious conversations about the advent of babies; periodic discovery by parents or teachers thrust these intriguing speculations still further underground, and led to that intensive searching for obstetrical details through the Bible and such school-library novels as *David Copperfield* and *Adam Bede* which appears to have been customary almost everywhere among the adolescents of my generation. Thanks to this composite enlightenment in addition to the decorous elucidations of *Household Medicine,* I had a fairly comprehensive though somewhat Victorian idea of the primitive fashion in which the offspring of even the most civilised parents make their appearance, but of how to rear infants and train small children I had not the slightest notion either in theory or in practice, since the influence of married women in the education of girls mostly destined for wifehood and maternity was then considered even less desirable than it is to-day. I was also, despite my stock of physiological information, still extremely hazy with regard to the precise nature of the sexual act.

This half-knowledge engendered in me so fierce an antipathy to the idea of physical relationship in so far as this happened to be separable from romance, that when, soon after I left school, I was proposed to by a neighbour of ours—a large, athletic young man with limited brains and evangelical principles, who strongly disapproved of my "unwomanly" ambitions, and could not possibly have been attracted by anything more substantial than my childish pretty-prettiness—my immediate and only reaction was a sense of intolerable humiliation and disgust.

---

*From *Testament of Youth* by Vera Brittain. Reprinted by permission of Vera Brittain. 1935, Macmillan Co. Pp. 47-48.

Ethel Mannin*
(1900-   )

At the board-school all the girls were morbidly interested in parturition, menstruation, and procreation. The older girls talked of little else. We raked the Bible for information, and those of us who came from homes in which there were books made endless research, looking up in encyclopedias and home medical works, such words as "confinement," "miscarriage," "after-birth," "puberty," "menses," "life, change of." We were both fascinated and horrified. At the age of twelve I ploughed through a long and difficult book on embryology. My brother did likewise at the same age. God knows what either of us got as a result of our search for knowledge. We had no one to guide our footsteps stumbling in the dark. Apart from the purely scientific aspect, which was beyond our comprehension, everything was "all along a dirtiness, all along a mess . . . all along of finding out, rather more or less." We had a number of obscene little rhymes which were passed by word of mouth to each other, and were written up in the lavatories by the more enterprising. Periodically there would be a campaign organized by the headmistress against these lavatory scribblings. Anyone found out was expelled, but it never occurred to anyone to clean up the mess by a little simple explanation, so it all went on, and as fast as the indecent words and rhymes were whitewashed over new ones would be written up, and along the walls and pavements and on the fences of the alleyways near the school, and nobody did anything.

Once we had a lesson on catkins, and the teacher boldly referred to the pollen from the male hazel catkin falling on the two pistils of the female catkin and fertilising it so that the ovaries swelled and developed into a nut. There was a good deal of sniggering over this: adolescence, with all its sexual instincts quickening, is not to be educated by delicate references to the pollination of flowers . . .

I was about eleven when I was informed by a girl of my own age coming home from Sunday School that she had found out where babies come from.

Breathlessly I asked, "Where?" for the great mystery was about to be unfolded at last. She nudged her sister who was with us, and they giggled, "Go on, you tell her."

"Oo—I can't—it's awful—you tell her!"

*From *Confessions and Impressions* by Ethel Mannin. Reprinted by permission of Hutchinson & Co., Ltd. 1930, Jarrolds Publishers, Ltd. Pp. 39-41.

At last nudging and whispering and giggling they opened their Bible and pointed to the line which held the supreme truth. I read, "Esau came forth from his mother's belly."

It seemed unspeakably dreadful, conjured up visions of sanguinary major operations. I was very miserable. I blurted out my discovery to the family at tea. I remember queerly that there was watercress for tea, and the best Doulton tea-pot was in use. A terrible anger was working in me as I gazed at my mother and father. All their stories of currant bushes, storks, and doctor's bags. . . . I burst out, "I know where babies come from. Mary told me."

My mother said drily, "Well, where do they come from?"

I said, "From their mothers' stomachs," and burst into tears.

My mother said, "Well, now you know. Get on with your tea. There's nothing to grizzle about. You've no business to be talking about such things."

After that Mary and I looked at every woman who passed us in the street to see if she were going to have a baby. Mary would be amused, and I would be grieved. I was unhappy for a long time about the whole thing, and not until I was fifteen did I know how parturition took place, and horror was heaped on horror's head. Menstruation was another shock. It all seemed dreadful. One took refuge more and more in one's secret self. . . .

For a long time I refused to believe that father had anything to do with the creation of a baby—in spite of all the funny little indecent rhymes and the assertions of the girls who had it on good authority from home medical books and older brothers and sisters. But the fact that mating did go on in the world was forced upon me by—silkworms. The moths got united. There was no denying the dreadful fact, and it bore out the truth of the distressing things I had been told by other girls concerning fathers and mothers. It was unspeakingly shocking. I had a friend who also bred silk-worms and had been similarly shocked into realisation by the conduct of the moths which hatched out of the cocoons.

"Then it's true about mothers and fathers," we whispered, and horror shook us. We swore great oaths that we would never, never marry. My friend thought that she would become a nun; I thought I would go to Africa and be a missionary—it being taken for granted that missionaries were holy and therefore did not coalesce. I got a box from Sunday School and began collecting for a fund to buy Bibles for the unenlightened heathen. It was tiring and dreary walking the streets and going from door to door, but I was glad about that. One needed to suffer to make up for the wickedness of the world. Jesus Christ had died for the sins of the world, and therefore it wasn't much to grow tired tramping the streets in the same cause.

REFERENCES

1. Bandura, Albert, & Walters, Richard H. *Adolescent Aggresssion.* New York: Ronald Press, 1959, p. 178.
2. Beauvoir, Simone de. *Memoirs of a Dutiful Daughter.* Cleveland: World Publishing Co., 1959, p. 92.
3. Brown, Fred, & Kempton, Rudolf T. *Sex Questions and Answers.* New York: McGraw-Hill Co., 1950, p. 37.
4. Catherine the Great. *Memoirs.* New York: Alfred A. Knopf, 1927, p. 67.
5. Freud, Sigmund. The sexual enlightenment of children. In *Collected Papers,* Vol. 2. New York: Basic Books, 1959, p. 36.
6. *Ibid.,* pp. 37-38.
7. *Ibid.,* pp. 41-42.
8. Gill, Eric. *Autobiography.* London: Jonathan Cape, 1940, p. 54.
9. Gorky, Maxim. *Autobiography: My Childhood; In the World; My Universities.* New York: Citadel Press, 1940, p. 195.
10. Kogan, David S. *The Diary of David S. Kogan.* Edited by Meyer Levin. New York: Beechhurst Press, 1955, p. 43.
11. Kuo, Helena. *I've Come a Long Way.* New York: D. Appleton-Century Co., 1942, p. 50.
12. Mannin, Ethel. *Confessions and Impressions.* London: Jarrolds, Ltd., 1930, pp. 39-41.
13. Monroe, Harriet. *A Poet's Life. Seventy Years in a Changing World.* New York: Macmillan Co., 1938, pp. 35-36.
14. Sinclair, Upton. *American Outpost. A Book of Reminiscences.* New York: Farrar & Rinehart, 1932, p. 40.
15. West, James. *Plainville, U.S.A..* In: Kardiner, Abram, *The Psychological Frontiers of Society.* New York: Columbia University Press, 1945, pp. 259-412.

Contradictions, Ambivalences, Polarities and Defenses

In puberty and adolescence the sameness and continuities relied on in childhood are questioned by the individual because of the rapid physical and physiological growth taking place. These changes force the adolescent to attempt to consolidate his social role. The massive disruption in personality development and the guilt aroused because of new impulses compel him to face up to new and stunning emotions. As a subsequent chapter will show, he is sometimes so morbidly bedeviled with what he feels and who he is that his preoccupation leads him to toy with the possibilities of suicide. In his search for a new sense of continuity and sameness, the adolescent has to struggle again with many of the crises of earlier years. Images of the persons who had guided him and were his source of norms are constantly retroprojected on persons surrounding him during his adult life. Accordingly, conflicts and struggles which had evolved during childhood repeat themselves albeit between other players and in a new shape (3). The precise way in which a given person will pass through the stages of development in adolescence is to a very great extent determined by the form of his infantile development (23). Jones (24) asserts there is possibly one difference between development in infancy and adolescence: in the former, greater emphasis seems to be laid on the acquirement of control over volitional motor outflow, while in the latter, it is laid on the acquisition of control over emotional outflow.

Pubescence is marked by the struggle to control the emotions. All authors, states Wittels (45), describe the ambivalence, the swinging pendulum that characterizes adolescence. Rebellion versus blind submission, cynicism versus idealism, optimism versus pessimism, may serve as examples of that polarity—which is the expression of the tendencies of the id versus those of the ego. Some youngsters cling to childhood, denying the signs of maturity as long as possible. Amiel (1), in his *Journal*, writes for the general populace what may be a specific for adolescence: " . . . strangely enough, what we think we are is just what we are not: what we desire to be is what suits us least; our theories condemn us, and our practice gives the lie to our theories. And the contradiction is to our advantage, for it is the source of conflict, of movement, and therefore a condition of progress. Every life is an inward struggle, every struggle supposes to contrary forces; nothing real is simple, and whatever thinks itself simple is in reality the farthest from simplicity. Therefore it would seem that every state is a moment in a series; every being a compromise between contraries."

From his sixteenth to his twentieth years, when he was in Sydney, Australia, away from his mother and father, Havelock Ellis felt particularly the force of the conflict and the growth Wittels and Amiel describe. "During all those years [1875-1879]", he wrote, "in the background of mental conflicts and in the intervals of depressed moods, there was a perpetual growth in intelligence, a constant broadening and deepening of culture. The conflicts and the moods were helpful, indeed, by adding intensity to my emotional nature and critical acuteness to my intellect [10]." But during the process, the viable emotional economy of the adolescent frequently does not permit him to enjoy the growth. Reality seems to be the loser in the struggle. The adolescent cannot decide what to do and that is why his clinical picture is sometimes reminiscent of an incipient psychosis. "To be an actor and a spectator," wrote John Cournos (8) in his *Autobiography*, "to suffer and to look at one's suffering, to be emotional and rationalize one's emotion, both at one and the same time, is a faculty which I think I had even as a child. It is a faculty which divided me against myself, and was to create a perpetual conflict in me."

This duality of feelings is remarked by Steffens (40): "Boys can despise and admire, resent and covertly hate and love at the same time; they are not consistent." The elusive mood swings of the adolescent—the height of elation or depth of despair, the quickly rising enthusiasms, the burning (or at other times sterile) intellectual and philosophical preoccupations, the yearning for freedom, the sense of loneliness and the avid desire for companionship, the rebellion against authority yet the pledge to some leader or idol of his own choosing, the marked selfishness and materialistic craving co-existent with high idealism, the inconsiderate behavior toward others and the extreme sensitivity toward himself—are all explained by the war between the id and the ego and the superego (16). The adolescent is more concerned with instinctual gratification than ever before because there is more libido at the id's disposal "and it cathects indiscriminately any id impulses which are at hand. Aggressive impulses are intensified to the point of complete unruliness, hunger becomes voracity and the naughtiness of the latency period turns into the criminal behavior of adolescence. Oral and anal interests, long submerged, come to the surface again. Habits of cleanliness, laboriously acquired during the latency period, give place to pleasure in dirt and disorder, and instead of modesty and sympathy we find exhibitionistic tendencies, brutality and cruelty to animals [18]." The adolescent fears the strength and quantity of his instincts rather than their quality, prompting him at one time to repudiate his instincts and subsequently to indulge in excesses. This process of alternation between denial and indulgence of the instincts is consistent with the inconsistencies of his behavior. Without this release the adolescent would soon kill the instinctual life within him, or, at least, paralyze it (19).

Thus, on the question of the inevitability of adolescent upset, its desirability, beneficence, and need, "psychoanalytic opinion is decisive and unanimous. . . . The so-called adolescent upheavals are no more than the external indications that such internal adjustments are in progress [17]." Such turmoil and difficulty in controlling impulses is seen in the diary of Elizabeth Fry (20), a Quaker and prison reformer. At the age of seventeen, in the year 1798, she entered in her journal, "I have known my faults and not corrected them and now I am determined I will once more try with redoubled ardour to overcome my wicked inclinations; I must not flirt; I must not ever be out of temper with the children; I must not contradict without a cause; I must not mump when my sisters are liked and I am not; I must not allow myself to be angry; I must not exaggerate which I am inclined to do. I must not give way to luxury; I must not be idle in mind, I must try to give way to every good feeling and overcome every bad."

About one hundred years later, two adolescent girls, one in New York, the other in Chicago, were exhibiting similar conflicts. Both felt they were so pulled apart as to have two personalities. "It was at this time that I became aware of the complexity of one's make-up," wrote Lucy S. Mitchell (32) of her adolescence. "When I acted in our stable theater, I seemed to be two people—one making up dramatic lines and rendering them with fine action—the other listening, approving and disapproving. I was actor and critic at the same time. I found that was disturbingly true whatever I did. When I talked with Father, when I helped Mother with household arrangements, I always heard and saw myself doing these things. I must be hopelessly insincere, I thought. But the sense of guilt did not change me a bit. So vivid did this onlooker self become that I called it sometimes 'the-thing-in-the-corner,' sometimes 'my other personality.' Among my old papers I find a curious document written at fourteen beginning,

'Tis seldom one Personality talks to another. Even more rare is it that One's Other Personality speaks to another's Personality. Too seldom, alas, for, more often than not, they speak in different tongues. . . .

I am no longer troubled by the critic within me. But I took myself very seriously in those days."

The other girl, Agnes Meyer (31), described her first contacts with the new and strange conventions of New York City life as "so overpowering that they threw me back upon myself. I was lost and unable to communicate what I could not find words to express. From that time for many years I became more and more a dual personality, which preserved outwardly the buoyancy of childhood as a successful disguise for the adolescent turmoil of mind and emotions. Instead of 'boasting' two soul-sides, as Browning put it, I suffered two soul-sides, one to face the world with, the other to show on only rare occasions to people whom I loved and trusted."

An ocean and a continent away, Martin Buber (2), one of the leading exponents of Hasidic philosophy and a student of the mystical religions of China and India, as well as that of medieval Christianity, found the surge of new impulses in adolescence and invigorated older drives debilitating and disorganizing. "So long as I lived [in my grandfather's] home, I was well-rooted, though some queries and doubts disturbed me. On my departure, the turbulence of the period assailed me. Until I was twenty, and to a lesser degree even afterward, my spirit was in constant and multiple flux. Tension and release followed one another, determined by manifold influences, forever assuming new forms, but remaining without a pivot and without cumulative substance. I really lived the *Olam Ha-tohu,* the world of confusion, the mythical limbo of lost souls. I experienced mobile spiritual fulfillment, but neither Judaism, nor humanity, nor the presence of the divine was in it. Zionism provided the first impetus for my release. I can only suggest here what it meant to me: revival of coherence, equilibrium and replacement in the community. No one needs the salvation of a racial bond so much as the youth gripped in spiritual search, and flung by his intellect into the ether. . . . " Buber used intellectualization to control his feelings.

It is not until the adolescent is in control of his id drives that he can channelize his disorganized energies into constructive goals. Because he has not yet determined his goals, he expresses his energy impulsively as it mounts. The adolescent, wrote William Ellery Leonard (28) in his autobiography, is "two individualities: the unfledged idealist, the sex-animal. Even his moonings about girls belongs to the idealist in him; for his sex-speculations and secret gloating he chooses feverishly some young wench of the plebs . . . whom he really despises." And G. K. Chesterton (7) explained, " . . . my only point for the moment is personal or psychological; my own private testimony to the curious fact that, for some reason or other, a boy often does pass, from an early stage, when he wants to know nearly everything, to a later stage when he wants to know next to nothing."

This changeableness of young people is commonplace. Helene Deutsch (9) has described the positive and negative aspects of adolescent narcissism: "In the first place, it has a certain unifying force that prevents dissolution of the young girl's personality as a result of too many identifications. In the second place, by increasing her self-confidence, it contributes considerably to strengthening the youthful ego. However, it also exerts a negative influence on the ego; and it is this double action that gives rise to movement back and forth, the ebb and tide of overweening pride and contrition, in brief, the whole picturesque medley that is the psychologic pattern of adolescence." The cyclic behavior of the adolescent, manifested in his periods of impulsivity followed by periods of inhibition, his individualism and rebelliousness and his need for direction and help, his know-it-all façade and his awful feelings of inadequacy, his restlessness and serenity, are all symptomatic of his fight between advance to maturity and retardation in childhood.

This conflict between the impulse to remain fixated at a childhood level of development and the urge to assume an adult role, and the positive and negative aspects of the function of ambivalence in the adolescent personality, are illustrated in the following passages from diaries and autobiographies.

Jean Jacques Rousseau
(1712-1778)

The mercurially labile personality of Rousseau is well known. His tumultuous emotions, his morbid vanity, his exhibitionism and sexual obsessions, his monstrous selfishness, his rancorous envy combine to make him detestable. Rousseau, himself, was extremely conscious of his vast ambivalences, for the *Confessions* reveal them time and again. The conflict between Rousseau's drives and his anxieties, both in childhood and adolescence, was perpetuated in adulthood. In the first excerpt, the French philosopher reveals his continued emotional duality as an adult and his inappropriate responses to minor distractions and irritations. In the second passage, he describes polarities and ambivalences occurring during his adolescence which undoubtedly laid the foundation for his adult difficulties in functioning.*

I am a man of very strong passions, and, while I am stirred by them, nothing can equal my impetuosity; I forget all discretion, all feelings of respect, fear and decency; I am cynical, impudent, violent and fearless; no feeling of shame keeps me back, no danger frightens me; with the exception of the single object which occupies my thoughts, the universe is nothing to me. But all this lasts only for a moment, and the

---

*From *Confessions* by Jean Jacques Rousseau. Reprinted by permission of Pocket Books, Inc. 1957. Pp. 20-21, 26.

following moment plunges me into complete annihilation. In my calmer moments I am indolence and timidity itself; everything frightens and discourages me; a fly, buzzing past, alarms me; a word which I have to say, a gesture which I have to make, terrifies my idleness; fear and shame overpower me to such an extent that I would gladly hide myself from the sight of my fellow-creatures. If I have to act, I do not know what to do; if I have to speak, I do not know what to say; if anyone looks at me, I am put out of countenance. When I am strongly moved I sometimes know how to find the right words, but in ordinary conversation I can find absolutely nothing, and my condition is unbearable for the simple reason that I am obliged to speak.

* * * *

I thus attained my sixteenth year, restless, discontented with myself and everything else, destitute at once of liking for my occupation, and of the enjoyments common to my age, devoured by desires of whose object I could form no conception, weeping without any cause for tears, and sighing for I knew not what;—in a word, fondly caressing my chimeras from the lack of seeing anything around me that I considered of equal value. On Sundays my comrades used to come after sermon-time to get me to go out and join them in their sports. Most gladly would I have avoided them had I been able; but when once really into their games, I was more ardent and went further than any. Difficult to shake, and difficult to restrain—such was ever my disposition.

Marie Bashkirtseff
(1860-1884)

The narcissistic preoccupation of Marie Bashkirtseff is evident on almost every page of the nearly five hundred that comprise her *Journal*. The diary, which she started at the age of twelve and kept until her death at twenty-four, shows a desperately deep concern with her desire for beauty, fame and recognition, and an unconscious desire to return to childhood. One entry reads, "At fifteen there was a childlike expression in my face. This, the most captivating of all expressions. . . . " Two months later, she wrote: "This morning Robert-Fleury was speaking to me, I listened like a baby. . . ." Marie was constantly looking at herself, comparing herself with statues, examining the qualities of her voice and her art, which may be interpreted, according to Freud, as a reversal of a scoptophilic into an exhibitionistic tendency. The masochistic trend in Marie Bashkirtseff reveals itself in the following passage,* which is replete with the ambivalences of pleasure derived from suffering: "I find myself happy in being miserable. . . . I love to weep. . . . I complain, and I take pleasure in doing so. . . . Everything in life pleases me. . . . "

Monday, September 6th, 1874

In this state of depression and incessant pain, I do not curse life; on the contrary I love it, and I find it good to live. Could one believe it? I find everything good and agreeable, even tears, even pain. I love to weep. I love to be in despair. I love to be sad and sorrowful. I look upon all that as so many diversions, and I love life in spite of all. I want to live. It would be cruel to make me die when I am so accommodating. I weep, I moan, and at the same time it pleases me; no, not that. . . . I do not know how to say it. . . . In fact everything in life pleases me. I find everything agreeable, and while demanding happiness, I find happiness in being miserable. I am no longer myself; my body weeps and laments, yet something within me, which is stronger than I am, rejoices at it all. It is not that I prefer tears to joy; but, far from cursing life in my moments of despair, I bless it, and say to myself: I am unhappy, I lament; still I find life so beautiful that everything appears to me beautiful and happy, and I wish to live. Apparently that something which rules me, which so rejoiced in weeping, has deserted me this evening, for I feel very unhappy.

I have never yet harmed anyone, but I have been already offended, calumniated, humiliated. How can I love men? I detest them, but God will not permit me to hate. God has forsaken me; God is trying me. Ah, well, if He is but trying me, He should cease those trials! He sees how I take it. I do not hide my sufferings under the mask of a cowardly hypocrisy, as the rogue Job, who, while mincing to our Lord, made Him his dupe.

One thing pains me more than all else. It is not the collapse of all my plans, but the regret which this series of misfortunes causes me. Not for myself—I do not know if I will be understood—because it pains me to see stains accumulate on a white gown which should have been kept spotless.

Each little sorrow wrings my heart. Not from self-love, but from

---

*From *Journal* by Marie Bashkirtseff. Translated by A. D. Hall. Chicago: Rand McNally, 1889.

pity, for each pang of sorrow is like a drop of ink falling into a glass of water, it can never be effaced and joined to its predecessors, but it turns the glass of clear water to a black and dirty grey. You may add more water, still the liquid remains impure. It wrings my heart because each time it leaves a stain on my life, in my soul. Do we not always feel a profound sorrow when we see something irreparable, even if insignificant in itself?

Jacob Wassermann
(1873-1934)

The great German novelist, Jacob Wassermann, recreates in this excerpt* a vivid picture of his confused and bewildering adolescent polarities. The quick transition between his attacks of ecstasy and silent forlornness left him "as if sundered." Sobriety alternated with demonic activity which kept him in a state of tension "that tormented and excited me and which the people around me mostly found incomprehensible." His predominant emotions were amazement and despair. All of these seemingly contradictory impulses Wassermann was never able to fathom. He suffered miserably from the treacherous stresses of adolescence and probably repressed so much from the period as to make it inaccessible to consciousness.

Between the ages of ten and twenty years I lived in a state of constant delirium; often I was so far away that only a shell devoid of all feeling remained for those who stood or walked beside me. Later I was told that people had to shout at me to arouse me, awake though I was. I had attacks of ecstasy, of wild, silent forlornness; and as a rule the break was so sudden and powerful that the connections snapped and I was left as if sundered; nor did I know what happened to me. In both spheres my powers of attention grew sharpened—indeed, attention is one of my fundamental traits—but there were no bridges. Here I could be entirely sober, there utterly beside myself, or vice versa; intercourse or communication between the two was completely lacking. This kept me in an extraordinary state of tension that tormented and excited me and which people around me mostly found incomprehensible. Amazement and despair were my predominant emotions; amazement at what I had seen and perceived and felt, despair be-

---

*From *My Life as a German Jew* by Jacob Wassermann. Translated by S. M. Brainin. Reprinted by permission of Coward McCann, Inc. 1933. Pp. 30-31.

cause it was incommunicable. What I really felt, I presume, was this: I knew that remarkable, unheard-of things were happening to me, with me, in me, but I was totally incapable of explaining them to myself or others. In a sense I was a Moses descending Mount Sinai, but without any recollection of what he had seen there and of what God had told him. Even today I have not the slightest idea of the true nature of that mystery, that hidden flame, that enigmatic other world. Though I feel tempted to explore some elements of it I must recognize that it is forever unfathomable. Yet it should be possible to determine what derives from one's ancestry and what from the earth, what lay in the blood and what entered through the eye, and from what depths the individual grows up into his predestined circle.

David S. Kogan
(1929-1951)

The 1945 New Year's resolutions of David S. Kogan, the Yonkers, New York boy who kept a diary during his adolescence, are reminiscent of the passage from the journal of the eighteenth-century Quaker girl, Elizabeth Fry, which was quoted earlier in this chapter. David, like Elizabeth, intellectually recognized the many problems of adolescence, as the ten resolutions show, but anxieties immobilized him. Although he recognized, for example, the importance of his school work, he had great ambivalence toward learning and frequently neglected it. The adolescent's dual nature does not always make congruent what he says and what he does. He may resent being told what to do by teachers, yet insist on being given clearly structured assignments that leave no room for independent planning. This bipolarity of feeling, based on the newly strengthened drives and the defenses against them, may have a frightening effect until the ego becomes familiar with the new phenomenon and learns to master it (15). Hence, anxiety compelled David to list resolution number six, "I shall endeavor to stabilize myself emotionally."*

This is the FIRST DAY OF THE NEW YEAR, 1945, and I think that the way to "start the year right" would be to offer ten resolutions for the coming year. Therefore, I hereby highly resolve that:

---

*From *The Diary of David S. Kogan*. Reprinted by permission of Beechurst Press. 1955. Pp. 81-82, 87-88.

1. Schoolwork is my most important job at present and I shall treat it as such.

2. I shall endeavor to keep guard over the words of my mouth so that falsehood, anger, and stupidity shall not emit therefrom.

3. I shall at all times endeavor to keep my abdomen in and my shoulders back, as the abdominal wall is the secret of strength.

4. I shall endeavor to use my time wisely to perform necessary action and not to procrastinate.

5. I shall make an intensive study of the several vocations.

6. I shall endeavor to stabilize myself emotionally.

7. I shall taste all manner of wholesome food in order that I might not be beset with the limitations of a picky eater.

8. I shall always think of the objects in my hands and be conscious of placing them in the various places, so that I might not be considered absent-minded and forgetful.

9. I shall try to live Judaism as a way of life. To this end I shall endeavor to learn the Hebrew language by speaking it whenever possible, and by daily study.

10. I shall attempt to improve my mind by listening attentively.

May the Almighty Jehovah enable me to have the strength of purpose to carry out these earnest resolutions. May I, at the close of this year 1945 in the Common Era, be a better boy and a better man than I was at its beginning. Amen.

Wednesday, January 3, 1945

Well, this is the third. I've lived three days under the New Regime, and I certainly made a mess of it. The change can even be seen from my style. I used Biblical inspirational style in the resolutions, and now I have fallen into my fault-finding depressing style. Maybe I am aiming too high. I think the trouble is that a sensitive high mind is ahead of a flaccid body, and, above all, a weak willpower.

My resolutions (a pocket copy for consultation) fell out of my pocket in Physics today, and now is a part of the knowledge of some of my fellow students. At first I had a feeling of anger, then shame. However, upon thought, I feel that if I do nothing to be ashamed of, all I can say is "So what!"

Monday, February 26, 1945

We returned to school today (after an absence of five days) an' I was as poorly prepared for work as I have ever been. Instead of concentrating on my dreary allotted task of schoolwork, I am "living an abundant life" with many outside activities ranging from studying the Bible to wrestling, and from saving pictures of famous personalities and semi-nude girls to preparing myself for a rabbinical seminary. This all might be fine and good, but still my conscience bothers me for slacking on the job.

It is the influence of Gil on my already weak will-power. I have had for the last few weeks as a fellow-traveler a fellow to whom homework is anathema. Gil is a slick article who laughs at honest boys. He barely passes his subjects with as little homework as he is physically able. He doesn't care—however—I feel I need some good school marks. I am not an adventurous rogue. I'm a "silky" type of young man. I need good marks and a good record in order to get into a fine college.

Anne Frank
(1929-1945)

The theme of the "double personality" runs through many of the autobiographical writings on adolescence. Elizabeth Fry, Lucy S. Mitchell and Agnes Meyer all dwelt on it. Anne Frank did too, as the very last entry in her diary shows.* There is an almost scientific detachment as the fifteen-year-old girl analyzes and dissects her own "little bundle of contradictions." The two Annes she reveals to the reader are marked by contradictions from within and contradictions from without, as she herself recognized with almost awesome insight. This passage is perhaps one of the most brilliant expositions of adolescent ambivalences in the literature, demonstrating the need for superego control during this period of life.

Tuesday, 1 August, 1944

Dear Kitty,

"Little bundle of contradictions." That's how I ended my last letter and that's how I'm going to begin this one. "A little bundle of contradictions," can you tell me exactly what it is? What does contradiction mean? Like so many words, it can mean two things, contradiction from without and contradiction from within.

The first is the ordinary "not giving in easily, always knowing best, getting in the last word," *enfin*, all the unpleasant qualities for which

*From *The Diary of a Young Girl*. Reprinted by permission of Doubleday & Co., Inc. Copyright 1952, Otto H. Frank. Pp. 235-237.

I'm renowned. The second nobody knows about, that's my own secret. I've already told you before that I have, as it were, a dual personality. One half embodies my exuberant cheerfulness, making fun of everything, my high-spiritedness, and above all, the way I take everything light. This includes not taking offense at a flirtation, a kiss, an embrace, a dirty joke. This side is usually lying in wait and pushes away the other which is much better, deeper and purer. You must realize that no one knows Anne's better side and that's why most people find me so insufferable.

Certainly I'm a giddy clown for one afternoon, but then everyone's had enough of me for another month. Really, it's just the same as a love film is for deep-thinking people, simply a diversion, amusing just for once, something which is soon forgotten, not bad, but certainly not good. I loathe having to tell you this, but why shouldn't I, if I know it's true anyway? My lighter superficial side will always be too quick for the deeper side of me and that's why it will always win. You can't imagine how often I've already tried to push this Anne away to cripple her, to hide her, because after all, she's only half of what's called Anne: but it doesn't work and I know, too, why it doesn't work.

I'm awfully scared that everyone who knows me as I always am will discover that I have another side, a finer and better side. I'm afraid they'll laugh at me, think I'm ridiculous and sentimental, not take me seriously. I'm used to not being taken seriously but it's only the "lighthearted" Anne that's used to it and can bear it; the "deeeper" Anne is too frail for it. Sometimes, if I really compel the good Anne to take the stage for a quarter of an hour, she simply shrivels up as soon as she has to speak, and lets Anne number one take over, and before I realize it, she has disappeared.

Therefore, the nice Anne is never present in company, has not appeared one single time so far, but almost always predominates when we're alone. I know exactly how I'd like to be, how I am too . . . inside. But, alas, I'm only like that for myself. And perhaps that's why, no, I'm sure it's the reason why I say I've got a happy nature within and why other people think I've got a happy nature without. I am guided by the pure Anne within, but outside I'm nothing but a frolicsome little goat who's broken loose.

As I've already said, I never utter my real feelings about anything and that's how I've acquired the name of chaser-after-boys, flirt, know-all, reader of love stories. The cheerful Anne laughs about it, gives cheeky answers, shrugs her shoulders indifferently, behaves as if she doesn't care, but, oh dearie me, the quiet Anne's reactions are just the opposite. If I'm to be quite honest, then I must admit that it does hurt me, that I try terribly hard to change myself, but that I'm always fighting against a more powerful enemy.

A voice sobs within me: "There you are, that's what's become of you: you're uncharitable, you look supercilious and peevish, people dislike you and all because you won't listen to the advice given you by your own better half." Oh, I would like to listen, but it doesn't work; if I'm quiet and serious, everyone thinks it's a new comedy and then I have to get out of it by turning it into a joke, not to mention my own family, who are sure to think I'm ill, make me swallow pills for headaches and nerves, feel my neck and my head to see whether I'm running a temperature, ask if I'm constipated and criticize me for being in a bad mood. I can't keep that up: if I'm watched to that extent, I start by getting snappy, then unhappy, and finally I twist my heart round again, so that the bad is on the outside and the good is on the inside and keep on trying to find a way of becoming what I would so like to be, and what I could be, if . . . there weren't any other people living in the world.

Yours, Anne

THE DEFENSE MECHANISMS

The defense mechanisms, which are part of the personality of every individual, become disrupted at adolescence because of the need of the youth to protect himself from the threats invoked by the resurgent, strong instinctual drives. The reactivation of the impulses prompts the adolescent to use the defense mechanisms more frequently and more obviously, perhaps, than at other times in his over-all development. These uses will be illustrated here by passages from personal documents dating from 1,000 A.D. to the present.

The adolescent, faced with the multitudinous problems brought on by the achievement of puberty, has to level up to the problems of establishing emotional equilibrium on a plane not hitherto required. His contradictions and ambivalences are symptomatic of the struggle. His two-sided personality exposes his difficulties, both to himself and to others, whether it is understood as such or not. Thus, Emily Shore (1819-1838), an English girl who started a diary at the age of eight, made this entry in it at sixteen: "There is completely a world within me, unknown, unexplored to any but myself. I see well that my feelings, my qualities, my character are understood by no one else. I am not what I am supposed to be; I am liked and loved more than I deserve. I hate—yes, I truly hate myself; for I see the depths of sin within me which are hidden from all other eyes [39]." The façade the adolescent presents, as illustrated from this diary as well as from the other sources in the preceding section, indicates the individual's need to mask himself from others, largely because he does not know yet who or what he himself is. Until he can assume his proper, acceptable and accepting role, until he finds himself, his emotional disequilibrium forces him to protect himself from all kinds of threats, real or imagined.

He employs the defense mechanisms for this purpose. A lady of rank in the Court at Saint Petersburg, who often saw young Princess Catherine (later, "the Great"), portrayed her as follows: "Her manners were always extremely good from infancy on; she was unusually well-developed and tall for her years. The cast of her features, without being beautiful, was very pleasing, and this impression was increased by the particular graciousness and friendliness she always showed [4]." However, Catherine did not consider herself attractive at all; rather, she was "firmly convinced" of her ugliness. In her *Memoirs* (5), she wrote, "I do not know whether I was really ugly as a child; but I remember very well that I was often told that I was and that for this reason I ought to strive for inward virtues and intelligence. Up to the age of fourteen or fifteen, I was firmly convinced of my ugliness and for that reason actually strove for inward excellence and was not so much concerned with my outward appearance." The compensatory mechanism functioned here and may well be responsible for her subsequent adult need for amatory conquests. Apparently, if the word of the lady of rank can be accepted, and as portraits of Catherine reveal, she was not ugly at all.

Another illustration of compensation comes from the pen of Sir Walter Scott (1771-1832). "My lameness," he explained in his *Memoirs* (36), "and the efforts which I made to supply that disadvantage, by making up in address what I wanted in activity, engaged the latter principle in my favour; and in the winter play hours, when hard exercise was impossible, my tales used to assemble an admiring audience round Lucky Brown's fireside, and happy was he that could sit next to the inexhaustible narrator." It is to be expected that the adolescent, particularly, will try to compensate for a real defect in order to maintain his self-esteem and ego integrity.

Yet, when the defect can be remedied but the individual is unwilling to correct it, he can protect himself by rationalization. In another illustration from Sir Walter Scott, he makes "reasonable" excuses for what he is going to do anyway: "At the Greek class, I might have made a better figure, for Professor Dalzell maintained a great deal of authority, and was not only himself an admirable scholar, but was always deeply interested in the progress of his students. But here lay the villainy. Almost all my companions who had left the High School at the same time with myself had acquired a smattering of Greek before they came to College [Scott was fifteen years old then]. I, alas! had none; and finding myself far inferior to all my fellow-students, I could hit upon no better mode of vindicating my equality than by professing my contempt for the language, and my resolution not to learn it [37]." Even though a classmate offered to tutor him and bring him up to the level of the others, the friend "was unable to prevail over my pride and self-conceit." He maintained his rationalistic defense even though he was called "The Greek Blockhead" by friends and "Dunce" by the Professor.

The popularly used "sour grapes" mechanism can also be called into play when the individual is threatened with some ego loss. In the Saturday, June 10, 1944 entry in his *Diary*, David S. Kogan (26) wrote: "This evening the fellers in the A.S.C. went to Phyllis' party. I stayed home, studied, and did a lot of Hebrew. Maybe I am better off. Tomorrow the party will be just an average memory. My Hebrew work will be an increase in my knowledge that will last forever. That is the trouble. A part of me is upon each side, and I feel cheated no matter what I do."

Eliza Southgate Bowne
(1783-1809)

When she was fourteen years old, Eliza Southgate Bowne left the security of her home for the first time to attend a boarding school in Medford, Massachusetts. In the letter below,* she revealed momentary regression when Mr. Boyd, a neighbor who had driven her to the school, left her and she realized she was all alone. The return to an infantile period of development, when she felt unqualifiedly

---

*From *A Girl's Life Eighty Years Ago* by Eliza Southgate Bowne. New York: Charles Scribner's Sons, 1887. P. 4.

loved and accepted by her parents, gave the adolescent girl some surcease from her feelings of possible rejection and loneliness.

Medford, May 12, 1797

Honored Parents:

With pleasure I sit down to the best of parents to inform them of my situation, as doubtless they are anxious to hear,—permit me to tell them something of my foolish heart. When I first came here I gave myself up to reflection, but not pleasing reflections. When Mr. Boyd left me I burst into tears and instead of trying to calm my feelings I tried to feel worse. I begin to feel happier and will soon gather up all my Philosophy and think of the duty that now attends me, to think that here I may drink freely of the fountain of knowledge, but I will not dwell any longer on this subject. I am not doing anything but writing, reading, and cyphering. There is a French Master coming next Monday, and he will teach French and Dancing. William Boyd and Mr. Wyman advise me to learn French, yet if I do at all I wish you to write me very soon what you think best, for the school begins on Monday. Mr. Wyman says it will not take up but a very little of my time, for it is but two days in the week, and the lessons only 2 hours long. Mr. Wyman says I must learn Geometry before Geography, and that I better not begin it till I have got through my Cyphering.

We get up early in the morning and make our beds and sweep the chamber, it is a chamber about as large as our kitchen chamber, and a little better finished. There's 4 beds in the chamber, and two persons in each bed, we have chocolate for breakfast and supper.

Your affectionate Daughter

Eliza Southgate.

San Kim
(1905-   )

The displacement of instinctual aims through the defense mechanism of sublimation is frequent during the adolescent period. By the time San Kim, the revolutionary Korean, was eighteen, he had decided never to marry. "My life was to be lived in revolutionary work and not in helping any woman." In the following passage* Kim reveals not only the process of sublimation at work but also

---

*From *Song of Ariran* by San Kim. Reprinted by permission of The John Day Company, Inc. 1941. Pp. 68-71.

the process of intellectualization. His study of physiology while in medical school gave him, he thought, the logical answers to the biological desires and necessities of the male and female which were able to buttress his sublimated ideational learning.

During my first year in medical school, I occasionally wrote to my proposed fiancée and received very affectionate replies. In 1923, however, I told her frankly that I could never marry any girl, for my life was to be entirely engrossed in revolutionary work and would have to be independent of any ties. I would have no money, and she could never live the hard life that was to be my voluntary lot. She seemed quite broken-hearted—but, nevertheless, only two years later, married someone else in Korea.

From the age of fifteen to the year 1923 I had had no decided opinions on the woman question, though I rebelled against arranged marriage. Those I had were determined by three influences: Christian idealistic training in respect for women; a natural human feeling for girls of my own age; and the inhibiting underlying thought that in a life of revolution I could never have a domestic life, so that, no matter if I loved a girl very much, it would be unfair to her to marry her. An Tung-hsi's daughter had first awakened my interest in girls, and after that I was shy and embarrassed in their company but secretly much interested in the opposite sex. In Shanghai there had been many Korean girls, but they were usually too much older or younger. I met several at gatherings of young people with An Ch'ang-ho and Li Kuang-ssu and sometimes took them roller skating in the parks. An Ch'ang-ho taught us not to marry early but to have a healthy, natural friendship with girls in the modern co-educational manner. He believed in keeping this relationship purely platonic, with friendship between boys and girls exactly as if of the same sex. He said that the traditional Oriental separation of the sexes was unnatural and created morbid curiosities and unhealthy attitudes; that it was designed to keep women helpless and an instrument of propagation or amusement only, denying their right to equality and mutual respect. Men must help in freeing women by protecting and guarding their equal status and encouraging them to enter into all activities in partnership with men. Marriage was to be such a partnership, when both were old enough to choose wisely and with understanding of each other as individual personalities.

I agreed with An Ch'ang-ho, but I was more idealistic and had a tendency to worship from afar. When I became acquainted with the girl in Korea I saw that I could easily learn to like her very much, even though she was not the ideal I had vaguely in mind. I did not then deny marriage absolutely but thought the matter could take care of itself in future. I was much interested in the general problem, however. There were several pairs of lovers in medical school, and I followed the course of these affairs with curiosity. They usually ended in jealousy and enmity, so I concluded that such love affairs were all nonsense.

Then—when I got into the study of physiology I saw that men's desires and necessities were not the same. The desires and necessities of animals were the same. But men could not make their wants and needs fit each other. And why should they? Rouseau taught the validity of the "natural man," but he influenced me in the opposite direction. The nature of man was not the same as that of the animal. It was natural only to itself. Animal desires are necessary to the animal but not to the man. Man can control his desires and thereby render them unnecessary, I decided. Man existed as such only when he had intellectual will and idea. In that he was not the same as the animal. His mind existed for the purpose of controlling his body as well as other forces of nature external to himself. Otherwise he failed to measure up to the stature of man as opposed to the beast.

I thought that women were physiologically passive and that their role in life was passive. They wanted peace and fulfillment. They were not active like men, and I did not like this. They were useful for their own purposes but not in a historical period demanding action and sacrifice external to material needs and the family group.

I decided that women and marriage were a biological and economic problem. In time of peace they were important. In time of fighting they were secondary and must be relegated to that position by will. I saw that no man can be independent if married and that to be in love was even greater bondage. In love a man loses, not only his freedom as an individual, but also the internal freedom of his own body. Girls were weaker than men, and I did not like any kind of weakness. My life was to be lived in revolutionary work and not in helping any woman. In 1923 I decided firmly never to marry and never to place myself in any position where I might become the victim of a love affair. For a long time after this I never talked with any girl and avoided coming into any contact with them whatsoever.

I did strong propaganda among the students in Peking on this subject though not all of it was effective. "Man is historical; woman is not. Woman is immediate," I would quote to them. I was very expert on women then—when I knew nothing about them.

"You are worse than a monk. You are a puritan," Kim Chung-chiang, the Kongosan ex-monk, would say to me.

" 'What is love?' " I would retort, quoting Tolstoy. " 'Love is only taking another baby's mother for your own child. One man takes a woman to save her from the arms of a cruel man into his own cruel arms.' "

"Ah, what a fine clean target you are for some girl." Kim would shake his head sagely. "You have no defense whatever. Don't you know that the only defense against women is more women? You are only keeping yourself vulnerable. Pity you when you fall in love some day. All the heavens will fall upon you. I think you should give up this theory before you are devoured by it. Come with me tonight."

"A great love is better than a mess of little ones, anyway," I would argue. "A great tragedy is not so harmful to a man as piece-meal destruction and demoralization. To be killed is better than to be ruined and still live."

"There is no more dangerous situation for any man to be in than to be virgin territory for the first woman," Kim would say. "I give you fair warning, for I was once a monk like you myself. I think that love may be either an injection, a transfusion, or a single blood stream. You can choose between them. I know nothing of real love myself, but I have decided that I must learn something of women."

"After his wife died when he was 25, Hegel refused ever to marry again. If I am no worse at dialectics than he, I shall not complain," I would remark. "To free the mind you must first free the body, even if handcuffs are necessary to do it in the dialectical manner."

"Hegel lived in abstractions. You must live and fight with the material men and women who are the real social forces. If you want to be a virgin ascetic go back to a cliff in the Kongosan," was Kim's argument.

But Kim agreed with me then that Korean revolutionaries should not marry. His argument was that you should let love destroy itself and thereby win freedom from it. All our close comrades pledged themselves to the principle of non-marriage because they knew our hard life and economic uncertainties in the future would be burden enough. We all lived together in one group in Peking and shared our problems in common. Most of us opposed having the others go out at night to nameless places and tried to prevent it. When they came back we said bitterly:

"It costs $6 or $7 a month for food for one of us, yet you spend $10 on women while we are half-starved."

"You have no soul," these students would reply. "You care only for meat, not even for flesh. Is one *chin* of mutton enough to satisfy you?" Our group finally had to take the position that it was a personal, secret problem. If the individual had money enough he could do as he pleased so long as he did not interfere with politics, but we watched those who spent it on such undesirable purposes with hawk eyes to detect the slightest political irregularity and made life unpleasant for them. If any one should contract a disease, this was to be considered an unpardonable crime against the revolution, so they had to go only to the best places which were very expensive, sometimes $10 a night, and few could afford to do this often.

"Sing-song girls are a defense against marriage," Kim would remark. "For this we can thank them. They leave our revolutionaries free agents. The price is not too high."

But I was personally a strict puritan and was never able to rationalize this question. I held that a strong man could and must suppress his body and we wanted only strong men in revolutionary work. An Ch'ang-ho had convinced me of this first, and Tolstoy's ideas influenced me greatly too. From Tolstoy I learned the philosophy of sacrifice, not only of life, but of desire. I felt that the truth lay somewhere between Tolstoyan asceticism and Rousseau. Tolstoy liked women at first, but after he became creative he had nothing to do with them. I thought to dispense with that first stage and go direct to my work.

Just as the defense mechanisms have been operative in adolescents of all times and in all cultures, so has the need to search for a personal identity always been present (35). A child has a number of opportunities to identify himself, more or less experimentally, with real or fictitious people of either sex in regard to habit traits, occupations, and ideas. Certain crises force him to make radical decisions. "However," states Erikson (11), "the historical era in which he lives offers only a limited number of socially meaningful models for workable combinations of identification fragments. Their usefulness depends on the way in which they simultaneously meet the requirements of the organism's maturational stage and ego habits of synthesis." Thus Erikson's emphasis is on the sequential psychosocial crises each individual experiences in order to achieve the full development of ego identity. This crisis is specific for each adolescent, as several of the illustrations in this section demonstrate.

The identification Catherine the Great (1729-1796) established with Frau von Bentinck when she was fourteen years old may have had a pervasive influence on her life. In her *Memoirs* (6), she wrote: "I went the next day under pretext of a visit again to Frau von Bentinck, whom I thought fascinating. And how could she seem otherwise? I was aged fourteen! She rode, danced, when she was in the mood, sang, laughed, skipped like a child, although she was at the time fully thirty years old. She was already living apart from her husband. I saw in her room a very beautiful three-year-old child and asked who it was. She said laughing that it was the brother of Fräulein Donop who lived with her; but to other acquaintances she said without formality that the child belonged to her and that she had it by her page."

Thomas Wolfe, the American novelist, was constantly involved in overly constricting personal relationships and subsequent struggles to break free from them as a result of what he called, "the search for a father." "The deepest search in life, it seemed to me," he wrote in *The Story of a Novel* (47), "the thing that in one way or another was central to all living, was man's search to find a father, not merely the father of his flesh, not merely the lost father of his youth, but the image of a strength and wisdom external to his need and superior to his hunger, to which the belief and power of his own life could be united." Wolfe's prolonged search for identity has been attributed to various causes: to nostalgia for the security of his early childhood which was disrupted by the partial separation of his parents; to bereavement at his father's death; to a desire to escape from the domination of his mother; to an unconscious Oedipal yearning for her; or to a search for the God-Father of a religion which he intellectually could not accept but for which he still had need (33). There is something to be said for all these interpretations, but it must also be remembered that the normal impulse of all adolescents is to attach themselves to people they admire, and that Wolfe retained many adolescent traits until comparatively late in life.

Erikson (12) characterized the great task of late adolescence as the establishment of a sense of identity, that is the striving of the individual to be and to feel most himself—and this in pursuits and roles which have meanings to others who are most significant to him (13). Common to the quest for identity is the enormous spurt of new needs, new energies and new faculties. In Thomas Wolfe's autobiographical novel, *Look Homeward, Angel,* the archetypal hero, Eugene Gant, was unable to identify with anyone. He acted out his need for identification extravagantly, knocking on strangers' doors in strange towns and identifying himself as a Carpenter, or as Thomas Chatterton looking for "a gentlemen by the name of Coleridge—Mr. Samuel T. Coleridge;" or else he would sign hotel registers as Ben Jonson, Robert Browning and other famous poets (46).

William Ellery Leonard
(1876-1944)

William Leonard, teacher, poet and autobiographer, was almost identically tormented during his adolescence by a need to relate himself to literary geniuses. In the next excerpt,* he describes his passion for and identification with Byron—among others. His need for Byron, he wrote, "was the nearest I ever came to that worship which the Christian heart and imagination experiences toward the divine Son of its creed." He imitated Byron's mood, theme and manner in his own verse. He wrote his doctoral dissertation at Columbia University on Byron. He became a leading authority on Byron. But out of the very pressures of the strong identifications with the English poet, Leonard was able, eventually, to recreate, broaden and synthesize his own, more individual identity.

I tormented myself in my very search for spiritual companionship, by the lives of those who had achieved, especially in scholarship and letters—Theodore Parker, Dr. Johnson, Milton, John Stuart Mill, Margaret Fuller, Macaulay, Wordsworth, and so on—I was always measuring what they knew and did at seventeen and eighteen with what I knew and did at seventeen and eighteen. Macaulay had read so much more Latin; Mill was an Aristotle at three; Shelley's "Queen Mab" and its recondite notes was only less great than the "Divine Comedy" (in Longfellow's translation), and Pope's heroics in the "Pastorals" were of a far more graceful and musical art at sixteen than I could achieve with an advantage of fourteen months. I did get some encouragement from Byron's "Hours of Idleness," and thought my

---

*From *The Locomotive-God* by William Ellery Leonard. Reprinted by permission of Appleton-Century-Crofts, Inc. Copyright 1927, Century Co.; 1942, D. Appleton-Century Co., Inc. Pp. 135-139.

own exercise in "Childish Recollections" in spots perhaps as good as Byron's. I was probably right. Or, with the unbalanced moods and judgments of this abnormal adolescent isolation, I would go to the other extreme. My rimed tale of the Persian Wars with its recurrent, "Master, remember the Athenians" (inserted in the original Greek . . . Athenaion . . . to rime with Aion, Bion, die on, lion, sigh on, etc.), I vowed was as good as "The Siege of Corinth"; my satire on Alexander the Great as good as the lines on Napoleon in "The Age of Bronze"— even as later in college my "Ode to Evening" was better, far better than Collins, far more like Keats and Shelley (for a fact, it was far more like Keats and Shelley). But did these realizing moments of conscious supremacy in precocious power bring me peace? They did not. They brought me further torment. They accentuated my rebellion and despair: here in this God-forsaken hole genius is doomed to rot away. Smile. I smile now too. It was Hell then. I was a fool? I was a fool. But I'm not talking about folly; I am talking about spiritual anguish.

I often, and more and more with the months, read not for spiritual support but for escape, to forget, to forget—yet always finding some unhappy image of myself on every other page. In mature years, I acquired indeed the resources of escape in books. Lucretius, Goethe, Dante, Cervantes, Abelard, Shakespere, Chaucer, Homer—how I thank you! For salvation again and again. For companionship too. Humbly content merely to walk by the sides of you. Finding exaltation enough in the elemental fact that I am man enough to understand the voices of you. I would have been dead long ago but for books. Yet back there in Bolton, if I could only have pitched hay, as I learned to do later in college vacations, and have sweated out on the sun-beat slopes the poisons my system then distilled even from books good and great!

Above all from Byron. I had already known Byron through "The Isles of Greece." Now "Childe Harold" became the companion of my lonely classical studies, "Childe Harold," "The Giaour," "The Curse of Minerva": Byron spoke out my emotions, Byron reinforced my imaginings, on Greece and Rome. We were together. Soon, however, the peculiarly Byronic in the classical mood became mine:

> O, Rome, my country, city of the soul,
> The orphans of the heart must turn to thee.

Byron . . . Rome . . . the Bolton exile. Then the Byronic mood itself, which had made increment of Greece (sad relic of departed worth) and of Rome (childless and crownless in her voiceless woe), became mine; or rather (without attempting a too subtle analysis) interpreted and reinforced my own moods, of self-conscious adolescence, of isolation from my kind, of world-pain, of the tragic grandeur of my fate. The Corsair had leaned beside a pillar in the hall, darkly scowling at the dancers. I visited a country dance under the oil-lamps in the upstairs of the Town-Hall and leaned and scowled too and withdrew into the night. I dramatized myself as Byron. This is the Byronic bane for adolescence, especially for an adolescence conditioned, as mine was, to meet the Byronic more than half-way on its own miserable ground. There was no bane for me in his so-called immoralities, either sentimental as in "Parisina" or farcical as in "Don Juan"; and I doubt if there is for anybody. I caught something of the veritable spirit of nature, of the heroic, of the sagacious in Byron; but the chief blessing, beside the bane, was the thoroughfares he opened to English literature around and before him. I followed one lead after another in his text or in the notes, and in the Byron biographies, to Shelley, Coleridge, Keats, Wordsworth, Crabbe, Gifford, and to Milton, Pope, Collins, Gray, Dryden, Johnson. And in their works, in turn (some of them of course already familiar to me in parts), I got other leads. I had no "Century Outlines" or "Century Readings"; no manuals. My mind did its own sorting out; and it got the chronology straighter than most students I have ever assisted in examining for their master's degrees. And, incidentally, I found that the simplest way to know *about* when a thing happened was to know *just* when it happened. And I knew just when it happened because the date meant to me a moment of Reality . . . 1688 . . . 1700 . . . 1744 . . . 1788 . . . 1809 . . . 1812 . . . 1815 . . . 1824 . . . 1850 . . . *1876*. I knew every line of Byron—this is not a figure of speech. I knew "Childe Harold" practically by heart—this is not a figure of speech. And reverence and pity and love for Byron, need for Byron, was the nearest I ever came to that worship which the Christian heart and imagination experiences toward the divine Son of its creed. A slighting comment on Byron by a professor in my freshman year made me flush and tremble and all but sob in my seat . . . (Byron, I'd like to talk this over with you sometime in the Elysian Fields.) Later Byron marked out for me much of my own pilgrimage through Europe—by the exulting and abounding river, by the castled crag where I became a university student, by Lake Leman mirroring the stars and mountains, in the pass where Jura answers from her misty shroud back to the joyous Alps who call to her aloud (where my own amazed ears heard the same thunder), even down to Italia. . . . And only not to Greece because too poor of purse. As I think of the great companion that led me through Europe, no longer a boy but still young, still free to follow light of mountain or sea or poet, of what his great voice did for my eyes, for my spirit, must I not forgive his part in the tragic buncombe of Bolton days? Byron too gave me my doctor's degree at Columbia. Byron made me an official examiner of Samuel Chew's Johns Hopkins dissertation a little later . . . which was so good that, in sad prescience, I realized my brief career as "perhaps the leading Byron authority of America" had about run its course. Yet when Drinkwater told me in Madison a few months ago of his new book on Byron, I said, "They'll ask Chew to review it, but they'll ask me too." And they did. "They" meant of course such people as Canby, Sherman, and Van Doren on Manhattan Isle.

My verses were obviously more and more Byronic; Byronic in mood, Byronic in theme, and manner. Worthless of course. Interesting, not for any outstanding poetic promise, but, possibly, for their part in fixating my morbidity, and for some suggestions on the psychology of composition. To re-create by self-identification as reader is a vital process, but not so vital as to re-create by self-identification as writer. And, worse, with me the re-creation found much stuff available inside myself. The Byronic imitation was not mere pose. I had, too, something more than Juvenal's *cacoethes scribendi*, scribbler's itch. I had the authentic need, the double urge behind all art—the urge to shape, to objectify, to get it off my chest; the urge to communicate, to propagandize for my state, to tell the world—the double urge that converts brute experience into human experience—to get it straight for yourself and to make it plain to your friend, whatever it be that has come home to you. I had too the external form of verse. I never learned meter and rime. Verse was for me only a specialized application of organized sound through speech, implicit in my original learning to talk. I had the stuff, not only an aching and a yearning heart, and a sense of human life, but a love of nature, first awakened in these hills, and wrought into my emotions of self and of life, a sense too of something far more deeply interfused. . . . Never again was I to vibrate so entirely as poet. But I failed to function as poet because I could not objectify and could not communicate. I lacked the stabilizations that come from the intellect and the self-reliance of an unmastered personality, using its own tongue on its own feet. I was undifferentiated splurge. There is no prophesying from youth. What the two urges become depends on the unforetellable nature of his future experience and what his intellect and his character can do with it. For every ten thousand at seventeen who scribble so-called promising verses, only one will be saying anything at thirty-seven. They really never transcend seventeen. And if they learn to *be,* they never learn to *speak.* Growing-up means getting the use of one's tongue as well as one's experience.

André Gide
(1869-1951)

One of the more spectacular and dramatic ways of coping with threat is the adolescent's use of the conversion symptom mechanism. André Gide made effective use of it when he came up against an intolerable situation at the *Ecole Alsacienne* which he attended. He was mocked, ridiculed, bullied and beaten by his classmates because of the perfection with which he recited poetry when called on by the teacher. Boys who had at first been his friends dropped him. The end of each schoolday found his enemies waiting in ambush for him. "There were days when I got home in a lamentable state, my clothes torn and muddy, my nose bleeding, my teeth chattering, haggard with fright. My poor mother was at her wits' end. Then at last, by some merciful providence, I fell seriously ill and my torture came to an end [22]." He had small-pox. But as he recovered and the time approached for him to return to school and his private and public hell, he conceived of the idea of simulating a kind of Saint Vitus dance performance. It succeeded; despite his shamming, the doctors advised André's mother to give him "the cure" at a spa. For ten months he and his mother remained there. "Cured," he was returned to the *Ecole,* but the threat he felt still persisted, and it was then that the actual conversion symptom took place. Persistent, chronic "sick headaches" disabled him from the time he was thirteen until twenty; there was a re-occurrence in 1916, when he was forty-six years old. In the following passage,* he describes how, at thirteen, his mother treated him like an invalid and finally removed him from the school: "I could not eat; I could not sleep."

When, after ten months of lying fallow, my mother brought me back to Paris and sent me to the *Ecole Alsacienne* once more, I had entirely lost the habit of work. I had not been there a fortnight before I added headaches to my repertory of nervous troubles, as being less startling and easier to manage at school. As these headaches left me

---

*From *If It Die* by André Gide. Translated by Dorothy Bussy. Reprinted by permission of Random House, Inc. Copyright 1935, The Modern Library, Inc. Pp. 97-100.

completely after the age of twenty, and even earlier, I looked upon them for some time with great severity and accused them of being, if not altogether feigned, at any rate greatly exaggerated. But now that they have begun again, I recognize them, at forty-six years old, as being exactly what they were when I was thirteen, and I admit they might very well have paralyzed my efforts to work. In truth, I was not lazy; and I approved with my whole heart, when I heard my uncle Emile say: "André will always love work."

But it was he too who called me "André the irregular." The fact is, I found great difficulty in working against the grain; even at that age, my steady hard work was done in short bouts—by repeating an effort I could not prolong. I was often overcome by sudden fits of fatigue— fatigue of the mind—interruptions of the current, so to speak; and this condition continued even after the sick headaches had left me, or, to be more accurate, succeeded the sick headaches and lasted for days, weeks, months at a time. Independently of all this, I experienced an unspeakable distaste for everything we did in class, for the class itself, for the whole system of lectures and examinations, even for the play hours; nor could I endure the sitting still, the lack of interest, the stagnation of the school régime. My headaches no doubt came in very conveniently; I cannot say how far I made the most of them.

Brouardel, who had originally been our doctor, was now so celebrated that my mother did not like to call him in, being hindered, I suppose, by the same kind of scruples which I have certainly inherited from her and which paralyze me too in my dealings with people of importance. There was no need to have any such fear regarding Monsieur Lizart, who succeeded him as our family doctor; one could rest assured that he, at any rate, would never be singled out for celebrity, for indeed there was nothing in him to single out. A good-natured creature he was; fair and foolish, with a gentle voice, a kind glance, a limp bearing; apparently harmless too—but nothing is more dangerous than a fool. How can his prescriptions be forgiven him? As soon as I felt nervy—bromides; as soon as I slept badly—chloral. And this for a growing child and an unformed brain! All my later weaknesses of will or memory I attribute to him. If one could take action against the dead, I would prosecute him. I remember with fury that for weeks together there was half a glass of solution of chloral (the bottle of little crystals was put entirely at my own disposal and I could measure out any dose I fancied)—of chloral, I repeat, placed by my bedside at night, in case of sleeplessness; that for weeks, for months together, when I sat down to table, I found beside my plate a bottle of "Sirop Laroze" (peel of bitter oranges and bromide of potassium). At every meal, I had to take one, two, and then three spoonfuls (not tea-spoons but table-spoons) of this mixture, and so on, in a rhythmical series of threes; and this treatment went on indefinitely, nor was there any reason it should ever stop, until it left the poor foolish patient—such as I was—completely stupefied. Especially as the syrup was very good! I cannot understand how I escaped perdition.

Decidedly the devil was on the watch for me; the shades of night were gathering thick and fast and no sign gave warning there was any rift through which a ray of light might reach me. It was then that occurred the angelic intervention that came to snatch me from the Evil One—an event infinitely slight in itself, but as important in my life as revolutions in the history of empires—the first scene of a drama which is not yet played out.

*   *   *   *

It must have been a little before the New Year. We were again at Rouen; not only because it was holiday time, but because, after a month's trial, I had again left the Ecole Alsacienne. My mother resigned herself to treating me as an invalid and to the inevitable necessity of my learning nothing except by accident; this meant another and prolonged interruption to my education.

I could not eat; I could not sleep. My aunt Lucile was all kindness and attention; in the morning, Adèle or Victor came to light the fire in my room; I used to lie in my big bed long after I woke, lazily listening to the great logs as they hissed and spurted their harmless sparks against the fireguard, sinking with a delicious feeling of torpor into the comfort that pervaded the house from top to bottom. I see myself sitting between my mother and aunt in the big, pleasant, stately dining-room, its four corners adorned with white statues of the four seasons; there they stood, decently lascivious, after the style of the Restoration, each statue in its niche, on a pedestal fitted up as a sideboard (in winter, provided with a hot-plate).

Séraphine used to prepare me special little dishes, but nothing tempted my appetite.

"You see, my dear," said my mother to my aunt, "all the saints in the calendar won't get him to eat."

"Juliette," my aunt would suggest, "do you think he might fancy oysters?"

Then Mamma:

"No, no, you're much too kind . . . Well, perhaps, one might try oysters."

I can honestly say that this was not mere fastidiousness on my part.

Everything was distasteful to me; I went to table as one might go to the scaffold; it was with the greatest difficulty that I swallowed a morsel or two; in vain my mother begged, scolded, and threatened, and nearly every meal ended in tears.

The "sick headaches" Gide manifested had at least two possible values for him. First, the headaches kept him close to his mother. Second, they kept him from going back to school where he might be symbolically castrated by the expression of intellect. The mechanism of conversion formed the basis of a conversion hysteria which was Gide's physical solution to his emotional conflict.

One of the purposes of the penetrating study Symonds made of adolescent fantasy was to reveal its nature. From the stories and autobiographies submitted by his population, as well as from the projective tests administered to them, Symonds concluded that themes of aggression and love are practically universal in adolescents. In few of the stories were there overt sexual fantasies. Rather they were kept on the level of social relationships and there was no particular atmosphere of guilt surrounding the love themes. Marriage was looked on by the young adolescent as a state of bliss. The aggressive themes, however, produced marked emotional responses. "In many of the aggressive stories there were fantasies of concealment and escape from the avenger. Generally punishment followed aggression in monotonous sequences. A sequence repeated over and over again was to have the aggression of robbery or personal attack followed by the arrival of the police, arrest, trial, conviction, and punishment. The punishments were of the severest kind—life imprisonment or the electric chair [42]."

Like Symonds' contemporary youth, almost all of the subjects in the passages which follow reveal the universal fantasies of either love or aggression. The adolescent is not limited to just these two varieties of daydreams, of course. He generally has a rich fantasy life. McCurdy, in his paper on the childhood patterns of genius, points out that the constant intercourse with the adult world which the young genius has may be especially important in the development of genius. "Not only is there an increase of knowledge, which is the usual aim of the instructors; there is also, in many cases, a profound excitement of imagination. Even John Stuart Mill confesses that he did not perfectly understand such grave works as the more difficult dialogs of Plato when he read them in Greek at seven. What, then, happens to such adult material pouring into the child's mind? Mill does not elucidate in his own case; but there is evidence in a number of the biographies before me that the dynamic processes of fantasy go to work on it and richly transform both what is understood and what is not [29]." McCurdy concludes, " . . . fantasy is probably an important aspect of the development of genius, not only in those cases where the chief avenue of fame is through the production of works of imagination in the ordinary sense, but also in those where the adult accomplishment is of a different sort. Instead of becoming proficient in taking and giving the hard knocks of social relations with his contemporaries, the child of genius is thrown back on the resources of his imagination, and through it becomes aware of his own depth, self-conscious in the fullest sense, and essentially independent [30]."

It is not only the genius who is so affected, but all adolescents, though perhaps to a lesser degree. In the progression from early to later adolescence, fantasy life undergoes a modification almost as abrupt and striking as the sudden acceleration of somatic growth which began with the puberty change (41). Fenichel (14) defines fantasy as thinking which is not followed by action and of which there are two types: creative fantasy, which prepares for some later action, and daydreaming fantasy, the refuge for wishes that cannot be fulfilled. Within these two categories there is a whole sub-classification in which the adolescent indulges, including oedipal fantasies, dreams of grandeur, homage, martyrdom, acts of daring such as saving someone's life to the applause of bystanders and relatives, and so on. Shaffer and Shoben (38) list some thirteen common daydreams.

During the entire period of adolescence, the individual shows a tendency to turn away from reality and indulge in fantasies (9). At times, he regards his fantasies as real so that he can deny the reality which is perhaps more dangerous to him. He derives comfort and security from them in the face of some threat, real or imaginary, or some unfulfilled wish. The daydreams give him a sense of satisfaction which he cannot achieve in real life and serve integrative as well as adjustive purposes.

Following the death of his mother, Yoshio Kodama, an extreme Japanese nationalist who wrote his autobiography in Sugamo

Prison, where he was incarcerated as a suspected war criminal, tasted the bitterness of poverty and the coldness of the world. As a child and adolescent, he had wandered up and down Korea looking for a place for himself and finding none. "And therefore," he wrote in his accurately titled autobiography, *I Was Defeated*, "I wanted to become a powerful man in order to make my way through the world. I did not want to become a merchant or salary man. I wanted to become someone engaged in some kind of work to help the weak. This was all I thought about and, although vaguely of course, I believed that the 'Kokusui' movement, which was becoming very active in Tokyo at that time, was heroic and grand [25]." An American youth of the same generation, David Kogan, experiencing feelings of loneliness, isolation and inferiority in athletic prowess, attempted to achieve some sort of integrated self-esteem through persistent daydreams. On July 31, 1942, he wrote in his *Diary:* "This is one part of my life which I have never until now touched—my thinking at night with my eyes closed. Thinking I am president of Palestine . . . great baseball player, manager, chess champ, greatest American in history, founder of modern housing projects. It has been going on night after night for a few years [27]."

The illustrations which follow point up the nature and function of the adolescent's daydreams. They include the romantic daydreams of an eleventh-century Japanese girl and the heroic fantasies of a Winnebago Indian youth.

The Sarashina Diary
(1009-1059)

The Sarashina Diary was kept by the daughter of a provincial Japanese governor, one Fujiwara Takasué, from the time she was twelve until near her death. In the entry reprinted below,* the girl was thirteen years old and reports a daydream of the "Shining Prince" who would some day come and marry her—identical with the daydreams, both in content and level of relationships, found in Symonds' (42) study of contemporary adolescents.

---

*From *Diaries of Court Ladies of Old Japan* edited by Annie Omori and Kochi Doi. Reprinted by permission of Houghton Mifflin Co. 1920. P. 20.

It may be interesting, for the purpose of satisfying curiosity, to indicate that the girl never found her Prince. An abortive love affair lightened her dreary life for a moment. "Who he was," the editors of the diary write, "we do not know, but she met him on an evening when 'there was no starlight, and a gentle shower fell in the darkness.' They talked and exchanged poems, but she did not meet him again until the next year; then, after an evening entertainment to which she had not gone, 'when I looked out, opening the sliding door on the corridor, I saw the morning moon very faint and beautiful,' and he was there. Again they exchanged poems and she believed that happiness had at last arrived. He was to come with his lute and sing to her. 'I waited to hear it,' she writes, 'and waited for the fit occasion, but there was none, ever.' A year later she has lost hope, she writes a poems and adds, 'So I composed that poem—and there is nothing more to tell.' Nothing more, indeed, but what is told conveys all the misery of her deceived longing [34]."

Although I was still ugly and undeveloped [I thought to myself] the time would come when I should be beautiful beyond compare, with long, long hair. I should be like the Lady Yugao [in the romance] loved by the Shining Prince Genji, or like the Lady Ukifuné, the wife of the General of Uji [a famous beauty]. I indulged in such fancies—shallow-minded I was indeed!

Could such a man as the Shining Prince be living in this world? How could General Kaoru [literal translation, "Fragrance"] find such a beauty as Lady Ukifuné to conceal in his secret villa at Uji? Oh! I was like a crazy girl.

While I had lived in the country, I had gone to the temple from time to time, but even then I could never pray like others, with a pure heart. In those days people learned to recite sutras and practise austerities of religious observance after the age of seventeen or eighteen, but I could scarcely even think of such matters. The only thing that I could think of was the Shining Prince who would some day come to me, as noble and beautiful as in the romance. If he came only once a year I, being hidden in a mountain villa like Lady Ukifuné, would be content. I could live as *heart-dwindlingly* as that lady, looking at flowers, or moonlight snowy landscape, occasionally receiving long-expected lovely letters from my Lord! I cherished such fancies and imagined that they might be realized.

Jean Jacques Rousseau
(1712-1778)

Rousseau's *Confessions* were presented by him as "unexampled truthfulness," the complete revelation of his "inmost self"; and perhaps that is what he thought he had achieved. We know better now, of course; the inmost self is not revealed through conscious processes, and besides being an exhibitionist, Rousseau was a pathological liar with strong masochistic tendencies. His *Confessions* are a classic in the literature of psychopathology.

However, it is tempting to believe implicitly the following passage because it reveals daydreams universally indulged in by adolescents. Rousseau described himself at sixteen as ready to give up everything—country, father, and a half-served apprenticeship—which would have given him some economic security. He imagined what would happen when he would run away. A whole galaxy of fantasies cropped up to give him some surcease from the adolescent frustrations and anxieties that accompanied this meaningful step.*

However mournful the moment, when terror suggested to me the idea of flight, had appeared—the moment when I carried it into execution appeared equally delightful. While still a child, to leave my country, my parents, my means of support, my resources; to give up an apprenticeship half-served, without a sufficient knowledge of my trade to earn my livelihood; to abandon myself to the horrors of want, without any means of saving myself from it; to expose myself, at the age of innocence and weakness, to all the temptations of vice and despair; to seek, in the distance, suffering, error, snares, servitude, and death, beneath a yoke far more unbending than that which I had been unable to endure—this was what I was going to do, this was the prospect which I ought to have considered. How different was that which my fancy painted! The independence which I believed I had gained was the only feeling which moved me. Free, and my own master, I believed I could do everything, attain to everything; I had only to launch myself forth, to mount and fly through the air. I entered the vast world with a feeling of security; it was to be filled with the fame of my achievements; at every step I was to find festivities, treasures, adventures, friends ready to serve me, mistresses eager to please me; I had

---

*From *Confessions* by Jean Jacques Rousseau. Reprinted by permission of Pocket Books, Inc. 1957. Pp. 28-29.

only to show myself, to engage the attention of the whole world—and yet not the whole world; to a certain extent I could dispense with it, and did not want so much. Charming society was enough for me, without troubling myself about the rest. In my modesty I limited myself to a narrow, but delightfully select circle, in which my sovereignty was assured. A single castle was the limit of my ambition. As the favourite of the lord and the lady, as the lover of the daughter, as the friend of the son and protector of the neighbours, I was content—I wanted no more.

Richard Henry Dana, Jr.
(1815-1882)

The aggressive theme which Symonds found to be universal in the fantasy life of the adolescent population in his study is also indicated in this passage from Dana's *Autobiographical Sketch.** Similarly, the exaggerated style and intensity of feeling Symonds' adolescents express are also to be found here. This is to be expected, for adolescence is a period of the intensification of drives. "The adolescent is driven by aggressive trends growing out of his frustrations and goaded by his need to assert independence and maturity [43]."

The fantasy related by Dana occurred in 1828, when he was in his fourteenth year. His need for revenge for the attack made on him by a teacher, which he felt was completely unjustified, met with some satisfaction through fantasy. He dreamed of the time when he would be big and strong and could demand nothing but a full apology—or else the teacher would suffer bodily harm.

The teachers following Mr. Sandford were, Henry S. McKean & Horatio Wood. Mr. Wood kept but a fortnight. He was very unfortunate in all his plans & notions. He made enemies of the boys & contrived to thin out the school more than one half, in those few days. His punishments were degrading. Among other things, he made the boys of the upper class, between 14 & 16 years of age, on the eye of entering college & thinking ourselves young gentlemen, stand out upon the middle of the floor for punishment, for the slightest offences. He also inflicted some violent corporal punishments. One in-

---

*From *Richard Henry Dana, Jr., An Autobiographical Sketch* edited by Robert G. Metzdorf. Reprinted by permission of Massachusetts Historical Society. Copyright 1953, The Shoe String Press. Pp. 46-48.

flicted upon myself was the cause of his being turned out of his office. He had placed me in the middle of the floor for some offence or other, & my station being near the stove, & the room very hot, I became faint. I asked to be allowed to go out & gave my reason, but to no purpose. In a few minutes we had our usual recess of a quarter of an hour, & I went out. Here I came very near fainting again, looked very pale, & asked leave to go home. This was refused. As I was really sick, at the suggestion of the boys, I went home, it was but a few minutes walk, to get a written excuse. My father saw that I was ill & kept me at home & sent me the next morning with a written excuse for non-appearance, alleging faintness & sickness. Mr. W. was mortified & angry at this & said that the excuse only covered my not returning, while the chief offence was my going home without leave, which he could not excuse, & calling me out, took his ferrule & ordered me to put out my left hand. (He also intimated that my sickness was all a sham.) Upon this hand, he inflicted six blows with all his strength, & then six upon the right hand. I was in such a phrenzy of indigation at his injustice & his insulting insinuation, that I could not have uttered a word, for my life. I was too small & slender to resist, & could show my spirit only by fortitude. He called for my right hand again & gave six more blows in the same manner, & then six more upon the left. My hands were swollen & in acute pain, but I did not flinch nor show a sign of suffering. He was determined to conquer & gave six more blows upon each hand, with full force. Still there was no sign from me of pain or submission. I could have gone to the stake for what I considered my honour. The school was in an uproar of hissing & scraping & groaning, & the master turned his attention to the other boys & let me alone. He said not another word to me through the day. If he had I could not have answered, for my whole soul was in my throat, & not a word could get out. For an hour after school was dismissed I could not articulate a whole word, solely from excitement & indignation. All my fostered notions of honour & personal character had been despised & outraged, & myself treated with indignity. I went in the afternoon to the trustees of the school, stated my case, produced my evidence, & had an examination made. The next morning but four boys went to school, & the day following the career of Mr. Wood ended. For several years after this affair, the notion of being revenged upon the perpetrator of this insult was frequently in my mind. As I grew larger & stronger, so as to be nearly a fair match for him, I determined that if I ever encountered him nothing but a full & unequivocal apology from the man should prevent my trying the utmost of my powers upon him. One evening, during the year before I entered college, I thought I saw him passing down a lane near where I was. I followed at a rapid pace, but on coming nearer, it proved to be another man. Had I been in a duelling country, I should have challenged him instantly, even the day I left his school; & I could understand, in this case, somewhat of the feeling of a duellist.

Hermann Sudermann
(1857-1928)

The fantasy life of thirteen-year-old Hermann Sudermann is reported here in a passage from the German novelist's autobiography, *The Book of My Youth*.* At the time, he was living with a maternal aunt and attending a local school, his own parents being too impoverished to support him. His imaginative dreams enabled him to transcend the barriers of time and space and poverty. Sudermann's daydreams centered on wealth, power and status, enabling him to live a glamorous life and dispelling some of the drabness and loneliness of actual circumstances. "Everything which I lacked in the other portion of my life," he wrote, "was given me here as a free dowry of destiny."

His dreams of greatness collapsed under the pressure of an almost unendurable anxiety which arose at this time. *He had lice!* And lice, for the status-conscious youth, meant being "low, neglected, looking like a beggar child, dirty. . . . " The lice reimposed reality on him; the vermin blasted his daydreams. For when the force of reality took over, the fantasies no longer worked.

My life became more and more divided into two halves. One I shared in common with all those around me, and there I was simply a harmless, quiet youngster who fought vigorously if he was beaten or jeered at, but who made it up quickly after every quarrel. But the higher portion of my life belonged to me alone. From it there arose a Jacob's ladder straight into heaven. There I was king, statesman, a sailor circumnavigating the world, and a prophet. There I held concourse with the great men of all times, and there a vast picture book was continually spread out before me. There I was noble, brave, generous, immeasurably rich, loved by all women, and the ruler of all. There I conquered the cleverest by the force of my speech, and was equal to the most learned in the fullness of my knowledge. In short,

*Reprinted by permission of The Bodley Head, Ltd. Copyright 1923. Pp. 102-105.

everything which I lacked in the other portion of my life was given me here as a free dowry of destiny. These dreams of greatness between the airy walls of which I was only too happy, one day collapsed miserably, in view of a discovery which robbed me of all self-respect and plunged me into despair.

For some time I had noticed a curious sensation on my head which was half painful and half a tickling, and which made me shudder far down my neck. It would usually disappear under pressure of my hand and with a little scratching. But if I had to sit still, as, for instance, at table or even at school, it bothered me so much that I often jumped up and ran to the door without asking for permission to do so. It was a disease, I felt, and certainly one which I could not talk about. An intuition which was more painful than the disease itself told me that. And one day I found out what it was—something too terrible and incomprehensible—*I had lice!* I, Hermann Sudermann, the son of respectable parents, and my mother's darling; I, the chosen genius who was at home with the highest in humanity, and as noble as the noblest in my feelings—I had lice! Lice like any beggar child, dirty and neglected, who would not have been allowed to come into our rooms at home.

It was at the municipal petroleum sheds, the control of which had been handed over to my "good aunt," that I made the crushing discovery in handing out the casks. When the carters had driven off I locked myself in so as not to be surprised, and ran from shed to shed, crying: "Mamma! Mamma! Mamma!"

But mamma was a long way off, and if I had ventured to confess to the "good aunt" instead, who knew no pardon for much smaller faults, I should have been turned out on the spot. I could not even think of confiding in Blechschmidt. I had with difficulty gained a certain amount of respect from my companions. The jeers which had so often tortured me and driven me to despair before were just beginning to be less frequent, and if he had laughed at my misfortune I would rather have thrown myself into the river Elbing than allow the floods of scorn which were sure to follow to be poured over my unfortunate head. And so the only thing to do was to bear the burden of my shame by myself, and wait for a miracle to happen which would relieve me. During the days and weeks which now followed, I learned to know all the tortures of a guilty conscience. A murderer who has to carry the knowledge of the blood which he has shed as a guilty secret for all his life cannot have much more to bear.

A few years later, when I was in the first class, one of my school friends, who was otherwise by no means very intimate with me, came to me one evening with a curiously shy look round my room, bolted the door behind him, and fell before me as if he had been felled by an ax, and sobbed into the hands he held before his face, "I am syphilitic." And when I picked him up and comforted him, and took him off to get the necessary advice, I thought continually, remembering my days of anguish, how happy he was in that he was able to confess.

I do not know what would have ultimately happened to me, owing to this daily increasing despair, if I had not suddenly been pushed into a chair one day by the "good aunt," and before I could protect myself found myself hopelessly betrayed by two or three strokes of a tooth comb. And how thankful I was to her! I was not hunted out of the house to join the criminals; I got only a good scolding because I had put up with the evil for so long, until traces of my disease had made themselves visible around me without my knowing it. In the period which followed she also endeavored to spread the mantle of love over my wickedness. But in the twilight when, as usual, she passed her terrible judgment over the wickedness of the world, she could not help remembering to give an occasional verbal castigation to those of her fellow creatures who suffered from vermin or the itch or other disgusting diseases. My cousin, however, nodded with an early developed malice at these passages, and scratched herself with the nail of her little finger, first behind her right ear, and, if I pretended not to notice this, then right behind at the back of her head. But what did I care? I was saved, and could raise my head again and look forward fearlessly to the future.

But I only received my full absolution during the long holidays which this year I was allowed to spend at home. How my cup ran over with happiness! Then I took my courage in both hands and confessed to my mother. And when she took my dishonored close-cropped head between both her hands, kissed it, and said no more than, "My poor boy," then I suddenly felt that everything was in order.

I have experienced many a prick of conscience, many times a sense of guilt, during my life, and been obliged to put up with them in my heart if they were not to be shaken off. But none has tortured me more than the horror which I experienced at thirteen at being infected by these vermin, and the fear of being outcast from the society of respectable people.

Crashing Thunder
(? - ?)

Paul Radin, the anthropologist and scholar, has edited the life of a remarkable man, Crashing Thunder, a Winnebago Indian. In the introduction to the autobiography, Radin gives some background to the dynamics of Crashing Thunder's behavior.*

As a child he was markedly nonsuggestible and he afterwards passes successively from the role of a man about town to that of a pimp, a thief, a murderer, and a coward, finally to develop into an excellent philosopher and something of a moralist. And yet he always feels himself the same, no better or worse at the end than at the beginning. He passes no judgment, he makes no evaluations on what he has done. In his own eyes he is no better when he finally succeeds in living up to a certain standard of self-restraint that would have made him a hero in any standard European biography than he was when, to save himself from imprisonment, he, in the most selfish fashion conceivable, betrays his companions who had participated in a murder which he had planned and for which he got all the glory. The question of good and bad simply does not present itself to him, because the task he had set himself did not entail the passing of judgments but the giving of as accurate an account of his life as was possible for him to give.

It would be both incorrect and stupid to imagine that he was either morally blunted or unintelligent or that he did not have many of those half-mystical strivings that so many of us have. All his life, in fact, can be said to have been spent in the search of an experience which his marked nonsuggestibility when a child prevented him from then obtaining. The fundamental religious experience of every member of the tribe to which he belonged was obtained in early youth. It consisted of fasting, of retiring at night to some lonely and inaccessible spot where one could commune undisturbed with the deities. Most youths got it. It was something of a disgrace not to. Yet he did not. In spite of his honestly persuading his father that he had been properly blessed, he never deluded himself about the matter. He always felt the stigma attached to his failure to experience what all the others had obtained, and in his inconsistent fashion he tried to find some substitute. When he finally got the experience he had been seeking, although it had come to him in the most devious and unexpected manner, he recognized it at once, was satisfied, and became a good man, even from the normal Christian standpoint.

In the passage which follows, Crashing Thunder describes the

*From *The Autobiography of a Winnebago Indian* edited by Paul Radin. Reprinted by permission of University of California Press. 1920.

War Bundle Feast, a ceremony of the Winnebago Indians consecrated to the spirits concerned with the bestowing of war powers. The fourteen-year-old boy was unable to keep his attention fixed firmly and exclusively on the fast or the rite as he was required to do. His mind centered on women all the time. He imagined that he had done something great and had risen thereby in their esteem. Because his thoughts were constantly deflected in other directions, he did not obtain the blessing of the spirits.*

Now the feasters were to eat again. A separate kettle had been put on for us (boys) and we were to eat first. They then called upon a man to eat out of our plate. The name of this man was *Blue-sitter*. He was to eat out of our plate first. He was a holy man, a doctor, and a brave man (one who had obtained war honors). Four deer-ribs were dished out to me in a wooden bowl. Then the one who was to eat out of my plate came and sat down near my dish and began to handle my food. He tore it up in small pieces for me. Then he began to tell me of his blessing.

He told me how all the great spirits had blessed him—the Sun, the Moon, the Thunder-birds, the Earth, the Heaven, the Day, and all the spirits that exist in the heavens. All these blessed him, he said. And the spirits who are on the earth, and those under the waters, all these talked to him, he said. (Thinking) of this power (he possessed) did he partake of my food. I was to go through battle unharmed and I was to obtain some war honor. My children, if I had any, were to enjoy a good and happy life. Thus he spoke.

Then he took a piece of my food in his mouth and placed some in my mouth four times. Then I continued eating and the rest of the feasters began to eat. For quite some time I was not able to eat much. Through it all I was not in the least conscious of any dreams or blessings. (All that I was aware of) was that all the people around were taking pity upon me.

I, on the contrary, had my mind fixed on women all the time. (In doing all these things) I imagined that I had accomplished something great and that I had risen greatly in their (women's) estimation. Even though I tried to render myself pitiable in the sight of the spirits, yet, through it all, my thoughts were centered upon women. I was never lowly at heart and never really desired the blessing of the spirits. All I thought of was that I was a great man and that the women would regard me as a great man.

---

*From *The Autobiography of a Winnebago Indian*. P. 397.

Ethel Waters
(1900-   )

The famous American Negro star of the stage and screen, Ethel Waters, begins her autobiography with the following startling declarative sentences:

"I was never a child. I was never coddled, or liked, or understood by my family. I never felt I belonged. I was always an outsider. I was born out of wedlock, but that had nothing to do with all this. To people like mine that just didn't mean much. Nobody brought me up. I just ran wild as a little girl. I was bad, always a leader of the street gang in stealing and general hell-raising. By the time I was seven I knew all about sex in the raw. I could outcurse any stevedore and took a sadistic pleasure in shocking people [44]."

With a childhood as depersonalized and lacking in love as hers, it was small wonder that when Ethel Waters worked as a chambermaid in a hotel in Philadelphia during her adolescence, she would spend a goodly portion of her time standing in front of a full-length mirror daydreaming of Miss Waters, the great actress, accepting the plaudits and adoration of the multitudes for her magnificent stage performances.*

I had the most fun at the Harrod Apartments on the days when I substituted for one of the chambermaids. I was allotted a half-hour to make up each room but soon became so efficient I could finish the work in ten minutes.

Then I'd lock the door, stand in front of the full-length mirror, and transform myself into Ethel Waters, the great actress. I played all sorts of roles and also the audience, mugging and acting like mad.

First of all I'd applaud vociferously. When I played the "other woman" in the play I'd pretend she was some girl enemy of mine and hiss her shamelessly. Was *she* a terrible performer!

When I'd finish portraying all the roles I'd seen played by Negro stock companies I'd imitate the acts I'd seen at the Standard Theatre in Philadelphia, great Negro actors like Drake and Walker; Sandy Burns, the comic; Sam Russell, the Bilow of Bilow and Ashes; Butterbeans and Susie, the Original Stringbeans; and the truly gifted Whit-

---

*From *His Eye Is on the Sparrow, An Autobiography* by Ethel Waters. Reprinted by permission of Doubleday & Co., Inc. Copyright 1950, 1951, Ethel Waters and Charles Samuels. Pp. 65-66.

man Sisters. I'd also imitate the performers I'd seen in the beer grottoes and rathskellers around Philadelphia where I sometimes extravagantly drank cream soda at twenty-five cents a bottle.

The vaudeville half of the entertainment started with an announcement by the master of ceremonies: "And now, folks, the famous and spectacular Miss Ethel Waters will sing!" Again there was wild applause from the eager audience, followed by joyful cries of:

"Come on, Miss Waters! Please sing for us, Miss Waters!"

After a slight and dignified pause I'd persuade myself to bow graciously before the mirror. Sometimes I'd be so carried away by my own magnificent performance that I'd forget where I was or what I was doing.

In spite of all this, my big ambition was not then show business. What I dreamed of was becoming the lady's maid and companion of some wealthy woman who was traveling around the world and would take me with her.

But it was about this time that I adopted a manner that caused people to mistake me for a theatrical performer. I was always pleased when they asked, "Are you a show person?" But I'd tell them, "No, I work as a scullion in the Harrod Apartments."

Sometimes I thought it must be my clothes that made them think I was an actress. I was still buying these at the welfare places and rummage sales and was convinced these secondhand outfits showed me off to great advantage. I told myself I didn't give a damn what others thought of my appearance, but I was delighted whenever complimented.

REFERENCES

1. Amiel, Henri-Frédéric. *Amiel's Journal.* New York: A. L. Burt Co., n.d., p. 68.
2. Buber, Martin. Mein Weg zum Chassidismus. In: Schwartz, Leo W. (Ed.), *Memoirs of My People.* New York: Farrar & Rinehart, 1943, p. 517.
3. Bychowski, Gustav. On relations between the ego and superego. *Psychoanal. Rev.,* 30:313, 1943.
4. Catherine the Great. *Memoirs.* New York: Alfred A. Knopf, 1927, p. 76.
5. *Ibid.,* p. 13.
6. *Ibid.,* p. 24.
7. Chesterton, G. K. *The Autobiography of G. K. Chesterton.* New York: Sheed & Ward, 1936, pp. 52-53.

8. Cournos, John. *Autobiography.* New York: G. P. Putnam's Sons, 1935, p. 14.
9. Deutsch, Helene. *The Psychology of Women, A Psychoanalytic Interpretation.* Vol. I. New York: Grune & Stratton, 1944, pp. 94, 130.
10. Ellis, Havelock. *My Life.* Boston: Houghton Mifflin Co., 1939, p. 132.
11. Erikson, Erik T. Ego development and historical change. In: *Identity and the Life Cycle. Psychol. Issues,* 1:26, 1959.
12. ————. Late adolescence. In: Funkenstein, Daniel H. (Ed.), *The Student and Mental Health.* Cambridge, Mass.: World Federation for Mental Health, 1959, p. 68.
13. *Ibid.,* p. 76.
14. Fenichel, Otto. *The Psychoanalytic Theory of Neurosis.* New York: W. W. Norton & Co., 1945, p. 50.
15. *Ibid.,* p. 111.
16. Freud, Anna. Adolescence. In Eissler, Ruth S., et. al. (Eds.), *The Psychoanalytic Study of the Child.* Vol. 13. New York: International Universities Press, 1958, p. 260.
17. *Ibid.,* p. 264.
18. Freud, Anna. *The Ego and the Mechanisms of Defence.* New York: International Universities Press, 1946, p. 159.
19. *Ibid.*
20. Fry, Elizabeth. *Memoir of the Life of Elizabeth Fry.* 2 Vols., 1847.
21. Gibbon, Edward. *The Autobiography of Edward Gibbon.* New York: Dutton Everyman's Library, 1911, p. 18.
22. Gide, André. *If It Die. An Autobiography.* New York: Modern Library Paperback, 1935, p. 91.
23. Jones, Ernest. Some problems of adolescence. *Brit. J. Psychol.,* 13:41, 1922.
24. *Ibid.,* p. 42.
25. Kodama, Yoshio. *I Was Defeated.* Japan: Robert Booth & Taro Fukuda, 1951, p. 12.
26. Kogan, David S. *The Diary of David S. Kogan.* New York: Beechhurst Press, 1955, p. 57.
27. *Ibid.,* p. 37.
28. Leonard, William Ellery. *The Locomotive-God.* New York: Century Co., 1927, p. 100.
29. McCurdy, Harold C. The childhood pattern of genius. In: *The Smithsonian Report for 1958.* Washington, D.C.: Smithsonian Institution, 1959, p. 538.
30. *Ibid.,* pp. 538-539.

31. Meyer, Agnes E. *Out of These Roots. The Autobiography of an American Woman.* Boston: Little, Brown & Co., 1953, pp. 30-31.

32. Mitchell, Lucy Sprague. *Two Lives. The Story of Wesley Clair Mitchell and Myself.* New York: Simon & Schuster, 1953, p. 66.

33. Nowell, Elizabeth (Ed.). *The Letters of Thomas Wolfe.* New York: Charles Scribner's Sons, 1956, p. xvi.

34. Omori, Annie Shepley, & Doi, Kochi (Eds.). *Diaries of Court Ladies of Old Japan.* Boston: Houghton Mifflin Co., 1920, p. xxxii.

35. Pearson, Gerald H. P. *Adolescence and the Conflict of Generations.* New York: W. W. Norton & Co., 1958, p. 82.

36. Scott, Sir Walter. *Memoirs of the Early Times of Sir Walter Scott, Written by Himself.* Vol. I. London: Macmillan Co., 1914, pp. 22-23.

37. *Ibid.,* p. 31.

38. Shaffer, Laurance F., & Shoben, Edward J., Jr. *The Psychology of Adjustment.* Boston: Houghton Mifflin Co., 1956, p. 206.

39. Shore, Emily. *Journal.* In Ponsonby, Arthur, *More English Diaries.* London: Methuen & Co., 1927, p. 206.

40. Steffens, Lincoln. *The Autobiography of Lincoln Steffens.* New York: Harcourt, Brace & Co., 1931, p. 99.

41. Sullivan, Harry Stack. *The Interpersonal Theory of Psychiatry.* New York: W. W. Norton & Co., 1953, p. 263.

42. Symonds, Peercival M. *Adolescent Fantasy.* New York: Columbia University Press, 1949, pp. 218-219.

43. *Ibid.,* p. 225.

44. Waters, Ethel. *His Eye Is on the Sparrow, an Autobiography.* Garden City, N.Y.: Doubleday & Co., 1951, p. 1.

45. Wittels, Fritz. The ego of the adolescent. In: Eissler, K. R. (Ed.), *Searchlights on Delinquency.* New York: International Universities Press, 1949, p. 259.

46. Wolfe, Thomas. *Look Homeward, Angel.* New York: Charles Scribner's Sons, 1929, pp. 596-598.

47. ———. *The Story of a Novel.* New York: Charles Scribner's Sons, 1936, p. 39.

CHAPTER FIVE

The Conflict of Generations

Perhaps more has been written about the conflict between adolescents and their parents than almost any other phase of adolescent development. Anyone who attempts to advise or help parents solve problems with their adolescent children finds himself in a situation fraught with peril, because there is no formula which can be applied. In regard to his parents, the adolescent is engaged in an emotional struggle of extreme urgency and immediacy. His libido is detaching itself from the parents and cathecting new love objects. His preoccupation with crushes, with homosexual or heterosexual relationships, or with his inability to resolve the original oedipal situation, provide some clues to the basic difficulties in parent-child relations. The struggle between the id and the ego during adolescence produces demonstrations of the upheaval which is universally observed, for the upset is no more than the external indication that internal adjustments are taking place.

Basic to the adolescent's struggle in emancipating himself from the primary love objects is not only the impulse for emotional expression of the struggle but also the active physical defense against the objects. Anna Freud (7) states that "It seems to be generally accepted that strong fixation to the mother, dating not only from the oedipal but from the preoedipal attachment to her, renders adolescence especially difficult." Her emphasis rests on the defenses the adolescent uses. By way of illustration, she cites the use of regression which may bring transitory relief to the ego by emptying the oedipal fantasies of their libidinal cathexis.

262

The adolescent's dependence on his parents is based not so much on his physical wants but rather on the need for love, a characteristic phenomenon of the oedipal phase. This phase normally diminishes during latency, but with the onset of puberty, it becomes vigorously re-established. "The regression which takes place during adolescence to the infantile oedipus relation to the parents," says Jones (10), "is chiefly manifested on the positive side only in relation to the father (with the boy), as hostility and rivalry; the attitude towards the mother at this period is mainly a negative one, a rejecting of caresses and intimacies that up till then had been permitted. At the same time greater activity begins to be shown towards other love objects and the desire to love increases at the expense of the desire to be loved. When the fully adult stage is reached the incestuous attachments are abandoned; a strange love object is found, who is loved not only with feelings of an 'inhibited' nature but also with those of a directly sexual kind. When this process is complete, then adult independence is achieved in all respects. Dependence can therefore be defined as persistent incestuous attachment of the libido and independence as the disposal of it in some other direction. The nonincestuous disposal of it may be either in relation to a love object or it may take the form of sublimation; most often it is both."

The universality of the recapitulation of the oedipal phenomenon in adolescence can be inferred from the investigation by Whiting, Kluckhohn and Anthony (21) in their study of the Kwoma, a primitive tribe of New Guinea. The Kwoma infant is held on the mother's lap all day and sleeps in her arms until he is weaned, at the age of two or three. During this time, the father sleeps by himself and has no intercourse with the wife. The child is weaned drastically—suddenly and all at once. He is put in his own bed and there is no more lap sitting. The parents resume intercourse. The inevitable trauma results: the child varies between sadness and anger, weeping and violent temper tantrums. The intense dependency of the boy on his mother and the rivalry with the father are evident. At puberty, the initiation ceremony includes circumcision, exposure to the wintry cold, the prohibition to drink a drop of water for three months, eating unpalatable food, and running the gauntlet between two rows of men who beat the adolescent with clubs. Any infraction of the ceremonial rites is punished severely. This type of initiation is necessary, the authors assert, because of the oedipal relationship previously established: "It is necessary (a) to put a final stop to [the boy's] wish to return to his mother's arms and lap, (b) to prevent an open revolt against his father who has displaced him from his mother's bed, and (c) to ensure identification with the adult males of the society. In other words, Kwoma infancy so magnifies the conditions which should produce oedipus rivalry that the specific cultural adjustment of ceremonial hazing, isolation from women, and symbolic castration, etc., must be made to resolve it."

The adolescent of New Guinea is not far removed from his cousins either emotionally or in time. Illustrations of oedipal conflict are given here, representing the old Roman Empire, Italy, Russia, the United States, France and Austria.

Saint Augustine
(354-430)

Monica, mother of Augustine, was emotionally alienated from her husband and had grown especially close to her son. Augustine tells us how she wept over him daily, pinned all her hopes on him and prayed for his soul. Kligerman (9a) states in his discussion of the Confessions, "It is not hard to detect an erotic quality in such behavior. Frigid hypermoral women frequently find concealed incestuous gratification in such stormy emotional scenes with their sons. For him it must have been an extremely seductive yet frustrating process, and sheds light on the turbulence of his adolescence. Augustine was a typically overstimulated child, culminating in a character type who seeks constantly to master his overwhelming tension and never finds adequate discharge—hence his violent emotionality and passionate fervor.

"When Augustine began to show his sexuality, his mother was filled with trembling anxiety and begged him not to fornicate and especially not to 'defile another's wife.' Whose wife did she have in mind? Apparently she was frightened by her own incestuous impulses which could scarcely have a reassuring effect on her son. On the other hand, she did not want to lose him and opposed his marriage. . . . If Augustine could not fornicate, commit adultery or marry, not much remained. In effect, then, Monica demanded that

Augustine relinquish sexuality in favor of the Church, which meant, at an unconscious level, that he should belong to her forever. . . . However, Augustine did not give up so easily. The *Confessions,* written ten years after his mother's victory in his conversion, praise her piety and castigate his own sinfulness, but the events at the time show vividly how desperately he struggled for his manhood."

It is notable that St. Augustine's father was a stimulant of his incestuous wishes rather than a help in repressing them. This is perhaps why he needed a stronger father, a god to command him. It is worthy of note, too, that Augustine considered his mother "God's handmaiden."*

Concerning his father, a freeman of Thagaste, the assister of his son's studies, and on the admonitions of his mother on the preservation of chastity. And for that year my studies were intermitted, while after my return from Madaura (a neighbouring city, whither I had begun to go in order to learn grammar and rhetoric), the expenses for a further residence at Carthage were provided for me; and that was rather by the determination than the means of my father, who was but a poor freeman of Thagaste. To whom do I narrate this? Not unto Thee, my God; but before Thee unto my own kind, even to that small part of the human race who may chance to light upon these writings. And to what end? That I and all who read the same may reflect out of what depths we are to cry unto Thee. For what cometh nearer to Thine ears than a confessing heart and a life of faith? For who did not extol and praise my father, in that he went even beyond his means to supply his son with all the necessaries for a far journey for the sake of his studies? For many far richer citizens did not the like for their children. But yet this same father did not trouble himself how I grew towards Thee, nor how chaste I was, so long as I was skilful in speaking —however barren I was to Thy tilling, O God, who art the sole true and good Lord of my heart, which is Thy field.

But while, in that sixteenth year of my age, I resided with my parents, having holiday from school for a time (this idleness being imposed upon me by my parents' necessitous circumstances), the thorns of lust grew rank over my head, and there was no hand to pluck them out. Moreover when my father, seeing me at the baths, perceived that I was becoming a man, and was stirred with a restless youthfulness, he,

---

*From *The Confessions of Saint Augustine.* Reprinted by permission of Liveright Publishers. 1942. Pp. 29-32.

as if from this anticipating future descendants, joyfully told it to my mother; rejoicing in that intoxication wherein the world so often forgets Thee, its Creator, and falls in love with Thy creature instead of Thee, from the invisible wine of its own perversity turning and bowing down to the most infamous things. But in my mother's breast Thou hadst even now begun Thy temple, and the commencement of Thy holy habitation, whereas my father was only a catechumen as yet, and that but recently. She then started up with a pious fear and trembling; and, although I had not yet been baptized, she feared those crooked ways in which they walk who turn their back to Thee, and not their face.

Woe is me! and dare I affirm that Thou heldest Thy peace, O my God, while I strayed farther from Thee? Didst Thou then hold Thy peace to me? And whose words were they but Thine which by my mother, Thy faithful handmaid, Thou pouredst into my ears, none of which sank into my heart to make me do it? For she despised, and I remember privately warned me, with a great solicitude, "not to commit fornication; but above all things never to defile another man's wife." These appeared to me but womanish counsels, which I should blush to obey. But they were Thine, and I knew it not, and I thought that Thou heldest Thy peace, and that it was she who spoke, through whom Thou heldest not Thy peace to me, and in her person wast despised by me, her son, "the son of Thy handmaid, Thy servant." But this I knew not, and rushed on headlong with such blindness, that amongst my equals I was ashamed to be less shameless, when I heard them pluming themselves upon their disgraceful acts, yea, and glorying all the more in proportion to the greatness of their baseness; and I took pleasure in doing it, not for the pleasure's sake only, but for the praise. What is worthy of dispraise but vice? But I made myself out worse than I was, in order that I might not be dispraised; and when in anything I had not sinned as the abandoned ones, I would affirm that I had done what I had not, that I might not appear abject for being more innocent, or of less esteem for being more chaste.

Behold with what companions I walked the streets of Babylon, in whose filth I was rolled, as if in cinnamon and precious ointments. And that I might cleave the more tenaciously to its very centre, my invisible enemy trod me down, and seduced me, I being easily seduced. Nor did the mother of my flesh, although she herself had ere this fled "out of the midst of Babylon,"—progressing, however, but slowly in the skirts of it,—in counselling me to chastity, so bear in mind what she had been told about me by her husband as to restrain in the limits of conjugal affection (if it could not be cut away to the quick) what she knew to be destructive in the present and dangerous in the future. But she took no heed of this, for she was afraid lest a wife should prove a hindrance and a clog to my hopes. Not those hopes of the future world, which my mother had in Thee; but the hope of learning, which both my parents were too anxious that I should acquire,—he, because he had little or no thought of Thee, and but vain thoughts for me— she, because she calculated that those usual courses of learning would not only be no drawback, but rather a furtherance towards my attaining Thee. For thus I conjecture, recalling as well as I can the dispositions of my parents. The reins, meantime, were slackened towards me beyond the restraint of due severity, that I might play, yea, even to dissoluteness, in whatsoever I fancied. And in all there was a mist, shutting out from my sight the brightness of Thy truth, O my God; and my iniquity displayed itself as from very "fatness."

Carlo Goldoni
(1707-1793)

Goldoni, in a burst of feeling which surprised even himself ("This is a digression foreign to these memoirs"), related the love he wanted from his mother and then discoursed on what mother love meant to him. In facile juxtaposition he described his own welcome home and his father's, the consolation he found in his mother's love "after having been seduced and deceived" by others, and the delight he felt in her tender attachment to him.* The mutuality of the tenderness and his mother's constant affection for him were the secure haven in Goldoni's life. He equated succoring love with genital love on an unconscious genital level. In his attempt to deny his sexual love and put it on a succoring basis, Goldoni was able to maintain his necessary, protective defenses.

On our arrival at Chiozza we were received as a mother receives her dear son, as a wife receives her dear husband after a long absence. I was delighted to see again that virtuous mother who was so tenderly attached to me; after having been seduced and deceived I required to be beloved. This was another sort of love; but till I could relish the pleasures of a respectable and agreeable passion, I found my consolation in maternal love; my mother and myself were very partial to each

*From *Memoirs* by Carlo Goldoni. Reprinted by permission of Alfred A. Knopf. 1926. P. 75.

other; but how different the love of a mother for her son from that of a son for his mother! Children love from gratitude; but mothers love by a natural impulse, and self-love has not a less share in their tender friendship; they love the fruits of their conjugal union, conceived by them with satisfaction, carried by them with pain in their bosom, and brought into the world with so much suffering. They have seen them grow up from day to day; they have enjoyed the first display of their innocence; they have been accustomed to see them, to love them, to watch over them . . . I am even disposed to believe that the last reason is the strongest of all, and that a mother would not be less fond of a child changed at nurse than of her own, provided she had *bonâ fide* received it for her own, had taken care of its first education, and been accustomed to caress and cherish it.

This is a digression foreign to these memoirs, but I like to gossip occasionally. . . .

Marie Bashkirtseff
(1860-1884)

The precocity of Marie Bashkirtseff is apparent in this resume of a conversation she had with her cousin (2). While her sixteen-year-old insight was superior to that of twenty-two-year-old Pascha, the latter was apparently fixated at the age when the initial oedipal phase usually occurs. Emotionally, Pascha was so attached to the primary love object that he could not see living without his mother. This passage illustrates the effect of the failure to cope with the repressed incestuous desire of the child for the opposite-sexed parent.

Although Marie had insight into Pascha's conflict, she had no awareness of her own similar problem. Her unbounded desire for fame as an artist replaced her desire for the love of her mother. Her diary is frequently suggestive of the desire for masculinity in order to vie for her mother's love. She also tells, repeatedly, of her longing and seeking for the childhood love attachments to her mother, frequent travel in a symbolic search for the mother, unsuccessful romantic attachments with young men, and falling in love with ineligible or unattainable men.

Wednesday, August 23rd, 1876

I have written to mamma almost as much as I have in my journal.

That will do her more good than all the doctors in the world. I pretend to be very happy, but I am not so yet. I have related everything in the most exact manner, but I shall not be sure of anything until the end of the story. We shall see some day. God is very good.

Pascha is my *real* cousin, the son of my father's sister. He puzzles me. This morning we were talking, and my father's name was mentioned. I said that sons always criticised the actions of their fathers, and once in their place, did the same things, to be in their turn criticised by their children.

"That is perfectly true," he said, "but my sons will not criticise me, for I shall never marry."

After a moment, I replied: "There has never been a young man who has not said the same thing."

"Yes, but it is not the same thing."

"Why not?"

"Because I am twenty-two, and I have never been in love, and no woman has ever even attracted me."

"That is quite natural. Before that age, a man ought not to fall in love."

"What! How about those boys who begin at fourteen?"

"Those affairs have nothing to do with real love."

"Perhaps, but I am not like everyone else. I am hot-headed, and proud, and conceited, and then—"

"But those qualities which you speak of—"

"Are good ones?"

"I think so."

Then, I don't remember why, he told me that, if his mother should die, he would go crazy.

"Yes, for a year, and then—"

"No, I should be crazy, I know it."

"For a year, for everything is effaced by new faces."

"Then you deny eternal sentiments and virtue?"

"Positively."

Agnes E. Meyer
(1887-   )

Agnes Meyer's family moved from Pelham, New York, to Manhattan coincident with, it would seem, the time of the recapitulation of the oedipal phase in her twelfth year. "The gap that springs up and steadily widens between parents and children during adolescence," she wrote in her autobiography, "appeared with a sudden shock for me because it was accentuated by a new environment which meant nothing but aridity to me. This whole transition period was sheer pain, all the more acute because a child of twelve, so suddenly uprooted, becomes inarticulate and suffers in silence a spiritual chaos which he cannot understand and which still defies my adult attempts at retrospection and analysis.*"

The girl's growing realization that the idealized father was a myth led to a hysterical reaction and to disillusionment. From the time she was thirteen until she was sixteen, Agnes "hoped that his metamorphosis was just a terrible nightmare from which we would both wake up and begin our common life anew." But this was just a hope and her love turned "into an exaggerated burning shame."

This disillusionment with the father is a natural development of the second oedipal phase. As the female adolescent grows up, the father is no longer fair game for her. His all-wisdom and behavior no longer appear so wonderful. The adolescent's love for the parent frequently turns to hate, a reaction formation because she is too afraid to love the father and must separate herself from him. The reaction formation defense might have been used by her father, as well, for by not giving his approval to Agnes' attending college, he betrayed his own expressed ideals and thus hurt her irreparably.

Throughout my four years in high school, with their social isolation, my relationship to the adored father of my childhood days had been steadily deteriorating. What actually happened to transform the model parent whom we children knew when we lived in the country into an ever more irresponsible human being has always remained a mystery to me. Years after my father had died I was told that even before we moved to New York, he had become emotionally involved with a beautiful young woman who was one of his law clients. Mercifully I knew nothing of this as a child; for even as an adult this revelation still had the power to tear open wounds I thought had been cicatrized by time. Perhaps this experience started him on the downward path. Perhaps the rigors of family life and heavy professional responsibilities had always been too exacting a burden for so artistic a temperament. Perhaps the city offered my father more opportunity to live the self-indulgent life that now absorbed him more and more to the

---

*From *Out of these Roots* by Agnes E. Meyer. Reprinted by permission of Little, Brown & Co. 1953. Pp. 39-43.

neglect of his law practice, his wife and his children.

Whatever the reasons, my growing realization that the idealized father of my childhood was a myth of my own making had a disastrous effect upon me. What aggravated my almost hysterical reaction to this disillusionment was the worry caused my mother by his Bohemian ways and by his growing indifference to his law clients and to the fact that butcher and grocer bills must be paid. Instead of earning a living for his family, he wrote books and dramas that were incredibly amateurish. One was a play about the German revolutionary, General Peter Muhlenberg, which was actually produced. In the last act the entire American and British forces seemed to be gathered on the stage. My brother Fred and I commented to each other that if there had been as many people in the audience as there were on the stage, the event would have been a success. Such experiments created mounting debts to which my father was sublimely indifferent. Failure after failure only encouraged him in the idea of being a misunderstood genius.

As an adult, I can appreciate the comedy of this development and realize that I took the situation too tragically. My poor mother, who should have been far more affected, could invent the most elaborate excuses for his conduct and even shared his illusion that an overwhelming artistic success was just around the corner. But it is one thing to read a Dickens novel and quite another to have a Micawber in the family. Because my father had been for me a knight in shining armor, I could make no compromise between my youthful hero and the harsh reality. For several years I still hoped that his metamorphosis was just a terrible nightmare from which we would both wake up and begin our common life anew. But when his irresponsibility became more and more pronounced, my love turned into an exaggerated burning shame that haunted me all the more because I was too proud and too deeply wounded to confess it even to my brothers.

What finally broke the golden cord that held me to him was the dawning realization that he no longer wanted me to go to college. He never expressed it in so many words, but from my mother I gleaned that he would be freer to pursue his fantastic mode of life, if I should begin remunerative work sooner than would be possible if I continued my academic career. The thought that the father who had inspired in me the love of learning was betraying the very ideals he had taught me to cherish was the chief cause of the deep wound in my soul that took so many years to heal. And then it healed only on the surface. For there are such things as mortal blows to which the heart can reconcile itself but from which it can never wholly recover.

To understand the anguish with which I lived for years afterward, it is necessary to remember not only my profound emotional involvement with my father but my Lutheran upbringing in a warmly religious household. The commandment "Honor thy father and thy mother" had been graven into my being not through the memorizing of mere words but through the happy family life I had lived as a child. This moral imperative was shattered and I was aghast. I was ashamed not only of my father but of myself.

I was also haunted by a sharp awareness that my father and I were two of a kind. In my heart I realized that I loved complete freedom and hated work, continuous effort and discipline as much as he did. This insight terrified me. He, on the other hand, was tortured by the knowledge that his only daughter, whom he could not help loving and protecting, had his own passionate nature and uncontrollable love of life. He suffered acutely, if unnecessarily, when some young man brought me home late at night from wholly innocent expeditions to the theater or concert or the most decorous parties. The scenes between us, when he tried to exert an authority which I was no longer willing to accept, were all the more searing because the distance, formality and restraints that had been so habitual between us as long as we understood each other, now broke down and gave way to the violence of emotion that was characteristic of both of us. And like all people who are "well brought up," these occasional bursts of temper left us both exhausted in mind and body and sick of ourselves and life in general.

Yet our silences, the things we never said, the fact that our eyes no longer met in glances of mutual understanding, these transformations tortured me and I am sure they tortured him more than the few open clashes that were my fault more than his. Occasionally my nerves were stretched to the breaking point, ordeals from which I recovered only because I was physically robust, and because my childhood sense of security had given me an indomitable love of life. But the lonely battle for self-control and survival was a heavy load for an adolescent youngster.

Years later I acquired a certain skepticism as to the perspicacity of psychiatrists when I spent a day entertaining the famous Dr. Jung. He interspersed his amusing conversation with questions that invited confidences. As I parried all of them, he finally beamed his radiant personality straight at me and made one last effort to conquer my reticence: "You show no wounds," he murmured. "Certainly not," I replied calmly. "I don't understand it," said the great healer of neuroses. Thereupon I turned toward him as if at last I was about to confess all and said in my most confidential manner: "I'll tell you why, Doctor. It's because, like a healthy dog, I licked them all until they got well."

Yet the estrangement that grew up between my father and me had an immediate effect of a salutary nature. Since he no longer really wished me to go to college, I refused henceforth to accept any financial assistance from him. That meant I had to win scholarships and earn enough money to pay all my expenses. It was the first sensible idea that I had had in four years. It brought me down to earth from my bookish and musical ivory tower at least now and then. It did more to strengthen a character that had all my father's weaknesses than anything else that happened to me throughout the next four years of college life.

Anonymous
(? - ?)

"Gretel," the anonymous writer of this diary (which was withdrawn from circulation after its publication in the United States because it was believed impossible for a child to have written it), creates in the three entries reproduced below the classical picture of the revived oedipal phase in adolescence (1).

In the first entry, the young girl makes plans for life with father, while her mother and sister are on a holiday, as would a bride. She will bring different flowers, and fresh ones, to the dinner table, she wrote, with the implied criticism of her mother quite clear. In the second entry, her father plays the incestuous game with her—innocently and unconsciously, of course, as do most fathers with their daughters. And in the last entry, the expressions of love which the father displayed are prolonged by Gretel as much as she can. Finally, the manifest dream content in the last paragraph can be readily interpreted, for dreams represent the fulfillment of a wish (9).

May 31st

They wanted me to go and stay with Hella [her best friend] for the month when Mother and Dora [her older sister] are away. It would be awfully nice, but I'm not going to, for I want to stay with Father. What would he do all alone at meal times, and whom would he have to talk to in the evenings? Father was really quite touched when I said this and he stroked my hair as he can and no one else, not even Mother. So I'm going to stay at home whatever happens. Flowers are very cheap now, so I shall put *different* flowers on the table every day, I shall go to the Market every day to buy a little posy, so that they can always be fresh. It would be stupid for me to go to the Brs., why should I, Resi [the servant] has been with us for such a long time, she knows how to do everything even if Mother is not there and everything else I can arrange. Father won't want for anything.

June 6th

Mother and Dora left early this morning. Mother has never gone away from us before for long at a time, so I cried a lot and so did she. Dora cried too, but I know on whose account. Father and I are alone now. At dinner he said to me: "My little housewife." It was so lovely. But it's frightfully quiet in the house, for 2 people don't talk so much as 4. It made me feel quite uncomfortable. . . .

June 9th

. . . Yesterday Father said: Poor little witch, it's very lonely for you now; but look here, Resi is no fit company for you; when your little tongue wants to wag, come to my room. And I was awfully stupid, I began to cry like anything and said: "Father, please don't be angry, I'll never think and never talk of such things any more." Father did not know at first what I meant, but afterwards it must have struck him, for he was so kind and gentle, and said: "No, no, Gretel, don't corrupt your youth with such matters, and when there's anything that bothers you, ask Mother, but not the servants. A girl of good family must not be too familiar with servants. Promise me." And then, though I'm so big he took me on his knee like a child and petted me because I was crying so. "It's all right, little Mouse, don't worry, you must not get so nervous as Dora. Give me a nice kiss, and then I'll come with you to your room and stay with you till you go to sleep." Of course I stayed awake on purpose as long as I could, till $\frac{1}{4}$ to 11.

And then I dreamed that Father was lying in Dora's bed so that when I woke up early in the morning I really looked across to see if he had not gone to bed there. But of course I'd only dreamed it.

Simone de Beauvoir

(1908-   )

The rivalry, impatience and bitter arguments which flare up
between the adolescent and the parent of the same sex during
the second oedipal phase are graphically illustrated in the following excerpts from a dutiful daughter's memoirs (3). At thirteen
and fourteen, Simone de Beauvoir's dissatisfaction with whatever
her mother said or did was abounding and seemingly abiding.
Although the arguments were violent, Simone was too dutiful to
break into open rebellion, perhaps because of the guilt feelings
she had. "I was jealous of the place [my mother] held in my father's
affections because my own passion for him had continued to grow."
Simone was dazzled by her father: he was misunderstood by others;
he told the wittiest stories; he was the most intelligent man she
knew; "he was the sovereign judge." She dreamed of having a more
intimate relationship with him but was rebuffed at every try.

I had lost the sense of security childhood gives, and nothing had
come to take its place. My parents' authority remained inflexible, but
as my critical sense developed I began to rebel against it more and
more. I couldn't see the point of visits, family dinners, and all those
tiresome social duties which my parents considered obligatory. Their
replies, "It's your duty" or "That just isn't done," didn't satisfy me at
all. My mother's eternal solicitude began to weigh me down. She had
her own "ideas" which she did not attempt to justify, and her decisions often seemed to me quite arbitrary. We had a violent argument
about a missal which I wanted to give my sister for her First Communion; I wanted to choose one bound in pale fawn leather, like
those which the majority of my schoolmates had; Mama thought that
one with a blue cloth cover would do just as well; I protested that the
money in my money box was for me to do what I liked with; she replied that one should not pay out twenty francs for a thing that could
be bought for fourteen. While we were buying bread at the baker's
and all the way up the stairs and in the house itself I held my own
against her. But in the end I had to give in, with rage in my heart,
vowing never to forgive her for what I considered to be an abuse of her
power over me. If she had often stood in my way, I think she would
have provoked me to open rebellion. But in the really important
things—my studies and the choice of my friends—she very rarely

meddled; she respected my work and my leisure too, only asking me to do little odd jobs for her like grinding the coffee or carrying the trash bin downstairs. I had the habit of obedience, and I believed that, on the whole, God expected me to be dutiful: the conflict that threatened to set me against my mother did not break out; but I was uneasily aware of its underlying presence. . . . In addition, I was jealous of the place she held in my father's affections because my own passion for him had continued to grow.

The more difficult life became for him, the more I was dazzled by my father's superior character; it did not depend on money or success, and so I used to tell myself that he had deliberately ignored these; that did not prevent me from being sorry for him: I thought he was not appreciated for his true value, that he was misunderstood and the victim of obscure cataclysms. I was all the more grateful to him now for his outbursts of gaiety, which were still quite frequent. He would tell stories, made wild fun of everybody, and said the wittiest things. When he stayed at home he would read us Victor Hugo and Rostand; he would talk about the writers he liked, about the theatre, great events of the past, and a host of other improving subjects which transported me far away from the everyday drabness of life. I couldn't imagine a more intelligent man than my father. In all the discussions at which I was present he always had the last word, and when he attacked people who were not present, he annihilated them. . . .

As long as he approved of me, I could be sure of myself. For years he had done nothing but heap praises on my head. But when I reached the awkward age, he was disappointed in me: he appreciated elegance and beauty in women. Not only did he fail to conceal his disillusionment from me, but he began showing more interest than before in my sister, who was still a pretty girl. He glowed with pride when she paraded up and down dressed as "The Queen of the Night." He sometimes took part in productions which his friend Monsieur Jeannot— a great advocate of religious drama—organized in the local church clubs; Poupette often played with him. Her face framed in her long fair hair, she played the part of the little girl in Max Maurey's *Le Pharmicien*. He taught her to recite fables, putting in gestures and expression. Though I would not admit it to myself, I was hurt by the understanding between them, and felt a vague resentment against my sister.

But my real rival was my mother. I dreamed of having a more intimate relationship with my father; but even on the rare occasions when we found ourselves alone together we talked as if she were there with us. When there was an argument, if I had appealed to my father, he would have said: "Do what your mother tells you!" I only once tried to get him on my side. He had taken us to the races at Auteuil; the course was black with people, it was hot, there was nothing happening, and I was bored; finally the horses were off: the people rushed toward the barriers, and their backs hid the track from my view. My father had hired folding chairs for us and I wanted to stand on mine to get a better view. "No!" said my mother, who detested crowds and had been irritated by all the pushing and shoving. I insisted that I should be allowed to stand on my folding chair. "When I say no, I *mean* no!" my mother declared. As she was looking after my sister, I turned to my father and cried furiously: "Mama is being ridiculous! Why can't I stand on my folding chair?" He simply lifted his shoulder in an embarrassed silence, and refused to take part in the argument.

At least this ambiguous gesture allowed me to assume that as far as he was concerned my father sometimes found my mother too domineering; I persuaded myself that there was a silent conspiracy between us. But I soon lost this illusion. One lunchtime there was talk of a wild-living cousin who considered his mother to be an idiot: on my father's own admission she actually was one. Yet he declared vehemently: "A child who sets himself up as a judge of his mother is an imbecile." I went scarlet and left the table, pretending I was feeling sick. I was judging my mother, and my father had struck a double blow at me by affirming their solidarity and by referring to me indirectly as an imbecile. What upset me even more is that I couldn't help passing judgment on the very sentence my father had just uttered: since my aunt's stupidity was plain to everyone, why shouldn't her son acknowledge it? It is no sin to tell oneself the truth, and besides, quite often, one tells oneself the truth unintentionally; at that very moment, for example, I couldn't help thinking what I thought: was that wrong of me? In one sense it was not, and yet my father's words made such a deep impression on me that I felt at once irreproachable and a monster of imbecility. After that, and perhaps partly because of that incident, I no longer believed in my father's absolute infallibility. Yet my parents still had the power to make me feel guilty; I accepted their verdicts while at the same time I looked upon myself with different eyes than theirs. My essential self still belonged to them as much as to me: but paradoxically the self they knew could only be a decoy now; it could be false. There was only one way of preventing this strange confusion: I would have to cover up superficial appearances, which were deceptive. I was used to guarding my tongue; I redoubled my vigilance. I took a further step. As I was not now admitting everything I thought, why not venture unmentionable acts? I was learning how to be secretive.

Parents and their adolescent children are generally separated by light-years of differences, regardless of the century in which they find themselves. Adolescence is regularly spoiled by adults who make the period more full of conflict than is necessary. Adults fear that the adolescent will not grow up to be a worker, that he will not be sufficiently obedient, co-operative or grateful, or that he will go astray sexually. Differences arise in philosophy about recreational and physical activities, educational choices, and values of certain habits and attitudes. These and many other anxieties on the part of adults cause the parent to be too frequently admonishing, scolding and criticizing. Not since early childhood has the adolescent been subjected to so many negative injunctions.

More likely than not, parental admonitions stem from feelings aroused by the children which touch upon their own repressed adolescence. For instance, "the knowledge or the suspicion that the adolescent son or adolescent daughter masturbates reminds the parent unconsciously of his own adolescent conflict and makes him incapable of dealing with it scientifically [16]." Thus, the strictness of the parents may be unnecessarily harsh.

In general, the parent acts too often as a brake on all the adolescent's strivings to choose a vocation and the educational preparation for it, to emanicipate himself, to make friends with the opposite sex, and to integrate himself. As an expected concomitant, rebellion against the parent is endemic among adolescents. But the rebellion is brought about not only by parental restraints, but also by those that exist within himself, which were developed so painstakingly during his latency years. Often, the adolescent attributes strictness to his parents which, as a matter of fact, is his own. For he is in militant opposition to his own self as well as to the outside world. This is one reason why the rebelliousness of adolescents is so confusing to their elders, and why the conflict with authority inevitably has an important and constant place in the psychology of adolescence. Infantile attitudes die hard, and the teenager fights many battles before he sloughs them off.

The main psychological fact about the adolescent is his continued helplessness and dependence. "In his efforts to achieve emotional independence he will often put on a great show of rebelliousness, whose violence only betrays his inner feelings of helplessness [12]." Montaigne (1533-1592) wrote in his autobiography, " . . . all I understand of the matter is that the gravest and hardest of human sciences is the rearing of children. It is easy enough to beget them; but once you have them, then the cares, troubles, and anxieties begin [14]." The literature of personal documents underscores this sentiment. Every age, as revealed in the memoirs which follow, has its serious sources of friction between parent and child. The daughter of Fujiwara Takasué, born in Japan in 1009, began her diary when she was twelve years old and mentioned in it that "Mother was a person of extremely antiquated mind [5]." Even the traditional Japanese delicacy of expression makes it pointedly clear that her "old lady was a square."

The adolescent is as prickly as a porcupine and the well-meaning adult who compares him unfavorably with others tends only to exasperate the youth. In 1794, when Mary Somerville was fourteen years old, she was visiting her aunt and uncle in Edinburgh. "Though kind in the main, my uncle and his wife were rather sarcastic and severe, and kept me down a good deal, which I felt keenly but said nothing. I was not a favorite with my family at that period of my life, because I was reserved and unexpansive, in consequence of silence I was obliged to observe on the subjects which interested me. Three Miss Melvilles, friends, or perhaps relatives, of Mrs. Chartres, were always held up to me as models of perfection, to be imitated in everything, and I wearied of hearing them constantly praised at my expense [18]."

Charles Leland, teacher and magazine editor, related that he was sixteen years of age (in 1840) and six feel tall "before I was allowed to leave off short jackets, go to the theatre, or travel alone, all of which was more injurious to me, I believe, than ordinary youthful dissipation would have been, especially in America. Yet, while thus repressed, I was being continually referred by all grown-up friends to enterprising youths of my own age, who were making a living in bankers' or conveyancers' offices, etc., and acting 'like men.' The result really being that I was completely convinced that I was a person of feeble and inferior capacity as regarded all that was worth doing or knowing in life . . . [11]."

The essence of the adolescent struggle for identity is the struggle for independence from the opinions of grownups. Adults are likely to assist unconsciously in this process, for they no longer have the closeness, the authority, nor the know-how to maintain the earlier parent-child relations. Parents do not know how to strike the right note of "chumminess" with those whom they have enjoyed as children, and children are literally helpless to accept their parents in a new role as big brothers or sisters (15). The autobiographical literature is replete with illustrations of the impossibility of adolescents communicating with and confiding in their parents. In 1826, John Stuart Mill felt ,"My father, to whom it would have been natural to me to have recourse in any practical difficulties, was the last person to whom, in such a case as this [he was feeling depressed], I looked for help. Everything convinced me that he had no knowledge of any such mental state as I was suffering from, and that even if he could be made to understand it, he was not the physician who could heal it [13]." John Clare (1793-1864) could not reveal to his parents how he spent his leisure hours. Marie Bashkirtseff could not remain with her mother "two minutes together without exasperating each other [2]." The former president of Hungary, Michael Karolyi, had little in common with his father and felt no affection for him. The adolescent author of *A Young Girl's Diary* (1) wrote that friendship between mother and daughter is impossible: "Mother has forbidden you to talk to me about certain things; do you call that a friendship?"

Only on occasion does the adolescent feel comfortable with his parents. Seldom do they have their moments together. When the adolescent is asserting himself, mother or father may be pulling him back to childhood status; and when his feeling is infantile, they are wishing for a young adult upon whom they can lean. Herbert Spencer (1820-1903) described himself as always argumentative with his parents and especially with his father. On a two-week visit to them in London when he was thirteen years old, he surprised himself by passing " a pleasant fortnight . . . there: one of the pleasures being the novel one of feeling myself an object of parental approval [19]." Ida M. Tarbell (1857-1944) wrote in her autobiography the unusual statement, "My mother always let me carry out my revolts, return when I would and no questions asked [20]." During a summer holiday at Lavarone, Martin Freud, son of Sigmund, wrote,

"Father, to my great delight, chose me as his companion for a walking and climbing expedition. . . . As it turned out, the trip was most enjoyable and my few days alone with father, who usually had to be shared with so many, remain my proudest and most precious memories. . . . " When father and son reached Trento and spent the night there, they found it difficult to sleep because of the ebullience of the Italian residents. Martin's diary, which he kept and preserved, and which he quotes in his recollections, continues: "What is one sleepless night against the pleasure and honor of being out on an excursion with father, and having him all to myself [8]?"

But most adolescents, because of the guilt feelings stemming from the second edition of the oedipus situation, as Freud phrased it, as well as many old unsolved elements to the father tie, do not experience the enjoyable relations indicated by Tarbell and Martin Freud. Dumas complained of his mother continuing to look upon him as a child, even though he was sixteen years old. Leon Trotsky's situation, at the age of seventeen, was intolerable. "My relations with my family were growing worse. On one of his trips to Nikolayev to market grain, my father somehow learned of my new acquaintances. He sensed the approach of danger, but hoped to prevent it by the power of his parental authority. We had several stormy scenes. I uncompromisingly defended my independence, my right to follow my own path. It ended with my refusing to accept material aid from home. I left my lodgings and went to live with Shvigovsky . . . "

The number of adolescents who leave home is legion. Deutsch states that a characteristic of puberty in the attempt to break ties with the parents is actual flight. "The flight from home is resorted to most often when the [adolescent's] relations with her friends has been disturbed or when the attempt to join a group has failed [4]." There are other causes, of course. Cellini ran away from home because his father's nagging was intolerable. William Stillman also ran away because of an impossible father. Throughout Rimbaud's boyhood there was constant friction with his mother. At the age of fifteen (1870), without any warning, he disappeared and took a train for Paris, a flight, perhaps, to escape unconscious incestuous desires. This was the first of a number of disappearances from home for Rimbaud. Benjamin Franklin left Boston for Philadelphia ostensibly because of the need to "assert my freedom" from his older brother James to whom he was indentured in the printing trade. Jean Jacques Rousseau, in his sixteenth year, "restless, dissatisfied with myself and everything, without any of the tastes of my condition of life, without any of the pleasures of my age, consumed by desires of the object of which I was ignorant, weeping without any cause for tears, sighing without knowing why—in short, tenderly caressing my chimeras [17]" ran away from his master, to whom he was apprenticed as an engraver, fleeing from Geneva to Turin.

The interior drama of the adolescent, acted out in these instances by flight from one's own incestuous wishes, or as a means of expressing resentment with the intent of isolating oneself, or as leaving an intolerable environment, has its counterpart in other manifestations. Adult sensitivities revolve frequently around projection. "Every father," wrote Goethe, "desires for his children that which he himself has not been privileged to attain." In the conscious effort to protect the adolescent, parents try to select his friends, censor his mail, maintain a vigil when the youth is out on a date, and engage in numberless other activities irritating to the adolescent. On the unconscious level, parents may not always be protecting their children so much as attempting to relive the sexual experiences of adolescence. Parental selection of friends may be prompted by feelings of jealousy directed against the friend who looms as a rival. Monica, Augustine's mother, tried to direct his friendships; so did Trotsky's father. Simone de Beauvoir's mother read her mail: "Clothilde and Marguerite sent me affectionate letters [of congratulations on passing the entrance examinations to the Sorbonne 'with distinction']; my mother rather spoiled my pleasure in them by bringing them to me already opened and regaling me with a full description of their contents; but this custom was so well-established that I made no protest [3]." Alexandre Dumas' mother was "greatly disturbed one night when, seated at the window watching for me, she saw no sign of me until three in the morning [6]."

The varieties of adolescent strife and parental sensitivities will be illustrated in the passages which follow. The similarities of feelings and behavior patterns of both parents and adolescents will be seen in the French bourgeosie, the Hungarian aristocracy and the English peasantry, the middle-class Jews of suburban New York and the intellectuals of literary England.

Thomas Moore
(1777-1852)

The anxiety of parents that their children do well in school is exemplified in this passage from Thomas Moore's memoirs.* Not only did Moore's mother examine him daily in all of his studies, but she also over-protected him from possible hurt. Moore shows the usual adolescent ambivalent feelings about her interest and her intellectual ambition for him.

My youth was in every respect a most happy one. Though kept closely to my school studies by my mother, who examined me daily in all of them herself, she was in every thing else so full of indulgence, so affectionately devoted to me, that to gain her approbation I would have thought no labour or difficulty too hard. As an instance both of her anxiety about my studies and the willing temper with which I met it, I need only mention that, on more than one occasion, when having been kept out too late at some evening party to be able to examine me in my task for next day, she had come to my bedside on her return home, and waked me (sometimes as late as one or two o'clock in the morning), and I have cheerfully sat up in my bed and repeated over all my lessons to her. Her anxiety indeed, that I should attain and keep a high rank in the school was ever watchful and active, and on one occasion exhibited itself in a way that was rather disconcerting to me. On our days of public examination which were, if I recollect, twice a year, there was generally a large attendance of the parents and friends of the boys; and on the particular day I allude to, all the seats in the area of the room being occupied, my mother and a few other ladies were obliged to go up into one of the galleries that surrounded the school, and there sit or stand as they could. When the reading class to which I belonged, and of which I had attained the first place, was called up some of the boys in it who were much older and nearly twice as tall as myself, not liking what they deemed the disgrace of having so little a fellow at the head of the class, when standing up before the audience all placed themselves above me. Though feeling that this was unjust, I adopted the plan which, according to Corneille, is that of *"l'honnête homme trompé,"* namely, *"ne dire mot,"*—and was

---

*From *Memoirs, Journals and Correspondence.* London: Longman, Brown, Green & Longmans, 1853, Vol. I. Pp. 15-16.

submitting without a word to what I saw the master himself did not oppose, when to my surprise and, I must say, shame, I heard my mother's voice breaking the silence, and saw her stand forth in the opposite gallery, while every eye in the room was turned toward her, and in a firm, clear tone (though in reality she was ready to sink with the effort), addressed herself to the enthroned schoolmaster on the injustice she saw about to be perpetrated. It required, however, but very few words to rouse his attention to my wrongs. The big boys were obliged to descend from their usurped elevation, while I—ashamed a little of the exhibition which I thought my mother had made of herself, took my due station at the head of the class.

John Clare
(1793-1864)

The adolescent's need for secrecy is manifested in innumerable ways, one of which is found in this excerpt from John Clare's sketch of his life.* Clare's parents had little understanding for their son's poetic efforts. They distrusted the written word, as many illiterates do. While patient with his ineptitude for any kind of trade, they belittled his poetry, which John then felt compelled to say was written by others. The need for secrecy was basic, in this instance, if the boy were to realize his own identity.

I cannot say what led me to dabble in rhyme. I made up many things before I ventured to commit them to writing; for I felt ashamed to expose them on paper, and after I ventured to write them down my second thoughts blushed over them. I burnt them for a long time, but as my feelings grew into song, I felt a desire to preserve some, and used to correct them over and over until the last copy had lost all kindred to the first, even in the title. I went on for some years in this way, wearing it in my memory as a secret to all; though my parents used to know that my leisure was occupied in writing, yet they had no knowledge of what I could be doing; for they never dreamed of me writing poetry.

At length I ventured to divulge the secret a little by reading imitations of some popular song floating among the vulgar at the markets and fairs till they were common to all; but these imitations they always laughed at, and told me I need never hope to make songs like

*From *A Life of John Clare* by J. W. Tibble and Anne Tibble. Reprinted by permission of The Bodley Head, Ltd. 1932. Pp. 40-41.

them. This mortified me often, and almost made me desist; for I knew that the excelling in such doggerel would be but a poor fame if I could do nothing better. But I hit upon a harmless deception by repeating my poems over a book as though I was reading it. This had the desired effect. They often praised them and said if I could write as good I should do. I hugged myself over this deception and often repeated it, and those which they praised as superior to others I tried to preserve in a hole in the wall; but my mother found out the hoard and unconsciously took them for kettle-holders and fire-lighters whenever she wanted paper, not knowing that they were anything further than attempts at learning to write; for they were written upon shop-paper of all colours, between the lines of old copy-books, and on any paper I could get at; for I was often wanting, though I saved almost every penny I had given me on Sundays and holidays to buy it instead of sweetmeats and fruit. I used to feel a little mortified after I discovered it, but I dared not reveal my secret by owning to it and wishing her to desist; for I feared if I did she would have shown them to someone to judge of their value, which would have put me to shame. So I kept the secret disappointment to myself and wrote on, suffering her to destroy them as she pleased; but when I wrote anything which I imagined better than others, I preserved it in my pocket, till the paper was chafed through and destroyed.

William J. Stillman
(1828-1901)

Many parents are prone to exercise their authority over children in an arbitrary, expedient and capricious manner, thus exacerbating the delicate equilibrium that exists between them. They may be prompted by their own rigid superego, as seen in this selection from Stillman's bitter adolescent experiences.* Not until an impasse had been reached between father and son and smoothed over by the mother was the hot war between the two to simmer down to a cold one. Once this was accomplished, Stillman learned never to risk reviving the father's habit of asserting his strong parental authority. Thus, in striving for his independence, the boy felt the need to repudiate the identifications he had made with his father.

---

*From *The Autobiography of a Journalist* by William J. Stillman. Reprinted by permission of Houghton Mifflin Co. 1901. Pp. 76-80.

I had a parrot given me by one of my brothers returning from the Southern States, and the bird took an extravagant fondness for my father rather than for me. He was allowed to go free about the house and garden, and would go and sit on the fence when my father should be coming back from the workshop to dinner and supper, and run to meet his footstep long before he was in sight, chuckling and chattering with delight. Early one morning the parrot got shut, by chance, in the cupboard, and, attempting to gnaw his way out, was mistaken for a rat, father took the shovel to kill him, while mother carefully opened the door so that the rat might squeeze his way out to be killed, but poor Poll got the blow instead, and had his neck broken. All that day my father stayed at home weeping for Polly, and no business misfortune in my recollection ever affected him as the death of the parrot did. He could flog me without mercy, but he could not see the suffering of a domestic or wild animal without tears, nor would he tolerate in us children the slightest tendency to cruelty to the least living thing.

I have alluded to the differences between him and my mother on the subject of education, the inutility of which, beyond a common-school standard, he made an article of faith, and the return to the workshop for the balance of the vacation, after my school-teaching failure, was the occasion of the final battle. As the vacation drew to an end, and the time which was still available for studying up the subjects of the last term, for the examination on reëntering, approached its imperative limit, I notified him that I must stop work. He said nothing until I had actually given it up and gone back to my study, about two weeks before the examination day. Coming home from the shop that day to dinner, in a very bad humor, he asked me why I had not been at work. I replied that I had barely the time absolutely necessary to make up my arrears of study to enter college for the next term. Then he broke out on me with a torrent of abuse as an idle, shirking boy, who only cared to avoid work, ending with the accusation that all I wanted was to "eat the bread of idleness," a phrase he was very fond of. I suppose I inherited some of his inequality of temper, and I replied by leaving the table, throwing my chair across the room as I did so; and, assuring him that when I ate another morsel of bread in his house he would know the reason why, I left the house in a towering rage. Having forewarned him days before that I must go, without his making the least objection, and having postponed the step to the latest possible moment, out of consideration for the work in hand, I considered this treatment as ungenerous, and was indignant.

I do not think that, weighing all the circumstances of the case, one could say that my father was entitled to impose his authority in a purely arbitrary interference with a matter in which the family council had decided on my course, and which involved all my future, or that my refusal to obey an irrational command implies any disrespect to him. At all events, I decided at once that I would not yield in this matter, and I made my preparations to seek another home, even with a modification in my career. If I must abandon the liberal education, I would not waste my life in a little workshop with three workmen, and no opportunity to widen the sphere of activity, or opening into a larger occupation. If I should be obliged to leave the college, it should be for something in the direction of art, and in this light I did not much regret the change. I had not, however, calculated on my mother's tenacity, or the imperceptible domination she exercised over my father.

When I returned to the house to get my clothes and make my preparations for leaving home for good, I had a most painful scene with my mother, and it was the only serious misunderstanding I ever had with her. She went through, in a rapid résumé, the history of my life, from the day when I was given her in consolation for the little brother before me, who died, with a word for each of the crises through which her care had carried me,—accidents, grave maladies, for I was apparently not a strong child, and at several conjunctures my life had been despaired of; all the story being told as she walked up and down rapidly in the chamber, with the tears running down her cheeks, and with a passionate vehemence I had never suspected her to be capable of, since she had the most complete self-restraint I ever knew in a woman. But it was an *impasse*—I neither could nor would go back from the career decided upon, nor would the family have consented, and to return to the workshop at my father's insistence was to lose everything. It seemed brutal to refuse mother's entreaties to ignore the collision of wills, and to go on as if nothing had happened, but to do this and remain in the house with my father, in the perpetual danger of another conflict, was impossible. The question had to be settled, and all I could do was to insist on father's making a distinct disavowal of any right or intention to demand my services in the shop at any future time, and leaving me free to follow the programme agreed on in the family council. It was in effect a frank apology that I wanted, but I knew him too well to suppose he would ever consent to make an apology in words, or to admit to me that he had made a mistake; and I left the solution in my mother's hands, with the understanding that the definite promise should be made to her, and I knew too that this would hold him as completely as if made to a public authority. Nothing could bring her to contradict him openly, and in all my life I never saw her make a sign of disrespect for his mastery in domestic things, but I knew that once this promise was made to her I could count on his being held to it sternly.

That evening the matter was settled, but of what had passed, or what was said, I never knew anything, for my mother never wasted words; and, while no apology was made, or any retraction expressed, neither my father nor myself ever alluded to the subject of my working in the shop again, nor did I ever, as before, go into it during the vacations, or offer to assist when affairs were hurried. The habit of asserting the paternal authority and the sense of it, in my father, were so strong that I never risked again reviving it.

Michael Karolyi
(1875-1955)

The preference of one child over another by a parent, whether it is real or imaginary, is very influential in the child's relationships at home. Michael Karolyi, who was President of the Hungarian Republic from 1918 to 1919, believed his father favored his sister. He believed, also, that his father resented his congenital cleft palate and wrongly opposed the operation to correct the condition. He felt, as he stated in the excerpt below,* that he was in contradiction with almost everything his father wanted for him, and vice versa: his schooling, vocational goals, philosophy, values and attitudes. He became more and more critical of his father's way of life.

The strength of Michael's repudiation of his father suggests this might be a repudiation of his oedipal feelings. Since the boy felt that his father was so critical of him, he thought perhaps his father did not want him to be more of a man. Seeing his father as hostile toward him was a projection of his own hostility toward his father.

> I was a weakly child and born with a defect of the palate. At the age of fourteen my grandmother had Doctor Billroth of Vienna operate on me. It was the first operation of this kind and was a matter of life and death. My father opposed it to the last minute. I thought this a weakness on his part. Ever since I have felt indebted to my grandmother for her initiative and strength of mind. I was big enough to

---

*From *Memoirs of Michael Karolyi*. Reprinted by permission of E. P. Dutton & Co., Inc. Copyright 1956, E. P. Dutton & Co., Inc. Pp. 21-23.

realize the danger and before the operation I made serious preparations for death. When lying on the operating table I asked for my sister Elisabeth and we prayed fervently together. Being deeply religious,
I was not afraid and trusted Providence. During my convalescence,
when for weeks I had to lie dumb in bed, it was this feeling of gratitude for being alive that comforted me and strengthened my faith.
When I recovered, there followed a strenuous and exhausting series of
exercises in speech, most exasperating and nerve-racking, but they increased my willpower. It was a valuable training for the struggle
against the setbacks of later years. It was often said that I was given a
golden palate. I may have been born with a golden spoon in my mouth
—but not a golden palate. I was surprised to find this legend in a recent book by a well-known writer.

I had little in common with my father and felt no affection for him.
I fancied, perhaps wrongly, that subconsciously he resented his son's
physical defect and preferred my sister to me. He opposed my studies
and wished me to become a country squire and manage the estate and
the stud. It was probably for this reason that I developed a special
antipathy to farming and country life. The only study he approved of
was that of the horse; he wished me to be an expert in this domain.
The head of the Veterinary College came regularly to lecture me on
the anatomy of that noble animal. My interest in horse-breeding rapidly waned in consequence. He also opposed my matriculation, saying: 'Let him learn to hunt.' But again my grandmother arranged for
me to be put surreptitiously through the secondary school course, thus
getting a chance of higher education.

My father was what one could call the typical *Grand seigneur*. Easy
and free in his ways, his proverbial charm acquired him friends wherever he went. He was President of the Hungarian Jockey Club and
Knight of the Golden Fleece, the emblem of which was erected on the
façade of our house in Budapest, enabling mass to be celebrated anywhere on the premises. But honours did not mean much to him. He
used to hang on his dog Fancy, a white fox terrier, a most distinguished decoration received from a foreign power, which gave us children great joy. He was very handsome and much loved by women, for
he had a detached and casual way of approach which was very attractive to them. He had also a great sense of fun.

In his youth my father had travelled a great deal and had visited the
U.S.A. during the civil war, in the company of the son of the 'greatest
Hungarian' as Count Stephen Szechenyi was called. Before they sailed,
they had to swear to my grandmother Caroline that they would not
change the Hungarian magnate's dress for a civilian's during their

whole stay in America. It was a most inconvenient way of travelling, this tight black and braided uniform with high boots, and rather warm during the summer months! I remember how he shocked me by telling me that all the *good* men were on the side of the South, that is, the slave owners, and against the liberation of the slaves. As I had just read *Uncle Tom's Cabin*, I was distressed to hear this opinion.

As I grew up, I became more and more critical of my father's way of life and his lack of interest in public affairs. I thus became estranged from him and most probably judged him unfairly; he wished to shelter me from the callous and cruel world, which he thought I was not fit to face.

How children at times misjudge their parents and how mistaken I was to believe him a weak man, I realized only later. Some worrying physical symptoms, about which the Hungarian doctors would not enlighten him, made him visit a doctor in Paris and request him to reveal to him in all sincerity the truth about his illness and how long he had to live. He was told that he was suffering from cancer of the throat and that a year was the maximum. I remember him sitting in his armchair in front of the open fireplace, silently brooding, for hours, with his forefinger between his teeth, and I never guessed what a tragedy was going on inside him; for no man could have had a happier life and a more difficult one to leave. I was fifteen years old when he died.

Sherwood Anderson
(1876-1941)

"You hear it said that fathers want their sons to be what they feel they cannot themselves be, but I tell you it also works the other way. A boy wants something very special from his father."

So wrote Sherwood Anderson in his *Memoirs*.* For many years, Sherwood was ashamed of his father, as many adolescents feel a sense of shame, for one reason or another, for their parents. While the shame usually dissipates as the adolescent matures into adulthood, the feeling of guilt about the shame generally persists. Anderson related how he "discovered" his father one rainy night after his father had "discovered" him: "Before that night my father had never seemed to pay any attention to me." For the first time, Anderson knew that he was the son of his father. The identification

---

*Reprinted by permission of Sherwood Anderson Estate. Copyright 1942, Harcourt, Brace & Co. Pp. 45-49.

process was operating on the conscious level. Up until that time, Anderson was ashamed of his father because the latter did not appear manly enough to him. Even though his father was apparently well-liked, everything he did had a ridiculous, gauche quality to it that had made it difficult for the boy to identify with him.

You hear it said that fathers want their sons to be what they feel they cannot themselves be, but I tell you it also works the other way. A boy wants something very special from his father. I know that as a small boy I wanted my father to be a certain thing he was not. I wanted him to be a proud, silent, dignified father. When I was with other boys and he passed along the street, I wanted to feel a flow of pride: "There he is. That is my father."

But he wasn't such a one. He couldn't be. It seemed to me then that he was always showing off. Let's say someone in our town had got up a show. They were always doing it. The druggist would be in it, the shoe-store clerk, the horse doctor, and a lot of women and girls. My father would manage to get the chief comedy part. It was, let's say, a Civil War play and he was a comic Irish soldier. He had to do the most absurd things. They thought he was funny, but I didn't.

I thought he was terrible. I didn't see how mother could stand it. She even laughed with the others. Maybe I would have laughed if it hadn't been my father.

Or there was a parade, the Fourth of July or Decoration Day. He'd be in that, too, right at the front of it, as Grand Marshal or something, on a white horse hired from a livery stable.

He couldn't ride for shucks. He fell off the horse and everyone hooted with laughter, but he didn't care. He even seemed to like it. I remember once when he had done something ridiculous, and right out on Main Street, too. I was with some other boys and they were laughing and shouting at him and he was shouting back and having as good a time as they were. I ran down an alley back of some stores and there in the Presbyterian Church sheds I had a good long cry.

Or I would be in bed at night and father would come home a little lit up and bring some men with him. He was a man who was never alone. Before he went broke, running a harness shop, there were always a lot of men loafing in the shop. He went broke, of course, because he gave too much credit. He couldn't refuse it and I thought he was a fool. I had got to hating him.

There'd be men I didn't think would want to be fooling around with him. There might even be the superintendent of our schools and a quiet man who ran the hardware store. Once I remember there was a

white-haired man who was a cashier of the bank. It was a wonder to
me they'd want to be seen with such a windbag. That's what I thought
he was. I know now what it was that attracted them. It was because
life in our town, as in all small towns, was at times pretty dull and he
livened it up. He made them laugh. He could tell stories. He'd even
get them to singing.

If they didn't come to our house they'd go off, say at night, to where
there was a grassy place by a creek. They'd cook food there and drink
beer and sit about listening to his stories.

He was always telling stories about himself. He'd say this or that
wonderful thing had happened to him. It might be something that
made him look like a fool. He didn't care.

If an Irishman came to our house, right away father would say he
was Irish. He'd tell what county in Ireland he was born in. He'd tell
things that happened there when he was a boy. He'd make it seem so
real that, if I hadn't known he was born in southern Ohio, I'd have
believed him myself.

If it was a Scotchman the same thing happened. He'd get a burr into
his speech. Or he was a German or a Swede. He'd be anything the
other man was. I think they all knew he was lying, but they seemed to
like him just the same. As a boy that was what I couldn't understand.

And there was mother. How could she stand it? I wanted to ask but
never did. She was not the kind you asked such questions.

I'd be upstairs in my bed, in my room above the porch, and father
would be telling some of his tales. A lot of father's stories were about
the Civil War. To hear him tell it he'd been in about every battle.
He'd known Grant, Sherman, Sheridan and I don't know how many
others. He'd been particularly intimate with General Grant so that
when Grant went East, to take charge of all the armies, he took father
along.

"I was an orderly at headquarters and Sim Grant said to me, 'Irve,'
he said, 'I'm going to take you along with me.' "

It seems he and Grant used to slip off sometimes and have a quiet
drink together. That's what my father said. He'd tell about the day
Lee surrendered and how, when the great moment came, they couldn't
find Grant.

"You know," my father said, "about General Grant's book, his
memoirs. You've read of how he said he had a headache and how,
when he got word that Lee was ready to call it quits, he was suddenly
and miraculously cured.

"Huh," said father. "He was in the woods with me.

"I was in there with my back against a tree. I was pretty well corned.
I had got hold of a bottle of pretty good stuff.

"They were looking for Grant. He had got off his horse and come into the woods. He found me. He was covered with mud.

"I had the bottle in my hand. What'd I care? The war was over. I knew we had them licked."

My father said that he was the one who told Grant about Lee. An orderly riding by had told him, because the orderly knew how thick he was with Grant. Grant was embarrassed.

"But, Irve, look at me. I'm all covered with mud," he said to father.

And then, my father said, he and Grant decided to have a drink together. They took a couple of shots and then, because he didn't want Grant to show up potted before the immaculate Lee, he smashed the bottle against the tree.

"Sim Grant's dead now and I wouldn't want it to get out on him," my father said.

That's just one of the kind of things he'd tell. Of course the men knew he was lying, but they seemed to like it just the same.

When we got broke, down and out, do you think he ever brought anything home? Not he. If there wasn't anything to eat in the house, he'd go off visiting around at farmhouses. They all wanted him. Sometimes he'd stay away for weeks, mother working to keep us fed, and then home he'd come bringing, let's say, a ham. He'd got it from some farmer friend. He'd slap it on the table in the kitchen. "You bet I'm going to see that my kids have something to eat," he'd say, and mother would just stand smiling at him. She'd never say a word about all the weeks and months he'd been away, not leaving us a cent for food. Once I heard her speaking to a woman in our street. Maybe the woman had dared to sympathize with her. "Oh," she said, "it's all right. He isn't ever dull like most of the men in this street. Life is never dull when my man is about."

But often I was filled with bitterness, and sometimes I wished he wasn't my father. I'd even invent another man as my father. To protect my mother I'd make up stories of a secret marriage that for some strange reason never got known. As though some man, say the president of a railroad company or maybe a Congressman, had married my mother, thinking his wife was dead and then it turned out she wasn't.

So they had to hush it up but I got born just the same. I wasn't really the son of my father. Somewhere in the world there was a very dignified, quite wonderful man who was really my father. I even made myself half believe these fancies.

And then there came a certain night. He'd been off somewhere for two or three weeks. He found me alone in the house, reading by the kitchen table.

It had been raining and he was very wet. He sat and looked at me for a long time, not saying a word. I was startled, for there was on his face the saddest look I had ever seen. He sat for a time, his clothes dripping. Then he got up.

"Come on with me," he said.

I got up and went with him out of the house. I was filled with wonder but I wasn't afraid. We went along a dirt road that led down into a valley, about a mile out of town, where there was a pond. We walked in silence. The man who was always talking had stopped his talking.

I didn't know what was up and had the queer feeling that I was with a stranger. I don't know whether my father intended it so. I don't think he did.

The pond was quite large. It was still raining hard and there were flashes of lightning followed by thunder. We were on a grassy bank at the pond's edge when my father spoke, and in the darkness and rain his voice sounded strange.

"Take off your clothes," he said. Still filled with wonder, I began to undress. There was a flash of lightning and I saw that he was already naked.

Naked, we went into the pond. Taking my hand he pulled me in. It may be that I was too frightened, too full of a feeling of strangeness, to speak. Before that night my father had never seemed to pay any attention to me.

"And what is he up to now?" I kept asking myself. I did not swim very well, but he put my hand on his shoulder and struck out into the darkness.

He was a man with big shoulders, a powerful swimmer. In the darkness I could feel the movement of his muscles. We swam to the far edge of the pond and then back to where we had left our clothes. The rain continued and the wind blew. Sometimes my father swam on his back and when he did he took my hand in his large powerful one and moved it over so that it rested always on his shoulder. Sometimes there would be a flash of lightning and I could see his face quite clearly.

It was as it was earlier, in the kitchen, a face filled with sadness. There would be the momentary glimpse of his face and then again the darkness, the wind and the rain. In me there was a feeling I had never known before.

It was a feeling of closeness. It was something strange. It was as though there were only we two in the world. It was as though I had been jerked suddenly out of myself, out of my world of the schoolboy, out of a world in which I was ashamed of my father.

He had become blood of my blood; he the strong swimmer and I the boy clinging to him in the darkness. We swam in silence and in silence we dressed in our wet clothes, and went home.

There was a lamp lighted in the kitchen and when we came in, the water dripping from us, there was my mother. She smiled at us. I remember that she called us "boys."

"What have you boys been up to?" she asked, but my father did not answer. As he had begun the evening's experience with me in silence, so he ended it. He turned and looked at me. Then he went, I thought, with a new and strange dignity out of the room.

I climbed the stairs to my own room, undressed in the darkness and got into bed. I couldn't sleep and did not want to sleep. For the first time I knew that I was the son of my father. He was a story teller as I was to be. It may be that I even laughed a little softly there in the darkness. If I did, I laughed knowing that I would never again be wanting another father.

John Lehmann
(1907-   )

When parents flout the taboos of adolescents, consciously or unconsciously, strife almost inevitably results. Adolescents are extremely sensitive—about their person, appearance, clothes, feelings, and especially about their families. They are extremely eager to impress their friends. John Lehmann describes some family visits to him at Eton when he was about sixteen years old.* The description illuminates these particular facets of adolescents' sensitivity. Lehmann's attempts to divorce himself from his relations were efforts to assert his own identity.

One of the most pleasant aspects of Eton for me was that I was never completely cut off from home. Fieldhead was only ten miles away and linked by the river. My mother, and my sisters when they were staying there—for both Helen and Rosamond were now married and Beatrix had started her life as an actress—would often motor over on a Sunday or a half-holiday afternoon and take me out with them; and I managed to get permission to pay many brief visits home in between "absences," and was sometimes even motored over by Marsden himself. This proximity also had its disadvantages: my relatives were apt to appear without due warning, and, growing to feel familiar with Eton, would ignorantly flout some of the most sacred taboos. There was a terrible afternoon when my mother brought Helen's eldest child, my

---

*From *The Whispering Gallery* by John Lehmann. Reprinted by permission of Harcourt, Brace & World, Inc. 1954. Pp. 119-120.

dear niece Maureen, then a small baby, over with her nurse. She came in to find me, and left nurse and child outside with the car parked by the low wall that runs between the yard outside Upper School and the road. No one was allowed to sit on this wall except the members of Pop: an electric wire of privilege, of the highest voltage but visible only to the Etonian eye, ran along it. As I emerged through the gateway of Upper School with my mother, a shock of the utmost consternation and dismay went through me. I would rather have sunk into the ground than see what I did see, and desperate plans of immediate escape and renunciation of my family for ever ran through my head: for Maureen's nurse had taken her out of the car and was encouraging her, with cooing baby noises, to toddle along the top of the holy wall. Nearly all schoolboys are, I believe, hyper-sensitive about the appearance and behaviour of their relatives, but perhaps I was peculiarly so: I remember how I boasted at Summer Fields about the beauty of my sisters and the smartness of the world they already moved in, and the disgrace I felt when Helen came to visit me soon after her marriage with her husband, Mountie, who was wearing—an old deer-stalker hat. But the disgrace about Pop Wall was far worse and far more profoundly disturbing.

Anonymous
(?-?)

"I must say that although I'm *awfully, awfully* fond of Mother, I really can't imagine having her as a *friend*. How can one have a true friendship with one's own mother?" So wrote thirteen-year-old Gretel (1) in her diary, nearly a thousand years after the Japanese author of the Sarashina diary had penned similar sentiments. Gretel pointed out the maternal qualities that seem to make it impossible for compatibility to exist between the two generations: the nagging, the overprotection, the constant orders and forbiddings, and the nonexistent line of communication. What she was protesting, basically, is the tamping down of the adolescent's attempt at self-identity and at independence from the parental bond which many parents are unwilling to loosen. The protest may be more than an effort at identity, it can also be the repudiation of a homosexual attachment.

August 3rd

I've found out now why Dora is so different, that is why she is again just as she was some time ago, before last winter. During the 4 weeks in Fr. she has *found a real friend in Mother!* To-day I turned the conversation to Viktor, and all she said at first was: Oh, I don't correspond with him any more. And when I asked: "Have you had a quarrel, and whose fault was it?" she said: "Oh, no, I just *bade him farewell.*" "What do you mean, bade him farewell; but he's not really going to America, is he?" And then she said: "My dear *Rita,* we had better clear this matter up; I parted from him upon the well-justified wish of our *dear Mother.*" I must say that though I'm *awfully, awfully* fond of Mother, I really can't imagine having her as a *friend.* How can one have a true friendship with one's own mother? Dora really can't have the least idea *what a true friendship* means. There are some things it's impossible for a girl to speak about to her mother, I could not possibly ask her: Do you know what, *something has happened,* really means? Besides, I'm not quite sure if she does know, for when she was 13 or 15 or 16, people may have used quite different expressions, and the modern phrases very likely did not then mean what they mean now. And what sort of a friendship is it when Mother says to Dora: You must not go out now, the storm may break at any moment, and just the other evening: Dora you *must* take your shawl with you. Friendship between mother and daughter is just as impossible as friendship between father and son. For between friends there can be no orders and forbiddings, and what's even more important is that one really can't talk about all the things that one would like to talk of. All I said last night was: "Of course Mother has forbidden you to talk to me about *certain things;* do you call that a friendship?" Then she said very gently: "No, Rita, Mother has not forbidden me, but I recognise now that it was thoughtless of me to talk to you about those things; one learns the seriousness of life quite soon enough." I burst out laughing and said: "Is *that* what you call the seriousness of life? Have you really forgotten how screamingly funny we found it all? It seems to me that your memory has been affected by the mud baths." She did not answer that. I do hope Ada will come. For *I* need *her* now just as much as *she* needs *me.*

Anne Frank
(1929-1945)

At the age of fifteen, Anne Frank had become the conscience of a ruthless era. Her diary, saved by the slightest chance, has been read or seen in stage and screen versions by millions of people all over the world. The passages from her diary selected for this section* are not intended to arouse the consciences of either parents or adolescents but rather to illuminate a difficult and trying situation as it exists.

Anne Frank wrote her diary with unsparing candor. In it she put down not only what might have been, or what should be, but what really happens when grace is put under the immeasurable pressure of disaster. Imprisoned in that fantastic hiding place, the "Secret Annexe" in Amsterdam, she showed how in Hitler's Europe the adolescent spirit, with all its contradictory grandeur, pettiness and cantankerousness survived from hour to hour, from day to day.

The inherent differences between generations, Anne shows us, are well matched by differences among men and women of the same generation. Thus, if she was sometimes driven to tears by the callous way her elders treated her or by their dreary inability to understand her, she was no less aware that those very elders were frequently at war with one another over large and small, trivial or fundamental, matters.

Wednesday, 2 September, 1942

. . . Mummy gave me another frightful sermon this morning; I can't bear them. Our ideas are completely opposite. Daddy is a darling, although he can sometimes be angry with me for five minutes on end. . . .

Sunday, 27 September, 1942

Dear Kitty,

Just had a big bust-up with Mummy for the umpteenth time; we simply don't get on together these days and Margot and I don't hit it off any too well either. As a rule we don't go in for such outbursts as this in our family. Still, it's by no means always pleasant for me. Margot's and Mummy's natures are completely strange to me. I can understand my friends better than my own mother—too bad!

Saturday, 7 November, 1942

Dear Kitty,

Mummy is frightfully irritable and that always seems to herald unpleasantness for me. Is it just a chance that Daddy and Mummy never rebuke Margot and that they always drop on me for everything? Yesterday evening, for instance: Margot was reading a book with lovely

---

*From *The Diary of a Young Girl* by Anne Frank. Reprinted by permission of Doubleday & Co., Inc. Copyright 1952, Otto H. Frank. Pp. 23, 27, 39-41, 58-60.

drawings in it; she got up and went upstairs, put the book down ready to go on with it later. I wasn't doing anything, so picked up the book and started looking at the pictures. Margot came back, saw "her" book in my hands, wrinkled her forehead and asked for the book back. Just because I wanted to look a little further on, Margot got more and more angry. Then Mummy joined in: "Give the book to Margot; she was reading it," she said. Daddy came into the room. He didn't even know what it was all about, but saw the injured look on Margot's face and promptly dropped on me: "I'd like to see what you'd say if Margot ever started looking at one of your books!" I gave way at once, laid the book down, and left the room—offended, as they thought. It so happened I was neither offended nor cross, just miserable. It wasn't right of Daddy to judge without knowing what the squabble was about. I would have given Margot the book myself, and much more quickly, if Mummy and Daddy hadn't interfered. They took Margot's part at once, as though she were the victim of some great injustice.

It's obvious that Mummy would stick up for Margot; she and Margot always do back each other up. I'm so used to that that I'm utterly indifferent to both Mummy's jawing and Margot's moods.

I love them; but only because they are Mummy and Margot. With Daddy it's different. If he holds Margot up as an example, approves of what she does, praises and caresses her, then something gnaws at me inside, because I adore Daddy. He is the one I look up to. I don't love anyone in the world but him. He doesn't notice that he treats Margot differently from me. Now Margot is just the prettiest, sweetest, most beautiful girl in the world. But all the same I feel I have some right to be taken seriously too. I have always been the dunce, the ne'er-do-well of the family, I've always had to pay double for my deeds, first with the scolding and then again because of the way my feelings are hurt. Now I'm not satisfied with this apparent favoritism any more. I want something from Daddy that he is not able to give me.

I'm not jealous of Margot, never have been. I don't envy her good looks or her beauty. It is only that I long for Daddy's real love: not only as his child, but for me—Anne, myself.

I cling to Daddy because it is only through him that I am able to retain the remnant of family feeling. Daddy doesn't understand that I need to give vent to my feelings over Mummy sometimes. He doesn't want to talk about it; he simply avoids anything which might lead to remarks about Mummy's failings. Just the same, Mummy and her failings are something I find harder to bear than anything else. I don't know how to keep it all to myself. I can't always be drawing attention to her untidiness, her sarcasm, and her lack of sweetness, neither can I believe that I'm always in the wrong.

We are exact opposites in everything; so naturally we are bound to run up against each other. I don't pronounce judgment on Mummy's character, for that is something I can't judge. I only look at her as a mother, and she just doesn't succeed in being that to me; I have to be my own mother. I've drawn myself apart from them all; I am my own skipper and later on I shall see where I come to land. All this comes about particularly because I have in my mind's eye an image of what a perfect mother and wife should be; and in her whom I must call "Mother" I find no trace of that image.

I am always making resolutions not to notice Mummy's bad example. I want to see only the good side of her and to seek in myself what I cannot find in her. But it doesn't work; and the worst of it is that neither Daddy nor Mummy understands this gap in my life, and I blame them for it. I wonder if anyone can ever succeed in making their children absolutely content.

Sometimes I believe that God wants to try me, both now and later on; I must become good through my own efforts, without examples and without good advice. Then later on I shall be all the stronger. Who besides me will ever read these letters? From whom but myself shall I get comfort? As I need comforting often, I frequently feel weak, and dissatisfied with myself; my shortcomings are too great. I know this, and every day I try to improve myself, again and again.

My treatment varies so much. One day Anne is so sensible and is allowed to know everything; and the next day I hear that Anne is just a silly little goat who doesn't know anything at all and imagines that she's learned a wonderful lot from books. I'm not a baby or a spoiled darling any more, to be laughed at, whatever she does. I have my own views, plans, and ideas, though I can't put them into words yet. Oh, so many things bubble up inside me as I lie in bed, having to put up with people I'm fed up with, who always misinterpret my intentions. That's why in the end I always come back to my diary. That is where I start and finish, because Kitty is always patient. I'll promise her that I shall persevere, in spite of everything, and find my own way through it all, and swallow my tears. I only wish I could see the results already or occasionally receive encouragement from someone who loves me.

Don't condemn me; remember rather that sometimes I too can reach the bursting point.

Yours, Anne

Saturday, 30 January, 1943

Dear Kitty,
I'm boiling with rage, and yet I mustn't show it. I'd like to stamp

my feet, scream, give Mummy a good shaking, cry, and I don't know what else, because of the horrible words, mocking looks, and accusations which are leveled at me repeatedly every day, and find their mark, like shafts from a tightly strung bow, and which are just as hard to draw from my body.

I would like to shout to Margot, Van Daan, Dussel—and Daddy too —"Leave me in peace, let me sleep one night at least without my pillow being wet with tears, my eyes burning and my head throbbing. Let me get away from it all, preferably away from the world!" But I can't do that, they mustn't know my despair, I can't let them see the wounds which they have caused, I couldn't bear their sympathy and their kindhearted jokes, it would only make me want to scream all the more. If I talk, everyone thinks I'm showing off; when I'm silent they think I'm ridiculous; rude if I answer, sly if I get a good idea, lazy if I'm tired, selfish if I eat a mouthful more than I should, stupid, cowardly, crafty, etc., etc. The whole day long I hear nothing else but that I am an insufferable baby, and although I laugh about it and pretend not to take any notice, I *do* mind. I would like to ask God to give me a different nature, so that I didn't put everyone's back up. But that can't be done. I've got the nature that has been given to me and I'm sure it can't be bad. I do my very best to please everybody, far more than they'd ever guess. I try to laugh it all off, because I don't want to let them see my trouble. More than once, after a whole string of undeserved rebukes, I have flared up at Mummy: "I don't care what you say anyhow. Leave me alone: I'm a hopeless case anyway." Naturally, I was then told I was rude and was virtually ignored for two days; and then, all at once, it was quite forgotten, and I was treated like everyone else again. It is impossible for me to be all sugar one day and spit venom the next. I'd rather choose the golden mean (which is not so golden), keep my thoughts to myself, and try for *once* to be just as disdainful to them as they are to me. Oh, if only I could!

Yours, Anne

Saturday, 27 February, 1943

. . . Lately Mummy and I have been getting on better together, but we still *never* confide in each other. Margot is more catty than ever and Daddy has got something he is keeping to himself, but he remains the same darling. . . .

David S. Kogan
(1929-1951)

The last three authors in this section, the anonymous Gretel, Anne Frank, and David S. Kogan, seem to have expressed themselves similarly in their diaries in relating experiences with their parents. How did an Austrian girl, a Dutch girl, and an American teenager from Yonkers, New York, arrive at such unanimity about their very different parents, who had very different cultural orientations, socioeconomic backgrounds, and who were so separated in space? The universality of adolescent experience is clearly exemplified in these instances. The excerpts from Kogan's diary*, which conclude this chapter, are very reminiscent of the others in their criticism of the adults, their lack of understanding and the inability to communicate.

Friday, June 19, 1942

Bob got a bike, not beautiful, but good and sturdy. For two years I have been fighting for a bike. I can't ride—that's a technicality. Mom thinks it isn't safe. If I get killed, Mom will commit suicide, Dad will be lonely.

I walked past a Yonkers used and new bicycle dealer, and he had a good used one with fairly good tires. They are rare these days. I made a big offensive. Dad said he would go. We couldn't buy without Ma. I talked for two hours, begged, argued, debated. Dad invited us to go for a "ride." The bike man convinced Ma. It is my first great victory.

We bought the bike. Two years of agitation is over, and I don't feel excited. I can't even ride it. But I like it. I love it. I have a bicycle.

Mom doesn't want me to ride the bike till I am admitted to the Bar.

Thursday, June 1, 1944

I have noticed that a breach has come between my parents and me. I don't tell them much and they resent it. I am sarcastic which shouldn't be; they use the same method and I can't take it. I know they are right, but I resent it, and they resent my resenting it.

Somehow I feel like a combo of the "Blues" and "Peck's Bad Boy."

The Diary of David S. Kogan. Reprinted by permission of Beechurst Press. 1955. Pp. 33, 56, 74-75, 90, 103, 113.

I feel I don't have a friend I can count on, who would help me in a pinch, who would wait for me. I also feel bad because Dad does not give me the freedom the fellers I go around with have. And to keep up with them I have to aggravate him, which burns. Then, too, although everybody likes to be liked, the girls do not like me enough to invite me anywhere.

Sunday, November 12, 1944

Mother fell down some stairs on Friday and envisioned spending the rest of her life in a wheel chair, but it is not as bad as that.

My mother is not easy to get along with. She has brains, illogical woman's brains, and is unhappy. She does have remorse for a lot of things she does, nevertheless she never learns. She is a woman of many talents, a good artist, fair musician, and a pretty good cook. She dabbles here and dabbles there. She does however love me. With a little change in her *Weltanschauung* she might be a fine woman. I only hope that someday she might treat her family as well as her friends.

Friday, November 24, 1944

I helped Mother quite a bit this morning, but as usual, the work did not receive grateful recognition.

Sunday, March 25, 1945

I'll say this: the parents say "no" a lot, but they don't know how to discipline me after I do something. However, they are good people (but nervous) an' the storm shall pass.

Monday, October 22, 1945

Mom had a real spat with me today. She said things like I'm throwing away my future; I never do any homework. I used my latest defense—look calmly sympathetic, and say that happiness is all that counts. She calmed down beautifully, and then bent over backwards. Still, I know she's right in many ways.

Saturday, February 9, 1946

Why don't I let my parents in on the bleak, proud, lonely, and desolate castle high on the moor which is my social life—perhaps they would not understand—of course they wouldn't.

REFERENCES

1. Anonymous. *A Young Girl's Diary*. New York: Thomas Seltzer, 1921, pp. 128-129, 151.
2. Bashkirtseff, Marie. *The Journal of a Young Artist*. New York: E. P. Dutton & Co., 1926, p. 178.
3. Beauvoir, Simone de. *Memoirs of a Dutiful Daughter*. Cleveland: World Publishing Co., 1959, pp. 111-115, 165.
4. Deutsch, Helene. *The Psychology of Women*. New York: Grune & Stratton, 1944, Vol. I, p. 37.
5. *Diaries of Court Ladies of Old Japan*. Boston: Houghton Mifflin Co., 1920, p. xxxii.
6. Dumas, Alexandre. *The Road to Monte Carlo*. Edited by Jules Eckert Goodman. New York: Charles Scribner's Sons, 1956, p. 43.
7. Freud, Anna. Adolescence. In: Eissler, Ruth S., et. al. (Eds.), *The Psychoanalytic Study of the Child*. New York: International Universities Press, 1959, Vol. XIII, p. 266.
8. Freud, Martin. *Sigmund Freud: Man and Father*. New York: Vanguard Press, 1958, pp. 126-127.
9. Freud, Sigmund. *The Interpretation of Dreams*. New York: Basic Books, 1958, p. 122.
9a. Kligerman, Charles. A psychoanalytic study of the *Confessions* of St. Augustine. *J. Amer. Psychoanal. Assoc.*, 5:469-484, 1957.
10. Jones, Ernest. Some problems of adolescence. *Brit. J. Psychol.*, 13:44-45, 1922.
11. Leland, Charles G. *Memoirs*. New York: D. Appleton & Co., 1893, pp. 65-66.
12. Linn, Louis, & Schwartz, Leo W. *Psychiatry and Religious Experience*. New York: Random House, 1959, pp. 52-53.
13. Mill, John Stuart. *Autobiography*. New York: Library of Liberal Arts, 1957, p. 88.
14. Montaigne, Michel de. *Autobiography*. Edited by Marvin Lowenthal. Boston: Houghton Mifflin Co., 1935, p. 29.
15. Murphy, Gardner. *Personality: A Biosocial Approach to Origins and Structure*. New York: Harper & Bros., 1947, p. 515.
16. Pearson, Gerald H. J. *Adolescence and the Conflict of Generations*. New York: W. W. Norton & Co., 1958, p. 62.
17. Rousseau, Jean Jacques. *Confessions*. New York: Modern Library, 1945, p. 41.
18. Somerville, Mary. *Personal Recollections, from Early Life to Old Age*. Boston: Robert Brothers, 1874, p. 42.
19. Spencer, Herbert. *An Autobiography*. New York: D. Appleton & Co., 1904, Vol. I, p. 120.

20. Tarbell, Ida M. *All in the Day's Work. An Autobiography*. New York: Macmillan Co., 1939, p. 7.

21. Whiting, John W. M., Kluckhohn, Richard, & Anthony, Albert. The function of male initiation ceremonies at puberty. In: Maccoby, Eleanor E., et al. (Eds.), *Readings in Social Psychology*. New York: Henry Holt & Co., 1958.

CHAPTER SIX

Sibling Feelings

Dating back to the Biblical stories of Cain and Abel and Joseph and his brothers, there is strong historical evidence for the traditional feelings of jealousy, rivalry and hostility that exist between siblings. The rivalry, both in its intrafamilial and dynastic forms, has remained an important feature of Middle Eastern family life to this day. A proverb, according to Patai (15), current in many variants in all Middle Eastern tongues, contains a reference to it: "I and my cousins against the world; I and my brothers against my cousins; I against my brothers." There is also evidence for the existence of such feelings in most cultures.

Adler (1) developed a systematized theory of sibling relationships and their effects on personality, temperament and behavior, based on sibling position in the family constellation. This has long been in practice through the widespread institution of primogeniture under which the oldest child inherits the major responsibilities of the household. "Under monarchies," Landis relates, "the oldest son becomes the prince. In many cultures the oldest son has inherited the family farm or the wealth of the family, or inherited the right to rule the younger children when the elders have passed from the scene. There still survives in American life something of this philosophy. Studies of occupation indicate that the oldest son more frequently than the others takes over the American family farm. Other studies of the social implications of sib position indicate that social advantages may be closely related to position in the family. Rowntree's famous studies of the poverty cycle among English workingmen indicated that the oldest child was at a disadvantage from the economic and social standpoints (16). In describing the life cycle of the poor family, Rowntree showed that when the couple married, they were able to get along fairly well until the first child came. After the birth of the first child the struggle with poverty began and continued in intensity as other children were added, only to be relieved when the oldest child reached an age when he could be forced out into the world of work to help support the family. As the older child added his income to the family, the economic burdens of the household were lightened, and the younger children profited by the advanced standard of living in the home and were the beneficiaries of better diet, better housing, and greater educational opportunity [13]."

In such a setting, resentment and hostility would be almost inevitable. The attempt by siblings to live comfortably together with such feelings would meet with insuperable obstacles. Repression, displacement and acting out, particularly during adolescence, would be some of the mechanisms used in order to avoid both painful competition with the rival and feelings of hatred and jealousy.

In the development of the Comanche Indian, whose whole culture was geared to war and performing manly acts of bravery, "classificatory sisters, who were often older than the boy, disciplined him by threatening to hang him or to use physical violence. The result of this was that the boy felt a thorough hostility toward older female relatives which lasted for life . . . [7]. The female child, though she is not most often the honored child, is not discriminated against. She has the same sexual freedom as the male, but occupies an unfavorable position as regards her brother; strict brother taboos and the fact that the classificatory sister is the disciplinarian, makes her the target of her brothers' dislike. She has no value to him [8]." Among the Alorese, who live on a small island of Indonesia about six hundred miles east of Java, and whose culture is predominantly Papuan, the rivalries between siblings customarily seen in our society "can not possibly develop to the same degree because little is expected from the parent and so there is little to fight about. On the contrary, the opportunities for strong attachments between siblings are very great. There are, however, many factors that militate against such attachments. The oldest sibling undoubtedly has the worst time of it, because it is compelled, as soon as it is able, to take over the maternal role without having enjoyed its benefits. The effects must be very uneven. A strong bond must undoubtedly be created by the fact that the siblings have common enemies and common grievances [9]."

Thus, even under favorable.environmental circumstances for developing good sibling relationships, frictions exist. Some brothers and sisters do get on together without damage to their emotional lives. With others, resentments and jealousies are of such intensity as to become sources of personality distortion in and of themselves. According to Josselyn (6), the smoothly established or stormy sibling relationships can be evaluated only when they are seen as a part of the total picture, not as a total picture. When the child has brothers or sisters, the family constellation becomes much more complex and the variety of interpersonal experiences becomes much richer and somewhat more hazardous, with the intensity and duration of the jealous reaction depending on the family factors (4).

Both Saint Augustine and Jean Jacques Rousseau give evidence in their *Confessions* of strong sibling problems and conflicts which were basic to each one's personality development. Saint Augustine, in his work, makes but one offhand reference to an unnamed younger brother; a younger sister is not mentioned at all. "In further describing the father in slighting terms, Augustine would have us believe that only his mother mattered [11]." (In the great majority of autobiographies selected for this volume, little or no reference is made to siblings.)

As for Rousseau, his seven-year-older brother was the only real rival for his father's affection. Rousseau wrote, "The extraordinary affection they lavished on me might be the reason he was too much neglected: this certainly was a fault which cannot be justified. His education and morals suffered by this neglect, and he acquired the habits of a libertine before he arrived at an age to be really one. . . . One day I remember when my father was correcting him severely, I threw myself down between them, embracing my brother whom I covered with my body, receiving the strokes designed for him; I persisted so obstinately in my protection that either softened by my cries and tears, or fearing to hurt me most, his anger subsided and he pardoned his fault." Kligerman asserts that in this episode,

"Rousseau demonstrates a reactive solicitude. We can easily imagine the brother's attitude toward him: after enjoying the mother's exclusive love for seven years, he was deprived first of her life, then of his father's affection by the little newcomer. There must have been intense mutual resentment which at least in the case of Jean Jacques was repressed with the reaction-formation of pity and tenderness [12]."

Rousseau's behavior was a characteristic resolution of a sibling rivalry situation motivated by the hatred of the sibling and the wish for his death. Rousseau's need to repress his hostility backfired, in the illustration cited, in the form of taking on the punishment he wished his rival to suffer, to the detriment of his own self-esteem and the suppression of all aggressive attitudes or actions. Throughout the *Confessions,* Rousseau refers constantly to his timidity, mildness, lack of aggression, and abhorrence of cruelty. Other characteristic resolutions of conflictual sibling relations include the wish to possess the attributes of the rival, which may lead to regressive longings, and the need to set up claims on the score of incapacity or illness, which compel one parent or the other to be attentive (10).

The following excerpts illustrate the characteristic manifestations and dynamics of sibling rivalry.

Benjamin Franklin
(1706-1790)

Franklin had been apprenticed by his father to his older brother, James, who in 1720 had started the second newspaper to be published in America, the *New England Courant*. The fourteen-year-old Ben composed type, printed the sheets and delivered the papers to customers. Anonymously, he submitted little essays for publication, which to his great delight were printed. Coincident with the revelation of the author, serious conflict between the two brothers arose. A judgment would be required of the father to settle the disputes—which were generally decided in favor of Ben. This infuriated James, who would beat him, which Ben "took extremely amiss." In a footnote, Franklin added this significant statement: "I fancy his harsh and tyrannical treatment of me might be a means of impressing me with that aversion to arbitrary power that has stuck to me through my whole life." Within the year, Ben ran away from the intolerable situation to begin a new life in Philadelphia.*

My brother had, in 1720 or 21, begun to print a newspaper. It was the second that appeared in America, and was called the *New England Courant*. The only one before it was the *Boston News-Letter*. I remember his being dissuaded by some of his friends from the undertaking, as not likely to succeed, one newspaper being, in their judgment, enough for America. At this time (1771) there are not less than five-and-twenty. He went on, however, with the undertaking, and after having worked in composing the types and printing off the sheets, I was employed to carry the papers through the streets to the customers.

He had some ingenious men among his friends, who amused themselves by writing little pieces for this paper, which gained it credit and made it more in demand, and these gentlemen often visited us. Hearing their conversations, and their accounts of the approbation their papers were received with, I was excited to try my hand among them; but, being still a boy, and suspecting that my brother would object to printing anything of mine in his paper if he knew it to be mine, I contrived to disguise my hand and, writing an anonymous paper, I put it in at night under the door of the printing-house. It was found in the morning and communicated to his writing friends when they called in as usual. They read it, commented on it in my hearing, and I had the exquisite pleasure of finding it met with their approbation, and that, in their different guesses at the author, none were named but men of some character among us for learning and ingenuity. I suppose now that I was rather lucky in my judges, and that perhaps they were not really so very good ones as I then esteemed them.

Encouraged, however, by this, I wrote and conveyed in the same way to the press several more papers which were equally approved; and I kept my secret till my small fund of sense for such performances was pretty well exhausted, and then I discovered it, when I began to be considered a little more by my brother's acquaintance, and in a manner that did not quite please him, as he thought, probably with reason, that it tended to make me too vain. And perhaps this might be one occasion of the differences that we began to have about this time. Though a brother, he considered himself as my master, and me as his apprentice, and accordingly expected the same services from me as he would from another, while I thought he demeaned me too much in some he required of me, who from a brother expected more indul-

---

*From *Autobiography* by Benjamin Franklin. New York: Rinehart & Co., 1948. Pp. 17-20.

gence. Our disputes were often brought before our father, and I fancy I was either generally in the right, or else a better pleader, because the judgment was generally in my favor. But my brother was passionate, and had often beaten me, which I took extremely amiss; and, thinking my apprenticeship very tedious, I was continually wishing for some opportunity of shortening it, which at length offered in a manner unexpected.

One of the pieces in our newspaper on some political point, which I have now forgotten, gave offense to the Assembly. He was taken up, censured, and imprisoned for a month, by the speaker's warrant, I suppose because he would not discover his author. I too was taken up and examined before the council; but, though I did not give them any satisfaction, they contented themselves with admonishing me, and dismissed me, considering me, perhaps, as an apprentice who was bound to keep his master's secrets.

During my brother's confinement, which I resented a good deal, notwithstanding our private differences, I had the management of the paper; and I made bold to give our rulers some rubs in it, which my brother took very kindly, while others began to consider me in an unfavorable light, as a young genius that had a turn for libeling and satire. My brother's discharge was accompanied with an order of the House (a very odd one), that "James Franklin should no longer print the paper called the *New England Courant*."

There was a consultation held in our printing-house among his friends what he should do in this case. Some proposed to evade the order by changing the name of the paper; but my brother seeing inconveniences in that, it was finally concluded on as a better way to let it be printed for the future under the name of *Benjamin Franklin*; and to avoid the censure of the Assembly, that might fall on him as still printing it by his apprentice, the contrivance was that my old indenture should be returned to me, with a full discharge on the back of it, to be shown on occasion; but to secure to him the benefit of my service, I was to sign new indentures for the remainder of the term, which were to be kept private. A very flimsy scheme it was; however, it was immediately executed, and the paper went on accordingly under my name for several months.

At length, a fresh difference arising between my brother and me, I took upon me to assert my freedom, presuming that he would not venture to produce the new indentures. It was not fair of me to take this advantage, and this I therefore reckon one of the first errata of my life; but the unfairness of it weighed little with me when under the impressions of resentment for the blows his passion too often urged him to bestow upon me, though he was otherwise not an ill-natured man; perhaps I was too saucy and provoking.

When he found I would leave him, he took care to prevent my getting employment in any other printing-house of the town, by going round and speaking to every master, who accordingly refused to give me work. I then thought of going to New York, as the nearest place where there was a printer; and I was the rather inclined to leave Boston when I reflected that I had already made myself a little obnoxious to the governing party, and, from the arbitrary proceedings of the Assembly in my brother's case, it was likely I might, if I stayed, soon bring myself into scrapes; and farther, that my indiscreet disputations about religion began to make me pointed at with horror by good people as an infidel or atheist. I determined on the point, but my father now siding with my brother, I was sensible that, if I attempted to go openly, means would be used to prevent me. My friend Collins, therefore, undertook to manage a little for me. He agreed with the captain of a New York sloop for my passage, under the notion of my being a young acquaintance of his, that had got a naughty girl with child, whose friends would compel me to marry her, and therefore I could not appear or come away publicly. So I sold some of my books to raise a little money, was taken on board privately, and as we had a fair wind, in three days I found myself in New York, near three hundred miles from home, a boy of but seventeen, without the least recommendation to, or knowledge of, any person in the place, and with very little money in my pocket.

Johann Wolfgang von Goethe
(1749-1832)

Goethe described his father as stern, severe, regulatory and demanding with his children. His mother was described as "still almost a child, who first grew up to consciousness with and in her two eldest children." The antagonism between the latter three and the father grew with the years since the mother and children could not give up their feelings and since the father followed out his views unshaken and uninterrupted. Goethe sought solace with his sister, one year younger than he, particularly after his first disappointment in love. What could be more natural, he asked, than that in these circumstances "brother and sister should cling close to each other and adhere to their mother?"*

*From *Goethe's Autobiography. Poetry and Truth from my own Life*. Reprinted by permission of Public Affairs Press. 1949. Pp. 194-195.

The child's oedipus complex reflects the parents' unsolved oedipus complex. Apparently this was operative in Goethe's case. Fenichel states, "Within the framework of the family, brothers and sisters represent persons who from the standpoint of the oedipus strivings are superfluous. First of all, they are objects of jealousy; individual circumstances determine whether their presence increases the unconscious hate toward the parent of the same sex or decreases it by means of diversion. But siblings may also serve as objects of the transference of love, especially older ones or those who are only a little younger, so that the world has never been experienced without them. If there are several older brothers and sisters, we may see 'doubles of the oedipus complex'; what is experienced with the parents is experienced with the older brother and sister a second time. This may have a relieving effect, but may also create new conflicts [2]."

From such excursions, undertaken partly for pleasure and partly for art, which could be completed in a short time and often repeated, I was again drawn home, and that by a magnet which always worked strongly upon me; this was my sister. She, only a year younger than myself, had lived my whole conscious period of life with me, and was thus bound to me by the closest ties. To these natural causes was added a forcible motive arising from our domestic condition; a father, certainly affectionate and well-meaning, but severe, who, because inwardly he cherished a very tender heart, externally with incredible consistency assumed a brazen sternness, that he might attain his object of giving his children the best education, building up, regulating, and preserving his well-founded house; on the other hand, a mother, still almost a child, who first grew up to consciousness with and in her two eldest children; these three, as they looked at the world with healthy eyes, capable of life, longed for present enjoyment. This antagonism floating over the family increased with years. My father followed out his views unshaken and uninterrupted; mother and children could not give up their feelings, their demands, and their wishes.

In these circumstances it was natural that brother and sister should cling close to each other and adhere to their mother, that they might at least snatch singly the pleasures forbidden them as a whole. But since the hours of seclusion and toil were very long compared with the moments of recreation and pleasure, especially for my sister, who could never leave the house for so long as I could, the necessity she felt for entertaining herself with me was still sharpened by the feeling of longing with which she accompanied me to a distance.

And so, as in the early years, playing and learning, growth and education, had been completely common to both of us, that we might well have been taken for twins; so did this mutual intercourse, this confidence, remain during the development of our physical and moral powers. That interest of youth, that amazement at the awakening of sensual impulses, which clothe themselves in mental forms, of mental necessities which clothe themselves in sensual images, all the reflections thereupon which obscure rather than enlighten us as the mist covers over and does not illuminate the valley from which it is going to rise, the many errors and aberrations which spring therefrom, the brother and sister shared and endured hand in hand, and were the less enlightened over their strange condition, as the nearer they wished to approach one another to clear up their minds, the sacred awe of their close relationship the more forcibly ever kept them apart.

Unwillingly do I mention this in general terms which I undertook years before to set forth, without being able to accomplish it. Since I lost this beloved, incomprehensible being all too soon, I felt sufficient inducement to represent her worth to myself, and so there arose in me the idea of a poetic whole, in which it would have been possible to exhibit her individuality, but I could think of no other form but that of the Richardsonian novels. Only by the minutest detail, by endless particular points which all bear vividly the character of the whole, and while springing from a wonderful depth give some feeling of that depth—only in such a way could one in some measure succeed in communicating a representation of this remarkable personality, for the spring can only be understood while it is flowing. But from this beautiful and pious resolve, as from so many other things, I was drawn away by the tumult of the world, and now nothing remains for me but to call up for a moment the shadow of that blessed spirit, as though by the help of a magic mirror. She was tall, well and delicately built, and had a natural dignity in her demeanour which melted away into a pleasing mildness. The lineaments of her countenance, neither striking nor beautiful, bespoke a being which was not and could not be at unity with itself. Her eyes were not the most beautiful which I have ever seen, but the deepest, behind which one expected the most, and when they expressed any affection, any love, had a brilliancy which was unequalled; and yet this expression was not exactly tender as that which comes from the heart and at the same time carries with it something of longing and desire; this expression came from the soul, it was full and rich, seemed only to wish to be giving, not needing to receive.

Thomas DeQuincey*
(1785-1859)

It was noted in the introduction to this chapter that one of the characteristic ways by which sibling rivalry is resolved is through the wish to possess the attributes of the rival. During the period described in this passage, DeQuincey's brother, William, was sixteen and Thomas was eight. DeQuincey presents a remarkable picture of the feelings his adolescent brother held. William despised the effeminacy of his delicate brother, domineered in the nursery, and compelled Thomas to take part in quarrels with the factory children of the district. Even more remarkable was DeQuincey's reaction to William's overt hostility and contempt: "I doted on it; and considered contempt a sort of luxury that I was in continual fear of losing."

Such a reaction formation was imperative were Tom to be allowed the company of his brother and to identify with him. Were he to lose the contempt, he would then lose his value to William. Thus his continued fear. The eight-year-old boy needed the identification, for their father had been in the West Indies on business for some time and had come home in 1793, only to die the same year.

DeQuincey's description of his eldest brother was glowing: "A remarkable boy"; "aspiring"; "immeasurably active"; "fertile in resources as Robinson Crusoe"—but he could also recall that William was "full of quarrel as it is possible to imagine." DeQuincey's feelings were undoubtedly colored because his brother died of typhus fever at the age of sixteen—the same year as their father.

My brother was a stranger from causes quite as little to be foreseen, but seeming quite as natural after they had really occurred. In an early stage of his career, he had been found wholly unmanageable. His genius for mischief amounted to inspiration: it was a divine *afflatus* which drove him in that direction; and such was his capacity for riding in whirlwinds and directing storms, that he made it his trade to create them, as a νεφεληγερετα Ζευς, a cloud-compelling Jove, in order that he *might* direct them. For this, and other reasons, he had

---

*From *The Collected Writings of Thomas DeQuincey* edited by David Masson. Edinburgh: Adam & Charles Black, 1889. Pp. 58-62.

been sent to the Grammar School of Louth, in Lincolnshire—one of those many old classic institutions which form the peculiar glory of England. To box, and to box under the severest restraint of honourable laws, was in those days a mere necessity of schoolboy life at *public* schools; and hence the superior manliness, generosity, and self-control, of those generally who had benefited by such discipline—so systematically hostile to all meanness, pusillanimity, or indirectness. . . .

Fresh from such a training as this, and at a time when his additional five or six years availed nearly to make *his* age the double of mine, my brother very naturally despised me; and, from his exceeding frankness, he took no pains to conceal that he did. Why should he? Who was it that could have a right to feel aggrieved by his contempt? Who, if not myself? But it happened, on the contrary, that I had a perfect craze for being despised. I doted on it; and considered contempt a sort of luxury that I was in continual fear of losing. Why not? Wherefore should any rational person shrink from contempt, if it happen to form the tenure by which he holds his repose in life? The cases, which are cited from comedy, of such a yearning after contempt, stand upon a footing altogether different: *there* the contempt is wooed as a serviceable ally and tool of religious hypocrisy. But, to me, at that era of life, it formed the main guarantee of an unmolested repose: and security there was not, on any lower terms, for the *latentis semita vitæ*. The slightest approach to any favourable construction of my intellectual pretensions alarmed me beyond measure; because it pledged me in a manner with the hearer to support this first attempt by a second, by a third, by a fourth—O heavens! there is no saying how far the horrid man might go in his unreasonable demands upon me. I groaned under the weight of his expectations. . . .

Still, with all this passion for being despised, which was so essential to my peace of mind, I found at times an altitude—a starry altitude— in the station of contempt for me assumed by my brother that nettled me. Sometimes, indeed, the mere necessities of dispute carried me, before I was aware of my own imprudence, so far up the staircase of Babel, that my brother was shaken for a moment in the infinity of his contempt: and, before long, when my superiority in some bookish accomplishments displayed itself, by results that could not be entirely dissembled, mere foolish human nature forced me into some trifle of exultation at these retributory triumphs. But more often I was disposed to grieve over them. They tended to shake that solid foundation of utter despicableness upon which I relied so much for my freedom from anxiety; and, therefore, upon the whole, it was satisfactory to my mind that my brother's opinion of me, after any little transient oscil lation, gravitated determinately back towards that settled contempt which had been the result of his original inquest. The pillars of Hercules upon which rested the vast edifice of his scorn were these two—1st, my physics: he denounced me for effeminacy; 2d, he assumed, and even postulated as a *datum*, which I myself could never have the face to refuse, my general idiocy. Physically, therefore, and intellectually, he looked upon me as below notice; but, *morally*, he assured me that he would give me a written character of the very best description, whenever I chose to apply for it. "You're honest," he said; "you're willing, though lazy; you *would* pull, if you had the strength of a flea; and, though a monstrous coward, you don't run away." My own demurs to these harsh judgments were not so many as they might have been. The idiocy I confessed; because, though positive that I was not uniformly an idiot, I felt inclined to think that, in a majority of cases, I really *was;* and there were more reasons for thinking so than the reader is yet aware of. But, as to the effeminacy, I denied it *in toto;* and with good reason, as will be seen. Neither did my brother pretend to have any experimental proofs of it. The ground he went upon was a mere *à priori* one—viz, that I had always been tied to the apron-string of women or girls; which amounted at most to this—that, by training and the natural tendency of circumstances, I *ought* to be effeminate: that is, there was reason to expect beforehand that I *should* be so; but, then, the more merit in me, if, in spite of such reasonable presumptions, I really were *not*. In fact, my brother soon learned, by a daily experience, how entirely he might depend upon me for carrying out the most audacious of his own warlike plans; such plans it is true that I abominated; but *that* made no difference in the fidelity with which I tried to fulfil them.

This eldest brother of mine was in all respects a remarkable boy. Haughty he was, aspiring, immeasurably active; fertile in resources as Robinson Crusoe; but also full of quarrel as it is possible to imagine; and, in default of any other opponent, he would have fastened a quarrel upon his own shadow for presuming to run before him when going westwards in the morning, whereas, in all reason, a shadow, like a dutiful child, ought to keep deferentially in rear of that majestic substance which is the author of its existence. Books he detested, one and all, excepting only such as he happened to write himself. And these were not a few. On all subjects known to man, from the Thirty-nine Articles of our English Church, down to pyrotechnics, legerdemain, magic, both black and white, thaumaturgy, and necromancy, he favoured the world (which world was the nursery where I lived amongst my sisters) with his select opinions.

Harriet Martineau
(1802-1876)

Harriet Martineau, long familiar to American readers, was a deaf Englishwoman who wrote fictionalized illustrations of economic theory and whose defense of the abolition of slavery in the United States made her a controversial figure. She was the peer of the Brownings, the Carlyles, the Darwins, Florence Nightingale, Wordsworth, Dickens and others. Herbert Spencer, in his *Autobiography*, made this comment about Miss Martineau: "About this period [he was fifteen years old and the date was 1835] we read aloud Miss Martineau's *Tales of Political Economy*. Years before, when at home, I had read sundry of them; and comments to my advantage had been made in consequence. I believe that these were but little deserved, and that I read for the stories and skipped the political economy. However, from remarks in my letters written in the spring of 1835, it appears that I had gathered something of a solid kind [17]."

Like Mrs. Trollope and Francis J. Grund, who also visited America and wrote about their experiences, Harriet Martineau felt herself the victim of a peculiarly nineteenth-century imbalance. "I had now plunged fairly into the spirit of my time," she wrote, "—that of self-analysis, pathetic self-pity, typical interpretation of objective matters, and scheme-making, in the name of God and Man [14]." In the following excerpt from her autobiography, some of the beginnings of this introspective self-pity are revealed in her description of the jealous rivalry she felt for a younger, presumably more favored, sister.*

I look back upon another scene with horror at my own audacity, and wonder that my family could endure me at all. At Mr. Perry's, one of our school-fellows was a clever, mischievous girl,—so clever, and so much older than myself as to have great influence over me when she chose to try her power, though I disapproved her ways very heartily. She one day asked me, in a corner, in a mysterious sort of way, whether I did not perceive that Rachel was the favourite at home, and treated with manifest partiality. Everybody else, she said, observed it. This

---

*From *Autobiography* by Harriet Martineau. Reprinted by permission of Houghton Mifflin Co. 1877. Pp. 65-67.

had never distinctly occurred to me. Rachel was handy and useful, and not paralysed by fear, as I was; and, very naturally, our busy mother resorted to her for help, and put trust in her about matters of business, not noticing the growth of an equally natural habit in Rachel of quizzing or snubbing me, as the elder ones did. From the day of this mischievous speech of my school-fellow, I was on the watch, and with the usual result to the jealous. Months,—perhaps a year or two—passed on while I was brooding over this, without a word to any one; and then came the explosion, one winter evening after tea, when my eldest sister was absent, and my mother, Rachel and I were sitting at work. Rachel criticised something that I said, in which I happened to be right. After once defending myself, I sat silent. My mother remarked on my "obstinacy," saying that I was "not a bit convinced." I replied that nothing convincing had been said. My mother declared that she agreed with Rachel, and that I ought to yield. Then I passed the verge, and got wrong. A sudden force of daring entering my mind. I said, in the most provoking way possible, that this was nothing new, as she always did agree with Rachel against me. My mother put down her work, and asked me what I meant by that. I looked her full in the face, and said that what I meant was that everything that Rachel said and did was right, and everything that I said and did was wrong. Rachel burst into an insulting laugh, and was sharply bidden to "be quiet." I saw by this that I had gained some ground; and this was made clearer by my mother sternly desiring me to practice my music. I saw that she wanted to gain time. The question now was how I should get through. My hands were clammy and tremulous; my fingers stuck to each other; my eyes were dim, and there was a roaring in my ears. I could easily have fainted; and it might have done no harm if I had. But I made a tremendous effort to appear calm. I opened the piano, lighted a candle with a steady hand, began, and derived strength from the first chords. I believe I never played better in my life. Then the question was—how was I ever to leave off! On I went for what seemed to me an immense time, till my mother sternly called to me to leave off and go to bed. With my candle in my hand, I said "Good-night." My mother laid down her work, and said, "Harriet, I am more displeased with you tonight than ever I have been in your life." Thought I, "I don't care: I have got it out, and it is all true." "Go and say your prayers," my mother continued; "and ask God to forgive you for your conduct tonight; for I don't know that I can. Go to your prayers." Thought I,— "No, I shan't." And I did not: and that was the only night from my infancy to mature womanhood that I did not pray. I detected misgiving in my mother's forced manner; and I triumphed. If the right was on my side (as I entirely believed) the power was on hers; and what the next morning was to be I could not perceive. I slept little, and went down sick with dread. Not a word was said, however, then or ever, of the scene of the preceding night; but henceforth, a most scrupulous impartiality between Rachel and me was shown. If the occasion had been better used still,—if my mother had but bethought herself of saying to me, "My child, I never dreamed that these terrible thoughts were in your mind. I am your mother. Why do you not tell me every thing that makes you unhappy?" I believe this would have wrought in a moment that cure which it took years to effect, amidst reserve and silence.

Fyodor Dostoevsky
(1821-1881)

The following letter from Dostoevsky to his brother Michael was written not too long after their father had been brutally murdered.* The shocking experience precipitated the novelist's epileptic seizures although it has been presumed they began in childhood in milder form (3). The murder of the father in *The Brothers Karamazov* is a direct recounting of what actually happened. Out of his misery, anxieties, and epileptic fits, Dostoevsky found the material for his novels.

This letter reflects Dostoevsky's misery. The effusiveness to Michael, his exaggerated gratitude for having received a letter from him, his fondling of the letter, examination of the envelope, and the postponement of its reading reflect the masochistic trait in Dostoevsky, his love of tormenting and his intolerance even toward the people he loved.

Petersburg, January 1, 1840

I thank you from my heart, good brother, for your dear letter. I am certainly quite a different sort of person from you; you could never imagine how delightfully my heart thrills when they bring me a letter from you, and I have invented a new sort of enjoyment: I put myself on the rack. I take your letter in my hand, turn it about for some minutes, feel it to see whether it's long, and when I've satiated myself with the sealed envelope, I put it in my pocket. You'd never guess what a

*From *Letters of Fyodor Michailovitch Dostoevsky to his Family and Friends* edited by Ethel Coburn Mayne. Reprinted by permission of Chatto & Windus, Ltd. Copyright Macmillan Co., n. d. Pp. 10-11.

pleasant state of heart and soul I thus procure for myself. I often wait a quarter of an hour; at last I fall greedily upon the packet, unseal it, and devour your lines—your dear lines! Countless feelings awake in my heart while I read your letter. So many tender and painful, sweet and bitter, emotions crowd into my soul—yes, dear brother, there are painful and bitter ones. You cannot dream how bitter it is for me when people don't understand me, when they mistake what I say, and see it in the wrong light. After I had read your last letter, I was quite *enragé* because you were not near me; I saw the dearest dreams of my heart, my most sacred principles, which I have won by hard experience, wholly distorted, mutilated, deformed. You said to me yourself: "Do write to me, contradict me, dispute with me." You anticipated some profit therefrom. Dear brother, it has not been of the least use! The only thing that you have got from it is, that in your egoism (we are all egoists, for that matter) you have formed just such an opinion of me, my views, ideas, and peculiarities, as happens to suit yourself. And that is an extremely insulting one! No—polemics in intimate letters are a subtle poison. How will it be now, when we see one another again? I believe that all this will be subject for endless contention. But enough of it.

Lincoln Steffens
(1866-1936)

Steffens wrote, in his *Autobiography*, with some astonishment as well as with perception, of the jealousy he felt toward his younger sisters when they arrived on the scene and he was no longer the object of the sole attention of his parents.* As Freud said in his paper on "Female Sexuality," "Childish love knows no bounds. It demands exclusive possession, is satisfied with nothing less than all. . . . Childish love has no real aim. It is incapable of complete satisfaction and this is the principal reason why it is doomed to end in disappointment and to give place to a hostile attitude." Steffens' analysis of the situation covered his early adolescent years, from about twelve to fourteen, and his reaction to discovering the depth of feeling his younger sister had for him. Toddlers regress, frequently, with the advent of a new baby in the family, reverting to more infantile ways of behaving. They whine or cry more easily, the speech becomes babyish, there is a clinging to the parents, and perhaps

---

*Reprinted by permission of Harcourt, Brace & World, Inc. 1931. P. 77.

a loss of bladder control. Steffens' reaction was on a more sophis-ticated level, as might be expected of an adolescent, but the feelings were identical.

One of the wrongs suffered by boys is that of being loved before loving. They receive so early and so freely the affection and devotion of their mothers, sisters, and teachers that they do not learn to love; and so, when they grow up and become lovers and husbands, they avenge themselves upon their wives and sweethearts. Never having had to love, they cannot; they don't know how. I, for example, was born in an atmosphere of love; my parents loved me. Of course. But they had been loving me so long when I awoke to consciousness that my baby love had no chance. It began, but it never caught up. Then came my sisters, one by one. They too were loved from birth, and they might have stayed behind as I did, but girls are different; my sisters seem to have been born loving as well as loved. Anyhow my first sister, though younger than I, loved me long before I can remember even noticing her, and I cannot forget the shock of astonishment and hu-miliation at my discovery of her feeling for me. She had gone to Stock-ton to visit Colonel Carter's family, and in a week was so homesick for me that my father and mother took me with them to fetch her. That was their purpose. Mine was to see the great leader of my father's wagon train across the plains and talk livestock with him. You can imagine how I felt when, as we walked up to the house, the front door opened and my little sister rushed out ahead, threw her arms around me, and cried—actually cried—with tears running down her cheeks, "My Len, my Len!"

I had to suffer it, but what would Colonel Carter think, and his sons?

Henry Handel Richardson
(1870-1946)

Henry Handel Richardson was the eldest daughter of Walter Linde-say Richardson, M.D., who emigrated to Australia in the 1850's and who died there in 1879. The family fortunes were low, but they improved when the mother began to earn a livelihood as a post-mistress. In 1882, Henry Handel, or Ethel Florence Lindesay Richardson, as she was christened, attended the Presbyterian Ladies College in Melbourne and began to show signs of musical talent. Five years later, the family, which included a younger daughter, Lil, left Australia for good to take up life in England, where it was hoped that Ethel would be able to pursue her musical studies. The passage over was a painful one, for the autobiographer relates she was not prepared for what took place on board ship: the passengers made Lil the object of their attention and left her in the unaccustomed role of second fiddle. Ethel's reaction was one of disbelief, incredulity and denial.*

To go back to the earlier voyage. Vividly as I recall it, I shall here do no more than pick out a few of the incidents that touch me nearly. For the rest, barring my inordinate fondness for the sea and the ability to stand up to any weather, I was in no way different from other girls; and I amused myself in typical girlish fashion.

One hindrance to this had mercifully been removed. Mother, with a little money to her credit—she got, I believe, something over four thousand for the house—was able to indulge her natural generosity and fit us out in style. Better still, she let us have a say in what we wore. For once I didn't need to blush for my clothes. They were now well cut and strictly neutral in tone.

As it was the off-season the number of passengers was small, and consisted for the most part of elderly men returning from business-trips to Australia. A few older women made up the list, but Lil and I were the only young girls on board. Thus we came in for a good deal of attention, by far the larger share of which however fell to her. For the first time in my life, I found myself reduced to playing second fiddle. And, incredible as it seemed, to no other than the unassuming little sister who had for so long trotted humbly at my heels. It was a bitter pill to swallow. Not that I rated my own looks high, I had heard too much about my nose for that; but I *was* accustomed to be picked on as the more important and to receive first notice. Henceforth the reverse was the case.

Pretty I had learnt to think Lil. But I was not prepared for seeing her the centre of attraction, or for the fulsome epithets now bestowed on her. By our Irish relatives, too, when we met. With the characteristic bluntness of their race they did not scruple to pronounce: "E. is very well, but Lil is a beauty." The men who clustered around her on the ship were of the same opinion, and found themselves further ensnared by a wistful naïveté of manner that went straight to their

---

*From *Myself When Young* by Henry Handel Richardson. Reprinted by permission of W. W. Norton & Co., Inc. 1948. Pp. 81-82.

elderly hearts. Wit and brilliance were not demanded of her: enough for them if she sat still to be looked at.

As a sister, it was difficult to see her with any but a sister's eye, and to understand the fuss made of her. I remained incredulous; and at the same time very fearful lest her young head should be turned by all this open flattery. However, except for a certain pernicketiness about her dress, which till now had not interested her, I couldn't detect any change.—In after years it was different. By then she had come to take admiration for granted, to accept it as her due; and, since it was invariably forthcoming, she developed a self-assurance, not to say complacency, that often made me wince. Looking back on her from this distance I can see that, added to all else, she must have inherited a good dose of Irish charm. Even when her prettiness faded, she had only to exchange a few casual words with a person to set them—him or her—singing her praises.

Helen Thomas Flexner
(1871-1956)

Brothers and sisters may have a particularly difficult time with each other during adolescence. Helen Flexner's older brother, Henry, was extremely critical of her, as these two passages,* the first when the girl was nearly thirteen, the second when she was fifteen, illustrate. He criticized her legs, her gaiters, her tone of voice, her posture, her attitude when with his male friends. This verbalization of criticism of her might have been a way of disguising a conflict he had that was similar to that centered about his relationship to his mother. In general, the adolescent boy may be "confused in his feeling towards a girl, with whom he has lived closely for most or all of his life, who is now developing into a woman. He must deny her attractiveness by dissertating on her limitations. This depreciation of her keeps him free of any awareness that he might find her attractive since she is just as is the mother, a forbidden sexual object. This depreciation may be very threatening to his sister. If her brother sees nothing charming in her, she has little confidence that other boys will either. She often needs a great deal of subtle support to maintain her own self-confidence against the brother's barrage. On the other hand, she is also reassured by his rejection because her

---

*From *A Quaker Childhood* by Helen T. Flexner. Reprinted by permission of Yale University Press. 1940. Pp. 168-169, 291-293.

brother is, for her, a forbidden sexual object [5]."

From time to time flashes of insight into my brother's feelings came to me and I saw the extreme sensitiveness from which under his gallant gaiety he suffered. On his side he was well aware of my secret emotions, childish feelings of inferiority and shame, personal vanities I tried to conceal, and sometimes he laid them bare with an acute comment in private or even in public before the assembled family, causing me agonies I have never forgotten.

My short fat legs were a dreadful trial to me and gaiters made them look even shorter and fatter. I avoided wearing gaiters whenever I could, so one wet morning when my mother told me to put them on before starting for school I protested.

"I really don't need gaiters, Mother," I said. "The rain is stopping already."

I saw my mother look at the windows down which the raindrops were pouring.

"Go right up to thy room and put thy gaiters on," she said. "It will take only a minute." Her voice was very firm.

As I pushed my chair back from the table to obey Harry remarked to the company in general, "Hellen is so proud of her legs, she hates to cover them up." Then speaking directly to me he said, "Thee looks very nice in gaiters. They really set off thy legs."

Though I did not glance about me I was well aware of the smiles his words excited.

This was not the first time Harry had teased me about my legs. He knew very well how I hated them. It hurt me terribly that he should put me to shame in this way. Perhaps he was not really fond of me, after all. Perhaps I only bothered him with my affection. I did not know what to think.

Later during the winter my equanimity was shattered by my brother Harry's unkindness, as it then seemed to me, though I did not hold it against him since I knew that he was genuinely fond of me. Like many clear-sighted, sensitive people, Harry had a way of exposing with devastating clarity the weaknesses of others, even the people he loved, when they annoyed him or when, as in my case no doubt, he felt it would do them good. He could not yet have had sufficient experience to know that the mistakes of young people, however annoying to their elders, should sometimes be passed over without comment.

One afternoon this brother of mine took me with him to visit the laboratory where he worked three times a week on some problem or other. As we entered the room the two young men seated at a long

table under high bare windows jumped up quickly and greeted me
with gallantry as if I were a young lady. One in particular showed me
the slide under his microscope and when I looked down the brass
tube, shutting my left eye as directed, he adjusted the focus for me and
pointed out to me the tiny object "in the center of the field." I really
did see it, though I had never looked into a microscope before, and I
managed to ask a shy question or two about it. We did not stay long,
but I was greatly pleased with the visit and the two handsome young
men who had been so charming to me.

After dinner Harry and I settled ourselves in the back parlor to talk
over the day's adventure. Harry expressed gratification that I had been
so much interested in the laboratory and then he proceeded to comment on my behavior.

"I cannot imagine what made thee speak in such an affected tone of
voice and stand with thy shoulders raised up almost to the level of thy
ears. Thee doesn't look particularly fascinating in that attitude."

The glance Harry fixed on me expressed not so much wonder as
annoyance. I felt my cheeks burn hotly under his eyes as I realized
that in my shyness and desire to make a good impression I had made a
fool of myself. I had been really interested and it had not entered my
head, consciously, that I could "fascinate" the young men, as Harry
said. My humiliation was intense. From that moment I avoided young
men, telling myself that they were no concern of mine and never
would be. Thus I constructed a suspension bridge of indifference to
walk on above the turmoils of humiliation.

Helena Morley
(1880-   )

At the age of thirteen, Helena Morley used the defense mechanisms
of intellectualization and rationalization to protect herself against
feelings of antagonism and resentment directed toward her younger
sister Luizinha. Intellectually, Helena recognized her own jealousy
toward Luizinha as well as her own character limitations. Nevertheless, she could not contain herself emotionally. In this passage,
Helena entered in her *Diary* a nasty trick she played on her sister,
making a point to deny that she was ashamed of her behavior.*

---

*From *The Diary of "Helena Morley"* edited by Elizabeth Bishop. Reprinted by
permission of Farrar, Straus & Cudahy, Inc. Copyright 1957, Elizabeth Bishop. Pp.
54-55.

Tuesday, August 29th, 1893

Why does everyone like to criticise the bad things we do and not to praise the good things? It doesn't seem as if my sister and I could be children of the same parents. I'm impatient, rebellious, impertinent, lazy, and incapable of being obedient and all the things they'd like me to be. Luizinha is as good as an angel. I don't know how anyone can be like her, so quiet. She never goes out of the house unless she's hanging on mama's arm. She never asks for anything. If I should say I'd ever heard her ask for a new dress, I'd be lying. And if she gets a dress and I want to take it away from her, she doesn't mind. Then everybody calls me a difficult child, but nobody praises Luizinha.

I'm going to write down here what I did to her, and not be ashamed, because only the paper's going to know.

For months she's been saving fifty *mil reis* that her godfather gave her, to buy a new dress. This year I've been thinking I should celebrate my birthday with a dinner party for my friends, because they invite me when they have birthdays. The Negro women at the *chácara* are all very good to me. Generosa, who's a very good cook, had already told me that if I could get the money to pay for the food she'd cook a very good dinner for me and I wouldn't have to bother about it at all. In my own imagination, I'm an only child. I'm already famous for it. The idea of Luizinha's money came to me. But because I didn't want to make her feel bad I prepared everything very well and I said to her, "Give me your fifty *mil reis* for my birthday party. If you make a dress with it, only you will get the benefit of it. But if you give me the money and I give the party, I'll get lots of presents and we'll divide everything." Luizinha agreed to do it. I gave the money to Generosa. She cooked a banquet and there even was a turkey. As presents I got: material for two dresses, a bottle of perfume, one of toilet water, a dozen handkerchiefs, a box of six cakes of soap, three pairs of stockings, and a tin of biscuits, besides the puddings and candies.

When the party was over my cousins began to butt in and take Luizinha's part, and wanted me to divide everything then and there the same night. But I didn't have the courage to deny myself anything and I said to them, "Tonight it's better just to divide the tin of biscuits and leave the rest for tomorrow."

Today Luizinha complained and I gave her one cake of soap, too, and one pair of stockings. She protested, but weakly. I know that eventually she'll forget about it. I know that I didn't keep my promise but I don't feel any remorse because I need the things more than she does. She almost never goes out of the house and then she only goes to the *chácara*, and I go out every day.

Anonymous
(? - ?)

From the very first entry in *A Young Girl's Diary*, written by an adolescent Austrian girl, evidence of rivalry with an older sister is apparent and seemingly of long duration. Nearly every one of the first dozen entries has a denigratory inference against Dora. Sarcasm, bitterness and jealousy flavor the entries and continue nearly to the end of the book, when, with more mature values asserting themselves, better understanding developed and the two sisters were able to establish a friendly *entente.**

July 12th

Hella and I are writing a diary. We both agreed that when we went to the high school we would write a diary every day. Dora keeps a diary too, but she gets furious if I look at it. I call Helene "Hella," and she calls me "Rita"; Helene and Grete are so vulgar. Dora has taken to calling herself "Thea," but I go on calling her "Dora." She says that little children (she means me and Hella) ought not to keep a diary. She says they will write such a lot of nonsense. No more than in hers and Lizzi's.

July 15th

Lizzi, Hella's sister, is not so horrid as Dora, she is always so nice! To-day she gave each of us at least ten chocolate-creams. It's true Hella often says to me: "You don't know her, what a beast she can be. *Your* sister is generally very nice to *me.*" Certainly it is very funny the way in which she always speaks of us as "the little ones" or "the children," as if she had never been a child herself, and indeed a much littler one than we are. Besides we're just the same as she is now. She is in the fourth class and we are in the first.

To-morrow we are going to Kaltenbach in Tyrol. I'm frightfully excited. Hella went away to-day to Hungary to her uncle and aunt with her mother and Lizzi. Her father is at manœuvres.

July 19th

It's awfully hard to write every day in the holidays. Everything is so new and one has no time to write. We are living in a big house in the

---

*From *A Young Girl's Diary* edited by Hermine von Hug-Hellmuth. New York: Thomas Seltzer, 1921. Pp. 11-17.

forest. Dora bagged the front veranda straight off for her own writing. At the back of the house there are such swarms of horrid little flies; everything is black with flies. I do hate flies and such things. I'm not going to put up with being driven out of the front veranda. I won't have it. Besides, Father said: "Don't quarrel, children!" (*Children* to *her* too!!) He's quite right. She puts on such airs because she'll be fourteen in October. "The verandas are common property," said Father. Father's always so just. He never lets Dora lord it over me, but Mother often makes a favourite of Dora. I'm writing to Hella to-day. She's not written to me yet.

July 23rd

It's awful. One has no time. Yesterday when I wanted to write the room had to be cleaned and D. was in the arbour. Before that I had not written a *single* word and in the front veranda all my pages blew away. We write on loose pages. Hella thinks it's better because then one does not have to tear anything out. But we have promised one another to throw nothing away and not to tear anything up. Why should we? One can tell a friend everything. A pretty friend if one couldn't. Yesterday when I wanted to go into the arbour Dora glared at me savagely, saying What do you want? As if the arbour belonged to her, she just wanted to bag the front veranda all for herself. She's too sickening.

Yesterday afternoon we were on the Kobler-Kogel. It was lovely. Father was awfully jolly and we pelted one another with pine-cones. It was jolly. I threw one at Dora and it hit her on her padded bust. She let out such a yell and I said out loud You couldn't feel it *there*. As she went by she said, Pig! It doesn't matter, for I knew she understood me and that what I said was true. I should like to know what she writes about every day to Erika and what *she* writes in her diary. Mother was out of sorts and stayed at home.

July 24th

To-day is Sunday. I do love Sundays. Father says: You children have Sundays every day. That's quite true in the holidays, but not at other times. The peasants and their wives and children are all very gay, wearing Tyrolese dresses, just like those I have seen in the theatre. We are wearing our white dresses to-day, and I have made a great cherry-stain upon mine, not on purpose, but because I sat down upon some fallen cherries. So this afternoon when we go out walking I must wear my pink dress. All the better, for I don't care to be dressed exactly the same as Dora. I don't see why everyone should know that we are sisters. Let people think we are cousins. She does not like it either; I wish I knew why. Oswald is coming in a week, and I am awfully pleased. He is older than Dora, but I can always get on with him. Hella writes that she finds it dull without me; so do I.

July 25th

I must write some more. I've had a frightful row with Dora. She says I've been fiddling with her things. It's all because she's so untidy. As if *her* things could interest me. Yesterday she left her letter to Erika lying about on the table, and all I read was: He's as handsome as a Greek god. I don't know who "he" was for she came in at that moment. It's probably Krail Rudi, with whom she is everlastingly playing tennis and carries on like anything. As for handsome—well, there's no accounting for tastes.

July 26th

It's a good thing I brought my dolls' portmanteau. Mother said: You'll be glad to have it on rainy days. Of course I'm much too old to play with dolls, but even though I'm 11 I can make dolls' clothes still. One learns something while one is doing it, and when I've finished something I do enjoy it so. Mother cut me out some things and I was tacking them together. Then Dora came into the room and said: Hullo, the child is sewing things for her dolls. What cheek, as if she had never played with dolls. Besides, I don't really play with dolls any longer. When she sat down beside me I sewed so vigorously that I made a great scratch on her hand, and said: Oh, I'm so sorry, but you came too close. I hope she'll know why I really did it. Of course she'll go and sneak to Mother. Let her. What right has she to call me child. She's got a fine red scratch anyhow, and on her right hand where everyone can see.

July 27th

Fräulein Prückl has written to me. The address on her letter to me was splendid, "Fräulein Grete Lainer, Lyzealschülerin." Of course Dora had to know better than anyone else, and said that in the higher classes from the fourth upwards (because she is in the fourth) they write "Lyzeistin." She said: "Anyhow, in the holidays, before a girl has attended the first class she's not a Lyzealschülerin at all." Then Father chipped in, saying that *we* (*I* didn't begin it) really must stop this eternal wrangling; he really could not stand it. He's quite right, but what he said won't do any good, for Dora will go on just the same.

Fräulein Prückl wrote that she was *delighted* that I had written. As soon as I have time she wants me to write to her again. Great Scott, I've always time for *her*. I shall write to her again this evening after supper, so as not to keep her waiting.

July 30th

To-day is my birthday. Father gave me a splendid parasol with a flowered border and painting materials and Mother gave me a huge postcard album for 800 cards and stories for school girls, and Dora gave me a beautiful box of notepaper and Mother had made a chocolate-cream cake for dinner to-day as well as the strawberry cream. The first thing in the morning the Warths sent me three birthday cards. And Robert had written on his: With deepest *respect your faithful R.* It is glorious to have a birthday, everyone is so kind, even Dora.

David Daiches
(1913-   )

David Daiches, second son of the Chief Rabbi of Scotland, devoted his autobiography to the two worlds in which he grew up and lived freely. Bagpipe music and synagogue melody represented the two poles between which his sensibilities moved. "I accepted this dualism as part of the nature of things, and looking back now I wonder at the ease with which I did so," he wrote.

The ambivalent feelings of brothers as they pass through their adolescent years together is expressed in this illustration from Daiches' *Two Worlds—An Edinburgh Jewish Childhood.** Lionel, the older brother, displayed toward David a mixture of teasing and loyalty which tended to throw the younger brother off balance. Daiches revealed the hard feelings he had when the brother deliberately got him involved in situations that were embarrassing and cruel, particularly when it seemed to him that justice and truth were on his side and when their father showed favoritism to Lionel.

Lionel, Sylvia, and I naturally played together a great deal, and Lionel and I alone to an even greater extent. His attitude to me was a mixture of loyalty and a most exasperating teasing. He teased me sometimes to distraction. I remember one occasion, when I was twelve

---

*Reprinted by permission of Harcourt, Brace & World, Inc. 1956. Pp. 134-137.

or thirteen, he amused himself by drawing up a contract in which I was made to hand over to him something of mine that he wanted. Naturally, I refused to sign it, so he secretly cut my signature out of the cover of my French notebook and gummed it onto the contract. This was, of course, a joke: he never intended to hold me to the contract; but when I found my French notebook mutilated—it was a new one, and I had prided myself on keeping it with scrupulous neatness— I was seized with a raging sense of injustice that vented itself in howling abuse. To my further infuriation, my parents reproved me for yelling and screaming, and seemed uninterested in the monstrous injustice I had suffered; to them, I was simply being very naughty and that was that. I remember the evening clearly: my father had been away, lecturing I think, somewhere in England, and had just returned, presenting both Lionel and me with a penknife. It was with his new penknife that Lionel cut out my name from the notebook. The atmosphere of happy family reunion was abruptly shattered by my raging on discovering the state of my notebook, and I recall thinking bitterly as, denied all redress, I went fuming upstairs to my room, that the incident had spoiled what would have been a happy evening.

On another occasion I remember that Lionel and a boy who lived in the next street (his name sticks in my mind as Bill Revans, but I may have got it wrong) jointly persuaded me to shake some pennies out of my little green money box and to spend the money on a large ice cream. Such behavior was unthinkable in our family; we children saved our weekly pennies (later, threepenny pieces) and the idea of spending them on sweets or ice cream was shocking. I allowed myself to be persuaded, bought the ice cream, and gave Lionel and Bill Revans the bulk of it. Later that day Lionel calmly informed my father of what I had done. I think it was sheer psychological curiosity on his part; he wanted to know how my father would react; but of course I was furious at this treachery. However, my father's reaction was surprisingly mild; he simply said that I shouldn't have done it and turned to his work, and that was the end of that.

But with all his teasing Lionel was fundamentally loyal. His sense of family unity was very deep—to this day I think he depends on it emotionally to a greater extent than any of us—and in a crisis he could always be depended on. I recall two incidents, widely separated in time, which illustrate his combination of day-to-day teasing with fundamental loyalty. The first occurred when I was about fourteen or fifteen, and was writing a great deal of verse, which I kept in a fat dark-blue notebook. Once, after I had entered a new composition in the book and was about to put it away in the drawer where I kept it,

Lionel noticed what I was doing and made some offensive remark about my "poems." I was angered, but instead of saying anything I calmly took up the notebook again and wrote down on the last page exactly what he had said. I headed the page: "Nasty remarks that people have made about my poems." Lionel's curiosity was aroused, and he demanded to know what I was doing. I told him, and explained that he would look a frightful fool when I was a famous poet and the disparaging remarks that he had made about my work were revealed. To my surprise, he took my words more seriously than I myself did, and reproved me for showing a mean spirit and bearing malice: it was unfair, he protested, that casual words spoken in haste should be recorded for posterity. I was touched, and tore out the page.

The other incident occurred either in my last year at school or in my first year at Edinburgh University. I had written a number of sketches, both words and music, songs from which Lionel and I often sang to entertain guests. Lionel had the idea that one of them should actually be presented publicly on a proper stage. I protested that this was not feasible, but Lionel persisted. He went round to all the boys of our own age that we knew—which meant, in fact, a handful of sons of members of the Edinburgh Jewish community—and aroused their interest by himself singing through the whole of one of the sketches, taking all the parts in turn. I was too shy to go into any of the boys' houses, but remained outside in the street while Lionel went through his performance. He convinced enough people of the merit of the piece to have it put on by a Jewish young people's club of which we were members (the Edinburgh Junior Jewish Club it was called, and later the name was changed to the Edinburgh Young Jewish Society). Lionel collected the cast, arranged for the hire of the hall, and produced the show, with an energy and fervor unusual for him. It was a great success, and was followed the next year by another. Never once did he show the slightest jealousy of my status as author and composer: for him, the whole thing showed what the family could do.

REFERENCES

1. Adler, Alfred. *The Practice and Theory of Individual Psychology.* New York: Harcourt, Brace & Co., 1923, p. 321.
2. Fenichel, Otto. *The Psychoanalytic Theory of Neurosis.* New York: W. W. Norton & Co., 1945, p. 93.
3. Freud, Sigmund. Dostoevsky and parricide. In: *Collected Papers,* Vol. 5. New York: Basic Books, 1959, p. 227.

4. Hutt, Max L., & Gibby, Robert G. *The Child. Development and Adjustment.* Boston: Allyn & Bacon, Inc., 1959, p. 145.

5. Josselyn, Irene M. *The Happy Child. A Psychoanalytic Guide to Emotional and Social Growth.* New York: Random House, 1955, pp. 338-339.

6. *Ibid.,* p. 339.

7. Kardiner, Abram, et al. *The Psychological Frontiers of Society.* New York: Columbia University Press, 1945, p. 75.

8. *Ibid.,* pp. 89-90.

9. *Ibid.,* pp. 154-159.

10. *Ibid.,* p. 360.

11. Kligerman, Charles. A psychoanalytic study of the *Confessions* of St. Augustine. *J. Amer. Psychoanal. Assn.,* 75:471, 1957.

12. ———. The character of Jean Jacques Rousseau. *Psychoanal. Quart.,* 20:241, 1951.

13. Landis, Paul H. *Adolescence and Youth.* New York: McGraw-Hill Book Co., 1952, pp. 238-239.

14. Martineau, Harriet. *Autobiography.* Boston: Houghton, Mifflin & Co., 1877, p. 119.

15. Patai, Raphael. *Sex and Family in the Bible and the Middle East.* Garden City, N.Y. Doubleday & Co., 1959, p. 218.

16. Rowntree, B. Seebohm. *Poverty: A Study of Town Life.* London: Macmillan & Co., 1902.

17. Spencer, Herbert. *An Autobiography,* Vol. I. New York: D. Appleton & Co., 1904, pp. 125-126.

CHAPTER SEVEN

The Peer Culture

The need to be liked, to be accepted, and to belong are universal feelings but perhaps at no time more emphatically felt than at adolescence. This is true because during this period the adolescent is undergoing many new and varied experiences involving the self-concept, physiological and physical changes, attempts to resolve the revived oedipal conflict, making a heterosexual adjustment and choosing a career. With such burdens, it is small wonder that the adolescent seeks his fellows out with such intensity of feeling. The need to succeed in these developmental tasks is primary and since, generally, he cannot relate to or communicate with his parents he finds refuge with those his own age.

Paralleling his detachment from his parents, the adolescent experiences a shift in ideals and standards based on his new associations. His friends now personify his ideals and his conscience. "Personalization is the métier of adolescence. Of all persons, adolescents are the most intensely personal; their intensity is often uncomfortable to adults. As cooperation and group adjustment become pervasive social norms; as tolerance supersedes passion as the basis for social action; as personalization becomes false-personalization, adolescence becomes more and more difficult [13]." The alienation from parental control generally compels the adolescent to externalize his conflicts and to control his behavior along standards determined by his group. Thus, for a time, the group criteria may dominate the adolescent's attitudes. Inevitably this brings about a sharp clash with the parents' ideas about life. "The subjective

335

struggle over standards is often bitter because of the adolescent's fear of losing control over his sexual and aggressive urges. The temptation to release these drives is intense, but the adolescent, dreading the loss of control, clings tenaciously to his childhood conscience and the parents from whom it was derived [1]." In effect, the conflict between his childhood superego and the new values imposed by the peer group creates a difficult situation for the adolescent.

How he copes with his problem of self-definition in relation to his peers will be illustrated in this chapter. For convenience, three areas will be scrutinized: 1. conformity and the peer culture; 2. the friendship pattern; and 3. social relationships.

CONFORMITY AND THE PEER CULTURE

The exaggerated patterns of conformity within the adolescent peer group, Ausubel states, constitute perhaps its most unique structural characteristic in comparison with the groupings of children and adults. "As adolescents become more and more resistive to adult suggestion and increasingly indifferent to adult approval and disapproval, the approval and disapproval of peers becomes progressively the most influential force motivating adolescent conduct [5]." The efforts of the adolescent are all directed at appearing alike, behaving alike, and doing what everyone in the group does.

This do-alike, act-alike, dress-alike proclivity is not a foible or a necessity of recent origin. In his *Autobiography,* Montaigne (1533-1592) wrote, "I loved to dress in finery when I was still under age, for the lack of other ornament; and it became me well. There are some people upon whom their rich clothes weep. I was always ready to imitate the negligent garb still to be seen among our young men —my cloak across the shoulder, my hood to one side, and a stocking in disorder, all of which was meant to show a proud disdain for these exotic trumperies and a contempt for everything artificial [23]." Catherine the Great (1729-1796) was also constrained to change her German dress styles to Russian. "In those days the ladies had no other occupation than dress; and their extravagance went so far that they changed their costume at least twice a day. The Empress herself loved adornment and changed her dress several times a day. Card-playing and dressing filled up the day. Since I tried on principle to please the people with whom I had to live, I adopted their habits and customs. I wished to be a Russian in order to be liked by the Russians. Besides I was fifteen years old and no one at that age dislikes adornment [7]."

Goethe (16), describing his student days at Leipzig in the year 1766, when he was seventeen years old, felt "that society had much to object in me . . . I had [to dress] myself in their fashion, and was obliged to talk according to their tongue." The same two factors of dress and speech affected Napoleon Bonaparte during his student days. At sixteen, in the year 1785, he wrote, "I did not remain long in the Paris Military School which I liked very much on account of the good discipline prevailing there. The physical exercises suited me well. I gradually lost my reserve, although I was still often laughed at on account of my foreign appearance and accent [24]." In the next century, Vyvyan Holland, the son of Oscar Wilde, also felt the pressure to conform. "My life at Cambridge was uneventful. I tried to be as much like other undergraduates as possible, wearing the same sort of clothes, using the same slang and getting into the same scrapes [18]." He was eighteen years old at the time. Mary Colum, the Irish poet, confessed that during her adolescence, "To try to act like everyone else became my constant preoccupation [9]."

Across the Pacific Ocean, Étsu-bo Sugimoto was as greatly entrapped by conformism as her counterparts in Ireland, Russia, Germany, France and England. Étsu-bo was fourteen years old—the year was 1888—when she left her village in the provinces to attend a missionary school in Tokyo. Her alien accent and dress precluded acceptance by her schoolmates: " . . . there was a dreaded something which constantly reminded me that I was still a daughter of Echigo [her rural home village]. My pronunciation of certain sounds, which was different from that of Tokyo, caused considerable amusement among the girls. Also, I suppose I used rather stately and stilted language, which, combined with the odd Echigo accent, must have sounded very funny to city-bred ears. The girls were so good-natured in their mimicry that I could not feel resentment, but it was a real trial to me, for it touched my deep loyalty to my own province. Since I did not quite understand where the difficulty lay, I was helpless, and gradually got in the habit of confining my conversation to few remarks and making my sentences as short as possible.

"Mrs. Sato noticed that I was growing more and more silent, and by tactful questioning she discovered the trouble. Then she quietly prepared a little notebook with a diagram of the troublesome sounds and, in the kindest way in the world, explained them to me.

"Brother was there that evening and he laughed.

" 'Etsu-bo,' he said, looking at me rather critically, "there is not such good reason to be ashamed by the accent of an honourable province as over your countrified dress. I must get you some different clothes.'

"I had already grown suspicious of the glances which my schoolmates had been casting at the sash that Toshi had so painstakingly made me of a piece of newly imported cloth called *a-ra-pac-a,* so I was glad to accept the garments which Brother brought the next day. They were surprisingly gay, and the sash, with one side of black satin, reminded me of the restaurant waiters of Magaoka, but the girls all said they had a 'Tokyo air,' so I wore them with a pride and satisfaction greater than I ever had felt about clothes [32]."

The exaggerated conformity to peer group standards forced Ethel Waters, when she was eleven and going around with girls of fourteen and fifteen, to feel "continually embarrassed because they had breasts and I was as flat as a board. I made many experiments with falsies, which I had seen prostitutes wearing. My luck was bad; half the time one falsie would be up around my shoulder and the other down on my hip [35]." And curiously enough, while there is this effortful striving toward conformity to the group pattern, there is a concomitant urge to be unique, to achieve individuality [34]. Philip O'Connor (25) relates this struggle: "I wore red trousers and bobbed hair, partly because other people didn't, and because I didn't want to be overlooked. Having made sure I wouldn't be overlooked, I complained heavily of people staring at me."

While these illustrations indicate, perhaps that the need to conform has always existed in the adolescent peer culture, they show too that distinctions exist in the modes of conforming, both from era to era and from culture to culture. The ways of conforming in a rigid class society or in a communal society are totally different from those in an inner-directed or acquisitive society. In the former, the mode is a behavioral conformity. The individual who does not conform is taunted and shamed; if he does not live up to the cultural values, he feels guilty. With the discoveries of new worlds by da Gama, Vespucci, Columbus, DeSoto, and others in the fifteenth and sixteenth centuries, and the subsequent expansion of new communities with new standards, came the beginnings of the internal gyroscope Riesman (27) discusses.

Today the adolescent conforms to peer group values without building in a strong conscience. The youngsters are told to succeed, to succeed by being sensitive to the standards of the peer group. This mode of conformity is insured through anxiety, which is one of the reasons the present has been called the age of anxiety. Where once the adolescent suffered from shame and guilt, now he experiences anxiety. Thus, while conformity has been a general mechanism used in all cultures and throughout history, standards have changed. Today, it would seem, the standard rests on the principle, "cheat if you have to, but get ahead, be successful." While we do not build strong superegos in our children, we try to establish greater flexibility, but usually in terms of "success."

The succeeding illustrations, which range from two centuries ago to the present and include both Oriental and Occidental cultures, will point up the differing affective responses to the adolescent's need to conform to the peer group.

Johann Wolfgang von Goethe*
(1749-1832)

. . . I had from my life many small unpleasantnesses, as one must always pay one's footing, when one changes one's place and enters into new conditions. The first thing that the ladies complained about in me related to my dress, for I had come from home to the university somewhat strangely equipped.

My father, who detested nothing so much as when anything happened to no purpose, when anyone did not know how to make use of his time, or found no opportunity for turning it to account, carried his economy of time and abilities so far that nothing gave him greater pleasure than to kill two birds with one stone. He therefore never had a servant who could not be useful in the house for something else. Now, as he had always written everything with his own hand and later had the convenience of dictating to that young friend of the

*From Goethe's Autobiography, Poetry and Truth from My Own Life. Reprinted by permission of Public Affairs Press. 1949. Pp. 213-215.

family, so he also found it most advantageous to have tailors as servants, who were obliged to employ their time well, as they had not only to make their own liveries, but also clothes for my father and the children, and to do all the mending. My father himself took trouble to have the best cloths and stuff, as he procured his wares at the fairs from foreign merchants and laid them up in store; as I can still well remember that he always visited the Herren from Lowenicht of Aix-la-Chapelle, and from my earliest youth made me acquainted with these and other eminent merchants. Care was also taken for the excellence of the stuff, and there was a sufficient stock of different kinds of cloth, serge, Göttingen stuff, as well as the necessary lining, so that, as far as the materials were concerned, we could well let ourselves be seen. But the cut spoiled almost everything; for if one of these domestic tailors was in any way a clever fellow at sewing and making up a coat which had been cut out in a masterly fashion, he now had also to cut out the dress himself, and this did not always succeed to perfection. In addition to this, my father kept everything which belonged to his clothing very well and neatly, and preserved it more than used it for many years; thus he had a predilection for certain old cuts and trimmings, whereby our dress sometimes acquired a strange appearance.

In the same way also my wardrobe, which I took with me to the university, was furnished; it was very complete and fine looking, and there was even a laced dress among the rest. Already accustomed to this kind of costume, I thought myself sufficiently well dressed, but it did not last long before my lady friends, first by gentle raillery, then by sensible remonstrances, convinced me that I looked as if I had been dropped down from another world. Though I felt much vexation at this, I did not at first see how I could help myself. But when Herr von Masuren, the favourite poetical country squire, once entered the theatre in a similar costume, and was heartily laughed at more on account of his outer than his inner lack of taste, I took courage and ventured at once to exchange my whole wardrobe for a new-fashioned one, suited to the place, by which, however, it shrunk considerably.

After this trial was surmounted, a new one made its appearance which for me was much more unpleasant, because it concerned a matter which one does not so easily put off and exchange. I had been born and bred in the Upper German dialect, and though my father was always studious of a certain purity of speech, and from youth up made us children attentive to what one really calls defects of that idiom and had prepared us for a better kind of speaking, I yet retained many deeper-seated peculiarities, which, because their *naïveté* pleased me, I brought out with pleasure, and thus every time I used them I drew down upon myself a severe reprimand from my new fellow-townsmen. The Upper German, and perhaps chiefly he who lives by the Rhine and Main (for great rivers have, like the seacoast, always something animating about them), expresses himself much in similes and allusions, and with a native, common-sense aptitude makes use of proverbial sayings. In both cases he is often blunt, yet when one sees the object of the expression, it is always appropriate; only, to be sure, something may often slip in which proves itself offensive to a more delicate ear.

Every province loves its own dialect, for it is, properly speaking, the element in which the soul draws its breath. But every one knows with what obstinacy the Meisnian dialect has managed to domineer over the rest, and even for a time to exclude them. We have suffered for many years under this pedantic tyranny, and only by frequent struggles have all the provinces again established themselves in these old rights. What a lively young man had to endure under this continual tutoring anyone will easily understand who considers that, with the pronunciation, which one at last consents to alter, has to be sacrificed at the same time the way of thinking, the imagination, feeling, and native character. And this intolerable demand was made by cultivated men and women whose convictions I could not adopt, whose injustice I seemed to feel, though I could not make it clear to myself. I was forbidden to make allusions to pithy biblical texts, as well as the use of the honest-hearted expressions from the Chronicles. I was to forget that I had read the "Geiler Von Kaisersberg," and dispense with the use of proverbs, which, however, instead of much fiddle-faddle, just hit the nail on the head—all this which I had appropriated with youthful ardour I was to do without; I felt myself paralysed to the core, and scarcely knew any more how I was to express myself about the commonest things. Then I heard that one should speak as one writes, and write as one speaks; while to me speaking and writing seemed once for all two different things, each of which might well maintain its own right. And I had yet to hear much in the Meisnian dialect which on paper would not have appeared particularly good.

Eliza Southgate Bowne*
(1783-1809)

June 12, 1800

Now Mamma, what do you think I am going to ask for?—a wig.

---

*From *A Girl's Life Eighty Years Ago* by Eliza Southgate Bowne. New York: Charles Scribner's Sons, 1887. P. 23.

Eleanor has got a new one just like my hair and only 5 dollars, Mrs. Mayo one just like it. I must either cut my hair or have one, I cannot dress it at all *stylish*. Mrs. Coffin bought Eleanor's and says that she will write to Mrs. Sumner to get me one just like it; how much time it will save—in one year we could save it in pins and paper, besides the *trouble*. At the assembly I was quite ashamed of my head, for nobody has long hair. If you will consent to my having one do send me over a 5 dollar bill by the post immediately after you receive this, for I am in hopes to have it for the next Assembly—do send me word immediately if you can let me have one. Tell Octavia she must write soon, and that there are many inquiries after her.

ELIZA

*Alfred Wallace**
(1823-1913)

One other case of this kind hurt me dreadfully at the time, because it exposed me to what I thought was the ridicule or contempt of the whole school. Like most other boys I was reckless about my clothes, leaning my elbows on the desk till a hole was worn in my jacket, and, worse still, when cleaning my slate using my cuff to rub it dry. Slate sponges attached by a string were unknown to our school in those days. As new clothes were too costly to be had very often, my mother determined to save a jacket just taken for school wear by making covers for the sleeves, which I was to wear in school. These were made of black calico, reaching from the cuff to the elbow, and though I protested that I could not wear them, that I should be looked upon as a guy and other equally valid reasons, they were one day put in my pocket, and I was told to put them on just before I entered the school. Of course I could *not* do it; so I brought them back and told my mother. Then, after another day or two of trial, one morning the dreaded thunderbolt fell upon me. On entering school I was called up to the master's desk, he produced the dreaded calico sleeves, and told me that my mother wished me to wear them to save my jacket, and told me to put them on. Of course I had to do so. They fitted very well, and felt quite comfortable, and I dare say did not look so very strange. I have no doubt also that most of the boys had a fellow-feeling for me, and thought it a shame to thus make me an exception to all the school. But to me it seemed a cruel disgrace, and I was miserable so long as I

---

*From *My Life* by Alfred Wallace. Reprinted by permission of Dodd, Mead & Co. 1906. Vol. I. Cap. 61.

wore them. How long that was I cannot remember, but I do not think
it was very long, perhaps a month or two, or till the beginning of the
next holidays. But while it lasted it was, perhaps, the severest punishment I ever endured.

Mohandas K. Gandhi*
(1869-1948)

We were to dine together at the Holborn Restaurant, to me a pala-
tial place and the first big restaurant I had been to since leaving the
Victoria Hotel. The stay at that hotel had scarcely been a helpful experience, for I had not lived there with my wits about me. The friend
had planned to take me to this restaurant evidently imagining that
modesty would forbid any questions. And it was a very big company
of diners in the midst of which my friend and I sat sharing a table between us. The first course was soup. I wondered what it might be made
of, but durst not ask the friend about it. I therefore summoned the
waiter. My friend saw the movement and sternly asked across the table
what was the matter. With considerable hesitation I told him that I
wanted to inquire if the soup was a vegetable soup. "You are too
clumsy for decent society," he passionately exclaimed. "If you cannot
behave yourself, you had better go. Feed in some other restaurant and
await me outside." This delighted me. Out I went. There was a vegetarian restaurant close by, but it was closed. So I went without food
that night. I accompanied my friend to the theatre, but he never said
a word about the scene I had created. On my part of course there was
nothing to say.

That was the last friendly tussle we had. It did not affect our relations in the least. I could see and appreciate the love by which all my
friend's efforts were actuated, and my respect for him was all the
greater on account of our differences in thought and action.

But I decided that I should put him at ease, that I should assure him
that I would be clumsy no more, but try to become polished and make
up for my vegetarianism by cultivating other accomplishments which
fitted one for polite society. And for this purpose I undertook the all
too impossible task of becoming an English gentleman.

The clothes after the Bombay cut that I was wearing were, I
thought, unsuitable for English society, and I got new ones at the
Army and Navy Stores. I also went in for a chimney-pot hat costing

---

*From *The Story of My Experiments with Truth* by Mohandas K. Gandhi. Reprinted by permission of Public Affairs Press. 1948. Pp. 69-71.

nineteen shillings—an excessive price in those days. Not content with this, I wasted ten pounds on an evening suit made in Bond Street, the centre of fashionable life in London; and got my good and noble-hearted brother to send me a double watchchain of gold. It was not correct to wear a ready-made tie and I learnt the art of tying one for myself. While in India, the mirror had been a luxury permitted on the days when the family barber gave me a shave. Here I wasted ten minutes every day before a huge mirror, watching myself arranging my tie and parting my hair in the correct fashion. My hair was by no means soft, and every day it meant a regular struggle with the brush to keep it in position. Each time the hat was put on and off, the hand would automatically move towards the head to adjust the hair, not to mention the other civilized habit of the hand every now and then operating for the same purpose when sitting in polished society.

As if all this were not enough to make me look the thing, I directed my attention to other details that were supposed to go towards the making of an English gentleman. I was told it was necessary for me to take lessons in dancing, French and elocution. French was not only the language of neighbouring France, but it was the *lingua franca* of the Continent over which I had a desire to travel. I decided to take dancing lessons at a class and paid down £ 3 as fees for a term. I must have taken about six lessons in three weeks. But it was beyond me to achieve anything like rhythmic motion. I could not follow the piano and hence found it impossible to keep time. What then was I to do? The recluse in the fable kept a cat to keep off the rats, and then a cow to feed the cat with milk, and a man to keep the cow and so on. My ambitions also grew like the family of the recluse. I thought I should learn to play the violin in order to cultivate an ear for Western music. So I invested £ 3 in a violin and something more in fees. I sought a third teacher to give me lessons in elocution and paid him a preliminary fee of a guinea. He recommended Bell's *Standard Elocutionist* as the text-book, which I purchased. And I began with a speech of Pitt's.

But Mr. Bell rang the bell of alarm in my ear and I awoke.

I had not to spend a lifetime in England, I said to myself. What then was the use of learning elocution? And how could dancing make a gentleman of me? The violin I could learn even in India. I was a student and ought to go on with my studies. I should qualify myself to join the Inns of Court. If my character made a gentleman of me, so much the better. Otherwise I should forego the ambition.

These and similar thoughts possessed me, and I expressed them in a letter which I addressed to the elocution teacher, requesting him to excuse me from further lessons. I had taken only two or three. I wrote a similar letter to the dancing teacher, and went personally to the violin teacher with a request to dispose of the violin for any price it might fetch. She was rather friendly to me, so I told her how I had discovered that I was pursuing a false idea. She encouraged me in the determination to make a complete change.

This infatuation must have lasted about three months. The punctiliousness in dress persisted for years. But henceforward I became a student.

Henry Handel Richardson* (1870-1946)

I must now go back to the child of twelve, the age at which I left home to become a pupil of the "Presbyterian Ladies' College."

Just how Mother contrived to meet the expense of my schooling I don't know, I never enquired. Nor would she have wanted me to. That was her own business. It may be that the rental drawn from the house at Hawthorn had been put by for the purpose. On the other hand, the authorities of the P.L.C. may have met her half-way. For the College, erected by those true lovers of learning, the Scotch, had been founded with a special eye to the daughters of unmoneyed Presbyterian ministers, and continued, I believe, to accept such girls at the original rates. I couldn't claim to be more than the niece of one; but his widow, my aunt, was a persuasively well-spoken woman, and I seem to have heard that she called on the Principal and laid my case before him. Well, however I got there it made no difference, either to me or to others in the same box. We mixed with the crowd on equal terms.—And a crowd it was; for the College had long outgrown its sectarianism. Various denominations were to be found among the horde of day-scholars; and, as it had the name of being the best school of its kind in Melbourne, the boarders included the rich, the very rich, as well as the less well-to-do.

At its massive grey-stone portals I arrived accompanied by a small tin trunk, battered and disreputable from much sea-voyaging, and as ill-suited to the surroundings as its owner. For about me everything was wrong. To save Mother the cost of a new outfit—the sensible fashion of a single uniform for all had not yet come in—a would-be kind friend handed over dresses worn by her daughter at the same school, when of my age. These were as ugly in colour as old-fashioned in

---

*From *Myself When Young* by Henry Handel Richardson. Reprinted by permission of W. W. Norton & Co., Inc. 1948. Pp. 63-64, 69-70.

make, and I dreaded each fresh appearance in one. Then, my hair. The curls, thank goodness, had been judged impracticable; but instead I was cut to a short bob—at a day when every other girl sported a long pigtail. Both it and my dowdy frocks brought me a great deal of unpleasant notice.

I owed my chief humiliation, however, to my manners, which were universally disapproved of. Lacking any form of restraint, I had sallied forth from home full of pep and assurance, not to say conceit; and teachers and schoolfellows alike felt it their duty to crush me. And as, for all my pertness, I was acutely sensitive to snubs and sneers, I came in for a very bad time. Only gradually did I learn to sink myself in the mass, instead of sticking out from it; to hide my knowledge, keep my opinions to myself. Once learnt, however, the lesson proved a lasting one; and the old innocent self-confidence never returned. Some of my faculties may have been blunted in the process, but it was certainly to the good in the long run. For the boy or girl who goes out into the world without knowing how to conform to its rules and standards is a creature to be pitied. The inevitable trimming and shaping are best got over early.

*   *   *   *

At school I was considered odd and unaccountable. Often to my own bewilderment, for I tried hard to adapt myself to my companions' way of thinking. On looking back I fancy I see one reason for this attitude. That I made good at tennis nobody took amiss. But to be able at the same time to turn out stuff like music smacked of the uncanny. I can still feel the oblique glances thrown at me as I sat, in what would have been my spare hour, over this unwanted task. They seemed to say plainer than words, we here, you there. And "there" I remained. I once, for instance, harmlessly invited a girl to write something in my album—we all possessed albums—and what I afterwards had to read was: "If ever you come down to earth again let me know, and I'll be friends with you." Oh, how that stung! For I had flattered myself I was already "friends" with this particular girl, who headed a clique I longed to join. Nor was I clear what she meant. Far from being off the earth I felt very much *on* it, thanks to pinpricks of this sort.

Mary Colum*
(1887[?]-1957)

To try to act like everyone else became my constant preoccupation.

---

*From *Life and the Dream* (9).

We had everything in common. We rose, washed, and dressed on the same minute; said the same prayers in unison; wore the same uniform; did our hair in the prescribed way, plaited down our backs and tied with a black silk ribbon. "Form ranks" or "Get into ranks"—that was the order several times a day whenever we went anywhere in a body. We walked in step in ranks of two and two going to the refectory, going to the little chapel. We first genuflected in pairs before the altar, then we turned to our seats, the girls to the right entering the right seats and those to the left, the left seats, all with drilled and trained precision, for the procedure had been rehearsed many times. A couple of times a week we had actual military drill by a drill sergeant. Perhaps drilling and conformity and totalitarianism are not so alien to the ideals of the human race as we in democracies consider. The supervision was ceaseless; everything we did or even thought, it seemed to me, was known to the heads of the school. Our letters were read coming and going, and the letters we sent out were thoroughly censored—not always, of course, for subject matter, but for style and manner. How to write a ladylike letter was the matter of a half hour's instruction from time to time. No criticism of the school in letters home, as I recall, was ever permitted, criticizing the sisters being considered a very serious breach of conduct and manners.

Nirad C. Chaudhuri*
(1897-   )

We left Kishorganj in February 1910, and went to Calcutta at the beginning of July. Within the four intervening months occurred one of the unhappiest experiences of my life and one of the happiest. The unhappy experience was a stay of about two months at Mymensingh, the district town, where my elder brother and I were sent provisionally to school while my father was making his final arrangements to settle down in Calcutta. My sufferings at Mymensingh were due to quite a number of causes, of which the following three were the ones most acutely felt. In the first place, I had never before been away from home, and the crowded and insanitary hostel in which I was lodged was not the place to reconcile me to the novel experience of being absent from home. Secondly, like all country towns in India, Mymensingh had all the worst features of town life—congestion, open drains full of filth, squalid streets and bazaars, flies and mosquitoes—unac-

---

*From *The Autobiography of an Unknown Indian* by Nirad Chaudhuri. Reprinted by permission of The Macmillan Co. 1951. P. 276.

companied by any of the amenities of big cities, of which I had gained some idea during my stay in Calcutta the previous year. Thirdly, my school fellows quizzed me. Although, with my experience of Calcutta, I thought nothing of their townsmen's airs the Mymensingh boys treated me as if I were a boor from some backward village. They teased me for my accent, which certainly was better than theirs, for their idea of smart speech did not go beyond an affectation of the accent of the city of Dacca, an accent notorious as the most uncultured and atrocious in all Bengal, whereas I could speak with a suggestion at least of the standard Calcutta accent. These boys behaved towards me with a superciliousness which I did not meet with even in Calcutta boys when only a few weeks later I went among them.

David Daiches*
(1913-   )

The school I went to—George Watson's Boys' College, which took boys from infancy right up to university entrance—was on the northern side of the Meadows, and the senior boys would use the Meadows as their playground during the lunch interval. In the late 1920's, when I was in the senior school, I would have to walk through groups of playing classmates on my way home from shul on a Jewish festival, for the way to the synagogue from our house ran through the Meadows and by the school, and by some unhappy coincidence the service on Passover or Tabernacles or other of the festivals would conclude just as the lunch interval commenced. My brother and sister and I were, of course, always absent from school on these festivals, and that did not worry us particularly—at least, not until our last years at school, when we were preparing for important competitive examinations, and missing a lesson might be serious. The teachers and the pupils accepted the fact that the Daiches boys were liable to be absent at odd times for religious reasons, and often on my return after such an absence someone would ask: "Was it a fast or a feast?" That side of it was perfectly all right, and I would enjoy myself explaining to teachers or classmates just what the particular festival was and wherein lay its historic significance (I am talking now of the time when I was fourteen or fifteen). Indeed, I remember several times explaining the difference between the Jewish and Christian religions to my classmates, especially to the son of the Prestonpans minister, with whom I went about a

---

*From *Two Worlds* by David Daiches. Reprinted by permission of Harcourt, Brace & World, Inc. 1956. Pp. 16-17.

great deal in my last years at school; and I remember lending him, and several of the masters, my pocket edition of Paul Goodman's *History of the Jews,* which I used to carry around with me in order to be able to answer questions and cite facts and figures whenever challenged. But walking through a group of boisterously playing classmates when I was dressed up in my festival clothes I found uncomfortable, particularly since my mother, who had the highest ideals for her children both sartorially and in other respects, insisted that Lionel and I wear suits consisting of black jackets and waistcoats and long striped trousers—a garb unknown among Edinburgh boys, who at that time always wore shorts (and sometimes the kilt) until they were fully grown. This battle of the suits played an important part in my childhood. My mother, who was born and brought up in Liverpool, remembered how gentlemanly little English boys had looked, and with the best of intentions tried to model us on them. Lionel seemed rather to take to this mode of dress (to which, being in the legal profession, he still clings), but I found it embarrassing. In my secret heart I wanted to wear a kilt, but I knew that I had no hereditary right to one, and never breathed a word of my ambition to anybody.

THE FRIENDSHIP PATTERN

The most remarkable phenomena in the life of adolescents, Anna Freud has stated, are at bottom connected with their object relations (15). Adolescents are inevitably disillusioned with the ideals they have held of their parents and society and thus seek innumerable new relationships, in part with contemporaries and in part with older people who are obviously substitutes for the renounced parents. They do so in accordance with the vicissitudes of their changing concept of self and the outer world (2). "These relationships are stormy, exclusive, and brief, and are repeated each time in identical form. They represent identifications of so primitive a type that the adolescent may change his beliefs, his style of clothing, his writing, with each new friend [30]." As a result, friendships become highly idealized, largely because the idealization is simply a reflection of the disquietude of the ego when it perceives the dissipation of all its new and passionate object relations (14).

Spiegel concurs with this theory. "Friendship, which is so strikingly an adolescent phenomenon, is an aspect of the struggle to attain a firm sense of self. As Anna Freud has pointed out, these relationships of adolescence are on a narcissistic basis and are in part restitution phenomena. The anxiety and guilt from the reanimated oedipus complex results in the withdrawal of cathexis from object to self-representations with subsequent oscillations of cathexis between self and object [29]." Once the adolescent has achieved a sense of identity to some degree, he can then progress to the next step in healthy personality development. This is the sense of intimacy, says Erikson, "intimacy with persons of the same sex or of the opposite sex or with one's self. The youth who is not fairly sure of his identity shies away from interpersonal relations and is afraid of close communion with himself. The surer he becomes of himself, the more he seeks intimacy, in the form of friendship, love and inspiration [11]. . . . Where a youth does not accomplish such intimate relations with others . . . in late adolescence or early adulthood, he may either isolate himself and find, at best, highly stereotyped and formal interpersonal relations (formal in the sense of lacking in spontaneity, warmth, and real exchange of fellowship), or he must seek them in repeated attempts and repeated failures [10]."

The desire to be liked and to make friends is recognized as a universal one. The author of the journal, *The Pillow Book of Sei Shōnagon,* which was written about the year 990 A.D., stated, "There is nothing in the whole world so painful as feeling that one is not liked [28]." Nearly a thousand years later, John Cowper Powys (26) was to write in his *Autobiography,* "I have, Heaven forgive me, a passion for being *liked* . . . by every child of Adam I meet!" Both writers had reason to say what they did. The author of *The Tale of Genji,* Murasaki Shikibu (978-1015), kept a diary in which she sketched portraits of prominent ladies of the Japanese court during the time when Heian culture was at its height. Among the women described was Lady Sei Shōnagon, of whom Murasaki Shikibu said: "A very proud person. She values herself highly, and scatters her Chinese writings all about. Yet should we study her closely, we should find that she is still imperfect. She tries to be exceptional, but naturally persons of that sort give offence. She is piling up trouble for her future. One who is too richly gifted, who indulges too much in emotion, when she ought to be reserved, and cannot turn aside from anything she is interested in, in spite of herself will lose control. How can such a vain and reckless person end her days happily! [21]." Powys (26) ascribed his neurotic need to be liked to fear: "I must resemble a cowardly dog in my conviction that the most negligible person, any sort of a poor devil, *could* be terribly dangerous. What I expect them to do to me I am sure I don't know, but when I meet their eyes—the eye of a peddler, of an organ-grinder, of a grocer's assistant, of a waiter, of a cab-driver, of the forlornest beggar— I feel as if I could not flatter this ferocious and terrifying being humbly enough, or get away quickly enough! Yes *that* is what it is. It is just *fear.*" Powys then related how this fear disgraced him time and again while he was at the Sherborne School and prevented him from achieving the respect and friendship of his peers.

A sensitive self-feeling brings adolescents to a state of isolation in which they cannot stand against the pressure of the environment growing out of and keeping pace with the development of self-consciousness; hence they seek trustworthy companions. "Adolescence," wrote William Ellery Leonard (22), "more than any years earlier or later, needs its own kind." Making friends is a major adolescent task, but unhappily the task occurs at a time when the youngster does not yet have the capacity to function independently on a mature level. This is apparent in the illustration from Richard Wagner's adolescence presented in this chapter. During Wagner's youth, he made many casual acquaintances but there was no deep bond between him and his comrades. He found it useful to have some comrade to whom he could pour out his views, but felt he never got any return from the comrade and when he tried to encourage such a return the relationship was usually broken off.

Such sudden and abrupt changes in friendships and attachments, with complete disregard for the feelings of the other person, are characteristic of the intermediary phase of social development which takes place at adolescence (6). The stability of adolescent friendships may prove transitory at best. The reasons can be capricious and arbitrary, meaningful and meaningless: interests and values may change; subtle or overt parental pressure may be brought to bear; other persons may prove more attractive; or one's needs for friendship may change. Whatever the cause, one of the deep troubles of adolescence is the instability of friendship (31). Ackerman feels that the tender quality of adolescent identity, the fragility of the borders of the adolescent self and with this, the extraordinary sensitivity to group pressures arising both within the family and in the wider community, make the adolescent

uniquely vulnerable to and readily torn by the conflicting requirements of his familial and extra-familial roles (3).

Since the adolescent's world is built on insecurity and its greatest
concern is for safety, the cost of safety is uniqueness of personality
and the measure of it is membership in the herd. Membership is
built on fragile friendships. "I was very fond of my friends," wrote
G. K. Chesterton (8) of his thirteenth year, "though, as is common
at such an age, I was much too fond of them to be openly emotional
about it." While the boy could not manifest his feelings openly, it
can be almost taken for granted that the cohesive force of the group
to which he belonged was the mutual emotional empathy that
existed. This is generally true for all adolescent groups for, since the
group is usually composed of individuals of approximately the same
emotional level of adjustment, it dominates his thinking and behavior (19).

The security he achieves in the group through his friendships is
of vast significance to the adolescent, for it helps to handle the panic
resulting from the unresolved conflicts of the adolescent period. It
is through his friendships that the individual learns how to modify
his infantile conscience and play an acceptable role in the culture
to which he belongs. "Frightened by his own impulses, and by the
hazardous choice between complete repression or free expression
of them, the adolescent turns to the group for support and for answers to his questions. He can there discuss his mixed feelings and
find solace in the identical sufferings of others. He can test tentative
answers to his perplexities against the equally tentative formulations of his friends. Most important, he can participate in the development of restrictions upon his behavior. This will assure him
of protection from a chaotic expression of impulses without risking the dangers inherent in the restrictions outlined by the parents
[20]." Thus, it is through the individual friendship and the group
membership, based on the close affectional ties to the parents whose
basic values he has introjected, that the adolescent formulates and
accepts a more mature, realistic superego.

Saint Teresa of Avila*
(1515-1582)

What I shall now speak of was, I believe, the beginning of great harm

---

*From *The Life of Saint Teresa of Jesus*. London: Thomas Baker, 1904. Pp. 6-9.

to me. I often think how wrong it is of parents not to be very careful that their children should always, and in every way, see only that which is good; for though my mother was, as I have just said, so good herself, nevertheless I, when I came to the use of reason, did not derive so much good from her as I ought to have done—almost none at all; and the evil I learned did me much harm. She was very fond of books of chivalry; but this pastime did not hurt her so much as it hurt me, because she never wasted her time on them; only we, her children, were left at liberty to read them; and perhaps she did this to distract her thoughts from her great sufferings, and occupy her children, that they might not go astray in other ways. It annoyed my father so much, that we had to be careful he never saw us. I contracted a habit of reading these books; and this little fault which I observed in my mother was the beginning of lukewarmness in my good desires, and the occasion of my falling away in other respects. I thought there was no harm in it when I wasted many hours night and day in so vain an occupation, even when I kept it a secret from my father. So completely was I mastered by this passion, that I thought I could never be happy without a new book.

I began to make much of dress, to wish to please others by my appearance. I took pains with my hands and my hair, used perfumes, and all vanities within my reach—and they were many, for I was very much given to them. I had no evil intention, because I never wished any one to offend God for me. This fastidiousness of excessive neatness lasted some years; and so also did other practices, which I thought then were not at all sinful; now, I see how wrong all this must have been.

I had some cousins; for into my father's house no others were allowed an entrance. In this he was very cautious; and would to God he had been cautious about them!—for I see now the danger of conversing, at an age when virtue should begin to grow, with persons who, knowing nothing themselves of the vanity of the world, provoke others to throw themselves into the midst of it. These cousins were nearly of mine own age—a little older, perhaps. We were always together; and they had a great affection for me. In everything that gave them pleasure, I kept the conversation alive—listened to the stories of their affections and childish follies, good for nothing; and what was still worse, my soul began to give itself up to that which was the cause of all its disorders. If I were to give advice, I would say to parents that they ought to be very careful whom they allow to mix with their children when young; for much mischief thence ensues, and our natural inclinations are unto evil rather than unto good.

So it was with me; for I had a sister much older than myself, from whose modesty and goodness, which were great, I learned nothing; and learned every evil from a relative who was often in the house. She was so light and frivolous, that my mother took great pains to keep her out of the house, as if she foresaw the evil I should learn from her; but she could not succeed, there being so many reasons for her coming. I was very fond of this person's company, gossiped and talked with her; for she helped me in all the amusements I liked, and, what is more, found some for me, and communicated to me her own conversations and her vanities. Until I knew her, I mean, until she became friendly with me, and communicated to me her own affairs—I was then about fourteen years old, a little more, I think—I do not believe that I turned away from God in mortal sin, or lost the fear of Him, though I had a greater fear of disgrace. This latter fear had such sway over me, that I never wholly forfeited my good name—and, as to that, there was nothing in the world for which I would have bartered it, and nobody in the world I liked well enough who could have persuaded me to do it.

This friendship distressed my father and sister exceedingly. They often blamed me for it; but, as they could not hinder that person from coming into the house, all their efforts were in vain; for I was very adroit in doing anything that was wrong. Now and then, I am amazed at the evil one bad companion can do—nor could I believe it if I did not know it by experience—especially when we are young: then is it that the evil must be greatest. Oh, that parents would take warning by me, and look carefully to this! So it was; the conversation of this person so changed me, that no trace was left of my soul's natural disposition to virtue, and I became a reflection of her and of another who was given to the same kind of amusements.

Colley Cibber*
(1671-1757)

However little worth notice the life of a school-boy may be supposed to contain, yet, as the passions of men and children have much the same motives, and differ very little in their effects, unless where the elder experience may be able to conceal them; as therefore what arises from the boy, may possibly be a lesson to the man, I shall venture to relate a fact or two that happened while I was still at school.

In February 1684-5, died King Charles II, who being the only king I

---

*From *An Apology for the Life of Colley Cibber.* Reprinted by permission of E. P. Dutton & Co., Inc. Everyman's Library. Pp. 20-22.

had ever seen, I remember (young as I was) his death made a strong impression upon me, as it drew tears from the eyes of multitudes, who looked no further into him than I did: but it was, then, a sort of school-doctrine to regard our monarch as a deity; as in the former reign it was to insist he was accountable to this world, as well as to that above him.

King Charles his death was judg'd, by our school-master, a proper subject to lead the form I was in, into a higher kind of exercise; he therefore enjoin'd us, severally, to make his funeral oration. This sort of task, so entirely new to us all, the boys received with astonishment, as a work above their capacity; and tho' the master persisted in his command, they one and all, except myself, resolved to decline it. But I, sir, who was ever giddily forward, and thoughtless of consequences, set myself roundly to work, and got through it as well as I could. I remember to this hour that single topick of his affability (which made me mention it before) was the chief motive that warmed me into the undertaking; and to shew how very childish a notion I had of his character at that time, I raised his humanity, and love of those who serv'd him, to such height, that I imputed his death to the shock he received from the Lord Arlington's being at the point of death, about a week before him. This oration, such as it was, I produc'd the next morning: all the other boys pleaded their inability, which the master taking rather as a mark of their modesty than their idleness, only seemed to punish by setting me at the head of the form: a preferment dearly bought! Much happier had I been to have sunk my performance in the general modesty of declining it. A most uncomfortable life I led among them for many a day after! I was so jeer'd, laugh'd at, and hated as a pragmatical bastard (school-boys' language) who had betray'd the whole form, that scarce any of them would keep me company; and tho' it so far advanced me into the master's favour that he would often take me from the school, to give me an airing with him on horseback, while they were left to their lessons; you may be sure such envy'd happiness did not increase their good-will to me: notwithstanding which, my stupidity could take no warning from their treatment. An accident of the same nature happen'd soon after, that might have frighten'd a boy of a meek spirit from attempting anything above the lowest capacity. On the 23rd of April following, being the coronation-day of the new king, the school petition'd the master for leave to play; to which he agreed, provided any of the boys would produce an English ode upon that occasion.—The very word "ode," I know, makes you smile already; and so it does me; not only because it still makes so many poor devils turn wits upon it, but from a more agreeable motive; from a reflection of how little I then thought that, half a century afterwards, I should be called upon twice a year, by my post, to make the same kind of oblations to an *unexceptionable* prince, the serene happiness of whose reign my halting rhimes are still so unequal to.— This, I own, is vanity without disguise; but, *Hæc olim meminisse juvat.* The remembrance of the miserable prospect we had then before us, and have since escaped by a revolution, is now a pleasure, which, without that remembrance, I could not so heartily have enjoyed. The ode I was speaking of fell to my lot, which in about half an hour I produced. I cannot say it was much above the merry stile of "Sing! Sing the Day, and sing the Song," in the farce; yet bad as it was, it served to get the school a play-day, and to make me not a little vain upon it; which last effect so disgusted my play-fellows, that they left me out of the party I had most a mind to be of in that day's recreation. But their ingratitude serv'd only to increase my vanity; for I considered them as so many beaten tits, that had just had the mortification of seeing my hack of a Pegasus come in before them. This low passion is so rooted in our nature, that sometimes riper heads cannot govern it. I have met with much the same silly sort of coldness, even from my contemporaries of the theatre, from having the superfluous capacity of writing myself the characters I have acted.

Vittorio Alfieri*
(1749-1803)

During the long and frequent intervals in which I was obliged from ill health to keep my chamber, one of the students, who, though somewhat older and much stronger, was yet more ignorant than myself, employed me occasionally in translating, extending, or composing verses for him. He compelled me to comply with his demands by this irresistible argument: "If you are willing to do my work, I will give you two balls to play with; here they are; you see they are large, of four colors, well made, of fine cloth, and extremely elastic; if you are not willing to do it, I will give you two *blows*," and he raised his athletic arm, which he held over my head. I chose the two balls, and proceeded with his work. At first I faithfully executed my task in the best manner I was able; and the master evinced not a little surprise at the unexpected progress of his scholar, who had been hitherto considered as extremely dull and stupid. For my own part I religiously kept the secret, more from the natural taciturnity of my temper than from any

---

*From his *Autobiography*. Boston: James R. Osgood & Co., 1877. Pp. 88-89.

dread of the threatened blows. Nevertheless, as I soon became tired of his balls, and disgusted with the fatigue, I began to pay less attention to the composition of these exercises, notwithstanding the praises bestowed on my talents, till at last I committed various solecisms, such as *potebam,* which at length drew on him the hisses of his comrades and the rod of the master. Though he found himself thus ridiculed in public, and forced to resume his *ass's skin,* he durst not openly vent his anger upon me; but he never afterwards employed me to execute his tasks. The disgrace with which he would have been loaded, had I discovered the secret, restrained the rage with which he was agitated. I never betrayed him; but I secretly laughed when others related that *potebam* and similar solecisms had found their way into his compositions, in which no one suspected I had the smallest share. I might probably be restrained within the limits of discretion, by the recollection of the hand which was held over my head, which I saw continually before my eyes, ready to take vengeance on me for so many balls expended to procure only ridicule. Hence I learned that mankind are only governed by mutual terror.

Napoleon Bonaparte*
(1769-1821)

In the middle of May 1779 I entered the Military School of Brienne, and was happy. All kinds of thoughts began to run through my head. I found the need to learn, to acquire knowledge, to make progress. I devoured books. Soon I was the only subject of conversation. I became an object of wonder and envy; I had confidence in my power, and enjoyed my superiority.

As I still spoke French badly, and found it hard to accustom myself to a completely different mode of living, I generally kept away from my companions at first, and preferred to occupy myself with my books. Extraordinarily sensitive as I was, I suffered infinitely from the ridicule of my schoolmates, who used to jeer at me as a foreigner. My pride and sense of honour would tolerate no insult to my country or to the beloved national hero Paoli. Once I had been guilty of some slight offense, whereupon a particularly severe master snorted out: "On your knees, Mr. Bonaparte, you will take your dinner kneeling." Greatly excited, I answered: "I will, if necessary, take my dinner standing, but not on my knees, for in our family we only kneel to God."

---

*From *Napoleon's Autobiography* (24). P. 13.

And as this brutal teacher still insisted on his demand, I uttered a cry of rage, and fell to the floor insensible.

In Brienne it was only in the exact sciences that I took an interest. Everyone used to say: "That is a boy whose talent is all for geometry." I lived apart from my comrades and had chosen a small corner of the courtyard to which I would retire in order to give myself up to my day-dreams, for I have always been fond of indulging in visions. When my companions tried to take this retreat from me I defended it with all my might. Already I had the feeling that my will was stronger than that of the others, and that whatever I fancied must belong to me. I was liked in the school; it takes time to be appreciated, and that I had not got. But even when there was nothing to do there always remained the indefinite feeling that I was losing nothing through the indiffer-ence of others.

Leigh Hunt* (1784-1859)

If I had reaped no other benefit from Christ Hospital, the school would be ever dear to me from the recollection of the friendships I formed in it, and of the first heavenly taste it gave me of that most spiritual of the affections. I use the word "heavenly" advisedly; and I call friendship the most spiritual of the affections, because even one's kindred, in partaking of our flesh and blood, become, in a manner, mixed up with our entire being. Not that I would disparage any other form of affection, worshipping, as I do, all forms of it, love in par-ticular, which, in its highest state, is friendship and something more. But if ever I tasted a disembodied transport on earth, it was in those friendships which I entertained at school, before I dreamt of any ma-turer feeling. I shall never forget the impression it first made on me. I loved my friend for his gentleness, his candour, his truth, his good repute, his freedom even from my own livelier manner, his calm and reasonable kindness. It was not any particular talent that attracted me to him, or anything striking whatsoever. I should say, in one word, it was his goodness. I doubt whether he ever had a conception of a tithe of the regard and respect I entertained for him; and I smile to think of the perplexity (though he never showed it) which he probably felt sometimes at my enthusiastic expressions; for I thought him a kind of angel. It is no exaggeration to say, that, take away the unspiritual part of it—the genius and the knowledge—and there is no height of con-cept indulged in by the most romantic character in Shakespeare,

*From *The Autobiography of Leigh Hunt, with Reminiscences of Friends and Contemporaries.* Westminster, England: Archibald Constable & Co., 1903, Vol. I. Pp. 92-94.

which surpassed what I felt towards the merits I ascribed to him, and
the delight which I took in his society. With the other boys I played
antics, and rioted in fantastic jests; but in his society, or whenever I
thought of him, I fell into a kind of Sabbath state of bliss; and I am
sure I could have died for him.

I experienced this delightful affection towards three successive
schoolfellows, till two of them had for some time gone out into the
world and forgotten me; but it grew less with each, and in more than
one instance became rivalled by a new set of emotions, especially in
regard to the last, for I fell in love with his sister—at least, I thought
so.

Richard Wagner*
(1813-1883)

I now entered into all the dissipations of raw manhood, the outward
ugliness and inward emptiness of which make me marvel to this day.
My intercourse with those of my own age has always been the result of
pure chance. I cannot remember that any special inclination or attraction determined me in the choice of my young friends. While I can
honestly say that I was never in a position to stand aloof out of envy
from any one who was specially gifted, I can only explain my indifference in the choice of my associates by the fact that through inexperience regarding the sort of companionship that would be of advantage to me, I cared only to have some one who would accompany
me in my excursions, and to whom I could pour out my feelings to my
heart's content without caring what effect it might have upon him.
The result of this was that after a stream of confidences to which my
own excitement was the only response, I at length reached the point
when I turned and looked at my friend; to my astonishment I generally found that there was no question of response at all, and as soon as
I set my heart on drawing something from him in return, and urged
him to confide in me, when he really had nothing to tell, the connection usually came to an end and left no trace on my life. In a certain
sense my strange relationship with Flachs was typical of the great majority of my ties in after-life. Consequently, as no lasting personal
bond of friendship ever found its way into my life it is easy to understand how delight in the dissipations of student life could become a
passion of some duration, because in it individual intercourse is entirely replaced by a common circle of acquaintances. In the midst of
rowdyism and ragging of the most foolish description I remained
quite alone, and it is quite possible that these frivolities formed a pro-

*From *My Life* by Richard Wagner. Reprinted by permission of Dodd, Mead & Co.
Copyright 1911, 1939. Pp. 45-46.

tecting hedge round my inmost soul, which needed time to grow to its natural strength and not be weakened by reaching maturity too soon.

Edmund Gosse*
(1849-1928)

Not one of my village friends attended the boarding-school to which I was now attached, and I arrived there without an acquaintance. I should soon, however, have found a corner of my own if my Father had not unluckily stipulated that I was not to sleep in the dormitory with boys of my own age, but in the room occupied by the two elder sons of a prominent Plymouth Brother whom he knew. From a social point of view, this was an unfortunate arrangement, since these youths were some years older and many years riper than I; the eldest, in fact, was soon to leave; they had enjoyed their independence, and they now greatly resented being saddled with the presence of an unknown urchin. The supposition had been that they would protect and foster my religious practices; would encourage me, indeed, as my Father put it, to approach the Throne of Grace with them at morning and evening prayer. They made no pretence, however, to be considered godly; they looked upon me as an intruder; and after a while the younger, and ruder, of them openly let me know that they believed I had been put into their room to "spy upon" them: it had been a plot, they knew, between their father and mine: and he darkly warned me that I should suffer if "anything got out." I had, however, no wish to trouble them, nor any faint interest in their affairs. I soon discovered that they were absorbed in a silly kind of amorous correspondence with the girls of a neighbouring academy, but, "what were all such toys to me?"

These young fellows, who ought long before to have left the school, did nothing overtly unkind to me, but they condemned me to silence. They ceased to address me except with an occasional command. By reason of my youth, I was in bed and asleep before my companions arrived upstairs, and in the morning I was always routed up and packed about my business while they still were drowsing. But the fact that I had been cut off from my coevals by night, cut me off from them also by day—so that I was nothing to them, neither a boarder nor day scholar, neither flesh, fish nor fowl. The loneliness of my life was extreme, and that I always went home on Saturday afternoon and returned on Monday morning still further checked my companionships at school. For a long time, round the outskirts of that busy throng of opening lives, I "wandered lonely as a cloud," and some-

---

*From *Father and Son* by Edmund Gosse. Reprinted by permission of Charles Scribner's Sons. Copright 1907, Charles Scribner's Sons; 1935, Philip Gosse. Pp. 293-297.

times I was more unhappy than I had ever been before. No one, however, bullied me, and though I was dimly and indefinably witness to acts of uncleanness and cruelty, I was the victim of no such acts and the recipient of no dangerous confidences. I suppose that my queer reputation for sanctity, half dreadful, half ridiculous, surrounded me with a non-conducting atmosphere.

We are the victims of hallowed proverbs, and one of the most classic of these tells us that "the child is father of the man." But in my case I cannot think that this was true. In mature years I have always been gregarious, a lover of my kind, dependent upon the company of friends for the very pulse of moral life. To be marooned, to be shut up in a solitary cell, to inhabit a lighthouse, or to camp alone in a forest, these have always seemed to me afflictions too heavy to be borne, even in imagination. A state in which conversation exists not, is for me an air too empty of oxygen for my lungs to breathe it.

Yet when I look back upon my days at boarding-school, I see myself unattracted by any of the human beings around me. My grown-up years are made luminous to me in memory by the ardent faces of my friends, but I can scarce recall so much as the names of more than two or three of my school-fellows. There is not one of them whose mind or whose character made any lasting impression upon me. In later life, I have been impatient of solitude, and afraid of it; at school, I asked for no more than to slip out of the hurly-burly and be alone with my reflections and my fancies. That magnetism of humanity which has been the agony of mature years, of this I had not a trace when I was a boy. Of those fragile loves to which most men look back with tenderness and passion, emotions to be explained only as Montaigne explained them, *"parceque c'était lui, parceque c'était moi,"* I knew nothing. I, to whom friendship has since been like sunlight and like sleep, left school unbrightened and unrefreshed by commerce with a single friend.

Sigmund Freud
(1856-1939)

The letter by Sigmund Freud which is reproduced here* requires a short explanation for full appreciation of the meaning and beauty of Freud's words. This explanation was originally tendered by Martin Grotjahn (17):

"Heinrich Braun, about whom Freud writes in this letter . . . [was] one and a half years older than Freud. He came from a family

---

*From *Letters of Sigmund Freud* edited by Ernst L. Freud. New York: Basic Books, 1960. Pp. 647-649.

of independent, liberal-thinking engineers. . . . He edited several scientific and political journals. . . . In the year 1903 he became a member of the German parliament. . . . He died on the 8th of February, 1927, in Berlin. After his death . . . his widow started to collect material as preparation for a book about her late husband. As a part of the research, she wrote a letter to Sigmund Freud asking him what he remembered about his former friend. Sigmund Freud, by then seventy-one years of age and still living in Vienna, Berggasse 19, wrote the following account of his associations and recollections. . . .

"One of the remarkable features of this letter is the style of almost free association in which it is written. Freud associated to the request for information and his mind at first turned to recollections of recent events before he reached far back to the beginning of his friendship with Heinrich Braun. Then he proceeded in chronological sequence. Once he interrupted his freely flowing associations with a reflection about the strange fact that he, Freud, later lived for more than thirty years in the same home in which he met Victor Adler. Freud put this thought in parenthesis. After some hesitation, so it seems, comes the report about what Freud calls the 'youthful friendship' with this fire-brand of a person, who was not a 'scholar' but a 'personality.'

"All the typical features of a boyhood friendship, with their deep feeling, their loyalties, their declaration of undying faith are implied in this recollection. It is remarkable to see how Freud attempts to combine the pride of being *Primus,* the first one in his class, with his admiration for the Promethean young man who was asked to leave school. In German-Austrian tradition such advice amounted to a deep shame and disaster to the whole family.

"Perhaps it is amusing to note how tactfully Freud mentions the fact that Heinrich Braun was thrown out of school. It seems that he was not quite sure whether he should mention it, and how Heinrich's widow would react to it. He is much less apologetic for his harsh judgment of Heinrich Braun's 'essentially negative aims' in his political philosophy.

"There is a slip of the pen or memory in Freud's letter when he calls the brother of Heinrich who interferes with the friendship by the awful name *Adolf;* his true name was Anton. Perhaps Freud did not like 'Adolf.' "

30 October, 1927
Wien IX, Berggasse 19

Hochgeehrte Frau:

No special introduction is required to make me fulfill your wish. I only fear that I cannot offer you as much as you expect. Our relationship, so strong during the years of the gymnasium, had already dissolved during the time at the University.

During the last 50 (!) years I have known hardly anything about him. During all these years of a long lifetime I met him several times accidentally on the streets of Vienna, once he may have visited me at my home. On another occasion I received a letter from him in which he asked me to treat analytically one of his sons who had caused him trouble. It must have been during the first decade of psychoanalysis. I refused because I was not equipped to guide adolescents and thought —rightfully—that personal relations are not favorable to the analytic situation.

I possess no letters from him. The last impressive meeting which we had may have taken place in 1883 (?) or 1884 (?). He came to Vienna then and invited me for lunch at his brother-in-law's, Victor Adler. I still remember that he was a vegetarian then and that I had a chance to see the little Fritz who must have been one or two years of age. (I think it is remarkable that this happened in the same rooms in which I have been living for thirty-six years.)

I know that I made the acquaintance of Heinrich Braun during the first year at the gymnasium on the day when we got our first "report card" and that we were soon inseparable friends. All the hours of the day which were left after school I spent with him, mostly at his home, especially as long as his family was not yet in Vienna and he lived with his next oldest brother Adolf and a private tutor. This brother tried to interfere with our relationship. We ourselves, however, got along marvelously. I hardly remember any quarrels between us or times during which we were "mad" at each other, which happens so frequently during such young friendships. What we did all those days and what we talked about is difficult to imagine after so many years. I believe he reinforced my aversion to school and to what was taught there; he awakened a multitude of revolutionary trends in me and we reinforced each other in the overestimate of our criticism and of our superior knowledge. He turned my interest to books like Buckle's *History of Civilization* and to a similar work by Lecky, which he admired greatly. I admired him: his self-confident poise; his independent judgment; I compared him secretly with a young lion and I was firmly convinced that sometime in the future he would assume a leading position in the world. A scholar he was not, but I did not mind that, though I myself soon became *Primus* and remained it; in the vague feeling of those years I understood that he possessed something which was more valuable than all success in school and which I have since learned to call "personality."

Neither the goals nor the means of our ambitions were very clear to us. Since then I have come to the assumption that his aims were essentially negative ones. But one thing was certain: that I would work with him and that I would never desert his "party." Under his influence I was also determined at that time to study law at the university.

Our relationship experienced its first interruption—I think it was during the Septima, the next to the last grade—when he left school, unfortunately not voluntarily. During the first year at the university he was there again. But I had become a student of medicine and he a student of law. Soon he made the acquaintance of Victor Adler, who later became his brother-in-law. Our ways separated slowly: he always had more relationships to people than I had and it was always easier for him to establish new ones. Contact with me had probably ceased to be a need to him long before. So it happened that I completely lost sight of him during the later years of study. I don't even know whether he took his doctor's degree in Vienna. I do not believe so. One day, perhaps in the year '81 or '82, I met him on the street, long after we had become strangers. As a matter of course we again immediately talked quite intimately. He showed me the picture of the girl whom he was engaged to marry; and I confessed that I was in the same situation. Perhaps it was then that he invited me to lunch at Adler's. And then there was nothing in common between us any more and no real relationship was ever established again.

In vorzüglicher Hochachtung

Ihr

(Signed) FREUD

Mohandas K. Gandhi*
(1869-1948)

Amongst my few friends at the high school I had, at different times, two who might be called intimate. One of these friendships did not last long, though I never forsook my friend. He forsook me, because I made friends with the other. This latter friendship I regard as a trag-

---

*From *The Story of My Experiments with Truth* by Mohandas K. Gandhi. Reprinted by permission of Public Affairs Press. 1948. Pp. 31-36.

edy in my life. It lasted long. I formed it in the spirit of a reformer.

This companion was originally my elder brother's friend. They were classmates. I knew his weaknesses, but I regarded him as a faithful friend. My mother, my eldest brother, and my wife warned me that I was in bad company. I was too proud to heed my wife's warning. But I dared not go against the opinion of my mother and my eldest brother. Nevertheless I pleaded with them saying, "I know he has the weaknesses you attribute to him, but you do not know his virtues. He cannot lead me astray, as my association with him is meant to reform him. For I am sure that if he reforms his ways, he will be a splendid man. I beg you not to be anxious on my account."

I do not think this satisfied them, but they accepted my explanation and let me go my way.

I have seen since that I had calculated wrongly. A reformer cannot afford to have close intimacy with him whom he seeks to reform. True friendship is an identity of souls rarely to be found in this world. Only between like natures can friendship be altogether worthy and enduring. Friends react on one another. Hence in friendship there is very little scope for reform. I am of opinion that all exclusive intimacies are to be avoided; for man takes in vice far more readily than virtue. And he who would be friends with God must remain alone, or make the whole world his friend. I may be wrong, but my effort to cultivate an intimate friendship proved a failure.

A wave of "reform" was sweeping over Rajkot at the time when I first came across this friend. He informed me that many of our teachers were secretly taking meat and wine. He also named many well-known people of Rajkot as belonging to the same company. There were also, I was told, some high-school boys among them.

I was surprised and pained. I asked my friend the reason and he explained it thus: "We are a weak people because we do not eat meat. The English are able to rule over us, because they are meat-eaters. You know how hardy I am, and how great a runner too. It is because I am a meat-eater. Meat-eaters do not have boils or tumours, and even if they sometimes happen to have any, these heal quickly. Our teachers and other distinguished people who eat meat are no fools. They know its virtues. You should do likewise. There is nothing like trying. Try, and see what strength it gives."

All these pleas on behalf of meat-eating were not advanced at a single sitting. They represent the substance of a long and elaborate argument which my friend was trying to impress upon me from time to time. My elder brother had already fallen. He therefore supported my friend's argument. I certainly looked feeble-bodied by the side of my brother and this friend. They were both hardier, physically stronger, and more daring. This friend's exploits cast a spell over me. He could run long distances and extraordinarily fast. He was an adept in high and long jumping. He could put up with any amount of corporal punishment. He would often display his exploits to me and, as one is always dazzled when he sees in others the qualities that he lacks himself, I was dazzled by this friend's exploits. This was followed by a strong desire to be like him. I could hardly jump or run. Why should not I also be as strong as he?

Moreover, I was a coward. I used to be haunted by the fear of thieves, ghosts, and serpents. I did not dare to stir out of doors at night. Darkness was a terror to me. It was almost impossible for me to sleep in the dark, as I would imagine ghosts coming from one direction, thieves from another and serpents from a third. I could not therefore bear to sleep without a light in the room. How could I disclose my fears to my wife, no child, but already at the threshold of youth, sleeping by my side? I knew that she had more courage than I, and I felt ashamed of myself. She knew no fear of serpents and ghosts. She could go out anywhere in the dark. My friend knew all these weaknesses of mine. He would tell me that he could hold in his hand live serpents, could defy thieves and did not believe in ghosts. And all this was, of course, the result of eating meat.

A doggerel of the Gujarati poet Narmad was in vogue amongst us schoolboys, as follows:

> Behold the mighty Englishman
> He rules the Indian small,
> Because being a meat-eater
> He is five cubits tall.

All this had its due effect on me. I was beaten. It began to grow on me that meat-eating was good, that it would make me strong and daring, and that, if the whole country took to meat-eating, the English could be overcome.

A day was thereupon fixed for beginning the experiment. It had to be conducted in secret. The Gandhis were Vaishnavas. My parents were particularly staunch Vaishnavas. They would regularly visit the *Haveli*. The family had even its own temples. Jainism was strong in Gujarat, and its influence was felt everywhere and on all occasions. The opposition to and abhorrence of meat-eating that existed in Gujarat among the Jains and Vaishnavas were to be seen nowhere else in India or outside in such strength. These were the traditions in which I was born and bred. And I was extremely devoted to my parents. I knew that the moment they came to know of my having eaten meat, they would be shocked to death. Moreover, my love of truth made me extra cautious. I cannot say that I did not know then that I should have to deceive my parents if I began eating meat. But my mind was bent on the "reform." It was not a question of pleasing the palate. I did not know that it had a particularly good relish. I wished to be strong and daring and wanted my countrymen also to be such so that we might defeat the English and make India free. The word "Swaraj" I had not yet heard. But I knew what freedom meant. The frenzy of the "reform" blinded me. And having ensured secrecy, I persuaded myself that mere hiding the deed from parents was no departure from truth.

So the day came. It is difficult fully to describe my condition. There were, on the one hand, the zeal for "reform," and the novelty of making a momentous departure in life. There was, on the other, the shame of hiding like a thief to do this very thing. I cannot say which of the two swayed me more. We went in search of a lonely spot by the river, and there I saw, for the first time in my life,—meat. There was baker's bread also. I relished neither. The goat's meat was as tough as leather. I simply could not eat it. I was sick and had to leave off eating.

I had a very bad night afterwards. A horrible nightmare haunted me. Every time I dropped off to sleep it would seem as though a live goat were bleating inside me, and I would jump up full of remorse. But then I would remind myself that meat-eating was a duty and so become more cheerful.

My friend was not a man to give in easily. He now began to cook various delicacies with meat, and dress them neatly. And for dining, no longer was the secluded spot on the river chosen, but a State house, with its dining hall, and tables and chairs, about which my friend had made arrangements in collusion with the chief cook there.

This bait had its effect. I got over my dislike for bread, forswore my compassion for the goats, and became a relisher of meat-dishes, if not of meat itself. This went on for about a year. But not more than half a dozen meat-feasts were enjoyed in all; because the State house was not available every day, and there was the obvious difficulty about frequently preparing expensive savoury meat-dishes. I had no money to pay for this "reform." My friend had therefore always to find the wherewithal. I had no knowledge where he found it. But find it he did, because he was bent on turning me into a meat-eater. But even his means must have been limited, and hence these feasts had necessarily to be few and far between.

Whenever I had occasion to indulge in these surreptitious feasts, dinner at home was out of the question. My mother would naturally ask me to come and take my food and want to know the reason why I did not wish to eat. I would say to her, "I have no appetite today; there is something wrong with my digestion." It was not without compunction that I devised these pretexts. I knew I was lying, and lying to my mother. I also knew that, if my mother and father came to know of my having become a meat-eater, they would be deeply shocked. This knowledge was gnawing at my heart.

Therefore I said to myself: "Though it is essential to eat meat, and also essential to take up food "reform" in the country, yet deceiving and lying to one's father and mother is worse than not eating meat. In their lifetime, therefore, meat-eating must be out of the question. When they are no more and I have found my freedom, I will eat meat openly, but until that moment arrives I will abstain from it."

This decision I communicated to my friend, and I have never since gone back to meat. My parents never knew that two of their sons had become meat-eaters.

Ernest Jones*
(1879-1959)

At puberty one begins life afresh and yet not anew. One of Freud's most interesting discoveries was that in the years immediately following puberty one is engaged in both reproducing and re-creating on another plane the stages of one's earlier development, of the first four years of life that are commonly blotted out from memory. The direction of one's path is inflexibly determined by the now unconscious past; and yet one is granted the opportunity of re-making it along more suitable and stable lines, of correcting earlier deviations in it, and of relating it more definitely to the environment. The vague, fantastic and irrational attributes of the first development now have a chance, on its repetition, of becoming better adapted to the world of reality.

A rich inner life of phantasy in infancy, one kept apart from the realistic contacts that went on side by side with it, reproduced itself at puberty after an almost dormant interval when I had been mainly concerned with the world of people. This brought about an inner disharmony, a sense of strain, with some unhappiness. Instead of throwing myself wholeheartedly into the new school life at Llandovery I

*From *Free Associations* by Ernest Jones. Reprinted by permission of Basic Books, Inc. Copyright 1959. P. 44.

compromised by making quite good external contacts with the other boys, but regarding this not as real life so much as a concession that had to be made to enable one to continue any inner personal life of emotional speculation. The main fault I found with them was that they were "too young," that they never seemed to think of anything beyond the actual moment and its doings. The greatest trial was, therefore, as it often is in Army life, that one got little or no time to oneself, no privacy.

Charles James Nowell
(? - ?)

Charley Nowell, a Kwakiutl Indian chief of Vancouver, illustrates here in his autobiography how he became a member of the ingroup by doing something admirable in its eyes. Hitherto he had been an outsider and the butt of its jokes.*

Sometime after Maggie died, I and Stephen Cook was sent up north to go to school. We stayed at the mission house where Bishop Ridley was. There was over twenty-four there—all boys. It was a kind of boardinghouse. We stayed there, slept there, and ate there. When we was there, we find that these boys are tough. They are fighting all the time, and they always want to tease us because we were strangers. One evening while we was having our supper, our cook, an Indian boy named Tlisk, he was mad with everybody, and he came along with a pot of stew to serve it out to all the boys. When he got to my plate, he bumped the pot against the side of my head. I took my elbow and jabbed it in his stomach, and he didn't give me any stew. He sat down and had his meal, and one of the other boys took the pot and came and gave me some of the stew. This cook boy was mad with us and talk and talk at us in his language. He was a humpback, and he look at me and talk at me. Finally, I says, "Shut up, you dirty humpback." He picked up his stew and threw it at me, and it got all over me and the other boys near me, and he took his tin mug and from where he sit— just across the table—he threw it at me hard. I put up my arm and the mug hit it. He was a short man, and I bent over the table and got hold of his shirt and pulled him right across the table, and picked him up and threw him right down the table, rattling all the dishes and spilling everything. All the boys cheered me and hollered out in fun.

*From *Smoke from Their Fires* edited by Clellan S. Ford. Reprinted by permission of Yale University Press. Copyright 1941.

Bishop Ridley came running and says, "What's the matter?" It was the other boys that told him how it was started. The cook was fired, and after that I got acquainted with the other boys.

Resat Güntekin
(1892-   )

Resat Güntekin is a Turkish national. Her mother died when she was six years old. She was then taken care of by her grandmother, who died when she was nine. Her father, of whom she saw very little, was a major in the cavalry—and he died when Resat, or Feridé, as she was nicknamed, was twelve, whereupon she was taken in by her aunts. Feridé was a tomboy. She describes herself as a scatterbrain, up to all sorts of deviltry and mischief right up to her wedding day. In the following passage,* Feridé relates her inability to develop friendships with her classmates and the resultant unpleasant feelings. She was fourteen years old.

At the end of the summer holidays the school was in a great state of ferment, which would only end when the terminal examinations began. The reason was this. My Catholic school friends who had reached their thirteenth or fourteenth year made their first communion at Easter; in white silk dresses down to the ground, with their heads wreathed in sheaves of muslin like brides' veils, they were betrothed to their prophet Jesus. The whole wedding ceremony was very impressive; it was performed in church, by candle-light, with prayers sung to an organ, amid clouds of incense which mingled with the scent of spring flowers and pervaded the air of the whole place.

The pity of it was, that during the holiday months which followed the ceremony, my faithless schoolmates were at once false to their betrothed, and betrayed the waxen-faced, blue-eyed Jesus with the first man they met; and indeed with more than one. When school reopened, what a number of letters, photographs, flowery keepsakes and the rest of it did they not bring with them, concealed in the corner of a trunk. When they took a stroll in the garden, in twos and threes, I used to know quite well what they were talking about. I had no difficulty in understanding that underneath those pictures of angels, and the coloured prints of their prophet (which had been presented to the

*From *Autobiography of a Turkish Girl* by Resat Güntekin. Reprinted by permission of George Allen & Unwin. 1949. Pp. 27-29.

most innocent and religious girls) were hidden the photographs of young men. The story one girl whispered in the ear of another in a corner of the garden, in a voice inaudible even to the insects buzzing around her in the air, did not escape me.

About this time, the girls would divide themselves off into groups of twos and threes, and stick to each other tenaciously. I, poor dear, was left all alone in the garden and in the class-room. The others seemed like so many mystery boxes to me. They avoided me even more than the nuns; you will ask why? Because I was a chatterbox, and (as my be-whiskered old uncle would say) I could not keep a secret. For instance, if I got to know that one of them had effected a little inno-cent exchange of flowers with one of the local young men through the garden railings, I would broadcast it all over the garden; and more than that, I was fanatical about things of that kind.

I shall never forget how one winter's evening, we were doing lessons in the class-room. A hard-working girl called Michelle had got per-mission from the Sister to study Roman history, and had gone to the seat at the back of the room. Suddenly, in the silence of the class-room, a sob was heard. The nun raised her head, and exclaimed: "What is the matter, Michelle? Are you crying?"

Michelle's face was wet with tears, and she covered it with her hand. I answered for her:

"Michelle has been moved by the defeat of the Carthaginians; that's why she's crying," I announced. The class burst out laughing.

The truth was, they were well advised not to admit me to their con-fidence. All the same, to be set apart from everyone, and for a girl of my age to be treated as a little chatterbox, was not a very pleasant experience.

Helena Kuo*
(1910-   )

Study was intensive. The bell called us to our lessons at eight. Class ended at twelve and began again at one in the afternoon, continuing to four or five. Ah Wei and I were in a section where the other stu-dents were boys of any age from fifteen to nineteen. Ah Wei was fif-teen. To look at her you would have said she was four or five years older. Her dreamy eyes were romantic enough to make even a sedate male teacher feel romantic. But that was only one of her diversions.

---

*From *I've Come a Long Way* by Helena Kuo. Reprinted by permission of Appleton-Century-Crofts, Inc. Copyright 1942, Helena G. C. Kuo. Pp. 60-64.

She had been to school in Shanghai and Peking, so she really was a creature from another world, as different from me as a New York girl would be from a farm girl in the Middle West.

As we worked together, ate together, and slept in the same dormitory, we had to get to know each other. She was a good test for my temper because she called for all my patience. Until I delivered myself of that weighty pronouncement on the campus, we had had many minor quarrels—not that they worried me much. I was conscious all the time that I would have to put a double effort into my studies because I was so far behind.

I shall always remember geography class, one morning after the first monthly exams. When the teacher, a kind friendly man with a smile always hanging around the corners of his fat genial face, walked in, the students began to ask him the usual questions. Who had passed, who had failed in the exams?

He always bore their impish conduct with more good humor than it deserved. You who haven't been in a Chinese classroom may not appreciate this, but we play twice as much as western children; in fact, we play and tease all our lives. Our sense of humor and our love of laughter are vital parts of our nature, so to teach us, masters have to have a double portion of patience.

I was busy writing a big "No" to a mash note that had been flipped across to me by Ah Wei pretending to be a boy, when I heard the teacher say: "I am not going to tell you who flunked, you unruly band of rascals, but I can tell you that at yesterday's meeting of the faculty, it was decided that this class tops the list for noise and naughtiness. However, it has been decided that one of you here shall get honors for exams as well as for behavior."

That started a rain of questions. All the boys were eager to know who the student was. Ah Wei and I sat in the back row taking no part in the discussion. Thoroughly enjoying the sensation he had created, the teacher proceeded steadily with the lesson and ignored the questions that kept coming up. All he would say was: "Some one is going to be proud, and the others are going to be mighty ashamed of themselves."

"I wish he would hurry up," whispered Ah Wei to me. "I want to know who it is. I hope he is presentable, as I do not mind talking to him if he asks me. I would like an intelligent sweetheart."

From our place in the back row we could see the whole class and observe their tricks far better than the master at the front. There was a reason for our being put in the back. On the first few days we had been put right in front of the class, but the boys teased us. They not

only poked fun at us, but prodded us with rulers in parts of our anatomy that are not meant to be prodded, so that the wise Dean decided
that our backs had better be protected by a wall. Sitting where we did,
we were not attacked with rulers when we were trying to answer questions and did not have to try to look cool and dignified when we sat
down suddenly on a thumb-tack that some wicked little devil-boy had
put on our seats.

I don't think Ah Wei liked that back seat very much, but I did, for I
could throw paper at the boys' ears by an elastic catapult, and they
never suspected it was I.

At the end of that lesson, the teacher was packing away his books as
if he had forgotten his secret, so the boys began to yell. "Now, Master
... tell us who has honors."

"You want to know? You are so interested in higher education?" the
teacher queried. "I am surprised. Well, I'll tell you: some have honors
for work, of course, but the one who has honors for both behavior and
the examination is a girl, Kuo Gin-Chiu."

There was a dead silence. The teacher told me to stand up. I
couldn't. Ah Wei dug me in the ribs, and I got up, blushing. I had
never meant to be as good as all that. If the faculty liked me that
much, the other students would hate me. They would be jealous.

"There she is, you little rascals," said the teacher. "Just a little girl,
and she has beaten you all. Kuo Gin-Chiu, I congratulate you."

I stammered and sat down—on a thumb-tack that some heartless
boy had put on my seat. I squealed, and the whole class roared with
laughter. I wept from sheer nerves. A message fell on my desk. I
opened it. Some one had written my new name on it: *Mai-Ka,* the
school slang for bookworm. Before that, they had called me Garbo—
because I was tall, slim, and seemed to want to be alone with my
books. Now I was the bookworm.

After class that morning, we had election for class president, vice-
president, secretary, and treasurer. When the office for president or
monitor was mentioned, the boys all stood up and yelled: "Old Mai-
Ka. We want old Mai-Ka as our judge. She knows how to behave." So I
was class judge. That was their joke on me. My duties were to preserve
discipline in the class when the master was not there and to have the
class ready to receive him. It was some job. How could a girl look after
a hundred mischievous and sometimes rough boys? I knew I could not
do it, and I wanted to resign. "Don't you do it," advised Ah Wei.
"You give them as much as they would give you. You must be hard on
men, else they will never respect you. Be very hard."

I took her advice and became a tyrant. I took their names every time anything was wrong, cracked down on them for everything, and pretended to be serious about it. They got what they never expected from a girl.

Eating in classrooms was forbidden. Any one guilty was fined by the students' committee and their food confiscated. I made a big collection of chewing-gum and peanuts, which Ah Wei and I enjoyed. The boys got mad, of course, but when they saw I was determined to be severe, they tried to soften me with stupid love notes. I would find "I love you" signed with a pigeon written on my desk, and I had to be more careful than ever about the thumb-tacks. However, when some one pointed out to them that thumb-tacks were too dangerous for girls, and must only be used on boys, they thought up a new idea. This was to sprinkle my seat with chalk. For a few days I went round all day with a white patch on my bottom which drew roars of laughter.

David S. Kogan*
(1929-1951)

Saturday, December 15, 1945

Called up Gordon this morning to ascertain if I could come over. Unfortunately he had homework, applications for college (sic) and company. About 6:00 P.M. I received a call from the boy—he wanted to spend the evening at my house. We had a very enjoyable time. Our friendship is a breathing reality and we pour out our hearts to each other. He quaintly proposed a perpetual partnership between us. Whenever we meet, I entertain him from the vast storehouse of my mind. I relate the foibles and psychologies of acquaintances, teachers, educational systems, Jewish problems, philosophy, economics, and the like. He loves it. If all his qualities and all mine were put in Ken Stone's body, endowed with Steve's health and Meltin's aggressiveness, the world's perfect man would be found.

SOCIAL RELATIONSHIPS

The social personality of the adolescent is based upon cultural definitions and group expectations. The group patterns set the standards of behavior; the adolescent is coerced into the group mold and acquires the set of attitudes and standards of behavior that bring him into line with the required behavior norms.

---

*From *The Diary of David S. Kogan*. Reprinted by permission of Beechurst Press. Copyright 1955. P. 107.

The adolescent is overwhelmingly preoccupied with social experience. The intensity of his passionate absorption in interpersonal relationships results from four factors: (a) his increasing concern with acquiring primary status as an independent entity; (b) his
newly won eemancipation from the home; (c) his greater mobility;
and (d) the opportunities the group provides for gratifying newly
acquired heterosexual needs and interests (4). It is through the
peer culture that the adolescent learns to clarify his social skills
and values, his sex role, and his ways of competing and co-operating.
In short, he learns about the social processes of the culture in which
he finds himself (33).

So seriously does the adolescent look upon his social participation
and so crucial is it for him, that the emotional tension accompanying his social life inevitably becomes heightened. It is Erikson's (12)
hypothesis that identity formation is the primary developmental
task in adolescence and that the acquisition of social roles is central
to identity formation. The adolescent who is mastering his appropriate sex role, both in affect and behavior, has generally had the
opportunity to observe, choose and learn the skills required for
appropriate sex role enactment. Essentially, successful mastery is
achieved if the adolescent participates in varied situations with different types of people and if there are individuals in the social life
who are appropriate models for sex role behavior. Conversely, if
the child is isolated and his models are inadequate or lacking, he
will tend in adolescence either to biologically primitive expressions of sexuality or to distortions of fantasy.

Many of the passages which follow illuminate the variety of situations with different types of people with whom the adolescent meets
and acts out his social needs. His ambivalences in the social situation—so characteristic of the adolescent—are manifested repeatedly. The progression from narcissism to mature libidinal sociality
also becomes evident; the enamels of propriety begin to harden;
radical changes in attitudes toward the self, which are reflected in
changes in social behavior, become apparent through the more
stable and more objective type of emotional interest in these social
relationships. And corresponding to the radical changes in social
behavior and attitudes toward the self are the physical changes occurring during the adolescent period. The illustrations below will
also show the narcissistic recrudescences of adolescence, even while

there is manifest the growing sexual sociality of the adolescent: pre-occupation with body and appearance, grooming, strength, size, skill and egocentric interests.

Margaret Cavendish*
(1624[?]-1674)

When the Queen was in Oxford, I had a great desire to be one of her maids of honour, hearing the Queen had not the same number she was used to have, whereupon I wooed and won my mother to let me go; for my mother, being fond of all her children, was desirous to please them, which made her consent to my request. But my brothers and sisters seemed not very well pleased, by reason I had never been from home, nor seldom out of their sight; for though they knew I would not behave myself to their or my own dishonour, yet they thought I might to my disadvantage, being unexperienced in the world; which indeed I did, for I was so bashful when I was out of my mother's, brothers', and sisters' sight, whose presence used to give me confidence, thinking I could not do amiss whilst any one of them were by, for I knew they would gently reform me if I did; besides, I was ambitious they should approve of my actions and behavior, that when I was gone from them, I was like one that had no foundation to stand, or guide to direct me, which made me afraid lest I should wander with ignorance out of the ways of honour, so that I knew not how to behave myself. Besides, I had heard that the world is apt to lay aspersions even on the innocent, for which I durst neither look up with my eyes, nor speak, nor be any way sociable, insomuch as I was thought a natural fool; indeed I had not much wit, yet I was not an idiot, my wit was according to my years; and though I might have learned more wit, and advanced my under-standing by living in a court, yet being dull, fearful, and bashful, I neither heeded what was said or practised, but just what belonged to my loyal duty, and my own honest reputation; and, indeed, I was so afraid to dishonour my friends and family by my indiscreet actions, that I rather chose to be accounted a fool, than to be thought rude or wanton; in truth, my bashfulness and fears made me repent my going from home to see the world abroad, and much I did desire to return to my mother again, or to my sister Pye, with whom I often lived when she was in London, and loved with a supernatural affection: but my

---

*From *A True Relation of the Birth, Breeding, and Life of Margaret Cavendish, Duchess of Newcastle* by Margaret Cavendish. London: Johnson & Warwick, 1814. Pp. 10-12.

mother advised me there to stay, although I put her to more charges than if she had kept me at home, and the more, by reason she and my brothers were sequestered from their estates, and plundered of all their goods; yet she maintained me so, that I was in a condition rather to lend than to borrow, which courtiers usually are not, being always necessitated by reason of great expenses courts put them to. But my mother said, it would be a disgrace for me to return out of the court so soon after I was placed; so I continued almost two years.

Carlo Goldoni*
(1707-1793)

Perhaps, my dear reader, I abuse your complaisance too much, in taking up your time with trifles, which can but little interest or amuse you; but I have a strong desire to mention this college to you, where I ought to have made my fortune, and where I met with a sad reverse. I wish to avow my errors, and to prove to you at the same time that at my age, and in my situation, the utmost virtue was requisite to avoid them. Listen to me with patience.

We were very well fed and lodged in this college; we had liberty to go out to the university, and we went where we pleased. The regulation allowed two to go out together, who were also to return together. We separated at the first turning, after appointing a rendezvous for our return, and when we returned alone, the porter took his money and said nothing. His place was worth that of the porter of a minister of state.

We were as elegantly dressed as the abbés who figure away in the world; English cloth, French silk, embroidery, lace, with a sort of robe-de-chambre, without sleeves, above the coat, and a velvet stole fastened to the left shoulder with the Ghislieri arms embroidered in gold and silver, surmounted by the pontifical tiara, and the keys of Saint Peter. This robe, called sovrana, which is the device of the college, gives an air of importance to the wearer very well calculated to inspire a young man with a high idea of himself. Our college was not, as you may perceive, a community of boys. We acted precisely as we pleased. There was a great deal of dissipation within, and a great deal of freedom without. I learned there fencing, dancing, music, and drawing; and I learned also all possible games of commerce and chance. The latter were prohibited, but they were none the less played, and that of primero cost me dear.

---

*From *Memoirs* by Carlo Goldoni. Reprinted by permission of Alfred A. Knopf, Inc. 1926. Pp. 34-35.

On going out, we looked at the university at a distance, and contrived to find our way into the most agreeable houses. Hence, the collegians at Pavia are viewed by the town's-people in the light of officers in garrison towns; they are detested by the men and welcomed by the women.

My Venetian jargon was agreeable to the ladies, and gave me some advantage over my comrades; my age and figure were not unpleasing, and my couplets and songs were by no means ill relished. Was it my fault that I did not employ my time well? Yes: for among the forty which our number consisted of, there were several wise and considerate individuals, whom I ought to have imitated; but I was only sixteen, I was gay, weak, fond of pleasure, and I yielded to seduction. But enough for my first year of college; the holidays are approaching; they begin about the end of June, and terminate with October.

Eliza Southgate Bowne*
(1783-1809)

Boston, Feb. 7th, 1800

After the toil, the bustle and fatigue of the week I turn towards home to relate the manner in which I have spent my time. I have been continually engaged in parties, plays, balls, &c. &c. Since the first week I came to town, I have attended all the balls and assemblies, one one week and one the next. They have regular balls once a fortnight, so that I have been to one or the other every Thursday. They are very brilliant, and I have formed a number of pleasing acquaintances there; last night, which was ball night, I drew No. 5, & 2nd sett drew a Mr. Snow, bad partner; danced voluntarily with Mr. Oliver, Mr. Andrews, Mr. McPherson; danced until 1 o'clock; they have charming suppers, table laid entirely with china. I had charming partners always. Today I intended going to Mrs. Codman's, engaged to a week ago, but wrote a billett I was indisposed, but the truth of the matter was that I wanted to go to the play to see Bunker hill, and Uncle (William King) wished I should—therefore I shall go. I have engagements for the greater part of next week. Tomorrow we all go to hear Fisher Ames' Eulogy. And in the morning going to look at some instruments; however we got one picked out that I imagine we shall take, 150 dollars—a charming toned one and not made in this country. I am still at Mrs. Frazier's, she treats me with the greatest attention. Nancy

---

*From *A Girl's Life Eighty Years Ago* by Eliza Southgate Bowne. New York: Charles Scribner's Sons, 1887. Pp. 21-22.

is indeed a charming girl,—I have the promise of her company the ensuing summer. I have bought me a very handsome skirt, white satin. Richard Cutts went shopping with me yesterday morn, engaged to go to the play next week with him. For mourning for Washington the ladies dress as much as if for a relation, some entirely in black, but now many wear only a ribbon with a line painted on it. I have not yet been out to see Mrs. Rawson and Miss Haskell, but intend to next week. Uncle William [King] has been very attentive to me—carried me to the play 3 or 4 times and to all the balls and assemblies excepting the last which I went with Mr. Andrews. Give my best respects to Pappa and Mamma, and tell them I shall soon be tired of this dissipated life and almost want to go home already. I have a line to write to Mary Porter and must conclude.

ELIZA

Alexandre Dumas*
(1802-1870)

"O youth! springtime of life! O spring! youth of the year!" So said Metastasio.

We have now reached the beginning of May 1818, and I should be sixteen in the month of July.

It was at this joyous time of renaissance that our town held its feast —a feast ever lavish and charming, for Nature took upon herself to defray its costs.

The feast, as I believe I have already said, lasted three days, and fell at Whitsuntide.

For three days the park was filled with pleasant sounds and happy murmurs, which began at early morning and did not die away until far on in the night. For three days the poor forgot their misery, and, much more extraordinary still, the rich forgot their riches. The whole town was gathered together in the park as one great family, and, as this family invited all its branches, relations, friends, acquaintances, the population increased fourfold. People came from la Ferté-Milon, from Crespy, from Soissons, from Château-Thierry, from Compiègne, from Paris! Every place in the coaches were booked for fifteen days in advance: and all kinds of other means of transport were devised; horses, cabs, tilburys, postcarts arrived and jostled each other in the only two hotels of the district, the *Dauphin* and the *Boule d'Or*. For

---

*From *My Memoirs* by Alexandre Dumas. Translated by E. M. Waller. New York: Macmillan Co., 1907. Pp. 499-507.

three days the little town was like a body over full of blood, whose heart was beating ten times as fast as it should.

Two strangers came to the pleasant feast of Whitsuntide, this particular year.

One was a niece of the Abbé Grégoire, named Laurence—I have forgotten her surname.

The other was a friend of hers. She made out that she was of Spanish extraction, and was called Vittoria.

The abbé had told me of her coming. One morning, he came into our house and quite frightened me.

"Come here, boy," he said to me.

And I went to him, not feeling very sure what he was going to do to me.

"Nearer," he said—"much nearer still; you know I am shortsighted ... there—that will do."

The poor abbé was really as blind as a mole.

"You can dance, can you not?"

"Why do you ask me that, M. l'abbé?"

"Why! don't you remember you accused yourself in your last confession of having been to the theatre, to the opera, and to a ball?"

And, indeed, in one of those examinations of conscience that are sold ready printed, to aid idle and recalcitrant memories, I had read that it was a sin to go to a comedy, to the opera, and to a ball; therefore, as during my journey to Paris with my father when I was three years old, I had seen *Paul et Virginie* played at the Opéra Comique; as I had since been to plays, if by chance any strolling players passed through Villers-Cotterets; as, finally, I had been to a ball at Madame Deviolaine's on the birthday of one of her daughters, I had naïvely accused myself of having committed these three sins, much to the amusement of the worthy Abbé Grégoire, who, as we see, had revealed the secrets of the confessional.

"Well,—yes, I can dance," I replied,—"but why?"

"Dance an *entrechat* for me."

The *entrechat* was my strong point. People really did dance at the time I learnt dancing: nowadays they are satisfied to walk; which is much more convenient ... and much easier to learn.

I danced a few steps there and then.

"Bravo!" said the abbé. "Now you shall dance with my niece, who is coming at Whitsuntide."

"But ... I do not like dancing," I rudely replied.

"Bah! you must pretend you do, out of politeness."

"It is no wonder your cousin Cécile says you are a bear in manners," added my mother, with a shrug of her shoulders.

This accusation set me thinking.

"I beg your pardon, M. l'abbé," I said; "I will do just what you wish."

"Very good," said the abbé; "and, to make the acquaintance of our Parisian visitors, come and have lunch with us after high mass on Sunday."

There were eight days in which to prepare myself for my office of attendant cavalier.

During those eight days an important event occurred.

When my brother-in-law left Villers-Cotterets he left part of his library behind.

Amongst these books, there was a work covered in smooth red paper, comprising some eight or ten volumes. My brother-in-law had remarked to my mother:

"You can let him read them all except that work."

I shot a furtive glance at the work, and determined that on the contrary it should be the very one I would read.

I waited some days after my brother-in-law's departure, then I set myself to find the famous red books he had forbidden me to read.

But, although I turned all the books upside down, I could not lay hands on it, and I had to renounce the search.

Suddenly the thought that I had to be the cavalier of a young lady of twenty-two or twenty-four made me look through my wardrobe. Nearly all my coats had patched elbows, and most of my trousers had darned knees.

The only presentable suit I had was the one I had worn at my first communion: nankeen breeches, a white piqué waistcoat, a light blue coat with gilt buttons. Luckily everything had been made two inches too long, so that now everything was but one inch too short.

There was a big chest in the loft which contained coats and vests and breeches belonging to my grandfather, and coats and breeches belonging to my father: all in very good condition.

These clothes were destined by my mother to form my wardrobe as I grew up, and they were protected against vermin by bottles of vétyver and sachets of camphor.

I had never troubled over my toilette, and consequently never taken it into my head to pay a visit to this chest.

But, promoted by the abbé, who looked upon me as a dancer whom he need not trouble about, to the dignity of squire to his niece, a new idea entered my head.

I felt myself seized by the desire to look smart.

Without saying a word to my mother, for I had my own plans in mind, I went up to the loft; I locked myself in there, so as to be undisturbed in my search; and then I opened the chest.

It contained clothing fashionable enough to satisfy the most fastidious taste: from a figured satin vest to a scarlet waistcoat braided
with gold; from rep breeches to pantaloons of leather.

But, of more importance still, at the bottom of that mysterious
press, under all these clothes, were the famous red paper-covered volumes which I had been so expressly forbidden to read.

I immediately opened the first that fell into my hands, and I read:

"*Adventures du Chevalier de Faublas.*"

The title did not convey much to my mind, but the engravings
taught me rather more.

A score of lines which I devoured taught me more than the engravings.

I gathered up the first four volumes, which I hid, carefully spread
out over my chest, over which I buttoned my waistcoat; and I went
down on tip-toe. I went along M. Lafarge's back lane rather than pass
by the shop, and I gained the park at a run. I hid myself in one of the
darkest and remotest parts of it, where I was quite certain I should not
be disturbed, and then I began to read.

Chance had sometimes put obscene books in my hands.

A travelling hawker who ostensibly sold pictures, but who concealed
forbidden literature under his cloak, used to go through Villers-
Cotterets two or three times a year, hobbling along with difficulty on
two wooden legs, and giving out he was an old soldier.

The money that I had managed to extort from my poor mother had
more than once been spent in these clandestine purchases; but a
feeling of delicacy which was innate in me, and by reason of which
there are not four out of the six hundred volumes I have written that
the most scrupulous of mothers need hide from her daughter—this
sentiment of delicacy, for which I give thanks to God, always caused
me to throw far away from me such books at the tenth page or at the
second picture.

But it was quite a different thing with *Faublas. Faublas* is, without
gainsaying, a bad book from the point of view of morality; a delightful
romance from the point of view of fancy; a romance full of originality,
depicting a variety of types, somewhat exaggerated, no doubt, but
which had their counterparts in the days of Louis xv.

So I felt as great an attraction towards *Faublas* as I had felt repugnance towards *Thérèse philosophe, Félicia ou mes fredaines,* those
dirty lucubrations which persistently polluted the press throughout
the latter part of the eighteenth century.

From that moment I discovered my vocation—one I had never

recognised or even suspected until then—I wanted to become a second Faublas.

It is true I soon renounced the idea, and that idiocy has never been put down on the list of the many failings with which I have been charged.

I had prepared a magnificent theory, all cut and dried, of seductiveness, by the time Sunday in Whitsuntide came, and I was introduced, clad in my light blue coat and nankeen breeches, to the two charming Parisian girls.

Mademoiselle Laurence was tall, thin, willowy in figure, and in character she was of a bantering and indolent disposition. She was fair-haired, clear-skinned, and possessed the graceful taste of a Parisian woman: she, as I have said, was the good abbé's niece.

Mademoiselle Vittoria was pale, stout, slightly pitted with small-pox, broad-bosomed, wide-hipped, bold in her looks, representing exactly the Spanish type from Madrid, with her dead white complexion, her velvety eyes, and her supple figure.

Although I knew it to be my duty, from M. Grégoire's previous choice of me, to give my special attention first to his niece, and although the expression of gentle candour on her face had won me from the very outset, it was to Mademoiselle Laurence that I first paid court.

It was to her I offered my arm for a walk in the park after dinner.

I will not hide the fact that I was dreadfully bored, and that I must therefore have behaved very awkwardly and very ridiculously. My appearance, besides, which was all right for a child attending his first communion in 1816, was slightly eccentric in the case of a young man making his first début into society in 1818. Breeches at that time were only worn by old-fashioned people, who almost all belonged to the previous century, so it came about that I, almost a child still, whom no one would have been surprised to see in a turn-down collar, a round waistcoat, and fancy knickerbockers, was dressed like an old man—an anachronism that made the charms of the coquettish young lady on my arm stand out to still greater advantage. She knew well enough that the ridicule that was being poured on her cavalier could not affect her, so she kept as calm a demeanour in the midst of the smiles we met and the curious looks that followed us, as Virgil's divinities, who passed in the midst of men unmoved by the looks of men, because they did not deign to notice them. But it was a different matter to me; I could feel myself blushing all the time; and, when anyone I knew came by, instead of meeting his glance proudly, I simply turned my head away.

Like the stag in the fable, I discovered that I had very poor legs.

My poor mother imagined that because I was heir to my father's breeches, I had also inherited his calves.

They have developed since, it is true, but they are a superfluous luxury at a time when short breeches are no longer worn.

Worse than this was the fact that the presence of the two strangers made me a centre of curiosity. Mademoiselle Vittoria walked immediately after us, giving her arm to the abbé's sister, who was a little hunchback, a most excellent housekeeper to her brother, but whose plain dress and deformity of figure stood out most conspicuously against the elegant dress and ample voluptuous figure of the Spanish woman.

Every now and again the two young girls exchanged looks and, although I did not catch them, I could feel, so to speak, the smiles that passed between them; smiles which sent the blood rushing up to my temples with shame, for they seemed to say, "Oh! my dear friend, what a bear garden have we stumbled upon!"

A word I heard increased my confusion and turned it to anger.

A young Parisian who had been employed for two or three years at the Castle, and who was gifted with all the qualities I lacked, that is to say, he was fair, pink, plump, and dressed in the latest fashion, crossed our path, and gazed after us through an eyeglass hung from a little steel chain.

"Ah! ah!" he said, "there is Dumas going to his first communion again, only he has changed his taper."

This epigram hit me straight to the heart; I went white, and almost dropped my companion's arm. She saw what was my trouble, no doubt, for she said, pretending she had not heard:

"Who is the young man who has just passed us?"

"He is a certain M. Miaud," I replied, "who is employed at the workhouse."

I must confess I dwelt on these last words with delight, hoping they might modify the good opinion my lovely companion seemed immediately to have formed of this dandy.

"Ah! how strange!" she said; "I should have taken him for a Parisian."

"By what?" I asked.

"By his style of dress."

I am sure the arrow was not shot intentionally, but, like Parthian barbed arrows, it went right to the depths of my heart, none the less.

"His style of dress!" So dress was a most important matter; by its means and in proportion to its good or bad taste, people could at the first glance at a man form an idea of his intelligence, his mind, or his heart.

This expression, "his style of dress," illuminated my ignorance at a flash.

He was indeed perfectly dressed in the fashion of 1818: he wore tight-fitting, light coffee-coloured trousers, with boots folded in the shape of a heart over his instep, a waistcoat of chamois leather with carved gilt buttons, a brown coat with a high collar. In his waistcoat pocket was a gold eyeglass fashioned to a fine steel chain, and a host of tiny charms and seals dangled coquettishly from the fob of his pantaloons.

I heaved a sigh, and vowed to dress like that some day, no matter what it cost me.

Theodore Dreiser*
(1871-1945)

Myrtle Trego's home was curiously like her. Small, neat, white, embowered. She lived with her mother and father and brother Charlie, in a white-sheathed, green-shuttered little house, in front of which a low white picket fence enclosed a green lawn, set with roses and small bushes. Once of a chill November evening, hanging about to see if I might catch a glimpse of her, I spied her through a window, reading a book, her head bowed, her smooth young cheek heightened by the shadow of the background against which she was outlined. Bitter sweet were my sensations, fire and ice, colored and tinted as are the dawns and evenings of spring in the eyes of youth.

But now, the fateful evening. I do not recall, but I must have dressed myself with extraordinary care. By some process, new suits for myself and Ed had been produced that winter. I wore mine, a dark, woolly blue. Perchance I wore a red tie—I hope so—the flag of my urgent disposition. But I recall that I suffered an intense nervous depression, springing from the feeling that I would prove unsuited to an occasion of this kind. My sister Trina was always insisting that I was awkward and ungainly, lacking this and that: looks, presence, courage, flair.

At any rate, my thoughts of myself shriveled me. Would I prove attractive to anyone, let alone *the* one? Would I not instead sit there, neglected, a hobbledehoy, destroyed by my own lacks? For think of it,

*From _Dawn, A History of Myself._ Reprinted by permission of World Publishing Co. Copyright 1931, Theodore Dreiser. Pp. 215-220.

I did not even have a girl to take! All the other boys were taking girls, even the erratic and not too handsome Croxton. But as for myself, and despite various glances and smiles in the past, I was still so restrained by my own conviction of want of skill as a gallant that I had never even approached one, never talked or laughed with any, had merely looked and looked. And so now I was compelled to escort my sister! And she angry with me for it, for she could have gone with a boy. Yet off we marched finally, and because of inexperience on the part of both, too early, a mere sprinkling of guests there when we arrived.

At first I sat frozen or freezing, my tongue leather, my hands unplaceable, trying to think of something to say, some intelligent, if not pleasing, way to look, some least move to make that would make it plain that I was not paralyzed. But no: only stiffness, an amazing conviction of mental as well as physical collapse. In vain it was that Mrs. Trego—an efficient, sensible little woman, as I recall her—and presently Myrtle, bustled here and there, speaking to each in turn and bidding us make ourselves at home. I stared as might a stone image. How did one feel at home? What did one do, say, under such circumstances?

And then, just as I was nearing coma, the entry appeared to be crowded with arriving guests. There were voices, laughter, the removing of wraps. Yet this merely complicated matters. From having no one to speak to, there were some twenty-five to whom one should make overtures, appear human! Someone—I believe it was Augusta Phillipson—came and sitting down beside me, said, quite warmly: "Hello, Theo!" but so terrorized me by so doing as to leave me tongue-tied. I could only twitch and fidget in speechless agony, until finding me hopeless, I presume, she arose and left me.

It was even worse with Cad Tuttle and her sister Maud, Nata Weyler, Lovie Morris, and indeed all of the others. However friendly and helpful they attempted to be, I was too much for them. Cad Tuttle—who had long taken note of my glances, as I had reason to believe—said: "Isn't it fun, Theo? Aren't you glad to be here?" But this from her red mouth and smiling eyes reduced me to sheer idiocy. If I said anything, it was stuttered, I am sure, for in such crises as this stammering usually descended upon me. Then Harry Croxton came over after a while and said: "Gee, what's the matter with you, anyhow? What do you want to sit here for? Why don't you come over and talk?" Terrorized by the suggestion, I actually shrank and asked him, and not too kindly, to let me alone. Whereupon, since we had been the best of friends up to this moment, he stared at me and said: "What's got into you?" I could not have told him myself.

Fortunately, and at last, a number of simple and all-inclusive games were begun, and I was part of the party. Apple-bobbing (it was Hallowe'en); word-making for forfeits, someone beginning with a single letter, the next adding a letter before or after until a word was completed, the last person adding the completing letter being the winner and receiving a prize. Another game was sentence-building or "histories." One wrote the name of a given person, male or female, at the head of a slip of paper, turning it under. Then each person added a sentence describing what the person said or did, also turning the paper under. The result, as may be guessed, was frequently ridiculous. "Demosthenes going to the hardware store told her mother to chew gum!"

The situation heightened considerably for me with the beginning of these games. I was a part of the life and recovered myself sufficiently to be able to interpolate an exclamation of gaiety now and then. But never for a moment unconscious of Myrtle. In a simple, demure little dress, she was here and there, and once in a game stood before me asking me the answer to something. Out of my rapturous, tongue-tied state I managed to speak, to answer. Perhaps it was because I saw that she, too, was as pale and nervous as myself.

Finally, about ten o'clock, when the trepidation of the majority— if it had ever existed—had almost completely worn off, the game of "post office" was proposed: a game which was nothing more nor less than a temporary license to kiss and embrace. Someone, a boy or girl, would go into a dark room and call for a favorite of the opposite sex to come and get his or her mail. This meant being kissed, and then remaining in the room as postmaster to call someone else. The only rules which seemed to govern the situation were these: no two persons could call each other back and forth, thus monopolizing the situation, nor could anyone remain more than a moment without creating a ripple of excitement outside, where others, no doubt, were anxious for their turn, the bolder spirits, anyhow. As the game was played here, a call to come and receive stamps, a post card or a letter (any number of one variety or all three at once, according to the wish of the acting postmaster) meant, in the case of a stamp, a stamp on the toe, and a post card or letter a kiss or a "hair-pull," according to the mood of the postmaster. Occasionally (very), some wag would send out for another boy to come and get "stamps," though in the main kisses and hugs were exchanged in the recesses of the darkened chamber.

I can only suggest the perturbation of spirit which seized upon me as this game began. I have been in many, many trying situations in my life; my spirit has been perturbed by anticipations of delight or pain that have not always materialized; but the clarity and vividness of this particular evening remain unmodified. I do not recall how long it was before I was called, but I do know that I watched the rout of gaiety with a hungry and yet frightened yearning. For the time being, no one seemed to want me, and I was becoming terrified lest I be passed over entirely, when presently Gusta Phillipson becoming postmistress, I was immediately sent for to receive a letter. I did not yearn for her as I did for some of the others, yet when she called, I went gaily, though nervously enough, glad that anyone had called me, yet ashamed at having sat uncalled for so long. When I entered I saw her outlined against the shadow, and the next moment with a "Poor Theo!" she put her arms around my neck and kissed me twice. It was so soothing to be sympathized with in this way that I was ready to cry; it was almost as though she were mothering me, and perhaps she was.

But when she left, as she did immediately, my own troubles began, for now the crier or messenger appeared to ask who was wanted. With a fainting heart I thought of Myrtle Trego, but I did not have the courage to send for her. The mere thought made me reel. I was really afraid she would not come. I compromised, therefore, on Cad Tuttle. Yet the moment I had done so, I was not only fearsome of the result but in addition sick with grief over my compromise. For had I not wanted Myrtle? And what might not she think of me, if she thought at all? But before I could speculate much, in fact, even as I thought, here was Cad before me, debonair, quick and warm, and saying, as she kissed me: "You're not so shy after all, are you?" I almost fainted with delight because of my success with her, for she embraced me warmly. I recall her thick hair, her warm, clinging lips, redolent of faint perfume. And yet, frozen by my own effrontery in calling her, I could not reply. Instead I thrilled from head to toe, for a word of commendation from her meant much; she liked me then a little. Yet as I came out, there was Myrtle, and in the midst of all this honeyed delight I paused to think on her. What a coward I had been not to call her! And I was regretting this deeply at quite the same time that I was experiencing a sense of triumph at having at last kissed or been kissed by two really pretty girls. Then I was not so hopeless after all!

But Cad Tuttle came out, having, to my chagrin, called another boy, one of the beaus of the school (whom Harry Croxton immediately told me she was "stuck on"). And he in turn called Nata Weyler, who called Charlie Trego, who in turn called Maud Tuttle, who called me. This second call precipitated a new crisis. For vaguely I sensed that Maud was fond of me, though such a fool was I that I could never bring myself to take advantage of the inviting smiles and knowing glances she occasionally turned in my direction. Now, though, I put my arms around her, trembling with excitement, and kissed her warm mouth. She yielded in so willing a way that I knew I was at liberty to take more than one, yet such was my shyness that even here my courage failed and I turned to go, when suddenly I recalled that it was my duty to stay and call another. And now, if I would, I might call Myrtle Trego. But would she come? Did she like me enough? Knowing there was no time to lose, I blurted out to the girl postmistress who looked in: "Myrtle Trego, a letter." And then my knees all but gave way. Myrtle! How I managed to remain standing I did not know, for in a moment she might be here, a moment which seemed to me an age. At the same time there was the thought of where to obtain sufficient courage to kiss her, touch her even, so remote from me and all that I was did she seem.

Yet as I pondered—a brief moment or two, I am sure—the door opened, and there she stood. A veritable shy mouse of a girl, gliding toward me, her head down, about her an atmosphere of shrinking unfamiliarity with life. I stood before her limp and choking, throat dry and body numb. I trembled so violently that I think she must have noticed. I tried to say something, but no sound came. She drew close to me, but I could do no more than lay my hands on her arms. As I bent to kiss her, her head slipped shyly into her arm and only her cheek was exposed. Even so, it seemed like the surface of the Cooba, that gate to paradise. I hurried out, weak and voiceless. When it came her turn to call someone, she called Etta Reed, a school chum of hers. Then more than ever I felt that I had shamelessly intruded on her, and at the same time felt glorified that she had not called a boy. She was not a boy's girl, that was plain. She had not wanted any boy to kiss her. And no other boy sent for her. After a while the game was dropped for taffy-pulling and refreshments, but I continued to seethe with the wonder of it.

Only when it came time to leave, I was thrown into an additional panic by the fact that I had no girl other than my sister to take home. I waited about nervously until the crowd thinned, when finding Trina, I slipped out and hurried away. But the shame of it! The loneliness and defeat!

But afterwards when it was over and I thought back on how I had kissed Myrtle and Maud and Cad and Gusta, my spirits rose and I did not feel so bad. I went over the details again and again: the call, each step, my trembling, all! In memory I kissed Myrtle a million times. Actually my lips quivered at the thought. I sat in our swing, studying the blue sky and the fleecy clouds, and the world seemed to me extremely beautiful. I swung and dreamed of the feel of Cad Tuttle's arms, the fragrance of Maud's personality. Gusta Phillipson's "Poor

Theo!" haunted me as a commentary on my social inefficiency, but always when I was nearing the danger point as to that, Myrtle's shy, delicate presence confronted me and all else was blotted out. I re-experienced the tingle of that paradisiacal moment. Once more I choked with delight. Would she speak to me now when we met? Would I ever be able to walk and talk with her? The thought haunted and frightened me. I knew I should never be able to build up the courage, nor she, even if she cared. But the splendor, the wonder of the dream!

John A. Rice*
(1888-   )

When I returned from the fitting school I was a grown-up young man, I told myself. My hands and feet had tentatively decided against secession, my voice no longer jumped suddenly out of register, and I wore long pants without confusion. My cousins could not now think of a good excuse to exclude me from their pursuits—that was, the girls. Besides, I hinted at experience and built up the picture with borrowed paint. There had been a girl in Bamberg, I said. There had been a girl in Bamberg in fact, but if I had told them the truth they would have thrown me across the gulf that now separated me from my brothers, for it was a noble, inglorious affair. On Saturday nights, while the big boys were in milltown, I sat in her respectable parlor listening to surprised feet scuttling across the floor above, the pouring of water into a bowl, and the sloshing of one having a good wash, while I waited moonily for the moment when she would come quickly down the stairs and burst into the room—sun-burst, for her face was red and shining from its recent soaping. When the end of the year came, and good-by, I asked if I might kiss her; but she said no, she thought it wouldn't be right, and I agreed. These things I did not tell my cousins.

During the week I was willing to play with my brothers, but with Sunday came all the cruelty of the child that was left in me and the arrogance of the coming man, and without so much as a look at their unhappy faces I climbed into the buggy, where I sat creased and starched between my cousins, ready for new and strange adventures, more thrilling than in their pale reality.

---

*From *I Came Out of the Eighteenth Century* by John A. Rice. New York: Harper & Bros., 1942. P. 149.

Buwei Yang Chao*
(1889-   )

Hitherto I had avoided meeting any boys who were not my relatives. There was no such thing as one-to-one dating—not for decades yet. Brothers and other members of the immediate family were the only men allowed to see the girls or take them out. I did not even go out when Third Brother and Kuanhung's brother Pingnan and Suchüan's brothers came to take us out together. But, after I heard about my being "a woman who sells songs," I promptly accepted all invitations to the parties. Seven or eight of us would go to Yuehsheng Company at the Four Elephants Bridge (Street) to eat ta-ts' ai, or foreign dinners, after which we would go into the houses of our schoolmates and their brothers to play. Those parties were very unorthodox for the times, though they were pretty well chaperoned.

Our house was quite a center of attraction for my schoolmates and their brothers. We played the new-fangled game of tennis. We played chess under an arbor between two big willows. We fished from the pond. We took photographs and developed them ourselves, since there was no place to send them to. Somebody brought a phonograph into our house, not one of those cylindrical things, heard through a sort of stethoscope at the temple fairs for two coppers a song, but a real His Master's Voice machine, with horn and all, which everybody could listen to at the same time. Occasionally, Grandfather would join our party and tell stories about foreign countries or explain the principles of some of the scientific gadgets we were playing with. The boys met almost every day. We girls joined them weekends.

When Aunt Ch'eng heard of what was going on, she got busy and sent my cousin to Nanking to enter the Huiwen Academy and instructed him to join our parties as much as he could. I did not avoid him, as it would have been proper and natural for a girl in my position to do, but continued to be as active in the group as ever. He was full of fun, but somehow was always afraid of me. So they teased him by parodying the nursery rhyme about the little mouse. Whenever they saw him, they would sing [it].

This teasing went on with my implicit approval. It compensated for my inferiority complex in not being a free person like most of my schoolmates.

Those were the happiest school days I ever had, not because I am

---

*From *Autobiography of a Chinese Woman* by Buwei Yang Chao. Reprinted by permission of the John Day Co., Inc. 1947. Pp. 68-69.

looking back from this distance through a time-filter, but because I told myself I was happy and everybody else told me so. I was successful in my studies, I had friends to play with. I was pampered by friends and family in every way. I thought nobody in any school, nobody in the world, could be as happy as I.

But a Chinese proverb says: "At the extreme end of happiness comes grief."

REFERENCES

1. Ackerman, Nathan. *The Psychodynamics of Family Life.* New York: Basic Books, 1958, p. 220.
2. *Ibid.,* p. 225.
3. *Ibid.,* p. 240.
4. Ausubel, David P. *Theory and Problems of Adolescent Development.* New York: Grune & Stratton, 1954, p. 302.
5. *Ibid.,* p. 353.
6. Blos, Peter. *The Adolescent Personality.* New York: Appleton-Century-Crofts, 1941, p. 301.
7. Catherine the Great. *Memoirs.* New York: Alfred A. Knopf, 1927, p. 60.
8. Chesterton, G. K. *Autobiography.* New York: Sheed & Ward, 1936, p. 63.
9. Colum, Mary. *Life and the Dream.* Garden City, N. Y.: Doubleday & Co., 1947, p. 24.
10. Erikson, Erik H. Growth and crises of the healthy personality. *Psychol. Issues,* 1:95, 1959.
11. ———. *A Healthy Personality for Every Child—Fact Finding Report: A Digest.* Midcentury White House Conference on Children and Youth. Raleigh, N. C.: Health Publications Institute, 1951, p. 21.
12. ———. Identity and the life cycle. *Psychol. Issues,* 1:18-164, 1959.
13. Friedenberg, Edgar Z. *The Vanishing Adolescent.* Boston: Beacon Press, 1959, p. 10.
14. Freud, Anna. *The Ego and the Mechanisms of Defense.* London: Hogarth Press, 1954, p. 177.
15. *Ibid.,* pp. 181-182.
16. Goethe, Johann Wolfgang von. *Goethe's Autobiography. Poetry and Truth from My Own Life.* Washington, D.C.: Public Affairs Press, 1949, p. 217.
17. Grotjahn, Martin. A letter by Sigmund Freud with recollections of his adolescence. *J. Amer. Psychoanal. Assn.,* 4:644-645; 649-650, 1956.

18. Holland, Vyvyan. *Son of Oscar Wilde*. New York: E. P. Dutton & Co., 1954.

19. Josselyn, Irene M. *The Happy Child*. New York: Random House, 1955, p. 124.

20. *Ibid.*, p. 147.

21. Keene, Donald. *Anthology of Japanese Literature*. New York: Grove Press, 1955, p. 152.

22. Leonard, William Ellery. *The Locomotive-God*. New York: Century Co., 1927, p. 150.

23. Montaigne, Michel de. *Autobiography*. Edited by Marvin Lowenthal. Boston: Houghton Mifflin Co., 1935, p. 26.

24. Napoleon. *Napoleon's Autobiography*. Edited by F. M. Kircheisen. New York: Duffield & Co., 1932, pp. 16-17.

25. O'Connor, Philip. *Memoirs of a Public Baby*. New York: British Book Centre, 1958, p. 165.

26. Powys, John Cowper. *Autobiography*. London: John Lane, 1934, p. 142.

27. Riesman, David. *The Lonely Crowd*. Garden City, N. Y.: Doubleday Anchor, 1953.

28. Sei Shōnagon. *The Pillow Book of Sei Shōnagon*. Boston: Houghton Mifflin Co., 1928, p. 93.

29. Spiegel, Leo A. Comments on the psychoanalytic psychology of the adolescent. In: Eissler, Ruth S., et al. (Eds.), *The Psychoanalytic Study of the Child*. Vol. XIII. New York: International Universities Press, 1958, p. 299.

30. ————. A review of contributions to a psychoanalytic theory of adolescence. In: Eissler, Ruth S., et al. (Eds.), *The Psychoanalytic Study of the Child*, Vol. VI. New York: International Universities Press, 1951, p. 381.

31. Strang, Ruth. *The Adolescent Views Himself*. New York: McGraw-Hill, 1957, p. 289.

32. Sugimoto, Etsu Inagaki. *A Daughter of the Samurai*. Garden City, N. Y.: Doubleday, Doran & Co., 1928, pp. 122-123.

33. Tryon, Carolyn M. The adolescent peer culture. In Henry, Nelson B. (Ed.), *The 43d Yearbook of the National Society for the Study of Education: Part I, Adolescence*. Chicago: University of Chicago Press, 1944, p. 217.

34. *Ibid.*, p. 223.

35. Waters, Ethel. *His Eye Is on the Sparrow: An Autobiography*. Garden City, N. Y.: Doubleday & Co., 1951, p. 44.

CHAPTER EIGHT

Socioeconomic Consciousness and Prejudice

Edward Gibbon, early in his *Autobiography*, noted the good fortune which was his by virtue of the accident of birth into a family
of rank and wealth. "I was born at Putney," he wrote, " . . . 27
April, 1737; the first child of the marriage of Edward Gibbon,
Esq., and of Judith Porten. My lot might have been that of a slave,
or a peasant; nor can I reflect without pleasure on the bounty of
nature, which cast my birth in a free and civilised country, in an
age of science and philosophy, in a family of honourable rank, and
decently endowed with the gifts of fortune [8]." One hundred and
one years later, Henry Adams, writing about himself in the third
person, stated, "Under the shadow of Boston State House, turning
its back on the house of John Hancock, the little passage called
Hancock Avenue runs, or ran, from Beacon Street, skirting the
State House grounds, to Mount Vernon Street, on the summit of
Beacon Hill; and there, in the third house below Mount Vernon
Place, February 16, 1838, a child was born, and christened later by
his uncle, the minister of the First Church after the tenets of Boston
Unitarianism, as Henry Brooks Adams. Had he been born in Jeru-
salem under the shadow of the Temple and circumcised in the
Synagogue by his uncle the high priest, under the name of Israel
Cohen, he would scarcely have been more distinctly branded, and
not much more heavily handicapped in the races of the coming
century, in running for such stakes as the century was to offer. . . .

Probably no child born in the year, held better cards than he. Whether life was an honest game of chance, or whether the cards were marked and forced, he could not refuse to play his excellent hand [1]."

The awareness of the rank and class into which he had been born was equally impressed into the consciousness of Stanley, a delinquent boy from Chicago, who wrote these words during his adolescence: "To start out in life, everyone has his chances—some good and some very bad. Some are born with fortunes, beautiful homes, good and educated parents; while others are born in ignorance, poverty and crime. In other words, Fate begins to guide our lives even before we are born and continues to do so throughout life. My start was handicapped by a no-good, ignorant, and selfish stepmother, who thought only of herself and her own kids. As far back as I can remember, my life was filled with sorrow and misery . . . [17]."

Gibbon, Adams, and young Stanley became conscious of the class to which they belonged within the first few years of their lives. The findings of anthropologists, sociologists and psychologists indicate that the individual expects to live and die in the social and economic class into which he was born. Perhaps this feeling is at its greatest during the period of adolescence when cliques and other closed forms of association develop that exclude one socioeconomic class from another. Adolescent groups are formed largely on the basis of the status of the family in the particular culture. Hollingshead, in his frequently cited study of the impact of social classes on adolescents, concluded that "children in the same class, living in the same neighborhood, learn similar definitions of acceptable and unacceptable behavior relative to the family, the job, property, money, the school, the government, men, women, sex, recreation. . . . In the neighborhood they also come into contact with persons, both children and adults, from other classes and neighborhoods. It is here that they first become aware that there are people socially different from themselves. . . . The specific behavior traits exhibited by adolescents tend to be along lines approved by their clique mates, who also tend to be members of the same class [11]."

The youth in Hollingshead's Elmtown rarely stray from one class to another, on pain of being ostracized by their class. Similarly in Plainville, U.S.A., the class system "provides natives with a master pattern for arranging according to rank every individual and every family, clique, club, lodge, church, and other association or organization in Plainville society. It provides also a set of patterns of expected behavior according to class, and a way of classifying and judging all norms and variations in individual behavior. . . . All children are obliged to learn complex rules regarding their proper relationship with socially inferior or superior children [19]." In another study made in England, it was ascertained that the social class views of adolescents are markedly influenced by their own position within the class structure and by the varying class environments (10).

It thus becomes apparent that the social classes into which people are born become mutually exclusive. Upper-class youth is so confirmed in its "natural" superiority, while lower class youth is so well indoctrinated with the sense of its social inferiority that the gulf between classes is seemingly so wide as to be unbridgeable. The effect on children of the lower social classes is marked: they feel disliked, inferior, conscious of personal and social deficiencies, and unhappy about their situation (9). They react with neurotic symptoms or with aggressive, defiant, and antisocial conduct. Upward social mobility is a rare phenomenon with such adolescents. George Moore (1853-1933) wrote in his *Confessions of a Young Man* that he "came into the world apparently with a nature like a smooth sheet of wax, bearing no impress, but capable of receiving any; of being moulded into all shapes. Nor am I exaggerating when I say I think that I might equally have been a Pharaoh, an ostler, a pimp, an archbishop, and that in the fulfillment of the duties of each a certain measure of success would have been mine [15]." While Moore's estimate of his probable success in these occupations might have been accurate, it was so because of the confidence engendered by his wealth and social position maintained through the years. Stanley, the Chicago delinquent, could have become a stableman or a procurer, but the likelihood of his achieving a position of legitimate power was unlikely. The Lynds, in their two studies of "Middletown" made in 1924 and 1935, indicate the difficulty, if not impossibility, of young people rising out of their class (13, 14).

The adolescent's feverish, anxious searching for identity, values and social orientation forces him to band together with others whom he believes to have the same standards he has. Erikson states:

Adolescents "become remarkably clannish, intolerant, and cruel in their exclusion of others who are 'different,' in skin color or cultural background, in tastes and gifts, and often in entirely petty aspects of dress and gesture arbitrarily selected as *the* signs of an in-grouper or out-grouper. It is important to understand . . . such intolerance as the necessary *defense against a sense of identity diffusion,* which is unavoidable at a time of life when the body changes its proportions radically, when genital maturity floods body and imagination with all manners of drives, when intimacy with the other sex approaches and is, on occasion, forced on the youngster, and when life lies before one with a variety of conflicting possibilities and choices. Adolescents help one another temporarily through such discomfort by forming cliques and by stereotyping themselves, their ideals, and their enemies [6]."

Such stereotypy profoundly influences the adolescent's affective life. In wresting symbols of identity from an impersonal environment, the adolescent is learning to stand aside from his impulse life, perceive it more nearly as if it were a part of external reality, and gain in his ability to channel its force toward his own ends. But until such time as he can achieve this, neither the cultural pecking order nor his own sense of identity permit him to respect his fellows always as human beings.

Some of the illustrations which follow show the effect of the socioeconomic class on the adolescent in terms of his emotional life, his sexual impulses, his interpersonal relations and his choice of vocation. Others will illustrate the effect of prejudice and discrimination to which the adolescent is exposed and its subsequent disruption of personality adjustment.

Napoleon Bonaparte
(1769-1821)

The comments of the editor of the volume from which this letter is taken are germane to the discussion at hand. "It is fitting," he wrote, "that the first extant letter of the young Napoleon, written at the age of twelve, should be so utterly Napoleonic. He knew well enough what it meant to his ambitious family to have a son at the exclusive military academy of Brienne. In effect, he was blackmailing his father. 'Let me come,' he cried, when what he really wanted was a larger allowance. He did not get it. In Charles Bonaparte's absence from home, Napoleon's strong-willed mother, Letizia, opened the letter. She was never one to coddle her children. Immediately she wrote a sharp reply: the impudence of him! Imagine his father's feelings if he should see such a letter! However—the maternal touch—a little money was enclosed, to ease the strain.

"Even more significant . . . than the precocity of the boy is the class-conscious feeling in these indignant lines. It was no ordinary schoolboy hatred that he felt for the boys who jeered at him. The hurt and rage got into his blood, and stayed with him forever. As an invisible gene in a tiny seed determines the form of the flowering tree, so Napoleon's state of mind at this time was to work a violent magic in his entire career. Long before the Revolution there was something revolutionary in him; he was 'against'; he had a cause. And in a way it was the cause of his time. The ferment in his brain was working also in millions of others, and preparing a bitter brew for his generation [4]."

Brienne, April 5, 1781

My Father,

If you, or my protectors, cannot give me the means of making a better appearance in this school, let me come home immediately. I am tired of living like a beggar and of having my insolent schoolmates, who have nothing but wealth to recommend them, make sport of my poverty. Not one of them is my equal, for not one of them can understand the lofty ideals which fill and inflame my heart.

What, sir! Shall your son be the butt of the sarcasms of these rich and impertinent young fellows who dare to make fun of the privations I endure! No, my Father, no—if nothing can be done to improve my circumstances, take me out of Brienne. Let me learn a trade, if necessary; place me with my equals and I promise you I shall soon be their superior.

By this offer you may judge how desperate I am. Let me repeat, I would rather be the first among the workmen in a factory than the laughing-stock of the best school in the world. Do not imagine that what I write is prompted by a desire to indulge in expensive amusements; they do not attract me; but I must be in a position to show my comrades that I too can afford them.

Your respectful and obedient son,
Napoleone

Leigh Hunt
(1784-1859)

The interfaith project Leigh Hunt set up for himself at the age of fifteen, and which he reports in the selection which follows,* started out as a search for God the Father, a deliberate exposure to the varieties of religious experience. Hunt's displacement of the feelings of adoration of and dependence on the father to the idea of God is familiar and typical of the behavior of the adolescent. His dislike of Catholic dogma and his pleasure in observing the "semi-Catholic pomp" of the Jewish service helped him, he felt, "to universalize [his] notions of religion and to keep them unbigoted." But in the last paragraph, Hunt points out the more typical pattern of childish and adolescent cruelty.

I mooted points of faith with myself very early, in consequence of what I heard at home. The very inconsistencies which I observed round about me in matters of belief and practice, did but the more make me wish to discover in what the right spirit of religion consisted: while, at the same time, nobody felt more instinctively than myself, that forms were necessary to preserve essence. I had the greatest respect for them, wherever I thought them sincere. I got up imitations of religious processions in the school-room, and persuaded my coadjutors to learn even a psalm in the original Hebrew, in order to sing it as part of the ceremony. To make the lesson as easy as possible, it was the shortest of all the psalms, the hundred and seventeenth, which consists but of two verses. A Jew, I am afraid, would have been puzzled to recognize it; though, perhaps, I got the tone from his own synagogue; for I was well acquainted with that place of worship. I was led to dislike Catholic chapels, in spite of their music and their paintings, by what I had read of Inquisitions, and by the impiety which I found in the doctrine of eternal punishment,—a monstrosity which I never associated with the Church of England, at least not habitually. But identifying no such dogmas with the Jews, who are indeed free from them (though I was not aware of that circumstance at the time), and reverencing them for their ancient connection with the Bible, I used to go with some of my companions to the synagogue in Duke's Place; where I took pleasure in witnessing the semi-Catholic pomp of their service, and in hearing their fine singing; not without something of a constant astonishment at their wearing their hats. This custom, how-

---

*From *The Autobiography of Leigh Hunt, with Reminiscences of Friends and Contemporaries*. Westminster, England: A. Constable & Co., 1903, Vol. I. Pp. 111-112.

ever, kindly mixed itself up with the recollection of my cocked hat and band. I was not aware that it originated in the immovable Eastern turban.

These visits to the synagogue did me, I conceive, a great deal of good. They served to universalize my notions of religion, and to keep them unbigoted. It never became necessary to remind me that Jesus was himself a Jew. I have also retained through life a respectful notion of the Jews as a body.

There were some school rhymes about "pork upon a fork," and the Jews going to prison. At Easter, a strip of bordered paper was stuck on the breast of every boy, containing the words "He is risen." It did not give us the slightest thought of what it recorded. It only reminded us of an old rhyme, which some of the boys used to go about the school repeating:—

> He is risen, he is risen,
> All the Jews must go to prison.

A beautiful Christian deduction; Thus has charity itself been converted into a spirit of antagonism; and thus it is that the antagonism, in the progress of knowledge, becomes first a pastime and then a jest.

John Clare
(1793-1864)

John Clare, the English poet and laborer, was himself the son of a laborer. A childish companionship with Mary Joyce, the daughter of a relatively prosperous farmer, ripened into idyllic love. "They met each other frequently during the winter of 1809 and the early spring of 1810, and they renewed their enthusiasm for flowers and fields. Clare's mind, already rich in love and observation, expanded happily under the new charm. Perhaps they parted in the following May-time, which would account for Clare's restlessness then, and his refusal to re-hire himself with Gregory [a local farmer] for a second year. Perhaps it was only after Clare had been absent from the village at his next situation, from which he returned penniless, that they became estranged. The blame for separating the boy and girl lovers has hitherto rested with the father of Mary. There is no evidence in any of Clare's known writings for this condemnation of him. It was Mary herself who realised the difference between her position and that of the poor labourer's son who had no prospects.

Clare says it was the world which 'choked the hope I had of thee, and made thee haughty, Mary'; and he was evidently too sensitive about his poverty to make any attempt to overcome the world's baleful influence . . . Before he even declared his love they parted, but during the years which followed, before the publication of his first book, he kept the half-smothered hope in his heart that he would one day be her equal and his dreams become reality [18]."

I was a lover very early in life; my first attachment, being a school-boy affection, was for Mary, who was beloved with a romantic or Platonic sort of feeling. If I could but gaze on her face or fancy a smile on her countenance, it was sufficient; I went away satisfied. We played with each other, but named nothing of love; yet I fancied her eyes told me her affections. We walked together as school-companions in leisure hours, but our talk was of play, and our actions the wanton nonsense of children. Yet, young as my heart was, it would turn chill when I touched her hand, and tremble, and I fancied her feelings were the same; for as I gazed earnestly in her face, a tear would hang in her smiling eye and she would turn to wipe it away. Her heart was as tender as a bird's. . . . I cannot forget her little playful fairy form and witching smile even now.

I remember an accident that roused my best intentions, and hurt my affection into the rude feelings of imaginary cruelty. When playing one day in the churchyard I threw a green walnut that hit her on the eye. She wept, and I hid my sorrow and my affection together under the shame of not showing regret, lest others might laugh it into love.

* * * *

She felt her station above mine; at least I felt that she thought so; for her parents were farmers, and farmers had great pretensions to something then. . . . I felt the disparagement in [my] situation, and, fearing to meet a denial, I carried it on in my own fancies to every extreme, writing songs in her praise, and making her mine with every indulgence of the fancy.

Anthony Trollope
(1815-1882)

The worst period of his life, wrote Anthony Trollope,* was the

*In *An Autobiography*. Reprinted by permission of The Clarendon Press. 1941. Pp. 10-12.

time when he was a sizar at a fashionable school. As a sizar, he was allowed certain deductible school expenses. This, coupled with the fact that he was the son of an unsuccessful tenant farmer living in a wretched, tumble-down farmhouse, made him the object of scorn by his peers. He was ignored, ostracized and held in odium by them, for they were the sons of noblemen and tycoons. "The indignities I endured," he wrote of the time from his fifteenth to his seventeenth birthdays, "are not to be described." But his feelings are certainly evident. The incitement to feelings of inferiority, shame and distrust led him eventually to aggressive rebellion as a protest against the stigmatization to which he had been cruelly subjected.

When I left Winchester, I had three more years of school before me, having as yet endured nine. My father at this time having left my mother and sisters with my younger brother in America, took himself to live at a wretched tumble-down farmhouse on the second farm he had hired. And I was taken there with him. It was nearly three miles from Harrow, at Harrow Weald, but in the parish: and from this house I was again sent to that school as a day-boarder. Let those who know what is the usual appearance and what the usual appurtenances of a boy at such a school, consider what must have been my condition among them, with a daily walk of twelve miles through the lanes, added to the other little troubles and labours of a school life!

Perhaps the eighteen months which I passed in this condition, walking to and fro on those miserably dirty lanes, was the worst period of my life. I was now over fifteen, and had come to an age at which I could appreciate at its full the misery of expulsion from all social intercourse. I had not only no friends, but was despised by all my companions. The farmhouse was not only no more than a farmhouse, but was one of those farmhouses which seem always to be in danger of falling into the neighbouring horse-pond. As it crept downwards from house to stables, from stables to barns, from barns to cowsheds, and from cowsheds to dung-heaps, one could hardly tell where one began and the other ended! There was a parlour in which my father lived, shut up among big books; but I passed my most jocund hours in the kitchen, making innocent love to the bailiff's daughter. The farm kitchen might be very well through the evening, when the horrors of the school were over; but it all added to the cruelty of the days. A sizar at a Cambridge college, or a Bible-clerk at Oxford, has not pleasant days, or used not to have them half a century ago; but his position was recognised and the misery was measured. I was a sizar at a fashionable school, a condition never premeditated. What right had a wretched

farmer's boy, reeking from a dunghill, to sit next to the sons of peers—
or much worse still, next to the sons of big tradesmen who had made
their ten thousand a year? The indignities I endured are not to be
described. As I look back it seems to me that all hands were turned
against me,—those of masters as well as boys. I was allowed to join in
no plays. Nor did I learn anything,— for I was taught nothing. The
only expense, except that of books, to which a house-boarder was then
subject, was the fee to a tutor, amounting, I think, to ten guineas. My
tutor took me without the fee; but when I heard him declare the fact
in the pupil-room before the boys, I hardly felt grateful for the charity.
I was never a coward, and cared for a thrashing as little as any boy, but
one cannot make a stand against the acerbities of three hundred tyrants without a moral courage of which at that time I possessed none.
I know that I skulked, and was odious to the eyes of those I admired
and envied. At last I was driven to rebellion, and there came a great
fight,—at the end of which my opponent had to be taken home for a
while. If these words be ever printed, I trust that some schoolfellow of
those days may still be left alive who will be able to say that, in claiming this solitary glory of my school-days, I am not making a false boast.

A. Henry Layard
(1817-1894)

Prejudice assumes a variety of faces. Sir A. Henry Layard, who was
to become Her Majesty's Ambassador to the Court at Madrid, had
been born in Paris, and until his thirteenth year had been brought
up primarily in Florence, Italy. His parents had reared him in the
gentlemanly, Old World tradition. He was precocious in matters
of art, being able to identify readily the masters of the art world
and the schools to which they belonged. He was fluent, as might be
expected, in French and Italian. When it was thought time to bring
him to his native England for his formal education, the boy found
it difficult to assume the behavior patterns of the ingroup sufficiently to be accepted by it. "We had little or nothing in common," wrote Layard. Their differences arose, apparently, not so
much because of his tastes and ideas but because of his knowledge
of the two foreign languages, a prejudice which survived in England
long after the end of the Napoleonic wars.*

---

*From *Autobiography and Letters from His Childhood until His Appointment as
H. M. Ambassador at Madrid* by A. Henry Layard. New York: Charles Scribner's Sons,
1903, Vol. I. Pp. 37-38.

Soon after our arrival in England, I was placed at a school kept by the Rev. James Bewsher, at Richmond. I found myself among seventy or eighty boys, who had been brought up differently from myself. We had little or nothing in common. I had tastes which seemed repugnant to them, and my head was crammed full of things and ideas which they despised. One of the first questions which I was asked was: "What do you know?" "French and Italian," I replied. A cuff on the head and a kick behind, with a "Take that, then," was the only mark of approval I received for the acquirements of which I was so proud. The report soon spread through the school that I spoke Italian. I was declared to be an "image-boy" or an "organ-grinder," my schoolfellows being persuaded that any one who spoke this foreign jargon must have been employed in carrying about on his head the then popular plaster representations of cats and rabbits, which were offered for sale in the streets, or in turning the handle of an organ. I was so unmercifully teased and bullied on this account, that I did my best to conceal my knowledge of this fatal language, and to avoid all allusion to Italy.

This contempt for foreign languages arose from the prejudice against Frenchmen which survived long after the close of the wars of Napoleon. It no longer, happily, exists in places where boys receive an education to fit them for the liberal professions or for commerce. But, at the time of which I am writing, it prevailed both in public and private schools. It was, however, considered necessary, even in such an establishment as Mr. Bewsher's, that there should be a French master. The unhappy wretch, who also taught us writing, was the butt of the boys, and the victim of those practical jokes and of that ingenious mischief which is characteristic of the English schoolboy. As for acquiring French from him—it was simply ridiculous to suppose it possible. There were, indeed, French lessons, and we were each furnished, at the expense of our parents, with a French Grammar and the "Adventures of Telemachus." But no one could learn to speak or even to understand the language from the use made of them.

Charlotte L. Forten
(1838-1914)

Charlotte Forten, born and raised in Philadelphia, was one of the first Negroes to receive a college education. She was welcomed into the liberal, freedom-loving atmosphere of Boston, but even in this climate, she and her friends met incidents of racial prejudice. The two entries from her *Journal* which follow relate events to which she was exposed when she was seventeen years old. Her feelings of contempt toward the "miserable doughfaces" who had given offense, her discouragement in the face of the continued "trifles," her weariness in meeting hatred with hatred, her wariness in loving or trusting any white person, and her exasperated plea for retribution are understandable under the circumstances. Her feelings express, perhaps, those of all colored peoples who have been subjected to prejudiced and discriminatory behavior by whites.*

Tuesday, September 5, 1855

. . . I have suffered much today,—my friends Mrs. Putnam and her daughters were refused admission to the Museum, after having tickets given them, solely on account of their complexion. Insulting language was used to them—Of course they felt and exhibited deep, bitter indignation; but of what avail was it? none, but to excite the ridicule of those contemptible creatures, miserable doughfaces who do not deserve the name of men. I will not attempt to write more.—No words can express my feelings. But these cruel wrongs cannot be much longer endured. A day of retribution must come. God grant that it may come very soon!

Wednesday, September 12, 1855

Today school commenced.—Most happy am I to return to the companionship of my studies,—ever my most valued friends. It is pleasant to meet the scholars again; most of them greeted me cordially, and were it not for the thought that *will* intrude, of the want of *entire sympathy* even of those I know and like best, I should greatly enjoy their society. There is one young girl and only one—Miss [Sarah] B[rown] who I believe thoroughly and heartily appreciates anti-slavery,—*radical* anti-slavery, and has no prejudice against color. I wonder that every colored person is not a misanthrope. Surely we have everything to make us hate mankind. I have met girls in the schoolroom[—]they have been thoroughly kind and cordial to me,—perhaps the next day met them in the street—they feared to recognize me; these I can but regard now with scorn and contempt,—once I liked them, believing them incapable of such meanness. Others give the most distant recognition possible.—I, of course, acknowledge no such recognitions, and they soon cease entirely. These are but trifles, cer-

*From *The Journal of Charlotte Forten* edited by Ray A. Billington. Reprinted by permission of Ray A. Billington. Copyright 1953, Dryden Press. Pp. 48, 62-63.

tainly, to the great, public wrongs which we as a people are obliged to endure. But to those who experience them, these apparent trifles are most wearing and discouraging; even to the child's mind they reveal volumes of deceit and heartlessness, and early teach a lesson of suspicion and distrust. Oh! it is hard to go through life meeting contempt with contempt, hatred with hatred, fearing, with too good reason, to love and trust hardly any one whose skin is white,—however lovable, attractive and congenial in seeming. In the bitter, passionate feelings of my soul again and again there rises the questions "When, oh! when shall this cease?" "Is there no help?" "How long oh! how long must we continue to suffer—to endure?" Conscience answers it is wrong, it is ignoble to despair; let us labor earnestly and faithfully to acquire knowledge, to break down the barriers of prejudice and oppression. Let us take courage; never ceasing to work,—hoping and believing that if not for us, for another generation there is a better, brighter day in store,—when slavery and prejudice shall vanish before the glorious light of Liberty and Truth; when the rights of every colored man shall everywhere be acknowledged and respected, and he shall be treated as a *man* and a *brother!*

Sigmund Freud
(1856-1939)

Notwithstanding his interest in instinctual drives, Sigmund Freud was essentially a rationalist. This is one of the basic reasons why Freud never forsook his Jewish origins although his attitude toward religion, per se, was negative. Toward Judaism, however, he vowed in a letter (July 23, 1882) to his fiancée, Martha Bernays, that "if the form wherein the old Jews were happy no longer offers us any shelter, something of the core, of the essence of . . . meaningful and life-affirming Judaism will not be absent from our home [7]." While Sigmund was not raised in a particularly observant Jewish household, his father Jacob was fond of reading the *Torah* and the boy was obliged to attend occasional lessons in the synagogue during his school days (12). At the age of seventeen, when Freud matriculated at the university, he encountered the virulent Viennese anti-Semitism common to the day. In his *Autobiographical Study,* Freud described his refusal to knuckle under to the attempts to make him feel inferior to his Christian classmates and indicated the great consequences which the anti-Semitic attacks had for him.* Freud's son, Martin, was also the victim of Viennese anti-Semitism in his student days. His reaction to it was more direct; for what he did, reference is made to the chapter on psychobiological development.

> When, in 1873, I first joined the University, I was met by some appreciable disappointments. Above all, I found that I was expected to feel myself inferior and an alien, because I was a Jew. I refused absolutely to do the first of these things. I have never been able to see why I should feel ashamed of my descent or, as people were beginning to say, of my race. I put up, without much regret, with my nonadmission to the community; for it seemed to me that in spite of this exclusion an active fellow-worker could not fail to find some nook or cranny in the frame-work of humanity. These first impressions at the University, however, had one consequence which was afterwards to prove important; for at an early age I was made familiar with the fate of being in the Opposition and of being put under the ban of the "compact majority." The foundations were thus laid for a certain degree of independence of judgment.
>
> I was compelled, moreover, during my first years at the University, to make the discovery that the peculiarities and limitations of my gifts denied me all success in many of the departments of science into which my youthful eagerness had plunged me. Thus I learned the truth of Mephistopheles' warning:
>
> > "Vergebens, dass ihr ringsum wissenschaftlich schweift,
> > Ein jeder lernt nur, was er lernen kann."**

Hermann Sudermann
(1857-1928)

Sudermann's description of the four classes of society in the Prussian village in which he grew up is very reminiscent of Hollingshead's Elmtown and the Lynds' Middletown. It was impossible to climb from one to the other class. Sudermann's family belonged to the middle class, and this was the greatest misery of his childhood, he wrote. It was the source of his ambition, obstinacy and industry.

---

*From *An Autobiographical Study* by Sigmund Freud. New York: Brentano's, 1927, pp. 192-193.

**"It is in vain that you range around from science to science: each man learns only what he can learn." *Faust*, Part I.

His family's genteel poverty necessitated his wearing home-made pants which were too big for him and which subjected him to the merciless taunting of his schoolmates. "These so-called school friends . . . were the first to saturate my sensitive soul with the corrosive poison of humiliation and bitterness, the first to give me the acrid draught of feeling that I was something inferior to the others, and to create in me a sense of being suppressed and bowed down. . . . " The effects on his later life were noted by Sudermann.*

What was more important for my development than my lessons, which at least gave me an elementary grounding of definite learning, was my intercourse with my fellows. It is gospel truth that it is not our teachers who educate us, but those with whom we are educated in common.

Who I was, *what* I was, what original characteristics I must confess to and which I must refuse to admit, I don't know, for my nature was a something which I took for granted. And consequently, as I saw it, everybody else must be like me at bottom. My mother says that I was a quiet, shy lad, easily elated and easily depressed, who wanted to "gang his ain gait."

That may be so. One thing is certain, that I was never beloved by my playmates. The girls, as a rule got on with me, but without showing any warm interest in me, but the boys gave me the cold shoulder and bullied me whenever they could.

There were two boys who were associated with almost the whole of my youth, for I met them again at home, until I met them permanently in the upper second class. One was called Louis Damarau, the other Albin Dobinsky; and there was a third, whose name I cannot mention, as he later showed himself very kind to a nephew of mine. I will give him the pseudonym of Hallgarten, which is not in the least like his real name. These so-called school friends, with whom I sat hundreds of times, first of all on the same bench at school and later at the same beer table, were the first to saturate my sensitive soul with the corrosive poison of humiliation and bitterness, the first to give me the acrid draught of feeling that I was something inferior to the others, and to create in me a sense of being suppressed and bowed down, which in later life had a damaging effect on me in every attack which I made on my surroundings. To this I trace many a defect in my character, for which I had to suffer as if it were a curse, and the worst features

*From *The Book of My Youth* by Hermann Sudermann. Reprinted by permission of The Bodley Head, Ltd. 1923. Pp. 47-50.

of which, slackness and lack of courage, I only conquered as I grew older.

That I was shut out from their games and walks, that they went bathing without me, that they made secret appointments with the girls which I was not permitted to hear, soon became habitual, and it did not hurt me the less because it was continually repeated. But they had a more subtle way of torturing me.

The straitness of the family's means made it necessary for my mother to make the clothes which we boys wore and one pair of trousers which she made for me were too broad, I suppose. Now the sawyers wore broad breeches because, otherwise, the continual bending would cause an ordinary pair to split in the back. My friends immediately noticed this similarity, and wherever I went or stood the word "sawyer" resounded behind me. And it was useless for me to defend myself furiously and fall blindly on my tormentors with my fists. They were bigger and therefore stronger than I was, and so I always got a licking into the bargain.

I cannot remember that any insult in the whole of my life ever hurt so much or plunged me into deeper despair. Probably it was the fact that I read into it some reflection on the family poverty which made it so painful, for even if my enemies had no such intention, the intimate connection of the gibe with our poverty pierced me to the most sensitive center of my soul, for it cut more deeply than anything else could do into my own flesh and blood. Society in every small Prussian town or larger village which is not purely agricultural in character is severely divided into four layers, the social structure and prevailing customs of which determine with an iron hand the education and career of the individual born in any one of these spheres. It is difficult, nay, almost impossible, to climb from one layer to another, and, as a rule, no ambition, no success, succeeds in bridging the gulf between one class and another.

The highest class is that of the "honoratorien," or gentry, which comprises those with a university education, landed proprietors, well-to-do businessmen, and a few others who, owing to their connections or by skillful maneuvering, have gained admission into the sacred circle. The second layer is composed of the middle class, which includes all those who are able to make some claim at least to a certain measure of education and respectability, such as the smaller officials, the landlords of the inns, most of the shopkeepers, and all those other people who do not feel themselves worthy to mix with the "upper class." Another gulf separates this class from the artisan class, the children of which are educated in the public schools and which finds its social amusement in rifle or gymnastic clubs. The fourth layer, that of the proletariat, the poor and the nameless, is not mentioned in good society and so I too will remain silent about it.

The fact that my family neither desired to belong to the first class, or gentry, nor was permitted to do so, but belonged to the middle class, was the greatest misery of my childhood. It was the source of my ambition, my obstinacy, my industry, and my efforts to reach the heights.

Lucy Sprague Mitchell
(1878-   )

Lucy Sprague's adolescent protest against her father's newly acquired social status, based on recently earned wealth, forms the basis for the following three passages from her autobiography.* Her protest "did not begin at once when we moved to Prairie Avenue. On the contrary, my first reaction to the new world into which I was plunged was a twelve-year-old's pleasurable excitement over new experiences. And they were many. I loved the spacious beauty of our new house. Nancy and I still roomed together, but we now had a dressing room with a washbasin and toilet. And we had a regular guest room—indeed we soon had several guest rooms. . . . The house was to Father a symbol of success and was planned for entertainment. Mother made an art of entertainment. Her table appointments were perfect. . . . " But the change in the Spragues' way of living coincided with the adolescent Lucy's awareness of a social world outside of, and much different from, her home.

> With our move from unpretentious, crowded quarters on Washington Boulevard to a grand new house on Prairie Avenue on the South Side, I entered a completely new phase in my life. I was then just twelve. The change in our way of living, coinciding as it did with my adolescence, brought an awareness of a social world outside my home —a social world which, at first, I saw through the eyes of my father. And Father saw the social world as one of a group of young men who had come to early Chicago and who had helped to build it into a city of big industries, big business and big finance. Through Father, Chicago history became a part of my family history. The story of my inner life during my three and a half years of adolescence in Chicago is largely of the protest that I gradually developed against the social

*From Two Lives by Lucy S. Mitchell. Reprinted by permission of Simon & Schuster, Inc. Copyright 1953, Lucy S. Mitchell. Pp. 55-56, 60, 65.

standards of my father and his friends and of the curious paths into which this struggle with myself led me.

* * * *

These were troubled years for me. Being at home so much, my role in the family became, more and more, that of the family nurse, for there was often someone sick in our home. Not only did I feel a failure in my own life. I began, too, to feel restless at being excluded from the "real" world. As a child I had thought of the world as made up of good people and bad people, and we, of course, belonged to the good people. I had known, of course, that there were rich people and poor people. But the idea that we belonged to the rich had never come home to me until we moved to our big Prairie Avenue house. At first this discovery merely embarrassed me. Gradually, I realized that Father had one attitude toward people who had money and another toward people who did not have money—that he thought of "success" largely in terms of the ability to make money. I was deeply disturbed. I had met a different attitude at Hull House, where, in earlier years, I had been taken by my parents. Now I began going to Hull House by myself. I had fallen under the spell of Jane Addams, that great and gracious woman who lived there—a spell which never lost its hold on me. She became for me a symbol of the "real" world—a world of work and of people that I longed to reach but could not. I felt I was a "pampered darling" bound by my father's wealth to a world of people whose standards I could not accept. My adolescent conflict of loyalties became acute. I developed a sense of shame and guilt at being rich which has never completely left me.

* * * *

Through the support of . . . businessmen, Chicago already had developed two cultural undertakings that ranked high in comparison with like institutions anywhere. Most of these wealthy men gave their financial support not because they themselves were interested in art or music but because of pride in "their" city. This, of course, was not true of them all. It was not true of the Martin Ryersons or of the "Charlie" Hutchinsons who lived across the street from us and who, more than others, were responsible for the fine collection at the beautiful new Art Institute on lower Michigan Avenue. Their houses had a lovely restraint, unusual in those days, with genuine "old masters" hung on uncrowded walls. But most of the patrons of the Art Institute, my father among them, knew little about art. Yet he took his family there to show us each new acquisition with a personal pride.

The same group of moneyed men were also responsible for the Chicago Symphony Orchestra, conducted by Theodore Thomas. The old Central Music Hall of my childhood was now superseded by a much larger hall in the new Auditorium—a fine new gray stone hotel on the corner of Michigan Avenue and Congress Street. To me, the Friday afternoon symphony concerts at which I sat alone in a balcony seat were high lights in my life. But at the Saturday evening concerts I had to sit with my parents in the family box, one of the impressive double tier of boxes that were filled with the patrons of music. There were, of course, some patrons who supported the symphony orchestra because they loved and understood music, but more gave their money because of civic pride. For box holders, the intermissions were social affairs. The men in swallowtails made the rounds of boxes while the wives in full evening dress stayed in the boxes to receive their husbands' business friends. Music was a serious matter to me. I resented the intrusion of these patrons with whom I had to shake hands, and who carried with them a proprietary air because their money supported music. Above all, I grieved that my father carried this air with him. Sitting exposed in a box—a symbol of wealth—increased my adolescent conflict—admiration for my forceful, urbane, witty father and disapproval of the exalted value he placed on money. I retired still further into an inner world that I created for myself.

Charles James Nowell
(? - ?)

Charles Nowell, or Tlakodlas as he was named by his older brother at a potlatch which is described in the next selection,* was a Kwakiutl Indian of Vancouver, Canada. The socioeconomic structure of the Kwakiutl has been compared to that of the United States in that the economic life is based on competitive, conspicuous consumption. The status jealousy of the Kwakiutl is seen predominantly in their feasts, called potlatches, at which chiefs outdo each other in providing food and in burning up blankets and sheets of copper which are the main indices of wealth in their society. Sometimes even a house or a canoe is sent up in flames in a final bid for dominant status. Riesman characterizes Kwakiutl society as a caricature of Veblen's thesis of conspicuous consumption (16). Charley Nowell's need to retain his status as son of a chief and brother of one

---

*From *Smoke from Their Fires* edited by Clellan S. Ford. Reprinted by permission of Yale University Press. 1941. Pp. 107-110.

is given support by the traditions of the tribe. The description of the potlatch contained here is a very real indication of this non-literate society's need to maintain social and economic distinctions.

Maybe I was twelve years old when my father took sick. He wanted to have a talk with me, so my brother came and took me out of school. My brother sent three of the boys to come and get me. He got one of the Hunt family to write a letter to Mr. Hall so I could go. Mr. Hall didn't seem to mind my going. He never even told me to come right back. I went to Fort Rupert, and, as soon as I get there, my father calls me to go to his bedside, and told me he is going to leave us, and told me to remember what he has taught me regarding potlatches. He told me to do the same as my brother does—that he is always loaning out blankets to other people, and that is the only way to get more blankets. "If you will spend your earnings foolishly, you will be no good. They will not look upon you as they are looking upon your brother. Most of all I want to say is, I know you have been to school, and I think the only way for you to remember the main positions and all the ancestors is for you to write them down, because it seems to me that everybody is forgetting all their ancestors and names. I have often heard people make mistakes. The first thing, you will write down our ancestors till now." So I did—all our ancestors right down to him. He then told me to write down the names we should use and told me about the positions in our clan, and told me who had that position and why we should use it. Then he began to talk about the dances and the dance names, and, when he finish that, he lay down and slept. He lose his breath talking to me, and, when he lay down to sleep, he died. He was going to talk about our relatives, but before he finished his breath gave out, and he died.

What became of those papers I wrote I don't know. It was my brother that looked after it. It must have been burnt when they burnt all my brother's clothing, according to the custom of the Indians, that they have to take everything that a man used for clothing and burn it after the funeral. I was so busy when my brother died, I didn't have a chance to go and watch.

After my father died, they put him in a long coffin, and it was cedar boards nailed together, and they buried him in the ground in back of the porch. My brother had to pay Mr. Hunt one pair of blankets for a place to bury him in the graveyard. Four days after, my brother gave the potlatch, and that is the time he put me in my father's position in our clan—number three position.

When my father died I was old enough to have my position in

my clan. My brother give a potlatch and announce my new name, Tlakodlas, which means "where you get your coppers from." After this two men are sent to go and invite me to a feast, and my brother gives them a blanket each. Then I go with these two men. I don't like to go —I would rather play than go to a feast. When the two men get to the front of the building where the feast is, one of them speaks to the people, saying that I have come to join the feast and that my seat should be open where I am going to sit. When I sit down, the chief of my clan gets up again, and tells the Kwekas to sit up and sing my brother's potlatch song. They begin to sing, and then after the singing, our chief announces that I am going to give a feast or a potlatch soon. After that, I am a man—not any more a child. They now have to remember me on every feast.

When I was in the third position in the first clan of the Kwekas, before I was married, a nephew of mine, Nulis, who was older than me and belonged to our clan, but his position was way lower, gave a potlatch after he sold a copper. When he was giving it to all the other tribes who came to Fort Rupert, he told the people of how we stand, and we are from one family in the olden days, that he has a right to be in one of our grandfather's positions, and that he wants to be put on the third position of our clan, and I was to be the fourth, which was a man called Likiosa who was a little older than me and was related to me, and we all just go down one so he can have my position. My brother wasn't at Fort Rupert. He was at Alert Bay working for the new Indian agent, Mr. Pidcock, and while he was talking to the people about this position, somebody told me to stand up and tell him I don't want him to come in front of me until my brother comes back, and agree to what he says.

When my brother comes back to Fort Rupert, there was another potlatch from other peoples to the Fort Ruperts, and this Nulis stood up and says, when the potlatch comes to my place, "Now give me my share on this position where I am now going to be." My brother stood up and told him he has heard about what he said, and that he doesn't agree with him. "If you had spoken to me beforehand," he says, "I might have agreed, but you have tried to steal the position away when I wasn't here, and so I am telling you by the face of all these people, that you are not going to get that position." Nulis says, "If you don't agree to that, then I'll be on the fourth position." Likiosa got up and says, "No, I'm not going to have you come in front of me." He then turned around to the Fort Ruperts and tells them to stand up and sing his potlatch song that he is going to give a potlatch. When we finish with this song, Nulis also told us to sing his song, that he is going to give another potlatch. They went on for so many years giving pot-latches, Likiosa and Nulis. When they went to other potlatches, they were given gifts—both together, so they wouldn't quarrel in the pot-latch. Finally Nulis won out and took the position away from Likiosa.*

When my brother wanted me to get my share, in anybody's potlatch, he gave a potlatch of blankets and told the people that this potlatch has been given away by his son. From now on I receive my gifts from the other people and use them for myself. That means that I am old enough to look after them myself. That was when I was quite grown up but before I was married. Maybe I was eighteen or twenty. At this potlatch he announced my name, Tlakodlas, the same as the second, and put me in my position in the clan. My brother was the first, and I was the third. I took my father's position, and the rest of our family was way down about thirty or more after me. My next oldest brother was on that place that I took, and he died about a year before this. If he hadn't died, I would have been in the lower position that I was in when I was called to the feast.

Ludwig Lewisohn
(1882-1955)

Ludwig Lewisohn, the son of German Jewish immigrants who set-tled in a southern community in the United States, made every effort as a youth to become acculturated to the local group. He was singularly unsuccessful, despite the fact that during these years he attended the Methodist Church, taught Sunday School, was a leader in the Epworth League, president of his college's literary society and editor-in-chief of its magazine. In the following two passages from his autobiography, symbolically entitled *Upstream,* Lewisohn relates his battle against the social, cultural and religious tides he was bucking, his naïve hopes, and his eventual sullen with-drawal from his gentlemen friends.** He overcompensated for his youthful negation of Judaism later in life when he immersed him-self in a thorough study of his people and their problems; and in

---

*With his brother supporting him, Charley retains his position. Note, too, that Nulis is censured for even the slightest deviation from the customary procedure. Any tentatives in the direction of stealing a position are immediately punished. Nulis is forced to fight his way according to traditional rules, and, when he does so, he wins an advancement.

**From *Upstream* by Ludwig Lewisohn. Reprinted by permission of Liveright Publishers. Copyright 1952, Ludwig Lewisohn. Pp. 73-74, 88-89.

such works as *Israel* and *The Last Days of Shylock* he became a Jew with a vengeance. As an apostle of Judaism, the stings of anti-Semitism hurt him no longer (3).

During my last year at High School, however, a difficulty beset me which during hours and days made life seem hideous and hopeless. There arose, very sharply and imperiously, the consciousness of sex. By a degrading and stupid convention the problem of sex is regarded as non-existent among Anglo-Americans. No doubt, men tell jokes. . . . So did the boys with whom I went to school—pointless, nasty jokes. But these boys, like many of my friends later, would have regarded a discussion of sex, the immense central problem of sex, as a little vulgar and more than a little disconcerting. And my Americanization was complete. I shared that point of view or, at least, very potently believed that I shared it. No power on earth could have dragged from me a hint of my emotions. I attended a Methodist church. I was a member of the Epworth league. Naturally I soon fell into a wretched conviction of sin and tried to double the zeal of my religious exercises. Yet all my inner life was like a clear pool that had been muddied and defiled. Neither prayer nor study were of much avail at certain hours. Relentlessly my mind drifted off into imaginings that filled me with terror, but that seem to me now, as I recall them, not only harmless but rather poetical. I was the more convinced of the wickedness of my thoughts by the absurd exaltation of woman which is so characteristic a note of Southern life. I had been taught by my whole social environment to believe that woman is a being without passion, without any feelings of the grosser sort. No one who has not lived in the South will credit the universality and blatancy of this preposterous folly. It imparts to the Southern gentleman a courtesy to "good" women which no self-sustaining human being needs; it makes his behavior to women who are not "good" literally currish. But these conventions had entered into the very texture of my life. Nothing could have persuaded me that I would ever have thoughts as "ungentlemanly" as those I have just set down. A gentleman believed that the South was in the right in the War between the States, that Christianity was the true religion—(to be merely suspected of liberality in points of doctrine added a bold, mysterious charm provided you were a man and over fifty)—that the Democratic party was the only means, under Providence, of saving the White Race from obliteration by the Nigger, that good women are sexless—"sweet and pure" was the formula—and that in a harlot's house you must keep on your hat. And we were trained to be "young gentlemen." Well, the good people succeeded with me. I shared their faith and their morals and my boyish soul was tormented and warped. . . . Some years later with a crowd of college-boys—all pretty drunk—I went into a harlot's house. We came out as we had gone in. I had wanted hard to take my hat off. The insult seemed so futile and so cruel. But I didn't dare risk the gibes of my comrades. I was a young gentleman.

* * * *

I still, during these years, attended the Methodist church, taught Sunday School and was a leader in the Epworth League. I did this partly because, up to my junior year, my Christian faith, though cooler, was still unshaken, partly through the influence and friendship of the physician whom I have mentioned, but also because I found a good deal of unreserved human friendliness among these people. And I needed this. The relations between my class-mates and myself were very cordial; several of them often visited me as I did them. Yet there always came a point at which I felt excluded. They themselves belonged to a definite social group. They neither drew me into this group nor did they have the good sense or good feeling to be silent before me concerning these more intimate affairs. I do not think their exclusion of me was at all a matter of reason or determination; it was quite instinctive. By virtue of my work on the college magazine and the attitude of the professors toward me, they respected me. Personally they liked me well enough and elected me, without hesitation, in due time, president of our literary society and editor-in-chief of the magazine. As tribesmen their resistance to me was tacit but final. A pushing or insinuating fellow might, assuredly, have made his way. But my sensitiveness was so alert that I, no doubt, at times created division by suspecting it and at once shrinking away. But of the fundamental fact there could be no doubt. It was terribly confirmed to me by an incident in my senior year. I was the most prominent student on the campus. My classmates called themselves my friends—voluntarily and without my seeking. And these very friends gathered to form the first chapter of a Greek letter fraternity at our college and—left me out. I did not know then that the fraternities do not admit Jews. I do not know now whether they practice this exclusion tacitly or by regulation. I never spoke of the incident either at school or at home. Our president who founded the chapter does not know to this day that I so much as observed the matter. I did, with a profound discouragement, with a momentary grim prevision of the future which I fought bitterly to blot out lest I should lose all my hopes and see all my life crumble before me at eighteen. I withdrew into myself with sullen pride and intensified ambition, convinced that the incident was local, exceptional, unrepresentative and un-American. Such was my simple faith. . . .

Floyd Dell
(1887-   )

Floyd Dell, the author of a number of autobiographical novels, has been called "a pre-eminent psychologist of adolescence," by virtue of the fact that he was "destined to endure a painful and protracted period of growing up, from the ill consequences of which he believes that psychoanalysis rescued him" (2), and as a result of which experiences he was able to produce the sensitive portrayal, for instance, of such an adolescent as the dreamy, introverted, egotistical Felix Fay in *Moon-Calf.*

As early as at the age of six, Dell resigned himself to a fate of suffering in deprivation. That was the panic year of 1893, "when my father was out of work, the older children had been sent away to stay with relatives in the country, I was kept indoors all winter because the soles of my shoes were worn through, and there was no money in the house as Christmas time approached. My parents must have believed that I would not know it was Christmas time if nothing was said about it; and since there was no money for presents, they kept silence. I was keeping count, however, by the kitchen calendar, and their silence on the subject of Christmas puzzled and frightened me; and, after one casual remark of mine about Christmas had been ignored, I kept silence, too. Christmas eve came, and still nothing was said. Then I asked, "This is the night before Christmas, isn't it?" My mother burst into tears, and my father, in a lamely humorous way, expressed surprise and ignorance—he hadn't been reading the newspapers, he said. I realized their humiliation, and went off to bed, to lie awake for hours paralyzed with the shock of what I had just learned—that we were poor [5]."

Dell's immediate reaction was one of stoicism. "I wanted nothing . . . I never asked my parents for money or toys, because we were too poor." But most particularly, he lost his father, "who because of his manifest financial inadequacy, could surely be no model or hero or influence. He had lost all identification with the masculine world that would make him wish to be a boy. . . . At twelve the identification with his mother and the rejection of his father took a different turn. Since the ostensible head of the house was inadequate, he would himself remedy the situation. Whereas he had formerly shown fixed ideas regarding his fate in the midst of poverty, and was ashamed of his home and family, he now began to search 'for grounds of emotional reconciliation' with his father. It was not that this parent was lazy or incompetent, but that he was a victim of the capitalistic system. Out of these thoughts arose his ideas of social rebellion [2]."

The two selections chosen from Floyd Dell's autobiography, *Homecoming*, reveal his search for some inner strength to save him from similar frightening experiences as those which occurred when he was six. The first passage, taking place when he was fourteen, indicates how he identified his father in verse with Lincoln, as well as in actual incident; the second, when he was sixteen, illustrates his extreme sensitivity to class distinctions.* It is significant to point out that with Dell's adherence to socialism in early adolescence came the resolution of the conflict with his father.

When we had moved to Quincy, the first thing that one of my new schoolmates said to me was, "My father is a doctor—what's yours?" I evaded answering, and told my mother about it. She said: "Tell them that your father is a retired butcher." I couldn't tell them that. I wanted to tell them to go to hell.

That next fall, in school, suddenly and with little outward reason, I wrote a poem—the second I had ever written. Again the lines poured out easily, rhymes and all. It was on the subject of Lincoln, the martyr President. But, underneath that (I am quite sure), I was praising and excusing my father. Heroism was enough; the hero did not have to be a good business man. What if my father had not supported his family in respectable style? I could be proud of him! That, certainly, was how I suddenly felt. American respectability had taken my father away from me. Socialism was giving me a chance to get him back.

And I had him back, not only in a poem, but, already that summer, in fact. In a rather silly but very satisfying way, it happened. As my father sat reading his Sunday paper, I began—strange behavior in so dignified a boy—to tickle his ear with a broomstraw. He thought it was a fly, and brushed at it. I kept it up until he turned and saw me. Even then I did not stop, but persisted in this silly trick until—"You seem to want a spanking," he said, "so I'll give it to you!"—and he did. I burst out laughing. I was happy.

---

*From *Homecoming, an Autobiography* by Floyd Dell. Reprinted by permission of Holt, Rinehart & Winston, Inc. 1933. Pp. 55-56, 70-71.

He seemed to understand, for he invited me to go fishing with him. I dug the worms, and we started. On the way to the creek we passed the 'Last Chance' saloon, and my father went in for a glass of beer, telling me that I might come in and have a glass of soda-pop if I liked.

But I was embarrassed, and stood waiting for him outside.

At that moment when I decided to stay outside, I was my mother's little boy.

But some new self within me made me feel ashamed. I wished I had gone in with him.

And after our fishing was done, on the way back, when we stopped there again, I marched in proudly and happily at his side. And when my soda-pop was served me in a bottle with a straw, I insisted on having it in a glass. I shyly pushed the glass along the bar till it touched my father's, and then drank deep.

*   *   *   *

Toward the end of my second year in high school, when I was all but sixteen years old, I found a fellow-Atheist and hence a friend. His name was Harry, and he was a year older than I, in the class above me in high school. One evening at the public library we discovered that we had a common enthusiasm for Haeckel's *History of Creation*. It was so almost incredible to each of us that there could really be another in the Quincy high school who held heretical views, that our preliminary conversation was shy and cautious. But it was true that we were kindred spirits; and a friendship blazed into existence like a star in the void.

Harry was a tall, rather quiet youth, whose clothes—and his house when I subsequently visited him there one Sunday—showed him to belong to a well-to-do family. I had no means of making accurate distinctions between the rich and the merely comfortable middle-class, then or for a long time afterward. But I knew what workingmen's homes looked like, and, what with boiled cabbage and codfish and the clothes-boiler, smelled like; I knew how workingmen's children were dressed, and the best achievement of maternal neatness in cleaning and patching an old blue serge suit that was shiny on the seat and too short in the sleeves could be instantly distinguished from an expensive cheviot suit however baggy and carelessly worn. Homes where there was space, and an atmosphere of serenity and leisure, however old the furniture (for that in a workingman's home might be shiny new, just bought on the instalment plan from the department store), homes in which Mother, however motherly and homey, did not come in with a red face from the kitchen stove, but had a maid to do the cooking;

homes in the back of which there wasn't a kitchen garden carefully cultivated to save the grocery bills, but a spacious lawn in front that the man of the house enjoyed cutting for exercise when he came home from his work, and flower-beds that the lady of the house had time to stoop over and watch and tend:—to me such places as these were all indistinguishably the homes of the upper class, of a kind of Aristocracy. My friend Harry had such a background, and I was uneasy in it, not knowing at table what some of the cutlery beside my plate was for, and conscious that the manners very carefully taught me by my mother were not quite the same as those which casually reigned in this dining-room and parlor.

It was requisite that I should invite my new friend in return to my house. I did not want to. I knew that a boy should not be ashamed of his home and family. But I did not wish to expose to the gaze of anyone of the "upper-class" a home that was in such painful contrast to the one to which he had so casually invited me. And my mother, a bent old woman, worn out in household drudgeries, weak in strength and health and all but spirit; eager to serve, sitting at table next to the kitchen door on the very edge of a tilted chair, so that she could rise and wait on the family; without even the dignity of age, for a pair of crooked brass-rimmed spectacles which she habitually wore (saving her gold ones, like her best dress, for grand occasions which never came) gave her thin face a sadly comic aspect: how could anyone else see in her the eager girl, the indomitable spirit, the angel with the flaming sword, that a son knows in his mother?

I think I did invite my friend; I have a vague impression of much uneasy suffering on my part, and of his behaving with perfect courtesy and ease, as though my house were like anybody else's house and my family like anybody else's family. But I cannot bring back the scene; and we were in one another's houses no more, but met in the perfect equality of the public library.

Vera Brittain
(1893-   )

Because of her socially and economically inferior position relative to the other girls who attended the fashionable St. Monica's School, thirteen-year-old Vera Brittain was made to feel inferior, separate and alone. She was able to attend the school only because her aunt was co-principal of it and she was therefore not charged the usual fees. Miss Brittain compensated for the second-class status afforded her by being ambitious and excelling in her studies.*

My classroom contemporaries regarded my ambitions, not unnaturally, with no particular interest or sympathy. Many of them were fashionable young women to whom universities represented a quite unnecessary prolongation of useless and distasteful studies, and they looked upon my efforts to reach the top of a form, and my naïve anxiety to remain there, as satisfactorily exonerating them from the troublesome endeavour to win that position for themselves.

Socially, of course, I was quite without standing among these wealthy girls, designed by their parents for London or Edinburgh society, with their town addresses in Mayfair or Belgravia, and their country houses of which the name "Hall" or "Park" was frequently a part. My parents could not afford the numerous theatres and concerts to which many of them were taken by request of their families; my "best" clothes were home-made or purchased from undistinguished shops in Buxton or Manchester; and the presents that I received at Christmas or on birthdays did not bear comparison with the many elegant gifts that my class-mates displayed for the admiration of contemporaries on returning to school after the holidays.

It is hardly surprising that few of the girls coveted the reputation unenthusiastically conceded to me for "brains," or even envied my comparative freedom from refused lessons, but regarded these assets as mere second-rate compensations for my obvious inferiority in the advantages that they valued most. In those days as in these, girls' private schools attracted but few parents possessed of more than a half-hearted intention to train their daughters for exacting careers or even for useful occupations. Both for the young women and their mothers, the potential occurrence that loomed largest upon the horizon was marriage, and in spite of the undaunted persistence with which both the Principals upheld their own progressive ideals of public service, almost every girl left school with only two ambitions—to return at the first possible moment to impress her school-fellows with the glory of a grown-up *toilette,* and to get engaged before everybody else.

Chiang Yee
(1903-   )

At the age of thirteen, Chiang Yee was sent by his family to collect

---

*From *Testament of Youth* by Vera Brittain. Reprinted by permission of Vera Brittain. Copyright 1935, Macmillan Co. Pp. 33-34.

the rents from tenant farmers who worked the land. For four years, the boy had been away from the farm where he had grown up and played, and had looked forward to playing again with his old friends. But upon his return, class differences prevented them from getting together.*

I wondered why the farmers spent so much money on this dinner, for I had never seen them eat and drink like this during my year among them, when their meals had invariably been simple, meat or chicken being included only very occasionally. Here there were two huge chickens besides other meats (chiefly pork), all beautifully cooked and with the flavour of the countryside. The meat and chickens were cut in slices about three inches square, which seemed enormous to me. All the farmers were very merry and talked cheerily. They played the game of guessing-fingers, and I remember that my relation lost a great deal at it, though he won several cups of wine; but then he did not drink, so the old farmer who had met me drained the cups for him.

My hosts kept pressing me to taste this and that dish and offering me tasty tit-bits. I knew it was not polite to refuse, so I asked for a second bowl and put into that all the food I could not eat. The farmers themselves ate enormously; further supplies of food were sent for from the kitchen. At the end of the dinner I asked that my extra bowl of food should be given to some of my old playfellows, who were not present at the dinner because they were too young, a circumstance which, as they were the same age as myself, surprised me until my relation explained that my position as family representative gave me special privileges. One of the old farmers seemed pleased that I should remember my old friends, but another teased me and said he would have put more into his own belly if he had known I was going to give my share away. After the dinner the farmers began to talk business, and I had to evade the issues by saying that it would be better to leave that to my uncle.

My duty done, I went to find my old playfellows. But they were shy of me, and I too felt embarrassed. How was it, I asked myself, that the short period of four years had brought about such a change in our relations? Perhaps it was the complete difference in environment and thought between the life of the country and the life of the city. My companions, no doubt, thought I would be too sophisticated for them.

I spent the night at the farm, and when, next morning, I was ready

---

*From *A Chinese Childhood* by Chiang Yee. Reprinted by permission of The John Day Co., Inc. 1952. Pp. 242, 244.

to leave, I found my playfellows helping their elders to beat the rice-grain on the open ground in front of the farm. They greeted me, but said nothing more. Some were gathering up the grains, some were taking the straw away and tying it in bundles to pile on the roof of the stables for the cows and buffaloes. One of the elders told me that the rice we had eaten the day before had only been beaten a few days previously. He then expressed his gratitude for the good harvest. I wanted to help with the beating, but they all said it was not suitable work for a long-gown wearer. So, I thought, I was a long-gown wearer! The long-gown is the sign of a scholar in China and its possession a source of pride to a Chinese. But not at my age! I saw now how my long-gown had deprived me of the pleasure of talking with my old playfellows.

When I got home I gave my elders a long account of the dinner and said how surprised I was at the rich food. My uncle roared with laughter. 'It is we, you know,' he said, 'who pay for this great dinner! It will all be put down on the bill which the tenants present to us.' I was astonished. My uncle explained, however, that it was traditional that a good dinner should be prepared for the farmers by the landlord, in order to thank them for their work with the harvest. To save trouble the landlord generally asked his tenants to prepare the meal for themselves and said that he would come and join them when it was ready. For generations this had been the arrangement.

REFERENCES

1. Adams, Henry. *The Education of Henry Adams*. Boston: Houghton Mifflin Co., 1918, pp. 3-4.
2. Bragman, Louis J. The case of Floyd Dell. *Amer. J. Psychiat.*, 93: 1401-1403, 1936.
3. Bragman, Louis J. The case of Ludwig Lewisohn. *Psychoanal. Rev.*, 21:300, 1934.
4. Carr, Albert (Ed.). *Napoleon Speaks*. New York: Viking Press, 1941, pp. 15-16.
5. Dell, Floyd. An autobiographical critique. *Psychoanal. Quart.*, 1:716, 1932.
6. Erikson, Erik H. Growth and crises of the healthy personality. *Psychol. Issues*, 1:92, 1959.
7. Freud, Ernst L. (Ed.). *Letters of Sigmund Freud*. New York: Basic Books, 1960, p. 22.
8. Gibbon, Edward. *Autobiography*. New York: Dutton Everyman's Library, 1911, p. 20.

9. Havighurst, Robert J., & Taba, Hilda. *Adolescent Character and Personality.* New York: John Wiley & Sons, 1949, p. 110.
10. Himmelweit, H. T., Halsey, A. H., & Oppenheim, A. N. The views of adolescents on some aspects of the social class structure. *Brit. J. Sociol.,* 3:148-172, 1952.
11. Hollingshead, August B. *Elmtown's Youth: The Impact of Social Classes on Adolescents.* New York: John Wiley & Sons, 1949, pp. 444-447.
12. Jones, Ernest. *The Life and Work of Sigmund Freud.* New York: Basic Books, 1957, Vol. III, p. 350.
13. Lynd, Robert S., & Lynd, Helen M. *Middletown.* New York: Harcourt, Brace & Co., 1929.
14. ——— & ———. *Middletown in Transition.* New York: Harcourt, Brace & Co., 1937.
15. Moore, George. *Confessions of a Young Man.* New York: Brentano's, 1915, p. 1.
16. Riesman, David, Glazer, Nathan, & Denney, Reuel. *The Lonely Crowd.* Garden City, N. Y.: Doubleday Anchor, 1953, p. 261.
17. Shaw, Clifford R. *The Jack-Roller. A Delinquent Boy's Own Story.* Philadelphia: Albert Saifer, 1930, p. 47.
18. Tibble, J. W., & Tibble, Anne. *John Clare. A Life.* New York: Oxford University Press, 1932, pp. 33-34, 57-58.
19. West, James. *Plainville, U.S.A.* In: Kardiner, Abram, *The Psychological Frontiers of Society.* New York: Columbia University Press, 1945, pp. 293,330.

CHAPTER NINE

The Adolescent Intellect

The ambivalent feelings of the adolescent are perhaps nowhere more clearly and generally perceptible than in the area of his intellectual development. He is almost simultaneously eager to learn and repelled by formal schooling. (He has a great desire for factual information but resorts to emotional argument to achieve his point.) He is perhaps at the peak of his intellectual powers but is inhibited by his defenses against his libidinal urgings. He wants to be a rational, poised thinker but the incompatible demands he inflicts upon himself tend to produce what John of Salisbury (18) described in 1159 as "Facetious folly, noisy volubility, empty loquacity, and puerile silliness."

In *The Ego and the Mechanisms of Defence,* Anna Freud (6) states that if " . . . we examine the diaries and jottings of adolescents, we are not only amazed at the wide and unfettered sweep of their thought but impressed by the degree of empathy and understanding manifested, by their apparent superiority to more mature thinkers and sometimes even by the wisdom which they display in their handling of the most difficult problems." But it seems probable that diaries are typically the work of those who are unusually intelligent (12). The diaries studied by Charlotte Bühler (2, 3) tend to bear this out, for all but one were written by adolescents who in adult life became learned persons.

More generally, the adolescent tends to intellectualize his instinctual life. This is an intensified necessity during adolescence because it "is simply part of the ego's customary endeavour to master the instincts by means of thought [7]." The adolescent, harassed as he is by his need for achieving identity, busy thinking about death and God and truth and sin, trying to commit the latter and being disappointed because of his usual lack of success in it, tries to connect the instinctual processes with ideas which can be dealt with consciously.

Napoleon, after a miserable period full of self-pity, addressed a monologue to a lady acquaintance which shows, typically, the exaggerated feelings, the boastings, and the bathos of adolescence, as well as the unfettered sweep of thought that Anna Freud writes about. "I have scarcely reached the age of eighteen, and I already hold the key of history in my hand. I know my weakness, but that is, perhaps, the best frame of mind in which to compose this kind of writing. I possess that enthusiasm which a deeper study of human nature often destroys in our hearts. The venality of a riper age will never smudge my pen. I breathe only truth, and I will also feel the strength to publish it. In the reading of this sketch of all our sufferings, I see, my dear fellow-countrymen, how your tears flow. Dear countrymen, we have always been unhappy! Today, as members of a powerful monarchy, all we get from its Government is the burden of its constitution, and perhaps, our troubles continuing, it will be only in the course of centuries that there will come a lessening of our misfortune [1]."

H. G. Wells, when he was eighteen and nineteen years old, found himself constantly dilating on the subjects "of atheism and agnosticism, of republicanism, of the social revolution, of the releasing power of art, of Malthusianism, of freedom and such-like liberating topics [24]." When Nehru was fourteen, nationalistic ideas filled his head. "I mused of Indian freedom and Asiatic freedom from the thraldom of Europe. I dreamt of brave deeds, of how, sword in hand, I would fight for India and help in freeing her [16]." Perhaps Jacob Wassermann (23), the great German novelist, summed up best the intellectualism of the adolescent when he tried to use that mechanism to deny the instinctual drives: "In my unquenchable thirst for intellectual intercourse I hurled myself into the cloaca of intellect. I hungered for corroboration and was pushed out of positions I had painfully gained."

The new strength of the drives in adolescence, unbalancing the previous equilibrium among the id, the ego and the superego, almost forces the young person to flee from feeling and to take refuge in thinking. This is a universal device in the struggle to master the intensification of the instinctual drives and in the attempt to re-establish equilibrium between the need for emotional outlets and social restrictions.

Most adolescents, according to Inhelder and Piaget (13), "have political or social theories and want to reform the world; they have their own ways of explaining all of the present-day turmoil in collective life. Others have literary or aesthetic theories and place their reading or their experiences of beauty on a scale of values which is projected into a system. Some go through religious crises and reflect on the problem of faith, thus moving toward a universal system—a system valid for all. Philosophical speculation carries away a minority, and for any true intellectual, adolescence is the metaphysical age *par excellence,* an age whose dangerous seduction is forgotten only with difficulty at the adult level." Examples of this kind of thinking—which furnishes the cognitive and evaluative bases for the assumption of adult roles—are given below.*

Closely allied to his intellectualism is the seemingly universal proclivity of the adolescent for arguing. In *The Metalogicon,* John of Salisbury (1115?-1180) gently but firmly suggested that the temerity of adolescence should be restrained. He explained, "Considerable indulgence should be . . . shown to the young, in whom verbosity should be temporarily tolerated, so that they may thus acquire an abundance of eloquence. As students mature and grow in understanding, our tolerance of unrestrained verbosity should diminish, and the impudence of sophistry (which Aristotle calls 'contentious,' but we refer to as 'deceitful' or 'cavilling') should be suppressed . . . Our tolerance of these exercises of the schools, which are, so to speak, games in the gymnasium of philosophy, indulged in for the purpose of developing proficiency [in the young], should not, however, be extended into more mature years and more serious studies. Facetious folly, noisy volubility, empty loquacity, and puerile silliness, should all be set aside, as soon as the first soft beard begins to appear on one's face. To indulge in the foregoing [on reaching maturity] is to throw away one's birthright as a philosopher, and to class oneself as a fool. According to the lesson of the allegory, as soon

---

*This chapter, section on Intellectual Ferment.

as he reached adolescence, Mercury, the god of eloquence, in accordance with the exhortations of his mother, wed Philology. For the fact that his cheeks were already beginning to show the down of manhood meant that he could no longer go about half naked, with only a short cape over his shoulders, without provoking Venus to peals of laughter. Venus, who represented the happy combination of wisdom and eloquence, derides the foolishness of nude, unarmed, windy eloquence [19]."

The nude, unarmed and windy eloquence of adolescents is given ample latitude in the debating societies which have existed since time immemorial. One of the early references was made by Lord Edward Herbert, who matriculated as a "gentleman-commoner" in 1596, according to the Oxford University Register, at the age of fourteen, and not twelve, as he himself recorded (11), "[I] attained to the knowledge of the Greek tongue and logic, insomuch, that at twelve years old my parents thought fit to send me to Oxford to University College, where I remember to have disputed at my first coming in logic. . . . "

The opportunities formal debating societies and informal argumentation among friends afford to adolescents help in the release of passions in a socially acceptable way, thus sublimating their instinctual drives. It is a safe conduit for repressed exhibitionistic impulses as well as for the release of hostile feelings against authority figures. It enables the individual to search out his self through verbal pyrotechnics. It helps the adolescent to develop competence in, and discover the limits of his capacity for, self-assertion and competition. It gives him comfort and esteem at a time when he desperately needs it. We see this in the passages from the writings of Benjamin Franklin, Jeremy Bentham, Sir Walter Scott, H. G. Wells and Albert Schweitzer.

Ambivalent feelings, the hallmark of the adolescent, are clearly manifest in his attitude toward learning. Adolescence is a period of renewal, of dynamism, of ardent energies not too well channelled. The individual loves and hates with what seems to be equal intensity. One moment he wants to possess all the available knowledge there is in the world, so that he can be sure of everything; the next moment he feels learning does not have the answers. The purpose of education is to train the ego in skills that will enable it to deal with the realities of life (5). But the adolescent, involved with his own narcissistic needs, concerned only with the present and unable to see beyond the morrow, frequently finds it impossible to sustain his interest in learning for a consistent length of time. Periods of elation with scholastic achievement follow periods of despair because of his "stupidity," or because of his anxiety about competing. When the ego-id-superego constellation is integrated and stabilized, the adolescent can then begin to learn effectively.

When this balance does not occur, the phenomenon of adolescent pseudostupidity may arise. This is an unconscious defense against the emergence into awareness of his instinctual desires and the recognition of his inability to gratify these desires in a personally satisfying and socially acceptable manner. So much time and energy are consumed in preventing the inappropriate expression of the adolescent's sexual and aggressive impulses that such intellectual capacities as abstract thinking and memory may be markedly impaired. All degrees of pseudostupidity occur, says Jones (15), which are not really expressions of a defect but of inhibition. The "stupidity" may be in the form of an infantile pattern of covert rebellion against giving parents what they want because of real or imaginary slights. Oberndorf (17) states that the symptom of stupidity usually develops in relation to deprivation of love by the parent of the same sex and is allied to feelings of unreality and depersonalization. The passage by Stillman (22) bears this out. The terrible gloom of Stillman's Puritan upbringing, at the instigation of his mother, "in which no light showed me promise of better things, only to be hoped for through a process of repentance and atonement for the sins of Adam, the fitness and method of which process were far beyond my capacity to comprehend, as beyond that of any child,—all these things made my intellectual life so sombre that I can but regard the long interval [from his seventh to his fourteenth year] of intellectual apathy as a fortunate provision against some form of mental malady consequent in the morbid development of my early childhood."

Hall, in his monumental work (10), catalogues nearly two dozen individuals of the seventeenth, eighteenth and nineteenth centuries who were considered "stupid" as adolescents.

> According to school standards, many [adolescents] were dull and indolent, but their nature was too large or their ideas too high to be satisfied with it. Wagner at the Nikolaischule at Leipzig was relegated

to the third form, having already attained to the second at Dresden, which so embittered him that he lost all taste for philology and, in his own words, "became lazy and slovenly." Priestley never improved by any systematic course of study. W. H. Gibson was very slow and was rebuked for wasting his time in sketching. James Russell Lowell was reprimanded, at first privately and then publicly, in his sophomore year "for general negligence in themes, forensics, and recitations," and finally suspended in 1838 "on account of continued neglect of his college duties." In early life Goldsmith's teacher thought him the dullest boy she had ever taught. His tutor called him ignorant and stupid. .... Humphry Davy was faithful but showed no talent in school, having "the reputation of being an idle boy, with a gift for making verses, but with no aptitude for studies of a graver sort." Later in life he considered it fortunate that he was left so much to himself. Byron was so poor a scholar that he only stood at the head of the class when, as was the custom, it was inverted, and the bantering master repeatedly said to him, "Now, George, man, let me see how soon you'll be at the foot." Schiller's negligence and lack of alertness called for repeated reproof, and his final school thesis was unsatisfactory. Hegel was a poor scholar, and at the university it was stated "that he was of middling industry and knowledge but especially deficient in philosophy." John Hunter nearly became a cabinetmaker. Lyell had excessive aversion to work. George Combe wondered why he was so inferior to other boys in arithmetic. Heine agreed with the monks that Greek was the invention of the devil. "God knows what misery I suffered with it." He hated French meters, and his teacher vowed he had no soul for poetry. He idled away his time at Bonn, and was "horribly bored" by the "odious, stiff, cut-and-dried tone" of the leathery professors. Humboldt was feeble as a child and "had less facility in his studies than most children." "Until I reached the age of sixteen," he says, "I showed little inclination for scientific pursuits." He was essentially self-taught, and acquired most of his knowledge rather late in life. At nineteen he had never heard of botany. Sheridan was called inferior to many of his schoolfellows. He was remarkable for nothing but idleness and winning manners, and was "not only slovenly in construing, but unusually defective in his Greek grammar." Swift was refused his degree because of "dullness and insufficiency," but given it later as a special favor. Wordsworth was disappointing. General Grant was never above mediocrity, and was dropped as corporal in the junior class and served the last year as a private. W. H. Seward was called "too stupid to learn." Napoleon graduated forty-second in his class. "Who," asks Swift, "were the forty-one above him?" Darwin was "singularly incapable of mastering any language." When he left school, he says, "I was considered by all my masters and by my father as a very ordinary boy, rather below the common standard in intellect. To my deep mortification, my father once said to me, 'You care for nothing but shooting, dogs and rat-catching, and you will be a disgrace to yourself and to all your family.' " Harriet Martineau was thought very dull.

Freud (8) illustrates, from the case history of a patient, how the psychic life becomes sensitive in a state of repression to the approach of the repressed material; very slight and subtle resemblances suffice to activate it again behind the agencies of repression and through them. "I once had occasion," he wrote, "to treat a young man, still almost a boy, who, after his first unwelcome notice of sexual processes, had taken flight from all desires rising up in him and used various means for their repression: he increased his zeal for study, overemphasized his childlike attachment to his mother, and in general assumed childish ways. I shall not detail here how his repressed sexuality broke forth again especially in his relationship to his mother, but should like to describe the less common and stranger case of the breaking down of another of his bulwarks from a cause that can hardly be recognized as sufficient. Mathematics enjoys the greatest reputation as a distraction from sexual matters. J. J. Rousseau once had to listen to this advice from a lady who was dissatisfied with him: 'Lascia le donne e studia le matematiche' ('Leave women alone and study mathematics'). Thus our fugitive tackled his mathematics and geometry in school with special zeal, until one day his mental powers weakened in the face of a few innocuous problems. The phrasing of the two could still be determined: 'Two bodies collide; one is travelling at a speed . . .' And: 'Inscribe a cone in a cylinder with the diameter m . . .' Because of these allusions to the sexual act, which are certainly not obvious to others, the young man felt let down by mathematics, too, and took flight from it as well."

Thus, while many adolescents experience comparable intellectual inhibition, many more respond to learning with a mixture of avidity and passivity. Probably not since his fifth or sixth year, when he first learned to read and the process of logical thinking became more ordered, has the adolescent found himself so intrigued by the world of knowledge. Illustrations from the fourth century—Saint Augustine and Saint Jerome, as well as the twentieth century—Anne Frank—reflect this eagerness.

In a letter addressed to a friend, Saint Jerome (14) described the inhibiting effect of his sexual drives on learning as well as his ambivalent feelings toward learning. At the time, he was a disciple of a monk in the Benedictine Order; the scene is the Egyptian desert. "In my youth, when I had taken shelter in the solitude of the desert, I was scarcely able to resist the temptation of vice and the natural fire; I tried to tame it by frequent fasting, but the thoughts flowed in my mind. In order to master them, I went to study with one of the brethren, who had been converted from Judaism; instead of the acuteness of Quintilian, the fluency of Cicero, the pomp of Fronto [Marcus Aurelius' tutor], and the pleasantness of Pliny, I learned the [Hebrew] alphabet and practised the sibilants and breathings. The labour I devoted to this, the difficulties I had to overcome, the frequent despair and abandonment of the work, followed by recommencement under the urge to learn, all this is testified to me by my conscience and can be attested by those who were living with me. But now I thank my Lord for it; for from the bitter seed of study, I am reaping sweet fruits."

In their eagerness to learn, Scaliger, Goethe, Maimon and Mary Somerville became fluent in several languages while still adolescents. Scaliger (1540-1609) wrote in his autobiography (20), "I had devoted two entire years to Greek literature, when an internal impulse hurried me away to the study of Hebrew. Although I did not even know a single letter of the Hebrew alphabet, I availed myself of no teacher other than myself in the study of the language." By the time Goethe had entered the university at Leipzig, he "had learnt Latin, like German, French, and English, only from practice, without rules and without comprehension [9]." When Mary Somerville (1780-1872) was thirteen, she and her family had spent the winter at Edinburgh to escape the rigors of their home seaport town. "On returning to Burntisland, I spent four or five hours daily at the piano; and for the sake of having something to do, I taught myself Latin enough, from such books as we had, to read Caesar's 'Commentaries' [21]." The eagerness of the adolescent's desire for learning, before it is hobbled by classmates or adults, can be seen in this excerpt from the autobiography of Lorenzo Da Ponte (4), who was Mozart's librettist and Casanova's friend: "Up to my fourteenth

year I was left completely ignorant in all branches of letters, and
while people kept exclaiming: 'Oh, how clever! How talented!' I
could inwardly feel only shame at being the least educated of all the
young boys in Ceneda, who used to call me in jest the 'clever dunce.'
I could not tell how deeply all this stung me, and how it made me
long for instruction!"

The passages which follow are classified topically: "Ambivalences
toward Learning," "Dislike for Schooling," "Intellectual Ferment,"
and "Argumentation and Debating." They reflect the universal feelings of adolescents over the past thousand years.

AMBIVALENCES TOWARD LEARNING

Guibert de Nogent
(1053-1124)

Guibert, Abbot of Notre Dame de Nogent, was born of noble
parents. His father died when he was eight. His mother was a fanatically pious woman, "who learned to loathe sin," Guibert tells us,
and who retired to a convent when he was twelve years old. Guibert
was destined by her for the church and he later—after great conflict
—took the vows.

He lived during a renaissance of thought and civilization which
was almost comparable to the Renaissance of two and a half centuries later. His *Gesta dei per Francos,* the history of the First
Crusade, is a remarkably modern, critical work. His autobiography,
De Vita Sua, from which the following passage is taken, is equally
contemporary in outlook, for he detailed his life not only with
psychological insight but with accurate descriptions of his time
and society which are the more remarkable because of their essential similarities with our own age.

Chapter XVI of Guibert's medieval *Autobiography* demonstrates
the libidinal conflict of the adolescent against "the promise of a
better hope." His eagerness for learning ran into many roadblocks
as we see in the difficulties and ambivalences he recorded during his
thirteenth and fourteenth years. In addition, Guibert makes clear
the adolescent's recourse to magical thinking. The duality of the
adolescent's personality frequently compels him to revert back to
the magical thinking of infancy, particularly when threatened by

aggressive and sexual impulses, or by some loss to his self-esteem, or as a defense against his infantile wishes. Guibert illustrates magical thinking when he alludes to the omniscient quality of both his mother and his master, as this passage* shows.

Now with the gradual growth of my little body, as its carnal life began to stir my itching heart with fleshly longings and lusts according to its stature, my mind oft fell to remembering and thinking on what and how great I might have been in the world, in which my imaginings often travelled beyond the truth. These thoughts, Gracious God, Thou didst reveal to Thy servant, my mother. Whatsoever the state, healthy or diseased, to which my unstable heart changed, thereafter there came to her in a vision by Thy will, O God, an image of the same. But whereas dreams are said to follow upon much care, and that is verily true, yet her cares were not aroused by the heat of greed, but were created by a real eagerness for inward holiness. Soon therefore when the troubling vision was impressed on her pious mind, as she was very subtle and clear sighted in the interpretation of such matters, soon, I say, when she had perceived that this trouble was betokened by her dream, she summoned me and in private questioned me how and what I was doing. And since I was in such submission to her that my will was one with hers, I readily confessed all those things which I had heard as in a dream, into which my mind seemed to relax and fall, and after her counsel concerning amendment, I at once gave her my promise with true affection.

O my God, oft did she declare in dark sayings that state in which I now am, and what she believed I had done or must do in that earlier condition, that I now experience every day and see it filling up the secret places of my heart. Nay, even my master himself with the same everpresent anxiety, enlightened by Thee, saw through many kinds of phantoms what was happening at the time and what might come to pass in the future. By God's goodness therefore in alarming, and again in comforting me, adversity and success were foretold, so that whether I would or not, I refrained from secret vice, because by Thy wonder-working so much was revealed to those who loved me; and sometimes I rejoiced in the promise of a better hope.

Now at a time when I was swayed by a spirit of sullenness by reason of the envy which I endured from my superiors and equals, I was eager with the aid of my kin to be transferred to other monasteries. For

---

*From *The Autobiography of Guibert, Abbot of Nogent-Sous-Coucy*. Reprinted by permission of Routledge & Kegan Paul, Ltd. Copyright 1925, E. P. Dutton & Co. Pp. 62-71.

some of our brotherhood, seeing me once far below them both in age and learning, in ability and understanding, and afterwards perceiving that I equalled them, or, if I may say so, altogether surpassed them through His gift alone who is the key of all knowledge instilling into my heart a hunger for learning, with such rage did their wrathful wickedness blaze forth against me, that, wearied with everlasting disputes and quarrels, I often regretted I had ever seen or known letters. Certainly my work was so much upset by them and so many brawls started, when occasion arose, about those letters by their constant questions, that they seemed to have this single object in view, to make me change my resolve and to embarrass my understanding. But as, when oil is poured on a fire, it bursts into a livelier flame with that which was supposed to put it out, the more that, like an oven, the capacity of my mind was overtaxed in such labours, the better it became, rendered stronger by its own heat. The questions by which they thought to crush me, gave exceeding keenness to my intelligence, and the difficulty of their objections, through much pondering to find answers and the turning over of various books, begat a strengthening of my wits and ability in debate. And so, although I was thus bitterly hated by them, yet Thou knowest, O Lord, how little, if at all, I hated them, and when they could not, as they wished, put any stigma upon me, they everywhere affirmed in disparagement that I was too proud of my little learning.

Amid these annoyances that I took very hardly, although by difficulties of this sort was begotten abundant good, yet my spirit grew weak, languishing under the endless torture of its thoughts. With fearful heart and failing powers of reason I began to consider what profit there was in hardship and eagerly decided to seek retreat whither my carnal weakness prompted me. When therefore I made my proposal that I should leave the place, not so much with the kindly permission of the Abbott, as at the suggestion and demand of my kinsfolk, the assent of my mother also being given in the belief that I was doing this from pious motives (for the place to which I wished to retire, was considered very holy). . . .

Meantime having steeped my mind unduly in the study of verse-making, so as to put aside for such worthless vanities the serious things of the divine pages, under guidance of my folly I went so far as to read the poems of Ovid and the Bucolics of Virgil and to aim at the airs and graces of a love poem in a critical treatise and in a series of letters. My mind therefore forgetting a proper severity and abandoning the modesty of a monk's calling, was led away by these enticements of a poisonous license, giving weight only to this, whether some courtly phrase could be referred to some poet, with no thought how much the toil which I loved might hurt the aims of our holy profession. By love of it I was doubly taken captive, being snared by the wantonness of the sweet words I found in the poets and those which I poured forth myself and caught by immodest fleshly stirrings through thinking on these things and the like.

For since my unstable mind, unaccustomed now to hard thinking, spent itself on these trifles, no sound could come from my lips, but that which my thought prompted.

Hence it came to pass that, from the boiling over of the madness within me, I fell into certain obscene words and composed brief writings, worthless and immodest, in fact bereft of all decency. . . .

I put no check on that irreverence I had within me, and refrained not from the vain jests of frivolous writers. Hammering out these verses in secret and daring to show them to no one, or at least only to a few like myself, yet I read them out when I could, often inventing an author for them and I was delighted when those which I thought it inconvenient to acknowledge as mine, were praised by those who shared such studies, but whereas their author gained no praise by them, he had to be content with the enjoyment, or rather the shame of making them. But these acts, O Father, in Thine own good time Thou didst punish; for misfortune coming on me for such work, Thou didst fence in my wandering soul with much affliction and hold me down by bodily infirmity. Therefore did a sword pierce through even to my soul, while trouble touched my understanding.

And so, when the punishment of sin had brought understanding to my hearing, then at last the folly of useless study withered away, yet since I could not endure to be idle, and was compelled, as it were, to cast aside vain imaginings, with renewal of my spiritual being I turned to more profitable exercises. I began therefore all too late to pant for that knowledge that so oft had been instilled in me by many good teachers, to busy myself, that is, with commentaries on the Scriptures, frequently to study the works of Gregory, in which are best to be found the keys to that art, and according to the rules of ancient writers to treat the words of the prophets and the Gospels in their allegorical, their moral and even their mystical meaning.

Sir Thomas Bodley
(1544-1613)

In the brief passage below, Sir Thomas describes the pre-Elizabethan period of religious persecution when his family had to flee

England because his father was "knowne and noted to be an enemie to Poperie [and] was so cruelly threatened. . . . " The family went first to Germany and then to Geneva. Thomas was twelve years old. While he does not dwell on his feelings concerning the intellectual fare he was subjected to during this time, it is interesting to note the regimen of his instruction.*

> Where, (as farre as I remember) the English Church consisted of some hundred persons. I was at time of 12 Yeares Age; but through my Fathers cost and care, suffitiently instructed to be Come an Auditor of Chevalerius in Hebrew, of Beroaldus in Greeke, of Calvin and Beza in devinitie; and of some other proffessors in that Universitie (which was newly then erected); besids my domesticall teachers, in the house of Phillibertus Saracenus a famous Phissition in that Cittie, with whome I was boarded: where Robertus Constantinus, that made the Greeke Lexicon, red Homer unto me. Thus I remayned there 2 yeares and more, untill such time as our Nation was advertised of the death of Queene Marie, and succession of Elizabeth, with the change of Religion; which caused my Father to hasten into England: Where he came with my Mother, and with all there Familie, within the first of the Queene, and settled there dwelling in the Citie of London. It was not long after, that I was sent away from thence to the Universitie of Oxon, recommended to the teaching and tuition of Doctor Humpherey, who was shortly after chosen the cheife Reader of divinitie, the President of Magdalen College. Their I followed my studies, till I tooke the degree of Batcheler of Art, which was in the year 1563.

Solomon Maimon
(1753-1800)

Solomon ben Joshua, a Pole who later took the name Maimon in homage to the famous Spanish-Jewish philosopher of the twelfth century, was a contemporary of Goethe but far removed during childhood and adolescence, indeed, from the social and economic advantages of the latter. However, like Goethe, he "burned with desire to acquire more knowledge." By the time he was eleven, he was a rabbi, with a full knowledge, of course, of Hebrew and Yiddish. Whereas Goethe's search for truth led him to a study of these

---

*From *The Life of Sir Thomas Bodley* in *Trecentale Bodleianum*. Reprinted by permission of The Clarendon Press. 1913. Pp. 4-5.

languages, Maimon's search led him to science, and thus a need to learn German and Latin, which he felt would open the doors for him. Goethe had to overcome the prejudices of his father and teacher, Maimon, the whole structure of Judaic life of the times. As a matter of fact, Maimon's life represents a constant conflict between the two streams of culture. He was accepted by neither Christian nor Jew. Although he was befriended by Moses Mendelssohn, accepted by the enlightened Jews of Berlin, and recognized by Kant and others as possessing a keen mind, he ended by being at odds with the respectable members of the community. His search for truth and a place in the world were unsuccessful and he died unfulfilled in both respects.*

By dint of instruction received from my father, but still more by my own industry, I had got on so well, that in my eleventh year I was able to pass as a full rabbi. I possessed besides some disconnected knowledge in history, astronomy, and other mathematical sciences. I burned with desire to acquire more knowledge, but how was this to be accomplished with the want of guidance, of scientific books, and of all other requisites? I was obliged to content myself with making use of any help that chance offered, without plan or method.

In order to gratify my desire of scientific knowledge, the only means available was to learn foreign languages. But how was I to begin? To study Polish or Latin with a Catholic teacher was for me impossible, on the one hand, because the prejudices of my own people prohibited all languages but Hebrew and all sciences but the Talmud and the vast array of its commentators, and on the other hand, because the prejudices of Catholics would not allow them to give instruction in such subjects to a Jew. Moreover, my temporal circumstances were disheartening. I was obliged to support a whole family by teaching, by correcting proofs of the Holy Scriptures, and by other work of a similar nature. For a long time I could only sigh in vain for the satisfaction of my natural inclination.

At last a fortunate accident came to my help. I observed in some stout Hebrew volumes that they contained several alphabets, and that the number of their signatures was indicated not merely by Hebrew letters, but that for this purpose the characters of a second and a third alphabet had also been employed, these being commonly Latin and German. Now I had not the slightest idea of printing. I imagined that

---

*From *An Autobiography* by Solomon Maimon. Reprinted by permission of Schocken Books, Inc. Copyright 1947, Schocken Books. Pp. 34-36.

books were printed like linen, each page being the impression of a separate form. I presumed, however, that the characters which stood in corresponding places must represent one and the same letter, and as I had already heard something of the order of the alphabet in these languages, I supposed that, for example, *a* standing in the same place as *aleph*, must likewise be an *aleph* in sound. In this way I gradually learnt the Latin and German characters.

By a kind of deciphering I began to combine various German letters into words; but as the characters corresponding to the Hebrew letters might be something quite different from the Hebrew, I was always in doubt whether the whole of my labor in this operation might not be in vain, till fortunately some leaves of an old German book fell into my hand. I began to read. How great were my joy and surprise when I saw from the connection, that the words completely corresponded with what I had learned. In my Jewish language, to be sure, many of the words were unintelligible; but from the context I was still able, even omitting such words, to comprehend the whole pretty well.

John Beattie Crozier
(1849-1921)

When John B. Crozier, a minor Canadian philosopher, was sixteen years old and about to graduate from high school in Galt, a Scotch settlement in the far west of Canada, he desperately wanted a university scholarship. But despite his serious resolve to give up all fun and sports in order to prepare himself for the examinations, adolescent ambivalences tended to check his forward progress, as this passage* tells us.

Nevertheless, he won his scholarship, entered the University, stayed for one or two weeks, and then left to return home. He had not yet recovered from the strain of preparing for the examinations. He felt "low and morbid in humour, oppressed with desolate forebodings of ill-health, and with my heart all in a ferment of confused passions and desires," a typical adolescent syndrome.

Crozier's is an expository autobiography, concerned with the effects of hereditary and environmental influences on his life. His purpose in writing it was to trace the development of an intellectual system. As he himself stated, his aim was "to indicate as succinctly and conscientiously as possible the successive stages through which

*From *My Inner Life: Being a Chapter in Personal Evolution and Autobiography.* London: Longmans Green & Co., 1898. Pp. 130-131.

I traveled in my mental evolution, with just sufficient illustration to make its course intelligible to the general reader."

Meanwhile the term of my scholarship was drawing to a close, having but three months to run. I was now head boy in the school, and the next stop would be to prepare to gain a scholarship at the University; but still the master remained severely reticent and gave no indication of what he intended to do with me. I began to feel very anxious and uncomfortable, when one afternoon in the autumn he called me up to him, and asked me if I were willing to prepare for the University Examination of the succeeding year. It was what I had been so long waiting and hoping for, and so overjoyed was I at the new prospect which opened out before me, that like another Hamlet, from that moment I resolved to renounce all fun and mischief, to wipe from my mind all trivial thoughts of play and to let the University Scholarship shine alone in my sky like a fixed constellation. I was now sixteen years of age, and except for the thorough grinding I had had in the rudiments and groundwork of Classics, the entire work of the curriculum was new to me. It was therefore with more than usual energy and determination that I set to work on it, under the personal supervision of the Master. The honour and passwork together, included certain books of Homer, Virgil, Livy, Horace, Cicero, Xenophon, Ovid, Lucian, and Sallust; but what with the radiant fancies and dreams of ambition with which I walked encompassed, and which threatened at times to push from my mind the very means by which they were to be achieved, the work itself; what with the tendency I had to keep chasing all kinds of meteoric fancies; what with the difficulty of keeping my mind steadily down to my work,—what with all this, together with the want of toughness in my mental fibre, and the nervous exhaustion which attended any sustained mental exertion, it was only a series of swoops and sallies, ever leaving the work and ever again returning to it, that I made any progress. Besides, in spite of my renunciation of sport, I was still too young for so heroic a resolve, and lost much of my time at play. But in the interim it too had changed with the silent revolutions of my mind, and was not to me what it had been before. It was now rather as a casual outsider that I took part in the games, than as an active participant; so that whereas formerly play was the ideal world which encompassed the hard and earthy work of the school like a gilded firmament, now it had become a mere relaxation, into which the romance of scholarships and examinations dipped and played, softly fading it in, and lending to it the greater part of its sweetness.

Anne Frank
(1929-1945)

Circumscribed though she was by the confined quarters of the "Secret Annexe" (as she called her family's hiding place from the Nazis in Amsterdam), Anne Frank nevertheless pursued as disciplined a regimen of study as conditions permitted. She was helped in her intellectual needs by sympathetic friends who brought her books from the library. She was "mad on" mythology and for more than a year pursued the subject avidly, despite the banal comments of the adults. Typical of the adolescent mentality is the commingling of serious studies with the need, recapitulated from middle childhood, to collect things—in this instance, pictures of film stars.*

Saturday, 27 March, 1943

Dear Kitty,

We have finished our shorthand course; now we are beginning to practice speed. Aren't we getting clever? I must tell you more about my time-killing subjects (I call them such, because we have got nothing else to do but make the days go by as quickly as possible, so that the end of our time here comes more quickly); I'm mad on Mythology and especially the Gods of Greece and Rome. They think here that it is just a passing craze, they've never heard of an adolescent kid of my age being interested in Mythology. Well, then, I shall be the first!

Thursday, 11 May, 1944

Dear Kitty,

I'm frightfully busy at the moment, and although it sounds mad, I haven't time to get through my pile of work. Shall I tell you briefly what I have got to do? Well, then, by tomorrow I must finish reading the first part of *Galileo Galilei,* as it has to be returned to the library. I only started it yesterday, but I shall manage it.

Next week I have got to read *Palestine at the Crossroads* and the second part of *Galilei.* Next I finished reading the first part of the biography of *The Emperor Charles V* yesterday, and it's essential that I work out all the diagrams and family trees that I have collected from it. After that I have three pages of foreign words gathered from various books, which have all got to be recited, written down, and learned.

---

*From *The Diary of a Young Girl* by Anne Frank. Reprinted by permission of Doubleday & Co., Inc. Copyright 1952, Otto H. Frank. Pp. 66-67, 206.

Number four is that my film stars are all mixed up together and are simply gasping to be tidied up; however, as such a clearance would take several days, and since Professor Anne, as she's already said, is choked with work, the chaos will have to remain a chaos.

Next Theseus, Oedipus, Peleus, Orpheus, Jason, and Hercules are all awaiting their turn to be arranged, as their different deeds lie criss-cross in my mind like fancy threads in a dress; it's also high time Myron and Phidias had some treatment, if they wish to remain at all coherent. Likewise it's the same with the seven and nine years' war; I'm mixing everything up together at this rate. Yes, but what can one do with such a memory! Think how forgetful I shall be when I'm eighty!

Oh, something else, the Bible; how long is it still going to take before I meet the bathing Suzanna? And what do they mean by the guilt of Sodom and Gomorrah? Oh, there is still such a terrible lot to find out and to learn. And in the meantime I've left Lisolette of the Pfalz completely in the lurch.

Kitty, can you see that I'm just about bursting?

DISLIKE FOR SCHOOLING

Saint Augustine
(340-430)

Perhaps the first of the great educational psychologists was not Thorndike but St. Augustine who preceded him by nearly 1600 years. St. Augustine traced the troubles he had in school up to his fifteenth year in terms of motivation, rewards and punishments. He tells why he disliked "Greek learning," and why Latin came so easily. " . . . a free curiosity hath more influence in our learning these things than a necessity full of fear."*

Concerning the hatred of learning, the love of play, and the fear of being whipped noticeable in boys: and of the folly of our elders and masters. O my God! what miseries and mockeries did I then experience, when obedience to my teachers was set before me as proper to my boyhood, that I might flourish in this world, and distinguish myself in the science of speech, which should get me honour amongst men, and deceitful riches! After that I was put to school to get learning of

---

*From *The Confessions of Saint Augustine*. Reprinted by permission of Liveright Publishers. 1942. Pp. 12-19.

which I (worthless as I was) knew not what use there was; and yet, if slow to learn, I was flogged! For this was deemed praiseworthy by our forefathers; and many before us passing the same course, had appointed beforehand for us these troublesome ways by which we were compelled to pass, multiplying labour and sorrow upon the sons of Adam. But we found, O Lord, men praying to Thee, and we learned from them to conceive of Thee, according to our ability, to be some Great One, who was able (though not visible to our senses) to hear and help us. For as a boy I began to pray to Thee, my "help" and my "refuge," and in invoking Thee broke the bands of my tongue, and entreated Thee though little, with no little earnestness, that I might not be beaten at school. And when Thou heardest me not, giving me not over to folly thereby, my elders, yea, and my own parents too, who wished me no ill, laughed at my stripes, my then great and grievous ill.

Is there any one, Lord, with so high a spirit, cleaving to Thee with so strong an affection—for even a kind of obtuseness may do that much —but is there, I say, any one who, by cleaving devoutly to Thee, is endowed with so great a courage that he can esteem lightly those racks and hooks, and varied tortures of the same sort, against which, throughout the whole world, men supplicate Thee with great fear, deriding those who most bitterly fear them, just as our parents derided the torments with which our masters punished us when we were boys? For we were no less afraid of our pains, nor did we pray less to Thee to avoid them; and yet we sinned, in writing, or reading, or reflecting upon our lessons less than was required of us. For we wanted not, O Lord, memory or capacity,—of which, by Thy will, we possessed enough for our age,—but we delighted only in play; and we were punished for this by those who were doing the same thing themselves. But the idleness of our elders they call business, whilst boys who do the like are punished by those same elders, and yet neither boys nor men find any pity. For will any one of good sense approve of my being whipped because, as a boy, I played ball, and so was hindered from learning quickly those lessons by means of which, as a man, I should play more unbecomingly? And did he by whom I was beaten do other than this, who, when he was overcome in any little controversy with a co-tutor, was more tormented by anger and envy than I when beaten by a playfellow in a match at ball?

Through a love of ball-playing and shows, he neglects his studies and the injunctions of his parents. And yet I erred, O Lord God, the Creator and Disposer of all things in Nature,—but of sin the Disposer only,—I erred, O Lord my God, in doing contrary to the wishes of my parents and of those masters; for this learning which they (no matter

for what motive) wished me to acquire, I might have put to good account afterwards. For I disobeyed them not because I had chosen a
better way, but from a fondness for play, loving the honour of victory
in the matches and to have my ears tickled with lying fables, in order
that they might itch the more furiously—the same curiosity beaming
more and more in my eyes for the shows and sports of my elders. Yet
those who give these entertainments are held in such high repute, that
almost all desire the same for their children, whom they are still willing should be beaten, if so be these same games keep them from the
studies by which they desire them to arrive at being the givers of them.
Look down upon these things, O Lord, with compassion, and deliver
us who now call upon Thee; deliver those also who do not call upon
Thee, that they may call upon Thee, and that Thou mayest deliver
them.

*Being compelled, he gave his attention to learning, but fully ac-
knowledges that this was the work of God.* But in this my childhood
(which was far less dreaded for me than youth) I had no love of learning, and hated to be forced to it, yet was I forced to it notwithstanding;
and this was well done towards me, but I did not well, for I would not
have learned had I not been compelled. For no man doth well against
his will, even if that which he doth be well. Neither did they who
forced me do well, but the good that was done to me came from Thee,
my God. For they considered not in what way I should employ what
they forced me to learn, unless to satisfy the inordinate desires of a
rich beggary and a shameful glory. But Thou, by whom the very hairs
of our heads are numbered, didst use for my good the error of all who
pressed me to learn; and my own error in willing not to learn, didst
Thou make use of for my punishment—of which I, being so small a
boy and so great a sinner, was not unworthy. Thus by the instrumen-
tality of those who did not well didst Thou well for me; and by my
own sin didst Thou justly punish me. For it is even as Thou hast appointed, that every inordinate affection should bring its own punishment.

*He delighted in Latin studies, and the empty fables of the poets, but
hated the elements of literature and the Greek language.* But what was
the cause of my dislike of Greek literature, which I studied from my
boyhood, I cannot even now understand. For the Latin I loved exceedingly—not what our first masters, but what the grammarians
teach; for those primary lessons of reading, writing, and ciphering, I
considered no less of a burden and a punishment than Greek. Yet

whence was this unless from the sin and vanity of this life? for I was "but flesh, a wind that passeth away and cometh not again." For those primary lessons were better, assuredly, because more certain; seeing that by their agency I acquired, and still retain, the power of reading what I find written, and writing myself what I will; whilst in the others I was compelled to learn about the wanderings of a certain Aeneas, oblivious of my own, and to weep for Dido dead, because she slew herself for love; while at the same time I brooked with dry eyes my wretched self dying far from Thee, in the midst of those things, O God, my life.

For what can be more wretched than the wretch who pities not himself shedding tears over the death of Dido for love of Aeneas, but shedding no tears over his own death in not loving Thee, O God, light of my heart, and bread of the inner mouth of my soul, and the power that weddest my mind with my innermost thoughts? I did not love Thee, and committed fornications against Thee; and those around me thus sinning cried, "Well done! Well done!" For the friendship of this world is fornication against Thee; and "Well done! Well done!" is cried until one feels ashamed not to be such a man. And for this I shed no tears, though I wept for Dido, who sought death at the sword's point, myself the while seeking the lowest of Thy creatures—having forsaken Thee—earth tending to the earth; and if forbidden to read these things, how grieved would I feel that I was not permitted to read what grieved me. This sort of madness is considered a more honourable and more fruitful learning than that by which I learned to read and write.

But now, O my God, cry unto my soul; and let Thy Truth say unto me, "It is not so, it is not so; better much was that first teaching." For behold, I would rather forget the wanderings of Aeneas, and all such things, than how to write and read. But it is true that over the entrance of the grammar school there hangs a vail; but this is not so much a sign of the majesty of the mystery, as of a covering for error. Let not them exclaim against me of whom I am no longer in fear, whilst I confess to Thee, my God, that which my soul desires, and acquiesce in reprehending my evil ways, that I may love Thy good ways. Neither let those cry out against me who buy or sell grammar-learnings. For if I ask them whether it be true, as the poet says, that Aeneas once came to Carthage, the unlearned will reply that they do not know, the learned will deny it to be true. But if I ask with what letters the name Aeneas is written, all who have learnt this will answer truly, in accordance with the conventional understanding men have arrived at as to these signs. Again, if I should ask which, if forgotten, would cause the greatest inconvenience in our life, reading and writing, or these poetical fictions, who does not see what every one would answer who had not entirely forgotten himself? I erred, then, when as a boy I preferred those vain studies to those more profitable ones, or rather loved the one and hated the other. "One and one are two, two and two are four," this was then in truth a hateful song to me; while the wooden horse full of armed men, and the burning of Troy, and the "spectral image" of Creusa were a most pleasant spectacle of vanity.

Why he despised Greek literature, and easily learned Latin. But why, then, did I dislike Greek learning, which was full of like tales? For Homer also was skilled in inventing similar stories, and is most sweetly vain, yet was he disagreeable to me as a boy. I believe Virgil, indeed, would be the same to Grecian children, if compelled to learn him, as I was Homer. The difficulty, in truth, the difficulty of learning a foreign language mingled as it were with gall all the sweetness of those fabulous Grecian stories. For not a single word of it did I understand, and to make me do so, they vehemently urged me with cruel threatenings and punishments. There was a time also when (as an infant) I knew no Latin; but this I acquired without any fear or tormenting, by merely taking notice, amid the blandishments of my nurses, the jests of those who smiled on me, and the sportiveness of those who toyed with me. I learnt all this, indeed, without being urged by any pressure of punishment, for my own heart urged me to bring forth its own conceptions, which I could not do unless by learning words, not of those who taught me, but of those who talked to me; into whose ears, also, I brought forth whatever I discerned. From this it is sufficiently clear that a free curiosity hath more influence in our learning these things than a necessity full of fear. But this last restrains the overflowings of that freedom, through Thy laws, O God,—Thy laws, from the ferule of the schoolmaster to the trials of the martyr, being effective to mingle for us a salutary bitter, calling us back to Thyself from the pernicious delights which allure us from Thee.

Carlo Goldoni
(1707-1793)

Goldoni, the Italian dramatist, was a reluctant schoolboy. When he learned that Perugia, where his father had brought him to study at a Jesuit school, had no theatre, the twelve-year-old boy remarked, "So much the worse; I would not remain here for all the gold in the world!" But remain he did. What he learned was minimal, enough to earn him the contempt of his classmates and the "Passage Latin," by which he could continue with his education. When an adolescent is consumed with a singular passion, as was Goldoni, anything that interferes with the need tends to suffer.*

My father determined that I should renew my studies; a very proper resolution, which accorded with my own wishes. The Jesuits were then in vogue, and on being proposed to them, I was received without difficulty.

The humanity classes are not regulated here as in France; there are only three, under-grammar, upper-grammar, or humanity properly so-called and rhetoric. Those who employ their time well may finish their course in the space of three years.

At Venice I had gone through the first year of under-grammar, and I might now have entered the upper, but the time which I had lost, the distraction occasioned by travelling, and the new masters under whom I was about to be placed, induced my father to make me recommence my studies; in which he acted very wisely, for you will soon see, my dear reader, how the vanity of the Venetian grammarian, who plumed himself on the composition of a play, was in an instant woefully mortified.

The literary season was well advanced, and I was received in the under class as a scholar properly qualified for the upper. My answers to the questions put to me were incorrect; I hesitated in my translations; and the Latin which I attempted to make was full of barbarisms and solecisms; in short, I became the derision of my companions, who took a pleasure in challenging me; and as every encounter with them ended in my defeat, my father was quite in despair, and I myself was astonished and mortified, and believed myself bewitched.

The time of the holidays drew near, when we had to perform a task, which in Italy is called the "Passage Latin"; for this little labour decides the fate of the scholar, whether he is to rise to a higher class, or continue to remain in the same. The latter alternative was all that I had a right to expect.

The day came: the regent or rector dictated; the scholars wrote down; and every one exerted himself to the utmost. I strained every nerve, and imagined to myself honour and ambition at stake, and the concern of my father and mother; I saw my neighbours bestowing a

---

*From *Memoirs* by Carlo Goldoni. Reprinted by permission of Alfred A. Knopf, Inc. 1926. Pp. 9-10.

side glance at me, and laughing at my endeavours:—*Facit indignatio versum*. Rage and shame spurred me on and inspired me; I read my theme, I felt my head cool, my hand rapid, and my memory fresh; I finished before the rest; I sealed my paper, took it to the regent, and departed very well pleased with myself.

Eight days afterwards the scholars were collected together and called on; the decision of the college was published. The first nomination was, "Goldoni to the upper"; at which a general laugh burst out in the class, and many insulting observations were made. My translation was read aloud, in which there was not a single fault of orthography. The regent called me to the chair; I rose to go; I saw my father at the door, and I ran to embrace him.

The regent wished to speak to me in private; he paid me several compliments, and told me that, notwithstanding the gross mistakes which I committed from time to time in my ordinary lessons, he had suspected that I was possessed of talents, from the favourable specimens he occasionally perceived in my themes and verses; he added that this last essay convinced him that I had purposely concealed my talents, and he alluded jocularly to the tricks of the Venetians.

"You do me too great an honour, reverend father," said I to him: "I assure you I have suffered too much during the last three months to amuse myself at such an expense. I did not counterfeit ignorance; I was in reality what I seemed, and it is a phenomenon which I cannot explain."

The regent exhorted me to continue my application, and as he himself was to pass to the upper class to which I had gained a right of entrance, he assured me of his favour and goodwill.

Henry James
(1843-1916)

The difficulties that beset the adolescent today in his pursuit of mathematical and scientific subjects is reflected in this passage from Henry James' *Autobiography*, wherein he describes a period in his life more than a hundred years ago.* His well-to-do parents had enrolled the twelve-year-old boy in the *Ecole Préparatoire aux Ecoles Spéciales* in Zurich. It was a polytechnic school, run by one

---

*From *Henry James: Autobiography* edited by Frederick W. Dupee. New York: Criterion Books, 1956. Pp. 240-241.

M. Rochette. James says that his parents had left him there "under a flattering misconception of my aptitudes that leaves me to-day even more thunderstruck than at that immediate season of my distress." And distress it was, not to be relieved until after his woebegone failure there prompted his removal to another academy where his older brother, William, was already a student.

I so feared and abhorred mathematics that the simplest arithmetical operation had always found and kept me helpless and blank—the dire discipline of the years bringing no relief whatever to my state; and mathematics unmitigated were at the Institution Rochette the air we breathed, building us up as they most officiously did for those other grim ordeals and pursuits, those of the mining and the civil engineer, those of the architectural aspirant and the technician in still other fields, to which we were supposed to be addressed. Nothing of the sort was indeed supposed of me—which is in particular my present mystification; so that my assault of the preliminaries disclosed, feeble as it strikingly remained, was mere darkness, waste and anguish. I found myself able to bite, as the phrase was, into no subject there deemed savoury; it was hard and bitter fruit all and turned to ashes in my mouth. More extraordinary however than my good parents' belief— eccentric on their part too, in the light of their usual practice and disposition, their habit, for the most part, of liking for us after a gasp or two whatever we seemed to like—was my own failure to protest with a frankness proportioned to my horror. The stiffer intellectual discipline, the discipline of physics and of algebra, invoked for the benefit of an understanding undisputedly weak and shy, had been accepted on my side as a blessing perhaps in disguise. It had come to me by I know not what perversity that if I couldn't tackle the smallest problem in mechanics or face without dismay at the blackboard the simplest geometric challenge I ought somehow in decency to make myself over, oughtn't really to be so inferior to almost every one else. That was the pang, as it was also the marvel—that the meanest minds and the vulgarest types approached these matters without a sign of trepidation even when they approached them, at the worst, without positive appetite. My attempt not therefore to remain abnormal wholly broke down, however, and when I at last withdrew from the scene it was not even as a conspicuous, it was only as an obscure, a deeply hushed failure. I joined William, after what had seemed to me an eternity of woe, at the Academy, where I followed, for too short a time but with a comparative recovery of confidence, such literary *cours* as I might.

William Butler Yeats
(1865-1939)

"The idea that I had come to school to work was too grotesque to cloud my mind for an instant. It was also too obvious a contrast with the facts and the results," wrote G. K. Chesterton about his schooling at St. Paul's. The situation was quite different with William Butler Yeats, the well-known Irish playwright. He learned in school but his nonconformity placed him at a disadvantage. He regretted that his father had not taught him at home, for if he had, he would have been "a properly educated man, and would not have to look in useless longings at books that have been, through the poor mechanism of translation, the builders of my soul, nor face authority with the timidity born of excuse and evasion."*

I was now fifteen; and as he did not want to leave his painting my father told me to go to Harcourt Street and put myself to school. I found a bleak eighteenth-century house, a small playing-field full of mud and pebbles, fenced by an iron railing, and opposite a long hoarding and a squalid, ornamental railway station. Here, as I soon found, nobody gave a thought to decorum. We worked in a din of voices. We began the morning with prayers, but when class began the headmaster, if he was in the humour, would laugh at Church and Clergy. "Let them say what they like," he would say, "but the earth does go round the sun." On the other hand there was no bullying and I had not thought it possible that boys could work so hard. Cricket and football, the collection of moths and butterflies, though not forbidden, were discouraged. They were for idle boys. I did not know, as I used to, the mass of my school-fellows; for we had little life in common outside the class-rooms. I had begun to think of my school work as an interruption of my natural history studies, but even had I never opened a book not in the school course, I could not have learned a quarter of my night's work. I had always done Euclid easily, making the problems out while the other boys were blundering at the blackboard, and it had often carried me from the bottom to the top of my class; but these boys had the same natural gift and instead of being in the fourth or fifth book were in the modern books at the end of the primer; and in place of a dozen lines of Virgil with a dictionary, I was expected to

*From *The Autobiography of William Butler Yeats*. Reprinted by permission of The Macmillan Co. 1953. Pp. 34-35.

learn with the help of a crib a hundred and fifty lines. The other boys
were able to learn the translation off, and to remember what words of
Latin and English corresponded with one another, but I, who it may
be had tried to find out what happened in the part we had not read,
made ridiculous mistakes; and what could I, who never worked when
I was not interested, do with a history lesson that was but a column
of seventy dates? I was worst of all at literature, for we read Shakespeare for his grammar exclusively.

One day I had a lucky thought. A great many lessons were run
through in the last hour of the day, things we had learnt or should have
learnt by heart over-night, and not having known one of them for
weeks, I cut off that hour without anybody's leave. I asked the mathematical master to give me a sum to work and nobody said a word.
My father often interfered, and always with disaster, to teach me my
Latin lesson. "But I have also my geography," I would say. "Geography," he would reply, "should never be taught. It is not a training for
the mind. You will pick up all that you need, in your general reading."
And if it was a history lesson, he would say just the same, and "Euclid,"
he would say, "is too easy. It comes naturally to the literary imagination. The old idea, that it is a good training for the mind, was long ago
refuted." I would know my Latin lesson so that it was a nine days'
wonder, and for weeks after would be told it was scandalous to be so
clever and so idle. No one knew that I had learnt it in the terror that
alone could check my wandering mind. I must have told on him at
some time or other for I remember the head-master saying, "I am going
to give you an imposition because I cannot get at your father to give
him one." Sometimes we had essays to write; and though I never got
a prize, for the essays were judged by handwriting and spelling, I
caused a measure of scandal. I would be called up before some master
and asked if I really believed such things, and that would make me
angry for I had written what I had believed all my life, what my father
had told me, or a memory of the conversation of his friends. I was
asked to write an essay on "Men may rise on stepping-stones of their
dead selves to higher things." My father read the subject to my mother
who had no interest in such matters. "That is the way," he said, "boys
are made insincere and false to themselves. Ideals make the blood
thin, and take the human nature out of people." He walked up and
down the room in eloquent indignation, and told me not to write on
such a subject at all, but upon Shakespeare's lines, "To thine own self
be true, and it must follow as the night the day thou canst not then be
false to any man." At another time, he would denounce the idea of
duty; "imagine," he would say, "how the right sort of woman would

despise a dutiful husband"; and he would tell us how much my mother would scorn such a thing. Maybe there were people among whom such ideas were natural, but they were the people with whom one does not dine. All he said was, I now believe, right but he should have taken me away from school. He would have taught me nothing but Greek and Latin, and I would now be a properly educated man, and would not have to look in useless longings at books that have been, through the poor mechanism of translation, the builders of my soul, nor face authority with the timidity born of excuse and evasion. Evasion and excuse were in the event as wise as the house-building instinct of the beaver.

INTELLECTUAL FERMENT

Eliza Southgate Bowne
(1783-1809)

In this letter to Moses Porter,* a favorite cousin who died in young manhood from a fever caught in boarding an infected vessel in the transaction of some business, Eliza Bowne attempted an intellectual exercise: the vindication of her sex. If she had lived her full share of days, she probably would have been in the forefront of the suffragette movement. But like Marie Bashkirtseff, Eliza died at the age of twenty-five of a "pulmonary disorder"—probably tuberculosis. She was born in Scarborough, Maine, the third in a family of twelve children. Her father was a physician as well as a Judge of the Common Court of Pleas.

Scarborough, June 1st, 1801

As to the qualities of mind peculiar to each sex, I agree with you that sprightliness is in favor of females and profundity of males. Their education, their pursuits would create such a quality even tho' nature had not implanted it. The business and pursuits of men require deep thinking, judgment, and moderation, while, on the other hand, females are under no necessity of dipping deep, but merely "skim the surface," and we too commonly spare ourselves the exertion which deep researches require, unless they are absolutely necessary to our pursuits in life. We rarely find one giving themselves up to profound

---

*From *A Girl's Life Eighty Years Ago* by Eliza Southgate Bowne. New York: Charles Scribner's Sons, 1887. Pp. 58-63.

investigation for amusement merely. Necessity is the nurse of all the great qualities of the mind; it explores all the hidden treasures and by its stimulating power they are "polished into brightness." Women who have no such incentives to action suffer all the strong energetic qualities of the mind to sleep in obscurity; sometimes a ray of genius gleams through the thick clouds with which it is enveloped, and irradiates for a moment the darkness of mental night; yet, like a comet that shoots wildly from its sphere, it excites our wonder, and we place it among the phenomenons of nature, without searching for a natural cause. Thus it is the qualities with which nature has endowed us, as a support amid the misfortunes of life and a shield from the allurements of vice, are left to moulder in ruin. In this dormant state they become enervated and impaired, and at last die for *want of exercise.* The little airy qualities which produce sprightliness are left to flutter about like feathers in the wind, the sport of every breeze.

Women have more fancy, more lively imaginations than men. That is easily accounted for: a person of correct judgment and accurate discernment will never have that flow of ideas which one of a different character might,—every object has not the power to introduce into his mind such a variety of ideas, he rejects all but those closely connected with it. On the other hand, a person of small discernment will receive every idea that arises in the mind, making no distinction between those nearly related and those more distant, they are all equally welcome, and consequently such a mind abounds with fanciful, out-of-the-way ideas. Women have more imagination, more sprightliness, because they have less discernment. I never was of opinion that the pursuits of the sexes ought to be the same; on the contrary, I believe it would be destructive to happiness, there would a degree of rivalry exist, incompatible with the harmony we wish to establish. I have ever thought it necessary that each should have a separate sphere of action,—in such a case there could be no clashing unless one or the other should leap their respective bounds. Yet to cultivate the qualities with which we are endowed can never be called infringing the prerogatives of man. Why, my dear Cousin, were we furnished with such powers, unless the improvement of them would conduce to the happiness of society? Do you suppose the mind of woman the only work of God that was "made in vain." The cultivation of the powers we possess, I have ever thought a privilege (or I may say duty) that belonged to the human species, and not man's exclusive prerogative. Far from destroying the harmony that ought to subsist, it would fix it on a foundation that would not totter at every jar. Women would be under the same degree of subordination that they now are; enlighten and expand their minds, and they would perceive the necessity of such a regulation to preserve the order and happiness of society. Yet you require that their conduct should be always guided by that reason which you refuse them the power of exercising. I know it is generally thought that in such a case women would assume the right of commanding. But I see no foundation for such a supposition,—nor a blind submission to the will of another which neither honor nor reason dictates. It would be criminal in such a case to submit, for we are under a prior engagement to conduct in all things according to the dictates of reason. I had rather be the meanest reptile that creeps the earth, or cast upon the wide world to suffer all the ills "that flesh is heir to," than live a slave to the despotic will of another.

I am aware of the censure that will ever await the female that attempts the vindication of her sex, yet I dare to brave that censure that I know to be undeserved. It does not follow (O what a pen!) that every female who vindicates the capacity of the sex is a disciple of Mary Wolstoncraft. Though I allow her to have said many things which I cannot but approve, yet the very foundation on which she builds her work will be apt to prejudice us so against her that we will not allow her the merit she really deserves,—yet, prejudice set aside, I confess I admire many of her sentiments, notwithstanding I believe should any one adopt her principles, they would conduct in the same manner, and upon the whole her life is the best comment on her writings. Her style is nervous and commanding, her sentiments appear to carry conviction along with them, but they will not bear analyzing. I wish to say something on your *natural refinement,* but I shall only have room to touch upon it if I begin, "therefore I'll leave it till another time."

Last evening, Mr. Samuel Thatcher spent with us; we had a fine "dish of conversation" served up with great taste, fine sentiments dressed with elegant language and seasoned with wit. He is really excellent company—a little enthusiastic or so—but that is no matter. In compassion I entreat you to come over here soon and make me some pens. I have got one that I have been whittling this hour and at last have got it to make a stroke (it liked to have given me the lie). I believe I must give up all pretension to *profundity,* for I am much more at home in my female character. This argumentative style is not congenial to my taste. I hate anything that requires order or connection. I never could do anything by rule,—when I get a subject I am incapable of reasoning upon, I play with it as with a rattle, for what else should I do with it? But I have kept along quite in a direct line; I caught myself "upon the wing" two or three times, but I had power to check my nonsense. I send you my sentiments on this subject as they really exist with me. I believe they are not the mere impulse of the moment, but founded on what I think truth. I could not help laughing at that part of your letter where you said the seal of my letter deprived you of some of the most interesting part of it. I declare positively I left a blank place on purpose for it, that you might not lose one precious word, and now you have the impudence to tell me that the most interesting part was the blank paper. It has provoked my ire to such a degree that I positively declare I never will send you any more blank paper than I possibly can avoid, to "spite you."

E. S.

John Stuart Mill
(1806-1873)

James Mill, father of John Stuart, refused to subject his son to what he felt was the corrupting influence of school and so taught the boy himself until his fourteenth year. The passage from Mill's *Autobiography* which follows* describes the method James Mill used in the rigid education he gave his son. (The substance of it is told, in part, in the chapter on "The Compulsion to Read.") This method had grave faults, as Mill indicates, as well as superb results. Among the latter was the intellectual stimulation and ferment to which the boy was subjected. For example, soon after Mill's trip to France, he read a history of the French revolution. "I learnt with astonishment, that the principles of democracy, then apparently in so insignificant and hopeless a minority everywhere in Europe, had borne all before them in France thirty years earlier, and had been the creed of the nation. . . . From this time, as was natural, the subject took an immense hold on my feelings. It allied itself with all my juvenile aspirations to the character of a democratic champion. What had happened so lately, seemed as if it might easily happen again: and the most transcendent glory I was capable of conceiving, was that of figuring, successful or unsuccessful, as a Girondist in an English Convention."

When I was about fourteen I left England for more than a year; and after my return, though my studies went on under my father's general direction, he was no longer my schoolmaster. I shall therefore pause here, and turn back to matters of a more general nature connected

---

*Reprinted by permission of The Liberal Arts Press, Inc. 1957. Pp. 21-25.

with the part of my life and education included in the preceding reminiscences.

In the course of instruction which I have partially retraced, the point most superficially apparent is the great effort to give, during the years of childhood, an amount of knowledge in what are considered the higher branches of education, which is seldom acquired (if acquired at all) until the age of manhood. The result of the experiment shows the ease with which this may be done, and places in a strong light the wretched waste of so many precious years as are spent in acquiring the modicum of Latin and Greek commonly taught to schoolboys; a waste, which has led so many educational reformers to entertain the ill-judged proposal of discarding these languages altogether from general education. If I had been by nature extremely quick of apprehension, or had possessed a very accurate and retentive memory, or were of a remarkably active and energetic character, the trial would not be conclusive; but in all these natural gifts I am rather below than above par; what I could do, could assuredly be done by any boy or girl of average capacity and healthy physical constitution: and if I have accomplished anything, I owe it, among other fortunate circumstances, to the fact that through the early training bestowed on me by my father, I started, I may fairly say, with an advantage of a quarter of a century over my contemporaries.

There was one cardinal point in this training, of which I have already given some indication, and which, more than anything else, was the cause of whatever good it effected. Most boys or youths who have had much knowledge drilled into them, have their mental capacities not strengthened, but overlaid by it. They are crammed with mere facts, and with the opinions or phrases of other people, and these are accepted as a substitute for the power to form opinions of their own: and thus the sons of eminent fathers, who have spared no pains in their education, so often grow up mere parroters of what they have learnt, incapable of using their minds except in the furrows traced for them. Mine, however, was not an education of cram. My father never permitted anything which I learnt to degenerate into a mere exercise of memory. He strove to make the understanding not only go along with every step of the teaching, but, if possible, precede it. Anything which could be found out by thinking I never was told, until I had exhausted my efforts to find it out for myself. As far as I can trust my remembrance, I acquitted myself very lamely in this department; my recollection of such matters is almost wholly of failures, hardly ever of success. It is true the failures were often in things in which success in so early a stage of my progress, was almost impossible. I remember at some time in my thirteenth year, on my happening to use the word idea, he asked me what an idea was; and expressed some displeasure at my ineffectual efforts to define the word: I recollect also his indignation at my using the common expression that something was true in theory but required correction in practice; and how, after making me vainly strive to define the word theory, he explained its meaning, and showed the fallacy of the vulgar form of speech which I had used; leaving me fully persuaded that in being unable to give a correct definition of Theory, and in speaking of it as something which might be at variance with practice, I had shown unparalleled ignorance. In this he seems, and perhaps, was, very unreasonable; but I think, only in being angry at my failure. A pupil from whom nothing is ever demanded which he cannot do, never does all he can.

One of the evils most liable to attend on any sort of early proficiency, and which often fatally blights its promise, my father most anxiously guarded against. This was self-conceit. He kept me, with extreme vigilance, out of the way of hearing myself praised, or of being led to make self-flattering comparisons between myself and others. From his own intercourse with me I could derive none but a very humble opinion of myself; and the standard of comparison he always held up to me, was not what other people did, but what a man could and ought to do. He completely succeeded in preserving me from the sort of influences he so much dreaded. I was not at all aware that my attainments were anything unusual at my age. If I accidentally had my attention drawn to the fact that some other boy knew less than myself—which happened less often than might be imagined—I concluded, not that I knew much, but that he, for some reason or other, knew little, or that his knowledge was of a different kind from mine. My state of mind was not humility, but neither was it arrogance. I never thought of saying to myself, I am, or I can do, so and so. I neither estimated myself highly nor lowly: I did not estimate myself at all. If I thought anything about myself, it was that I was rather backward in my studies, since I always found myself so, in comparison with what my father expected from me. I assert this with confidence, though it was not the impression of various persons who saw me in my childhood. They, as I have since found, thought me greatly and disagreeably self-conceited; probably because I was disputatious, and did not scruple to give direct contradictions to things which I heard said. I suppose I acquired this bad habit from having been encouraged in an unusual degree to talk on matters beyond my age, and with grown persons, while I never had inculcated in me the usual respect for them. My father did not correct this ill-breeding and impertinence, probably from not being aware of it, for I was always too much in awe of him to be otherwise than extremely subdued and quiet in his presence. Yet with all this I had no notion of any superiority in myself; and well was it for me that I had not. I remember the very place in Hyde Park where, in my fourteenth year, on the eve of leaving my father's house for a long absence, he told me that I should find, as I got acquainted with new people, that I had been taught many things which youths of my age did not commonly know; and that many persons would be disposed to talk to me of this, and to compliment me upon it. What other things he said on this topic I remember very imperfectly; but he wound up by saying, that whatever I knew more than others, could not be ascribed to any merit in me, but to the very unusual advantage which had fallen to my lot, of having a father who was able to teach me, and willing to give the necessary trouble and time; that it was no matter of praise to me, if I knew more than those who had not had a similar advantage, but the deepest disgrace to me if I did not. I have a distinct remembrance, that the suggestion thus for the first time made to me, that I knew more than other youths who were considered well educated, was to me a piece of information, to which, as to all other things which my father told me, I gave implicit credence, but which did not at all impress me as a personal matter. I felt no disposition to glorify myself upon the circumstance that there were other persons who did not know what I knew; nor had I ever flattered myself that my acquirements, whatever they might be, were any merit of mine: but, now when my attention was called to the subject, I felt that what my father had said respecting my peculiar advantages was exactly the truth and common sense of the matter, and it fixed my opinion and feeling from that time forward.

It is evident that this, among many other of the purposes of my father's scheme of education, could not have been accomplished if he had not carefully kept me from having any great amount of intercourse with other boys. He was earnestly bent upon my escaping not only the ordinary corrupting influence which boys exercise over boys, but the contagion of vulgar modes of thought and feeling; and for this he was willing that I should pay the price of inferiority in the accomplishments which schoolboys in all countries chiefly cultivate. The deficiencies in my education were principally in the things which boys learn from being turned out to shift for themselves, and from being brought together in large numbers. From temperance and much walking, I grew up healthy and hardy, thought not muscular; but I could do no feats of skill or physical strength, and knew none of the ordinary bodily exercises. It was not that play, or time for it, was refused me. Though no holidays were allowed, lest the habit of work should be broken, and a taste for idleness acquired, I had ample leisure in every day to amuse myself; but as I had no boy companions, and the animal need of physical activity was satisfied by walking, my amusements, which were mostly solitary, were in general of a quiet, if not a bookish turn, and gave little stimulus to any other kind even of mental activity than that which was already called forth by my studies: I consequently remained long, and in a less degree have always remained, inexpert in anything requiring manual dexterity; my mind as well as my hands, did its work very lamely when it was applied, or ought to have been applied, to the practical details which, as they are the chief interest of life to the majority of men, are also the things in which whatever mental capacity they have, chiefly shows itself: I was constantly meriting reproof by inattention, inobservance, and general slackness of mind in matters of daily life. My father was the extreme opposite in these particulars: his senses and mental faculties were always on the alert; he carried decision and energy of character in his whole manner and into every action of life: and this, as much as his talents, contributed to the strong impression which he always made upon those with whom he came into personal contact. But the children of energetic parents, frequently grow up unenergetic, because they lean on their parents, and the parents are energetic for them. The education which my father gave me, was in itself much more fitted for training me to *know* than to *do*. Not that he was unaware of my deficiencies; both as a boy and as a youth I was incessantly smarting under his severe admonitions on the subject. There was anything but insensibility or tolerance on his part towards such shortcomings: but, while he saved me from the demoralizing effects of school life, he made no effort to provide me with any sufficient substitute for its practicalizing influences. Whatever qualities he himself, probably, had acquired without difficulty or special training, he seems to have supposed that I ought to acquire as easily. He had not, I think, bestowed the same amount of thought and attention on this, as on most other branches of education; and here, as well as in some other points of my tuition, he seems to have expected effects without causes.

Fyodor Dostoevsky
(1821-1881)

Freud described Dostoevsky as distinguished by four facets of a rich personality: the creative artist, the neurotic, the moralist and the sinner. Dostoevsky had a great need for love and an enormous capacity for love, as the following two letters* to his brother Michael show. Yet in his writings, Dostoevsky singled out from all others violent, murderous and egoistic characters, and so indicated like qualities in himself.

Some of these destructive tendencies are shown in these highly intellectual, self-pitying letters. The first one begins with explanations of why Dostoevsky had not written to his brother for so long: he had not had a kopeck to his name. He was sixteen years old at the time and felt that "our world has become one immense Negative, and that everything noble, beautiful, and divine, has turned itself into a satire." In the second letter, he discourses on Nature, the soul, love and God, which "one recognizes through the heart and not through reason." He tried to develop a logical and systematic rationale for poetry and philosophy, and when he completed his argument, stated, in typical adolescent fashion, "I have jabbered enough," and then proceeded to wallow in miserable self-pity.

Petersburg, August 9, 1838

It is true that I am idle—very idle. But what will become of me, if everlasting idleness is to be my only attitude towards life? I don't know if my gloomy mood will ever leave me. And to think that such a state of mind is allotted to man alone—the atmosphere of his soul seems compounded of a mixture of the heavenly and the earthly. What an unnatural product, then, is he, since the law of spiritual nature is in him violated. . . . This earth seems to me a purgatory for divine spirits who have been assailed by sinful thoughts. I feel that our world has become one immense Negative, and that everything noble, beautiful, and divine, has turned itself into a satire. If in this picture there occurs an individual who neither in idea nor effect harmonizes with the whole—who is, in a word, an entirely unrelated figure—what must happen to the picture? It is destroyed, and can no longer endure.

Yet how terrible it is to perceive only the coarse veil under which the All doth languish! To know that one single effort of the will would suffice to demolish that veil and become one with eternity—to know all this, and still live on like the last and least of creatures. . . . How terrible! How petty is man! Hamlet! Hamlet! When I think of his

---

*From *Letters of Fyodor Michailovitch Dostoevsky to His Family and Friends* translated by Ethel Coburn Mayne. Reprinted by permission of Chatto & Windus, Ltd. (n.d.) Macmillan Co. Pp. 3-9.

moving wild speech, in which resounds the groaning of the whole numbed universe, there breaks from *my* soul not one reproach, not one sigh. . . . That soul is then so utterly oppressed by woe that it fears to grasp the woe entire, lest so it lacerate itself. Pascal once said: He who protests against philosophy is himself a philosopher. A poor sort of system!

But I have talked enough nonsense. Of your letters I have had only two, besides the last of all. Now, brother, you complain of your poverty. I am not rich either. But you will hardly believe that when we broke up camp I had not a kopeck. On the way I caught cold (it rained the whole day and we had no shelter), was sick with hunger as well, and had no money to moisten my throat with so much as a sip of tea. I got well in time, but I had suffered the direst need in camp, till at last the money came from Papa. I paid my debts, and spent the rest.

However, it is time to speak of other things. You plume yourself on the number of books you have read. . . . But don't please imagine that I envy you that. At Peterhof I read at least as many as you have. The whole of Hoffman in Russian and German (that is, "Kater Murr," which hasn't yet been translated), and nearly all Balzac. (Balzac is great! His characters are the creations of an all-embracing intelligence. Not the spirit of the age, but whole millenniums, with all their strivings, have worked towards such development and liberation in the soul of man.) Besides all these, I read Goethe's "Faust" and his shorter poems, Polevois' History, "Ugolino" and "Undine" (I'll write at length about "Ugolino" some other time), and finally, Victor Hugo, except "Cromwell" and "Hernani." Farewell. Write to me, please, as often as you possibly can, for your letters are a joy and solace. Answer *this* at once. I shall expect your reply in twelve days at the very latest. Do write, that I may not utterly languish.

Thy brother,

F. Dostoevsky

I have a new plan: to go mad. That's the way: for people to lose their heads, and then be cured and brought back to reason! If you've read all Hoffmann, you'll surely remember Alban. How do you like him? It is terrible to watch a man who has the Incomprehensible within his grasp, does not know what to do with it, and sits playing with a toy called God!

Petersburg, October 31, 1838

How long since I've written to you, dear brother! That hateful examination—it prevented me from writing to you and Papa, and from looking up I. N. Schidlovsky. And what came of it all? I have not yet been promoted. O horror! to live another whole year in this misery! I should not have been so furious did I not know that I am the victim of the sheerest baseness. The failure would not have worried me so very much, if our poor father's tears had not burned into my soul. I had not hitherto known the sensation of wounded vanity. If such a feeling had got hold of me, I might well have blushed for myself. . . . But now you must know that I should like to crush the whole world at one blow. . . . I lost so much time before the examination, and was ill and miserable besides; but *underwent* it in the fullest and most literal sense of the word, and yet have failed. . . . It is the decree of the Professor of Algebra, to whom, in the course of the year, I had been somewhat cheeky, and who was base enough to remind me of it to-day, while ostensibly explaining to me the reason for my failure. Out of ten full marks I got an average of nine and a half, and yet I'm left. . . . But hang it all, if I must suffer, I will. . . . I'll waste no more paper on this topic, for I so seldom have an opportunity to talk with you.

My friend, you philosophize like a poet. And just because the soul cannot be for ever in a state of exaltation, your philosophy is not true and not just. To *know* more, one must *feel* less, and *vice versa*. Your judgment is feather-headed—it is a delirium of the heart. What do you mean precisely by the word *know?* Nature, the soul, love, and God, one recognizes through the heart, and not through the reason. Were we spirits, we could dwell in that region of ideas over which our souls hover, seeking the solution. But we are earth-born beings, and can only guess at the Idea—not grasp it by all sides at once. The guide for our intelligences through the temporary illusion into the inner-most centre of the soul is called *Reason.* Now, Reason is a material capacity, while the soul or spirit lives on the thoughts which are whispered by the heart. Thought is born in the soul. Reason is a tool, a machine, which is driven by the spiritual fire. When human reason (which would demand a chapter for itself) penetrates into the domain of knowledge, it works independently of the *feeling,* and consequently of the *heart.* But when our aim is the understanding of love or of nature, we march towards the very citadel of the heart. I don't want to vex you, but I do want to say that I don't share your views on poetry or philosophy. Philosophy cannot be regarded as a mere equation where nature is the unknown quantity! Remark that the poet, in the moment of inspiration, comprehends God, and consequently does the philosopher's work. Consequently poetic inspiration is nothing less than philosophical inspiration. Consequently philosophy is nothing but poetry, a higher degree of poetry! It is odd that you reason quite in the sense of our contemporary philosophy. What a lot of crazy systems have been born of late in the cleverest and most ardent brains! To get a right result from this motley troop one would have to subject them all to a mathematical formula. And yet they are the "laws" of our contemporary philosophy! I have jabbered enough. And if I look upon your flabby system as impossible, I think it quite likely that my objections are no less flabby, so I won't bother you with any more of them.

Brother, it is so sad to live without hope! When I look forward I shudder at the future. I move in a cold arctic atmosphere, wherein no sunlight ever pierces. For a long time I have not had a single outbreak of inspiration. . . . Hence I feel as the Prisoner of Chillon felt after his brother's death. The Paradise-bird of poetry will never, never visit me again—never again warm my frozen soul. You say that I am reserved; but all my former dreams have long since forsaken me, and from those glorious arabesques that I once could fashion all the gilding has disappeared. The thoughts that used to kindle my soul and heart have lost their glow and ardency; or else my heart is numbed, or else. . . . I am afraid to go on with that sentence. I won't admit that all the past was a dream, a bright golden dream.

Brother, I have read your poem. It urged some tears from my soul, and lulled it for a while by the spell of memories. You say that you have an idea for a drama. I am glad of that. Write your drama, then. If you had not these last crumbs from the Elysian feast, what would be left you in life? I am so sorry that these last few weeks I have not been able to look up Ivan Nikolayevitch (Schidlovsky); I was ill. Now listen. I think that the poet's inspiration is increased by success. Byron was an egoist; *his* longing for fame was petty. But the mere thought that through one's inspiration there will one day lift itself from the dust to heaven's heights some noble, beautiful human soul; the thought that those lines over which one has wept are consecrated as by a heavenly rite through one's inspiration, and that over them the coming generations will weep in echo . . . that thought, I am convinced, has come to many a poet in the very moment of his highest creative rapture. But the shouting of the mob is empty and vain. There occur to me those lines of Pushkin, where he describes the mob and the poet:

> "So let the foolish crowd, thy work despising, scream,
> And spit upon the shrine where burns thy fire supreme,
> Let them in childish arrogance thy tripod set a-tremble. . . . "

Wonderful, isn't it? Farewell.

Your friend and brother,
F. Dostoevsky

By the way, do tell me what is the leading idea in Châteaubriand's work, "Génie du Christianisme." I read lately in *Ssyn Otetschestva* an attack by the critic Nisard on Victor Hugo. How little the French esteem him! How low does Nisard rate his dramas and romances! They are unfair to him; and Nisard (though he is so intelligent) talks nonsense. Tell me, too, the leading motive of your drama; I am sure it is fine.

I pity our poor father! He has such a remarkable character. What trouble he has had. It is so bitter that I can do nothing to console him! But, do you know, Papa is wholly a stranger in the world. He has lived in it now for fifty years, and yet he has the same opinions of mankind that he had thirty years ago. What sublime innocence! Yet the world has disappointed him, and I believe that that is the destiny of us all. Farewell.

Marie Bashkirtseff
(1860-1884)

These two entries from Marie Bashkirtseff's diary, the first when she was sixteen years old, the second when she was eighteen, reveal, among other things, the process of intellectualization through repression of the sexual impulses.* Marie reports the arrival of an attractive male guest to her home; she greets him and then immediately excuses herself. On her return she is dressed in an exotic, diaphanous gown with a revealing, open bodice, which she takes great care to describe. Marie then goes on—from an exhibition of her body—to an exhibition of her mind, discussing knowingly all subjects so that the company cries out that she is wonderful, that there is nothing about which she cannot talk, no subject of conversation in which she does not find herself at home. In this way, Marie attempted to sublimate her repressed exhibitionistic tendencies. Similarly, the second entry, which shows her desire to see, to hear and to learn everything, may exemplify sublimations of her repressed sexual curiosity.

Wednesday, August 23rd, 1876

My father was waiting for us under the colonnade, and viewed us with a look of contentment.

---

*From *Journal* by Marie Bashkirtseff. Translated by A. D. Hall. Chicago: Rand McNally, 1889.

"Well, did I deceive you? Do I look bad in a riding habit? Ask Pacha how I ride. Do I look well?"

"Yes—humph—very well, really."

And he looked at me with evident satisfaction.

I am far from regretting that I brought thirty gowns; my father must be captured through his vanity.

At this moment, M— arrived with a bag and a servant. When he had saluted me, I answered the usual compliments, and went to change my dress, saying: "I shall be back soon." I returned dressed in a gown of Oriental gauze with two yards of train, a corsage of silk open before in the Louis XV style and fastened by a large knot of white ribbon. The skirt is all of one piece and the train square.

M— spoke of my toilet and admired it.

He is said to be stupid, but he conversed on several subjects—music, art, and science. It is a fact, however, that it was I who did the talking and he only said: "You are perfectly right; it is true."

I was silent as to my studies, fearing to alarm him. But I forgot myself at dinner; I quoted a Latin verse and discoursed with the doctor on classical literature and the modern imitations of it.

They cried out that I was astonishing, and there was nothing in the world of which I could not speak, no subject of conversation where I was not at my ease.

Papa made heroic efforts to conceal his pride in me. Then, a chicken with truffles started a culinary discussion, in which I showed a gastronomic knowledge which made M—'s eyes and mouth open still more.

And then, passing to *sophistication,* I explained all the utility of good cooking, maintaining it made men virtuous.

Wednesday, September 4th, 1878

Kant pretends that things exist only through our own imagination. That is going too far; but I admit his system in the domain of sentiment. In fact, our sentiments are produced by the impression made upon us by persons or things; and since Kant says that objects are not such, or such, that in a word they have no objective value, and no reality, except in our mind, why— But to follow out this line of thought, I ought not to be in a hurry to go to bed, nor to have to think of the hour I must commence drawing to finish for Saturday.

Ordinarily, imagination is considered to be something different from what I think it; people use the word imagination to express folly and stupidity; but can love exist otherwise than in the imagination? It is thus with all other sentiments. This philosophical scaffold-

ing is certainly admirable, but a simple woman like me can demonstrate its falsity.

Things have a reality only in our mind! Well, and I—I say to you
that the object strikes the sight, and sound the hearing, and that these
(let us say *things*) determine everything—otherwise nothing would
need to exist, we would *invent* everything. If, in this world nothing
exists, where then, does anything exist? For, to affirm that nothing
exists, we must have knowledge of the real existence of something or
other, no matter where, were it only to demonstrate the difference
between objective and imaginary values. Indeed—inhabitants of another planet, perhaps, see otherwise than we do, and in that case we
are right; but we are on the earth, let us remain on it, and study what
is above or under, and that is quite enough.

I become enthusiastic for these learned, patient, extraordinary,
tremendous follies—these reasonings, these deductions, so concise, so
learned. There is but one thing which grieves me, and that is, I feel
them to be false, and I have not the time nor the inclination to find out
why.

I should like to converse about it with someone. I am all alone; but
I assure you that what I advance is not intended to impose on people.
I candidly give my ideas and I would willingly accept all the good
arguments that anyone else could make.

I long, without making myself ridiculous by too much pretension
—I long to listen to the discourse of learned men. I want so much, so
much, to penetrate into the learned world; to see, to hear, to learn—
but I know not to whom, nor how to ask it, and I remain here stupid,
amazed, not knowing what direction to take, and catching glimpses on
all sides of treasures of interest—histories, languages, science, all the
world, in fact. I want to see all together and to know all, to learn all!

Helen Thomas Flexner
(1871-1956)

The ardent idealism of the adolescent is reflected in this passage
written by a member of one of the outstanding Quaker families in
the United States.* Helen Thomas' father was a physician and
preacher; her sister, Carey, was Dean of Bryn Mawr College; her
renowned aunt was Hannah Pearsall Smith; her husband was Dr.
Simon Flexner.

---

*From *A Quaker Childhood* by Helen T. Flexner. Reprinted by permission of Yale
University Press. 1940. Pp. 260-264.

Helen's intellectual need to know American history as it related to her own sense of pride and shame, her identification with her father and with George Fox, and her discontent with the haphazard information she gleaned, as well as her desire for more knowledge, are typical manifestations of the adolescent.

During this holiday I was preparing a paper for my history teacher on the rise of democracy in Rome, an *original* paper to be put together from big standard histories. With much trepidation I had made my first visit to the Peabody Library to hunt out my authorities. Mounting the wide stone steps all alone, consulting the catalogue, handing in my slip to the young men behind the desk, taking my seat at a corner table and waiting for my books to be brought—every incident of the adventure had terrified me, in spite of Miss Harrison's careful instructions; and when the books came I had been too much excited to understand what I read. But on my second visit I settled down quickly to work with the agreeable ease of an initiate and was soon absorbed in the struggle between the common people of Rome and the senators. On the side of the Tribunes of the People from the first, I adored the Gracchi who remained for years my favorite heroes.

Up to this time I had taken little interest in the past. A year of English history at Miss Bond's school had, it is true, left in my mind certain picturesque figures like King Alfred, the Black Prince, Henry VIII, and Mary, Queen of Scots. In American history I had not had, and as it turned out was never to have, a particle of instruction. I knew of course the most famous stories about our national heroes and had picked up a few general facts, but my ignorance and my lack of curiosity about my own country were appalling and had already brought disgrace down on my head.

During Yearly Meeting the autumn before, I had been assigned to guide a visiting English Friend down our street to Cousin Francis King's house. As I walked along beside him in silence I felt very proud of companioning such a tall, handsome man, a distinguished stranger. But, alas, the street sign on a lamppost we were passing caught his eye!

"Why do Americans honor Madison so greatly?" he asked me, gazing at the sign. "In every town I have visited there is an avenue or a public square named after Madison. What did he do to become such a hero?"

He smiled down at me, waiting for my answer.

With burning cheeks I gazed up at my Englishman. The pause

seemed hours long before I managed to stammer out the information that Madison was a very great man in American history.

Though my companion did not insist, though he dropped the subject at once, I remembered the walk with horror. How could I have lived all my life on a street named after Madison and know absolutely nothing about him? The surprised face of that Englishman had a trick of flashing up in my mind to make my cheeks burn.

Not for worlds would I have mentioned my disgrace to anyone, least of all to my father, but by questioning him discreetly I learned that Madison had been the fourth President of the United States. This discovery did little to comfort me.

What general knowledge I possessed I had picked up from my father. He liked to read out to us Burke's speeches in defense of the American colonists, so that our Revolution was first presented to me as a quarrel between liberals and conservatives in England as well as in the Colonies. Lincoln my father revered as the emancipator of the slaves and the preserver of the Union, but he revered almost as much the English Quaker, John Bright, who had supported the side of the Northern States in our Civil War. Inevitably I thought of Americans and English as essentially one people though I knew of course that we in the United States were American, not English, citizens. It never occurred to me that English literature was not part of my birthright, that Shelley, Swinburne, and Tennyson were not as much mine as Longfellow, Whittier, and Poe. Thus when I first met it in England, the repudiation of Americans as legitimate sharers in the glories of English literature gave me a severe shock. I resented especially the scornful denial of our right even in Chaucer and Shakespeare, who lived long before the Declaration of Independence.

Only my information about the history of the Society of Friends was at all detailed. I knew a great deal about George Fox, its founder, and loved him in part because of an old engraving we possessed of him with eyes up-rolled and hands uplifted in an ecstasy. I liked to laugh over Charles II's witty rebuke to him for wearing his hat in the royal presence. William Penn, surrounded by his feathered savages and himself so primly and carefully dressed, was a far less sympathetic figure; still I was proud of William Penn's justice to the Indians, unconsciously reckoning it up for righteousness in the sum of our own family inheritance. On the other hand, I boiled with indignation against the early Pilgrims for their persecution of peaceable Quakers, their whipping at cart tails of decent Quaker women, and their shameful expelling of them from towns. The burning of witches also flamed on the Northern horizon in my imagination. The Puritans, it seemed, had fled from bigotry and intolerance in England only to establish their own kind of bigotry and intolerance in New England. Our Catholic founders of Maryland, Englishmen too, had done better than that, Catholics though they were. I felt very critical of the Yankees and very superior to them, and no doubt I enjoyed sharing in this way the local hatred of the North without disloyalty to the Union.

Thus my ideas of the world had been formed at haphazard by family and local prepossessions. In that old quarrel between the Roman senators and the Tribunes of the People I could not have failed to be on the side of the common people against the aristocrats, of the poor against the rich. And yet investigating for myself a question so remote from my daily life gave me the sense of arriving at my own judgments. This study of the past, superficial and biased as it was, initiated a slight change in my mental attitude, hard to define and yet very real. It was not exactly a sense of historical sequence that I acquired, though I was amazed to find democratic ideals and Christian virtues in pagans born long before Christ; rather it was the dawning in my mind of a suspicion that many surprising and important things had happened in the past, of which I was ignorant. They were written down and recorded in books, waiting for me to discover them. At the moment, busy as I was, I could not follow the trail.

When the holidays were over and school began again, my Greek and my Latin and my French lessons pressed upon me day by day. Nor could my algebra and English composition be neglected. Science, too, claimed its toll of time. At no point in all this studying could I linger for a moment, since I had to get over so much ground in so short a time. To wander from the direct path was to risk falling behind, and this risk I was unwilling to take.

Floyd Dell
(1887-   )

Radical ideas have a great appeal for the adolescent. The recent waves of revolutions and upheavals in Hungary, Cuba, Haiti, South Korea, Turkey, and Japan had strong support and impetus from college youth. When Floyd Dell was seventeen years old and unemployed, he was willing to embark on a career as a revolutionary poet—provided he could write as good revolutionary poetry as Swinburne's *Songs Before Sunrise*. "On the other hand, my admiration for the novels of Frank Norris, Jack London and Upton Sinclair moved me to write prose fiction which should be at least a help in the Liberation War of Humanity. And, as a necessary step to such a career, I deliberately stopped being a poet."

Dell's socialistic activity at this time was due to his need for a father surrogate as well as to his adolescent hunger for new intellectual contacts, a reaching out for new friendships to replace the inadequacy of associating with mere schoolboys. Dell had just graduated from high school, and had been fired from a series of factory jobs. His friendship with Fred Feuchter, a leader in the socialist local, "was the most important thing that happened in my life." Feuchter treated the seventeen-year-old boy like an adult, drank beer with him, made him his lieutenant in Socialist affairs. Certainly the intellectual appeal and the identification were great.*

One evening in that fall of 1904 there was a Socialist meeting on a down-town street-corner; and Michael Kennedy, who had not shown up at the Colored Baptist Church that spring, occupied the soap-box. I was in the edges of the crowd, an enthusiastic seventeen-year-old listener to Comrade Kennedy's speech, which told, among other things, of the growing forces of the revolutionary working class throughout the world, mentioning with especial pride the great German Social-Democratic Party. . . . Taking advantage of some pause, a burly stranger asked a courteous question—whether the speaker had ever been in Germany. The speaker had not; and it appeared that the burly stranger had, and had become well acquainted with the workings of the Social-Democratic party organization, and was willing to tell something about it, if requested. The invitation was heartily extended, and the burly stranger mounted the soap-box.

The German Social-Democratic Party, he said, was indeed a large and very efficient organization. But, he went on to say, it was not a revolutionary organization, and the Socialists here ought to know what it was like. It was a liberal and reform party, something like the Democratic Party in the United States. It had no hope of any revolution, nor any belief in one. At this point, Comrade Kennedy, who had been making agitated interruptions, mounted the soap-box beside him, and denounced him for the trickery by which he had gained possession of it. The burly stranger announced that he would continue his remarks on the opposite corner for all who cared to hear him, and then courteously gave the soap-box back to Comrade Kennedy. The amused crowd followed the burly stranger to the opposite corner, where another soap-box was quickly set up for him; and Comrade Kennedy found himself addressing only the dispirited committee of five or six who were in charge of the meeting. It was a poor evening for the Davenport Socialists.

But it was to be a fine evening for me. I maintained my stand among the faithful few, until Comrade Kennedy gave up his attempt to win back the crowd and bitterly went away. The rest of us joined the crowd at the other corner, and I listened in indignation to the malicious libels which were being uttered against my German Socialist comrades. The speaker then went on to discuss and confute Socialist theory. I was quite familiar with the Communist Manifesto, with Engels' *Socialism, Utopian and Scientific,* and other small books in red paper covers; and I had read some of the more readable parts of *Capital.* When the speaker gave something as Marx's view, referring to *Capital,* I was quite sure it was not there, and dashed to the public library, a block away. Back I came breathlessly with Karl Marx's *Capital* under my arm. I tried to break up this fellow's meeting with questions, as he had broken up the other, but he ignored me. Not until he had finished did I have a chance to challenge his statements, and offer him *Capital* to find his proof in if he could; he smiled, and declined the opportunity. Furious, I told him he had lied about Marx; he snubbed me casually, and went away, leaving me in my chagrin.

But a big, florid man from the group of the Socialist faithful came over and talked to me; and presently, to my delight, I found myself invited to accompany the group to Turner hall for a glass of beer. I sat at a large table with five men who believed in another kind of world than the one we lived in, and were helping to bring it about— a world of justice and beauty and order. I drank beer with them. Beer, before that, had been a bitter drink; but now it was flavored with the splendor of talk and ideas. Afterward I walked with the big man to the place where he lived, and he asked me to drop in to see him the next evening. So began my great friendship with Fred Feuchter— Fritz, as I was proud to call him. He was a mail-carrier, a big, florid, dynamic man, large-minded and eloquent, and wiser in great things and small than anyone I had ever known.

The Socialist local, on his assurance, took me in as a member, though I was still a year too young by the rules. I thought the meetings dull, and no one disputed that; I was put on a program committee, and the meetings became lively, for after all I did know how to run a club. As fall turned to winter, I worked overtime at the factory, till nine; and I would hurry on the Friday evenings of our meetings from the factory to Turner hall, to be in time to take part

in some discussion, or contribute an essay to the program. Our meetings had a large attendance, now that "business" was not droned out
boringly at indefinite length; wives came with their Socialist husbands,
and a few Socialist girls showed up from high school. We discussed
ideas, and my friend Fred Feuchter shone in that. If the energies of
the Socialist local were, under the influence of my youthful enthusiasm, turned in cultural directions, there were none the less, and
possibly more, votes for Eugene V. Debs—who was, I suppose, the
candidate that year. I distributed literature at factories, and took a
hand in odd jobs during the campaign. My friend Fred Feuchter
had helped me magnificently in my program activities; and gradually
I became his lieutenant in the practical and tactical management of
the local. I discovered in myself a capacity for faithful henchmanship
under an able leader, with no poetic shrinking from harsh measures.

A young enthusiast had his chance to try his hand at anything. The
youngest convert may aspire to leadership, and often does; but I never
did. I did try, and fail, to be an efficient impersonal cog in the Party
organization. I was financial secretary for a while; and it is doubtful if
they ever did get the books straightened out afterward. It was conceded that I was better in writing platforms and manifestoes than in
keeping track of the vouchers.

My friendship with Fred Feuchter was the most important thing
that happened in my life. I had found a man whom I truly admired,
and wished to follow, a man who had wisdom and courage, a man—
and the first man—whose advice I could ask about anything. Not
that I asked much advice: which was a good thing, for no human
being could have been as infallible as I deemed my friend Fritz to be.
But I learned many things from him of the greatest importance in
the conduct of life. . . . Under his influence I began to learn not to
attach to situations emotional values which were not there for the
other persons involved; to live as though the outside world were real,
whether I liked it or not; and not to pre-judge life, but to take it as it
came and see it as it was.

Since this was the first time anybody had ever taken serious note
of my belief that I had to earn a living in factory work, his consideration of, and dismissal of, this belief was impressive. What my "bourgeois" friends—I know that blessed word "bourgeois" now—what they
had tried to assure me was that I might have a great career as a writer;
what he conveyed to me was that I didn't have a dog's chance as a
factory worker.

I was, in fact, after the Christmas rush, fired from the factory. I got
work in a job-printing shop, at a hand press; but I had some objection

to running the normal risk of having my right hand crushed to a mash in the iron jaws of the machine (my eldest brother had just lost part of another finger at the sash-and-door factory, leaving him a total of four whole fingers and one whole thumb on both hands); and I was transferred to the lithographing department. There it was my duty to feed beer-labels into a bronzing machine. I had also to breathe bronze-dust for eight hours a day. I became rather bitter about a civilization which could find no better task for a youth than that; a civilization in which the gilt on beer-labels—Very good, suggested Fred Feuchter, for a poem. "But *you*—quit! Your family will not starve." That was true; I had never thought of it that way. I did quit. It was now spring. I put on my best suit, and went to look for a job. Pausing to look at the new printing press in the windows of the Times, the idea occurred to me that I might get a job washing the ink off the rollers, or something like that. I went in. By one of those coincidences which make real life so utterly unlike realistic fiction, there had been, in the edition I had just seen run off, an advertisement for a cub reporter. It was supposed that I had come in answer to this advertisement, and I was sent to the city room, where I was given the job and told to report in the morning.

Although my friend Fritz had refused to prophesy the way in which I would be able to make a living by using my brains, this was the answer so pat that I felt as though he had not only pulled me out of a factory but pushed me into a newspaper office.

ARGUMENTATION AND DEBATING

Benjamin Franklin
(1706-1790)

Benjamin Franklin's father, Josiah, in order to retain his freedom of conscience, left the England of Charles II for New England. Benjamin, appropriately named, was the youngest of seventeen children. Probably, as the youngest, he learned early and quickly how to protect himself. The sophistry he displays in the excerpt below gives some indication of how he went about it.* Inspired by Xenophon's *Memorable Things of Socrates,* Franklin dropped his usual adolescent "abrupt contradiction and positive argumentation, and

---

*From *Autobiography* by Benjamin Franklin. New York: Rinehart & Co., 1948. Pp. 14-16.

put on the humble inquirer and doubter." His success with this method prompted him to continue with it all his life, he relates, and to great advantage. The fourth point of Franklin's *Plan for Future Conduct* states, "I resolve to speak ill of no man whatsoever, not even in a minute of truth; but rather by some means excuse the faults I hear charged upon others, and upon proper occasions speak all the good I know of everybody." The oral aggression which prompted this resolve undoubtedly gave rise to feelings of anxiety. He reacted against the oral aggression by saying only kind things about other people.

When about sixteen years of age I happened to meet with a book, written by one Tryon, recommending a vegetable diet. I determined to go into it. My brother, being yet unmarried, did not keep house, but boarded himself and his apprentices in another family. My refusing to eat flesh occasioned an inconvenience, and I was frequently chid for my singularity. I made myself acquainted with Tryon's manner of preparing some of his dishes such as boiling potatoes or rice, making hasty pudding, and a few others, and then proposed to my brother, that if he would give me, weekly, half the money he paid for my board, I would board myself. He instantly agreed to it, and I presently found that I could save half what he paid me. This was an additional fund for buying books. But I had another advantage in it. My brother and the rest going from the printing-house to their meals, I remained there alone and dispatching presently my light repast, which often was no more than a biscuit or a slice of bread, a handful of raisins or a tart from the pastry-cook's, and a glass of water, had the rest of the time till their return for study, in which I made the greater progress, from that greater clearness of head and quicker apprehension which usually attend temperance in eating and drinking.

And now it was that, being on some occasion made ashamed of my ignorance in figures, which I had twice failed in learning when at school, I took Cocker's book of arithmetic, and went through the whole by myself with great ease. I also read Seller's and Sturmy's books of navigation, and became acquainted with the little geometry they contain; but never proceeded far in that science. And I read about this time Locke *On Human Understanding,* and the *Art of Thinking,* by Messrs. du Port Royal.

While I was intent on improving my language, I met with an English grammar (I think it was Greenwood's), at the end of which there were two little sketches of the arts of rhetoric and logic, the latter finishing with a specimen of a dispute in the Socratic method; and soon after I procured Xenophon's *Memorable Things of Socrates,* wherein there are many instances of the same method. I was charmed with it, adopted it, dropped my abrupt contradiction and positive argumentation, and put on the humble inquirer and doubter. And being then, from reading Shaftesbury and Collins, become a real doubter in many points of our religious doctrine, I found this method safest for myself and very embarrassing to those against whom I used it; therefore I took a delight in it, practiced it continually, and grew very artful and expert in drawing people, even of superior knowledge, into concessions, the consequences of which they did not foresee, entangling them in difficulties out of which they could not extricate themselves, and so obtaining victories that neither myself nor my cause always deserved. I continued this method some few years, but gradually left it, retaining only the habit of expressing myself in terms of modest diffidence; never using, when I advanced anything that may possibly be disputed, the words *certainly, undoubtedly,* or any others. that give the air of positiveness to an opinion; but rather say, I conceive or apprehend a thing to be so or so; it appears to me, or I should think it so or so, for such and such reasons; or I imagine it to be so; or it is so, if I am not mistaken. This habit, I believe, has been of great advantage to me when I have had occasion to inculcate my opinions and persuade men into measures that I have been from time to time engaged in promoting. . . .

Jeremy Bentham
(1748-1832)

Jeremy Bentham, the founder of utilitarianism, took his views from Adam Smith, and these were expanded by such loyal disciples and friends as James Mill and his son, John Stuart Mill. Bentham stated that "Nature has placed mankind under the governance of two sovereign masters, *pain* and *pleasure.* . . . The principle of utility recognizes this subjection, and assumes it for the foundation of that system, the object of which is to rear the fabric of felicity by the hands of reason and law." The principle of utility is further defined by Bentham as "the principle which approves or disapproves of every action whatsoever, according to the tendency which it appears to have to augment or diminish the happiness of the party whose interest is in question." John Stuart Mill was to modify this principle, for happiness, he wrote, was something more than Bentham's mathematical excess of pleasure over pain: one had to consider the quality of pleasure as well as its quantity; happiness must preserve the sense of dignity; and pleasure had to do with caring for somebody else, with a "fellow-feeling with the collective interests of mankind."

Bentham had considerable boyhood experience in convincing others of his philosophy, as the passage below shows.* At thirteen he was attending Oxford University, declaiming and disputing regularly and successfully with his classmates. He graduated from Oxford in 1763, at the age of sixteen.

June 30, 1761

Dear Poppa,

I have sent you a declamation I spoke last Saturday, with the approbation of all my acquaintances, who liked the thing itself very well, but still better my manner of speaking it. Even a bachelor of my acquaintance went so far as to say that he never heard but one speak a declamation better all the time he has been in College; which, indeed, is not much to say, as, perhaps, you imagine, for sure nobody can speak worse than we do here; for, in short, 'tis like repeating just so many lines out of a *Propria quae Maribus.* I have disputed, too, in the Hall once, and am going in again tomorrow. There also I came off with honour, having fairly beat off, not only my proper antagonist, but the moderator himself; for he was forced to supply my antagonist with arguments, the invalidity of which I clearly demonstrated. I should have disputed much oftener, but for the holidays or eves, that happen on Mondays, Wednesdays, and Fridays; and, besides, we went three times into the Hall before we disputed ourselves, that we might see the method. Indeed, I am very sorry it did not come to my turn to dispute every disputation day; for, for my own part, I desire no better sport. [Then, at the end of the letter, the orator and logician suddenly became the thirteen-year-old small boy.]

I wish you would let me come home very soon, for my clothes are dropping off my back; and if I don't go home very soon, to get new ones, I must not go down stairs, they are so bad; for as soon as one hole is mended, another breaks out again; and, as almost all the commoners either are gone for the vacation, or will go in a day or two's time, very little business will be going forward. Pray, give me an answer very soon, that I may know whether I am to wear clothes or go

---

*From *Collected Works* edited by John Bowring. London: Simpkin, Marshall & Co., 1843. P. 31.

in rags. Pray, give my duty to grand-mama, and love to dear Sammy, and represent the woful condition of one who is, nevertheless, your dutiful and affectionate son, J. Bentham.

Sir Walter Scott
(1771-1832)

Sir Walter Scott describes below the debating societies of his day to which the adolescent belonged.* He spells out the kind of mind and personality necessary to withstand the assaults of friends and opponents alike. Not much has changed in the past two hundred years. Adolescents still need to test their ideas and the way they express them and they do these things best with peers.

Scott was particularly grateful for the literary society he joined at the age of seventeen since, because of his illness, he "had had little or no intercourse with any of my class-companions, one or two only excepted." It gave him the opportunity to identify with others and to explore his own self-identity further.

In other points . . . I began to make some amends for the irregularity of my education. It is well known that in Edinburgh one great spur to emulation among youthful students is in those associations called *literary societies,* formed not only for the purpose of debate, but of composition. These undoubtedly have some disadvantages, where a bold, petulant, and disputatious temper happens to be combined with considerable information and talent. Still, however, in order for such a person being actually spoiled by mixing in such debates, his talents must be of a very rare nature, or his effrontery must be proof to every species of assault; for there is generally in a well-selected society of this nature, talent sufficient to meet the forwardest, and satire enough to penetrate the most undaunted. I am particularly obliged to this sort of club for introducing me about my seventeenth year into the society which at one time I had entirely dropped; for, from the time of my illness at college, I had had little or no intercourse with any of my class-companions, one or two only excepted. Now, however, about 1788, I began to feel and take my ground in society. A ready wit, a good deal of enthusiasm, and a perception that soon ripened into tact and observation of character, rendered me an acceptable companion to

---

*From *Memoirs of the Early Life of Sir Walter Scott, Written by Himself.* Reprinted by permission of Macmillan & Co., Ltd. Copyright 1914. Pp. 41-44.

many young men whose acquisitions in philosophy and science were infinitely superior to anything I could boast.

In the business of these societies—for I was a member of more than one successively—I cannot boast of having made any great figure. I never was a good speaker unless upon some subject which strongly animated my feelings; and, as I was totally unaccustomed to composition, as well as to the art of generalizing my ideas upon any subject, my literary essays were but very poor work. I never attempted them unless when compelled to do so by the regulations of the society, and then I was like the Lord of Castle Rackrent, who was obliged to cut down a tree to get a few faggots to boil the kettle; for the quantity of ponderous and miscellaneous knowledge, which I really possessed on many subjects, was not easily condensed, or brought to bear upon the object I wished particularly to become master of. Yet there occurred opportunities when this odd lumber of my brain, especially that which was connected with the recondite parts of history, did me, as Hamlet says, "yeoman's service." My memory of events was like one of the large, old-fashioned stone-cannons of the Turks—very difficult to load well and discharge, but making a powerful effect when by good chance any object did come within range of its shot. Such fortunate opportunities of exploding with effect maintained my literary character among my companions, with whom I soon met with great indulgence and regard. The persons with whom I chiefly lived at this period of my youth were William Clerk, already mentioned; James Edmonstoune, of Newton; George Abercromby; Adam Ferguson, son of the celebrated Professor Ferguson, and who combined the lightest and most airy temper with the best and kindest disposition; John Irving, already mentioned; the Honourable Thomas Douglas, now Earl of Selkirk; David Boyle—and two or three others, who sometimes plunged deeply into politics and metaphysics, and not unfrequently "doffed the world aside, and bid it pass."

Looking back on these times, I cannot applaud in all respects the way in which our days were spent. There was too much idleness, and sometimes too much conviviality: but our hearts were warm, our minds honourably bent on knowledge and literary distinction; and if I, certainly the least informed of the party, may be permitted to bear witness, we were not without the fair and creditable means of attaining the distinction to which we aspired. In this society I was naturally led to correct my former useless course of reading; for—feeling myself greatly inferior to my companions in metaphysical philosophy and other branches of regular study—I laboured, not without some success, to acquire at least such a portion of knowledge as might enable me to maintain my rank in conversation. In this I succeeded pretty well; but unfortunately then, as often since through my life, I incurred the deserved ridicule of my friends from the superficial nature of my acquisitions, which being, in the mercantile phrase, *got up* for society, very often proved flimsy in the texture; and thus the gifts of an uncommonly retentive memory and acute powers of perception were sometimes detrimental to their possessor, by encouraging him to a presumptuous reliance upon them.

H. G. Wells
(1866-1946)

Wells recalls a hilarious incident he was party to during his eighteenth year while at college.* The debating society he belonged to had tabooed the subjects of politics and religion, taboos which Wells abjured. When someone began a discussion on superstitution, Wells took up the cue and mentioned "a certain itinerant preacher." For the better part of an hour, the youths raged and stormed. Wells finally had to be carried out forcibly. In what period, other than adolescence, could such a discussion be held, with such seriousness and such ferment!

The startled guffaws of Jennings had already persuaded me that I was something of a wit, and my rather unconventional contributions to the discussions in the Debating Society were also fairly successful and attracted one or two appreciative friends. There were three men, Taylor and Porter and E. H. Smith in that early group, of whom I have lost sight; there were also my life-long friends, A. T. Simmons and William Burton, Elizabeth Healey and A. M. Davies. We loitered in the corridors, made groups in the tea-shop at lunch-time, lent each other books and papers and developed each other's conversational powers.

Curiously enough, though I remember the Debating Society very vividly, I do not remember anything of the speeches I made. I did make speeches because my friends remember them and say they were amusing. The meetings were held in an underground lecture theatre used by the mining school. It was lit by a gas jet or so. The lecturers' platform and the students' benches were surrounded by big models

*From *Experiment in Autobiography* by H. G. Wells. Reprinted by permission of Executors of the Estate of H. G. Wells. Copyright 1934, Macmillan Co. Pp. 189-191.

of strata, ore crushers and the like which receded into a profound obscurity, and austere diagrams of unknown significance hung behind the chairman. The usual formula was a paper for half an hour or so, a reply and then promiscuous discussion. Those who lacked the courage to speak, interjected observations, made sudden outcries or hammered the desks. The desks indeed were hammered until the ink jumped out of the pots. We were supposed to avoid religion and politics; the rest of the universe was at our mercy.

I objected to this taboo of religion and politics. I maintained that these were primary matters, best beaten out in the primary stage of life. I did all I could to weaken and infringe those taboos, sailing as close to the wind as possible, and one or two serious-minded fellow students began to look out for me with an ever ready cry of "Or-der." One evening somebody read an essay on *Superstitions* and cited among others the thirteen superstitions. I took up the origin of that. "A certain itinerant preacher whom I am not permitted to name in this gathering," I began, "had twelve disciples. . . . "

The opposition was up in arms forthwith and we had a lovely dispute that lasted for the better part of an hour. I maintained that the phrase "itinerant preacher," was an exact and proper description of the founder of Christianity, as indeed it was. But the vocabulary of the ordinary Englishman is sticky with stereotyped phrasing and half dried secondary associations. It seemed that "itinerant preacher" connoted a very low type of minister in some dissenting bodies. So much the worse, I said, for the dissenting bodies. The sense of the meeting was against me. Even my close friends looked grave and reproachful. I was asked to "withdraw" the expression. I protested that it was based on information derived from the New Testament, "a most respectable compilation." This did not mend matters. Apparently they could not have it that the New Testament was "respectable" or "compiled." I was warned by the chair and persisted in my insistence upon the proper meaning of words.

I was carried out struggling. To be carried out of an assembly in full fight had recently been made splendid by Charles Bradlaugh. Irish members of parliament were also wont to leave that assembly by the same laborious yet exhilarating method of transport. Except that my hair was pulled rather painfully by someone, a quite momentary discomfort, that experience was altogether bright and glorious.

But I will not expand into this sort of anecdotage. That sample must serve. The Debating Society was a constant source of small opportunities for provocation and irreverence. And about the schools, in lecture theatres, I became almost an expert in making strange unsuitable noises, the wailing of a rubber blowpipe tube with its lips stretched, for example, and in provoking bursts of untimely applause.

Albert Schweitzer
(1875-   )

To argue for argument's sake, to be considered insolent by adults when one is questioning fundamentals, to reason through in supposedly systematic and orderly fashion when affect precludes such a possibility, all seem to be characteristic of adolescence. Albert Schweitzer highlights these aspects of his youth, a period which he calls "an unpleasant phase of development." His passion for discussion led him into all kinds of familial difficulties and opprobrium. Discussion was an intoxicant for him, leading him to disturb every conversation and to be considered an *agent provocateur* within the home.*

Between my fourteenth and sixteenth years I passed through an unpleasant phase of development, becoming an intolerable nuisance to everybody, especially to my father, through a passion for discussion. On everyone who met me in the street I wanted to inflict thoroughgoing and closely reasoned considerations on all the questions that were then being generally discussed, in order to expose the errors of the conventional views and get the correct view recognised and appreciated. The joy of seeking for what was true and serviceable had come upon me like a kind of intoxication, and every conversation in which I took part had to go back to fundamentals. Thus I emerged from the shell of reserve in which I had hitherto concealed myself, and became the disturber of every conversation which was meant to be merely conversation. What a number of times at both Mülhausen and Günsbach, did I bring the conversation at meals into stormy water! My aunt scolded me as being insolent, because I wanted to argue out my ideas with grown-up people as though they were of my own age. If we went to pay a visit anywhere, I had to promise my father not to spoil the day for him by "stupid behavior during conversations."

I must confess to having been as intolerable as a well-brought up young man, half-way through his education, ever can be, but it was not in the least any egotistic disputatiousness which made me so; it

---

*From *Memories of Childhood and Youth* by Albert Schweitzer. Reprinted by permission of The Macmillan Co. 1950. Pp. 54-55.

was a passionate need of thinking, and of seeking with the help of others for the true and the serviceable. The light and truth-seeking spirit of my grandfather Schillinger had awoke in me. The conviction that human progress is possible only if reasoned thought replaces mere opinion and absence of thought had seized hold of me and its first manifestations made themselves felt in this stormy and disagreeable fashion.

REFERENCES

1. Bonaparte, Napoleon. *Napoleon's Autobiography*. Edited by F. M. Kircheisen. New York: Duffield & Co., 1932, p. 24.
2. Bühler, Charlotte. *Das Seelenleben des Jugendlichen*. Jena: G. Fischer, 1923.
3. ———. *Tagebuch eines jungen Mädchens*. Jena: G. Fischer, 1922.
4. Da Ponte, Lorenzo. *Memoirs*. Philadelphia: J. B. Lippincott Co., 1929, p. 32.
5. English, O. Spurgeon, & Pearson, Gerald H. J. *Emotional Problems of Living*. New York: W. W. Norton & Co., 1955, p. 300.
6. Freud, Anna. *The Ego and the Mechanisms of Defence*. New York: International Universities Press, 1946, p. 175.
7. *Ibid.*, p. 179.
8. Freud, Sigmund. *Delusion and Dream*. Boston: Beacon Press, 1956, pp. 56-57.
9. Goethe, Johann Wolfgang von. *Goethe's Autobiography. Poetry and Truth from My Own Life*. Washington, D. C.: Public Affairs Press, 1949, p. 204.
10. Hall, G. Stanley. *Adolescence*. New York: Appleton-Century-Crofts, 1904, Vol. I, pp. 541-542.
11. Herbert, Edward. *Life*. New York: E. P. Dutton & Co. (n. d.), p. 21.
12. Hollingsworth, Leta S. *The Psychology of the Adolescent*. New York: D. Appleton & Co., 1928, p. 189.
13. Inhelder, Bärbel, & Piaget, Jean. *The Growth of Logical Thinking from Childhood to Adolescence*. New York: Basic Books, 1958, p. 340.
14. Jerome, Saint. *Select Letters of Saint Jerome*. Cambridge, Mass.: Harvard University Press, 1933. Epistle 125, 12, pp. 419-421.
15. Jones, Ernest. Some problems of adolescence. *Brit. J. Psychol.*, 13:37, 1922.
16. Nehru, Jawaharlal. *An Autobiography*. London: John Lane, 1936, p. 16.
17. Oberndorf, C. P. The feeling of stupidity. *Int. J. Psychoanal.*, 20: 443-451, 1939.

18. Salisbury, John of. *The Metalogicon.* Berkeley, Calif.: University of California Press, 1955, p. 245.
19. *Ibid.,* pp. 244-246.
20. Scaliger, Joseph. *Autobiography.* Cambridge, Mass.: Harvard University Press, 1927, p. 31.
21. Somerville, Mary. *Personal Recollections from Early Life to Old Age.* Boston: Roberts Brothers, 1874, pp. 36-37.
22. Stillman, William J. *The Autobiography of a Journalist.* Boston: Houghton Mifflin & Co., 1901, p. 44.
23. Wasserman, Jacob. *My Life As German and Jew.* New York: Coward-McCann, Inc., 1933, p. 67.
24. Wells, H. G. *Experiment in Autobiography.* New York: Macmillan Co., 1934.

CHAPTER TEN

The Compulsion to Read

A universal phenomenon of adolescence, notable particularly in the early years of the period, is the passion for reading. The individual consumes books with a voracious appetite. He indulges in indiscriminate reading, usually, taking on everything and anything within reach.

In autobiographical literature, there is recorded evidence of the existence of this phenomenon from the time of Libanius, born in 314 A. D., to the present. Libanius tells us, according to Misch, how at the age of fifteen he was filled with such love of *litterae* that he threw himself entirely into the reading of the classics and gave up all the childish pleasures with which, as the pampered son of a rich and distinguished family in Antioch, he had occupied himself—gladiatorial fights, horse-racing, sight-seeing, and pigeon-racing during his frequent stays in the countryside. He learned classical texts by heart, and strictly forbade himself all declamation and writing in order to concentrate on memorizing; he continued this for five years, and so acquired his astonishingly wide range of reading (17).

In *An Apology for Smectymnuus*, John Milton (1608-1674) wrote, "I was so allured to read, that no recreation came to me better welcome." Edward Gibbon, born in 1737, "read, with application and pleasure, *all* the epistles, *all* the orations, and the most important treatises of rhetoric and philosophy" of Cicero in his eighteenth year (11). When Thomas Bewick was sixteen years old in 1769, he "had few that I could call intimate acquaintances. My almost only ones were books, over which I spent my time, mornings and evenings, late and early. This too intense application to books, together with the sedentary employment, and being placed at a very low work bench, took away my healthy appearance, and I put on a more delicate look, and became poorly in health [2]." But the doctor who subsequently examined Tom told him he "was as healthy as a horse," gave him an expectorant, and told the boy's master, an engraver, not to work him so hard.

In the United States, Sam Houston at the age of fourteen (in the year 1807) described "an Academy established in that part of East Tennessee . . . [that] I went to . . . for a while. I had got possession of two or three books, among them Pope's translation of the *Iliad*, which I read so constantly that I could repeat it almost entire from the beginning to the end [13]." The American physicist, John Henry (1797-1878), one day "followed a rabbit under the Public Library at Albany, found a hole in the floor that admitted him to the shelves, and unknown by any one, read all the fiction the library contained, then turned to physics, astronomy, and chemistry, and developed a passion for the sciences [12]." In the 1860's, Edison undertook to read the Detroit Free Library through, and read fifteen solid feet as the books stood on the shelves before he was stopped. Walt Whitman described himself during his teens as "a most omnivorous novel-reader . . . devour'd everything I could get . . . [25]."

John Strachey, born in 1859, wrote, "I did not read till I was nearly nine, and even then did not use the power of reading. The book habit did not come till I was twelve or thirteen—though then it came, as far as poetry was concerned, with a rush. By fifteen I had read all the older English poets and most of the new . . . [21]." The Russian girl, Marie Bashkirtseff, entered in her *Journal* for January 8, 1881, "I have genuine passion for my books: I arrange them on the shelves, I count them, I gaze at them; only to look at these shelves filled with old books rejoices my heart. I stand back from them to look at them admiringly, as I would a picture. I have only seven hundred volumes, but as they are almost all large ones, they are equivalent to a much greater number of ordinary ones [1]." By the time Edith Wharton was seventeen in 1879, she recalled, " . . . although I had not read every book in my father's library, I had looked into them all [24]."

Theodore Dreiser's family, in 1886, when he was fifteen years old, "was by now convinced that I had distinct intellectual tendencies. My father, coming home from Terre Haute on one occasion, for instance, and finding me reading so much, actually approved of the purchase of a set of Washington Irving's works . . . [5]." In 1871, at the age of twelve, Havelock Ellis discerned his "real self . . . emerging, but it was discovering itself along lines that I never revealed at school and could never even dream of revealing . . . During the years I was at Merton College reading was my constant delight during all my spare hours and moments. In the holidays it was only with difficulty that my mother, anxious for my health, drove me out of the house for solitary walks in the dreary suburb that contained nothing that appealed to me. . . . At that time my mind was an empty treasure-house into which every precious thing I could find was eagerly poured. I bought cheap editions of Milton and Burns and religiously read them through at the age of twelve, though as yet with no great relish [6]."

In 1873, Freud recalled, "I had developed a passion for collecting and owning books. . . . And I had already discovered, of course, that passions often lead to sorrow. When I was seventeen I had run up a largish account at a bookseller's and had nothing to meet it with; and my father had scarcely taken it as an excuse that my inclinations might have chosen a worse outlet [10]."

The only pleasure John Cowper Powys experienced at the Sherborne School was "to sit for hours in the school library, a lovely, old, medieval building, with deep window seats that had leather cushions, searching through all manner of ancient and modern volumes, if so be it that I might find some paradise passage of sweet immorality [18]." And in 1903, when Floyd Dell was about sixteen years old, he described his passion for reading in the following passage:

> However, at that time the only American authors who existed for me were Frank Norris and Mark Twain; and Frank Norris had died last year, while Mark Twain was only a boyhood memory. Fiction did not interest me much.
>
> But I retained from Frank Norris's "Octopus" a picture of a girl that was to haunt me always—a sturdy, earth-strong girl, with hair as yellow as the ripe wheat, serene, calm-browed, happy-hearted. I was in love with her image in my mind.

And now I was reading poetry. Back in Quincy a footnote in Prescott's "Conquest of Peru" had sent me to Southey's "Thalaba"; I had read all of Southey, and admired it all. But Byron now swept Southey out of existence. Keats came next, a never-to-be-forgotten delight. I read, in a five-and-ten-cent store, standing on one foot and then the other, the "Rubaiyat," and carried home in dazed wonder that casket of enchantments. Browning's poems became mine at the same price; my library was growing. I was reading English and some other poetry at the rate of one great poet a week; I read and knew vastly by heart Wordsworth, Shelley, Walt Whitman, Kipling, Wilde, the Rossettis, Tennyson, Wilfred Scawen Blunt, Herrick, Milton, Heine, Swinburne, John Donne, Marvell, Drayton, Shakespeare's Sonnets; some Persian and Chinese poetry of which I made my own rhymed versions; among living Americans I was enthusiastic about Bliss Carman and William Vaughn Moody; then came a magnificent discovery that for a long time no one in Davenport would share—A. E. Housman's "Shropshire Lad," bought with a dollar that was being saved to buy shoes with; and with an appetite geared to that pitch, the world has seemed, ever since, in this respect, a poor barren starveling place, which cannot produce more than two or three great poets in a century [4].

What is the meaning behind this seemingly compulsive absorption in reading to the exclusion of almost all other activities? There is no one answer to this question but rather a number of causative factors. The adolescent's unconscious motivation in this area may be prompted by his equally unconscious search for identity; it may be a means of channeling and sublimating his libidinal energy, as the excerpt from Powys' *Autobiography* suggests; or he may find reality testing too dangerous and the vicarious experience he garners through books safer, helping to see him through the period of threat. Other factors involve the renewal and intensification of curiosity at adolescence; the need for privacy which can be achieved through the isolation of reading; or, perhaps, an attempt to crystallize, synthesize, and integrate his concepts into universal systems valid for all.

This last point has been emphasized by Inhelder and Piaget (14) and is illustrated in Leon Trotsky's autobiography (22), where he describes his behavior in this respect at the age of seventeen, in the year 1894: "I swallowed books, fearful that my entire life would not be long enough to prepare me for action. My reading was nervous, impatient and unsystematic. After wading through the illegal pamphlets of the preceding period, I passed on to *Logic* of John Stuart Mill, then took up Lippert's *Primitive Culture* without completing *Logic*. The utilitarianism of Bentham seemed to me the last word in human thought. For several months I was a stanch Benthamist. In the same manner I was carried away by the realistic aesthetics of Chernyshevsky. Without having finished Lippert, I threw myself upon the history of the French Revolution by Mignet. Each book lived separately for me, with no place in a unified system. My striving for a system became tense, sometimes savage. At the same time, I would be repelled by Marxism partly because it seemed a completed system."

Not only the adolescent's need to derive and construct a system is apparent here, but also his contradictoriness in terms of verbalizing the need but pursuing it in an unsystematic, even disordered, manner. "Boys and girls alike are voracious for factual information and obtain it from whatever sources they can . . . [20]." The craving for knowledge is a renewal of his intellectual needs and broadening horizons which are first seen in the child at about the age six. In childhood, the earliest disciplined learning is reading, and through it are discovered new worlds far removed from the narrow confines of home. This is recapitulated in adolescence but on a more sophisticated level. Like the acquisition of a new name, noted in the chapter on the Language of the Adolescent, this is a kind of intellectual rebirth, and very meaningful.

The compulsive nature of the reading may stem, as indicated previously, from the adolescent's need for self-identity. "Learning to read novels, we slowly learn to read ourselves," stated one critic (19). Another was more specific: "Although [books] are separate, together they add up to something; they are connected with each other and with other cities. The same ideas, or related ones, turn up in different places; the human problems that repeat themselves in life repeat themselves in literature, but with different solutions according to different authors who wrote at different times. Books influence each other; they link the past and the present and the future and have their own generations, like families. Wherever you start reading you connect yourself with one of the families of ideas, and, in the long run, you not only find out about the world and the people in it: you find out about yourself, too [3]."

This is precisely what the adolescent is searching: his self and his relatedness. He is constantly preoccupied with his physical being, his sexual character, his anticipated occupational role. "The most apparent symptom naturally is a paralysis of workmanship in the form of an inability to concentrate on required or suggested tasks; or a self-destructive pre-occupation with some one-sided activity, i.e., excessive reading, listening to music, exercising to exhaustion, etc. [7]." Kris (15) indicated that the adolescent tends to use heightened productivity as a defense against threatening upheaval.

To withdraw into the world of books may be a denial of the threatening reality the adolescent fears in the world of life to be. Since he is uncertain of himself, the world about him is too threatening and dangerous for him to test—at least for a while. During this quiescent period, the adolescent, it would seem, is gathering strength for the arduous reality tasks ahead. At the age of twelve, Liszt made a great success in Paris as a keyboard prodigy and became quite fashionable. At fourteen, his opera *Don Sancha* was given at the Grand Opera in Paris. After this period of great activity and success, there was a period of exhaustion, a craving for solitude and for reading.

In pursuit of self-identity, the boy and girl indulge in a rich fantasy life precipitated, or perhaps reinforced, through reading. Unable to cope with the everyday world, adolescents achieve otherwise unattainable satisfactions through daydreams and reading. Characters in books may serve as useful objects for identification and imitation (23) in terms of incorporating certain qualities into the adolescent's ideal self. "I lost my identity in that of the individual whose life I was reading," Rousseau acknowledged. Through reading, he may bring his own feelings to the surface, enabling him to recognize and identify himself in what he has read and thereby helping to bring about the reintegrated personality and self-actualization he is seeking.

The excerpts which follow—beginning with an entry in the diary of a Japanese girl written in 1021, and ending with an autobiographical passage by a contemporary Chinese woman—illustrate the dynamics involved in the adolescent's passion for, and involvement in, reading. They cover nearly a thousand years of recorded human history, spanning both Eastern and Western cultures, and including scientists, literary figures, artists, an educator, and a court lady.

The Sarashina Diary
(1009-1059)

The name of the author of the *Sarashina Diary* is unknown. However, Omori and Doi tell us she was the daughter of Fujiwara Takasué and was born in 1009. In 1017, Takasué was appointed governor of a province, and went with his daughter to his new post. It is the return journey, made in 1021, with which the *Diary* opens.

During the Heian Period, the position of women was very different from what it later became in the feudal era. They were educated, and much of the best literature of Japan has been written by women, as *The Tale of the Genji* testifies. In the passage which follows,* the thirteen-year-old girl entered in her diary how she had to tease her mother into giving her "books of stories" and her "strange passion" for them. "My joy knew no bounds and I read them day and night. . . . " She prayed for the opportunity to read all fifty of the books of Genji-monogatari and when she finally did secure them, "All day and all night, as late as I could keep my eyes open, I did nothing but look at the books."

It was dark when I arrived at the residence on the west of the Princess of Sanjo's mansion. Our garden was very wide and wild with great, fearful trees not inferior to those mountains I had come from. I could not feel at home, or keep a settled mind. Even then I teased mother into giving me books of stories, after which I had been yearning for so many years. Mother sent a messenger with a letter to Emon-no-Myōgu, one of our relatives who served the Princess of Sanjo. She took interest in my strange passion and willingly sent me some excellent manuscripts in the lid of a writing box, saying that these copies had been given her by the Princess. My joy knew no bounds and I read them day and night; but I soon began to wish for more, but as I was an utter stranger to the Royal City, who would get them for me?

My stepmother [meaning one of her father's wives] had once been a lady-in-waiting at the court, and she seemed to have been disap-

---

*From *Diaries of Court Ladies of Old Japan* edited by Annie Omori and Kochi Doi. Reprinted by permission of Houghton Mifflin Co. Copyright 1920. Pp. 16-20.

pointed in something. She had been regretting the World [her marriage], and now she was to leave our home. She beckoned her own child, who was five years old, and said, "The time will never come when I shall forget you, dear heart"; and pointing to a huge plum-tree which grew close to the eaves, said, "When it is in flower I shall come back"; and she went away. I felt love and pity for her, and while I was secretly weeping, the year, too, went away. . . .

When I had first arrived at the Capital I had been given a book of the handwriting of this noble lady for my copy-book. In it were written several poems, among them the following:

> When you see the smoke floating up the valley of
> Toribe Hill,*
> Then you will understand me, who seemed as shadow-like
> even while living.

I looked at these poems which were written in such a beautiful handwriting, and I shed more tears. I sat brooding until mother troubled herself to console me. She searched for romances and gave them to me, and I became consoled unconsciously. I read a few volumes of Genji-monogatari and longed for the rest, but as I was still a stranger here I had no way of finding them. I was all impatience and yearning, and in my mind was always praying that I might read all the books of Genji-monogatari from the very first one.

While my parents were shutting themselves up in Udzu-Masa** Temple, I asked them for nothing except this romance, wishing to read it as soon as I could get it, but all in vain. I was inconsolable. One day I visited my aunt, who had recently come up from the country. She showed a tender interest in me and lovingly said I had grown up beautifully. On my return she said: "What shall I give you? You will not be interested in serious things: I will give you what you like best." And she gave me more than fifty volumes of Genji-monogatari put in a case, as well as Isé-monogatari, Yojimi, Serikawa, Shirara, and Asa-udzu. How happy I was when I came home carrying these books in a bag! Until then I had only read a volume here and there, and was dissatisfied because I could not understand the story.

Now I could be absorbed in these stories, taking them out one by one, shutting myself in behind the kicho. To be a Queen were nothing compared to this!

---

*Place where cremation was performed.
**It is a Buddhist custom to go into retreat from time to time.

All day and all night, as late as I could keep my eyes open, I did nothing but look at the books, setting a lamp close beside me.

Soon I learnt by heart all the names in the books, and I thought that a great thing.

Jean Jacques Rousseau
(1712-1778)

Rousseau, when he was sixteen years old, experienced precisely what Erikson (7) has described as belonging to the psychopathology of everyday adolescence. "Cases of severe identity diffusion regularly . . . suffer from an acute upset in the sense of workmanship, and this either in the form of an inability to concentrate on required or suggested tasks, or in a self-destructive preoccupation with some one-sided activities, i.e., excessive reading."

Miserable in his apprenticeship to an engraver, and weary of the antics of his companions, Rousseau found solace in books. Reading became a passion for him "and soon a regular madness." He read indiscriminately and avidly. "I read at the work-table, I read on my errands, I read in the water-closet, and forgot myself for hours together; my head became giddy with reading; I could do nothing else." This interference with his work prompted Rousseau's master to beat him and destroy some of the books, but to no avail. For a year, Jean Jacques maintained the pace, and then abruptly seemed to have quit. The books had "filled my heart with nobler sentiments," an indication of the conscious level of the identification process, but another defense mechanism cropped up, sublimation, an outgrowth of developing sensuality in the boy. "This consisted in feeding myself upon the situations which had interested me in the course of my reading, in recalling them, in varying them, in combining them, in making them so truly my own that I became one of the persons who filled my imagination."*

> I should never finish these details if I were to follow all the paths along which, during my apprenticeship, I descended from the sublimity of heroism to the depths of worthlessness. And yet, although I adopted the vices of my position, I could not altogether acquire a

---

*From *Confessions* by Jean Jacques Rousseau. Reprinted by permission of Pocket Books, Inc. 1957. Pp. 24-26.

taste for them. I wearied of the amusements of my companions; and when excessive restraint had rendered work unendurable to me, I grew tired of everything. This renewed my taste for reading, which I had for some time lost. This reading, for which I stole time from my work, became a new offense which brought new punishment upon me. The taste for it, provoked by constraint, became a passion, and soon a regular madness. La Tribu, a well-known lender of books, provided me with all kinds of literature. Good or bad, all were alike to me; I had no choice, and read everything with equal avidity. I read at the work-table, I read on my errands, I read in the water-closet, and forgot myself for hours together; my head became giddy with reading; I could do nothing else. My master watched me, surprised me, beat me, took away my books. How many volumes were torn, burnt, and thrown out of the window! how many works were left in odd volumes in La Tribu's stock! When I had no more money to pay her, I gave her my shirts, neckties and clothes; my three sous of pocket-money were regularly taken to her every Sunday. . . .

In consequence of quarrels, blows, and secret and ill-chosen reading, my disposition became savage and taciturn; my mind became altogether perverted, and I lived like a misanthrope. However, if my good taste did not keep me from silly and insipid books, my good fortune preserved me from such as were filthy and licentious; not that La Tribu, a woman in all respects most accommodating, would have made any scruple about lending them to me; but, in order to increase their importance, she always mentioned them to me with an air of mystery which had just the effect of making me refuse them, as much from disgust as from shame; and chance aided my modest disposition so well, that I was more than thirty years old before I set eyes upon any of those dangerous books which a fine lady finds inconvenient because they can only be read with one hand.

In less than a year I exhausted La Tribu's little stock, and want of occupation, during my spare time, became painful to me. I had been cured of my childish and knavish propensities by my passion for reading, and even by the books I read, which, although ill-chosen and frequently bad, filled my heart with nobler sentiments than those with which my sphere of life had inspired me. Disgusted with everything that was within my reach, and feeling that everything which might have tempted me was too far removed from me, I saw nothing possible which might have flattered my heart. My excited senses had long clamoured for an enjoyment, the object of which I could not even imagine. I was as far removed from actual enjoyment as if I had been sexless; and, already fully developed and sensitive, I sometimes thought of my crazes, but saw nothing beyond them. In this strange situation, my restless imagination entered upon an occupation which saved me from myself and calmed my growing sensuality. This consisted in feeding myself upon the situations which had interested me in the course of my reading, in recalling them, in varying them, in combining them, in making them so truly my own that I became one of the persons who filled my imagination, and always saw myself in the situations most agreeable to my taste; and that, finally, the fictitious state in which I succeeded in putting myself made me forget my actual state with which I was so dissatisfied. This love of imaginary objects, and the readiness with which I occupied myself with them, ended by disgusting me with everything around me, and decided that liking for solitude which has never left me. In the sequel we shall see more than once the curious effects of this disposition, apparently so gloomy and misanthropic, but which is really due to a too affectionate, too loving and too tender heart, which, being unable to find any in existence resembling it, is obliged to nourish itself with fancies. . . .

Edward Gibbon
(1737-1794)

Gibbon wrote with a great deal of self-satisfaction about the vast number of books he read as an adolescent. He became so immersed in Roman literature and history that his identification with Quintilian, for example, enabled him to breathe "the spirit of freedom, and I imbibed from his precepts and examples the public and private sense of a man." His readings in the Roman field are so extensive as to make us marvel. Small wonder he was able to produce his masterpiece, *The History of the Decline and Fall of the Roman Empire,* in eight detailed volumes.

The first time Gibbon went to Rome, in 1764, he stated in his *Autobiography,* he approached it with "strong emotions which agitated my mind." The morning after his arrival, following a sleepless night, "I trod," he wrote, "with a lofty step, the ruins of the Forum; each memorable spot where Romulus stood, or Tully spoke, or Caesar fell, was at once present to my eye."* His inspirational visit to the ruins of pagan glory, intellectually grounded as it was during his adolescent years of reading, started him off on a twenty-seven-year labor of love, the writing of his *Decline and Fall.*

---

*From *The Autobiography of Edward Gibbon.* Reprinted by permission of E. P. Dutton & Co., Inc. Everyman's Library. Pp. 67-69.

I am tempted to distinguish the last eight months of the year 1755 as the period of the most extraordinary diligence and rapid progress. In my French and Latin translations I adopted an excellent method, which, from my own success, I would recommend to the imitation of students. I chose some classic writer, such as Cicero and Vertot, the most approved for purity and elegance of style. I translated, for instance, an epistle of Cicero into French; and, after throwing it aside till the words and phrases were obliterated from my memory, I re-translated my French into such Latin as I could find; and then compared each sentence of my imperfect version with the ease, the grace, the propriety of the Roman orator. A similar experiment was made on several pages of the Revolutions of Vertot; I turned them into Latin, returned them after a sufficient interval into my own French, and again scrutinised the resemblance or dissimilitude of the copy and the original. By degrees I was less ashamed, by degrees I was more satisfied with myself; and I persevered in the practice of these double translations, which filled several books, till I had acquired the knowledge of both idioms, and the command at least of a correct style. This useful exercise of writing was accompanied and succeeded by the more pleasing occupation of reading the best authors. The perusal of the Roman classics was at once my exercise and reward. Dr. Middleton's History, which I then appreciated above its true value, naturally directed me to the writings of Cicero. The most perfect editions, that of Olivet, which may adorn the shelves of the rich, that of Ernesti, which should lie on the table of the learned, were not within my reach. For the familiar epistles I used the text and English commentary of Bishop Ross; but my general edition was that of Verburgius, published at Amsterdam in two large volumes in folio, with an indifferent choice of various notes. I read, with application and pleasure, *all* the epistles, *all* the orations, and the most important treatises of rhetoric and philosophy; and as I read, I applauded the observation of Quintilian, that every student may judge of his own proficiency by the satisfaction which he receives from the Roman orator. I tasted the beauties of language, I breathed the spirit of freedom, and I imbibed from his precepts and examples the public and private sense of a man. Cicero in Latin, and Xenophon in Greek, are indeed the two ancients whom I would first propose to a liberal scholar; not only for the merit of their style and sentiments, but for the admirable lessons, which may be applied almost to every situation of public and private life. Cicero's *Epistles* may in particular afford the models of every form of correspondence, from the careless effusions of tenderness and friendship, to the well-guarded declaration of discreet and dignified resentment.

After finishing this great author, a library of eloquence and reason, I formed a more extensive plan of reviewing the Latin classics, under the four divisions of, 1, historians; 2, poets; 3, orators; and 4, philosophers, in a chronological series, from the days of Plautus and Sallust to the decline of the language and empire of Rome: and this plan, in the last twenty-seven months of my residence at Lausanne (January 1756—April 1758), I *nearly* accomplished. Nor was this review, however rapid, either hasty or superficial. I indulged myself in a second and even third perusal of Terence, Virgil, Horace, Tacitus, etc., and studied to imbibe the sense and spirit most congenial to my own. I never suffered a difficult or corrupt passage to escape, till I had viewed it in every light of which it was susceptible: though often disappointed, I always consulted the most learned or ingenious commentators, Torrentius and Dacier on Horace, Catrou and Servius on Virgil, Lipsius on Tacitus, Meziriac on Ovid, etc.; and in the ardour of my inquiries I embraced a large circle of historical and critical erudition. My abstracts of each book were made in the French language: my observations often branched into particular essays; and I can still read, without contempt, a dissertation of eight folio pages on eight lines (287-294) of the fourth *Georgic* of Virgil. Mr. Deyverdun, my friend, whose name will be frequently repeated, had joined with equal zeal, though not with equal perseverance, in the same undertaking. To him every thought, every composition, was instantly communicated; with him I enjoyed the benefits of a free conversation on the topics of our common studies.

Charles Leland
(1824-1903)

Leland described in his *Memoirs** a flash of insight, "to me it was more like an apocalypse," his first stealthy and brief reading of Rabelais when he was fourteen years old. The fifteen-minute dip into the volume made him realize, "like a young giant just awakened, that there was in me a stupendous mental strength to grasp and understand that magnificent mixture of ribaldry and learning, fun and wisdom, deviltry and divinity." A year later, when he came across the poems of François Villon, he experienced a comparable sensation. "Never shall I forget the feeling, which Heine compares to the unexpected finding of a shaft of gold in a gloomy

---

*From *Memoirs* by Charles Leland. Reprinted by permission of Appleton-Century-Crofts, Inc. Copyright 1893. Pp. 70-71.

mine, which shot through me as I read for the first time these *bal-lades.*"

The life-long influence of books showed its mark on Leland. From the high school of Philadelphia, he went on to Princeton, became the editor of a magazine and the friend of Emerson, Holmes, Lowell, and Louis Agassiz.

One day I saw Mr. Hunt and Mr. Kendall [his teachers] chuckling together over a book. I divined a secret. Now, I was a very honourable boy, and never pried into secrets, but where a quaint old book was concerned I had no more conscience than a pirate. And seeing Mr. Hunt put the book into his desk, I abode my time till he had gone forth, when I raised the lid, and . . .

Merciful angels and benevolent fairies! it was Urquhart's translation of Rabelais! One short spell I read, no more; but it raised a devil which has never since been laid. Ear hath not heard, it hath not entered into the heart of man to conceive, what I felt as I realised, like a young giant just awakened, that there was in me a stupendous mental strength to grasp and understand that magnificent mixture of ribaldry and learning, fun and wisdom, deviltry and divinity. In a few pages' time I knew what it all meant, and that I was gifted to understand it. I replaced the book; nor did I read it again for years, for from that hour I was never quite the same person. The next day I saw Callot's *Temptation of St. Anthony* for the first time in a shop-window, and felt with joy and pride that I understood it out of Rabelais. Two young gentlemen—lawyers apparently—by my side thought it was crazy and silly. To me it was more like an apocalypse.

I am speaking plain truth when I say that that one quarter of an hour's reading of Rabelais—standing up—was to me as the light which flashed upon Saul journeying to Damascus. It seems to me now as if it were the great event of my life. It came to such a pass in after years that I could have identified any line in the Chronicle of Gargantua, and I also was the suggester, father, and founder in London of the Rabelais Club, in which were many of the best minds of the time, but beyond it all and brighter than all was that first revelation.

It should be remembered that I had already perused Sterne, much of Swift, and far more comic and satiric literature than is known to boys, and, what is far more remarkable, had thoroughly taken it all into my *cor cordium* by much repetition and reflection.

*   *   *

Something took place which cast a marvellous light into this darkened life of mine. For one day my father bought and presented to me a share in the Philadelphia Library. This was a collection which even then consisted of more than 60,000 well-chosen volumes. And then began such a life of reading as was, I sincerely believe, unusual in such youth. My first book was *Arthur of Little Britaine,* which I finished in a week; then *Newes from New Englande, 1636,* and the *Historie of Clodoaldus.* Before long I discovered that there were in the Loganian section of the library several hundred volumes of occult philosophy, a collection once formed by an artist named Cox, and of these I really read nearly every one. Cornelius Agrippa and Barret's *Magus,* Paracelsus, the black-letter edition of Reginald Scot, Glanville, and Gaffarel, Trithemius, Baptista Porta, and God knows how many Rosicrucian writers became familiar to me. Once when I had only twenty-five cents I gave it for a copy of *Waters of the East* by Eugenius Philalethes, or Thomas Vaughan.

All of this led me to the Mystics and Quietists. I read Dr. Boardman's *History of Quakerism,* which taught me that Fox grew out of Behmen; and I picked up one day Poiret's French work on the Mystics, which was quite a handbook or guide to the whole literature. But these books were but a small part of what I read; for at one time, taking another turn towards old English, I went completely through Chaucer and Gower, both in black letter, the collections of Ritson, Weber, Ellis, and I know not how many more of mediæval ballads and romances, and very thoroughly and earnestly indeed Warton's *History of English Poetry.* Then I read Sismondi's *Literature of Southern Europe* and Longfellow's *Poets and Poetry of Europe,* which set me to work on Raynouard and other collections of Provençal poetry, in the knowledge of which I made some progress, and also St. Pelaye's, Le Grand's, Costello's, and other books on the Trouveurs. I translated into rhyme and sent to a magazine, of which I in after years became editor, one or two *lais,* which were rejected, I think unwisely, for they were by no means bad. Then I had a fancy for Miscellanea, and read the works of D'Israeli the elder and Burton's *Anatomy.*

One day I made a startling discovery, for I took at a venture from the library the black-letter first edition of the poems of François Villon. I was then fifteen years old. Never shall I forget the feeling, which Heine compares to the unexpected finding of a shaft of gold in a gloomy mine, which shot through me as I read for the first time these *ballades.* Now-a-days people are trained to them through second-hand sentiment. Villon has become—Heaven bless the mark!—*fashionable!* and æsthetic. I got at him "straight" out of black-letter reading in boyhood as a find of my own, and it was many, many years ere

I ever met with a single soul who had heard of him. I at once translated the "Song of the Ladies of the Olden Time"; and I knew what
bon bec meant, which is more than one of Villon's great modern
translators has done! Also *heaulmière,* which is *not* helmet-maker, as
another supposes.

I went further in this field than I have room to describe. I even read
the rococo-sweet poems of Joachim du Bellay. In this year my father
gave me *The Doctor,* by Robert Southey, a work which I read and reread assiduously for many years, and was guided by it to a vast amount
of odd reading, Philemon Holland's translation of Pliny being one of
the books. This induced me to read all of Southey's poems, which I
did, not from the library, but from a bookstore, where I had free run
and borrowing privileges, as I well might, since my father lost £ 4,000
by its owner.

While at Mr. Greene's school I had given me Alsopp's *Life and Letters of Coleridge,* which I read through many times; then in my thirteenth year, in Philadelphia, I read with great love Charles Lamb's
works and most of the works of Coleridge. Mr. Alcott had read Wordsworth into us in illimitable quantities, so that I soon had a fair all-
round knowledge of the Lakers, whom I dearly loved. Now there was
a certain soupçon of Mysticism or Transcendalism and Pantheism
in Coleridge, and even in Wordsworth, which my love of rocks and
rivers and fairy lore easily enabled me to detect by sympathy.

Santiago Ramón y Cajal
(1852-1934)

Ramón y Cajal was born in Petilla de Aragon near Navarre in
northeast Spain. His father was generally severe with him, as will
be seen in the description which follows,* particularly when it
came to the boy's studies and reading matter. Recreational books
were not permitted in the home, so that when the twelve-year-old
Ramón discovered a cache of forbidden novels, histories, collections of poetry and books on travel in a neighbor's garret, he took
advantage of the treasure. "Who could enhance the enjoyment
which I experienced in reading these delightful books! So great
were my enthusiasm and pleasure that I forgot entirely the common occupations of everyday life." The passion for reading had

---

*From *Recollections of My Life* translated by E. Horne Craigie. Reprinted by permission of American Philosophical Society. 1937. Pp. 98-103.

overtaken this Spanish boy, as it had the Japanese girl, the French Rousseau and the other adolescents to be described subsequently.

I write of the joyful and hilarious enthusiasm with which I cele-brated the summer of 1864 after the June examinations, in which, if I did not deserve honour diplomas, neither did I encounter the dreaded failure.

Upon my arrival at Ayerbe, my first thought was to get into touch with my old playmates, to whom I proudly related my adventures and exhibited my drawings and sketches.

When I had satisfied my thirst for friendly expression of welcome and for running wildly about the town, my father called me to order and informed me of his decision that I must give up foolish pastimes and absurd artistic caprices and devote the summer to study, first re-viewing all the work in which I had recently passed the examinations, though I had learned it but mediocrely, and then attacking the texts prescribed for the following session. He believed that this exercise which he had planned would make the next year's tasks much easier. Such a decision was like a jug of cold water poured over my head, which was aflame with eagerness to give joyful rein to my natural inclinations.

I had no alternative but submission to the paternal advice and I even believe that I sincerely intended to comply with it; but the demon of rebellion, which had never been overcome, and my deter-mined and troublesome artistic tendencies broke down these sensible intentions.

It often happens that wilful boys, even though fundamentally good, are transformed into artful hypocrites by the desire to spare their parents pain. On the pretext that my assiduous reading required ab-solute silence and freedom from disturbance, which could not be had in the study, I asked and obtained my father's permission to equip as a work room the pigeon house, a room adjoining the barn, which had a window opening upon the roof of the next house. From the door of my retreat I could conveniently keep a lookout for those who were watching my conduct. The stratagem succeeded perfectly, as we are about to see.

As the ultimate step in caution, I constructed a sort of confessional or niche out of boards, rough sticks, and brushwood on the roof of the neighbouring house, behind a chimney, where it was screened from prying eyes; and beneath the seat in this I secreted the forbidden papers, pencils, colours, and novels. From time to time, in order to carry out the deception, I returned to the pigeon house (especially when I heard the sound of footsteps) and began very seriously to translate Cornelius Nepos, or to study the psychology of Monlau and the algebra of Vallín y Bustillo. Apart from these brief moments, my retreat was the cage on the roof, where I spent my time drawing, my favourite amusement. I do not remember exactly the subjects which my brush profaned that summer, but I recall that for the time my work had mostly a lugubrious and melancholy atmosphere.

It is manifest to the world that in the fickle interests of youth an important part is played by suggestion and imitation. Someone (I think it was in Huesca) had lent me a volume of gloomy and funereal poetry, among which I remember the hackneyed and commonplace verses attributed groundlessly to Espronceda and entitled "Despair" and the famous "Mournful nights" of Cadalso.

Influenced by such depressing reading, I imagined it to be my inevitable duty to attune myself with the sombre temper of the poets, affecting the deepest melancholy in both my words and my sketches. And so my brush, which showed the fluctuations of my morbid sensibilities as the pointer of a galvanometer indicates the direction of electric currents, dwelt joyfully upon winter landscapes, desolate wastes, the sufferings of the shipwrecked, and macabre views of cemeteries.

If my memory does not deceive me, it was at the end of that summer that there happened an event which had a decisive influence in directing my future literary and artistic tastes.

I have already mentioned that in my home books of recreation were not permitted. It is true that my father possessed a few works of fiction, but he concealed them from our wild curiosity, as if they were deadly poison. In his opinion, young people should not distract their imagination with frivolous reading during the formative period. In spite of the prohibition, my mother, unknown to the head of the house, allowed us to read some cheap romantic novels which she had kept in the bottom of a trunk since before she was married. There were, I well remember, *El solitario del monte salvaje, La extranjera, La cana* of Balzac, *Catalina Howard, Genoveva de Brabante,* and a few others which have slipped my memory. It is superfluous to say that my brothers and sisters as well as I read them with immediate enthusiasm, evading the jealous vigilance of the head of the family.

Aside from these novels, my reading for pleasure up to that time had been reduced to some poems of Espronceda, of whom I was a fervent admirer, and a certain collection of old time ballads and stories of knight errantry which in those days were sold for a few coppers by the blind and by the dealers in religious prints and writing materials. At that period, as I have already said, I was a romantic though ignorant of romanticism. No book by Rousseau, Chateaubriand, Victor Hugo, etc., had fallen into my hands.

But accident often becomes the accomplice of our desires. One day, when I was exploring at random my secret domain above the tiles, I looked in at the window of a garret belonging to the neighbouring confectioner and beheld—oh, delightful surprise!—beside old pieces of furniture and frames covered with sweetmeats and dried fruits, a rich and varied collection of novels, stories and histories, collections of poetry, and books of travel. There were to be seen, tempting my burning curiosity, the celebrated *Count of Monte Cristo* and *The Three Musketeers* of Dumas père; *Maria or the daughter of a laborer* by E. Sué; *Men Rodríguez de Sanabria* by Fernándex y González; *The Martyrs, Atala and Chactas,* and *René* by Chateaubriand; *Graziella* by Lamartine; *Notre Dame de Paris* and *Ninety-three* by Victor Hugo; *Gil Blas de Santillana* by Le Sage; *History of Spain* by Mariana; *The comedies of Calderón;* several books and poems by Quevedo; *The Voyages of Captain Cook, Robinson Crusoe, Don Quixote,* and innumerable books of less importance of which I have not a detailed recollection. It was obvious that the confectioner was a man of taste and that he did not reckon his happiness solely in terms of making caramels and cakes.

Excitement at such a fortunate occurrence held me spellbound for several minutes. Then, recovering from my surprise, I determined to make the most of my good luck and considered how best to take advantage of that inestimable treasure. It was essential to obviate all suspicions of the owner and to avoid leaving any tell-tale traces of my visits to the garret. The most elementary caution told me to leave alone, for the present, the delicious and appetizing candies on the frames, for I was sure, that, if the manufacturer missed any of his candied pears and plums, he would close the window or put a grating over it and leave me out in the cold. After careful consideration I decided to strike the first blow early in the morning, while the occupants of the house were asleep, and to take the coveted books one at a time, replacing each volume in its own place on the shelves.

Thanks to these precautions, I enjoyed in peace the most interesting works in the library, without the worthy pastry-cook being aware of the abuse, and without my parents discovering my absences from the pigeon house. Who could enhance the enjoyment which I experienced in reading these delightful books! So great were my enthusiasm and pleasure that I forgot entirely the common occupations of everyday life.

What exquisite artistic sensations those admirable novels brought
me! What fascinating new types of humanity they revealed to me!
The brilliant descriptions in *Atala* of the virgin forests of America,
where the abounding plant life seems to smother man in his insignificance; the tender and chaste loves of Cimodocea in *The Martyrs;*
the exquisite and angelic form of *Graziella;* the exalted and almost
monstrous passion of Quasimodo, in *Notre Dame de Paris;* the nobility, magnanimity, and punctilious bravery of the incomparable
d'Artagnan, Porthos, and Aramis, in *The Three Musketeers;* and
finally the cold, inexorable, and carefully planned vengeance of the
leading character in the *Count of Monte Cristo,* captivated and
aroused my sympathies in an extraordinary fashion.

At last, though by illicit means, I made the acquaintance of the
splendid creatures of the imagination; superb and magnificent beings,
all energy and determination, with overgrown hearts shaken by super-
human passions. It is true that nearly all the novels which I devoured
at that time belonged to the romantic school, which was then in
fashion, and of which the heroes seem to be designed expressly to
carry away the young, who are always thirsty for extraordinary events
and marvellous adventures.

It would be difficult for me to tell now, after the passage of so many
years, the books which impressed me most. I believe, however, that I
am not going far astray when I state that I was most excited and fascinated by the delightful novels of action and intrigue of Dumas
(père) and the ultra-romantic stories of Victor Hugo, which I then
rated higher than *Faust, Gil Blas de Santillana* and even— I blush
to confess it—the marvellous *Don Quixote.*

Maxim Gorky
(1868-1936)

During Gorky's twelfth year of life, he was a slavey, working in the
household of his grandmother's sister. He had to make the beds,
sweep the floor, keep the stoves going, run errands and perform
other menial tasks. Both his parents were dead; a stepfather, still
alive, was ill and living with his mistress; the maternal grandmother, while loving, could not maintain the boy.

The only brightness in his bleak and cheerless lot was reading.
Gorky tells us the lengths he was willing to go to in order to get
books. Like young Freud, he went into debt to the local bookseller;
he was almost forced to steal in order to pay that gentleman back:

since he had no funds for buying candles, he collected tallow drip-
pings to provide himself with sufficient light to enable him to read
at night.

For Gorky, books made living bearable. They brought him far
afield from the miserable Russian village and the existence circumstances found him in. "They placed in my ken a world which
widened every day, a world splendid like the cities of romance."
The "vacuous melancholia" of adolesence was dissipated—for a
time—under the impact of the new worlds he discovered through
reading.*

For certain lugubrious reasons I well remember the mortification,
the indignities, the alarms I incurred in the precipitate growth of my
literary appetites. The books belonging to the cutter's wife had a
costly look, and since I feared their immolation in the oven by the
old woman, I did my best to forget them and turned instead to small,
paper-bound volumes on sale in the shop where I made my morning
purchase of bread.

Its owner was an unhandsome, thick-lipped individual, whose skin
was continually agleam with sweat, whose pallid, wrinkled face was
sown with eruptions and their scars, whose eyes were white, and whose
bloated hands terminated in stubby, clumsy fingers. His place served
as a club for the grown men and the flightier girls on our street. It
was my boss' brother's hangout for a nightly glass of beer and a hand
of cards. Sent there to summon him to supper, I saw him, or some other
young gallant, more than once, in the tiny, airless back room, with
the shopkeeper's pink, coquettish wife on his knee. The shopkeeper
seemed to take no offense, nor did he seem to mind that his sister,
who helped tend shop, lavished her caresses on drunken soldiers, or
anybody else, for that matter, who suited her whim.

Business was poor, for which the shopkeeper gave the explanation
that it was a new venture, although he had actually opened in the
fall. His services to his customers included exhibits of pornographic
pictures, and permission to copy the salacious rhymes underneath.

I read the trivial little tales by Misha Yevstigneyev at a rental of a
kopeck or so apiece. This was high, while the pleasure I got out of
them was nil. As also such literature as *Gouak,* or *Truth Unconquerable, The Venetian, The Battle Between the Russians and the Khab-
ardins,* or *The Moslem Beauty Who Died on Her Husband's Grave*—

*From *Autobiography* by Maxim Gorky. Reprinted by permission of The Citadel
Press. 1940. Pp. 276-279.

books that, in fact, annoyed me. I felt laughed at, by these books, for my gullibility; their matter was so incredible and their manner so insipid.

More satisfying were such tales as *The Marksman, Yury Miloslavsky, The Mysterious Monk, Yapancha,* and *The Tatar Raider.* Such reading enriched me. But my favorites were the *Lives of the Saints.* These had substance that made them credible, and roused responsive emotion in me. I found resemblances in all the martyrs to Good Idea, and, in the women martyrs, to grandma; and in the hermits to grandpa at his best.

My reading was done in the cold shed, when I went out to split firewood; or in the attic, which I found hardly any warmer or more convenient. When I became absorbed in a book, or had to finish it by a certain time, I would wait till the rest were asleep, and read by candle. Observing the diminution of the candles, the old woman took to measuring them with a piece of wood. And if, in the morning, I had failed to find her measuring rod and notch it to the burned-down length, her outcries would ring through the kitchen.

Once Victor stormed at her, "Cut out that yelling, mama. Sure—he uses up the candles reading books. I know where he gets them—in the store. You'll find them in his stuff in the attic."

Up to the attic the old woman leaped, hunted out a book, and burned it. As you can well understand, this made me furious, but only sharpened my appetite. I realized that if a saint strayed into that household, my employers would have gone to work on him, to tune him to their own key. And the attempt would be made just to give themselves something to do. Had they stopped making judgments on people, nagging them, deriding them, they would have lost the faculty of speech, become mutes, been themselves no longer. One becomes conscious of himself through his contacts with others. No relationship with others was possible to my employers, except that of censorious mentors. Had they educated somebody to their identical way of living, feeling, thinking, then they would have reproached him for that. That was the sort they were.

I kept up my secret reading. This meant the annihilation of several books at the hands of the old woman and I found myself the shopkeeper's debtor for the staggering sum of forty-seven kopecks. He demanded it from me, threatening to withhold it when he made change for me on purchases I made for my employers. "What'll you do then," he scoffed.

I found him intolerably coarse. He knew it, and retaliated by tormenting me with his threats. He greeted me with a broad leer on his pustular face and the bland inquiry, "Have you come to settle your debt?"

"I can't."

He appeared startled, and frowned. "How come? Are you looking for charity from me? I see I'll have to get my money by fixing up a trip to the reformatory for you."

There was no way I could put my hands on the money, my wages being turned over to grandpa. I got into a panic. What was to become of me? To my pleas for more time, the storekeeper replied by stretching out his greasy, bladder-like hand and saying, "I'll wait if you'll kiss my hand."

Instead, I picked up a weight from the counter and aimed it at his head. He ducked and yelled, "What's the matter? I was only fooling!"

I knew very well he wasn't fooling, and to be quit of him, I decided to steal that sum.

Brushing the boss' clothes in the morning, I heard coins jingling in the trouser pockets, and some, at times, fell out and rolled over the floor. Once two had rolled under the staircase, which I forgot about. Finding them several days later, I had given them back to the boss, and his wife had remarked, "See! Better count the money you leave in your pockets."

With a smile at me he had replied, "I know he won't steal."

Having decided to steal, the recollection of these words and his confiding smile made it hard for me. Several times I took coins out of his pocket, counted them, and then put them back. For three days I kept torturing myself this way, when the problem was solved for me, simply and at once.

The boss surprised me by asking, "What's wrong with you, Peshkov? You've grown so listless, lately. Don't you feel well, or what?"

I gave him a candid report of what was on my mind. Frowning, he said, "See what your books have gotten you into? Sooner or later books are bound to get people into trouble."

He gave me a half a ruble, cautioning me, "Look, you, not a word about this to my wife or my mother, or there'll be a scandal." With a kind smile, he added, "The devil, but you're persistent! And that's good. Just the same, no books. Come New Year, I'll subscribe to a good journal, so there'll be reading for you."

Henry Handel Richardson
(1870-1946)

The leaden-footed months Miss Richardson spent in her fourteenth year just prior to leaving her native Australia for England were painful and desolate. Her break with a girl friend, Evelyn, had left open scars which would take a long time to heal. For what had transpired, the reader is referred to the section on homosexuality in the chapter on psychosexual development.

It was extremely difficult for young Miss Richardson to give up the immediate love object, particularly since, as is true in adolescence, her libido was engaged in an emotional struggle of extreme urgency and immediacy and had detached itself from the parents and cathected a new object. According to Anna Freud (9), "Some mourning for the objects of the past is inevitable; so are the 'crushes,' i.e., the happy or unhappy love affairs with adults outside the family, or with other adolescents, whether of the opposite or the same sex; so is, further, a certain amount of narcissistic withdrawal which bridges the gap during periods when no external object is cathected."

The excerpt below from Miss Richardson's autobiography* is an illustration of this narcissistic withdrawal. In the attempt to drown the hurt and sorrow she felt, she turned to books. She fell on everything that came her way and even stole a work of Longfellow.

But until the sum my uncle stood out for was agreed to and the house disposed of, months dragged by. To me they seemed like years. Seldom have I been so miserable. I was still raw and bleeding from the break with Evelyn. I couldn't forget her, or forgive fate for making our worldly lots so unequal. The result was a quantity of doggerel verse—afterwards fortunately consigned to the fire—in which I railed my fill at life's injustices. And as if all this weren't enough, it was now thought only fair that, after the many sacrifices made on my behalf, I should at least earn my own pocket-money. And so, outwardly calm but stewing inwardly, I found myself installed as morning-governess in a small private school at Toorak. I loathed the job, and was of course a blank and utter failure as a teacher. But I stuck it out. And it was well I did. For though I left my pupils where I found them, I myself learned that there was *nothing* I would not rather do than impart, or try to impart knowledge to others. I should no doubt have been ignominiously dismissed at the end of the term, had I not been

*From *Myself when Young* by Henry Handel Richardson. Reprinted by permission of W. W. Norton & Co., Inc. 1948. Pp. 74-78.

beforehand and announced that we were leaving Australia.

I drowned my sorrows in books. For the afternoons were my own, readable books, so scarce at school, to hand in plenty. On the shelves stood my father's pocket-edition of Scott, till then unread, and this I fell upon, blotting out the unlovely present in one after another of the great romances. I can see myself of a wintry evening, my feet on the fender, poring over the microscopic print by the light of a single gas-jet—for in those days we knew no better. Or at a solitary lunch, consisting, God save the mark, of strong tea and a dish of cucumber, with a vigorous love-story by Rhoda Broughton propped up against the pot. Or in bed, a flickery candle at my elbow, struggling through Tom Paine's *Rights of Man*.

For poetry I had a six-volumed edition of Tennyson, won as a dux-prize for English and History in my last year at school. There, we had learned a fair amount of Milton, Wordsworth, Gray, Cowper and so on; but Tennyson was not yet accounted a classic, and stray scraps were all I knew of him. From the complete works I had promised my-self much—overmuch it seemed, when I came to read them. For except in the lyrics, parts of *Maud,* and the whole of *Ulysses,* which I take some credit for even then thinking flawless, Tennyson failed to grip me. I felt old and, in my small way, too sophisticated for his village maidens—they recalled early browsings in *The Family Herald*—and at the same time was still too young and too ignorant to see where he excelled. Indeed it was often the very smoothness and polish of this verse that told against it.

In those days Tennyson's name was usually bracketed with—and after—Longfellow's. And so I too would have ranked them. Long-fellow I thought the world of, and had done ever since somebody presented me, while still at school, with a sixpenny paper-copy of *Hiawatha*. Here, the rushing metre and the music of the Indian words took my ear by storm. I remember, at a first reading, finding it so heady that I spent a coach-journey between Castlemaine and Maldon shouting out melodious bits to myself, for sheer joy in the sound. There were of course no other passengers, and the elderly driver snoozed on his box. Subsequently I managed to get hold of the short poems, and these too were greedily lapped up. I used to bombard poor Lil with them, in the hope, the vain hope, of awakening a fellow spark. For neither she nor Mother had any feeling for verse. Things one assimilates with such gusto in childhood are not easily forgotten; and many a line from this now neglected poet still runs in my head. *"How beautiful is the rain! After the dust and heat."* Or *"I heard the trailing garments of the Night, Sweep through her marble halls!"* or

"Peace! Peace! Orestes-like I breathe this prayer." Or *"Spanish sailors with bearded lips, And the beauty and mystery of the ships, And the magic of the sea."* Let alone the lovely refrain: *"For a boy's will is the wind's will, and the thoughts of youth are long, long thoughts."* As for his rendering of Salis's *Silent Land,* then a particular favourite, reflecting as it did my own world-weary mood, it still seems to me a finer poem than the original.

In the room at Toorak where I gave my so-called music-lessons stood a number of books on open shelves. I couldn't keep my eyes off them, and soon spotted a volume by Longfellow that was new to me. A request for the loan of it would have been looked on as "sauce"; so I took French leave, pocketed it by stealth, and carried it home. I had intended to keep it for a night only; but the one ran to three or four. It was called, I think, *Hyperion,* and included a translation of E. T. A. Hoffmann's *Kreisleriana,* purporting to relate the musical sufferings of a certain Kapellmeister Johannes Kreisler. Nothing like them had ever come my way, and they so intrigued me that in bed at night I surreptitiously copied out chapter after chapter. The old exercise book containing them still exists; and I wonder alike at my zeal and at the ugliness of my huge, untidy hand.—Such was my earliest contact with a writer of the Romantic School.

John Cowper Powys
(1872-1963)

The adolescent frequently resorts to sublimation of his libidinal drives through the reading of erotic literature. The strength of the sex drive as well as availability undoubtedly determine the nature of the reading. According to Powys, the pornographic and the salacious left him cold and disgusted. But more delicate reading matter left him with "a kind of quivering poetry of lust [18]."

Adolescents turn to literature to satisfy their sexual needs, not only because of physical promptings, but out of their craving for knowledge of what it is like for the opposite sex. Stone and Church (20) remark that in the folklore, and in the literature found in scientific publications—written largely by men—there is an amazing ignorance of female sexuality. Boys are inclined either to project their own sexuality onto girls or to see girls as indifferent or hostile to sex; in any case, they are uncertain what to believe. So far as girls are concerned, they often do not know what to think about their own sexuality.

For the adolescent, as was true for Powys, books can provide relief from the physical tensions under which he functions.

I have forgotten what book I was so absorbed in, the day when the little Llewelyn, with the hot sun all about him, peeped in upon me with such quizzical wonder; but I well remember how my erotic obsession drove me to search through all the *Addisonian Spectators* in that drawing-room. I can now see the delicate rosewood of the bureau where these volumes stood, as I hunted feverishly for fuel for the fever that consumed me. I can recall some particular passage now, two or three of them, to which I would turn; but I will let those of my readers who possess these volumes pursue their own quest! Certainly some of the happiest hours of my whole life—and when I think of the tenuous atmosphere of enchanted glamour that suffused them I cannot find it in me to be ashamed—have been occupied in this cult of cerebral eroticism.

Very, very slowly in those days I was learning to get pleasure from the exposed limbs of young women as well as of lovely boys; but, so far, this was confined to their representation in pictures. Descriptions of ordinary amorous scenes I disliked. They left me, and still do, cold and disgusted. And as for the least approach to gross or lewd bawdiness—such things froze, like the touch of ice, the very roots of lechery in me! These were the days of that fantastical publication, known as *Ally Sloper,* and although the comic portions of this periodical were abhorrent to me, I soon found that it contained daintily sketched outlines of the feminine form most perfectly adapted to satisfy my exacting senses. These *Ally Sloper* young ladies I would cut out with trembling hands and carry about with me in my pocket. Is it not strange how moralists forget their own early feelings in such matters, how entrancing, and also how harmless, they were! My own feelings, I know, were touched with a kind of quivering poetry of lust, a soft, melting, ravishing, spring-like tenderness of lust, that was at the extreme opposite pole from all indecency. I can remember exactly how I felt when, during my first visit to London, staying with a most friendly clergyman there who was my father's closest friend at Corpus, I was taken to the Covent Garden Pantomime, and beheld a whole galaxy—so it seemed to my dazzled and swimming eyes—of girl-angels straight from the well-loved section of my egregious periodical.

Lucy Sprague Mitchell
(1878-   )

The compulsive nature of the adolescent's reading is strikingly seen in the twelfth, thirteenth and fourteenth years of Lucy Sprague's life.* She had set for herself the herculean task of "reading right around Father's library systematically." The compulsivity is seen not only in the over-all task Lucy assigned herself but in her method as well. Not only did she proceed to take the books off the shelves in a prescribed manner, but she also "stinted" herself a certain number of pages to read per day.

In her own cool and detached tone, Mrs. Mitchell ascribes two possible motives for this behavior: seeking Father's approval by her studious ways and escaping from an unsatisfying life. The reader can make his own oedipal inferences. McCurdy (16), in tracing the childhood pattern of twenty geniuses, found that "books themselves, to which these children are so much attached, are representatives of the adult world. This is true in the superficial sense that they are provided by adults and, more significantly, may be drawn from a father's sacred library."

> I decided to use those long days at home to read right around Father's library systematically. That was no light task, for Father had greatly increased his library. I began on the top shelf in the section near the bay window and read through to the bottom shelf. Then I started on the next section. This meant that I got great doses of one author after another, for Father had many sets. Tolstoy and Victor Hugo took me a long time, but time is what I had too much of. My hardest job among the novelists was with Dickens. I couldn't stand him—his people seemed like caricatures. Scott, Bulwer-Lytton, Trollope, the Brontës, Jane Austen and particularly George Eliot—all these went swiftly. The archaeological section slowed me down, but I made a thorough job of it. Green's *Short History of the English People* and Guizot's *History of France,* also John Fiske's *The Discovery of America,* I loved best of all. I read them over and over, probably three or four times each. History and archaeology released me from my little world into a *real* world of *real* people. I got something out of Plato's *Republic* and the allegory of Rasselas sent me off writing al-

---

*From *Two Lives* by Lucy S. Mitchell. Reprinted by permission of Simon & Schuster, Inc. Copyright 1953, Lucy S. Mitchell. Pp. 58-60.

legories of my own. The only books I skipped were encyclopedias or duplicates. There were many duplicates, for Father had brought back from England hundreds and hundreds of the classics in the pirate Tauchnitz edition. They were small, closely printed little books bound in blue with a red back. We took quantities away on summer vacations. I didn't like the Tauchnitz. It took weeks to read a single shelf of them. I kept track of how far I had read on the shelves and sandwiched in a poetry book whenever I finished some long hard book. I never did get the whole way around the room, but I reached the last wall.

As I look back at the long pig-tailed girl who was myself, curled up in the sunny corner of the great bay window seat, I wonder what were the impulses that kept me reading, reading, reading. I am sure that I was attempting to get educated in this abnormal way since I always made a failure when I tried the normal way of going to school. I am sure, too, that I sought Father's approval by my studious ways and unexpected pieces of information that I brought out from time to time. Otherwise I think I would hardly have been so systematic in my attack. Mine was no leisurely browsing. I stinted myself—so many pages a day—and kept reckoning what percentage of my stint I had accomplished. Yet I am sure other impulses were at work, too. I was trying to escape an unsatisfactory life. For a few hours after the crowd of children on our block were home from school, I lived a normal, happy life. But that is not enough when you are twelve, thirteen, fourteen. Books provided me with adventure, friends, new people, new problems. My child's body sat reading in Father's library, yes. My child's spirit ranged boldly over the world, while Chicago and Prairie Avenue faded.

Theodor Reik
(1885-   )

Although Reik's main thesis in his *Fragment of a Great Confession** deals ostensibly with the experience of false shame, it is of interest here because of the compulsive involvement of the author with reading Goethe. Reik explores the dynamics of motivation for the reasons which prompted him to read, in his eighteenth year, every line Goethe wrote. This was no mean accomplishment, for it meant reading 55 volumes of poetry, 13 volumes of scientific papers,

---

*Reprinted by permission of Farrar, Straus & Cudahy, Inc. Copyright 1949, Theodor Reik. Pp. 8-14.

50 volumes of letters and 15 volumes of diaries, for a total of 133!

The death of his father, for which Reik had unconsciously felt responsible, precipitated this effort. In an attempt to expiate his sin and cope with his guilt feelings, Reik devised a self-punitive measure by taking up a near-impossible task. In the accomplishment of something extraordinary, he felt he would have satisfied his father who had been concerned about his achievement in school. Upon self-analysis, Reik discovered that his worship of Goethe resulted from a neurotic urge to realize and also to resist the wishes of his own father. Reik also reports a similar process with regard to the father substitute of his later life, Freud. It is interesting to remember in this connection that Freud considered the death of the father the most important experience in the life of a man. Reik was freed from his Goethe cult only when he was emancipated from his unconscious hatred and contempt (8).

Here is an instance from personal experience of false shame. For many years I carefully hid a fact which other people might have mentioned with harmless pride, namely, that in my eighteenth year I had read every line Goethe had published. I went through the *Weimarer*, or *Sophien*, edition, which consists of 55 volumes of poetic works, 13 volumes of scientific papers, the diaries in 15 volumes, and the letters in 50 volumes. I also read the many collections of Goethe's conversations, as well as most books and papers on Goethe which the Vienna University Library then had, and that was a considerable number of books. It is, of course, not important that I read all these volumes, but why did I never mention the fact? Why did I keep it secret as if I were ashamed of it?

There were many opportunities later on, for instance in conversations with literary friends and writers, to drop a remark about my Goethe reading. I remember such an occasion which came rather late. It must have been about 1926 or 1927—that is, more than twenty years after my Goethe obsession. One summer afternoon, Franz Werfel, Alma Maria, the widow of Gustav Mahler and now Werfel's wife, a friend, and I sat in the library of the beautiful cottage which the composer had bought in Breitenstein on the Semmering near Vienna. Mrs. Werfel pointed to the many volumes containing Goethe's letters and told me that Mahler used to say, "I reserve this reading for the years of my old age." During the ensuing conversation on Goethe I felt for a second the temptation to reveal that in my eighteenth year I had read all of Goethe in print, but the impulse disappeared immediately. There were other such occasions, but with the exception of my own analysis I never spoke of my compulsive reading of Goethe when I was a youth. Why was I ashamed of it?

To understand my secrecy, I must revive an important part of my young years, and awaken painful memories of grief and repentance. I do not agree with those writers who assert that such resurrection of the past is not difficult. To change the tenses is easy only on paper, but not in emotional experience. To recall feelings and impulses one is ashamed of, to admit emotions to others which one has not even admitted to oneself, is by no means an easy task. Our memories are conveniently derelict in such matters and we are only too apt to forget not only events, but also feelings and tendencies we did not like in ourselves. The dialogue which Nietzsche once imagined should be varied in this sense: "Thus I felt and thought," says my memory. "This I could not have felt and thought," says my pride. And my memory gives in. Such compliance of our memories with regard to unpleasant recollections is unavoidable. When one endeavors with all moral courage and sincerity to reconstruct what has been suppressed and repressed, one should be satisfied with incomplete results and not expect to attain the impossible and complete reconstruction of the past.

As for my compulsive Goethe study, more than forty years ago, my memory is somewhat bolstered by reference to a concrete event of those days. The event and the emotional experiences out of which my strange labor emerged are vividly recalled in reading a paper about them I wrote a few years later. In this paper I tried in retrospect to understand my odd behavior by means of the newly learned method of self-analysis. The paper lies on my desk now, as I write. It is entitled, "On the Effect of Unconscious Death-Wishes" ("*Ueber die Wirkungen unbewusster Todeswünsche*"). I wrote it in 1913, seven years after the experiences out of which my Goethe study emerged. This article was published anonymously in 1914 in Volume II of the *Internationale Zeitschrift für Aerztliche Psychoanalyse* edited by Sigmund Freud. A short footnote contains the following sentences: "Most of the following analysis is made on a person whose mental good health I have no reason to doubt: on myself. It would be petty, if we analysts would refrain from the analysis of our own fantasies after our master and some of his students have published interpretations of their own dreams. The personal sacrifice appears small compared with the profit which could accrue to research out of such reports. It is to be hoped that the intellectual interest of the reader in these complex problems will lead him to forget that the person analyzed is the analyst himself."

The spirit of these sentences would be more commendable if the author had signed his name to his paper. I can partly excuse him, since in his analytic report some persons were mentioned who were then still alive. Reasons of discretion made it necessary to remain anonymous, but I suspect that discretion appeared to him then as the better part of valor. The young man however has become an old man in the meantime, and he thinks it is never too late for moral courage and for overcoming the fright we feel in facing up to our own thoughts. He still believes in what he wrote then, thirty-five years ago, as his creed for psychological explorers. In the following paragraphs I shall follow that fragmentary analysis of 1913 as it was then published, supplementing it only as it concerns my Goethe study, which is, of course, not mentioned in the paper. Here are the events and experiences which preceded it, the soil from which this strange plant grew.

My father died of arterio-sclerosis on June 16, 1906. I was eighteen years old. This blow hit me a few days before the final examinations that open the doors of the university to the students. In those days this final examination did not signify merely the completion of high school. In keeping with its name *(Maturitätsprüfung)*, it marked the student's arrival at maturity, in addition to academic achievement.

(The subject in which I had been least successful during my high school years had been mathematics. When I returned to school, after my father's funeral, I often felt the glance of my mathematics instructor resting on me. I must have looked rather miserable because the old man, who resembled my father in figure and bearing, looked at me as though he felt sorry for me. On the day before the examination, he stopped me on the stairs of the school, said a few casual words, and slipped a little paper into my hand. On it were the questions he would ask me the next day. He said, shortly, "Adieu" and went downstairs. He died two days after the examination, of the same disease as my father. This episode was also woven into the pattern of my obsession-thoughts later on.)

The death of my father threw me into an emotional turmoil of the strangest kind. I did not understand then what had happened to me and in me. I was unable to grasp the meaning of the emotions and thoughts which beset me, and I searched in vain for a solution, groping about as does a blind man for the exit from a room. The first faint notion of the concealed meaning occurred to me a few years later. I was then a student of psychology, and Professor Jodl, who was especially interested in the studies of Wundt, Fechner, Mach, and Ziehen, once mentioned casually the name of a neurologist living in Vienna,

Sigmund Freud, who asserted that forgetting does not follow the laws of mechanical association and that dreams have a secret meaning. I read, then, the *Interpretation of Dreams.*

The emotional conflict in me had its point of departure in the rejection of a thought which emerged on the evening of the day my father died. The beloved man sat breathing heavily and groaning in an easy chair. Two physicians were at his side and one of them ordered me to go to the pharmacy to get camphor for an injection. The pharmacy was about fifteen minutes distant, with no bus or tram available. I was well aware of the urgency of the order. I knew the injection should be life-saving. I ran as if for my own life. I soon had to stop and catch my breath, and then I ran on again through the streets. Suddenly, the image of my father already dead emerged in my mind. As I passed from running to quick walking, I excused myself because I was out of breath. But then it occurred to me how much depended on my speed and I ran the more quickly to make up for the lost seconds. I reached the pharmacy, and then I ran back. Near collapse, I stormed into our apartment. My father was dead. I still know that I was in a terrible panic as if stunned by a strong electric shock, and I threw myself before the body, in despair.

The next days were filled with grief and mourning. An increasing longing for the familiar face, for his voice and smile, for his kind words, tortured me. When I came home from school, I expected to see him in the living room and was again and again painfully reminded that he was not there. When I heard a funny remark or when I got a good grade, I thought, "I shall tell father," and only after some minutes, in which I imagined he would enjoy it, did I become aware that he was dead. Then there emerged that doubt which had first occurred on the terrible evening. Could I have saved father's life if I had run more quickly? The doubt soon changed into self-reproaches and guilt feeling. I asked myself often in those days whether I would trade my own life for his. I answered at first that I would, of course, gladly die, if he could live again. But this was internally rejected by the sophistical argument that my longing for him would not be appeased if I were to die.

The stake was then diminished in my thoughts and I said to myself that I would gladly sacrifice a few years of my life if I could have prolonged his. Inner sincerity forbade that I make myself believe that I was ready to bring about this sacrifice. At the end of such trains of thoughts and fantasies I had to admit to myself, with terror, that I was unwilling to sacrifice a single year of my life for him.

In the following weeks my guilt feeling increased when I caught myself laughing at a witty remark or enjoying a stimulating conversation. I thought it was wrong to forget even for a moment that my father had died so recently. The worst of all self-reproaches came soon afterward. To my consternation, a wave of sexual excitement swept over me, against which I fought with all my might. I could not fall asleep because the power of the sexual drive tortured me, and though only a few days after my father's death, I searched for any opportunity to have sexual intercourse. When at last I found this opportunity, my self-reproaches became intolerable. They had the form: Now, when all my thoughts and feelings should be directed to the dear departed, I am indulging in sexual pleasure. The power of the sexual drive was, however, stronger than my will; each sexual act was followed by depression, self-reproach, and repentance. I remember that I shuddered then at myself. I did not consciously believe in immortality, or in a life in the beyond, yet I could not rid myself of the thought that my dead father knew all about me: that I had slowed my running in the hour of his dying and that I felt sexual excitement in these weeks of mourning.

I often had a kind of expectancy of impending calamity as if my father would punish me for my deeds. All this is too sharply expressed, too definitely stated. It really had the character of fleeting thoughts, of vague ideas that occurred to me again and again. But this is just the nature of incipient obsessions; it is in this typical form that obsessive thoughts first transgress the threshold of the conscious. Thus I feared or thought it possible that my father would let me become ill (and eventually die), and this obsession-idea made me especially afraid of venereal diseases. All these thoughts and fears were, of course, contradicted from within and rejected by reason; but what could reason do against the emotional powers which forced me to think and act as I did? I first realized how much method was in this madness; soon afterward, how much madness was in this method. When I began to study psychoanalysis a few years later, I recognized how many typical traits were in my attitude and that they had almost the clinical character of an obsessional neurosis. Obsessions and counter-obsessions fought each other in me, and I was for many weeks a victim of those strange thoughts, compulsions, and emotions.

Out of this situation emerged a compulsive way of working as the most conspicuous symptom. It was accompanied by the conscious wish to accomplish something extraordinary for my years. During my high school years I had been rather easygoing concerning my studies. With the exception of a few subjects in which I was at the top I had been lazy and careless. My father had often been worried about me when I had bad grades in mathematics, physics, and chemistry. He expressed his anxiety that I would not amount to much, if I continued to take life so lightly.

The thought that I had caused him grief in this direction had, of course, occurred among my self-reproaches, but the decision to give myself entirely to study and work seemed to emerge independently from my remorse. I still remember that it suddenly occurred to me that I wanted to become famous—the connection of my ambition with the memory of my father emerged through a detour later on. I thought that I wanted to give honor to his name in making my own name well known.

I can recapture only rarely, and for a fleeting moment, a faint echo of the emotions I felt then. Some years ago, a playwright in psycho-analysis described to me the first night of his first play. His parents had been poor immigrants and had lived poverty-stricken on the Lower East Side of New York, but they had made every sacrifice to give their children a good education. When the cheering first-nighters called the playwright to the stage, his glance fell at once on his parents. They sat motionless and cried. My patient said this moment was the greatest triumph of his life. Other successes followed, but nothing approached the satisfaction experienced in those few moments when he looked at the two old people while bowing to the applauding audience.

While I listened to him, I had a vivid feeling of envy, and on this detour I recaptured the memory of an old emotion. During the last illness of my father I had studied for that final examination with all my energy. I wanted to prove to him that I was capable of a great effort. I wanted to show him that I could achieve something. I had often studied secretly in the night because I wished to surprise him with the results of the examination. During the weeks after his death I had the bitter feeling that I had been too late. Destiny had not al-lowed me this chance to convince him that I could make a place for myself in the world of men.

Sheila Kaye-Smith
(1887-   )

The superego can play all kinds of tricks on the adolescent. Until it becomes more or less stabilized, it can leave the adolescent be-wildered, uncertain, confused, and sometimes frightened. While reading books during her adolescence, Sheila Kaye-Smith was torn between the injunctions of an overly prudish schoolmistress and the more liberal attitudes of her parents. In her youthful anxiety, the superego played the "safe" side so that "when anything suggesting deviation from strict propriety occurred or seemed likely to occur in a book . . . my conscience would cry 'Stop'!" Yet she could not stop; she had to read on. "The result was a mental conflict that reduced me to a trembling state of fear, as I risked, I thought, my eternal salvation just to find out what had happened in a book." This conflict pursued the fifteen-year-old Sheila clear through to the "magical" age of twenty-one, when she felt she would be free of such inhibitions. Until that time, she took her prohibitions in the narrowest possible sense. For example, because her mother had put a literary taboo on *Jane Eyre,* and had never allowed herself to read it, it followed that Sheila should not read it. "My conscience would not allow me to disobey hers."* The censorship was highly effective.

The third trail laid in the college library seems in some ways the most unlikely, and I shall never know how *Sir Charles Grandison* found its way on to those shelves. I do not think it was there at the beginning, for I could not have been much younger than sixteen or seventeen when I read it, and at fifteen had developed that conscientious desire to improve my reading which I have already mentioned. If it had been there I should have read it earlier as part of my campaign with the classics, so I can only surmise the date as well as the cause of its appearance.

I had not till then given much attention to eighteenth-century literature—that is literature of a later date than Pope and Addison. It is true that I had followed Gulliver in a safely expurgated edition to Laputa and the land of the Houyhnhnms as well as to Lilliput and Brobdingnag, but Defoe was still only the author of *Robinson Crusoe,* and Richardson, Sterne, Fielding and Smollett were no more than names. I associated Richardson with *Clarissa Harlowe* and his authorship of *Grandison* came as a surprise. I had also associated him and the other authors of that period with shocking impropriety, and in spite of its place of origin, which would have been enough to reassure most people, I opened the volume with much the same air of suspicious inquiry as that with which a cat approaches a saucer of milk he is not quite sure about.

*From *All the Books of My Life* by Sheila Kaye-Smith. Reprinted by permission of Sir Penrose Fry and Estate of Sheila Kaye-Smith. Copyright 1956, Harper & Bros. Pp. 34-47.

I had no sooner begun to read than I was seized. Seized is the only word that expresses the intensity of my interest. This was not like reading Scott or even Dickens—it was sheer possession. It is hard to tell at this long range what it was exactly that so held me. Richardson is no stylist and the society he describes is in many ways more remote from ours than that of Dickens or Scott, but there is an extraordinary lifelikeness about him and also a feminine smother which for me was something new. I shared the being of Harriet Byron as I had never shared that of Jeanie Deans or Amy Robsart or Dora Copperfield. I could almost see and smell her gown. Her story, too, seemed to come straight off her pen, as if her letters had been written to *me*. Be causes what they may, I can in this case say literally that I could not put the book down. I could not, but I feared I ought.

I was at this time going through a phase of extreme prudery. It is not uncommon at the present day for adolescents to develop peculiarities of conscience, strange compulsions and inhibitions. These may often be mere superstition—sevenfold repetitions, touches, charms —but even today the abnormality may be moral, though it is unlikely to take the same form as mine. My generation was in many ways more inhibited than those immediately before it, and as I moved up through my teens I collected quite a load of taboos.

Very few of these can have originated in my own home. My parents were sensible and the French influence persisted in the form of a sewing maid until I was well over fifteen. I think my school must take some of the blame. We are none of us, especially in our teenage, blank slates on which other people can inscribe their follies, but I cannot help believing that a greatly loved and admired hierarchy of spinsters had something to do with my morbid attitude towards childbirth.

My class was frequently called upon to read aloud from Shakespeare, and every now and then the mistress would cry, "Stop! Don't read what follows. Start again at the bottom of the page." We always had a special school edition of whatever play we were studying, one that had already been revised in the interests of decorum. But the reviser had not always, it seems, gone far enough. For instance in *A Midsummer Night's Dream* he had left the whole of the lovely passage beginning:

> Set your heart at rest
> The fairy-land buys not the child of me.

I can clearly remember being made to "Stop!" before I could get as far as—

When we have laughed to see the sails conceive
And grow big-bellied with the wanton wind.

—missing out everything till Oberon's "How long within this wood intend you stay?" restored the play to decency.

As a result of all this, I must be almost the only one of her readers who has ever detected impropriety in Charlotte Yonge. It was that perfect lady's treatment of childbirth which made me suspend my reading of *The Heir of Redclyffe*. Fortunately I told my mother that I had done so and even repeated the shocking words: "She is to be confined in the Spring." Her reaction was not that of my form mistress. "But there's nothing improper in *that!* How could there be? It's *natural!*"

"Natural" was her word of praise and comfort—I have heard her reassure a kittening cat with "It's all right dear, it's natural"—and when she spoke it one was taken back to Genesis and the early hours of the world's morning when "God saw that it was good." I sometimes wonder if it was as a result of my strictures on *The Heir of Redclyffe* that when my sister Thea came to our home for the birth of her first child, I was not, like Mona, sent to spend the birthday with neighbours, but remained in the house throughout it all, being even taken upstairs and shown the baby when she was only an hour old. The sight of the tiny child and my sister, flushed and happy and exhausted, broke down the very last of that especial kind of nonsense in my mind. I seemed at last to see for myself that these things were "natural."

Unfortunately other kinds of nonsense remained, and like the schoolmistress my conscience would cry "Stop!" when anything suggesting deviation from strict propriety occurred or seemed likely to occur in a book. I had read *David Copperfield* with grave misgivings on account of the story of Little Em'ly, and only my mother's casual statement that she had seen it once as a play in Edinburgh made me feel that a breach of the seventh commandment had not been made both by Dickens and by me. *Sir Charles Grandison* threatened something much worse. It is true that Harriet's abduction was meant to lead to a forced marriage, but I was terrified of what might possibly happen *en route,* and I had all the evil fame of eighteenth-century novelists in general and Richardson in particular to take into account.

Yet I could not stop reading. I must learn what happened to Harriet, whether she was married or seduced or rescued, and the hero, Sir Charles himself, had not yet appeared. The result was a mental conflict that reduced me to a trembling state of fear, as I risked, I thought, my eternal salvation just to find out what happened in a book. Luckily when I could endure no more I had enough sense to apply to the person who had already resolved similar conflicts for me. My mother, no doubt believing that my school library was not a likely source of corruption, took the whole thing very calmly. "If you find anything that's improper you can always skip it. It seems a pity not to read the book when you're enjoying it so much."

So I read *Sir Charles Grandison* right through to the end, and as it happened found nothing to shock me; which does not mean that it could not have been there, for apart from the scruples I had picked up at school I was amazingly innocent.

*   *   *   *

When at the age of fifteen I started my period of conscientious reading, I received one piece of very good advice. A friend of my mother's advised me not to read Thackeray until I was grown up. "You wouldn't understand him now. You'd miss a lot."

This was perfectly true and I only wish her advice had been applied more widely, for I spoilt a number of books and authors for myself by reading them too early. I was, in the first place, young for my age, I had lived a very sheltered life, I knew nothing of the world and hardly any men besides my father. Nor had I at that time had any contacts with good literature except the Bible and Shakespeare's plays, which were already spoilt for me by being "lessons." If I were ever asked to guide a young person in a similar situation I should put Dickens and Jane Austen with Thackeray on the waiting list, also the whole of George Eliot except *Adam Bede* and the whole of the Brontës except *Jane Eyre.* I should insert the thin end of the literary wedge with Scott's *Ivanhoe* and *Quentin Durward;* Stevenson's romances and Charles Kingsley's *Water Babies,* though I should not seriously expect a girl of fifteen (if she were at all like myself) to enjoy the latter, and then build up on Mrs. Gaskell, Mark Twain, or Fenimore Cooper, according to the tastes revealed.

But I had nobody to guide me, and I cannot remember who or what first put the idea of conscientious reading into my head. I use the word conscientious because the entire course was directed by the compulsion of Ought and Ought Not. I was convinced that there was a number of books that I ought to read if I meant to become an author in my own right. L. T. Meade had long ago withered as an inspiration, and though I was at that time passionately devoted to the works of Edna Lyall, I realized that these had not about them that immortal glow I wished my own to display. I had heard of course all the great names, and it was now my ambition to bring the gods to earth.

This shows that Ought was not an exclusively moral compulsion. Ought Not, on the other hand, was the direct voice of conscience, my own and other people's. I have shown that my mother was not unduly puritanical, but she had her literary taboos, one of which was *Jane Eyre*. She could remember all the fuss there had been when it first appeared, and how frightening and shocking everyone had thought it. She herself had never been allowed to read it, so, according to her logic, it followed that I should not. My conscience would not allow me to disobey hers, and the very book that I myself would have chosen to start a beginner on the literary trail was deliberately pushed aside —or rather ahead, for I fully intended to read *Jane Eyre* as soon as I was twenty-one. I attributed almost magical properties to my twenty-first birthday, believing that it would set me free from all obligation to obey my parents or accept their point of view. I saw myself on that day as an independent being, no longer bound by prohibitions which until then I would not dream of defying. Before that day of liberation dawned *Jane Eyre* had been joined by *Adam Bede* and *Tom Jones*.

So short a list does not point to any very drastic literary censorship. *Adam Bede,* which is another of my would be introductions, went on it at the instance of my sister Dulcie. She told my mother she did not think I ought to read it. She had heard of a subscriber to some library who had found it so shocking that she had torn out all the last pages —which seemed much more drastic than my familiar experience of finding them gummed together. *Tom Jones* was no individual ban, but a book which I had been led to believe unreadable by anyone with any modest feelings. I provided myself with a copy some weeks before my twenty-first birthday, but I did not open it till then.

Nirad C. Chaudhuri
(1897-   )

When he was thirteen years old, the Calcutta schoolboy, Nirad Chaudhuri, like the Spanish schoolboy, Santiago Ramón y Cajal, discovered the wonderful world of books. Both boys had to practice deception in order to read, but Chaudhuri relates " . . . the unlocked basket [of books] served only to relieve the conscience and not to prevent . . . corruption." He, like the other, read indiscriminately and hungrily.[*]

In another sense, however, we stepped into a more lively and gener-

*From *The Autobiography of an Unknown Indian* by Nirad Chaudhuri. Reprinted by permission of The Macmillan Co. (New York). 1951. Pp. 282-283.

ous literary atmosphere in Calcutta. This had nothing to do with our school life, but resulted from the wider literary life of Calcutta. The city was the centre of the literary, as of every other, activity in our cultural and political life, and in those days it had a very lively literary society. We did not, indeed, go into this society, but its tidings were brought to us by an uncle who was a university student. This uncle was a distant cousin of our mother and came to live with us after our arrival in Calcutta. He was not a very good student in the usual meaning of the phrase, for he got plucked in his B.A. examination twice, but he was a young man with genuine literary enthusiasm and real taste. He was a regular buyer of books even on his modest allowance, and had already formed a fair collection of English classics in the Everyman's Library and Nelson's sixpenny series, while his Bengali books comprised nearly the whole of our contemporary literature. It was by looking at the titles of his English books that I learned the names of Jane Austen, Charlotte Brontë, and George Eliot as the greatest women writers in English literature. My brother gave me the additional information that they were novelists of a new kind—"psychological novelists," which sounded very impressive. Where and how he had picked up that idea I cannot say, but he did give the explanation, "Look at the titles—*Pride and Prejudice, Sense and Sensibility.*"

While my uncle's English books were kept on open shelves, the Bengali volumes snuggled in the privacy of a wicker basket, guarded both against "pinching," the common fate of all things printed among us, and unauthorized reading by young people. Bengali parents considered juvenile addiction to fiction as the equivalent of juvenile addiction to smoking. But the unlocked basket served only to relieve the conscience and not to prevent our corruption. What I did was to take out one book at a time and read it sitting on a windowsill while my uncle was out. If by any chance Uncle Anukul—his full name was Anukul Roy—came home unexpectedly I just sat on the book and pretended to watch the street, and when he had gone for tea quietly replaced it in its box. It was thus that I read, among other things, all the novels by Tagore and all the plays of D. L. Roy. But certainly I did not succeed in deceiving my uncle. He noticed the traces of rummaging among his books and suspected me, although he never flatly accused me.

Helena Kuo
(1910-   )

The same craze for reading that marks the occidental adolescent holds constant for the oriental boy and girl, as this illustration from Helena Kuo's autobiography shows.* This Chinese girl marks her "development" from the time she began to "read like mad" as a freshman in college. "I went through the books available like a human panzer," she wrote, and expressed the idea to one of her professors that she wanted to read "everything." She was goaded to this ambition, she stated, in an attempt to compensate for the inferior role women played in China.

My development really began when I became a Freshman in second year. I had learned to use the library, and I read like mad. Nothing was too dull, nothing too difficult. I went through the books available like a human panzer. If I read everything written, I shall learn to write, I told myself.

One of the professors became so used to seeing me sitting in the library that he became interested in the bookworm. He was a little cynical when I told him I wanted to read everything, but he was kind enough to get me special permission to work in the stack room of the library building. I soon found the English books too difficult for me. I got angry with them, for English seemed a stupid language that I would master later, I decided. I would tackle my own language first. The demon was at work again. I fell on the liberal arts shelf and worried it until I knew every book by heart. Sun had whetted my appetite for philosophy. He had confused me a little with his own philosophy and Schopenhauer, so I wanted to find out the middle way for myself.

I was dissatisfied. I had read a great deal of contemporary writing in which young Chinese writers had criticized the social, political, and economic conditions in China. Communism was still a name for me, and a danger. Every day students and older people were being executed by the Gendarmerie without trial for being Communists, yet the movement was growing. The intellectual Communists were publishing numerous periodicals and secret newspapers.

I decided to leave it till I was older. Sun had told me that China's four thousand years of history would give me plenty to read even if so many of our precious manuscripts had been destroyed by the tyrant Emperor Chin.

The first few books I read, in Chinese text, were *History of European Philosophy,* of which Nietzsche and Schopenhauer appealed most to me, and Dr. Hu Shih's *History of Chinese Philosophy.*

When I read Dr. Hu Shih's scholarly and fascinating work little did I think that one day I was to sit in a New York hotel and be given

*From *I've Come a Long Way* by Helena Kuo. Reprinted by permission of Appleton-Century-Crofts, Inc. 1942. Pp. 89-92.

friendly and devastating criticism by this same Dr. Hu Shih, now Chinese Ambassador to the United States. Little did I dream then that I should be typing a book in the English language on a typewriter that came as a surprise present from the same scholarly diplomat, who found time in the middle of his onerous duties to remember me and to encourage me in my puny struggle to go a long way.

These two books stimulated me. They gave me ideas that now may seem ridiculous. I discovered one cogent thing in ferreting with my immature brain among those literary treasures. All great thinkers have a standard of greatness and a directness of language. I decided for myself that thought controls language, not that language directs thought, as I had been imagining. Before I read in that library I had always imagined that a writer was a kind of juggler with words, a weaver of spells, but in that dingy stack room I extracted a gem of thought for myself. I examined logic. I reasoned out problems and enjoyed myself in a way that to-day seems queer and immature.

One of the men students who also came to study in the stack room gave me some books and periodicals issued by a publisher called *Chuang Tsao She* (Creative Society). This was run by a group of progressive thinkers, many of whom were intellectual Communists. Their best magazine was *Yu Sse* (Threads of Chatter), a kind of highbrow review distinguished for its verity of thought and liberal discussion. I was enchanted to find so much intellectual leadership in modern print. The Creative Society, I learned afterwards, was run by one Kuo Mo-Jo who later had to flee China and take refuge in Japan because he was accused of being a Communist. He is now head of the Cultural Committee of the Political Department of the Military Commission. Kuo Mo-Jo has written many novels, plays, and poems and translated many of the great works of European and Japanese literature. His translations of Goethe's *Sorrow of Young Werther* and *Faust* I read over and over again and quoted in many of my youthful writings. His play called *The Three Rebellious Females,* based on stories of three brave women who lived in the Warring States and Han Dynasty of the Third Century, B.C. to the Second Century, A.D., gave me food for much thought. Since I was a little girl, I had hated the idea of being a typical Chinese woman, intellectually, socially, and economically inferior to men. This strange resentment at being a woman, I am convinced, goaded me to strive to compensate for what inferiority nature and custom had laid on me. What Mr. Kuo Mo-Jo said in his notes on his *The Three Rebellious Females* impressed me so much that it became the inspiration and purpose of my struggle. He said that woman labored under a double injustice. First, she had to combat the injustice of her sex that was abused by man, and, second, she was a perpetual victim of class distinction.

Kuo Mo-Jo's translations of foreign literature interested me in the study of the history of European literature since the Renaissance, and I read everything on the subject that I could lay my hands on.

From the early and superficial study of the history of European literature, I began to interest myself in the works of Tolstoy, Ibsen, Oscar Wilde, Victor Hugo, and some others. Tolstoy's *War and Peace* impressed me as a masterpiece. In all his novels and stories, there is always a woman, young and serene, named Helene or Helena, which pleases me. His dissertation on woman's beauty, in which he said that a woman's lips were the part a man should notice first, has been my beauty rule ever since. I liked Ibsen because he was revolutionary and most understanding of woman. Oscar Wilde appealed to me as a hopelessly sentimental wit. I liked Victor Hugo for his grandeur and nobleness.

All these books were in Chinese text. If I ever have time to read them again in the English version, I wonder what I shall think of them.

REFERENCES

1. Bashkirtseff, Marie. *The Journal of a Young Artist*. New York: E. P. Dutton & Co., 1919, p. 250.
2. Bewick, Thomas. *Memoirs of Thomas Bewick, Written by Himself, 1822-1828*. New York: Dial Press, 1925, p. 58.
3. Cerf, Bennett. It's fun to read. In: Stefferud, Alfred (Ed.), *The Wonderful World of Books*. New York: New American Library, 1953, pp. 24-25.
4. Dell, Floyd. *Homecoming. An Autobiography*. New York: Farrar & Rinehart, 1933, p. 81.
5. Dreiser, Theodore. *Dawn. A History of Myself*. New York: Horace Liveright, Inc., 1931, p. 202.
6. Ellis, Havelock. *My Life*. Boston: Houghton Mifflin Co., 1939, pp. 71-73.
7. Erikson, Erik H. Late adolescence. In: Funkenstein, Daniel H. (Ed.), *The Student and Mental Health*. Cambridge, Mass.: World Federation for Mental Health, 1959, p. 81.
8. Feldman, Harold. Tragic comedy of great men. *Psychoanal. & Psychoanal. Rev.*, 46:7, 1959.
9. Freud, Anna. Adolescence. In: Ruth S. Eissler et al. (Eds.), *The Psychoanalytic Study of the Child*, Vol. XIII. New York: International Universities Press, 1958, p. 263.

10. Freud, Sigmund. *The Interpretation of Dreams.* New York: Basic Books, 1958, pp. 172-173.
11. Gibbon, Edward. *The Autobiography of Edward Gibbon.* New York: Dutton Everyman's Library, 1911, p. 68.
12. Hall, G. Stanley. *Adolescence,* Vol. I. New York: Appleton-Century-Crofts, 1904, p. 539.
13. Houston, Sam. *The Autobiography of Sam Houston.* Norman, Okla.: University of Oklahoma Press, 1954, p. 5.
14. Inhelder, Bärbel, and Piaget, Jean. *The Growth of Logical Thinking from Childhood to Adolescence.* New York: Basic Books, 1958, p. 340.
15. Kris, Ernst. *Psychoanalytic Explorations in Art.* New York: International Universities Press, 1952, p. 94.
16. McCurdy, Harold C. The childhood pattern of genius. *Smithsonian Report for 1958.* Washington, D.C.: Smithsonian Institution, 1959, p. 538.
17. Misch, Georg. *A History of Autobiography in Antiquity,* Vol. II. Cambridge, Mass.: Harvard University Press, 1951, p. 557.
18. Powys, John Cowper. *Autobiography.* London: John Lane The Bodley Head, 1934, pp. 118-119, 123.
19. Schorer, Mark. An interpretation. In: Ford, Ford Madox, *The Good Soldier.* New York: Alfred A. Knopf, 1951, p. v.
20. Stone, L. Joseph, and Church, Joseph. *Childhood and Adolescence.* New York: Random House, 1957, p. 312.
21. Strachey, John St. Loe. *The Adventure of Living. A Subjective Autobiography.* London: Hodder & Stoughton, Ltd., 1922, p. 74.
22. Trotsky, Leon. *My Life. An Attempt at an Autobiography.* New York: Charles Scribner's Sons, 1931, p. 99.
23. Weingarten, Samuel. Reading as a source of the ideal self. *Reading Teacher,* 8:159-164, 1955.
24. Wharton, Edith. *A Backward Glance.* New York: D. Appleton-Century Co., 1936, p. 71.
25. Whitman, Walt. *Autobiographia or the Story of a Life.* New York: Charles L. Webster & Co., 1892, p. 27.

CHAPTER ELEVEN

The Influence of Teachers

"Every man," wrote Gibbon in his *Autobiography,* "who rises above the common level has received two educations: the first from his teachers; the second, more personal and important, from himself [8]." A century later, Cardinal Newman (16) declared in almost identical words, "No matter how much a faculty can do for a student it is as nothing compared to what he can do for himself."

The role and influence the teacher assumes is secondary only to that of the parents in the adolescent's life. The teacher is frequently a parent substitute who not only guides the individual in his learning process but also has an understanding and alert interest in the total personality of the adolescent. The good teacher has the same goal as the good psychiatrist: to help the adolescent develop his ego to solve satisfactorily the conflicts between his basic instinctual drives and the restrictions imposed on the methods of gratification of these drives by reality.

The revival of the oedipal conflict in pubescence prompts the adolescent to forsake temporarily his parents and seek identification elsewhere. The approval of another adult often becomes a necessity. The close connection between the ebbing off of the oedipal conflict and readiness for more systematic learning in school has frequently been observed and stated (Plank, 20). "As one watches children through their years of growth, one is impressed by the fact that the motive of learning in order to be rewarded by the teacher's love is very important and powerful and continues not only through grade school but also into senior high school and college. . . . If, to the child, the teacher seems to be interested in learning, he too must become interested in learning in order to be like the teacher and so be liked by him. . . . The reward which is most gratifying to the child is that of love from the adult, whether this be the parent or a professional educator. When the child loves the teacher he will do anything to please him, even to learning the most uninteresting subject, but he anticipates a real expression of love from the teacher in return and as long as he gets it, he will continue to learn [Pearson, 19]."

These mechanisms of identification with the teacher and intro-jection of the latter's attitudes, help the adolescent in the process of resolving the second phase of the oedipal conflict. They serve the function of helping him to develop a healthy ego which is able to evaluate, direct, and control instinctual impulses so that he is able to live with comfort in a particular society (Pearson, 18). Everyone can remember a few magnificent teachers in his school career whose function far transcended the mere imparting of information. Through some special, indefinable gift, they were able not only to bring to life the high drama of ideas but also to bring out within the individual his best efforts. It is true too that, as Giacomo Leopardi (1798-1837) wrote, "As touching the persons to whom we commit the education of our children, we very well know that in many cases, and in many respects, they themselves are uneducated. Yet we never doubt their ability to give that which they have not received [11]." The inadequacy of such teachers doubles their burden, since adolescent behavior is unstable, inconsistent, and unpredict-able. Teachers are confronted with a shifting situation that is often extremely difficult to handle (Blos, 2), no matter how dedicated they might be. In order to handle their own anxieties, they tend to inhibit the adolescent and restrict his freedom. Here, too, the prin-ciples held up to the child by his parents and teachers—their wishes, requirements and ideals—are introjected (A. Freud, 7).

As Fenichel (4) points out, a person's self-esteem, as well as the content and extent of his defenses, depends upon his ideals, which are developed less by direct teaching than by the general spirit that surrounds the growing child. "Soap and education are not as sud-den as a massacre," said Mark Twain, "but they are more deadly in the long run." In the entrance hall of one of the buildings at the University of Delhi there is the following quotation from Rabindranath Tagore: "A teacher can never truly teach unless he is still learning himself. A lamp can never light another lamp unless it continues to burn its own flame. The teacher who has come to the end of his subject, who has no living traffic with his knowledge but merely repeats his lesson to his students can only load their minds; he cannot quicken them. Trust must not only inform but also inspire; if the inspiration dies out and the information only accumulates, then truth loses its infinity. The greater part of our learning in the schools has been waste because for most of our teachers their subjects are like dead specimens of once living things with which they have a learned acquaintance but no communication of life and love [Cantril & Bumstead, 3]."

It has been said that the proper comparison of an education is not with filling up an empty pot but rather with lighting a fire. The proper test of an education is whether it teaches the pupil to think and whether it awakens his interest in applying his faculties to the various problems and opportunities that life presents. In analytic terms, all learning is a transmutation of libido from early id sources, and as differentiation into ego and superego takes place, diversification and elaboration of symbol also take place (Liss, 12). Thus, as Aichhorn (1) stated, "Education is no more than a means of unfolding existing potentialities and cannot add anything new to the individual."

To Montaigne (15), education was a training of judgment. He quotes Cicero as saying, "The authority of the teachers is generally prejudicial to those who desire to learn." The student must be permitted to pour everything through a sieve, and "store nothing in his head on mere authority and trust. To him Aristotle's principles should be no more principles than those of the Stoics and Epicureans; let their various theories be put to him, and he will choose, if he is able; if not he will remain in doubt. Only fools are certain and cocksure." The kind of attitude the teacher has and the kind of emotional atmosphere he creates are primary to the learning process. The active encouragement of a teacher has frequently played a decisive role in the adolescent's life. In the 1960 Walter Van Dyke Bingham Memorial Lecture, Wolfle (24) recalled that Bingham "once told me that he approached the end of high school with no thought of entering college. One day one of his teachers took him aside and planted the idea that led him to enroll at Kansas

University the following fall. I wonder how often a similar scene has occurred in the early lives of men and women who later entered the professional or learned fields. George Beadle, who was awarded the 1958 Nobel Prize in Physiology and Medicine, tells an almost identical story: a Nebraska farm boyhood, a father uninterested in higher education, and an inspiring teacher who urged the future Nobel laureate to enter the University of Nebraska. There must be many other eminent men and women who could tell similar stories: bright and industrious students with potentialities far exceeding the range of vision acquired from home and community, whose sights were lifted by a teacher or an older friend who took the trouble to encourage talent."

Wolfle is correct in his assumption that there are others who can tell comparable stories. From the days of Marcus Aurelius to the twentieth century, testaments by the famous and the unknown are to this effect, as illustrated in the following selections. In many of the excerpts, it will be seen that the common contributions of the teachers to their adolescent students include a deepening of their perception of moral truth, a broadening of the horizons of their social obligations, a sensitizing of their feelings toward others, the developing of real independence of mind and a fundamental respect for intellectual integrity and devotion to the pursuit of knowledge. While these characteristics vary from individual to individual, culture to culture, and generation to generation, they were the core and the basis for the pervasive influence of teachers on the lives of the adolescents represented here.

Marcus Aurelius
(121-180)

The Emperor Marcus Antoninus, commonly called Marcus Aurelius, was seventeen years old when Antoninus Pius adopted him and so made him heir to the throne. The Emperor chose as his totur the most famous representative of forensic eloquence in Rome at the time, Fronto, an orator full of mannerisms (Misch, 14). Among Fronto's writing are his correspondence with Marcus during the student years of the crown prince. The modern editor of this correspondence (9) describes Fronto's role thus:

Fronto began by taking his pupil through a course of old farces, comedies, ancient orators, and poets, and Marcus was encouraged to make extracts from the authors that were read. . . . Verse-making was regularly practised as an aid towards oratory. . . . Similes formed an important part of his oratorical armoury. . . . The next step was to use the "Commonplaces of Theodorus" (a rhetorician of Gadara) for the manufacture of maxims. One aphorism a day was the allotted task. . . . Translation from one language into another formed part of the curriculum. Original composition was also recognized by Fronto, and Marcus himself seems to have had some aspirations in that direction. . . . Fronto's eyes, however, were not on the facts, but on the best way to show his rhetorical skill in commonplace or panegyric. . . . Finally came the writing of themes and *controversiae,* in which the pros and cons of any question, historical or fictitious, are discussed as by a forensic speaker.

At the height of his career, in his fifties, about a decade after his accession, the Emperor Marcus began the notes out of which the *Meditations* came. The beginning of Book I, which is quoted here,* is a personal acknowledgement of lessons learned and good gifts received from the men and women who seemed in retrospect to have had the most influence on his life, especially on his intellectual and moral training.

1. From my grandfather Verus: the lessons of noble character and even temper.

2. From my father's reputation and my memory of him: modesty and manliness.

3. From my mother: piety and bountifulness, to keep myself not only from doing evil but even from dwelling on evil thoughts, simplicity too in diet and to be far removed from the ways of the rich.

4. From my mother's grandfather: not to have attended public schools but enjoyed good teachers at home, and to have learned the lesson that on things like these it is a duty to spend liberally.

5. From my tutor: not to become a partisan of the Green jacket or the Blue in the races, nor of Thracian or Samnite gladiators; to bear pain and be content with little; to work with my own hands, to mind my own business, and to be slow to listen to slander.

6. From Diognetus: to avoid idle enthusiasms; to disbelieve the professions of sorcerers and impostors about incantations and exorcism

---

*Reprinted by permission of the Clarendon Press. 1906. P. 5.

of spirits and the like; not to cock-fight or to be excited about such sports; to put up with plain-speaking and to become familiar with philosophy; to hear the lectures first of Baccheius, then of Tandasis and Marcian, in boyhood to write essays and to aspire to the camp-bed and skin coverlet and the other things which are part of the Greek training.

Guibert
(1053-1124)

Guibert, Abbot of Nogent-Sous-Coucy, relates in his *Autobiography* the oppressive and severe lessons he learned under the tutelage of a master whom his mother had secured for him.* The boy's father died when he was eight years old and the Abbot complained that the tutor so directed every aspect of his life for the six years he remained with him "that he was regarded as exercising the guardianship not of a master, but of a parent, and not over my body only, but my soul, too." Despite the beatings the boy received and despite the inadequacy of the teaching, Guibert felt that his tutor loved him. He points this out, as well as several other principles of teaching and learning that sound remarkably like a modern textbook in educational psychology. For example, Guibert makes a strong case for proper spacing of learning materials and for variety rather than dull repetition.

Placed under him I was taught with such purity and checked with such honesty in the excesses which are wont to spring up in youth, that I was kept well-guarded from the common wolves and never allowed to leave his company, or to eat anywhere than at home, or to accept gifts from anyone without his leave; in everything I had to shew self-control in word, look or act, so that he seemed to require of me the conduct of a monk rather than a clerk. For whereas others of my age wandered everywhere at will and were unchecked in the indulgence of such inclinations as were natural to their age, I, hedged in with constant restraints, would sit and look on in my clerical chasuble at the troops of players like a beast awaiting sacrifice.

Even on Sundays and Saints' Days I had to submit to the severity of school exercises; on no day, and hardly at any time, was I allowed to

*Reprinted by permission of Routledge & Kegan Paul, Ltd. Copyright 1925. Pp. 19-23.

take holiday; in fact, in every way and at all times I was driven to study. But he, on the other hand, gave himself up solely to my education, being allowed to have no other pupil.

And whilst he was working me so hard, and anyone looking on might suppose my little mind was being exceedingly sharpened by such driving, the hopes of all were being defeated. For he was utterly unskilled in prose and verse composition. Meantime I was pelted almost every day with a hail of blows and hard words, whilst he was forcing me to learn what he could not teach.

With him in this fruitless struggle I passed nearly six years, but got no reward worth the expenditure of time. Yet otherwise in all that is supposed to count for good training in the behaviour of a gentleman, he spared no effort for my improvement. Most faithfully and lovingly did he steep me in all that was temperate and pure and outwardly refined. But I clearly perceived that at my expense he had no consideration and restraint in urging me on without intermission and at much pains under show of teaching. For by the strain of undue application, the natural powers of grown men, as well as of boys, are blunted and the hotter the fire of their mental activity in unremitting study, the sooner is the strength of their understanding weakened and chilled by excess and its energy turned to sloth. . . .

Now the love that this man had for me was of a savage sort and excessive severity was shewn by him in his unjust floggings; and yet the great care with which he guarded me was evident in his acts. Clearly I did not deserve to be beaten, for if he had had the skill in teaching which he professed, it is certain that I was, for a boy, well able to grasp anything that he taught correctly. But because his elocution was by no means pleasing and what he strove to express was not at all clear to himself, his talk rolled ineffectively on and on in a commonplace, but by no means obvious, circle, which could not be brought to any conclusion, much less understood. For so uninstructed was he that he retained incorrectly what he had, as I have said before, once badly learnt late in life, and if he let anything slip out (incautiously, as it were), he maintained and defended it with blows, regarding all his own opinions as certainly true; but I think he would certainly have been spared such folly . . . for before, says the same teacher, a man's nature has absorbed knowledge, he may win greater praise by keeping silence on that he knows not than by telling of what he knows. . . .

Although, therefore, he crushed me by such severity, yet in other ways he made it quite plain that he loved me as well as he did himself. With such watchful care did he devote himself to me, with such foresight did he secure my welfare against the spite of others and teach me on what authority I should beware of the dissolute manners of some who paid court to me, and so long did he argue with my mother about the elaborate richness of my dress, that he was regarded as exercising the guardianship not of a master, but of a parent, and not over my body only, but my soul, too. As for me, considering the dull sensibility of my age and my littleness, great was the love I conceived for him in response, in spite of the many weals with which he marked my tender skin so that not through fear, as is common in those of my age, but through a sort of love deeply implanted in my heart, I obeyed him in utter forgetfulness of his severity.

Arai Hakuseki
(1657-1725)

"Arai Hakuseki, whose 'true' name was Minamoto Kimiyoshi, was a Confucian author and statesman of the enlightened Genroku period. Among his contemporaries were some of Japan's foremost cultural figures, including the painter Hishikawa Moronobu, the poet Matsuo Basho, the erotic novelist Ibara Saikaku, and the playwright Chikamatsu Monzaemon. Hakuseki himself was a prolific writer of poems, histories, economics and politics. He rose to a high position at the court of the Shogun, becoming the official scholar and finally the chief minister under the Shogun Ienobu.

"In this autobiographic account, Hakuseki tells about his intellectual preparation for his career. As a boy he was too poor to buy books and he had wretched teachers, but he overcame obstacles by sheer hard work. Upon his retirement from public service at the age of sixty, he wrote the history of his career in order, he said, to remind his descendants 'of our family's laborious rise in rank [Padover, 17].' "

This sketch points up the great contemporary need to encourage talent, whether by parents or other interested individuals, or through building encouragement into the customs and traditions that characterize a particular social group.

When three years old, I was sitting one day tracing the pictures and ideographs in the *Ueno-monogatari* of people going to see the flowers, and mother said several of the ideographs were well made, and showed my work to father. Others thought it extraordinary, and it was shown to a number. I saw it in Kadzusa when I went there in my seventeenth year. I also wrote my name on a screen and two of the ideographs were well made. The screen burned in a conflagration. From that time I constantly amused myself reading and writing but had no teacher and so studied the pictured guide books. . . .

When six years old I was taught a Chinese poem with its explanation and music, so that I could comment on it, by a scholar named Uematsu, who also taught me two others. He advised sending me to some good master, but the old conservatives said: "No one can become a scholar without talent, diligence and wealth. The boy has talent, but whether diligent or no we do not know. He surely has not wealth." And father said, "The Kobu is too fond of him to send him away to school." But still the Kobu took pride in my writing and wanted me to learn, and when, in my eighth year, he went to Kadzusa, he set me this task, to write three thousand ideographs every day and one thousand every evening. When the winter days were too short for my task, I moved my table out on the verandah so as to finish by daylight, and when I grew sleepy at night I put two pots of water by my side. Then as I began to nod I threw back my gown and my friend emptied one of the pots over me, and as I gradually grew dry and warm and sleepy again, he threw the other over me and so I got through the task. This was in the winter and autumn of my ninth year, and from that time I conducted father's correspondence.

In the autumn of my eleventh year I learned the *Tekinorai* by heart in ten days, wrote it out and presented it to the Kobu who was greatly pleased. From my thirteenth year I conducted his correspondence. When I was eleven father had a friend named Seki, whose son was a clever fencer, and taught the art. I asked for lessons, but was refused as too young, when I replied, "If I cannot use my sword why should I wear it?" Then he consented, and taught me one style so well that in a contest with wooden swords with a youth of sixteen three times I was beaten and thrice victorious, the lookers laughing in their interest. So I took up martial exercises and read all the old war stories to the neglect of my writing.

In my seventeenth year I saw a copy of the *Okina-Mondō* in the house of a fellow page and borrowed it. Out of it I first learned of the "Way of the Sages." I liked it at once and wished to study it, but had no teacher. However, a physician of some attainments heard of my desire. He came daily to the Kobu's mansion, and taught me the "Introduction to the Little Learning," and then the history by Chūki. Day and night I studied the "Little Learning" and the "Four Classics." So far the physician helped me but as I went on to the "Five Books" I had no teacher and worked at them with a lexicon and made many mistakes as I now know. So I studied by myself, and understood only in part and took up composition and rhetoric and poetry, making my first poem of fifty-six characters in the twelfth month of that year. Then I wrote an essay, my first attempt at prose, in explanation of my verse, as I had heard a man ridicule and criticise it. I kept these boyish studies from the knowledge of father and his friends, but as I needed books I made a confidante of my mother.

When twenty-one I left the Kobu's mansion and continued my studies with congenial friends but, for reasons of my own, without a teacher. The scholar Ahiru of Tsushima was one of my friends and when, in the autumn of my 26th year, I was in service again, and a Korean ambassador arrived, I sent an hundred verses of my own to him by Ahiru with a request for an introduction for the book. He liked the verses, and asked to meet me, and so I had an evening with him and his two attendants, writing poetry, and, at the close, the ambassador wrote the Introduction to my verses, as I had asked.

The same year Kinoshita first took office from the Shogun (1682). Later I went to Yamagata and kept a journal which Ahiru showed to Kinoshita who was his master. Ahiru also showed Kinoshita my book of poems and he liked the books and asked to see me, and so I met him. When Ahiru died he asked me to request Kinoshita to prepare his epitaph, and I acted as amanuensis.

So I became a disciple of Kinoshita and very intimate with him though the usual ceremonies of initiation were omitted. For years he had many distinguished disciples, but I was put at their head and he sent me to teach the heir apparent of the Shogun.

As I review my life it would appear that I should have made much greater progress had I had good teachers, when I began to write at three years, study poetry at six, and the "Way" at seventeen. When employed by the Shogun I bought many books and was given many, but was so pressed by my duties that I found little time for reading. Before that I was so poor that my books were borrowed or copied and therefore few. In this matter of study no one has been more unfortunate. That I have so far succeeded is because I have followed father's advice and done the most difficult task first. What others learn at once, I master only with ten repetitions and what others with ten, I with a hundred repetitions.

John Stuart Mill
(1806-1873)

Mill, under his father's personal and unremitting tutelage, began hard intellectual work before he was three years old. The type of training he received is famous in the annals of education. It was completely and rigorously intellectual, permitting him little or no contact with youngsters his own age. "The education which my father gave me," wrote Mill, "was in itself much more fitted for training me to know than to do. . . . He was earnestly bent upon my escaping not only the corrupt influences which boys exercise over boys but the contagion of vulgar modes of thought and feeling; and for this he was willing that I should pay the price of inferiority in the accomplishments which schoolboys in all countries chiefly cultivate. . . . As I had no boy companions, and the animal need of physical activity was satisfied by walking, my amusements, which were mostly solitary, were in general of a quiet, if not a bookish turn, and gave little stimulus to any other kind even of mental activity than that which was already called forth by my studies [13]." The influence of his father-tutor was very deeply stamped on Mill and throughout his life he hesitated to express fully and decisively opinions which conflicted with those of his father.*

It would have been wholly inconsistent with my father's ideas of duty, to allow me to acquire impressions contrary to his convictions and feelings respecting religion: and he impressed upon me from the first, that the manner in which the world came into existence was a subject on which nothing was known: that the question, "Who made me?" cannot be answered, because we have no experience or authentic information from which to answer it; and that any answer only throws the difficulty a step further back, since the question immediately presents itself, Who made God? He, at the same time, took care that I should be acquainted with what had been thought by mankind on these impenetrable problems. I have mentioned at how early an age he made me a reader of ecclesiastical history; and he taught me to take the strongest interest in the Reformation, as the great and decisive contest against priestly tyranny for liberty of thought.

I am thus one of the very few examples, in this country, of one who has, not thrown off religious belief, but never had it: I grew up in a negative state with regard to it. I looked upon the modern exactly as I did upon the ancient religion, as something which in no way concerned me. It did not seem to me more strange that English people

---

*From *Autobiography* by John Stuart Mill. Reprinted by permission of The Liberal Arts Press, Inc. (New York). 1957. Pp. 28-35.

should believe what I did not, than that the men I read of in Herodotus should have done so. History had made the variety of opinions among mankind a fact familiar to me, and this was but a prolongation of that fact. This point in my early education had, however, incidentally one bad consequence deserving notice. In giving me an opinion contrary to that of the world, my father thought it necessary to give it as one which could not prudently be avowed to the world. This lesson of keeping my thoughts to myself, at that early age, was attended with some moral disadvantages; though my limited intercourse with strangers, especially such as were likely to speak to me on religion, prevented me from being placed in the alternative of avowal or hypocrisy. I remember two occasions in my boyhood, on which I felt myself in this alternative, and in both cases I avowed my disbelief and defended it. My opponents were boys, considerably older than myself: one of them I certainly staggered at the time, but the subject was never renewed between us: the other who was surprised, and somewhat shocked, did his best to convince me for some time, without effect. . . .

But though direct moral teaching does much, indirect does more; and the effect my father produced on my character, did not depend solely on what he said or did with that direct object, but also, and still more, on what manner of man he was.

In his views of life he partook of the character of the Stoic, the Epicurean, and the Cynic, not in the modern but the ancient sense of the word. In his personal qualities the Stoic predominated. His standard of morals was Epicurean, inasmuch as it was utilitarian, taking as the exclusive test of right and wrong, the tendency of actions to produce pleasure or pain. But he had (and this was the Cynic element) scarcely any belief in pleasure; at least in his later years, of which alone, on this point, I can speak confidently. He was not insensible to pleasures; but he deemed very few of them worth the price which, at least in the present state of society, must be paid for them. The greater number of miscarriages in life, he considered to be attributable to the overvaluing of pleasures. Accordingly, temperance, in the large sense intended by the Greek philosophers—stopping short at the point of moderation in all indulgences—was with him, as with them, almost the central point of educational precept. His inculcations of this virtue fill a large place in my childish remembrances. He thought human life a poor thing at best, after the freshness of youth and of unsatisfied curiosity had gone by. This was a topic on which he did not often speak, especially, it may be supposed, in the presence of young persons: but when he did, it was with an air of settled and profound conviction. He would sometimes say, that if life were made what it might be, by good government and good education, it would be worth having: but he never spoke with anything like enthusiasm even of that possibility. He never varied in rating intellectual enjoyments above all others, even in value as pleasures, independently of their ulterior benefits. The pleasures of the benevolent affections he placed high in the scale; and used to say, that he had never known a happy old man, except those who were able to live over again in the pleasures of the young. For passionate emotions of all sorts, and for everything which has been said or written in exaltation of them, he professed the greatest contempt. He regarded them as a form of madness. "The intense" was with him a bye-word of scornful disapprobation. He regarded as an aberration of the moral standard of modern times, compared with that of the ancients, the great stress laid upon feeling. Feelings, as such, he considered to be no proper subjects of praise or blame. Right and wrong, good and bad, he regarded as qualities solely of conduct—of acts and omissions; there being no feeling which may not lead, and does not frequently lead, either to good or to bad actions: conscience itself, the very desire to act right, often leading people to act wrong. Consistently carrying out the doctrine, that the object of praise and blame should be the discouragement of wrong conduct and the encouragement of right, he refused to let his praise or blame be influenced by the motive of the agent. . . .

It will be admitted, that a man of the opinions, and the character, above described, was likely to leave a strong moral impression on any mind principally formed by him, and that his moral teaching was not likely to err on the side of laxity or indulgence. The element which was chiefly deficient in his moral relation to his children was that of tenderness. I do not believe that this deficiency lay in his own nature. I believe him to have had much more feeling than he habitually showed, and much greater capacities of feeling than were ever developed. He resembled most Englishmen in being ashamed of the signs of feeling, and by the absence of demonstration, starving the feelings themselves. If we consider further that he was in the trying position of sole teacher, and add to this that his temper was constitutionally irritable, it is impossible not to feel true pity for a father who did, and strove to do, so much for his children, who would have so valued their affection, yet who must have been constantly feeling that fear of him was drying it up at its source. This was no longer the case later in life, and with his younger children. They loved him tenderly: and if I cannot say so much of myself, I was always loyally devoted to him. As regards my own education, I hesitate to pronounce whether I was more a loser or gainer by his severity. It was not such as to prevent me from having a happy childhood. And I do not believe that boys can be induced to apply themselves with vigour, and what is so much more difficult, perseverance, to dry and irksome studies, by the sole force of persuasion and soft words. Much must be done, and much must be learnt, by children, for which rigid discipline, and known liability to punishment, are indispensable as means. It is, no doubt, a very laudable effort, in modern teaching, to render as much as possible of what the young are required to learn, easy and interesting to them. But when this principle is pushed to the length of not requiring them to learn anything *but* what has been made easy and interesting, one of the chief objects of education is sacrificed. I rejoice in the decline of the old brutal and tyrannical system of teaching, which, however, did succeed in enforcing habits of application; but the new, as it seems to me, is training up a race of men who will be incapable of doing anything which is disagreeable to them. I do not, then, believe that fear, as an element in education, can be dispensed with; but I am sure that it ought not to be the main element; and when it predominates so much as to preclude love and confidence on the part of the child to those who should be the unreservedly trusted advisers of after years, and perhaps to seal up the fountains of frank and spontaneous communicativeness in the child's nature, it is an evil for which a large abatement must be made from the benefits, moral and intellectual, which may flow from any other part of the education.

Richard Henry Dana, Jr.
(1815-1882)

Richard Henry Dana was suspended, in 1831, from Harvard College for a six-month period. In order to make good use of the time, his father sent him to Andover to study privately under a Rev. Leonard Woods, Jr., who later became President of Bowdoin College. In the excerpt found here,* Dana writes glowingly of his experience with Woods and compares the latter's way of teaching with Harvard's system of emphasis on grades and the disinterest of its professors in the students as individuals. Woods seems to have been an educator who fulfilled the Tagore criteria quoted earlier in this chapter.

---

*From *Richard Henry Dana, Jr.: An Autobiographical Sketch* edited by Robert G. Metzdorf. Reprinted by permission of Massachusetts Historical Society. Copyright 1953, The Shoe String Press. Pp. 58-61.

... I was placed under the charge of a man who did more than any instructor I had ever had to interest me in learning & to direct my ambition & industry to worthy objects. This person was the Rev. Leonard Woods Jr., then a resident licentiate of the Andover Theological Seminary, & now, at a very early age, President of Bowdoin College. Mr. Woods was then only about four & twenty years old, yet had completed his course of college & professional education, was giving his time to a system of comprehensive scholarship, chiefly theological, & had already become a ripe scholar. Beside his Latin & Greek & Hebrew, with which he [was] sufficiently conversant for the purposes of his reading, he both read & wrote with ease, German, French, &, I think, Italian. He was an indefatigable & enthusiastic student, with a heart full of noble & kind sentiments, with a manner which won the confidence & love of all, with remarkable purity of spirit, & with a firm religious faith & a complete religious personal experience. He was also more free from prejudice, opinionatedness & exclusiveness than most students of theological systems. Indeed, I never saw that he had any [of] those faults. More than any person whom I ever knew he seemed to read, study, think & converse for the purpose of developing fairly all his powers & coming to a knowledge of truth. He was not only a fair but a favourable critic, & his society was very agreeable to the most unlearned & simple, & much sought after by them, a thing not usual with the learned & accomplished. For a student of abstractions, he was uncommonly familiar with every variety of polite literature. Poetry he studied as high philosophy & enjoyed as answering to a soul tuned for harmony, in love with beauty, & alive to noble & graceful sentiments. Novels & romances of every school he read with interest, & kept himself acquainted with the current literature of the day, & with so much of the lighter literature of other times which has survived to us.

To do all this required system & quiet application; & both of these he certainly had. He never lost a moment. His books, nature, or society & his hours set apart for retirement employed all his time, & whatever he did was done with his might.

Under the instruction & in the society of such a man my six months' banishment at Andover passed in a most delightful & improving manner. I can hardly describe the relief I felt at getting rid of the exciting emulation for college rank, & at being able to study & recite for the good of my own mind, not for the sixes, sevens & eights, which, at Cambridge, were put against every word that came out of a student's mouth. I studied to get the meaning of the author & to acquaint myself with the language, & we read over the lesson together as friends look at a beautiful picture. The books we were upon were Horace in Latin & Demosthenes in Greek, so that the peculiar character of my instructor's mind, had opportunity to show itself for my advantage. He also put me upon the study of German, & so much of his own enthusiasm did he communicate to me, that I went through the grammar & the preliminary readings with the eagerness & pleasure with which one makes his preparations for a journey through a delightful country to be prosecuted with [a] clear & intelligent companion. As soon [as] I sufficiently advanced, we went upon the ballads & shorter poems of Schiller, Goethe & others, & reading & repeating them over & conversing upon them at the recitations & in our walks, I became more familiar with the sound & character of the language, & with the minds of its great writers, than I could in double the time spent in the mechanical writing of college exercises.

My mathematics I studied with a friend of Mr. Woods, a Mr. Thompson, a student of theology. With him, too, I could converse familiarly upon the problems of solid & spherical geometry, which we were then investigating. This was a contrast, indeed, with the mode of teaching the same science at Cambridge. For I state it as a fact that during the whole time we were studying plane geometry, which was our introduction to the whole science, & which it was essential we should comprehend, in order to go forward intelligently, I never heard a word of explanation or illustration from our tutor. If a student recited well, he received a high mark. If his recitation showed that he did not understand the problem, he received a low mark & was left to his ignorance. No explanation was offered, & the student was unwilling to detain the instructor after the exercise, with questions; & furthermore, so injurious was the effect of the rank system, that if a student conversed at all with the tutor, he was suspected of fishing, & would be hissed by the class as he came down. Consequently, from a misunderstanding of a single problem which [by] a few words would be made clear, many students were left in confusion & darkness in all their future progress.

Mr. Woods set learning & the cultivation of the intellect, the feelings & the whole moral nature, in a most attractive light. They became objects worthy of, & beyond the powers of the greatest intellectuals. In this view the strife for college rank, & for rank in the world, professional, political & social, took its right, & a very low, place. What a man is, & not merely what he has done, became the standard of emulation & effort.

Peter Kropotkin
(1842-1921)

Prince Peter Kropotkin was born in the Equerries Quarter of Moscow, the equivalent of the Faubourg Saint-Germain of Paris. It was where the elite of the Moscow nobility lived. Kropotkin's father was an officer of the Tzar Nicholas I, a vast landowner with over 1200 serfs to command. Kropotkin lived the first fifteen years of his life in this atmosphere, until he was sent to the Corps of Pages school in St. Petersburg. At this institution, whose function is explained by Kropotkin in the following passage,* he came under the tyranny of one Colonel Giradot. So fearful were the cadets of the Colonel that they turned on one another in order to release their aggression and hostility. One is reminded by Kropotkin's description of the recent findings of Kurt Lewin and his associates (10) in their experiment with authoritarian, laissez-faire and democratic leaders working with groups of youngsters.

The long-cherished ambition of my father was thus realized. There was a vacancy in the corps of pages which I could fill before I had got beyond the age to which admission was limited, and I was taken to St. Petersburg and entered the school. Only a hundred and fifty boys— mostly children of the nobility belonging to the court—received education in this privileged corps, which combined the character of a military school endowed with special rights and of a court institution attached to the imperial household. After a stay of four or five years in the corps of pages, those who had passed the final examinations were received as officers in any regiment of the guard or of the army they chose, irrespective of the number of vacancies in that regiment; and each year the first sixteen pupils of the highest form were nominated *pages de chambre;* that is, they were personally attached to the several members of the imperial family,—the emperor, the empress, the grand duchesses, and the grand dukes. That was considered, of course, a great honor; and, moreover, the young men upon whom this honor was bestowed became known at the court, and had afterward every chance of being nominated aides-de-camp of the emperor or of one of the grand dukes, and consequently had every facility for making a brilliant career in the service of the state. Fathers and mothers

---

*From *Memoirs of a Revolutionist.* Reprinted by permission of Houghton Mifflin Co. 1899. Pp. 71-77.

of families connected with the court took due care, therefore, that their boys should not miss entering the corps of pages, even though entrance had to be secured at the expense of other candidates who never saw a vacancy opening for them. Now that I was in the select corps my father could give free play to his ambitious dreams.

The corps was divided into five forms, of which the highest was the first, and the lowest the fifth, and the intention was that I should enter the fourth form. However, as it appeared at the examinations that I was not sufficiently familiar with decimal fractions, and as the fourth form contained that year over forty pupils, while only twenty had been mustered for the fifth form, I was enrolled in the latter.

I felt extremely vexed at this decision. It was with reluctance that I entered a military school, and now I should have to stay in it five years instead of four. What should I do in the fifth form, when I knew already all that would be taught in it? With tears in my eyes I spoke of it to the inspector (the head of the educational department), but he answered me with a joke. "You know," he remarked, "what Cæsar said,—better to be the first in a village than the second in Rome." To which I warmly replied that I should prefer to be the very last, if only I could leave the military school as soon as possible. "Perhaps, after some time, you will like the school," he remarked, and from that day he became friendly to me.

When I entered the corps of pages, its inner life was undergoing a profound change. All Russia awakened at that time from the heavy slumber and the terrible nightmare of Nicholas I.'s reign. Our school also felt the effects of that revival. I do not know, in fact, what would have become of me, had I entered the corps of pages one or two years sooner. Either my will would have been totally broken, or I should have been excluded from the school with no one knows what consequences. Happily, the transition period was already in full sway in the year 1857.

The director of the corps was an excellent old man, General Zheltúkhin. But he was the nominal head only. The real master of the school was "the Colonel,"—Colonel Girardot, a Frenchman in the Russian service. People said he was a Jesuit, and so he was, I believe. His ways, at any rate, were thoroughly imbued with the teachings of Loyola, and his educational methods were those of the French Jesuit colleges.

Imagine a short, extremely thin man, with dark, piercing, and furtive eyes, wearing short clipped mustaches, which gave him the expression of a cat; very quiet and firm; not remarkably intelligent, but exceedingly cunning; a despot at the bottom of his heart, who was capable of hating—intensely hating—the boy who would not fall under his fascination, and of expressing that hatred, not by silly persecutions, but unceasingly, by his general behavior,—by an occasionally dropped word, a gesture, a smile, an interjection. His walk was more like gliding along, and the exploring glances he used to cast round without turning his head completed the illusion. A stamp of cold dryness was impressed on his lips, even when he tried to look well disposed, and that expression became still more harsh when his mouth was contorted by a smile of discontent or of contempt. With all this there was nothing of a commander in him; you would rather think, at first sight, of a benevolent father who talks to his children as if they were full-grown people. And yet, you soon felt that every one and everything had to bend before his will. Woe to the boy who would not feel happy or unhappy according to the degree of good disposition shown toward him by the Colonel.

The words "the Colonel" were continually on all lips. Other officers went by their nicknames, but no one dared to give a nickname to Girardot. A sort of mystery hung about him, as if he were omniscient and everywhere present. True, he spent all day and part of the night in the school. Even when we were in the classes he prowled about, visiting our drawers, which he opened with his own keys. As to the night, he gave a good portion of it to the task of inscribing in small books,—of which he had quite a library,—in separate columns, by special signs and in inks of different colors, all the faults and virtues of each boy.

Play, jokes, and conversation stopped when we saw him slowly moving along through our spacious rooms, hand in hand with one of his favorites, balancing his body forward and backward; smiling at one boy, keenly looking into the eyes of another, casting an indifferent glance upon a third, and giving a slight contortion to his lip as he passed a fourth: and from these looks every one knew that he liked the first boy, that to the second he was indifferent, that he intentionally did not notice the third, and that he disliked the fourth. This dislike was enough to terrify most of his victims,—the more so as no reason could be given for it. Impressionable boys had been brought to despair by that mute, unceasingly displayed aversion and those suspicious looks; in others the result had been a total annihilation of will, as one of the Tolstois—Theodor, also a pupil of Girardot—has shown in an autobiographic novel, *The Diseases of the Will*.

The inner life of the corps was miserable under the rule of the Colonel. In all boarding-schools the newly entered boys are subjected to petty persecutions. The "greenhorns" are put in this way to a test.

What are they worth? Are they not going to turn "sneaks"? And then the "old hands" like to show to newcomers the superiority of an established brotherhood. So it is in all schools and in prisons. But under Girardot's rule these persecutions took on a harsher aspect, and they came, not from the comrades of the same form, but from the first form,—the pages de chambre, who were non-commissioned officers, and whom Girardot had placed in a quite exceptional, superior position. His system was to give them carte blanche; to pretend that he did not know even the horrors they were enacting; and to maintain through them a severe discipline. To answer a blow received from a page de chambre would have meant, in the times of Nicholas I., to be sent to a battalion of soldiers' sons, if the fact became public; and to revolt in any way against the mere caprice of a page de chambre meant that the twenty youths of the first form, armed with their heavy oak rulers, would assemble in a room, and, with Girardot's tacit approval, administer a severe beating to the boy who had shown such a spirit of insubordination.

Accordingly, the first form did what they liked; and not further back than the preceding winter one of their favorite games had been to assemble the "greenhorns" at night in a room, in their night-shirts, and to make them run round, like horses in a circus, while the pages de chambre, armed with thick india-rubber whips, standing some in the centre and the others on the outside, pitilessly whipped the boys. As a rule the "circus" ended in an Oriental fashion, in an abominable way. The moral conceptions which prevailed at that time, and the foul talk which went on in the school concerning what occurred at night after circus, were such that the least said about them the better.

The Colonel knew all this. He had a perfectly organized system of espionage, and nothing escaped his knowledge. But so long as he was not known to know it, all was right. To shut his eyes to what was done by the first form was the foundation of his system of maintaining discipline.

However, a new spirit was awakened in the school, and only a few months before I entered it a revolution had taken place. That year the third form was different from what it had hitherto been. It contained a number of young men who really studied and read a good deal; some of them became, later, men of mark. My first acquaintance with one of them—let me call him von Schauff—was when he was reading Kant's *Critique of Pure Reason*. Besides, they had amongst them some of the strongest youths of the school. The tallest member of the corps was in that form, as also a very strong young man, Kóshtoff, a great friend of von Schauff. The third form did not bear the yoke of the pages de chambre with the same docility as their predecessors; they were disgusted with what was going on; and in consequence of an incident, which I prefer not to describe, a fight took place between the third and the first form, with the result that the pages de chambre got a very severe thrashing from their subordinates. Girardot hushed up the affair, but the authority of the first form was broken down. The india-rubber whips remained, but were never again brought into use. The circuses and the like became things of the past.

George Santayana
 (1863-1952)

Santayana, the son of a Spanish father and an American mother, was born in Madrid. He came to the United States in 1872 at the age of nine and was enrolled in the Latin School in Boston. In this passage, he describes the teachers of that school during the period of his adolescence.* They were, for the most part, drones, dull fellows who were bored and boring. A few, however, were respected and struck a responsive chord in the boy who was not—and never would be—at home in America. Although Santayana himself became an influential professor at Harvard and an outstanding philosopher and novelist, the Spanish tradition corresponded more to his inclinations. He spent the last years of his life as a guest in a convent in Italy.

The teachers, though it is not possible for me now to distinguish them all in memory, were surely not out of keeping with their surroundings: disappointed, shabby-genteel, picturesque old Yankees, with a little bitter humor breaking through their constitutional fatigue. I daresay that for them as for me, and for all the boys who were at all sensitive, the school was a familiar symbol of fatality. They hadn't chosen it, they hadn't wanted it, they didn't particularly like it; they knew no reason why it should be the sort of school it was: but there it stood, there they somehow found themselves entangled; and there was nothing else practicable but to go on there, doing what was expected and imposed upon them. You may say that for the teachers at least, in that age of individual initiative and open careers, a thousand alternatives were, or had been, possible; and you may say that they could not have been altogether insensible of their high vocation

---

*From *Persons and Places* by George Santayana. Reprinted by permission of Charles Scribner's Sons. Copyright 1944, Charles Scribner's Sons. Pp. 154-157.

and the high vocation of their country to create gradually and securely a better world, a world free from superstition, from needless hatreds, from unjust inequalities, and from devastating misery. Yes: but all that was negative; it consisted of things to be got rid of and avoided, and in America the more obvious of them had actually been escaped. Officially, especially now that slavery had been abolished, everything was all right. Everybody was free. Everybody was at work. Almost everybody could be well educated. Almost everybody was married. Therefore almost everybody was, or ought to be, perfectly happy. But were the teachers at the Latin School, perhaps the best of American schools, happy? Or were the boys? Ah, perhaps we should not ask whether they were happy, for they were not rich, but whether they were not enthusiastically conscious of a great work, an endless glorious struggle and perpetual victory, set before them in the world. And I reply, not for myself, since I don't count, being an alien, but in their name, that they decidedly were conscious of no such thing. They had heard of it; but in their daily lives they were conscious only of hard facts, meagerness, routine, petty commitments, and ideals too distant and vague to be worth mentioning.

Those teachers were stray individuals; they had not yet been standardized by educational departments and pedagogy. Some were like village schoolmasters or drudges; elderly men, like Mr. Capen, with crotchets, but good teachers, knowing their particular book and knowing how to keep order, and neither lax nor cruel. Others, especially Mr. Fiske, afterwards headmaster, and Mr. Groce, were younger, with a more modern education. They might have been college professors; they loved their subjects, Greek and English, and allowed them to color their minds out of school hours. In a word, they were *cultivated* men. I was an unprofitable though not unappreciative pupil to Mr. Fiske, because I didn't learn my Greek properly. That was not his fault. If I could have had him for a private tutor I should have become a good Grecian: it would have added immensely to my life and to my philosophy. But I was only one of forty; I was expected to study dryly, mechanically, without the side-lights and the stimulus of non-verbal interest attached to the words. In Latin, I could supply these side-lights and non-verbal interests out of my own store. Latin was the language of the Church, it was old Spanish. The roots were all my roots. But Greek roots were more often foreign and at first unmeaning; they had to be learned by hammering, to which my indolence was not inclined. And there was another difficulty. My apprehension of words is auricular; I must *hear* what I read. I knew, with small variations, what was the sound of Latin. I had heard it all my life;

slovenly and corrupt as the Spanish pronunciation of it may be, at least it is something traditional. But what of Greek pronunciation? How should Homer sound? How should Sophocles? How should Xenophon or Plato? The artificial German Greek that we were taught —without even a proper o—was impossible. I tried many years later, when I was in Greece, to learn a little of the modern language, in hopes that it might react on my sense for the ancient texts and make me feel at home in them: but the time was too short, my opportunities limited, and I was too old to be quick in such a matter.

Even as it was, however, I learned a little Greek at School after my fashion, and one day surprised Mr. Fiske by reciting a long speech out of *Oedipus Tyrannus* for my ordinary declamation. He couldn't believe his ears, and afterwards privately congratulated me on my pronunciation of the o's. But that didn't make me master of the Greek vocabulary or the Greek inflections. I didn't *study* enough. I learned and remembered well what I could learn from Mr. Fiske without studying. He was an exceedingly nervous, shy man; evidently suffered at having to address any one, or having to find words in which to express his feelings. His whole body would become tense, he would stand almost on tiptoe, with two or three fingers in the side pocket of his trousers, and the other two or three moving outside, as if reaching for the next word. These extreme mannerisms occasioned no ridicule: the boys all saw that there was a clear mind and a goodwill behind them; and Mr. Fiske was universally liked and admired. This, although his language was as contorted as his gestures. He always seemed to be translating literally and laboriously from the Greek or the German. When he wished to fix in our minds the meaning of a Greek word he would say, for instance: "χαράδρα, a ravine, from which our word *character,* the deeply graven result of long-continued habit." Or "χαταρρέω, to flow down, whence our word *catarrh,* copious down-flowings from the upper regions of the head." We didn't laugh, and we remembered.

Very different was dapper Mr. Groce, our teacher of English composition and literature, a little plump man, with a keen, dry, cheerful, yet irritable disposition, a sparkling bird-like eye, and a little black mustache and diminutive chin-beard. I suspect that he was too intelligent to put up patiently with all the conventions. Had he not been a public-school teacher, dependent on the democratic hypocrisies of a government committee, he might have said unconventional things. This inner rebellion kept him from being sentimental, moralistic, or religious in respect to poetry; yet he *understood* perfectly the penumbra of emotion that good and bad poetry alike may drag after them in an untrained mind. He knew how to rescue the structural and rational beauties of a poem from that bog of private feeling. To me this was a timely lesson, for it was precisely sadness and religiosity and grandiloquence that first attracted me in poetry; and perhaps I owe to Mr. Groce the beginnings of a capacity to distinguish the musical and expressive charm of poetry from its moral appeal. At any rate, at sixteen, I composed my first longish poem, in Spenser's measure, after *Childe Harold* and *Adonais,* full of pessimistic, languid, Byronic sentiments, describing the various kinds of superiority that Night has over Day. It got the prize.

Rudyard Kipling
(1865-1936)

Kipling had been sent by his father to England from India to get a college education. He attended the United Services College which was "largely a caste-school—some seventy-five per cent of us had been born outside England and hoped to follow their fathers in the Army. . . . The college was in the nature of a company promoted by poor officers and the like for the cheap education of their sons, and set up at Westward Ho! near Bedford."* Kipling delighted in his Classics Master, a man with a "splendid physique," an athlete, customarily given to direct speech and the possessor of a ready temper—characteristics which appeal to many adolescents. Kipling used this man as the prototype for one of his *Stalky* characterizations, so great an impression did he make on him. This admiration has been satirized by Max Beerbohm and Lionel Trilling, the latter declaring (23) that "It is the emotion of a boy—he lusts for the exclusive circle, for the sect with the password, and he profoundly admires the technical, secret-laden adults who run the world, the overalled people, majestic in their occupation, the dour engineer and the thoughtful plumber. To this emotion, developed not much beyond a boy's, Kipling was addicted all his life, and eventually it made him silly and a bore."

My main interest as I grew older was C——, my English and Classics Master, a rowing-man of splendid physique, and a scholar who

*From *Something of Myself* by Rudyard Kipling. Reprinted by permission of Mrs. George Bambridge and Doubleday & Co., Inc. Copyright 1927, Caroline Kipling. Pp. 35-37.

lived in a secret hope of translating Theocritus worthily. He had a violent temper, no disadvantage in handling boys used to direct speech, and a gift of schoolmaster's 'sarcasm' which must have been a relief to him and was certainly a treasure-trove to me. Also he was a good and House-proud House-master. Under him I came to feel that words could be used as weapons, for he did me the honour to talk at me plentifully; and our year-in year-out form-room bickerings gave us both something to play with. One learns more from a good scholar in a rage than from a score of lucid and laborious drudges; and to be made the butt of one's companions in full form is no bad preparation for later experiences. I think this 'approach' is now discouraged for fear of hurting the soul of youth, but in essence it is no more than rattling tins or firing squibs under a colt's nose. I remember nothing save satisfaction or envy when C—— broke his precious ointments over my head.

I tried to give a pale rendering of his style when heated in a 'Stalky' tale, 'Regulus,' but I wish I could have presented him as he blazed forth once on the great Cleopatra Ode—the 27th of the Third Book. I had detonated him by a very vile construe of the first few lines. Having slain me, he charged over my corpse and delivered an interpretation of the rest of the Ode unequalled for power and insight. He held even the Army Class breathless.

There must be still masters of the same sincerity; and gramophone records of such good men, on the brink of profanity, struggling with a Latin form, would be more helpful to education than bushels of printed books. C—— taught me to loathe Horace for two years; to forget him for twenty, and then to love him for the rest of my days and through many sleepless nights.

Lincoln Steffens
(1866-1936)

In this powerfully eloquent portrayal of the functions of a teacher, Steffens examines his own intellectual development and the rising excitement within him as he came under the sway of one Evelyn Nixon.* Here was a teacher who opened up the beauty and meaning of Greek, Latin and English; who did not have the "answers" for the boy's question but who shouted at him: "I will answer no questions of yours. Men know no answers to the natural questions

---

*From *Autobiography* by Lincoln Steffens. Reprinted by permission of Harcourt, Brace & World, Inc. 1931. Pp. 111-116.

of a boy, of a child. We can only underline your questions, make you mad yourself to answer them, and add ours to whip, to lash you on to find out yourself—one or two; and tell us! That is what youth is for: to answer the questions maturity can't answer. . . . Go to, boy. The world is yours. Nothing is done, nothing is known. The greatest poem isn't written, the best railroad isn't built yet, the perfect state hasn't been thought of. Everything remains to be done —right, everything." With this kind of approach, with the aliveness and interest Nixon had in teaching and in scholarship, and with the opportunities he gave Steffens to participate in the free, passionate and witty conversations of his friends, the eager student was "inspired to be, like him, not a hero nor even a poet, but a Greek scholar, and thus an instrument on which beautiful words might play."

The year 1884-85 was a period of great adventure for me. When I came up to Berkeley for the entrance examinations at the University of California I failed in Greek, Latin, and enough other subjects to be put off for a year. My father was alarmed. I was eighteen years old, and he thought, I think, that my failure was his fault; he had chosen the wrong school for me. He had, but the right school for me and my kind did not exist. There were schools that put boys into the colleges, east and west, and at a younger age than mine. I came to know these boys well. They are the boys (and they become the men) that the schools, colleges, and the world are made for. Often I have envied them; more often I have been glad that I was not one of them.

The elect were, for the most part, boys who had been brought up to do their duty. They memorized whatever their teachers told them to learn. Whether they wanted to know it, whether they understood it or no, they could remember and recite it. Their own driving motives were, so far as I could make out, not curiosity; they rarely talked about our studies, and if I spoke of the implications of something we had read or heard, they looked dazed or indifferent. Their own motives were foreign to me: to beat the other fellows, stand high, represent the honor of the school.

My parents did not bring me up. They sent me to school, they gave me teachers of music, drawing; they offered me every opportunity in their reach. But also they gave me liberty and the tools of quite another life: horses, guns, dogs, and the range of an open country. As I have shown, the people, the businesses, and the dreams of this life interested me, and I learned well whatever interested me. School subjects which happened to bear on my outside interests I studied in school and out; I read more than was required, and I read for keeps, too. I know these subjects to this day, just as I remember and love still the men and women, the boys and girls, who let me be friends with them then and so revealed to me some of the depths and the limitations of human nature. On the other hand I can remember few of my teachers and little of the subjects which seemed to me irrelevant to my life.

These other subjects are interesting, and they might have been made interesting to me. No one tried to interest me in them; they were put before me as things that I had to have to get into college. The teachers of them did not appeal to my curious, active mind. The result was that I did not really work at them and so got only what stuck by dint of repetition: the barest rudiments of a school education. When I knocked at the college gates, I was prepared for a college education in some branches; my mind was hungry enough for the answers to some profound questions to have made me work and develop myself, especially on lines which I know now had no ready answers, only more and ever more questions: science, metaphysics, etc. I was not in the least curious about Greek, Latin, mathematics, and the other "knowledge" required by the standardization of that day.

My father discovered and put me into the best private school in San Francisco as a special student to be crammed for Berkeley—and he retained one of the teachers there, Mr. Evelyn Nixon, to tutor me on the side. Characteristically, too, my father gave me liberty: a room to sleep and work in, with no one to watch over and care for me. I could go and come as I pleased. And I came and went. I went exploring and dreaming alone around that city as I had the country around Sacramento, and the place I liked best was the ocean shore; there I lived over the lives of the Greek heroes and the Roman generals and all the poets of all the ages, sometimes with ecstasy, but never, as in my boyhood, with myself as the hero. A change had come over me.

Evelyn Nixon formed it. He was the first teacher I ever had who interested me in what I had to learn—not in myself, but in the world outside, the world of conscious culture. He was a fanatic of poetry, especially of the classic poets. When he read or recited Greek verse the Greeks came to life; romance and language sang songs to me, and I was inspired to be, like him, not a hero nor even a poet, but a Greek scholar, and thus an instrument on which beautiful words might play. Life filled with meaning, and purpose, and joy. It was too great and too various for me to personify with my boyish imitations and heroism. I wrote verses, but only to learn the technique and so feel poetry more perfectly. I wanted to read, not to write; I wanted to know, not to do and be, great things—Mr. Nixon expressed it.

"I'm nobody," he used to say. "I'm nothing but one of the unknown beings Homer and Dante, Shakespeare, Caesar, and the popes and the generals and statesmen have sung and fought and worked for. I'm the appreciator of all good words and deeds."

A new, a noble rôle, and Evelyn Nixon was a fine example of it: the receiver, not the giver, of beautiful inventions. He was an Englishman; he took a double first at Oxford, I heard, and came for his health to San Francisco. There was a group of such men, most of them with one story. They were athletes, as well as scholars at Oxford and Cambridge; they developed muscles and a lung capacity which they did not need and could not keep up in the sedentary occupations their scholarship put them into. Lung troubles exiled them.

"Keep out of college athletics," they advised. "Don't work up any more brawn there than you can use every day afterward."

Nixon taught me Greek, Latin, and English at school, and at his house he opened up the beauty and the meaning of the other subjects I had to cram up for entrance. I worked for him; I worked more, much more, for myself. He saw this, he saw my craving for the answers to questions, and he laughed.

"I will answer no questions of yours," he shouted. "Men know no answers to the natural questions of a boy, of a child. We can only underline your questions, make you mad yourself to answer them, and add ours to whip, to lash you on to find out yourself—one or two; and tell us! That is what youth is for: to answer the questions maturity can't answer." And when I looked disappointed and balked, he would roar at me like a demon.

"Go to, boy. The world is yours. Nothing is done, nothing is known. The greatest poem isn't written, the best railroad isn't built yet, the perfect state hasn't been thought of. Everything remains to be done—right, everything."

This said, he said it again and again, and finally, to drive me, he set our private hour from seven till eight o'clock Saturday evenings, so that I could stay on into the night with his group of friends, a maddening lot of cultivated, conflicting minds. There were from four to ten of them, all Englishmen, all Oxford and Cambridge men, all exiles and all interested in any and all subjects, which they discussed with knowledge, with the precise information of scholarship, but with no common opinions on anything apparently. There were Tories among them and liberals and one red: William Owen, a grandson, I think, certainly a descendant, of Robert Owen, the first of the early

English socialists. There was at least one Roman Catholic, who showed me so that I never forgot it the Christianity of that church; his favorite thesis was that the Protestant churches were Old Testament, righteous sects and knew nothing really of Christ's teachings of love and forgiveness. And there were Protestants there, all schooled in church history, and when a debate came to a clinch, they could quote their authorities with a sureness which withstood reference to the books. I remember one hot dispute of the Catholic's reference to some certain papal bull. Challenged, he quoted it verbatim in the original Latin. What they knew was amazing to me, and how they knew it, but what they did not know struck me harder still. They could not among them agree on anything but a fact. With all their knowledge they knew no essential truth.

It was conversation I was hearing, the free, passionate, witty exchanges of studied minds as polished as fine tools. They were always courteous; no two ever spoke together; there were no asides; they all talked to the question before the house, and while they were on the job of exposition any one, regardless of his side, would contribute his quota of facts, or his remembrance of some philosopher's opinion or some poet's perfect phrase for the elucidation or the beautification of the theme. When the differences rose the urbanity persisted. They drank their Californian wine with a relish, they smoked the room thick, and they pressed their views with vigor and sincerity and eloquence; but their good temper never failed them. It was conversation. I had never heard conversation before; I have heard conversation sometimes since, but rarely, and never like my remembrance of those wonderful Saturday nights in San Francisco—which were my preparation for college.

For those conversations, so brilliant, so scholarly, and so consciously unknowing, seemed to me, silent in the background, to reveal the truth that even college graduates did not know anything, really. Evidences they had, all the testimony of all the wise men in the historical world on everything, but no decisions. None. I must myself go to college to find out more, and I wanted to. It seemed as if I had to go soon. My head, busy with questions before, was filled with holes that were aching voids as hungry, as painful, as an empty stomach. And my questions were explicit; it was as if I were not only hungry; I was hungry for certain foods. My curiosity was no longer vague.

When on Sundays I would take the gatherings I had made out of the talk of the night before down to the Cliff House with me and sit there on the rocks and think, I formed my ignorance into a system. I was getting a cultivated ignorance, a survey not of the solved but of the unsolved problems in every science from astronomy to economics, from history to the next tricks in versification. I thought of them; I thought, rejoicing, that there were things to do for everybody in every science, every art, every business. Why, men did not know even how to love, not technically, not beautifully! I learned of the damage done me by having my sex feelings separated from love and poetry, and as for astronomy, government, conversation, play and work, men were just crawling on their hands and knees out of their caves.

But the best that I got out of it all was objectivity. Those men never mentioned themselves; apparently they never thought of themselves. Their interest was in the world outside of themselves. I caught that. No more play-acting for me. No more dreaming I was Napoleon or a trapper, a knight, a statesman, or the younger son of a lord. It is possible that I was outgrowing this stage of a boy's growth; the very intensity of my life in subjective imagination may have carried me through it, but whether I would have come out clearly impersonal or no by myself, I don't know. All I am sure of is that their conversations, the attitude and the interest of those picked Englishmen, helped and, I think, established in me the realization that the world was more interesting than I was. Not much to see? No, but I have met men since, statesmen, scholars, business men, workers, and poets, who have never made that discovery. It is the scientific attitude, and some scientists have it—not all; and some others, too.

When I went up for my examination this time in Berkeley I passed, not well in all subjects, but I was admitted to the University, and that fall I entered the University of California with a set of examination questions for the faculty, for the professors, to answer.

Theodore Dreiser
(1871-1945)

Two high-school teachers, both women, evinced a personal interest in Theodore Dreiser and in his views and aspirations at a time when the little town of Warsaw was buzzing with malicious gossip about the Dreiser family. Amy, Theodore's older sister, had just had an illegitimate baby and his unforgiving father lay seriously ill with bladder trouble. The interest these teachers had in Theodore, prompted perhaps by their own frustrations, not only helped the boy over a very difficult time but also inspired him to "progress as fast intellectually . . . as I ever did at any time." He exclaims, "But the thrill of it! The bracing, encouraging thrill! Instantly and because of this strong, affectionate support, I felt so much better about everything."*

There were two women teachers in this High School at the time who came to exercise a most hopeful and helpful influence over me, to make for somewhat more of optimism in connection with myself than hitherto had been. One of these was a tall old maid from Malden, Massachusetts, a certain Mildred Fielding, who at thirty-three or thereabouts was for the first time in her life finding herself moderately attractive, and thinking, no doubt, therefore, that the world was not so bad. As I afterwards learned from her, she had had a very hard life. In her youth she had been poor, socially nobody, cursed with an ungainly form, protruding teeth, in short, every physical disadvantage which could afflict a young and otherwise healthy girl. At last she had fought her way up to being a teacher and in addition had had her teeth straightened, her hair properly dressed, had learned to wear appropriate clothes and only now was beginning to reap the fruits of her long struggle. In spite of all her difficulties, she had retained a sweet, gentle and lovable disposition. Her attitude now was one of broad tolerance and generosity. At thirty-five, her light brown hair, grey-blue eyes, and pink complexion made her seem younger than she was. It was this woman who was destined to come to my aid in a very curious way some two years later. Just then, as director of the High School recitation room, she was in touch with me, my studies in connection with algebra, physical geography, general history, botany, and so on, being recited to and corrected or directed by her.

The other teacher—Alvira Skarr, I think her name was—who controlled the study room, was a very different type. Small, red-haired, finicky, and showy in a material and yet conservative way, she was at the same time lively, friendly and attractive. She wore gold-bridge glasses and a showy gold watch fastened at her breast by a jeweled pin. A taste for appearing in new dresses of rich material and talking of her family in Erie, Pennsylvania, indicated either a plentiful supply of money or a good salary. I think it was the former, for her salary could not have been more than twelve hundred dollars a year.

Both of these women, soon after my entrance into first year High, evinced a genial personal interest in me and my views and aspirations, which flattered me not a little, and by degrees seriously affected my personal estimate of myself. It must be remembered that I was then at the age when one is most easily influenced. Miss Fielding, to my

---

*From *Dawn. A History of Myself* by Theodore Dreiser. Reprinted by permission of World Publishing Co. Copyright 1931, Theodore Dreiser. Pp. 274-276.

surprise and embarrassed pleasure, frequently assisted me after school with my algebra, with which I had some difficulty. More, and at the same time, she appeared to be aware of our local history, and while this troubled me not a little, at the same time it was coupled with, in her case, a tender and quite obvious solicitude as well as desire to fortify me against any depressing effect our home troubles might be having on me.

Thus, one afternoon, and quite out of a clear sky, in the midst of an explanation in connection with an alegbra problem, she paused and said: "Theodore, I want to say something to you. It is not prompted by anything but a real interest in you and your welfare." I instantly shivered with the thought that she was going to tell me I was not sufficiently trained as yet for the work I was undertaking and would need to return to the previous grade. But instead she went on: "I can see that you are not like the other boys and girls here. You are different, Theodore. Very sensitive. Your mind is very different. You understand well enough where you are interested. It is only where you aren't that you do so poorly. But you mustn't let that worry you. You must study and go on, for your mind will find its way. I know it!" And then looking directly into my eyes, her own lit with a warm, tender, even affectionate, glow, she concluded: "But there is some-thing else. You mustn't mind my saying this, Theodore, because I am fond of you and want you to succeed in life. And you will, if you wish. Please don't mind anything that is said or done in a small town like this, and don't let it hurt you. I was brought up in one, and I know how small people can be and how they talk. But please don't let it affect you. You will soon grow up and go away and then all that has. happened here will seem as nothing to you. It is only you that can hurt yourself, not the actions or words or opinions of anyone else. You understand me, Theodore, don't you?"

I was moved almost to tears, and so grateful that though I wished to speak, I could not. Instead I merely looked. But she must have gath-ered what I felt, for she laid a gentle, caressing hand on my arm and added, smilingly: "Now shall we see if we can solve this?" I tried to follow her, but seeing that I could not, she said: "Well, we'll put it over until to-morrow. You might look it over tonight. It will come to you." And—reluctantly, as it seemed to me—she walked away, and I gathered up my books and hurried out.

But the thrill of it! The bracing, encouraging thrill! Instantly and because of this strong, affectionate support, I felt so much better about everything. Pooh! Warsaw and its people! What of them? Who were they? Had I not just been told that I had a different and good mind and that once I was out in the world I could get along? Supposing our family was talked about—evidently it was, since she chose to refer to it—was that certain to affect me? She seemed to think not, had practically assured me that it could not. I felt so much braver, stronger, walked with an air, a trifle of vanity swelling in me.

And better—if such things really are better—this was added to, if in a lesser degree, by Miss Skarr. My interest in English and world literature seemed to appeal to her. As busy as she was—and she was in charge of a very large roomful of scholars—she too (possibly at Miss Fielding's behest) managed to find time to talk to me and to point out books in which I might be interested, some lectures that were occasionally given on literature at the home of Professor Saunders, our school superintendent, and lastly, after learning I was half German, urged me to take a German course which she was conducting and which would open the door to Schiller, Goethe, Heine and others. I could read a little German, and here was all this superior wisdom at my hand. At once, my estimate of my father's native land (hitherto, because of his religious dogmatizing, exceedingly low) rose. I joined the course, and during the remainder of that year, along with ten others (one of them Nata Weyler, if you please) scanned—cursorily, as one may guess—a history of German literature.

Grant Richards
(1872-   )

Grant Richards, a British publisher who was born in Glasgow of English parents, pays tribute to an uncle of his, Grant Allen. He "was an influence in my life because, to begin with, he paid a little attention to the fact that I existed, and because I came to look to him and to my aunt, his wife, for sympathy and for assistance in my little troubles, and because I found in his company a ready understanding and in his surroundings a degree of comfort which I had not hitherto tasted [21]." His uncle helped the fifteen-year-old boy put his mind into some kind of ordered relation to the world. Unlike Steffens' tutor, he answered questions put to him. Many adolescents need authoritative answers to give them a sense of stability in their chaotic world and apparently Allen satisfied this need for his nephew.

But, whether consciously or unconsciously, Grant Allen began to teach me. He put my young mind into some kind of ordered relation to the world. Nobody else showed the slightest signs of doing that. Moreover, he was a realist. If I asked a question he answered it, and took trouble that his answer should be both intelligible and truthful. He used to open my eyes to things. Soon enough he despaired of my ever taking any real interest in science as a whole, or even in Natural History, and it was very much out of his way to try to set me on any definite path of reading. Read what you like, seemed to be his idea of what he should say to a child, and I did read what I liked in his very miscellaneous collection of books, a reviewer's collection, most of it. I might and did read volumes in the series known as "The Family Herald Story-Teller," and some large and frank volume dealing with human physiology. Grant Allen had cared for the classics himself, and knew as much as he had had time to know about the English standard authors, but he was quite indifferent as to whether I read them, and I must confess that I only read them now and again. Rather did I read and very much enjoy reading "penny dreadfuls." There was *Jack Harkaway,* and in a shop just on the Surrey side of Blackfriars Bridge I could have my choice of "bloods" of all sorts. My favourite was *Lost in a London Sewer,* or a story with some such title. The idea of caves, caverns or subterranean passages has always had attraction for youth.

G. K. Chesterton
(1874-1936)

In a hilarious chapter entitled "How To Be a Dunce," taken from his *Autobiography,** G. K. Chesterton describes the difficulties some of his teachers at St. Paul's experienced with the boys. The peer culture demanded the appearance of stupidity on the part of the students and the absolute prohibition of showing off. To give a correct answer in response to the teacher's question was tantamount to treason. But two of Chesterton's teachers were able to get past his guard and "discover the horrible secret that I was, after all, endowed with the gift of reason above the brutes."

But I do remember coming, almost seriously, to the conclusion that a boy must go to school to study the characters of his schoolmasters. And I still think that there was something in it. After all, the schoolmaster is the first educated grown-up person that the boy comes to

---

*Reprinted by permission of Sheed & Ward, Inc. (New York) and Miss D. E. Collins. Copyright 1936. Pp. 63-65.

see constantly, after having been introduced at an early age to his father and mother. And the masters at St. Paul's were very interesting; even those of them who were not so obviously eccentric as the celebrated Mr. Elam. To one very distinguished individual, my own personal debt is infinite; I mean the historian of the Indian Mutiny and of the campaigns of Caesar—Mr. T. Rice Holmes. He managed, heaven knows how, to penetrate through my deep and desperately consolidated desire to appear stupid; and discover the horrible secret that I was, after all, endowed with the gift of reason above the brutes. He would suddenly ask me questions a thousand miles away from the subject in hand, and surprise me into admitting that I had heard of the Song of Roland, or even read a play or two of Shakespeare. Nobody who knows anything of the English schoolboy at that date will imagine that there was at the moment any pleasure in such prominence or distinction. We were all hag-ridden with a horror of showing off, which was perhaps the only coherent moral principle we possessed. There was one boy, I remember, who was so insanely sensitive on this point of honour, that he could hardly bear to hear one of his friends answer an ordinary question right. He felt that his comrade really ought to have invented some mistake, in the general interest of comradeship. When my information about the French epic was torn from me, in spite of my efforts, he actually put his head in his desk and dropped the lid on it, groaning in a generous and impersonal shame and faintly and hoarsely exclaiming, "Oh, shut it. . . . Oh, shut up!" He was an extreme exponent of the principle; but it was a principle which I fully shared. I can remember running to school in sheer excitement repeating militant lines of "Marmion" with passionate emphasis and exultation; and then going into class and repeating the same lines in the lifeless manner of a hurdy-gurdy, hoping that there was nothing whatever in my intonation to indicate that I distinguished between the sense of one word and another.

Nobody, I think, ever got past my guard in this matter except Mr. T. R. Holmes and Mr. R. F. Cholmeley, who afterwards became the house-master of my two intimate friends, and who, I am glad to say, has often joined us in later years in our reunions of remembrance. But, somehow or other, a rumour must have begun to circulate among the authorities that we were not such fools as we looked. One day, to my consternation, the High Master stopped me in the street and led me along, roaring in my deafened and bewildered ears that I had a literary faculty which might come to something if somebody could give it solidity. Some time after that, to my cowering terror, he bellowed aloud to a whole crowd of parents and other preposterous intruders, on the occasion of a prize day, that our little magazine showed signs of considerable talent, though it was an unofficial publication on which he "might have hesitated to set his *Imprimatur*". Somehow we felt it would have been even more crushing if he had set his *Imprimatur*. It sounded like the thumb of a giant.

Adolf Hitler
(1889-1944)

Shortly after Hitler's argument with his father about becoming a painter (see the chapter on Vocation and Identification), his work at the Linz high school began to suffer. His marks were so poor that he was dismissed from the school, a fact that rankled him all through life. He developed a contempt for teachers and professors. In *Mein Kampf* he wrote, "When I think of the men who were my teachers, I realize that most of them were slightly mad." And again, "I have the most unpleasant recollections of the teachers who taught me." And still again, "Our teachers were absolute tyrants. They had no sympathy with youth. . . . "

But there was one instructor at the Linz high school who exercised a stong and fateful influence on the young Adolf Hitler. This was a history teacher, Dr. Leopold Poetsch, who, as reported by William L. Shirer, "came from the southern German-language border region where it meets that of the South Slavs and whose experience with the racial struggle there had made him a fanatical German nationalist. Before coming to Linz he had taught at Marburg, which later, when the area was transferred to Yugoslavia after the First World War, became Maribor. Though Dr. Poetsch had given his pupil marks of only 'fair' in history, he was the only one of Hitler's teachers to receive a warm tribute in *Mein Kampf*. Hitler readily admitted his debt to this man [22]."

It was perhaps decisive for my whole later life that good fortune gave me a history teacher who understood, as few others did, this principle . . . of retaining the essential and forgetting the nonessential . . . In my teacher, Dr. Leopold Poetsch of the high school in Linz, this requirement was fulfilled in a truly ideal manner. An old gentleman, kind but at the same time firm, he was able not only to hold our attention by his dazzling eloquence but to carry us away with him. Even today I think back with genuine emotion on this gray-haired man who, by the fire of his words, sometimes made us forget the present; who, as if by magic, transported us into times past and, out of the millennium mists of time, transformed dry historical facts into vivid reality. There we sat, often aflame with enthusiasm, sometimes even moved to tears . . . He used our budding national fanaticism as a means of educating us, frequently appealing to our sense of national honor. This teacher made history my favorite subject. And indeed, though he had no such intention, it was then that I became a young revolutionary.

Esther C. Dunn
(1891-   )

Esther Dunn was forced by her status-conscious father to take up Greek during her high school days. She was reluctant and unhappy about it, for almost all of her girl friends were studying German. But it was her Greek teacher who did more for her ideas and method of learning than any other single force in her life. He was the kind of teacher who felt "his way, day by day, hour by hour, adapting his specific matter to the mood and need of particular pupils on particular days." Miss Dunn compares the great teacher with a gardener who does not force-feed, nor overfeed nor underfeed his tender plants, but treats each one individually and acknowledges the variations he finds.* Professor Dunn should know the qualities of a real teacher, for she taught English at Smith College for many years. Among her published texts are *Ben Jonson's Art, The Literature of Shakespeare's England, Shakespeare in America,* and *The Trollope Reader.*

I took Greek and it was a great cross to me. No one I knew took Greek. There were four others in the class; three were sons of doctors and obviously were heading for the same profession. They would need Greek for medical terms and prescriptions. There was one girl beside myself, the daughter of a minister. She and I, with the sudden intimacy born of misery, compared notes on the first day. Her father had forced her to take Greek, too. Our common experience of parental tyranny made the predicament more bearable. The boys turned out to be of a good sort. Perhaps the whole experience wouldn't be so ostracising as we feared.

---

*In *Pursuit of Understanding.* Reprinted by permission of Esther Cloudman Dunn. Copyright 1945, Macmillan Co. Pp. 49-53.

But as we walked home from school, unhappiness settled down upon me again. "The girls" were full of their German class. It was large; the teacher talked to them in German. Though they could not understand a word she said, they expected they would before long. They bandied a few German words about in a knowing way. With the mere mention of *der Apfel* they left me in outer darkness. Besides, German was the language of music and the notion of going to Germany some summer had already brushed them with its gleaming wings. Gone was that comfortable solidarity of doing what the others did. I was isolated and miserable.

I said nothing to "the girls" but besought Mother to beg Father to let me transfer from Greek to German. "If Father has put his foot down, perhaps you can get him to take it up again." But she was not successful. The stalwart boot, size eleven and a half and well-polished, stayed where it was. A more powerful *advocatus diaboli* had been before her.

While Father did not know Greek, he could not have lived in New England among lawyers and judges without feeling its prestige. It marked off a group of old-fashioned classical aristocrats. It was, in his view, one source of the power of our New England orators and statesmen. He had seen, or thought he had seen, its enriching, mellowing effect among the older members of the county bar at which he had practised. But he knew the value of Greek only by hearsay. So he had gone to a friend, lawyer and Harvard man, for his opinion. It was this man's eulogy of Greek, pronounced while pacing up and down his library with his hands behind him, that confirmed Father in his decision that, come what would, I should study Greek. Neither Mother's tactful efforts nor my feeling of ostracism from my fellows had any effect.

The room where our first Greek class met is not clear in my memory nor, at first, the teacher; though it was this man who would do more for my ideas and method of learning than any other single figure in what now seems a lifetime of teachers. But the textbook we used, *Ball's Elements of Greek,* I took to myself at once. It was bound in yellow-green cloth and my copy was significantly clean and white. In 1907 the Greek books did not have hard usage in public schools; not one of the five copies we used had been rebound. The paper had a smooth finish and took with precision the imprint of the delicate Greek letters.

I remember the Greek coin, the two sides of which were reproduced on one of the early pages. It was an Athenian obol; on one side stared Athena's owl with its crude round eyes and meticulously placed feathers; on the other the helmeted goddess in profile looked out imperiously from her Olympian height. The imperfect circle of that coin, with the bevel worn off on one side like a waning moon, made Greek feel real. I saw and believed in a world where Greek was the only language in which to whisper, sing, buy and sell, make jokes, order one's shoes re-soled. Avaricious thumbs had clasped that coin, light fingers had picked it from a pocket, extravagant hands had let it slip through them, all in the ordinary course of the days. Enough of those days, enough of those fingers handling it over greedily or generously, had worn it off. If this coin had been so actually and mercilessly used, so had those strange words in unfamiliar letters which surrounded it on the page.

Thus Greek became a live language with human voices shouting it to one another across streets in the noonday glare, just as "the girls'" German was live to them. Let them proclaim *"der Apfel auf dem Tisch"; I* knew something, too. As we mounted the hill going home from school, we looked out across the harbour. I knew that it was ϑάλασσα, the ageless, timeless wine-dark element that lapped the shores of ancient Athens. Athens had a harbour, too, not unlike the bay below me with its six-masters and its lighthouses.

The incident of the Greek coin with the worn edge shows what magic is in the greatest teaching. I do not remember how the unevenness of the obol was called to our attention. It was done so naturally and so vividly that it was just there in our consciousness, a part of our equipment, a talisman by which all at once, then and forever after, the Greek world became alive and ours to return to, to roam about in, to love as long as we lived.

Gradually bit by bit the person and personality of the Greek teacher were borne in upon us. He spoke to us in his own variation of a Harvard accent. It had been Maine's best, to begin with. It staunchly refused to give up entirely a fastidious reverberation through his high-cut nostrils. The words came out elegantly tinged with Maine nasality. He was my first teacher who maintained his authority without speaking to us as if we were an audience in a public hall. The class seemed rather like a meeting in a hotel lobby or a club. There was no chasm that separated teacher from taught.

The desk itself was merely a point of reference, not a fixed centre. He would stray to the window, pull aside the cord on the shade and look out. He knew just as we did, even in the midst of recitation, that there was another world, our actual world, waiting just outside. Some of his brightest flashes came back over his shoulder as he looked across the roofs to the clanging trolley cars on the main street. Or he would lean slightly sideways, the fingers of one hand brushing the bottom of his coat aside and tipping themselves into the slit of his trousers' hip pocket.

He was thus elegantly at ease in the midst of a fine point of Greek grammar. His authority rested on deeper foundations than the maintenance of a rigid upright position in front of a class. He was always blowing the chalk-dust from his lean fingers as if it were an element with which he had only a casual contact. Teaching Greek, writing with chalk on blackboards was merely one of the many ways in which his knowledge of the meaning of life, of the scope of human achievement, past with present in unbroken continuity, expressed itself, made contact with the particular human lives around him.

The rest of my high-school career, three years of it, becomes in memory a single piece of experience. I still was one of the quartet; we still shared adolescent pleasures in clothes, beaux, dances and houseparties. But along with this outward conformity to the usual pattern of the middle 'teens, went something immediately and continuously my own. It was so with all four of us; we each began to show at that moment in our lives the faint beginnings of our individual pattern, as differentiated from the pattern which we shared in common with others of our generation. Gertrude began to think of herself as a potential musician; Adelaide as a potential woman of the world. The focus of our private lives became clearer; the choice among the immediate alternatives of each day, week and month, was made by each of us half consciously, in accordance with its usefulness in achieving this ultimate individual pattern.

The centre for me was an idea of knowing the ancient world of Greece and Rome, mastering it, living by it, and probably teaching it. The idea was always there gradually disclosing vistas toward which it and I might go. The only thing needed was patience to acquire a gradually increasing power to read Greek and Latin. It was like the glimpse of ultimate perfection that flashes upon an amateur golfer. He sees himself and the ball and the necessary sticks moving, on some happy future day,. with brilliant rightness over the most beautiful and difficult golf course in the world. Just so I might some day move with facility among the Greek words which waited there in their black grace upon the white page. I could then re-create the Greek world and exist within it. As it seemed to me the most beautiful, witty and right world, no price was too high to pay to win my way into it.

This idea with its beckoning power was the creation of the Greek teacher. He did not put it into words. Neither he nor any great teacher could or would do that. Rather a real teacher feels his way, day by day, hour by hour, adapting his specific matter to the mood and need of particular pupils on particular days. He is like a gardener to whom the summer's task has regular stages and series of things to do; planting, weeding, spraying, staking, pruning. No gardener could tell at the beginning of the summer the order and date when each of these things should be done. He must feel his way; consider the weather, the unexpected in shade or light, in quality of soil, in presence of unsuspected rock at root. The variation between one plant and another, set in the same row and at the same time, would not escape his flexible garden knowledge. So it was with my Greek teacher.

I remember less of the actual business of vocabulary, grammar and translation, in the early stages, than of the teacher's asides. They illumined with vision the long grind of learning to read Greek. The day we found the Greek word for "red" in the vocabulary, the teacher seemed to take it up in his hand. He turned it over, like the faceted jewel it was, and showed us its hidden brilliance. The word, he said, showed in its origin how the Greeks made their red-purple dye from a shell fish. It was precious, used for the garments and carpets of kings.

Nirad C. Chaudhuri
(1897-   )

The Bengali Hindu, Nirad Chaudhuri, was influenced in early adolescence first by his father and uncle and then by a Moslem schoolmaster who wore Western clothes. Despite the nonconformity of the teacher and the vexing schoolboy pranks played on him, he not only communicated to the thirteen-year-old Nirad his love of literature but also taught him the discipline of writing. Here is illustrated the fact that learning and interests become vehicles of emotional import and the teacher is in a stunning position to enhance the affective aspects of learning.*

Shortly afterwards a second personal influence entered my life. It was that of a teacher. Our headmaster one day entered the class with an almost boyish young man by his side and introduced him as our new teacher of English. He was very dark, but possessed of decidedly handsome features, his eyes particularly being very fine. Though short and plump, he was not so much so as to repel me with a suggestion of

*From *The Autobiography of an Unknown Indian* by Nirad Chaudhuri. Reprinted by permission of The Macmillan Co. (New York). 1951. P. 284.

corpulence. He provoked notice and criticism by being dressed in a navy-blue striped suit instead of in *dhoti* and shirt. He drew on himself greater criticism by introducing an unwonted fervour into his teaching of poetry. It was reported that he moved in literary circles and even contributed to magazines. The general opinion of his pupils was that he was no good, for literary enthusiasm was considered bad form in teaching and useless, if not worse, for examinations. One day some boys wrote *ass* in reverse with chalk on the back of his chair, and the word imprinted itself right and distinct on the blue-black coat. The offence was discovered and the culprits punished, but only too many thought that the practical joke had not been undeserved. He particularly scandalized one of my best friends in the school, a boy Gangadhar by name, by teaching us the "Ode to a Nightingale." Gangadhar indicted our new teacher as a champion of booze, on the strength of the famous stanza on the blushful Hippocrene. For my brother and me, however, this teacher completed what my father and Uncle Anukul had begun. He not only communicated to us his love of literature but also taught us to be exacting in writing the two languages we used. I remember him as something more than one of my teachers, for as Mr. Mohitlal Mazumdar, the distinguished contemporary poet and critic, he exerted a very strong and beneficial influence on my later life. He introduced me to the literary society of Calcutta and made a writer of me almost by main force.

Robin George Collingwood
(1889-1943)

R. G. Collingwood was for many years Waynflete Professor of Metaphysical Philosophy at Oxford University. He was the author of such diverse works, ranging from aesthetics to political philosophy, as *The Idea of History, The Principles of Art, Roman Britain and the English Settlements, The Three Laws of Politics,* and *An Essay on Philosophical Method.* In the passage which follows from Collingwood's *Autobiography,** he describes the pallid and incompetent teaching to which he and his bored classmates were subjected at Rugby. Unchallenged, unmotivated, and unfulfilled, young Collingwood endured—however contemptuously—between the ages of fourteen and nineteen, the inhibitory and punitive qualities of the majority of his teachers. It was not until he attended Univer-

---

*Reprinted by permission of The Clarendon Press. 1939. Pp. 7-12.

sity College, Oxford, that his almost morbid, long-balked craving
for knowledge began to be appeased, and this occurred not so much
because of his tutors but rather because of the freedom to arrange
his own studies which the College afforded him.

... I went on, a year later, to Rugby; a school which then had a high
reputation, owing (as I found out in time) to the genius of one first-
rate teacher, Robert Whitelaw, a man who touched nothing that he
did not adorn. Because one of my five years there was spent in his
form, it would be untrue to say that my time at Rugby was altogether
wasted. And there were other things. I was in the Sixth Form for
three years and head of my house for two; thus for the first time I
tasted the pleasure of doing administrative work, and learnt once for
all how to do it. In addition to Whitelaw, whose obviously sincere
assumption that you knew as much as he did stimulated his pupils to
incredible feats, I worked for a time under one other good teacher, C.
P. Hastings, from whom I learnt a good deal of modern history.
Among those of the other masters who did not have to teach me I
made a few good friends; and with my contemporaries my relations
were always of the happiest.

These were benefits conferred by the school itself: others I obtained
rather in spite of it. I discovered Bach, learned to play the violin,
studied harmony and counterpoint and orchestration, and composed
a great deal of trash. I taught myself to read Dante and made the
acquaintance of many other poets, in various languages, hitherto unknown to me. These unauthorized readings (for which, in summer
time, I used to perch in a willow tree overhanging the Avon) are my
happiest recollection of Rugby; but not my most vivid.

That description must apply to the pigsty conditions of our daily
life and the smell of filth constantly in our nostrils. Second to that
comes the frightful boredom of being taught things (and things
which ought to have been frightfully interesting) by weary, absent-
minded or incompetent masters; then the torment of living by a time-
table expressly devised to fill up the day with scraps and snippets of
occupation in such a manner that no one could get down to a job
of work and make something of it, and, in particular, devised to prevent one from doing that "thinking" in which, long ago, I had
recognized my own vocation.

Nor did I get any compensating satisfaction out of the organized
games which constituted the real religion of the school; for at football
in my first year I suffered an injury to the knee which the surgery of
those days rendered incurable. This was a crucial point in my school

life. The orthodox theory of public-school athletics is that they distract the adolescent from sex. They do not do that; but they give
him a most necessary outlet for the energies he is not allowed to use
in the class-room. Apart from a few eccentrics like Whitelaw, the
public school masters of my acquaintance were like the school-master
in the *Dunciad:*

> Plac'd at the door of learning, youth to guide
> We never suffer it to stand too wide.

The boys were nothing if not teachable. They soon saw that any
exhibition of interest in their studies was a sure way to get themselves
disliked, not by their contemporaries, but by the masters; and they
were not long in acquiring that pose of boredom towards learning and
everything connected with it which is notoriously part of the English
public school man's character. But they must have some compensation
for their frustrated and inhibited intellects; and this they got in
athletics, where nobody minds how hard you work, and the triumphs
of the football field make amends for the miseries of the class-room.
If I had retained the use of my limbs I should no doubt have become
an athlete and stopped worrying my head about the crack of that
door and what was hidden behind it. As it was, I could not reconcile
myself to the starvation imposed on me by the teaching to which I was
subjected; and as time went on I learnt to devote my time more and
more to music and to reading in subjects of my own choice like medieval Italian history or the early French poets, not because I preferred
them to Thucydides and Catullus, but because I could work at them
unhampered by masters.

These habits were not undiscovered, and I became a rebel, more
or less declared, against the whole system of teaching. I did not rebel
against the disciplinary system, and with my housemaster (my immediate superior in the disciplinary hierarchy) I remained on excellent terms; I did not even neglect my work to the extent of incurring
punishment for idleness; but my masters were quite able to discern
the difference between my abilities and my performance, and were
justifiably annoyed by it; especially, I seemed to notice, when they had
to send up my compositions, or as we called them "copies," to the headmaster for distinction. I could not prevent that from happening; for
my plan was ca' canny, not sabotage, and I would not wilfully write
bad "copies." But I could and did refuse to enter for the prizes which
decorated the career of a good boy. To make this refusal more pointed,
I would enter now and then for a prize that had nothing to do with my
proper subjects of study: one for English literature, which I remember

with gratitude because it introduced me to Dryden, one for astronomy, which entailed many nights with the four-inch equatorial and the transit instrument in the school observatory, one for musical theory and composition, and one (which I failed to win) for reading aloud . . .

To apportion blame for mishaps is seldom worth doing. If my five years at Rugby were mainly waste, the fault lies partly with the obvious faults of the English public-school system; partly with Rugby as a bad example of that system, though among its faults I do not reckon the institution of fagging or that of government by members of the sixth form, both of which I count as virtues; partly with my father, who gave me an adult scholar's attitude towards learning while I was still a child, realizing, as I now think, what the results would be, but judging the game worth the candle; and partly with myself, for being a conceited puppy and an opinionated prig.

To show that I mean these epithets seriously, I will describe one incident of the feud between that form-master and myself. Reading to his form a note by some modern scholar, as it might be Jebb, on a passage in a Greek text, he came to the word floret, and said 'Floret? I don't believe there is such a word. Has any of you heard of it?' All the rest held their tongues, and so should I have done if I had learnt to be a proper schoolboy; but something inside me whispered "for God's sake, speak up and put an end to this silly game of hide-and-seek"; and I said "It means one of the little things that make up a flower of the order compositae; I expect he got it from Browning's description of the sunflower, 'with ray-like florets round a disk-like face.' " And I still remember, with bitter shame, the contemptuous tone in which I said it, and the disconcerted face with which the poor man complimented me on my learning.

Going up to Oxford was like being let out of prison. In those days, before the anthology habit infected Classical Moderations, a candidate for honours was expected to read Homer, Vergil, Demosthenes, and the speeches of Cicero more or less entire, in addition to a special study of other texts, among which I chose Lucretius, Theocritus, and the *Agamemnon*. This was not only leading a horse to the water, but (hardly less important) leaving him there. The happy beast could swill and booze Homer until the world contained no Homer that he had not read. After long years on a ration of twenty drops a day, nicely medicated from a form-master's fad-bottle, I drank with open throat. One hour a week I had to spend showing compositions to my tutor; and there were a few lectures which he had advised me to attend: otherwise my time was my own. Nor were these exceptions very serious. If I had shut myself up in my rooms for a week together, to do some work of my own choosing, my tutor would only have passed it off, when I emerged very apologetic, with an erudite but good-humoured joke. In short, I had come to a place where, even if it was not actually assumed that one had an adult attitude towards learning, at any rate one was not penalized for having such an attitude; and all I had to do was to forget my school life and let myself go.

Yet it was not quite so simple as that. The ill effects of my school years could not be removed by a mere change of environment. My long-balked craving for knowledge was now almost morbid. I could think of nothing else. Perched in my tower in the garden quadrangle of University College, I read all day and most of the night. All the good easy social life that was going on around me I brushed aside. Even my friendships were few. Long experience of hostility between myself and the system under which I lived had made me cynical, suspicious, and eccentric; caring little for my relations with my neighbours; quick to take offence and not unready to give it. But, for all that, there were many long walks in the country, many idle afternoons on the river, many evenings spent playing and hearing music, many nights talking until dawn; and more than one lifelong friendship in the making.

Russell Criddle
(1916-   )

Blinded at the age of twelve by an errant dirty snowball which hit him in, and infected, his eyes, Russell Criddle spent the following two years trying to learn to adjust to and accept his handicap. At fourteen, he returned to school and fortunately entered the class of an insightful and sympathetic teacher. Criddle writes, "I will never know what gave Miss Baudendistel her insight into my problem. To understand me so completely she must have identified with me, and that she could do so without suffering a natural horror of blindness amazes me."* His teacher, apparently, exemplified most of the characteristics associated with the good instructor: a student of motivation, a promoter of learning, an observer of growth, a craftsman and technician, an experimenter, administrator and therapist (5).

---

*From *Love Is Not Blind* by Russell Criddle. Reprinted by permission of W. W. Norton & Co., Inc. 1953. Pp. 44-49.

In January of 1930, after missing approximately two years of school, I entered Sight-saving Class. My attitude toward blindness after my own experience without sight was that of a sighted person: I believed it to be horrible, because of its inconveniences; I believed it to be thoroughly incapacitating.

I knew, however, and had proved, that I was not thoroughly incapacitated. Therefore I was not blind.

But I did not know that in blind schools all over the land there were hundreds of children with as much vision as I had, and more, or that I had little enough vision to be classified as blind by the industrial laws.

All the people I had met considered me blind. Mrs. Decker had refused to give me the paper job; another neighbor had called the authorities because Mother let me run the streets with the gang. Perfect strangers, seeing me reading with my eye a bare two inches from the paper, had reprimanded me violently for not wearing glasses, and one had complained to the health authorities. As a fourteen-year-old I had learned what few people will admit—that the distress that a blind man causes a sighted person provokes in him a negative reaction, ranging from casual rejection to inhuman cruelties.

I had learned to fear blindness intensely.

Only after Mother's continual assurances that the Sight-saving Class was not a school for blind kids, did I agree to attend. In deference to my pride, Mother did not go into the schoolroom with me that first day, but left me at the door. I found the teacher's desk without too much difficulty, and told her my name.

"Oh, yes, you're the new boy. My name is Miss Baudendistel. Russell," she said, "you understand that this is not a school for the blind, don't you?"

Was Miss Baudendistel telling me that I was blind, and did not belong in a Sight-saving Class? I had not expected this from her, because I believed that teachers were not wrong about such things. Teachers were like parents: they understood; they were always right and just. The shock of thinking that they were just the same as anyone else was terrible.

Never before had I been in a position where I needed understanding from anyone other than my mother and father. I had learned that little could be done to convince adults that I was not blind, and it had always been easy for me to walk away from what I have come to call the negative reaction.

But I wanted to go to school. I wanted to go to school even if I had to go to a sissy Sight-saving School, for I had found life outside, in the world of adults, unbearably lonely.

"I ain't blind," I blurted. "I just have to get close, that's all." Miss Baudendistel, taken aback by my passion, did not speak for a moment, and I interpreted her silence as disbelief. In despair I said, "I ain't blind, and I don't want to go to any sissy Sight-saving Class anyway."

I turned, and was halfway out of the building when Miss Baudendistel caught up with me.

"You misunderstood, Russell. I wanted you to know that this was not a class where you learned Braille. I know you have to get close, and bless you child, that is just why you are here, so you can get just as close as you wish."

I stood there for a moment, trying to search her face for confirmation of what her words implied.

Had Miss Baudendistel not been one person in a thousand, she would have reasoned that my eyes were too bad for me to attend Sight-saving Class, that my attitude was far too defensive, and that I should be educated in a school for the blind, and I would have walked out, back to the lonely world of adults where self-preservation might have required me to conform to the helpless concept of blindness.

"You see," Miss Baudendistel said, "I know you are not blind." In her voice was the compassionate smile I could not see on her face and I felt such affection for her that I could not hold back the tears. She led me to the boys' room, where I composed myself before returning to my first lesson, which was on saving sight.

Freda Baudendistel pioneered the Sight-saving Class of Binghamton. With the indomitable spirit of a meek woman with a purpose, she forced the school authorities to face the fact that children were going blind because of the eyestrain of normal classroom work. She bullied, cajoled, and flattered service clubs into supporting her program. It is impossible to estimate how many she has spared the tragedy of blindness.

Her pupils were not students, they were sight savers. Academic advancement was secondary to the welfare of their eyes. The only lesson she required us to learn perfectly was the first one: Never strain your eyes.

This rule Miss Baudendistel impressed upon me by reprimanding me for trying to read the textbook with my eyes too far away from it.

"Russell," she said sternly, "I know that you need to get the page very close to your eye to see it. You are embarrassed to let the others see you get so close."

"It makes them feel sorry for me," I said defensively. ·

"That is one of the things you must learn to accept. It is the most difficult thing about being different, but you just remember that no two people in the world are alike. Some people's differences are obvious, like yours. It's all right to pretend you can see when it doesn't strain your eyes."

I will never know what gave Miss Baudendistel her insight into my problem. To understand me so completely she must have identified herself with me, and that she could do so without suffering a natural horror of blindness amazes me.

I grinned as though I had been caught in some childish mischief and put my eye close, where I could see three or four of the large letters at a time. I felt no embarrassment in having to move my head along the page, for I sensed that this woman did not pity me.

"You can read fine," she commented. "Now try this."

She handed me a sheet of off-white paper, upon which were written in large, black handwriting the rules of sight saving. "Never strain your eyes. Eat good food, get plenty of sleep." She had tactfully omitted the fourth rule, "Always wear your glasses." With scholarship secondary in importance to our eyes it was no more than incidental that we learned at all. Because sleepiness is the first symptom of eye-strain, we were encouraged to rest our heads in our arms and take a nap if possible whenever we felt like it. We were not allowed to study at home, which meant no homework. If a child was failing, Miss Baudendistel could not apply pressure for harder study, for that meant eye-strain. She could only work harder herself.

I had been failing in the seventh grade when the snowball interrupted my schooling. I hadn't wanted to get high marks, because the gang considered model pupils sissies. The only reason I had ever studied at all was that I had feared failing and the resulting dissatisfaction it provoked in my teachers and my parents. Now the restrictions that sight saving placed upon my endeavor and the excuse my handicap offered for failure would make it seem logical that I should continue to fail academically. However, paradoxical though it seems, my handicap had a beneficial effect upon my scholarship. We sight savers were required to pass standard Regents Board examinations and my marks were rather good for each of the three semesters I spent with Miss Baudendistel.

Probably the answer to this phenomenon lies in the psychological effect my handicap had in abolishing the fears that I had unconsciously associated with school work. Nor did I need to fear excellence, because there was no one else in the seventh grade—no one for me to excel. In this connection, Miss Baudendistel, as part of her sight-saving program, made as light of excellence as she did of failure so as not to give an incentive for harder study.

Now, with all unpleasantnesses removed from the subject matter, with all personal conflicts relieved, my mind was free to absorb academic facts as a sponge absorbs water, and I knew the thrill of learning.

REFERENCES

1. Aichhorn, August. *Wayward Youth*. London: Imago Publishing Co., 1951, p. 7.
2. Blos, Peter. *The Adolescent Personality*. New York: Appleton-Century-Crofts, 1941, p. 495.
3. Cantril, Hadley, & Bumstead, Charles H. *Reflections on the Human Venture*. New York: New York University Press, 1960, pp. 181-182.
4. Fenichel, Otto. The means of education. In: Eissler, Ruth S., et al. (Eds.), *The Psychoanalytic Study of the Child*. New York: International Universities Press, Vol. I, p. 291.
5. Fleming, C. M. *Teaching: A Psychological Analysis*. New York: John Wiley & Sons, 1959.
6. Friedenberg, Edgar Z. *The Vanishing Adolescent*. Boston: Beacon Press, 1959, p. 5.
7. Freud, Anna. *The Ego and the Mechanisms of Defence*. New York: International Universities Press, 1946, p. 157.
8. Gibbon, Edward. *Autobiography*. New York: Dutton Everyman's Library, 1911, p. 60.
9. Haines, C. R., (Ed.). *The Correspondence of M. Corn. Fronto*. Cambridge, Mass.: Harvard University Press, 1955, Vol. I, p. xxxv.
10. Lewin, Kurt. Experiments in social space. In *Resolving Social Conflicts*. New York: Harper & Bros., 1948, pp. 71-83.
11. Leopardi, Giacomo. *Essays, Dialogues and Thoughts of Count Giacomo Leopardi*. Edited by Patrick Maxwell. London: Walter Scott, Ltd., 1893, p. 252.
12. Liss, Edward. The ego ideal role in learning. In: Krugman, Morris (Ed.), *Orthopsychiatry and the School*. New York: American Orthopsychiatric Association, 1958, p. 103.
13. Mill, John Stuart. *Autobiography*. New York: Library of Liberal Arts, 1957, pp. 21-25.
14. Misch, Georg. *A History of Autobiography in Antiquity*. Cambridge, Mass.: Harvard University Press, 1951, Vol. II, p. 447.
15. Montaigne, Michel de. *Essays*. Translated by E. J. Trechmann. New York: Modern Library, 1946, p. 149.
16. Newman, John Henry Cardinal. *Apologia Pro Vita Sua, Being a History of His Religious Opinions*. New York: Sheed & Ward, 1946.
17. Padover, Saul K. (Ed.). *Confessions and Self-Portraits. 4600 Years of Autobiography*. New York: John Day Co., 1957, pp. 347-349.

18. Pearson, Gerald H. J. The most effective help a psychiatrist can give to the teacher. In: Krugman, Morris (Ed.), *Orthopsychiatry and the School*. New York: American Orthopsychiatric Association, 1958, p. 5.

19. ———. *Psychoanalysis and the Education of the Child*. New York: W. W. Norton & Co., 1954, pp. 148-149.

20. Plank, Emma N., & Plank, Robert. Emotional components in arithmetical learning as seen through autobiographies. In: Eissler, Ruth S., et al. (Eds.), *The Psychoanalytic Study of the Child*. New York: International Universities Press, 1954, Vol. IX, p. 274.

21. Richards, Grant. *Memories of a Misspent Youth, 1872-1896*. New York: Harper & Bros., 1933, pp. 71, 75-76.

22. Shirer, William L. *The Rise and Fall of the Third Reich. A History of Nazi Germany*. New York: Simon & Schuster, 1960, p. 13.

23. Trilling, Lionel. *The Liberal Imagination*. Garden City, N. Y.: Doubleday Anchor Books, 1950, p. 121.

24. Wolfle, Dael. Diversity of talent. *Amer. Psychol.*, 15:537, 1960.

CHAPTER TWELVE

The Uses of Language

Adolescence has been recognized, particularly in primitive cultures, as a kind of rebirth of personality. Along with the rebirth and the emerging "new" persona, there develop new orientations and interests, new perceptions and values. The world becomes a different place, full of threats and contradictions as well as of ambivalent joys and hopes.

In the coping process the adolescent attempts to find his role and self-identity as best he can. In the ordinary daily world of human contacts he may be curiously like a foreigner, uneasily not at home, finding it difficult if not impossible to enter into communication with any but those who can speak his native intellectual language of ideas. The intrinsic relationship of speech, says Erikson (7), not only to the world of communicable facts, but also to the social value of verbal commitment and uttered truth is strategic among the experiences which support—or fail to support—a sound ego development.

Language may reflect the intellectual disturbances seen in adolescence. "It is as if the magical use of words of the phallic period is again revived. These changes in thought also have a positive side. The violent disruption of language, the all-too-free flow of thought and imagination unhindered by facts permit the 'winged word' to appear in the poetry and drama of adolescence [Spiegel, 26]." This is why the adolescent delights in employing such artificial elegance of language as "Mortals who abide in vitreous edifices should not possess morbid propensities toward disestablishmentarianism," when he could more easily use, "People who live in glass houses shouldn't throw stones."

The adolescent's language may be a sign of revolt against convention, against adults, or the need to grow up. He uses "pig Latin" or "sparrow language," imitating the secret but meaningful babbling of the infant and child, as if unwilling to leave behind the freedom and irresponsibility of childhood.

The regressive lallation of the adolescent through his use of pig or dog Latin may be a rebellion against words which are the means whereby a situation is controlled. Language starts as an order and a submission to it and it then becomes conversation. Schachtel (24) states, "The fact that language is adult language, the language of an adult civilization, and that the infant and small child is moulded only very gradually from its natural existence into a member of the civilization into which it is born makes the discrepancy between his precivilized, unschematized experience and the categories of civilized, conventional language much greater." The recapitulation of this infantile and childhood experience is here, too, manifested in adolescence.

Among the developments that become conspicuous as a child approaches and enters adolescence is a desire to exercise control over his privacy. One sign of maturity, according to Josselyn (15), is an ability to choose to keep things to himself or to share them at will. Pig Latin has preserved many secrets from inquisitive adults. The adolescent uses it to conceal something from outsiders because he wants to safeguard his privacy or perhaps because of his illicit conduct or intentions. Further, in his deep need to belong, he must speak the language of his peers. Outsiders always want to be insiders; thus the adolescent will pick up and use the *lingua franca* of groups to which he does not belong but wishes he did. In his urgency to belong, the adolescent seeks tacit approval of the group by adopting its vocabulary. The group's language creates a state of feeling among its members. Obviously to know the language is first of all to show oneself "hep," to give evidence of that knowingness and belongingness. It is a passport to his "new" world, indicative of a freedom from authority, a measure of ego integrity, and promising of a voyage of excitement. And, as is so typical of adolescence, this gesture toward freedom and self-identity is marked by his entrapment in conformism, for the secret language he converses in common with his fellows unwittingly imprisons him for a time in the very area from which he is trying to escape. "The desire to be inconspicuous," says Barzun (2), "that is, to take on the color of one's surroundings, encourages the use of vogue words and phrases."

Hirshberg (13) describes the use of "dog Latin" by Baltimore children in 1913 and suggests that the use of such language indicates a response to something more than mere mystery or secretiveness. "There are included elements of responsibility, dignity, and superior knowledge." Jamgotchian (14) analyzed, at the turn of the century, the use of "sparrow language" by Armenian boys, who from the ages of twelve to twenty-two resorted frequently to the device. Every syllable includes a vowel and every vowel represents only one sound so that it is very easy to adapt to the alterations of a secret. Adding a suffix or a prefix to each syllable insures the adolescent a privacy and belongingness he feels he needs.

One of the most heartening facts reported by Iona and Peter Opie (20), in *The Lore and Language of School Children,* is the long-lived vitality of the rhymes and rites which pass between school children and so vividly color their lives. "Children," they state, "remain tradition's warmest friends. . . . Boys continue to crack jokes that Swift collected from his friends in Queen Anne's time; . . . they ask riddles which were posed when Henry VIII was a boy. . . . " The authors report one nonsense rhyme first heard in England in 1850, the echoes of which are still heard in Maryland and California. "Conscious as we were of the economy of human invention, and the tenacity of oral tradition (the two elements without which there would be no folklore), we were not prepared for quite the identity of ritual and phraseology which has been revealed throughout the land in children's everyday witticisms, and in the newer of their self-organized amusements."

Trumbull (27) has reported on the resemblance between American and Japanese teen-age slang. "Although the words are different, the slick corruptions of the standard language in teen talk [in Japan] indicate the same insouciant disregard of convention that makes American campus argot so colorful. The Japanese, however, form slang not only by twisting their own mother tongue but also by borrowing and adapting English, French, and German expressions learned in school or elsewhere (for instance, a part-time job is *arubeito,* from the German *arbeit,* and money is *gereto,* from *gelt;* to go steady is to be *avec,* from the French for with; a recently coined term for the Japanese equivalent of the American hipster is *mambo boy)."*

That the continuity in language exists cannot be denied. Nor does distance mean much. For example, the secret language of the adolescent is not confined to Western or sophisticated cultures. The use of a special language and magically potent terms, state Bloch and Niederhoffer (3), may become zealously guarded as the cult secret of one sex and age group as compared with another. They cite the sharp distinctions made between the reproductive functions of the Arapesh women and the food-getting responsibilities of the male which are pointed up in the sounds and sights to which the two sexes are exposed during puberty ceremonials. With the Bakongo in Africa, an isolated stockade or *vela* is erected to which the groups of youths retire for initiation rites and where they are forced to learn a new and secret language. "Common objects [are] referred to by impressive titles—the eye as the 'possessor of sight,' for example—and ordinary words [are] obscured by the use of special prefixes. . . . The entire effect of such devices, apparently, is to convince the outsider that the experience has actually produced a new revelation and outlook, an experience which signifies the emergence of a renascent individual."

The universal use of a secret, private language, unintelligible except to the *cognoscenti,* fills seemingly universal needs for adolescents. In 1790, when he was almost fifteen years old, DeQuincey (5) and his friend Lord Westport communicated their thoughts "by means of a language which we, in those days, found useful enough at times, and which bore the name of *Ziph."* Chopin's youthful letters are replete with foreign phrases interspersed with his native Polish. At the age of thirteen (1882), André Gide (11) "exchanged odd, mysterious letters in cypher, which could only be read with the help of a key or a grille." In 1919, John Lehmann (17) describes how his sister "Beatrix had evolved a kind of secret society called 'The Witus' at home, with a silly language private to the four of us which disconcerted my mother and made her sometimes feel (I suspect) that she had given birth to four village idiots." And Anne Frank (10) recorded in her diary on October 1, 1942, when she was thirteen years old, "Elli has written to some secretarial school or other and ordered a correspondence course in shorthand for Margot, Peter and me. You want to see what perfect experts we shall be by next year. In any case it's extremely important to be able to write in a code."

In his search for self, the adolescent will use not only a private language but also language which is raucous, coarse, and vulgar if not replete with throaty, four-letter Anglo-Saxon expletives. This represents an attempt to identify with adults and may also be experienced consciously as an assertion of masculinity. The adolescent's humor, too, tends to be Rabelaisian and scatological, indicating a renewal of infantile anal interests. Some of the letters of young Mozart, reproduced in this chapter, are evidence of this. A milder example is found in Chopin's (21) letter to his friend Jan Bialoblocki, written in 1825, when Chopin was sixteen years old. It is addressed with the nickname, "Dear Jasia!" and concludes with the sentence, "I'll write more by post; and now, only that we all embrace you, especially I, your sin (cerest) fr (iend) F. F. Chopin." Adolescents the world over have probably ended letters to friends in similar fashion at some time or other.

Nicknames and name-calling are additional evidence of infantile recapitulation in adolescence. Given names, surnames, nicknames, and assumed names have numerous important significances in the ego development of the adolescent (Murphy, 18). An unpleasant emotional reaction to personal names may result from an unconscious feeling on the part of the adolescent bearing the name that it in some way reveals an inherent weakness in personality which the individual wishes to conceal (Oberndorf, 19). Orgel and Tuckman (22) think of the nickname as "a verbal caricature or condensation of the outstanding physical, intellectual or personality characteristic of an individual," whereas the evidence collected by Habbe (12) indicates that while nicknames based on psychological anomalies are as numerous among the hated names as those dealing with the usual physical characteristics, "nicknames most frequently are simply name adaptations without significance as caricatures or condensations of outstanding characteristics of the individual."

For the adolescent, both of these points are valid. For some, the nickname may well be an innocuous name-shortening or adaptation rather than an instrument of verbal caricature. On the other hand, the name-calling or the pet names used by the youngster may be an irrational attempt at relieving tension, undertaken as a means of defense by a person in conflict with the outside world. It may be symptomatic of the presence of fear and of a weakness which is due to the lack of harmony among the ego, superego and id. Smythe (25) suggests that hostility is inherent in name-calling, that name-calling serves as an expression of guilt projection and helps to maintain self-esteem by focusing blame on another. While many Americans call male Chinese "Charlie," which may be a deliberate affront or an unconscious expression of disdain, the Chinese call Westerners *Fan Kuai,* "foreign devils," a term coined to express a feeling of contempt.

Adolescents are usually more direct and cruel in their use of language. John Milton complained of the epithet, "The Lady of Christ's College," by which he was known at Cambridge while a student there in the 1620's. Vittorio Alfieri was twelve years old in 1761 and attending a school noted for its sparse diet and the poor quality of the food served. He was constantly sick and his body was covered with sores and ulcers because of it, he tells us in his autobiography (1). "I became the constant sport of my companions, who bestowed on me the nickname of *Carcase;* while those among them who wished to appeal still more witty added the epithet *rotten.*" Heine speaks, as we shall see below, of the "embittered and empoisoned . . . fairest years of the springtime of my life," because of the homonymitic relationship of his first name to that of a local four-legged jackass. Auguste Forel, about the middle of the nineteenth century, felt deeply mortified because of the appellation given him of *Rebhuhn,* or "Partridge." Havelock Ellis (6) described what happened to him during his early adolescence: "There is . . . a peculiarity in the profile of [my] lower jaw which is probably characteristic. I have never been able to analyse it precisely, nor to say definitely that it is due to prognathism, but when the head is raised there is, in some aspects, a slightly apelike suggestion. Boys are quick to catch the faintest abnormalities, and my school-fellows at Mitcham sometimes, quite good-naturedly, would call me 'Baboon.' " Yen Liang, a Mongolian raised in Peiping, was taunted with "Barbarian!" by her Chinese schoolmates during all of her formative years.

The adolescent's propensity to scribble his name all over his notebook is a frequently observed phenomenon. He will write his name with a caressing flourish, print it in a variety of styles, scramble the letters, make anagrams from it, add honorific titles and embroider it, and invent countless other ingenious devices. He enjoys and gets a measure of comfort out of this activity for at least he can identify himself with his own name.

His name is something the young person can never choose for himself. It is significant that with the "rebirth" attendant at adolescence, the individual should find such fascination with his name and such a universal desire to alter it in some way, while simultaneously marvelling at the beauty with which he fashions its letters over and over again. Typically, the ambivalence of the adolescent is manifested here. On the one hand, he is in rebellion against the name arbitrarily bestowed on him by his parents; the temptation to make a free choice is an overpowering one. But on the other hand, the adolescent feels secure in his name. At the very least, it is *his*. In his quest for identity, his name can be a solid support, an anchor, something he knows exists. If he is unsure of everything else in his universe, he is at least sure of his name.

In 1770, at the age of fourteen, beneath a dignified and adult letter to his sister, Nannerl, telling her about some opera singers he had heard, Mozart signed his letter, "Wolfgang de Mozart, the Honourable Highdale, Friend of the Counting House." In other letters to her and to his mother, his signature reads, "De Mozartini"; or "Wolfg. Mozart"; or, "Wolfgango Amadeo"; and, "Wolfgango in Germania." Napoleon (4), in a letter written to his uncle in 1784 when he was fifteen years old, signed his name, "Napoleon di Buonaparte," prompted, it is believed, not by a sense of fun but rather by patriotic feelings concerning the Corsican fight with France and by the social pressures he felt strongly at the aristocratic military academies he attended at Brienne and the Ecole Royale Militaire in Paris.

More recent evidence comes from the personal letters of Franklin Delano Roosevelt (23). Letters to his mother from age eleven to age fifteen (1883-1887) reveal his preoccupation with his name until he settled, finally, on Franklin D. Roosevelt. At eleven, he delighted in closing a letter with this reversed spelling, "Tlevesoor D. Nilknarf." At fourteen, in one letter addressed to "Dear Mommerr and Popperr," he used his initials, which were later to become a Roosevelt trademark, to sign off. That year, too, he ended a letter with his name spelled—erroneously—in Greek, "Upavkλlv Deλavw Pwoeveλt," and another one with the formal "Franklin D. Roosevelt." This one apparently pleased him most, for a year later, in a letter to "mama," he postscripted, "Do you like this signature better than the other?"

According to Bloch and Niederhoffer (3), the formalizing of this process of adolescent name-giving is well established in other cultures and provides a highly rational basis in the acceptance of the natural stages of each individual's growth. They quote Fletcher's (9) study of the Pawnee, in whose culture the child's life is a continuing search for new levels of growth and, consequently, the recognition of the emergent personality is designated by a new name.

Conferring of a personal name, in many cultures, whether it is "Tarzan," "Running Horse," "Titty," "The Bulpington of Blup," "Le Petit Ami," "Duke," "Useless," "The Poet," or "Spike," constitutes a symbolic landmark in the adolescent's quest for self-identity. In *Totem and Taboo,* Freud noted that "in the view of primitive man one of the most important parts of a person is his name." This is equally true in literate societies, as will be seen in many of the illustrations which follow.

John Milton
(1608-1674)

Milton's own explanation of the epithet, "The Lady of Christ's College," applied to him while at Cambridge, is probably intuitively closer to the truth than is Aubrey's, who said, "He was so fair that they called him" by that nickname. Milton is a magnificent defense against the probable projection of his taunters' own ambivalent sexual feelings.

By the end of the summer term of 1628, Milton's popularity with his fellows was in the ascendancy. He had been chosen to give the oration to mark the end of school and deliver it before the entire university. His function in this address was to provide "comic entertainment," and Milton explains the "looseness" and "licentiousness" of his oratorical buffoonery in terms of the taste of his audience and the genius of Cambridge.*

---

*In *Milton on Himself* edited by John S. Diekhoff. Reprinted by permission of John S. Diekhoff. Copyright 1939, Oxford University Press. Pp. 70-71.

From some I have lately heard the epithet 'Lady.' But why do I seem to those fellows insufficiently masculine? Was it any disgrace to Priscian? Really, the silly grammaticasters attribute to the feminine gender signs which belong to the masculine! Doubtless it was because I was never able to gulp down huge bumpers in pancratic fashion; or because my hand has not become calloused by holding the plough-handle; or because I never lay down on my back under the sun at midday, like a seven-year ox-driver; perhaps, in fine, because I never proved myself a man in the same manner as those gluttons. But would that they could as easily lay aside their asshood as I whatever belongs to womanhood.

But notice how stupidly, how thoughtlessly they have taunted me about that which I, on the best authority, shall turn to my honour. For truly, even Demosthenes was called by his rivals and opponents a little man. Likewise Quintus Hortensius, most renowned of all the orators, after Marcus Tullius, was called by Lucius Torquatus "Dionysia the citharess." To him he replied: "I would prefer indeed to be Dionysia than what you are, Torquatus—unrefined, boorish, ill-bred." But I put far away and repel from me whatsoever pertains to Lord and Lady; I do not desire to be a "Lord," fellow students, except on your rostrum and in your tribunal. Who now will stop me from enjoying an omen so auspicious and happy, and from exulting with joy that I have been united in company with such great men under the same reproach! Meanwhile, as I think that all good and excellent men are placed above envy, so I believe these malicious fellows are so far the lowest down of all that they are not worth reviling.

* * * *

But I fear, fellow students, that I have spun out the thread of my discourse longer than is proper. I shall not present excuses, as I might, lest, by apologizing, the fault should be accentuated. Now, freed from oratorical laws, we will break forth into comic licence; in which, if by chance I should swerve from my habit, if from the rigid laws of modesty, as they say, a finger's breadth, be it known, fellow students, that I have stripped off and laid aside for a short time my former custom out of good feeling for you; or, if anything shall be said loosely, if anything licentiously, you may consider that not my mind and disposition, but the procedure of the occasion and the genius of the place has indeed suggested it to me. Accordingly, like that which the comic actors used to beg at their exit, I at the very beginning entreat: Clap your hands and laugh.

Wolfgang Amadeus Mozart
(1756-1791)

Mozart's precocity is too well known to bear retelling. It is a fact that Mozart was musically active before most children are able to read, and was composing short pieces for the clavier at the age of five.

His father, Leopold, was entirely responsible for the young Mozart's education. Like John Stuart Mill, Wolfgang never went to school but identified completely with his father. An expression commonly attributed to him in childhood is, "After God, Papa." Leopold has been characterized as an overmethodical, pedantic, inquisitive parent, extremely religious, regarding work as a cardinal virtue. In his youth, Wolfgang observed Catholicism in orthodox fashion, and in many other areas submitted to his father's will.

According to Esman's (8) study of Mozart "the orderliness and meticulousness of Leopold is clearly reflected in Wolfgang's music which, more than any other of the generally orderly classical period, is distinguished by its clarity, precision, and economy. . . . As Wolfgang matured, and particularly traveled about Europe with his father, signs of rebellion became increasingly evident. Even as he was composing the delicate, precise music of his late adolescence, he was writing to his female cousin in Augsburg the famous 'Bäsle' letters. These fascinating documents throw a good deal of light on Mozart's character. They are replete with nonsense, neologisms, wordplay, and innumerable references to feces, defecation, the anus and buttocks, reiterated lovingly and interminably. Granted the greater freedom of the eighteenth century in permitting such expressions, these letters are nonetheless unusual, and it is difficult to doubt the evidence of a marked anal pre-occupation, breaking through the reaction-formations imposed by his rigid, anal father and representing the first sign of restiveness."

In the six letters reproduced here which were written to his sister, we see the early manifestation of Mozart's anal preoccupation, as well as the silly word play typically found in many adolescent letters.*

---

*From *The Letters of Mozart and His Family* edited by Emily Anderson. Reprinted by permission of Emily Anderson. Copyright 1938, Macmillan Co., Ltd. Vol. I. Pp. 169, 197, 281, 282, 283, 323, 345-346.

Milan, February 17th, 1770

Here I am, now you have me. Dear little Marianne, with all my arse I rejoice that you had such a frightfully good time. Tell Nurse Ursula, the one, I mean, with the cold arse, that I still maintain that I sent back all her songs to her. But *in any case* if, engrossed in my high and important thoughts, I swept the song off to Italy, I shall not fail, should I find it, to stuff it into a letter. Addio. Farewell, my children. I kiss Mamma's hands a thousand times and send you a hundred kisses or smacks on your marvellous horseface. Per fare il fine, I am your, etc.

Rome, May 2nd, 1770

Praise and thanks be to God, I am well and kiss Mamma's hand and my sister's face, nose, mouth, neck and my bad pen and arse, if it is clean.

WOLFGANGO MOZART. ROME, 1770

Verona, August 18th, 1771

Dearest Sister,

I have only slept an hour, for I do not care much about sleeping after a meal. You may trust, believe, opine, hold the opinion, cherish the constant hope, consider, imagine, think and be confident that we are well, but I can assure you of the fact. Well, I must hurry. Addio. My greetings to all our good friends. Wish Herr von Hefner from me a prosperous journey and ask him if he has seen anything of Annamiedl? Addio. Keep well. I kiss Mamma's hand. What beautiful handwriting mine is!

WOLFGANG

Milan, August 24th, 1771

Dearest Sister,

We suffered greatly from the heat on our journey and the dust worried us most impertinently the whole time, so that we should certainly have been choked to death, if we had not been too clever for that. Here it has not rained for a whole month (or so the Milanese say). To-day it began to drizzle a little, but now the sun is shining and it is very hot again. What you promised me (you know what, you dear one!) you will surely do and I shall certainly be most grateful to you. The Princess had an attack of diarrhoea the other day. Apart from that I have no news. Do send me some. My greetings to all our good friends, and I kiss Mamma's hand. I am simply panting from the heat! So I am tearing open my waistcoat. Addio. Farewell.

WOLFGANG

Milan, December 18, 1772*

I hope that you are well, my dear sister. When you receive this letter, my dear sister, that very evening my opera will have been performed, my dear sister. Think of me, my dear sister, and try as hard as you can to imagine that you, my dear sister, are hearing and seeing it too, my dear sister. That is hard, I admit, as it is already eleven o'clock. Otherwise I believe and do not doubt at all that during the day it is brighter than at Easter. We are lunching to-morrow, my dear sister, with Herr von Mayr, and why, do you think? Guess! Why, because he has asked us. The rehearsal to-morrow is at the theatre, but Signor Castiglione, the impresario, has begged me not to tell anyone about it; otherwise a whole crowd of people will come running in and we do not want this. So, my child, I beg you not to mention it to anyone, my child, otherwise too many people will come running in, my child. That reminds me. Have you heard what happened here? I shall tell you. We left Count Firmian's to-day to go home and when we reached our street, we opened the hall door and what do you think we did? Why, we went in. Farewell, my little lung. I kiss you, my liver, and remain as always, my stomach, your unworthy

$$\left\{ \begin{array}{l} \text{frater} \\ \text{brother} \end{array} \right.$$

WOLFGANG

Please, please, my dear sister, something is biting me. Do come and scratch me.

August 14th, 1773

I hope, my queen, that you are enjoying the highest degree of health and that now and then or rather, sometimes, or, better still, occasionally, or, even better still, qualche volta, as the Italians say, you will sacrifice for my benefit some of your important and intimate thoughts, which ever proceed from that very fine and clear reasoning power, which in addition to your beauty, and although from a woman, and particularly from one of such tender years, almost nothing of the kind is ever expected, you possess, O queen, so abundantly as to put men and even greybeards to shame. There now, you have a well-turned sentence. Farewell.

WOLFGANG MOZART

---

*A postscript to his father's letter. In the autograph, lines 2, 4 and 6 are written upside down.

Thomas DeQuincey
(1785-1859)

DeQuincey here gives the amusing history of the secret language, *Ziph*, which he and his fourteen-year-old-friend, Lord Westport, used as a means of communicating their private thoughts (5). As DeQuincey would have us understand it, *Ziph* was first published early in the reign of Charles II, in the 1650's. Its oral use unquestionably predates this; and its currency by the two adolescents as well as the story told by Dr. Mapleton suggest the widespread application of this secret language by English adolescents as far back as the sixteenth century and perhaps earlier.

. . . As respected myself individually, I had reason to be grateful: every kindness and attention were shown to me. My invitation I was sensible that I owed entirely to my noble friend. But, *having* been invited, I felt assured, from what passed, that it was meant and provided that I should not, by any possibility, be suffered to think myself overlooked. Lord Westport and I communicated our thoughts occasionally by means of a language which we, in those days, found useful enough at times, and which bore the name of *Ziph*. The language and the name were both derived (that is, were *immediately* so derived; for *remotely* the Ziph language may ascend to Nineveh) from Winchester. Dr. Mapleton, a physician in Bath, who attended me in concert with Mr. Grant, an eminent surgeon, during the nondescript malady of the head, happened to have had three sons at Winchester; and his reason for removing them is worth mentioning, as it illustrates the well-known system of *fagging*. One or more of them showed to the quick medical eye of Dr. Mapleton symptoms of declining health; and, upon cross-questioning, he found that, being (as juniors) *fags* (that is, bondsmen by old prescription) to appointed seniors, they were under the necessity of going out nightly into the town, for the purpose of executing commissions; but this was not easy, as all the regular outlets were closed at an early hour. In such a dilemma, any route, that was barely practicable at whatever risk, must be traversed by the loyal fag; and it so happened that none of any kind remained open or accessible, except one; and this one communication happened to have escaped suspicion, simply because it lay through a succession of temples and sewers sacred to the goddesses Cloacina and Scavengerina. That of itself was not so extraordinary a fact: the wonder lay in the number —viz., seventeen. Such were the actual amount of sacred edifices, which, through all their dust, and garbage, and mephitic morasses, these miserable vassals had to thread all *but* every night of the week. Dr. Mapleton, when he had made this discovery, ceased to wonder at the medical symptoms; and, as *faggery* was an abuse too venerable and sacred to be touched by profane hands, he lodged no idle complaints, but simply removed his sons to a school where the Serbonian bogs of the subterraneous goddess might not intersect the nocturnal line of march so *very* often. One day, during the worst of my illness, when the kind-hearted doctor was attempting to amuse me with this anecdote, and asking me whether I thought Hannibal would have attempted his march over the Little St. Bernard, supposing that he and the elephant which he rode had been summoned to explore a route through seventeen similar nuisances, he went on to mention the one sole accomplishment which his sons had imported from Winchester. This was the *Ziph* language, communicated at Winchester to any aspirant for a fixed fee of one half-guinea, but which the doctor then communicated to me—as I do now to the reader—*gratis*. I make a present of this language without fee, or price, or entrance-money, to my honoured reader; and let him understand that it is undoubtedly a bequest of elder times. Perhaps it may be co-eval with the Pyramids. For in the famous "Essay on a Philosophical Character" (I forget whether *that* is the exact title), a large folio written by the ingenious Dr. Wilkins, bishop of Chester, and published early in the reign of Charles II, a folio which I, in youthful days, not only read but studied, this language is recorded and accurately described amongst many other modes of cryptical communication, oral and visual, spoken, written, or symbolic. And, as the bishop does not speak of it as at all a *recent* invention, it may probably at that time have been regarded as an antique device for conducting a conversation in secrecy amongst by-standers; and this advantage it has, that it is applicable to all languages alike; nor can it possibly be penetrated by one not initiated in the mystery. The secret is this (and the grandeur of simplicity at any rate it has)—repeat the vowel or diphthong of every syllable, pre-fixing to the vowel so repeated the letter G. Thus, for example:—Shall we go away in an hour? Three hours have we already staid. This in Ziph becomes:—*Shagall wege gogo agawagay igin agan hougour? Threegee hougours wege hagave agalreageadygy stagaid.* It must not be sup-posed that Ziph proceeds slowly. A very little practice gives the greatest fluency; so that even now, though certainly I cannot have practised it for fifty years, my power of speaking the Ziph remains unimpaired. I forget whether in the Bishop of Chester's account of this cryptical lan-guage the consonant intercalated be G or not. Evidently any consonant will answer the purpose. F or L would be softer, and so far better.

In this learned tongue it was that my friend and I communicated our feelings; and having staid nearly four hours, a time quite sufficient to express a proper sense of the honour, we departed; and, on emerging into the open high-road, we threw up our hats and huzzaed, meaning no sort of disrespect, but from uncontrollable pleasure in recovered liberty.

Heinrich Heine
(1799-1856)

During his early adolescence, Heinrich Heine experienced some exquisite anguish at the hands of his school mates. They taunted him because of the similarity between his name and that of a scavenger's donkey.

In the introduction to his autobiography (16), Heine wrote, "You will find in rich abundance those biographical notes which may be interesting to you, all that is important and characteristic is honestly communicated here, and the combined effect of exterior events and of occurrences in the inner life of my soul will reveal to you the stamp of my being and myself. The veil has fallen from my soul, and you may look at it in all its beautiful nakedness. There are no blemishes, only wounds. And alas! wounds made not by the hands of my enemies but by those of my friends." In the passage below, Heine's best school chums—Franz and Dietrich, whom he loved dearly—betray him cruelly, adding salt to the wounds inflicted by his other tormenting school mates.

Because my father's friend who was a very skilled buyer of velveteen, bore the name of Harry, I received this name and I was called Harry in my family and by intimate friends and neighbours.

Even now it gives me great pleasure to be called by that name, although I owe to it much mortification and perhaps the most grievous of my childhood.

Only now that I no longer live among the living and all social vanity is blotted out from my soul am I able to speak of it controlledly.

Here in France immediately on my arrival in Paris my German name "Heinrich" was translated into "Henri," and I had to adapt myself to it and had even so to style myself here in this country, for the word Heinrich is not pleasing to Frenchmen and the French do make everything in the world pleasant for themselves. Even the name "Henri Heine" they were unable to pronounce, and most of them called me M. Enri Enn: many contracted this to Enrienne and some called me M. Un Rien.

I suffer by it in many of my literary relations, but I do gain certain advantages. For instance among my noble fellow countrymen who come to Paris there are many who would gladly slander me, but as they always pronounce my name in German it does not occur to the French that the villain, the poisoner of the wells of innocence, who is so roundly abused, is no other than their friend, M. Enrienne, and these noble souls in vain give rein to their virtuous zeal: the French do not know that they are speaking of me, and transrhenish virtue has in vain shot the bolts of its calumny.

But there is, as I have said, a sort of embarrassment in hearing one's name mispronounced. There are men who are extremely touchy when it occurs.

For myself, I have never felt anything of the sort.

Heinrich, Harry, Henri—all of these names sound well when they come tripping from pretty lips. Best of all sounds Signor Enrico. So was I called in those clear blue summer nights, spangled with great silver stars, of that noble and unhappy land which is the home of beauty, and brought forth Raphael Sanzio of Urbino, Joachim Rossini and Princess Christiana Belgiojoso.

As my physical condition robs me of all hope of ever again living in society, and as society in truth no longer exists for me, I have stripped myself of the fetters of that personal vanity which imprisons every man who has to go among men, into the world, as it is called.

I can therefore speak unreservedly of the mishap which was bound up with my name of Harry, and embittered and empoisoned the fairest years of the springtime of my life. The facts of the case are these. In my native town there lived a man who was called the Scavenger because every morning he drove through the streets of the town with a cart to which a donkey was harnessed, and stopped before every house to take up the refuse which the servants gathered together in orderly heaps, and carried it out to the dumping-ground. The man looked like his trade, and the donkey, who resembled his master, stood still in front of the houses or moved on according to the tone of voice in which the scavenger cried the word *Haarüh*.

Was that his real name or only a catchword? I know not, but this much is certain that I had to endure an extraordinary amount of suffering at the hands of my school-mates, and the children of our neighbours because of the resemblance of the word to my name Harry. To tease me they pronounced it exactly as the scavenger called to his donkey, and when I grew angry the rascals would take on an expression of innocence and asked me to teach them, in order to avoid confusion, how my name and the donkey's should be pronounced; but they were deliberately dense and would have it that the scavenger usually drew out the first syllable and cut short the second, while sometimes on the contrary his call sounded exactly like my name, and while the brats practised the most nonsensical variations, mixing up the donkey and myself, there were mad *coqs à l'ane,* at which everybody else laughed, while I was brought to tears.

When I complained to my mother, she said that I must try to learn much and to be discreet, and nobody would take me for an ass.

But my homonymity with the despised long ears remained my bugbear. The big boys used to pass me, greeting me with *Haarüh,* and the small boys did the same though from a distance. In school the same theme was turned to account with subtle cruelty; whenever a donkey cropped up they squinted at me and I always blushed, and it is incredible how skilful schoolboys are in discovering or bringing personalities into prominence upon the least occasion.

For example, one would ask another: "What is the difference between the zebra and the ass of Balaam, son of Boaz?" Came the answer: "One speaks the zebraic, the other Hebraic tongue." Then came the question: "What is the difference between the scavenger's donkey and his namesake?" and the impertinent answer was: "We do not know the difference between them." Then I wished to make an onslaught on them, but I was restrained, and my friend Dietrich, who drew very beautiful holy pictures, and has since become a celebrated painter, used, on such occasions, to try and comfort me by promising me a picture. He painted a Saint Michael for me—but the rascal wickedly made game of me. The archangel had the features of the scavenger, his steed looked like his donkey, and instead of a dragon his lance pierced the carcase of a dead cat.

And fair-haired, gentle, girlish Franz, whom I loved so dearly, betrayed me also. He took me in his arms, and laid his cheek tenderly against mine and we remained for a long time sentimentally breast to breast—suddenly he whispered a mocking *Haarüh!*—and as he ran away shouted the contemptuous word so that it rang through the cloisters of the monastery.

I came in for even more scurvy treatment at the hands of some of the children of our neighbourhood, guttersnipes of the lowest class, who are known as *Haluten* in Düsseldorf, a word which would certainly lead etymologists away from the helots of Sparta.

Such a *Halut* was little Jupp, whose name was Joseph, and I will also give his patronymic, Hader, so that he may not be confused with Jupp Rörsch, who was quite a jolly infant, and, as I am glad to learn, is still living as postmaster at Bonn. Jupp Hader always carried a long fishing-rod with which he struck at me when we met. He took a delight in throwing horse dung at my head, picking it up in the street piping hot just as it came from nature's oven. But he never ceased to call in every possible tone of voice the fatal *Haarüh!*

Frederic Chopin
(1810-1849)

Like the precocious Mozart, Chopin started his musical career very early in life. By the time he was sixteen, he was the pride and joy of the Warsaw Conservatory. At eighteen he had triumphed in Vienna. At twenty, he reached his goal, Paris, the intellectual capital of the world of the eighteen-thirties and forties. There he met Heine, Liszt, George Sand, Delacroix, Lamartine, Rossini, Gautier, Balzac, Meyerbeer, and Eugene Sue, among others. And there he was to die, like Mozart, before his time and in his thirties.

The anal quality noted in some of Mozart's letters is also noticeable in this one written by Chopin* to his friend Jan Bialoblocki. The schoolboy pun on the word "enema," tied in with the coarse humor, the interlarding of French with his native Polish, and the extravagant language he employed, are all marks of the adolescent.

To Jan Bialoblocki in Sokolowo
Warsaw, 27 November 1825

Mon Cher!

La lettre que vous m'avez écrite, rejoiced me, although, comme je vois, it contains sad news. Votre jambe vous fait mal; I grieve for that; not que vous êtes assez gai, as I see from the letter, ça m'a donné de la sauce, and leaves me in the best of humours.

Demain nous finissons notre examination. Je ne prendrai pas de prix, car les lavements le prennent—When I come to you, I will explain this riddle—est-ce possible qu'on donne un prix à un lavement?** It would need a long explanation to make this clear in a letter; but one

---

*From *Chopin's Letters* edited by Henryk Opienski. Reprinted by permission of Alfred A. Knopf, Inc. 1931. Pp. 8-9.

**Tomorrow we finish our examinaion. I shan't take a prize for the enemas take it . . . Is it possible that a prize should be given to an enema?

spoken word will show you all the finesse of this expression.

On Monday, as Panna Ludwika has decided, we leave here, and arrive in Szafarnia on Wednesday. Si vous voulez me voir, venez le premier, car autrement my good Guardian Lady will not allow me to go to you.

Tomorrow at this hour quel bonheur quel plaisir; when I go to bed, I shan't get up early on Friday. I have new breeches with [undecipherable] well cut (though this last is not true); a new muffler on my neck—you can call it by some other name, as perhaps you don't understand that one,—a tie for je ne me souviens plus, how many zlotys, je le paie avec l'argent et la main de ma chère soeur Louise.

Ecoutez, ecoutez, ma'mzelle Dorothée

Adolf Szydlowski in the Servant's part.

Ecoutez, here I begin the end of my letter, we shall soon meet; you know that I don't like to scribble much (except with 4 hands); so forgive me for stopping now. We are all well, I have had 3 letters from you; examination tomorrow; Panna Leszczńska sends you greetings; Pan Domowicz has been in Warsaw; Zywny is still wearing the old wig; Pani Dekert shakes your hand; Barciński embraces you; I'll bring you a book for Okunio. All the household sends love to you; same to your Papa. Give your muzzle! I love you.

F. F. Chopin

August Forel
(1848-1931)

Although Forel could never bring himself to accept Freudian psychology, he was one of the pioneer psychiatrists who advocated a public informed about sex. In 1909, his book *Die sexulle Frage,* was published and became the forerunner of many of the more popular texts with which we are familiar today.

Forel's miserably unhappy childhood was reinforced when he entered the Latin school at Morges, in Switzerland, where he remained until his fourteenth year when he entered the cantonal school at Lausanne. "Without exaggeration," he recalled in his autobiography, "I can say that these school years were the most dismal years of my life." Nearly all his schoolfellows treated him with derision, while the boys of the Volksschule stoned him. On his very first appearance at the school, he was nicknamed "The Partridge" and was "deeply mortified" by it.*

---

*From *Out of My Life and Work* by August Forel. Reprinted by permission of W. W. Norton & Co., Inc. 1937. Pp. 31-32.

The Latin school at Morges, in the Rue Couvaloup, was truly a school of the old pattern. Our classes were held in a small, low-ceilinged, badly-lit schoolroom, where we sat on narrow benches in a stuffy atmosphere. A small court-yard, closely hemmed in by houses, had to serve as our playground, and here we spent the ten minutes' intervals for recreation, which were passed mainly in mutual hostilities.

The masters were mostly pedants. Among the praiseworthy exceptions I will name the pioneer Alexandre Yersin and the very gifted mathematician and astronomer Charles Dufour. The greatest stress was laid upon the study of the dead languages, of course by the most boring method conceivable.

I was consigned to the lower fourth form. Without exaggeration I can say that these school years were the most dismal years of my life. I was shooting upwards, had little muscular strength, and in all physical exercises—even in running away—I displayed an absolute inferiority. To this must be added my timidity and prudishness. It was no wonder that I became the principal victim of my schoolfellows' ridicule, and was constantly bullied. I was literally predestined to such a fate. In these fledgling years it is customary to respect only audacity, agility, and muscular strength, and it was just in these that I was so peculiarly defective, so that I regarded myself as the most wretched and stupidest fellow in the world. Now the delight which my uncle's pronouncement gave me will be comprehensible. My misery was aggravated by my inexpertness in drawing and calligraphy, and also by a then almost absolute lack of musical ear and musical faculty, so that I seemed to be quite incapable of singing. Only by applying myself to my tasks with unwearying industry did I succeed, in spite of my bad memory for merely learning things by heart, in becoming a good scholar, and finally the head of my class. On account of this industry I was something of a favourite with my teachers. On the other hand, nearly all my schoolfellows treated me with derision, and bullied me, and the rough boys of the Volksschule pelted me with stones that drew blood. Even little boys of half my size could safely venture to strike me, and in the end I ceased to offer any resistance. On my first appearance I was given the nickname of *Rebhuhn,* "Partridge," and was foolish enough to feel deeply mortified.

I was all the more thankful, therefore, to win the friendship of a good-natured and muscular schoolfellow, Adrien Reymond, from Aclens, who often rescued me from the hands of my tormentors, and for whom I conceived a warm affection. Later I became even more intimate with another boy, who remained my friend until his death:

Giovanni Rochat, from Florence, whose parents, as Protestants, had been compelled to take refuge in Switzerland on account of religious persecution.

In one thing I was superior to my schoolfellows: I had a better knowledge of the German language, of which I had learned enough, from my mother and a maidservant, to enable me to express myself fairly well in German.

Santiago Ramon y Cajal*
(1852-1934)

By contrast to Forel, who complained bitterly of his "absolute inferiority . . . even in running away," the Spanish youth, Ramón y Cajal, was stung and humiliated by the opprobrious nicknames given him by his classmates and older boys, but he fought them for three years until he was big enough and strong enough to threaten them with physical reprisal.

Cajal, like Forel, went on to become a physician. Although during his lifetime Cajal made many discoveries of great histological significance, his importance in medical history rests chiefly on his fundamental work on the neuron. His painstaking research completely revolutionized the existing concepts of the nerve cell and its function, and laid the foundation for twentieth-century investigations in neurohistology and neurophysiology. In 1906 he received the Nobel Prize.

In spite of the best intentions, my artistic tendencies, as well as the urge for incessant activity and dramatic excitement, rose with a crescendo, since I found in Huesca many companions who shared my tastes and were ready to join in the most preposterous mischief. Dreamy sentimentality and a proud, punctilious character which did not readily brook insults or humiliations, were the cause of several mischances, and even of real dangers, from which only my robust constitution was able to save me.

I shall pass over most of the unfortunate episodes of that year, otherwise my narrative would be interminable. In order not to try the reader's patience too much, and to adhere to the plan adopted, I shall confine myself to relating some of the events and incidents which remained most deeply engraved upon my memory.

*From *Recollections of My Life* translated by E. Horne Craigie. Reprinted by permission of American Philosophical Society. 1937. Pp. 85-89.

Fortunately, initiations were not customary at the Institute of Huesca, but instead there was something as deplorable as they are; namely, the irritating abuse of strength against the weak, with bullying which regulated the games and the mutual relations of the boys. Every recent arrival who displeased the coxcombs of the upper years, whether by his appearance, by his attire, or by his character, found himself obliged, if he would escape persecution, either to remain prudently indoors during the hours of play or to solicit the protection of some big fellow who could stand up against the insolent bullies.

I had the misfortune to appear unpleasing to the aforesaid braves, so that, for no particular reason, they maltreated me by word and deed from my first appearance in the courtyards of the Institute, forcing me to take part in rows and disputes, from which I nearly always emerged in bad condition. Among those who most abused their strength with me, I recall a fellow called Azcón, a native of Alcalá de Gállego, a chronic loafer, whose studies had been interrupted several times in consequence. He was eighteen or nineteen years old, and his square and robust figure, his coarse red neck, and his vigorous brown arms betrayed at a glance the rustic who had hardened his muscles by guiding the plough and wielding the spade.

This savage recognized at once the weakness in my character and, always ready to cast slurs and in any way amuse himself at my expense, whenever he met me about the Institute he loaded me with insults. Among other epithets which I, in my simplicity, deemed mortifying, he applied to me those of Dago and Goatflesh. (The latter term was at that time applied in ridicule to everyone from Ayerbe.)

The term Dago requires explanation. My good mother, extraordinarily frugal and economical, made for me a roomy winter overcoat from the cloth of an old great-coat of my father's. The unfortunate part was that, considering my rapid growth and foreseeing a continuation thereof, she left the skirts of the coat considerably longer than was fashionable at the time. It must be acknowledged that my appearance was somewhat reminiscent of that of the strolling Savoyards who at that time used to wander about the Peninsula playing the harp or making bears or monkeys dance to the sound of the drum.

Among those young gentlemen, dressed in *le dernier cri,* the sudden apparition of my strange overcoat produced delighted amazement. One harsh and dominating voice—that of the above-mentioned Azcón—put into words the vague idea which welled up in that chorus of wags—"Look at the Dago."

"That is what he is," repeated his laughing cronies.

"He only needs the harp," cried one. "Where has he left his monkey?" exclaimed another.

The crescendo of jokes and jests would have gone on if anger and desperation, which I had with difficulty restrained hitherto, had not impelled me to fight for what I considered my outraged dignity. Without a word of response, I sprang like a tiger upon Azcón and his insolent friends, dealing blows and kicks on all sides.

A wiser and less hot-headed lad would have adopted the procedure, which is best in such cases, of saying nothing or taking it all as a joke. In this case the epithet would soon have been forgotten; but I, who was unacquainted with the well-known counsel, "be the first to laugh at your own defects, if you would not have them flung in your face," took the matter very seriously. The result was that, once they had recovered from their surprise, those whom I had attacked retaliated with interest, and gave me a never-to-be-forgotten beating. Thoroughly did they revenge themselves! For not only did they pound me with kicks, but flinging me to the ground, they rolled on my back, crushing me for a long time, until I was in danger of suffocation. When they were tired of thrashing me, I picked myself up as well as I could, collected the remains of my books, cleaned myself, and went home, aching all over, limping and vowing vengeance.

The reader will probably expect that after such an impressive lesson my bile would remain pacified, taking up thenceforth an attitude of submission and meekness. Quite the contrary. A few days afterwards, upon leaving the classroom, I came upon the same group of wags who, taking advantage of the presence of Azcón, hurled the hated nickname in my face in cowardly fashion. Seized with blind fury, I boldly attacked the insolent fellows, who closed in upon me with the same deplorable results as in the previous case. And this went on for two or three months. My chums did not know which to be most surprised at, the cruelty of Azcón and his followers or the persistence and impetuosity with which I responded to their abuse. How often, as I returned home sad and depressed, with my hat dented, my chest heaving with excitement, and my eyes red and damp with passion and hatred, I said to myself philosophically, "And to think that all this happens to me on account of a few inches of cloth which could have been cut off in the first place!"

In making this sad reflection I was entirely mistaken. What happened to me occurred also, although in a less degree—thanks to their prudence—to other beginners in the lower years, although they were dressed in the latest fashion. A pretext was never lacking, only there were combined in me two features which sooner or later would have attracted to me the animosity of those savages: the well earned fame for boldness and daring which I had brought from Ayerbe, the home of madcaps and a regular hotbed of bullies, and the indignation which injustice and the abuse of strength had always produced in me.

All these boyish conflicts, which to many will appear mere childishness, have a decisive importance not only for the formation of character but even for later conduct in adult life. The most proper and peaceable student, obliged to suffer such iniquitous attacks, ends in adopting according to his temperament one of three attitudes; either fawning and flattery towards his persecutors, the invocation of superior authority, or the most violent use of the muscles accompanied by cunning. The last was the method chosen by me. The two former I considered dishonorable. "In order to keep the strong at bay," I thought, "it is necessary to surpass them, or at least to equal them in vigour."

But how was I to attain this superiority and especially to attain it quickly? My insolent enemies admittedly were older than I, and besides they were many and I was one. Bah! I said to myself, if I can only beat Azcón all the rest will become my allies. And that is exactly what happened.

Fortunately, I knew well the highly strengthening effects of gymnastics and of obligatory work. I had observed how great an advantage in contests, fights, races, and jumping, had the strong and swarthy boys who had recently arrived from the villages and were accustomed to the weight of the spade compared with the tall, pale, young gentlemen with narrow chests and long slender shanks brought up in the sheltered city streets and in the gentle warmth of their mothers' laps.

Consequently, I resolved to engage in systematic physical exercises, to which end I spent hours and hours alone in the groves and thickets of the Isuela, climbing trees, jumping over ditches, lifting heavy stones by hand, and performing, in fact, all the actions which I believed would tend to hasten my muscular development, raising it to the greatest strength possible at my age. I hoped that by the end of a few months, or at any rate by the next scholastic year, things would change radically and that even the proudest bullies would have to treat me with respect. This consoling hope, though illusory at first sight, was largely realized in the succeeding sessions.

As the reader will see further on, persistent gymnastics and exasperated self-love performed miracles. With all my serious defects, I was always ready to learn by experience, which, in connection with this and other similar cases, is summed up in the common maxim, "If you wish to triumph in difficult undertakings, put into them your whole will, preparing yourself with more time and work than are obviously necessary." In the long run, surplus strength is never a loss but rather finds an adequate use in other ways, while an insufficiency, even if very slight, exposes one to distressing failures.

The results of my physical training were splendid. From the third year, my ability with my fists and my skill in the use of the sling and the cudgel inspired respect in the bullies of the upper years, and even the athletic Azcón had to capitulate and finally made friends with me. The fact of the matter is that I had informed him that whenever he was insolent towards me, I should imbed a stone in his skull. And my threat did not sound to him like an idle boast because he observed my prowess with the sling every day and so was convinced that I was capable of making good my promise. Needless to say, my humiliating nickname was forgotten.

Yen Liang
(1917-   )

Yen Liang is a Mongolian who was born and raised in Peiping. Her father was a well-to-do professor of classical Chinese, a scholar of the highest rank, and a descendant of Genghis Khan.

When she was six years old, as the following passage* shows, Miss Liang was subjected to the usual name-calling by the other kindergarten tots because of her strange appearance: "Straight Nose!" and "Yellow Hair!" they would cry. Epithets pursued her into high school, and while they were not as derisive, she was never really accepted by the others.

When I was six (a child in China, by the way, is a year old at birth and adds another year at New Year's) I was sent to kindergarten. I recall little except that we did a lot of singing, were forever carrying stools from one spot to another, and were always proclaiming we were hungry. I do recall, too, that when the class was taught simple characters written in a sandbox, I was usually a proud first to shout recognition of *shou, san, jen,* and the others.

After only a few days the teacher accompanied me home in the afternoon.

"Have you been naughty again, Daughter?" Mother asked at once.

The teacher hastened to speak. "It isn't that, *Tai Tai*—it's just that perhaps your daughter should skip kindergarten and go directly to

---

*From *Daughter of the Khans* by Yen Liang. Reprinted by permission of W. W. Norton & Co., Inc. 1955. Pp. 16-17.

primary school. She is ahead of the other children."

Father, told of this, smiled on me for the first time I could remember, and I smiled delightedly back.

I was then sent to first grade at a school for girls, since parents in China frowned then on the mixing of sexes after the age of five or six. It was a public school; I was the only child in our family to go to one. "It's much cheaper than a private school," I overheard Father tell Mother. "Besides, she is only a girl." To me he said: "You are too used to luxury. It will do you good to learn what life really is."

I was the only girl who came to the big gray brick building in a carriage, and with a man to hold the reins of the big horse and another to open the carriage door. At noon, noodles, Chinese rolls and other simple foods were served in the school cafeteria; but a servant from home set before me a dinner pail of four or five layers that often contained crab or shrimp—food such as the others had never even smelled. Naturally there was jealousy among my schoolmates, jealousy that grew with each arrival of the carriage, each serving of lunch. My schoolmates' uniforms were of cotton, while mine was of silk, Mother subscribing to a Chinese superstition that cotton, the mourning cloth, brought bad luck. And my shoes were of leather, a gift from Mother that I couldn't very well ignore, while my schoolmates' were of felt.

The girls saw that I was different in still another way: My nose was straighter than theirs and had more of a bridge; my cheekbones were higher, and my hair, though dark, wasn't their jet-black. *"Kao Pi-tze!"* they shouted—"Straight Nose!" It was a common name among the flat-nosed Chinese for Tibetan lamas, Sinkiang traders and other outlanders of China who came into their midst. A Westerner was "Big Nose" to them, for his nose usually is not only straight like an outlander's but even bigger. And my schoolmates jeered *"Whang Mao!"* (yellow hair) at me the way they jeered "Red Hair!" at Westerners on the streets.

Before long the girls learned from their parents why I looked different. "Tartar!" they hooted. "Barbarian!" In China, as perhaps in much of the world, another people is looked on with distrust, with hostility—especially a people who once were China's conquerors.

*   *   *   *

The girls who entered high school came from better families [than the ones she met in public school]; prejudice was less deeply imbedded. If I was a "Barbarian" to them, it was in gentle fun. Still, they never let me become really one of them. Would a day of belonging ever come? I wondered.

David S. Kogan
(1929-1951)

David Kogan, like Marie Bashkirtseff and Anne Frank, never lived
out the promise of his youth. He was born the same year as Anne
Frank and lived five years longer than she. Although their political
environments were obviously of a different kind, the institutional
patterns of their lives were quite similar. It is almost possible to
match parallel entries in Kogan's diary and Anne's. In the following brief entry,* the plaintive cry of David is one that is echoed by
many adolescents when they are called by pet names.

Saturday, August 15, 1942

At the Barbeque at Bernice's I acted like "Biff" Kogan, mascot and
court jester of the A.S.C. Why must I do that? When I keep thinking
"I will not make a fool of myself," I do not, but I do that thinking
at night, and all my grand plans of behavior, athletics, society, and
school evaporate in the morning, not to be a reality that day.

Arty's argument includes the point I do not look like a ninth
grader. I think he is right. Am I really too young for a ninth grader?
Am I licked?

Bernice has a slam book—pages for everyone, and you write what
you think of that person. Bernice was peeved when I refused to write
in her pages. My page has a lot of "cute" and "adorable" and an
"l'enfant." I didn't get one really bad, but the "l'enfant" gets me mad.

REFERENCES

1. Alfieri, Vittorio. *Autobiography*. Boston: James R. Osgood, 1877,
   p. 115.
2. Barzun, Jacques. *The House of Intellect*. New York: Harper, 1959.
3. Bloch, Herbert A., and Niederhoffer, Arthur. *The Gang*. New York:
   Philosophical Library, 1958, pp. 63-65.
4. Carr, Albert (Ed.). *Napoleon Speaks*. New York: Viking Press, 1941,
   p. 21.
5. DeQuincey, Thomas. *Autobiography from 1785 to 1803*. In: Masson,
   David (Ed.), *The Collected Writings of Thomas DeQuincey*. Edinburgh: Adams & Charles Black, 1889, pp. 200-203.
6. Ellis, Havelock. *My Life*. Boston: Houghton Mifflin, 1939, p. 103.

---

*From *The Diary of David S. Kogan*. Reprinted by permission of Beechurst Press.
1955. P. 39.

7. Erikson, Erik H. The problem of ego identification. *Psychol. Issues,* 1:115, 1959.

8. Esman, Aaron H. Mozart: a study of genius. *Psychoanal. Quart.,* 20:603-612, 1951.

9. Fletcher, A. C. The Hako: a Pawnee ceremony. *Bur. Amer. Ethnol., Ann. Rep.,* 22, 1900-1901, p. 365.

10. Frank, Anne. *The Diary of a Young Girl.* New York: Pocket Books, 1953, pp. 33-34.

11. Gide, André. *If It Die.* New York: Modern Library, 1935, p. 142.

12. Habbe, Stephen. Nicknames of adolescent boys. *Amer. J. Orthopsychiat.,* 7:375, 1937.

13. Hirshberg, L. K. "Dog Latin" and sparrow-languages used by Baltimore children. *Ped. Sem.,* 20:258, 1913.

14. Jamgotchian, Mesrob K. Sparrow language (junjugheren) the secret language among the Armenian children. *Ped. Sem.,* 20:98, 1913.

15. Josselyn, Irene. *Psychosocial Development of Children.* New York: Family Service Association of America, 1948.

16. Karpeles, Gustav (Ed.). *Heinrich Heine's Memoirs.* London: John Lane Co., 1910, pp. 40-44.

17. Lehmann, John. *The Whispering Gallery. Autobiography I.* New York: Harcourt, Brace, 1954, p. 103.

18. Murphy, William F. A note on the significance of names. *Psychoanal. Quart.,* 26:91-106, 1957.

19. Oberndorf, C. P. Reaction to personal names. *Int. J. Psycho-Anal.,* 1:223, 1920.

20. Opie, Iona, and Opie, Peter. *The Lore and Language of Schoolchildren.* London: Oxford University Press, 1959, pp. 2-4.

21. Opienski, Henryk (Ed.). *Chopin's Letters.* New York: Alfred A. Knopf, 1931, p. 18.

22. Orgel, Samuel Z., and Tuckman, Jacob. Nicknames of institutional children. *Amer. J. Orthopsychiat.,* 5:276, 1935.

23. Roosevelt, Elliott (Ed.). *F. D. R. His Personal Letters.* New York: Duell, Sloan & Pearce, 1947, Vol. I, pp. 35, 73.

24. Schachtel, Ernest G. On memory and childhood amnesia. *Psychiat.,* 10:10, 1947.

25. Smythe, Hugh H., and Seidman, Myrna. Name calling: a significant factor in human relations. *J. Human Relations,* 6:75, 1957.

26. Spiegel, Leo A. Comments on the psychoanalytic psychology of the adolescent. In: Eissler, Ruth S., et al., (Eds.), *The Psychoanalytic Study of the Child.* New York: International Universities Press, 1958, Vol. XIII, p. 304.

27. Trumbull, Robert. Children of Japan's "broken family." *New York Times Magazine,* August 30, 1959, p. 67.

CHAPTER THIRTEEN

God, Father and the Adolescent

The child's earliest concept of God is molded by his image of his parents. In early childhood, there is a tendency to equate God with the father and this tendency is repeated in adolescence—but this time frequently with antireligious results. The antagonistic response to religion may have nothing to do with any real skepticism concerning religion, but rather stems from basic hostility directed toward the parents, which has been projected onto the religious area. As has often been pointed out, the youngster who rejects his parents may reject all that his parents stand for, including, of course, religion. According to psychoanalytic theory, authoritarian religion is the internalized voice of authority, having the same restrictive effect as had the father. Freud (7) stated, "Psychoanalysis has made us aware of the intimate connection between the father complex and the belief in God, and has taught us that the personal God is psychologically nothing other than a magnified father; it shows us every day how young people can lose their religious faith as soon as the father's authority collapses. We thus recognize the root of religious need as lying in the parental complex."

Actually, there is great diversity in the dynamics of the adolescent's interest in, or rejection of, religion. Sudden eruptions of religiosity in the adolescent may be a reawakening of his oedipal wishes. Religious perplexity may be all mixed up with a disturbed relationship with a boy friend or girl friend. Often, religion is not a source of distress at all to the adolescent. However, the readoption in adolescence of attitudes that were originally symptoms of infantile conflicts may manifest itself in this sphere. No general inference can be made except that this area appeals to certain adolescents as a medium for orienting themselves, and often reflects the adolescent's attempt to establish himself as an individual (Blos, 5).

Numerous studies have indicated that "overtly expressed disbelief in God is more frequently encountered at the start of adolescence than at any other age, yet it is typical of the paradox of adolescence that it is also characterized as the most religious period of all. The fact is that these extremes may be encountered at different times in the same youngsters [Linn & Schwarz, 10]." In their search for God, the Father, many youngsters deliberately expose themselves to a variety of religious experiences.

Ernest Jones was doing this for the two years between 1895 and 1897. "Those years," he recalled in his autobiography (9), "from sixteen to eighteen, were indubitably the most stirring and formative of my life. The starting point was the problem of religion, which covered more personal sexual ones. Since the age of ten I had never been able to give my adherence to any particular creed, but my conscience troubled me badly and impelled me to seek in every direction for enlightenment. I prayed earnestly, frequented the diverse religious services available, and read widely on both sides. From that time dates my lasting interest in religious phenomena and the meaning of their importance to the human soul."

Nearly a century and a half earlier, another Englishman, Thomas Bewick (3), an artist and wood engraver, described his religious search at the age of fifteen. The year was 1768. "I feel it as a misfortune, that a bias, somehow or other, took place in my mind at this time, which led me deeply into the chaos of what is called religious works; and, for the purpose of getting into a thorough knowledge of all matters of this important kind, I spent much time, and took great pains, to obtain information; but, instead of this, I got myself into a labyrinth—bewildered with dogmas, creeds, and opinions, mostly the fanatical reveries, or the bigoted inventions, of interested or designing men, that seemed to me to be without end; and, after all my pains, I left off in a more unsettled state of mind than when I began."

William James, in *The Varieties of Religious Experience* (8), cited a letter written by Edward Everett Hale, a Unitarian minister, in which Hale wrote, "I observe, with profound regret, the religious struggles which come into many biographies, as if almost essential to the formation of the hero. I ought to speak of these, to say that any man has an advantage, not to be estimated, who is born, as I was, into a family where the religion is simple and rational. . . . I always knew God loved me, and I was always grateful to him for the world he placed me in. . . . I can remember perfectly that when I was coming to manhood, the half-philosophical novels of the time had a deal to say about the young men and maidens who were facing the 'problem of life.' I had no idea whatever what the problem of life was. To live with all my might seemed to me easy; to learn where there was so much to learn seemed pleasant and almost of course; to lend a hand, if one had a chance, natural; and if one did this, why, he enjoyed life because he could not help it, and without proving to himself that he ought to enjoy it."

Should this sound like an ingenuous statement, it can still be accepted at face value, for it is acknowledged that some adolescents survive their adolescence without being confronted with religion as a problem. But more than half of the people whose works have been used in this text have taken some pains to describe their religious conflictual difficulties as adolescents.

The author of the Sarashina diary (11) said of her feelings as a young lady of seventeen in Japan: " . . . I was somehow restless and forgot about novels. My mind became more sober and I passed many years without doing any remarkable thing. I neglected religious services and temple observances." She was describing herself in the year 1026. And from that date until 1947, the year of the last entry in this chapter, the refrain and burden of the adolescent's brooding and moodiness, bewilderment, disbelief, revulsion, depression, morbid introspection, and feelings of sinfulness and guilt about religion as seen in diaries and autobiographies are continuous and universal.

In these passages, we shall see how the adolescent, looking for peace within himself, that is, his own identity, projects his inner pubertal struggle onto the outer world; or rejects religion, as did Freud (6), as a negative element in the culture, an illusion that exists until mankind achieves emotional maturity; or finds in the institution of religion a restoration of the trust in existence that had been damaged or lost in earlier childhood; or converts to a religion other than his parents' as an expression of one kind of need or another, perhaps primarily a heresy which emancipates him from his family. These passages reveal the stark, confused religious conflicts of generations of adolescents in a variety of cultural milieus.

Richard Baxter
(1615-1691)

In the seven years between 1625 and 1632, when he bridged his tenth to seventeenth years, Richard Baxter was much troubled in conscience because of his guilt feelings and "sinfulness." A Puritan, and the son of a Puritan, he described his sinfulness in terms which even from a Puritan seem severe.* He became a man of strong convictions, although they were marked by a moderation in an age of extremism and violent antagonisms. He lived in the time of the Cavaliers and the Roundheads; he survived the plague of 1665 when 100,000 inhabitants of London died; and he survived the Great Fire of London. He was witness to the St. Bartholomew's Day order, when two thousand ministers were silenced and cast out of the established church. It was the time when the Dutch fleet destroyed some of England's greatest ships in the Thames. He needed to be fortified by religion, it would seem, and the rigid training in his youth prepared him for the upheavals and disasters of his adulthood.

> At first my father set me to read the historical part of the Scripture, which suiting with my nature greatly delighted me; and though all that time I neither understood nor relished much of the doctrinal part and mystery of redemption, yet it did me good by acquainting me with the matters of fact, drawing me on to love the Bible and to search by degrees into the rest.
>
> But though my conscience would trouble me when I sinned, yet divers sins I was addicted to, and oft committed against my conscience; which for the warning of others I will confess here to my shame.
>
> 1. I was much addicted, when I feared correction, to lie, that I might scape.
>
> 2. I was much addicted to the excessive gluttonous eating of apples and pears; which I think laid the foundation of that imbecility and

---

*In *The Autobiography of Richard Baxter*. Reprinted by permission of E. P. Dutton & Co., Inc. Everyman's Library. Pp. 5-6.

flatulency of my stomach which caused the bodily calamities of my life.

3. To this end, and to concur with naughty boys that gloried in evil, I have oft gone into other men's orchards and stolen their fruit, when I had enough at home.

4. I was somewhat excessively addicted to play, and that with covetness, for money.

5. I was extremely bewitched with a love of romances, fables and old tales, which corrupted my affections and lost my time.

6. I was guilty of much idle foolish chat, and imitation of boys in scurrilous foolish words and actions (though I durst not swear).

7. I was too proud of my masters' commendations for learning, who all of them fed my pride, making me seven or eight years the highest in the school, and boasting of me to others, which, though it furthered my learning, yet helped not my humility.

8. I was too bold and unreverent towards my parents.

These were my sins, which, in my childhood, conscience troubled me with for a great while before they were overcome.

Thomas Shepard *(1605-1649)*

A contemporary of Baxter, and also a Puritan, was Thomas Shepard. The Puritan of those days was in constant struggle for Grace. The sins of the best men were terribly visible. The Puritan had to account to God for his sins and he had to be an example to man. "Almost every Puritan," Perry Miller wrote in *The American Puritans,* "kept a diary, not so much because he was infatuated with himself but because he needed a strict account of God's dealing with him, so that at any moment, and above all at the moment of death, he could review the long transaction. Or if he himself could not get the benefit of the final reckoning, then his children could; they might find help in their own affairs by studying those of their parent. In this spirit, and for the edification of his children, Thomas Shepard told his story."*

The first two years I spent in Cambridge was in studying and in my neglect of God and private prayer, which I had sometime used. I did

---

*From *The American Puritans: Their Prose and Poetry* edited by Perry Miller. Reprinted by permission of Doubleday & Co., Inc. Copyright 1956, Perry Miller. Pp. 225, 226-227.

not regard the Lord at all unless it were at some fits. The third year wherein I was sophister, I began to be foolish and proud and to show myself in the public Schools, and there to be a disputer about things which now I see I did not know then at all, but only prated about them. Toward the end of this year, when I was most vile (after I had been next unto the gates of death by the smallpox the year before), the Lord began to call me home to the fellowship of His grace, which was in this manner:

I do remember that I had many good affections (but blind and inconstant) oft cast into me since my father's sickness, by the spirit of God wrestling with me, and hence I would pray in secret. Hence when I was at Cambridge, I heard old Dr. Chadderton, the master of the College when I came; the first year I was there to hear him upon a sacrament day, my heart was much affected, but I did break loose from the Lord again. Half a year after, I heard Mr. Dickinson commonplace in the chapel upon those words, "I will not destroy it for ten's sake" (Gen. 19), and then again was much affected. But I shook this off also, and fell from God to loose and lewd company, to lust and pride and gaming and bowling and drinking; and yet the Lord left me not, but a godly scholar walking with me, fell to discourse about the misery of every man out of Christ, *viz.* that whatever they did was sin. This did much affect me. And at another time, when I did light in godly company, I heard them discourse about the wrath of God and the terror of it, and how intolerable it was, which they did present by fire: how intolerable the torment of that was for a time, what then would eternity be? This did much awaken me, and I began to pray again. But then by loose company, I came to dispute in the Schools and there to join loose scholars of other colleges, and was fearfully left of God and fell to drink with them. I drank so much one day that I was dead drunk, and that upon a Saturday night, and so was carried from the place I had drunk at and did feast at unto a scholar's chamber, one Basset of Christ's College, and knew not where I was until I awakened late on that Sabbath, and sick with my beastly carriage. When I awakened, I went from him in shame and confusion, and went out into the fields, and there spent that Sabbath lying hid in the cornfields, where the Lord, who might justly have cut me off in the midst of my sin, did meet me with much sadness of heart and troubled my soul for this and other my sins, which then I had cause and leisure to think of. Now when I was worst, He began to be best unto me, and made me resolve to set upon a course of daily meditation about the evil of my sin and my own ways; yet although I was troubled for this sin, I did not know my sinful nature all this while. . . .

Hester Ann Rogers
(1756-1806)

"I was born at Macclesfield, in Cheshire," wrote Hester Ann Rogers in her autobiography, "Jan. 31, 1756, of which place my father was minister for many years; being a clergyman of the church of England. He was a man of strict morals, and as far as he was enlightened, of real piety. . . . I was trained up in the observance of all outward duties, and in the fear of sins, which in these modern times are too often deemed accomplishments. I was not suffered to name God but with the deepest reverence; and once for telling a lie, I was corrected in such a manner as I never forgot. We had constantly family prayer; the sabbath was kept strictly sacred; and as far as outward morality, my parents lived irreproachably, and in all social duties were regular and harmonious."

Hester Ann Rogers' autobiography (12) is a religious tract of a pious woman who relates primarily her sense of sinfulness and ultimate conversion to Methodism. In the account which follows there is a passionate recollection of the bewilderment she felt as an adolescent because of the religious demands forced on her and her own conflicting youthful desires for such sinful pleasures as reading novels, attending plays and dances, and wearing frilly clothes.

My grief [for her father who died April 1, 1765] for some time would not suffer me to take recreation of any kind; but I would sit and read to my mother, or weep with her. But after a season, I was invited to the houses of relations and friends; and as I soon became a laughing stock among them for my seriousness, and dislike to their manners and their plays, I began to be ashamed of being so particular! My mother was also now prevailed on to let me learn to dance, in order to raise my spirits and improve my carriage, &c. This was a fatal stab to my seriousness and divine impressions; it paved the way to lightness, trifling, love of pleasure, and various evils. As I soon made a proficiency, I delighted much in this ensnaring folly. My pride was fed by being admired, and began to make itself manifest with all its fruits. I now aimed to excel my companions, not in piety, but in fashionable dress! and could not rest long together without being engaged in parties of pleasure, and especially in this (what the world calls) innocent amusement. I also obtained all the novels and romances I possibly could, and spent some time every day in reading them; though at first it was unknown to my mother, who would not then suffer it. After this, I attended plays also. In short, I fell into all the vain customs and pleasures of a delusive world, as far as my situation would admit; and even beyond the proper limits of that station God had placed me in. Thus was my precious time mispent, and my foolish heart wandering far from happiness and God; yea, urging on to endless ruin! Yet in all this, I was not left without keen convictions, gentle drawings, and many short-lived good resolutions, especially till fifteen years of age. God often wrought strongly upon my mind, and that various ways, of which I come now to speak. But O! how did I grieve and resist the Holy Ghost! How justly might he have given me up; yea, and sealed me over to eternal destruction.

At thirteen years old, namely, in the year 1769, the bishop of Chester being to hold a confirmation at Macclesfield, I resolved to attend that ordinance, though it was with many fears and much trembling; for I believed till persons were confirmed, they were not alike accountable to God for their own conduct. But when this solemn renewal of the baptismal covenant was made in their own persons, then whosoever did not keep that covenant must perish everlastingly! I therefore endeavored seriously to understand the import of it, and was deeply convinced I was neither inwardly nor outwardly what it required. The knowledge of this wrought much sorrow; and I formed strong resolutions to lead a new life. Yet sin had so blinded my eyes, that I could not at this time believe, or at least I would not, that dancing, cards, or attending plays, were sinful. These therefore, I did not even resolve against. But I resolved against anger, pride, disobedience to my parent; also the neglect of secret prayer and church-going; with all the wanderings in those duties, and a variety of other evil tempers &c. which I knew myself guilty of. Having humbled myself before God, fasted and prayed, and (as I vainly thought) fortified myself by these resolutions, of keeping all God's commands in future, I ventured to take upon me the solemn vow. But such was my fear and trembling at the time, that when I approached the altar I was near fainting; and when returned to the pew, burst into a flood of tears. This was on Whitsunday; and I intended to receive the holy sacrament the follow-ing Sunday. But before I came, I was conscious I had already broken my solemn vows; and on the reflection, my distress was great, and I had many doubts whether partaking of the Lord's Supper would not be sealing my own damnation. However, one day as I was praying, it came into my mind, this holy sacrament is called a mean of grace; surely then it is just what so sinful, so helpless a soul wants: I will go to it then as a means whereby to receive strength and grace to conquer sin in future. In this view of that blessed ordinance I found much comfort; and I am now assured it was from the Lord, whom ignorantly I was feeling after. I approached the Lord's table therefore, with renewed vows, and renewed hopes: but alas! these also were as the "morning cloud, and as the early dew, which passeth away." For several months I thus repented and sinned, resolved and broke all my resolutions; sinned and repented again. I dared not to receive the Lord's Supper without resolving on a new life; neither dared I to stay from it; nor did I ever attend without being wrought on by the Spirit of God.

The latter end of this year I had a malignant fever, and believed I should die. I felt myself totally unprepared to appear before a holy God, and was in great distress: I earnestly entreated him to spare me a little longer, and resolved I would then spend a new life indeed. A patient forbearing God of love listened to my request, and did not cut the fig tree down. One night during this illness, I dreamed my soul was departed out of the body, and I, with three of my cousins (with whom I had a close intimacy, and who I thought had left the body also) were waiting in dreadful expectation of being summoned to the bar of God; and we all believed our doom would be everlasting darkness! My sins all appeared as in array against me, in the court of conscience, and my mouth was stopped: I had no plea whatever, no hope: for it seemed the justice of God must unavoidably sentence me to endless misery, which I felt to be my real desert; and was bewailing my own folly with bitter cries and lamentations. Their employ I thought was the same; each for ourselves, dreading "the worm that dieth not, and the fire which never shall be quenched!" When suddenly there appeared a cloud of uncommon brightness, and soon after a glorious angel descended in the cloud and stood before us, clothed in white, with a majesty and beauty not to be described. We beheld his approach with trembling awe, and almost an agony of despair, believing he was sent to summon us to appear and receive the deserved but dreadful sentence, "Depart ye accursed!" But to our inconceivable surprise, he smiled on us with heavenly sweetness, and said, "The Lord Jesus Christ has forgiven all your sins, and washed you in his own blood, and I am come to bid you enter into the joy of your Lord, and to conduct you into his blissful presence!" Being now suddenly transported from depths of misery into joy unspeakable, love beyond compare, and extreme delight; I thought I sprung up, clapped my hands, leaped for joy, and praised my God in extacies unknown before: so that it awoke me! Never did I feel anything like what I felt in this dream, sleeping or waking, before or after, till the Lord did truly speak my sins forgiven. This made a deep impression on my mind for some time. For a month or two I was very serious and circumspect; and read all the religious books I could meet with.

* * * *

It was some time however before I had so resisted the convictions of the Spirit of God, as to remain at ease: he strove with me various ways, till I was a little more than fifteen. But I so repeatedly grieved and quenched the motions of that Holy Spirit, that I was then in some measure given up to my own foolish rebellious heart. Dress, novels, plays, cards, assemblies and balls, took up the most of my time, so that mother began to fear the consequences of my living so much above my station in life. But I would not now listen to her admonitions. I loved pleasures, and after them I would go.

What increased my vanity and pride was, that I was much beloved by my god-mother, a lady of very considerable fortune, and often spent most of the summer months at Aldington with her; where I was always treated as if she intended to bestow a handsome fortune on me. She introduced me into the company of those in high life, and enabled me, by large presents, to dress in a manner suitable to such company. O how fatal in general are such prospects to a young mind! Yet in all this, I still wished to preserve a religious appearance. I still frequented church and sacraments, still prayed night and morning, fasted sometimes, and especially in lent; and because I did these things, esteemed myself a far better christian than my neighbors. Yea, so blind was I, that I had a better opinion now of my own goodness than formerly, when I was far more earnest about salvation. What a proof that sin darkens the understanding!

Richard Henry Dana, Jr. (1815-1882)

From his fifteenth to his twentieth years, Richard Henry Dana, Jr. suffered from "a deep depression . . . with a sinking of the heart, which I could feel physically as well as mentally." His gloomy sensations were generally precipitated by his "struggle against the spirit of God," according to his self-diagnosis. It was an unequal battle for the unexperienced adolescent. In an eerie moment, he felt the presence of "Another Being" and for a year he preserved "an excellent character for morality and good conduct in all the relations of life." But no one really knew the real state of his heart and affliction, because despite the revelation, he rebelled against the belief of the inevitable doom of the impenitent.*

It is understandable, perhaps, that no one really suspected what was in the heart of the youthful Richard, for the boy came from an illustrious family, in which no such problems were supposed to exist. His grandfather was the Chief Justice of the State of Massachusetts and the first minister to represent the United States at the Russian Court in Saint Petersburg. His father was a distinguished lawyer. Richard ultimately became a lawyer too, but only after he had sailed around Cape Horn and subsequently written the autobiographical *Two Years Before the Mast.*

I had never doubted the truths of revealed religions. I had always been aware that in the sight of a perfectly pure God, I was a miserable sinner. Believing the gospel declaration to [be] true that the gate to life is narrow & few there be that find it, & that everlasting punishment awaits those who do not repent & trust alone in Jesus Christ, I had often fearful misgivings; no, they were not misgivings, they were certainties which were only now & then made real to me. I had from my boyhood been the subject of deep religious impressions, but they had always gone off with little abiding effect. I had been religiously taught, but very early gave up prayer & estranged myself entirely from God. I can hardly recollect the time when I did give up prayer, I was so very young; but from that time on to the time of which I write, I had never prayed, except in moments of alarm or of awaked conscience. The first instance I can recollect of my being called back to a sense of my duties, was when reading the story of "Little Henri & his bearer" while at Westford. It was of a Sunday afternoon. I walked into the orchard in tears & with a full heart; but the effect was gone on the morrow. Afterwards, during the year before I entered college, under the preaching of the Rev. Mr. Adams at Cambridge, I became the subject of deep religious convictions. I felt in my inmost heart the truth of the doctrines he preached. I felt that if God should condemn me, I could have nothing to say. The convictions both of my understanding & of my heart were right, but my will was not conquered. I determined to let the subject go. This I could not do without a struggle; & I did struggle against the spirit of God, & for a season I prevailed. When now after the lapse of eleven years I call those times to mind, I calmly & seriously

---

*From *Richard Henry Dana, Jr., An Autobiographical Sketch* edited by Robert G. Metzdorf. Reprinted by permission of Massachusetts Historical Society. Copyright 1953, The Shoe String Press. Pp. 69-71.

believe that at certain moments, which I can distinctly point out, remembering where I stood & what I was doing, the spirit of God was at work as directly upon my spirit as when man converses with man. I recollect being seated at a desk practicing a lesson in drawing, by myself, when I felt in my heart something calling to me. I felt the presence of another being, though I knew that nothing was visible to my bodily senses. I was aware that I had praying friends, & the prevailing thought in my mind was that I was at that very instant the subject of a fervent effectual prayer to God, & that God was allowing me to be especially visited. I felt held as by a chain. I was obliged to give up what I was about. Thoughts crossed my mind of falling on my knees & giving myself up entirely to God & asking pardon through Jesus Christ, & devoting myself to the love & service of God. But this involved a religious life, renunciation of sin, & a coming out before the whole world as a servant of God: & these I could not make up my mind to do. The feeling passed off; how, I do not recollect, but probably from some one interrupting me, or my going off into the street, or into a room with others, in desperation. Since this season, which lasted about a year, I had but slight awakenings of conscience, & once or twice had serious doubts whether I had not sinned against the Holy Ghost & been given up by God's Spirit. During all this time & indeed throughout my whole life, I preserved an excellent character for morality & good conduct in all the relations of life, & all of my friends who were not evangelized in their views thought I had nothing to fear or repent of. Unitarian preaching justified me & passed over my head. Orthodox preaching sounded in my ears like the knell of judgment, but I knew it to be true, & that no other would lead me to salvation. During all these struggles, not a soul knew of the real state of my heart, except from suspicions of their own. For myself, I lived five years with a conviction that should I be taken out of life I had nothing to expect but the doom of the impenitent. This was the settled conviction of my mind. I knew too that there was a way of escape, but I refused to walk in it. It may be thought that I must have been melancholy & desponding. Not at all. On the contrary I was remarkably bright & buoyant. Everything & every body interested & excited me. It was only when alone & when religious subjects forced themselves upon me, that I felt gloomy. Then the struggle was usually short. I never in a single instance mastered these feelings, but always fled from them. During these five years I was subject to a deep depression which seized me when alone, & from which I fled as from a nightmare. Sometimes I went to books, but if the fit was a severe one, books failed. My own mental resources always failed. Walking & diversion upon natural objects sometimes succeeded, but not always, & I was almost invariably obliged to join myself to some one in conversation, unless relieved by some accident. The subject upon my mind was not always nor usually religion. Indeed, I generally had no particular subject before me, but was affected with a sinking of the heart, which I could feel physically as well as mentally.

Maharshi Devendranath Tagore (1817-1905)

At the same time that Richard Henry Dana, Jr. was experiencing his religious depression in Massachusetts, in Calcutta, a youth of comparable family background and wealth was feeling much the same way. He was Devendranath Tagore, the father of Rabindranath, Indian poet and founder of the school at Santinetekan.

Devendranath's melancholy, however, unlike Richard's was precipitated by a specific event—his grandmother, Didima's death. The boy had been very attached to Didima and nothing could assuage his grief or give him solace. "I knew not where to turn," he wrote. "I found happiness in nothing, peace in nothing." His desire to learn Sanskrit led him to the study of the Mahabharata wherein he hoped to find truths regarding the Godhead. But for all his search, "the sense of emptiness of mind remained just the same; nothing could heal it, my heart was being oppressed by that gloom of sadness and feeling of unrest."[*]

One day, after Didima's death, whilst sitting in my *boythakkhana* (drawing-room) I said to those around me, "To-day I have become a *kalpataru* (the wishing-tree which grants all desires). Whoever will ask of me anything that it is in my power to give, that will I give to him." Nobody else asked me for anything except my cousin Braja Babu, who said, "Give me those two big mirrors, give me those pictures, give me that gold-laced dress suit." I immediately gave him all these. The next day he brought men and took away all the *boythakkhana* things. There were some good pictures and other valuable articles of furniture; he took them all away. In this manner I got rid of all my things. But the grief in my heart remained just the same; nothing could dispel it. I knew not where to turn for solace. Some-

[*]From *Autobiography* by Maharshi Devendranath Tagore. Reprinted by permission of Macmillan & Co., Ltd. 1914. Pp. 44-48.

times, lying on a sofa and pondering over problems about God, I used
to become so absent-minded that I did not know when I had got up
from my couch, and taken my meals, and lain down again. I used to
feel as if I had been lying there the whole time. I would go alone to
the Botanical Gardens in the middle of the day, whenever I got a
chance. It was a very unfrequented, lonely spot. I used to take my seat
on a tombstone in the middle of the gardens. Great grief was in my
heart. Darkness was all around me. The temptations of the world had
ceased, but the sense of God was no nearer; earthly and heavenly happiness were alike withdrawn. Life was dreary, the world was like a
graveyard. I found happiness in nothing, peace in nothing. The rays
of the midday sun seemed to me black. At that time this song suddenly
broke from my lips, "Vain, oh! vain is the light of day; without knowledge all is dark as night." This was my first song. I used to sing it out
loud sitting alone on that tombstone.

I then felt a strong desire to learn Sanskrit. From my boyhood I had
been fond of Sanskrit. I used carefully to commit to memory the verses
of *Chanakya*. Whenever I heard a good *sloka* (verse) I learnt it by
heart. There was then in our house a family pundit. His name was
Kamalakanta Chudamani, his home Bansberia. Formerly he was attached to the family of Gopimohun Tagore, then he came to us. He
was a learned man of strong character. I was then young, and he was
very fond of me, whilst I looked up to him with reverence. One day I
said to him, "I will read *Mugdhabodha Vyakarana* with you." He said,
"Do, by all means. I will teach it to you." Then I commenced the
Mugdhabodha with Chudamani, and began learning by heart, *ja, da,
ga, ba, jha, dha, gha, bha*. It was as a means of acquiring the knowledge
of Sanskrit that I first threw myself enthusiastically into the study of
Mugdhabodha with Chudamani. One day he quietly took out a piece
of paper with his writing on it, and putting it into my hand, said, "Put
your signature to this." "What is this writing?" I asked. On reading it,
I found it said I would have to support his son Shyamacharan for
life. I signed it then and there. I had a great love and respect for Chudamani, so I put my signature at his request without any hesitation. I
gave no thought at the time to what it meant. Shortly afterwards our
sabha pundit Chudamani died. Then Shyamacharan came to me, with
that bit of signed paper, and said, "My father is dead, I am helpless;
you will now have to support me. See here, you have already promised
to do so." I agreed to this, and from that time Shyamacharan lived with
me. He knew some Sanskrit. I asked him where I could find truths
regarding the Godhead. "In the Mahabharata," he answered. Then I

began reading the Mahabharata with him. On opening the book, one particular *sloka* struck my eye, which says:

> May you have faith in religion, may you ever be devoted to religion; religion alone is the friend of him who has entered the next world.
> However well you may serve mammon and woman, you can never bring them into subjection, nor will they ever be faithful to you.

On reading this *sloka* of the Mahabharata, I felt greatly inspirited.

I had an idea that in all languages, as in Bengali and English, adjectives preceded nouns. But in Sanskrit I found the noun was here, and the adjective right away over there. It took me some time to master this. I read through a good portion of the Mahabharata. I remember quite well Upamanyu's reverence for his guru in the story of Dhaumya Rishi. Now that voluminous book has become accessible to the reading public through translation, but in those days very few people used to read it in the original. My thirst for spiritual knowledge led me to read a great deal of it.

As on the one hand there were my Sanskrit studies in the search after truth, so on the other hand there was English. I had read numerous English works on philosophy. But with all this, the sense of emptiness of mind remained just the same; nothing could heal it, my heart was being oppressed by that gloom of sadness and feeling of unrest. Did subjection to Nature comprise the whole of man's existence? I asked. Then indeed are we undone. The might of this monster is indomitable. Fire, at a touch, reduces everything to ashes. Put out to sea in a vessel, whirlpools will drag you down to the bottom, gales will throw you into dire distress. There is no escape from the clutches of this Nature-fiend. If bowing down to her decree be our end and aim, then indeed are we undone. What can we hope for, whom can we trust? Again I thought, as things are reflected on a photographic plate by the rays of the sun, so are material objects manifested to the mind by the senses; this is what is called knowledge. Is there any other way but this of obtaining knowledge? These were the suggestions that Western philosophy had brought to my mind. To an atheist this is enough, he does not want anything beyond Nature. But how could I rest fully satisfied with this? My endeavour was to obtain God, not through blind faith but by the light of knowledge. And being unsuccessful in this, my mental struggles increased from day to day. Sometimes I thought I could live no longer.

August Forel
(1848-1931)

Forel was born in Switzerland, in the famous year of the Revolution. His autobiography* reveals a lonely, disturbed child of a melancholy, Calvinistic mother, a child whose only friends were some ants. He became a rebellious son, but in his rebellion remained obedient to the ascetic ideals of his mother. However, he could not abide the confirmation ceremony and refused to go through with it.

In Morges, as I have said, I was obliged to attend church with absolute regularity. I had usually to struggle hard in order to keep myself awake. The sermons were extremely boring, often without any real coherence, so that they were greatly inferior to my mother's religious teaching. Now, since I was fourteen years of age, I had to attend the confirmation class. It was my mother's ardent hope that this would affect my conversion, and all her prayers were directed to this end. She thought the pastor would be able to explain matters better than she could. What an illusion! The result was the very contrary of what she had hoped.

I went to Pastor Bridel for instruction. He was a celebrated preacher, especially revered by the ladies, but he was really a superficial orator. Vainly, for my mother's sake, I endeavoured to receive the grace of God from his teaching. This pastor allowed the members of his confirmation class to ask him anonymous questions in writing, more particularly towards the end of the course. I was very glad of the opportunity. Instead of asking trivial questions, as most of my schoolfellows did, I went straight to the heart of the problem, and unbosomed myself of my increasing doubts by asking the most insidious questions; for example, questions concerning original sin and human responsibility. But every time Pastor Bridel had to answer one of my questions it was as though a snake had bitten him. He wrinkled his forehead, and gave unwilling and evasive answers, without assuaging my thirst for knowledge. His embarrassment did not escape me. I felt that I had scored; I noted his inability to give me a clear, reassuring answer, which would confirm my faith in Christianity. Words, words, nothing but words and phrases! I thought to myself. And so, little by little, the remnant of my faith perished.

---

*Out of My Life and Work. Reprinted by permission of W. W. Norton & Co., Inc. 1937. Pp. 39-40, 46-47.

My love and reverence for my mother remained unshaken, but I began to realize more and more clearly that she was allowing herself to be deluded by the mystical hocus-pocus of Christianity. Once an uncle of mine came to see us from Paris, a bombastic pastor, Georges Fisch. He was the very type of the unconscious egoist. His sermons were as empty as they were noisy. Since his dogmatic, pompous delivery and his sanctimonious tone annoyed me, I contradicted him and allowed my unbelief to become apparent. I shall never forget the irritable passion and simulated grief with which he answered me. Of course, I was thoroughly scolded by my father, who always complained that "arguing" was my chiefest fault. Meanwhile my Italian friend Giovanni Rochat (afterwards Protestant pastor in Florence, where, following my example, he was the first to introduce the total abstinence movement in Italy), who, unlike myself, had remained a pious believer, was preparing for his theological course. With him I had the most violent discussions on matters of belief, and on the way from Vaux to Morges we often had heated arguments, which, of course, left each of us entirely unconvinced.

* * * *

At the end of the year 1864 came the confirmation I had dreaded so. I dreaded it because I saw a gulf yawning between the faith which I was then supposed to confess, and my unbelief, a gulf which, in spite of my good intentions, could no longer be bridged. Before the first communion Pastor Bridel invited each of us to a tête-à-tête. I felt that for me this was to be decisive: *Hic Rhodus, hic salta!* Trembling and shuddering, I went to the pastor's room on that memorable day, entered, and was silent. I take it that he suspected me of being the writer of the insidious anonymous questions of which I have spoken. I can still see the stern gaze which he bent upon me, a miserable sinner. I was silent, because my words seemed to stick in my throat. It was a painful situation. At last he spoke: "Well, what have you to say to me?" I sought for words, but could only stammer stupidly: "I can't believe." The pastor's expression became even more sombre, and he asked me, to the best of my recollection, whether I did not believe in God and the divinity of Christ, to which I repeated, in a stifled voice: "I can't." Thereupon he gazed at me with angry contempt, and said: "Come again when you are in a better frame of mind!" I did not wait for more, but promptly disappeared, never to return. My head was in a whirl. So this was the result of the confirmation classes on which my mother had set all her hopes! This was all the consolation which God's servant could offer me! My gorge rose against the man, and against Christianity, and I remember as though it were yesterday how I cried aloud: "I shake the dust of your house from my feet!" And I added: "You have seen me for the last time!"

I had indeed had more than enough of all this hypocrisy. In the quiet meadows round my home I had often cried in despair to the so-called personal God: "If you really exist, destroy me here and now; then I shall know that you exist, but otherwise I cannot believe in your existence!" But all was silent; I was not destroyed.

I went to my mother, and without circumlocution told her of my resolve: "I can't lie to you, because you have always quite rightly taught me to hate lies. And I had to be honest with the pastor too. Well, you see the charity with which he treated me. I can't share your religious beliefs, so I can't be confirmed. That would be the worst of lies." My mother was in despair, but she was also disappointed in Pastor Bridel. She even backed me up in my resolve that I would not be confirmed without faith. Nevertheless, she insisted on making a last attempt, and begged me to listen to the views of Pastor Cuénod in Morges, for whom she had a great respect, and whom I too esteemed. This clergyman was a good, upright, honourable man. He agreed with me that one cannot compel oneself to believe, but he hoped that belief would come in the course of time, and he prayed for me fervently. Encouraged by his kindness, I spoke to him openly and explained all my doubts and their reasons. Of course, he could not remove my doubts, but we parted on the friendliest of terms. For my mother's sake I regretted the turn which this business had taken, and the outcome of it, but I could not honestly do otherwise than I had done. However, to please my mother I continued to go to church from time to time, but there was an end of prayer and worship. There was one very clever and talented boy in the college, Biaudet by name, with whom I discussed these matters. He praised my critical judgment, and confessed that he too was an unbeliever. The others, whether they believed or not, all allowed themselves to be confirmed in obedience to convention and tradition.

Beatrice Webb
(1858-1943)

The young adolescent's doubts and ambivalence about religion, the guilt feelings, martyrdom, self-pity and maundering, are reflected in this passage from Beatrice Webb's manuscript diary which she later incorporated in her autobiography.* It is dated December 23, 1872, when she was fourteen years old.

Because she felt she had transgressed deeply and "trifled with the Lord," she resolved to give up any pleasure rather than go into society. But, alas, as with many resolutions, Beatrice was not very successful with this one, for later in her autobiography she relates how the following season she spent a good deal of her time in the Ladies' Gallery of the House of Commons listening to the debates between Gladstone and Disraeli. And the following autumn and winter she travelled with her father and sister Kate to the United States.

> This autumn unsatisfactory to me in many ways. I have hardly learned anything in the way of lessons; honestly speaking, I have been extremely idle, especially during and after the company. But one thing I have learnt is, that I am exceedingly vain, to say the truth I am very disgusted with myself; whenever I am in the company of any gentleman, I cannot help wishing and doing all I possibly can to attract his attention and admiration; the whole time I am thinking how I look, which attitude becomes me, and contriving everything to make myself more liked and admired than my sisters. The question is, how can I conquer it, for it forwards every bad passion and suppresses every good one in my heart; the only thing I can think of, is to avoid gentlemen's society altogether. I feel I am not good enough to fight any temptation at present, I have not enough faith. Talking about faith, I don't know what to think about myself. I believe, and yet I am always acting contrary to my belief, when I am doing any silly action, when I am indulging my vanity, I hear a kind of voice saying within me, "It doesn't matter at present what you say and do, if there is a God, which I very much doubt, it will be time to think of that when you are married or an old maid," and what is worse still I am constantly acting on that idea. Meanwhile I feel my faith slipping from me, Christ seems to have been separated from me by a huge mass of worldliness and vanity. I can no more pray to Him with the same earnest faith as I used to do, my prayers seem mockeries. I pray against temptations, which I run into of my own accord, and then I complain secretly that my prayers are not answered. And intellectual difficulties of faith make it impossible to

---

My Apprenticeship. Reprinted by permission of The Passfield Trustees and Longmans Green & Co., Ltd. (London). 1926. Pp. 61-62.

believe. I am very very wicked; I feel as if Christ can never listen to
me again.

Vanity, all is vanity. I feel that I have transgressed deeply, that I
have trifled with the Lord. I feel that if I continue thus I shall become a frivolous, silly, unbelieving woman, and yet every morning
when I wake I have the same giddy confident feeling and every night
I am miserable. The only thing is to give up any pleasure rather than
go into society; it may be hard, in fact I know it will, but it must be
done, else I shall lose all the remaining sparks of faith, and with
those all the chances of my becoming a good and useful woman in
this world, and a companion of our Lord in the next.

May God help me to keep my resolution.

Marie Bashkirtseff
(1860-1884)

One of the truly revealing journals of adolescence, rivaling, in our
time, *The Diary of Anne Frank,* is Marie Bashkirtseff's *Journal* (2).
Marie was of rich and noble Russian birth and lived most of her
short life in France. The *Journal* was begun in her twelfth year and
maintained until shortly before she died of what Charcot, her celebrated physician, diagnosed as "laryngeal phthisis," or consumption.
Her diary seems to be frank, pretentious, affected, obtuse, exaggerated, deliberately written for posterity, engaging, insightful, witty,
depressing. It reveals all the symptoms one would expect in a gifted
adolescent who is able to express herself effectively. Some critics
have called Marie's diary the feminine counterpart of Rousseau's
confessions, but Hall feels it is a more precious psychological document than Rousseau's because of its sustained elucidation of adolescent ferment in an unusually vigorous and gifted—and less neurotic—individual.

Marie belonged to the Russian Orthodox Church. Her prayers
were largely self-centered, consisting of promises to God for favors
requested. She would pray to God "to preserve, strengthen, and
develop" her voice; she promised God "to sing no more (a resolution that I have since broken a hundred times) until I take lessons";
she pleaded with God to grant the return of her passionate love for
a Duke who had no knowledge of her existence. "O my God," she
cried out in her twelve-year-old misery, "at the thought that he
will never love me I am ready to die of grief!" As the passages pro-

ceed, her religious feelings, her ambivalences, her rejection of religion, and finally, with the knowledge of impending death, her return to and acceptance of faith are depicted.

Friday, December 30, 1872

This evening we spent at church; it is the first day of our Holy Week, and I performed my devotions. I must say that there are many things about our religion which I do not like; but it is not for me to reform them; I believe in God, in Christ, and in the Holy Virgin. I pray to God every night, and I have no wish to trouble myself about a few trifles that have nothing to do with true religion—with true faith. I believe in God, and He is good to me; He gives me more than I need. Oh, if He would only give me what I desire so much! The good God will have pity on me, although I might do without what I ask. I should be so happy if the Duke would only take notice of me, and I would bless God.

May 6, 1873

... Then we went to the Russian church—the Church of the Trinity. The whole church was decorated with flowers and plants. Prayers were offered up, in which the priest asked pardon for sins, mentioning each one separately. Then he knelt down and prayed again. Everything he said was so applicable to me that I remained motionless, listening to and echoing his prayer. This is the second time that I have prayed with so much fervor in church. The first time was on New Year's day. The service has become so banal, and then the things spoken of are not those of everyday life—things that concern every one. I go to mass, but I do not pray. The prayers and the hymns they sing find no response either in my heart or in my soul. They prevent me from praying with freedom, while the *Te Deum,* in which the priest prays for every one (where every one finds something applicable to himself) penetrates my soul.

Thursday, June 24, 1874

All last winter I could not sing a note. I was in despair; I thought I had lost my voice, and I blushed and remained silent when I was spoken to. Now it has come back again, my voice, my treasure, my fortune! I receive it with tears in my eyes, and I thank God for it on my knees. I said nothing, but I was truly grieved. I did not dare speak of it. I prayed to God, and He has heard me! What happiness! What a pleasure it is to sing well!

Friday, October 1, 1875

God has not done what I asked him to do; I am resigned; (not at all, I am only waiting). Oh, how tiresome it is to wait, to do nothing but wait!

Tuesday, December 28, 1875

... It appears that God does not hear me. Yet I cry to Him loudly enough.

Wednesday, December 29, 1875

My God, if you will make my life what I wish it to be, I make a vow, if you will but take pity on me, to go from Kharkoff to Kieff, on foot, like the pilgrims. If, along with this, you will satisfy my ambition and render me completely happy, I will take a vow to make a journey to Jerusalem, and to go a tenth part of the way on foot. Is it not a sin to say what I am saying? Saints have made vows; true, but I seem to be setting conditions. No; God sees that my intention is good, and if I am doing wrong He will pardon me, for I desire to do right. . . .

Monday, June 12th, 1876—Tuesday, June 13th

I longed to live seven lives at once, and I do not live a quarter of a life. I am chained down.

God will have pity upon me; but I know that I am weak and it seems to me that I am going to die.

This is the truth of the matter: Either I must have all that God has permitted me to discern and to comprehend, in which case I shall be worthy of having it, or I shall die!

For God, if He can not justly grant me all, will not have the cruelty to impose life upon an unhappy creature to whom He has given comprehension and the ambition to acquire what she comprehends.

God has not made me what I am, without design. He can not have endowed me with the faculty of *seeing everything,* only to torment me by giving me nothing. Such a supposition is not in accordance with the nature of God, Who is a Being of justice and mercy.

I must have what I want, or I must die. There is no question of that. Let Him do as He thinks best! I love Him, I believe in Him, I bless Him, and I beg Him to forgive me for the wrong I do.

He has given me my comprehension of things to satisfy my longings, if I am worthy. If I am not worthy, He will let me die!

Saturday, March 31st, 1877

What is the use of complaining? My tears will effect nothing. I am doomed to be unhappy. That always, and then artistic fame. And if I fail! Ah, have no fear, I will not live to rust somewhere in the practice of the domestic virtues.

I do not care to speak of love, because I have done so without avail. I will no longer appeal to God to bless me, for I want to die.

My God, Lord Jesus Christ, let me die! My life has been short, but the lesson learned has been a hard one. I want to die. I am as incoherent and as disordered as what I write, and I detest myself as I detest everything that is miserable. Let me die! My God! Let me die! I have had enough of it!

Let me have a peaceful death! Let me die singing some beautiful air of Verdi's. No rebellious feeling rises within me as before, when I wished to live *expressly* that *others* might not rejoice and triumph. Now it is a matter of supreme indifference to me; I suffer too much.

Saturday, January 11th, 1879

I worked honestly all the week until 10 o'clock at night on Saturday, then I returned home and wept. Until now I have always carried my sorrows to God, but as He has not heard me, I believe in Him—very little.

Those alone who have experienced this feeling can understand it in all its horror. It is not that I wish to virtuously preach religion, but God is something very convenient at times. When there is no one to appeal to, when we are at the end of our resources, God remains. To pray to God pledges you to nothing, troubles no one, and is a supreme consolation.

Whether He exists or not, *we must believe in Him absolutely,* unless our life is a very happy one. In the latter case, we can do without Him. But in all sorrows, in misfortune, in all disagreeable things, it were better to die than not to believe.

God is an invention which saves us from absolute despair. Imagine, then, what it is when we invoke Him, as our last, our only resource, and even as we do so, realize that we do not believe in Him!

Tuesday, February 18th, 1879

Just now I fell on my knees at my bedside to ask God for justice, pity, pardon! If I have not deserved such tortures, let Him give me justice! If I have committed abominable crimes, let Him pardon me! If He exists at all, if He is such as they teach us to believe, He should be just, pitiful, and forgiving. I have but Him; it is but natural that I should seek Him, and that I should beg Him not to abandon me to despair, not to cause me to sin, nor to allow me to doubt, blaspheme, or die.

My sin is, without doubt, like my torment, I probably commit every instant little infamies which form a frightful total.

Just now I answered my aunt rudely, but I could not help it; she came in at a time when I was weeping, with my head buried in my hands, and begging God to notice me. Oh, misery of miseries!

No one must see me weep, they would think that I weep from disappointed love, and I—should weep at their mistake.

Paris, Sunday, August 22, 1880

. . . And then, mamma talks all the time about God: "If it is God's will!" "With the help of God!" When one invokes God so often, it is only to excuse the neglect of all sorts of little duties.

This is not faith, nor even religion; it is a mania, a weakness, the cowardice of the lazy, the incapable, and the indolent. What more indelicate than to cover all one's shortcomings by the word "God?" It is not only indelicate, it is more, it is criminal, if one believes in God. "If it is ordained that such a thing shall happen, it will happen," she says, to avoid the trouble of exerting herself and to ward off remorse.

If everything were foreordained, God would be only a constitutional president, and free-will, vice, virtue, meaningless words.

Friday, October 29th, 1880

A passage I have read in the New Testament is so extraordinarily in accord with the thoughts that were guiding me, that I have returned once more to the religious fervor, the miracles, Jesus Christ, and my passionate prayers of the old days. For some time I have contented myself with one God, and my belief has been very pure, very severe, very simple; but now I return to a more familiar, more consoling religion, one more in consonance with the fears, the miseries, and the meanness of my nature.

The Man-God and the Virgin Mary seem to hear you more than the real God.

Tuesday, November 16th, 1880

I believe I exaggerated the other day in regard to the Church, my remorse afterward almost drove me out of bed to make my apology here; for the Church teaches us to know God, the Church has made tremendous efforts for the preservation of morals, the Church has carried to savage nations the name of God and civilization. Without offense to God, I believe they might have been civilized without Catholicism; but then the Church, like feudalism, has been useful, and like it, has run, or nearly run, its course. There are too many things inadmissible and revolting, not to say odious, in Catholicism. The divine has been confused with the legendary; there are too many enlightened people nowadays for those venerable falsehoods to be respected. But we are traversing an epoch of transition, and, unfortunately, the masses are not as yet sufficiently enlightened not to pass from vain superstitions to contempt, and the negation of God.

There are men who are sincerely religious, but are there any who are sincere monarchists? There are people, to be sure, who believe that monarchy is necessary to the prosperity of certain countries. There, I had forgotten that, the other day, when I said that to love monarchy, one must have the soul of a lackey. . . .

Thursday, March 3d, 1881

I am very ill. I cough very much, breathe with difficulty, and there is a sinister rattling in my throat. I believe it is called phthisis laryngitis.

I opened lately the New Testament, neglected for some time past, and twice, in the space of a few days, I have been struck by the appropriateness with which the lines my eye happened to fall upon answered my thoughts. I pray again to Christ. I have returned to the Virgin; to miracles, after having been a deist—after days of absolute atheism. But the religion of Christ, according to His own words, resembles but little your Catholicism, or our own orthodoxy, which I abstain from following, limiting myself to following the precepts of Christ, without embarrassing myself with allegories, which pass for realities, superstitions, and various absurdities, introduced later into religion, by men, for political or other motives.

Lucy Sprague Mitchell
(1878-   )

Lucy Sprague Mitchell, one of the leading educators in the United States, was the founder and first president of the Bank Street School and Bank Street College, two institutions in the forefront of American education.

Her adolescence was not entirely a happy one, for she was disturbed by her father's new-found wealth, her mother's ill-health, and her own maturational problems. At that time—she was then thirteen—she "sought for help in the age-old refuge of religion," and found in Christian Science a temporary comfort. The remarkable understanding of her parents during this time is worthy of note.*

In these years, I sought for help in the age-old refuge of religion. The Presbyterian church that we all attended, dressed in our Sunday clothes, which meant high silk hats for Father and Uncle Albert, left me entirely unmoved. I thought I'd investigate other churches. I went to Catholic mass for a time. I went to Jewish synagogues for a time. I enjoyed the pageant and strangeness in these unfamiliar houses of worship, but otherwise they left me unmoved. I went to the Central Music Hall, the big downtown auditorium where, as a young child, I had sometimes heard David Swing preach. Now, Dr. Gunsaulus held Sunday services there. I knew him as a friend of Father's. But he was a different man behind the pulpit—I almost said on the stage, for he treated a pulpit pretty much as a theater stage. His oratory flowed with wild beauty and earnestness. Here at last, I thought, is what I want. But I found myself thinking how skillfully he chose his words, how he timed his vivid climaxes and followed them by a hushed, tired voice. He has a "thing-in-the-corner" who is admiring him mightily, I decided. And I turned down Dr. Gunsaulus.

Once I attended a great Salvation Army meeting in Central Music Hall. Evangeline Booth herself spoke. She swept me out of my self-conscious, critical attitude. But the audience began weeping and calling out hysterically. My sense of privacy was outraged. I was embarrassed by these emotional exhibitions all around me. No, revivalist methods could not reach me.

And still I pondered over the problem of sin, which had worried me since my real childhood days. If God were good, if God were all-powerful, why had he permitted sin and sickness? Finally, I took the last complete step of escape. God had never created sin and sickness. He couldn't by his very nature. Sin and sickness did not really exist. God was good, God was All; therefore, All was good. I had stumbled upon the Christian Science formula for negation. I became a Christian Scientist.

At the time, I thought I had evolved this philosophy all by myself. As I look back now, I can see the subtle hand of Mrs. Milward Adams

---

*From *Two Lives* by Lucy S. Mitchell. Reprinted by permission of Simon & Schuster, Inc. Copyright 1953, Lucy S. Mitchell. Pp. 67-69.

in my new faith. She was a well-known teacher in Chicago, though what she taught never got a name so far as I can remember. She had developed her own system of teaching young people to use their bodies efficiently and with ease, to use their voices to express the words they were saying, to love poetry—to read it aloud and to write it. She had an almost hypnotic effect upon her pupils. They simply swallowed her teachings whole. I was sent to Mrs. Adams because of my extreme shyness, which made me silent with strangers. Mrs. Adams was a Christian Scientist, though she was careful not to let me know this until I had apparently worked out the whole philosophy by myself. Then she put Mary Baker Eddy's *Science and Health* into my hands. I was then thirteen.

For two years I lived in a state of exalted negation. I remember concrete events in a haze of denial. I denied Mother's increasing headaches. I denied crimes I read about in the newspapers. I even denied Otho's death when it came—Otho whom I loved better than anyone else. I not only denied illness, I treated it mentally. No one ever told me how to do this, though I knew a number of Christian Scientists by this time, and my method of treatment was probably utterly unlike that of professional healers. This is how I did it. I withdrew into myself so that I was scarcely conscious of where I was. I rhythmically pulsed, thinking with intense concentration, "Mother has no headache, Mother has no headache. God is good, All is good," over and over again. Yet all the time I might be wringing out hot wet cloths and laying them on Mother's closed eyes.

I never spoke of Christian Science to any member of the family. They must have known of my faith for I left tracts around freely hoping someone might see the light! Tolerance meant "Hands off," to Father and Mother. I had a right to my own thoughts and beliefs. They never talked to me. They just left me alone.

Edwin Muir
(1887-1959)

Probably no subject within the psychology of religion has been more extensively studied than conversion. The great variety of mental conflicts and cultural pressures that bedevil the adolescent are etiologically at the root of his religious reorientation.

Allport (1) describes three forms of religious awakening: (1) the definite crisis or conversion experience; (2) the emotional stimulus type of awakening, wherein the individual is able to designate some single event which serves as the effective stimulus to his conversion; and (3) a gradual awakening, with no specifiable occasion being decisive. Usually, after the conversion experience, the adolescent is invaded by a new energy, by feelings of ecstatic fulfillment that defy description, by visions of rebirth and cosmic vistas of sublime beauty.

The change that came over Edwin Muir when he converted at the age of fourteen is reported below.* It would seem that the subtle but ever-present pressure from his mother, combined with the feeling of rejection by her because of his original unwillingness to experience conversion, prompted the boy's step. "I felt alone in the house," he wrote. "I felt impelled towards the only act which would make me one with my family again; for my father and mother and sister were saved, and I was outside, separated from them by an invisible world."

Muir's conversion created a change in him that was undeniable and purifying. It was also temporary, for at the age of twenty-one he became a convert to socialism. This was, in essence, a recapitulation of his earlier conversion.

That winter a revivalist preacher, a thin, tense young man called Macpherson, came to Kirkwall and began to make converts. While we were at Garth the famous John McNeill, a large-scale evangelist, had made a short visit to Orkney, and had preached in the church we attended in Kirkwall. I can remember him dimly; a big, stout, genial man with a black beard, who greatly embarrassed the congregation by keeping them laughing during the whole service, for he was a great wit. He did not make many converts; our people refused to be chaffed into salvation. Later two other revivalists appeared together: one of them, thin, small, and tense, preached hell fire, and the other, tall, stout, and expansive, radiated the love of God. We all went in to hear them one Sunday evening; many people at the end of the service rose from their seats when the preachers summoned them to Christ: I looked on with excitement, but did not understand the glad perturbation of the people round me. As we left the church the two preachers, standing at the door, shook hands with the congregation. It was the big, benevolent preacher who was at our side of the door, and as he took my hand in his large, comforting one he looked down at me and

---

*From *An Autobiography* by Edwin Muir. Reprinted by permission of William Sloane Associates. 1954. Pp. 84-88, 113.

said to my father, "Will not this little fellow come to Christ?" My father, to shield me, murmured something to the effect that perhaps I was too young and tender yet. "What! Too young and tender to come to gentle Jesus!" the preacher said in a shocked voice. My father was much impressed by this answer, and often repeated it afterwards; but I felt that the preacher was not really so shocked as he appeared to be.

This must have happened when I was ten or eleven; I was now fourteen, and, except when I was reading, very unhappy. I paid no attention to the visit of Mr. Macpherson; the boys I went about with jeered at his converts whenever they met them; some of their acquaintances had already been saved. Then my sister Clara was converted, and my mother in her delight drew closer to her. I felt alone in the house; but I was reading *Les Misérables,* and consoled myself with the thought that I too was capable of loving noble things. Yet gradually, by a power independent of myself, I felt impelled towards the only act which would make me one with my family again; for my father and mother and sister were saved, and I was outside, separated from them by an invisible wall. A tremor of the fear which had cut me off in a world of my own at Helye returned, and I began to listen to Mr. Macpherson's outdoor services at the head of the pier, standing well back in the crowd so as not to be seen by my friends. Then one dark cold night—how it happened I do not know—I found myself in the crowd which marched after the preacher, all the length of Kirkwall, to the mission hall. As we passed through the narrow streets groups standing there turned round and stared at us: the unredeemed, whom I still feared so much that I slipped for safety deeper into the heart of the crowd. The people round me marched on side by side, ignoring one another in a sort of embarrassment at still being lost sinners, their eyes fixed straight before them. At last we reached the hall; after the darkness outside the white-washed walls and the yellow benches were so bright that they dazzled me; the worshippers entered, ordinary men and women and children now, smiling at one another as if in secret understanding; the doors were shut; the service began. I remember nothing of it; I probably did not listen, for I was filled with an impatience which did not have anything to do with the words the preacher was saying; all round me people were bursting into sobs and loud cries, as if they too felt the same agonized anticipation and could wait no longer for redemption; and when Mr. Macpherson stopped at last and asked those who had accepted Christ to rise in their places the whole audience rose, lifting me with them, and I found myself on my feet with a wild sense of relief. But the great majority of the audience had accepted Christ already, and the difficult moment came now, for when we had all sat down again the new converts, a mere handful, were asked to walk up to the platform and kneel down at the penitent form, a long wooden bench set there in full view. I hesitated; I was appalled by this naked exposure before people whom I did not know; but when a small group—men, women, boys, and girls—had risen, I rose too and followed them and knelt down. The preacher went along the bench where we were kneeling and asked each of us in turn, "Do you accept Jesus Christ as your personal Saviour?" and when my turn came and I replied, "I do," I felt that these words, which were the seal of my salvation, yet were uttered deliberately, not torn from me, must bring with them an overwhelming assurance; and I was deeply disappointed when they did not, for they seemed merely to be two words. The preacher asked me to offer up a prayer, but I could not think of one, and felt that it would be presumptuous of me, so newly converted, to address God out of my own invention. Beside me was kneeling a red-haired, spectacled young man who served in a shop. He had been the most conspicuous groaner during the service, exclaiming so emphatically that people had looked round at him with surprise and respect; he now burst into a loud and rapid prayer, as if he were already resolved to make a record in the world of the saved. My exaltation did not keep me from feeling slightly annoyed with him for his forwardness; but I suppressed the feeling, telling myself that I must love him. When I got up at last, dazzled, an involuntary smile of joy on my face, and returned to my seat with the others, all the faces of the congregation melted into one great maternal face filled with welcome and wonder, and I felt I was walking straight into a gigantic pair of loving arms.

I went home and told my mother, and returned with a sense of absolute security to Les Misérables, which now seemed a new and holy book, with meanings which I had never guessed at before. But a doubtful look came into my mother's face when she saw me returning so eagerly to a profane story; she stood and thought for a moment, then smiled whimsically, glancing at the book and then at me. I felt she doubted that my conversion was real, and was deeply offended.

What was the nature of my experience that night? For some time afterwards I certainly felt a change within myself; coarse thoughts and words to which I had become hardened during the last year became unendurable to me; I was perpetually happy, and found it easy to reply gently to insults and sneers. The slightest suggestion of evil pierced me to the heart; yet I remained unaffected in some part of myself, as if I were invulnerable. At the same time I found myself often reflecting with relief that I should be leaving Kirkwall in a fortnight, so that I should not have to testify for long before those who had known me: in Glasgow, I told myself, I should associate with the saved from the start; they would be all round me. At times I actually felt ashamed of my new state, belittling it to my friends instead of proclaiming it loudly like the ardent, red-haired shop assistant. I made friends with the Kirkwall boys of my own age who had been saved, and avoided my old companions. Among the saved were some of the roughest boys at the school; they were now incapable of speaking a rude word, and their faces shone with grace. A sort of purification had taken place in us, and it washed away the poisonous stuff which had gathered in me during that year; but it was more a natural than a spiritual cleansing, and more a communal than a personal experience, for it is certain that if the whole audience had not risen that night I should not have risen. To pretend that it was a genuine religious conversion would be ridiculous; I did not know what I was doing; I had no clear knowledge of sin or of the need for salvation; at most I wished to be rescued from the companions among whom I had fallen and to be with the good, with my father and my mother and my sister. Yet the change itself was so undeniable that it astonished me. I was not trying to be changed; I was changed quite beyond my expectation; but the change did not last long.

* * * *

By now I was twenty-one, and though I did not know it, my conversion to Socialism was a recapitulation of my first conversion at fourteen. It was not, that is to say, the result of an intellectual process, but rather a sort of emotional transmutation; the poisonous stuff which had gathered in me during the past few years had found another temporary discharge. I read books on Socialism because they delighted me and were an escape from the world I had known with such painful precision. Having discovered a future in which everything, including myself, was transfigured, I flung myself into it, lived in it, though every day I still worked in the office of the beer-bottling factory, settling the accounts of the lorry-men and answering the jokes of the slum boys. My sense of human potentiality was so strong that even the lorry-men and the slum boys were transformed by it; I no longer saw them as they were, but as they would be when the society of which I dreamed was realized. I felt for them the same love as I had felt for the audience that night in Kirkwall when I returned from the penitent form, but it was a lighter, more hygienic love, by which the future had already purified in anticipation what it would some time purify in truth. For the first time in my life I began to like ordinary vulgar people, because in my eyes they were no longer ordinary or vulgar, since I saw in them shoots of the glory which they would possess when all men and women were free and equal. In spite of its simplicity, this was a genuine imaginative vision of life. It was a pure, earthly vision, for I had now flung away, along with my memories of my squalid youth, everything connected with it, including religion. It was false in being earthly and nothing more; indeed, that alone was what made it false. But I could not have seen it in any other terms then; my horror of my past life was too great. I realized for the first time how I should live with other men and women, and what I should look for in them, and, as after my conversion in Kirkwall, I seemed again to become invulnerable, so that no jealousy among those who were working along with me for Socialism, no weakness or vice, could disgust me or lessen the stationary affection I felt for all of them. It was a state which did not last for long; but having once known it I could sometimes summon it back again.

Jawaharlal Nehru
(1889-   )

At the age of thirteen, under the influence of an English tutor, Jawaharlal Nehru turned to the Theosophism of Mrs. Annie Besant. This was not a true conversion but rather an intellectual one, titillated by the smug feeling of being one of the elite. Although Brahmins of the Hindu faith, neither Nehru nor his father ever followed its rigid codes. When Nehru asked his father for permission to join the Theosophical Society, "he laughingly gave it; he did not seem to attach importance to the subject either way."*

When I was about eleven a new resident tutor, Ferdinand T. Brooks, came and took charge of me. He was partly Irish (on his father's side) and his mother had been a Frenchwoman or a Belgian. He was a keen theosophist who had been recommended to my father by Mrs. Annie Besant. For nearly three years he was with me and in many ways he influenced me greatly. The only other tutor I had at the time was a dear old Pandit who was supposed to teach me Hindi and Sanskrit. After many years' effort the Pandit managed to teach me extraordinarily little, so little that I can only measure my pitiful knowledge of Sanskrit with the Latin I learnt subsequently at Harrow. The fault,

*From *Toward Freedom* by Jawaharlal Nehru. Reprinted by permission of The John Day Co., Inc. 1936. Pp. 14-16.

no doubt was mine. I am not good at languages, and grammar has had no attraction for me whatever.

F. T. Brooks developed in me a taste for reading and I read a great many English books, though rather aimlessly. I was well up in children's and boys' literature; the Lewis Carroll books were great favourites, and *The Jungle Books* and *Kim*. I was fascinated by Gustave Doré's illustrations to *Don Quixote,* and Fridtjof Nansen's *Farthest North* opened out a new realm of adventure to me. I remember reading many of the novels of Scott, Dickens and Thackeray, H. G. Wells's romances, Mark Twain, and the Sherlock Holmes stories. I was thrilled by the *Prisoner of Zenda,* and Jerome K. Jerome's *Three Men in a Boat* was for me the last word in humour. Another book stands out still in my memory; it was Du Maurier's *Trilby,* also *Peter Ibbetson*. I also developed a liking for poetry, a liking which has to some extent endured and survived the many other changes to which I have been subject.

Brooks also initiated me into the mysteries of science. We rigged up a little laboratory and there I used to spend long and interesting hours working out experiments in elementary physics and chemistry.

Apart from my studies, F. T. Brooks brought a new influence to bear upon me which affected me powerfully for a while. This was Theosophy. He used to have weekly meetings of theosophists in his rooms and I attended them and gradually imbibed theosophical phraseology and ideas. There were metaphysical arguments, and discussions about reincarnation and the astral and other super-natural bodies, and auras, and the doctrine of *Karma,* and references not only to big books by Madame Blavatsky and other Theosophists but to the Hindu scriptures, the Buddhist *"Dhammapada,"* Pythagoras, Apollonius of Tyana, and various philosophers and mystics. I did not understand much that was said but it all sounded very mysterious and fascinating and I felt that here was the key to the secrets of the universe. For the first time I began to think, consciously and deliberately, of religion and other worlds. The Hindu religion especially went up in my estimation; not the ritual or ceremonial part, but its great books, the *"Upanishads"* and the *"Bhagavad Gita."* I did not understand them, of course, but they seemed very wonderful. I dreamt of astral bodies and imagined myself flying vast distances. This dream of flying high up in the air (without any appliance) has indeed been a frequent one throughout my life; and sometimes it has been vivid and realistic and the countryside seemed to lie underneath me in a vast panorama. I do not know how the modern interpreters of dreams, Freud and others, would interpret this dream.

Mrs. Annie Besant visited Allahabad in those days and delivered several addresses on theosophical subjects. I was deeply moved by her oratory and returned from her speeches dazed and as in a dream. I decided to join the Theosophical Society, although I was only thirteen then. When I went to ask father's permission he laughingly gave it; he did not seem to attach importance to the subject either way. I was a little hurt by his lack of feeling. Great as he was in many ways in my eyes, I felt that he was lacking in spirituality. As a matter of fact he was an old theosophist, having joined the Society in its early days when Madame Blavatsky was in India. Curiosity probably led him to it more than religion, and he soon dropped out of it, but some of his friends, who had joined with him, persevered and rose high in the spiritual hierarchy of the Society.

So I became a member of the Theosophical Society at thirteen and Mrs. Besant herself performed the ceremony of initiation, which consisted of good advice and instruction in some mysterious signs, probably a relic of freemasonry. I was thrilled. I attended the Theosophical Convention at Benares and saw old Colonel Olcott with his fine beard.

It is difficult to realise what one looked like or felt like in one's boyhood, thirty years ago. But I have a fairly strong impression that during these theosophical days of mine I developed the flat and insipid look which sometimes denotes piety and which is (or was) often to be seen among theosophist men and women. I was smug, with a feeling of being one-of-the-elect, and altogether I must have been a thoroughly undesirable and unpleasant companion for any boy or girl of my age.

Soon after F. T. Brooks left me I lost touch with Theosophy, and in a remarkably short time (partly because I went to school in England) Theosophy left my life completely. But I have no doubt that those years with F. T. Brooks left a deep impress upon me and I feel that I owe a debt to him and to Theosophy. But I am afraid that theosophists have since then gone down in my estimation. Instead of the chosen ones they seem to be very ordinary folk, liking security better than risk, a soft job more than the martyr's lot. But, for Mrs. Besant, I always had the warmest admiration.

Crashing Thunder
(? - ?)

The Winnebago Indian of Nebraska passes from the period of childhood—*ninkdjck'*—to that of youth—*hodjána*—at about the age of twelve or thirteen. At this time he performs the ritual described below. The fasting, the fear of the spirits "from the heavens and from the earth," their blessings, and the telling of the sacred stories have their counterparts in the religions of more literate societies. Similarly, the feelings that the Indian youth expresses in this passage* are akin to those of his more sophisticated peers. Crashing Thunder reveals his dread of subterfuge and his guilt feeling about deceiving his elders so that he might seem to fulfill their expectations for him.

When the girls with whom I used to play moved away I became very lonesome. In the evenings I used to cry. I longed for them greatly, and they had moved far away!

After a while we got fairly well started on our way back. I fasted all the time. We moved back to a place where all the leaders used to give their feasts. Near the place where we lived there were three lakes and a black hawk's nest. Right near the tree where the nest was located they built a lodge and the war-bundle that we possessed was placed in the lodge.[1] We were to pass the night there, my older brother and myself. It was said that if anyone fasted at such a place for four nights he would always be blessed with victory and the power to cure the sick. All the spirits would bless him.

"The first night spent there one imagined oneself surrounded by spirits whose whisperings were heard outside of the lodge," they said. The spirits would even whistle. I would be frightened and nervous, and if I remained there I would be molested by large monsters, fearful to look upon. Even (the bravest) might be frightened, I was told. Should I, however, get through that night, I would on the following night be molested by ghosts whom I would hear speaking outside. They would say things that might cause me to run away. Towards morning they would even take my blanket away from me. They would grab hold of me and drive me out of the lodge, and they would not stop until the sun rose. If I was able to endure the third night, on the fourth night I would really be addressed by spirits, it was said, who would bless me, saying, "I bless you. We had turned you over to the (monsters, etc.) and that is why they approached you, but you over-

---

*From *The Autobiography of a Winnebago Indian* edited by Paul Radin. Reprinted by permission of University of California Press. 1920. Pp. 388-391.

[1] Every Winnebago clan has at least one war-bundle; most of them have more. The father of S. B. possessed one, and most of the "power" resident in this particular bundle was supposed to have been bestowed by the thunder-birds and night-spirits. Perhaps that is why a black-hawk's nest was selected for the fasting-lodge, the black-hawk being regarded as a thunder-bird, although my interpreter was uncertain about the matter.

came them and now they will not be able to take you away. Now you may go home, for with victory and long life we bless you and also with the power of healing the sick.[2] Nor shall you lack wealth (literally, 'people's possessions'). So go home and eat, for a large war-party is soon to fall upon you who, as soon as the sun rises in the morning, will give the war whoop and if you do not go home now, they will kill you."[3]

Thus the spirits would speak to me. However if I did not do the bidding of this particular spirit, then another one would address me and say very much the same sort of thing. So they would speak until the break of day, and just before sunrise a man in warrior's regalia would come and peep in. He would be a scout. Then I would surely think a war-party had come upon me, I was told.

Then another spirit would come and say, "Well, grandson, I have taken pity upon you and I bless you with all the good things that the earth holds. Go home now for the war-party is about to rush upon you." And if I then went home, as soon as the sun rose the war whoop would be given. The members of the war party would give the war whoop all at the same time. They would rush upon me and capture me and after the fourth one had counted coup, then they would say, "Now then, grandson, this we did to teach you. Thus you shall act. You have completed your fasting." Thus they would talk to me, I was told. This war party was composed entirely of spirits, I was told, spirits from the heavens and from the earth; indeed all the spirits that exist would all be there. These would all bless me. They also told me that it would be a very difficult thing to accomplish this particular fasting.

So there I fasted, at the black hawk's nest where a lodge had been built for me. The first night I stayed there I wondered when things would happen; but nothing took place. The second night, rather late

[2] It was customary for parents, generally grandparents, to tell youths who were fasting what kind of an experience they were to expect, and particularly how they were to recognize the true spirit when he should appear and thus guard against being deceived by an evil spirit. Apparently S. B.'s father told the youth in considerable detail what he was to expect on this particular occasion. The supernatural experience given here is peculiar in a number of respects; first, because it contains many elements distinctly intended to frighten the faster, and secondly, because it contains a well-known motif taken from the origin myth of the Four Nights' Wake. In practically all the fasting experiences I collected among the Winnebago the spirits are pictured simply as offering their blessings and having them refused or accepted by the faster. The test theme so prominent here does not occur at all. Apart from these facts, the experience is a good example of the type one would expect to find among the Winnebago, and perhaps the Woodland-Plains tribes in general.

[3] Practically every Winnebago fasting experience contains an attempt of an evil spirit to deceive the faster.

in the night, my father came and opened the war-bundle and taking a gourd out began to sing. I stood beside him without any clothing on me except the breech-clout, and holding tobacco in each hand I uttered my cry to the spirits as my father sang. He sang war bundle songs and he wept as he sang. I also wept as I uttered my cry to the spirits. When he was finished he told me some sacred stories, and then went home.

When I found myself alone I began to think that something ought to happen to me soon, yet nothing occurred so I had to pass another day there. On the third night I was still there. My father visited me again and we repeated what we had done the night before. In the morning, just before sunrise, I uttered my cry to the spirits. The fourth night found me still there. Again my father came and we did the same things, but in spite of it all, I experienced nothing unusual. Soon another day dawned upon us. That morning I told my elder brother that I had been blessed by spirits and that I was going home to eat. However I was not telling the truth. I was hungry and I also knew that on the following night we were going to have a feast and that I would have to utter my cry to the spirits again. I dreaded that. So I went home. When I got there I told my people the story I had told my brother; that I had been blessed and that the spirits had told me to eat. I was not speaking the truth, yet they gave me the food that is carefully prepared for those who have been blessed. Just then my older brother came home and they objected to his return for he had not been blessed. However, he took some food and ate it.

That night we gave our feast. There, however, our pride received a fall,[4] for although it was supposedly given in our honor, we were placed on one side (of the main participants). After the kettles of food had been put on twice, it became daylight.

The following spring we moved to the Mississippi in order to trap. I was still fasting and ate only at night. My brothers used to flatter me, telling me I was the cleverest of them all. In consequence I used to continue to fast although I was often very hungry. However, (in spite of my desire to fast) I could not resist the temptation to be around girls. I wanted always to be near them and was forever looking for them, although I had been strictly forbidden to go near them, for they were generally in their menstrual lodges when I sought them out. My parents most emphatically did not wish me to go near them, but I did nevertheless.

My parents told me that only those boys who had had no connec-

---

[4] It was a common practice for the older people to treat the younger men in this way, in order to train them in humility.

tion with women, would be blessed by the spirits. However, all that I desired was to appear great in the sight of the people. To be praised by my fellow-men was all that I desired. And I certainly received all I sought. I stood high in their estimation. That the women might like me was another of the reasons why I wanted to fast. However, as to being blessed, I learned nothing about it, although I went around with the air of one who had received many blessings and talked as such a one would talk.

Hsieh Pingying was born in Hunan province and Yen Liang, a decade later, in Peiping. They are coupled here because they have much in common. Miss Pingying was a rebel all her life who fought in early adolescence against the double standard for men and women in China. Miss Liang, of Mongolian parentage, came from a traditional Buddhist family, but she too rebelled against the restrictions of "genteel" women working and against arranged marriages.

At eighteen, Miss Liang's father wanted her to be married. She wanted to study in the United States. In desperation, she managed to secure a tutoring job to the two sons of a prince, but when her father discovered this, she was forced to resign. In her misery, she turned to religion.*

In the second selection, Hsieh Pingying had won her battle with her mother for an education and was placed in a missionary school. She was fourteen at the time, full of doubts about religion, and refused to join her classmates in prayer at mealtime.**

Yen Liang
(1917-   )

On the third evening of my teaching, Mother came to my quarters. "Your father has learned. He feels it is terrible for him that you are out earning money. He demands that you stop."

My body tightened. "What's wrong with it? I'm proving I can take care of myself." My lips trembled. "What's wrong—"

"I know, Daughter. I have said that."

---

*From *Daughter of the Khans* by Yen Liang. Reprinted by permission of W. W. Norton & Co., Inc. 1955. Pp. 56-57.

**From *Girl Rebel* by Hsieh Pingying. Reprinted by permission of The John Day Co., Inc. 1940. Pp. 41-43.

I was in tears. "They have been so kind. . . . How will I have face to tell them?"

"Your father says to tell them you are ill."

Next morning I telephoned that message. The old prince must have understood, for he never called to ask when I would be back.

I turned to religion.

Refusing to leave my quarters, I read Buddhist scripture, kept an incense burner lighted, prayed kneeling before a picture of Kwan Yin. Since Buddhists were vegetarians, I passed up meat, fowl, even the sea food that was my favorite fare, and lived on noodles and greens.

I thought: I will become a Buddhist nun—or as nearly one as possible without taking vows. They cannot draw me back from this path of purity into their dirty world. They cannot marry me off.

And so it was. There was opposition, yes—with Father and Mother sending in relatives to talk about the virtues of marriage, the hardships of nunhood. But there was no dragging me out of my courtyard, for it would be unrighteous thus to prevent a search for purity.

I never smiled, never wept either, never said more than: "Yes," "No," "I don't know." I even neglected the flowers and stopped admiring the butterflies in the garden outside my windows.

But after about three months I gave up my nun-like life. I was growing afraid that I would really become a nun.

Hsieh Pingying
(1907-   )

No one knew that from the day I entered the school I had a heavy weight pressing on my heart. It was that I did not believe in God, and I did not like to read the Bible. I did not like saying the Lord's Prayer before meals, "Our Father, Who art in Heaven . . . " I liked singing the hymns, but I did not like singing:

> The love of God is perfect,
> When we die, He will protect us.

Wanting to avoid the prayer, I would sit in the privy and suffer every morning and evening or at meal times. Miss Wu discovered that I was being late to meals and told me to go to the matron's office.

"Why are you always late in going to meals?" she asked me.

"I did not hear the bell."

"What were you doing?"

"Reading the Bible."

"Are you really so hard-working?" she asked. "Isn't it true that you don't like the Bible?"

"Why shouldn't I speak the truth?" I replied. "Who said that I did not like the Bible? I was not interested in reading the Bible before, but now I know that God is the only Savior of the world. I believe in Him and worship Him."

She smiled and patted my head. "Don't tell lies before God. Henceforth, come to the prayer before meals."

"Certainly!" I muttered with my mouth, but in my heart I said, "Ha, ha! God knows . . ."

My knowledge was childish and my mind was simple; I had no profound reasons for not believing in God. I just felt that there was no such thing as God. "Anyone who believes in God is saved." That seemed really a joke. Why did the people who came to church on Sundays in poor dresses always stay poor? God could not give them dresses, food, board, could not heal their sicknesses, and what is more could not find them jobs. As for saying that God would punish these poor people by making them poor because they had sinned, this was "nasty talk." I did not think there was a God anyway. I only knew that men were the gods who were building the world and must depend entirely on themselves.

The news of my not believing in God and not going to church soon got to my brother's ears. He came to warn me and said, "Sister, don't cause trouble or the school will dismiss you. Then I will have to take you home, and good-by to your dream of studying again!"

That night I could not sleep. What was there for me to do? No matter what, I could not believe in God; if they really would expel me for that, then let them expel me.

Simone de Beauvoir
(1908-   )

Simone de Beauvoir, the brilliant author of *The Second Sex* and *Memoirs of a Dutiful Daughter,* was a very proper, if willful, girl in a well-ordered bourgeois Parisian household. She dreamed of entering a convent even as her young mind began to question the black-and-white laws of obedience and convention that surrounded her. Her defection from the Catholic church is graphically illustrated in this section from her autobiography,* from the crucial

Memoirs of a Dutiful Daughter translated by James Kirkup. Reprinted by permission of World Publishing Co. Copyright 1959, World Publishing Co. Pp. 141-142, 146-148.

confessional in the school chapel to the self-discovery that God had no influence on her behavior. We see her marked spiritual turmoil and the heavy burden of carrying her religious defection all alone. Even though "I had done nothing wrong," she cried out in her anguish, "I felt guilty. I was the victim of a spell which I couldn't manage to exorcise." All her attempts to regain faith failed and she resigned herself "to the life of an outcast."

All nature spoke to me of God's presence. But quite definitely it seemed to me that He was a total stranger to the restless world of men. Just as the Pope, away inside the Vatican, hadn't to bother his head about what was going on in the world, so God, high up in the infinity of heaven, was not supposed to take any interest in the details of earthly adventures. I had long since learned to distinguish His law from secular authority. My insolence in class, and my furtive reading of banned books did not concern Him. As year followed after year, my growing piety was purified and I began to reject dry-as-dust mortality in favor of a more lively mysticism. I prayed, I meditated, I tried to make my heart aware of the divine presence. About the age of twelve I invented mortifications: locked in the water closet—my sole refuge—I would scrub my flesh with pumice stone until the blood came, and beat myself with the thin golden chain I wore around my neck. My fervor did not bear fruit. In my devotional books there was much talk about spiritual progress and exaltation; souls were supposed to stagger up rugged paths and overcome obstacles; one moment they would be trudging across barren wildernesses and then a celestial dew would fall for their refreshment: it was quite an adventure; in fact, whereas intellectually I felt I was moving ever onward and upward in my quest for knowledge, I never had the impression that I was drawing any closer to God. I longed for apparitions, ecstasies; I yearned for something to happen inside or outside me: but nothing came, and in the end my spiritual exercises were more and more like make-believe. I exhorted myself to have patience and looked forward to the day when, miraculously detached from the earth, I would find myself ensconced at the heart of eternity. Meanwhile I was able to go on living unconstrainedly on earth because my efforts set me up on spiritual peaks whose serenity could not be troubled by worldly trifles.

My complacency received a nasty shock. For the last seven years I had been making my confession to Abbé Martin twice a month; I would expatiate upon the state of my immortal soul; I would accuse myself of having taken Holy Communion without any true religious fervor, of not having thought often enough of God, and of having

paid Him only lip service in my prayers; he would reply to these ethe-
real shortcomings with a sermon couched in very elevated terms. But
one day, instead of going through the usual rigmarole, he began to
speak to me in a more familiar tone of voice: "It has come to my ears
that my little Simone has changed . . . that she is disobedient, noisy,
that she answers back when she is reprimanded . . . From now on you
must be careful about these things." My cheeks were aflame; I gazed
with horror upon the impostor whom for years I had taken as the
representative of God on earth; it was as if he had suddenly tucked up
his cassock and revealed the skirts of one of the religious bigots; his
priest's robe was only a disguise; it covered an old busybody who fed
on gossip. With burning face I left the confessional, determined never
to set foot in it again: from that moment on, it would have been as
repugnant to me to kneel before Abbé Martin as before "the Old
Scarecrow." Whenever I caught a glimpse of his black skirts swishing
along a school corridor, my heart would begin to thump and I would
run away: they made me feel physically sick, as if the abbé's deceit had
made me his accomplice in some obscene act.

I suppose he must have been very surprised; but probably he felt
himself bound by the secret of the confessional; I never heard that he
told anyone of my defection; he did not attempt to have it out with
me. The break had been sudden, but complete.

. . . My changed attitude did not affect my daily life. I had stopped
believing in God when I discovered that God had no influence on my
behavior: so this did not change in any way when I gave Him up. I had
always imagined that the logical necessity of moral laws depended on
Him: but they were so deeply engraved on my spirit that they remained unaltered for me after I had abolished Him. It was my respect
for her which gave my mother's rulings a sacred character, and not the
fact that she might owe her authority to some supernatural power. I
went on submitting myself to her decisions. Everything was as before:
the concept of duty; righteousness; sexual taboos.

I had no intention of revealing my spiritual turmoil to my father:
it would have put him in a terribly embarrassing situation. So I bore
my secret all alone and found it a heavy burden: for the first time in
my life I had the feeling that good was not necessarily the same thing
as truth. I couldn't help seeing myself through the eyes of others—my
mother, Zaza, my school friends, my teachers even—and through the
eyes of the girl I once had been. The year before, in the philosophy
class, there had been an older pupil of whom it was rumored that she
was an "unbeliever"; she worked well, she never expressed subver-
sive notions, and she had not been expelled; but I would feel a sort of

terror whenever, in the school corridors, I caught sight of her face, which was all the more disturbing because of the fixed intensity of a glass eye. Now it was my turn to feel I was a black sheep. My case was aggravated by deception: I still went to Mass and took Holy Communion. I would swallow the Host with complete indifference, and yet I knew that, according to the faith, I was committing a sacrilege. I was making my crime all the worse by concealing it; but how could I have dared confess it? I would have been pointed at with the finger of scorn, expelled from the school; I would have lost Zaza's friendship; and how terribly upset my mother would have been! I was condemned to live out a lie. It was no harmless fib: it was a lie that cast a shadow over my whole life, and sometimes—especially with Zaza whose forthrightness I admired—it weighed upon my spirits like a secret disease. Once again I was the victim of a spell which I couldn't manage to exorcise: I had done nothing wrong, and I felt guilty. If the grownups had called me a hypocrite, a blasphemer, an unnatural and crafty child, their verdict would have seemed to me at once horribly unjust and perfectly well-deserved. I could be said to be living a double life; there was no relationship between my true self and the self that others saw.

Sometimes I suffered such distress at feeling myself a marked person, an accursed outcast, that I longed to fall into error again. I had to return the *Handbook of Ascetic and Mystical Theology* to Abbé Roullin. I went back to Saint-Sulpice, knelt down in his confessional, and told him that I had not partaken of the sacraments for several months because I had lost my faith. Seeing the *Handbook* and measuring the heights from which I had fallen, the abbé was astounded, and with a disconcerting brutality asked me: "What mortal sin have you committed?" I protested that I had not committed any sin. He did not believe me and advised me to pray hard. I resigned myself to the life of an outcast.

Najmeh Najafi
(c. 1932-   )

Najmeh Najafi was born in Persia. When she was fifteen, she was shocked to hear her very rich and very religious uncle declare that she was not a good Moslem. It was then that "I first went outside myself and looked inside at my soul."

Although she read the Koran daily, kept the fast of Ramazon, made pilgrimages to the sacred shrines, and prayed at dawn, twice at noon, and again in the evenings, she wanted to believe but wondered what to believe.*

I do not know when I first went outside myself and looked inside at my soul. Perhaps it was the evening at my uncle's home when he said, "Najmeh is not a good Moslem."

I could not believe that he had really said these words. I could not believe, even if the words had been spoken by my very good uncle, that they were true. I felt his wife's eyes on my face, and looking toward her I saw there was understanding and deep affection on her sweet face, but she did not say a word to refute my uncle's harsh statement.

We, my mother and I, were guests in her half-brother's home. Often the two of us spent an evening there; since I had grown up I could spend fewer and fewer days with this aunt who loved me. My uncle, who was very rich and very religious, was also very warm toward my mother and her children. This evening we had been talking of the pilgrimage to Mecca. In the Islamic religion every one longs to go one time at least to the holy city of Mecca. It takes a great deal of money to do this, not for the traveling alone, but for the alms one must give on this holy pilgrimage. When my father died my mother had enough money to give the alms and go to Mecca. However, she chose to sell her property a parcel at a time to rear her family, to make a home for us, and to educate us.

This evening by uncle was saying that she should have gone to Mecca and I said, more politely than it can be said in English, of course, "Uncle, why do you give alms to the shrines that already have very much money instead of helping the poor of Teheran or the starving people of the villages?"

He looked at me as if I had said a very evil thing. He did not answer the question, just said flatly, "Najmeh is not a good Moslem."

I did not answer. Maybe he was right. But I now had my eyes on something that before had been hidden.

At first I felt anger at my uncle for speaking such words. If I were not a good Moslem, whose fault was it. It was in his home that I had seen people living devotedly according to the ancient customs. It was there that my brother Mosen had learned to join in the call to prayer —"Allah Akbar, Allah Akbar, Allah Akbar." It was his wife who had first taught me the devotions, bribing me to learn them with candy

---

*From *Persia is My Heart* by Najmeh Najafi as told by Helen Hinckley. Reprinted by permission of Harper & Bros. Copyright 1953, Najmeh Najafi and Helen Hinckley Jones. Pp. 159-164.

and cookies and fruits. She had taught me the mohbah, the mostahab, the makruh, the haram, and the vajeb.

But now my uncle had said, "Najmeh is not a good Moslem."

Going home I studied his words. I read the Koran every day, most often aloud to my mother, and found in every word enough to live for many years. I kept the fast of Ramazon. Although I had never been to Mecca I had been to the sacred shrines closer to Teheran. I thought now of the shrine of Imam Riza in Meshed. I remembered going at midnight to pray. A most beautiful voice ringing like a deep gong from the minaret had announced the time for praying—a beautiful voice that shook my soul—and the camels coming under the deep blue sky to bring food for the city. God had been with me in Meshed, though I had never been to Mecca.

I was clean. I prayed before dawn, twice at noon, and again in the evenings, and while I did not give regular alms I was still young and gave of what I had to those I saw in need. I thought of the vajeb, the mohbah, the mostahab, the makruh, and the haram. I could not think of sins which I had committed, only good things that I had left undone, sometimes, perhaps.

"Mother," I said, troubled, "am I a good Moslem?"

"Think nothing of those words," my mother said, and I knew she had been concerned by them, too. "You are an angel. We do not need to go to that home again."

But I knew how much the closeness of her brother had meant to her since the death of my father so I said, "It is all right. He has not broken my feelings."

But I could not forget his words and perhaps they were good for me, because I searched my mind and my heart, and I studied and read more religious books, trying to measure my own soul. This sounds unusual for a young girl, but in my country the religious life is important. For the first time I really saw Mohammed, the prophet, as a young man, wanting to believe, but wondering what to believe.

*   *   *   *

After my uncle's words I spent more time than ever with the Koran. The words took on deeper and deeper meaning.

Praise be to God, Lord of the worlds
The compassionate, the merciful
King on the day of reckoning!

Thee only do we worship and to Thee we cry for help.
Guide Thou us on the straight path,
The path of those to whom Thou hast been gracious;
With whom Thou are not angry, and who go not astray.

But there were other things which I had read carelessly before which now began to trouble me. For the first time I began to think of religion as a matter of chance and of geography.

I was born in Persia, in a Moslem home, so I was what the Koran calls a "believer." But I was a believer not because of any special quality in my own heart but because my mother taught me these things. Had I been born in another country perhaps a Christian mother would have led me to a different church telling me different things.

In the Koran I read that all unbelievers are destined to hell; but as I read other books I found that Catholics, for example, believe that the unbaptized go to hell. I was worried. I had said so often in my devotions that God is compassionate and merciful, and it was hard for me to add in my thoughts, "to Moslems, only."

Maybe that is why I am not a "good Moslem." I do not have strongly enough the feeling that we are a special people. I think of the world worshiping God in different ways but God being compassionate to all.

Often, here in America, people ask me if I believe the Koran. Of course I believe the Koran, but I believe—what do you call it?—historically. Besides, I am not wise enough to say I do believe or I don't believe every special thing.

REFERENCES

1. Allport, Gordon. *The Individual and His Religion, a Psychological Interpretation*. New York: Macmillan, 1950.
2. Bashkirtseff, Marie. *Journal*. Translated by A. D. Hall. Chicago: Rand McNally, 1889.
3. Bewick, Thomas. *Memoirs of Thomas Bewick, Written by Himself, 1822-1828*. New York: Dial Press, 1925, p. 57.
4. Bishop, Elizabeth (Ed.). *The Diary of "Helena Morley."* New York: Farrar, Straus & Cudahy, 1957, p. xxvi.
5. Blos, Peter. *The Adolescent Personality*. New York: Appleton-Century-Crofts, 1941, p. 420.
6. Freud, Sigmund. *The Future of an Illusion*. London: Hogarth Press, 1943.
7. ——. Leonardo Da Vinci and a memory of his childhood. In: *Standard Edition*. London: Hogarth Press, pp. 59-137.

8. James, William. *The Varieties of Religious Experience. A Study in Human Nature.* New York: New American Library, 1958, p. 79.

9. Jones, Ernest. *Free Associations. Memories of a Psycho-Analyst.* New York: Basic Books, 1959, p. 57.

10. Linn, Louis, & Schwarz, Leo W. *Psychiatry and Religious Experience.* New York: Random House, 1958, p. 49.

11. Omori, Annie Shepley, and Doi, Kochi (Trans.). *Diaries of Court Ladies of Old Japan.* Boston: Houghton Mifflin, 1920, p. 33.

12. Rogers, Hester Ann. *A Short Account of the Experiences of Mrs. Hester Ann Rogers.* New York: Daniel Hitt & Thomas Ware, 1815, pp. 3, 7-12, 14-15.

CHAPTER FOURTEEN

Vocation and Identification

In all cultures, the primary status of the individual is achieved through his occupational role. It is recognized, of course, that there are varying degrees of emphasis placed upon the acquisition of superior status or competence. As Ausubel (2) states, "The universal fact [remains] that considerable variability is found in the relative status needs of different individuals *within* a homogeneous cultural setting and that such differences in urgency and magnitude of need are largely a function of the pressure or absence of intrinsic feelings of adequacy." Thus he concludes that whenever socioeconomic roles are differentiated by a functional division of labor or a hierarchy of social prestige values, the typical occupation of the individual defines and symbolizes his relative position in the stratified social organization that almost inevitably results.

Not until the adolescent assumes a productive occupational role is he generally considered to be an adult. Inhelder and Piaget (12) put it this way: "On a naive global level, without trying to distinguish between the student, the apprentice, the young worker, or the young peasant in terms of how their social attitudes may vary, the adolescent differs from the child above all in that he thinks beyond the present. The adolescent is the individual who commits himself to possibilities—although we certainly do not mean to deny that his commitment begins in real-life situations. In other words, the adolescent is the individual who begins to build 'systems' or 'theories,' in the largest sense of the term. . . . But this does not mean that the adolescent takes his place in adult society merely in terms of general theories and without personal involvement. Two other aspects of his entrance into adult society have to be considered —his life program, and his plans for changing the society he sees. ... The focal point of the decentering process [from the egocentrism of the adolescent] is the entrance into the occupational world or the beginning of serious professional training. The adolescent becomes an adult when he undertakes a real job. It is then he is transformed from an idealistic reformer into an achiever."

"When I gaze back," wrote Ernest Jones (13) in *Free Associations, Memories of a Psycho-Analyst,* "through the mists of more than half a century, at that youth of seventeen I am persuaded that the picture I conjure up is not very far from the truth. It is that of a youth who, though bright, quick and intelligent somewhat above the average, had no special endowment of facility, aptitude, or mental powers; he had to work hard for everything he acquired. Outwardly merry and friendly, inwardly he was over-earnest for his age. There was a good supply of self-confidence, still more of hopefulness, but stronger still was a deep sense of duty—not so much of obligation towards the world as the benevolent desire to do something for its good. This desire, or ideal, was surely the dominating influence in his nature, one that must have been transmitted, in different forms, from both parents. It had, of course, its narcissistic components as well. There was the confident belief that he had it within him to achieve some lofty aim and, further, the worldly ambition to reach some position in life that would give him the necessary opportunity for influencing his fellow-men. But these components were harmonized with the altruistic ones, to which they were definitely subordinated. Clearly a nature exposed in an unusual degree to the inevitable blows and disappointments of life, but one with enough resilience not to be broken by them. And so it proved."

For the adolescent, the question, "What shall I be?" actually means, "With whom shall I identify?" Central to his problem of vocational choice is the problem of identification. Work mastery in any culture, states Erikson (5), is the backbone of identity formation. The adolescent's feelings about vocation and work are reflected in his feelings about his independent masculine role. A healthy approach to this area requires successful masculine identifications, which must necessarily involve the functions of the father and sexual privileges. "Work goals," says Erikson, "by no means only support or exploit the suppression of infantile instinctual aims; they also enhance the functioning of the ego, in that they offer constructive activity with actual tools and materials in a communal reality. The ego's tendency to turn passivity into activity here thus acquires a new field of manifestation, in many ways superior to the mere turning of passive into active in infantile fantasy and play; for now the inner need for activity, practice, and work completion is ready to meet the corresponding demands and opportunities in social reality."

The turning of passivity into activity is seen in August Forel's late childhood experiences. "Apart from my visits to my grandparents," wrote Forel (6), who was later to become an authority on entomology, "I was cut off from all human intercourse. My mother would not even let me go into the garden alone; a maid had always to go with me. Completely isolated from other children, I grew shyer than ever, and I gradually came to regard myself as a sort of exception, an inferior being, unfitted for life. With my sister, who was very self-willed and unruly, I was on the worst of terms. It was no wonder that my imagination sought nourishment where it could find it. And it found it in my physical environment, in Nature. To begin with, I took an enthusiastic interest in snails, which were crawling about everywhere; it delighted me to observe their deliberate wanderings, and to watch them at last laboriously climbing a tree. . . . They were my first love." At the age of eleven, Forel's grandmother gave him Pierre Huber's *History of the Ants* "which literally became my Bible." August's inability to identify with his father led him to his uncle who was a naturalist and who, significantly, supported the boy in his fights with his parents.

When the adolescent complains that he cannot find himself, vocationally, it is usually symptomatic of the incompleteness of mastery of feeling about himself, his sexual orientation, and his social role (16). The subtle and overt pressures brought to bear on him by his family are great and pervasive. Goethe (9) wrote nearly two hundred years ago in his autobiography, "It is a laudable wish of all fathers to see realised in their sons what they themselves have failed to attain, almost as if they lived for a second time and wished to use aright the experiences of their first career." Lorenzo da Ponte (17), a contemporary of Goethe, verified the latter's analysis:

"My father, being deceived in the choice of my career, and allowing himself to be guided rather by his circumstances than by his parental duty, was thinking of turning me to the Altar; though that was utterly contrary to my vocation and my character. I was therefore trained after the manner of the priests, though inclined by taste and, as it were, made by nature for different pursuits."

In 1819, when George Borrow (3) was sixteen years old, his "parents deemed it necessary that I should adopt some profession, they named the law; the law was as agreeable to me as any other profession within my reach, so I adopted the law." Strikingly casual as this choice may seem, the startling declaration of John Stuart Mill leaves the reader breathless. "In May, 1823 [he was seventeen years old], my professional occupation and status for the next thirty-five years of my life, were decided by my father's obtaining for me an appointment from the East India Company, in the office of the Examiner of India Correspondence, immediately under himself [15, p. 53]." With this abrupt sentence, Mill tells us his destiny. No glimmer of his feelings at the time emerges, and in retrospect, it would seem, he rationalized. "I do not know any one of the occupations by which a subsistence can now be gained, more suitable than such as this to any one who, not being in independent circumstances, desires to devote a part of the twenty-four hours to private intellectual pursuits." However, Mill touched on his difficulty in expressing feelings, commenting on the coldness of the English people and the unreal, extravagant sentiment of the poets. For him, logic and reason predominated. " . . . My father's teachings tended to the undervaluing of feelings." There seems to be a wistfulness here, but he hurried on to a defense of his father. "It was not that he was himself cold-hearted or insensible; I believe it was rather from the contrary quality; he thought that feeling could take care of itself. . . . " But in his early twenties, after painfully surviving a period of profound depression, Mill was able to write, "The cultivation of the feelings became one of the cardinal points in my ethical and philosophical creed. And my thoughts and inclinations turned in an increasing degree towards whatever seemed capable of being instrumental to that object [15, p. 93]." It is interesting to speculate about Mill's choice of career had he been able to achieve self-identity through the freedom to express himself during adolescence and had he not been so dominated by his strong-willed father.

A more reasonable parent was Theodore Roosevelt's. "When I entered college," toward the end of the 1870's, Roosevelt (18) wrote, "I was devoted to out-of-doors natural history, and my ambition was to be a scientific man of the Audubon, or Wilson, or Baird, or Coues type—a man like Hart Merriam, or Frank Chapman, or Hornaday, today. My father had from the earliest days instilled into me the knowledge that I was to work and to make my own way in the world, and I had always supposed that this meant that I must enter business. But in my freshman year (he died when I was a sophomore) he told me that if I wished to become a scientific man I could do so. He explained that I must be sure that I really intensely desired to do scientific work, because if I went into it I must make it a serious career; that he had made enough money to enable me to take up such a career and do non-remunerative work of value if I intended to do the very best work there was in me; but that I must not dream of taking it up as a dilettante."

Trotsky's revolutionary career began in his home and very early in life. When he was seventeen, "in the autumn of 1896, I visited the country [his father's farm] after all; but the visit resulted only in a brief truce. Father wanted me to become an engineer, whereas I hesitated between pure mathematics, to which I was very strongly attached, and Revolution, which little by little was taking possession of me. Every time this question arose there was an acute family crisis. Everybody looked depressed, and seemed to suffer intensely; my elder sister would weep furtively and nobody knew what to do about it. One of my uncles, an engineer and owner of a plant in Odessa, who was staying in the country with us, persuaded me to come and visit him in the city. This was at least a temporary relief from the *impasse* [22]."

In *Mein Kampf*, Hitler (11) made much of a dramatic conflict between himself and his father over his ambition to become an artist. According to Shirer, the story of the bitter unrelenting struggle of the boy against a hardened and domineering father is one of the few autobiographical items which Hitler set down in great detail and with apparent sincerity and truth in *Mein Kampf*. "The conflict aroused the first manifestation of that fierce, unbending will which later would carry [Hitler] so far despite seemingly insuperable obstacles and handicaps and which, confounding all those who stood in his way, was to put an indelible stamp on Germany and Europe [19]."

"I did not want to become a civil servant," wrote Hitler (11), "no, and again no. All attempts on my father's part to inspire me with love or pleasure in the profession by stories of his own life accomplished the exact opposite. I . . . grew sick to my stomach at the thought of sitting in an office, deprived of my liberty; ceasing to be master of my own time and being compelled to force the content of my whole life into paper forms that had to be filled out. . . . One day it became clear to me that I would become a painter, an artist. . . . My father was struck speechless. 'Painter? Artist?' He doubted my sanity, or perhaps he thought he had heard wrong or misunderstood me. But when he was clear on the subject, and particularly after he felt the seriousness of my intention, he opposed it with all the determination of his nature. 'Artist! No! Never as long as I live!' . . . My father would never depart from his 'Never!' And I intensified my 'Nevertheless!' "

Identification is both conscious and unconscious with the like-sexed parents who usually are the first models. The pantheon of reasons why the boy breaks away from identifying with the father has been discussed in previous chapters. What is relevant to note here is that the rebelliousness of the boy against the parental vocational desire is primarily a manifestation of asserting self-identity. In choosing an occupation, according to Super (20), one is in effect choosing a means of implementing a self-concept. Nevertheless, while the adolescent generally resists the specific vocational suggestion of the parent, he achieves ultimately an occupational status commensurate with the family and social class background. But it is primarily the inability to settle on an occupational identity which disturbs young people (5).

All of these factors are demonstrated in the illustrations which follow. The history of adolescent rebellion against parental vocational dictates goes back nearly two thousand years. The need to achieve a self-identity is relevant in all cultures and in all ages.

Lucian
(120[?]-200[?])

The Dream, or *Lucian's Career,* as the following selection is dually known, is a parable followed by its application.* Lucian had re-

---

*From *Lucian* edited by A. M. Harmon. Reprinted by permission of Harvard University Press and the Loeb Classical Library. 1947. Vol. III. Pp. 215-229.

turned to his native town of Samosata in Syria after a successful visit to Gaul, and this was his homecoming speech. He starts it by giving us a glimpse of his early life and professes to tell how he chose the career which brought him social advancement. Lucian deals with his choice with reference to the difference of outlook between the educated and the uneducated, a fundamental difference that formed the main social distinction between freeborn men. His parents were uneducated manual workers. He had run away from them and was admitted to the school of rhetoric in Ionian Asia Minor. His subsequent career as a lawyer and public speaker took him to Athens, Rome and Gaul where he had become rich and famous. *The Dream,* in which he recounts these events, was written after the end of his wanderings and before his fortieth year.

What is of special interest is the way Lucian describes his choice of profession, how in spite of his lowly origin he rose to distinction, and how he attributes his success to his own initiative. In his dream, two women, one representing Sculpture, in dirty work clothes, the other Culture, noble to look at, were the forces which inspired his career choice. But the petty nature of the man is betrayed in the statement he makes about the advantage of his profession: it will "inspire envy and jealousy in all men."

No sooner had I left off school, being then well on in my teens, than my father and his friends began to discuss what he should have me taught next. Most of them thought that higher education required great labour, much time, considerable expense, and conspicuous social position, while our circumstances were but moderate and demanded speedy relief; but that if I were to learn one of the handicrafts, in the first place I myself would immediately receive my support from the trade instead of continuing to share the family table at my age; besides, at no distant day I would delight my father by bringing home my earnings regularly.

The next topic for discussion was opened by raising the question, which of the trades was best, easiest to learn, suitable for a man of free birth, required an outfit that was easy to come by, and offered an income that was sufficient. Each praised a different trade, according to his own judgement or experience; but my father looked at my uncle (for among the company was my uncle on my mother's side, who had the reputation of being an excellent sculptor) and said: "It isn't right that any other trade should have the preference while you are by.

Come, take this lad in hand"—with a gesture toward me—"and teach him to be a good stone-cutter, mason, and sculptor, for he is capable of it, since, as you know, he has a natural gift for it." He drew this inference from the way in which I had played with wax; for whenever my teachers dismissed me I would scrape the wax from my tablets and model cattle or horses or even men, and they were true to life, my father thought. I used to get thrashings from my teachers on account of them, but at that time they brought me praise for my cleverness, and good hopes were entertained of me, on the ground that I would soon learn the trade, to judge from that modelling.

So, as soon as it seemed to be a suitable day to begin a trade, I was turned over to my uncle, and I was not greatly displeased with the arrangement, I assure you; on the contrary, I thought it involved interesting play of a sort, and a chance to show off to my schoolmates if I should turn out to be carving gods and fashioning little figures for myself and for those I liked best. Then came the first step and the usual experience of beginners. My uncle gave me a chisel and told me to strike a light blow on a slab that lay at hand, adding the trite quotation, "Well begun, half done." But in my inexperience I struck too hard; the slab broke, and in a gust of anger he seized a stick that lay close by and put me through an initiation of no gentle or encouraging sort, so that tears were the overture to my apprenticeship.

I ran away from the place and came home sobbing continuously, with my eyes abrim with tears. I told about the stick, showed the welts and charged my uncle with great cruelty, adding that he did it out of jealousy, for fear that I should get ahead of him in his trade. My mother comforted me and roundly abused her brother, but when night came on, I fell asleep, still tearful and thinking of the stick.

Up to this point my story has been humorous and childish, but what you shall hear next, gentlemen, is not to be made light of; it deserves a very receptive audience. The fact is that, to use the words of Homer, "a god-sent vision appeared unto me in my slumber Out of immortal night," so vivid as not to fall short of reality in any way. Indeed, even after all this time, the figures that I saw continue to abide in my eyes and the words that I heard in my ears, so plain was it all.

Two women, taking me by the hands, were each trying to drag me toward herself with might and main; in fact, they nearly pulled me to pieces in their rivalry. Now one of them would get the better of it and almost have me altogether, and now I would be in the hands of the other. They shouted at each other, too, one of them saying, "He is mine, and you want to get him!" and the other: "It is no good your claiming what belongs to someone else." One was like a workman, masculine, with unkempt hair, hands full of callous places, clothing tucked up, and a heavy layer of marble-dust upon her, just as my uncle looked when he cut stone. The other, however, was very fair of face, dignified in her appearance, and nice in her dress.

At length they allowed me to decide which of them I wanted to be with. The first to state her case was the hard-favoured, masculine one.

"Dear boy, I am the trade of Sculpture which you began to learn yesterday, of kin to you and related by descent; for your grandfather" —and she gave the name of my mother's father—"was a sculptor, and so are both your uncles, who are very famous through me. If you are willing to keep clear of this woman's silly nonsense"—with a gesture toward the other—"and to come and live with me, you will be generously kept and will have powerful shoulders, and you will be a stranger to jealousy of any sort; besides you will never go abroad, leaving your native country and your kinsfolk, and it will not be for mere words, either, that everyone will praise you.

"Do not be disgusted at my humble figure and my soiled clothing, for this is the way in which Phidias began, who revealed Zeus, and Polycleitus, who made Hera, Myron, whom men praise, and Praxiteles, at whom they marvel. Indeed, these men receive homage second only to the gods. If you become one of them, will you not yourself be famous in the sight of all mankind, make your father envied, and cause your native land to be admired?"

Sculpture said all this, and even more than this, with a great deal of stumbling and bad grammar, talking very hurriedly and trying to convince me: I do not remember it all, however, for most of it has escaped my memory by this time.

When she stopped, the other began after this fashion:

"My child, I am Education, with whom you are already acquainted and familiar, even if you have not yet completed your experience of me. What it shall profit you to become a sculptor, this woman has told you; you will be nothing but a labourer, toiling with your body and putting in it your entire hope of a livelihood, personally inconspicuous, getting meagre and illiberal returns, humble-witted, an insignificant figure in public, neither sought by your friends nor feared by your enemies nor envied by your fellow-citizens—nothing but just a labourer, one of the swarming rabble, ever cringing to the man above you and courting the man who can use his tongue, leading a hare's life, and counting as a godsend to anyone stronger. Even if you should become a Phidias or a Polycleitus and should create many marvellous works, everyone would praise your craftsmanship, to be sure, but none of those who saw you, if he were sensible, would pray to be like you; for no matter what you might be, you would be considered a mechanic, a man who has naught but his hands, a man who lives by his hands.

"If you follow my advice, first of all I shall show you many works of men of old, tell you their wondrous deeds and words, and make you conversant with almost all knowledge, and I shall ornament your soul, which concerns you most, with many noble adornments—temperance, justice, piety, kindliness, reasonableness, understanding, steadfastness, love of all that is beautiful, ardour towards all that is sublime; for these are the truly flawless jewels of the soul. Nothing that came to pass of old will escape you, and nothing that must now come to pass; nay, you will even foresee the future with me. In a word, I shall speedily teach you everything that there is, whether it pertains to the gods or to man.

"You who are now the beggarly son of a nobody, who have entertained some thought of so illiberal a trade, will after a little inspire envy and jealousy in all men, for you will be honoured and lauded, you will be held in great esteem for the highest qualities and admired by men preeminent in lineage and in wealth, you will wear clothing such as this"—she pointed to her own, and she was very splendidly dressed—"and will be deemed worthy of office and precedence. If ever you go abroad, even on foreign soil you will not be unknown or inconspicuous, for I will attach to you such marks of identification that everyone who sees you will nudge his neighbour and point you out with his finger, saying, 'There he is!' If anything of grave import befalls your friends or even the entire city, all will turn their eyes upon you; and if at any time you chance to make a speech, the crowd will listen open-mouthed, marvelling and felicitating you upon your eloquence and your father upon his good fortune. They say that some men become immortal. I shall bring this to pass with you; for though you yourself depart from life, you will never cease associating with men of education and conversing with men of eminence. . . . "

While these words were still on her lips, without waiting for her to finish what she was saying, I stood up and declared myself. Abandoning the ugly working-woman, I went over to Education with a right good will, especially when the stick entered my mind and the fact that it had laid many a blow upon me at the very outset the day before. When I abandoned Sculpture, at first she was indignant and struck her hands together and ground her teeth; but at length, like Niobe in the story, she grew rigid and turned to stone. Her fate was strange, but do not be incredulous, for dreams work miracles.

Guibert
(1053-1124)

Guibert was orphaned at eight and bereft of his mother, who "divorced herself from the world" by entering a nunnery, when he was twelve. The boy grew up under the tutelage of a master who was not always able to control him. The youthful excesses Guibert described, the Abbot's "entreaties daily repeated to become a monk," his seemingly unpremeditated and unconditional acceptance of the pleas, his mother's surprising objection to this choice of career, and the sudden abatement of his "sinfulness" once he made the decision, are factors frequently found in the adolescent's vocational development.*

Why say more? Whilst she was thus divorcing herself from the world, I was left deserted by mother, guide and master. For he who had so faithfully trained and taught me, fired by my mother's example, love and counsel, betook himself to the monastery of Ely. And I, now possessed of a baneful liberty, began most immoderately to abuse my power, to laugh at churches, to hate school, to love the company of my young lay cousins devoted to knightly pursuits, and, whilst cursing the clerk's garb, to promise remission of sins, to indulge in sleep in which formerly I was allowed little relaxation, so that by unaccustomed excess of it my body began to waste. Meantime the agitating news of my doings fell on my mother's ears, and surmising from what she heard, my immediate ruin, she was half-dead with fear. For the fine clothing which I had in the church processions, provided by her in the hope that I might be the more eager for the clerk's life, I wore everywhere in wanton pursuits unnatural at my age, rivalling the boldness of older youths, utterly careless and intemperate.

Whilst therefore the looseness, ay, the madness of my behaviour was all the worse, because I had lived before a strict and guarded life, my mother, unable to endure what she heard, had recourse to the Abbot and begged him and the brotherhood that my master might be allowed to resume my training. The Abbot, brought up by my grandfather and under obligation for benefits received from his house, gave me a ready welcome, when I went to him, and followed up his kind reception with still kinder treatment thereafter. I call Thee to witness,

---

*From *The Autobiography of Guibert, Abbot of Nogent-Sous-Coucy.* Reprinted by permission of Routledge & Kegan Paul. E. P. Dutton & Co., 1925. Pp. 55-57.

Holy God and Disposer, that from the moment I entered the monastery church and so soon as I saw the monks sitting there, at that sight a longing for the monk's life seized me, which never grew cold, and my spirit had no rest until its desire was fulfilled. And so living with them in the same cloister and thinking on their whole existence and condition, as the flame increases when fanned by the wind, so by contemplation of them my soul yearning to be made like unto them, could not but be on fire. Lastly I was urged by the Abbot of the place by entreaties daily repeated to become a monk there, and although I passionately desired so to do, yet could not my tongue be loosed by the prayer of those who desired me to make such a promise and what would be most difficult now that I am older, to be silent with a full heart, yet boy as I was, that silence I kept without much difficulty.

At length I opened the matter to my mother, and she fearing the instability of boyhood, tried by reasoning to dissuade me from my purpose, which made me not a little sorry I had revealed my intention; and when I also told my master, he opposed it still more. Deeply annoyed at the opposition of both, I determined to turn my mind elsewhere; and so I began to act as if I had never had such a desire. Having put the matter off from the week of Pentecost until Christmas day, and being both eager and anxious to bring the matter to an end, I impatiently threw off my respect for my mother and my fear of my master, and betaking myself to the Abbot, who was eager for this to happen but had failed to draw any promise from me, I cast myself at his feet, begging him earnestly and with tears in such terms as a sinner would use, to be received by him. He gladly granting my prayer provided the necessary habit, as soon as he could, that is, on the next day, and invested me with it, my mother in tears looking on afar off, and ordered that alms should forthwith be offered that day.

Meanwhile my former master, not being able to teach me any longer because of the strict rule of the brotherhood, at least took care to urge me to search diligently those holy books which I was reading, to study those less known by more learned men, to compose short pieces of prose and verse, warning me to apply myself the more closely because less care was being expended by others on my instruction. And, O Lord, True Light, I well remember the inestimable bounty Thou didst then bestow on me. For so soon as I had taken Thy habit at Thy invitation, a cloud seemed to be removed from the face of my understanding and that wherein I had wandered blindly and in error, began to be apprehended by it. Besides I was suddenly inspired with such love of learning that for this above all I yearned and thought the day was lost on which I did not engage in some such work. How often did they think me asleep and resting my little body under the coverlet, when my mind was concentrated on composition, or I was reading under a blanket, fearful of the rebuke of the others.

Benvenuto Cellini
(1500-1571)

The struggle between Benvenuto Cellini and his father over whether the boy should be a goldsmith or a musician was a crucial and bitter one, lasting from 1515 to 1520. The pressures Cellini senior put on the boy were powerful and painful, forcing the latter to succumb to him in moments of tremendous guilt feelings, only to override the feelings when his needs for identity and self-expression became dominant. Benvenuto made several attempts to please his father but each time the goldsmith's trade lured him away. He ran away from home to escape his father. In "piteous" letters to him, the father pleaded for him to return and "not to lose the music he had taught me with such trouble." But the letters had only the force of compelling Benvenuto to stay where he was and to "hate that accursed music." His guilt feelings are evident in the frequent references he made to his father: "My poor father," "My good father," or "I went on working with Pagolo Arsagno, and earned a good deal of money, the greater part of which I always sent to my good father." The passage to follow* will strike a responsive and familiar chord with many parents and adolescents today.

When I reached the age of fifteen, I put myself, against my father's will, to the goldsmith's trade with a man called Antonio, son of Sandro, known commonly as Marcone the goldsmith. He was a most excellent craftsman and a very good fellow to boot, high-spirited and frank in all his ways. My father would not let him give me wages like the other apprentices; for having taken up the study of this art to please myself, he wished me to indulge my whim for drawing to the full. I did so willingly enough; and that honest master of mine took marvellous delight in my performances. He had an only son, a bastard, to whom he often gave his orders, in order to spare me. My liking for the art was so great, or, I may truly say, my natural bias, both one and

---

*From *Autobiography* translated by John Addington Symonds. Reprinted by permission of Doubleday & Co., Inc. Garden City Publishing Co., 1927. Pp. 14-17, 39.

the other, that in a few months I caught up with the good, nay, the best young craftsmen in our business, and began to reap the fruits of my labours. I did not, however, neglect to gratify my good father from time to time by playing on the flute or cornet. Each time he heard me, I used to make his tears fall accompanied with deep-drawn sighs of satisfaction. My filial piety often made me give him that contentment, and induced me to pretend that I enjoyed the music too. . . .

To please my father, I went to Pierino's house and played the cornet and the flute with one of his brothers. . . . On one of those days my father came to Piero's house to hear us play, and in ecstasy at my performance exclaimed: "I shall yet make you a marvellous musician against the will of all or any one who may desire to prevent me." To this Piero answered, and spoke the truth: "Your Benvenuto will get much more honour and profit if he devotes himself to the goldsmith's trade than to this piping." These words made my father angry, seeing that I too had the same opinion as Piero, that he flew into a rage. . . . Thereupon we left the house, muttering words of anger on both sides. I had taken my father's part; and when we stepped into the street together, I told him I was quite ready to take vengeance for the insults heaped on him by that scoundrel, provided he permit me to give myself up to the art of design. He answered: "My dear son, I too in my time was a good draughtsman; but for recreation, after such stupendous labours, and for the love of me who am your father, who begat you and brought you up and implanted so many honourable talents in you, for the sake of recreation, I say, will not you promise sometimes to take in hand your flute and that seductive cornet, and to play upon them to your heart's content, inviting the delight of music?" I promised I would do so, and very willingly for his love's sake. . . .

All this while I worked as a goldsmith, and was able to assist my good father. His other son, my brother Cecchino, had, as I said before, been instructed in the rudiments of Latin letters. It was our father's wish to make me, the elder, a great musician and composer, and him, the younger, a great and learned jurist. He could not, however, put force upon the inclination of our nature, which directed me to the arts of design, and my brother, who had a fine and graceful person, to the profession of arms. . . .

Cellini at seventeen had left his father to go to Pisa.

My father, in the meanwhile, kept writing piteous entreaties that I should return to him; and in every letter bade me not to lose the music he had taught me with such trouble. On this, I suddenly gave up all

wish to go back to him; so much did I hate that accursed music; and
I felt as though of a truth I were in paradise the whole year I stayed at
Pisa, where I never played the flute. . . .

Shortly afterward, Cellini left Pisa to study in Florence. A friend,
Giovan Battista, suggested that they go to Rome, to which Cellini
agreed, "being angry with my father for the same old reason of
music."

When Cellini was nineteen, he consented to play at a music
festival for the Pope, Clement, who admired the excellence of his
soprano cornet and invited him to become a member of the papal
orchestra.

When I left them, I went meditating whether I ought to accept the
invitation, inasmuch as I could not but suffer if I abandoned the noble
studies of my art. The following night my father appeared to me in a
dream, and begged me with tears of tenderest affection, for God's love
and his, to enter upon this engagement. Methought I answered that
nothing would induce me to do so. In an instant he assumed so horrible an aspect as to frighten me out of my wits, and cried: "If you do
not, you will have a father's curse; but if you do, may you be ever
blessed by me!" When I woke, I ran, for very fright, to have myself
inscribed. Then I wrote to my old father, telling him the news, which
so affected him with extreme joy that a sudden fit of illness took him,
and wellnigh brought him to death's door. In his answer to my letter,
he told me that he too had dreamed nearly the same as I had.

Jerome Cardan
(1501-1576)

Prior to Cardan, autobiographies were either religious confessions,
such as St. Augustine's, Suso's, or Guibert's, or historical memoirs,
as Caesar's or Josephus'. Cardan attempted a scientific self-study; it
was his avowed aim to examine himself "as if he were a new species
of animal which he never expected to see again." He is perhaps the
first manifestation of what we today term the scientific spirit, deeply
interested in the brain and the nervous system and their relation to
the physical and intellectual life. Cardan has been sometimes referred to as the first psychologist.

He was a contemporary of Cellini, born in Pavia, Italy, the son of a renowned lawyer. His father wanted him to follow in his footsteps, but young Girolamo persistently held to his goal: "that I should make it my duty to care for human life." The father was bitterly disappointed but Cardan became a celebrated physician in Milan and a professor at the University of Pavia. *De Vita Propria Liber,** from which this reference comes, was written in 1575, a year before he died.

From my early youth I persistently held to this purpose—that I should make it my duty to care for human life. The study of medicine seemed to point more clearly to such a career than did the study of law, as being more appropriate to the end I had in view, and as of more common concern to all the world in every age. I deemed medicine a profession of sincerer character than law, and a pursuit relying rather upon reason and nature's everlasting law, than upon the opinions of men.

Accordingly, I embraced this pursuit and not jurisprudence. Thereupon, deliberately, I not only rejected the advances of friends engaged in the law, contemning riches, power, and honors, but even shunned these influences. My father actually wept in my presence when he learned that I had given over jurisprudence to follow the study of philosophy, and felt deeply grieved that I would not apply myself to his same interests. He considered jurisprudence a more ennobling discipline—repeatedly he quoted Aristotle on this point—and a profession better adapted to the acquisition of wealth and influence, and to the improvement of the family position. He realized that his office of lecturing in the law schools of the city, together with the honorarium of an hundred crowns which he had enjoyed for so many years, would not, as he had hoped, fall to me, but that another would succeed him in his post. Nor would that commentary of his ever be published, which I was to annotate. For not long before this there had dawned a faint hope that he might achieve some renown as the critic of *The Commentaries of John, Bishop of Canterbury, on Optics and Perspective*. The following couplet had even been published for this work:

Hoc Cardano viro gaudet domus: omnia novit
Unus; habent nullum sæcula nostra parem.

This might rather be considered in the manner of prophecy for one

---

The Book of My Life translated by Jean Stoner. Reprinted by permission of E. P. Dutton & Co., Inc. 1930. Pp. 39-41.

who was then about to set out upon his life's labors, than as applying to my father himself, who, beyond the law—which, I understand, he practiced with extraordinary brilliance—had mastered only the elements of mathematics; he was in no wise given to original thinking, nor had he availed himself of the resources of the Greek language. This situation came about, in his case, more because of his many-sided interests, and his inconstancy of purpose, than because he was not naturally gifted, or because of sloth or faulty judgment; for he was subject to none of these defects. However, because my will was firmly set to my purpose on account of the reasons which I have already advanced, together with other motives, I was not moved by my father's advices, especially since I saw that he, although he had met with practically no reverses, had succeeded but indifferently.

Saint Teresa of Avila
(1515-1582)

Saint Teresa was born in Avila on March 28, 1515. Her father was Don Alfonso Sanchez de Cepeda, and her mother Dona Beatriz Davila y Ahumada. Dona Beatriz, the second wife of Don Alfonso, died young, and the eldest daughter, Maria de Cepeda, took charge of her two younger sisters and acted as a second mother to them until her marriage, which took place when Teresa was sixteen years old. It was felt she was too young to be placed in charge of her father's house, and as her education was not finished, she was sent to the Augustinian nunnery. The Saint's own account is that she was too giddy and careless to be trusted at home, and that it was necessary to put her under the care of those who would watch over her and correct her ways.

St. Teresa remained with the nuns eighteen months, during which time there was only a faint glimmer, if anything, of her future vocation. In actuality, Teresa was seriously conflicted about becoming a nun. She struggled to "remove some of the great dislike which I had for being a nun, and which had become deeply engrained in me." Furthermore, her father opposed her choice. She wrote, "He was so fond of me that I was never able to get his consent." The conflict within herself and between herself and Don Alfonso lasted several months. Curiously enough, Teresa outlined the argument by which she convinced herself to follow the calling and we see here how she achieved her goal (21).

I began gradually to like the good and holy conversation of this nun. How well she used to speak of God! for she was a person of great discretion and sanctity. I listened to her with delight. I think there never was a time when I was not glad to listen to her. She began by telling me how she came to be a nun through the mere reading of the words of the Gospel: "Many are called, and few are chosen." She would speak of the reward which our Lord gives to those who forsake all things for His sake. This good companionship began to root out the habits which bad companionship had formed, and to bring my thoughts back to the desire of eternal things, as well as to banish in some measure the great dislike I had to be a nun, which had been very great; and if I saw any one weep in prayer, or devout in any other way, I envied her very much; for my heart was now so hard, that I could not shed a tear, even if I read the Psalm through. This was a grief to me.

I remained in the monastery a year and a half, and was very much the better for it. I began to say many vocal prayers, and to ask all the nuns to pray for me, that God would place me in that state wherein I was to serve Him; but, for all this, I wished not to be a nun, and that God would not be pleased I should be one, though at the same time I was afraid of marriage. At the end of my stay there, I had a greater inclination to be a nun, yet not in that house, on account of certain devotional practices which I understood prevailed there, and which I thought overstrained. Some of the younger ones encouraged me in this my wish; and if all had been of one mind, I might have profited by it. I had also a great friend in another monastery; and this made me resolve, if I was to be a nun, not to be one in any other house than where she was. I looked more to the pleasure of sense and vanity than to the good of my soul. These good thoughts of being a nun came to me from time to time. They left me very soon; and I could not persuade myself to become one.

At this time, though I was not careless about my own good, our Lord was much more careful to dispose me for that state of life which was best for me. He sent me a serious illness, so that I was obliged to return to my father's house.

When I became well again, they took me to see my sister in her house in the country village where she dwelt. Her love for me was so great, that, if she had had her will, I should never have left her. Her husband also had a great affection for me—at least, he showed me all kindness. This too I owe rather to our Lord, for I have received kindness everywhere; and all my service in return is, that I am what I am.

On the road lived a brother of my father—a prudent and most excellent man, then a widower. Him too our Lord was preparing for Himself. In his old age, he left all his possessions and became a religious. He so finished his course, that I believe him to have the vision of God. He would have me stay with him some days. His practice was to read good books in Spanish; and his ordinary conversation was about God and the vanity of the world. These books he made me read to him; and, though I did not much like them, I appeared as if I did; for in giving pleasure to others I have been most particular, though it might be painful to myself—so much so, that what in others might have been a virtue was in me a great fault, because I was often extremely indiscreet. O my God, in how many ways did His Majesty prepare me for the state wherein it was His will I should serve Him! —how, against my own will, He constrained me to do violence to myself! May He be blessed for ever! Amen.

Though I remained here but a few days, yet, through the impression made on my heart by the words of God both heard and read, and by the good conversation of my uncle, I came to understand the truth I had heard in my childhood, that all things are as nothing, the world vanity, and passing rapidly away. I also began to be afraid that, if I were then to die, I should go down to hell. Though I could not bend my will to be a nun, I saw that the religious state was the best and the safest. And thus, by little and little, I resolved to force myself into it.

The struggle lasted three months. I used to press this reason against myself: The trials and sufferings of living as a nun cannot be greater than those of purgatory, and I have well deserved to be in hell. It is not much to spend the rest of my life as if I were in purgatory, and then go straight to Heaven—which was what I desired. I was more influenced by servile fear, I think, than by love, to enter religion.

The devil put before me that I could not endure the trials of the religious life, because of my delicate nurture. I defended myself against him by alleging the trials which Christ endured, and that it was not much for me to suffer something for His sake; besides, He would help me to bear it. I must have thought so, but I do not remember this consideration. I endured many temptations during these days. I was subject to fainting-fits, attended with fever,—for my health was always weak. I had become by this time fond of good books, and that gave me life. I read the Epistles of St. Jerome, which filled me with so much courage, that I resolved to tell my father of my purpose,— which was almost like taking the habit; for I was so jealous of my word, that I would never, for any consideration, recede from a promise when once my word had been given.

My father's love for me was so great, that I could never obtain his consent; nor could the prayers of others, whom I persuaded to speak to him, be of any avail. The utmost I could get from him was that I might do as I pleased after his death. I now began to be afraid of myself, and of my own weakness—for I might go back. So, considering that such waiting was not safe for me, I obtained my end in another way.

Abraham Cowley
(1618-1667)

Before he was twelve years old, wrote Abraham Cowley in his brief autobiography, *Of My Self,** he was "made a Poet as irremediably as a Child is made an Eunuch." The precocity of the boy was undeniable, probably stimulated by his mother who read frequently to him during early childhood. In this sketch, Cowley tells us how he preferred to construct the rules of Latin grammar from the authors he read rather than learn them by rote; how he spent his holidays in quiet country walks with a book rather than indulge in sports; and how his poetic fancy and ambition were sparked through finding Spenser's *Faerie Queene* in his house and reading it through completely before he was twelve. In such a way, perhaps, is a poet made.

Cowley belongs to the group of poets between Milton and Dryden and to the generation of Lovelace and Marvell. He is remembered today primarily for his graceful and simple prose, a sample of which is seen here.

It is a hard and nice Subject for a man to write of himself, it grates his own heart to say any thing in disparagement, and the Readers Eares to hear any thing of praise from him. There is no danger from me of offending him in this kind; neither my Mind, nor my Body, nor my Fortune, allow me any materials for that Vanity. It is sufficient, for my own contentment, that they have preserved me from being scandalous, or remarkable on the defective side. But besides that, I shall here speak of myself, only in relation to the subject of these precedent discourses, and shall be likelier thereby to fall into the contempt, than rise up to the estimation of most people. As far as my

*In *Abraham Cowley. The Essays and Other Prose Writings* edited by A. B. Gough. Reprinted by permission of The Clarendon Press. 1915. Pp. 215-218.

Memory can return back into my past Life, before I knew, or was capable of guessing what the world, or glories, or business of it were, the natural affections of my soul gave me a secret bent of aversion from them, as some Plants are said to turn away from others, by an Antipathy imperceptible to themselves, and inscrutable to mans understanding. Even when I was a very young Boy at School, instead of running about on Holy-daies and playing with my fellows; I was wont to steal from them, and walk into the fields, either alone with a Book, or with some one Companion, if I could find any of the same temper. I was then too, so much an Enemy to all constraint, that my Masters could never prevail on me, by any perswasions or encouragements, to learn without Book the common rules of Grammar, in which they dispensed with me alone, because they found I made a shift to do the usual exercise out of my own reading and observation.

... I was even then acquainted with the Poets and perhaps it was the immature and immoderate love of them which stampt first, or rather engraved these Characters in me: They were like Letters cut into the Bark of a young Tree, which with the Tree still grow proportionably. But, how this love came to be produced in me so early, is a hard question: I believe I can tell the particular little chance that filled my head first with such Chimes of Verse, as have never since left ringing there: For I remember when I began to read, and to take some pleasure in it, there was wont to lie in my Mothers Parlour (I know not by what accident, for she her self never in her life read any Book but of Devotion) but there was wont to lie *Spencers* Works; this I happened to fall upon, and was infinitely delighted with the Stories of the Knights, and Giants, and Monsters, and brave Houses, which I found every where there: (Though my understanding had little to do with all this) and by degrees with the tinckling of the Rhyme and Dance of the Numbers, so that I think I had read him all over before I was twelve years old, and was thus made a Poet as irremediably as a Child is made an Eunuch. With these affections of mind, and my heart wholly set upon Letters, I went to the University.

Colley Cibber
(1671-1757)

Accident and chance frequently play a decisive factor in the adolescent's choice of occupation. Colley Cibber, an actor who also wrote plays, humorously speculates, in this earliest of reminiscent autobiographies, on the fates of King James and the Prince of Orange, had he entered upon a military career as his father wanted

—or had he gone into the ministry. "Providence thought fit to postpone [my fortune], 'till that of those great rulers of nations was
justly perfected." As Cibber relates it,* had his father's sculpting
schedule permitted him to bring his son to Winchester College one
month earlier, he might very well have been commissioned in the
military or ministry. But Colley's love affair with the theater, begun at about this time, took him permanently into its world.

I am now come to that crisis of my life when fortune seem'd to be at
a loss what she should do with me. Had she favour'd my father's first
designation of me, he might then, perhaps, have had as sanguine hopes
of my being a bishop as I afterwards conceived of my being a general,
when I first took arms at the Revolution. Nay, after that, I had a third
chance too, equally as good, of becoming an underpropper of the state.
How, at last, I became to be none of all these, the sequel will inform
you.

About the year 1687, I was taken from school to stand at the election
of children into Winchester College; my being, by my mother's side, a
descendant of William of Wickham, the founder, my father (who knew
little how the world was to be dealt with) imagined my having that advantage would be security enough for my success, and so sent me simply
down thither, without the least favourable recommendation or interest, but that of my naked merit, and a pompous pedigree in my pocket.
Had he tack'd a direction to my back, and sent me by the carrier to the
mayor of the town, to be chosen member of Parliament there, I might
have had just as much chance to have succeeded in the one as the other.
But I must not omit in this place to let you know that the experience
which my father then bought, at my cost, taught him, some years after,
to take a more judicious care of my younger brother, Lewis Cibber,
whom, with the present of a statue of the founder, of his own making,
he recommended to the same college. This statue now stands (I think)
over the school-door there, and was so well executed that it seem'd to
speak—for its kinsman. It was no sooner set up than the door of preferment was open to him.

'Twas about this time I first imbib'd an inclination, which I durst
not reveal, for the stage; for, besides that I knew it would disoblige my
father, I had no conception of any means, practicable, to make my way
to it. I therefore suppress'd the bewitching ideas of so sublime a station,
and compounded with my ambition by laying a lower scheme, of only

*In *An Apology for the Life of Colley Cibber*. Reprinted by permission of E. P. Dutton & Co., Inc. Everyman's Library. Pp. 34-37.

getting the nearest way into the immediate life of a gentleman collegiate. My father being at this time employed at Chattsworth in Derbyshire, by the (then) Earl of Devonshire, who was raising that seat from a Gothic to a Grecian magnificence, I made use of the leisure I then had, in London, to open to him, by letter, my disinclination to wait another year for an uncertain preferment at Winchester, and to entreat him that he would send me, *per saltum*, by a shorter cut, to the university. My father, who was naturally indulgent to me, seem'd to comply with my request, and wrote word, that as soon as his affairs would permit, he would carry me with him, and settle me in some college, but rather at Cambridge, where (during his late residence at that place, in making some statues that now stand upon Trinity College new library) he had contracted some acquaintance with the heads of houses, who might assist his intentions for me. This I lik'd better than to go discountenanc'd to Oxford, to which it would have been a sort of reproach to me not to have come elected. After some months were elaps'd, my father, not being willing to let me lie too long idling in London, sent for me down to Chattsworth, to be under his eye, till he cou'd be at leisure to carry me to Cambridge. Before I cou'd set out on my journey thither, the nation fell in labour of the Revolution, the news being then just brought to London, that the Prince of Orange, at the head of an army, was landed in the west. When I came to Nottingham, I found my father in arms there, among those forces which the Earl of Devonshire had raised for the redress of our violated laws and liberties. My father judg'd this a proper season for a young stripling to turn himself loose into the bustle of the world; and being himself too advanc'd in years to endure the winter fatigue, which might possibly follow, entreated that noble lord that he would be pleas'd to accept of his son in his room, and that he would give him (my father) leave to return and finish his works at Chattsworth. This was so well receiv'd by his lordship, that he not only admitted of my service, but promis'd my father, in return, that when affairs were settled, he would provide for me. Upon this my father return'd to Derbyshire, while I, not a little transported, jump'd into his saddle. Thus, in one day, all my thoughts of the university were smother'd in ambition! A slight commission for a horse officer was the least view I had before me. At this crisis you cannot but observe that the fate of King James, and of the Prince of Orange, and that of so minute a being as myself, were all at once upon the anvil. In what shape they wou'd severally come out, tho' a good guess might be made, was not then *demonstrable* to the deepest foresight; but as my fortune seem'd to be of small importance to the publick, Providence thought fit to postpone it, 'till that of those great rulers of nations was justly perfected. Yet, had my father's business permitted him to have carried me one month sooner (as he intended) to the university, who knows but, by this time, that purer fountain might have wash'd my imperfections into a capacity of writing (instead of plays and annual odes) sermons, and pastoral letters. But whatever care of the church might so have fallen to my share, as I dare say it may be now in better hands, I ought not to repine at my being otherwise dispos'd of.

Benjamin Franklin
(1706-1790)

Franklin relates here the step-by-step procedure by which it was determined that he should become a printer (7). His deep dislike for the tallow-chandler trade led his father to explore a variety of trades with him: carpentering, bricklaying, wood-turning, and so on. Although Benjamin vetoed all of these occupations, the impressions he received from his explorations give the reader a clue to his scientific experiments and inventions. It was Benjamin's love for reading that determined his father to make him a printer, and although the boy hankered for the sea, he signed the indenture papers as an apprentice to his brother as the best compromise among several unappealing choices.

... I continued thus employed in my father's business for two years, that is, till I was twelve years old;—and my brother John, who was bred to that business, having left my father, married, and set up for himself at Rhode Island, there was all appearance that I was destined to supply his place and be a tallow-chandler. But my dislike to the trade continuing, my father was under apprehensions that if he did not find one for me more agreeable, I should break away and get to sea, as his son Josiah had done, to his great vexation. He therefore sometimes took me to walk with him, and see joiners, bricklayers, turners, braziers, etc., at their work, that he might observe my inclination and endeavor to fix it on some trade or other on land. It has ever since been a pleasure to me to see good workmen handle their tools; and it has been useful to me, having learned so much by it as to be able to do little jobs myself in my house when a workman could not readily be got, and to construct little machines for my experiments, while the intention of making the experiment was fresh and warm in my mind. My father at last fixed upon the cutler's trade, and my uncle

Benjamin's son Samuel, who was bred to that business in London, being about that time established in Boston, I was sent to be with him some time, on liking. But his expectations of a fee with me displeasing my father, I was taken home again.

From a child I was fond of reading, and all the little money that came into my hands was ever laid out in books. Pleased with the *Pilgrim's Progress,* my first collection was of John Bunyan's works in separate little volumes. I afterwards sold them to enable me to buy R. Burton's *Historical Collections;* they were small chapman's books, and cheap, forty or fifty in all. My father's little library consisted chiefly of books in polemic divinity, most of which I read and have since often regretted that at a time when I had such a thirst for knowledge, more proper books had not fallen in my way, since it was now resolved I should not be a clergyman. *Plutarch's Lives* there was, in which I read abundantly, and I still think that time spent to great advantage. There was also a book of Defoe's, called an *Essay on Projects,* and another of Dr. Mather's, called *Essays to do Good,* which perhaps gave me a turn of thinking that had an influence on some of the principal future events of my life.

This bookish inclination at length determined my father to make me a printer, though he had already one son (James) of that profession. In 1717 my brother James returned from England with a press and letters to set up his business in Boston. I liked it much better than that of my father, but still had a hankering for the sea. To prevent the apprehended effect of such an inclination, my father was impatient to have me bound to my brother. I stood out some time, but at last was persuaded, and signed the indentures when I was yet but twelve years old. I was to serve as an apprentice till I was twenty-one years of age, only I was to be allowed journeyman's wages during the last year. In a little time I made great proficiency in the business and became a useful hand to my brother. I now had access to better books. An acquaintance with the apprentices of booksellers enabled me sometimes to borrow a small one, which I was careful to return soon and clean. Often I sat up in my room reading the greatest part of the night, when the book was borrowed in the evening and to be returned early in the morning, lest it should be missed or wanted.

Carlo Goldoni
(1707-1793)

Like Cibber a third of a century before him, Goldoni, from early adolescence, had a passion for the theater. But his father, a physician, "destined me for medicine," and, he continues in his *Memoirs*,* "I durst not be refractory, for I should have been told that I wished to do neither one thing nor another." The unhappy fifteen-year-old was ordered to accompany his father on the daily rounds of patients, a chore made endurable only because of the anticipation of seeing the touring company of actors which had extended its stay in the town. When his true feelings caught up with him, depression set in. Remission from the "violent fit of this lethargic disease" came after his mother interposed for him, and it was "settled" that Carlo become an advocate.

"Where is the [acting] company gone to?"—"It is here."—"Here?" —"Yes, father."—"Do they act here?"—"Yes, father."—"I shall go to see them."—"And I also, father?"—"You, rascal! What is the name of the principal actress!"—"Clarice."—"O, Clarice! . . . excellent, ugly, but very clever."—"Father . . . "—"I must go to thank them."—"And I, father?"—"Wretch!"—"I beg your pardon."—"Well, well, for this time . . . "

My mother, who had heard everything, now entered: she was very glad to see me on good terms with my father.

She mentioned the Abbé Gennari to him, not with the view of preventing me from going to the play (for my father was as fond of it as myself); but for the sake of informing him that the canon, suffering under different diseases, was anxious to see him; that he had spoken to the whole town of the famous Venetian physician, pupil of the great Lancisi, who was instantly expected; and that he had only to show himself to receive more patients than he could desire.

This is what really happened. Everybody wanted this one doctor, Goldoni; rich and poor flocked to him, and the poor paid better than the rich.

He took more commodious apartments, and settled at Chiozza, to remain there so long as fortune should continue favourable to him, or till some other physician should supplant him in vogue.

Seeing me unoccupied, and in want of good masters in town, my father wished himself to make something of me.

He destined me for medicine, and till he should have the letters announcing my nomination to the college of Pavia, he ordered me to accompany him in his daily visits. He thought that a little practice before the study of the theory would give me a superficial acquaint-

---

*Reprinted by permission of Alfred A. Knopf, Inc. 1926. Pp. 23-24.

ance with medicine, which I might find very useful for the understanding of technical terms and the first principles of the art.

I was not over fond of medicine; but I durst not be refractory, for I should have been then told that I wished to do neither one thing nor another.

I therefore followed my father, and saw the greatest number of his patients along with him. I felt their pulse, I looked at their urine, I examined their saliva, and did many other things equally disgusting to me. Patience: so long as the company continued their representations, which were prolonged to thirty-six, I thought myself indemnified.

My father was very well satisfied with me, and my mother still more so. But one of the three enemies of man, perhaps two, or all the three together, began to attack me and disturb my tranquility.

* * * *

I was naturally gay, but subject from my infancy to hypochondriacal or melancholy vapours, which threw a dark shade over my mind.

Attacked with a violent fit of this lethargic disease, I sought for relief, but could find none. The players were gone; Chiozza had no longer any amusement to my taste; I was discontented with medicine; I became gloomy and thoughtful, and fell away more and more every day.

My parents soon perceived my state; and my mother was the first to question me. I confided my uneasiness to her.

One day, when we were partaking of a family dinner, without strangers or the presence of servants, my mother turned the conversation to me. There was a debate of two hours. My father was absolutely resolved that I should pursue medicine. It was in vain for me to agitate myself, make wry faces, and look gloomy; he would not yield. My mother at length proved to my father that he was wrong, and she did it in this way.———

"The Marquis Goldoni," said she, "wishes to take our child under his care. If Charles be a good physician, his protector may favour him, it is true; but can he give him patients? Can he persuade people to prefer him to so many others? He may procure him the place of professor in the University of Pavia; but then, what an immense time and labour before he can get it; whereas, if my son were to study law and become an advocate, it would be easy for a senator of Milan to make his fortune without the smallest trouble or difficulty."

My father made no answer; he remained silent for a few minutes.

At length, turning to me, he said jocularly: "Would you like the Code and Digest of Justinian?"—"Yes, father," I replied, "a great deal better than the Aphorisms of Hippocrates."—"Your mother," said he, "is a sensible woman; her reasons are good, and I may acquiesce in them; but in the meantime you must not remain idle, but continue to accompany me."

I was still, therefore, where I was. My mother then took up my cause with warmth. She advised my father to send me to Venice and settle me with my uncle Indric, one of the best attorneys of the capital, and she proposed to accompany me herself and to remain with me there till my departure for Pavia. My aunt supported her sister's project. I held up my hands and wept for joy. My father consented, and I was to go instantly to Venice.

I was now contented, and my vapours were immediately dissipated.

Sir Walter Scott
(1771-1832)

The fundamental process by which the ego acquires efficiency is identification with the parents, their attitudes, values and feelings. The ego can learn not only from its own trial and errors but also from the experience of others.

In the following passage from Scott's *Memoirs*,* this fundamental process is seen. Although Scott detested the drudgery of the barrister's work and the confinement of an office, he loved his father and "felt the rational pride and pleasure of rendering myself useful to him." He went along with his father's wish, and when his father proposed further preparation for the more ambitious profession of the bar, Scott again could not disappoint him even though he felt strongly antagonistic toward such a career. And so for four more years, he prepared himself.

The identification led, ultimately, to independence. In assuming the attitudes of his father, Scott dispensed gradually with his support and became self-sufficient. It was then that he turned to his successful writing career.

I imagine my father's reason for sending me to so few classes in the College, was a desire that I should apply myself particularly to my legal studies. He had not determined whether I should fill the situa-

---

*Reprinted by permission of Macmillan & Co., Ltd. 1914. Vol. I. Pp. 34, 43-44.

tion of an Advocate or a Writer; but judiciously considering the
technical knowledge of the latter to be useful at least, if not essential,
to a barrister, he resolved I should serve the ordinary apprenticeship
of five years to his own profession. I accordingly entered into indentures with my father about 1785-6, and entered upon the dry and
barren wilderness of forms and conveyances.

I cannot reproach myself with being entirely an idle apprentice—
far less, as the reader might reasonably have expected,

A clerk foredoom'd my father's soul to cross.

The drudgery, indeed, of the office, I disliked, and the confinement
I altogether detested; but I loved my father, and I felt the rational
pride and pleasure of rendering myself useful to him. I was ambitious
also; and among my companions in labour, the only way to gratify
ambition was to labour hard and well. Other circumstances reconciled
me in some measure to the confinement. The allowance for copy
money furnished a little fund for the *menus plaisirs* of the circulating
library and the Theatre; and this was no trifling incentive to labour.
When actually at the oar, no man could pull it harder than I, and I
remember writing upwards of 120 folio pages with no interval either
for food or rest. Again, the hours of attendance on the office were
lightened by the power of choosing my own books and reading them
in my own way, which often consisted in beginning at the middle or
the end of a volume.

*   *   *   *

Amidst these studies, and in this society, the time of my apprenticeship elapsed; and in 1790, or thereabouts, it became necessary that I
should seriously consider to which department of the law I was to
attach myself. My father behaved with the most parental kindness.
He offered, if I preferred his own profession, immediately to take me
into partnership with him, which, though his business was much diminished, still afforded me an immediate prospect of a handsome independence. But he did not disguise his wish that I should relinquish
this situation to my younger brother, and embrace the more ambitious
profession of the bar. I had little hesitation in making my choice—for
I was never very fond of money; and in no other particular do the
professions admit of a comparison. Besides, I knew and felt the inconveniences attached to that of a writer; and I thought (like a young
man) many of them were 'ingenio non subcunda meo.' The appearance of personal dependence which that profession requires was
disagreeable to me; the sort of connexion between the client and the

attorney seemed to render the latter more subservient than was quite agreeable to my nature; and, besides, I had seen many sad examples while overlooking my father's business, that the utmost exertions, and the best meant services, do not secure the *man of business,* as he is called, from great loss, and most ungracious treatment on the part of his employers. The bar, though I was conscious of my deficiencies as a public speaker, was the line of ambition and liberty; it was that also for which most of my contemporary friends were destined. And, lastly, although I would willingly have relieved my father of the labours of his business, yet I saw plainly we could not have agreed on some particulars if we had attempted to conduct it together, and that I should disappoint his expectations if I did not turn to the bar. So to that object my studies were directed with great ardour and perseverance during the years 1789, 1790, 1791, 1792.

Marie-Henri Beyle (Stendahl)
(1783-1842)

The July 12, 1801 entry in Stendahl's private diary, when he was eighteen years old, reveals the third period in the individual's choice of profession: the reality phase. In the entry, the French author showed his youthful determination to improve and to acquire worldly experience, to learn how to converse with ease and fluency, all for the expressed purpose of furthering his writing career. He based his confidence on the plays he had written or was planning to write.*

At the same time, the adolescent's intellectual bravura, his philosophical maunderings and easy generalizations are embodied in this passage. But Stendahl's ability and perseverance enabled him to fulfill his ambition, as his later novels certify.

July 12, 1801

Let us put the present to good use, for our minutes are numbered. The hours I've spent fretting have nonetheless brought me that much nearer death. Let us work, for work is the father of pleasure, but let us never fret. Let us reflect sanely before deciding our course; once our decision is taken, we ought never to change our minds. With a

---

*From *The Private Diaries of Stendahl* translated by Robert Sage. Reprinted by permission of Doubleday & Co., Inc. Copyright 1959, Robert Sage. Pp. 11-12.

steadfast heart, anything can be attained. Give us talent; the day will come when I'll regret the time I've wasted.

A major source of consolation is the fact that you can't simultaneously be an expert in everything. You formulate an elevated idea of yourself by observing your superiority in a certain line, your mind is stimulated by this reflection, you compare yourself to those who are inferior to you, you develop a feeling of superiority to them; then you are mortified to see that they are more successful than you in some other line that often is the principal subject of their attention. It would be too cruel for the same man to have every kind of superiority; I even wonder if the apparent happiness he'd get from this wouldn't quickly fade into boredom. It's essential, however, to try to attain this superiority, because, though never absolute, it does exist, more or less, and usually is the source of success; moreover, it gives a feeling of assurance that it is almost always the decisive factor in success.

I believe, for instance, that one of these days I'll do something in the theatrical line. The draft of *Selmours*, of *Le Ménage à la Mode*, of *Les Quiproquos,* the ideas of *L'Aventurier* Nocturne, the tragedies of *Le Soldat Croisé Revenant chez ses Parents* and *Ariodant* seem to justify this confidence. My mind, which is constantly occupied, always drives me to seek instruction which may justify my hopes. As soon as there is an opportunity to improve myself and have a good time, I need to remind myself that I must acquire worldly experience to be able to choose my pleasures. After that, how can I be surprised to be awkward with women, not to succeed with them and to shine in society only when the argument gets heated or the conversation turns on the multitude of characters or passions that form my continual subject of study?

Benjamin Robert Haydon
(1786-1846)

The start of Benjamin Haydon's tragic career as a painter is brushstroked for us in the pages below. He paints the fierce battles he had with his father who opposed his artistic ambitions and the tearful scenes with his mother who tried to reconcile the two. But nothing would stop the eighteen-year-old boy from his chosen profession, not even near-blindness which visited him twice, nor any other "tortures of the rack." His stubborn determination, abetted by the repugnance he felt toward his apprenticeship to a merchant and his detestation of his father's business, overcame the heavy pressures brought to bear on him. His rebellion was complete and final.

All of Haydon's life was a struggle for recognition which never quite came his way. Nor, despite his extremely industrious habits, was he ever able to provide himself a firm financial foothold. At the age of sixty, his courage at length snapped, and he completed his diary with a pathetic farewell message:

> 22d—God forgive me. Amen.
> **Finis**
> of
> B. R. Haydon.

After which he abandoned the struggle, vainly attempted to shoot himself and then successfully cut his throat (10).

With my schooling at Plympton concluded my classical education. I returned home, and was sent to Exeter to be perfected in merchants' accounts. Here I did little. The master's son taught crayon-drawing, and I drew under him for a short time, but was more celebrated for electrifying the cat, killing flies by sparks, and doing everything and anything but my duty. At the end of six months I came back for life— unhappy in mind, disgusted with everything but drawing, yet prepared to do what my father thought right, and resolved to make the best of it.

I was bound to him for seven years, and now began that species of misery I have never been without since—ceaseless opposition. Drawing for amusement was one thing, but studying the art for a living was another. My father's business realised a handsome income; I had nothing to do but pursue his course and independence was certain.

Now that I was bound by law, repugnance to my work grew daily. I rose early and wandered by the sea; sat up late and pondered on my ambition.

I knew enough of form to point out with ridicule the misshapen arms, legs, feet, and bodies of various prints of eminent men in my father's windows, and was censured for my presumption.

I hated day-books, ledgers, bill-books, and cash-books; I hated standing behind the counter, and insulted the customers; I hated the town and people in it. I saw my father had more talent than the asses he was obliged to bend to; I knew his honourable descent, and I despised the vain fools that patronised him. Once, after a man had

offered me less than the legitimate price for a Latin dictionary, I
dashed the book on its shelf and walked out of the shop. My father
restored his customer to good humour by explaining to him the impropriety of expecting a respectable tradesman to take less than the
market price. The man, convinced, paid the full sum and took the
book.

I never entered the shop again. Now what was to be done? Into the
shop I would not go, and my father saw the absurdity of wishing it.
He was a good, dear, fond father. We discussed my future prospects,
and he asked me if it was not a pity to let such a fine property go to
ruin, as I had no younger brother? I could not help it. Why? Because
my whole frame convulsed when I thought of being a great painter.

"Who has put this stuff in your head?" "Nobody: I always have had
it." "You will live to repent." "Never, my dear father; I would rather
die in the trial."

After that we were silent—at dinner, at tea, at bedtime. Friends
were called in; aunts consulted, uncles spoken to; my language was
the same; my detestation of business unaltered; my resolution no
tortures of the rack would have altered.

Luckily, I had an illness, which in a few weeks ended in chronic
inflammation of the eyes. For six weeks I was blind, and my family
were in misery. At last, fancying I could see something glittering I put
out my hand and struck it against a silver spoon. That was a day of
happiness for us all. My mind, always religious, was deeply affected.
I recovered my sight, but never perfectly; had another attack, slowly
recovered from that, but found that my natural sight was gone, and
this too, with my earnest and deep passion for art. "What folly! How
can *you* think of being a painter? Why, you can't see," was said. "I can
see enough," was my reply; "and, see or not see, a painter I'll be, and
if I am a great one without seeing, I shall be the first." Upon the
whole, my family was not displeased that I could only see sufficiently
for business. I could still keep accounts and post the cash-books. It
would have been quite natural for an ordinary mind to think blindness a sufficient obstacle to the practice of an art, the essence of which
seems to consist in perfect sight, but "when the divinity doth stir within us," the most ordinary mind is ordinary no longer.

It is curious to me *now*, forty years after, to reflect that my dim sight
never occurred to me as an obstacle; not a bit of it: I found that I
could not shoot as I used to do, but it never struck me that I should
not be able to paint.

The moment my health recovered I went to see an apprentice of my father's who had set up for himself and who had brought down from town some plaster casts of the Discobolos and Apollo—the first I had ever seen. I looked at them so long that I made my eyes ill, and bought them out of a two-guinea piece given to me by my godfather. I doted over them; I dreamt of them; and when well, having made up my mind how to proceed, I wandered about the town, in listless agony, in search of books on art.

My father's apprentice (Johns), a man of considerable talent and ingenuity, possessed a library in which I used to read. Accidentally tumbling his collection over I hit upon Reynolds' *Discourses*. I read one. It placed so much reliance on honest industry, it expressed so strong a conviction that all men were equal and that application made the difference, that I fired up at once. I took them all home and read them through before breakfast the next morning. The thing was done. I felt my destiny fixed. The spark which had for years lain struggling to blaze, now burst out for ever.

I came down to breakfast with Reynolds under my arm, and opened my fixed intentions in a style of such energy that I demolished all arguments. My mother, regarding my looks, which probably were more like those of a maniac than of a rational being, burst into tears. My father was in a passion and the whole house was in an uproar. Everybody that called during the day was had up to bait me, but I attacked them so fiercely that they were glad to leave me to my own reflections. In the evening I told my mother my resolution calmly, and left her. My friend Reynolds (a watchmaker) backed me. I hunted the shop for anatomical works, and seeing Albinus among the books in the catalogue of Dr. Farr's sale at Plymouth hospital, but knowing it was no use asking my father to buy it for me, I determined to bid for it and then appeal to his mercy. I went to the sale and the book was knocked down to me at two pounds ten shillings. I returned home, laid the case before my dear mother, who cried much at this proof of resolution, but promised to get my father to consent. When the book came home my father paid with black looks. Oh, the delight of hurrying it away to my bedroom, turning over the plates, copying them out, learning the origin and insertion of the muscles, and then getting my sister to hear me! She and I used to walk about the house, with our arms round each other's neck—she saying, "How many heads to the deltoid?" "Where does it rise?" "Where is it inserted?" and I answering. By these means, in the course of a fortnight, I got by heart all the muscles of the body.

My energy was incessant. My head whirled at the idea of going to

London and beginning life for myself. My father had routed me from the shop, because I was in the way with my drawings; I had been driven from the sitting-room, because the cloth had to be laid; scolded from the landing-place, because the stairs must be swept; driven to my attic, which now became too small, and at last I took refuge in my bedroom.

One morning as I lay awake very early, musing on my future prospects, the door slowly opened, and in crept my dear mother with a look of sleepless anxiety. She sat down on my bedside, took my hand, and said that my father blamed her very much for promising that I should go up to London, that he had been talking all night to her, and had said that I should have everything I wished, if I would only give up my scheme. She added: "My dear Benjamin, you are our only support, and in the delicate state of your poor father's health God only knows how soon I may be left alone and unaided. It will break my heart if, after all my care and anxiety for your infancy, you leave me just as you are becoming able to comfort and console me."

I was deeply affected, but checking my tears I told her, in a voice struggling to be calm, that it was of no use to attempt to dissuade me. I felt impelled by something I could not resist. "Do not," said I, "my dear mother, think me cruel; I can never forget your love and affection; but yet I cannot help it—I must be a painter." Kissing me with wet cheeks and trembling lips she said in a broken voice: "She did not blame me; she applauded my resolution, but she could not bear to part with me."

I then begged her to tell my father that it was useless to harass me with further opposition. She rose sobbing as if to break her heart and slowly left my room, borne down with affliction. The instant she was gone I fell upon my knees and prayed God to forgive me if I was cruel, but to grant me firmness, purity, and piety to go on in the right way for success.

My father's opposition arose from the peculiarity of his situation. In early life he had been most basely treated by a man whom he had assisted in every possible way, and who returned this lavish generosity by a blow from which my father never recovered.

Disgusted with the world, he plunged into dissipation to forget himself. The society of the educated and virtuous was not stimulating enough, and from one class to another he gradually sunk till nothing pleased or gratified him but the company of players.

This neglect of his duties soon led him to embarrassment, embarrassment to law costs, and law costs, as a matter of course, to ruin and bankruptcy. However, he recommenced business, and then took into partnership a brother of my mother's, a Mr. Cobley, who was the friend of Prince Hoare and Kelly. He was fond of reading, accustomed to the best society, had passed his early life in Italy and acquired a taste for art, but with all these accomplishments and advantages was so habitually indolent that when he came to see my mother on a six weeks' visit he never had energy to remove, got imbedded in the family, stayed thirty years and died. Prince Hoare told me that he was the "pleasantest idle man he had ever known."

His mother left him an estate in Devonshire, which he sold to Sir Lawrence Palk, but he was so hideously indifferent to the future, that instead of investing what would have been an independence for life, he kept the money in his portmanteau for many years, taking it out, guinea by guinea, until it was all gone.

In this condition he came to us on a visit, and, finding every comfort, remained until he became a partner and died in possession of the business. Cobley had lived to see the folly of passing a youth at whist and watering-places, associating with actors and actresses, selling a maternal estate, and living on the money till it was spent. As he had suffered by his extreme folly in doing nothing but enjoy himself when he was young, he thought the soundest morality to preach was the danger of young people enjoying themselves at all. He was always talking of economy and expense, whilst economy and expense did not interfere with his enjoyments; and after expatiating on the prudence of eating cold meat the second day would pretend an engagement and dine at an inn, forgetting that his dinner and the cold meat both came from the profits of the business.

As a boy I soon saw through this, and gave him hints to that effect, which, of course, he did not relish.

My father had rapidly regained his lost credit, and was getting on well, when my determination to be a painter threw the whole family into confusion and anxiety. Cobley saw a continuance of expenditure on me, when it was hoped I should have been a help. My sister's education was not over, and I was still to be supplied. Remonstrances, quarrels, scoldings took place without end; till at last, seeing all was useless and cursing my firmness, they agreed to let me go and gave me twenty pounds to start upon.

Profound indeed were the predictions that I would be glad to return to papa and mamma before a month was over.

My poor father worn down with long sickness, the sad effect of trying to drown remembrance in wine, tottered about me. I collected my books and colours—packed my things—and on the 13th of May, 1804, took my place in the mail for the next day. The evening was passed in silent musing. Affection for home was smothered, not extinguished, in me: I thought only of London—Sir Joshua—Drawing —Dissection—and High Art.

The next day I ate little, spoke less, and kissed my mother many times. When all my things were corded and packed ready for the mail, I hung about my mother with a fluttering at my heart, in which duty, affection and ambition were struggling for the mastery.

As evening approached I missed my mother. At last the guard's horn announced the coming mail; I rushed upstairs, called her dear name, and was answered only by violent sobbings from my own bedroom. She could not speak—she could not see me. "God bless you, my dear child," I could just make out in her sobbings. The guard became impatient; I returned slowly downstairs with my heart too full to speak, shook my father by the hand, got in, the trunks were soon on the top, the whip cracked, the horses pranced and started off—my career for life had begun!

Hector Berlioz
(1803-1869)

Parental projection is once more in evidence in this excerpt from Berlioz' *Memoirs.** Berlioz' father, himself a physician, considered the profession "the finest in the world," and insisted Hector follow it, despite the boy's predilection for, and obvious talent in, music. Bribery (a flute), and mingled respect and fear which his father inspired in him, compelled him to accede to his father's demand.

Berlioz attended medical school in Paris but he was so drawn to music that "when I learnt that the library of the Conservatoire, with its wonderful wealth of scores, was open to the public, I could not resist the longing to become better acquainted with Gluck's works, for which I had an instinctive love, and which were not then being played at the Opéra. Once I entered that sanctuary I never quitted it. It was the death-blow to my medical career, and the dissecting room was finally abandoned."

While engaged in these experiments, and absorbed in reading, geography, religion, and the storms and calms of my first love affair,

---

*Reprinted by permission of Alfred A. Knopf, Inc. 1932. Pp. 15-17.

the time approached for me to choose a career. My father intended me to follow his profession, which he considered the finest in the world; and had told me so long before. I had often expressed my contrary views on the subject most emphatically, and he thoroughly disapproved of them. I had as yet no very definite ideas; but I felt a strong presentiment that I was not intended to spend my life at the bedsides of sick people, in hospitals, or in dissecting-rooms, and was firmly determined to resist all attempts to make a doctor of me. About this time I read the lives of Gluck and Haydn in the *Biographie universelle,* and they excited me immensely. "What a glorious existence!" I said to myself, as I thought of their illustrious careers; "what an art, and what happiness to be able to live for it!" An apparently trifling incident strengthened my bent in this direction, and shot a sudden light into my soul that revealed to me a thousand strange and splendid musical horizons.

I had never seen a full score. The only pieces of music I knew were *solfeggios* accompanied by a figured bass, solos for the flute, or bits of operas with pianoforte accompaniment. One day, however, I found a sheet of paper with twenty-four staves ruled upon it. I realised in a moment the wondrous instrumental and vocal combinations to which they might give rise, and I cried out, "What an orchestral work one might write on that!" From this moment the musical fermentation in my head went on increasing, and my distaste for medicine redoubled. But I was far too much afraid of my parents to venture to impart my wild dreams to them, and one day my father suddenly determined to use my love of music as a lever for removing what he called a "childish aversion," and by one masterstroke to embark me at once on the study of medicine.

In order to familiarise me with the things I was soon to have constantly before my eyes, he spread out in his study Munro's enormous treatise on osteology, with life-size illustrations of the structure of the body.

"This is the work you are to study," he said to me. "I do not suppose you will persist in your prejudice against medicine, for it is unreasonable and wholly unfounded, and if you promise to work earnestly at osteology I will get you a splendid flute, with all the new keys, from Lyons."

I had long coveted such an instrument, and what could I say? . . . The earnestness of the proposal, the mingled respect and fear with which, in spite of all his kindness, my father inspired me, and the promised reward, were too much for me. I stammered out a faint Yes, fled into my room, and threw myself on my bed overwhelmed with grief.

Become a doctor! study anatomy! dissect! witness horrible operations! instead of throwing myself heart and soul into the glorious and beautiful art of music! Forsake the empyrean for the dreary realities of earth! the immortal angels of poetry and love and their inspired songs for filthy hospitals, dreadful medical students, hideous corpses, the shrieks of patients, the groans and death rattle of the dying! ... It seemed to me the utter reversal of the natural conditions of my life; horrible and impossible. Yet it came to pass.

My osteological studies were undertaken in company with my cousin, A. Robert, since become a great Paris doctor, who had also become my father's pupil. Unfortunately Robert played the violin very well, and was one of my performers in the quintets, so that we spent more time at music than at anatomy. But he worked so hard at home that he always knew his demonstrations much better than I did. This called forth severe rebukes and even fierce bursts of anger from my father. Still, partly by my own efforts, partly by coercion, with the aid of prepared skeletons, I at last learnt in a kind of way all my father could teach me about anatomy; and at [seventeen], encouraged by my fellow-student, I decided to go with him to Paris, and there enter upon my medical studies in earnest.

Hans Christian Andersen
(1805-1875)

The Danish fairy tale master began his career in an almost fairy-like manner. Armed with no more than a letter of recommendation from a neighbor, thirteen rigsdalers he had saved over several years, and a naive but determined ambition to make good in the theater, the fourteen-year-old boy left his mother and grandmother to seek fame and fortune in the big city, Copenhagen. It was only after a " 'wise woman' had been fetched from the asylum" and told his fortune in the cards and coffee grounds—and a remarkably accurate prophecy it was—that his mother permitted him to go (17).

> When I turned fourteen my mother thought I should be confirmed, so that I could be apprenticed to a tailor and have some sensible occupation. She loved me with her whole heart, but she did not understand my aspirations and hankerings, and neither did I at the time. The neighbours were always passing remarks about the way I lived and spent my time, and that grieved and pained her.

For several years I had been saving up all the little coins I received on different occasions, and when I now counted these I had thirteen rigsdalers. It was overwhelming to find myself in possession of so large a sum, and as my mother was now insisting that I become a tailor's apprentice, I begged and pleaded with her that instead I might be allowed to try my luck in Copenhagen.

"What will become of you?" asked my mother.

"I shall be famous!" I replied and told her about all the famous men of whom I had read who had been born in poverty. "You first go through an awful lot of bad things," said I, "and so you become famous!" It was an entirely inexplicable urge which possessed me. I wept and pleaded and in the end my mother gave way, but not till a so-called "wise woman" had been fetched from the asylum and she had told my fortune in the cards and coffee grounds.

"Your son will become a great man," the old woman said, "and one day Odense town will be illuminated in his honour!" My mother wept when she heard this and after that had nothing against my going. All the neighbours and any who heard of it told my mother that it was a dreadful thing to allow me, who was only fourteen and such a child over everything, to go off to Copenhagen which was so far away and a large city where I knew no one and would get lost. "He won't let me have any peace," replied my mother, "and I have had to give him permission to go, but it doesn't matter, because I'm sure that he will get no farther than Nyborg. When he sees the wild seas there, he will be afraid and turn back, and then he shall become a tailor's apprentice."

The summer before my confirmation part of the Royal Theatre company had come to Odense and performed a number of operas and tragedies. Being well in with the bill-poster, I had not only seen all the performances from the wings, but I had myself appeared both as a page and as a shepherd boy, and in one piece I had even had a couple of lines to say. All the praise I had had of my singing voice and the way I recited poetry and monologues made me now realize quite clearly that I was born for the stage and that it was here I should become famous. Therefore it was the theatre in Copenhagen which was the object of my aspirations. The presence of the actors in Odense was to many people, and especially to me, the great event of their lives. There were some who had been in Copenhagen and gone to the theatre there, and they spoke of something they called "ballet" which was said to surpass opera and comedy. Madame Schall, the dancer, was, they said, the first and the greatest, and so I took her to be like the queen of it all, and in my imagination I regarded her as the one person who, when I had won her kindness and protection, would be able to help me to honours and fortune.

Filled with this idea, I went to old Iversen, the book printer, one of Odense's most respected citizens, whom I knew the actors had visited daily while they were in Odense, and who, knowing them all, must also know the dancer. I wanted to ask him to give me a letter to her, and after that God would do the rest.

It was the first time the old man had ever seen me, but he was friendly and listened to me, but he advised me most strongly not to venture on such a journey. "You ought to learn a trade," he told me. "That would really be a great pity!" I replied, and he was amazed at the way I said it, and it won him over. He told me that he did not know the dancer personally, but he would give me a letter to her all the same. I was given it and thought that now fortune's door was open to me.

My mother packed a little bundle of clothes, spoke with the diligence man to see whether I couldn't be given a "lift" to Copenhagen, and it was arranged that I was to pay only three rigsdalers for the whole journey. At last came the afternoon when I was to leave. Sorrowfully mother went with me outside the town gate; there stood my old grandmother. Latterly her pretty hair had turned grey; she put her arms round my neck, weeping and unable to utter a word; I was sad myself —and so we parted. I never saw her again, for she died the following year.

The postillion blew his horn. It was a lovely sunny afternoon, and soon my fickle childish mind had forgotten its sadness. I rejoiced in all the new things I was seeing, and then too I was journeying to the goal of my longings. When we left Nyborg and came out on to the Great Belt and sailed away from my native island, however, I realized how alone and left to my own resources I was, and how I had no other than God in heaven. As soon as I stepped ashore in Zealand I went behind a shed on the beach, fell on my knees and prayed to God to help and guide me. After that I felt comforted, put my trust in God and in my luck and so drove all that day and the next night through towns and villages. While the horses were being changed, I stood nearby and ate my bread. It was all so strange, that I seemed to be far out in the wide world.

W. P. Frith
(1819-1909)

A different kind of father-son relationship is depicted in the following illustration from W. P. Frith's autobiography (8). In this instance we see a father encouraging a reluctant and frightened son to enter the art profession even though the century considered it a "disreputable calling," and relatives thought the parents "insane." Frith, senior, however, had great faith in his son's talent, and in a methodical way set out to determine if that talent was great enough to justify him in starting his boy on a career in art.

Frith was human enough, modest enough, and realistic enough to be able to say, "I know very well that I never was, nor under any circumstances could have become, a great artist; but I am a very successful one. . . . " As an art student, he was friendly with Edward Lear. He later became a Member of the Royal Academies of Belgium, Stockholm, Vienna and Antwerp.

The motivation of parents in directing their children's careers is varied and familiar, although not usually recognized by the people concerned. Projection, compensation, and rationalization are probably the most frequent factors. Parental needs for status and security may over-ride the children's needs, for if the progeny fulfills the parents' wishes, the latter can live out their lives through the children.

I now go back to my own career. On returning home from school with my bundle of specimens, a family council was called, with friends to assist. There was no doubt in the mind of any one of them, I verily believe, that I was a great genius.

"Why, just look," said an old woman in the shape of a man, "you can't tell one from t'other!" showing a print of Teniers' and my chalk copy from it; and they certainly were, and are (for they still hang and can be compared on my staircase), very much alike.

I was the wonder of High Harrogate, then my home. People came and asked for a sight of the wonderful works, which my dear mother showed with a pardonable pride. She could not and did not ask her guests to wash their hands—a treatment, as I remember, desirable for some of them; but she would never let the drawings leave her own hands, for fear of the precious things being rubbed or otherwise injured.

"If I was you," said one wiseacre, "I'd never let him have any teaching; they'd spoil him. Look at Mr. Wilkie now, the man that did the 'Blind Fiddler' and that; he was self-taught."

"No, he wasn't," said my father. "Don't you talk of what you know nothing about."

I may remark here that my father was a gruff, silent man, but by no means such a fool as to think that a self-taught artist had anything but a fool for both master and pupil. At this time I was in my fifteenth year, and it was thought desirable that my future career should be determined. My eldest brother had died, my youngest one was intended for the law, and I for the arts if I decided on that profession. Parents, in nearly all instances that have come within my experience, have shown marked and often angry opposition to the practice of art as a profession for their children; naturally and properly, I think, considering the precarious nature of its pursuit. My parents were exceptions to that rule, and I shall never forget my father's look of disappointment when, on his asking me if I should like to go to London and learn to be a real artist, I replied:

"I don't care much about it."

"Well, what would you like to be? You must do something for your living, you know."

"I think I should like to be an auctioneer, or something of that kind."

"An auctioneer be——!" said my father, who used strong language sometimes. . . .

As my father and I returned home after seeing the H—— collection, he recurred to the subject of my future destiny.

"Surely you would like to be able to paint such pictures as H——'s," said he.

"Yes, but I never could; still, I will try if you wish it."

Not much of the sacred fire in all this, not much of the passion for art which Constable once stigmatized in a man who painted very poor pictures, and who claimed a right to have them exhibited because painting had been all his life a passion that possessed him. "Yes," said Constable, "a *bad* passion."

Soon after this my father showed me a letter from Sir Launcelot Shadwell, who was, I think, vice-chancellor, and who had been one of the visitors at The Dragon for several seasons. The letter was in reply to an inquiry as to the best way of proceeding in the event of my studying as an artist. Sir Launcelot had seen my drawings, and, being pardonably ignorant, had seen, or fancied he saw, not only promise, but such performance in them as would make much instruction unnecessary! Mr. Phillips, R.A., however, a friend of the vice-chancellor's, informs all and sundry that the kind of drawing described to him meant nothing; that if I intended to follow the profession seriously I had best go to London and place myself under a Mr. Sass, who had a school of art in Charlotte Street, Bloomsbury; and after I had worked hard there for two or three years, I might possibly become a student of the Royal

Academy, where I should find ample and gratuitous instruction. I was a light-minded, rather idle, flighty youth, not at all fond of serious work, and this letter frightened me. I told my father I did not think my health would stand such work as that.

"What do you mean—your health? What's the matter with your health? You have never been ill in your life, except when you had measles. Don't talk such stuff! Now look here," he added; "I want to talk to you seriously" (he seldom talked, and always seriously). "You have your living to get; everybody says you show ability for the artist business; will you follow it? If you will, I shall take you to London, and am willing to spend some money on it; and if you won't do this, what will you do? If you are not an artist, what will you be?"

I had been two or three times to an auction-room, and the business seemed a very easy and, I had heard, a profitable one; so instead of saying I would rather die than not be a painter, I reiterated to my father that I thought I should like auctioneering better. Again the blank look of disappointment; then, after a pause, he said,

"Very well, will you agree to this? You and I will go to London. I will take your drawings and show them to Sir Launcelot Shadwell's friend the R.A. If he says you ought to be an artist, will you go to this Mr. What's-his-name in Bloomsbury and learn the business? If he thinks nothing of your drawings, I will apprentice you to Oxenham's in Oxford Street, and you can learn auctioneering. Now, what do you say?"

"Very well, I will."

"You agree to what I propose?"

"Yes, I do."

"Now go and tell your mother; she will be pleased, I know."

William J. Stillman
(1828-1901)

The folly and injustice of parents arbitrarily deciding what course of vocational action their children must take is nowhere more bitterly described, perhaps, than in the words of William J. Stillman.* Stillman was the youngest of nine children, five of whom died before his mother. One brother became a physician, another a leading engineer, a third a school principal and a fourth a foreman in a factory. It was these siblings who sided with their mother in insist-

---

*From *The Autobiography of a Journalist*. Reprinted by permission of Houghton Mifflin Co. 1901. Pp. 61-63.

ing that William go to Union College and prevailed over their father, who was tenacious in his intention of apprenticing the boy to his workshop. Sixteen-year-old William was hardly consulted, for he wanted neither choice. His choice was art.

He describes here the effect of this decision on his adult life: the compromises necessarily made, the foreboding sense of frustration, and the dissatisfaction of the dilettante. Later in life, Stillman renounced his United States citizenship to become a British subject. He worked in the diplomatic service and from 1876 to 1898, as a correspondent for the *London Times*.

Returning to Schenectady, I found that the family had begun to discuss the future of my career, which had arrived at the point of divergences. My father, who had no opinion of the utility of advanced education for boys in our station, was tenacious in his intention to have me in his workshop, where he needed more apprentices, but my mother was still more obstinate in hers that I should have the education; and in the decision the voices of my brothers were too potent not to hold the casting vote. In the stern, Puritanical manner of the family, I had been more or less the *enfant gâté* of all its members, except my brother Paul, the third of my brothers, who, coming into the knowledge of domestic affairs at the time when the family was at its greatest straits, had expressed himself bitterly at my birth, over the imprudence of our parents' increasing their obligations when they were unable to provide for the education of the children they had already, and had always retained for me a little of the bitterness of those days. On the whole, the vote of the family council was for the education. My own wishes were hardly consulted, for I differed from both opinions, having an intense enthusiasm for art, to which I wished to devote myself.

The collective decision, in which my father and myself were alike overruled, was that I should go to Union College, in Schenectady, as the collegiate education was supposed to be a facilitation for whatever occupation I might afterwards decide on. This was, so far as I was concerned, a fatal error, and one of a kind far too common in New England communities, where education is estimated by the extent of the ground it covers, without relation to the superstructure to be raised on it. I had always been a greedy reader of books, and especially of histories and the natural sciences,—everything in the vegetable or animal world fascinated me,—and I had no ambition for academic honors, nor did I ever acquire any, but I passionately desired a technical education in the arts, and the decision of the family deferred the first steps in that direction for years, and precisely those years when facility of hand is most completely acquired and enthusiasm against difficulties is strongest—the years when, if ever, the artist is made.

In my case the result of the imposed career was a disaster; I was diverted from the only occupation to which I ever had a recognizable calling, and ultimately I drifted into journalism, as the consequence of a certain literary facility developed by the exercises of the college course. The consequences were the graver that I was naturally too much disposed to a vagrant life; and the want of a dominant interest in my occupation led to indulgence, on every occasion that offered in later life, of the tendency to wander. I came out of the experience with a divided allegiance, enough devotion to letters to make it a satisfaction to occupy myself with them, but too much interest in art to be able to abandon it entirely. Before entering college, art was a passion, but when, at the age of twenty, the release gave me the liberty to throw myself into painting, the finer roots of enthusiasm were dead, and I became only a dilettante, for the years when one acquires the mastery of the hand and will which make the successful artist were past.

Hannah Smith
(1832-1911)

The fantasy life of the adolescent is usually a full one and frequently a comforting one. To daydream about one's future accomplishments while still dependent, to pretend to be all-powerful when one is still helpless, and to dream of multitudes paying homage when reality says he is low man on the totem pole, give the adolescent a private sanctuary to which he can retreat in time of need.

Hannah Whitall Smith, one of the leading Quakers in American religious history, describes in this letter to her cousin, Annie Whitall, the several "air castles" she built for herself one day during her eighteenth year.*

Thee cannot imagine, cousin, Annie, what a splendid air castle I built today (I won't say where). I imagined that on a certain time Thomas Evans should preach to me, and all of a sudden in some unaccountable manner I should get perfectly good, just like Mme. Guyon. I should dress like mother in a cap and handkerchief, and sugarscoop bonnet and hooded cloak, and should preach at the very

*From *Philadelphia Quaker: The Letters of Hannah W. Smith* edited by Logan P. Smith. Reprinted by permission of Harcourt, Brace & World, Inc. 1950. Pp. 4-5.

next meeting I attended. And oh! what a *splendid* voice I gave to my-self; I pictured the whole meeting as almost ready to fall down and worship me, I was so magnificently eloquent, so grandly sublime.

And next I went on a religious visit to England when only 19, where the whole nation even the Queen herself crowded to hear the "young eloquent Quaker girl," and next I went to France—but here my visions were cut short, most fortunately perhaps, or I might next have gone on a religious visit to the moon. Is it not queer, cousin Annie, but does thee know nearly all my air castles are on that subject, I have always had such an idea even from a little child that I *would* preach some day. As far back as I can remember I used to sit in meeting and look at the ministers and wonder how I would feel when I sat up there and preached, as I fully expected to do: and once, at Yearly Meeting-time when it snowed, and we waited for the carriage, I tried it. I stood in Elizabeth Evans's place and imagined myself with a cap and handkerchief on and all the benches full of people, and began "my dear friends." But I could go no further, my feelings were really awful. I was frightened and hurried down as fast as possible. Foolish, foolish child! Of course I know now that such a thing is utterly out of the question, but I cannot help the feeling once in a while passing through my mind. I have always said that I expected to be a minister —to be as fat as aunt Scattergood—and to be married and have 13 great children; but don't for the world let anyone know that last expectation;—it was the folly of my younger years, I don't expect such things now.

Joseph Conrad *(1857-1924)*

From the age of fourteen, Conrad had secretly longed to be a sailor. At the age of sixteen, in 1872, he confided this ambition to his uncle. The following account, assembled by Frank W. Cushwa* from "a personal record," shows the strength of Conrad's desire, the ex-tremity of the opposition, and the almost mystical influence of a stranger. It should be noted that the "unforgettable Englishman" spoke no word to Conrad, or Conrad to him; that it was the stran-ger's "striving-forward" appearance at a critical moment which emboldened the youth at the top of the Alpine pass—where he was

---

*In *An Introduction to Conrad*. Reprinted by permission of J. M. Dent & Sons, Ltd. and Trustees of the Joseph Conrad Estate. Pp. 25-30.

visiting in 1873—not to capitulate. A little more than a year later, Conrad was on the docks at Marseilles and a decade or so after that was a Master in the British Merchant Service.

   ... It was the year in which I had first spoken aloud of my desire to go to sea. At first, like those sounds that, ranging outside the scale to which men's ears are attuned, remain inaudible to our sense of hearing, this declaration passed unperceived. It was as if it had not been. Later on, by trying various tones, I managed to arouse here and there a surprised momentary attention—the "What was that funny noise?" sort of inquiry. Later on it was—"Did you hear what that boy said? What an extraordinary outbreak!" Presently a wave of scandalized astonishment (it could not have been greater if I had announced the intention of entering a Carthusian monastery) ebbing out of the educational and academical town of Cracow spread itself over several provinces. It spread itself shallow but far-reaching. It stirred up a mass of remonstrance, indignation, pitying wonder, bitter irony, and downright chaff. I could hardly breathe under its weight, and certainly had no words for an answer. . . .

   ... I don't mean to say that a whole country had been convulsed by my desire to go to sea. But for a boy between fifteen and sixteen, sensitive enough, in all conscience, the commotion of his little world had seemed a very considerable thing indeed. So considerable that, absurdly enough, the echoes of it linger to this day. I catch myself in hours of solitude and retrospect meeting arguments and charges made thirty-five years ago by voices now for ever still; finding things to say that an assailed boy could not have found, simply because of the mysteriousness of his impulses to himself. I understood no more than the people who called upon me to explain myself. There was no precedent. I verily believe mine was the only case of a boy of my nationality and antecedents taking a, so to speak, standing jump out of his racial surrounding and associations.

   ... People wondered what Mr. T. B. would do now with his worrying nephew and, I dare say, hoped kindly that he would make short work of my nonsense.

   What he did was to come down all the way from Ukraine to have it out with me and to judge by himself, unprejudiced, impartial, and just, taking his stand on the ground of wisdom and affection. As far as is possible for a boy whose power of expression is still unformed, I opened the secret of my thoughts to him and he in return allowed me a glimpse into his mind and heart; the first glimpse of an inexhaustible and noble treasure of clear thought and warm feeling, which through life was to be mine to draw upon with a never deceived love and confidence. Practically, after several exhaustive conversations, he concluded that he would not have me later on reproach him for having spoiled my life by an unconditional opposition. But I must take time for serious reflection. And I must not only think of myself but of others; weigh the claims of affection and conscience against my own sincerity of purpose. "Think well what it all means in the larger issues, my boy," he exhorted me finally with special friendliness. "And meantime try to get the best place you can at the yearly examinations."

The scholastic year came to an end. I took a fairly good place at the exams, which for me (for certain reasons) happened to be a more difficult task than for other boys. In that respect I could enter with a good conscience upon that holiday which was like a long visit *pour prendre congé* of the mainland of old Europe I was to see so little of for the next four-and-twenty years. Such, however, was not the avowed purpose of that tour. It was rather, I suspect, planned in order to distract and occupy my thoughts in other directions. Nothing had been said for months of my going to sea. But my attachment to my young tutor and his influence over me were so well known that he must have received a confidential mission to talk me out of my romantic folly. It was an excellently appropriate arrangement, as neither he nor I had ever had a single glimpse of the sea in our lives. That was to come by-and-by for both of us in Venice, from the outer shore of Lido. Meantime he had taken his mission to heart so well that I began to feel crushed before we reached Zurich. He argued in railway trains, in lake steamboats, he had argued away for me the obligatory sunrise on the Rigi, by Jove! Of his devotion to his unworthy pupil there can be no doubt. He had proved it already by two years of unremitting and arduous care. I could not hate him. But he had been crushing me slowly, and when he started to argue on the top of the Furca Pass he was perhaps nearer a success than either he or I imagined. I listened to him in despairing silence, feeling that ghostly, unrealized, and desired sea of my dreams escape from the unnerved grip of my will.

We sat down by the side of the road to continue the argument begun half a mile or so before. I am certain it was an argument because I remember perfectly how my tutor argued and how without the power of reply I listened with my eyes fixed obstinately on the ground. A stir on the road made me look up—and then I saw my unforgettable Englishman. There are acquaintances of later years, familiars, shipmates, whom I remember less clearly. He marched rapidly towards the east (attended by a hangdog Swiss guide) with the mien of an ardent and fearless traveler. He was clad in a knicker-bocker suit, but as at the same time he wore short socks under his laced boots, for reasons which, whether hygienic or conscientious, were surely imaginative, his calves, exposed to the public gaze and to the tonic air of high altitudes, dazzled the beholder by the splendor of their marble-like condition and their rich tone of young ivory. He was the leader of a small caravan. The light of a headlong exalted satisfaction with the world of men and the scenery of mountains illumined his clean-cut, very red face, his short silver-white whiskers, his innocently eager and triumphant eyes. In passing he cast a glance of kindly curiosity and a friendly gleam of big, sound, shiny teeth towards the man and the boy sitting like dusty tramps by the roadside, with a modest knapsack lying at their feet. His white calves twinkled sturdily, the uncouth Swiss guide with a surly mouth stalked like an unwilling bear at his elbow; a small train of three mules followed in single file the lead of this inspiring enthusiast. . . .

I tell you it was a memorable year! One does not meet such an Englishman twice in a lifetime. Was he in the mystic ordering of common events the ambassador of my future, sent out to turn the scale at a critical moment on the top of an Alpine pass, with the peaks of the Bernese Oberland for mute and solemn witnesses? His glance, his smile, the inextinguishable and comic ardor of his striving-forward appearance helped me to pull myself together. . . .

The enthusiastic old Englishman had passed—and the argument went on. What reward could I expect from such a life at the end of my years, either in ambition, honor, or conscience? An unanswerable question. But I felt no longer crushed. Then our eyes met and a genuine emotion was visible in his as well as in mine. The end came all at once. He picked up the knapsack suddenly and got on to his feet.

"You are an incorrigible, hopeless Don Quixote. That's what you are."

I was surprised. I was only fifteen and did not know what he meant exactly. But I felt vaguely flattered at the name of the immortal knight turning up in connection with my own folly, as some people would call it to my face. Alas! I don't think there was anything to be proud of. Mine was not the stuff the protectors of forlorn damsels, the redressers of this world's wrongs are made of; and my tutor was the man to know that best. Therein, in his indignation, he was superior to the barber and the priest when he flung at me an honored name like a reproach.

I walked behind him for full five minutes; then without looking back he stopped. The shadows of distant peaks were lengthening over the Furca Pass. When I came up to him he turned to me and in full view of the Finster-Aarhorn, with his band of giant brothers rearing their monstrous heads against a brilliant sky, put his hand on my shoulder affectionately.

"Well! That's enough. We will have no more of it."

And indeed there was no more question of my mysterious vocation between us. There was to be no more question of it at all, nowhere or with any one. We began the descent of the Furca Pass conversing merrily. Eleven years later, month for month, I stood on Tower Hill on the steps of the St. Katherine's Dockhouse, a master in the British Merchant Service.

Simone de Beauvoir
(1908-   )

Miss de Beauvoir, in the two excerpts found here,* illustrates the tentative vocation choice of the early adolescent and the more realistic choice of the later adolescent. When she was twelve and thirteen, Simone was a pious Catholic child who would slip into the school chapel between classes and offer up lengthy prayers, who would each year enter a retreat for several days, who would maintain silent meditations at home, and whose "conduct left so little to be desired that I could hardly be any better than I already was." What could be more natural than for the girl to decide to become a nun?

Three years later, when the "celestial radiance" had dimmed from her eyes, and more worldly visions appeared, Simone decided on the field of writing. On this point she had no doubts at all. The reasons? "My father rated [writers] far higher than scholars, philosophers, and professors." Simone was experiencing a very difficult revived oedipal complex, as is seen in the excerpt in that section, and part of the problem was worked on through its vocational component. Another reason for her choice was compensation. Writing "would guarantee me an immortality that would compensate for the loss of heaven and eternity; there no longer was a God to love me, but I would burn as a beacon in millions of hearts."

---

*From *Memoirs of a Dutiful Daughter*. Reprinted by permission of World Publishing Co. Copyright 1959, World Publishing Co. Pp. 77-80, 148-150.

I was very pious; I made my confession twice a month to Abbé
Martin, received Holy Communion three times a week, and every
morning read a chapter of *The Imitation of Christ;* between classes,
I would slip into the school chapel and, with my beads in my hands,
I would offer up lengthy prayers; often in the course of the day I
would lift up my soul to my Maker. I was no longer very interested in
the Infant Jesus, but I madly adored Christ. As supplements to the
Gospels, I had read disturbing novels of which He was the hero, and
it was now with the eyes of a lover that I gazed upon His grave, tender,
handsome face; I would follow, across hills covered with olive groves,
the shining hem of His snow-white robe, bathe His naked feet with my
tears; and He would smile down upon me as He had smiled upon the
Magdalene. When I had clasped His knees and sobbed on His blood-
stained corpse long enough, I would allow Him to ascend into heaven.
There he became one with that more mysterious Being to whom I
owed my existence on earth, and whose throne of glory would one
day, and forever, fill my eyes with a celestial radiance.

Each year I went into retreat for several days; all day long, I would
listen to my priest's instructions, attend services, tell my beads, and
meditate; I would remain at school for a frugal repast, and during the
meal someone would read to us from the life of a saint. In the
evenings, at home, my mother would respect my silent meditations.
I wrote down in a special notebook the outpourings of my immortal
soul and my saintly resolutions. I ardently desired to grow closer to
God, but I didn't know how to go about it. My conduct left so little
to be desired that I could hardly be any better than I already was;
besides, I wondered if God was really concerned about my general
behavior. The majority of faults that Mama reprimanded my sister
and me for were just awkward blunders or careless mistakes. . . . It was
perplexing that God forbade so many things, but never asked for
anything positive apart from a few prayers or religious practices
which did not change my daily course in any way. I even found it most
peculiar to see people who had just received Holy Communion
plunging straight away into the ordinary routine of their lives again;
I did the same, but it embarrassed me. Fundamentally it seemed to me
that believers and nonbelievers led just the same kind of life; I became
more and more convinced that there was no room in the secular world
for the supernatural life. And yet it was that otherworldly life that
really counted: it was the only kind that mattered. It suddenly became
obvious to me one morning that a Christian who was convinced of his
eternal salvation ought not to attach any importance to the ephemeral

things of this world. How could the majority of people go on living in the world as it was? The more I thought about it, the more I wondered at it. I decided that I, at any rate, would not follow their example: my choice was made between the finite and the infinite. "I shall become a nun," I told myself. The activities of sisters of charity seemed to me quite useless; the only reasonable occupation was to contemplate the glory of God to the end of my days. I would become a Carmelite. But I did not make my decision public: it would not have been taken seriously. I contented myself with the announcement that I did not intend to marry. My father smiled: "We'll talk about that again when you're fifteen years old." In my heart of hearts I resented his smile. I knew that an implacable logic led me to the convent: how could you prefer having nothing to having everything?

This imaginary future provided me with a convenient alibi. For many years it allowed me to enjoy without scruple all the good things of this world.

* * * *

I had long ago decided to devote my life to intellectual labors. Zaza shocked me when she declared, in a provocative tone of voice: "Bringing nine children into the world as Mama has done is just as good as writing books." I couldn't see any common denominator between these two modes of existence. To have children who in their turn would have more children was simply to go on playing the same old tune ad infinitum; the scholar, the artist, the writer, and the thinker created other worlds, all sweetness and light, in which everything had a purpose. That was where I wished to spend my life; I was quite determined to carve out a place for myself in those rarefied spheres. As soon as I had renounced heaven, my worldly ambitions increased: it became necessary for me to be somebody. Stretched out in a meadow I could see at eye level the endless waves of grass, each blade identical, each submerged in a miniature jungle that concealed it from all the rest. That unending repetition of ignorance and indifference was a living death. I raised my eyes and looked at the oak tree: it dominated the landscape and there was not another like it. That, I decided, is what *I* would be like.

Why did I decide to be a writer? As a child, I had never taken my scribblings very seriously; my real aim had been to acquire knowledge; I enjoyed doing French compositions, but my teachers objected to my stilted style; I did not feel I was a "born" writer. Yet at the age of fifteen when I wrote in a friend's album the plans and preferences which were supposed to give a picture of my personality, I answered without hesitation the question "What do you want to do later in life?" with "To be a famous author." As far as my favorite composer and my favorite flower were concerned I had invented more or less factitious preferences. But on that one point I had no doubts at all: I had set my heart on that profession, to the exclusion of everything else.

The main reason for this was the admiration I felt for writers: my father rated them far higher than scholars, philosophers, and professors. I, too, was convinced of their supremacy: even if his name was well-known, a specialist's monograph would be accessible to only a small number of people; but everyone read novels: they touched the imagination and the heart; they brought their authors universal and intimate fame. As a woman, these dizzy summits seemed to me much more accessible than the lowlier slopes; the most celebrated women had distinguished themselves in literature.

I had always had a longing to communicate with others. In my friend's album I cited as my favorite hobbies reading and conversation. I was a great talker. I would recount, or try to, everything that had struck me in the course of the day. I dreaded night and oblivion; it was agony to condemn to silence all that I had seen, felt, and liked. Moved by the moonlight, I longed for pen and paper and the ability to describe my feelings. When I was fifteen I loved volumes of letters, intimate journals—for example, the diary of Eugénie de Guérin—books that attempted to make time stand still. I had also realized that novels, short stories, and tales are not divorced from life but that they are, in their own way, expressions of it.

If at one time I had dreamed of being a teacher it was because I wanted to be a law unto myself; I now thought that literature would allow me to realize this dream. It would guarantee me an immortality that would compensate for the loss of heaven and eternity; there no longer was a God to love me, but I would burn as a beacon in millions of hearts. By writing a work based on my own experience I would re-create myself and justify my existence. At the same time I would be serving humanity: what finer offering could I make to it than books? I was concerned at the same time with myself and with others; I accepted the individuality of my "incarnation," but I did not wish to surrender membership in the universal. This writing project reconciled everything; it gratified all the aspirations which had been unfolding in me during the past fifteen years.

Yoshio Kodama
(1911-   )

Yoshio Kodama was a Japanese extremist, a nationalist who wrote his autobiography (14) in Sugamo Prison as a World War II Class A war crimes suspect. He had spent a good deal of his boyhood and adolescence in Korea with his father and younger brother. They were bitter and painful years, as he describes them.

In the passage used here, Kodama covers the two years between his sixteenth and eighteenth birthdays. It gives the reader an inkling of the hardships he endured and some understanding of the reasons for his subsequent political behavior. In 1929, he wrote, he was eighteen years old and "had finally crossed the threshold from boyhood into youthdom." That year was an ill-chosen one for such a major event.

I had attained the age of sixteen. I worked at this factory in Mukojima from 1927 to 1929, commuting from Imado-cho in Asakima. In the evenings, I attended night school at Mitoshiro-cho in Kanda. It was in those days that I gradually came to understand the functionings of society. And though in gradual stages, I also came to understand ideological and political issues.

During my life as a factory worker, a life of two years and more spent amid the din of flapping belts, two years of eating lunch with the stench of oil-stained hands striking my nostrils, I began to understand that the interests of the laborers and the capitalists were diametrically opposed. I was also to learn that the big capitalists were always in conspiracy with politicians and that the whole administration was centered around the capitalists.

In order to go to the iron factory in Mukojima from Imado-cho, where I lived, I used to take the shortest way by crossing the Sumida River over the Shirashige Bridge. At that time, the Shirashige Bridge was a dangerous half-broken construction. In the middle of the bridge there was a small stall kept by an old woman selling "daifuku-mochi." I often bought these cakes on my way home from the factory and it was one of my greatest pleasures to eat these cakes on the bridge, while looking down upon the Sumida River and pondering over life's problems. Down below, small steamboats churned the greasy surface of the river leaving behind trails of ripples as they passed. In this environment I often turned to the past, remembering my departed parents, reliving my life in Korea. Always my meandering thoughts returned to the question: What should I become?

"One thing is certain, I shall never again submit myself to suffering caused by others." And each time I reiterated this determination, I felt my youthful blood course through my body as deep unnamed anger surged within me. What then was my future to be? What course was I to take?

My trip to Korea with my father and younger brother after my mother's death at Takatanobaba, the poverty-stricken life in my birthplace, the struggles of a child laborer at a spinning factory, my hardships as a wanderlust in Korea and finally my life as a laborer at an iron factory attending night school—all this had gone into the making of my boyhood days. But now the year changed. It was 1929 and I was 18 years of age. I had finally crossed the threshold from boyhood into youthdom.

David S. Kogan
(1929-1951)

Most adolescents have a rich fantasy life, replete with magical beliefs and a *deus ex machina* rescuing them from an intolerable situation. One of the fondest magical beliefs of contemporary adolescents in the United States is in the so-called aptitude tests which will tell them "what they are best suited for."

This excerpt from David Kogan's *Diary** illustrates the dependency of many on the supposedly objective, scientific test. "It's amazing," David exclaims in awe, "what human engineering does!" The "engineering," as he reported it, gave him the superstructure but not the underpinning. The battery of tests he took revealed his I.Q., told him he had an "inferiority complex," and that he was interested in half a dozen fields. But it still left him troubled with the need to choose and prepare for a vocation, as was Lucian nearly two thousand years before him in ancient Syria—without benefit of tests—and most of the others whose vocational lives we have examined.

Thursday, October 3, 1946

Took a vocational guidance test today at the Jewish Vocational Guidance office, and had a long interview with Miss Potash, who was

---

*Reprinted by permission of Beechurst Press. 1955. Pp. 122-123.

very sympathetic. They are on scholastic aptitude, intelligence, personality, and interests. The results will be known Monday. Among the questions were hundreds of this type—"Would you rather visit a slum, dissect a frog, sell a fur coat?" The personality test was very personal, they even solicited an answer on crying! It's amazing what human engineering does!

Mom was interested in such questions as whether I would prefer being a barber or book reviewer, taking it for granted that I filled out "book reviewer, of course."

"Why, the 'of course'?" I had to disillusion her. Would I enjoy discussing day after day what other people wrote? It would kill my own thoughts. I would much rather be a barber. How colorful is the life of Sam—his place is practically an American institution. There politics are discussed together with current events, and local gossip is sprinkled with a fine sense of humor. Why, I am always glad his haircuts are not too close—gives me a chance to come back oftener.

Monday, October 7, 1946

Of importance were the results of the vocational guidance tests which I took: My I.Q. is 139; I have an inferiority complex; am primarily interested in the social, literary, and service fields, with things mechanical, musical, and computational secondary. Mine is a hard case—I should continue to explore—have good language power. Rabbi might be fine. Miss Potash was very kind.

REFERENCES

1. Andersen, Hans Christian. *The Mermaid Man. The Autobiography of Hans Christian Andersen.* New York: Library Publishers, 1955, pp. 22-25.
2. Ausubel, David P. *Theory and Problems of Adolescent Development.* New York: Grune & Stratton, 1954, pp. 437-438.
3. Borrow, George. *Lavengro—The Scholar—The Gypsy—The Priest.* London: Constable & Co., 1923, p. 190.
4. Erikson, Erik H. Growth and crises of the healthy personality. *Psychol. Issues,* 1:92, 1959.
5. ——. The problem of ego identity. *Psychol. Issues,* 1:128, 163, 1959.
6. Forel, August. *Out of My Life and Work.* New York: W. W. Norton & Co., 1937, pp. 22-23.
7. Franklin, Benjamin. *Autobiography.* New York: Rinehart & Co., 1948, pp. 10-11.

8. Frith, W. P. *My Autobiography and Reminiscences.* New York: Harper & Bros., 1889, Vol. I, pp. 7-11.
9. Goethe, Wolfgang von. *Goethe's Autobiography. Poetry and Truth from My Own Life.* Washington, D. C.: Public Affairs Press, 1949, p. 121.
10. Haydon, Benjamin Robert. *The Autobiography and Memoirs of Benjamin Robert Haydon (1768-1846).* New York: Harcourt Brace, 1926, Vol. I, pp. 12-16.
11. Hitler, Adolf. *Mein Kampf.* New York: Reynal & Hitchcock, 1941, pp. 8-10.
12. Inhelder, Bärbel, & Piaget, Jean. *The Growth of Logical Thinking: From Childhood to Adolescence.* New York: Basic Books, 1958, pp. 339, 342, 346.
13. Jones, Ernest. *Free Associations. Memories of a Psychoanalyst.* New York: Basic Books, 1959, pp. 63-64.
14. Kodama, Yoshio. *I Was Defeated.* Japan: Robert Booth & Taro Fukuda, 1951, p. 11.
15. Mill, John Stuart. *Autobiography.* New York: Library of Liberal Arts, 1957, pp. 53, 71, 93.
16. Mohr, George J., & Despres, Marian A. *The Stormy Decade: Adolescence.* New York: Random House, 1958.
17. Ponte, Lorenzo da. *Memoirs.* Philadelphia: J. B. Lippincott, 1929, p. 34.
18. Roosevelt, Theodore. *An Autobiography.* New York: Macmillan Co., 1914, pp. 25-26.
19. Shirer, William L. *The Rise and Fall of the Third Reich. A History of Nazi Germany.* New York: Simon & Schuster, 1960, p. 11.
20. Super, Donald, et al. *Vocational Development. A Framework for Research.* New York: Bureau of Publications, Teachers College, 1957.
21. Teresa (Saint). *The Life of St. Teresa of Jesus.* London: Thomas Baker, 1904, pp. 12-15.
22. Trotsky, Leon. *My Life. An Attempt at an Autobiography.* New York: Charles Scribner's Sons, 1931, p. 103.

CHAPTER FIFTEEN

Morbidity and the Suicidal Impulse in Adolescence

Fairly commonly, psychoneurotic depression and suicidal fantasies and impulses break out in adolescence. In the psychopathology of everyday pubescence, the ambivalent feelings of the gloriousness of life and the comforting fantasies of death provide the simple answers to the questionable human condition. Adolescents are prone to feel a sense of futility about life, a kind of *Weltschmertz*, a vast sorrow for the unrealizable and the indefinable, and for the injustices in their world and the world.

The revival of the oedipal conflict during adolescence leads to castration anxiety and it is this anxiety which precipitates the young person's morbid feelings and depression. The hostility intended for the parents is deflected back on the self. Self-depreciatory trends are inevitably related to the adolescent's hostile need to destroy the idealized image of his parents, by whom he feels he has been betrayed (1). His excessive feelings of disgust, brought about by deep disappointments in loved persons or by the breakdown of parental idealizations, are largely responsible for the adolescent's morbid preoccupation (23). Jacobson (14) suggests that the superego becomes endowed with the archaic omnipotence of early parental images, which accounts for the pathological tension arising between an overpowerful superego and a bent-down ego. Such people, she concludes, have not given up clinging to a magical power, which, if its favor is gained, can still be changed from bad to good and which promises support and protection as did originally the mother's breast. While the child can still hope to gain back love and security from the punishing God-like parents by atonement, he cannot expect anything more from the devalued parents. Thus, one of the dynamics in suicide and suicidal fantasy is aggression, an aggression turned against the self, in which both self and the hated incorporated objects are annihilated, while death is the punishment for the wish to kill. Moss and Hamilton (17) state that suicidal fantasy is an effort at problem solving, albeit misdirected or unrealistic, an effort to gain status in a situation of great emotional stress.

The problem solving for the adolescent revolves around his need for self-identity. Schmideberg (23) believes that every action which implies giving up an old life and starting a new one, which is implicit in adolescent development, is unconsciously linked with suicidal fantasies. In keeping with the belief that the adolescent represents a new emergent personality, ceremonials and rituals have been developed in many cultures to indicate the death or passing away of the previous personality and the emergence or rebirth of the new adult form (5). "In puberty and adolescence," writes Erikson (7), "all sameness and continuities relied on earlier are questioned again because of a rapidity of body growth which equals that of early childhood and because of the entirely new addition of physical genital maturity. The growing and developing young people, faced with this physiological revolution within them, are now primarily concerned with attempts at consolidating their social roles."

In achieving the new role, the adolescent must have an identity, and this of course is central to his whole problem. He could bear some of his frustrations more readily and utilize his own resources more effectively in overcoming some of his difficulties if his self-concept were clear, realistic and positive. Despair turns to productivity once he knows who he really is, for once he knows who he is, he knows who he is going to be. Suicidal ideation in adolescence frequently occurs when there is a crisis, which is suffused with hostility, for identity. When angry, adolescents' deeds may be seen to contain not only anger directed against the environment, but the punishment for their acts as well. "In these suicidal children may be seen not only the attempt to fulfill aggressive, hostile impulses and superego prohibitions, but also the return of omnipotent, magical means of avoiding punishment by escaping through death [29]."

This position is upheld by Zilboorg (31), who considered suicide an archaic form of response to inner conflict, a psychologic phenomenon whose force is derived from the instinct for self-preservation, since through suicide man achieves fantasied immortality and an uninterrupted fulfillment of his hedonistic ideals.

In his transitional, search-for-identity state, the adolescent vacillates between the roles of a dependent child and an independent adult. Schechter (22) states that in the adolescent, "the impulses can more easily take the form of overt suicidal acts because of the lessened dependence on the love object (accompanied by the heightened emotional stresses of reawakened oedipal conflicts) and also because he is now a person physically more capable of hurting himself. In addition, in the actions of suicidal children can be seen not only the hostility against the frustrating parents turned inward, but also the desperate attempts at regaining contact with the lost gratifying love object. In other words, the suicidal act also represents a type of restitutional phenomenon. It is in this psychoanalytic framework—the attack of the introjected object and the attempts to recover it as a love object—that we can best understand some of the suicides or suicidal equivalents of children." The adolescent who is uncomfortable with his memories of a past in which he played a role that he is now trying to transcend may have, as Jung (15) states, a panic-fear of life, although at the same time he intensely desires it. He may be so overwhelmed by the adolescent process that he is immobilized.

Conscious suicidal ideation among adolescents has been found to consist of thoughts about punishment, being separated from parents, criticism, ridicule, deprivation, being unloved and unwanted by parents, being beaten by parents, hurting and killing parents and siblings, jealousy of siblings, rape, defective sexual identity, coercive and dramatized bids for attention and getting rid of auditory hallucinations (24). Feelings of inadequacy in attempts to satisfy maturational problems and the new demands put on the adolescent may be of such oppressive weight as to be depressing. Moodiness, irritability, self-pity, fantasies of a martyr's death, anguish and despair plague him. The new strength of the drives, reawakened in exacerbated form during adolescence, tends to unbalance the previous equilibrium between the drives and the social forces in the individual and gives rise to reactions of anxiety and depression. There is a renewal of the unresolved infantile conflicts in terms of the tendency to reidentify with the ambivalently loved object and achieve reunion with the mother. There is the individual's regressive behavior, in terms of a revival of anality manifesting itself in sloppy dressing and general untidiness, as well as a renewal of the oral drive. It is seen, too, in the asceticism of the adolescent, his intellectualism, and in the lessening of ego function in terms of his magical thinking of omnipotence.

Psychoanalytically dynamic factors such as turning of aggression against the self, killing the internalized hated object, and joining the lost object were found operative among eighty-four adolescents, ages twelve to sixteen, who were admitted for suicidal behavior to Kings County Hospital in Brooklyn, New York during 1956 and 1957. Schneer and his colleagues (24), who made the study, state that "the period of adolescence shows a remarkable rise in suicidal behavior from childhood. It is our impression that the crisis of identity, in the sense of fulfilled identification as male or as female, as it is for the age of adolescence, is particularly significant for suicidal behavior among adolescents as compared with children. The genital awareness and continuing confrontation with the oedipal struggle at adolescence, for the adolescents in our study, led to a revival of unbearable memories of old frustrations; and through the loss or rejection at the hands of the parents, an interference with realization of the self as male or female. Suicidal behavior, furthermore, provided the primitive, magical, omnipotent, infantile solution for the enraged, guilt-laden but desperate wish for fusion with the mother. The biological father, while usually the object actually lost to the child or adolescent in one way or another, had a role secondary and based on frustration caused by the mother, who, however, physically was more or less present throughout the child's life. Stengel indicated an 'appeal function' for attempted suicide. If the family recognized the appeal for attention, repetition of attempts or threats would not occur. Our study indicates that the 'appeal' of the suicidal behavior among adolescents, attempted or threatened, represents a specific plea for help in dealing with the problem of sexual identification and its associated libidinal and hostile impulses aimed at the parents."

Some form of these problems is found universally among adolescents. While statistics on adolescent suicides are neither complete

nor wholly accurate, some of the figures which are available are illuminating. In Prussia, during the fourteen years from 1884 to 1898,
936 youths between the ages of ten and fifteen committed suicide.
A later study, for the years 1917-1920, showed 239 boys and 57 girls
committed suicide in that state. Between 1867 and 1875, there were
482 suicides of youths in France. In the Federal District of Mexico
City alone, there were 67 reported suicides of adolescents for a scattered twelve-month period about a decade ago (1). For the twenty-
seven years covering 1904-1931, 1251 cases of suicide in Baden, Germany by persons under the age of twenty were recorded (19). A
morbidity study for the three-year period, 1947-1949, at Oxford
University, indicated a suicide rate eleven times that of the general
population aged 15 to 24 (16). In India, Murphy (18) reported, if
students appear likely to fail, they often threaten suicide. "Year
after year, there is a genuine wave of suicides after examination
results come out."

In the United States, figures for child and adolescent deaths by
suicide are high. At least thirty boys and girls under the age of ten
kill themselves each year. Between ten and fourteen, the number
rises to about fifty. In the fifteen- to nineteen-year-old group there
are some 290 successful attempts. The suicide rate in colleges is
high, too. One study sets the figure at 13 per 100,00 students. These
are the reported figures. They do not include the "hidden suicides," those denied by families and classed as accidents. New York
health officials feel that probably ten per cent of all fatal car accidents and fifteen per cent of home accidents (usually by poisoning)
are actually suicide attempts.

One of the Dionysian Indian tribes of the Northwest coast of
America is the Kwakiutl of Vancouver Island. Ruth Benedict observed, "The characteristic Kwakiutl response to frustration was
sulking and acts of desperation. If a boy was struck by his father . . .
he retired to his pallet and neither ate nor spoke. When he had determined upon a course which would save his threatened dignity, he
rose and distributed his property, or went head-hunting, or committed suicide. One of the commonest myths of the Kwakiutl is
that of the young man who is scolded by his father or mother and
who after lying for four days motionless upon his bed goes out into
the woods intent on suicide. He jumps into waterfalls and from prec-
ipices, or tries to drown himself in lakes, but he is saved from death

by a supernatural who accosts him and gives him power. Thereupon he returns to shame his parents by his greatness [4]."

How similar the dynamics are here to the findings of Rubinstein et al. (21), in their recent clinical study of forty-four patients who attempted suicide. They suggest that attempted suicide is not an effort to die but rather is a communication to others in an effort to improve one's life. Thirty-four of the forty-four cases studied brought about desired changes in the life situation as a result of their attempted suicide. And in 1898, G. Stanley Hall (11) cited Lancaster's observation that "we are constantly told by adults past thirty that they never had this or that experience, and that those who have had them are abnormal. . . . [However,] not a single young person with whom I have had free and open conversation has been free from serious thoughts of suicide . . . but these are forgotten later on."

Referring again to the above-mentioned psychoanalytic study of eighty-four suicidal adolescents, Schneer and his co-workers (24) described the dynamics underlying the action of a fifteen-year-old girl which relates to the behavior of Graham Greene (to be illustrated in this chapter). Charlotte was a tomboy who felt rejected by her mother. She had attended a beer party which had been forbidden. Further, she was threatened with expulsion from school. At this point, she had taken her mother's gun and threatened to shoot herself. Schneer explained, "As the girl with the gun, the tomboy, she would appear regressively attempting to repair the damage brought on by the miscarried bid for femininity. The damage consisted of loss of love and threat of expulsion. But it is mother's gun. She is now like her mother, the phallic woman. Only this identity is no longer acceptable. Thus her wish to be a 'big shot' with the gun and threatening to shoot herself goes beyond the idea of destroying the hated introject (mother) to the stage of infantile omnipotence and fusion with the mother as a final solution. In this way she would lose her identity as such and no longer need to cope with the oppressive, guilt-laden problems of sexual identification and aggression. . . . The patient's passion was to photograph or 'shoot pictures' of the women teachers on whom she had developed 'crushes.' Herein can be recognized the libidinal and aggressive impulses to the introjected object, the mother, displaced onto the teachers. In regard to the omnipotence factor and fusion with the mother, B. Lewin had noted that psychologically, suicide may represent a fusion of ego and superego, or a return to the mother. He suggested also that suicide need not necessarily be depressive, but could be manic just as well,—a consideration where the moodiness of adolescents is concerned [24, p. 511]."

Of the two hundred-odd autobiographies and diaries cited in this volume, more than a third deal meaningfully, and sometimes at length, with the morbid preoccupations and suicidal impulses of adolescence. Early in Goethe's career as a student at the University of Leipzig—this was in the year 1766—the meaningless need to conform in dress and speech, his boredom with the instruction and his disappointment with the intellectual life there led him to write, "This uncertainty of taste and judgment disturbed me more every day, so at last I fell into despair. I had brought with me those of my youthful works which I thought best, partly because I hoped to get some credit by them, partly in order to be able to test my progress more surely; but I found myself in the completely wretched condition in which one is placed when a complete change of mind is required—a renunciation of all that I hitherto loved and found good. After some time, however, and many a struggle, I felt so great a contempt for my works begun and ended, that one day on the kitchen hearth I burnt up poetry and prose, plans, sketches, and designs altogether, and by the smoke which filled the whole house threw our good landlady into no small fright and anxiety [10]." Goethe's renunciation of all that he had previously loved and found good was necessary because he was facing a more naked castration anxiety and less superego anxiety. Thus Goethe's superego seemed to act for itself without functional continuity with the ego. Anna Freud attributed this alienation of the superego to its libidinization and subsequent ascetic treatment by the ego; that is, the ego treats the superego as if it were an incestuous object. This segregation of the superego shows itself in a variety of ways: in dissocial behavior, in the use of new defense mechanisms, and in a feeling of extreme isolation. The superego is no longer an ally, for the adolescent is confronted periodically with situations reminiscent of earlier childhood (27). With Goethe, there was a derivative need to get away from the unconscious love objects.

When the self-pitying, "misunderstood" attitude of the narcissistic adolescent begins to give rise to negative symptoms, the vacuum between the two object worlds is expressed in depressive moods. The adolescent realizes he is not equal to his own high demands; the need for solitude and isolation becomes primary; morbid introspection follows. Thus Marie Bashkirtseff (3) wrote amidst her self-glorification, "Shall I ever find a dog on the streets, famished and beaten by boys . . . a poor devil of any kind, sufficiently crushed, sufficiently miserable, sufficiently sorrowful, sufficiently humiliated, sufficiently depressed, to be compared with me?"

William Stillman, born in 1828, a reporter for the London *Times*, described his whole early adolescence "as dreary and void, except when I got to nature, and the delight of my hours in the fields and woods is all that remains to me of a childhood tormented by burdens of conscience laid on me prematurely, and by a domestic discipline the severity of which, with all the reverence and gratitude I bear my parents, I can hardly consider otherwise than gravely mistaken and disastrous to me [28]." Stillman's adolescence was depressing and tormenting because of the superego conflict brought about by the increased drives and the need to revolt against his archaic parents and to achieve independence.

The great French novelist, Romain Rolland, described his life between the ages of sixteen and eighteen as "two tragic years, unimportant only to those who would have seen nothing but *der Stoff*, the familiar schoolboy existence of a restless youth. But they concealed the voracious monsters of a deadly despair. Those were the days when I plumbed the very depths of total emptiness [20]." Don C. Talayesva, the Hopi Sun Chief, related, "It was in Moenkopi that I quarreled with my mother and nearly committed suicide [26]." At one point in Havelock Ellis' adolescence, his "attitude towards life was embodied in an 'Ode to Death' in which I implored Death to bear me away from the world on gentle wings, although at the same time I had no thought of taking any steps to aid Death in this task [6]."

Jacob Wasserman, the German novelist, wrote about the "bleakness, fear, oppression, desolation [and] torpor" during his adolescence. "I remember that I suffered from morbid fears: fear of ghosts, of people, of dreams. In everything about me lay a sinister sorcery, always baneful, always boding disaster and always confirmed. I was often invited to an old house where lived an old couple. The husband was a scholar; in his room stood a bookcase behind whose glass door were numerous editions of the works of Spinoza; and these had a curious fascination for me. When, one day, I asked the mistress of the house to give me a volume she told me, in a tone of sibylline gloom, that whoever read these books must become insane. For years the name of Spinoza was associated in my mind with the sound and sense of her words. More or less the same thing happened with everything gay and playful and festive that tried to reach me or that I tried to reach. All these things were thrust aside, suspected, made joyless. Pleasure was forbidden [29]." Behold the ascetic adolescent. Everything Wasserman "tried to reach" was made joyless and pleasure was forbidden. The repudiation of his instinctual drives is manifest.

Yarmolinsky, in piecing together Ivan Turgenev's adolescent suicidal preoccupations, wrote, "The pricking of the [sensual] senses was accompanied for Ivan, as for most adolescents, by an atrabilious complexion of the spirit. Sixteen is a melancholy, metaphysical age, and if there was a little dalliance in the garden, there was much vexation in the closet. One may readily believe, however, that he sucked on the thought of suicide as a small boy does on a lemon-stick, and that he played with transcendental platitudes concerning the use of life and the meaning of death as he used to play with new puppies [30]."

Two final, short illustrations remain. Both are American, one the account of a young Negro girl, the other of a juvenile delinquent. Charlotte Forten (1838-1914) was one of the first Negroes admitted to a white teacher-training institute in Massachusetts. Her diary, which is primarily a factual account of her experiences, occasionally reveals flashes of feeling. The following passage is one of them (8). The year is 1854; Charlotte is seventeen. She is the adolescent in the eternal pursuit of new ideals and who, in her quest, questions the new ideals and feels she has been unfairly put upon. Inherent in these feelings is the masturbatory conflict with its depressing concomitant.

Friday, August 11

I have been thinking lately very much about death,—that strange, mysterious, awful reality, that is constantly around and among us, that power which takes away from us so many of those whom we love and honor, or those who have persecuted and oppressed us, our bitter enemies whom we vainly endeavor not to hate. Oh! I long to be good, to be able to meet death calmly and fearlessly, strong in faith and holiness. But this I know can only be through One who died for us, through the pure and perfect love of Him, who was all holiness and love. But how can I hope to be worthy of His love while I still cherish this feeling towards my enemies, this unforgiving spirit? This is a question which I ask myself very often. Other things in comparison with this seem easy to overcome. But hatred of oppression seems to me so blended with hatred of the oppressor I cannot separate them. I feel that no other injury could be so hard to bear, so very hard to forgive, as that inflicted by cruel oppression and prejudice. How *can* I be a Christian when so many in common with myself, for no crime suffer so cruelly, so unjustly? It seems in vain to try, even to hope. And yet I still long to resemble Him in the last degree, for I know that it must be so ere I can accomplish anything that is really good and useful in life.

Stanley, the delinquent, was one of seven children. His mother had died, his father had remarried, this time to a brutal woman who neglected him. "Becoming disgusted, I left home, without knowing where to go. I roamed a few days and became hungry, dirty and lonesome. But nothing could force me to go back to the stepmother. I found my way to the Madison Street bridge, and half resolved to throw myself over, but my youth belied the idea. So I roamed the street, finding that better than returning to the 'house of hell.' I was between two hells. Being on parole, I was supposed to live at home, so if arrested I'd be returned to St. Charles [25]."

These brief illustrations demonstrate the peculiarly universal phenomenon of adolescent morbidity. Goethe's renunciation and symbolic self-immolation, Ellis' melancholy poetry, Turgenev's intellectualization, Wasserman's obsessions, and Charlotte Forten's preoccupation with death, all reveal the dark and unresponsive world in which they felt they lived. The lengthier passages which follow cover the past 1500 years and provide illustrations from China, India, and Italy, in addition to the countries represented above.

Saint Augustine
(354-430)

The first section of *The Confessions* deals with St. Augustine's childhood and youth, revealing his feelings toward his mother and father, his juvenile acts of depredation and his growing involvement with the world. What is most remarkable here is not so much the facts St. Augustine reveals as his feelings. For this is a book without a precedent: Augustine was the first to produce the autobiography of introspection, the self-registered subjective account of the inner man. In Book X, he stated his theme: "What am I myself inwardly?" And this Augustine searches rigorously throughout the text. In offering himself up as an example, he did not spare himself on account of his "vile" conduct, his "base" motives, his "erroneous" thinking.

St. Augustine spent his seventeenth, eighteenth, and nineteenth years in Carthage, where he completed his course of studies. In the passage which follows,* he described how he was caught "in the snares of a licentious passion and fell into the snares of the Manichaeans." But despite the physical and intellectual pleasures he had been wallowing in, Augustine was miserable, moved to tears, and loved grief in his ambivalent, preoccupied, adolescent morbidness.

Deluded by an insane love, he, though foul and dishonourable, desires to be thought elegant and urbane. To Carthage I came, where a cauldron of unholy loves bubbled up all around me. I loved not as yet, yet I loved to love; and, with a hidden want, I abhorred myself that I wanted not. I searched about for something to love, in love with loving, and hating security, and a way not beset with snares. For within me I had a dearth of that inward food, Thyself, my God, though that dearth caused me no hunger; but I remained without all desire for incorruptible food, not because I was already filled thereby, but the more empty I was the more I loathed it. For this reason my soul was far from well, and, full of ulcers, it miserably cast itself forth, craving to be excited by contact with objects of sense. Yet, had these no soul, they would not surely inspire love. To love and to be loved was sweet to me, and all the more when I succeeded in enjoying the person I loved. I befouled, therefore, the spring of friendship with the

*From *The Confessions of St. Augustine.* Reprinted by permission of Liveright Publishers (New York). 1942. Book III. Pp. 41-44.

filth of concupiscence, and I dimmed its lustre with the hell of lustfulness; and yet, foul and dishonourable as I was, I craved, through an excess of vanity, to be thought elegant and urbane. I fell precipitately, then, into the love in which I longed to be ensnared. My God, my mercy, with how much bitterness didst Thou, out of Thy infinite goodness, besprinkle for me that sweetness! For I was both beloved, and secretly arrived at the bond of enjoying; and was joyfully bound with troublesome ties, that I might be scourged with the burning iron rods of jealousy, suspicion, fear, anger, and strife.

In public spectacles he is moved by an empty compassion. He is attacked by a troublesome spiritual disease. Stage-plays also drew me away, full of representations of my miseries and of fuel to my fire. Why does man like to be made sad when viewing doleful and tragical scenes, which yet he himself would by no means suffer? And yet he wishes, as a spectator, to experience from them a sense of grief, and in this very grief his pleasure consists. What is this but wretched insanity? For a man is more affected with these actions, the less free he is from such affections. Howsoever, when he suffers in his own person, it is the custom to style it "misery;" but when he compassionates others, then it is styled "mercy." But what kind of mercy is it that arises from fictitious and scenic passions? The hearer is not expected to relieve, but merely invited to grieve; and the more he grieves, the more he applauds the actor of these fictions. And if the misfortunes of the characters (whether of olden times or merely imaginary) be so represented as not to touch the feelings of the spectator, he goes away disgusted and censorious; but if his feelings be touched, he sits it out attentively, and sheds tears of joy.

Are sorrows, then, also loved? Surely all men desire to rejoice? Or, as man wishes to be miserable, is he, nevertheless, glad to be merciful, which, because it cannot exist without passion, for this cause alone are passions loved? This also is from that vein of friendship. But whither does it go? Whither does it flow? Wherefore runs it into that torrent of pitch, seething forth those huge tides of loathsome lusts into which it is changed and transformed, being of its own will cast away and corrupted from its celestial clearness? Shall, then, mercy be repudiated? By no means. Let us, therefore, love sorrows sometimes. But beware of uncleanness, O my soul, under the protection of my God, the God of our fathers, who is to be praised and exalted above all for ever, beware of uncleanness. For I have not now ceased to have compassion; but then in the theatres I sympathized with lovers when they sinfully enjoyed one another, although this was done fictitiously in the play. And when they lost one another, I grieved with them, as if pitying them, and yet had delight in both. But now-a-days I feel much more pity for him that delighteth in his wickedness, than for him who is counted as enduring hardships by failing to obtain some pernicious pleasure, and the loss of some miserable felicity. This, surely, is the truer mercy, but grief hath no delight in it. For though he that condoles with the unhappy be approved for his office of charity, yet would he who had real compassion rather there were nothing for him to grieve about. For if good-will be ill-willed (which it cannot), then can he who is truly and sincerely commiserating wish that there should be some unhappy ones, that he might commiserate them. Some grief may then be justified, none loved. For thus dost Thou, O Lord God, who lovest souls far more purely than do we, and art more incorruptibly compassionate, although Thou art wounded by no sorrow. "And who is sufficient for these things?"

But I, wretched one, then loved to grieve, and sought out what to grieve at, as when, in another man's misery, though feigned and counterfeited, that delivery of the actor best pleased me, and attracted me the most powerfully, which moved me to tears. What marvel was it that an unhappy sheep, straying from Thy flock, and impatient of Thy care, I became infected with a foul disease? And hence came my love of griefs—not such as should probe me too deeply, for I loved not to suffer such things as I loved to look upon, but such as, when hearing their fictions, should lightly affect the surface; upon which, like as with empoisoned nails, followed burning, swelling, putrefaction, and horrible corruption. Such was my life! But was it life, O my God?

Napoleon Bonaparte
(1769-1821)

In September 1785, Napoleon was gazetted as Second Lieutenant to the La Fere Artillery Regiment, which was then quartered in Valence. He was sixteen years old, and an orphan (for his father had died a short time previously). Although he was sent to Valence with his friend Des Mazis, and was comfortably billeted with a "worthy" Mademoiselle Bou, an "old maid aged fifty," and her father, and although he wrote he could never forget his stay in Valence, the following passage* reveals the self-pity of the morbid

---

*From *Napoleon's Autobiography* edited by F. M. Kircheisen. Reprinted by permission of Dodd, Mead & Co. Duffield & Co., 1931. Pp. 17-18.

adolescent. His attitudinizing and intellectualizing seem to be typical. His exaggerated patriotism has been explained as a projection of his love for mother onto a love for mother country. Much later in his career, he found in Talleyrand a symbol of the father, thus projecting his jealousy of the male parent upon his political rival. In this passage and in the one used in the chapter on socioeconomic consciousness, we see Napoleon's strong inferiority feeling and his self-punishing attitude.

Later on in his life, when he was at the height of his success, Napoleon was to issue the often cited Order of the Day in which he censured a soldier who had committed suicide because of frustrated love: "A French soldier ought to show as much courage in facing the adversities and afflictions of life as he shows in facing the bullets of a battery. Whoever commits suicide is a coward; he is a soldier who deserts the battlefield before victory." But in April, 1814, Napoleon himself made an unsuccessful suicide attempt.

As I was poor I gave myself up completely to my duties and my books. My relatives, my country, and my veneration for Paoli and Rousseau were my only passion. Far from home and those I loved a repugnance to life often overcame me so that I thought of suicide. At this time—it was the beginning of May 1786—I wrote the following words:

"Always alone in the midst of people, I return home in order to give myself up with unspeakable melancholy to my dreams. How do I regard life today? I give way to thoughts of death. I stand at the dawn of life and may hope to live long. For six or seven years now I have been absent from my country. What pleasure shall I feel when, in four months' time, I see my countrymen and my relatives again? Can I conclude from this tender recollection of my youthful enjoyment that my happiness will be complete? What madness then drives me to wish to kill myself? Why am I really in the world? As I must die some time it would perhaps be better if I killed myself! If I had already sixty years behind me I would respect the prejudices of my contemporaries and wait patiently for nature to complete her work. But, as I am beginning to feel the seriousness of life, and nothing any longer gives me pleasure, why should I suffer the days from which I can promise myself no further good? What a gap there is between mankind and nature! How cowardly, base, and crawling men are! What tragedy awaits me in my country? My fellow-countrymen are loaded with chains! and have to bear, trembling, the weight of the oppressor's hand! Gone are the brave Corsicans whom a hero once inspired with his virtues, those enemies of tyrants, luxury, and base courtiers. Proud, and filled with the noble feeling of his worth, the Corsican led a happy life when he had devoted the day to public affairs. Then he spent the night in the tender arms of a loved spouse. Good sense and enthusiasm caused all the cares of the day to be forgotten. Love and nature created divine nights. But they also have vanished like the dreams of those happy days! You Frenchmen! It is not enough that you have robbed us of what we loved most, you have even destroyed our manners and customs! The present condition of my country and the impossibility of altering it are a further reason for leaving a world in which I am compelled by duty to love people whom I should naturally hate. What attitude shall I adopt, how shall I speak when I arrive in my country? When his country no longer exists a good citizen should die. If one man could save my country- men by sacrificing his life, I would at once rise and thrust the avenging sword into the breast of the tyrant in order to revenge my country and its injured rights.

"Life has become a burden to me, for I no longer enjoy any pleasure, and everything causes me pain. It is a burden to me because the people with whom I live, and probably always shall live, have manners and customs which are as different from mine as the light of the moon from that of the sun. I cannot, therefore, live as I should wish to, and thence arises an aversion to everything."

Benjamin Constant
(1767-1830)

A contemporary of Napoleon—and a supporter while it suited his purpose—was Henri Benjamin Constant de Rebecque, author, politician, and at his death, President of the Council of the French State. Constant was an ardent champion of freedom of the press, the author of a substantial number of novels (*Adolphe* is probably his best known), and a massive *History of Religion*.

Harold Nicholson, in his introduction to Constant's autobiog- raphy, *The Red Notebook,* described the chaotic and motherless childhood he experienced. "He was given French tutors, German tutors and English tutors; these pedagogues seem to have been selected almost by chance and without discrimination. Benjamin was a precocious child; he mastered the rudiments of Greek grammar at the age of five; the letters which he wrote at the age of ten are so mature that Sainte-Beuve . . . pronounced them to be forgeries. They were, in fact, authentic. 'I wish,' he wrote while still a boy, 'that someone could stop my blood circulating so rapidly and impart to it a calmer rhythm. I have tried to see whether music could produce this effect; I have been playing adagios and largos such as would send thirty cardinals to sleep.' The feverish impatience, which in adult years amounted to a gambler's recklessness, was a cause of worry to Benjamin even as a child. His father did little to render him more quiescent. He dragged him off to Paris, he took him over to Oxford for a while, he sent him to the German university of Erlangen. From Germany, on a sudden impulse, Benjamin went to Edinburgh where he enrolled as a student. The year and a half which he spent in Scotland appeared to him in later life as the happiest of his many interludes. In 1786, at the age of nineteen, he crossed again to Paris; there followed a period of gaming and debauchery. . . . "

It is at this juncture that we pick up Constant's life and his attempt at suicide. Here, too, we see the morbid self-pity, the fantasy, "If I die . . . all will be over; and if I am saved, Mademoiselle Pourras will be bound to feel tenderly towards a man who has sought to kill himself for her." But, at bottom, Constant had not the slightest desire to kill himself.*

This new passion did not occupy my whole time. I still had enough, unfortunately, in which to incur a deal of debt. A woman who used to write from Paris to my father informed him of my behaviour, but wrote to him also that I could make all well if I succeeded in marrying a young person who belonged to the set in which I habitually moved, and who was said to have an income of ninety thousand francs. This idea, very naturally, had a great attraction for my father. He communicated it to me in a letter which also contained a great number of very just reproaches, and at the end of which he declared that he would not allow me to prolong my stay at Paris unless I endeavoured to realize this advantageous project, and unless I believed that I had some chance of success.

The person in question was sixteen years of age, and very pretty. Her mother had received me, ever since my arrival in Paris, with much

*From *The Red Notebook* translated by Norman Cameron. Reprinted by permission of Hamish Hamilton. 1949. Pp. 127-131.

friendship. I saw myself placed between the necessity of at least attempting a thing that might result greatly to my advantage, and that of leaving a city where I found much entertainment, to rejoin a father who had announced great disapproval of me. I did not hesitate to take the risk. In accordance with custom, I began by writing to the mother to ask her daughter's hand. She answered in a very friendly fashion, but with a refusal, for which she offered the explanation that her daughter was already promised to another, whom she was to marry within a few months. Nevertheless, I do not believe that the mother herself regarded this refusal as irrevocable: for, on the one hand, I have since learnt that she made inquiries in Switzerland concerning my fortune; and, on the other hand, she gave me every opportunity of speaking with her daughter *tête-à-tête*.

I behaved, however, like a real fool. Instead of profiting by the benevolence of the mother, who even whilst refusing me had shown me good will, I sought to embark upon a romance with the daughter, and began it in the most absurd fashion. I made no attempt to win her favour, I said to her not a single word of endearment. But I wrote her an eloquent letter, as if to a person whose parents wished to marry her against her will to a man whom she did not love, and I proposed that we should elope. Her mother, to whom she doubtless showed this strange letter, had the indulgence towards me to allow her daughter to answer as if she had told the mother nothing of the matter.

Mademoiselle Pourras—such was her name—wrote to me that it was for her parents to decide her future, and that it was not proper for her to receive letters from a man. I would not take this for an answer, and handsomely renewed my proposals of elopement, deliverance and protection against the marriage that was being forced upon her. One might have thought that I was writing to a victim who had implored my help, and to a person who had for me all the passion that I persuaded myself that I felt for her. The truth was that all my letters were addressed to a very reasonable little person, who loved me not at all, who had no repugnance against the man proposed for her, and had given me neither the occasion nor the right to address her in this fashion. But I had committed myself to this path, and not for the devil would I leave it.

What was even more inexplicable was that when I saw Mademoiselle Pourras I said not a word to her that had any connection with my letters. Her mother always left me alone with her, despite the extravagant proposals of which she surely knew: this strengthens my belief that I might yet have succeeded. But, far from profiting by these opportunities, I fell victim, each time I found myself alone with Mademoiselle Pourras, to an extreme shyness. I spoke to her only of insignificant matters, and did not even allude to the letters that I wrote her daily, nor to the sentiment that dictated them.

At length a circumstance with which I was not in the least involved caused a crisis that ended the whole affair. Madame Pourras, who all her life had carried her heart on her sleeve, still had a regular lover. Ever since I had asked her for her daughter's hand she had continued to show me friendship, and had always maintained the appearance of knowing nothing of my absurd correspondence. Thus, whilst I daily wrote to the daughter with proposals of elopement, I made the mother the confidante of my passion and sorrow. I did all this, I may say, spontaneously, and without the least bad faith; but such was the course to which I had committed myself with each of the two women.

It thus came about that Madame Pourras and I often had long conversations *tête-à-tête*. Her lover took umbrage. There were violent scenes, and Madame Pourras, who was nearly fifty and unwilling to lose a lover who might be her last, resolved to reassure him. I suspected nothing, and was one day making my usual lamentations to Madame Pourras, when in came M. de Sainte-Croix—this was the lover's name—and evinced much ill humour. Madame Pourras took me by the hand, led me up to him and asked whether I would solemnly declare to him that it was her daughter whom I loved and had asked in marriage, and that she herself was entirely unconnected with my assiduous visits to her home.

Madame Pourras had regarded the declaration that she demanded of me only as a means of putting an end to the resentment of M. de Sainte-Croix. I, however, viewed the matter in another light. I saw myself dragged before a stranger to confess to him that I was a disappointed lover, a man rejected by both mother and daughter. My wounded vanity threw me into a real fever. I happened to have in my pocket a small phial of opium, which I had for some time been carrying about with me. This was a result of my relationship with Madame de Charrière. She took a deal of opium to soothe her distress, thus giving me the idea of also obtaining some; and her conversation, always abundant and vigorous but very fantastic, kept me in a sort of mental drunkenness, which was in no small degree responsible for all the follies I committed at this period.

I had been in the habit of saying that I wished to kill myself, and had almost persuaded myself of this, although at bottom I had not the slightest desire to do so. Having my opium in a pocket, therefore, at the moment when, as I thought, I was being made a spectacle in the eyes of M. de Sainte-Croix, I felt an embarrassment from which it seemed easier to extract myself by a scene than by a quiet conversation. I foresaw that M. de Sainte-Croix would ask me questions and evince an interest in me. Since I considered myself humiliated, I could not endure the prospect of these questions or this interest, or of anything that might prolong the situation. I was confident that by swallowing my opium I would create a diversion from all this. Moreover, I had long entertained the notion that to seek to kill oneself for a woman is a method of pleasing her.

This notion is not exactly correct. When one already pleases a woman, and she only asks to give herself, it is good to threaten her with suicide, because one thus furnishes her with a decisive, rapid and honourable pretext. But when one is not loved, neither the threat nor the act has any effect. Throughout my whole adventure with Mademoiselle Pourras, my fundamental error was that I acted the drama entirely by myself.

Accordingly, when Madame Pourras had finished speaking, I replied that I thanked her for having put me in a situation which left only one course of action open to me. I then brought out my little phial and carried it to my lips. I remember that, in the brief instant that elapsed whilst I performed this operation, I presented myself with an alternative that finally decided me. "If I die," I said to myself, "all will be over; and if I am saved, Mademoiselle Pourras will be bound to feel tenderly towards a man who has sought to kill himself for her."

So I swallowed my opium. I do not think that there was enough of it to do me great harm; and since M. de Sainte-Croix precipitated himself upon me, I spilt more than half of it. There was great consternation, and I was made to take acids to destroy the opium's effect. I did what was asked of me with perfect docility, not because I was afraid, but because they would have insisted, and I should have found it too tedious to argue. When I say that I was not afraid, I do not mean that I knew how small the danger was. I was not at all acquainted with the effects of opium, and believed them much more terrible than they are. But after considering my alternative I was quite indifferent to what might happen. Nevertheless, my complaisance in allowing myself to be given anything that might prevent the effect of my action must have persuaded the spectators that there was nothing serious about the whole tragedy.

This was not the only time in my life that after a dramatic action I have been suddenly unable to support the tedious solemnity necessary to keep it up, and have out of sheer boredom undone my own work. They administered to me all the remedies that they thought proper, and preached me a little sermon, half compassionate and half magisterial, to which I listened with a tragic air. Mademoiselle Pourras, who had not been present whilst I was playing the fool for her, now entered the room, and I illogically had the delicacy to aid the mother in her efforts to prevent the daughter from noticing anything. The latter was dressed to go to the Opera, where there was a first performance of *Tarare* by Beaumarchais. Madame proposed that I should accompany them, and I accepted. In order that everything about this affair should be tragi-comic, my attempt upon my life ended in an evening at the Opera. I was actually in a state of wild gaiety, whether because the opium had produced this effect upon me, or because—which seems to me more probable—I was disgusted with all the previous lugubrious events, and felt a need of entertainment.

William Hazlitt
(1778-1830)

Across the sea from Napoleon and Constant was an Englishman named William Hazlitt. The excesses of the French Revolution, perpetrated during the time Hazlitt was an adolescent of thirteen to fifteen, profoundly affected the boy and he writes of it in the succeeding passage (12). "The dumb and brutish trouble of adolescence" hobbled him, preventing him from speaking his intellectual torment, making him feel smothered and wishing for "the strong embrace of the King of Terrors."

At other times it seems to me as if I had set out in life with the French Revolution, and as if all that had happened before that were but a dream. Certainly there came to me at that time an extraordinary acceleration of the pulse of being. Youth then was doubly Youth. It was the dawn of a new era; a new impulse had been given to men's minds, and the sun of Liberty rose upon the sun of life in the same day, and both were proud to run their race together. Little did I dream in those two years, while my first hopes and wishes went hand in hand with the human race, that before long that dawn would be overcast, and set once more in the night of despotism—"total eclipse." Happy that I did not! Two years I had of unsullied joy! Then the storms that I have never since been able to escape, began to break.

I think it was just after July 14th, 1791, and the firing of Dr. Priestley's house by the Birmingham mob, the burning of the books and papers that were his life-work, that I first became a man in feeling, and realized the strength of the forces of destruction, realized that a battle for the liberty of the human mind had begun, and that it was necessary for me to take my place in the fight. Afterwards I realized that even then the main issues began to be lost sight of in the inflammation of mob passion on both sides of the Channel. It was Burke, who professed to despise mobs, who did more than any man to inflame mob fury in England, in the heat of which all true issues were melted down to nothingness and forgotten, leaving only the worm that dieth not to work its will on Man. In France, it was the Duke of Brunswick's manifesto, just over a year later, also in July, that brought the terrible cauldron of men's passions to the boilng-point. And who can wonder? ... It was this insult, this outrage to the image of man's nature, that produced and called aloud for retaliation and defiance to the *outrance* that called "to strike and spare not;" that made the eye start and the brain split; that filled every faculty with fear and shame and hate; that made the fountain of their tears run blood, and the glow of passion sear the heart. This is the true version of the horrors and excesses of that period, of the massacres that presently were to pollute the streets of Paris. It is from hence that we may fairly date the excesses of the French Revolution. This proclamation, which showed in burning daylight the degradation from which they had escaped, the crying injustice with which they were threatened, and which was not even attempted to be glossed over, exasperated their passions and exhausted their patience, as well it might; and the contrast between what they had hoped and what they feared almost turning their brain, they struck at the spectre of power which haunted them like a filthy nightmare, wherever they could encounter it in a tangible shape, with fear and hatred, without mercy and without remorse.

These things came to pass while I was yet in my boyhood and dwelt in my father's house. I read of them while all around me was peace; I could still turn my eyes to the long line of blue hills, and see the sunset wash their tops in gold and caress the red leaves of the dwarf-oaks as they rustled in the evening breeze. And I could still rejoice. The light of the Revolution, dabbled though it now was with drops of crimson gore, still circled my head like a glory. Yet I was not at peace because I had no words to express and so to win release from the thoughts that went pouring through my mind. Because, too, I was in the dumb and brutish trouble of adolescence and could speak to no one of what I suffered, I was obsessed by a stifling sense of oppression and confinement, as if I were in a prison-house from which I could not burst. It was this which made me do things that seemed troublesome and strange to those around me. It was this which sent me scampering through the fields at night like a wild thing trying to outrun its own heart-beats. It was this that made me walk in my sleep. If I were troublesome to others, I was far more troublesome to myself. I thought sometimes, although yet the thought of death smote cold upon my mind, that if only I could have burst through the nameless constriction that agonized me, I would have been contented to grasp the whole of existence in one strong embrace, to sound the mystery of life and death in one moment, to confront, in horrible fascination, the King of Terrors in his grisly palace!

In the outset of life, all that is to come seems to press with double force upon the heart. The first ebullitions of hope and fear lift us to heaven or sink us into the abyss. I was perilously poised. Well it was for me perhaps, when in the autumn—it was then the persecuting year of 1793—there came a certain redirection of interests, as a new phase of my life began. It was then that I left my father's house and turned my steps towards London.

John Stuart Mill
(1806-1873)

Like Athena who sprang full-bloomed from Jupiter's head, John Stuart Mill was apparently the offspring of the pure intellect of his father. "I was born in London, on the 20th of May, 1806, and was the eldest son of James Mill, the author of *The History of British India*." Not once, in his intellectual and austere autobiography, did Mill mention his mother!

Under his father's determined and watchful tutelage, Mill began the study of Greek when he was three years old. Between his fourth and seventh years, he read Hume, Gibbon and other historians; from his eighth to his twelfth year, he read—in Latin—Virgil, Horace, Phaedrus, Livy, Sallust, Ovid, Terence, Cicero and Lucretius. He did as much in Greek. In addition, he learned algebra and geometry. When he was thirteen, his father took him "through a complete course of political economy." He spent his fourteenth year in France as the guest of Jeremy Bentham's brother, General Sir Samuel Bentham. He became caught up in the study of the French

Revolution and democracy, in Benthamism and the Utilitarian Society.

In the autumn of 1826, Mill fell into "a dull state of nerves," where he could no longer enjoy life, and what had produced pleasure seemed insipid. From the time he was fifteen, Mill's object in life was to reform the world. But he asked himself the question, "Suppose that all your objects in life were realized; that all the changes in institutions and opinions which you are looking forward to could be completely effected at this very instant, would this be a great joy and happiness to you? And an irrepressible self-consciousness distinctly answered, 'No.' At this my heart sank within me: the whole foundation on which my life was constructed fell down. . . . I seemed to have nothing left to live for."

Taught as he had been by his father to repress instinctual feeling, Mill sought relief in books and in intellectualizing, but with no surcease, until "I now saw, or thought I saw, what I had always before received with incredulity—that the habit of analysis has a tendency to wear away the feelings: as indeed it has, when no other mental habit is cultivated, and the analysing spirit remains without its natural complements and correctives. . . . The very excellence of analysis (I argued) is that it tends to weaken and undermine whatever is the result of prejudice." More than a hundred years later, Ernest Jones was to write, "Truths painfully won are apt to be defended with great tenacity. . . . What began as a piece of insight hardens into a conviction and may at the end petrify into a prejudice."

Freud (in 1883, before he turned to psychoanalysis) termed Mill's *Autobiography* "so prudish or so unearthy that one would never learn from it that humanity is divided between men and women [9]." When finally Mill permitted himself the luxury of accepting his emotions, he was never again quite as miserable, as this chapter from his *Autobiography* shows.*

From the winter of 1821, when I first read Bentham, and especially from the commencement of the Westminster Review, I had what might truly be called an object in life; to be a reformer of the world. My conception of my own happiness was entirely identified with this object. The personal sympathies I wished for were those of fellow

*Reprinted by permission of The Liberal Arts Press. 1957. Pp. 86-93.

labourers in this enterprise. I endeavoured to pick up as many flowers as I could by the way; but as a serious and permanent personal satisfaction to rest upon, my whole reliance was placed on this; and I was accustomed to felicitate myself on the certainty of a happy life which I enjoyed, through placing my happiness in something durable and distant, in which some progress might be always making, while it could never be exhausted by complete attainment. This did very well for several years, during which the general improvement going on in the world and the idea of myself as engaged with others in struggling to promote it, seemed enough to fill up an interesting and animated existence. But the time came when I awakened from this as from a dream. It was in the autumn of 1826. I was in a dull state of nerves, such as everybody is occasionally liable to; unsusceptible to enjoyment or pleasurable excitement; one of those moods when what is pleasure at other times, becomes insipid or indifferent; the state, I should think, in which converts to Methodism usually are, when smitten by their first "conviction of sin." In this frame of mind it occurred to me to put the question directly to myself: "Suppose that all your objects in life were realized; that all the changes in institutions and opinions which you are looking forward to, could be completely effected at this very instant: would this be a great joy and happiness to you?" And an irrepressible self-consciousness distinctly answered, "No!" At this my heart sank within me: the whole foundation on which my life was constructed fell down. All my happiness was to have been found in the continual pursuit of this end. The end had ceased to charm, and how could there ever again be any interest in the means? I seemed to have nothing left to live for.

At first I hoped that the cloud would pass away of itself; but it did not. A night's sleep, the sovereign remedy for the smaller vexations of life, had no effect on it. I awoke to a renewed consciousness of the woeful fact. I carried it with me into all companies, into all occupations. Hardly anything had power to cause me even a few minutes oblivion of it. For some months the cloud seemed to grow thicker and thicker. The lines in Coleridge's "Dejection"—I was not then acquainted with them—exactly describe my case:

> A grief without a pang, void, dark and drear,
> A drowsy, stifled, unimpassioned grief,
> Which finds no natural outlet or relief
> In word, or sigh, or tear.

In vain I sought relief from my favourite books; those memorials of past nobleness and greatness from which I had always hitherto drawn strength and animation. I read them now without feeling, or with the accustomed feeling *minus* all its charm; and I became persuaded, that my love of mankind, and of excellence for its own sake, had worn itself out. I sought no comfort by speaking to others of what I felt. If I had loved any one sufficiently to make confiding my griefs a necessity, I should not have been in the condition I was. I felt, too, that mine was not an interesting, or in any way respectable distress. There was nothing in it to attract sympathy. Advice, if I had known where to seek it, would have been most precious. The words of Macbeth to the physician often occurred to my thoughts. But there was no one on whom I could build the faintest hope of such assistance. My father, to whom it would have been natural to me to have recourse in any practical difficulties, was the last person to whom, in such a case as this, I looked for help. Everything convinced me that he had no knowledge of any such mental state as I was suffering from, and that even if he could be made to understand it, he was not the physician who could heal it. My education, which was wholly his work, had been conducted without any regard to the possibility of its ending in this result; and I saw no use in giving him the pain of thinking that his plans had failed, when the failure was probably irremediable, and, at all events, beyond the power of *his* remedies. Of other friends, I had at that time none to whom I had any hope of making my condition intelligible. It was however abundantly intelligible to myself; and the more I dwelt upon it, the more hopeless it appeared.

My course of study had led me to believe, that all mental and moral feelings and qualities, whether of a good or of a bad kind, were the results of association; that we love one thing, and hate another, take pleasure in one sort of action or contemplation, and pain in another sort, through the clinging of pleasurable or painful ideas to those things, from the effect of education or of experience. As a corollary from this, I had always heard it maintained by my father, and was myself convinced, that the object of education should be to form the strongest possible associations of the salutary class; associations of pleasure with all things beneficial to the great whole, and of pain with all things hurtful to it. This doctrine appeared inexpungable; but it now seemed to me, on retrospect, that my teachers had occupied themselves but superficially with the means of forming and keeping up these salutary associations. They seemed to have trusted altogether to the old familiar instruments, praise and blame, reward and punishment. Now, I did not doubt that by these means, begun early, and applied unremittingly, intense associations of pain and pleasure, especially of pain, might be created, and might produce desires and aversions capable of lasting undiminished to the end of life. But there must always be something artificial and casual in associations thus produced. The pains and pleasures thus forcibly associated with things, are not connected with them by any natural tie; and it is therefore, I thought, essential to the durability of these associations, that they should have become so intense and inveterate as to be practically indissoluble, before the habitual exercise of the power of analysis had commenced. For I now saw, or thought I saw, what I had always before received with incredulity—that the habit of analysis has a tendency to wear away the feelings: as indeed it has, when no other mental habit is cultivated, and the analysing spirit remains without its natural complements and correctives. The very excellence of analysis (I argued) is that it tends to weaken and undermine whatever is the result of prejudice; that it enables us mentally to separate ideas which have only casually clung together: and no associations whatever could ultimately resist this dissolving force, were it not that we owe to analysis our clearest knowledge of the permanent sequences in nature; the real connexions between Things, not dependent on our will and feelings; natural laws, by virtue of which, in many cases, one thing is inseparable from another in fact; which laws, in proportion as they are clearly perceived and imaginatively realized, cause our ideas of things which are always joined together in Nature, to cohere more and more closely in our thoughts. Analytic habits may thus even strengthen the associations between causes and effects, means and ends, but tend altogether to weaken those which are, to speak familiarly, a *mere* matter of feeling. They are therefore (I thought) favourable to prudence and clear-sightedness, but a perpetual worm at the root both of the passions and of the virtues; and, above all, fearfully undermine all desires, and all pleasures, which are the effects of association, that is, according to the theory I held, all except the purely physical and organic; of the entire insufficiency of which to make life desirable, no one had a stronger conviction than I had. These were the laws of human nature, by which, as it seemed to me, I had been brought to my present state. All those to whom I looked up, were of opinion that the pleasure of sympathy with human beings, and the feelings which made the good of others, and especially of mankind on a large scale, the object of existence, were the greatest and surest sources of happiness. Of the truth of this I was convinced, but to know that a feeling would make me happy if I had it, did not give me the feeling. My education, I thought, had failed to create these feelings in sufficient strength to resist the dissolving influence of analysis, while the whole course of my intellectual cultivation had made precocious and premature analysis the inveterate habit of my mind. I was thus, as I said to myself, left stranded at the commencement of my voyage, with a well-equipped ship and a rudder, but no sail; without any real desire for the ends which I had been so carefully fitted out to work for: no delight in virtue, or the general good, but also just as little in anything else. The fountains of vanity and ambition seemed to have dried up within me, as completely as those of benevolence. I had had (as I reflected) some gratification of vanity at too early an age: I had obtained some distinction, and felt myself of some importance, before the desire of distinction and of importance had grown into a passion: and little as it was which I had attained, yet having been attained too early, like all pleasures enjoyed too soon, it had made me *blasé* and indifferent to the pursuit. Thus neither selfish nor unselfish pleasures were pleasures to me. And there seemed no power in nature sufficient to begin the formation of my character anew, and create in a mind now irretrievably analytic, fresh associations of pleasure with any of the objects of human desire.

These were the thoughts which mingled with the dry heavy dejection of the melancholy winter of 1826-7. During this time I was not incapable of my usual occupations. I went on with them mechanically, by the mere force of habit. I had been so drilled in a certain sort of mental exercise, that I could still carry it on when all the spirit had gone out of it. I even composed and spoke several speeches at the debating society, how, or with what degree of success, I know not. Of four years continual speaking at that society, this is the only year of which I remember next to nothing. Two lines of Coleridge, in whom alone of all writers I have found a true description of what I felt, were often in my thoughts, not at this time (for I had never read them), but in a later period of the same mental malady:

> Work without hope draws nectar in a sieve,
> And hope without an object cannot live.

In all probability my case was by no means so peculiar as I fancied it, and I doubt not that many others have passed through a similar state; but the idiosyncrasies of my education had given to the general phenomenon a special character, which made it seem the natural effect of causes that it was hardly possible for time to remove. I frequently asked myself, if I could, or if I was bound to go on living, when life must be passed in this manner. I generally answered to myself, that I did not think I could possibly bear it beyond a year. When, however, not more than half that duration of time had elapsed, a small ray of light broke in upon my gloom. I was reading, accidentally, Marmontel's "Mémoires," and came to the passage which relates his father's death, the distressed position of the family, and the sudden inspiration by which he, then a mere boy, felt and made them feel that he would be everything to them—would supply the place of all that they had lost. A vivid conception of the scene and its feelings came over me, and I was moved to tears. From this moment my burthen grew lighter. The oppression of the thought that all feeling was dead within me, was gone. I was no longer hopeless: I was not a stock or a stone. I had still, it seemed, some of the material out of which all worth of character, and all capacity for happiness, are made. Relieved from my ever present sense of irremediable wretchedness, I gradually found that the ordinary incidents of life could again give me some pleasure; that I could again find enjoyment, not intense, but sufficient for cheerfulness, in sunshine and sky, in books, in conversation, in public affairs; and that there was, once more, excitement, though of a moderate kind, in exerting myself for my opinions, and for the public good. Thus the cloud gradually drew off, and I again enjoyed life: and though I had several relapses, some of which lasted many months, I never again was as miserable as I had been.

The experiences of this period had two very marked effects on my opinions and character. In the first place, they led me to adopt a theory of life, very unlike that on which I had before acted, and having much in common with what at that time I certainly had never heard of, the anti-self-consciousness theory of Carlyle. I never, indeed, wavered in the conviction that happiness is the test of all rules of conduct, and the end of life. But I now thought that this end was only to be attained by not making it the direct end. Those only are happy (I thought) who have their minds fixed on some object other than their own happiness; on the happiness of others, on the improvement of mankind, even on some art or pursuit, followed not as a means, but as itself an ideal end. Aiming thus at something else, they find happiness by the way. The enjoyments of life (such was now my theory) are sufficient to make it a pleasant thing, when they are taken *en passant*, without being made a principal object. Once make them so, and they are immediately felt to be insufficient. They will not bear a scrutinizing examination. Ask yourself whether you are happy, and you cease to be so. The only chance is to treat, not happiness, but some end external to it, as the purpose of life. Let your self-consciousness, your scrutiny, your self-interrogation, exhaust themselves on that; and if otherwise fortunately circumstanced you will inhale happiness with the air you breathe, without dwelling on it or thinking about it, without either forestalling it in imagination, or putting it to flight by fatal questioning. This theory now became the basis of my philosophy of life. And I still hold to it as the best theory for all those who have but a moderate degree of sensibility and of capacity for enjoyment, that is, for the great majority of mankind.

The other important change which my opinions at this time underwent, was that I, for the first time, gave its proper place, among the prime necessities of human well-being, to the internal culture of the individual. I ceased to attach almost exclusive importance to the ordering of outward circumstances, and the training of the human being for speculation and for action.

I had now learnt by experience that the passive susceptibilities needed to be cultivated as well as the active capacities, and required to be nourished and enriched as well as guided. I did not, for an instant, lose sight of, or undervalue, that part of the truth which I had seen before; I never turned recreant to intellectual culture, or ceased to consider the power and practice of analysis as an essential condition both of individual and of social improvement. But I thought that it had consequences which required to be corrected, by joining other kinds of cultivation with it. The maintenance of a due balance among the faculties, now seemed to me of primary importance. The cultivation of the feelings became one of the cardinal points in my ethical and philosophical creed. And my thoughts and inclinations turned in an increasing degree towards whatever seemed capable of being instrumental to that object.

Anthony Trollope
(1815-1882)

The prolific British novelist, Anthony Trollope, author of such works as *Barchester Towers, Orley Farm,* and *The Warden,* had as depressing and wretched a boyhood as Charles Dickens might have described. The son of an eccentric and irritable father who failed in everything he touched, young Anthony was sent to Harrow and Winchester, fashionable schools which his father could not afford.

There, the boy endured such years of social ostracism that he was moved to think about finding his way "up to the top of the college tower, and from thence put an end to everything."*

After a while my brother left Winchester and accompanied my father to America. Then another and a different horror fell to my fate. My college bills had not been paid, and the school tradesmen who administered to the wants of the boys were told not to extend their credit to me. Boots, waistcoats, and pocket-handkerchiefs, which, with some slight superveillance, were at the command of other scholars, were closed luxuries to me. My schoolfellows of course knew that it was so, and I became a Pariah. It is the nature of boys to be cruel. I have sometimes doubted whether among each other they do usually suffer much, one from the other's cruelty; but I suffered horribly! I could make no stand against it. I had no friend to whom I could pour out my sorrows. I was big, and awkward, and ugly, and, I have no doubt, skulked about in a most unattractive manner. Of course I was ill-dressed and dirty. But, ah! how well I remember all the agonies of my young heart; how I considered whether I should always be alone; whether I could not find my way up to the top of that college tower, and from thence put an end to everything? And a worse thing came than the stoppage of the supplies from the shopkeepers. Every boy had a shilling a week pocket-money, which we called battels, and which was advanced to us out of the pocket of the second master. On one awful day the second master announced to me that my battels would be stopped. He told me the reason,—the battels for the last half-year had not been repaid; and he urged his own unwillingness to advance the money. The loss of a shilling a week would not have been much, —even though pocket-money from other sources never reached me,— but that the other boys all knew it! Every now and again, perhaps three or four times in a half-year, these weekly shillings were given to certain servants of the college, in payment, it may be presumed, for some extra services. And now, when it came to the turn of any servant, he received sixty-nine shillings instead of seventy, and the cause of the defalcation was explained to him. I never saw one of those servants without feeling that I had picked his pocket.

---

*From *An Autobiography* by Anthony Trollope. Reprinted by permission of The Citadel Press. 1941. Pp. 8-9.

Beatrice Webb
(1858-1943)

Beatrice Webb, the English economist and sociologist, was one of nine sisters. Her father, the president of two railroad companies in Canada and England, was away a good deal of the time. Her mother felt Beatrice was the lowest in intelligence of all her children and entrusted her largely to the care of nurses. In her autobiography,* Mrs. Webb described her relationship with her mother.

My mother was nearing forty years of age when I became aware of her existence, and it was not until the last years of her life, when I was the only grown-up daughter remaining in the home, that I became intimate with her. The birth of an only brother when I was four, and his death when I was seven years of age, the crowning and devastating sorrow of my mother's life, had separated me from her care and attention; and the coming of my youngest sister, a few months after my brother's death, a partial outlet for my mother's wounded feelings, completed our separation. "Beatrice," she wrote in a diary when I was yet a child, "is the only one of my children who is below average in intelligence," which may explain her attitude of indifference. Throughout my childhood and youth she seemed to me a remote personage discussing business with my father or poring over books in her boudoir; a source of arbitrary authority whose rare interventions in my life I silently resented. I regarded her as an obstacle to be turned, as a person from whom one withheld facts and whose temper one watched and humored so that she should not interfere with one's own little plans. This absence of affection between us was all the more pitiful because, as we eventually discovered, we had the same tastes, we were puzzling over the same problems; and she had harbored, deep down in her heart, right up to middle life, the very ambition that I was secretly developing, the ambition to become a publicist.

The three excerpts which follow describe the melancholy state Beatrice experienced as a sixteen-year-old. The need for attention and love, her mother's neglect, her father's frequent and long absences from home, her jealous carping of her older sisters and their

---

*My Apprenticeship. Reprinted by permission of The Passfield Trustees and Longmans Green & Co., Ltd. (London). 1926. Pp. 11-12, 58-59, 74.

admirers, and her psychosomatic ailments, all contributed to her misery.

> ... almost continuous illness, bouts of neuralgia, of indigestion, of inflammation of all sorts and kinds, from inflamed eyes to congested lungs, marred my happiness; and worse than physical pain was boredom, due to the incapacity of ill-health, the ever-recurring problem of getting rid of the time between the meals, and from getting up to going to bed; and, worst of all, the sleepless hours between going to bed and getting up. I have a vivid memory of stealing and secreting a small bottle of chloroform from the family medicine-chest as a vaguely imagined alternative to the pains of life and the ennui of living; and of my consternation when one day I found the stopper loose and the contents evaporated.

Beatrice added a footnote to this, an excerpt from her manuscript diary, dated April 8, 1874:

> My childhood was not on the whole a happy one. Ill-health and starved affection, and the mental disorders which spring from these, ill-temper and resentment, marred it. Hours spent in secret places, under the shade of shrub and tree, in the leaf-filled hollows of the wood and in the crevices of the quarries, where I would sit and imagine love-scenes and death-bed scenes and conjure up the intimacy and tenderness lacking in my life, made up the happy moments. But dreary times of brooding and resentfulness, sharp pains of mortified vanity and remorse for untruthfulness, constant physical discomfort and frequent pain absorbed the greater part of my existence; and its loneliness was absolute.

A short time later, when she was "down in the depths of egotistical misery," Beatrice wrote in her diary:

> I think that the great benefit one receives from keeping a diary is that it often leads one to examine oneself and that it is a vent for one's feelings, for those feelings in particular that one cannot communicate to other people. Since I have been poorly this autumn I have been thinking of nothing but myself, and I am sure that it is the most unhealthy state of mind. I am suffering from an indisposition which is decidely trying to one's health of mind as it prevents one from doing

depressed.

much, and that always makes one discontented and low-spirited. I have never felt so low-spirited as I have this autumn. I have felt for the first time in my life how much unhappiness there is in life. But one has not been given the choice of existing or not existing, and all one has to think of is how to live the best and most useful and the happiest life. I have come to the conclusion that the only real happiness is devoting oneself to making other people happy. I feel that it is very discouraging to lose so much valuable time when I might be studying, but I believe that if I take this ill-health in a proper way, and bear it bravely and cheerfully, I shall improve my character more than I should have improved my mind in the same time. And character weighs more than intellect in the scales of life.

Harriet Monroe
(1860-1936)

Freud, in "The Psychogenesis of a Case of Homosexuality in a Woman" (9a), stated, "Analysis has explained the enigma of suicide in the following way: probably no one finds the mental energy required to kill himself unless, in the first place, in doing this he is at the same time killing an object with whom he has identified himself, and, in the second place, is turning against himself a death-wish which has been directed against someone else." For five years during her adolescence, Harriet Monroe, destined to become one of America's leading poets and editors, experienced a very conscious death-wish. One of Harriet's classmates had committed suicide, which precipitated a crisis in the impressionable and sensitive girl. "Five years passed," Miss Monroe wrote, "before I could say to myself that the dread temptation to suicide no longer haunted me." She eloquently described, both in verse and prose, the pathology of her adolescent neurosis.*

More and more, during the formative period of childhood, my little feelings were shut up within myself—I could not tell anything to anybody. My father was a hail-fellow playmate, enjoying his children when not absorbed with work—as he often was, even at home, until the wee small hours—or with chummy poker parties, which, on an evening or two each week, drove us out of our beloved library. My

*In *A Poet's Life* by Harriet Monroe. Reprinted by permission of Henry S. Monroe. Macmillan Co., 1938. Pp. 28-36.

mother, usually tucking away at the sewing machine, adored her children, but was a somewhat Spartan disciplinarian, little given to softness and quite unaware of what was going on inside us. My all-powerful sister continued to express her affection in sidelong teasing sallies which shut me up tighter than a lock and key. She had New York *Ledger* secrets with Hannah, the Irish cook, but my own real affection for the latter took a cruel delight in torture; I used to mount the kitchen table and orate a school-reader piece—"Shame upon you!" —about Ireland's disgrace in not fighting for freedom. I was never on confidential terms with my schoolmates or the two or three girls of my own age in the neighborhood; and as for boys, they were a separate awesome species, and I was emotionally afraid of them.

Thus there was no one to help me through a severe emotional crisis which struck me unaware when I was ten years old. Half a century later I put it into a free-verse monologue which presents the whole experience with such exactness that I can do no better than repeat it here:

> I hear them whispering—what is it?
> "Lizzie Wescott—hush!"
> Where is she? Yesterday she was here—
> So nice, so pretty, with curly hair—
> Here at her desk, like me.
> It's something awful—where is she?
> "Hush—Lizzie Wescott is dead."
> Dead.
> What is it to be dead?
>
> It is to be white—and still—
> And to lie in a coffin
> And to be buried in the ground.
> Lizzie Wescott will be buried in the ground.
>
> To be sure she was old, six years older than me—
> Sixteen.
> But that wasn't so very old.
> Her curly hair will be buried in the ground.
>
> Can we see her lying white and still
> Before they put her in the ground?
> Can we go to see her in her coffin?
>
> No, they won't let us.

It was hard to go to bed,
And think of her in the dark.
And it's hard to come to school and hear them whispering.
It's something more—oh, tell me!
Tell me!

"She did it—she took a poison,
She committed suicide."

Oh hush—don't say it—why must I listen?
What do they call it?—
"Suicide."

Then she wanted to lie white and still, curly hair and all,
And be buried forever in the ground.
Why?
But we mustn't ask why—nobody will tell.
We can crowd around her house—where she is lying
    white and still,
But nobody comes out—nobody will ever tell us.
Why?

How could she do it!—she liked to dance in the sun!
How could she lie down stiff, and sin so great a sin,
And send her little soul to burn in hell forever!

Suicide—even God could not forgive her!
"Think where she is now!"

It's awful—too awful to think of.
Why do I have to think of it?
It's too awful for God to think of, sitting there happy
    on His Great White Throne,
With angels around Him.
How could He send her little soul to burn in hell forever!
He couldn't.

It's easy then—
Between day-time and day-time she did it,
In one little night,
And she never told anybody—of course she couldn't.
In the morning they found her—they thought
    she was sleeping in her bed,

But she was lying white and still.

It's easy—anybody might do it—
Yes, even me!

Why do I think of it all the time,
God?
Please take the thought away from me—
I don't want to!
It's too dark for a little girl down there,
And too cold.
Take it away!
He doesn't take it away.
If I step on that crack in the sidewalk I'll have to do it—
Oh awful, if I should step on that crack!
Help me over it, God—surely You don't want me to do it!
Thank You!
Oh, help me!

I couldn't tell Wezie—no, never!—
She would laugh.
Nor Mama, nor anybody.
There's only God to help me, and He's very far away,
And very old.
I couldn't tell anybody.

Why am I running so fast—
Running away!
Oh, why did I see it—
That big blue bottle with *Poison* on it, and a skull—
    and two bones!
Now I'll have to do it—
It's right there—so near!
How can I help it now?

If I step on that red rose in the carpet I'll have to take it—
One swallow would be enough.
If I step on that rose I'll have to open the closet door,
And take out the bottle and drink some.
Oh, help me not to!—
I don't want to fall white and still,

And be buried in the ground.

Why did they put it there so near—
For me?
I'm afraid to pass that closet—
I'm afraid, afraid!
I'm afraid all the time of the skull on it—
When I wake up in the night it laughs at me.
God, surely You don't want a little girl to sin so great a sin,
And shut You out in the sky,
And be put out of Your sight in the ground.

Every day and every night just the same.
That rose in the carpet is always there—
I don't want to step on it.
If I have to do it, what will You say to my
        little flying soul—
When I am lying white and still
Down in the ground?

What did You say to her soul?—she didn't want to either.
What did You say?

I remember the horror whispers that flew through our classroom at the Moseley School; our questions, never answered, as to why Lizzie Wescott killed herself. I remember precisely that old Sunday-school room, the hysterical agony of the minister's talk, and the sobs of us weeping children. That any educated man could be so illiberal, and so ignorant of child psychology, seems incredible today; yet so it was —his exhortation went on and on with orotund repetitions, until our little hearts were torn to pieces and our minds, already severely shocked, were shaken out of balance. For me the crisis was dangerous; no doubt the cause of my frail health at that period, for five years passed before I could say to myself that the dread temptation to suicide no longer haunted me. Sunday school, and even church, had always been minor observations in our family, and from that time my mind began to question them. Gradually I followed my father toward liberal thinking, but I was thirty or more before I had lost entirely all allegiance to old creeds.

I don't know how far my overwrought nervous condition was responsible for the vivid sensations which used to seize me from my thirteenth to seventeenth years. They may have been pathological, and again I could not confide in anyone; but in later life I have often thought that in this period of earliest awakening youth I lived through many philosophies. Suddenly I would feel that the world did not exist, that the next step would plunge me into a void. Or I would know that only I of all mankind was alive, that these people around me were shadows without substance. Or I myself was a dream with all the rest, deluding myself into seeming speech and action in an abyss of nothingness. Or everything around me would vanish, and I would seem to realize the infinite in immensities of astronomical space. Such sensations as these, disturbing but almost sublime, which seemed to shake the very bases of life, were not reasonings of the mind, or even emotions of the heart, but deep upward surgings of the blood, tidal waves of life, not to be controlled or explained.

At last all this mental and emotional excitement was lulled by illness. The summer of 1876 was eventful in our family—almost our first experience of travel, for in June we went luxuriously in a body to the Centennial Exposition at Philadelphia, where I fear the Corliss engine, turning its great wheels massively, impressed me more vividly than the art gallery. Throughout this brief journey I was well enough, and some weeks later went for my usual summer fortnight with "Aunt Emma and Uncle Dave" and certain younger Dickinsons in Waukegan; but gradually a strange lassitude prostrated me, and when I was brought home, all white and trembling, our beloved long-bearded Dr. Allen thought I had set out to die of pernicious anemia. The next three or four months were deliciously restful as I lay on the Turkish lounge dressed in a scarlet-and-black Scotch-plaid flannel wrapper which was my only affliction. All my youthful troubles seemed to straighten out amid the prevailing kindness, and if I had really ceased to breathe, as my schoolmates heard one November morning, it would have been a gentle and painless death.

Mohandas K. Gandhi
(1869-1948)

Mahatma Gandhi, "the great soul," was a rebellious son, stubborn and arbitrary, Hitschmann (13) observed in his "New Varieties of Religious Experience." He had to take care of his sick father for several years, and the main reason for his intense guilt feelings was that by having intercourse with his wife, he missed being present at his father's death. At one time he attacked his wife and drove her away. His dietetic asceticism was hidden behind health theories, but the doctors advised him at least to take goat's milk in addition to his vegetables. His principle of 'non-violence' in politics, by its fundamental and overemphasized nature, looks suspiciously like a reaction to a very strong personal aggression impulse. His methods of hunger strike and civil disobedience are aggression under a new mask. His fight against the English government had a rare tenacity; he was the admired leader of the Indians, he who fought for them as a martyr.

"Gandhi proves once again that a very aggressive boy may, by repression and reaction formation, develop into the most altruistic, ascetic and pious man. But the repressed aggression of the 'original sin' will return, accompanied by feelings of guilt, manifesting itself by submission to God and reactive masochistic traits, such as the preference of a simple life, asceticism, periods of silence or fasting. He did not mind being imprisoned many times. Thus he represented 'the fighting soul of India' and aroused in the Indians a sense of nationhood and courage."

If we recall that the dynamic of suicide is aggression turned against the self, a primitive impulsive result of frustrated genital wishes, then Gandhi's chapter on "Stealing and Atonement" validates this postulate as well as Hitschmann's statement. Gandhi described his feelings between the ages of thirteen and fifteen, when he felt unbearably oppressed by the restrictions imposed on him by his parents.*

I have still to relate some of my failings during this meat-eating period and also previous to it, which date from before my marriage or soon after.

A relative and I became fond of smoking. Not that we saw any good in smoking, or were enamoured of the smell of a cigarette. We simply imagined a sort of pleasure in emitting clouds of smoke from our mouths. My uncle had the habit, and when we saw him smoking, we thought we should copy his example. But we had no money. So we began pilfering stumps of cigarettes thrown away by my uncle.

The stumps, however, were not always available, and could not emit much smoke either. So we began to steal coppers from the servant's pocket money in order to purchase Indian cigarettes. But the question was where to keep them. We could not of course smoke in the presence

---

*In *The Story of My Experiments with Truth.* Reprinted by permission of Public Affairs Press. 1948. Pp. 39-40.

of elders. We managed somehow for a few weeks on these stolen coppers. In the meantime we heard that the stalks of a certain plant were porous and could be smoked like cigarettes. We got them and began this kind of smoking.

But we were far from being satisfied with such things as these. Our want of independence began to smart. It was unbearable that we should be unable to do anything without the elders' permission. At last, in sheer disgust, we decided to commit suicide!

But how were we to do it! From where were we to get the poison? We heard that *Dhatura* seeds were an effective poison. Off we went to the jungle in search of these seeds, and got them. Evening was thought to be the auspicious hour. We went to *Kedarji Mandir,* put ghee in the temple-lamp, had the *darshan* and then looked for a lonely corner. But our courage failed us. Supposing we were not instantly killed? And what was the good of killing ourselves? Why not rather put up with the lack of independence? But we swallowed two or three seeds nevertheless. We dared not take more. Both of us fought shy of death, and decided to go to *Rama Mandir* to compose ourselves, and to dismiss the thought of suicide.

I realized that it was not as easy to commit suicide as to contemplate it. And since then, whenever I have heard of someone threatening to commit suicide, it has had little or no effect on me.

The thought of suicide ultimately resulted in both of us bidding good-bye to the habit of smoking stumps of cigarettes and of stealing the servant's coppers for the purpose of smoking.

Romain Rolland
(1866-1944)

During the very time when the young Gandhi made his semi-serious, abortive suicidal attempt, a teen-age French boy, later to become a staunch admirer and biographer of Gandhi, was experiencing much of the same terrible crisis as the Hindu boy. But Rolland, as he retrospected in his autobiography, was much more perceptive than Gandhi, for he was able to put his finger on the central problem of adolescence, that of identity: " . . . not only did I have no vocation whatever for any of those great 'Schools,' of which I knew absolutely nothing, but I knew even less about myself, nothing about what I wanted, nor what I was. Was I anything? . . . "

The sentimental exaltation and humanitarianism of Rolland is evident in his *Journey Within,* a passage of which follows.* Any one who has read his classic novel, *Jean-Christophe,* will recognize the autobiographical material contained in it, particularly the material relevant to the young Jean-Christophe, who, like Rolland, experienced much the same torments in trying to crystallize his feelings about himself.

When I was almost fourteen, my nest in the province was destroyed. My mother had knocked it down by one of her bold decisions, that cast prudence to the winds, but that nothing could shake, risking all to gain all—which is, for certain lives, like hers and my own, fundamentally wise. Clamecy was not good enough for the completion of my studies. But instead of sending me alone to Paris, like my father and grandfather, to serve life's apprenticeship, she had decided to follow me and to transplant the whole family. She did not want the child, a slender reed, to which all her hopes in life was attached, to be delivered over to the uncertain hazards of the great city that lie in wait for young bodies and untried souls. Besides, she wanted to break the accursed circle inside of which she felt herself dying in rebellion against the strangulation of the drowsy province. Everything gave way before her decision. In France, woman's energy has always compensated for her legal inferiority in the eyes of the law, and for the lowly place to which the sly, blustering, very questionable dictum of "Omnipotence on the male side . . . " seeks to assign her. Man or woman, whoever wills what he wants, can do it.

My father held a privileged position in his little city. He directed the municipal affairs along with his notary's practice, the most successful in the district. For miles around the entire region, he enjoyed a popularity that was balm to my childish heart. He gave up everything; sold his practice and, without taking the time to procure an adequate position in Paris, he buried himself in the office of the Crédit Foncier, where he was obliged to accept a subordinate position. He suffered deeply because of it, but never complained.

Overnight, we five found ourselves piled up with the monumental, provincial furniture, that had to be decapitated to get it in—and you bruised your sides going around the corners—located in a second-floor apartment up on the rue de Tournon, where the prehistoric omnibuses, thundering along like a herd of mammoths, shook the glasses in the buffet, and upset my fitful sleep in the little iron bedstead.

It was a terribly risky game that was being played. Even today when

*Reprinted by permission of Philosophical Library. 1947. Pp. 83-90.

I look back upon it, it depresses me as it did then through the long, restless nights. For I was conscious, to an exaggerated degree perhaps, of my family's sacrifice, that I felt I had to repay with success. Now, there was nothing less certain of accomplishment. The merciless clarity of my self-knowledge that I was never able to deceive, kept repeating to me night and day:

"You are not of those who conquer. Are you even equal to life?"

The moral wretchedness of those years was the stupid, iron-clad rule governing the choice of a career, which decreed that, in four or five years, I must force the door (which would immediately swing to behind me for life) of one of the principal Schools to which I was blindly destined by chance. Now, not only did I have no vocation whatever for any of those great "Schools," of which I knew absolutely nothing, but I knew even less about myself, nothing about what I wanted, nor what I was. Was I anything? . . .

I was going through a terrible crisis of personality disintegration. The shock of adolescence increased the upheaval of the exodus. Transplanted at the age of fourteen from my native Nivernais to the asphalt pavements of Paris where holes are made for the trees to breathe, like fish under the ice, my bruised roots tried feebly to attach themselves again. Everything eluded me, all security in life; the good, comfortable, social position upset; mental equilibrium unbalanced; confidence in study lost. From the small-town college, sleepy and old-fashioned, where I had easily been a little king, thrown into the croaking pond of sixty little Parisians, frogs and tadpoles—(nor were eels, leeches and little pike lacking)—I disappeared under this swarming mass that cut off my air and light. There was no longer any question of coming out first. I had scarcely room to exist at all. In spite of myself, they had made out of me one cell in an anonymous and formless body that was repulsive to me. In the college of Clamecy, I had already been incorporated into the classes; but the bonds were loosely tied because there were only a few of us, because eight out of ten of my comrades were a foreign substance to me, rude little peasants, only half awake, caring nothing about the intellectual world, and, because in that intellectual world, there were only two or three of us (including the young teacher, our elder brother), quite free to wander about, with the silence of the province around us, and space and time our own. In Paris, it was a culture-medium, swarming with corpuscles, with the larva of intelligence, twisting and darting, always in motion. Big cities are monstrous organisms, where, like the microbes of all maladies, those of the mind multiply rapidly. New-comers, if they do not succumb at once (like the water of the Seine, full of typhoid), must undergo a long and painful period to acclimatize their blood to these poisons. My blood absorbed them—it had to, or die—but my spirit never accepted them. But it is not good to be your guinea-pig. And I was. And so are all your children, more or less. Those who are born in you, do not know it. They are born immunized, and they play in the experimental cage. But I was not playing; I was defending my life. It took me years to accustom myself to the poisons. And for years, I was just one leap ahead of death.

I was a mountain of confused weaknesses and strengths; of attacks that blindfolded me; of giddy spells that sapped my strength; of desires, aversions, of fever, of debility of the flesh and of the spirit. Everything for me was an abyss: love, that inspired a holy fear in me, and whose heavy breath, thrown back from the baking walls and pavements, hit me full in the face. Everything for me was an abyss: ideas, where I could no longer find my provincial footpath, that twisted slowly and surely through the monotonous fields and between the blooming hedges. Here, in the lycées, in the word of the masters and that of books, in conversations with comrades, in the talk of the streets, nothing but a chaos of contradictory directions, a thicket of broken lines, of winding, slippery roads leading toward a vacuum, like the threads of a spider-web. . . . Universal Doubt, at a time when I needed a firm hand to grasp my fingers, about to let go their hold on the earth that I could hear crumbling away under my body suspended in midair. Nothing to hold on to. I was lost in my studies where I had to unlearn everything that I had learned: style, way of thinking, all my Burgundy currency that was not legal tender here; and I swung, a ridiculous figure, from second or third place to the fortieth, without understanding why the seesaw placed me here or there: for what I thought good was considered bad, and for something that I did without understanding it at all, they said to me: "That's good." Despairing of ever understanding, I regarded it as a game of heads or tails.

But the confusion at school was as nothing compared to that of my mental life. God was dead. To tell the truth, when I thought I believed in him in the provinces, I had never seen him living. When I prayed to him as best I could, he was never there. But I kept telling myself that he was probably in the next room. A few months in Paris opened all the doors. Behind them there was nothing. The Master had left the house in ruins and semi-darkness. (How could I know it was that of the dawn, and not of night?) I cannot tell you how completely the minds of all about me: masters and comrades, the whole moral atmosphere of Paris around 1880, was *deicidal*. And as, without my suspecting it, the essence of my whole being was—was always—religious, a daughter of God—*it was I they were killing*. My being was dissolving: my spirit into the nothingness of the air, and my flesh into the stream of the cemetery. I was falling. Several times, in the street— I can still recall the place—rue de Buci;—or, while I was descending the steps of a stairway, now destroyed (at the corner of the rue Monsieur-le-Prince and the boulevard Saint-Michel)—I suddenly had to clench my teeth and my fists to hold myself on the incline: I felt my head heavy as a rock pulling my body forward, and I jerked myself back, terrified, on the point of falling. I went on walking. Who was walking? A ghost, among other ghosts. Nothing was there. . . .

Between the ages of fifteen and seventeen, I breathed in the sulphurous vapors of the abyss. And so, what a temptation it was when I, leaning over the iron railing on the sixth floor of number 31, rue Monge, (our new home), as from a high promontory that juts out over the steep slope of Mount Saint-Genevieve, what a temptation to let myself be sucked in by the lips of the gaping emptiness below! No effort was needed! Just let oneself go! But with my flesh prickling, I tore myself away, by a tremendous effort, from the monster who was lying in wait. At any rate, the unknown God, the Force, my Destiny, seized me by the nape of the neck and deposited me again on the bank. The command to live!

"But how can I go on living, God in whom I do not believe, I in whom I do not believe?"

"By denying you."

No is an affirmation of life just as *yes* is. Only falsehood is death. Lying to oneself, a defect of the spirit.

My whole salvation was attained by my spiritual sincerity, absolute and constant, at every moment of my life, and on all occasions. Because of love or hatred, desire or fear, passion for life or weariness of living— even when I was not very brave or frank with the world, through fear —never have I tried to deceive myself; never have I been my own dupe.

My first act of strength, during this period of my adolescence when I was sinking without God, was to break with my religion. It was my most religious act. (I shall come back to that.) Out of respect for myself and the hidden God, I did not wish to pretend, to imitate the appearance of faith, to whitewash the outside, to persist in conforming. God! I am honest with you! I don't go to Mass any more. I know it is too solemn for me to incline before your bleeding body, a body deprived of its soul, whose lips pronounce empty prayers. I don't believe in you.

"Not to believe is still to believe! You would not deny me, were we not adversaries. . . ."

My break with Catholicism hurt my mother deeply. My father, a non-believer, was affronted. He was one of those who consider religion good for children. The Church, indifferent, made not the slightest effort to keep me in the fold; she waited until doomsday for me to return to her.

David Garnett
(1892-   )

The prickly, sensitive ego of the adolescent is frequently a difficult thing for the adult to discern. Despite the adult assumption that the adolescent has nearly everything he would want, some almost unrelated spark can set the youth down in the darkest depths. In fact, states Ballesteros (2), it seems that the adolescent is ready to take his life for any seemingly unimportant vexation or upset.

Such a youngster was David Garnett, the brilliant author of the imaginative novel, *Lady Into Fox*. Visitors to his home, when he was a child and adolescent, were such greats of the literary world as W. W. Hudson, Joseph Conrad, Stephen Crane and John Galsworthy. His neighbor was Ford Madox Ford. David was a frequent visitor to the theater and in the passage below,* he describes the series of melancholy events which followed his witnessing of the famous actress, Eleonora Duse, in *La Dame aux Camélias*. This performance triggered off in the impressionable fifteen-year-old boy a morbidly sensitive period, during which he felt the world "as not fit to be lived in," and for a blinding moment thought suicide was the answer.

About this time I went with my Mother to see Eleonora Duse, in *La Dame aux Camélias*. The effect she produced on me was overwhelming, and I can remember her face, her voice, her gestures far more vividly than the actress I saw a year or two ago. No doubt this was partly because she was the first great actress that I ever saw, possibly the only great actress I have ever seen.

Every moment that Duse was on the stage I was living more intensely than I had ever lived before. I was transported out of myself, caring nothing that I was a boy of fourteen and not a man. For those wonderful hours nothing mattered but that supremely tragic woman, and it was happiness enough to have seen her and heard that wonderful voice.

*From *The Golden Echo*. Reprinted by permission of Harcourt, Brace & World, Inc. 1954. Pp. 123-124.

Afterwards, in a daze, Constance and I went round to the stage door and waited for her. Across the road was another theatre, the stage door of which was surrounded by a throng of exquisitely dressed young men, in shining top hats, morning coats, striped trousers and spats. The play over there was *The Spring Chicken,* and they were waiting to see Lily Elsie. There were scarcely half a dozen of us waiting for the plainly dressed and tired-looking Italian woman.

Duse and Lily Elsie both came out together, so that the first thing that Duse saw was the heroine of *The Spring Chicken,* all frills and flounces, parasol and picture hat, being fêted by an adoring throng of gilded youths on the opposite side of the street. Then she looked round and saw us and burst out laughing, waved her hand and thanked us very prettily and graciously, but when she had got into her cab and was being driven away I could see her fall back against the cushions to laugh again.

I was at this stage morbidly sensitive, and the impact of real tragedy was as overwhelming as that of Duse's interpretation of the dying consumptive girl. An old lady dearly beloved by us all had died suddenly, while staying with her daughter who was expecting a child. Shock and grief were disastrous, and when the baby was born it proved to be mentally deficient. Though not an idiot, its intelligence never developed but was arrested. My mother explained to me this tragic story: mother and child were close at hand, and I wandered away alone into the woods, thinking the matter over and seeing clearly for the first time the insane cruelty of cause and effect. The intensity of one great sorrow had bred another more terrible and lasting. As I thought it over, it seemed to me that the world in which such things were normal and natural was not fit to be lived in: that life in such an environment and on such terms was unendurable, and that I should be wise to be quit of it.

"Suicide is the answer," I said to myself, and I drew my keen little black-handled Finnish knife and looked at it. "Only drive that in between your ribs and you will be free of all sorrows," and I lay for a long time undecided, holding the knife in my hand.

Hsieh Pingying
(1907-   )

Hsieh Pingying called her autobiography, appropriately, *Girl Rebel.** She was born in Hunan province at a time when the clearly defined relationships between husband and wife, parents and chil-

---

*Reprinted by permission of The John Day Co., Inc. 1940. Pp. 28-32.

dren, elder brother and younger brother, and so on through every aspect of personal contact, was the sustaining force in Chinese society. It was these factors that Hsieh rebelled against and which we see spelled out below. At the age of twelve, Hsieh was determined to go on with her education, but equally determined to prevent her was her castrating mother. It was only after the young girl had chosen fasting as the least painful attempt at suicide that the mother relented.

In the winter Mother received a letter from Elder Brother, and in it there were a few sentences concerning me: "My sister Phoenix has quite rare ability, worthy of a good education. Next Spring we should send her to Tatung Girls' School, and prepare for her to go to the Girls' Normal School in the future. Nowadays girls are beginning to go out, and there are schools all around. Our family was always one of scholars. I hope Mother will not object just because she is a girl."

For this I was very grateful to Elder Brother and I really did not understand at that time why he was so kind. My future looked bright and hopeful! I was happy, and did not close my eyes all that night. I wanted only to get through this year quickly and go to Tatung Girls' School. "When I get there I shall study very hard. I shall read more books than my brothers." Such was my dream.

At that time, Father, Second Brother, and Third Brother were not at home. Sister was staying at home with her baby. She cried all day until her eyes were swollen, because she wanted to hire a wet nurse, and Mother strictly forbade it.

In the evening Mother was weaving beside the fire, and Sister was feeding her baby at her breast. I was studying and thinking of Elder Brother's letter. I said hopefully, "Mother, I do want to go to Tatung Girls' School next year."

"Still thinking of studying?" she said, casually. "What you have learned already is enough for a girl. You are not a boy. What is the use of reading so many books?" She did not even take my words seriously!

"Didn't Elder Brother write and say that he wanted me to go to school?" I said, still softly.

"What does he know? Training girls is my business. You will start embroidering next year. Your feet are still too big, and I haven't finished with them yet. If you are like this when you marry, people will say that your mother did not bring you up properly."

"But I want to study," I said. "Am I not a human being like my brothers?"

"What a joke! Like your brothers! They study to become officials and earn money, but you are a girl. You can only be a good wife and good mother, and learn to serve your parents-in-law and run a home. What is the use of your studying?"

At that time I really could not give a reason for studying. I did not know about equality between men and women, much less did I know how an educated woman could be useful to society. I only felt that I wanted knowledge just as I wanted to eat and dress, and I did not see why girls had only to be wives, to give birth to children for their husbands, and to be ill-treated by the parents-in-law as Sister was.

Two shining tears ran from my eyes. How could my mother treat me so? I saw that her face was really ferocious as she looked at me out of the corners of her eyes and continued:

"Moreover, you are not like a girl. You are worse than boys. Everyone in the school says that you are very naughty. Even such a strict teacher can do nothing with you. If you continue to read more books, you will get worse and worse!"

From then on, I dared not mention the question again. I knew that Mother could not be persuaded. There might be some hope when my father came back, but I knew that Father was afraid of Mother and listened to her in everything. Grandmother and Father did try to persuade Mother to let me go for one year, but she would not yield. Sister-in-law and my aunts all came to plead with her, but still she would not. So I lost all hope of continuing school. When I realized this my heart was broken and I decided to commit suicide.

When the spirit of spring came to the earth again, there was life and growth everywhere; only I was planning to tread the road of death.

In our village, all the ways I knew of committing suicide were:

1. Hanging by a rope.
2. Jumping into the river.
3. Swallowing matches.
4. Eating opium.
5. Swallowing a ring.
6. Cutting my throat with a knife.

I was after all only a child; I wanted to commit suicide, but I was afraid of pain. I realize now that it was quite funny! Every day I debated with myself as to the best way of suicide. The results were as follows:

As for the first way, I had seen how frightful Yiti's wife looked when she hanged herself and her tongue stuck out; so I dared not.

Second, jumping in the river would cause my stomach to swell like a big drum and men would have to take my dress off and pump the water out. I was not willing to permit that. My mind was so poisoned with ancient ideas!

Third, matches had an awful smell.

Fourth, there was no way of buying opium.

Fifth, I had no rings, and even if I had one, I would not dare swallow it, for I remembered the suffering when a penny had stuck in my throat.

Sixth, if the knife did not cut clean through my throat, and I did not die, it would be terrible.

At last I decided to starve myself to death in bed.

I stayed two whole days in bed, and everyone thought I was sick. Mother immediately called the nearsighted teacher who was also a doctor. "She is not sick," he said.

My sister came to my bed and tried to comfort me. She wept with me. She had been feeling very sad because she had no milk for her baby, and my illness made her feel worse.

"Good Sister," she said, "tell me if there is anything you wish that I can do."

"No one can do it!" I said.

"Tell me what is the matter," she persisted.

"I want . . . I want to study," I said at last.

Mother seemed to know that I was fasting because I wanted to study, and purposely paid no attention to me, which made me all the more determined to die. "Mother loves her children so much, and yet why does she still refuse to consent when I am about to die?" I said, and I doubted her love.

But on the third day, when she saw I was so stubborn, Mother consented. She said that for two years she was going to watch my behavior. If I improved after those two years, then I could go to school. If not, she would marry me off.

Through this ray of hope my small life was saved.

Graham Greene
(1905-   )

By the time he was sixteen years old, Graham Greene, the gifted English author of *The End of the Affair*, *The Heart of the Matter*, and *The Quiet American*, as well as of the international intrigues, *The Ministry of Fear* and *Our Man in Havana*, had "completed" his psychoanalysis, brought about by his running away from school. His analysis left him wrung dry, he tells us, bored to an intolerable depth, a boredom as deep, perhaps, as we saw in Beatrice Webb. Greene recalled the comment of the German poet, Rainer Maria Rilke and applied it to himself: "Psychoanalysis is too fundamental a help for me, it helps you once and for all, it clears you up, and to find myself finally cleared up one day might be even more helpless than this chaos."

In this mood, and to escape his insufferable boredom, Greene played Russian roulette with himself. But even the sense of jubilation and "the crude kick of excitement" he got from pulling the trigger palled on him after the fifth try and he put the revolver away in the corner cupboard. "One campaign was over, but the war against boredom had got to go on."*

I can remember very clearly the afternoon I found the revolver in the brown deal corner cupboard in the bedroom which I shared with my elder brother. It was the early autumn of 1922. I was seventeen and terribly bored and in love with my sister's governess—one of those miserable, hopeless, romantic loves of adolescence that set in many minds the idea that love and despair are inextricable and that successful love hardly deserves the name. At that age one may fall irrevocably in love with failure, and success of any kind loses half its savour before it is experienced. Such a love is surrendered once and for all to the singer at the pavement's edge, the bankrupt, the old school friend who wants to touch you for a dollar. Perhaps in many so conditioned it is the love for God that mainly survives, because in his eyes they can imagine themselves remaining always drab, seedy, unsuccessful, and therefore worthy of notice.

The revolver was a small genteel object with six chambers like a tiny egg stand, and there was a cardboard box of bullets. It has only recently occurred to me that they may have been blanks; I always assumed them to be live ammunition, and I never mentioned the discovery to my brother because I had realized the moment I saw the revolver the use I intended to make of it. (I don't to this day know why he possessed it; certainly he had no licence, and he was only three years older than myself. A large family is as departmental as a Ministry.)

My brother was away—probably climbing in the Lake District—and until he returned the revolver was to all intents mine. I knew what to do with it because I had been reading a book (the name Ossendowski

*From *The Lost Childhood* by Graham Greene. Reprinted by permission of The Viking Press, Inc. 1952. Pp. 173-176.

comes to mind as the possible author) describing how the White Russian officers, condemned to inaction in South Russia at the tail-end of the counter-revolutionary war, used to invent hazards with which to escape boredom. One man would slip a charge into a revolver and turn the chambers at random, and his companion would put the revolver to his head and pull the trigger. The chance, of course, was six to one in favour of life.

How easily one forgets emotions. If I were dealing now with an imaginary character, I would feel it necessary for verisimilitude to make him hesitate, put the revolver back into the cupboard, return to it again after an interval, reluctantly and fearfully, when the burden of boredom became too great. But in fact I think there was no hesitation at all, for the next I can remember is crossing Berkhamsted Common, gashed here and there between the gorse bushes with the stray trenches of the first Great War, towards the Ashridge beeches. Perhaps before I had made the discovery, boredom had already reached an intolerable depth.

I think the boredom was far deeper than the love. It had always been a feature of childhood: it would set in on the second day of the school holidays. The first day was all happiness, and, after the horrible confinement and publicity of school, seemed to consist of light, space and silence. But a prison conditions its inhabitants. I never wanted to return to it (and finally expressed my rebellion by the simple act of running away), but yet I was so conditioned that freedom bored me unutterably.

The psycho-analysis that followed my act of rebellion had fixed the boredom as hypo fixes the image on the negative. I emerged from those delightful months in London spent at my analyst's house—perhaps the happiest months of my life—correctly orientated, able to take a proper extrovert interest in my fellows (the jargon rises to the lips), but wrung dry. For years, it seems to me, I could take no aesthetic interest in any visual thing at all: staring at a sight that others assured me was beautiful, I would feel nothing. I was fixed in my boredom. (Writing this I come on a remark of Rilke: "Psycho-analysis is too fundamental a help for me, it helps you once and for all, it clears you up, and to find myself finally cleared up one day might be even more helpless than this chaos.")

Now with the revolver in my pocket I was beginning to emerge. I had stumbled on the perfect cure. I was going to escape in one way or another, and because escape was inseparably connected with the Common in my mind, it was there that I went.

The wilderness of gorse, old trenches, abandoned butts was the unchanging backcloth of most of the adventures of childhood. It was to the Common I had decamped for my act of rebellion some years before, with the intention, expressed in a letter left after breakfast on the heavy black sideboard, that there I would stay, day and night, until either I had starved or my parents had given in; when I pictured war it was always in terms of this Common, and myself leading a guerilla campaign in the ragged waste, for no one, I was persuaded, knew its paths so intimately (how humiliating that in my own domestic campaign I was ambushed by my elder sister after a few hours).

Beyond the Common lay a wide grass rise known for some reason as Cold Harbour to which I would occasionally with some fear take a horse, and beyond this again stretched Ashridge Park, the smooth olive skin of beech trees and the thick last year's quagmire of leaves, dark like old pennies. Deliberately I chose my ground, I believe without any real fear—perhaps because I was uncertain myself whether I was play-acting; perhaps because so many acts which my elders would have regarded as neurotic, but which I still consider to have been under the circumstances highly reasonable, lay in the background of this more dangerous venture.

There had been, for example, perhaps five or six years before, the disappointing morning in the dark room by the linen cupboard on the eve of term when I had patiently drunk a quantity of hypo under the impression that it was poisonous: on another occasion the blue glass bottle of hay fever lotion which as it contained a small quantity of cocaine had probably been good for my mood: the bunch of deadly nightshade that I had eaten with only a slight narcotic effect: the twenty aspirins I had taken before swimming in the empty out-of-term school baths (I can still remember the curious sensation of swimming through wool): these acts may have removed all sense of strangeness as I slipped a bullet into a chamber and, holding the revolver behind my back, spun the chambers round.

Had I romantic thoughts about the governess? Undoubtedly I must have had, but I think that at the most they simply eased the medicine down. Boredom, aridity, those were the main emotions. Unhappy love has, I suppose, sometimes driven boys to suicide, but this was not suicide, whatever a coroner's jury might have said of it: it was a gamble with six chances to one against an inquest. The romantic flavour—the autumn scene, the small heavy compact shape lying in the fingers— that perhaps was a tribute to adolescent love, but the discovery that it was possible to enjoy again the visible world by risking its total loss was one I was bound to make sooner or later.

I put the muzzle of the revolver in my right ear and pulled the trigger. There was a minute click, and looking down at the chamber I could see that the charge had moved into place. I was out by one. I remember an extraordinary sense of jubilation. It was as if a light had been turned on. My heart was knocking in its cage, and I felt that life contained an infinite number of possibilities. It was like a young man's first successful experience of sex—as if in that Ashridge glade one had passed a test of manhood. I went home and put the revolver back in the corner cupboard.

The odd thing about this experience was that it was repeated several times. At fairly long intervals I found myself craving for the drug. I took the revolver with me when I went up to Oxford and I would walk out from Headington toward Elsfield down what is now a wide arterial road, smooth and shiny like the walls of a public lavatory. Then it was a sodden unfrequented country lane. The revolver would be whipped behind my back, the chambers twisted, the muzzle quickly and surreptitiously inserted beneath the black and ugly winter tree, the trigger pulled.

Slowly the effect of the drug wore off—I lost the sense of jubilation, I began to gain from the experience only the crude kick of excitement. It was like the difference between love and lust. And as the quality of the experience deteriorated so my sense of responsibility grew and worried me. I wrote a very bad piece of free verse (free because it was easier in that way to express my meaning without literary equivocation) describing how, in order to give a fictitious sense of danger, I would "press the trigger of a revolver I already know to be empty." This piece of verse I would leave permanently on my desk, so that if I lost my gamble, there would be incontrovertible evidence of an accident, and my parents, I thought, would be less troubled than by an apparent suicide—or than by the rather bizarre truth.

But it was back at Berkhamsted that I paid a permanent farewell to the drug. As I took my fifth dose it occurred to me that I wasn't even excited: I was beginning to pull the trigger about as casually as I might take an aspirin tablet. I decided to give the revolver—which was six-chambered—a sixth and last chance. Twirling the chambers round, I put the muzzle to my ear for the last time and heard the familiar empty click as the chambers revolved. I was through with the drug, and walking back over the Common, down the new road by the ruined castle, past the private entrance to the gritty old railway station—reserved for the use of Lord Brownlow—my mind was already busy on other plans. One campaign was over, but the war against boredom had got to go on.

I put the revolver back in the corner cupboard, and going downstairs I lied gently and convincingly to my parents that a friend had invited me to join him in Paris.

REFERENCES

1. Ackerman, Nathan W. *The Psychodynamics of Family Life*. New York: Basic Books, 1958, p. 231.
2. Ballesteros, Antonio. Suicides in adolescence. In: Millan, Alfonso (Ed.), *Proceedings of the Fourth International Conference on Mental Health*.
3. Bashkirtseff, Marie. *Journal*. Chicago: Rand McNally, 1889.
4. Benedict, Ruth. *Patterns of Culture*. New York: New American Library, 1934, p. 202.
5. Bloch, Herbert A., & Niederhoffer, Arthur. *The Gang*. New York: Philosophical Library, 1959, p. 82.
6. Ellis, Havelock. *My Life*. Boston: Houghton Mifflin Co., 1939, p. 112.
7. Erikson, Erik H. Growth and crises of the healthy personality. *Psychol. Issues,* 1:89, 1959.
8. Forten, Charlotte. *Journal*. New York: Dryden Press, 1953, p. 47.
9. Freud, Ernst L. (Ed.). *Letters of Sigmund Freud*. New York: Basic Books, 1960.
9a. Freud, Sigmund. The psychogenesis of a case of homosexuality in a woman. *Collected Papers,* 2:202-231, 1924.
10. Goethe, Johann Wolfgang von. *Goethe's Autobiography. Poetry and Truth from My Own Life*. Washington, D. C.: Public Affairs Press, 1949, pp. 220-221.
11. Hall, G. Stanley. *Adolescence*. New York: Appleton-Century-Crofts, 1904, Vol. I, p. 535.
12. Hazlitt, William. *Hazlitt Painted by Himself*. London: C. & J. Temple, 1948, pp. 20-24.
13. Hitschmann, Edward. New varieties of religious experience. In: Róheim, Géza (Ed.), *Psychoanalysis and the Social Sciences*. New York: International Universities Press, 1947, pp. 226-228.
14. Jacobson, Edith. Depression; the oedipus complex in the development of depressive mechanisms. *Psychoanal. Quart.,* 12:541-560, 1943.
15. Jung, Carl G. The soul and death. In: Feifel, Herman (Ed.), *The Meaning of Death*. New York: McGraw-Hill, 1959, p. 4.
16. Malleson, Nicholas. The ecological concept in British student health services. In: Funkenstein, Daniel H. (Ed.), *The Student and Mental Health, an International View*. Cambridge, Mass.: World Federation for Mental Health, 1959, p. 443.

17. Moss, Leonard M., & Hamilton, Donald M. Psychotherapy of the suicidal patient. *Amer. J. Psychiat.*, 112:814-820, 1956.
18. Murphy, Henry B. M. National and cultural variations: Ceylon, Hong Kong, India, Malaya, Thailand. In: Funkenstein, Daniel H. (Ed.), *The Student and Mental Health, an International View.* Cambridge, Mass.: World Federation for Mental Health, 1959, p. 38.
19. Obermüller. Beitrag sum Jugendselbstmord in Baden (A study of adolescent suicide in Baden). *Z. Kinderforsch*, 45:149-156, 1936.
20. Rolland, Romain. *Journey Within.* New York: Philosophical Library, 1947, p. 15.
21. Rubenstein, Robert, Moses, Rafael, & Lidz, Theodore. On attempted suicide. *AMA Arch. Neurol. Psychiat.*, 79:103-112, 1958.
22. Schechter, Marshall D. The recognition and treatment of suicide in children. In: Shneidman, Edwin S., & Farberow, Norman L. (Eds.), *Clues to Suicide.* New York: McGraw-Hill Book Co., 1957, pp. 132, 136.
23. Schmideberg, Melitta. A note on suicide. *Int. J. Psycho-Anal.*, 17:1-5, 1936.
24. Schneer, Henry I., Kay, Paul, & Brozovsky, Morris. Events and conscious ideation leading to suicidal behavior in adolescence. *Psychiat. Quart.*, 35:507-508, 511, 1961.
25. Shaw, Clifford. *The Jack-Roller. A Delinquent Boy's Own Story.* Philadelphia: Albert Saifer, 1930, p. 71.
26. Simmons, Leo W. (Ed.). *Sun Chief. The Autobiography of a Hopi Indian.* New Haven: Yale University Press, 1942, p. 93.
27. Spiegel, Leo A. Comments on the psychoanalytic psychology of adolescence. In: Eissler, Ruth S., et al. (Eds.), *The Psychoanalytic Study of the Child.* New York: International Universities Press, 1958, Vol. XIII, p. 306.
28. Stillman, William J. *The Autobiography of a Journalist.* Boston: Houghton Mifflin Co., 1901, p. 43.
29. Wassermann, Jacob. *My Life As a German and As Jew.* New York: Coward McCann, 1933, pp. 21-22.
30. Yarmolinsky, Avrahm. *Turgenev. The Man, His Art and His Age.* New York: Orion Press, 1959, p. 28.
31. Zilboorg, Gregory. Considerations on suicide, with particular reference to that of the young. *Amer. J. Orthopsychiat.*, 7:15-31, 1937.

CHAPTER SIXTEEN

Juvenile Delinquency

The concern over the rise of juvenile delinquency in the past two decades has been a justified one. It has reached such proportions in the United States that a Senate Investigating Committee was established in 1960 to explore its causes and recommend preventive measures. But familiar as we are through the newspapers of sensational acts of delinquency perpetrated by adolescents in the United States, the problem is a world-wide one. Furthermore, although the facts are available, it has not always been recognized that delinquency has been a general problem since the early days of history.

In West Germany today, delinquents are called *halb-starken,* literally, the "half-strong," a colloquial term for youth in rebellion against stern social disciplines. In England, the "teddy boys" riot in racial antagonism against the influx of West Indian Negroes. The *teppisti* (hooligans) of Italy slash automobile tires, break windows, annoy women on the street, rough up their escorts, and make the night hideous with the noise of their motor-scooters. The French *blousons noirs* (black leather jackets) have sprung up to molest people and damage storefronts and automobiles. The delinquents in Africa, known as *tsotsis,* terrorize the populace and run the gamut of crime from theft to murder. And so it goes in all the nations, regardless of political faith, racial stock, religion, economic status or geographical location.

The practices of infanticide and exposure as well as the selling of infants were widespread among the Chinese and Japanese until fairly recently and were common, too, in ancient Greece and Rome.

"How common," write authorities on these cradles of civilization (19), "was the dreadful exposure of children who were physically imperfect or for any causes disagreeable to their parents, so that crowds of these little unfortunates were to be seen exposed around a column near the Velebrum at Rome—some being taken to be raised as slaves, others as prostitutes, others carried off by beggars to be maimed for exhibition, or captured by witches to be murdered, and their bodies to be used in their magical preparations."

On February 14, 1960, the following item appeared in *The New York Times (13)*: "There are countless child victims of India's criminal masters, who employ professional kidnappers to bring in young recruits of both sexes. Small girls who fall into their clutches are trained as prostitutes, boys as thieves and swindlers. Schools for beggars exist, where tots learn to feign physical disabilities or are deliberately maimed." Almost the identical words are used to describe identical situations separated in time by almost two thousand years. In-between, by way of illustration, the court records of eighteenth-century England indicate the numerous cases in which thieves and prostitutes "adopted" children to aid them in their business or hired them out as beggars. In 1859, James Burn wrote his autobiographical experiences as a beggar boy (4), and as recently as 1956, Emma Smith, in her autobiography, *A Cornish Waif's Story* (14), deals with the same subject.

The problem of destitute, dependent and delinquent children was recognized by the Emperor Trajan (110 A.D.) who established the first asylum for their care. Nerva, Constantine the Great, and the Emperors Valentinian and Justinian all promulgated laws protecting children. But even so, Juvenal (60? A.D.-140? A.D.) in his *Third Satire* on the city of Rome bewailed the "young hoodlums, all steamed up on wine," who started street fights for no reason at all (9). By the fourth century, the influence of the Christian religion —in part due to the thesis that every individual was acceptable to God—had started in the ascendancy. While foundling homes and asylums were established, the institution of feudalism, the sale of children, the general callousness and scant attention paid children, the brevity of childhood—and delinquency—persisted.

Delinquency had reached such a state in the early eighteenth century that Pope Clement IX found it imperative to establish the first specific institution for delinquent youth, the Hospice of San

Michele in Rome. In England in the same century, juvenile offenders from the ages of six to fourteen were imprisoned, flogged, put in solitary confinement or hung for vagrancy, theft and other less serious offenses with which probation officers now deal. Charles Lamb, in one of his *Essays of Elia,* described the cruelty imposed on the children who had been committed for petty offenses to Christ's Hospital in London. As late as 1833, a child of nine who broke a window pane was tried and sentenced to death in England (20). Gangs, too, abounded in early days. One of them was the "Pinking Dindies," who flourished in Dublin at the beginning of the nineteenth century. These youths were, "to a man . . . skillful swordsmen," who "amused themselves by going about the place prodding at citizens with the points of swords. . . . The Dindies were too gallant to pink ladies, but the gentleman upon whose arm one walked might at any time suffer this indignity [3]." At the same time the Dindies were riding high in Dublin, the first known gang in New York City, according to Asbury (1), was formed. In his book Asbury chronicles the typical development of teen-age gangs of the nineteenth and early twentieth centuries into a kind of "farm system" that fed graduated members into adult criminal gangs.

This cursory and very rudimentary treatment of the history of juvenile delinquency gives, perhaps, some concept of its historical precedents. As we shall see, the characteristic behavior of the juvenile delinquent today differs little from that of his ancient forebear. Swords and daggers have given way to switchblade knives and zip guns. Rampaging gangs of hoodlums on horseback have been usurped by motorcycle brigades. Even the almost universal scarification ceremony in primitive puberty rites finds its parallel in the tattooing practice of contemporary adolescents, the dueling scars of the German student *mensuren* and the knife scars proudly worn by Negro and Puerto Rican gang members.

But scarification among American youth assumes a far more formalized pattern. Bloch and Niederhoffer (2) have discovered teen-age boys and girls of both low- and middle-class economic groups willingly submitting to scarification.

> . . . two fourteen-year-old girls were found to be engaged in a fight as champions of opposing gangs. Having been separated, one of the girls, in displaying her injuries, rolled up her sleeve to show finger

nail scratches. The name, George, was indelibly scarred into her upper arm. She explained it by saying that most of the girls in her set branded themselves in this fashion. They produced the scars by pricking their flesh with bobby pins until blood appeared, thereby forming a permanent scar. Her opponent in the fight, upon being questioned, proudly exhibited a scar clearly spelling out the name, Paul, on the upper thigh in the vicinity of the genital region. Both girls asserted that their boy friends had scarred themselves in the same manner as a sign of solidarity. Further investigation has indicated the wide prevalence of this specific type of practice which, incidentally, is not confined to working class children or to gang members of either sex. Similar practices have been widely found among middle class boys and girls removed from the atmosphere of the socially condemned and predatory neighborhood gang.

While the behavior of the delinquent differs little from that of his predecessors, the connotation of the term, juvenile delinquency, has changed considerably. Robert M. MacIver (12), director of the New York City Juvenile Delinquency Evaluation Project (1960), proposed the elimination of the "juvenile delinquency" label. "Because of the newspaper publicity given to serious offenses committed by children under sixteen, the term juvenile delinquency has taken on a secondary meaning generally associated with serious criminality. . . . In the popular mind, the juvenile delinquent more often connotes a gang killer or auto thief than a child who is truant or disobedient to his parents. . . . Since the term juvenile delinquency covers a wide range of acts of all degrees of seriousness, including some that if committed by adults would have no legal consequences at all, it appears desirable to eliminate the designation altogether."

Thus, to define juvenile delinquency in terms of contemporary connotations and for general application involves many variables, as would a discussion on its etiology, on the various moral and legal issues that arise out of the disorder, on methods of dealing with delinquency, and on its prevention. It is commonly accepted by most authorities that the roots of juvenile delinquency can be traced to disturbance within the individual family constellation combined with social pressures which confront the youngster. Kanner (10) takes the approach of multiple causation and develops three types of predatory delinquency in childhood. These are (a) delinquency founded on brain pathology, (b) delinquency seemingly originating in the "pathology" of relationships in the family, and (c) delinquency which can be described to "social dislocation." Prime contributors to delinquency have been variously diagnosed as personal tension, defective discipline, insecurity, lack of home guidance, and emotional instability. Johnson and Szurek (8) have long argued the thesis that the delinquent acts out the unconscious desires of his parents, particularly the destructive impulses of his mother. All of these factors are symptoms of deep-seated emotional problems and disturbances in interpersonal relations, whether or not the delinquency is explained as a result of poor home life, neighborhood groups, or inadequate social conditions.

The too permissive or too primitive superego of the delinquent becomes manifest in his acting out of his emotional tensions and difficulties rather than thinking them out. The delinquent is usually far more defiant of social custom and far less submissive to authority than others. His pattern is consistently that of the uninhibited, unreflective, undisciplined child. Wirt and Briggs (18), in their study of personality and environmental factors in the development of delinquency, found that "most delinquents do not appear to be motivated by special desires or needs for antisocial acts, but rather are only incidentally delinquent. We have found that these boys are superficial, sensual, and selfish. Their relations with others are casual and their chief interests are self-indulgent and characterized by needs for excitement and changes. They achieve poorly in terms of the social mores." Where identity diffusion is based on a strong previous doubt of one's ethnic and sexual identity, delinquent incidents are not uncommon (6).

One of the defining factors in the phenomenon of delinquency concerns aggression. In the delinquencies, aggression is always directed toward the outside and can be carried out in thoughts, looks, gait, and actions, and is usually allied to and even fused with its counterpart: love (5). In the excerpts which follow, starting with the remarkable delinquency revelations of St. Augustine, this fusion of aggression and love will be noted, as will the variety of other causal factors. Tolstoy (born in 1828) unscientifically but with great feeling wrote in his autobiography, "I have read somewhere that children between twelve and fourteen years of age—that is the transition stage from childhood to adolescence—are especially apt to become murderers or incendiaries. When I recall my own adolescence (and the state of mind I was in one day) I can understand the incentive to the most dreadful crimes committed without aim or purpose, without any precise desire to harm others—done simply out of curiosity, out of an unconscious need of action. There are moments when the future looks so gloomy that one fears to look forward to it [16]."

In reading many of the passages used in this section, it should be kept in mind that today's popular conception of the juvenile delinquent is not necessarily the correct or only one. It is hoped that the broader perspective suggested by these introductory paragraphs will help. Most of the passages will point up the contemporary meaning of delinquency. G. Stanley Hall (1846-1924), the American psychologist and president of Clark University, described in his *Life and Confessions of a Psychologist* (7) a situation which is prevalent today: "In the treatment of the schoolhouse and its surroundings we were vandals. The first schoolhouse I attended is still standing as it was. The desks were carved by the jackknives of generations of pupils, especially on the boys' side. There were rude initials deeply indented, and the walls had to be whitewashed often to obliterate pencil marks and drawings. At the end of the term the rounded ceiling of the room was covered with chewed paper wads which it was a favorite diversion to throw and make stick there. We tore up the floor in the wood-room and raised havoc in the cellar, while the outhouses, both that of the girls and boys, were indescribable."

Sudermann (15), a major German literary figure (1857-1927), wrote with assumed naïvete mixed with guilt about his juvenile escapades—which today would be handled in a juvenile offenders' court. "Who was it," he asked rhetorically, "who broke the street lamps on the *Speicher Insel* fifty years ago? Who has the cat murder on the Junkerstrasse on his conscience? Who was it who broke into the Kasino gardens one night and took the garlands, which were provided for the summer festival the next day, to adorn the bathing place where we used to go swimming? Oh, my dear citizens of Elbing, I could reveal secrets to you which would make your eyes open. But I should be boasting if I were to maintain that I really enjoyed these scrapes. My heart always beat too fast, and it was far too difficult to get out and return secretly to give me any comfort in playing robber, or even at being captain of the band. And if it had not been for my uncle Heinrich, who concealed many a crime, the 'good aunt' would probably have soon turned me out."

Still another variety of what we would term today "juvenile delinquency" is reported, almost predictably, by Leon Trotsky (1877-1940). The year was 1892 and he was fifteen years old (17).

> There was but one municipal boys' school in Bobrinetz. The nearest *gymnasium* was in Elizavetgrad, fifty kilometres away. There was a junior girls' high school in Bobrinetz, and during the school season the girls recruited their friends from among the students of the municipal school. In the summer things were different. The high-school boys would return from Elizavetgrad, and the magnificence of their uniforms and the finesse of their manners would push the municipal pupils into the background. The antagonism was bitter. The offended Bobrinetz schoolboys would form fighting groups and on occasion would resort not only to sticks and stones but to knives as well. As I was sitting nonchalantly eating berries in the branch of a mulberry-tree in the garden of some friends, some one threw a stone at me from behind a fence, hitting me on the head. This was but one small incident in a long and not entirely bloodless warfare, interrupted only by the departure of the privileged class from Bobrinetz. Things were different in Elizavetgrad. There the high-school students dominated both streets and hearts. In the summer, however, the university students would arrive from Kharkoff, Odessa and more distant cities, and shove the high school boys into their backyards. Here the struggle was likewise fierce, and the perfidy of the girls was indescribable.

The three examples cited in this introduction all concern children from middle-class homes. The final brief sample to be shown here also concerns a middle-class youngster, David Kogan, from whose diary the following selection is taken (11). "I participated in something that was essentially a rowdy gang war. The Rams 'attacked' our clubhouse and we 'defended' it. No one thought much of its consequences before the fight; now, afterwards, I view it with the feeling that the A. S. C. is continuing its course of self-degradation; I also noticed the disgusted looks of the Gentiles and Jews in the neighborhood. Well, to return to the struggle. Ed, Hank, and I manned the slanted roof, where a stiff battle ensued. I don't remember much, except being punched in the mouth. However, the whole school is giving me credit for pushing one of the attackers off the roof. After 35 min. the Rams left. We surveyed the damage: four broken windows, the work of six months decorating and furnishing the clubhouse, cuts, bruises, and a broken arm. We rejoiced in our 'glorious' victory."

Ten longer illustrations from the autobiographical literature conclude this chapter. The first one dates from the fourth century, the last from the twentieth. The countries include Italy, Britain, the United States, Russia, Venezuela, Germany and Korea. In them, we shall see the role of play activities in delinquency patterns, the inability of family influences to counteract the forces of the surrounding social world, the disorganized neighborhood factors, and the importance of cultural conflict in the life of the adolescent.

Saint Augustine
(354-430)

One of the remarkable aspects of these chapters from Augustine's *Confessions* is the clarity with which he sees the motivations for his acts of delinquency as a youth of sixteen. The thievery itself was nothing, he declares. "By what feelings, then, was I animated?" He answers in terms of the love of the companionship of his accomplices, although in his self-abasement, he says it was the enjoyment of the crime itself.* In actuality, Augustine's delinquency was only incidental and not central to the need to commit an antisocial act. If the Johnson-Szurek hypothesis (8) has validity, it can be applied successfully to Augustine's case. Behind a façade of mildness and obedience to his father, the willful, hot-tempered and pagan Patricius, his mother, the devout Monnica, had a fanatical determination that her son should be a Catholic Christian. Augustine presents this as the burning mission of her life. The parental conflict thus engendered about his religious upbringing was one factor, perhaps, in his delinquency. Monnica's outward submissiveness to her husband undoubtedly must have concealed much resentment which was communicated to Augustine and which is seen throughout the book in his bitterly depreciatory attitude toward his father. Monnica can be viewed as a castrating female, with destructive impulses

---

*From *The Confessions of Saint Augustine*. Reprinted by permission of Liveright Publishers (New York). 1942. Pp. 32-40.

concerning her son's development—except in the religious sphere. Augustine's difficulty in identifying with his father, and his mother's unconscious destructive impulses are two additional factors which probably prompted his delinquent acts.

He commits theft with his companions, not urged on by poverty, but from a certain distaste for well-doing. Theft is punished by Thy law, O Lord, and by the law written in men's hearts, which iniquity itself cannot blot out. For what thief will suffer a thief? Even a rich thief will not suffer him who is driven to it by want. Yet had I a desire to commit robbery, and did so, compelled neither by hunger, nor poverty, but through a distaste for well-doing, and a lustiness of iniquity. For I pilfered that of which I had already sufficient, and much better. Nor did I desire to enjoy what I pilfered, but the theft and sin itself. There was a pear-tree close to our vineyard, heavily laden with fruit, which was tempting neither for its colour nor its flavour. To shake and rob this some of us wanton young fellows went, late one night (having, according to our disgraceful habit, prolonged our games in the streets until then), and carried away great loads, not to eat ourselves, but to fling to the very swine, having only eaten some of them; and to do this pleased us all the more because it was not permitted. Behold my heart, O my God; behold my heart, which Thou hadst pity upon when in the bottomless pit. Behold, now, let my heart tell Thee what it was seeking there, that I should be gratuitously wanton, having no inducement to evil but the evil itself. It was foul, and I loved it. I loved to perish. I loved my own error—not that for which I erred, but the error itself. Base souls, falling from Thy firmament to utter destruction—not seeking aught through the shame but the shame itself!

Concerning the motives to sin, which are not in the love of evil, but in the desire of obtaining the property of others. There is a desirableness in all beautiful bodies, and in gold, and silver, and all things; and in bodily contact sympathy is powerful, and each other sense hath his proper adaptation of body. Worldly honour hath also its glory, and the power of command, and of overcoming; whence proceeds also the desire for revenge. And yet to acquire all these, we must not depart from Thee, O Lord, nor deviate from Thy law. The life which we live here hath also its peculiar attractiveness, through a certain measure of comeliness of its own, and harmony with all things here below. The friendships of men also are endeared by a sweet bond, in the oneness of many souls. On account of all these, and such as these, is sin committed; while through an inordinate preference for these goods of a lower kind, the better and higher are neglected,—even Thou, our Lord God, Thy truth, and Thy law. For these meaner things have their delights, but not like unto my God, who hath created all things; for in Him doth the righteous delight, and He is the sweetness of the upright in heart.

Why he delighted in that theft, when all things which under the appearance of good invite to vice, are true and perfect in God alone. What was it, then, that I, miserable one, so doted on in thee, thou theft of mine, thou deed of darkness, in that sixteenth year of my age? Beautiful thou wert not, since thou wert theft. But art thou anything, that so I may argue the case with thee? Those pears that we stole were fair to the sight, because they were Thy creation, Thou fairest of all, Creator of all, Thou good God—God, the highest good, and my true good. Those pears truly were pleasant to the sight; but it was not for them that my miserable soul lusted, for I had abundance of better, but those I plucked simply that I might steal. For, having plucked them, I threw them away, my sole gratification in them being my own sin, which I was pleased to enjoy. For if any of these pears entered my mouth, the sweetener of it was my sin in eating it. And now, O Lord my God, I ask what it was in that theft of mine that caused me such delight; and behold it hath no beauty in it—not such, I mean, as exists in justice and wisdom; nor such as is in the mind, memory, senses, and animal life of man; nor yet such as is the glory and beauty of the stars in their courses; or the earth, or the sea, teeming with incipient life, to replace, as it is born, that which decayeth; nor, indeed, that false and shadowy beauty which pertaineth to deceptive vices. . . .

Thus doth the soul commit fornication when she turns away from Thee, and seeks without Thee what she cannot find pure and untainted until she returns to Thee. Thus all pervertedly imitate Thee who separate themselves far from Thee, and raise themselves up against Thee. But even by thus imitating Thee they acknowledge Thee to be the Creator of all nature, and so that there is no place whither they can altogether retire from Thee. What, then, was it that I loved in that theft? And wherein did I, even corruptedly and pervertedly, imitate my Lord? Did I wish, if only by artifice, to act contrary to Thy law, because by power I could not, so that, being a captive, I might imitate an imperfect liberty by doing with impunity things which I was not allowed to do, in obscured likeness of Thy omnipotency? Behold this servant of Thine, fleeing from his Lord, and following a shadow! O rottenness! O monstrosity of life and profundity of death! Could I like that which was unlawful only because it was unlawful? ...

In his theft he loved the company of his fellow-sinners. "What fruit had I then," wretched one, in those things which, when I remember them, cause me shame—above all in that theft, which I loved only for the theft's sake? And as the theft itself was nothing, all the more wretched was I who loved it. Yet by myself alone I would not have done it—I recall what my heart was—alone I could not have done it. I loved, then, in it the companionship of my accomplices with whom I did it. I did not, therefore, love the theft alone—yea, rather, it was that alone that I loved, for the companionship was nothing. What is the fact? Who is it that can teach me, but He who illuminateth mine heart and searcheth out the dark corners thereof? What is it that hath come into my mind to inquire about, to discuss, and to reflect upon? For had I at that time loved the pears I stole, and wished to enjoy them, I might have done so alone, if I could have been satisfied with the mere commission of the theft by which my pleasure was secured; nor needed I have provoked that itching of my own passions, by the encouragement of accomplices. But as my enjoyment was not in those pears it was in the crime itself, which the company of my fellow-sinners produced.

It was a pleasure to him also to laugh when seriously deceiving others. By what feelings, then, was I animated? For it was in truth too shameful; and woe was me who had it. But still what was it? "Who can understand his errors?" We laughed, because our hearts were tickled at the thought of deceiving those who little imagined what we were doing, and would have vehemently disapproved of it. Yet, again, why did I so rejoice in this, that I did not alone? Is it that no one readily laughs alone? No one does so readily; but yet sometimes, when men are alone by themselves, nobody being by, a fit of laughter overcomes them when anything very droll presents itself to their senses or mind. Yet alone I would not have done it—alone I could not at all have done it. Behold, my God, the lively recollection of my soul is laid bare before Thee—alone I had not committed that theft, wherein what I stole pleased me not, but rather the act of stealing; nor to have done it alone would I have liked so well, neither would I have done it. O Friendship too unfriendly! thou mysterious seducer of the soul, thou greediness to do mischief out of mirth and wantonness, thou craving for others' loss, without desire for my own profit or revenge; but when they say, "Let us go, let us do it," we are ashamed not to be shameless.

With God there is true rest and life unchanging. Who can unravel that twisted and tangled knottiness? It is foul. I hate to reflect on it. I hate to look on it. But thee do I long for, O righteousness and innocency, fair and comely to all virtuous eyes, and of a satisfaction that never palls! With thee is perfect rest, and life unchanging. He who enters into thee enters into the joy of his Lord, and shall have no fear, and shall do excellently in the most Excellent. I sank away from Thee, O my God, and I wandered too far from Thee, my stay, in my youth, and became to myself an unfruitful land.

Benvenuto Cellini
(1500-1571)

The Renaissance, to which Cellini belonged and which he helped make great, was an age of individualism. Prior to this period, people thought of themselves as members of groups—of the knighthood, clergy, nobility, serfs, and so on. But with the Renaissance, the individual came to the fore spurred on by the rapid growth of humanism and science. The individualism of Cellini is manifested in this excerpt from his *Autobiography*,* but it is expressed in delinquent behavior. We see in the excerpt the bullying, the provocation, the physical attack, the retaliation, and then the sequence of events when the law takes over. Not only are Cellini's feelings of outrage, anger, frustration and defiance typical of the adolescent, but so are his actions and behavior.

It chanced one day that I was leaning against a shop of one of these men, who called out to me, and began partly reproaching, partly bullying. I answered that had they done their duty by me, I should have spoken of them what one speaks of good and worthy men; but as they had done the contrary, they ought to complain of themselves and not of me. While I was standing there and talking, one of them, named Gherardo Guasconti, their cousin, having perhaps been put up to it by them, lay in wait till a beast of burden went by. It was a load of bricks. When the load reached me, Gherardo pushed it so violently on my body that I was very much hurt. Turning suddenly round and seeing him laughing, I struck him such a blow on the temple that he fell down, stunned, like one dead. Then I faced round to his cousins, and said: "That's the way to treat cowardly thieves of your sort"; and when they wanted to make a move upon me, trusting to their numbers, I,

*Reprinted by permission of Doubleday & Co., Inc. 1927. Pp. 27-30.

whose blood was now well up, laid hands to a little knife I had, and cried: "If one of you comes out of the shop, let the other run for the confessor, because the doctor will have nothing to do here." These words so frightened them that not one stirred to help their cousin. As soon as I had gone, the fathers and sons ran to the Eight, and declared that I had assaulted them in their shops with sword in hand, a thing which had never yet been seen in Florence. The magistrates had me summoned. I appeared before them; and they began to upbraid and cry out upon me—partly, I think, because they saw me in my cloak, while the others were dressed like citizens in mantle and hood; but also because my adversaries had been to the houses of those magistrates, and had talked with all of them in private, while I, inexperienced in such matters, had not spoken to any of them, trusting in the goodness of my cause. I said that, having received such outrage and insult from Gherardo, and in my fury having only given him a box on the ear, I did not think I deserved such a vehement reprimand. I had hardly time to finish the word box, before Prinzivalle della Stufa, who was one of the Eight, interrupted me by saying: "You gave him a blow, and not a box, on the ear." The bell was rung and we were all ordered out, when Prinzivalle spoke thus in my defence to his brother judges: "Mark, sirs, the simplicity of this poor young man, who has accused himself of having given a box on the ear, under the impression that this is of less importance than a blow; whereas a box on the ear in the New Market carries a fine of twenty-five crowns, while a blow costs little or nothing. He is a young man of admirable talents, and supports his poor family by his labour in great abundance; I would to God that our city had plenty of this sort, instead of the present dearth of them."

Among the magistrates were some Radical fellows with turned-up hoods, who had been influenced by the entreaties and the calumnies of my opponents, because they all belonged to the party of Fra Girolamo; and these men would have had me sent to prison and punished without too close a reckoning. But the good Prinzivalle put a stop to that. So they sentenced me to pay four measures of flour, which were to be given as alms to the nunnery of the Murate. I was called in again; and he ordered me not to speak a word under pain of their displeasure, and to perform the sentence they had passed. Then, after giving me another sharp rebuke, they sent us to the chancellor; I muttering all the while, "It was a slap and not a blow," with which we left the Eight bursting with laughter. The chancellor bound us over upon bail on both sides; but only I was punished by having to pay the four measures of meal. Albeit just then I felt as though I had been massacred, I sent for one of my cousins, called Maestro Annibale, the surgeon, father of Messer Librodoro Librodori, desiring that he should go bail for me. He refused to come, which made me so angry, that, fuming with fury and swelling like an asp, I took a desperate resolve. At this point one may observe how the stars do not so much sway as force our conduct. When I reflected on the great obligations which this Annibale owed my family, my rage grew to such a pitch that, turning wholly to evil, and being also by nature somewhat choleric, I waited till the magistrates had gone to dinner; and when I was alone, and observed that none of their officers were watching me, in the fire of my anger, I left the place, ran to my shop, seized a dagger and rushed to the house of my enemies, who were at home and shop together. I found them at table; and Gherardo, who had been the cause of the quarrel, flung himself upon me. I stabbed him in the breast, piercing doublet and jerkin through and through to the shirt, without however grazing his flesh or doing him the least harm in the world. When I felt my hand go in, and heard the clothes tear, I thought that I had killed him; and seeing him fall terror-struck to earth, I cried: "Traitors, this day is the day on which I mean to murder you all." Father, mother, and sisters, thinking the last day had come, threw themselves upon their knees, screaming out for mercy with all their might; but I perceiving that they offered no resistance, and that he was stretched for dead upon the ground, thought it too base a thing to touch them. I ran storming down the staircase; and when I reached the street, I found all the rest of the household, more than twelve persons; one of them had seized an iron shovel, another a thick iron pipe, one had an anvil, some of them hammers, and some cudgels. When I got among them, raging like a mad bull, I flung four or five to the earth, and fell down with them myself, continually aiming my dagger now at one and now at another. Those who remained upright plied both hands with all their force, giving it me with hammers, cudgels, and anvil; but inasmuch as God does sometimes mercifully intervene, He so ordered that neither they nor I did any harm to one another. I only lost my cap, on which my adversaries seized, though they had run away from it before, and struck at it with all their weapons. Afterwards, they searched among their dead and wounded, and saw that not a single man was injured.

George Borrow
(1803-1881)

Street-fighting and the gang rumble of the present day are not recent phenomena. They were as common and as frequent in previous

centuries as they seem to be now. George Borrow, the son of an
English army captain, lived in many countries with his peripatetic
father. One of them was Scotland, and Borrow describes the "bickers" in which he participated there. He says—with hindsight—that
while no harm came to him, there was at least one time when he
could have had his brains beaten in with stones if his gang hadn't
stayed by him. He describes gang fights in which eyes were gouged,
jaws broken, and teeth knocked out. He never forgot one bicker
which was so furious that subsequently "the authorities of the town,
alarmed by the desperation of its character, stationed forthwith a
body of police on the hill-side to prevent, in future, any such
breaches of the peace."*

The Scotch are certainly a most pugnacious people; their whole
history proves it. Witness their incessant wars with the English in the
olden time, and their internal feuds, highland and lowland, clan with
clan, family with family, Saxon with Gael. In my time, the schoolboys,
for want, perhaps, of English urchins to contend with, were continually fighting with each other; every noon there was at least one pugil-
istic encounter, and sometimes three. In one month I witnessed more
of these encounters than I had ever previously seen under similar
circumstances in England. After all, there was not much harm done.
Harm! what harm could result from short chopping blows, a hug, and
a tumble? I was witness to many a sounding whack, some blood shed,
"a blue ee" now and then, but nothing more. In England, on the
contrary, where the lads were comparatively mild, gentle, and pacific,
I had been present at more than one death caused by blows in boyish
combats, in which the oldest of the victors had scarcely reached
thirteen years; but these blows were in the jugular, given with the full
force of the arm shot out horizontally from the shoulder.

But the Scotch—though by no means proficient in boxing (and
why should they box, seeing that they have never had a teacher?)—are,
I repeat, a most pugnacious people; at least they were in my time. Anything served them, that is, the urchins, as a pretence for a fray, or,
Dorically speaking, a *bicker;* every street and close was at feud with its
neighbour; the lads of the school were at feud with the young men of
the college, whom they pelted in winter with snow and in summer
with stones; and then the feud between the Old and New Town!

One day I was standing on the ramparts of the Castle on the south-

---

*From *Lavengro—The Scholar—The Gypsy—The Priest* by George Borrow. London: Constable & Co., Ltd. 1923. Pp. 79-85.

western side which overhangs the green brae, where it slopes down into what was in those days the green swamp or morass, called by the natives of Auld Reekie the Nor' Loch; it was a dark, gloomy day, and a thin veil of mist was beginning to settle down upon the brae and the morass. I could perceive, however, that there was a skirmish taking place in the latter spot. I had an indistinct view of two parties—apparently of urchins—and I heard whoops and shrill cries. Eager to know the cause of this disturbance, I left the Castle, and, descending the brae, reached the borders of the morass, where was a runnel of water and the remains of an old wall, on the other side of which a narrow path led across the swamp; upon this path at a little distance before me there was a "bicker." I pushed forward, but had scarcely crossed the ruined wall and runnel when the party nearest to me gave way, and in great confusion came running in my direction. As they drew nigh, one of them shouted to me, "Wha are ye, man? are ye o' the Auld Toon?" I made no answer. "Ha! ye are o' the New Toon; Deil tak ye, we'll moorder ye"; and the next moment a huge stone sung past my head. "Let me be, ye fule bodies," said I, "I'm no of either of ye, I live yonder aboon in the Castle." "Ah! ye live in the Castle; then ye're an auld tooner; come, gie us your help, man, and dinna stand there staring like a dunnot, we want help sair eneugh. Here are stanes."

For my own part I wished for nothing better, and, rushing forward, I placed myself at the head of my new associates, and commenced flinging stones fast and desperately. The other party now gave way in their turn, closely followed by ourselves; I was in the van and about to stretch out my hand to seize the hindermost boy of the enemy, when, not being acquainted with the miry and difficult paths of the Nor' Loch, and in my eagerness taking no heed of my footing, I plunged into a quagmire, into which I sank as far as my shoulders. Our adversaries no sooner perceived this disaster than, setting up a shout, they wheeled round and attacked us most vehemently. Had my comrades now deserted me, my life had not been worth a straw's purchase, I should either have been smothered in the quag, or, what is more probable, had my brains beaten out with stones; but they behaved like true Scots, and fought stoutly around their comrade until I was extricated, whereupon both parties retired, the night being near at hand.

"Ye are na a bad hand at flinging stanes," said the lad who first addressed me, as we now returned up the brae; "your aim is right dangerous, man, I saw how ye skelpit them; ye maun help us agin thae New Toon blackguards at our next bicker."

So to the next bicker I went, and to many more, which speedily followed as the summer advanced; the party to which I had given my help on the first occasion consisted merely of outliers, posted about half-way up the hill, for the purpose of overlooking the movements of the enemy.

Did the latter draw nigh in any considerable force, messengers were forthwith despatched to the "auld toon," especially to the filthy alleys and closes of the High Street, which forthwith would disgorge swarms of bare-headed and bare-footed "callants," who, with gestures wild and "eldrich screech and hollo," might frequently be seen pouring down the sides of the hill. I have seen upwards of a thousand engaged on either side in these frays, which I have no doubt were full as desperate as the fights described in the Iliad, and which were certainly much more bloody than the combats of modern Greece in the war of independence. The callants not only employed their hands in hurling stones, but not unfrequently slings, at the use of which they were very expert, and which occasionally dislodged teeth, shattered jaws, or knocked out an eye. Our opponents certainly laboured under considerable disadvantage, being compelled not only to wade across a deceitful bog, but likewise to clamber up part of a steep hill before they could attack us; nevertheless, their determination was such, and such their impetuosity, that we had sometimes difficulty enough to maintain our own. I shall never forget one bicker, the last indeed which occurred at that time, as the authorities of the town, alarmed by the desperation of its character, stationed forthwith a body of police on the hill-side to prevent, in future, any such breaches of the peace.

It was a beautiful Sunday evening, the rays of the descending sun were reflected redly from the grey walls of the castle, and from the black rocks on which it was founded. The bicker had long since commenced, stones from sling and hand were flying; but the callants of the New Town were now carrying everything before them.

A full-grown baker's apprentice was at their head; he was foaming with rage, and had taken the field, as I was told, in order to avenge his brother, whose eye had been knocked out in one of the late bickers. He was no slinger or flinger, but brandished in his right hand the spoke of a cart-wheel, like my countryman Tom Hickathrift of old in his encounter with the giant of the Lincolnshire fen. Protected by a piece of wickerwork attached to his left arm, he rushed on to the fray, disregarding the stones which were showered against him, and was ably seconded by his followers. Our own party was chased half-way up the hill, where I was struck to the ground by the baker, after having been foiled in an attempt which I had made to fling a handful of earth into his eyes. All now appeared lost, the Auld Toon was in full retreat. I myself lay at the baker's feet, who had just raised his spoke, probably to give me the *coup de grâce*—it was an awful moment. Just then I heard a shout and a rushing sound. A wild-looking figure is descending the hill with terrible bounds: it is a lad of some fifteen years; he is bare-headed, and his red, uncombed hair stands on end like hedgehogs' bristles; his frame is lithy, like that of an antelope, but he has prodigious breadth of chest; he wears a military undress, that of the regiment, even of a drummer, for it is wild Davy, whom a month before I had seen enlisted on Leith Links to serve King George with drum and drumstick as long as his services might be required, and who, ere a week had elapsed, had smitten with his fist Drum-Major Elzigood, who, incensed at his inaptitude, had threatened him with his cane; he has been in confinement for weeks, this is the first day of his liberation, and he is now descending the hill with horrid bounds and shoutings; he is now about five yards distant, and the baker who apprehends that something dangerous is at hand, prepares himself for the encounter; but what avails the strength of a baker, even full grown?—what avails the defence of a wicker shield?—what avails the wheel-spoke, should there be an opportunity of using it, against the impetus of an avalanche or a cannon ball?—for to either of these might that wild figure be compared, which, at the distance of five yards, sprang at once with head, hands, feet and body, all together, upon the champion of the New Town, tumbling him to the earth amain. And now it was the turn of the Old Town to triumph. Our late discomfited host, returning on its steps, overwhelmed the fallen champion with blows of every kind, and then, led on by his vanquisher, who had assumed his arms, namely, the wheel-spoke and wicker shield, fairly cleared the brae of their adversaries, whom they drove down headlong into the morass.

Richard Wagner
(1813-1883)

The almost annual spring battles between the students of Yale University and the police force of New Haven, Connecticut have their precursors in hoary traditions. Richard Wagner described such an episode which took place in Leipzig in 1830.* There is a twist to Wagner's story that is now a commonplace with some educators: making the bad boy the monitor of the class. Some students had been arrested in a street brawl and had to be rescued. The rest-

*In *My Life* by Richard Wagner. Reprinted by permission of Dodd, Mead & Co. Copyright 1911, 1939. Pp. 48-52.

less undergraduates, singing *Gaudeamus igitur,* marched through the streets to release the imprisoned students, only to be frustrated in their goal by the Rector who announced that they had already been set free. "But the tense expectation of a revolution had grown too great not to demand some sacrifice." The hooliganism, house-breaking, and property damage by the students led to excesses and violence by the populace in general. When this happened, the students were called in as a task-force to prevent further looting and rioting!

Before I was able to develop my politico-musical conceptions further, disorders broke out in Leipzig itself which summoned me from the precincts of Art to take a direct share in national life. National life in Leipzig at this time meant nothing more than antagonism between the students and the police, the latter being the arch-enemy upon whom the youthful love of liberty vented itself. Some students had been arrested in a street broil who were now to be rescued. The under-graduates, who had been restless for some days, assembled one even-ing in the Market Place and the Clubs, mustered together, and made a ring round their leaders. The whole proceeding was marked by a certain measured solemnity, which impressed me deeply. They sang *Gaudeamus igitur,* formed up into column, and picking up from the crowd any young men who sympathised with them, marched gravely and resolutely from the Market Place to the University buildings, to open the cells and set free the students who had been arrested. My heart beat fast as I marched with them to this "Taking of the Bastille," but things did not turn out as we expected, for in the courtyard of the Paulinum the solemn procession was stopped by Rector Krug, who had come down to meet it with his grey head bared; his assurance that the captives had already been released at his request was greeted with a thundering cheer, and the matter seemed at an end.

But the tense expectation of a revolution had grown too great not to demand some sacrifice. A summons was suddenly spread calling us to a notorious alley in order to exercise popular justice upon a hated magistrate who, it was rumoured, had unlawfully taken under his protection a certain house of ill-fame in that quarter. When I reached the spot with the tail-end of the crowd, I found the house had been broken into and all sorts of violence had been committed. I recall with horror the intoxicating effect this unreasoning fury had upon me, and cannot deny that without the slightest personal provocation I shared, like one possessed, in the frantic onslaught of the undergraduates, who madly shattered furniture and crockery to bits. I do not believe that the ostensible motive for this outrage, which, it is true, was to be found in a fact that was a grave menace to public morality, had any weight with me whatever; on the contrary, it was the purely devilish fury of these popular outbursts that drew me, too, like a madman into their vortex.

The fact that such fits of fury are not quick to abate, but, in accordance with certain natural laws, reach their proper conclusion only after they have degenerated into frenzy, I was to learn in my own person. Scarcely did the summons ring out for us to march to another resort of the same kind than I too found myself in the tide which set towards the opposite end of the town. There the same exploits were repeated, and the most ludicrous outrages perpetrated. I cannot remember that the enjoyment of alcoholic drinks contributed to the intoxication of myself and my immediate fellows. I only know that I finally got into the state that usually succeeds a debauch, and upon waking next morning, as if from a hideous nightmare, had to convince myself that I had really taken part in the events of the previous night by a trophy I possessed in the shape of a tattered red curtain, which I had brought home as a token of my prowess. The thought that people generally, and my own family in particular, were wont to put a lenient construction upon youthful escapades was a great comfort to me; outbursts of this kind on the part of the young were regarded as righteous indignation against really serious scandals, and there was no need for me to be afraid of owning up to having taken part in such excesses.

The dangerous example, however, which had been set by the undergraduates incited the lower classes and the mob to similar excesses on the following nights, against employers and any who were obnoxious to them. The matter at once assumed a more serious complexion; property was threatened, and a conflict between rich and poor stood grinning at our doors. As there were no soldiers in the town, and the police were thoroughly disorganised, the students were called in as a protection against the lower orders. An undergraduate's hour of glory now began, such as I could only have thirsted for in my schoolboy dreams. The student became the tutelar deity of Leipzig, called on by the authorities to arm and band together in defence of property, and the same young men who two days before had yielded to a rage for destruction now mustered in the University courtyard. The proscribed names of the students' clubs and unions were shouted by the mouths of town councillors and chief constables in order to summon curiously equipped undergraduates, who thereupon, in simple mediæval array of war, scattered throughout the town, occupied the guard-rooms at the gates, provided sentinels for the grounds of various wealthy merchants, and, as occasion demanded, took places which seemed threatened, more especially inns, under their permanent protection.

Though, unluckily, I was not yet a member of their body, I anticipated the delights of academic citizenship by half-impudent, half-obsequious solicitation of the leaders of the students whom I honoured most. I had the good fortune to recommend myself particularly to these "cocks of the walk," as they were styled, on account of my relationship to Brockhaus, in whose grounds the main body of these champions were encamped for some time. My brother-in-law was among those who had been seriously threatened, and it was only owing to really great presence of mind and assurance that he succeeded in saving his printing works, and especially his steam presses, which were the chief object of attack, from destruction. To protect his property against further assault, detachments of students were told off to his grounds as well; the excellent entertainment which the generous master of the house offered his jovial guardians in his pleasant summer-house enticed the pick of the students to him. My brother-in-law was for several weeks guarded day and night against possible attacks by the populace, and on this occasion, as the mediator of a flowing hospitality, I celebrated among the most famous "bloods" of the University the true saturnalia of my scholarly ambition.

For a still longer period the guarding of the gates was entrusted to the students; the unheard-of splendour which accordingly became associated with this post drew fresh aspirants to the spot from far and near. Every day huge chartered vehicles discharged at the Halle Gate whole bands of the boldest sons of learning from Halle, Jena, Göttingen, and the remotest regions. They got down close to the guards at the gate, and for several weeks never set foot in an inn or any other dwelling; they lived at the expense of the Council, drew vouchers on the police for food and drink, and knew but one care, that the possibility of a general quieting of men's minds would make their opportune guardianship superfluous. I never missed a day on guard or a night either, alas! trying to impress on my family the urgent need for my personal endurance. Of course, the quieter and really studious spirits among us soon resigned these duties, and only the flower of the flock of undergraduates remained so staunch that it became difficult for the authorities to relieve them of their task. I held out to the very last, and succeeded in making most astonishing friends for my age. Many of the most audacious remained in Leipzig even when there was no guard duty to fulfil, and peopled the place for some time with champions of an extraordinarily desperate and dissipated type, who

had been repeatedly sent down from various universities for rowdyism
or debt, and who now, thanks to the exceptional circumstances of the
day, found a refuge in Leipzig, where at first they had been received
with open arms by the general enthusiasm of their comrades.

In the presence of all these phenomena I felt as if I were surrounded
by the results of an earthquake which had upset the usual order of
things. My brother-in-law, Friedrich Brockhaus, who could justly
taunt the former authorities of the place with their inability to maintain peace and order, was carried away by the current of a formidable
movement of opposition. He made a daring speech at the Guildhall
before their worships the Town Council, which brought him popularity, and he was appointed second-in-command of the newly constituted Leipzig Municipal Guard. This body at length ousted my adored
students from the guard-rooms of the town gates, and we no longer had
the right of stopping travellers and inspecting their passes. On the
other hand, I flattered myself that I might regard my new position as
a boy citizen as equivalent to that of the French National Guard, and
my brother-in-law, Brockhaus, as a Saxon Lafayette, which, at all
events, succeeded in furnishing my soaring excitement with a healthy
stimulant. I now began to read the papers and cultivate politics enthusiastically; however, the social intercourse of the civic world did
not attract me sufficiently to make me false to my beloved academic
associates. I followed them faithfully from the guard-rooms to the
ordinary bars, where their splendour as men of the literary world now
sought retirement. My chief ambition was to become one of them as
soon as possible.

William J. Stillman
(1828-1901)

Bullies hung around school-yards in the last century as well as this
one. William Stillman, who attended one of the earliest free schools
in New York City, was appointed a "yard monitor" by his teacher
because he was tall and strong for his thirteen years. He needed to
be, because like his Scot contemporary, George Borrow, he nearly
had his head pounded in. The "stone fights" that Stillman recounts
seem to be a universal method of carrying on schoolboy warfare.*

There was a gang of young ruffians, street boys, who used to hang

---

*From *The Autobiography of a Journalist*. Reprinted by permission of Houghton
Mifflin Co. 1901. Pp. 55-56.

around the school gates and maltreat the stragglers and even the boys in the yard, if the gate was left open, and I remember one day three or four of them invading the school-yard after I had dismissed the boys to go upstairs at the end of the intermission, thinking that they would have a fine game with the monitor. One made a pretext to quarrel with me, and, gripping me round the body, called to his companions to go and get some stones to pound me on the head with, this being the approved manner of the young roughs of New York. Finding that I could not extricate myself from his grip, I dragged him to the wall, and, catching him by the ears, beat his head against the rough stones until he dropped insensible, when, to the astonishment of his comrades, instead of stamping on him and finishing him at once, I ran upstairs as fast as my legs could carry me, so that when they came with their stones they had only their champion to carry out.

On the holidays there were generally stone-fights between the boys of our quarter and one of the adjoining quarters, and I shall carry to my grave the scars on my head of cuts received in one of these field combats, in which I refused to follow my party in flight, and took the onslaught of the whole vanguard of the enemy, armed with stones, and had my head pounded yellow, being only saved from worse by the intervention of the men of the vicinity. This fight gave me the unmerited reputation of courage and fighting power, and I was thereafter unmolested by the young roughs, though, in fact, I was timid to a degree and only stood my ground from nervous obstinacy; I never provoked a quarrel, and only revolted against a bully when the position became intolerable. I can remember the amazement of a companion older than myself, who had been in the habit of bullying me freely, until one day he went too far and I took him by the collar and shook and swung him till he was dizzy and begged for mercy, for of downright pugilistics I knew nothing, and a deliberate blow in the face with my fist in cold blood was a measure too brutal to enter into my mind.

Maxim Gorky
(1868-1936)

Born in extreme poverty, orphaned early, and rejected by his avaricious maternal grandfather, Gorky at twelve resorted to acts of delinquency for which he surely would have been institutionalized had he committed them today. However, the morals of the entire Russian village, as Gorky tells it,* condoned thievery as a means of

---

*In *Autobiography*. Reprinted by permission of The Citadel Press. 1940. Pp. 161-163.

keeping body and soul together. Stealing planks from the lumber yards, salvaging timber borne downstream by the current, picking pockets of tipsy factory hands, truckmen and other workers, and snaring pigeons were all accepted practices. "Children did it in the sight of their parents." Gorky organized a gang of five boys who, while shying away from the more vicious acts, did not consider it sinful to make away with lumber.

On holidays and in the early mornings I went through the streets and the backyards with a sack, collecting rags, paper, bones and metal scraps. Junkmen paid me two greven for a forty-pound bundle of rags, paper and metal junk, and eight to ten kopecks for the same weight of bones. I carried on my junk-collecting after school hours as well, and Saturdays. For specially lucky finds I got from thirty kopecks to half a ruble, and sometimes even more. When grandma accepted the money from me, she hastily stuffed it into her skirt pocket, looked down, and commended me, "Ah, thanks, darling. This will get us our food. You've made out well."

I saw her once, weeping as she gazed at a five-kopeck coin I had given her; a grimy tear wobbled on the tip of her grainy nose, that looked like a bar of pumice stone.

More profitable than ragpicking was stealing from the lumber yards on the banks of the Oka or on Pesk Island, where during the Fair, the temporary booths where metal articles had been sold were dismantled at the end of the Fair, and the posts and boards stored on the piers, until the approach of the spring floods. A good board would fetch ten kopecks from cottagers, and one might make away with two such boards a day. But the job required bad weather, snow or a heavy rain that would send the watchmen to cover.

I got together a small gang; ten-year-old Sanka Vyakhir, son of a Mordvin beggarwoman, a boy marked by serene good nature; Kostrom, a tall, skinny orphan with strikingly big black eyes who, at thirteen, was committed to a reformatory for the theft of two pigeons; the Tatar boy Khabi, a twelve-year-old "giant," genial and frank; snubnose Yaz, eight-year-old son of a cemetery caretaker, wordless as a fish and an epileptic; and the oldest, Gregory Churka, a widowed dressmaker's son, an honest and judicious lad and formidable with his fists. We all came from the same street.

In our village stealing did not count as crime; it was a way of life, indeed, almost the only livelihood of villagers ever on the verge of starvation. The six-week Fairs did not bring enough to keep them through the year. Even "respectable citizens" engaged in a little "river work," that is, salvaging logs or finished timbers borne downstream by the current, securing them piece by piece, or in loads. But, in the main, this "river work" took the form of robbing barges or a general marauding along the Volga and Oka River banks, making off with whatever was not tied down. On Sundays adults bragged about their hauls; and the small-fry eavesdropped and learned.

During the hot spell before the Fair, children picked the pockets of tipsy factory hands, truckmen and other workers lurching through the village streets. This, too, went disregarded; children did it in sight of their parents. A carpenter might be stripped of his tools, a cabman of his keys; harness might be stripped from the cart horse and metal parts from axles.

Our gang did not do that sort of stealing. Churka declared, "I won't steal. Mama forbids me." And Khabi said, "I'm scared to." Kostrom loathed the child thieves; and he enunciated the word "thief" with scornful vehemence. When he saw a little thief at the pockets of a drunk, he interfered, giving the pickpocket a beating, if he caught him. This big-eyed, melancholy boy aped grownups, adopted the longshoreman's swaggering gait, spoke in the gruffest voice he could manage, and put on a taciturn, composed manner as if he were an old man. Vyakhir believed stealing was a sin.

However, we didn't consider it sinful to make away with lumber from Pesk Island. None of us had any twinges of conscience over that. Our chief concern was to so plan our forays as to make sure of success. At night, or by day in bad weather, Vyakhir and Yaz would openly cross the creek to Pesk over the thawing ice. This was done to divert the attention of the watchmen; the rest of us crossed unobserved, one by one. With the watchmen's eyes on Yaz and Vyakhir, who decoyed them out of range, we got to the timber, picked out what we wanted and made away with it. We each carried a small length of rope with a bent nail at the tip, which we hooked into plank or post, dragging it over the snow and ice. We were hardly ever seen by the watchmen, and then we were too far off for pursuit.

On disposal of our booty, we divided the money into six parts, about five to seven kopecks apiece. That provided for a satisfactory day's meals; but Vyakhir got a beating from his mother if he failed to bring something extra for a drop of liquor. Kostrom was putting his money by in order to start a pigeon coop. Churka's mother was an invalid, and for that reason he was always on the lookout for more work. Khabi, too, was saving his money—for fare back home. The uncle who had brought him to Nizhny had drowned almost immediately after their arrival. Khabi had forgotten the name of his home town; all he remembered was that it was on the Kama River, near its junction with the Volga. We chose to make fun of the town, making up a rhyme to tease him:

> Oh, the town's on the Kama, there,
> But nobody knows where.

Khabi's first reaction was one of anger, but when Vyakhir, in his cooing voice which earned him his nickname, Dove, said, "Come on, now. You don't get mad on comrades," it so shamed the Tatar that, from then on, he joined in when the ditty was sung.

We favored ragpicking, however, to timber stealing. It was especially interesting in the springtime when the thaws and the rains washed the pavements. On the Fair grounds there were sure to be nails and other metal scrap; and our finds sometimes included coppers and even silver. The watchman had to be appeased either with bribes of a few coins or obsequious bows and salutations, or he would chase us and confiscate our sacks. All in all money was hard to come by. Just the same we boys kept on good terms, and despite occasional flareups, I cannot recall one serious dispute.

T. R. Ybarra
(1880-   )

T. R. Ybarra, the former *New York Times* reporter, was the son of a Venezuelan army officer and a Yankee mother. He received much of his schooling in Caracas where warfare and revolution—in the schools—seemed to be the order of the day. "There was no need to go in search of the school's lawlessness," he wrote in his autobiography.* "It jumped up and smacked you in the face." The lawlessness expressed itself in fights between teachers and pupils, in pitched battles with stones and more refined weapons, and in extortion for protection and for promised services never rendered. The blackboard jungle of the Venezuelan school of the 1890's has its duplicate in many other countries, in different cultures and in different times.

Lawlessness walked hand in hand with unscrupulousness at the Colegio Villegas. One day, a big boy, Arias by name, suggested that my knowledge of arithmetic needed special treatment.

"I'm going to get up a supplementary class in arithmetic—*un paso*

Young Man of Caracas. Reprinted by permission of Ives Washburn, Inc. 1941. Pp. 203-205.

de aritmética," he informed me. "Several other little boys have already signed up. I've got Coronil's permission. Come on and join."

I did. Instead of going to some class under the Old Man, or Coronil, or Mariña, or Dr. Montenegro (who taught Latin) a small troop of little boys marched into one of the classrooms, under the wing of Arias. He promptly locked the door.

"And now," he said, with a grin, "for the *paso de aritmética.* Who has any money?"

I had a few cents. A couple of the others were similarly endowed. Arias collected. Then he went to the barred window, opening onto the corner of Piñango. He whistled and shouted until he attracted the attention of the man who ran the *pulpería* opposite our school. The man sent a minion across the street.

"Twelve conservas de coco," said Arias. The minion returned to the grocery shop and reappeared with twelve sticky messes, which he handed in between the bars. After levying generous tribute, our self-appointed teacher of arithmetic divided what was left among us small urchins. We spent the next quarter of an hour munching and licking our sticky fingers. Then Arias pulled himself together.

"Now, boys, for the *paso de aritmética.* Who's got any money?"

Having exacted another forced contribution, he again went to the window and summoned the grocer's minion.

"Pan he horno—six," he ordered.

The minion returned with six circular things, like crumbly, dry doughnuts—indigestion in visible, tangible form. We proceeded to eat them.

That, with insignificant variations, was the *paso de aritmética.* It was held three or four times. Then Old Man Villegas got suspicious.

One afternoon there was a thundering knock on the door. Arias was in the midst of financial negotiations with the grocer's minion. Canceling them abruptly, he unbarred the door. The Vice-President of Venezuela strode into the room, his white goatee bristling with unfriendliness. On his face was the look that usually preceded an outbreak of palmeta.

"What's this all about?"

"Un paso de aritmética," explained Arias, in a wavering voice.

Old Man Villegas looked at him. Arias looked at the floor.

"Follow me!"

Preceded by our formidable headmaster, we trooped miserably back to the main schoolroom. The *paso de aritmética* was never held again. Instead, at the hour when I had been eating indigestible sweets, my ears rang again to enraged shouts of:

"La mano!"

San Kim
(1905-   )

Because there were no good colleges at home, Korean students flocked to Japan for their studies. Usually they were extremely poor, and tried to work their way through college by getting jobs in low-status occupations such as pulling rickshaws, working in sweatshops, and acting as delivery boys. Kim tells of the desperate struggle to earn enough money to pay for a day's food, of the terror the students instilled in more favorably circumstanced classmates, of their outrageous conduct in restaurants, and their treatment of landlords.*

Shortly after the March First movement had subsided, I decided to try to earn my way through college in Japan. Tokyo then was the Mecca for students all over the Far East and a refuge for revolutionaries of many kinds. Every Korean student wanted to go there for higher education, as no good colleges existed at home and Japanese schools were at that time liberal and full of postwar intellectual excitement.

Father had no money, however, and strongly opposed my desire. I decided that if no one should help me I would run away secretly. In the end, my second brother came to the rescue, as always—and was blamed again for making a rebel of me. He wanted me to study medicine and gave me 100 yen, which was enough for about five months' schooling.

I found a room with a friend named Pak Kun and another student. We paid twelve yen a month for this. I soon found a job delivering eighty newspapers before eight o'clock in the morning, for which I received ten yen a month. Another student tutored me in chemistry and algebra while I prepared to enter Tokyo Imperial University.

Over a third of the Korean students in Tokyo then earned their way through school by part-time jobs. Usually they pulled jinrickshas, delivered newspapers or milk, or corrected proof at printing houses. (So many hungry students stole the milk off the streets in the morning while still warm, however, that the Japanese installed little milk boxes with keys to prevent this.) Other students worked in the many little sweatshop factories. These Korean boys were a picturesque element in the life of Tokyo, though most of the Japanese thought them a very bad element. Six hundred of the students pulled jinrickshas. Several

---

*In *Song of Ariran*. Reprinted by permission of The John Day Co., Inc. 1941. Pp. 32-34.

times I myself pulled one to meet the trains, and the fare from a single ride was enough to live on for a whole day. It was good money, but no Chinese or Japanese students would stoop to do this work. We bought their cast-off clothes at secondhand shops. Since 1910 Korean students had migrated to Tokyo and struggled through school in this manner. They were menials for the Japanese, but these wages made Japan pay for their education.

We poor Korean students sometimes went out in small groups to ask for old books and magazines and clothing at people's houses. All the Japanese housewives and girls were kind. They liked the Korean students and often even gave us new things. We did not beg but always paid a little for what was given us. If a pretty Japanese girl came to the door, the group usually tried to be invited in to sit down awhile—and got a very good bargain. If the owner of the house were rude and refused them, the students would become impudent and demand to examine the house to see if he were not lying. We divided all the old books, magazines, and newspapers collected in this way and sold them to secondhand bookshops and stalls.

I delivered my eighty newspapers early in the morning, went to school, then every afternoon at four put on working clothes for whatever job I happened to have.

Once when Pak Kun and I went to a house to "buy" old books, we got into a fight with the owner because he swore at us. This Japanese happened to be good at jiujitsu, and Pak Kun received a broken nose. After that we always tried to call when the husbands were not at home.

Pak Kun was put into prison in 1929. Even in 1919 his attitude, often expressed to the Japanese, was that "we should confiscate the property of the Japanese to pay for all they have looted from Korea."

There were two definite classes among the Korean students in Japan —those who worked and those who had money. The one-third of the students who were poor "work-and-study" students were called by the others the "*Lumpen*-proletariat." We, however, usually referred to ourselves as the "*Lumpen*-intelligentsia" and called them "Eggshells," meaning that they had pretty white skin and nothing but softness inside. Korean workers traditionally refer to the upper class as "eggshells," and we borrowed this from them.

"One blow of the fist is enough to smash their pretty faces in," we said.

We also referred to them scornfully as the "hot-house class."

We 800 "*Lumpens*" dominated the entire body of Korean students and called our rule the "dictatorship of the proletariat." We ran all student meetings and lectured the "Eggshells" at will, with plentiful doses of proletarian philosophy. Our work-and-study section was far more advanced intellectually than the others. All studied Marxism. Poverty and struggle sharpen the brain and give reality to knowledge. The rich "Eggshells" were terrified of us and privately referred to us as "bandits."

Once, at a big festival, many rich students spent a good deal of money for a feast. We *"Lumpens"* went in a body to the restaurant, ordered chopsticks, and sat down to eat with them without being invited. Some rich students were smart enough to pay us tribute and often invited us specially to birthday dinners and such feasts—just as gangsters are paid off.

Sometimes we were more romantic. We would burst in on a feast and in high Tolstoyan phrases demand to know how the rich could eat while we hundreds were starving. Then we overturned the tables and walked out in great disdain—nursing our hunger and pride.

The Japanese hated to rent rooms to the *"Lumpens"* because they seldom paid their rent but moved out in a high dudgeon whenever it was suggested by the landlord, caring nothing about being arrested. We called the police station "the only free hotel."

The Jack Roller
(? - ?)

The following is a fourteen-year-old boy's story which reveals an intense emotional conflict between his father and mother.* The boy had been referred to a child-study clinic because of much petty stealing in the neighborhood, sex practices, repeated truancy from home, indifference to schoolwork, and frequent conflicts with his father.

Clifford Shaw, the editor of the book from which this excerpt comes, feels that "it is in the personal document that the child reveals his feelings of inferiority and superiority, his fears and worries, his ideals and philosophy of life, and antagonisms and mental conflicts, his prejudices and rationalizations. . . . The child's 'own story' is of particular importance in the diagnosis and treatment of cases of delinquency. The attitudes and intimate situations revealed in the life story not only throw light upon the fundamental nature of the behavior difficulty, but, along with the other case material,

---

*From *The Jack Roller* edited by Clifford R. Shaw. Reprinted by permission of Clifford R. Shaw, Henry D. McKay, and Albert Saifer. 1930. Pp. 8-10.

afford a basis for devising a plan of treatment adapted to the attitudes, interests and personality of the child."

What is reproduced here is the adolescent's own words—and spelling. His story was confirmed by verifiable material obtained from independent sources.

There has always been trouble in our family as long as I can remember. My father and mother quarrel and find fault with each other over almost everything. Most of the time my father nags and finds fault with my mother. He nags about her friends, what she reads, her religious ideas and opinions, the way she dresses and talks, just about everything that she does. He says to her, "Why do you go out with such and such a person, she's dumb," "Why do you read novels and newspapers and cheap trash instead of fundamental books like Wells, *Outline of History*, and the *Book of Knowledge*," "You wear too flashy clothes," "Your ideas are dumb and show you are not well read," "You're too sentimental and emotional about things, be more rational," etc. When he says these things it starts a quarrel. After the quarrel my mother cries and begs his pardon and everything is all right for a while. I can't remember any time that they didn't have quarrels like these.

My dad is very peculiar and not like any other man I have ever known. He is one-sided in his opinions and very dogmatic. He always insists that he is right although he is proved wrong. He is proud of himself, but he is very critical of people and always finds fault with what they say or do. But if anyone should criticize him there is trouble, he doesn't like it. He wants you to do everything just as he says, and sets himself up as a model. He is precise and particular about how he talks and the way he dresses. Once when I started to wash in warm water after he had told me to use cold water, he got mad and grabbed me by the throat with one hand, and started to hit me with the other but my mother took my part and then he got mad at her and told her to mind her own affairs.

I can't figure him out, so I just accept him at face value and let it go at that. He is sarcastic and belittles me in every way. He calls me "a giddy goat," "a silly ass," "a bad egg," and makes remarks about my dumness and says I have a "child's mind." And the looks he can give you! He makes you feel miserable by just his peculiar, synical expression. He doesn't approve of anything I do. My friends are all "bad characters and thieves," I read "trashy books," I'm not "dependable or truthful," I'm "vulgar," go to "cheap shows," "have too much interest in girls," "can't grasp fundamental things," "have wrong ideas about religion and everything." He thinks everything about me is wrong.

Everything will be nice in the house until my dad comes home from work, then the atmosphere changes. It soon feels like a morgue. He's cold and synical and turns up his nose at everything. If I say a word about something that happened at school or read in the newspaper, he'll look at me as if to say, "Oh, is that all you've got to talk about? Why don't you get interested in something worth while?" So soon the whole atmosphere is changed and we just sit at the table without saying a word. If there is conversation it's always an argument and dad has to be right or there's trouble.

My mother is altogether different from my dad. She is sympathetic and patient. If I do a wrong she scolds like most mothers, but in a nice way. She confides in me and even talks to me about her trouble with dad. She takes my part against him. I usually go out to shows with my mother. The whole family doesn't do things together very often. Usually my dad works or reads, my brother works in his shop and mother and I go out together. She tells me that she has always had trouble with dad and that when my brother and me get out of school we will leave him. The trouble with the situation is that neither side ever gets together. My mother is religious and wants to go to church, but my dad objects and won't let her go. He thinks he is too intelligent to be religious. She likes movies and novels but he refuses to let her enjoy these things.

Now to discuss the last but not least member of the family, my brother. He is altogether different from me not only in looks but in disposition. He generally sides with both my father and my mother so as to be safe. I have learned through painful experience that this is a wise thing to do. Our tastes do not agree with each other except in the picking of girls. He doesn't like to work very well except at the work bench where he can work with tools. He is very clever with his hands when it comes to making things. He doesn't seem to be disturbed about the family situation. He cusses at my dad behind his back, and sympathizes with my mother when my dad is not around. We hardly ever play together like brothers.

So our family is not like any other family; it is like dog eat dog, every fellow for himself. We never enjoy ourselves together or do things like other families. My mother has her own ideas and my dad has his, and they never agree. They never get together. I side with my mother, and that makes my dad sore, then he thinks I am a double-crosser. My brother plays up to both of them and they both think he is a double-crosser.

REFERENCES

1. Asbury, Herbert. *The Gangs of New York.* Garden City, N.Y.: Doubleday & Co., 1928.
2. Bloch, Herbert A., & Niederhoffer, Arthur. *The Gang.* New York: Philosophical Library, 1958, p. 97.
3. Bowen, Elizabeth. *The Shelbourne Hotel.* New York: Alfred A. Knopf, 1951, pp. 50-51.
4. Burns, James. *Autobiography of a Beggar Boy.* London: Smith, Elder & Co., 1859.
5. Eissler, K. R. General problems of delinquency. In: *Searchlights on Delinquency.* New York: International Universities Press, 1949, p. 8.
6. Erikson, Erik H. Growth and crises of the healthy personality. *Psychol. Issues,* 1:91, 1959.
7. Hall, G. Stanley. *Life and Confessions of a Psychologist.* New York: D. Appleton & Co., 1927, p. 111.
8. Johnson, Adelaide M., & Szurek, S. A. The genesis of antisocial acting out in children and adults. *Psychoanal. Quart.,* 21:323-343, 1952.
9. Juvenal. *The Satires of Juvenal* (translated by Ralph Humphries). Bloomington: Indiana University Press, 1958, p. 44.
10. Kanner, Leo. In: *Symposia on Child and Juvenile Delinquency.* Washington, D. C.: Psychodynamics Monograph Series, 1959.
11. Kogan, David S. *The Diary of David S. Kogan.* New York: Beechhurst Press, 1955, pp. 77-78.
12. MacIver, Robert M. *Report of the New York City Delinquency Evaluation Project,* 1960.
13. Samuels, Gertrude. World-wide story—juvenile delinquency. *The New York Times Magazine,* February 14, 1960, p. 86.
14. Smith, Emma. *A Cornish Waif's Story. An Autobiography.* New York: E. P. Dutton, 1956.
15. Sudermann, Hermann. *The Book of My Youth.* London: The Bodley Head, 1923, p. 10.
16. Tolstoy, Leo. *Childhood, Boyhood, Youth.* New York: Wiley, 1904.
17. Trotsky, Leon. *My Life. An Attempt at an Autobiography.* New York: Charles Scribner's Sons, 1931, pp. 56-57.
18. Wirt, Robert D., & Briggs, Peter F. Personality and environmental factors in the development of delinquency. *Psychol. Mongr.,* 73:41, 1959.
19. Wynkoop & Hallenbeck. Quoted In: Teeters, Negley K., & Reinemann, John O., *The Challenge of Delinquency.* New York: Prentice-Hall, 1950, p. 42.
20. Zilboorg, Gregory. Historical sidelights on the problem of delinquency. *Amer. J. Psychiat.,* 100:759, 1944.

CHAPTER SEVENTEEN

Gambling, Lying, Cheating and Stealing

GAMBLING

Gambling and games of chance have been a part of man's history from the time the first human being figured that three and four added up to lucky seven. That was a long time ago: dice much like ours have been uncovered in ancient Egyptian tombs and in the ruins of Babylon. "Artifacts and relics pertaining to various games of chance, such as paired cubes, throwing stones, drawing sticks, gaming boards, and similar contrivances, have been found in the archeological remains of the Sumerian, Egyptian, and Chinese cultures. The Greeks were particularly familiar with games of chance, and the casting of paired and multiple cubes was an especially favored pastime among the Romans. Primitive cultures, from the ancient Peruvian to the Bantu in Africa and the Eskimo in North America, have regaled themselves with such amusements as matching fingers or rolling pebbles or other objects, in which the elements of chance constituted one of the principal attractions. Early magic and religious rituals relied heavily upon chance, as in the study of the entrails of sacrificial animals among the Romans, although divine intervention was employed as an explanatory device in order to impose some sense of order upon the unknown and the unpredictable. Card-playing has a lengthy history, many of the forms of our modern card games predating the medieval era in European history [5]." The lure of gambling has always been so powerful, apparently, that neither moral censure, nor restrictive legislation, nor financial losses have ever been able to dampen it.

In Chafetz's unique view of history (7), it was the gambler's restlessness that helped push America westward, his flamboyant character that gave luster to frontier individualism, and his legerdemain and quick gun that often forced the coming of law and order. How did an Indian squaw pick her brave? By how good a gambler he was; otherwise she and her papoose might find themselves the pawns of a sharper peach-stone roller. What did Thomas Jefferson meditate on while composing the Declaration of Independence? His losses at backgammon, cards and lotto. Who caused the Great Chicago Fire? Not Mrs. O'Leary's cow but Mrs. O'Leary's crap-shooting son, who was rolling the bones in the barn when an opponent rolled over a lantern.

That gambling is related to emotions has long been recognized by the writers of autobiographies and diaries, as the passages which follow show. But the distinctive pathologies which characterize gambling became meaningful and understandable only within the last thirty years. The illustrations used here go back nearly four hundred years, involve a variety of cultures, and substantiate the findings of these recent psychoanalytic theories.

The first of the modern thinkers about gambling was Ernest Simmel who wrote in 1920 that gambling "serves the unfolding or the substitute formation of the exceedingly pre-genital anal-sadistic libido in the unconscious. The insatiable inordinate desire that will not rest in the endless vicious circle until the loss becomes gain and the gain once more loss, originates in the narcissistic desire of the anal birth phantasies, to fructify himself, to devour his own excrement, gold, and to give birth to himself out of himself in immeasurable increase, replacing and surpassing his father and mother. The passion for gambling therefore gratifies ultimately the inclination for the bisexual idea, which the narcissist finds in himself; it serves the compromise formed of man and woman—active and passive—sadism and masochism—and finally the unsettled decision between genital and anal libido, for which the gambler battles in the well known colour symbol, 'rouge et noir.' The passion for gambling thus serves the auto-erotic gratification, whereby the playing is fore-pleasure, the gaining orgasm, and the loss ejaculation, defecation and castration [30]."

Eight years later, in his analysis of Dostoevsky's passion for gambling, Freud related the pathological compulsion to the pervasive conflict over masturbation. "The 'vice' of masturbation is replaced by the mania for gambling. ... The passion for play is an equivalent of the old compulsion to masturbate; 'playing' is the actual word used in the nursery to describe the activity of the hands upon the genitals. The irresistible nature of the temptation, the solemn resolutions, which are nevertheless invariably broken, never to do it again, the numbing pleasure and the bad conscience which tells the subject that he is ruining himself—all these elements remain unaltered in the process of substitution [13]."

In a critical study of this essay by Freud, Reik related gambling to obsessional symptoms and recognized its oracular origins in ancient history, for marked sticks and pebbles were used by seers and diviners who cast them as a means of determining the will of the gods. In the modern form of oracle, Reik believes the gambler tries to divine the future in order to obtain the answer to the question, Will I be punished or forgiven for my trespasses (masturbation)? "Destiny, the ultimate father surrogate, is thus besought for an answer through the vicissitudes of the play and its chance-determined outcome [27]."

Jones (21), in his discussion of the chess wizard, Paul Morphy, dealt with gambling as a sublimation of oedipal aggression toward the father. Bergler believes that in gambling, since it has a certain recognized social status, the pleasure principle can coexist with the reality principle. The underlying quality is the gambler's illusion of omnipotence. The pleasure-complex, consisting of this omnipotence allied with aggression and exhibitionism, opposes a punishment mechanism which involves the desire to lose, acknowledgement of homosexual tendencies, and social defamation. These two opposed triple mechanisms are common to gamblers. "All gambling is at bottom a desire to compel love through an unconscious masochistic attitude. Hence the gambler always loses in the long run [4]."

Greenson (16) agrees with Jones that gambling provides an opportunity for the revival of unconscious oedipal fantasies and with Simmel in that it "offers satisfaction possibilities for latent and unconscious homosexual, anal-sadistic, oral-receptive drives, and gratification of unconscious needs for punishment." Further, gambling is a socially acceptable activity which is used to prevent impending depression, which seemingly arises out of the threatened breakthrough into consciousness of such intolerable sexual and aggressive impulses. Lindner (23) defined the gambler as "an obsessional neurotic engaged in what might be called the making of magic." Gambling is an addiction with a fantasy component dominated by a feeling of omnipotence.

In summary, psychoanalytic theory holds that gambling is an obsessional neurosis rooted in (1) the repressed incestuous desires of the gambler (2) the substitution of gambling for masturbation (3) the fantasy of omnipotence and (4) rebellion against an authoritarian father. While the obsessional element in gambling during adolescence is generally transient, the relevancy of these four factors is clear.

The adolescent, faced with the revived oedipal phase, corresponds to the gambler who asks the two questions, according to Lindner: Are my wishes powerful enough to cause the death of my father and, Will I be punished or rewarded for my secret sexual desires (incest)?

Gambling and masturbation, the latter activity associated primarily with adolescence, present a wide variety of parallels. Both are repetitive acts, wrote Lindner, "both are compulsively driven, and the nervous and mental states accompanying the crucial stages in the performing of each are almost impossible to differentiate. The parallels between the two are remarked upon consistently by patients under analysis. One, whom I am analyzing at this time, is a habitual slot-machine player. He has called my attention to the rhythmic-repetitive nature of his preoccupation with the 'one-armed bandits' and to the correspondence between his mental and physical states when indulging in this pastime and his recollections from adolescence. This patient has also related 'hitting the jackpot' to orgasm, and believes the 'teasing' nature of each play is equivalent to the masturbating youth's manipulation of the genitals with the unexpressed question, How far can I go without having an ejaculation [23]?"

The third factor, the fantasy of omnipotence, is readily related to the adolescent's rich fantasy life. Through gambling, the adolescent finds a rich vein of gold to mine, for with the spectacular successes which he daydreams about he can become a monarch unlimited in power and unrestricted in ambition.

Thus, the adolescent, in the height of experiencing the struggle of the revived oedipal situation, sublimating his sexual needs through masturbation, enjoying a rich fantasy life, and attempting to become free from the control of his parents, seems to encompass all of the symptoms of the neurotic adult gambler while falling prey actively but transiently to the passion for gambling.

The earliest autobiographical reference bearing on gambling in adolescence is culled from Jerome Cardan (1501-1576). Cardan, Professor of Medicine at Pavia, enjoyed a wide reputation as a physician and as a mathematician. He was the illegitimate son of an eccentric jurist and mathematician already advanced in years. His mother, who did her best to abort, had a difficult and protracted confinement, and he was at once put out to nurse. His foster mother died within a month of his birth. He suffered from rickets as well as a whole catalogue of infantile complaints. He was weaned at three. By this time his parents had married, but unhappily so, and the effect on the highly strung, nervous child was lasting. In addition to the quarreling, the father was always in financial troubles, constantly moving from one house to another. The boy had no companionship with other children and was thrown entirely on himself. As he grew older, the father set him to doing tasks of a menial order until he fell ill. Upon recovery, he was released from his servile duties. Adolescence found him untrained, uneducated, sensitive, ever conscious of the slur of illegitimacy, introspective, all undergirding the feeling of rejection by his parents. It was not until he was nineteen that his father allowed him to become a serious student of Latin. At the same time his capacity for mathematics stirred him to attempt two treatises, one on astronomical calculations, the other on the theory of chance in relation to card-playing. His love of gambling, which lasted throughout his life, no doubt dated from this period of repression, and it would appear that, added to his skill and knowledge of the mathematical aspects of gambling, the excitement which it provided offered an escape from reality and from his feelings of inferiority into a realm where the dice-box placed all on an equal footing (1). "From my youth," Cardan wrote in *De Vita Propria Liber* (6), "I was immoderately given to gambling; and in this way I became known to Francesco Sforza, a prince of Milan, and made many friendships for myself among the nobles. . . . I was inordinately addicted to the chessboard and the dicing table . . . I gambled at both for many years [and] I say it with shame—every day and with the loss at once of thought, of substance, and of time."

Thomas Shepard (1605-1649) and Richard Baxter (1615-1691) both confess to uncontrolled craving for gambling during their youth. In 1813, Leopold Zunz was planning to go ahead with his studies. "With this end in view I bought a lottery ticket for the first time and lost five thaler on No. 19367 [32]." Two years later he admitted to playing dice. But these admissions are in the more normative run of events. Many adolescents play poker or other games of chance for less devious and less complex reasons than heretofore stated. The type of wagering between friends, merely to whet the competition of the game, is not gambling in the full sense. Here the gambling is harnessed to several other overriding motives; a large part of the interest resides not in the amount of money wagered but in the friendly social contact within which the game takes place (22). Gambling has been classified too as an escape from reality (24). Galdston asserts that gamblers retain within their psychic economy certain atavistic components that impede their effective operation. What they have retained is the early pre-causal patterns of comprehending and dealing with reality and experience (14).

But for the most part, analytic theory concerning gambling and applied to adolescents holds true, as the excerpts which follow illustrate. Included are examples of a young French dandy, a boy who subsequently became a backwoods preacher, a Papago Indian girl, the greatest German composer of opera, an Irish *bon vivant*, a Russian reared in incredible poverty, a middle-class Japanese boy, an American teenager of the 1880's and, last, a fourteen-year-old Siamese boy of the twentieth century.

Benjamin Constant
(1767-1830)

Henrietta de Chandieu Constant, mother of Henri Benjamin Constant de Rebecque, died a few days after giving birth to him in Lausanne, Switzerland. Colonel Juste de Constant, the boy's father, combined the tolerance of the eighteenth century with a cold Protestantism. While condoning the follies of his son and encouraging his vices, he was unable to accord him either his confidence or his affection. During the Colonel's almost continuous absence on military duty, Benjamin was raised by a series of tutors. His feverish impatience, says Nicholson (25), which in adult years amounted to a gambler's recklessness, was a cause of worry to Benjamin even as a child. In 1786, at the age of nineteen, he crossed to Paris; there followed a period of gaming and debauchery. A part of this period is described in the following excerpt from Constant's autobiography,* in which will be seen not only the difficulties his gambling involved him in but also the unconscious oedipal involvement.

Gaming, which had already got me into so much trouble, and has got me into so much trouble since, now again began to disturb my life and to spoil all that my father's kindness had done for me.

In Switzerland, at Mrs. Trevor's house, I had made the acquaintance of an elderly French lady, Madame de Bourbonne, who played to excess but was in other respects a kindly and rather original person. She played in her carriage, in bed, in her bath, morning, night, evening, always and everywhere, at every opportunity. I visited her in Paris, where she daily received a *quinze,* which she urged me to join. I regularly lost all the money that I brought there, and what I brought was the whole of my allowance from my father, and all I could borrow; which latter was, fortunately, not a great sum, although I neglected no means of running into debt.

I had in this connection a somewhat curious adventure with one of the oldest women of Madame Suard's set. She was Madame Saurin, wife of Saurin the philosopher and author of *Spartacus.* She had been very beautiful, and was the only person who remembered it, since she was sixty-five years old. She had shown me much friendship, and, although I was foolish enough to mock at her a little, I had more confidence in her than in any other person in Paris. One day I lost at Madame de Bourbonne's house all the money that I had, and all that I could lose on credit. Not knowing how to pay, it occurred to me to have recourse to Madame Saurin for a loan of the sum that I lacked. Since I myself, however, disapproved of this manœuvre, I wrote to her instead of speaking to her of the matter. I told her that I would come for her answer after dinner. This I did, and found her alone. My natural shyness, enhanced by the circumstances, caused me to wait a long time for her to be the first to mention my letter. At length, when she had said nothing about it, I resolved to break the silence. Blushing, with lowered eyes and in a voice of great emotion, I began to

---

The Red Notebook translated by Norman Cameron. Reprinted by permission of Hamish Hamilton. 1949. Pp. 123-125.

speak. "You will perhaps be astonished," I said, "at my having approached you thus. I would be most unhappy to have given you an ill impression of myself by a thing that I would not have confided to you, had not your sweet kindness towards me encouraged me to do so. The confession which I have made to you, and which, as I fear from your silence, has wounded you, was extracted from me by an irresistible impulse of trust in you."

I said all this with a pause after each word, not looking at Madame Saurin. Since she did not answer, however, I raised my eyes, and saw by her air of surprise that my harangue had utterly perplexed her.

I asked her if she had received my letter, and found that she had not. This was still more of a facer, and I would willingly have had all my words unsaid, provided only that I could find some other means of escaping from my financial embarrassment. But I had no choice: I had to go on. I therefore resumed: "You have been so kind to me, you have taken so much interest in me—perhaps I have presumed too much upon it. But there are moments when a man loses his head. I should never console myself if I had impaired your friendship. Allow me to speak to you no more of this unhappy letter. Let me conceal from you what escaped from me only in a moment of distress."

"No," she said to me. "Why do you doubt my feelings? I wish to know all; go on, go on." And she covered her face with her hands and trembled throughout her body. I clearly saw that she had taken all I had said to her as a declaration of love. This misunderstanding, her emotion and a great bed of red damask that was within two paces of us —these things filled me with an inexpressible terror. However, with the furious courage of a coward in revolt, I hastened to dispel her mistake. "In truth," I said to her, "I know not why I should continue to annoy you so long with a matter of very little importance. I have been so foolish as to gamble, I have lost more than I at the moment possess, and I wrote to you to know if you could do me the service of lending me what I lack to pay my debt."

Madame Saurin was for a moment motionless. Then her hands descended from her face, which it was no longer necessary to cover. She arose without saying a word, and counted out the money for which I had asked her. We were so confounded, she and I, that not a word passed between us. I did not open my mouth even to thank her.

Peter Cartwright
(1785-1872)

Like adolescents of all times, Peter Cartwright, a Kentucky frontier boy, exhibited ambivalent feelings. On the one hand, he was held in thrall by the devil: he loved race horses and gambling. Despite daily remonstrances by his mother, his fascination and captivation with cards made him break his frequent vows. On the other hand was religion. One day when he was sixteen he was overcome by an acute consciousness of sin and heard a voice from heaven saying, "Peter, look at me." Some time later, as he tells in his autobiography, God revealed Himself to him in a flash and gave him religion.*

Henceforth, Padover (26) relates, Cartwright was a dedicated soul and his active life spanned a major period in American history. He began preaching in the first year of Jefferson's administration, ran for Congress against Abraham Lincoln, and died during the presidency of General Grant. For almost three quarters of a century, he carried his vigorous Methodism into the backwoods of Kentucky, Ohio, Tennessee, and Illinois, and became the most famous exponent of "muscular Christianity" in the United States.

> I was naturally a wild, wicked boy, and delighted in horse-racing, card-playing, and dancing. My father restrained me but little, though my mother often talked to me, wept over me, and prayed for me, and often drew tears from my eyes; and though I often wept under preaching, and resolved to do better and seek religion, yet I broke my vows, went into young company, rode races, played cards and danced.
>
> At length my father gave me a young race-horse, which well-nigh proved my everlasting ruin; and he bought me a pack of cards, and I was a very successful young gambler; and though I was not initiated into the tricks of regular gamblers, yet I was very successful in winning money. This practice was very fascinating, and became a special besetting sin to me, so that, for a boy, I was very much captivated by it. My mother remonstrated almost daily with me, and I had to keep my cards hid from her; for if she could have found them, she would have burned them, or destroyed them in some way. O, the sad delusions of gambling! How fascinating, and how hard to reclaim a practiced gambler! Nothing but the power of Divine grace saved me from this wretched sin.

Richard Wagner
(1813-1883)

Although religion did not "get" seventeen-year-old Richard Wagner

---

*From *Autobiography of Peter Cartwright, the Backwoods Preacher.* New York: Eaton & Mains, 1856. Pp. 27.

as it did Preacher Cartwright, it is relevant to note the religious significance given a gambling experience he relates. For several months during his student life, Wagner devoted himself passionately to gambling and lost heavily. The obsessive nature of the gambler is illustrated in the theft of his mother's pension in order to recoup previous losses. Wagner's excitement was so intense that he had to leave the gaming table several times in order to vomit, despite the fact that he had had nothing to eat or drink. By taking great risks, he changed his luck and won enough to pay back his debts to his mother and others. While Theodor Reik describes gambling as a "kind of question addressed to destiny," Wagner wrote, ". . . suddenly it dawned upon me that this was destined to be my last day with the cards." He concluded the episode on a mystical note: "My sensations during the whole of this process were of the most sacred nature: I felt as if God and His angels were standing by my side and were whispering words of warning and of consolation into my ears."*

I cannot clearly recall the incidents that removed from Leipzig the few remaining fire-eaters to whom I had pledged myself since that fatal vacation-time; I only know that this side of my fame as a student yielded to another. We celebrated the 'freshmen's gathering,' to which all those who could manage it drove a four-in-hand in a long procession through the town. After the president of the club had profoundly moved me with his sudden and yet prolonged solemnity, I conceived the desire to be among the very last to return home from the outing. Accordingly I stayed away three days and three nights, and spent the time chiefly in gambling, a pastime which from the first night of our festivity cast its devilish snares around me. Some half-dozen of the smartest club members chanced to be together at early dawn in the Jolly Peasant, and forthwith formed the nucleus of a gambling club, which was reinforced during the day by recruits coming back from the town. Members came to see whether we were still at it, members also went away, but I with the original six held out for days and nights without faltering.

The desire that first prompted me to take part in the play was the wish to win enough for my score (two thalers): this I succeeded in doing, and thereupon I was inspired with the hope of being able to

*From *My Life* by Richard Wagner. Reprinted by permission of Dodd, Mead & Co. Copyright 1911, 1939. Pp. 60-62.

settle all the debts I had made at that time by my winnings at play. Just as I had hoped to learn composition most quickly by Logier's method, but had found myself hampered in my object for a long period by unexpected difficulties, so my plan for speedily improving my financial position was likewise doomed to disappointment. To win was not such an easy matter, and for some three months I was such a victim to the rage for gambling that no other passion was able to exercise the slightest influence over my mind.

Neither the *Fechtboden* (where the students' fights were practised), nor the beer-house, nor the actual scene of the fights, ever saw my face again. In my lamentable position I racked my brains all day to devise ways and means of getting the money wherewith to gamble at night. In vain did my poor mother try everything in her power to induce me not to come home so late at night, although she had no idea of the real nature of my debauches: after I had left the house in the afternoon I never returned till dawn the next day, and I reached my room (which was at some distance from the others) by climbing over the gate, for my mother had refused to give me a latch-key.

In despair over my ill-luck, my passion for gambling grew into a veritable mania, and I no longer felt any inclination for those things which at one time had lured me to student life. I became absolutely indifferent to the opinion of my former companions and avoided them entirely; I now lost myself in the smaller gambling dens of Leipzig, where only the very scum of the students congregated. Insensible to any feeling of self-respect, I bore even the contempt of my sister Rosalie; both she and my mother hardly ever deigning to cast a glance at the young libertine whom they only saw at rare intervals, looking deadly pale and worn out: my ever-growing despair made me at last resort to foolhardiness as the only means of forcing hostile fate to my side. It suddenly struck me that only by dint of big stakes could I make big profits. To this end I decided to make use of my mother's pension, of which I was trustee of a fairly large sum. That night I lost everything I had with me except one thaler: the excitement with which I staked that last coin on a card was an experience hitherto quite strange to my young life. As I had had nothing to eat, I was obliged repeatedly to leave the gambling table owing to sickness. With this last thaler I staked my life, for my return to my home was, of course, out of the question. Already I saw myself in the grey dawn, a prodigal son, fleeing from all I held dear, through forest and field towards the unknown. My mood of despair had gained so strong a hold upon me that, when my card won, I immediately placed all the money on a fresh stake, and repeated this experiment until I had won quite a considerable amount. From that moment my luck grew continuously. I gained such confidence that I risked the most hazardous stakes: for suddenly it dawned upon me that this was destined to be my last day with the cards. My good fortune now became so obvious that the bank thought it wise to close. Not only had I won back all the money I had lost, but I had won enough to pay off all my debts as well. My sensations during the whole of this process were of the most sacred nature: I felt as if God and His angels were standing by my side and were whispering words of warning and of consolation into my ears.

Once more I climbed over the gate of my home in the early hours of the morning, this time to sleep peacefully and soundly and to awake very late, strengthened and as though born again.

No sense of shame deterred me from telling my mother, to whom I presented her money, the whole truth about this decisive night. I voluntarily confessed my sin in having utilised her pension, sparing no detail. She folded her hands and thanked God for His mercy, and forthwith regarded me as saved, believing it impossible for me ever to commit such a crime again.

And, truth to tell, gambling had lost all fascination for me from that moment. The world, in which I had moved like one demented, suddenly seemed stripped of all interest or attraction. My rage for gambling had already made me quite indifferent to the usual student's vanities, and when I was freed from this passion also, I suddenly found myself face to face with an entirely new world.

To this world I belonged henceforth: it was the world of real and serious musical study, to which I now devoted myself heart and soul.

Maria Chona
(1854-1937)

The Papago Indians are found in southwest Arizona, on the Mexican border. One of them was Maria Chona, whose autobiographical account was taken down and edited by the noted anthropologist, Ruth Underhill.

Maria Chona was ninety years old when she told her story to Dr. Underhill. Her father, José Maria, the village chieftain, was nicknamed "The Gambler." In the episodes which are described here, Maria was about thirteen years old. As in the previous illustration cited, Maria's passion for gambling seems obsessive. She would bet everything she possessed, from the shell beads her father brought her from the River Country to her own wearing apparel. But unlike the parents in the previous excerpts, Maria's never said a word; and unlike Richard Wagner, Maria's ethics would not permit her to bet anything which did not belong to her.*

I was a good housekeeper. I did all the cooking and I fetched the water and ground the corn. I could catch the horses, too, and saddle them for my brothers. But I could not go out alone on the desert as they did. Why should I want to? That is man's work and no woman with a right heart wants to be a man. But I was excitable. My heart was not cool. When I had finished my work, I always wanted to race, and I was a good racer; the fastest of all the girls. And I was a gambler. Yes, always I have been a gambler and a lucky one. When I had ground the corn and fetched the firewood for the day, I used to run out to the houses where my girl cousins lived: "Come on. Let's throw dice."

We had dice which we made of sticks, painted black on one side with charcoal from the fire. Every girl had four, and we kept them always with us as we kept our red paint. We sat in a circle, and all the people gathered to watch us and bet on the game. Each girl in turn tapped her sticks on a stone and threw them. Two points if all black, one if all white. And if of different colors, let the next girl throw!

We bet everything on that game. I had baskets which I had made and a mat. My father had brought me shell beads from the River Country and all those things I wagered. My mother did not mind; she was looking on. She would not say a word if I bet everything I had, even my clothes. But I never bet her things or my sisters'. Neither did my father. He bet his own things and he gambled all the time. That was his name, the Gambler.

Once I played against a grown woman from another village. First, I won her red woven girdle, then a whole red dress, then a Mexican scarf. She went back to her house and got everything she had, a basket, a mat, a big water jar. She said she wanted to bet them all, but she would race me on the race track.

So we went to the track and all the people came with us, betting. We chose two men to take charge; a relative of mine for the starter, one of hers for the finisher. I started from one end, she from the other and all the people yelled. But then hers stopped yelling and mine went on. She was not winning. I reached her relatives who stood at the end of the track where she had started, and she was still far from the rope. Her relative had to make mine stop yelling and then he said I had won.

---

*From *The Autobiography of a Papago Woman* edited by Ruth M. Underhill. Reprinted by permission of American Anthropological Association & Dr. Ruth M. Underhill. 1936. Vol. 46. Pp. 29-30.

I heard her crying that night in the desert because she had lost everything.

My father was a gambler, too. He used to go all over our country playing against the men. Beads and necklaces he used to bring me back from the River people. And sometimes he took all the family with him when there were races between the villages and all our young men ran. But he would not let me run at those races nor bet on them.

"Wait till you are married," he said. "When you have a husband he will take you to the feasts. They are for married people, not for young girls."

George Moore
(1853-1933)

In comparison with the other illustrations used in this chapter, the following excerpt from the *Confessions of a Young Man** shows Moore's gambling to be but a peccadillo. Shumaker characterizes Moore's autobiography as "completely brazen and rather flaunting than remorseful." From the single paragraph reproduced here, the brazenness of the work becomes apparent. At sixteen, Moore was expelled from school "for idleness and general worthlessness." Back at home, his ideal became the stable, race-horses and betting. The latter continued when the family removed to London and the boy surreptitiously made small bets at a tobacconist's.

Moore's main theme, as he took pains to explain, was praise of the unrespectable—jockeys, gamblers, actors, "even" actresses. The point he continually emphasized was that respectability had wound itself about society as a "sort of octopus" and that his main business in life (he was thirty when he wrote the *Confessions*) was to break the hold.

The natural end to such school-days as mine was expulsion. I was expelled when I was sixteen, for idleness and general worthlessness. I returned to a wild country home, where I found my father engaged in training race-horses. For a nature of such intense vitality as mine, an ambition, an aspiration of some sort was necessary; and I now, as I have often done since, accepted the first ideal to hand. In this instance it was the *stable*. I was given a hunter, I rode to hounds every week, I rode gallops every morning, I read the racing calendar, stud-book,

*Reprinted by permission of Coward McCann, Inc. 1915, Brentano's. Pp. 4-5.

latest betting, and looked forward with enthusiasm to the day when I should be known as a successful steeplechase rider. To ride the winner of the Liverpool seemed to me a final achievement and glory; and had not accident intervened, it is very possible that I might have succeeded in carrying off, if not the meditated honor, something scarcely inferior, such as—alas, *eheu fugaces!* I cannot now recall the name of a race of the necessary value and importance. About this time my father was elected Member of Parliament; our home was broken up, and we went to London. But an ideal set up on its pedestal is not easily displaced, and I persevered in my love, despite the poor promises London life held out for its ultimate attainment; and surreptitiously I continued to nourish it with small bets made in a small tobacconist's. Well do I remember that shop, the oily-faced, sandy-whiskered proprietor, his betting-book, the cheap cigars along the counter, the one-eyed non-descript who leaned his evening away against the counter, and was supposed to know some one who knew Lord ———'s footman, and the great man often spoken of, but rarely seen—he who made "a two-'undred pound book on the Derby"; and the constant coming and going of the cabmen—"Half an ounce of shag, sir." I was then at a military tutor's in the Euston Road; for, in answer to my father's demand as to what occupation I intended to pursue, I had consented to enter the army. In my heart I knew that when it came to the point I should refuse—the idea of military discipline was very repugnant, and the possibility of an anonymous death on a battle-field could not be accepted by so self-conscious a youth, by one so full of his own personality. I said Yes to my father, because the moral courage to say No was lacking, and I put my trust in the future, as well I might, for a fair prospect of idleness lay before me, and the chance of my passing any examination was, indeed, remote.

Lincoln Steffens
(1866-1936)

The neurotic gambler, according to analysts who have studied the subject, plays not only to win but to *lose*. This trenchant paradox, originally established by Bergler and elaborated upon by Lindner, is explained by the latter thus: "The two-pronged fork on which [the gambler] is impaled is forged of the necessity *to win and lose at the same time* for his sanity's sake, and this can never be done. His psyche is a battleground on which irreconcilable opposites strive. If he should win, the omnipotence of his wishes is thereby proved and his incestuous aims condoned, *but*—he is at the same time rendered and adjudged guilty of parricide and vulnerable to the tortures consequent thereon. If he should lose, he is relieved of the burden of unconscious murder which is too much for sanity to bear, *but*—he forfeits the omnipotence on which he has based his life and exposes himself to the terrible penalty to be exacted for his incestuous desires. . . . In short, he plays both [to win and lose (23, p. 217)]."

Lincoln Steffens began playing cards at the age of nineteen while at college in order to pay for "extra-curricular" activities in the city. He played for the "excitement" of the game—and for money. He was not a true neurotic gambler but rather one who found a fascination in the danger of the game and whose emotions were accelerated and accentuated by it.

> . . . and some of us gambled. We had to get money for theaters, operas, and other expenses in the city. I had only my board, lodging, and clothes paid for by my father, and others had not even that. We played cards, therefore, among ourselves, poker and whist, so that a lucky few got each month about all the money all of the other hard-ups had, and so had all the fun. We played long, late, and hard, and for money, not sport. The strain was too great.
>
> One night my roommate, sunk low in his chair, felt a light kick on one of his extended legs; a second later there were two kicks against his other leg. Keeping still and watching the hands shown down, he soon had the signal system of two men playing partners, the better hand staying in the game. We said nothing but, watching, saw that others cheated, too. We knew well an old professional gambler from the mining-camps who was then in San Francisco. We told him all about it.
>
> "Sure," he said, "cheating will sneak into any game that's played long enough. That's why you boys oughtn't to gamble. But if you do, play the game that's played. Cards is like horse-racing. I never bet a cent except I know, and know how, the game is crooked."
>
> Having advised against it, he took us around to the gambling-houses and the race course and showed us many of the tricks of his trade, how to spot and profit by them—if we must play. "Now you won't need never to be suckers," he said. "And ye needn't be crooks either," he added after a pause. But we had it in for our opponents. We learned several ways to cheat; we practiced them till we were cool and sure. After that our "luck" was phenomenal. We had money, more than we

needed. In my last two years at the university I had a salary as military instructor at a preparatory school in the town, and my roommate, the adopted son of a rich gold-miner, had a generous allowance. But we went on playing and cheating at cards for the excitement of it, we said, but really it was for the money. And afterward, when I was a student in Germany, I played on, fair, but hard—and for money I did not need, till one night at the Café Bauer in Berlin, sitting in a poker game that had been running all night, an American who had long been playing in hard luck, lost a large amount, of which I carried away more than my share. The next day we read in the papers that when he got home he had shot himself. I have never gambled since—at cards [31].

Maxim Gorky
(1868-1936)

Clinical findings confirm that in the history of neurotic gamblers either severe deprivation or over-gratification in childhood is present. Gorky's childhood and adolescence were dominated by extreme poverty, which might very well have been one of the factors prompting his unrestrained indulgence in gambling at the ages of twelve and thirteen. In the following passage,* Gorky describes his feelings about his prowess at jacks, billiards and bowling for which he had become renowned among adolescents and adults alike in the little Russian village where he lived. The unconscious, contrapuntal motif that runs throughout the selection deals with his feelings of guilt and need for expiation. He confesses to the priest that he has robbed from the church collection in order to gamble but the priest ignores him; instead of putting his contribution into the plate, he keeps it to buy jacks with which to indulge his "mania"; he gambles all through mass and even misses mass to pursue his craving; he runs home to grandma (both parents are dead), "dreading a quiz" that will find him out and perhaps expose his gambling as a compulsive acting out, pleading with the surrogate figure for the affirmative response to the questions, "Do you love me?" "Do you approve of me?" "Do you think I am good, and smart, and strong?"

I stayed away from mass, too, particularly in the spring, which held me back from church with an irresistible power. A seven-kopeck piece given to me to put into the collection was my ruin. I bought jacks with

---

*From *Autobiography*. Reprinted by permission of Citadel Press. 1940. Pp. 229-231.

it, played all through the mass, and got home late, of course. And once I managed to lose the coins given to me for prayers for the dead and for the sacramental bread; and when the priest distributed it, I had to take some other person's share.

I developed quite a mania for gambling. I was equipped with skill and strength, and was soon renowned through the streets for my prowess at jacks, billiards and bowling.

During Lent I was told to get ready for communion, and I went to confess to the neighbor priest, Father Pokrovsky. He impressed me as a stern sort, and many of my sins had been at his expense. I had stoned his flimsy summer house in the garden, and I had fought with his children. Such sins, if he chose, he could himself recall. This made me fearful; and standing in his poor little church, waiting my turn in the confession box, my heart skipped some beats.

But Father Pokrovsky gave me a cheerful greeting, "Oh, it's my neighbor. Kneel down, my boy, what sins have you committed?"

Over my head he laid a piece of heavy velvet. The odors of wax and incense reached my nostrils. I found it hard to speak, and I did so reluctantly.

"Have you obeyed your elders?"

"No."

"Say, 'I have sinned.' "

Then, startling myself, I came out with, "I stole."

"How? Where?" asked the priest, slowly and reflectively.

"At the church of the Three Saints, at Pokrov, at Nikol . . . "

"So, in all the churches! That was wrong, my child, a sin, do you understand?"

"I understand."

"Say, 'I have sinned.' And why did you steal? For something to eat?"

"Sometimes; and other times it was because I lost money at games; and since I had to bring home some sacramental bread, I stole."

Father Pokrovsky said something in a tired and almost inaudible whisper; then, after a few more questions, he suddenly asked me, and his face was now very solemn, "Did you read any banned books?"

That question, of course, was beyond me, and I asked, "What books?"

"Banned books. Did you read any?"

"No. Not one."

"Rise; your sins are remitted."

I gave him an astonished glance. His look was abstracted, but kind, which intensified my bad conscience, and added to my uneasiness. By way of preparation for the confessional, my employers had stressed its

terrors, and harped on the necessity of baring even the most trivial sin.
So I added to my testimony, "I threw rocks at your summer house."

Still looking past me, the priest raised his head and said, "That was
very bad. You can go, now."

"I stoned your dog, too."

"Next!" Father Pokrovsky called, ignoring me.

And off I went, feeling cheated and neglected. To have been subjected to such apprehension over the confessional ordeal, only to discover that it was so harmless, even dull. The only thing about it that
interested me was the matter of the banned books, of which I was entirely ignorant. I recalled the basement room reading scene, the student reading to the two women; and Good Idea's shelves of squat,
black tomes with their incomprehensible diagrams.

The following day I was given fifteen kopecks and dispatched to
my communion. Easter was late; the snow had thawed off sometime
ago; I walked through dry streets; dust already blew over the high-
ways; and the weather was bright and genial. Close to the church some
workers were rolling jacks. I said to myself, "There's still time for
communion," and asked to be let into the game.

"A kopeck's the ante," said a ruddy pock-marked man, cockily.

As cockily, I began with a three-kopeck bet. I had a run of luck; two
tries by an adult player, at the pair of jacks I had bet on went amiss,
which brought me six kopecks winnings from grown men, and I felt
elated. Then one of the players said, "Keep an eye on that kid, or he'll
scoot off with his winnings."

Taking this as an insult, I showed my defiance by placing a nine-
kopeck bet. The players seemed unimpressed, except for a boy of about
my own age who said, "What luck he's got, that little devil from Zvez-
drinsky; I know all about him."

A thin man, a furrier by the reek from his clothes, said cuttingly, "A
little devil? Good!"

With a careful throw, he won my nine kopecks and turned to me,
"Howl, little devil!"

My reply was a three-kopeck bet, which he accepted and lost. By the
rules of the game, one could not bet on the same jacks more than three
times in succession. I picked another pair and garnered four more kopecks. But there my luck ran out, and I lost my next three bets. In the
meanwhile mass had been finished, the church bells rang the close of
services, and the congregation began pouring out.

The furrier asked me, "Are you married?" and made a grab at my
hair, but I dodged and got away. I came to a boy, all dressed up in his

holiday best, and asked him, very mealy-mouthed, "Were you at communion?"

"Suppose I was? What's it to you?"

I asked him to describe the communion rite, what the priest recited, and what my part in it would have been. He took hold of me, gave me a shaking, and terrified me with his yelling. "You heretic, staying away from communion! You won't get a thing out of me. I hope you get a thrashing from your father!"

I ran home, dreading a quizzing, certain that my truancy would be fished out of me. But after receiving their congratulations, all the old woman asked me was, "What did you give the clerk?"

"Five kopecks," I replied, brazenly.

"And three kopecks for the other; you got away with seven kopecks, you beast!"

Seiji Noma
(1878-1938)

Seiji Noma was for many years the president of the Dai Nippon Yubenkai Kodansha (Great Japan Oratorical Society) and owner of the Hochi Newspaper Company in Tokyo. He was born in Kiryu, and raised in a traditional Japanese household where the father's idea of family organization was that it should be sustained in unity by the combined efforts of all and under his personal and exacting direction. The looser social policy under which the son grew up perhaps prompted his rebellion against the authoritarian father figure through gambling. In every case, according to Lindner, the father of the gambler conforms to type. He is strong, domineering, moralistic, sustained by his convictions of self-importance, lacking in warmth or the expression of warmth toward his offspring, and niggardly in money matters (23). All of these qualities do not necessarily apply to Noma's father, but most of them are present.*

When I had advanced to the third-year class, in my twelfth year, my naughtiness took on a slightly priggish or conceited colour and I began to think and talk about becoming a big man, a General or a Minister of State. Sometimes I fell into a state of melancholy reflection about my future. I had heard some of my teachers or family friends say that I

*From *The Nine Magazines of Kodsansha* by Seiji Noma. Reprinted by permission of Methuen & Co., Ltd. 1934. Pp. 20-24.

might become a "somebody" in the future, so I began to look after the little corner of the room which formed my study, arranging books and magazines neatly on the desk and sitting before it, book in hand, making such a pose as a great writer might make in his library. I did not like the flavour of tobacco but thought that smoking was a sign of future greatness, so I tried to smoke such brands as "Hero" and "Pinhead," which were then in vogue. Two or three other boys in the same class were secretly smoking also. I began also to think about girls.

In those days a boy nearing graduation from the Senior Primary School was popularly supposed to have had a high course of education and was regarded much as graduates of colleges are regarded to-day.

One afternoon my father was passing a house known as "Enjudo," a confectioner's shop, owned by a friend. The latter happened to be sitting in the forefront of the shop and as my father passed he beckoned and asked him to come in for a chat. Both sat down, after the manner of country people, to a cup of tea and a talk. The master of "Enjudo" began by complimenting my father on having a clever, bright boy, and added, as if casually: "Your Seiji San seems to have extraordinary skill in archery. He can fairly beat many adult would-be archers, I am told." My father, highly flattered, said something in modest derogation of my merits, but as their talk progressed he was abashed to find that the compliment was a piece of bitter irony, and was given as a friendly warning to the father about the future of his son.

Archery was one of the hobbies I had acquired in the latter part of my Senior Primary career. It was not the archery that had been practised by the *samurai* of old, but was mere pleasure archery done for amusement at a vulgar establishment run for money with female "arrow-collectors" in attendance.

There was one such house between the school and my home and I had been going there regularly with some other boys after school was over. I had soon acquired a moderate degree of skill. If the target was a large one, say eight inches in diameter, I was able to hit eight times out of ten, or, if it was a seven-inch target, I could hit six or seven times with ten arrows. So far so good. The objectionable thing was the mild gambling that went with it.

I was a favourite with some of the gamblers and when I won they sometimes treated me to a savoury dish ordered from a neighbouring restaurant. I had learned to visit a macaroni restaurant near the archery shop where I could get a bowl of macaroni with fried lobster for three *sen*. Only two or three out of the third-year boys dared visit such a restaurant, and this, added to the fact that I was a favourite of the gambling archers, had shocked the master of "Enjudo" into giving timely warning to my father. He must have painted a horrible picture, giving the impression of a boy who mingled with adult profligates and was on the road to damnation.

One afternoon a few days later, while I was busy plying my bow and arrows in an exciting game on which probably hung a heavy stake, a voice of thunder sounded from behind me: "Seiji!" I looked round and beheld the gigantic form of my father bolt upright, grim and terrible. Instinct told me that he was not the usual benevolent parent and before I had time to speak came the stern command, "Seiji, come home with me immediately."

I laid down my bow and arrow and followed my parent out into the street. He walked with big, solemn strides; I followed behind like a sheep. He uttered not a word, nor did I. I could not understand and thought something dreadful must have happened at home or somewhere.

There was nobody at home and my father and I sat face to face. He gave me a long, earnest sermon. He explained that gambling was the root of all evil, of idleness, hatred of serious occupation and other vices. It was a pathetic sermon; my father blanched in the face and shivered as he spoke as if horror-struck at the enormity of my sin. I was more frightened at his manner than at his words. It was altogether different from his usual custom when angry with my sister or me of giving vent to his displeasure in one or two thunderous words of reprimand. Now he spoke in a slow, measured tone, and in a mood more sad than angry.

"I am not condemning archery itself," my father said towards the end. "On the contrary I think it is a good, healthful practice, and if you really like it I will make room for archery practice at the back of our house, so that you may play with your friends, but for heaven's sake never go again to that disgraceful shop." I gave him my word never again to cross the threshold of the bow-and-arrow house.

"That is right," my father exclaimed, the tension relaxed, "but a mere verbal promise to a human being will not prove effectual when you are assailed by strong temptation. If I were you, I would go to our tutelary deity and make the same promise before the august shrine. Now go at once lest you forget."

I left home immediately and walked toward the local *Shinto* shrine. As I was approaching the gate in front I saw a slender middle-aged woman and a girl of twelve or thirteen walking this way and that on the paved ground, marking the "hundred-time-walking-pathway" after the manner of devout pilgrims making the "hundred-time-prayer" (that is, walking the prescribed distance in the temple compound and worshipping the deity each time the shrine is faced). On walking farther up and taking a closer view, I found the two persons to be my mother and sister, and our eyes met. In a flash as we exchanged glances I read the whole dreadful situation. They were praying for the redemption of my sins!

My father was as good as his word. He constructed a little embankment at the back of our house suitable for archery exercise and bought me a bow and arrows. Though the house itself was small and shabby, it had a background of fruit trees and flowering shrubs with ample space for an archery ground for boys to practise.

Kumut Chandruang
(1914-   )

Kumut Chandruang was born and brought up in Siam (now Thailand) at a time when the country was making a slow and nonviolent transition from a sleepy agrarian economy to a semiwesternized industrial one. A short forty years before Kumut was born, the King had abolished slavery. However, polygamy was still permitted. Kumut's father had three wives, and the boy, two younger brothers and one sister grew up under this system.

When the boy was in his early adolescence, Kumut's father, the First Justice of Nakorn Sawanka Province, sent him to Bangkok for his education. The adjustment to city life was difficult for Kumut as was the separation from family and friends. When, in the ninth grade, the fourteen-year-old boy was beaten by a teacher, his reaction was to play truant. It was at this juncture that his gambling activities began, flourished and got him into the temporary difficulties which he describes in this passage.*

In spite of the poor accommodations at home, which discouraged my studying, I was not a poor student. Although I never came first in examinations, I was always among the Class-A students. We studied geometry and algebra in English. I was not good in penmanship, drawing, geography, and history, but I surpassed my friends in Siamese composition, English grammar, English translation and moral philosophy.

I became a bad boy in my ninth grade, as I had a fierce teacher who whipped me when I came to school late. I was a good student as far as

---

*From *My Boyhood in Siam*. New York: John Day. 1940. Pp. 164-165.

studying was concerned, but I did not have a good sleeping place. The noise of the factories bothered me at night, and sometimes I had to stay up late chaperoning the sisters. I came to school late. When the teacher started to whip me, I debated whether I should strike him on the face or run away from school. I chose the latter—and I stayed away from school for weeks.

No one in the house knew that I skipped school. I pretended to dress up and leave the house with my books every morning, but instead of reaching my class, I stopped at the pool halls, playing billiards and gambling with the older men. Sometimes I lost all my monthly allowance which my father sent me; I had to lie to the family in many ways. They believed me, because I had been a good boy—but I gradually became unhappy losing the bets, and I even fell into debt to the other gamblers, who threatened to report my case to the family if I did not pay off. I was forced to give them my diamond rings, ruby rings, and expensive jewels which my mother had given me, and then lie to the sisters and the aunts about how I had lost them. They began to suspect my behavior—and I was worried.

One day the teacher came to the house—and all my sins were exposed. My father came down from the country to settle my case. Everybody scolded me; I was ashamed and cried, but remained obstinate about returning to school. Father begged the teacher not to whip me, because I was the kind of boy who was not used to punishment. The teacher felt that Father's request was against his principles. But Father was a good friend of the superintendent of the school, who therefore ordered the teacher never to punish me.

LYING, CHEATING AND STEALING

Adolescence serves as a rigorous testing and proving ground for the adequacy of personality structure laid down in childhood. Existing defects in adolescence are glaring, states Ausubel (2), but in most instances are not basic enough to lead to more than transitory disturbances. The textbooks of psychopathology describe at length the deficiencies of the superego in persons who lie, cheat or steal. These three forms of behavior are common in childhood and adolescence but are more frowned on in the latter period because by that time the superego is supposedly more highly developed. At the time of the initial coping with the oedipal conflict, which usually occurs between the fourth and sixth years of the child's life, the superego comes into being. With the second phase of the oedipal conflict, recapitulated in adolescence, the superego becomes more exacting. Since the adolescent experiences so much that is new—almost too much—the moral standards that have been established are not always handled effectively.

True morality begins when the internalized criticism, now embodied in the standard exacted by the superego, coincides with the ego's perception of its own fault. From that moment, the severity of the superego, says Anna Freud (12), is turned inwards instead of outwards. The superego has a double aspect. It represents a protective power which prevails under normal circumstances and a punitive power, under which occasional punishments are accepted for purposes of conciliation. The most frequent complication in the triad of lying, cheating and stealing is represented by conflicts between the ego and the superego. Fenichel (11) describes the conflict thus: "The patients try to convince themselves that since they did not get enough affection, they have a right to steal. But, as a rule, they do not succeed. Instead they feel guilty, try to fight this guilt feeling in different ways, and may even become 'criminals out of guilt feeling,' stealing more and more, thus becoming enmeshed in a vicious circle. Stealing (like wandering) may also have a direct sexual significance. For example, it may represent 'doing a forbidden thing secretly,' and thus mean masturbation."

Thus the dual function of the conscience involves both the inhibition of the impulse and feelings of guilt when restraints have temporarily broken down. By adolescence, internalized controls have begun, to a large extent, to replace the purely external controls of childhood. For most adolescents, when conscience has developed adequately, even the mere thought of a transgression is sufficient to arouse feelings of guilt. As the adolescent widens his range of behavior and with more and more consistency, his actions "become subject to a new kind of restraint, that of conscience or control by guilt. The anticipation of guilt feelings, self-criticism, and loss of self-esteem, now deter him from acting in socially disapproved ways [3]."

But in the inextricably interwoven struggle for identity and self-esteem, the adolescent is compelled to learn the new standards of socially approved behavior expected of him. He is confronted not only with the transformation from childhood to adult conscience, but also the struggle to contain his aggressive impulses, the control of his sexual needs and the tendency to externalize the functions of conscience with the resulting urges to act out. His aggressive behavior is frequently if not inevitably the reaction to frustration (9). "During adolescence . . . frustration is commonplace. In learning to handle his resurging drives and to become more socialized, the adolescent meets with frequent failures or partial successes before he is able to deal comfortably with his adult role. The whole process of becoming more independent, with the conflicting psychological and social needs of elders, makes it difficult for the young person *not* to rebel on occasion. . . . Aggressive behavior is not pathological of itself and may be an indication of the adolescent's attempts to develop initiative and independence. When it takes extreme forms, or persists in spite of opportunities for other and more effective ways of coping with the problems of growth and development, it is likely to be psychopathological. When it results in the breaking of laws and in apprehension by civil authorities and conviction, it becomes delinquency [18]."

This chapter is not concerned with the latter form of aggression, but with the former—the adolescent striving for initiative and independence and acting out his needs through lying, cheating or stealing. For example, William Cowper (1731-1800), out of his feeling of rejection when sent away to school at the age of six, wrote in his memoirs that by the time he was thirteen, "I became such an adept in the infernal art of lying, that I was seldom guilty of a fault for which I could not invent an apology capable of deceiving the wisest [8]." A child's lies are usually motivated by feelings of humiliation and inadequacy, and an underlying fear that he cannot be accepted on his own merits. So the child tries to make himself appear grander or smarter or more influential or even more guilty (when this enhances status) than he is. A lying child's fear that he cannot succeed or be accepted on his own merits is based on his inability to accept himself. This, in turn, is usually based on his parents' failure in accepting him, which is traceable ultimately to their inability to accept themselves.

The causal factors in cheating are basically the same. Cheating is an infantile, manipulative level of adaptation to the environment. In an investigation carried out by Havighurst and Taba (17), the authors found that adolescents of sixteen are underdeveloped in the ability to apply moral beliefs to their daily experiences and tend to resolve their conflicts by using stereotyped slogans rather than value judgments. Although the purpose of education is to train the ego in skills that will enable it to deal with the realities of life, the reason for cheating most commonly given is that the pressure to succeed, reinforced by the fear of failure, overwhelms considerations of honor. Jacobs, in his recent study of values among university and college students in the United States, found the principal causes of cheating to be overemphasis on grade-examination procedures and a widespread student tradition of tolerance toward the practice. "The traditional moral virtues are valued by almost all students. They respect sincerity, honesty, loyalty, as proper standards of conduct for decent people. But they are not inclined to censor those who choose to depart from these canons. Indeed they consider laxity a prevalent phenomenon, even more prevalent than the facts seem to warrant. Nor do they feel personally bound to unbending consistency in observing the code, especially when a lapse is socially sanctioned. For instance, standards are generally low in regard to academic honesty, systematic cheating being a common practice rather than the exception at many major institutions [19]."

The social sanction of cheating by students is not a phenomenon peculiar to institutional life in the United States. It is to be found also in China, Russia, India, France, England, Brazil and Scotland, as the illustrations to follow will show. Gandhi, Trotsky, Milne and the others demonstrate the prevalence of cheating in their respective countries, indicating the similar needs of certain adolescents irrespective of the country or age in which they live. In at least two of the excerpts (Helena Morley and Simone de Beauvoir), there seems to be a very real need on the part of the two youthful offenders to be caught in their cheating. A frequent explanation for this is that the adolescent is motivated by an unconscious sense of guilt. "Since the guilt is deeply repressed, the evidence on which this explanation is based is usually that some antisocial acts are performed so inefficiently that apprehension is inevitable. While it is true that some offenders appear to invite detection, it does not necessarily follow that they or other repeated offenders are motivated by a sense of guilt [3, p. 365]." Thus, when Helena Morley was caught in the act of cribbing on an examination, the entry in her diary reads, "It was my bad luck. What can I do?" But no mention of remorse or guilt is made.

For our purpose, one final point should be made about cheating. This deals with the unconscious and conscious attitudes of the examiner toward the examinee and vice versa. English and Pearson (10) have universalized the problem in this manner: "Examinations are a testing, a tormenting of the younger by the older. If assessment of knowledge were in fact the motive for examinations, then they would be given throughout life. . . . Examinations can be compared to initiation ceremonies which express the elder's envy and jealousy mixed with love and the younger's fear mixed with reverence and gratitude. In the initiation rites the hostility against the young men is based on the fear of retaliation which stems from the elder's guilt towards his own parents. 'I rebelled against my parents and therefore anticipate that I will be paid back in kind by having my children rebel against me.' While inflicting the cruelties, the elders also attempt to appease the youngsters and thus to forestall any retaliation. The appeasement is accompanied by impressing the initiates with the awesomeness and secrecy of the proceedings and by imposing upon them vows of silence concerning the rites, thus binding them in a bond of secrecy. . . . It is therefore not surprising that the same tendencies should stand out in the relationship between the student and the teacher and examiner. An examiner, particularly a neurotic examiner, may make himself a severe, overstrict father, or a loving and over lenient father; he may insist narcissistically that the student's views and methods of expression be like his own; or he may fear the candidate." Gandhi's, Trotsky's, Morley's and de Beauvoir's experiences reflect the variety of attitudes of examiner and examinee in the light of this quotation.

Stealing, the last of the casual delinquent behavioral patterns to be considered in this chapter, is perhaps predictable in adolescence. The experimental stealing the adolescent engages in is not serious and is usually outgrown as the superego develops greater stability. Among the pranks Lincoln Steffens and his college chums practiced was stealing some chickens from a University of California professor. "We liked to steal," he confessed in his *Autobiography* (31), "but we didn't care to think about it, not as stealing." Two hundred years earlier, Rousseau wrote (28), "I did not exactly want to steal the money, I wanted to steal the employment of it; the less of a theft it was, the greater its disgracefulness." Most adolescents develop their own inhibitions and control without any outside action, but when the inner tensions are overpowering, they may be expressed through stealing.

Stealing has its basis in a multiplicity of adjustive causes. Sometimes the youngster feels a real sense of deprivation, as MacKinley Kantor described in a passage from his autobiography, and in order to compensate for this feeling, steals. The things he takes bring him satisfactions which he never had from people, and thus for many years, he persisted in this infantile behavior. But honesty is not a consistent general trait. "Knowing whether a child will steal pennies is of little aid in predicting whether he will cheat in school. Each situation has its own particular determiners of behavior. . . . Honest or dishonest acts may arise from different causes in different persons, and yet be consistent in each case with the individual's personality. One child may steal to show off; another, to get money or support a hobby, a third, to express aggression against the person from whom he steals. Each child reveals his personality but does not have a clearcut trait that can be labelled 'dishonesty' [29]."

Gallagher and Harris (15) state bluntly that "it is unlikely that anyone can truly say that he has *never* stolen. Most of us can remember taking something in order to appear generous by giving it to someone we admired, or to make ourselves appear more important by having such a special possession or to replace something lost and thereby avoid punishment." And Jersild states that if all adolescents who committed overt misdeeds in the legal sense were reported, as well as those who were held strictly to account in a psychological sense, practically all adolescents would be classed as delinquents. Many adolescents who are law-abiding in their overt behavior commit violent acts of aggression in their fantasies (20). The adolescent who persistently gambles, lies, cheats or steals is expressing a symptom of an acute personality disorder. The adolescent who manifests such behavior occasionally has not yet established fully effective controls to prevent the outbreaks. The superego lacunae that crop out from time to time in adolescence are illustrated in the examples which follow.

Jean Jacques Rousseau (1712-1778)*

She left a year's wages to her underservants. I received nothing, not

---

*From *The Confessions of Jean Jacques Rousseau.* Reprinted by permission of Pocket Books, Inc. 1957. Pp. 51-55.

having been entered on the list of her establishment. However, the Comte de la Roque ordered thirty *livres* to be given me, and left me the new suit which I was wearing, and which M. Lorenzi wanted to take from me. He even promised to try and find a place for me, and gave me leave to go and see him. I went there two or three times without being able to speak to him. Being easily rebuffed, I did not go again. It will soon be seen that I was wrong. Would that I had finished all that I had to say about my stay at Madame de Vercellis's! But, although my condition apparently remained the same, I did not leave the house as I entered it. I carried away from it lasting recollections of crime and the insupportable weight of remorse, which, after forty years, still lies heavy on my conscience; while the bitterness of it, far from growing weaker, makes itself more strongly felt with my advancing years. Who would believe that a childish fault could have such cruel consequences? For these more than probable consequences my heart is inconsolable. I have, perhaps, caused the ruin of an amiable, honest, and estimable girl, who certainly was far more worthy than myself, and doomed her to disgrace and misery.

It is almost unavoidable that the break up of an establishment should cause some confusion in the house, and that several things should get lost; however, the servants were so honest, and the Lorenzis so watchful, that nothing was missing when the inventory was taken. Only Mademoiselle Pontal had lost a piece of old red and silver-coloured ribbon. Many other things of greater value were at my disposal; this ribbon alone tempted me; I stole it, and, as I took no trouble to conceal it, it was soon found. They wanted to know how it had come into my possession. I became confused, stammered, blushed, and at last said that Marion had given it to me. Marion was a young girl from Maurienne, whom Madame de Vercellis had taken for her cook, when she left off giving dinners and discharged her own, as she had more need of good soup than of fine stews. Marion was not only pretty but had a fresh colour, only found on the mountains, and, above all, there was something about her so gentle and modest, that it was impossible for anyone to see her without loving her; in addition to that, she was a good and virtuous girl, and of unquestionable honesty. All were surprised when I mentioned her name. We were both equally trusted and it was considered important to find out which of us two was really the thief. She was sent for; a number of people were assembled, amongst them the Comte de la Roque. When she came, the ribbon was shown to her. I boldly accused her; she was astounded, and unable to utter a word; looked at me in a manner that would have disarmed the Devil himself, but against which my barbarous heart was proof. At last, she denied the theft firmly, but without anger, addressed herself to me, exhorted me to reflect, and not to disgrace an innocent girl who had never done me any harm; but I, with infernal impudence, persisted in my story, and declared to her face that she had given me the ribbon. The poor girl began to cry, and only said to me: "Ah! Rousseau, I thought you were a good man. You make me very unhappy, but I should not like to be in your place." That was all. She proceeded to defend herself with equal simplicity and firmness, but without allowing herself to utter the slightest reproach against me. This moderation, contrasted with my decided tone, did her harm. It did not seem natural to suppose, on the one side, such devilish impudence, and, on the other, such angelic mildness. Although the matter did not appear to be absolutely settled, they were prepossessed in my favour. In the confusion which prevailed, they did not give themselves time to get to the bottom of the affair; and the Comte de la Roque, in dismissing us both, contented himself with saying that the conscience of the guilty one would amply avenge the innocent. His prediction has been fulfilled; it fulfills itself every day.

I do not know what became of the victim of my false accusation; but it is not likely that she afterwards found it easy to get a good situation. She carried away with her an imputation upon her honesty which was in every way cruel. The theft was only a trifling one, but still it was a theft, and, what is worse, made use of to lead a young man astray; lastly, lying and obstinacy left nothing to be hoped from one in whom so many vices were united. I do not even consider misery and desertion as the greatest danger to which I exposed her. At her age, who knows to what extremes discouragement and the feeling of ill-used innocence may have carried her? Oh, if my remorse at having succeeded in making her unhappy is unendurable, one may judge what remorse I feel at the thought of having, perhaps, made her worse than myself!

This cruel remembrance at times so sorely troubles and upsets me, that in my sleepless hours I seem to see the poor girl coming to reproach me for my crime, as if it had been committed only yesterday. As long as I have lived quietly, it has tormented me less; but in the midst of a stormy life it robs me of the sweet consolation of persecuted innocence, it makes me feel what I think I have said in one of my books, that "Remorse goes to sleep when our fortunes are prosperous, and makes itself felt more keenly in adversity." However, I have never been able to bring myself to unburden my heart of this confession to a friend. The closest intimacy has never led me so far with anyone, not even with Madame de Warens. All that I have been able to do has been to confess that I had to reproach myself with an atrocious act, but I have never stated wherein it consisted. This burden has remained to this day upon my conscience without alleviation; and I can affirm that the desire of freeing myself from it in some degree, has greatly contributed to the resolution I have taken of writing my Confessions.

I have behaved straightforwardly in the confession which I have just made, and it will assuredly be found that I have not attempted to palliate the blackness of my offence. But I should not fulfil the object of this book, if I did not at the same time set forth my inner feelings, and hesitated to excuse myself by what is strictly true. Wicked intent was never further from me than at that cruel moment; and when I accused the unhappy girl, it is singular, but it is true, that my friendship for her was the cause of it. She was present to my thoughts; I threw the blame on the first object which presented itself. I accused her of having done what I meant to do, and of having given me the ribbon, because my intention was to give it to her. When I afterwards saw her appear, my heart was torn; but the presence of so many people was stronger than repentance. I was not afraid of punishment, I was only afraid of disgrace; and that I feared more than death, more than crime, more than anything else in the world. I should have rejoiced if the earth had suddenly opened, swallowed me up and suffocated me; the unconquerable fear of shame overcame everything, and alone made me impudent. The greater my crime, the more the dread of confessing it made me fearless. I saw nothing but the horror of being recognised and publicly declared, in my own presence, a thief, liar, and slanderer. Complete embarrassment deprived me of every other feeling. If I had been allowed to recover myself I should have assuredly confessed everything. If M. de la Roque had taken me aside and said to me: "Do not ruin this poor girl; if you are guilty, confess it to me," I should have immediately thrown myself at his feet, of that I am perfectly certain. But, when I needed encouragement, they only intimidated me. And yet it is only fair to consider my age. I was little more than a child, or rather, I still was one. In youth real crimes are even more criminal than in riper years; but that which is only weakness is less so, and my offence was at bottom scarcely anything else. Thus the recollection of it afflicts me not so much by reason of the evil in itself as on account of its evil consequences. It has even done me the good of securing me for the rest of my life against every act tending to crime, by the terrible impression which I have retained of the only offence that I have ever committed; and I believe that my horror of a lie is due in great measure to my regret at having been capable myself of telling one so shameful. If it is a crime that can be expiated, as I venture to believe, it must be expiated by all the unhappiness which has overwhelmed the last years of my life, by forty years of honourable and up-

right conduct in difficult circumstances; and poor Marion finds so
many avengers in this world, that, however great my offence against
her may have been, I have little fear of dying without absolution. This
is what I have to say on this matter: permit me never to speak of it
again.

Santiago Ramón y Cajal*
(1852-1934)

In connection with these studies of colour, I conceived a childish project at which I worked ardently for some time. As an exercise, I undertook to reproduce in a large sketchbook all the various tints presented
by natural objects, making a sort of pictorial dictionary in which,
though lacking a name, each complex colour would appear with a
number indicating its position in the scale. By way of example I added
a picture of the corresponding object. It was something like the well
known colour scale of Chevreuil (with which I was not then acquainted), but more complete, since it contained, besides the simple
colours in various degrees of saturation, the products of mixing all the
colours, including naturally white and black.

The making of this album was carried out just as I desired so long as
I chose for reproduction rocks, insects, and wild flowers; but when I
came to cultivated flowers, I met unexpected difficulties. Carnations,
roses, hyacinths, geraniums, zinnias, pansies, gillyflowers, etc., were
not free, they had owners and were private property, and since I had
no money, I had to pilfer them from gardens and from flower pots.

As was to be expected, some disagreeable experiences came to me in
consequence. Of these I shall mention only two, related, by the irony
of fate, to the preparation of the chapter on roses. One of my chums, to
whom I had confided my tastes and aspirations, when he saw that I
was vexed because of the lack of specimens of a beautiful variety called
in Huesca the rose of Alexandria,—a flower notable alike for its colour
and for its fragrance—proposed to me a raid upon a certain garden
where this and other very fine flowers were abundant. I agreed readily
to the suggestion, which held for me the added attraction of a dangerous adventure, and we arranged to carry it out at nine o'clock the next
night. When the time came, my friend appeared punctually, accompanied by two playmates who were likewise attracted by the innocent

*From *Recollections of My Life* translated by E. Horne Craigie. Reprinted by permission of American Philosophical Society. 1937. Pp. 93-96.

and poetic booty, and we stole silently and cautiously up to the walls
of the garden, above which a high grape-trellis extended and sprays of
magnificent climbing roses shone at intervals. It was important, before
commencing to break in, to ascertain whether the owners, or possibly
the gardener, were living in the house; so, in order to make sure, we
resorted to the simple expedient of throwing two or three stones at the
roof. There was no response to the clatter, not a voice, not a sound.
Encouraged by the silence, we approached the wall at a place where
it was easily scaled, clambered up quickly, got over the bars of the
trellis, and jumped down, not without a thrill, upon the path round
the garden.

Hardly had we grasped a few of the coveted roses when there
emerged from the house two peasants, each armed with a stick, who
rushed at us furiously. Recovering from the disagreeable surprise, we
started to run round and round through the avenues of the garden.
But how were we to escape? The gates were closed and the walls of the
enclosure were so high that it was impossible to climb out of reach
before the enraged gardeners should catch us with their formidable
cudgels. In this critical situation, instinct suggested to us the strategy
of running breathlessly about the garden so as to tire its custodians, or
at least to gain such an advantage over them as would allow us the
few seconds necessary for scaling the wall. But, alas, we fed ourselves
with vain hopes! In truth, for the first quarter of an hour things did
not go badly at all; much practice in running and the spur of fear
enabled us to preserve an advantage over our enemies of perhaps
twenty metres or more. But after fifteen minutes had passed the distance grew progressively less; in twenty minutes or so it was less than
ten metres. We were wracked with terror. Nevertheless, we did not
despair in the desperate struggle for space and time. In such an extreme danger, it seemed that our spirits had entered into our muscles,
and our hearts, which are muscles too, worked at full capacity, pre-
ferring to burst rather than surrender.

But alas! The sturdy musculature of our rustic pursuers was not yet
wearied, and our forces, on the other hand, began to flag; our hearts
palpitated dizzily and our parched throats cried out for unobtainable
refreshment. And still the distance diminished alarmingly. Paralyzed
with exhaustion, one of my comrades fell, and his cries and howls in
our ears served as the final spur. The capture of our playmate gave us
a respite, allowing us to get our breath and to regain some of our advantage. Hope was born anew, but only, alas, to vanish again soon; for
our enemies, exasperated by such persistence and anxious to trap us
surely, divided their forces; one of them kept running straight on,

while the other went round in a circle. We were going to be caught between two fires.

There was no time to lose. I had a plan which I had developed during the brief moments, when, as I turned the corners, I was out of sight of my pursuers and could examine conveniently the trees and walls of the place. Taking advantage, then, of one of these pauses, I made a supreme effort and jumped up into the branches of an apple tree, from which I gained the wall and so reached freedom. This was real good fortune, for only a few seconds later heartrending groans were heard. It was my poor companions in misfortune who had been caught by the fierce gardeners and bit the dust beneath a rain of blows. Indignant at the abuse of which I considered my friends the victims, I had the impudence to climb back to the top of the wall for long enough to hurl four or five heavy stones at the enraged wielders of the cudgels, some of which must have reached their mark, for the men turned towards me furiously. I had, naturally, the prudence to escape.

Thus was concluded the famous adventure of the roses of Alexandria. The beating which my companions received was so severe that they were absent from school for several days: one of the victims, if I remember correctly, was seriously ill. In truth it was a dreadful whipping and was entirely out of proportion to the insignificance of the offence.

Mohandas K. Gandhi*
(1869-1948)

I must have been about seven when my father left Porbandar for Rajkot to become a member of the Rajasthanik Court. There I was put into a primary school, and I can well recollect those days, including the names and other particulars of the teachers who taught me. As at Porbandar, so here, there is hardly anything to note about my studies. I could only have been a mediocre student. From this school I went to the suburban school and thence to the high school, having already reached my twelfth year. I do not remember having ever told a lie, during this short period, either to my teachers or to my school-mates. I used to be very shy and avoided all company. My books and my lessons were my sole companions. To be at school at the stroke of the hour and to run back home as soon as the school closed,—that was my daily habit. I literally ran back, because I could not bear to talk to anybody. I was even afraid lest anyone should poke fun at me.

*From *The Story of My Experiments with Truth*. Reprinted by permission of Public Affairs Press. 1948. Pp. 15-16.

There is an incident which occurred at the examination during my first year at the high school and which is worth recording. Mr. Giles, the Educational Inspector, had come on a visit of inspection. He had set us five words to write as a spelling exercise. One of the words was "kettle." I had mis-spelt it. The teacher tried to prompt me with the point of his boot, but I would not be prompted. It was beyond me to see that he wanted me to copy the spelling from my neighbour's slate, for I had thought that the teacher was there to supervise us against copying. The result was that all the boys, except myself, were found to have spelt every word correctly. Only I had been stupid. The teacher tried later to bring this stupidity home to me, but without effect. I never could learn the art of "copying."

Marie Lenéru
(1875-1918)

June 27, 1887

The sins that I have to overcome in myself are: lying for although I find I lie a good deal less I often disguise the truth for example to give more interest to a story I am telling. . . .

September 25, 1887

I have just examined my conscience and I am very sad when I see that I always fall back into the same faults, it is true I am not so bad as I used to be for example when I lie it is more exaggeration or dressing up a fact and the same way for everything, but what I should do is to break myself of it completely. Well I don't despair. . . .

1888

. . . I have spoiled my day by lying oh lying very badly indeed (surely), Fernande, putting that in my diary knowing that you will read it, will be penance enough for me) well then, I said I had ridden horseback and that I had a riding-habit, then telling a lot of things about Pierre Loti [who was actually on friendly terms with the Lenéru family] and about his dinner, I said that he had promised to dedicate a book to me, that his son was disguised as a minstrel (I don't even know what that is) then I made believe I knew a certain lady of Gif whose name I had only seen in *L'Illustration* and a whole lot of other things. I have said only what was hardest for me to tell, but I told a lot of others. *Mon Dieu* what an ugly thing it is to lie, but how hard it is to tell the truth, even in one's diary.

Leon Trotsky*
(1877-1940)

The sixth grade passed without incident. Everybody was anxious to escape from the school drudgery as soon as possible. The matriculation examinations were staged with all pomp in the great hall, and with the participation of university professors sent especially by the educational authorities. The head master would open with great solemnity the package received from the inspector-general, which contained the subject for the papers. Its announcement was usually followed by a general sigh of fear, as if everybody had been dipped into icy water. The nervous suspense made one think that the task was utterly beyond one's powers. But further consideration soon revealed that the fears were much exaggerated. As the time drew toward the end of the two hours allotted for each paper, the teachers themselves would help us deceive the vigilance of the regional authorities. Having finished my paper, I did not hand it in immediately but remained in the hall, by a tacit agreement with the inspector Krizhanovsky, and engaged in animated correspondence with those who found themselves in difficulties.

Helena Morley**
(1880-   )

Saturday, December 9th, 1893

I didn't pass the first year and it was entirely due to bad luck and nothing else.

In the geography examination almost all of us cheat. We make concertinas [narrow strips of paper, folded concertina-style on which the students wrote notes in order to cheat in their examinations]; it's so much easier. I made them all with the greatest care and I went to the examination with my pockets full of them.

The subject for the written exam turned out to be "Rivers of Brazil." Marvelous! I took out my little concertina and started to copy it, and told the others out loud that they should copy, too. I think that's what caught his eye. Seu Artur Queiroga came down from the platform and stood near my desk and I couldn't possibly go on writing. I

---

*From *My Life. An Attempt at Autobiography.* New York: Charles Scribner's Sons. 1931. Pp. 13-14.

**From *The Diary of "Helena Morley"* edited by Elizabeth Bishop. Reprinted by permission of Farrar, Straus & Cudahy, Inc. Copyright 1957, Elizabeth Bishop. Pp. 87-88, 120-121.

put my concertina in my desk and put my hands on top. He said, "All right; go on!" I'd just been describing the Amazon River. I don't know what gave me the idea of saying what I said, that was what spoiled everything. He repeated, "Go on! Write!" I answered, "I can't, Seu Artur. I am drowned in the Amazon River." He gave a loud laugh that attracted the attention of the other examiners and they came to my desk, too. Seu Artur said, "I'm going to rescue you. Let's see if you can go on if I get you out of the Amazon." And then he said, "Run this way; receive these tributaries; debouch here . . . " But it was impossible to follow him. It only amused the teachers and the others went on cheating in peace and I and my class couldn't do the exam.

I had to hand over the concertina and Seu Artur only asked me to explain why I made that instead of studying. I answered that I didn't know; that that was the way I'd been taught and I thought it was a good system.

After this exam others went the same way. The teachers came and distracted me while my schoolmates were peacefully cheating away.

It was my bad luck. What can I do?

Saturday, May 5th, 1894

Today I went to see Cecília and because I had to go home again to do my composition, the only compulsory thing at School, I said to her, "I can't stay with you because I still haven't done my composition, and early tomorrow I'm going to Palha for two days and I shan't have time."

She said, "Don't go home for that. I'll loan you my book and you can copy out a letter in a second, and take it."

I took the book and was amazed! I asked her where she'd bought it. "Such nice letters, so well-written! That's why you always have such nice exercises. Oh! If I'd only been able to buy this book, too!" Cecília said, "You don't have to. When you want it I'll loan it to you." I said, "Then I'm going to want it every day. You can bring it to school, because I can copy it there and get it done, and have the evenings for studying."

She agreed. I copied a letter I thought was a beauty, folded it up small and put it in the front of my dress. I came home well satisfied. I kept thinking of the moment when Seu Sebastião would read the compositions in class, the way he does when he finds one well-written, and would praise me. "How beautifully you're writing! Congratulations!"

I handed in the exercise yesterday. Today when I got to class he had a pile of exercises on top of the table and he was calling off the names,

the way he does, to give them back. When it was my turn: "Helena
Morley!" He looked at me and stopped for a minute. My heart was
pounding, waiting for compliments. Then he yelled, "Where did you
find the manual?" The pupils began to roar with laughter.

How mean of Seu Sebastião!

A. A. Milne*
(1882-1956)

In my French set at this time I had my first experience of "cheating."
To the average boy there are two kinds of cheating: that which gives
you the advantage of another boy, and that which enables you to hold
your own against a master. The first is "not done"; the second may
have to be done. The master in charge of this set had the longest and
most beautiful pair of moustaches (one could only think of them as a
pair) which I have seen. He was also, as I discovered later, one of the
most delightful of men. But he over-estimated the capacity of his form
for absorbing French. At every lesson he would dictate twenty-four
questions to which we had to write down the answers. Anybody who
got less than twenty correct answers was "sent up-School"—which
meant that he had to work in the afternoon instead of playing games.
To be sent up-School more than fifteen times in a term brought you
in danger of a public "handing" (with birch) by the Headmaster. For
a Queen's Scholar to be sent up-School even once a term was considered disgraceful.

When we had written down our answers, we changed papers with
the boy next to us, so that each boy was correcting somebody else's
paper. This, which was supposed to prevent cheating, made cheating
more certain, for one was now doing it with an easy conscience on
another boy's behalf. We sat alphabetically, and I was next to a boy
called Moon. Leonard Moon was almost then, and was to become,
the hero of every Westminster boy. He was just getting into the school
elevens; he became a double Blue, made a century against the Aus-
tralians, played cricket for Middlesex, played football for Corin-
thians and the South of England, was extraordinarily good-looking,
and was, with it all, an extremely modest, charming person. Could I
let this paragon, who was even worse at French than I, go up-School?
Of course not. Could I, as a loyal Westminster, handicap the school

by denying him his cricket and football practice? Unthinkable. When his name was read out, I said "Twenty-one" firmly. And when my own name was read out, and he said "Twenty-two," it was equally unthinkable that I should rise in my place and say, "Sir, I suspect this charming boy on my left of uttering falsehoods. I doubt very much if I got more than seven answers right. I insist on a re-count." Instead I looked modestly down my nose. In a few weeks I had settled down happily to a life of deception.

Simone de Beauvoir*
(1908-   )

But one incident reminded me how much I still depended on [grownups'] judgment. It exploded unexpectedly just as I was beginning to enjoy a carefree existence.

Just as I did every week, I made a careful word-for-word translation of my Latin text; I wrote it in a column opposite the original. Then I had to put it into "good French." As it happened, this particular piece of prose had been translated in my textbook on Latin literature, and with an elegance which I felt could not be equaled: in comparison, all the expressions which came to my mind seemed painfully clumsy. I had not made any mistake in the meaning; I was certain to get a good mark, and I had no ulterior motives; but the words, the phrases, were demanding: each sentence had to be perfect. It was repugnant to me to substitute my heavy-handed inventions for the ideal model furnished by the textbook. Then and there I copied it straight out of the book.

We were never left alone with Abbé Trécourt; one of our old schoolmarms would sit at a little table near the window and watch over us; before he handed us back our translations, she entered our marks in a register. On that day the task had fallen to Mademoiselle Dubois, the one with the degree, whose Latin classes I would have normally attended the year before but which Zaza and I had scorned in favor of the abbé's: she did not like me. I could hear her making a fuss behind my back; she was whispering furious protests. In the end she drafted a note which she placed on top of the pile of exercise books before giving them back to the abbé. He wiped his eyeglasses, read the message and smiled: "Yes," he said mildly, "this passage from Cicero was already translated in your textbook and many of you apparently noticed

it. I have given the highest marks to those of you whose work showed
the most originality." Despite his indulgent tones, Mademoiselle Dubois' furious face and the uneasy silence of my classmates filled me
with terror. Whether through force of habit, absent-mindedness, or
simple affection, the abbé had given me the best mark: I had got 17.
In any case, no one had got less than 12. Doubtless in order to justify
his partiality he asked me to construe the text word by word: I kept
my voice steady and did so without a mistake. He congratulated me
and the tension eased a little. Mademoiselle Dubois didn't dare ask
me to read out my final version; Zaza, sitting next to me, didn't so
much as glance at it: she was scrupulously honest and I think refused
to entertain any suspicions about me. But when the lesson was over
certain other classmates of mine started whispering together and Mademoiselle Dubois took me to one side: she felt she would have to inform Mademoiselle Lejeune of my dishonesty. And so the thing I had
often dreaded was finally going to happen: an act performed innocently and in secret would, by being brought to light, disgrace me. I
still felt some respect for Mademoiselle Lejeune: the idea that she
would despise me was torture. It was impossible to turn back the
clock, to undo what I had done: I was marked for life! I had had a
presentiment of danger: the truth can be unjust, unfair; all that evening and part of the night I tried to fight a way out of the trap into
which I had so thoughtlessly fallen and which would not let me go.
Usually I evaded difficulties by running away from them, or keeping
silent, or forgetting them; I rarely took any initiative; but this time I
decided to fight it out. Lies would be needed to cover up the circumstances which conspired against me; so lie I must. I went to see Mademoiselle Lejeune in her study and I swore to her, with tears in my eyes,
that I hadn't copied my Latin translation: only some involuntary recollections of the textbook version had slipped into mine. Convinced
that I had done nothing wrong, I defended myself with all the fervor
of an injured innocent. But my tactics were absurd: had I been guiltless, I would have taken my work with me as the chief evidence in my
defense; but I merely gave my word. The principal did not believe me,
told me so, and added impatiently that the subject was now closed. She
did not give me a talking-to, and she did not reproach me for what I
had done: this indifference and the crisp tone of her voice made me
realize that she hadn't an ounce of affection for me. I had been afraid
that my mistake would ruin the good opinion she had of me: but for a
long time now I had had nothing more to lose. I recovered my equanimity. She had so categorically withheld her respect that I no longer
wished for it.

Helena Kuo*
(1910-   )

My fellow-students at Shanghai were not nearly so neatly dressed as those in Lingnan University. Neither were they as honest in their examinations. I could not believe my eyes when I saw how they contrived to cheat the professors. I was infuriated at the injustice of a system that allowed those who cheated to get good marks, while those who did not—which meant myself—failed to gain the professor's favor.

David Daiches**
(1913-   )

I found the work in Class "B" easy enough, for I could already read and write and do simple sums with slapdash speed, but it took me some time to get used to the formality and regularity of the classroom. For some reason, the idea of starting work promptly at nine o'clock each morning distressed me, and I explained to Miss Don, the teacher, that I did not think I should be able to manage it. She smiled, and said that I must do my best, and I earnestly replied that I would. Shortly afterward, Miss Don left to get married and her place was taken by Miss Barron or Miss Barrons, a name which the boys in the class for some reason found themselves unable to enunciate clearly. Miss Barn, Miss Barmy, and Miss Barley were favorite variants, and I remember myself that when I first heard her called Miss Barley I decided at once that that was the simplest and most convenient form of the name and that I would therefore stick to it. I do not think that there was any deliberate mockery involved in this playing about with Miss Barron's name: "Barron" just seemed to be difficult or at least implausible.

In the autumn of 1919 I moved up to Class "D," taught by one of the numerous Miss Smiths at Watson's. She was popularly known among the boys as "Smiggles o'D," which distinguished her from "Smiggles of H," the Miss Smith who was to teach me the following year when I moved up into Class "H." Smiggles o'D was an old war horse of a teacher, who had got the teaching of seven- and eight-year-olds systematized into a well-tried routine. She was efficient in a tired sort of way, and had a cut-and-dried list of basic offenses for which punish-

*From *I've Come a Long Way*. Reprinted by permission of Appleton-Century-Crofts, Inc. Copyright 1942, Helena Kuo. P. 83.

**From *Two Worlds*. Reprinted by permission of Harcourt, Brace & World, Inc. 1956. Pp. 53-55.

ment by the "tawse" (a leather strap, used on the palm of the hand) was obligatory. If, for example, you handed in your writing exercise (which was done at home) smudged and filthy with dirty finger marks you got the tawse. And of course you got the tawse for cheating. One morning, after she had marked the sums that we had been doing in class, she discovered that both I and the boy sitting next to me had got one sum wrong, and that we both had the same wrong answer. She decided that I had copied my answer from the boy beside me. This decision outraged me, for in fact I had not copied the answer, and I was better at arithmetic than the boy whom she assumed I had copied from. She insisted that the evidence proved that I had cheated, yet, since she refrained from giving me the tawse and contented herself with a tongue lashing, she must have realized that there was just as much chance of the other boy's having cheated. (As a matter of fact, I was convinced then and I still am that neither of us cheated: our getting the same wrong answer was simply a coincidence.) Throughout the rest of the day she would interrupt what she was saying to refer to me as the boy who had cheated. After a while I ceased to deny it, and, with the extraordinary resilience of childhood, shrugged the whole thing off. But I knew from that moment that Miss Smith was a wickedly irresponsible woman, and I never forgave her. I cannot bring myself to forgive her yet, though she has been dead now for some years. She destroyed forever my trust in teachers.

The following year, when I was in Class "H," I really did cheat, in a curiously lighthearted way without any sense of sin. Why I did it still puzzles me. One day I could not be bothered memorizing my geography homework, so I carefully wrote out the names of the rivers and the populations of the cities and the other facts and figures I was expected to learn by heart, and when next morning we were asked to write down the answers to questions on these matters I quietly took out the piece of paper on which I had written down the answers and copied them into my exercise book. As far as I can remember, I made no great effort to conceal what I was doing, and congratulated myself on having discovered a simple and efficient way of getting good marks. Of course I was soon spotted, and Smiggles of H was horrified at my criminal behavior—all the more criminal because I was regarded as a bright boy who had no need of such wicked tricks. I got two strokes of the tawse—my first experience of that instrument of torture—and was sent to the bottom of the class. I felt neither worried nor aggrieved, moving through the whole experience in a sort of trance, but I was astonished at the amount of real pain inflicted by the tawse and by the length of time it lasted. For over half an hour my hand felt as though it were about a foot thick and the tips of my fingers, which felt as large as balloons, pulsed with agony. Then suddenly the pain changed into a warm glow, and everything was very pleasant. I never bore any grudge against Smiggles of H; she was, of course, only doing her duty.

Shih-Hua Tan*
(? - ?)

On the first of June the school year ended and the examinations began. The class rooms were no longer quiet during lesson hours. They resounded with studying pupils. The lazy ones, kindled with belated diligence, buried their noses in their books, put their fingers in their ears, and swayed from side to side, learning names, words, and rules. The good students had a much easier time. During the school year they had learned all that was required. Now it was necessary for them to stay away from the buzzing class rooms, because there they were immediately attacked by the lazy pupils who swarmed around them.

"Please, explain it to me! Show me how! Solve this problem! Help me!"

Some of the head pupils earned a lot during this examination fever. These enterprising boys tutored the backward pupils in exchange for new notebooks, paper, money, or a fine dinner in a restaurant.

Four different classes were to sit together during the examinations in order to prevent pupils from copying from one another. Because of this arrangement the inventors of "ponies" had been working at full speed. They cut up a great number of long narrow strips of paper, narrow as telegraph tape, and covered them from top to bottom with the tiniest hieroglyphics. They worked day and night like diligent ivory carvers, not even using a magnifying glass. This first task done, they folded the tape like an accordion and placed it between their fingers. Then they practised the involved technique of reading from this complicated apparatus.

Some of the students wrote their subjects down on class-tables, in the hope they might have the good luck to sit at the same table. Others tattooed the formulae and rules on the palms of their hands and would refrain from washing for fear of destroying their learning. The disadvantage of this system lay in the fact that during the examinations they were likely to perspire from excitement, and their hands, tattooed with such care and effort, might then present only a picture of stormy clouds.

*From *A Chinese Testament*. Reprinted by permission of Simon & Schuster, Inc. Copyright 1934, Simon & Schuster, Inc. Pp. 111-112.

The inspector walked about on his noiseless soles, watching, remembering, moving his fingers. On the day of examinations, the possessors of "ponies" and the "cuff-writers" might be thrown out of the class by those fingers.

REFERENCES

1. Auden, G. A. Jerome Cardan: a study in personality. *J. Ment. Sci.*, 75:220-233, 1929.
2. Ausubel, David P. *Theory and Problems of Adolescent Development*. New York: Grune & Stratton, 1954, p. 511.
3. Bandura, Albert, & Walters, Richard H. *Adolescent Aggression*. New York: Ronald Press, 1959, pp. 249, 365.
4. Bergler, Edmund. *The Psychology of Gambling*. New York: Hill & Wang, 1957.
5. Bloch, Herbert A. The sociology of gambling. *Amer. J. Sociol.*, 57: 215, 1951.
6. Cardan, Jerome. *The Book of My Life*. New York: E. P. Dutton & Co., 1930, pp. 54, 73.
7. Chafetz, Henry. *Play the Devil: A History of Gambling in the U. S.* New York: Clarkson N. Potter, 1961.
8. Cowper, William. *Memoirs of the Early Life of William Cowper, Esq.* Newburgh, N. Y.: Phil B. Pratt, 1817, p. 5.
9. Dollard, John, et al. *Frustration and Aggression*. New Haven: Yale University Press, 1939.
10. English, O. Spurgeon, & Pearson, Gerald, H. J. *Emotional Problems of Living*. New York: W. W. Norton & Co., 1955, pp. 302-303.
11. Fenichel, Otto. *The Psychoanalytic Theory of Neurosis*. New York: W. W. Norton & Co., 1945, p. 321.
12. Freud, Anna. *The Ego and the Mechanisms of Defence*. New York: International Universities Press, 1946, p. 128.
13. Freud, Sigmund. Dostoevsky and parricide. In: Strachey, James (Ed.), *Collected Papers*. New York: Basic Books, 1959, Vol. V, pp. 240-241.
14. Galdston, Iago. The psychodynamics of the triad, alcoholism, gambling, and superstition. *Ment. Hyg.*, 35:293, 1951.
15. Gallagher, J. Roswell, & Harris, Herbert I. *Emotional Problems of Adolescents*. New York: Oxford University Press, 1958, p. 160.
16. Greenson, Ralph R. On gambling. *Amer. Imago*, 4:61-77, 1947.
17. Havighurst, Robert J., & Taba, Hilda. *Adolescent Character and Personality*. New York: John Wiley & Sons, 1949, pp. 83-87.
18. Hutt, Max L., & Gibby, Robert G. *The Child*. Boston: Allyn & Bacon, 1959, p. 178.

19. Jacob, Philip E. *Changing Values in College*. New York: Harper & Bros., 1957, p. 2.
20. Jersild, Arthur T. *The Psychology of Adolescence*. New York: Macmillan Co., 1957, p. 363.
21. Jones, Ernest. The problem of Paul Morphy. A contribution to the psycho-analysis of chess. *Int. J. Psychoanal.*, 12:1-23, 1931.
22. Kiell, Norman. The behavior of five adolescent poker players. *J. Human Relations*, 3:80, 1957.
23. Lindner, Robert. The psychodynamics of gambling. In: *Explorations in Psychoanalysis*. New York: Julian Press, 1953, pp. 212, 215, 217.
24. McGlothlin, William H. A psychometric study of gambling. *J. Consult. Psychol.*, 18:149, 1954.
25. Nicolson, Harold. Introduction to Benjamin Constant's *The Red Notebook*. New York: New American Library, 1959, pp. vii-xxvi.
26. Padover, Saul K. (Ed.). *Confessions and Self-Portraits. 4600 Years of Autobiography*. New York: John Day Co., 1957.
27. Reik, Theodor. The study of Dostoevsky. In: *Thirty Years with Freud*. New York: International Universities Press, 1940.
28. Rousseau, Jean Jacques. *Confessions*. New York: Modern Library, 1945, p. 38.
29. Shaffer, Laurance, & Shoben, Edward J., Jr. *The Psychology of Adjustment*. Boston: Houghton Mifflin Co., 1956, p. 357.
30. Simmel, Ernst. Psycho-analysis of the gambler. *Int. J. Psychoanal.*, 1:353, 1920.
31. Steffens, Lincoln. *Autobiography*. New York: Harcourt, Brace & Co., 1931, p. 122-123.
32. Zunz, Leopold. *Diary*. In: Schwarz, Leo W. (Ed.), *Memoirs of My People*. New York: Farrar & Rinehart, 1943, p. 321.

CHAPTER EIGHTEEN

Toward Adulthood

The primary task of adolescence is to achieve maturity. This is true for all cultures, although societies differ in the degrees to which they accord adult status to the adolescent. These variations tend to confuse the question, when does an adolescent become an adult? A society may permit considerable freedom in one sphere, e.g., sexual behavior, but be highly restrictive in another, e.g., permitting the youngster to attain full economic status (4, pp. 11-12). In other societies, the adolescent may be barred from participating in ceremonial rites while granted nearly complete sexual and economic freedom of expression. To compound the complication, even when certain adult privileges are granted, the major sphere of adult activity may be denied to the adolescent because of competitive reasons, with the result that the remaining granted privileges may pale into insignificance or become vitally affected.

However, as Bloch and Niederhoffer emphasize, "The adolescent period in all cultures, visualized as a phase of striving for the attainment of adult status, produces experiences which are much the same for all youths, and certain common dynamisms for expressing reaction to such subjectively held experiences. The intensity of the adolescent experience and the vehemence of external expression depend on a variety of factors, including the general societal attitudes toward adolescence, the duration of the adolescent period itself, and the degree to which the society tends to facilitate entrance into adulthood by virtue of institutionalized patterns, ceremonials, rites and rituals, and socially supported emotional and intellectual preparation. When a society does not make adequate preparation, formal or otherwise, for the induction of its adolescents to the adult status, equivalent forms of behavior arise spontaneously among adolescents themselves, reinforced by their own group structure, which seemingly provides the same psychological content and function as the more formalized rituals found in other societies [5]." From their findings, Bloch and Niederhoffer conclude "that the strains toward adulthood in all cultures provide only a limited number of alternatives—a limitation of possibilities—in which the adolescent may express himself, irrespective of how widely such expressive forms may differ in content. Thus, what we may be observing is a universal psychodynamic pattern during the adolescent stage which is present in all cultures but which may assume a wide variety of expressive forms [4, p. 140]."

Nearly every current text dealing with the problems of adolescence stresses the difficulty the individual has in closing the gap between youth and maturity, putting the major responsibility for it on the highly developed, rapidly changing industrial and technical society in which the adolescent lives. The rapidity of change tends to produce confusion and to prolong the age period. "Many of the mechanisms of adjustment," Erikson (8) writes, "which once made for evolutionary adaptation, tribal integration, national or class coherence, are at loose ends in a world of universally expanding identities. Education for an ego identity which receives strength from changing historical conditions demands a conscious acceptance of historical heterogeneity on the part of adults, combined with an enlightened effort to provide human childhood anywhere with a new fund of meaningful continuity."

That there is evidence for such continuity can be seen, for example, in the *Autobiography* of Thomas DeQuincey, written more than a hundred years ago. Like the current textbooks, DeQuincey (6, p. 317) asks, "When, by what test, by what indication, does manhood commence? Physically by one criterion, legally by another, morally by a third, intellectually by a fourth—and all indefinite. Equator, absolute equator, there is none. Between the two spheres of youth and age, perfect and imperfect manhood, as in all analogous cases, there is no strict line of bisection." Nearly two hundred years ago, a sixteen-year-old Quaker girl, Elizabeth Fry (1780-1845), entered in her diary, "I feel by experience how much entering the world hurts me; worldly company I think materially injures, it excites a false stimulus, such a love of pomp, pride, vanity, jealousy and ambition; it leads to think about dress and such trifles and when out of it we fly to novels and scandal or something of that kind for entertainment [12]."

Thus, the difficulty the adolescent faces in his quest for mature status is not peculiar to this century or generation—nor to Western culture. In Margaret Mead's description of coming of age in Samoa (16), the adolescent passes from puberty into adulthood without protracted conflict. But the Samoans reveal little of an affective nature; there is such a paucity of affect they seem undifferentiated and insufficiently characterized, which, in and of itself, presents difficulties. "In other simple cultures, in which the role of the adult is likewise thoroughly familiar to the child by the time he reaches puberty, the young are initiated into adult life much more harshly. Sometimes the process is more loving than it appears to be, though the very fact that adults find it necessary to inflict it is conclusive evidence of some hostility toward the young. . . . Some of these cultures are primitive; others are relatively stable subcultures of the Western world like that of the British coal miners whose sons are hazed into adult status by their elders when they first enter the mines themselves. But in these as well, the adults seem curiously indistinguishable by our criteria of personality. Differences of temperament and attitude toward life may be very conspicuous indeed. But they stop short of what we regard as normal variation of human personality; the range is wide, but not as deep [11]."

Societies in every culture have certain definite expectations in regard to the conduct of adolescents. Even though there is no consensus of values and no consistency in adult behavior, roughly the same characteristics mark adolescence in all civilizations. The period of puberty represents the first powerful forward thrust into the previously barred world of adulthood, for which all else has been preparation; this seems to be well established in all societies irrespective of the age level at which adolescence is officially recognized and whether the age level coincides naturally with the physiological changes of puberty (4, p. 68). The nature of the barrier between adolescence and adulthood is determined partly by the behavioral limitations of the individual adolescent and partly by the social pressure from adults and other adolescents (2). While puberty appears at about the same ages in all races and in all societies, the ages at which adult roles are assumed vary considerably among societies and even among social milieus (13).

The discrepancy between the requirements of childhood and those of adulthood can create conflicts which may become severe in adolescence. In all societies, adolescents achieve new privileges, but they must also assume new responsibilities. "They must prove their worth sexually, socially, economically. They are expected to pursue and control their sexual drives according to modes predetermined by the given culture. They must evolve into approved versions of men and women [1]." According to Inhelder and Piaget (13), "the adolescent manifestation of egocentrism stems directly from the adoption of adult roles, since the adolescent not only tries to adapt his ego to the social environment but, just as emphatically, tries to adjust the environment to his ego. In other words, when he begins to think about the society in which he is looking for a place, he has to think about his own future activity and about how he himself might transform this society. The result is a relative failure to distinguish between his own point of view as an individual called upon to organize a life program and the point of view of the group which he hopes to reform."

The drive toward adulthood necessarily implies emancipation, involving a drastic change in the adolescent's relationship with the very people toward whom he felt the strongest dependency in his childhood years (17). The adolescent process is conclusively complete only when "the individual has subordinated his childhood identifications to a new kind of identification, achieved in absorbing sociability and in competitive apprenticeship with and among his age-mates. These new identifications are no longer characterized by the playfulness of childhood and the experimental zest of youth: with dire urgency they force the young individual into choices and decisions which will, with increasing immediacy, lead to a more final self-definition, to irreversible role pattern, and thus to commitments 'for life' [9]."

This final self-definition is achieved when the incestuous attachment to the parent is abandoned and a strange love object is found who is loved, as Jones indicated, not only with feelings of an "inhibited" nature but also with those of a directly sexual kind. "When this process is complete, then adult independence is achieved in all

respects. Dependence can therefore be defined as persistent incestuous attachment of the libido and independence as the disposal of
it in some other direction [14, p. 45]." Deutsch amplifies this view-
point when she signifies that the task of adolescence is above all else
to develop from the phase of intensified narcissism to that of object
relations and to achieve in these a favorable unification of the affections and instinctual drives. "The fact that, shortly before the new
objects are found, the rising instinctual drives turn for a time to the
old objects, creates a characteristic difficulty in adolescence. Affective struggles take place between an intense desire to 'get away'
and an equally intense urge to 'go back,' and this backward movement, which is now endowed with sexual force, actually arises from
the re-establishment of an old situation that existed before the beginning of the latency period. For this reason adolescence has been
called a new edition of the oedipus complex, and its task has been
defined as the sloughing off of this complex. . . . Thus the task of
adolescence is not only to master the oedpius complex, but also to
continue the work begun during prepuberty, that is, to give adult
forms to the old, much deeper, and much more primitive ties with
the mother, and to end all bisexual wavering in favor of a definite
heterosexual orientation [7]."

The achievement of maturity is attained by the adolescent in a
variety of ways, as the illustrations from the personal documents
which follow will show. The process is generally a painful one and
success is usually achieved with some residual emotional scar tissue.
The Dutch boy, David DeJong (5), reports about himself that "innocence seemed to be fleeing almost visibly away from me, looking
over her shoulder like a shy filly but also showing no real inclination
to return. I marvelled at this, and regretted it, but could do nothing
to prevent it." The American novelist, MacKinley Kantor (15),
remembers, "My first maturity was like a blended liqueur distilled
from the wines of worry and of pain. While in the role of coltish boyhood I rambled, shouted and scampered along with a pack of other
rapscallions not yet dressed in the fuzz of puberty, still I was conscious of the agonies experienced by unglimpsed people all thousands of miles distant. I lay suffering with them in my dreams; in
waking moments, personal problems were nettles on my skin." The
eloquent Frenchwoman, Simone de Beauvoir (3), recalls, "Bathed
in the sunset glow, with the world crouched at my feet like a big

friendly animal, I smiled to myself at the adolescent who would die on the morrow only to rise again in all her glory: no other life, no moment in any other life could hold all the promises which were thrilling to my credulous heart."

Perhaps there is some significance to the fact that each of these three authors used the analogy of animal life to their own stage of development. DeJong conjured up a shy filly, Kantor a colt, and de Beauvoir a big, friendly animal. Besides being powerful phallic representations equated with the father, are these animal figures a symbolic plea for kindness to the dumb, equine-like, marginal adolescent who is on the periphery of two groups, the animal and the human—childhood and adulthood—belonging to both yet belonging to neither? Is this period of transition, in which the individual is shifting his identification from childhood to maturity so uncomfortable that the adolescent is forced to construct a (nonhuman) world of his own? Still another contemporary writer, Herman Wouk, the creator of *The Caine Mutiny* and the autobiographical novel, *City Boy*, associated with the equine world to define his feelings about adolescence: "I do not think I am wrong in remembering the teens as an uncomfortable, on the whole, a wretched, time. To the staggering colt, the world around him must seem a drunkenly reeling nightmare of sights and sounds. I understood very little of what was happening around me. It was like living in a foreign country, vainly pretending to be a native and getting mocked at and fleeced from all sides. And there was this brutal joke that nature had played, springing the feverish puzzle of sex at a time when I was barely learning to read and write and to navigate among the common dangers of existence. Girls were half marvels and half horrors. Adults were unfriendly, nagging nuisances. Education was an old man of the sea, and the social code existed to make a lout of me. I felt I would be a lumpy, pimply fifteen forever. Maybe I had a high old time and was a glamorous, enviable figure. I do not remember it that way [19]."

Ernest Jones (14), in his paper, "Some Problems of Adolescence," attempted to get at the essence of the business of "growing up," to assess the forces bringing it about or impeding it, and to what extent, and with what results, it is usually achieved. "What," he asked, "is actually effected during this transitional stage of adolescence, when the child becomes the man? . . . One might think that it would be no very formidable task to establish the most notable differences between a child and an adult, but I can only say that on attempting it I found it extremely difficult." Nevertheless, Jones did cite certain evidence to distinguish the two age groups: (1) the greater intellectual powers of the adult; (2) the higher degree of integration in the adult; (3) a higher form of fantasy life, more closely related to reality; (4) specific changes in the individual's relationship to others; and (5) sexual maturity. These, then, would seem to be the important changes that must be effected for the child to become an adult, and which are transmitted through the transitional stage of adolescence.

Thomas DeQuincey
(1785-1859)

In this blistering chapter from his *Autobiography* (6), Thomas De-Quincey asks—several times—"How, under so variable a standard, both natural and conventional of everything almost that can be received for a test or a presumption of manhood, shall we seize upon any characteristic feature, sufficiently universal to serve as a *practical* use, as a criterion of the transition from the childish mind to the dignity (relative dignity, at least) of that mind which belongs to conscious maturity?"

The single criterion DeQuincey established lay "in the reverential feeling, sometimes suddenly developed, towards woman, and the idea of woman." This is remarkably akin to psychoanalytic theory as stated by Freud and as expressed by Jones in the introduction to this chapter. The human being progresses in his sexual life from autoerotism, narcissism, and homosexuality to heteroerotism; the adult stage is reached when the incestuous attachments are abandoned. It is then that full adult independence is achieved.

DeQuincey brings up, in his first paragraph, an area of the problem of achieving maturity which is receiving especial attention today, but which, even one hundred years ago, he recognized. This deals with the prolongation of adolescence because of the lengthening years spent in college. Erikson has spoken directly to this point. "Among the special institutions designed for (late adolescence), college education is probably the greatest organized artificial postponement of adulthood, emotionally speaking, that could be imagined.

There were always periods of apprenticeship, in any cultural system, in any culture, which would lead at a reasonable date to the individual entering the life of his people as a worker, earner and homemaker, and thus emancipating himself from his parents' home. College education is one among many of those long apprenticeships of our time, which are getting longer and more specialized, and constitutes a most radical postponement of some emotional satisfactions and a replacement of them by others. It fosters particular forms of extended childishness even as it cultivates certain forms of one-sided precocity. This is so whether or not college education is more a means to an end, such as a trade or profession, or whether it is more an end in itself, as it becomes in some of our alumni who acquire a kind of college identity for life. In some cultures the pursuit of knowledge is the only decent way to escape from one's childhood home and yet to postpone establishing one's own. It offers . . . a 'psychological moratorium' [10]."

This present chapter, it may seem, promises something of the same episodical or parenthetic character. But in reality it does not. I am now returning into the main current of my narrative, although I may need to linger for a moment upon a past anecdote. I have mentioned already that, on inquiring at the Birmingham Post-office for a letter addressed to myself, I found one directing me to join my sister Mary at Laxton, a seat of Lord Carbery's in Northamptonshire, and giving me to understand, that, during my residence at this place, some fixed resolution would be taken and announced to me in regard to the future disposal of my time, during the two or three years before I should be old enough on the English system for matriculating at Oxford or Cambridge. In the poor countries of Europe, where they cannot afford double sets of scholastic establishments,—having, therefore, no splendid schools, such as are, in fact, peculiar to England,— they are compelled to throw the duties of such schools upon their universities; and consequently you see boys of thirteen and fourteen, or even younger, crowding such institutions, which, in fact, they ruin for all higher functions. But England, whose regal establishments of both classes emancipate her from this dependency, sends her young men to college not until they have ceased to be boys—not earlier, therefore, than eighteen.

But when, by what test, by what indication, does manhood commence? Physically by one criterion, legally by another, morally by a third, intellectually by a fourth—and all indefinite. Equator, absolute equator, there is none. Between the two spheres of youth and age, perfect and imperfect manhood, as in all analogous cases, there is no strict line of bisection. The change is a large process, accomplished within a large and corresponding space; having, perhaps, some central or equatorial line, but lying, like that of our earth, between certain tropics, or limits widely separated. This *intertropical* region may, and generally does, cover a number of years; and, therefore, it is hard to say, even for an assigned case, by any tolerable approximation, at what precise era it would be reasonable to describe the individual as having ceased to be a boy, and as having attained his inauguration as a man. Physically, we know that there is a very large latitude of differences, in the periods of human maturity, not merely between individual and individual, but also between nation and nation; differences so great, that, in some southern regions of Asia, we hear of matrons at the age of twelve. And though, as Mr. Sadler rightly insists, a romance of exaggeration has been built upon the facts, enough remains behind a real marvel to irritate the curiosity of the physiologist, as to its efficient, and, perhaps, of the philosopher, as to its final cause. Legally and politically, that is conventionally, the differences are even greater on a comparison of nations and eras. In England we have seen senators of mark and authority, nay, even a prime minister, the haughtiest, the most despotic, and the most irresponsible of his times, at an age which, in many states, both ancient and modern, would have operated as a ground of absolute challenge to the candidate for offices the meanest. Intellectually speaking, again, a very large proportion of men *never* attain maturity. Nonage is their final destiny; and manhood, in this respect, is for them a pure idea. Finally, as regards the moral development—by which I mean the whole system and economy of their love and hatred, of their admirations and contempts, the total organisation of their pleasures and their pains—hardly any of our species ever attain manhood. It would be unphilosophic to say that intellects of the *highest* order were, or could be, developed fully, without a corresponding development of the whole nature. But of such intellects there do not appear above two or three in a thousand years. It is a fact, forced upon one by the whole experience of life, that almost all men are children, more or less, in their tastes and admirations. Were it not for man's latent tendencies—were it not for that imperishable grandeur which exists by way of germ and ultimate possibility in his nature, hidden though it is, and often all but effaced—how unlimited would be the contempt amongst all the wise for his species; and misanthropy would, but for the angelic ideal buried and imbruted in man's sordid race, become, amongst the noble, fixed, absolute, and deliberately cherished.

But, to resume my question, how, under so variable a standard, both natural and conventional, of everything almost that can be received for a test or a presumption of manhood, shall we seize upon any characteristic feature, sufficiently universal to serve a *practical* use, as a criterion of the transition from the childish mind to the dignity (relative dignity, at least) of that mind which belongs to conscious maturity? One such criterion, and one only, as I believe, there is—all others are variable and uncertain. It lies in the reverential feeling, sometimes suddenly developed, towards woman, and the idea of woman. From that moment when women cease to be regarded with carelessness, and when the ideal of womanhood, in its total pomp of loveliness and purity, dawns like some vast aurora upon the mind, boyhood has ended; childish thoughts and inclinations have passed away for ever; and the gravity of manhood, with the self-respecting views of manhood, have commenced.

> Mentemque priorem
> Expulit, atque hominem toto sibi cedere jussit
> Pectore.—*Lucan*

These feelings, no doubt, depend for their development in part upon physical causes; but they are also determined by the many retarding or accelerating forces enveloped in circumstances of position, and sometimes in pure accident. For myself, I remember most distinctly the very day—the scene, and its accidents—when that mysterious awe fell upon me which belongs to woman in her ideal portrait: and from that hour a profounder gravity coloured all my thoughts, and a "beauty still more beauteous" was lit up for me in this agitating world. Lord Westport and myself had been on a visit to a noble family about fifty miles from Dublin; and we were returning from Tullamore by a public passage-boat on the splendid canal which connects that place with the metropolis. To avoid attracting an unpleasant attention to ourselves in public situations, I observed a rule of never addressing Lord Westport by his title: but it so happened that the canal carried us along the margin of an estate belonging to the Earl (now Marquis) of Westmeath; and on turning an angle we came suddenly in view of this nobleman taking his morning lounge in the sun. Somewhat loftily he reconnoitred the miscellaneous party of clean and unclean beasts crowded on the deck of our ark, ourselves amongst the number, whom he challenged gaily as young acquaintances from Dublin; and my friend he saluted more than once as "My Lord." This accident made known to the assembled mob of our fellow-travellers Lord Westport's rank, and led to a scene rather too broadly exposing the spirit of this world. Herded together on the deck (or roof of that den denominated the "*state*-cabin") stood a party of young ladies, headed by their governess. In the cabin below was mamma, who as yet had not condescended to illuminate our circle, for she was an awful personage —a wit, a bluestocking (I call her by the name then current), and a leader of *ton* in Dublin and Belfast. The fact, however, that a young lord, and one of great expectations, was on board brought her up. A short cross-examination of Lord Westport's French valet had confirmed the flying report, and at the same time (I suppose) put her in possession of my defect in all those advantages of title, fortune, and expectation which so brilliantly distinguished my friend. Her admiration of him, and her contempt for myself, were equally undisguised. And in the ring which she soon cleared out for public exhibition, she made us both fully sensible of the very equitable stations which she assigned to us in her regard. She was neither very brilliant nor altogether a pretender, but might be described as a showy woman, of slight but popular accomplishments. Any woman, however, has the advantage of possessing the ear of any company: and a woman of forty, with such tact and experience as she will naturally have gathered in a talking practice of such duration, can find little difficulty in mortifying a boy, or sometimes, perhaps, in tempting him to unfortunate sallies of irritation. Me, it was clear, that she viewed in the light of a humble friend, or what is known in fashionable life by the humiliating name of a "toad-eater." Lord Westport, full of generosity in what regarded his own pretensions, and who never had violated the perfect equality which reigned in our deportment to each other, coloured with as much confusion as myself at her coarse insinuations. And, in reality, our ages scarcely allowed of that relation which she supposed to exist between us. Possibly, she did *not* suppose it: but it is essential to the wit and the display of some people that it should have a foundation in malice. A victim and a sacrifice are indispensable conditions in every exhibition. In such a case, my natural sense of justice would generally have armed me a hundredfold for retaliation; but at present—chiefly, perhaps, because I had no effectual ally, and could count upon no sympathy in my audience—I was mortified beyond the power of retort, and became a passive butt to the lady's stinging contumely, and the arrowy sleet of her gay rhetoric. The narrow bounds of our deck made it not easy to get beyond talking-range; and thus it happened that for two hours I stood the worst of this bright lady's feud. At length the tables turned. Two ladies appeared slowly ascending from the cabin, both in deepest mourning, but else as different in aspect as summer and winter. The elder was the Countess of Errol, then mourning an affliction which had laid her life desolate, and admitted of no human consolation. Heavier grief—grief more self-occupied and deaf to all voice of sympathy—I have not happened to witness. She seemed scarcely aware of our presence, except it were by placing herself as far as was possible from the annoyance of our odious conversation. The circumstances of her loss are now forgotten; at that time they were known to a large circle in Bath and London, and I violate no confidence in reviewing them. Lord Errol had been privately instrusted by Mr. Pitt with an official secret—viz., the outline and principle details of a foreign expedition; in which, according to Mr. Pitt's original purpose, his lordship was to have held a high command. In a moment of intoxication, the earl confided this secret to some false friend, who published the communication and its author. Upon this, the unhappy nobleman, under too keen a sense of wounded honour, and perhaps with an exaggerated notion of the evils attached to his indiscretion, destroyed himself. Months had passed since that calamity, when we met his widow; but time appeared to have done nothing in mitigating her sorrow. The younger lady, on the other hand, who was Lady Errol's sister—Heavens! what a spirit of joy and festal pleasure radiated from her eyes, her step, her voice, her manner! She was Irish, and the very impersonation of innocent gaiety, such as we find oftener, perhaps, amongst Irish women than those of any other country. Mourning, I have said, she wore; from sisterly consideration, the deepest mourning: that sole expression there was about her of gloom or solemn feeling—

> But all things else about her drawn
> From May-time and the cheerful dawn.

Odious bluestocking of Belfast and Dublin! as some would call you, how I hated you up to that moment! half-an-hour after, how grateful I felt for the hostility which had procured me such an alliance. One minute sufficed to put the quick-witted young Irishwoman in possession of our little drama, and the several parts we were playing. To look was to understand, to wish was to execute, with this ardent child of nature. Like Spenser's Bradamant, with martial scorn she couched her lance on the side of the party suffering wrong. Her rank, as sister-in-law to the Constable of Scotland, gave her some advantage for winning a favourable audience; and, throwing her ægis over me, she extended that benefit to myself. Road was now made perforce for me also; my replies were no longer stifled in noise and laughter. Personalities were banished; literature was extensively discussed; and that is a subject which, offering little room to argument, offers the widest to eloquent display. I had immense reading; vast command of words, which somewhat diminished as ideas and doubts multiplied; and, speaking no longer to a deaf audience, but to a generous and indulgent protectress, I threw out, as from a cornucopia, my illustrative details and recollections; trivial enough, perhaps, as I might now think, but the more intelligible to my present circle. It might seem too much the case of a storm in a slop-basin, if I were to spend any words upon the revolution which ensued. Suffice it that I remained the lion of that company which had previously been most insultingly facetious at my expense; and the intellectual lady finally declared the air of the deck unpleasant.

Never, until this hour, had I thought of women as objects of a possible interest, or of a reverential love. I had known them either in their infirmities and their unamiable aspects, or else in those sterner relations which made them objects of ungenial and uncompanionable feelings. Now first it struck me that life might owe half its attractions and all its graces to female companionship. Gazing, perhaps, with too earnest an admiration at this generous and spirited young daughter of Ireland, and in that way making her those acknowledgments for her goodness which I could not properly clothe in words, I was roused to a sense of my indecorum by seeing her suddenly blush. I believe that Miss Bl—— interpreted my admiration rightly; for she was not offended; but, on the contrary, for the rest of the day, when not attending to her sister, conversed almost exclusively, and in a confidential way, with Lord Westport and myself. The whole, in fact, of this conversation must have convinced her that I, mere boy as I was (viz., about fifteen), could not have presumed to direct my admiration to *her,* a fine young woman of twenty, in any other character than that of a generous champion, and a very adroit mistress in the dazzling fence of colloquial skirmish. My admiration had, in reality, been addressed to her moral qualities, her enthusiasm, her spirit, and her generosity. Yet that blush, evanescent as it was—the mere possibility that I, so very a child, should have called up the most transitory sense of bashfulness or confusion upon any female cheek, first—and suddenly as with a flash of lightning penetrating some utter darkness—illuminated to my own startled consciousness, never again to be obscured, the pure and powerful ideal of womanhood and womanly excellence. This was, in a proper sense, a *revelation;* it fixed a great era of change in my life; and, this new-born idea being agreeable to the uniform tendencies of my own nature—that is, lofty and aspiring—it governed my life with great power, and with most salutary effects. Ever after, throughout the period of youth, I was jealous of my own demeanour, reserved and awe-struck in the presence of women; reverencing, often, not so much *them,* as my own ideal of woman latent in them. For I carried about with me the idea, to which often I seemed to see an approximation, of

> A perfect woman, nobly plann'd,
> To warn, to comfort, to command.

And from this day I was an altered creature, never again relapsing into the careless, irreflective mind of childhood.

Charles Leland
(1824-1903)

Charles Leland's evocation of his emancipation—at the age of sixteen—from short jackets and pants, and of the finally found freedom to go about the city of Philadelphia alone is typical of the experience of many city-bred adolescents with overprotective parents. The repression of his personal freedom, he felt, was particularly harmful to him. He was confused by well-meaning adults who pointed out to him other youths who were earning money and acting like men. He was made to feel inferior and stupid. When the adolescent's status in the culture is ambiguous, such feelings seem to be almost inevitable.*

How happy I was again to see my mother and father and Henry! And then came other joys. My father had taken a very nice house in Walnut Street, in the best quarter of the city, below Thirteenth Street, and this was a source of pleasure, as was also a barrel of apples in the cellar, to which I had free access. They had been doled out to us very sparingly at school, and I never shall forget the delight with which I one day in December at Jamaica Plain discovered a frozen apple on a tree! Then there was the charm of being in a great city, and familiar old scenes, and the freedom from bad marks, and being ruled

*From *Memoirs* by Charles Leland. Reprinted by permission of Appleton-Century-Crofts, Inc. 1893. Pp. 65-66.

into bounds, and sent to bed at early hours. There is, in certain cases, a degree of moral restraint and discipline which is often carried much too far, especially where boys are brought up with a view to pushing themselves in the world. I was sixteen years of age and six feet high before I was allowed to leave off short jackets, go to a theatre, or travel alone, all of which was more injurious to me, I believe, than ordinary youthful dissipation would have been, especially in America. Yet, while thus repressed, I was being continually referred by all grown-up friends to enterprising youth of my own age, who were making a living in bankers' or conveyancers' offices, &c., and acting "like men." The result really being that I was completely convinced that I was a person of feeble and inferior capacity as regarded all that was worth doing or knowing in life, though Heaven knows my very delicate health and long illnesses might of themselves have excused all my failings. The vast majority of Americans, however kind and generous they may be in other respects, are absolutely without mercy or common-sense as regards the not succeeding in life or making money. Such, at least, was my experience, and bitter it was. Elders often forget that even obedience, civility, and morality in youth are luxuries which must be paid for like all other extravagances at a high price, especially in children of feeble constitution. The dear boy grows up "as good as pie," and, being pious, "does not know one card from another," nor one human being from another. You make of him a fool, and then call him one—I mean, what you regard as a fool. I am not at all sure that one or two cruises in a slaver (there were plenty of them sailing out of New York in those days) would not have done me far more good of a certain kind than all the education I had till I left college in America. I am not here complaining, as most weak men do, as if they were specially victims to a wretched fate and a might-have-been-better. The vast majority of boys have not better homes or education, kinder parents, or advantages greater than mine were. But as I do not recall my boyhood's days or my youth till I left college with that *joyousness* which I find in other men without exception, and as, in fact, there always seems as if a cloud were over it all, while from below there was a low continual murmur as of a patient soul in pain, I feel that there was something wrong in it all, as there indeed was.

W. H. Hudson
(1841-1922)

The author of the idyllic *Green Mansions*, the locale of which is the remote, lush jungles of South America, was himself born and raised in the back country of Argentina. Up to the time in his adolescence when he became ill, his life was an idyll, too, in many ways. He recalled his reluctance, at the age of fifteen, to accept his growing maturity and the apprehension with which he faced it. The greater part of him wanted to persist in the childhood freedoms he enjoyed, particularly through his delight in nature which he felt to be an "enchanted realm . . . at once natural and supernatural." He dreaded the thought of becoming more and more absorbed in the dull business of life, which adulthood inevitably enforced on one.*

Fifteen years old! This was indeed the most memorable day of my life, for on that evening I began to think about myself, and my thoughts were strange and unhappy thoughts to me—what I was, what I was in the world for, what I wanted, what destiny was going to make of me! Or was it for me to do just what I wished, to shape my own destiny, as my elder brothers had done? It was the first time such questions had come to me, and I was startled at them. It was as though I had only just become conscious; I doubt that I had ever been fully conscious before. I had lived till now in a paradise of vivid sense-impressions in which all thoughts came to me saturated with emotion, and in that mental state reflection is well-nigh impossible. Even the idea of death, which had come as a surprise, had not made me reflect. Death was a person, a monstrous being who had sprung upon me in my flowery paradise and had inflicted a wound with a poisoned dagger in my flesh. Then had come the knowledge of immortality for the soul, and the wound was healed, or partly so, for a time at all events; after which the one thought that seriously troubled me was that I could not always remain a boy. To pass from boyhood to manhood was not so bad as dying; nevertheless it was a change painful to contemplate. That everlasting delight and wonder, rising to rapture, which was in the child and boy, would wither away and vanish, and in its place there would be that dull low kind of satisfaction which men have in the set task, the daily and hourly intercourse with others of a like condition, and in eating and drinking and sleeping. I could not, for example, think of so advanced an age as fifteen without the keenest apprehension. And now I was actually at that age—at that parting of the ways, as it seemed to me.

What, then, did I want?—what did I ask to have? If the question

*From *Far Away and Long Ago* by W. H. Hudson. Reprinted by permission of E. P. Dutton & Co., Inc. Copyright 1918, E. P. Dutton & Co., Inc.; 1946, Royal Society for the Protection of Birds. Pp. 292-295.

had been put to me then, and if I had been capable of expressing what was in me, I should have replied: I want only to keep what I have; to rise each morning and look out on the sky and the grassy dew-wet earth from day to day, from year to year. To watch every June and July for spring, to feel the same old sweet surprise and delight at the appearance of each familiar flower, every new-born insect, every bird returned once more from the north. To listen in a trance of delight to the wild notes of the golden plover coming once more to the great plain, flying, flying south, flock succeeding flock the whole day long. Oh, those wild beautiful cries of the golden plover! I could exclaim with Hafiz, with but one word changed: "If after a thousand years that sound should float o'er my tomb, my bones uprising in their gladness would dance in the sepulchre!" To climb trees and put my hand down in the deep hot nest of the Bierte-veo and feel the hot eggs—the five long pointed cream-coloured eggs with chocolate spots and splashes at the larger end. To lie on a grassy bank with the blue water between me and beds of tall bulrushes, listening to the mysterious sounds of the wind and of hidden rails and coots and courlans conversing together in strange human-like tones; to let my sight dwell and feast on the *camaloté* flower amid its floating masses of moist vivid green leaves—the large alamanda-like flower of a purest divine yellow that when plucked sheds its lovely petals, to leave you with nothing but a green stem in your hand. To ride at noon on the hottest days, when the whole earth is a-glitter with illusory water, and see the cattle and horses in thousands, covering the plain at their watering-places; to visit some haunt of large birds at that still, hot hour and see storks, ibises, grey herons, egrets of a dazzling whiteness, and rose-coloured spoonbills and flamingoes, standing in the shallow water in which their motionless forms are reflected. To lie on my back on the rust-brown grass in January and gaze up at the wide hot whitey-blue sky, peopled with millions and myriads of glistening balls of thistle-down, ever, ever floating by; to gaze and gaze until they are to me living things and I, in an ecstasy, am with them, floating in that immense shining void!

And now it seemed that I was about to lose it—this glad emotion which had made the world what it was to me, an enchanted realm, a nature at once natural and supernatural; it would fade and lessen imperceptibly day by day, year by year, as I became more and more absorbed in the dull business of life, until it would be lost as effectually as if I had ceased to see and hear and palpitate, and my warm body had grown cold and stiff in death, and, like the dead and the living, I should be unconscious of my loss.

It was not a unique nor a singular feeling: it is known to other boys, as I have read and heard; also I have occasionally met with one who, in a rare moment of confidence, has confessed that he has been troubled at times at the thought of all he would lose. But I doubt that it was ever more keenly felt than in my case; I doubt, too, that it is common or strong in English boys, considering the conditions in which they exist. For restraint is irksome to all beings, from a black-beetle or an earthworm to an eagle, or, to go higher still in the scale, to an orang-u-tan or a man; it is felt most keenly by the young, in our species at all events, and the British boy suffers the greatest restraint during the period when the call of nature, the instincts of play and adventure, are most urgent. Naturally, he looks eagerly forward to the time of escape, which he fondly imagines will be when his boyhood is over and he is free of masters.

Henry M. Stanley
(1841-1904)

Henry M. Stanley has become immortal for most people because of his highly formal greeting in the heart of the wild African jungle, "Dr. Livingstone, I presume?" Stanley's whole life was a search for identification and for a father. He was an illegitimate child who never knew his father's name; the one he made famous had been given him by an American benefactor. John Rowlands, by which name Stanley was baptized, was brought up first by his maternal grandfather and after the latter's death was boarded out with a maternal uncle at half a crown a week. When he was six years old, the boy was tricked into being placed at The Workhouse at St. Asaph in Wales, where he remained until he ran away at fifteen.

Stanley's *Autobiography* reveals his feelings, particularly during childhood and adolescence, of rejection and abandonment, his detachment from others, and his desperate need for affection, friendship and a sense of belonging. At St. Asaph's Workhouse, Stanley was subjected to its rigid discipline which was one of such severity that most of its population seemed molded into homogeneous, obedient, brain-washed robots, with few differentiated personality traits.

A kind of maturity came to Stanley abruptly and without warning, precipitated by the folly and brutality of his teacher at the orphanage, one James Francis. Francis had been working as a collier at Mold until he met with an accident which deprived him of his left hand. As he had some education he was appointed Master at St. Asaph Union, where he remained for many years. He became more and more savage, until it was discovered he was psychotic and he later died in a mental institution. This is the man Stanley is describing in the following excerpt* and who unwittingly helped the youth achieve a certain independence.

Not many weeks after Francis had returned from Mold, an event occurred which had a lasting influence on my life. But for the stupid and brutal scene which brought it about, I might eventually have been apprenticed to some trade or another, and would have mildewed in Wales, because, with some knowledge of my disposition, I require great cause to break away from associations. Unknown to myself, and unperceived by anyone else, I had arrived at the parting of the ways. Unconsciously I had contracted ideas about dignity, and the promise of manhood was manifest in the first buds of pride, courage, and resolution; but our school-master, exposed to moods of savage temper, and arbitrary from habit, had failed to notice the change.

In May, 1856, a new deal table had been ordered for the school, and some heedless urchin had dented its surface by standing on it, which so provoked Francis that he fell into a furious rage, and uttered terrific threats with the air of one resolved on massacre. He seized a birch which, as yet, had not been bloodied, and, striding furiously up to the first class, he demanded to know the culprit. It was a question that most of us would have preferred to answer straight off; but we were all absolutely ignorant that any damage had been made, and probably the author of it was equally unaware of it. No one could remember to have seen anyone standing on the table, and in what other manner more dents had been impressed in the soft deal wood was inexplicable. We all answered accordingly.

"Very well, then," said he, "the entire class will be flogged, and, if confession is not made, I will proceed with the second, and afterwards with the third. Unbutton."

He commenced at the foot of the class, and there was the usual yelling, and writhing, and shedding of showers of tears. One or two of David's oaken fibre submitted to the lacerating strokes with a silent squirm or two, and now it was fast approaching my turn; but instead of the old timidity and other symptoms of terror, I felt myself har-

---

*From *Autobiography* by Henry Morton Stanley. Boston: Houghton Mifflin Co. 1909. Pp. 32-34.

dening for resistance. He stood before me vindictively glaring, his spectacles intensifying the gleam of his eyes.

"How is this?" he cried savagely. "Not ready yet? Strip, sir, this minute; I mean to stop this abominable and barefaced lying."

"I did not lie, sir. I know nothing of it."

"Silence, sir. Down with your clothes."

"Never again," I shouted, marvelling at my own audacity.

The words had scarcely escaped me ere I found myself swung upward into the air by the collar of my jacket, and flung into a nerveless heap on the bench. Then the passionate brute pummelled me in the stomach until I fell backward, gasping for breath. Again I was lifted, and dashed on the bench with a shock that almost broke my spine. What little sense was left in me after these repeated shocks made me aware that I was smitten on the cheeks, right and left, and that soon nothing would be left of me but a mass of shattered nerves and bruised muscles.

Recovering my breath, finally, from the pounding in the stomach, I aimed a vigorous kick at the cruel Master as he stooped to me, and, by chance, the booted foot smashed his glasses, and almost blinded him with their splinters. Starting backward with the excruciating pain, he contrived to stumble over a bench, and the back of his head struck the stone floor; but, as he was in the act of falling, I had bounded to my feet, and possessed myself of his blackthorn. Armed with this, I pushed at the prostrate form, and struck him at random over his body, until I was called to a sense of what I was doing by the stirless way he received the thrashing.

I was exceedingly puzzled what to do now. My rage had vanished, and, instead of triumph, there came a feeling that, perhaps, I ought to have endured, instead of resisting. Some one suggested that he had better be carried to his study, and we accordingly dragged him along the floor to the Master's private room, and I remember well how some of the infants in the fourth room commenced to howl with unreasoning terror.

After the door had been closed on him, a dead silence, comparatively, followed. My wits were engaged in unravelling a way out of the curious dilemma in which I found myself. The overthrow of the Master before the school appeared to indicate a new state of things. Having successfully resisted once, it involved a continued resistance, for one would die before submitting again. My friend Mose asked me in a whisper if I knew what was to happen. Was the Master dead? The hideous suggestion changed the whole aspect of my thoughts. My heart began to beat, as my imagination conjured up unknown consequences of the outrage to authority; and I was in a mood to listen to the promptings of Mose that we should abscond. I assented to his proposal, but, first, I sent a boy to find out the condition of the Master, and was relieved to find that he was bathing his face.

Mose and I instantly left the school, for the ostensible purpose of washing the blood from my face; but, as a fact, we climbed over the garden-wall and dropped into Conway's field, and thence hastened through the high corn in the Bodfari direction, as though pursued by bloodhounds.

This, then, was the result of the folly and tyranny of Francis. Boys are curious creatures, innocent as angels, proud as princes, spirited as heroes, vain as peacocks, stubborn as donkeys, silly as colts, and emotional as girls. The budding reason is so young and tender that it is unable to govern such composite creatures. Much may be done with kindness, as much may be done with benevolent justice, but undeserved cruelty is almost sure to ruin them.

We ran away with a boundless belief that beyond the walls lay the peopled South that was next to Heaven for happiness. The singing birds, the rolling coaches, the tides of joyous intercourse, the family groups, the happy hearths, the smiling welcome of our kind, all lay beyond the gates, and these we fled to meet, with the innocence of kids.

John A. Rice
(1888-   )

John Rice, the inspired founder of Black Mountain College in North Carolina and a leading educator, rebelled against the "Shinto" tradition of the genteel South. The title of his autobiography, *I Came Out of the Eighteenth Century,* indicates the measure of his rebellion and the many gallant and unpopular stands he took during his career. His rebelliousness started early in life, predicated as it was on a search for mature, honest and contemporary values. When he was thirteen, he "lived in a between-world, no longer a small boy and not nearly a man." At sixteen, the time he describes in the following passage, Rice was experiencing the ambivalent feelings of yearning to regress to his childhood and regain his "lost wholeness" or to plunge forward toward adulthood, looking for meaning in life, not just knowledge, for merely to know was not enough (18).

In the eighteenth century an awaited illness among young girls was the "green sickness"—the words convey the meaning. The cure was marriage. When the bride turned from the altar and hooked herself to her new husband through the crook of his arm, parents and relatives accepted the symbol with gratitude and dismissed her from their thoughts; for them she ceased to be a person at the moment she became a wife. So it was in the South; a fiction, of course, but fictions are fertilizers of culture.

For a boy, however, there was no such fiction, no easy step into oblivion. He had to become a man, whatever that might mean, and the eventual crook of an arm would only add to his troubles. It was as if he stood, not at the fork of the roads—that figure is too simple—but on the depot platform of any Southern city, surrounded by bawling hack drivers inviting him to perfect destinations; or, to bring him up to date, at a clover-leaf intersection with hundreds of signs and no time to read them, honked at by impatient travelers who think they know where they want to go. It is now that he would like a little peace and quiet, but there is none. Awkward, stumbling, aching, with voice and limbs that fly incontinently out of register, every morning he wakes to the shock of change, and at night, when he reluctantly drags himself to bed, he knows that even his dreams will italicize his fears. This is the time when wise elders will surround a boy with unsolicitous love and leave him to find his own way into manhood. This is the time when nobody lets him alone. He cuts a swath through the room stumbling over chairs and rugs and thoughts, and his father glares. This awful thing was an infant, then he was a boy, now he is a monster. Even his mother may love him too much.

While he was an infant he absorbed knowledge, taking it in through his tissues, with thought or care. Then, in boyhood, he became a collector, of birds' eggs, stamps, tobacco tags, baseball averages, dates— anything that can be arranged in series. But if he is to become a man —some do—he grows tired of counting and collecting, and a terrifying thing happens: he ceases to be a scientist; he begins to ask, "What does it mean?" and with the coming of this question there comes the first step into manhood. To know is not enough.

It hit me about the time we moved to Montgomery. Until then I had been a whole, a self-contained universe; but now when voice and shape and thoughts began to change, this other change came, this disrelish for mere knowledge, this hesitant desire for meaning. At times I scrambled back into childhood, searching for my lost wholeness, wondering whether I should ever be whole again; then there were other, frightening, moments of certainty that I would never be whole again, not in that wholeness.

My father could not understand. No blame to him; he had leapt from childhood into middle age and had forgotten or never known the torture of second birth, of birth into meaning. He thought he knew meaning because he thought he had found final meaning; he had become a Christian and elected to be a preacher at the time when other boys were mere collectors; thought, in fact, that there was only one meaning and, somehow or other, everything must be packed into that. Music had no meaning to him, for music eludes dogma, as painting, and literature, and every created thing. Meaning for him meant purpose, and there was only one purpose. For me, religion had already proved an ineffectual midwife.

The ordeal of parenthood is to admit new premises for old conclusions. In the multiple premises of the nineteenth century there was one constant, God; in the twentieth, none. As to conclusions there was no argument—they were deep in all of us, these old conclusions—we were only seeking new constants; but, by the irony of conflict, there was the center of alienation.

This lapse of communication, long preparing, now became clear to me. I had just made the disturbing discovery, new to me as to every generation but old as Adam, that experiment and experience were not the same thing, that there is in action a quality beyond the reach of the imagination. I hung around my father's study, a very small Lady Macbeth, in manly hope and boyish fear that he would ask me why I was troubled. At last he turned in his swivel chair and said, "What's the matter with you this morning, John Andrew? Why are you so restless? Why aren't you at school?" I told him what had happened. It was like striking him in the face. He sat looking at me through twisted muscles and heard me silently to the end. Then, to my horror, I saw him getting down on his knees and as they touched the floor, heard the familiar words, "Our Heavenly Father ... "

A man may remember his childhood with pleasure, but where is one who does not wince at the memory of his adolescence?

I came sodden to the breakfast table and nibbled where once I had gorged, apologetic because my tossing had rattled the parsonage bedsprings and again waked my father, apologetic when my reports came from school, apologetic for being alive. The doctors were called in. My father remembered, as I more vividly, the year I had spent in bed not long ago, kept firmly there on doctor's orders, and he became afraid. I was in a panic; a year in bed was just what I did not want. They came, looked me over hurriedly—we were preacher's family and there would be no fee—and said, "Take him out of school." What was I to do out of school? "Get him a job," they said, and went.

Arturo Barea
(1897-1957)

The Spanish journalist and essayist, Andrea Barea, several of whose works have been published in the United States (among them are *Lorca, the Poet and His People,* and *Unamuno,* studies in modern European literature and thought), traces through in these four passages* his struggle to receive recognition as an adult. His resentment of the untenable position he was put in by the adults in his world is manifested repeatedly. "The people I knew stopped treating me as a child, but nobody thought of treating me as a man," he complains. He is made to feel ashamed when he becomes interested in raising silkworms because they were considered a child's toy. He cannot order a suit of clothes until he brings his mother to sanction the purchase. The only satisfaction he derives is to storm out of the tailor's shop. He bitterly resents the disposition of an inheritance he comes into because he was not consulted. To give expression to his feeling, he smokes a cigarette in front of his mother. He vows, "I'm going to speak my mind to my mother. If I'm a boy, then let them send me to school, bring me up, and pay for my keep. If I'm grown up, let them treat me as a grown-up. And if I'm neither, then let them go to hell, all of them, but I won't be played with like a kitten!"

After the end of the lesson I followed Father Joaquín back to his room. "What do you think of it?" he asked me.

"It's difficult to say." I found it hard to speak. With my hat between my fingers, I was standing on the other side of the desk, facing him. Father Joaquín rose, walked round the desk, put his hand on my shoulder and drew me gently nearer.

"Now come, tell me. What's the matter with you?"

"I don't know. It's very funny. Everything seems changed. Even the stones of the cloisters, which I know by heart, one by one. Everybody seems changed to me, the boys, you, the school. Even Mesón de Paredes Street. When I walked through it this morning I found it changed. To me, the men, the women, the kids, the houses, everything—absolutely everything—seems changed. I don't know how, and I can't explain it."

Father Joaquín looked straight into my eyes for a short while.

*From *The Forging of a Rebel*. Reprinted by permission of Barea Estate. Reynal & Hitchcock. 1946. Pp. 126-128, 177-178, 183-187.

"Of course, you see everything changed. But everything is just the same as before, only you have changed. Let's see what you've got in your pockets—show me." I was bewildered, but he insisted. "Yes, I mean it, show me everything you carry in your pockets."

In confusion, I pulled a silk handkerchief out of my breast pocket, then my smart, new leather wallet, the silver watch, the folded handkerchief, two pesetas, a fancy magazine pencil, a small notebook. There was nothing else.

"Haven't you anything else?"

"No, sir."

"Well, well. And what have you done with your marbles and your spinning-top? Don't you carry brass chips, or matchboxes, or printed pictures, or string for playing thieves and robbers? Haven't you a single torn pocket, isn't there a button missing somewhere, haven't you got ink-stains on your fingers?"

I must have made a very silly face. He took the things piece by piece, mockingly, and stowed them back into my pockets.

"Here's the nice silk handkerchief, to look elegant. So you ogle the girls already, do you? The nice wallet to keep the money safe. There aren't any banknotes in it yet, but they'll come, never mind. Everything takes time. Here's the silver watch so you know the time, and you don't have to look at the clocks in shops any more and then sprint through the streets because it's getting late. And you don't have to wait for the clock in the bell tower to strike any more."

He put both hands on my shoulders, the two big hands of a man, and again looked straight into my face.

"Do you understand now what has happened to you?"

"Yes, sir," I said.

"If you go now to see Father Vesga," he added quizzically, "he'll tell you that you have lost the condition of purity. I tell you simply that you're no longer a child."

*   *   *   *

I was separated from everybody else, except Father Joaquín. I saw this very clearly. The people I knew stopped treating me as a child, but nobody thought of treating me as a man. I realized that there were many things of which they could not talk to me. Yet I needed to talk, I needed people to talk to me, I needed to understand things. The grown-up people never realized that their behavior to me was ridiculous. If they were talking of women when I happened to come in, they stopped and changed the conversation, so that I should not hear that kind of thing, since I was still a child. They did not realize that I knew everything they could have told me. They were hypocrites and fools, all of them. Didn't they see that I was lonely?

I needed to play. I bought a heap of tools and started to construct a small steam engine. I made the drawings and cut out the pieces from sheet-brass. I had bought a treatise on steam engines and copied its drawings. The book was old and described engines of thirty years ago, but it suited me. I wanted to make a very simple engine. My aunt was annoyed because I stained my hands and made a mess in the flat.

*   *   *   *

On my way home I went into the Experimental Farm which the Institute of Agricultural Engineers kept in the Moncloa. It had rabbit hutches, chicken coops, cowsheds, and pigsties with every kind of breed, and it had beehives and a breeding station for silkworms. They let me have a packet of fresh mulberry leaves, and when I came home I spent my time watching the assault my silkworms made on them. Concha laughed at my worms and said they were a toy for children, but I was a man now. She made me feel ashamed of them and I almost gave them away. But then I found out at the Experimental Farm that she was quite wrong. They were by no means children's toys. The silk industry used to be one of the most important industries of Spain, but it had gone to rack and ruin. One of the professors showed me the various breeds of silkworms, their diseases and the cures for them, and the way to extract silk. He gave me a leaflet; I had the right to get free stock from the station and to sell all my cocoons to them, by weight, before they opened and the moths crept out. It might be a good business to breed silkworms. Then the laugh would be on Concha. We could go to Méntrida, where mulberry trees grew along the river, and breed silkworms and chickens. We could do it on the ten thousand pesetas and still have money left to live on for a year. Whenever we wanted to go to Madrid we could do it without difficulty, it was near enough.

One of the Sundays when I went to the station for mulberry leaves I told the professor my plan. He listened to me very kindly, asked me details about my family, and, when I had explained everything, he said:

"My dear boy, that is all very nice, but you're still a minor and will have to do what your mother wishes. And she won't wish to plunge into this maze which needs a lot of experience and a lot of money."

So my mother can do whatever she likes with the money? I am a minor. Every time one has got something which belongs to one, one

turns out to be a minor, but all the others are of age, always, and have
the right to snatch away what belongs to one, just because one is a
minor. But as far as working is concerned one is already of age. One is
a minor when it comes to cashing in. One is paid as a minor. The
family has the right to pocket what one has earned; so it happened to
Gros, whose father came to the Bank and asked for his son's wages to
be paid out to him, because young Gros had spent something out of his
pay one month. Even when one wants to buy something people always
take one's age into account. For years I've had my suits made by the
same tailor. I didn't want him to make my last suit and asked my
mother to give me the money to buy it for myself. I went to a tailor in
the Calle de la Victoria. The good man looked me up and down,
showed me his patterns, and when I told him to take my measurements, he said most politely that I should ask my papa or my mama to
come with me to the shop. "You see, we're not allowed to serve
minors."

I came back to him with my mother. The tailor was extremely polite
to us, took out the cloth I had chosen and showed it to my mother.
The two discussed the price between them as though I did not even
exist. Then my mother asked: "Do you like it?" "Yes," I said. "All
right, then, will you take his measurements?" The tailor armed himself with his tape: "Would you be so kind as to take off your coat?"

I burst out: "I don't want to! Put your old suit where there's a hole
for it. That's the only right I've got as a minor, not to have the suit
made and to tell you to go to hell."

My mother was frightfully upset and I was sorry for it afterwards.
But I had to tell that fellow what I thought of him.

I went by myself to my old tailor and he made me a suit which I
liked.

*　*　*　*

My mother and I went up the Calle del Arenal to the Puerta del
Sol. I walked beside her, but not with her. I did not take her arm as I
always had done when we went out together. I walked abreast of her,
but at two feet's distance. Neither of us spoke. She went with short
steps, the steps of a nervous little woman. I strode out with my long
legs, one step for two of hers. I was full of resentment. I started by
feeling resentment against some of the others and finished by feeling
it against my mother. Nobody was excepted. I resented the relatives
because of their suspicious, meticulous scrutiny of the accounts down
to the last centimo, their adding up of all the sums, their asking ten

times for an explanation of the difference between 69 and 100 per cent, their fingering of the receipts, the certificates, the Bank of Spain deposit receipt, with faces contracted by anger. I resented Don Primo because he acted in agreement with my mother, because they both did as they liked without taking me into account, without even saying a word to me. I did not think it a bad thing for the money to stay in the bank, but I thought it wrong of them to have done it behind my back. "There is no need for the boy to sign." Why should he? The boy is a boy, and they are grown people who can do what they like with boys. They can make them work and cash in on them, they can buy State Loan Bonds or a new suit, and that's all right for them. In his time the boy will be a man, and when he is grown up he can protest, if he still feels like it.

No, no, and no. As soon as we are at home there will be a row. I'm going to speak my mind to my mother. If I'm a boy, then let them send me to school, bring me up, and pay for my keep. If I'm grown up, let them treat me as a grown-up. And if I'm neither, then let them go to hell, all of them, but I won't be played with like a kitten!

I wanted to smoke a cigarette to get over my nervousness. I carried cigarettes in my pocket, my mother knew that I smoked, but I had never smoked in her presence so far, and I did not care to start it now. But so much the better if she gets angry, so much the better. In the Puerta del Sol I made up my mind, pulled out a cigarette and lighted it. My mother looked at me and walked on with short even steps as though it were nothing. I began to feel annoyed because she said nothing. If she had scolded me, I could have exploded, I needed to shout, to quarrel, to get rid of what I felt inside.

In the Calle de Carretas she asked me at long last:

"What are you thinking about?"

"Nothing."

"So much the better for you."

"Of course, if the other people do all the thinking for one, what should one think about?"

"Why do you say that?"

"Why? You know as well as I do." I stopped and faced her. "Because I'm fed up with being treated like a child and now you know it."

We fell back into a sulky silence, and so we came home.

Just as I had imagined, Señora Pascuala followed us along the corridor and came with us into the attic when we opened the door.

"Well, is everything nicely settled, Leonor?"

My mother sighed, took the black handkerchief from her head and sat down.

"Yes, it's all settled. I'm glad the whole thing is over and done with. I must say, if it hadn't been for the boy. . . . People go crazy as soon as they see a banknote. I almost thought they were coming to blows in the Notary's office. And what for? Only to snatch at a pittance which isn't even enough to lift you out of poverty. Now look here. José's brothers had been working together thirty years. José sold the grain for them, lent them money for mules and land, and made them the wealthiest people in the whole village. Well, because of the inheritance they've separated, they've gone to law against each other about the mules and the land. The brothers and their children look as if they wanted to knife one another. And they're all the same. Even he! (She pointed at me.) Here you've got him in a fury because I've done what I thought best for him. Even the children go crazy when they see money. I've been through a lot so that the four of them should get on in life—you know something about it, Pascuala—but for myself I prefer my stew and my warmed-up coffee. So I've lived all my life and so I want to die. I'll be content if they let me die in peace in my bed and not take me to hospital. And that's not asking for much, I think."

"I haven't said anything," I retorted peevishly.

"No, you haven't said anything, but don't you think I've got eyes in my head? You walked beside me the whole way like an altar-boy, a few steps apart. And then the young gentleman lights a cigarette for himself in the Puerta del Sol, quite brazenly. What did you expect—that I would make a row? No, my boy, no. You can smoke as much as you like. And now, let's have it out. What is the matter?"

"You ask what's the matter?—well, it's just that I—I'm fed up with being treated like a child or a little boy and having my belongings disposed of without any consideration for me. Who told you to buy State Bonds? You may have your views about the money, but so have I. And after all, it's my money and nobody else's."

"And what are your views about the money?"

"That doesn't concern anybody but me. You had to collect the money, because they wouldn't let me have it while I'm a minor, but afterwards we should have thought out together what to do with it. And you shouldn't have got together with the Notary and bought State Bonds. Do you know what State Bonds are? I'm working in a bank, precisely in that department which handles securities, and I must know about them. State Loan! If you'd bought Convertible Loan, then we would at least have a chance of getting a premium. But State Loan, which no one wants! But of course, you think I'm just a little boy who doesn't understand anything about anything."

"Of course I do, you silly." She stroked my tousled hair, her fingers twisted its strands and soothed my taut nerves. "Of course I think it. Listen. I'm your guardian until you stop being a minor. That doesn't mean that I can do what I like, it means that it's my responsibility to administer your money and that I must give you an account of what I've done the day you come of age. We can't spend your money now just as you like, because then you might come when you're a man and ask me: 'Where's my money?' If I then said 'You've spent it,' you might answer: 'I? But I couldn't have spent it, I was a child. You must have spent it yourself, because you were the only person with a right to do so.' And you could even send me to prison as a thief. No, your money is going to stay in the bank until you can give the order to withdraw it—and then you may spend it as you like, on business or on women, and may it bring you joy. I don't need anything. I've been poor all my life and I'll die poor. You have your life still before you, and I'm an old woman."

Her fingers in my hair and her last words dispelled all my anger, and my eyes filled with water.

"Now, d'you see that you're a little boy and a silly?"

She wiped my face as she used to do when I was a child and kissed me on the forehead. She took out a hundred peseta note and gave it to me.

"Here, treat your friends and buy yourself something, but don't do anything foolish."

Señora Pascuala sighed. "Goodness me, these children, Leonor, these children! What they make us suffer! And what are you going to do now?"

"Well, nothing. Just go on as always."

"I thought you were going to move out. I've been saying to myself, as soon as Leonor's boy gets his money they'll move. I've been sorry, because by now it's a good sixteen years that we've been living side by side, with nothing but a partition between us."

"Of course we're going to move," I said. "I don't want to stay in the attic."

"Now look here, my dear, let's be sensible. This money"—she took up the deposit receipt—"doesn't make us rich. It gives you exactly one peseta twenty-five centimos interest a day. Do you think that one twenty-five more or less settles all our difficulties? No; here we pay nine pesetas a month and don't get into debt. If we take a flat we only spend your interest and a bit over. In the end we should be in debt, and then what? When you earn more, and your brother and sister too, then we can see what we can do about it. But, as things are now, you know very well that all of us together just earn what we need to live as we do live. The only thing I'd like to do is to take another attic room, like the cigar-woman's or Señora Paca's, as soon as one of them gets empty. I'd like it for your sake because you're getting older and if Concha comes home to live with us one day we can't all sleep in one room. We could do that, because the two rooms together would mean twenty pesetas rent a month, and that much we can manage."

"All right," I said, "but there's something I want, and it will be done."

"Tell me."

"I want to install electric light in our attic. I'm sick of having my eyebrows singed by the oil lamp every time I want to read for a while."

The electric light was granted and I promised to arrange with the company. It would have to be a lamp screwed on in the middle of the sloping ceiling, with a very long cord so that it would light the table, but could be hung on a hook over my head when I was in bed and wanted to read; and it would need a switch in the socket so that I could turn it off without having to get up.

Simone de Beauvoir
(1908-   )

The senseless cruelties and embarrassments adults sometimes inflict on adolescents can turn out to be propellants for the latter in their quest for maturity. Simone de Beauvoir illustrates this in the following excerpt from her insightful *Memoirs of a Dutiful Daughter.** Emancipation from the control of adults, the psychological freeing of oneself from childish bonds and an ever-increasing degree of autonomy in place of the heteronomy which distinguishes the immature mind generally, characterize the movement toward adulthood. Sometimes the adolescent is not aware of what is transpiring. "I realized vaguely that my childhood was coming to an end," de Beauvoir wrote. The beginnings of conscious separation from authority had, at last, begun.

The majority of the boys I knew seemed to me uncouth and of very limited intelligence; yet I knew that they belonged to a privileged category. If they had charm and a ready wit I was prepared to put up with them. My cousin Jacques had never lost his prestige in my eyes. He lived alone with his sister and an old nurse in the house in the

*Reprinted by permission of World Publishing Co. Copyright 1959, World Publishing Co. Pp. 128-131.

Boulevard Montparnasse and he often came to spend the evening with us. At thirteen he already had the assurance of a young man; his independent way of life and his authority in discussions had turned him into a precocious adult and I thought it was quite natural that he should treat me as a little girl. My sister and I were delighted whenever we heard his ring at the door. One evening he arrived so late that we were already in bed; we rushed into the study in our nighties. "What a way to behave!" my mother exclaimed. "You're big girls now!" I was taken aback. I looked upon Jacques as a sort of older brother. He helped me with my Latin prose, criticized my choice of books, and recited poems to me. One evening, on the balcony, he recited Hugo's *Tristesse d'Olympio,* and I suddenly remembered, with a pang in my heart, that we had been "engaged." But now the only real conversations he ever had were with my father.

He was a day student at the Collège Stanislas, where he was a brilliant pupil; between the ages of fourteen and fifteen he became infatuated with his French literature teacher, who taught him to prefer Mallarmé to Rostand. My father shrugged his shoulders, then grew angry. Since Jacques would run down *Cyrano* without being able to explain its weak points to me, and would recite obscure poems with great relish but without showing me why they were beautiful, I agreed with my parents that he was posing. All the same, while deploring his tastes I admired the highhanded way he defended them. He knew a host of poets and writers of whom I knew nothing at all; the distant clamor of a world that was closed to me used to come into the house with him: how I longed to explore that world! Papa used to say with pride: "Simone has a man's brain; she thinks like a man; she *is* a man." And yet everyone treated me like a girl. Jacques and his friends read real books and were abreast of all current problems; they lived out in the open; I was confined to the nursery. But I did not give up all hope. I had confidence in my future. Women, by the exercise of talent or knowledge, had carved out a place for themselves in the universe of men. But I felt impatient of the delays I had to endure. Whenever I happened to pass by the Collège Stanislas my heart would sink; I tried to imagine the mystery that was being celebrated behind those walls, in a classroom full of boys, and I would feel like an outcast. They had as teachers brilliantly clever men who imparted knowledge to them with all its pristine glory intact. My old school marms only gave me an expurgated, insipid, faded version. I was being crammed with an ersatz concoction; and I felt I was imprisoned in a cage.

In fact I no longer looked upon the schoolmistresses as the august high priestesses of Knowledge but as absurd bigots. More or less affiliated with the Jesuit Order, they parted their hair on the side while they were still novices and in the middle when they had taken their final vows. They thought it their duty to give witness to their devoutness in the eccentricity of their garb: they wore dresses of shot silk with leg-of-mutton sleeves and whaleboned collars; their skirts swept the floor; their qualifications were Christian virtues rather than degrees and diplomas. It was considered a great triumph when Mademoiselle Dubois, a dark bewhiskered lady, managed to scrape through a degree in English; Mademoiselle Billon, who was at least thirty, had been seen at the Sorbonne, all buttoned up and blushing, trying to get through the oral of her bachot. My father made no secret of the fact that he found these pious old frauds a little backward. It exasperated him that I should be obliged, at the end of any composition in which I described an outing or a party, to "thank God for a pleasant day." He thought highly of Voltaire and Beaumarchais, and knew Victor Hugo by heart: he wouldn't admit that French literature came to a stop in the seventeenth century. He went as far as to suggest to my mother that my sister and I should attend the *lycée;* there we would enjoy a better and more liberal grounding and at much less cost. I rejected this proposal with all the vehemence I could muster. I should have lost all desire to go on living if I had been separated from Zaza. My mother supported my objections. But I was divided over this question too. I wanted to stay on at the Cours Désir and yet I didn't like it there any more. I went on working zealously, but my behavior was changing. The lady in charge of higher studies, Mademoiselle Lejeune, a tall, gaunt woman with a ready tongue, was rather intimidating; but with Zaza and a few other fellow pupils I used to make fun of the rest of our teachers' foibles. The assistant mistresses just couldn't keep us in order. We used to spend free time between classes in a large room known as "the lecture-study room." There we would talk and giggle and plague the life out of the poor creature left in charge whom we had nicknamed "the Old Scarecrow." My sister, who had thrown all discretion to the winds by now, had decided that she would behave in the most outrageous way. With a friend she had chosen herself, Anne-Marie Gendron, she founded *The Cours Désir Gazette;* Zaza lent her some hectograph jelly and from time to time I contributed to it; we turned out some bloodthirsty numbers. We were no longer given marks for good conduct; our mistresses lectured us and complained to our mother. She became rather worried, but as my father always laughed at our escapades she disregarded the complaints. I never dreamed of attaching any moral significance to our naughty pranks; as soon as I found out how stupid they were, our schoolmistresses could no longer speak with any authority on what was right and wrong.

Stupidity: at one time my sister and I used to accuse other children of stupidity when we found them dull and boring; now there were many grown-ups, and in particular our schoolteachers, who were so accused. Unctuous sermons, all kinds of solemn twaddle, grand words, inflated turns of phrase, and any pompous affectation was "stupidity." It was stupid to attach importance to trifles, to persist in observing conventions and customs, to prefer commonplaces and prejudices to facts. The very height of stupidity was when people fatuously believed that we swallowed all the righteous fibs that were dished out to us. Stupidity made us laugh; it was one of our never-failing sources of amusement; but there was also something rather frightening about it. If this duncelike dullness had won the day we would no longer have had the right to think, make fun of people, experience real emotion, and enjoy real pleasures. We had to fight against it, or else give up living.

In the end my teachers got fed up with my insubordination and they let me know their displeasure. The Institut Adeline Désir took great care to distinguish itself from secular establishments where the mind is cultivated at the expense of the soul. At the end of the year, instead of awarding prizes for scholastic success—which would have run the risk of encouraging worldly rivalry among the pupils—we were presented at the end of March, in the presence of a bishop, with certificates and medals which were mainly rewards for industriousness and good behavior and also for long attendance at the school. The ceremonies took place, with tremendous pomp, at the Salle Wagram. The highest distinction was called "the certificate of honor" awarded to only a few pupils from each class who had excelled in everything. The rest only had a right to "special mentions." That year, after my name had reverberated in the solemn silence of the hall, I was startled to hear Madame Lejeune announce: "Special mentions in mathematics, history, and geography." From my assembled schoolmates came a murmur of consternation; and also of satisfaction because not all of them were my friends. I took this affront without turning a hair. At the end of the ceremony, my history teacher approached my mother: Zaza had a bad influence upon me; we would no longer be allowed to sit next to each other at school. I tried hard to steel myself, but in vain: my eyes filled with tears, to the great delight of Mademoiselle Gontran who thought I was weeping because I had only got a special mention; I was choking with rage because they were going to take me away from Zaza. But my distress had a more profound significance. In that sad corridor

I realized vaguely that my childhood was coming to an end. The grown-ups still had me under their thumb, but peace had gone forever from my heart. I was now separated from them by this freedom that was no source of pride to me, but that I suffered in solitary silence.

REFERENCES

1. Ackerman, Nathan. *The Psychodynamics of Family Life*. New York: Basic Books, 1958, p. 209.
2. Barker, Roger G., Wright, Beatrice A., & Gonick, Mollie R. *Adjustment to Physical Handicaps and Illness: A Survey of the Social Psychology of Physique and Disability*. New York: Social Science Research Council, 1946, p. 36.
3. Beauvoir, Simone de. *Memoirs of a Dutiful Daughter*. Cleveland: World Publishing Co., 1959, p. 156.
4. Bloch, Herbert A., & Niederhoffer, Arthur. *The Gang. A Study in Adolescent Behavior*. New York: Philosophical Library, 1958, pp. 11-12, 17, 68, 140.
5. DeJong, David. *With a Dutch Accent*. New York: Harper & Bros., 1944, p. 244.
6. DeQuincey, Thomas. *Autobiography from 1785 to 1803*. In: Masson, David (Ed.), *The Collected Writings of Thomas DeQuincey*. Edinburgh: Adam & Charles Black, 1889, pp. 316-325.
7. Deutsch, Helene. *The Psychology of Women. A Psychoanalytic Interpretation*. New York: Grune & Stratton, 1944, Vol. I, pp. 115-116.
8. Erikson, Erik H. Ego development and historical change. *Psychol. Issues,* 1:40, 1959.
9. ———. The problem of ego identity. *Psychol. Issues,* 1:110-111, 1959.
10. ———. Late adolescence. In: Funkenstein, Daniel H. (Ed.), *The Student and Mental Health. An International View*. Cambridge, Mass.: World Federation for Mental Health, 1959, pp. 74-75.
11. Friedenberg, Edgar Z. *The Vanishing Adolescent*. Boston: Beacon Press, 1959, p. 12.
12. Fry, Elizabeth. *Memoir of the Life of Elizabeth Fry*. Vol. I, 1847.
13. Inhelder, Bärbel, & Piaget, Jean. *The Growth of Logical Thinking: From Childhood to Adolescence*. New York: Basic Books, 1958, pp. 335-336, 343.
14. Jones, Ernest, Some problems of adolescence. *Brit. J. Psychol.,* 13: 33-39, 45, 1922.
15. Kantor, MacKinley. *But Look, The Morn. The Story of a Childhood*. New York: Coward-McCann, 1947, p. 288.

16. Mead, Margaret. *Coming of Age in Samoa.* New York: New American Library, 1949, p. 146.
17. Redl, Fritz, & Wineman, David. *Controls from Within.* Glencoe, Ill.: Free Press, 1952, p. 91.
18. Rice, John A. *I Came Out of the Eighteenth Century.* New York: Harper & Bros., 1942, pp. 184-187.
19. Wouk, Herman. The terrible teens. *Good Housekeeping,* 146:60, 1958.

Psychology, Psychoanalysis and Personal Documents

This list of 1,063 items deals not only with the psychology of the adolescent in autobiographies, diaries, memoirs and letters but the whole range of human development and personality. One of the introductory chapters of this book is concerned with the relationship between psychology and human documents; many of the listings here reflect this unity. Included are a number of autobiographies by, and biographies about, professional people in the fields of psychology and psychoanalysis.

While it is not intended that this list be considered exhaustive, it is as thorough and complete as patience and energy could make it. The earliest document to be found in the bibliography dates from 1870, and there are perhaps two dozen items from the nineteenth century. Obviously, the great preponderance of entries is from our own times, clustering around the 1930's and continuing to the present. Twenty-four countries are represented, and nineteen languages: Arabic, Czech, Danish, Dutch, English, French, German, Hebrew, Hungarian, Italian, Japanese, Latvian, Norwegian, Polish, Portuguese, Russian, Spanish, Swedish and Yiddish. For translating the foreign language titles, I am indebted to several friends in the Modern Language Department of Brooklyn College.

Abegg, W. *Aus Tagebüchern und Briefen junger Menschen. (From the Diaries and Letters of Young People)*. Basel: Ernst Reinhart, 1954.

Abely, Paul. En relisant Balzac psychiatre occasionnel. (On reading Balzac as a psychiatric study). *Ann. Med.-psychol.*, 2:751-761, 1958.

Abenheimer, Karl M. The diary of Vaslov Nijinsky; a patho-graphical study of a case of schizophrenia. *Psychoanal. Rev.*, 33:257-284, 1946.

Aberle, David F. The reconciliation of divergent views of Hopi culture through the analysis of life-history material. *Microfilm. Abstr.*, 11 (1): 9-10, 1951.

Abraham, Karl. Amenhotep IV. A psychoanalytic contribution to the understanding of his personality and the monotheistic cult of Aton. *Psychoanal. Quart.*, 4:537-569, 1935.

———. Giovanni Segantini: a psychoanalytic essay. *Psychoanal. Quart.*, 6: 453-512, 1937.

———. Giovanni Segantini. Ein psychoanalytischer Versuch. (Giovanni Segantini: a psychoanalytic essay). *Schr. z. angew. Seelenk.*, 11:1-65, 1911.

Abrahamsen, David. *The Mind and Death of a Genius.* New York: Columbia University Press, 1946.

———. Otto Weininger—and bisexuality; a psychoanalytic study. *Amer. J. Psychother.*, 1:25-44, 1947.

Achille-Delmas, G. A propos du Père Surin et de M.-Th. Noblet. (Apropos of Père Surin and Marie Thérèse Noblet). *Etud. Carmélit.*, 23: 235-239, 1938.

Adam, Antoine. *Le Vrai Verlaine; Essai Psychoanalytique. (The Real Verlaine; A Psychoanalytic Essay).* Paris: E. Droz, 1936.

Adam, K. *Die geistige Entwicklung des heiligen Augustine. (The Intellectual Development of St. Augustine).* Augsburg: Haas & Grabherr, 1931.

Adams, L. Sigmund Freud's correct birthday. *Psychoanal. Rev.*, 41:359-362, 1954.

Adler, Alfred. *The Case of Miss R.: the Interpretation of a Life Story.* New York: Greenberg, 1929.

———. Dostoevsky, in *Individual Psychology.* Paterson, N. J.: Littlefield, Adams & Co., 1959. Pp. 280-290.

———. How I chose my career. *Indiv. Psychol. Bull.*, 6:9-11, 1947.

Adler, C. A. Richard III—his significance as a study in criminal life-style. *Int. J. Indiv. Psychol.*, 2:55-60, 1936.

Adolf, E. Knut Hamsun's Veranlagung und Weltbild. (The outlook and world picture of Knut Hamsun), in Beth, K., & Braunmüller, W. (Eds.), *Religionspsychologie*, Vol. III. Wien und Leipzig. Pp. 22-28.

Agneiv, M. The auditory imagery of great composers. *Psychol. Monographs.*, 31:279-287, 1922.

Alajouanine, Th. Aphasia and artistic realization. *Brain*, 71:229-241, 1948.

Albrecht, M. C. A study of Julian Green. *J. abnorm. soc. Psychol.*, 41: 169-188, 1946.

Allen, Clifford. Homosexuality and Oscar Wilde: a psychoanalytic study. *Int. J. Sexol.*, 2:205-215, 1949.

———. The personality of Radclyffe Hall. *Int. J. Sexol.*, 4:95-98, 1950.

———. The problem of John Ruskin: a psycho-sexological analysis. *Int. J. Sexol.*, 4:7-14, 1950.

Allendy, René Felix. *Journal d'un Médicin Malade; ou Six Mois de Lutte avec la Mort. (Diary of a Sick Doctor; or Six Months of Struggle with Death)*. Paris: Denoël, 1944.

Alexander, Franz. A jury trial of psychoanalysis. *J. abnorm. soc. Psychol.*, 35:305-323, 1940.

———. Psychology and the interpretation of history, in Ware, C. F. (Ed.), *The Cultural Approach to History*. New York: Columbia University Press, 1940. Pp. 48-57.

———. *The Western Mind in Transition. An Eyewitness Story*. New York: Random House, 1960.

Allport, Floyd H., Walker, L., & Lathers, E. Written compositions and characteristics of personality. *Arch. Psychol.*, Vol. 26, 1934.

Allport, Gordon W., (Ed.). Letters from Jenny. *J. abnorm. soc. Psychol.*, 41:315-350, 449-480, 1946.

———. Personality: a problem for science or a problem for art? *Revista de Psicologie*, 1:488-502, 1938.

———. Personalistic psychology as science: a reply. *Psychol. Rev.*, 53:132-135, 1946.

———. The study of personality by the intuitive method. An experiment in teaching from *The Locomotive-God. J. abnorm. soc. Psychol.*, 24: 14-27, 1929.

———. *The Use of Personal Documents in Psychological Science*. New York: Social Science Research Council, 1945.

Allport, Gordon W., Bruner, J. S., & Jandorf, E. M. Personality under social catastrophe: nine life-histories of the Nazi revolution. *Character & Pers.*, 10:1-22, 1941.

Al-Meligui, A. [Psychology of adolescence through diaries.] *Egypt. J. Psychol.*, 6:173-184, 1950-51.

Alvarez, Walter C. *Minds That Came Back*. Philadelphia: J. B. Lippincott, 1961.

Anastasi, Anne, Cohen, N., & Spatz, D. A study of fear and anger in college students through the controlled diary method. *J. Genetic Psychol.*, 73:243-249, 1948.

Anderson, Camilla M. *Saints, Sinners and Psychiatry.* Philadelphia: J. B. Lippincott & Co., 1950.

Anonymous. *Autobiography of a Schizophrenic Girl.* With analytic interpretation by Marguerite Sechehaye. New York: Grune & Stratton, 1951.

———. Magna est verita. *Psychiat. Quart.,* 20:150-156, 1946.

———. [Marcel Proust as data for psychology.] *Int. Zsch. f. Indiv.-Psychol.,* 7:57-58, 1929.

———. My life as a dissociated personality. *J. abnorm. Psychol.,* 3:240-260, 311-334, 1908.

Anthony, Katherine S. *Margaret Fuller: A Psychological Biography.* New York: Harcourt, Brace & Co., 1920.

Antonini, G. Psicopatologia di Vittorio Alfieri. (The psychopathology of Vittorio Alfieri). *Arch. di. Psichiat.,* 19:177-252, 1898.

Antonini, G., & Cognetti De Martiis, L. *Vittorio Alfieri. Studi psicopatologici. (Vittorio Alfieri. A Psychopathological Study).* Turin: Frat. Bocca, 1898.

Apperly, F. L. A study of American Rhodes scholars. *J. Hered.,* 30:493-495, 1939.

Armaingaud, ———. Montaigne était-il hypocondriaque? (Was Montaigne hypochondriacal?). *Chron. Méd.,* 15:177-184, 1908.

Aron, Willy. Fartsaykhnungen vegn opshtam fun Freud un vegn zayn Yiddishkeyt. (Notes on Freud's ancestry and his Jewishness). *Yivo Bleter,* 40:166-174, 1956.

Asselineau, Roger. *The Evolution of Walt Whitman. The Creation of a Personality,* Part I. Cambridge, Mass.: Harvard University Press, 1960.

Auden, G. A. Jerome Cardan: a study in personality. *J. Ment. Sci.,* 75: 220-233, 1929.

Aviles Robalino, A. El perfil psiquico de Rossolimo; su aplicacion en los aliendos. (The psychological profile of Rossolimo; its application in cases of insanity). *An. Univ. Ecuador,* 66:83-134, 1941.

Baade, W., Lipmann, O., & Stern, W. Fragment eines psychographischen Schemas. (Fragment of a psychographic pattern). *Zsch. f. Ang. Psychol.,* 3:191-315, 1909.

Bachler, Karl. Alfred Kubin und die Flucht ins Traumreich; ein Beitrag zur Deutung des künstlerischen Schaffens. (Alfred Kubin and the flight into the realm of dreams; a contribution to the interpretation of artistic creativeness). *Psychoanal. Bewegung,* 5:53-65, 1933.

———. August Strindberg. Eine psychoanalytische Studie. (August Strindberg. A psychoanalytic study). *Psychoanal. Bewegung,* 2:365-381, 555-579, 1930.

Bader, H. Der Lebensstil des Kindes in Erzähling, Traum und Spiel. (The life pattern of the child as revealed in his own stories, dreams and play). *Int. Zsch. f. Indiv.-Psychol.*, 10:224-230, 1932.

Bahle, Julius. *Hans Pfitzner und der Geniale Mensch: eine Psychologische Kulturkritik. (Hans Pfitzner and the Man of Genius: A Study in Social Psychology)*. Konstanz: Curt Weller, 1949.

Baillie, J. B. The mind of John Bunyan. *Hibbert J.*, 27:385-405, 1929.

Bain, R. The impersonal confession and social research. *J. appl. Sociol.*, 9:356-361, 1925.

——. Man is the measure; writing, neurotic and normal. *Sociometry*, 7: 332-337, 1944.

——. Spencer's love for George Eliot. *Psychoanal. Rev.*, 14:37-55, 1926.

Balaban, N. I. [The pathological in the personality of Leo Tolstoi.] *Sovet. psikhonevr.*, 3:108-112, 1933.

Balcolm, Lois. The value of a comparative analysis of an author's autobiographical and fictional writings for interpretation of aspects of his personality: a study based on selected works of William Dean Howells. *Dissert. Abstr.*, 16:373, 1956.

Balderston, Katherine C. Johnson's vile melancholy, in *The Age of Johnson: Essays Presented to Chauncy Brewster Tinker*. New Haven: Yale University Press, 1949. Pp. 3-14.

Baldwin, Alfred L. Personal structure analysis: a statistical method for investigating the single personality. *J. abnorm. soc. Psychol.*, 37:163-183, 1942.

——. The statistical analysis of the structure of a single personality. *Psychol. Bull.*, 37:518-519, 1940.

Barine, A. *Névrosés: Hoffmann; Quincey; Edgar Poë; G. de Nerval. (Neuroses)*. Paris: Hachette, 1898.

Barker, Roger G., Wright, Beatrice A., & Gonick, Mollie R. *Adjustment to Physical Handicap and Illness: A Survey of the Social Psychology of Physique and Disability*. New York: Social Science Research Council, 1946. Pp. 38-42, 71-72, 82.

Barker, Roger G., & Wright, Herbert S. *One Boy's Day; A Specimen Record of Behavior*. New York: Harper & Bros., 1951.

Barnes, Harry E. Psychology and history. *Amer. J. Psychol.*, 30:337-376, 1919.

——. Some reflections on the possible services of analytical psychology to history. *Psychol. Rev.*, 8:22-37, 1921.

Baruch, Dorothy. *One Little Boy*. New York: Julian Press, 1952.

Barzun, Jacques. Truth in history: Berlioz. *Univ. Rev.*, 5:275-280, 1939.

Baudoin, Charles. Anatole France. Genèse d'un scepticism. (Anatole

France. The origin of a skeptic attitude). *Psyché-Paris,* 2:1075-1082, 1947.

——. *The Birth Of Psyche.* New York: E. P. Dutton & Co., 1923.

——. Petite suite pascalienne. (Reflections on Pascal). *Action et Pensée,* 17:33-39, 1941.

——. *Psychanalyse de Victor Hugo. (Psychoanalysis of Victor Hugo).* Geneva: Edit. do Mont-Blanc, 1943.

——. *Tolstoi Educateur. (Tolstoi the Teacher).* New York: E. P. Dutton & Co., 1923.

Bäumer, G., & Droescher, L. *Von der Kindesseele. Beiträge zur Kinderpsychologie aus Dichtung und Biographie. (Of the Soul of the Child. Contributions to Child Psychology from Fiction and Biography).* Leipzig: Voigtländer, 1922.

Baumgärtel, Knut. [The Youth of Stendhal.] *Int. Z. Indiv.-Psychol.,* 18: 130-133, 1949.

Baumgarten, Franziska. Character traits derived from biographies. *Character & Pers.,* 6:147-149, 1937.

Bayon, H. P. A medico-psychological revision of the story of Jehanne, la Purcelle de Domrémy (Joan of Arc). *Proc. R. Soc. Med.,* 34:161-170, 1941.

Beck, Walter. Die Biographische Methode in der Sozial-Psychologie. (The biographical method in social psychology). *Psychol. Rundschau,* 3:203-213, 1952.

Becker, Carl. The memoirs and the letters of Madame Roland. *Amer. Hist. Rev.,* 33:784-803, 1928.

Becker, Jacob R. [*A Psychoanalytic Study of Rabbi Nachman of Bratislaw.*] Jerusalem: Deah, 1928.

Beers, Clifford W. *A Mind that Found Itself; An Autobiography.* New York: Doubleday, Doran & Co., 1928.

Behn, Siegfried. Biographie und Psychoanalyse. (Biography and psychoanalysis). *Psychol. Beitr.,* 2:375-389, 1956.

Belcher, E. L. A technique for diary analysis. *Child Devel.,* 3:53-56, 1932.

Bellezza, P. *Genio e follia di Alessandro Manzoni. (The Genius and Madness of Alessandro Manzoni).* Milan: Cogliati, 1898.

Beltran, Juan R. El complejo psicologico de Lope de Vega. (The psychological complex of Lope de Vega). *An. Inst. Psicol. Univ. B. Aires,* 3: 81-93, 1941.

Bem, A. L. *Dostoevskij. Psichoanaliticeskie Etjudy. (Dostoeevsky. A Psychoanalytic Study).* Berlin: Petropolis Verlag, 1938.

Benedict, Ruth. Journals: 1912-1916; 1915-1934, in *An Anthropologist at Work. Writings of Ruth Benedict.* Edited by Margaret Mead. Boston: Houghton Mifflin Co., 1959. Pp. 118-155.

——. Mary Wollstonecraft. *Ibid.,* pp. 491-519.

——. The story of my life. *Ibid.,* pp. 97-112.

——. Two diaries. *Ibid.,* pp. 55-79.

Bennett, Edward. The case of Eric Riddal. A biographical sketch, in *Personality Assessment and Diagnosis.* New York: Ronald Press, 1961.

Benson, Arthur C. *Ruskin. A Study in Personality.* New York: G. P. Putnam's Sons, 1911.

Berendsohn, W. A. Knut Hamsun und die Psychoanalyse. (Knut Hamsun and psychoanalysis). *Psychoanal. Bewegung,* 2:60-68, 1930.

Beres, David. The contribution of psychoanalysis to the biography of the artist: a commentary on methodology. *Int. J. Psycho-Anal.,* 40:26-37, 1959.

Bergler, Edmund. Die Biographik macht der Psychoanalyse Konzessionen. (Biography makes concessions to psychoanalysis). *Psychoanal. Bewegung,* 5:501-512, 1933.

——. Psychoanalysis of writers and of literary production, in Roheim, Géza. (Ed.), *Psychoanalysis and the Social Sciences,* Vol. 5. New York: International Universities Press, 1947. Pp. 247-296.

——. The relation of the artist to society: a psychoanalyst's comment on the exchange of letters among V. S. Pritchett, Elizabeth Bowen and Graham Greene. *Amer. Imago,* 5:247-258, 1948.

——. [*Talleyrand-Napoleon-Stendhal-Grabbe. Psychoanalytic Biographic Essays.*] Vienna: Internationaler Psychoanalytischer Verlag, 1934.

——. Unbewusste Motive im Verhalten Napoleons zu Talleyrand. (Unconscious motives in the attitude of Napoleon toward Talleyrand). *Psychoanal. Bewegung,* 5:319-369, 1933.

——. *The Writer and Psychoanalysis.* Garden City, N. Y.: Doubleday & Co., 1950.

Berguer, Georges. *Some Aspects of the Life of Jesus from the Psychological and Psychoanalytical Point of View.* New York: Harcourt, Brace & Co., 1923.

Berkeley-Hill, Owen. A short study of the life and character of Mohammed. *Int. J. Psycho-Anal.,* 2:31-53, 1921.

Bernabei, M. *Maria Baskirtserva—l'Eroina dell'io. (Marie Bashkirtseff—the Heroine of the Ego).* Milan: Ed. Dante Alighieri, 1932.

Bernfeld, Siegfried. Freud's scientific beginnings. *Amer. Imago,* 6:163-196, 1949.

——. (Ed.). *Vom Gemeinschaftsleben der Jugend. (Community Life of*

Youth). Leipzig: Internationaler Psychoanalytischer Verlag, 1922.

——. Sigmund Freud, M.D., 1882-1885. *Intl. J. Psycho-Anal.*, 32:204-217, 1951.

——. Trieb und Tradition im Jugendalter: kulturpsychologische Studien an Tagebüchern. (Impulse and tradition in adolescence. Psycho-cultural studies of diaries). *Beihefte z. Asch. f. Angew. Psychol.*, 54:1-181, 1931.

——. An unknown biographical fragment written by Freud. *Amer. Imago,* 4:3-19, 1946.

Bernfeld, Siegfried, & Bernfeld, Suzanne C. Freud's early childhood. *Bull. Menninger Clinic,* 8:107-115, 1944.

——. Freud's first year in practice, 1886-1887. *Bull. Menninger Clinic,* 16:37-49, 1952.

Bett, W. R. *The Infirmities of Genius.* New York: Philosophical Library, 1952.

Bibl, V. *Thronfolger. (The Crown Prince).* Munich: Musarion Verlag, 1931.

Bien, Ernst. Tagebuchblätter einer Zwölfjährigen. (Diary of a twelve-year-old girl). *Psychoanal. Praxis,* 3:59-68, 1933.

Bienenfeld, Elsa. Edvard Grieg und seine Vorfahren. (Edward Grieg and his ancestors). *Arch. Rass.-u.-GesBiol.,* 28:409-413, 1935.

Binet, Alfred. La création littéraire. Portrait psychologique de M. Paul Hervieu. (Literary creation. A psychological portrait of Paul Hervieu). *Année Psychol.,* 10:1-62, 1903.

——. The paradox of Diderot. *Pop. Sci. Mo.,* 51:539-543, 1897.

Binet-Sanglé, C. La maladie de Blaise Pascal. (The illness of Blaise Pascal). *Ann. Méd.-Psychol.,* 9:177-199, 1898.

Binswanger, Ludwig. Studien zum Schizophrenieproblem: der Fall Suzanne Urban; der Fall Jean Jacques Rousseau. (Studies in the problem of schizophrenia: the case of Suzanne Urban; the case of Jean Jacques Rousseau). *Archiv. f. Neurologie u. Psychiatrie,* 70:1-32, 1952.

Bjerre, P. Hitler som psykoterapeut. (Hitler as psychotherapist). *Hygiea, Stockholm,* 96:81-93, 1934.

Blalock, A. A boyhood portrait of William Stewart Halsted, 1852-1922. *Bull. Hist. Med.,* 35:195-198, 1960.

Blanchard, Phyllis M. A psychoanalytic study of August Comte. *Amer. J. Psychol.,* 29:159-181, 1918.

Blanck, Karl. *Heine und die Frau. (Heine and Woman).* Munich: Müller, 1913.

Blanton, Margaret Gray. *Bernadette of Lourdes.* New York: Longmans, Green & Co., 1939.

Blatz, W. E. *The Five Sisters*. New York: William Morrow & Co., 1938.

Blondell, C. *La Psychographie de Marcel Proust. (Psychograph of Marcel Proust)*. Paris: Vrin, 1932.

Blum, Harold P. Van Gogh's chairs. *Amer. Imago,* 13:307-318, 1956.

Blumer, Herbert. *An Appraisal of Thomas and Znanieki's "The Polish Peasant in Europe and America."* New York: Social Science Research Council, 1939.

Boder, D. P. The adjective-verb quotient: a contribution to the psychology of language. *Psychol. Record,* 3:310-343, 1940.

Bonaparte, Marie. A defense of biography. *Int. J. Psycho-Anal.,* 20:231-240, 1939.

———. *Life and Works of Edgar Allen Poe: A Psychoanalytic Interpretation*. New York: Anglobooks, 1951.

———. La structure psychique d'Edgar Poë. (The psychic make-up of Edgar Poe). *Hyg. ment.,* 28:193-201, 1933.

Bondy, Curt. *Die proletarische Jugendbewegung in Deutschland. (The Proletarian Youth Movement in Germany)*. Lauenberg, 1922.

Borde, M. *La Maladie et l'Oeuvre de Chopin. (The Illness and the Work of Chopin)*. Lyon: Bosc & Rion, 1932.

Boring, Edwin G. Great men and scientific progress. *Proc. Amer. Phil. Soc.,* 94:339-351, 1950.

———. Was this analysis a success? *J. abnorm. soc. Psychol.,* 35:4-10, 1940.

Boring, Edwin G., et al. (Eds.). *A History of Psychology in Autobiography,* Vol. IV. Worcester, Mass.: Clark University Press, 1952.

Boring, Mollie D., & Boring, Edwin G. Masters and pupils among the American psychologists. *Amer. J. Psychol.,* 61:527-534, 1948.

Bose, Nirmal Kumar. Some facts of psychoanalytic interest of Gandhiji's life. *Samiksa,* 6:163-175, 1952.

Bottome, Phyllis. *Alfred Adler*. New York: Vanguard Press, 1957.

Bousfield, E. G. Paul. *The Omnipotent Self; A Study in Self-Deception and Self-Cure*. New York: E. P. Dutton & Co., 1923.

Boutonier, Juliette. Réflexions sur l'autobiographie d'un criminal. (Reflections on the autobiography of a criminal). *Rev. Française de Psychanal.,* 14:182-214, 1950.

Boven, William. Alexander der Grosse. (Alexander the Great). *Imago,* 8:418-439, 1922.

Bowerman, W. G. *Studies in Genius*. New York: Philosophical Library, 1947.

Boyd, Ernest. Sex in biography. *Harper's Mag.,* 165:757-759, 1932.

Boyer, L. Bryce. Sculpture and depression: a psychiatric study of the life and productions of a depressed sculptress. *Amer. J. Psychiat.,* 106:606-615, 1950.

Brachfeld, O. André Gides Werdegang. (The development of André Gide). *Int. Zsch. f. Indiv. Psychol.*, 8:376-389, 1930.

Bradford, Gamaliel. The art of biography. *Sat. Rev. Lit.*, 1:769-770, 1925.

——. The art of psychography. *Lit. Digest*, April 28, 1923.

——. The art of psychography. *New York Post Lit. Rev.*, 3:641-642, 1923.

——. Psychography, in *A Naturalist of Souls*. Boston: Houghton Mifflin Co., 1917.

Bradley, C. Biography of a schizophrenic child. *Nerv. Child.*, 1:141-171, 1942.

Bragman, Louis J. The case of Algernon Charles Swinburne: a study in sadism. *Psychoanal. Rev.*, 21:51-74, 1934.

——. The case of Arthur Symons. The psychotherapy of a man of letters. *Brit. J. Med. Psychol.*, 12:346-362, 1932.

——. The case of Dante Gabriel Rossetti. *Amer. J. Psychiat.*, 92:1111-1122, 1936.

——. The case of Floyd Dell. A study in the psychology of adolescence. *Amer. J. Psychiat.*, 93:1401-1411, 1937.

——. The case of John Aldington Symonds. A study in aesthetic homosexuality. *Amer. J. Psychiat.*, 93:375-398, 1936.

——. The case of Ludwig Lewisohn. *Amer. J. Psychiat.*, 11:319-331, 1931.

——. Ludwig Lewisohn on *The Creative Eros*. *Psychoanal. Rev.*, 20:5-9, 1933.

——. Ludwig Lewisohn: psychoanalyst of literature. *Psychoanal. Rev.*, 21:300-315, 1934.

Brain, W. Russell. Authors and psychopaths. *Brit. Med. J.*, 2:1949.

——. A post-mortem on Dr. Johnson. *London Hosp. Gazette*, 37:225-230, 288-289, 1934.

Bramwell, W. G. Galton's *Hereditary Genius* and the three following generations since 1869. *Eugenics Rev.*, 39:146-153, 1948.

Brandwein, Paul F., Friedenberg, Edgar Z., Roe, Anne, and Stone, Solomon. Creativity and personality in the scientist, in Henry, Nelson B. (Ed.), *Rethinking Science Education*. The 59th Yearbook of the National Society for the Study of Education, Part I. Chicago: National Society for the Study of Education, 1960.

Braunschvig, M. & G. *Notre Enfant; Journal d'un Père et d'une Mère. (Our Child; Journal of a Father and Mother)*. Paris: Hachette, 1913.

Brèdif, L. *Du charactère intellectuel et moral de J. J. Rousseau. (On the Intellectual and Moral Character of J. J. Rousseau)*. Paris: Hachette, 1906.

Breuer, Josef. Autobiography. *Int. J. Psycho-Anal.*, 34:64-67, 1953.

Brink, Louis. *Women Characters in Richard Wagner*. Nervous and

Mental Disease Monograph Series No. 37. New York: Nervous & Mental Disease Publ. Co., 1924.

Brodie, Fawn M. *Thaddeus Stevens*. New York: W. W. Norton & Co., 1959.

Brower, Judith F. Personal documents, in Brower, Daniel, & Abt, Lawrence E., (Eds.), *Progress in Clinical Psychology*, Vol. I. New York: Grune & Stratton, 1952. Pp. 63-66.

Brown, M. W. Washington's strange interest in sickness and death. *Med. J. & Rec.*, 135:201-202, 1932.

Brown, Norman O. *Life against Death: The Psychoanalytic Meaning of History*. Middletown, Conn.: Wesleyan University Press, 1959.

Brown, R. A., & Brown, M. R. Biography in the social sciences: changing concepts. *Soc. Educ.*, 17:30-32, 1954.

——. Biography and the social studies: another harvest of American lives. *Soc. Educ.*, 19:213-217, 1955.

Brunot, Henriette. Balzac et les femmes. (Balzac and women). *Psyché-Paris*, 6:206-223, 1951.

Bühler, Charlotte. The curve of life as studied in biographies. *J. Appl. Psychol.*, 19:405-409, 1935.

——. Drei Generationen im Jugendtagebuch. (Three generations in a youth diary). In *Quellen und Studien zur Jugendkunde (Sources and Studies in Youth)*, Vol. II. Jena: Fischer, 1934.

—— (Ed.). Jugendtagebuch und Lebenslauf. Zwei Mädchen-Tagebücher mit einer Einleitung. (Youth diary and life. Two girls' diaries with an introduction). In *Quellen und Studien zur Jugendkunde (Sources and Studies in Youth)*, Vol. II. Jena: Fischer, 1934.

——. *Der menschliche Lebenslauf als psychologisches Problem. (Human Life as a Psychological Problem)*. Leipzig: Hirzel, 1933. 2nd. Ed. Göttingen: Verlag für Psychologie, Dr. C. J. Hogrefe, 1959.

Bühler, Charlotte, & Frenkel, Else (Eds.). *Psychologische Forschungen uber den Lebenslauf. (Psychological Studies on the Course of Life)*. Vienna: Gerold, 1937.

Burchell, Samuel C. Dostoiefsky and the sense of guilt. *Psychoanal. Rev.*, 17:195-207, 1930.

——. Marcel Proust, an interpretation of his life. *Psychoanal. Rev.*, 15:300-303, 1928.

Burks, Barbara S., Jensen, Dortha W., & Terman, Lewis M. *The Promise of Youth; Follow-Up Studies of a Thousand Gifted Children*, Vol. III in *Genetic Studies of Genius*. Stanford, Calif.: Stanford University Press, 1930.

Burns, Wayne. His mother's son: the emotional development of Charles Reade. *Lit. & Psychol.*, 4:31-47, 1954.

Burr, Charles W. The biography of a patient with paranoid dementia praecox. *Amer. J. Insanity*, 69:107-118, 1912-1913.

Burrow, Trigant. *A Search for Man's Sanity: The Selected Letters of Trigant Burrow, with Biographical Notes*. New York: Oxford University Press, 1958.

Burt, Cyril L. An autobiographical sketch. *Occupational Psychol., London*, 23:9-20, 1949.

Busemann, A. *Die Jugend im eigenen Urteil. (Self Estimates of Young People)*. Langensalza: J. Beltz, 1926.

Büttner, A. *Buddha, eine psychologische Studie. (Buddha, a Psychological Study)*. Halle: Gebauer-Schwetschke, 1906.

Bychowski, Gustav. *Dictators and Disciples from Caesar to Stalin: A Psychoanalytic Interpretation of History*. New York: International Universities Press, 1948.

——. Dictatorship and paranoia, in Muensterberger, Warner, & Axelrad, Sidney (Eds.), *Psychoanalysis and the Social Sciences*, Vol. V. New York: International Universities Press, 1955. Pp. 127-134.

——. Marcel Proust als Dichter der psychologischen Analyse. (Marcel Proust as writer of psychological analysis). *Psychoanal. Bewegung*, 4:323-344, 1932.

——. Oliver Cromwell and the Puritan revolution. *J. clin. Psychopath. Psychother.*, 7:281-309, 1945.

——. *Slowacki i Jego Dusza-Studjum Psychoanalityczne. (Slowacki and His Soul: A Psychoanalytic Study)*. Warsaw: J. Mortkowicz, 1930.

——. Walt Whitman: a study in sublimation, in Roheim, Géza (Ed.), *Psychoanalysis and the Social Sciences*, Vol. III. New York: International Universities Press, 1951. Pp. 223-261.

Campbell, C. Macfie. Psychology and biography. *Amer. J. Psychiat.*, 10: 855-872, 1931.

Campbell, Joseph. *The Hero with a Thousand Faces*. New York: Meridian Books, 1959.

Cannon, Dorothy F. *Explorer of the Human Brain; The Life of Santiago Ramón y Cajal (1852-1934)*. New York: Henry Schuman, 1949.

Cantril, Hadley. *The Psychology of Social Movements*. New York: John B. Wiley, 1941.

Cantril, Hadley, & Bumstead, Charles H. *Reflections on the Human Venture*. New York: New York University Press, 1960.

Capgras, Joaki. Autobiographie d'un pervers érotique. (The autobiography of an erotic pervert). *Encéphale et Hygiène Mentale*, 7:367, 1921.

Carlson, E. T. Amariah Brigham: life and works. *Amer. J. Psychiat.*, 112:831-836, 1956.

Carrère, J. *Degeneration in the Great French Masters; Rousseau, Chateaubriand, Balzac, Stendhal, Sand, Musset, Beaudelaire, Flaubert, Verlaine, Zola.* New York: Brentano's, 1922.

Cartwright, Dorin, & French, John R. P., Jr. The reliability of life-history studies. *Character and Pers.,* 8:110-119, 1939.

Castle, Cora S. A statistical study of eminent women, in *Columbia University Contributions to Philosophy and Psychology,* Vol. 22. New York: Science Press, 1913.

Cattell, James. McK. Families of American men of science. *Pop. Sci. Mo.,* 86:504-515, 1915.

——. Families of American men of science, III. Vital statistics and the composition of the families. *Scientific Mo.,* 5:368-377, 1917.

——. A statistical study of eminent men. *Pop. Sci. Mo.,* 62:359-377, 1903.

Cattell, Raymond B. La Vida y la Obra de Charles Spearman. (The life and work of Charles Spearman). *Rev. Psicol. Gen. Apl., Madrid,* 2:337-348, 1947.

Cavan, Ruth Shonle. The diaries of two suicides, in *Suicide.* Chicago: University of Chicago Press, 1928. Pp. 198-220.

Cavan, Ruth Shonle, Hauser, P. M., & Stouffer, S. A. Note on the statistical treatment of life history material. *Social Forces,* 9:200-203, 1930.

Cellerino, A. [Benvenuto Cellini in the guise of patient. Points from his "Vita"]. *Minerva Med.,* 51:1567-1570, 1960.

Cesio, Fidias. R. El cáracter de Sigmund Freud. (Sigmund Freud's character). *Rev. Psicoanal., Buenos Aires,* 15:386-397, 1958.

Chamberlain, Frederick. *The Private Character of Queen Elizabeth.* London: The Bodley Head, 1921.

Choisy, Maryse. Gandhi dans le monde moderne. (Gandhi in the modern world). *Psyché-Paris,* 3:2-12, 1948.

Chrapovitski, M. L. [Materials on the pathogenesis of the personality of Gleb Uspensky.] *Klin. arkh. genialn. i odaren.,* 4:69-73, 1928.

Christensen, Erwin O. Freud on Leonardo da Vinci. *Psychoanal. Rev.,* 31:153-164, 1944.

——. Infantile sources of artistic interests in the neurosis of Marie Bashkirtseff. *Psychoanal. Rev.,* 30:277-312, 1943.

Clark, E. T. *Psychology of Religious Awakening.* New York: Macmillan Co., 1929.

Clark, Kenneth. *America's Psychologists.* Washington, D. C.: American Psychological Association, 1957.

Clark, L. Pierce. *Lincoln: A Psycho-Biography.* New York: Charles Scribner's Sons.

——. The narcissism of Napoleon. *Med. J. & Rec.,* 129:440-442, 520-525, 1929.

——. A psycho-historical study of the epileptic personality in genius. *Psychoanal. Rev.,* 9:367-401, 1922.

——. Unconscious motives underlying the personalities of great statesmen. I. A psychological study of Abraham Lincoln. *Psychoanal. Rev.,* 8:1-21, 1921.

——. Unconscious motives underlying the personalities of great statesmen and their relation to epoch-making events; the narcissism of Alexander the Great. *Psychoanal. Rev.,* 10:56-69, 1923.

Clark, P. *Napoleon, Self-Destroyed.* New York: Cape & Smith, 1929.

Clark, W. H. A study of some of the factors leading to achievement and creativity with special reference to religious skepticism and belief. *J. soc. Psychol.,* 41:57-69, 1955.

Clarke, E. L. *American Men of Letters: Their Nature and Nurture.* New York: Columbia University Press, 1916.

Claparède, E. J.-J. Rousseau et la signification de l'enfance. (J. J. Rousseau and the meaning of childhood). *Ann.-suisses d'Hygiène scol.,* 13:525-553, 1912.

Cohen, John. Individuality of thought. *Bull. John Rylands Library,* 37: 103-119, 1954.

Cohen, M. J. *Jacob Emden: A Man of Controversy.* Philadelphia: Jewish Publication Society, 1937.

Coleman, Stanley M. August Strindberg: the autobiographies. *Psychoanal. Rev.,* 23:248-273, 1936.

——. The dual personality of Philip Heseltine. *J. Ment. Sci.,* 95:456-466, 1949.

——. The phantom double. Its psychological significance. *Brit. J. Med. Psychol.,* 14:254-273, 1934.

Cololian, Paul. Psychopathologie. Gustave Flaubert et la psychanalyse. (Psychopathology. Gustave Flaubert and psychoanalysis). *Hippocrate,* 5:488-495, 1937.

Combs, Arthur W. A method of analysis for the Thematic Apperception Test and autobiography. *J. clin. Psychol.,* 2:167-174, 1946.

——. The use of personal experience in Thematic Apperception Test story plots. *J. clin. Psychol.,* 2:357-363, 1946.

Constable, F. C. *Poverty and Hereditary Genius: A Criticism of Mr. Francis Galton's Theory of Hereditary Genius.* London: Arthur C. Fifield, 1905.

Corner, George W. (Ed.). *The Autobiography of Benjamin Rush; His "Travels through Life" together with His Commonplace Book for 1789-1813.* Princeton: Princeton University Press, 1948.

Cosack, H. Tagebuch eines Autistischen Jugendlichen. (The diary of an autistic adolescent). *Z. ges. Neurol. Psychiat.,* 154:258-264, 1936.

Courbon, ———. *Etude psychiatrique sur Benvenuto Cellini. (A Psychiatric Study of Benvenuto Cellini).* Thèse méd. Lyon: 1906.

Cox, Catherine M., et al. *The Early Mental Traits of Three Hundred Geniuses,* Vol. II in *Genetic Studies of Genius.* Stanford, Calif.: Stanford University Press, 1926.

Cox, David. *Jung and St. Paul.* New York: Association Press, 1959.

Coy, L. G. The mentality of a gifted child. *J. appl. Psychol.,* 2:299-307, 1918.

Crandall, Norma. *Emily Brontë. A Psychological Portrait.* Rindge, N.H.: Richard R. Smith Publ., Inc., 1957.

Crawshaw, William H. *Literary Interpretation of Life.* New York: Macmillan Co., 1900.

Crook, Guy H. A memory of infantile life; a scrap of personal experience. *J. abnorm. soc. Psychol.,* 20:90-91, 1925.

Culpin, Millais. An autobiography. *Occupational Psychol., London,* 23:140-152, 1949.

Dalbiez, Roland. Marie-Thérèse Noblet considérée du point de vue Psychologique. (A psychological view of Marie Thérèse Noblet). *Etud. Carmélit.,* 23:201-209, 1938.

Darlington, H. S. The confessions of sins. *Psychoanal. Rev.,* 24:150-164, 1937.

Darroch, Jane. An interpretation of the personality of Jesus. *Brit. J. Med. Psychol.,* 21:75-79, 1947.

Darwin, Charles. A biographical sketch of an infant, in Dennis, Wayne, (Ed.), *Readings in Child Psychology.* New York: Prentice-Hall, 1951. Pp. 54-67.

Davenport, C. B. *Naval Officers: Their Heredity and Development.* Washington, D.C.: Carnegie Institution, 1919.

David, Gilbert. The stability of biographical predictors. *Dissert. Abstr.,* 12:778-779, 1952.

Debesse, M. *Comment Étudier les Adolescents: Examen Critique des Confidences Juvéniles. (How to Study Adolescents: A Critical Examination of Confidential Statements of Young People).* Paris: Alcan, 1937.

DeGreef, E. Succédanes et Concomitances Psychopathologiques de la "Nuit Obscure." (Psychopathological substitutes and concomitants of the "Dark Night"). *Etud. Carmélit.,* 23:152-176, 1938.

Delacroix, Henri. *Les Grand Mystiques Chretiens. (Eminent Christian Mystics).* Paris: Alcan, 1938.

De la Mare, Walter. *Early One Morning in the Spring: Chapters on Children and on Childhood As It Is Revealed in Particular in Early Memories and in Early Writings.* New York: Macmillan Co., 1935.

Del Greco, Francesco. Le "Confessioni" e le "Autobiografie" nel Giro delle Mentalità Communi e Abnormali. ("Confessions" and "Auto-biographies" in normal and abnormal subjects). *Ann. Osp. Psichiat. Perugia,* 3-4:119-131, 1936.

———. Sulle anormalita di carattere di alcuni grandi intellettuali. (On the character abnormalities of some great intellectuals). *Arch. gen. Neurol. Psichiat.,* 10:182-189, 1929.

Dell, Floyd. An autobiographical critique. *Psychoanal. Quart.,* 1:715-730, 1932.

Delvolve, J. L'histoire mentale d'August Comte. (The mental history of August Comte). *J. de Psychol.,* 28:749-768, 1931.

Dennis, Wayne. The age decrement in outstanding scientific contributions: fact or artifact? *Amer. Psychol.,* 13:457-460, 1958.

———. Age and productivity among scientists. *Science,* 123:724-725, 1956.

———. A bibliography of baby biographies. *Child Devel.,* 7:71-73, 1936.

Dennis, Wayne, & Dennis, M. G. Behavorial development in the first year as shown by forty biographies. *Psychol. Rec.,* 1:349-361, 1937.

Deri, M. Caligula. *Psychoanal. Bewegung,* 2:400-407, 1930.

De Sanctis, S. Studio clinico e psicologico di Anna Giuseppini in Monaro. (A clinical and psychological study of Anna Giuseppini Monaro). *Ric. sci.,* 2:190-235, 1934.

Deutsch, Felix. Artistic expression and neurotic illness. I. The respiratory neurosis of Charles Kingsley's *The Water Babies* and Anton Locke's *Dream. Amer. Imago,* 4:64-102, 1947.

Deutsch, Helene. George Sand—ein Frauenschicksal. (George Sand—fate of a woman). *Imago,* 14:334 ff., 1928.

De Voto, Bernard. *Mark Twain at Work.* Cambridge, Mass.: Harvard University Press, 1942.

———. The skeptical biographer. *Harper's Mag.* 166:181-192, 1933.

Diether, Jack. Mahler and psychoanalysis. *Psychoanal. & Psychoanal. Rev.,* 45:3-14, 1958.

Dillingham, Louise B. The creative imagination of Théophile Gautier. *Psychol. Monographs,* 37:1927.

Dilthey, Wilhelm. *Das Erlebnis und die Dichtung. Lessing, Goethe, Novalis, Hölderlin. (Experience and Fiction).* Leipzig: Teubner, 1910.

Dobree, B. Modern biography. *Nat. Rev.,* 99:128, 1932.

———. Some aspects of biography since Strachey. *Britain Today,* 152:16-20, 1948.

Dollard, John. *Criteria for the Life History—with Analysis of Six Notable Documents.* New Haven: Yale University Press, 1935.

——. The life history in community studies. *Amer. Sociol. Rev.*, 3:724-737, 1938.

Dollard, John, & Mowrer, O. H. A method of measuring tension in personal documents. *J. abnorm. soc. Psychol.*, 42:3-32, 1947.

Dooley, Lucile. Psychoanalysis of the character and genius of Emily Brontë. *Psychoanal. Rev.*, 17:208-239, 1930.

——. Psychoanalysis of Charlotte Brontë as a type of woman genius. *Amer. J. Psychol.*, 31:221-272, 1920.

——. Psychoanalytic studies of genius. *Amer. J. Psychol.*, 27:363-416, 1916.

Dracoulidès, N. N. Profil Psychoanalytique de Charles Baudelaire. (A psychoanalytic profile of Charles Baudelaire). *Psyché-Paris*, 8:461-485, 1953.

Drever, James, Sr. An autobiography. *Occupational Psychol., London*, 22:20-30, 1948.

Du Bois, Cora, *The People of Alor.* Minneapolis: University of Minnesota Press, 1944.

Dudycha, George J., & Dudycha, Martha M. Childhood memories, a review of the literature. *Psychol. Bull.*, 38:668-682, 1941.

Duff, I. F. Grant. Die Beziehung Elisabeth-Essex; eine psychoanalytische Betrachtung. (The relationship between Elizabeth and Essex; a psychoanalytic observation). *Psychoanal. Bewegung*, 3:457-474, 1931.

——. Die Geschichte der Phantasie einer Heiligen. (The history of the imagination of a saint) . *Imago*, 16:487-501, 1930.

——. A one-sided sketch of Jonathan Swift. *Psychoanal. Quart.*, 6:238-259, 1937.

Dugas, L. Auguste Comte: Étude critique et psychologique. (Auguste Comte: a critical and psychological study). *Rev. Philos.*, 40:225-251, 360-398, 1895.

Dumas, G. L'état mental d'Auguste Comte. (The mental state of Auguste Comte). *Rev. Philos.*, 45:30-60, 151-180, 387-414, 1898.

——. La folie d'Auguste Comte. (The madness of Auguste Comte). *Rev. d. Paris*, 4:321-346, 1897.

Dumaz, J. Psychologie de Jeanne d'arc. (The psychology of Joan of Arc). *Ann. Méd.-Psychol.*, 19:353-376, 1904.

Dupouy, R. Charles Baudelaire toxicomane et opiomane. (Charles Baudelaire, toxic and opium addict). *Ann. Méd.-Psychol.*, 11:353, 1911.

——. Coleridge. Opiumisme et psychose périodique. (Coleridge's addiction to opium and periodic psychosis). *J. de psychol. norm. et path.*, 7:226-247, 1910.

——. L'opiumisme d'Edgard Poë. (Edgar Allen Poe's addiction to opium). *Ann. Méd.-Psychol.,* 13:5-19, 1911.

Earnest, Ernest. *S. Weir Mitchell: Novelist and Physician.* Philadelphia: University of Pennsylvania Press, 1950.

Ekstein, Rudolf. A biographical account on Freud's dual instinct theory. *Amer. Imago,* 6:211-216, 1949.

Edel, Leon. *Henry James, the Untried Years: 1843-1870.* Philadelphia: J. B. Lippincott, 1953.

——. Hugh Walpole and Henry James. *Amer. Imago,* 8:3-21, 1951.

——. *Literary Biography.* Garden City, N. Y.: Doubleday Anchor Books, 1959.

——. That one may say this was the man. *New York Times Book Rev.,* June 24, 1956, pp. 1, 12.

Eisele, Carolyn. Charles S. Pierce, nineteenth century man of science. *Scripta Mathematica,* 24:305-324, 1959.

Eissler, Kurt R. An unknown autobiographical letter by Freud and a short comment. *Int. J. Psycho-Anal.,* 32:319-324, 1951.

——. Goethe and science: a contribution to the psychology of Goethe's psychosis, in Muensterberger, Warner, & Axelrad, Sidney, (Eds.), *Psychoanalysis and the Social Sciences,* Vol. V. New York: International Universities Press, 1958. Pp. 51-98.

——. Notes on the environment of a genius, in Eissler, Ruth S., et al., (Eds.), *The Psychoanalytic Study of the Child,* Vol. XIV. New York: International Universities Press, 1959. Pp. 267-313.

Ellery, R. S. *The Cow Jumped over the Moon.* Melbourne: Cheshire, 1956.

Ellis, Havelock. *From Rousseau to Proust.* Boston: Houghton Mifflin Co., 1935.

——. *A Study of British Genius.* London: Hurst & Blackett, 1904.

——. *Views and Reviews.* London: Harmsworth, 1932.

Eng, Erling. Cellini's two childhood memories. *Amer. Imago,* 13:189-203, 1956.

Eng, H. Dr. Parrs dagbok over utviklingen av sine barns tale. (Dr. Parr's diary on development of speech in his children). *Norsk pedagog. Årsb.,* 12:105-117, 1944.

Engle, Bernice & French, Thomas M. Some psychodynamic reflections upon the life and writings of Solon. *Psychoanal. Quart.,* 20:253-274, 1951.

Erikson, Erik H. The first psychoanalyst. *Yale Rev.,* 1:40-62, 1956.

——. Hitler's imagery and German youth. *Psychiatry,* 5:475-493, 1942.

——. The legend of Hitler's childhood, in *Childhood and Society.* New York: W. W. Norton & Co., 1950. Pp. 284-315.

——. The legend of Maxim Gorky's youth, in *Ibid.* Pp. 316-358.

——. Observations on the Yurok: childhood and world image. *Univ. Calif. Publ. Amer. Arch. & Ethnology,* 35:257-301, 1943.

——. The problem of ego identity. *Psychol. Issues,* 1:101-164, 1959.

——. *Young Man Luther, a Study in Psychoanalysis and History.* New York: W. W. Norton & Co., 1958.

Esman, Aaron H. Mozart: a study in genius. *Psychoanal. Quart.,* 20:603-612, 1951.

Esselbrügge, K. Die Struktur des Humors bei Gottfried Keller. (The nature of humor in Gottfried Keller). *Jahrb. f. Charakterol.,* 6:177-213, 1929.

Esteve, P. L. Marcel Proust. *Psychol. et vie,* 2:21-25, 1928.

Evans, Jane. *Three Men; An Experiment in the Biography of Emotion.* New York: Alfred A. Knopf, 1954.

Evlachow, A. Léonard de Vinci. N'était-il pas un Épileptoide? (Was Leonardo da Vinci an epileptoid?). *Arch. Gen. Neurol. Psichiat.,* 18:343-357, 1937.

Fabricant, Noah. *Thirteen Famous Patients.* Philadelphia: Chilton Co., 1960.

Fantham, H. B. Charles Dickens: a biological study of his personality. *Character & Pers.,* 2:222-230, 1934.

Farnsworth, P. R. Musical eminence and year of birth. *J. Aesthet.,* 4:107-109, 1945.

Fearing, Franklin. Psychological studies of historical personalities. *Psychol. Bull.,* 24:521-539, 1927.

Federov, I. V. [The curator's registration card of the student Chekhov (from archival material)]. *Klin. Med. (Moscow),* 41:148-153, 1960.

Feis, Oswald. *Hector Berlioz, eine pathographische Studie. (Hector Berlioz, a Pathographical Study).* Wiesbaden: Bergmann, 1911.

Feldman, A. Bronson. Doestoevsky and father love. *Psychoanal. & Psychoanal. Rev.,* 45:84-98, 1958.

——. Franklin, an anal-erotic personality. *Psychoanal.,* 5:33-54, 1957.

——. *The Unconscious in History.* New York: Philosophical Library, 1959.

Feldman, Eugene S. Sherwood Anderson's search. *Psychoanal.,* 3:44-51, 1955.

Feldman, Harold. Tragic comedy of great men. *Psychoanal. & Psychoanal. Rev.,* 46:3-16, 1959.

Ferenczi, Sandor. Cornelia, die Mutter der Gracchen. (Cornelia, the mother of the Gracchi). *Int. Zeitschr. f. Psychoanal.,* 5:117-120, 1919.

Ferguson, L. W. The evaluative attitudes of Jonathan Swift. *Psychol. Rec.,* 3:26-44, 1939.

Ferrari, G. C. Autobiografia. (Autobiography). *Riv. Psicol. norm. patol.*, 29:2-11, 69-85, 1933.

Fiedler, Leslie A. Archetype and signature. The relationship of poet and poem, in *No! in Thunder*. Boston: Beacon Press, 1960, pp. 309-328.

Fischell, E. *Untersuchungen über die Entwicklung Weiblicher Interessen auf Grund von Selbstdarstellung. (Investigations on the Development of Feminine Interests on the Basis of Autobiographies)*. Paderborn: Schoningh, 1932.

Fishman, Leo. A pathography of August Comte. *Psychoanal. Rev.*, 37: 66-70, 1950.

Flugel, J. C. *Men and their Motives; Psycho-Analytical Studies*. New York: International Universities Press, 1947.

——. On the character and married life of Henry VIII. *Int. J. Psycho-Anal.*, 1:24-55, 1920.

Folly, ——. Elisabeth d'Austriche. Étude historique et psychiatrique. (Elizabeth of Austria. An historical and psychiatric study). *Hyg. ment.*, 29:73-98, 1934.

Fontes, Vítor. Notas à Margem de Dois Diarios-Intimos de Adolescentes. (Notes on two intimate diaries of adolescents). *Criança Portug.*, 5: 67-91, 1945-46.

Forel, August. Autobiographie subjective et inductive de troubles psychiques après une thrombose du cerveau. (A subjective and inductive autobiography of psychic disturbance after a thrombosis of the brain). *Prog. med.*, 54:7-9, 126-138, 245-247, 1927.

Foulkes, S. H. Some remarks on a chapter of Helen Keller's book: *The World I Live In*. *Psychoanal. Rev.*, 28:512-519, 1941.

Frade Correia, Joao. *Dinamene ou o Drama Psicológico de Camões. (Dinamene or the Psychological Drama of de Camöens)*. Oporto, Portugal: Castelo Branco, 1946.

Freedman, Burrill. Italo Svevo: a psychoanalytic novelist. *Psychoanal. Rev.*, 18:434-443, 1931.

——. H. R. Lenormand: a psychoanalytical dramatist. *Psychoanal. Rev.*, 19:64-71, 1932.

Freedman, Burrill, & Freedman, Sumner. The psychology of Casanova. *Psychoanal. Rev.*, 20:73-78, 1933.

Freimark, H. *Robespierre. Eine historisch-psychologische Studie. (Robespierre. A Historical-Psychological Study)*. Wiesbaden: Bergmann, 1913.

——. *Talstoj als Charakter. Eine Studie auf Grund seiner Schriften*. (The Personality of Tolstoi. A Study Based on His Writings). Wiesbaden: Bergmann, 1909.

Freistadt-Lederer, A. Eine Frau Allein. (A woman alone). *Psychol. Rund-schau*, 4:215-219, 1933.

French, R. S. *From Homer to Helen Keller: A Social and Educational Study of the Blind.* New York: American Foundation for the Blind, 1932.

Frenkel, Else. Studies in biographical psychology. *Character & Pers.,* 5:1-34, 1936.

Frenkel-Brunswick, Else. Psychoanalysis and personality research. *J. abnorm. soc. Psychol.,* 35:176-197, 1940.

———. Mechanisms of self-deception. *J. soc. Psychol.,* 10:409-420, 1939.

Freud, Ernst L. (Ed.). *Letters of Sigmund Freud.* Translated from the German by Tania and James Stern. New York: Basic Books, 1960.

Freud, Sigmund. A childhood recollection from *Dichtung und Wahrheit,* in Strachey, James (Ed.), *Collected Papers,* Vol. IV. New York: Basic Books, 1959. Pp. 357-367.

———. Dostoevsky and parricide, in *Ibid.,* Vol. V. Pp. 222-242.

———. Entwurf zu einem Brief on Thomas Mann von Sigm. Freud. [1936] (Sketch of a letter by Freud to Thomas Mann). *Int. Z. Psychoanal. Imago,* 26:217-219, 1941.

———. *Leonardo da Vinci: A Psycho-Sexual Study of an Infantile Reminiscence.* New York: Dodd, Mead & Co., 1932.

———. *Moses and Monotheism.* London: Hogarth Press, 1951.

———. *On Creativity and the Unconscious.* New York: Harper & Bros., 1958.

———. Psycho-analytic notes upon an autobiographical account of a case of paranoia (dementia paranoides), in Strachey, James, (Ed.), *Collected Papers,* Vol. III. New York: Basic Books, 1959. Pp. 387-470.

Friedländer, Kate. Charlotte Brontë: a study of a masochistic character. *Int. J. Psycho-Anal.,* 24:45-54, 1943.

Friedlander, Rudolph. Wilhelm II. Eine psychologische Studie. (A psychological study of Wilhelm II). *Die Umschau,* No. 13-17, 1919.

Friedmann, A. Die Kindheit Gandhis. (Gandhi's childhood). *Int. Zsch. f. Indiv.-Psychol.,* 11:1-7, 1933.

Frisch, Fritz, & Hettzer, Hildegard. Die religiöse Entwicklung des Jugendlichen auf Grund von Tagebüchern. (The religious development of children as judged from personal diaries). *Arch. f. d. ges. Psychol.,* 62:409-442, 1928.

Fromm, Erich. *Sigmund Freud's Mission: An Analysis of His Personality and Influence.* New York: Harper & Bros., 1959.

Fronz, E. *Babys Briefe und Tagebuch über das erste Lebenjahr. (Baby's Letters and Diaries about the First Year of Life).* Graz: Leykam, 1926.

Fruhock, W. M. Thomas Wolfe: Of time and neurosis. *Southwest Rev.*, 33:349-360, 1948.

Fry, C. L. The religious affiliations of American leaders. *Scientific Mo.*, 36:241-249, 1933.

Fuchs, H. Die Sprache des Jugendlichen im Tagebuch. (The language of the adolescent as revealed in diaries). *Zsch. f. angew. Psychol.*, 29: 74-120, 1927.

Fuess, C. M. Debunkery and biography. *Atlant. Mon.*, 151:347-356, 1933.

Gabel, Joseph. Swift et la schizophrénie. Le point de vue du psychiatre. (Swift and schizophrenia. The point of view of the psychiatrists). *Psyché-Paris*, 4:253-258, 1949.

Galant, I. B. [The psychopathological figure of L. Andreyev]. *Klinicheski arkhiv genialnosti i odarennosti*, 2:147-165, 1927.

Galant, Johann S. Die prägenitale Sexualität nach einem Kindheitserlebnis Leonid Andrejews. (Pregenital sexuality after a childhood experience of Leonid Andreyev). *Arch. Kinderhk.*, 81:262-280, 1927.

Gallot, H. M. Psychanalyse de Huysmans. (Psychoanalysis of Huysmans). *Evolut. Psychiat.*, 4:53-72, 1948.

Galton, Francis. *English Men of Science, Their Nature and Nurture*. London: Macmillan Co., 1874.

——. *Hereditary Genius*. New York: D. Appleton Co., 1870.

——. *Memories of My Life*. New York: E. P. Dutton & Co., 1909.

Garma, Angel. Essai de psychanalyse d'Arthur Rimbaud. (Essay on the psychoanalysis of Arthur Rimbaud). *Rev. Franç. Psychanal.*, 10:383-420, 1938.

Garraty, John A. How should you tell a man's story? *New York Times Book Rev.*, July 5, 1959, pp. 1, 10.

——. The interrelations of psychology and biography. *Psychol. Bull.*, 51: 569-582, 1954.

——. *The Nature of Biography*. New York: Alfred A. Knopf, 1957.

——. Preserved Smith, Ralph Volney Harlow, and psychology. *J. Hist. Ideas*, 15:456-465, 1954.

Garrison, Charlotte G., Burke, Agnes, & Hollingworth, Leta S. The psychology of a prodigious child. *J. Appl. Psychol.*, 1:101-110, 1917.

George, Alexander L., & George, Juliette L. *Woodrow Wilson and Colonel House. A Personality Study*. New York: John Day Co., 1956.

Gerling, R. Dr. Martin Luther. Eine Charakteranalyse. (Dr. Martin Luther. A character analysis). *Zsch. f. Menschenkd.*, 2:6-18, 1926.

Gesell, Arnold. The biography of a wolf-child. *Harper's Mag.*, 182:183-193, 1941.

——. *Wolf Child and Human Child*. New York: Harper & Bros., 1941.

Gesell, Arnold, Castner, B. M., Thompson, H., & Amatruda, C. S. *Biog-*

raphies of Child Development. The Mental Careers of Eighty-Four Infants and Children. New York: Paul Hoeber, 1939.

Giese, Fritz. Das freie literarische Schaffen bei Kindern und Jugendlichen. (Free literary creativity in children and adolescents). *Beiheft Zsch. f. Angewandte Psychol., Leipzig,* 1914. Pp. vi-vii.

Gilbert, Gustave M. Hermann Goering, amiable psychopath. *J. abnorm. soc. Psychol.,* 43:211-229, 1948.

——. *Psychology of Dictatorship.* New York: Ronald Press, 1950.

Gilbert, M. S. *Biography of the Unborn.* Baltimore: Williams and Wilkins, 1938.

Gillespie, James M., & Allport, Gordon W. *Youth's Outlook on the Future.* New York: Random House, 1955.

Glaser, R. *Goethes Vater. Sein Leben nach Tagebüchern und Zeitberichten. (Goethe's Father. His Life Based on Diaries and Contemporary Accounts).* Leipzig, 1929.

Goertzel, Mildred G., & Goertzel, Victor H. Intellectual and emotional climate in families procuring eminence. *Gifted Child Q.,* 4:59-60, 1960.

Goitein, P. Lionel. Diary of fellatio: terrorization and its unconscious counterpart. *J. crim. Psychopath.,* 5:95-113, 1943.

——. The diary of a self slasher. *J. crim. Psychopath.,* 5:521-540, 1944.

Golan, Shmuel (Ed.). Introduction to *Yoman (A Diary). Ofakim,* 8:259-288, 1954.

Goldenweiser, A. Some contributions of psychoanalysis to the interpretation of social facts, in Barnes, Harry E. (Ed.), *Contemporary Social Theory.* New York: Century Co., 1940. Pp. 391-430.

Gottfried, Alex. The use of psychosomatic categories in a study of political personality. *Western Political Quart.,* 8:234-247, 1955.

Gottschalk, Louis, Kluckhohn, Clyde, & Angell, Robert. *The Use of Personal Documents in History, Anthropology and Sociology.* New York: Social Science Research Council, 1945.

Gould, G. M. A biographic clinic on Gustave Flaubert. *Med. Record,* 69:569-578, 1906.

——. *Biographic Clinics. The Origin of the Ill-Health of DeQuincey, Carlyle, Darwin, Huxley and Browning.* Philadelphia: Blakiston, 1903.

——. Lafacadio Hearn. A study of his personality and art. *Fortn. Rev.,* 80:685-695, 881-892, 1906.

Graf, Max. [Richard Wagner in the *Flying Dutchman.* A contribution to the psychology of artistic creation.] *Schriften,* Vol. 1, 1911.

Graucot, K. Hans Carossas Selbstdarstellung seiner Kindheit und Jugend in ihrer Entwicklungs-und typenpsychologischen Bedeutung. (Hans

Carossa's description of his childhood and youth in their genetic and typological significance). *Zsch. f. Angew. Psychol.,* 44:217-244, 1933.

Graves, A. *The Eclipse of a Mind.* New York: Medical Journal Press, 1942.

Gray, H. Brother Klaus; with a translation of Jung's commentary. *J. nerv. ment. Dis.,* 103:359-377, 1946.

Grazia, Sebastian de. Mahatma Gandhi: the son of his mother. *Political Quart.,* 19:336-348, 1948.

Green, F. C. *Jean-Jacques Rousseau.* Cambridge: Cambridge University Press, 1955.

Greenacre, Phyllis. The childhood of the artist: libidinal phase development and giftedness, in Eissler, Ruth S., et al. (Eds.), *The Psychoanalytic Study of the Child,* Vol. XII. New York: International Universities Press, 1957. Pp. 47-72.

——. The family romance of the artist, in *Ibid.,* Vol. XIII. New York: International Universities Press, 1958. Pp. 9-43.

——. The imposter. *Psychoanal. Quart.,* 27:359-382, 1958.

——. "It's my own invention"; a special screen memory of Mr. Lewis Carroll, its form and history. *Psychoanal. Quart.,* 24:200-244, 1955.

——. The relation of the imposter to the artist, in Eissler, Ruth S., et al., (Eds.), *The Psychoanalytic Study of the Child,* Vol. XIII. New York: International Universities Press, 1958. Pp. 521-540.

——. *Swift and Carroll. A Psychoanalytic Study of Two Lives.* New York: International Universities Press, 1955.

Gregory, Hoosag K. *The Prisoner and His Crimes: A Psychological Approach to William Cowper's Life and Writings.* Unpublished Ph.D. thesis. Cambridge, Mass.: Harvard University, 1951.

Grotjahn, Martin. A letter by Sigmund Freud with recollections of his adolescence. *J. Amer. Psychoanal. Assoc.,* 4:644-652, 1956.

Gruhle, H. W. Selbstbiographie und Personlichkeitsforschung. (Autobiography and personality investigation). *Ber. ü. d. Kongr. f. exper. Psychol.,* 8:165-167, 1924.

Guerin, J. G. E. *Pathologie de Honoré de Balzac. (The Pathology of Honoré de Balzac).* Paris: Thèse de Méd., 1938.

Gurrier, P. *Etude médico-psychologique sur Thomas de Quincey. (A Medico-Psychological Study of Thomas de Quincey).* Lyon: Rey, 1908.

Gutheil, Emil A. (Ed.). *The Autobiography of William Stekel.* New York: Liveright, 1950.

Guttmacher, Manfred S. *America's Last King: An Interpretation of the Madness of George III.* New York: Charles Scribner's Sons, 1941.

Hahn, L. Psycho-pathologie de Goethe. (The psychopathology of Goethe). *Chron. Méd.,* 11:10, 1904.

Haldane, Charlotte. *Alfred: The Passionate Life of Alfred de Musset.* New York: Roy Publishers, 1961.

Hale, William B. *The Story of a Style. A Psychoanalytic Study of Woodrow Wilson.* New York: Viking Press, 1920.

Hall, G. Stanley. Adolescence in literature, biography and history, in *Adolescence: Its Psychology,* Vol. I. New York: D. Appleton & Co., 1904. Pp. 513-589.

——. A study in anger. *Amer. J. Psychol.,* 10:516-591, 1899.

——. A study of fears. *Amer. J. Psychol.,* 8:147-249, 1897.

Holliday, James L. *Mr. Carlyle, My Patient: A Psychosomatic Biography.* New York: Grune & Stratton, 1950.

Hamilton, A. M. Psychopathic rulers. *No. Amer. Rev.,* 187:378-386, 1908.

Hariga, J. A propos de la psychologie de Van Gogh. (About the psychology of Van Gogh). *Acta neurol. psychiat., Belg.,* 59:215-227, 1959.

Harlow, Ralph V. A psychological study of Samuel Adams. *Psychoanal. Rev.,* 9:418-428, 1922.

——. *Samuel Adams.* New York: Henry Holt & Co., 1923.

Harms, Ernest. Die Psychologische Bedeutung des Tagesbuches. (The psychological significance of diaries). *Psyche, Schweiz,* No. 9, 1934.

Harrington, M. R. The life of a Lenape boy. *Pennsylvania Archaeologist,* 3:3-8, 1933.

Hartman, D. A. The psychological point of view in history. Some phases of the slavery struggle. *J. abnorm. Psychol.,* 17:261, 1922-23.

Hartmann, W. *Richelieu; eine psychologische Studie. (Richelieu; a Psychological Study).* Berlin: Junker & Dünnhaupt, 1940.

Havighurst, Robert J., & Taba, Hilda. *Adolescent Character and Personality.* New York: John Wiley & Sons, 1949.

Haviland, C. M. An autobiography. *Psychoanal. Rev.,* 8:284-313, 1921.

Heidenhain, Adolf. J. J. Rousseau; Personlichkeit, Philosophie und Psychose. (J. J. Rousseau; his personality, philosophy and psychosis). *Grenzfrag. d. Nerv. u. Seelenl.,* 117:1-84, 1924.

Heider, Fritz. The description of the psychological environment in the work of Marcel Proust. *Character & Pers.,* 9:295-314, 1941.

Heimann, J. Die Heilung der Elisabeth Browning in ihren Sonetten. (The cure of Elizabeth Browning by her sonnets). *Imago-Leipzig,* 21:227-254, 1935.

Heilbrunn, E. Stendhal. *Jahrb. f. Charakterol.,* 6:155-177, 1929.

Helwig, H. Den maniodepressive Psykoses Betydning for historiske Personligheder. (The importance of the manic-depressive psychosis for historic personalities). *Hospitalstid*, 77:1-21, 1934.

———. *Soren Kierkegaard. En Psykiatrisk-Psykologisk Studie. (Soren Kierkegaard. A Psychiatric and Psychological Study)*. Copenhagen: Hagerup, 1933.

Henry, G. W. *Sex Variants: a Study of Homosexual Patterns*. New York: Paul Hoeber, 1941.

Hermann, Imré. Benvenuto Cellinis dichterische Periode. (Benvenuto Cellini's poetical period). *Imago*, 10:418-423, 1924.

———. Charles Darwin. *Imago*, 13:57-82, 1927.

———. *Gustav Theodor Fechner. Eine psychoanalytische Studie über individuelle Bedingtheiten wissenschaftlicher Ideen. (Gustav Theodor Fechner. A Psychoanalytic Study of the Extent an Author's Personality Influences His Theories)*. Vienna: Internationaler Psychoanalytischer Verlag, 1925.

———. Die Regression zum zeichnerischen ausdruck bei Goethe. (Goethe's regression to drawing as means of expression). *Imago*, 10:424-430, 1924.

———. Zwei Überlieferungen aus Pascals Kinderjahren. (Two episodes from Pascal's childhood). *Imago*, 11:346-351, 1925.

Hermann-Cziner, Alice. Die Grundlagen der Zeichnerischen Begabung bei Marie Bashkirtseff. (The basis of Marie Bashkirtseff's drawing talent). *Imago*, 10:434-438, 1924.

Hentig, H. V. *Robespierre. Studien zur Psycho-Pathologie des Machttriebes. (Robespierre. Studies about the Psychology of the Desire for Power)*. Stuttgart: Julius Hoffmann, 1924.

Hetzer, H. Zur Geschichte des Kindertagebuches. (Contributions to the history of childhood diaries). *Kleine Kinder*, 4:1-3, 1930.

Hillpern, Else P., Spaulding, Irving A., & Hillpern, Edmund P. *Bristow Rogers: American Negro. A Psychoanalytical Case History*. New York: Hermitage House, 1949.

Hillyer, Jane. *Reluctantly Told*. New York: Macmillan Co., 1926.

Hirth, G. *Er pathologisch? Ein Beitrag zur Feier von Goethes 150. Gebrurstag. (Was He Pathological? A Contribution to the Celebration of Goethe's 150th Birthday)*. Munich: G. Hirth, 1899.

Hitschmann, Edward. Die Bedeutung der Psychoanalyse für die Biographik. (The meaning of psychoanalysis for biography). *Psychoanal. Bewegung*, 2:305-313, 1930.

———. Die Binding Eckermanns an Goethe. (Eckermann's attachment to Goethe). *Psychoanal. Bewegung*, 5:520-526, 1933.

———. Ein Dichter und sein Vater (Dauthendey). (A poet and his father—Dauthendey). *Imago*, 4:337-345, 1916.

——. Franz Schubert's grief and love. *Amer. Imago,* 7:67-75, 1950.

——. *Ein Gespenst aus der Kindheit Knut Hamsuns. (A Ghost from Knut Hamsun's Childhood).* Vienna: Internationaler Psychoanalytischer Verlag, 1926.

——. *Gottfried Keller: Psychoanalyse des Dichters, seiner Gestalten und Motive. (Gottfried Keller: Psychoanalysis of the Writer, His Characters and Themes).* Leipzig: Bach, 1915.

——. *Great Men. Psychoanalytic Studies.* New York: International Universities Press, 1956.

——. Johann Peter Eckermann. *Psychoanal. Bewegung,* 5:392-414, 1933.

——. Knut Hamsun und die Psychoanalyse. (Knut Hamsun and psychoanalysis). *Psychoanal. Bewegung,* 1:318-324, 1929.

——. *Psychoanalytisches zur Persönlichkeit Goethes. (Psychoanalytic Comments on Goethe's Personality).* Vienna: Internationaler Psychoanalytischer Verlag, 1932.

——. Schopenhauers Versuch einer Psychoanalyse des Philosophen. (Schopenhauer's attempt to psychoanalyze the philosopher). *Imago,* 101-174, 1913.

——. Selma Lagerlöf, ihr Wesen und ihr Werk. (Selma Lagerlöf, the person and her work). *Imago,* 24:304-332, 1939.

——. Some psycho-analytic aspects of biography. *Int. J. Psycho-Anal.,* 37:265-269, 1956.

——. Von, um and über Knut Hamsun. (Knut Hamsun). *Imago,* 14:358-363, 1928.

——. Zum Werden eines Romandichters. (About the development of a novelist). *Imago,* 1:49-55, 1912.

Hobman, J. B. (Ed.). *David Eder. Memoirs of a Modern Pioneer.* London: Victor Gollancz, 1945.

Hoffer, Willi. Diaries of adolescent schizophrenics (hebephrenics), in Eissler, Ruth S., et al., (Eds.), *The Psychoanalytic Study of the Child,* Vol. II. New York: International Universities Press, 1946. Pp. 293-312.

——. Die Onaniekampf im Tagebuch des Jugendlichen. (The fight against masturbation in the diary of a youth). *Ztschr. f. psychoanal. Pädagogik,* 5:35-38, 1931.

Holland, John L. Undergraduate origins of American scientists. *Science,* 126:433-437, 1957.

Hollingworth, H. L. *Leta Stetter Hollingworth; A Biography.* Lincoln, Nebr.: University of Nebraska Press, 1943.

Hollingworth, Leta S. Introduction to biography for young children who test above 150 I.Q. *Teachers College Record,* 24:277-287, 1924.

Holmes, A. *The Mind of St. Paul: A Psychological Study.* New York: Macmillan Co., 1929.

Holstijn, A. J. Westerman. The psychological development of Vincent Van Gogh. *Amer. Imago,* 8:239-273, 1951.

Hopkins, P. Observations on some criminal and pathological traits in the dictators. *J. crim. Psychopath.,* 4:243-251, 1942.

Hopkirk, Mary. *Nobody Wanted Sam. The Story of the Unwelcomed Child, 1930-1948.* London: Murray, 1949.

Hoppe, A. Psychopathologisches bei Schiller und Ibsen. (Psychopathological traces in Schiller and Ibsen). *Zentbl. f. Nervenhk. u. Psychiat.,* 18:223-228, 1907.

Horsfield, E. Charles II: the bewitched; last Hapsburg king of Spain; he was infirm of body with probable mental deficiency. *Amer. J. ment. Def.,* 46:175-180, 1941.

Horst, L. Van Der. *Das Tagebuch eines Knaben. (A Boy's Diary).* Berlin: Kultur Verlag, 1920.

Hubble, D. Charles Darwin and psychotherapy. *Lancet,* 244:129-133, 1943.

Hug-Hellmuth, Hermine von. [The true nature of the child psyche. Letters of children.] *Imago; Zsch. f. Aniv. d. Psychoanal. auf. d. Geisteswiss.,* 1920 (?), Vol. 4, No. 1.

Hunt, Morton M. *The Natural History of Love.* New York: Alfred A. Knopf, 1959.

Hurlock, Elizabeth B., & McHugh, G. Use of the biographical method in the study of motor coordination. *Child Devel.,* 7:161-168, 1936.

Hurlock, Elizabeth B., & Schwartz, R. Biographical records of memory in pre-school children. *Child Devel.,* 3:230-239, 1932.

Huth, A. Grundsätzliches über Personalbogen. (Fundamental principles concerning personal data sheets). *Zsch. f. päd. Psychol.,* 22:117-125, 1921.

Hyslop, T. B. *The Great Abnormals.* London: Phillip Allan & Co., 1925.

Iovetz-Tereschenko, N. M. *Friendship-Love in Adolescence.* London: Allen & Unwin, 1936.

Ireland, W. W. Friedrich Nietzsche: a study in mental pathology. *Alien. & Neurol.,* 22:223-267, 1901.

——. On the mental state of Auguste Comte. *J. Ment. Sci.,* 46:30-42, 1900.

Israeli, N. *Abnormal Personality and Time.* New York: Science Press, 1936.

Jacobson, A. C. *Genius: Some Revaluations.* New York: Greenberg, 1926.

——. Tuberculosis and the creative mind. *Med. Library & Hist. J.,* 5:225-249, 1907.

————. Tuberculosis and genius: with particular reference to Francis Thompson, in *Recent Studies of Tuberculosis*. St. Louis: Interstate Medical Journal Co., 1914. Pp. 131-138.

James, William. *The Varieties of Religious Experience: A Study in Human Nature*. New York: New American Library, 1958.

Jaspers, K. *Strindberg und van Gogh. Versuch einer pathographischen Analyse unter vergleichender Heranziehung von Swedenborg und Hölderlin. (Strindberg and Van Gogh. An Attempt at a Pathographic Analysis and Comparison with Swedenborg and Hölderlin)*. Berlin: J. Springer, 1926.

Jastrow, Joseph. Helen Keller: a psychological autobiography. *Pop. Sci. Mo.*, 43:71-83, 1903.

————. The withered arm and what it did for the Kaiser. *Cent. Mag.*, 114: 398-406, 1927.

Jekels, Ludwig. The turning point in the life of Napoleon I, in *Selected Papers*. New York: International Universities Press, 1952. Pp. 1-73.

————. Der Wendepunkt im Leben Napoleons I. (See *supra*). *Imago*, 3: 313-381, 1914.

Jentsch, E. *Das Pathologische bei Otto Ludwig. (The Pathological Element in Otto Ludwig)*. Wiesbaden: Bergmann, 1913.

Johnson, A. Tendencies in recent American biography. *Yale Rev.*, 1:390-403, 1912.

Johnson, G. W. *Randolph of Roanoke: A Political Fantastic*. New York: Minton, Balch, 1929.

Johnson, H. K. Thomas Lovell Beddoes. *Psychiat. Quart.*, 17:447-469, 1943.

Johnston, James C. *Biography: The Literature of Personality*. New York: Century Co., 1927.

Jones, Ernest. Andrea del Sartos Kunst und der Einfluss seiner Gattin. (The art of Andrea del Sarto and the influence of his wife). *Imago*, 2:468-480, 1913.

————. The birth and death of Moses. *Int. J. Psychiat.*, 39:1-14, 1958.

————. The case of Louis Bonaparte, King of Holland. *J. abnorm. Psychol.*, 8:289-301, 1914.

————. How to tell your friends from geniuses. *Sat. Rev.*, 40:9-10, 39-40, 1957.

————. The influence of Andrea del Sarto's wife on his art, in *Essays in Applied Psycho-Analysis*. London: International Psychoanalytic Press, 1923. Pp. 227-244.

————. *The Life and Work of Sigmund Freud*. New York: Basic Books, 1953, 1955, 1957. 3 Vols.

————. Das Problem des "Gemeinsamen Sterbens," namentlich mit Bezug auf den Selbstmord Heinrich von Kleists. (The problem of a joint death, particularly in respect to the suicide of Heinrich von Kleist). *Zentralbl. f. Psychoanal.,* 1:563-567, 1911.

——. The problem of Paul Morphy. A contribution to the psychoanalysis of chess. *Int. J. Psycho-Anal.,* 12:1-23, 1931.

——. Psycho-Analyse Roosevelts. (A psychoanalysis of T. Roosevelt). *Zentralbl. Psychoanal. u. Psychother.,* 2:675-677, 1912.

Jones, Howard Mumford. Methods in contemporary biography. *English J.,* 21:113-122, 1932.

Jones, Lucy. A Propos de Lewis Carrol. (On Lewis Carroll). *Rev. Franç. Psychanal.,* 14:511-522, 1950.

Josephson, Matthew. Historians and mythmakers. *Virginia Quart. Rev.,* 16: 92-109, 1940.

Juda, Adele. The relationship between highest mental capacity and psychic abnormalities. *Amer. J. Psychiat.,* 106:296-307, 1949.

Judge Baker Foundation. *Twenty Case Studies.* Boston: Judge Baker Foundation, 1922.

Jung, E. J. J. Rousseau als Psychoanalytiker. (Rousseau as a psychoanalyst). *Zentralbl. Psychoanal. u. Psychother.,* 3:52, 1912-1913.

Jury, Paul. Descartes, psychanalyste avant la lettre. (Descartes, psychoanalyst before the advent of analysis). *Psyché-Paris,* 5:150-164, 1950.

——. La fessée de Jean-Jacques Rousseau. (The spanking of Jean Jacques Rousseau). *Psyché-Paris,* 2:159-182, 1947.

——. George Sand et Musset. *Psyché-Paris,* 4:229-252, 626-636, 1949.

——. Mère et fils. (Mother and son). *Psyché-Paris,* 5:557-579, 1950.

——. Une Nuit de Racine. (A night with Racine). *Psyché-Paris,* 2:1480-1500, 1947.

Kafka, G. Géza Révész: Erinnerungen eines Jugenfreundes. (Géza Révész: recollections of a friend of adolescence). *Acta Psychol.,* 7: 121-125, 1950.

Kahle, M. Beziehungen weiblicher Fürsorgezöglinge zur Familie. (Relationships of female foster children to the family). *Beihefte z. Zsch. f. Angew. Psychol.,* No. 60, 1931.

Kahn, S. Is Hitler insane? *Med. Rec.,* 155:409-414, 1942.

Kanzer, Mark. Autobiographical aspects of the writer's imagery. *Int. J. Psycho-Anal.,* 40:52-58, 1959.

——. Dostoyevsky's matricidal impulses. *Psychoanal. Rev.,* 35:115-125, 1948.

——. Dostoyevsky's *Peasant Marey. Amer. Imago,* 4:78-88, 1947.

——. Gogol: a study of wit and paranoia. *J. Amer. Psychoanal. Assoc.,* 3: 110-125, 1955.

——. The self-analytic literature of Robert Louis Stevenson, in Wilbur,

George B., & Muensterberger, Warner, (Eds.), *Psychoanalysis and Culture*. New York: International Universities Press, 1951.

——. Writers and the early loss of parents. *J. Hillside Hosp.*, 2:148-151, 1953.

Kapp, Julius. *Richard Wagner and die Frauen, Eine erotische Biographie. (Richard Wagner and Women. An Erotic Biography)*. Berlin: 1921.

Kardiner, Abram. The biography as social source material, in *The Psychological Frontiers of Society*. New York: Columbia University Press, 1945. Pp. 35-38.

Karinthy, Frigyes. *A Journey Round My Skull*. New York: Harper & Bros., 1939.

Karpas, M. J. Socrates in the light of modern psychopathology. *J. abnorm. Psychol.*, 10:185-200, 1915.

Karpman, Benjamin. From the autobiography of a bandit; toward the psychogenesis of so-called psychopathic behavior. *J. crim. Law Crimin.*, 36:305-325, 1945.

——. From the autobiography of a liar: toward the clarification of the problem of psychopathic states. *Psychiat. Quart.*, 23:497-521, 1949.

Kästner, A. Goethes Bild der Kindheit. (Goethe's picture of childhood). *Zsch. f. päd. Psychol.*, 40:100-107, 1939.

Katz, Joseph. Balzac and Wolfe: a study of self-destructive overproductivity. *Psychoanal.*, 5:3-20, 1957.

Kaus, Otto. *Der Fall Gogol. (The Case of Gogol)*. Zsch. d. Ver. f. freie psychoanalyt. Forsch. No. 2. Munich: Reinhardt, 1912.

Kazin, Alfred. The conquistador: Freud in his letters. *Griffin*, 9:2-8, 1960.

Kearney, J. F. The psychological biography. *Catholic World*, 129:96-98, 1929.

Kelley, D. M. The autobiographical study as an aid to psychotherapy. *Amer. J. Psychiat.*, 102:375-377, 1945.

——. Preliminary studies of the Rorschach records of the Nazi war criminals. *Rorschach Res. Exch.*, 10:45-48, 1946.

Kempf, Eward J. Abraham Lincoln's organic and emotional neurosis. *Arch. Neurol. Psychiat.*, 67:419-433, 1952.

——. Charles Darwin—the affective sources of his inspiration and anxiety neurosis. *Psychoanal. Rev.*, 15:151-192, 1918.

Kenney, William. Dr. Johnson and the psychiatrists. *Amer. Imago*, 17: 75-82, 1960.

King, Arden R. The dream biography of a Mountain Maidü. *Character & Pers.*, 11:227-234, 1943.

Klages, Ludwig. *Goethe als Seelenforscher. (Goethe as Psychologist)*. Leipzig: Barth, 1932.

Klette, Werner. Louis Pergaud: 'La Guerre des Boutons, Roman de ma Douzième Année.' (Louis Pergaud. 'The Button War, the Story of the 12th Year of My Life'). *Imago:* 2:527-530, 1913.

Kligerman, Charles. The character of Jean Jacques Rousseau. *Psychoanal. Quart.,* 20:237-252, 1951.

———. A psychoanalytic study of the *Confessions* of St. Augustine. *J. Amer. Psychoanal. Assoc.,* 5:469-484, 1957.

Klossowski, P. Éléments d'une étude psychanalytique sur le Marquis de Sade. (Elements of a psychoanalytic study of the Marquis de Sade). *Rev. Franç. Psychanal.,* 6:458-474, 1933.

Kluckhohn, Clyde. Needed refinements in the biographical approach, in Sargent, S. Stansfeld, & Smith, Marian W., (Eds.), *Culture and Personality.* New York: Viking Fund, 1949.

Knapp, Robert H., & Goodrich, H. B. *Origins of American Scientists.* Chicago: University of Chicago Press, 1952.

Knight, G. Wilson. *Lord Byron's Marriage.* New York: Macmillan Co., 1957.

Knight, John. *The Story of My Psychoanalysis.* New York: McGraw-Hill Book Co., 1950.

Kobylinski. M. La malattia di Dostojewski. (The illness of Dostoevsky). *Ill. med. ital.,* 8:75-77, 1926.

Kohn, Edwin. *Lassalle—der Fuhrer. (Lassalle—the Leader).* Leipzig: Internationaler Psychoanalytischer Verlag, 1926.

Kolle, Kurt (Ed.). [*Great Physicians of the Mind and Nerves. 21 Biographies.*] Stuttgart: Georg Thieme, 1956.

Krapf, E. Eduardo. *Tomas de Aquino y la Psicopatologia. (Thomas Aquinas and Psychopathology).* Buenos Aires: Editorial Index, 1943.

Kretschmer, E. *The Psychology of Men of Genius.* New York: Harcourt, Brace & Co., 1931.

Kris, Ernst. Ein geisteskranker Bildhauer. Die Charakterköpfe des Franz Xaver Messerschmidt. (A mad artist. Character of Franz Xaver Messerschmitt). *Imago,* 19:384-411, 1933.

———. The image of the artist. A psychological study of the role of tradition in ancient biographies, in *Psychoanalytic Explorations in Art.* New York: International Universities Press, 1952. Pp. 64-86.

———. The personal myth; a problem in psychoanalytic technique. The autobiography as screen. *J. Amer. Psychoanal. Assoc.,* 4:653-681, 1956.

———. A psychotic artist of the middle ages, in *Psychoanalytic Explorations in Art.* New York: International Universities Press, 1952. Pp. 118-127.

——. A psychotic sculptor of the eighteenth century, in *Ibid*. Pp. 128-150.

Kronfeld, Arthur. August Forel, der Mann und sein Werk. (August Forel: the man and his work). *Psychotherapeutische Praxis*, 1:227-228, 1934.

Kronhausen, Eberhard, & Kronhausen, Phyllis. *Pornography and the Law. The Psychology of Erotic Realism and "Hard Core" Pornography*. New York: Ballantine Books, 1959.

Krueger, E. T. *Autobiographical Documents and Personality*. Unpublished. Chicago: Chicago University Library, 1925.

Krug, Josef. Kritische Bemerkungen zu dem "Tagebuch eines halbwüchsigen Mädchens." (Critical remarks on *A Young Girl's Diary*). *Ztschr. angew. Psychol.*, 27:370-381, 1926.

Kruif, Paul de. *Man Against Insanity*. New York: Harcourt, Brace & Co., 1957.

Krutch, Joseph Wood. *Edgar Allen Poe*. New York: Alfred A. Knopf, 1926.

Kunemann, G. *E. T. W. Hoffmann. Études médico-psychologiques. (E. T. W. Hoffmann. Medico-Psychological Studies)*. Thèse lett. Paris: 1911.

Künzli, Arnold. *Die Angst als abendländische Krankheit; dargestellt am Leben und Denken Soeren Kierkegaards. (Anxiety as an Accidental Illness; Presented through the Life and Thinking of Soeren Kierkegaard)*. Zurich: Rascher, 1948.

Kupky, O. *The Religious Development of Adolescents*. New York: Macmillan Co., 1928.

——. Tagebücher von Jugendlichen als Quellen zur Psychologie der Reifezeit. (Diaries of adolescents as sources for the psychology of puberty). *Päd. Psychol. Arbeit.*, 13:132-163, 1924.

Laborde, J. V. *Léon Gambetta. Biographie psychologique. (Leon Gambetta. A Psychological Biography)*. Paris: Reinwald, 1898.

Lacombe, Pierre. *Le Cas de Borodine, Musicien du Dimanche. (The Case of Borodin, a Sunday Musician)*. Paris: Malvine, 1936.

——. The enigma of Clemenceau. *Psychoanal. Rev.*, 33:165-176, 1946.

Ladell, R. Macdonald. The neurosis of Dr. Samuel Johnson. *Brit. J. Med. Psychol.*, 9:1929.

LaForgue, René. *L'échec de Baudelaire. Étude psychanalytique. (Baudelaire's Downfall. A Psychoanalytic Study)*. Paris: Denoel & Steele, 1931.

——. *The Defeat of Baudelaire; A Psycho-Analytic Study of the Neurosis of Charles Baudelaire*. London: Hogarth Press, 1932.

——. Devant la Barrière de la Névrose. Étude Psychanalytique sur la

Nevrose de Charles Baudelaire. (In front of the barrier of neurosis. A psychoanalytic study of the neurosis of Charles Baudelaire). *Rev. Franç. Psychanal.*, 31:4, 274-406, 1930.

——. *Étude sur Jean-Jacques Rousseau. (A Study of Jean Jacques Rousseau).* Paris: Gaston Doin et Cie, 1927.

——. *Talleyrand, L'Homme de la France; Essai Psychanalytique sur la Personnalité Collective Française. (Talleyrand, Man of France; A Psychoanalytic Study of the French Collective Personality).* Geneva: Editions du Mont-Blanc, 1947.

Lagriffe, L. Guy de Maupassant. Étude de psychologie pathologique. (Guy de Maupassant. A pathological and psychological study). *Ann. med. psychol.*, 8:203-238, 353-372, 1908; 9:5-14, 177-193, 1909.

——. Un probleme psychologique.—Les deux aspects d'Arthur Rimbaud (1854-1891). (A psychological problem.—The two aspects of Arthur Rimbaud). *J. Psychol. norm. path.*, 7:499-523, 1910.

Laird, D. A. Diaries of earlier generations in the study of sleep. *Science,* 80:382, 1934.

Lalo, C. Eugène Delacroix. Esquisse d'un type psycho-esthétique. (Eugene Delacroix; an outline sketch of a psychoesthetic type). *J. Psychol. norm. path.*, 37/38: 161-184, 1940-41.

Lamb, Charles. On the sanity of true genius, in Hutchinson, Thomas (Ed.), *The Works of Charles Lamb.* London: Milford, 1924.

Lamm, M. Strindberg. *Zsch. f. Aesth.*, 20:141-156, 1926.

Lancaster, E. G. The psychology and pedagogy of adolescence. *Pedagogical Seminary,* 5:61-128, 1897.

Lancaster, Evelyn, & Poling, James. *The Final Face of Eve.* New York: McGraw-Hill Book Co., 1958.

Landauer, Karl. Die Gemeinschaft mit sich selber. (The union with oneself). *Psychoanal. Bewegung,* 2:260ff, 1930.

Landis, Carney. Psychoanalytic phenomena. *J. abnorm. soc. Psychol.,* 35:17-28, 1940.

Lange, W. *Die Psychose Maupassants. Ein kritischer Versuch. (The Psychosis of Maupassant. A Critical Analysis).* Leipzig: Barth, 1909.

Lange-Eichbaum, W. *The Problem of Genius.* New York: Macmillan Co., 1932.

Langer, Walter C., Kris, Ernst, & Lewin, Bertram D. *A Psychological Analysis of Adolph Hitler.* Washington, D. C., Office of Strategic Services, 1944.

Lasswell, Harold D. Life-histories and political science, in *Psychopathology and Politics.* New York: Viking Press, 1960. Pp. 1-27.

——. The scientific study of human biography. *Scient. Mo.,* 30:79-80, 1930.

Lauter, Paul. Walt Whitman: lover and comrade. *Amer. Imago,* 16:407-435, 1959.

Lauvriere, E. *Un génie morbide, Edgar Poe. (A Morbid Genius—Edgar Allen Poe).* Paris: Alcan, 1904.

Lawton, George. *Straight to the Heart; A Personal Account of Thoughts and Feelings while Undergoing Heart Surgery.* New York: International Universities Press, 1956.

Leeper, Robert, & Madison, Peter. *Toward Understanding Human Personalities.* New York: Appleton-Century-Crofts, 1959.

Legewie, B. *Augustinus, eine Psychographie. (St. Augustine. A Psychographic Portrait).* Bonn: Marcus u. Weber, 1925.

Lehman, H. C. *Age and Achievement.* Princeton, N. J.: Princeton University Press, 1953.

Lehman, H. C., & Witty, P. A. Scientific eminence and church membership. *Scientific Mo.,* 34:544-549, 1931.

Lehner, Fritz. Zum Thema Biographik und Psychoanalyse. (On the writing of biographies and psychoanalysis). *Psychoanal. Bewegung,* 5: 201-202, 1933.

Lehnhoff, Wilhelm. *Spiele und Streiche aus den Kindheitstagen der Dichter und Meister. (Games and Tricks from the Childhood days of Poets and Great Men).* Leipzig: Brandstetter, 1913.

Leighton, Alexander H., & Leighton, Dorothea C. *Gregorio, the Hand-Trembler: A Psychobiological Personality Study of a Navaho Indian.* Cambridge, Mass.: Peabody Museum, 1949.

Leschnitzer, Adolf F. Faust and Moses. *Amer. Imago,* 6:229-243, 1949.

LeSenne, René. *Traité de Caractérologue. (Treatise on Characterology).* Paris: Presses Universitaires de France, 1946.

Leux, I. *Hermann Sudermann (1857-1928). Eine individualanalytische und schaffenspsychologische Studie. (Hermann Sudermann. An Analytic and Creative Psychological Study).* Leipzig: Barth, 1931.

Levey, H. B. A theory concerning free creation in the inventive arts. *Psychiatry,* 3:229-294, 1940.

Levi Bianchini, Marco. *Diario di Guerra di un Psichiatra nella Campagna contro l'Austria (1915-1918). (War Diary of a Psychiatrist in the Campaign against Austria, 1915-1918).* Nocera Superiore: Bibl. Psichiat. Interbaz, 1920.

Lewin, L. *Friedrich Hebbel. Beitrag zu einem Psychogramm. (Friedrich Hebbel. Contributions to a Psychological Portrait).* Berlin-Steglitz: Behr, 1913.

Ley, A. Les methodes de pathographie historique et biographique. (The methods of historical and biographical pathography). *J. belge Neurol. Psychiat.,* 34:438-444, 1934.

Lhermitte, Jean. De l'angoisse au Genié. De l'anxieté de Lucrèce, l'angoisse de Pascal. (Concerning anxiety in genius. Lucretius' anger and Pascal's anxiety). *Encéphale et Hyg. Mentale,* 36:60-64, 1946-47.

——. Marie-Thérèse Noblet considérée du point du vue Neurologique. (A neurological view of Marie Thérèse Noblet). *Edut. Carmélit.,* 23:201-209, 1938.

Liber, B. Hitler's mind. *Med. Rec.,* 156:414-416, 1943.

Lind, Sidney E. Poe and mesmerism. *Publ. Mod. Lang. Assoc.,* 57:1077-1094, 1947.

Lindenau, Heinrich. Eine Tagebucheintragung Goethes über Fehlleistungen. (An entry on parapraxis in Goethe's diary). *Psychoanal. Bewegung,* 4:86, 1933.

Llinás, Pablo A. La Personalidad psiquica del liberatador Simón Bolívar. (The psychic personality of the liberator Simon Bolivar). *Rev. Med. Legal, Colombia,* 8:33-43, 1946.

Lloyd, J. H. The case of William Cowper, the English poet. *Arch. Neur. Psychiat.,* 24:682-689, 1930.

Lodge, Helen C. The influence of the study of biography on the moral ideology of the adolescent at the eighth grade level. *J. educ. Res.,* 50:241-255, 1956.

Loeb, Laurence. Psychopathology and Toulouse-Lautrec. *Amer. Imago,* 16:213-234, 1959.

LoGotto, E. Il problema religioso in Dostojeoskij. (The religious problem in Dostoevsky). *Bilychnis,* 16:333-346, 1927.

Lombard, A. Guy de Maupassant, sa vie, son oeuvre, sa maladie, sa mort. Les tentatives de suicide de G. de Maupassant. (Guy de Maupassant, his life, his work, his illness, his death, his attempts at suicide). *Chron. méd.,* 15:34-40, 1908.

Lombroso, Cesare. Emile Zola in the light of researches by Dr. Toulouse and recent theories of genius. *Med. Week.,* 5:25-29, 1897.

——. *The Man of Genius.* London: Scott, 1891.

——. Osservazioni sul Mondo esterno e Sull'io. Diario Giovanile (1854-1857). (Observations on the external world and the self. A youthful diary). *Quad. dell'arch. Antrop. Crim. e Med. Leg.,* No. 9, 1932.

——. La psychopathologie de Manzoni. (The psychopathology of Manzoni). *Rev. Psychol. Clin. et Thèr.,* 5:71-82, 103-112, 1901.

Lomer, G. *Ignatius von Loyola. Vom Erotiker zum Heiligen. Eine pathographische Geschichtsstudie. (St. Ignatius of Loyola. The Development from Sensuality to Sainthood. A Pathographic-Historical Study).* Leipzig: Barth, 1913.

Lorenz, Emil F. Die Kindheitserinnerung des Baron de la Motte Fouriqué. (The childhood memories of Baron de la Motte Fouriqué). *Imago,* 2:513-519, 1913.

———. Leo N. Tolstoi, Kindheit. (Childhood). *Imago,* 2:93-96, 1913.

Lorge, Irving, & Hollingworth, Leta S. Adult status of highly intelligent children. *J. genet. Psychol.,* 49:215-226, 1936.

Lowes, John Livingston. *The Road to Xanadu.* Boston: Houghton Mifflin & Co., 1927.

Lowtzky, Fanny. *Sören Kierkegaard. Das subjektive Erlebnis und die religiöse Offenbarung. Eine psychoanalytische Studie. (Sören Kierkegaard: Subjective Experience and Religious Revelation. A Psychoanalytic Study).* Vienna: Internationaler Psychoanalytischer Verlag, 1935.

Ludwig, E. *Bismarck. Ein psychologischer Versuch. (Bismarck. An Attempt at a Psychological Portrait).* Berlin: Fischer, 1911.

Macalpine, Ida, & Hunter, Richard A. (Eds.). *Daniel Paul Schreber—'Memoirs of My Nervous Illness'.* Cambridge, Mass.: Robert Bentley, Inc., 1955.

———. *Schizophrenia 1677. A Psychiatric Study of an Illustrated Autobiographical Record of Demoniacal Possession.* Psychiatric Monograph Series No. 2. London: William Dawson & Sons, Ltd., 1956.

Magri, F. Biopsicologia del Genio Politico. (The biopsychology of political genius). *G. clin. Med.,* 18:1277-1286, 1937.

Maller, J. B. Studies in character and personality in German psychological literature. *Psychol. Bull.,* 30:209-232, 1933.

Malone, Dumas. Biography and history, in Strayer, J. R. (Ed.), *The Interpretation of History.* Princeton, N. J.: Princeton University Press, 1943. Pp. 121-148.

Mamlock, G. Zur Psychographie von Marat. (Contribution to the psychography of Marat). *Zsch. f. Psychother.,* 8:200-207, 1922.

Manheim, Leonard F. The personal history of David Copperfield: a study in psychoanalytic criticism. *Amer. Imago,* 9:21-43, 1952.

Mann, M. B. Studies in language behavior. III. The quantitative differentiation of samples of written language. *Psychol. Monographs,* 56: 41-74, 1944.

Mann, Thomas. *Freud, Goethe, Wagner.* New York: Alfred A. Knopf, 1937.

Marañon, G. *Amiel. Un estudo de la timidiez. (Amiel. A Study of Timidity).* Madrid: Espasa-Calpe, 1932.

Marcuse, M. Lenz, Vater und Sohn. (Lenz, father and son). *Zsch. f. Sex.-Wiss.,* 14:395-397, 1928.

Margis, P. Psychologische Analyse E. Th. Hoffmanns—auf Grund eines psychographischen Schemas. (A psychographic analysis of E. Th.

Hoffmann—based on a psychographic system). *Zsch. f. angew. Psychol.*, 1911.

Mariani, C. E. *L. N. Tolstoï. Studio psicologico. (L. N. Tolstoi. A Psychological Study)*. Torino: Bocca, 1903.

Märker, F. *Autokraten und Demokraten. Characterologische Bildnisse. (Autocrats and Democrats. Characterological Portraits)*. Zurich: Rentsch, 1931.

Markgraf, B. *Der junge Luther als Genie. (The Genius of Young Luther)*. Leipzig: Fröhlich, 1928.

Marone, Silvio. Homosexuality and art. *Int. J. Sexol.*, 7:175-190, 1954.

Martin, Everett D. A psychoanalytic study of Friedrich Nietzsche. *Int. J. Psycho-Anal.*, 2:484-485, 1921.

Martin, Louis C. A note on Hazlitt. *Int. J. Psycho-Anal.*, 1:414-419, 1920.

Masini, M. U. Paolina Bonaparte. *Illus. med. ital.*, 7:65-72, 1925.

Matthews, R. *English Messiahs*. London: Methuen, 1936.

Mauron, Charles. *Introduction à la Psychanalyse de Mallarmé. (Introduction to the Psychoanalysis of Mallarmé)*. Neuchâtel: La Baconnière, 1950.

Mayer, W. Zur Problem des Dichters Lenz. (A contribution to the case of the poet Lenz). *Arch. f. Psychiat. u. Nervenkr.*, 63:889-890, 1921.

Mayer-Gross, W. *Selbstschilderungen der Verwirrtheit; die Oneiroide Erlebnisform. (Self Portraits of the Confused State; The Dream-like Form of Existence)*. Berlin: Springer, 1924.

McCurdy, Harold C. The childhood patterns of genius. *Smithsonian Report for 1958*. Washington, D. C.: Smithsonian Institution, 1959. Pp. 527-542.

——. *The Personality of Shakespeare. A Venture in Psychological Method*. New Haven: Yale University Press, 1953.

McKown, Robin. *Pioneers in Mental Health*. New York: Dodd, Mead & Co., 1961.

Mead, Margaret. The study of national character, in Lerner, Daniel, & Lasswell, H. D. (Eds.), *The Policy Sciences*. Stanford, Calif.: Stanford University Press, 1951. Pp. 70-85.

Mecklin, J. M. *The Passing of the Saint; A Study of a Cultural Type*. Chicago: University of Chicago Press, 1941.

Medico, H. E. Del. Ein Oedipuskomplex im elften Jahrhundert. Michael Psellos. (An Oedipus complex in the 11th century. Michael Psellos). *Imago*, 18:214-242, 1932.

Mendousse, Pierre. *L'Ame de l'Adolescent. (The Soul of the Adolescent)*. Paris: Alcan, 1930.

Menninger, Karl. The historian of psychiatry, in *A Psychiatrist's World*. New York: Viking Press, 1959. Pp. 811-878.

Merriam, Charles E. The significance of psychology for the study of politics. *Amer. polit. Sci. Rev.*, 18:469-488, 1924.

Merrill, M. A. Rosalind's diary: a study in temperament of a social misfit. *J. Delinq.*, 5:95-116, 1920.

Michel, André. L'Analité de Stravinsky. (The anal character of Stravinsky). *Psyché-Paris*, 5:363-368, 1950.

———. Chopin et le sein maternel. (Chopin and the maternal breast). *Psyché-Paris*, 5:491-496, 1950.

———. Claude Debussy. *Psyché-Paris*, 5:427-446, 1950.

Middleton, W. C. The psychopathology of George Fox, founder of Quakerism. *Psychol. Rev.*, 38:296-316, 1931.

Migliorino, G. Profili psicologico di Goethe. (A psychologic profile of Goethe). *Riv. Psicol. norm. pat.*, 39:162-165, 1943.

Miles, Catherine C., & Wolfe, Lillian S. Childhood physical and mental health records of historical geniuses. *Psychol. Monographs*, 47:390-400, 1936.

Miles, George H. An autobiography. *Occupational Psychol., London*, 23:193-211, 1949; 24:31-39, 1950.

Miller, Milton L. *Nostalgia: A Psychoanalytic Study of Marcel Proust.* Boston: Houghton Mifflin & Co., 1956.

Milner, Marion. *On Not Being Able to Paint.* New York: International Universities Press, 1957.

Minkowska, F. Van Gogh; de samenhang tusschen zijn leven, zijn ziekte en zijn werk. (Van Gogh; the connection between his life, his illness and his work). *Nederlands Tijdschrift voor Psychol.*, 3:155-178, 1935.

Misch, Georg. *A History of Autobiography in Antiquity.* Cambridge, Mass.: Harvard University Press, 1951. 2 Vols.

Mitchell, John D. André Gide, rebel and conformist. *Amer. Imago*, 16:148-153, 1959.

Möbius, P. J. *Über J. J. Rousseaus Jugend. (On J. J. Rousseau's Youth).* Langensalza: Beyer u. Söhne, 1899.

Money-Kyrle, R. A psycho-analytic study of the voices of Joan of Arc. *Brit. J. Med. Psychol.*, 13:63-81, 1933.

Montmorand, B. de. Saint Vincent de Paul: essai de psychologie religieuse. (Saint Vincent de Paul: a religious psychological essay). *Rev. de Phil.*, 14:44-67, 1909.

Moore, Thomas V. The hound of heaven. *Psychoanal Rev.*, 5:345-363, 1915.

———. Percy Bysshe Shelley: an introduction to the study of character. *Psychol. Monographs*, 31:1-62, 1922.

———. A study in sadism: the life of Algernon Charles Swinburne. *Character & Pers.*, 6:1-15, 1937.

Moorman, L. J. *Tuberculosis and Genius.* Chicago: University of Chicago Press, 1940.

Moxon, C. The development of libido in Friedrich Nietzsche. *Psychoanal. Rev.*, 10:170-183, 1923.

Muensterberger, Warner, & Axelrad, Sidney. Psychobiography, in *Psychoanalysis and the Social Sciences,* Vol. V. New York: International Universities Press, 1959.

Müller, E. Die alten römaischen Kaiserbiographien sind weder Märchen noch Romane. (The biographies of the ancient Roman emperors are neither fairy tales nor novels). *Psychiat.-neurol. Wschr.*, 42:492-496, 1940.

———. Das Constantinische Kaiserhaus, eine Porträt-und Charakterstudie. (The royal family of Constantine, a portrait and character study). *All. Z. Psychiat.*, 99:438-444, 1933.

Müller-Freienfels, Richard. *Tagebuch eines Psychologen. (The Diary of a Psychologist).* Leipzig: Seemann, 1931.

Mumford, E. E. R. *Joan: A Study from Life.* London: Longmans, Green, 1931.

Münzer, A. Dostojewski als Psychopathaloge. (Dostoevski as a psychopathologist). *Berl. klin. Woch.*, 51:1943-1945, 1914.

Murchison, Carl (Ed.). *A History of Psychology in Autobiography.* Worcester, Mass.: Clark University Press, 1930-36. 3 Vols.

Murphy, Gardner. Notes for a parapsychological autobiography. *J. Parapsychol.*, 21:165-178, 1958.

Murray, Henry A., et al., (Eds.). *Explorations in Personality. A Clinical and Experimental Study of Fifty Men of College Age.* New York: Oxford University Press, 1938.

Murray, Henry A. What should psychologists do about psychoanalysis? *J. abnorm. soc. Psychol.*, 35:150-175, 1940.

Mussolini, Benito. Diario di guerra. (War diary). *Riv. di psicol.*, 12:16-67, 1916.

Myers, Robert C. Biographical factors and academic achievement: an experimental investigation. *Educ. psychol. Measmt.*, 12:415-426, 1952.

Naesgaard, Sigurd. *En Psykoanalyse af Søren Kierkegaard. (A Psychoanalysis of Søren Kierkegaard).* Odense, Denmark: Psykoanalytisk Forlag, Paul Høymark, 1950.

Natenberg, Maurice. *The Case History of Sigmund Freud; a Psychobiography.* Chicago: Regent House, 1955.

Neilon, Patricia. Shirley's babies after fifteen years: a personality study. *J. genet. Psychol.,* 73:175-186, 1948.

Neufeld, Jolan. *Dostojewski; Skizze zu seiner Psychoanalyse. (Dostoevski. Sketch for His Psychoanalysis).* Leipzig: Internationaler Psychoanlytischer Verlag, 1923.

Nicola, Pietro de. Sulla Presunta Psicoptia Ossessiva e Dissociativa del Poeta R. M. Rilke. (On the alleged obsessive and dissociative psychopathy of the poet, R. M. Rilke). *Arch. Psicol. Neurol. Psiciat.,* 9: 363-374, 1948.

Niederland, William G. The 'miracled-up' world of Schreber's childhood, in Eissler, Ruth, et al., (Eds.), *The Psychoanalytic Study of the Child,* Vol. XIV. New York: International Universities Press, 1959.

——. Three notes on the Schreber case. *Psychoanal. Quart.,* 20:579-591, 1951.

——. Schreber: father and son. *Psychoanal. Quart.,* 28:151-169, 1959.

Nissen, I. *Sjelelige kriser i menneskets liv. Henrik Ibsen og den moderne psykologi. (Mental Crises of Human Life. Henrik Ibsen and the Modern Psychology).* Oslo: Aschehoug, 1931.

Noad, K. B. Young laurels: the brief lives of John Irvine Hunter, Rene Laennec and John Keats. *Med. J. Australia,* 47:521-527, 1960.

Nötzel, Karl. Das Gatten—und Elternerlebnis in Dostojewski. (Dostoievski's experiences with parents and wife). *Vivos Voco, I,* 1921(?).

Nuttall, W. The memoir of a stammerer. *Psyche, London,* 17:151-184, 1937.

Nyirö, C. Kötözseni és pszichiátria. (Poet geniuses and psychiatry). *Magyar Psychol. Szemle,* 6:63-86, 1933.

Oakeshott, Edna. *Childhood Experience in Autobiography.* London: Cambridge University Press, 1960.

Oberndorf, Clarence P. (Ed.). The autobiography of Josef Breuer (1842-1925). *Int. J. Psycho-Anal.,* 34:64-67, 1953.

O'Brien, Barbara. *Operators and Things: The Inner Life of a Schizophrenic.* Cambridge, Mass.: Arlington Books, 1959.

O'Connor, Len. *They Talked to a Stranger.* New York: St. Martin's Press, 1959.

Odinot, R. *Étude médico-psychologique sur Alfred de Musset. (A Medico-Psychological Study of Alfred de Musset).* Lyon: Storck, 1908.

O'Higgins, H. & Reede, E. H. *The American Mind in Action.* New York: Harper & Bros., 1924.

Oka, S. [A diary of the growth of a girl.] *Trans. Inst. Child Stud., Hiroshima,* 16:755-810, 1934.

Oppeln-Bronckowski, Friedrich. Eros als Schicksal bei Friedrich dem Grossen und bei Stendhal. Ein sexualpsychologischer Vergleich. (Eros as fate in Frederick the Great and in Stendhal. A psychosexual comparison). *Psychoanal. Bewegung*, 2:314-325, 1930.

Orgler, Hedda. *Alfred Adler: The Man and His Work*. Ashington, England: C. W. Daniel Co., 1947.

Ossipow, N. Über Leo Tolstois Seelenleiden. (On Leo Tolstoy's emotional sufferings). *Imago*, 9:495-498, 1923.

——. *Tolstois Kindheitserinnerungen. Ein Beitrag zu Freuds Libidotheorie. (Tolstoy's Childhood Memories. A Contribution to Freud's Theory of the Libido)*. Leipzig: Internationaler Psychoanalytischer Verlag, 1923.

Ostwald, Wilhelm. *Auguste Comte, der Mann und das Werk. (August Comte, the Man and His Work)*. Leipzig: Verlag Unesma, 1914.

——. *Grosse Männer. (Great Men)*. Leipzig: Akad Verlagsgesellsch., 1910.

——. Psychographische Studien. (Psychographic studies). *Annalen der Naturphilo.*, Vols. VI, VII, VIII, 1907, 1908, 1909.

Paden, W. D. *Tennyson in Egypt*. University of Kansas Publ., No. 27, 1942.

Pannenborg, W. A. Een vergelijkend biografisch onderzvek naar eenige psychische eigenschappen van de tragedie-en comedieschrijvers. (A comparative biographical study on some psychological characteristics of authors of tragedy and comedy). *Alg. Neder. Tijdschr. Wijsbegeert. Psychol.*, 36:107-123, 1943.

Papini, G. *San Agostino. (St. Augustine)*. Florence: Vallechi, 1929.

Partridge, G. E. Psychopathological study of Jean-Nicolas-Arthur Rimbaud. *Psychoanal. Rev.*, 17:401-425, 1930.

Pascal, B. Les malades mentales de Robert Schumann. (The mental illness of Robert Schumann). *J. de Psychol.*, Vol. V, 1908.

Pascal, Roy. *Design and Truth in Autobiography*. Cambridge, Mass.: Harvard University Press, 1960.

Paul, Sherman. *The Shores of America: Thoreau's Inward Exploration*. Urbana, Ill.: University of Illinois Press, 1958.

Paulhan, F. Herbert Spencer d'après son autobiographie. (Herbert Spencer as shown in his autobiography). *Rev. de Phil.*, 64:145-158, 1907.

Paulus, Jean. Les deux Visages de Stendhal. (Two views of Stendhal), in *Miscellanea Psychologica Albert Michotte*. Paris: Libraire Philosophique, 1947. Pp. 429-439.

Pauly, Robert. L'Épilepsie de Dostoievsky; Realité de l'Épilepsie; Épilepsie et Travail Intellectuel; Épilepsie et Mysticisme. (The epilepsy of Dostoevsky; reality of the epilepsy; epilepsy and intellectual work; epilepsy and mysticism). *J. méd. Bordeaux*, 125:337-345, 1948.

Peck, E. M. A study of the personalities of five eminent men. *J. abnorm. soc. Psychol.*, 26:37-57, 1931.

Perry, Isabella H. Vincent Van Gogh's illness. *Bull. Hist. Med.*, 21:146-172, 1947.

Pfister, Oskar. Hysterie und Mystik bei Margaretha Ebner, 1291 bis 1351. (The hysteria and mysticism of Margaretha Ebner—1291 to 1351). *Zentralbl. f. Psychoanal.*, 1:468-485, 1911.

——. [The piety of Count Ludwig von Zinzendorf.] *Schriften*, Vol. 8, 1910.

Pichon-Rivière, Arminda A. de. Balzac, un caracter oral. (Balzac; an oral character). *Rev. Psicoanál., B. Aires,* 4:705-717, 1947.

Plank, Emma N. Memories of early childhood in autobiographies, in Eissler, Ruth S., et al., (Eds.), *The Psychoanalytic Study of the Child,* Vol. VIII. New York: International Universities Press, 1953. Pp. 381-393.

Plank, Emma N., & Plank, Robert. Emotional component in arithmetical learning as seen through autobiographies, in Eissler, Ruth S., et al. (Eds.), *The Psychoanalytic Study of the Child,* Vol. IX. New York: International Universities Press, 1954. Pp. 274-293.

Plesso, G. I. [Concerning the psychopathy of I. S. Turgenev.] *Klin. arkh. genialnosty i odarennosty,* 4:54-68, 1928.

Polansky, Norman A. How shall a life-history be written. *Character and Pers.,* 9:188-207, 1941.

Polla-Caselli. *La psicologia del bambino nelle autobiografie: medaglioni. (The Psychology of the Infant in Autobiographies: Medallions).* Pisa: Mariotti, 1921.

Once, Anibal. *Diario Intimo di Una Adolescente. (The Intimate Diary of an Adolescent Girl).* Buenos Aires: Editorial El Ateneo, 1934 (?).

Popovic, S. [*Self-Reports as a Means of Exercising the Introspection of Adolescents.*] Belgrad: 1933.

Popper-Lynkeus, J. *Voltaire, eine Charakteranalyse. (Voltaire, a Character Analysis).* Vienna: Löwit, 1925.

Portenier, Lillian G. Personality as revealed through autobiographies. *J. Colo.-Wyo. Acad. Sci.,* 4:68-69, 1950.

Portnoy, Julius. *A Psychology of Art Creation.* Doctoral dissert. Philadelphia: University of Pennsylvania, 1942.

Potter, G. Analytic suggestions about Alfred W. McCann. *Psychoanal. Rev.,* 19:454-461, 1932.

Prätorius, Numa. Die Homosexualität des Prinzen Heinrich von Preussen, des Bruders Friedrichs des Grossen. (The homosexuality of

Prince Henry of Prussia, brother of Frederick the Great). *Ztsch. f. Sexualwsschft,* 15 (7), 1929.

——. Ein Homosexueller Dichter des 17. Jahrunderts: Saint-Pavin, der "Koenig von Sodom." Eine Sexuell-psychologische Studie. (A homosexual poet of the 17th century: Saint-Pavin, the "King of Sodom"). *Ztsch. f. Sexualwsschft.,* 5:261-271, 1918.

Preyer, W. *Die Seele des Kindes. (The Soul of the Child).* Leipzig: T. Grieben, 1882.

Prince, C. A psychological study of Stalin. *J. soc. Psychol.,* 22:119-140, 1945.

Prince, Morton H. *The Dissociation of a Personality: A Biographical Study in Abnormal Psychology.* New York: Longmans, Green, 1957.

——. *The Psychology of the Kaiser; A Study of His Sentiments and His Obsession.* Boston: Badger, 1915.

——. Roosevelt analyzed through the new psychology. *New York Times,* March 24, 1912.

Proal, L. *La psychologie de J. J. Rousseau.* Paris: Alcan, 1923.

Proudfit, I. The big round world. A psychiatric study of Louis Stevenson. *Psychoanal. Rev.,* 23:121-148, 1936.

Pruette, L. A psychoanalytic study of Edgar Allen Poe. *Amer. J. Psychol.,* 31:370-402, 1920.

Pulido, Martin A. [Memories of youth. At the side of Albarran.] *Boletin Cultural e Informativo (Madrid),* 23:80-81, 1960.

Puner, Helen Walker. *Freud: His Life and His Mind, a Biography.* New York: Howell, Soskin, 1947.

Püschmann, H. Gefühlsbestimmtes Denken von Jugendlichen in ihrer Selbstbetrachtung. (Emotionalized thinking of adolescents in self-observations). *Zsch. f. päd. Psychol.,* 27:65-72, 1926.

Racker, Enrique. [A psychoanalytic essay on the personality and dramatic works of Richard Wagner.] *Rev. Psicoanál.,* 6:32-81, 1948.

Ramos, Mejia, Jose Maria. *Las Neurosis de los Hombres Celebres en las Historia Argentina. (Neurosis in Men Famous in Argentine History).* Buenos Aires: La Cultura Argentina, 1915.

Ranald, Josef. *Pens and Personalities.* London: Vision Press, 1959.

Rank, Otto. Zu Baudelaires Inzestkomplex. (On Baudelaire's incest complex). *Zentralbl. f. Psychoanal. u. Psychother.,* 1:275, 1911.

——. [The Lohengrin Saga.] *Schriften,* Vol. 13, 1911.

——. Ein Selbstbekenntnis Wilhelm Buschs. (A confession of Wilhelm Busch). *Zentralbl. f. Psychoanal. u. Psychother.,* 1:523, 1911.

Raskin, Evelyn. A comparison of scientific and literary ability: a biographical study of eminent scientists and men of letters of the nineteenth century. *J. abnorm. soc. Psychol.,* 31:20-35, 1936.

Rasmussen, Vilhelm. *Diary of a Child's Life from Birth to the Fifteenth Year.* London: Gyldendal, 1931.

——. *Ruth. Tagebuch über die Entwicklung eines Mädchens von der Geburt bis zum 18. Lebensjahr. (Ruth. A Diary of the Development of a Girl from Birth to 18 Years).* Munich u. Berlin: Oldenbourg, 1934.

Ratchford, Fannie E. *The Brontës Web of Childhood.* New York: Columbia University Press, 1941.

Rathlef, E. *Goethe pathologisch. (Goethe as a Pathological Person).* Riga: Jonck & Poliewsky, 1904.

Raviar, G. Le Génie de Balzac. (The genius of Balzac). *Ann. Méd.-Psychol., Paris,* 4:481-503, 1954.

Ravn, J. [The psychic constitution of Selma Lagerlof.] *Acta Psychiat. Scand.* 34:321-324, 1959.

Redfield, C. L. The ancestors of eminent men. *J. educ. Psychol.,* 7:548-552, 1916.

Régis, E. Étude médicale sur J. J. Rousseau. (A medical study of J. J. Rousseau). *Chron. Méd.,* 7:65-76, 132-140, 173-178, 194-206, 1900.

Rees, H. E. *A Psychology of Artistic Creation as Evidenced in Autobiographical Statements of Artists.* New York: Bureau of Publications, Teachers College, Columbia University, 1942.

Reik, Theodor. Aus den Denkwürdigkeiten der Glückel von Hameln. (From the *Memoirs of Glückel of Hameln*). *Int. Zsch. f. Psychoanal.,* 3:235-239, 1915.

——. Flauberts Jugendregungen. Der liebende Flaubert. (Emotional impulses of young Flaubert. Flaubert as a lover). *Pan,* 2 (3, 4), 1911.

——. *Flaubert und seine Versuchung des heiligen Antonius. (Flaubert and His Temptation of St. Anthony).* Minden: J. C. Bruns, 1912.

——. Freuds Studie über Dostojewski. (Freud's study on Dostoevsky). *Imago,* 15:233ff, 1929.

——. Eine Kindheitserinnerung Alexander Dumas. (A childhood recollection of Alexander Dumas). *Imago,* 5:128-219, 1917.

——. Aus dem Leben Guy de Maupassants. (From the life of Guy de Maupassant). *Imago,* 2:519-521, 1913.

——. Eine psychoanalytische Studie über Caligula. (A psychoanalytic study of Caligula). *Imago,* 17:130-132, 1931.

——. *The Secret Self: Psychoanalytic Experiences in Life and Literature.* New York: Farrar, Straus & Young, 1952.

——. *Warum verliess Goethe Friederike? (Why Did Goethe Leave Friederike?)* Vienna: Internationaler Psychoanalytischer Verlag, 1930.

——. Zwei Träume Flauberts. (Two dreams of Flaubert). *Zentralbl. f. Psychoanal.,* 3:222-224, 1913.

Rein, David M. Conrad Aiken and psychoanalysis. *Psychoanal. Rev.*, 42: 402-411, 1955.

——. *S. Weir Mitchell as a Psychiatric Novelist.* New York: International Universities Press, 1952.

Reiter, P. J. *Martin Luthers Umvelt, Charakter und Psychose; sowie die Bedeutung dieser Factoren für seine Entwicklung und Lehre; eine historisch-psychiatrische Studie. I. Teil. Die Umwelt. II. Teil. Luthers Persönlichkeit, Seelenleben und Krankheiten. (Martin Luther's Environment, Character and Psychosis; together with the Influence of these Factors on his Development and Doctrines. Part I. The Environment. Part II. Luther's Personality, Inner Life and Illnesses).* Copenhagen: Munksgaard, 1941. 2 Vols.

Reitman, F. Goya: a medical study. *Character & Pers.*, 8:1-17, 1939.

Reuter, E. B. The sociology of adolescence. *Amer. J. Sociol.*, 43:414-427, 1937.

Révész, Geza. *Erwin Nyiregyházi: Psychologische Analyse eines musikalisch hervorragen Kindes. (Erwin Nyiregyhazi: A Psychological Analysis of a Musically Outstanding Child).* Leipzig: Veit u. Co., 1916.

——. *The Psychology of a Musical Prodigy.* New York: Harcourt, Brace & Co., 1925.

Révész-Alexander, M. Portret en Zelfportret als Menselijk Document. (Portrait and self-portrait as a human document). *Nederlands Tijdschrift voor Psychol.*, 9:372-384, 1954.

Reznikoff, Phillip. A note on Washington. *Int. J. Psycho-Anal.*, 15:301-302, 1934.

Rîbnikov, N. A. [Adolescent diaries and their study.] *Psikhol.*, 1:83-95, 1928.

——. [Autobiographies as psychological documents.] *Psikhol.*, 3:440-458, 1930.

——. [Psychology and the study of biography.] *Psikhol.*, 2:215-225, 1929.

Rieff, Philip. *Freud. The Mind of the Moralist.* New York: Viking Press, 1959.

Riesman, Evelyn T. Childhood memory in the painting of Joan Miro. *ETC: A Rev. of General Semantics,* 6:160-168, 1949.

Rinaker, Clarissa. A psychoanalytical note on Jane Austen. *Psychoanal. Quart.,* 5:108-115, 1936.

Rittmeister, John. In Memoriam. Aus den Tagebuchblättern des Dr. John Rittmeister, aufgezeichnet im Gefängnis in der Zeit vom 26.9. 1942 bis zum Tage seiner Hinrichtung am 13.5.1943. (In memoriam. From the diary of Dr. John Rittmeister, written in prison from Sept.

26, 1942 to the day of his execution on May 13, 1943). *Z. Psychoanal.,* 1:60-68, 1949.

Roback, A. A. *I. L. Peretz. Psychologist of Literature.* Cambridge, Mass.: Sci-Art Publishers, 1935.

——. *William James, His Marginalia, Personality and Contribution.* Cambridge, Mass.: Sci-Art Publishers, 1942.

Roberts, Donald R. A Freudian view of Jonathan Swift. *Lit. & Psychol.,* 6:8-17, 1956.

Robinson, C. Historical pathology: the case of King Louis XI of France. *Amer. J. Insanity,* 75:155-186, 1918.

Roe, Anne. Artists and their work. *J. Personality,* 15:1-40, 1946.

——. Early differentiation of interests, in Taylor, C. W. (Ed.), *The Second (1957) Research Conference on the Identification of Creative Scientific Talent.* Salt Lake City: University of Utah Press, 1958. Pp. 98-108.

——. *The Making of a Scientist.* New York: Dodd, Mead & Co., 1953.

——. The personality of artists. *Educ. psychol. Msmt.,* 6:401-408, 1946.

——. Personality and vocation. *Transac. N. Y. Acad. Sci.,* 9:257-267, 1947.

——. Psychological examinations of eminent biologists. *J. consult. Psychol.,* 13:225-246, 1949.

——. A psychological study of eminent biologists. *Psychol. Monographs,* 65:1951.

——. A psychological study of eminent psychologists and anthropologists, and a comparison with biological and physical scientists. *Psychol. Monographs,* 67:1953.

Roe, Janet. I was born at 18 in America. *Psychiat. Quart. Suppl.,* 21:94-107, 1947.

Rohleder, Hermann. Das Sexuelle in Leben Napoleons I. (The sexual element in the life of Napoleon I). *Sexualprobleme,* 1913.

Roncoroni, ——. Il carattere di Ricardo Wagner. (The character of Richard Wagner). *Ann. di Freniat.,* 9:1-37, 101-122, 1899.

Rorschach, Hermann. *Zwei schweizerische Sektenstifter. (Two Swiss Founders of Sects).* Vienna: Internationaler Psychoanalytischer Verlag, 1927.

Rorschach, O. Über das Leben und die Wesenart von Hermann Rorschach. (The life and essential nature of Hermann Rorschach). *Schweiz. arch. Neurol. Psychiat.,* 53:1-11, 1944.

Rosen, Ephraim. George X: the self-analysis of an avowed fascist. *J. abnorm. soc. Psychol.,* 44:528-540, 1949.

Rosenzweig, Saul. The idiocultural dimension of psychotherapy: pre- and posthistory of the relations between Sigmund Freud and Josef Popper-Lynkeus, in Muensterberger, Warner, and Axelrad, Sidney,

(Eds.), *Psychoanalysis and the Social Sciences,* Vol. V. New York: International Universities Press, 1959. Pp. 9-50.

Rossman, J. *The Psychology of the Inventor: A Study of the Patentee.* Washington, D. C.: Inventors Publishing Co., 1931.

——. A study of the childhood, education and age of 710 inventors. *J. Patent Office Soc.,* 17:411-421, 1935.

Rubin, Louis D., Jr. *Thomas Wolfe. The Weather of His Youth.* Baton Rouge, La.: Louisiana State University Press, 1955.

Rubinow, Olga. The course of man's life—a psychological problem. *J. abnorm. soc. Psychol.,* 28:207-215, 1933.

Rubinstein, M. M. [*Youth According to Diaries and Autobiographies.*] Moscow: 1928.

Runner, J. R. Social distance in adolescent relationships. *Amer. J. Sociol.,* 43:428-439, 1937.

Rusu, L. *Goethe.* Cluj: Tipografia Viata, 1932.

Ruttkay-Nedecký, Ivan, & Zigmund, Vladislav. *Psychobiografický rozbor životopiso. (Psychobiographic analysis of curricula vitae).* Bratislava: Slovak Acad. of Sciences, 1957.

Sachs, Hanns. Baudelaire, der Verfluchte. (Baudelaire, the damned). *Almanach,* 191-194, 1932.

——. *Caligula.* London: Matthews & Marriot, 1932.

——. Caligulas Geliebten. (Caligula's mistresses). *Pschoanal. Bewegung,* 2:248-255, 1930.

——. Edgar Allen Poe. *Psychoanal. Quart.,* 4:294-306, 1935.

——. *Freud, Master and Friend.* Cambridge, Mass.: Harvard University Press, 1944.

——. The man Moses and the man Freud, in *The Creative Unconscious: Studies in the Psychoanalysis of Art.* Cambridge, Mass.: Sci-Art Publishers, 1942.

——. Was this analysis a success?—Comment. *J. abnorm. soc. Psychol.,* 35:11-16, 1940.

——. What would happen if... *Amer. Imago,* 3:61-66, 1946.

Sachs, Wulf. *Black Hamlet. The Mind of an African Negro Revealed by Psychoanalysis.* London: Bles, 1937.

Sadger, J. *Conrad Ferdinand Meyer. Eine pathographisch-psychologische Studie. (Conrad F. Meyer. A Pathographic-Psychological Study).* Wiesbaden: Bergmann, 1908.

——. *Friedrich Hebbel: ein psychoanalytischer Versuch. (Friedrich Hebbel: An Attempt at a Psychoanalytic Portrait).* Vienna: Deuticke, 1920.

——. *Aus dem Liebesleben Nikolaus Lenaus. (About the Love Life of Nikolaus Lenau).* Vienna: Deuticke, 1909.

——. *Heinrich von Kleist. Eine Pathographic-Psychologische Studie.*

(Heinrich von Kleist. A Pathographic-Psychological Study). Wiesbaden: Bergmann, 1910.

——. Über den Wert der Autobiographie sexuell Perverser. (On the value of autobiographies of sexual perverts). *Fortsch. Med.,* 1913.

——. Welcher Wert kommt den Erzählungen und Autobiographien der Homosexuellen zu? (What value can be attributed to the stories and autobiographies of homosexuals?) *Arch. Krim. Anthrop.,* 53: 179, 1913.

Sanchez-Perez, J. M. Cajal, the philosopher as revealed by his literary works. *Bull. Los Angeles Neurol. Soc.,* 17:47-53, 1952.

Sanford, Filmore H. Speech and personality. *Psychol. Bull.,* 39: 811-845, 1942.

——. Speech and personality: a comparative case study. *Character & Pers.,* 10:168-198, 1942.

Sarkar, Sarasi Lal. A conversion phenomenon in the life of dramatist Girish Chandra Ghose. *Int. J. Psycho-Anal.,* 11:228-231, 1930.

——. A study of the psychology of sexual abstinence from the dreams of an ascetic. *Int. J. Psycho-Anal.,* 24:170-175, 1943.

Saslow, G., & Chapple, E. D. A new life history form, with instructions for its use. *Appl. Anthrop.,* 4:1-18, 1945.

Saupe, W. Aus Nietzsches Jugend und früher schöpfenzeit. (Nietzsche's youth and early productive period). *Zsch. f. päd. Psychol.,* 39:295-300, 1938.

Saveth, E. N. The historian and the Freudian approach to history. *N. Y. Times Book Rev.,* Jan. 1, 1956, p. 7.

Schacht, W. *Nietzsche. Eine psychiatrisch-philosophische Untersuchung. (Nietzsche. A Psychiatric and Philosophical Investigation)*. Berne: Schmid & Francke, 1901.

Schaefer, P. *Das Schuldbewusstsein in den Confessiones des heiligen Augustinus. (The Feeling of Guilt in the Confessions of St. Augustine)*. Wuerzburg: Becker, 1930.

Schliebe, G. Selbstberichte Jugendlicher Ausreisser. (Young runaways' own reports of themselves). *Z. Jugendk.,* 4:275-280, 1934.

Schmidl, Fritz. Sigmund Freud and Ludwig Binswanger. *Psychoanal. Quart.,* 28:40-58, 1959.

Schnabel, Ernst. *Anne Frank. A Portrait in Courage*. New York: Harcourt, Brace & Co., 1958.

Schneider, Daniel E. *The Psychoanalyst and the Artist*. New York: International Universities Press, 1950.

Schneider, J. Class origin and fame: eminent English women. *Amer. Sociol. Rev.,* 5:700-712, 1940.

Schnier, Jacques. The blazing sun: a psychoanalytic approach to Van Gogh. *Amer. Imago:* 7:143-162, 1950.

Schramek, R. Franz Liszt, Eine psychologische Untersuchung über Leben und Werk. (Franz Liszt. A psychological investigation of his life and work). *Arch. ges. Psychol.*, 92:45-84, 1934.

Schuckmann, ——. Die Analyse der Tagebücher von Jugendlichen. (Analysis of diaries of adolescents). *Päd. Warte*, 34:8, 97-103, 1927.

Schueter, J. Religionpsychologische Biographienforschung. (The religious-psychological investigation of biographies). *Arch. f. Religious-psych.*, 1:202-210, 1914.

Schulhof, H. Zur Psychologie Strindbergs. (Contribution to the psychology of Strindberg). *Int. Zsch. f. Individualpsychol.*, 2:20-25, 1924.

Schweitzer, Albert. *The Psychiatric Study of Jesus.* Boston: Beacon Press, 1958.

Scupin, G. *Lebensbild eines Deutschen Schuljungen. Tagebuch einer Mutter. (Biography of a German Schoolboy. The Diary of a Mother).* Leipzig: Durr, 1931.

Séailles, G. *Ernest Renan; Essai de biographie psychologique. (Ernest Renan; An Attempt at a Psychological Biography).* Paris: Perrin et Cie., 1895 (?). 2 Vols.

Sechehaye, M. A. *Die Symbolische Wunscherfülling: Darstellung einer neuen psychotherapeutischen Methode und Tagebuch der Kranken. (Symbolic Realization: Presentation of a New Psychotherapeutic Method and the Patient's Diary).* Berne: Hans Huber Verlag, 1955.

Seillière, E. L'égotisme pathologique chez Stendhal. (The pathological egotism of Stendhal). *Rev. deux mondes*, 31:334-361, 650-679, 1906.

Selling, L. S. The autobiography as a psychiatric technique. *Amer. J. Orthopsychiat.*, 2:162-171, 1932.

——. *Men Against Madness.* New York: Greenberg, 1940.

Shakow, David. One psychologist as analysand. *J. abnorm. soc. Psychol.*, 35:198-211, 1940.

Shapira, R. Al Hayomanim shel b'ne Han' Urim. (About adolescents' diaries). *Ofakim*, 4:40-45, 1947.

Sharpe, Ella Freeman. Francis Thompson: a psychoanalytical study. *Brit. J. Med. Psychol.*, 5:329-344, 1925.

Shiff, Nathan A. *Diary of a Nymph.* New York: Lysle Stuart, Inc., 1961.

Shinn. M. W. *The Biography of a Baby.* Boston: Houghton Mifflin Co., 1900.

Shirley, M. *The First Two Years: A Study of Twenty-five Babies.* Minneapolis: University of Minnesota, 1933. 3 Vols.

Sibéril, ——. *Histoire médicale de Jean-Jacques Rousseau. (Medical History of Jean-Jacques Rousseau).* Thèse. Bordeaux: 1900.

Siegel, Laurence. A biographical inventory of students: I. Construction and standardization of the instrument. *J. appl. Psychol.*, 40:5-10, 1956.

——. Note on a biographical inventory for students. *J. couns. Psychol.,* 1:116-118, 1954.

Singh, J. A. L., & Zingg, R. M. *Wolf-Children and Feral Man.* New York: Harper & Bros., 1942.

Sinthern, P. *Werden einer Heiligenseele. Ein Blick in das Seelenleben der hl. Therese vom Jesuskind. (The Development of a Saint. A Glance into the Inward Life of St. Theresa of Jesus).* Innsbruck: Marianischer Verlag, 1930.

Skaggs, E. B. Personalistic psychology as science. *Psychol. Rev.,* 52:234-238, 1945.

Smith, L. Aaron Burr. *Psychoanal. Quart.,* 12:67-99, 1943.

Smith, Mapheus. Eminent men. *Sci. Mon.,* 48:554-562, 1939.

——. Racial origins of eminent personages. *J. abnorm. soc. Psychol.,* 32:63-73, 1937.

Smith, May. An autobiography. *Occupational Psychol., London,* 23:74-80, 1949.

Smith, Preserved. Luther's early development in the light of psychoanalysis. *Amer. J. Psychol.,* 24:260, 1913.

Smith, S. S., & Isotoff, A. The abnormal from within: Dostoevsky. *Psychoanal. Rev.,* 22:361-391, 1935.

Spearman, C. The life and work of William McDougall. *Character & Pers.,* 7:175-183, 1939.

Sperber, Alice. Von Dantes unbewussten Seelenleben. (On Dante's unconscious). *Imago,* 3:205-249, 1914.

Sperber, M. Knut Hamsun. *Int. Zsch. f. Indiv.-Psychol.,* 7:447-450, 1929.

Squires, Paul C. The clairpsychism of Strindberg. *Psychoanal. Rev.,* 29:50-70, 1942.

——. The creative psychology of César Franck. *Character & Pers.,* 7:41-49, 1938.

——. Fyodor Dostoevsky; a psychopathological sketch. *Psychoanal. Rev.,* 24:365-385, 1937.

——. Jean Paul Friedrich Richter: a psychoanalytic portraiture. *Psychoanal. Rev.,* 26:191-218, 1939.

——. Mozart: the Janus of music. *J. Musicol.,* 3:53-59, 1941.

——. Peter Ilich Tschaikowsky: a psychological sketch. *Psychoanal. Rev.,* 28:445-465, 1941.

Starbuck, E. D. *The Psychology of Religion: An Empirical Study of the Growth of Religious Consciousness.* New York: Charles Scribner's Sons, 1899.

Stead, Philip J. (Ed.). *The Memoirs of Lacenaire.* New York: Roy, 1955.

Stein, Morris I., & Heinze, Shirley J. *Creativity and the Individual. Summaries of Selected Literature in Psychology and Psychiatry.* Chicago: Free Press, 1960.

Stekel, Hilda. Autobiography by Wilhelm Stekel, M.D. Introductory note. *Amer. J. Psychother.*, 1:183-188, 1947.

Stekel, Wilhelm. Aus Gerhart Hauptmanns Diarium. (From Gerhart Hauptmann's diary). *Zentralbl. f. Psychoanal. u. Psychother.*, 1:431, 1911.

——. Autobiography. *Amer. J. Psychother.*, 1:338-346, 479-494, 1947; 2:82-107, 256-282, 417-437, 624-649, 1948; 3:46-73, 1949.

——. *Autobiography. The Life Story of a Pioneer Psychoanalyst.* New York: Liveright, 1950.

——. Goethe äussert sich über die Macht infantiler Eindrücke. (Goethe expresses himself on the power of infantile impressions). *Zentralbl. f. Psychoanal. u. Psychother.*, 2:106, 1912.

——. Kinderbriefe. (Children's letters). *Zentralbl. f. Psychoanal. u. Psychother.*, 4:111, 1913.

——. Nietzsche und Wagner. Eine sexual-psychologische Studie zur Psychogenese des Freundschaftsgefühles und des Freundschaftsverrates. (Nietzsche and Wagner. A sexual-psychological study about the psychogenesis of friendship feelings and friendship betrayed). *Zsch. f. Sexualwisschft.*, 4:22-28, 58-65, 1917.

——. Aus dem Tagebuch eines Neurotikers. (From the diary of a neurotic). *Zentralbl. f. Psychoanal. u. Psychother.*, 2:89-90, 1912.

——. Ein Traumbild des Benvenuto Cellini. (A dream picture of Benvenuto Cellini). *Zentralbl. f. Psychoanal. u. Psychother.*, 4:322-323, 1914.

Sterba, Editha, & Sterba, Richard F. *Beethoven and His Nephew. A Psychoanalytic Study of Their Relationship.* New York: Pantheon Books, 1954.

Sterba, Richard, & Sterba, Editha. The anxieties of Michelangelo Buonarotti. *Int. J. Psycho-Anal.*, 37:325-329, 1956.

——. Beethoven and his nephew. *Int. J. Psycho-Anal.*, 33:47-478, 1952.

Stern, William. *Anfänge der Reifezeit. Ein Knabentagebuch in psychologischer Bearbeitung. (Beginnings of Puberty. A Boy's Diary Considered Psychologically).* Leipzig: Quelle & Meyer, 1925.

——. Helen Keller—persönliche Eindrucke. (Helen Keller—personal impressions). *Zsch. f. angew. Psychol.*, 3:321-333, 1910.

——. (Ed.) Jugendliches Seelenleben und Krieg. (Adolescent psychic life and war). *Zsch. f. angewandte Psychol.*, 1915.

Stevens, G. C. Autobiographical material concerning the childhood environments and the effects on the after-adjustment of one hundred college freshmen. *Amer. J. Orthopsychiat.*, 2:279-303, 1932.

Stewart, H. L. Tolstoy as a problem in psycho-analysis. *Proc. & Tr. Roy. Soc. Canad., Ottawa*, 17:29-39, 1923.

Stifter, Adalbert. *Betrachtungen und Bilder. (Reflections and Portraits).* Vienna: Amalthea, 1923.

Still, Robert. Gustav Mahler and psychoanalysis. *Amer. Imago,* 17:217-240, 1960.

Storch, Alfred. *August Strindberg in Lichte seiner selbstbiographie. Eine psychopathologische Persönlichkeitanalyse. (August Strindberg in the Light of His Autobiography. A Psychopathologic Personality Analysis).* Wiesbaden: Bergmann, 1921.

Storfer, Adolf J. (Ed.) Beitrag zur Bibliographie der Psychoanalytischen Biographik. (Contribution to the bibliography of psychoanalytic biography). *Psychoanal. Bewegung,* 2:385-393, 1930.

Strachey, James. Preliminary notes upon the problem of Akhenaten. *Int. J. Psycho-Anal.,* 20:33-42, 1939.

Strang, Ruth. *The Adolescent Views Himself: A Psychology of Adolescence.* New York: McGraw-Hill Book Co., 1959.

Stroup, Herbert H. Social work and the attainment of historical perspective. *Amer. J. Econ. & Sociol.,* 13:297-303, 1954.

Stümcke, Heinrich. Strindberg und die Frauen. (Strindberg and women). *Zeitsch. Sexualwisschft,* 5:367-375, 1919.

Sully, J. *My Life and Friends: a Psychologist's Memories.* New York: E. P. Dutton & Co., 1922.

Susmann-Galant, J. Leo Tolstoi und seine Bezeihungen zur Psychiatrie. (Leo Tolstoi's relationship to psychiatry). *Psychiat.-Neur. Woch.,* 31:31-34, 1929.

Symonds, Percival M. *Adolescent Fantasy.* New York: Columbia University Press, 1949.

——. The needs of teachers as shown in autobiographies. *J. educ. Res.,* 36:662-667, 1943; 37:641-655, 1944.

——. Personality adjustment of women teachers. *Amer. J. Orthopsychiat.* 11:14-21, 1941.

——. Psychoanalysis, psychology, and education. *J. abnorm. soc. Psychol.,* 35:139-149, 1940.

Symonds, Percival M., & Jensen, Arthur R. *From Adolescent to Adult.* New York: Columbia University Press, 1961.

Szilágyi, Géza. Freud Öneletrajza. (Freud's autobiography). *Plesti Naplo,* 1925.

Szirmay Pulszky, H. Bolyai János életének és munk asságának lélektani értelmezése. (The psychological significance of John Bolyai's life and work). *Magyar Psychol. Szemle,* 5:86:104, 1932.

Taft, Jessie. *Otto Rank.* New York: Julian Press, 1958.

Talbert, E. L. On the enigmatic personality of Amiel. *J. abnorm. soc. Psychol.,* 34:129-132, 1939.

Taylor, William S., & Culler, E. The problem of *The Locomotive-God*. *J. abnorm. soc. Psychol.*, 24:342-399, 1929.

Terman, Lewis M. The discovery and encouragement of exceptional talent. *Amer. Psychol.*, 9:221-230, 1954.

———. The intelligence quotient of Francis Galton in childhood, in Dennis, Wayne (Ed.), *Readings in Child Psychology*. New York: Prentice-Hall, Inc., 1951. Pp. 371-377.

———. *Mental and Physical Traits of a Thousand Gifted Children*, Vol. I in *Genetic Studies of Genius*. Stanford, Calif.: Stanford University Press, 1925.

———. Scientists and nonscientists in a group of 800 gifted men. *Psychol. Monographs*, 58:1954.

Terman, Lewis M., & Chase, Jessie M. The psychology, biology and pedagogy of genius. *Psychol. Bull.*, 17:397-409, 1920

Terman, Lewis M., & Fenton, Jessie C. Preliminary report on a gifted juvenile author. *J. appl. Psychol.*, 5:163-177, 1921.

Terman, Lewis M., & Oden, Melita H. *The Gifted Child Grows Up; Twenty-Five Years' Follow-Up of a Superior Group*, Vol. IV in *Genetic Studies of Genius*. Stanford, Calif.: Stanford University Press, 1947.

———, & ———. *The Gifted Group at Mid-Life: Thirty-Five Years' Follow-Up of the Superior Child*, Vol. V in *Genetic Studies of Genius*. Stanford, Calif.: Stanford University Press, 1959.

Theilhaber, F. A. *Goethe, Sexus und Eros. (Goethe, Sex and Eros)*. Berlin: Horen Verlag, 1929.

Thigpen, Corbett H., & Cleckley, Hervey M. *The Three Faces of Eve*. New York: McGraw-Hill Book Co., 1957.

Thimme, W. *Augustins Selbstbildnis in den Konfessionen. Eine religionpsychologische Studie. (Augustine's Self-Portrait as Revealed in the Confessions. A Religious-Psychological Study)*. Guetersloh: Bertelsmann, 1929.

Thomae, Hans. Biographie und psychologie. *Sammlung*, 6:443-455, 1951.

Thomas, William I., & Znaniecki, Florian. *The Polish Peasant in Europe and America*. New York: Dover Press, 1959. 2 Vols.

Thompson, D. *A Mind that Was Different*. Oklahoma City: Harlow Publishing Co., 1931.

Thorn, K. F., & Bryngelson, B. An analytic study of the social and speech adjustment of good and poor speakers by means of the autobiographic method. *Speech Monographs*, 12:61-73, 1945.

Thorndike, Edward L. The origin of superior men. *Sci. Mon.*, 56:424-432, 1943.

——. Traits of personality and their intercorrelations as shown in biographies. *J. educ. Psychol.*, 41:193-216, 1950.

Thrift, Inez E. Religion and madness. The case of William Cowper. *Psychoanal. Rev.*, 13:312-317, 1926.

Tissi, Silvio. *Au Microscope Psychanalytique: Pirandello, Shakespeare, Tolstoi, Shaw, Bourget, Gide. (In the Psychoanalytic Microscope)*. Milan: Ulrico Hoepli, 1932.

Tozzer, Alfred M. Biography and biology. *Amer. Anthrop.*, 35:418-432, 1933.

Towne, Jackson E. Carlyle and Oedipus. *Psychoanal. Rev.*, 22:297-305, 1935.

Tramer, M. Diary of a psychotic child. *Nerv. Child*, 1:232-249, 1942.

——. Tagebuch über ein geisteskrankes Kind. (Diary of a psychotic child). *Z. Kinderpsychiat.*, 1:91-97, 123-126, 154-161, 1934; 1:187-194, 1935; 2:17-28, 86-90, 114-124, 1935; 10:115-121, 1943.

Triplett, M. L. Influences in the adolescent years of artists. *Sch. Rev.*, 51:300-308, 1943.

Trueblood, C. K. Saint-Beuve and the psychology of personality. *Character & Pers.*, 8:120-143, 1939.

Tumin, Melvin. Some fragments from the life history of a marginal man. *Character & Pers.*, 13:261-296, 1945.

Uher, J. [The diary in the life of students.] *Psychologie, Brno*, 1:128-140, 1935.

Ulin, C. *Personlighetsbildningen hos unga flickor. (Formation of Personality in Young Girls)*. Stockholm: Natur och Kultur, 1944.

Upvall, Axel. *August Strindberg. A Psychoanalytic Study with Special Reference to the Oedipus Complex*. Boston: Richard G. Badger, 1920.

Urstein, M. *Leopold and Loeb: A Psychiatric-Psychological Study*. New York: New York & Chicago Medical Book Co., 1924.

Vallejo Nagera, A. [Psychological study of Nero]. *An. Acad. Nac. Med. (Madrid)*, 76:97-131, 1959.

——. [Psychopathology of the Caesars: psychopathological study of the Julian family.] *An. Acad. Nac. Med. (Madrid)*, 76:85-96, 1959.

Van Tuyl, M. C. T. A study in student thinking. *Rel. Educ.*, 32:255-262, 1937.

——. Where do students 'lose' religion? *Rel. Educ.*, 33:19-29, 1938.

Velikovsky, Immanuel. *Oedipus and Akhnaton. Myth and History*. Garden City, N. Y.: Doubleday, 1960.

——. Tolstoy's Kreutzer Sonata and unconscious homosexuality. *Psychoanal. Rev.*, 24:18-25, 1937.

Vernon, Horace M. An autobiography. *Occupational Psychol., London*, 22:73-82, 1948.

Vernon, W. H. D. Hitler, the man—notes for a case history. *J. abnorm. soc. Psychol.*, 37:295-308, 1942.

Vineberg, O. *August Strindberg och Hans Kvinnohat. (August Strindberg and His Hatred against Women).* Stockholm: Chelius, 1929.

Visher, Stephen S. The education of the younger starred scientists. *J. Higher Educ.*, 10:124-132, 1939.

——. Environmental backgrounds of leading American scientists. *Amer. Sociol. Rev.*, 13:65-72, 1948.

——. Scientists starred 1903-1943, in *American Men of Science: A Study of Collegiate and Doctoral Training, Birthplace, Distribution, Backgrounds, and Developmental Influences.* Baltimore: Johns Hopkins University Press, 1947.

——. Sources of great men. *Eugenics Quart.*, 2:103-109, 1955.

Voizard, F. *Sainte-Beuve, l'homme et l'oeuvre. Étude médico-psychologique.* ¡Sainte-Beuve, the Man and His Work. A Medical-Psychological Study). Lyon: 1912.

Vooys, C. J. Psychische Achtergrond bij Descartes. (Psychic background of Descartes). *Psychol. Achtergr.*, 17/18:219-221, 1952.

Vorberg, Gaston. Der Fall Jean-Jacques Rousseau. (The case of Jean-Jacques Rousseau). *Zeitschr. f. Sexualwisschft,* 10:37-40, 1923.

——. Martin Luthers skatologische Ausdrucksweise und ihre Beziehungen zur Persönlichkeit. (Martin Luther's scatalogical expressions and relations to his personality). *Fortschr. Sexualw. Psychoan.*, 2: 526-528, 1926.

Vorwahl, H. Zu Goethes Liebesleben. (On Goethe's love life). *Zeitschr. f. Sexualwisschft,* 18:503-507, 1932.

——. Die Sexualität bei Luther. (Sexuality in Luther). *Zeitschr. f. Sexualwisschft,* 15 (5), 1928.

Wagner, Lydia E. Coleridge's use of laudanum and opium, as connected with his interest in contemporary investigations concerning stimulation and sensation. *Psychoanal. Rev.*, 25:309-334, 1938.

Wallace, William J. Personality variation in a primitive society. *J. Personality*, 15:321-328, 1947.

Wallin, John E. W. *Minor Mental Maladjustments in Normal People; Based on Original Autobiographies of Personality Maladjustments.* Durham, N. C.: Duke University Press, 1949.

Wangh, Martin. The scope of the contribution of psychoanalysis to the biography of the artist. *J. Amer. Psychoanal. Assoc.*, 5:564-575, 1957.

Warren, Louis A. *Lincoln's Youth. Indiana Years; Seven to Twenty-One.* New York: Appleton-Century-Crofts, 1959.

Watson, Goodwin. Clio and Psyche: some interrelations of history and psychology, in Ware, C. F. (Ed.)., *The Cultural Approach to History.* New York: Columbia University Press, 1940. Pp. 34-47.

Wechniakoff, T. *Savants, penseurs et artistes; Biologie et pathologie comparées. (Scholars, Thinkers and Artists; Biology and Pathology Compared)*. Paris: Alcan, 1899.

Weichbrodt, R. Der Dichter Lenz. Eine Pathographie. (The poet Lenz. A pathographic study). *Arch. f. Psychiat. u. Nervenkr.*, 62:153-187, 1920.

Weidel, K. *Jesu Persönlichkeit. Eine psychologische Studie. (The Personality of Jesus. A Psychological Study)*. Halle: Marhold, 1908.

Weiss, Karl. Strindberg über Fehlleistungen. (Strindberg on parapraxes). *Int. Zeitschr. f. Psychoanal.*, 1:268, 1913.

Weissman, Philip. The childhood and legacy of Stanislavsky, in Eissler, Ruth S., et al. (Eds.), *The Psychoanalytic Study of the Child*, Vol. XII. New York: International Universities Press, 1957. Pp. 399-417.

———. Conscious and unconscious autobiographical dramas of Eugene O'Neill. *J. Amer. Psychoanal. Assoc.*, 5:432-441, 1957.

———. Shaw's childhood and Pygmalion, in Eissler, Ruth S. et al. (Eds.), *The Psychoanalytic Study of the Child*, Vol. XIII. New York: International Universities Press, 1958.

———. Why Booth killed Lincoln: a psychoanalytic study of a historical tragedy, in Muensterberger, Warner, & Axelrad, Sidney, (Eds.), *Psychoanalysis and the Social Sciences*, Vol. V. New York: International Universities Press, 1959. Pp. 99-118.

Wellek, Albert. Goethe und die Psychologie. (Goethe and Psychology). *Schweiz. Z. Psychol. Anwend.*, 9:1-24, 1950.

Wells, F. L. Hölderlin: greatest of "schizophrenics." *J. abnorm. soc. Psychol.*, 41:199-206, 1946.

Wells, Henry W. Poet and psychiatrist. Merrill Moore, M. D. *J. Nerv. & Ment. Dis.*, 122:595-602, 1955.

———. *Poet and Psychiatrist. Merrill Moore, M. D.* New York: Twayne Publishers, 1955.

Wells, Walter A. *A Doctor's Life of John Keats*. New York: Vantage Press, 1959.

Westermann, D. *Afrikaner Erzahlen ihr Leben. (Africans Tell Their Life Stories)*. Essen: Essener Verlagsanstalt, 1938.

Weymouth, A. *A Psychologist's War-Time Diary*. New York: Longmans, 1940.

Weyr, H. Grosse Männer. (Great men). *Int. Zsch. f. Indiv.-Psychol.*, 10: 216-223, 1932.

White, John S. The character development of Ernest Psichari. A study of fascism in France. *Psychiat.*, 7:409-423, 1944.

White, Ralph K. Black Boy: a value-analysis. *J. abnorm. soc. Psychol.*, 42:440-461, 1947.

———. Note on the psychopathology of genius. *J. soc. Psychol.*, 1:311-315, 1930.

———. *Value Analysis: The Nature and Use of the Method.* Glen Gardner, N. J.: Society for the Psychological Study of Social Issues, 1951.

———. The versatility of genius. *J. soc. Psychol.*, 2:460-489, 1931.

White, Robert W. *Lives in Progress.* New York: Dryden Press, 1952.

———. The personality of Joseph Kidd. I. History of an adolescent crisis in the development of ego-structure. II. Psychological appraisal at eighteen and a half years. III. Three years of ego-reconstruction. *Character & Pers.*, 11:183-208, 318-338, 339-360, 1943.

White, W. A. *Autobiography of a Purpose.* New York: Doubleday, Doran & Co., 1938.

Wight, F. Picasso and the unconscious. *Psychoanal. Quart.*, 13:208-216, 1944.

Winterstein, Alfred R. F. *Adalbert Stifter, Persönlichkeit und Werk; eine tiefenpsychologische Studie. (Adalbert Stifter, His Personality and His Work; A Depth-Psychological Study).* Vienna: Phönix, 1946.

———. *Dürers Melancholie im Lichte der Psychoanalyse. (Dürer's Melancholia as Viewed in the Light of Psychoanalysis).* Vienna: Internationaler Psychoanalytischer Verlag, 1929.

———. Rousseaus Bekenntnisse. (Rousseau's Confessions). *Zentralbl. f. Psychoanal. u. Psychother.*, 2:225, 1912.

———. Swedenborgs religiöse Krise und sein Traumtagebuch. (Swedenborg's religious crisis and his dream diary). *Imago*, 22:292-338, 1936.

Wittels, Fritz. Economic and psychological historiography. *Amer. J. Sociol.*, 51:527-532, 1946.

———. Le grand amour. (The great love). *Psychoanal. Bewegung*, 1:242ff, 1929.

———. Heinrich von Kleist—Prussian Junker and creative genius. *Amer. Imago*, 11:11-31, 1954.

———. Revision of a biography. *Amer. J. Psychol.*, 45:745-749, 1933.

———. *Sigmund Freud, His Personality, His Teaching, and His School.* New York: Dodd, Mead & Co., 1924.

Witty, P. A., & Lehman, H. C. Nervous instability and genius: military and political leaders. *J. soc. Psychol.*, 3:212-234, 1932.

Wizel, Adam (Ed.). *Memoiren einer Patientin. Psychoanalytisches Studium. (Memoirs of a Female Patient. A Psychoanalytic Study).* Warsaw: Hoesick Verlag, 1926.

Wolberg, Lewis R. The *Divine Comedy* of Dante. *Psychoanal. Rev.*, 30: 33-46, 1943.

Wolf, E. Arthur Rimbaud fut-il Schizophrenie? (Was Arthur Rimbaud schizophrenic?) *Ann. Méd.-Psychol.*, 2:429-444, 1956.

Wolfenstein, Martha. Analysis of a juvenile poem, in Eissler, Ruth S., et al., (Eds.), *The Psychoanalytic Study of the Child*, Vol. XI. New York: International Universities Press, 1956. Pp. 450-472.

Wolffheim, Nelly. Friedrich Fröbel. *Psychol. Berater Gesunds Prakt. Lebensgestalt.*, 4:294-309, 1952.

Wolters, Albert W. An autobiography. *Occupational Psychol., London*, 22:180-189, 1948.

Wood, Austin B. Another psychologist analyzed. *J. abnorm. soc. Psychol.*, 36:87-90, 1941.

Wood, Clement. *Amy Lowell*. New York: Vinal, 1926.

Woods, Frederick A. *The Influence of Monarchs*. New York: Macmillan Co., 1913.

——. *Mental and Moral Heredity in Royalty*. New York: Henry Holt & Co., 1906.

Wulff, M. (Ed.). *Max Eitingen in Memoriam*. Jerusalem: Israel Psychoanalytic Society, 1950.

Wyatt, Stanley. An autobiography. *Occupational Psychol., London*, 24: 65-74, 1950.

Yoda, A. [A psychological study of diaries.] *Rep. 6th Cong. Jap. psychol. Assoc.*, 268-279, 1938.

Yoder, A. H. The study of the boyhood of great men. *Pedagogical Seminary*, 3:134-156, 1894.

Ziemer, M. *Schillers Charakter*. Breslau: Brieg, 1934.

Zilboorg, Gregory. Psychological sidelights on Andreas Vesalius. *Bull. Hist. Med.*, 14:562-575, 1943.

Zink, H. A case study of a political boss. *Psychiat.*, 1:527-533, 1938.

Zohar, Zvi. Dostoyevski Be'Eyney Avi Hapsikohanlaiza. (Dostoevsky as seen by the father of psychoanalysis). *Ofakim*, 10:290-294, 1956.

Zuccarelli, A. *Gli "uomini di genio" e la loro biografia clinica. (Men of Genius and Their Clinical Biography)*. Naples: Melfi & Joele, 1898.